D0115045

California

Andrea Schulte-Peevers

Sara Benson, Tom Downs, Robert Landon,
Suzanne Plank, Ryan Ver Berkmoes, John A Vlahides

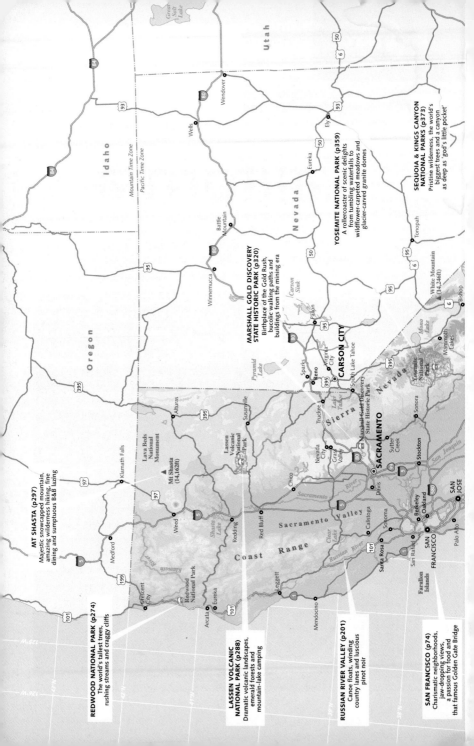

MT SHASTA (p297)
Majestic snowcapped mountain, amazing wilderness hiking, fine dining and sumptuous B&B lazing

MARSHALL GOLD DISCOVERY STATE HISTORIC PARK (p320)
Birthplace of the Gold Rush, bucolic walking paths and buildings from the mining era

YOSEMITE NATIONAL PARK (p359)
A rollercoaster of scenic delights from tumbling waterfalls to wildflower-carpeted meadows and glacier-carved granite domes

SEQUOIA & KINGS CANYON NATIONAL PARKS (p373)
Pristine wilderness, the world's biggest trees and a canyon as deep as 'god's little pocket'

REDWOOD NATIONAL PARK (p274)
The world's tallest trees, rushing streams and craggy cliffs

LASSEN VOLCANIC NATIONAL PARK (p288)
Dramatic volcanic landscapes, emerald forests and mountain-lake camping

RUSSIAN RIVER VALLEY (p201)
Canoe floats, winding country lanes and luscious pinot noir

SAN FRANCISCO (p74)
Charismatic neighborhoods, jaw-dropping views, a passion for food and that famous Golden Gate Bridge

Utah

Idaho

Oregon

Nevada

Mountain Time Zone

Pacific Time Zone

Wendover

Wells

Ely

Eureka

Battle Mountain

Winnemucca

Tonopah

White Mountain (14,246ft)

Bishop

Mammoth Lakes

Mono Lake

Yosemite National Park

Sonora

Carson Sink

Fallon

Pyramid Lake

Reno

Sparks

Virginia City

CARSON CITY

South Lake Tahoe

Lake Tahoe

Truckee

Sierra

Marshall Gold Discovery State Historic Park

Nevada City

Grass Valley

SACRAMENTO

Sutter Creek

Stockton

San Joaquin River

SAN JOSE

Palo Alto

Oakland

Berkeley

SAN FRANCISCO

San Rafael

Farallon Islands

Santa Rosa

Sonoma

Calistoga

Davis

Chico

Sacramento River

Sacramento Valley

Clear Lake

Russian River

Mendocino

Leggett

Coast Range

Red Bluff

Redding

Shasta Lake

Mt Shasta (14,162ft)

Weed

Klamath River

Lava Beds National Monument

Lassen Volcanic National Park

Alturas

Susanville

Klamath Falls

Medford

Crescent City

Redwood National Park

Arcata

Eureka

Great Salt Lake

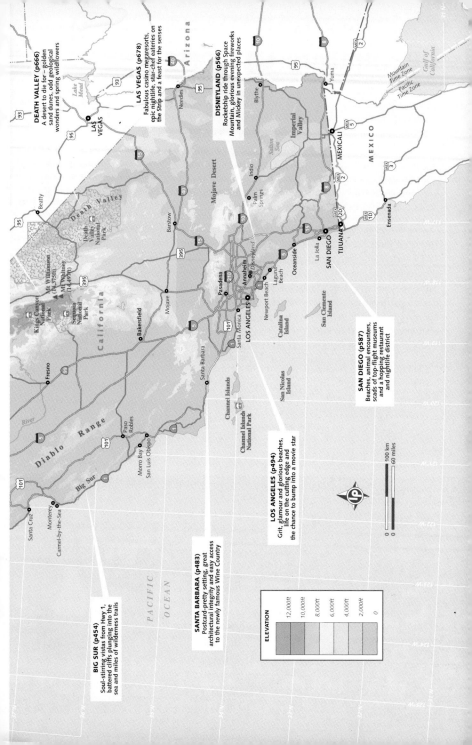

DEATH VALLEY (p666)
A desert to die for – golden sand dunes, odd geological wonders and spring wildflowers

LAS VEGAS (p678)
Fabulous casino megaresorts, epic nightlife, star-chef eateries on the Strip and a feast for the senses

DISNEYLAND (p566)
Rocketship ride through Space Mountain, glorious evening fireworks and Mickey in unexpected places

SAN DIEGO (p587)
Beaches, animal encounters, scads of top-flight museums and a hopping restaurant and nightlife district

LOS ANGELES (p494)
Grit, glamour and glorious beaches, life on the cutting edge and the chance to bump into a movie star

SANTA BARBARA (p483)
Postcard-pretty setting, great architectural integrity and easy access to the newly famous Wine Country

BIG SUR (p454)
Soul-stirring vistas from Hwy 1, battered cliffs plunging into the sea and miles of wilderness trails

ELEVATION
12,000ft
10,000ft
8,000ft
6,000ft
4,000ft
2,000ft
0

0   100 km
0   60 miles

Destination California

Buff, bronzed and beautiful, California is a sly seductress who tempts you with her bountiful riches. She's a creative genius who bowls you over with ideas and trends poised to take the world by storm. She's a bon vivant, passionately feasting on the smorgasbord of life, never taking things – or herself – too seriously. California is all that and then some to those who live here and to the millions of visitors eager to experience her mythology or, put more prosaically, to find out what all the fuss is about.

One thing's for sure: the Golden State could not possibly have been more aptly named. The Gold Rush may have inspired this moniker, but treasures abound wherever you go. You'll find them in the surf crashing against blissful beaches and fog-shrouded cliffs, in big-shouldered mountains chiseled into rugged splendor by glaciers and the elements, and in giant trees whose graceful limbs reach for the heavens. Uncover them in zigzagging canyons tracing pathways once trod by native inhabitants, explorers and pioneers, and in the ghost towns of the rough-and-tumble frontier days. Treasures are served on the dinner tables of edgy restaurants in the great cities of San Francisco and Los Angeles, and awaiting in the shapely dunes, sculpted boulders and proud cacti of the vast desert.

California, of course, gave birth to the film industry. And now it's up to you to make your own movie of memories. Will it be a noir mystery? A romantic comedy? An action adventure? California provides the set. You bring the vision.

DAVID PEEVERS

Highlights California

GREG GAWLOWSKI

The iconic, art deco Golden Gate Bridge stands sentinel at the entrance to San Francisco Bay from the Pacific Ocean (p92)

DAVID PEEVERS

Join glam shoppers, Rodeo Drive (p516), Los Angeles

OTHER HIGHLIGHTS

- Take the time to sip and savor California's fine wines (p187).

- Place your trust in Lady Luck and meet some larger-than-life characters along the Strip (p681) in Las Vegas.

- Forestiere Underground Gardens (p426) in Fresno are a testament to the will of one man to overcome nature's harsh realities.

RICK GERHARTER

Come out for all the color and fun at the Gay Pride Parade (p108), San Francisco

6

PHILIP & KAREN SMITH

Hike boulder outcrops of Joshua
Tree National Park (p654)

Hot air rises at Bumpass Hell thermal area
(p289), Lassen Volcanic National Park

JOHN ELK III

Breathe in the air and drink in the views of Yosemite Valley (p359)

ROB BLAKERS

JUDY BELLAH

Imagine life with your own Greco-Roman temple and Charles Cassou's statuary at Hearst Castle (p461)

LEE FOSTER

Lake Tahoe (p335) is the place to ski and be seen

Santa Cruz's 1906 boardwalk offers good, old-fashioned amusement activities (p434)

RICK GERHARTER

ROB BLAKERS

Sand dunes near Stovepipe Wells (p670)
extend far into Death Valley

Challenge your stomach on the Boomerang
Roller Coaster, Knott's Berry Farm (p573)

RICHARD CUMMINS

Catch the ultimate wave on the Pacific coast off Santa Cruz (p436)

RICK GERHARTER

Contents

Regional Map Contents

NORTHERN MOUNTAINS p283

NORTH COAST p233

WINE COUNTRY p189

GOLD COUNTRY p311

SAN FRANCISCO p78-9

SIERRA NEVADA p332

SAN FRANCISCO BAY AREA p137

CENTRAL VALLEY p408

CENTRAL COAST p433

LAS VEGAS VALLEY p678

CALIFORNIA DESERTS p636

ORANGE COUNTY p565

LOS ANGELES p498-9

SAN DIEGO AREA p587

The Authors

ANDREA SCHULTE-PEEVERS
Coordinating Author,Getting Started, Itineraries, California Outdoors, Los Angeles, Sierra Nevada, Directory, Transportation

Andrea fell in love with California – its pizzazz, people and sunshine – almost the instant she landed in the Golden State. She grew up in Germany, lived in London and traveled the world, but settled in Los Angeles, got a degree from UCLA and embarked on a career in travel writing. Andrea has written or contributed to nearly 30 Lonely Planet books, including several earlier editions of this one and the guide to Los Angeles & Southern California. She's explored nearly every nook and cranny of California and still thinks it's a perfect place to live.

My California
While I love California's endless beaches, craggy mountains and classy cities, it's the desert's energy-restoring qualities that pull me in time and again. A perfect getaway would start with a day sipping margaritas poolside in Palm Springs (p638). Then it's goodbye to civilization and hello to Joshua Tree National Park (p654), whose grand scale and raw beauty always enthrall me. While in the vicinity, I'd squeeze in a raucous night of ribs and rock at Pioneertown's Pappy's and Harriet's (p659), the ultimate desert honky tonk, and indulge in a mental-cobweb-clearing 'sound bath' at the outta-this-world Integratron (p657), near Joshua Tree. To finish, I'd stop in Desert Hot Springs (p643) for a soothing dip in its balmy natural mineral waters.

SARA BENSON
The Culture, Environment, California Deserts, Las Vegas Valley

After graduating with a liberal arts degree in Chicago, Sara jumped on a plane to the West Coast with just one suitcase and $100 in her pocket. She landed in San Francisco. A decade later, she's still there, but she'll defend LA and Las Vegas to the death against any silly Bay Area prejudices. Already the author of several travel and nonfiction books, Sara has also written Lonely Planet's *Las Vegas* and *Road Trip: Route 66* guides.

LONELY PLANET AUTHORS
Why is our travel information the best in the world? It's simple: our authors are independent, dedicated travellers. They don't research using just the Internet or phone, and they don't take freebies in exchange for positive coverage. They travel widely, to all the popular spots and off the beaten track. They personally visit thousands of hotels, restaurants, cafés, bars, galleries, palaces, museums and more – and they take pride in getting all the details right, and telling it how it is. For more, see the authors section on www.lonelyplanet.com.

TOM DOWNS — San Francisco, San Francisco Bay Area, Central Valley

Tom is a California native, born in Silicon Valley, schooled in Los Angeles, married in Vegas (somewhere outside California). He lived in San Francisco for eight years before settling with his family in Oakland. Tom has covered San Francisco and the Bay Area for Lonely Planet on and off since 1998. For this book's Central Valley chapter he also took a spin down Hwy 99. It's one of his favorite routes through the state. 'I always was interested in the non-public face of places, the part that doesn't update itself all the time,' he says. 'Hwy 99 is the back alley of California, but there's more to it than utility trucks and feral cats.'

ROBERT LANDON — Food & Drink, Orange County, San Diego

When he left the East Coast for California in 1985, Robert's mother wept with the knowledge he would never move back home. So far she's been right. After completing his BA at Stanford in 1989, Robert knocked around San Francisco until 1992, then spent two years at UC Irvine in Orange County, where he earned a highly marketable master's degree in English literature. Since 1994, Robert has made Berkeley his base, though he has traveled extensively.

SUZANNE PLANK — Northern Mountains

Suzanne Plank is a freelance writer living and working in the San Francisco Bay Area. Arriving in a covered wagon, Suzanne's ancestors first settled in the Sierra Nevada over 150 years ago. Genetic predeterminism and many years of backroad roaming have inspired Suzanne's great love of Northern California's mountains. Outside of California, Suzanne has explored many parts of the globe; she's written about some of her travels and been touched by all of them. She has an MA from Stanford in Latin American Studies and has lived and worked in Mexico and South America.

RYAN VER BERKMOES — Snapshot, History, Gold Country, Central Coast

Ryan Ver Berkmoes grew up in Santa Cruz County, right near the beach. As a child he used his innocent charm to bamboozle tourists by giving out wrong directions to points of interest. He's worked to make amends to travelers ever since. Ryan attended one of America's worst (and now defunct) private high schools on the cliffs overlooking Steamers Lane. Later, as life, work and love have taken him to various spots around the globe, he always looks forward to returning to the place he considers home. And where he never asks a small kid for directions.

JOHN A VLAHIDES   Wine Country, North Coast

Freelance travel writer John Vlahides is a French-trained chef and former Clefs d'Or luxury-hotel concierge. He regularly writes about the West, lives in San Francisco, and spends his free time touring the California coast by motorcycle, sunning beneath the Golden Gate Bridge, skiing in Utah and the Sierra Nevada, and singing tenor with the San Francisco Symphony Chorus.

CONTRIBUTING AUTHORS

Dr David Goldberg provided information for the Health chapter. David completed his training in internal medicine and infectious diseases at Columbia-Presbyterian Medical Center in New York City, where he has also served as voluntary faculty. At present, he is an infectious diseases specialist in Scarsdale, New York State, and the editor-in-chief of the website MDTravelHealth.com.

Mark Morford wrote the What Is Burning Man? boxed text (p354). A columnist for sfgate.com and the *San Francisco Chronicle*, he is also a yoga teacher and fiction writer, outstanding parallel parker, fervent wine devotee, former smoker, frequent skeptic and sporadic true believer. Mark has been to Burning Man five times.

Getting Started

California has an extremely well-organized tourism infrastructure; visitors, from backpackers to families to jet-setters, will all find their needs and expectations met. Room and travel reservations are a good idea during peak season (June to early September and around major holidays), but otherwise you can keep your advance planning to a minimum.

WHEN TO GO

Any time is a good time to be *somewhere* in California, but the *best* time to visit pretty much depends on what type of vacation you envision. Most people arrive in summer, between June and September, when accommodations are scarce and costly, and you'll be competing for space at major attractions like Disneyland and Yosemite National Park. Still, summer is fabulous for frolicking on the beaches, enjoying alfresco dinners and attending festivals and outdoor events. The mountains are gorgeous and perfect for hiking, camping, biking and other outdoor pursuits. Summer is not ideal for venturing into the desert, however, where the mercury can soar as high as 120°F, although low lodging prices and sparse crowds do have a certain appeal. If San Francisco and the Northern California (NoCal) coast are on your itinerary, bring warm clothes as thick summer fog makes the region surprisingly chilly. A similar phenomenon occurs in late spring in Southern California (SoCal), but by July the coast is clear, so to speak.

See Climate Charts (pp702–3) for more information.

The shoulder seasons (March to May and September to November) bring smaller crowds and lower prices. In spring, wildflowers brighten meadows, mountains and desert, while in fall it can still be warm enough to swim in the Pacific (at least in SoCal). Unless you're planning a beach vacation, winter (December to February) is a great time to visit. The desert is beautiful and temperatures are mild and pleasant. The mountains, meanwhile, turn into a winter wonderland, drawing skiers and snowboarders to the slopes. Chances of rain are greatest in the winter months, of course, but they're still pretty slim unless you're traveling in NoCal. But just about everywhere the cultural calendars are in full swing and lines are as short as they'll ever be (except around holidays).

For information on holidays see p706, while festivals and special events are discussed on p705.

DON'T LEAVE HOME WITHOUT...

- Checking the latest passport and visa requirements (p707)
- Valid travel and health insurance (p707)
- Hotel or camping reservations, especially in summer (p698)
- Classic California tunes for road-tripping in style (p18)
- Nerves of steel for driving on the freeways, especially in LA (p725)
- A raincoat, rainproof shoes and clothing for those days when the sun is a no-show
- Some spiffy clothes and shoes for hitting big-city clubs, the opera or nice restaurants
- This book and a curious mind

COSTS & MONEY

California ain't a bargain destination. Most people here earn rather handsome incomes and appreciate the good life, which drives up the overall standard of living. What you spend depends largely on what kind of traveler you are, what experiences you wish to have and the season in which you're visiting.

In summer and around holidays, renting a car, staying in midrange hotels, enjoying two sit-down meals a day, spending some money on sightseeing, activities and going to bars or clubs will cost between $150 and $250 per day (per person, traveling as an adult couple). Families can save by booking hotels that don't charge extra for children staying in the same room as their parents and by taking advantage of discounts at museums, theme parks and other sights. (For information on traveling with children, see p701.) For mere survival, you probably won't be able to spend less than $50 to $70 per day – this will have you sleeping in hostels, riding buses, preparing your own meals or eating snacks and fast food, and limiting your entertainment. For more detail on costs and ways to save, see information about accommodations (p698), discount cards (p705) and food (p706).

Comfortable midrange accommodation starts at around $90 for a double room, not accounting for regional and seasonal variations. A two-course meal in an average restaurant without alcoholic drinks costs between $20 and $30, plus tax and tip. Drinks at a bar are usually in the $3 to $10 range (from bottled beers in a dive bar to top-shelf martinis at an upscale lounge). Museums charge anything up to $15, while attractions such as Disneyland will set you back $50 per person. Car rentals start at $20 per day, excluding tax and insurance.

HOW MUCH?

Pack of cigarettes $4.40

Cappuccino $2.50-3

Movie ticket $8-11

Theme park admission $43-60

Internet access per hour $5-12

TRAVEL LITERATURE

To get you in the mood for your trip, read some of these titles, which paint vivid pictures of the land and society you're about to visit.

My California: Journeys by Great Writers (2004) is an insightful collection of stories about the Golden State by 27 of its finest chroniclers, including Pico Iyer, Rubén Martinez, Patt Morrison and Carolyn See. Proceeds benefit the California Arts Council.

If you're headed for the Sierra Nevada, whet your appetite with any book written by John Muir. *My First Summer in the Sierra* (1911) is an especially inspiring and infectious account of how he first fell in love with this glorious region in 1869.

In *Where I Was From* (2003), Joan Didion's thoughts on California shatter palm-fringed fantasies as she skewers the rancidly rich, the violence and shallowness and describes her pioneering family's own history on this warped shore.

Desert rats should pick up Mary Austin's *The Land of Little Rain* (1903), an eloquent and poetic portrait of a harsh country and its intimate yet profound beauty.

Charles Phoenix' *Southern California in the '50s* (2001) and *Southern Californialand* (2004) are colorful, high-spirited pictorial romps taking you back to the era that gave birth to car culture, suburbia and Disneyland.

One of the first travelers to record his impressions of California was Richard Henry Dana, who visited the state in 1835 during the Mexican Rancho period. He recounts his thoughts in *Two Years Before the Mast*, a classic read that's still in print.

The Dharma Bums is Jack Kerouac's California-experiential book where he meets with bohemian San Franciscans, befriends a Buddhist

TOP TENS
Adventures
With its great ocean, mountains and deserts, California is pretty much tailor-made for adrenaline junkies. Whether you're young or not, single or family, novice or expert, there's certainly no shortage of exciting things to do. For more ideas, see p58 and the destination chapters.

- Scream your head off while rafting the ferocious American River (p319)
- Hang with the dawn patrol at Malibu's mythical Surfrider beach (p531)
- Go off-trail spelunking among the marble formations of Crystal Cave (p386) in Sequoia National Park
- Dangle from a ledge in the rock-climbing mecca of Joshua Tree National Park (p657)
- Traipse amidst the steamy landscape of Lassen Volcanic National Park (p288)
- Travel back in time along legendary Route 66 (p664)
- Brave the sensory onslaught (and potent margaritas) on Avenida Revolución in Tijuana (p632)
- Battle thin air on your way to the roof of the lower USA, Mt Whitney (p405)
- Party like a rock star and put your paycheck on the poker table in Vegas (p678)
- Try to stay sober while following the path of the *Sideways* crew (p482) in the Santa Barbara Wine Country

Festivities
Everybody loves a good party and Californians are especially keen on letting their hair down at festivals and special events year-round. Here's a list of favorites, but also have a look at the Festivals & Events sections in the destination chapters.

- Rose Parade (Pasadena, p532) January 1
- Coachella Valley Music & Arts Festival (Indio, p644) April/May
- Cinco de Mayo (Los Angeles, p532, and elsewhere) May
- Kinetic Sculpture Race (Arcata, p270) May
- Bay to Breakers Run (San Francisco, p108) May
- Pride Parades (San Francisco, p109, Los Angeles, p533) June
- Laguna Art Festivals (Laguna Beach, p583) July to August
- Reggae on the River (Garberville, p259) August
- Monterey Jazz Festival (Monterey, p447) September
- National Finals Rodeo (Las Vegas, p687) December

Tunes
What better way to get in the mood for your California adventure than with songs celebrating the Golden State in all its grit and glory?

- 'California Girls' (1965) Beach Boys
- 'California Dreamin'' (1966) The Mamas and the Papas
- 'California' (2002) Phantom Planet, theme from The *OC*
- 'Californication' (1999) Red Hot Chili Peppers
- 'California Love' (1996) 2Pac
- 'California' (1996) Tom Petty & the Heartbreakers
- 'It Never Rains in Southern California' (1973) Albert Hammond
- 'Back to California' (2004) Sugar Cult
- 'Streets of Bakersfield' (1988) Dwight Yoakam with Buck Owens
- 'Get Your Kicks on Route 66' (1976) Asleep at the Wheel

poet/roustabout and discovers the tranquil lessons and beauty of the High Sierra.

In *Road Angels* (2001) Kent Nerburn rediscovers his youthful West Coast haunts during a coastal trek where Steinbeck-ian characters divulge their insights into his Americana obsessions. It's a ride well worth sharing.

California Uncovered (2004), edited by Chitra Banerjee Divakaruni and sponsored by the California Council for the Humanities, is an insightful anthology of poems, profiles and essays by seasoned authors and fresh new voices about California's many different faces and complex, constantly evolving identity.

For a little more light-hearted reading, try Dianna Gessler's *Very California: Travels Through the Golden State* (2001), in which she captures her adventures and the state's character in whimsical watercolors and short vignettes.

INTERNET RESOURCES

California Department of Transportation (www.dot.ca.gov) Packed with tourist assistance, route planning, mapping assistance, highway information and weather conditions.

California State Parks (www.parks.ca.gov) Indispensable site for history, information and reservations at all state parks.

California Tourism (www.visitcalifornia.com) Links to all visitors centers throughout the state.

LonelyPlanet.com (www.lonelyplanet.com) Travel news and summaries, the Thorn Tree travel forum and links to other Web resources.

Roadside America (www.roadsideamerica.com) The 'online guide to offbeat attractions' covers lots of stuff they won't tell you about at the local tourist office.

Theme Park Insider (www.themeparkinsider.com) Visitors rate and evaluate rides and attractions at major theme parks in California and elsewhere.

Itineraries

CLASSIC ROUTES

GOLDEN STATE GRAND TOUR   Three to Four Weeks

Kick off your epic California adventure in **Los Angeles** (p494), where you'll be spoiled for choice with top-notch sights, legendary beaches and Southern California's (SoCal) best cuisine scene. Following a couple of metro-intense days, exchange urbanity for nature in **Sequoia and Kings Canyon National Parks** (p373) to gaze in awe at the world's biggest trees and a gorge deeper than the Grand Canyon. Nothing, though, can prepare you for the off-the-charts splendor of **Yosemite National Park** (p359), where your camera will have a love affair with thunderous waterfalls, chiseled

California is a rich quilt of spirit-lifting coast, mysterious deserts, exciting cities and awe-inspiring mountains. This grand, 2000-mile loop route can be 'done' in three weeks, but adding one, or even two, more will allow you to immerse yourself more deeply in the Golden State and its treats, treasures and temptations.

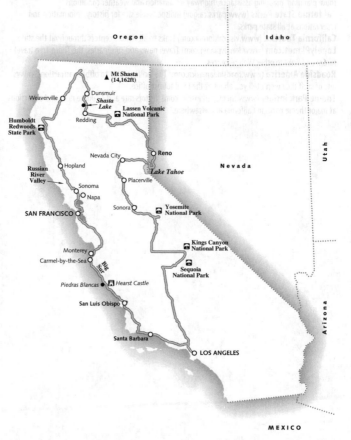

monoliths and meadows smothered in wildflowers. From here, head north on Hwy 49 through the heart of the mother lode, where the spirit of the Gold Rush still permeates such weathered towns as **Sonora** (p328), **Placerville** (p320) and **Nevada City** (p315).

A short drive east is **Lake Tahoe** (p333), a deep-blue jewel cradled by jutting peaks decorated with rugged hiking trails and the slopes of world-famous ski resorts. Veer north on Hwy 395, perhaps stopping in **Reno** (p351) for a spot of gambling, then cut west to unearthly **Lassen Volcanic National Park** (p288), a hellishly beautiful world of churning hot springs, odiferous fumaroles and steamy mud pots. Continue west to **Redding** (p284), then north on I-5, bisecting **Shasta Lake** (p287) on its way to mystical **Mt Shasta** (p297), which you'll spot edging into the sky from afar. Pay your respects to this majestic mountain, perhaps spending a night in **Dunsmuir** (p295), then prepare for the long, winding but scenic journey south on Hwy 3, through lake-studded Trinity Alps, to Gold Rush-era **Weaverville** (p306) with its famous Chinese temple.

Work your way southwest to fragrant and junglelike **Humboldt Redwoods State Park** (p260), where you'll encounter the tallest trees on earth while strolling on fern-fringed trails or driving along the imposing Avenue of the Giants. Following Hwy 101 south takes you from redwood country to wine country. **Hopland** (p249) is the gateway to the vineyards of Mendocino County, where the local drop is worth a tasting. The more famous grapes, though, grow south of here in **Sonoma Valley** (p191), **Napa Valley** (p215) and the **Russian River Valley** (p201).

After all this rural meandering you'll likely be ready for a dose of big-city culture, and what better place to find it than in **San Francisco** (p74), sitting proud and pretty on its gorgeous bay. South of here awaits a supremely beautiful stretch of coast starting in historic **Monterey** (p440), where a stop at the Monterey Bay Aquarium is de rigueur. From Monterey it's off to pint-sized **Carmel-by-the-Sea** (p451), the gateway to beguiling **Big Sur** (p454), whose timeless charms have inspired poets, painters, photographers, mystics and untold numbers of visitors. Take your own sweet time as you meander south along Hwy 1, stopping perhaps for a tour of impressive **Hearst Castle** (p461), watching elephant seals in **Piedras Blancas** (p460) or checking out the lively university town of **San Luis Obispo** (p466). Make **Santa Barbara** (p483) – a symphony of red-tile roofs, great architecture and restaurants – your final stop off before arriving back in LA.

COASTAL MEANDERINGS   Two Weeks

Start your coastal tour in **San Diego** (p587), where Balboa Park, the zoo and SeaWorld will capture your attention, before heading north to Riviera-like **Laguna Beach** (p581) and the überposh **Newport Beach** (p577). Perhaps make a quick detour to **Disneyland** (p568) before swooping down on **Los Angeles** (p494) for a spot of stargazing in Venice, Malibu and Santa Monica. North of here, posh and pretty **Santa Barbara** (p483) is the gateway to the wine country immortalized in the movie *Sideways*. In the college town of **San Luis Obispo** (p466) pick up Hwy 1, which skirts by agreeable beach towns, including **Morro Bay** (p463), and fantastical **Hearst Castle** (p461) on its way to soul-stirring **Big Sur** (p454), the Central Coast's boho heart. From there it's a quick drive to **San Francisco** (p74), which woos you with a cosmopolitan yet relaxed vibe.

North of San Francisco, the Pacific coast turns increasingly raw and untamed but remains drop-dead scenic as Hwy 1 skirts rocky shores, secluded coves, sweeping beaches and sandstone cliffs. The stretch between **Jenner** (p236) – the gateway to the **Russian River Valley** (p201) – and artsy, tiny **Mendocino** (p240) is especially scenic. **Fort Bragg** (p245) is worth a stop, perhaps for a ride on its vintage Skunk Train. Beyond here, Hwy 1 hooks inland, bypassing the remote **Lost Coast** (p261) and merging with Hwy 101 in Leggett. This is the start of 'Redwood Country,' home of the world's tallest trees, which are protected by a string of state and national parks, including **Humboldt Redwoods State Park** (p260), **Redwood National Park** (p274) and **Jedediah Smith Redwoods State Park** (p280). The latter is near fairly utilitarian **Crescent City** (p278), the northernmost coastal town, just shy of the Oregon border.

A ride along California's magical coast reveals eye candy at every bend of the road. Take your time as you travel along this 1000-mile-long rollercoaster of urban and natural delights. Resist the temptation to race through; its true charms want to be savored.

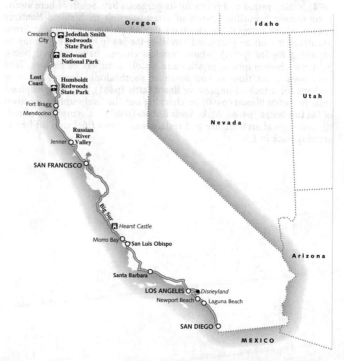

DESERT RAMBLINGS   10 Days to Two Weeks

Start your trip with a couple of days in dynamic **Los Angeles** (p494), then head east to retrochic **Palm Springs** (p638), the in-then-out-then-hip-again former hangout of Elvis and Sinatra. Sip margaritas poolside, hike along palm-studded canyons, then head up to a pine-scented alpine wonderland, all in one day. North of here, near-mystical **Joshua Tree National Park** (p654), with its piles of battered boulders and whimsically twisted namesake trees, has inspired many artists, most famously the band U2. Take time to linger and absorb the stark beauty of this land, then continue north to the **Mojave National Preserve** (p662), an empty and wonderfully quiet pastiche of sand dunes, mountains, volcanic cinder cones and sculpted rocks.

Ready for a change of pace? Step on it, then, and head northeast for **Las Vegas** (p678), baby. Sin City is exciting, seductive, outrageous and abso-lutely unique. Where else can you climb the Eiffel Tower, kiss your sweetie in a gondola and visit an Egyptian pyramid all in a couple of hours? Be-fore you gamble away your life savings, get back in the car for the drive west to **Death Valley National Park** (p666), where the desert puts on a truly spectacular show. Singing sand dunes, desert floor covered in saw-toothed miniature mountains, hills erupting in fireworks of color and mysteriously moving boulders are just some of the amazing features you'll see.

Heading west from Death Valley will take you from the lowest point in the country to the highest in the lower 48 states: **Mt Whitney** (p405). The drive along Whitney Portal Rd from the teensy town of **Lone Pine** (p404) takes you through the Alabama Hills, where many a Hollywood western was shot. From here it's about four hours back to LA.

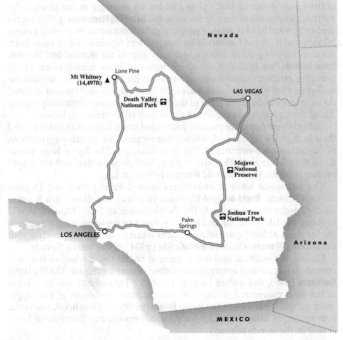

Open roads, big skies and breath-taking scenery await you on this 900-mile magical mystery tour through the California desert and the two great glamour capitals of Los Angeles and Las Vegas. Pack a good camera, a keen eye and an open mind.

TAILORED TRIPS

MILESTONES IN HISTORY

Think history is boring? Not in California, where it's been shaped by a colorful, often ingenious, sometimes ragtag bunch of friars, miners, charlatans, pioneers and visionaries. And let's not forget the land's original caretakers, the Native Americans who demonstrated amazing creative flourishes long before Hollywood arrived on the scene in the early 20th century. Just have a look at the pictographs in the **Chumash Painted Cave State Historic Park** (p483) near Santa Barbara.

It was Junípero Serra, a Spanish friar on a mission to bring God to the Indians, who paved the way for European settlement of California. And missions he built, 21 of them all told, starting with **Mission San Diego de Alcalá** (p600) in San Diego. Those in **San Juan Capistrano** (p584), **Santa Barbara** (p485) and **Carmel-by-the-Sea** (p451) are especially impressive.

Settlers soon arrived from Mexico and across America, many enduring long and arduous journeys. For a sense of just how treacherous things could get, visit the **Donner Memorial State Park** (p347) at the east end of Donner Lake. A museum here chronicles the fateful journey of the Donner Party, who became trapped in the Sierra in the harsh winter of 1846–47 and ended up resorting to cannibalism for survival. Southwest of here, in Sonoma, the **Bear Flag Monument** (p195) marks the brief period in 1846 when a gaggle of gutsy frontiersmen revolted against Mexico and declared California an independent republic. Three years later, the discovery of gold at Sutter's Mill, now part of the **Marshall Gold Discovery State Historic Park** (p320) touched off waves of mass immigration. Other evocative places to relive the rough-and-tumble Gold Rush era include the well-preserved ghost town of **Bodie** (p392), which sits in a state of arrested decay on a wind-battered plain in the Eastern Sierra, and **Virginia City** (p359), site of the Comstock Lode, one of the richest silver strikes in history.

Entirely new populations now descended upon California to try to find their luck in the mines and, when those petered out, in came agriculture, oil, aviation and, eventually, the film industry. The horse barn where Cecil B DeMille shot *The Squaw Man*, Hollywood's first feature-length movie, is inside the **Hollywood Museum** (p512) in LA.

The last major wave of newcomers arrived during the Great Depression via historic **Route 66** (p664), which you can still follow from Needles on the border with Arizona to the Pacific Ocean in Santa Monica. WWII brought hardship abroad and at home. For a heart-wrenching glimpse of life for the 120,000 Japanese Americans taken to internment camps, visit the stirring **Manzanar National Historic Site** (p404) in the Sierra Nevada.

During the political and social turmoil of the second half of the 20th century San Francisco emerged as a hotbed of counterculture. The **City Lights Bookstore** (p96), still owned by poet Lawrence Ferlinghetti, was the center of the Beat movement in the '50s. Across town, remnants of the hippie spirit survive – barely – in the funky **Haight** (p102) neighborhood, where the intersection of Haight and Ashbury Sts still evokes the 'Summer of Love' (1967) in the minds of many.

Map labels: Marshall Gold Discovery State Historic Park; Donner Lake; Nevada; Virginia City; Sonoma; Bodie; San Francisco; Manzanar National Historic Site; Carmel-by-the-Sea; Chumash Painted Cave State Historic Park; Santa Barbara; 66; Los Angeles; Arizona; San Juan Capistrano; San Diego

READY FOR YOUR CLOSE-UP?

Filmmakers were drawn to California for many of the same reasons visitors still are today – near-perfect weather and a rich tapestry of landscapes resembling everything from extragalactic space to steaming jungles. The capital of moviemaking is, of course, Los Angeles, where a gazillion movies have been shot, including the 1955 James Dean cult hit *Rebel Without a Cause* at the **Griffith Observatory** (p513), Ridley Scott's darkly futuristic 1982 *Blade Runner* in the **Bradbury Building** (p523) and the 1970 Robert Altman film version of *M*A*S*H* in **Malibu Creek State Park** (p518). South of here, in San Diego, the venerable **Hotel del Coronado** (p603) co-starred with Marilyn Monroe, Tony Curtis and Jack Lemmon in the timeless 1959 Billy Wilder comedy classic *Some Like It Hot*. To travel in the footsteps of Miles and Jack, the antiheroes of the surprise 2004 hit *Sideways,* head to the undulating roads meandering through the hilly **Santa Barbara Wine Country** (p482). Up the coast, the undulating **Guadalupe Dunes** (p473) starred in Cecil B DeMille's 1923 epic silent version of the *Ten Commandments*, while **Hearst Castle** (p461) stood in as the villa of Crassus in Stanley Kubrick's 1960 extravaganza *Spartacus*. The famously sexy beach scene between Burt Lancaster and Deborah Kerr in *From Here to Eternity* (1953) was not filmed in Hawaii but in **Big Sur** (p454). In nearby Monterey, the **Monterey Bay Aquarium** (p443) had a bit part in *Star Trek IV: The Voyage Home* (1986).

Film buffs can spend days tracking down locations in **San Francisco** (p74). The first talkie, Al Jolson's 1927 *The Jazz Singer,* was filmed near Union Sq. The 1979 *Escape from Alcatraz* with Clint Eastwood and the 1996 *The Rock,* starring Sean Connery, were both shot on location at the famous prison. And Frisco's vertiginous streets also formed the ideal backdrop for Hitchcock's 1958 nail-biter, *Vertigo*.

North of here, **Bodega Bay** (p234) will forever be associated with the creepy 1963 Hitchcock mystery *The Birds*. Still further north pretty **Ferndale** (p263) saw its 15 minutes of fame in the 1994 killer-virus thriller *Outbreak* starring Dustin Hoffman.

Lake Tahoe (p333) featured in Coppola's 1974 *The Godfather, Part II,* which was filmed on the west shore, and Mick Jackson's 1992 *The Bodyguard,* which was shot at Fallen Leaf Lake in South Lake Tahoe. South of here, scores of classic Westerns were made in the boulder-studded Alabama Hills in the Eastern Sierra town of **Lone Pine** (p404). The long list includes the 1938 *Yellow Sky* starring Gregory Peck, who returned in 1962 to shoot John Ford's *How the West Was Won*. The most famous Western of them all, *High Noon* (1952) with Gary Cooper, was partly filmed in the well-preserved Gold Rush town of **Columbia** (p327) in the Gold Country, as was Clint Eastwood's 1985 *Pale Rider*.

Fans of Percy Adlon's 1988 cult hit *Bagdad Café* still make the pilgrimage to this wind-battered roadside stop in **Newberry Springs** (p665), on legendary Route 66.

IT'S KIDDIE TIME

It's no secret: kids love California with its glorious beaches, reliable sunshine and bevy of theme parks, outdoor adventures and cool museums. Topping most of their must-do lists is, of course, **Disneyland** (p568), the original 'mouse house.' Here they can meet Mickey, Minnie and other classic Disney characters, scream at the top of their lungs on thrill rides and watch the sky catch fire during a spectacular fireworks show. The park's new neighbor, **Disney's California Adventure** (p569), celebrates the natural and cultural glories of the Golden State and also has some fun rides. Both Disney parks are in Anaheim not far from **Knott's Berry Farm** (p573), which gets

high marks for its neat Old West theme, several fun-but-scary thrill rides and the spookiest Halloween party around. Preteens adore the rainbow-colored fantasy world of rides, shows and attractions at **Legoland California** (p627), a quick drive south in Carlsbad. Tots can dig for dinosaur bones, pilot helicopters, earn their driver's license and do scores of other fun activities. San Diego, meanwhile, is all about animal magnetism. The famous **San Diego Zoo** (p599) has an entire Noah's Ark worth of critters, from cuddly koalas to playful pandas. **SeaWorld** (p606) is a watery zoo where you'll be entertained by the antics of Shamu, the killer whale, and his finned friends. Another highlight is the safari-style **San Diego Wild Animal Park** (p623), where large mammals such as giraffes and zebras roam 'freely' in large enclosures. Los Angeles, meanwhile, lets you take a peek at movie magic at **Universal Studios Hollywood** (p528), one of the world's largest film studios. Its movie-based theme park offers an entertaining mix of thrill rides, live action and audience-participation shows, plus a studio-backlot tram tour peppered with special effects. Rides at Universal are tame, though, compared to what awaits at **Six Flags Magic Mountain** (p559), where hair-raising rollercoasters should satisfy even the most speed-crazed teen.

Rides are a lot less frenzied at the nostalgic **Santa Cruz Beach Boardwalk** (p434), whose wooden rollercoaster and Louff carousel have brought smiles to generations of kids' faces. Along the coast, the awesome **Monterey Bay Aquarium** (p443) is a must-stop for encounters with sharks, sardines, jelly fish, sea otters and other aquatic creatures. Little ones can actually handle – carefully – slimy sea cucumbers and elegant starfish in the touch tanks.

San Francisco has plenty going on for tots, who'll love the novelty of riding a **cable car** (p134), the challenge of figuring out how to escape **Alcatraz** (p92) and the chance of pushing and pulling knobs at the interactive **Exploratorium** (p99) and **Zeum** (p100), both museums with a techno-science bent.

In the far north, swing by the **Turtle Bay Exploration Park** (p284) in Redding, which has a mesmerizing walk-through river aquarium and butterfly house. Inland, a wacky spot is the **Forestiere Underground Gardens** (p426) in Fresno, the subterranean home and garden of an Italian immigrant with a lot of verve and imagination.

Kids love the great outdoors and finding ways to keep them entertained should not be terribly challenging. Among the national parks, **Yosemite** (p359) does a great job of catering to kids with storytelling sessions, photography walks, nature exhibits and other 'wild' programs.

BIGGER, BETTER, BEST

California is truly a land of superlatives, no matter whether you're drawn to the desert, the mountains, the coast or the cities. You can climb to the top of 14,497ft **Mt Whitney** (p405), the tallest mountain in the lower 48 states, which dominates the sweeping massif of the Sierra Nevada. Only 80 miles east, you can stand 282ft below sea level in a foreboding landscape of crinkly salt flats called **Badwater** (p670), the lowest elevation in all of North America. It's in the heart of **Death Valley National Park** (p666), a timeless medley of canyons, sand dunes, oases and sculpted mountains that also holds the record for driest spot in the USA and for the highest temperature ever measured in the country: 134°F in July 1913. And at more than 5200 sq miles, it is also the largest national park outside Alaska.

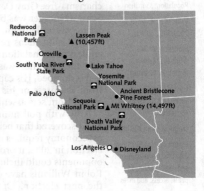

Between Mt Whitney and Death Valley, the stark and barren White Mountains are home to the **Ancient Bristlecone Pine Forest** (p403), which harbors the world's oldest tree, a gnarled and wind-battered specimen named Methuselah believed to have been a mere sapling some 4700 years ago. The world's biggest tree in terms of volume is not far from here in the Giant Forest of **Sequoia National Park** (p386). Called the General Sherman Tree, this massive conifer soars an impressive 275ft and has a base diameter of 36.5ft. To see the world's tallest trees, though, you'll have to travel north of San Francisco to the rugged North Coast, where behemoths taller than the Statue of Liberty can be found in **Redwood National Park** (p275) and elsewhere.

The state is also home to the world's longest aqueduct: the 444-mile California Aqueduct which includes the 770ft **Oroville Dam** (p417), the tallest in the USA. California also has the highest waterfall in North America: **Yosemite Falls** (p363) in Yosemite National Park, which plummets 2425ft in three tiers.

Want more records? Then head north to **Lassen Peak** (p288), the world's largest plug-dome volcano and still considered active even though the most recent eruption took place in 1915. At the **South Yuba River State Park** (p314) in the Gold Country, you can cross all 251ft of the longest single-span, wooden-truss covered bridge in the country, while Atherton near **Palo Alto** (p173) has the nation's most expensive zip code, based on a survey of real-estate values by *Forbes* magazine. **Lake Tahoe** (p333), meanwhile, lays claim to being the continent's largest 'alpine' lake and the highest in the country.

But California can't always be number one and there are at least a couple of near-misses. **Disneyland** (p568) ranks behind Orlando's Magic Kingdom in terms of visitor numbers and **Los Angeles** (p494) with four million people is 'only' the second-biggest city in the country after New York.

Snapshot

Electing a movie-star governor has its own tradition in California (remember Ronald Reagan?) and it continues with Arnold Schwarzenegger. In fact, given his recent string of flops, you might say that the state has its own tradition of electing *fading* movie stars as governor.

Arnold Schwarzenegger became the governor in 2003 through a weird quirk in the election laws (after a recall of the recently re-elected and charisma-free Gray Davis). As might be expected in this home of celebrity, Schwarzenegger was big news right from the start. His initial popularity ratings were sky-high, largely on his promise of bipartisan leadership.

But Californians seduced by his charm (and choosing to ignore his endless pronunciation of the state name as 'Cawl-lee-forna') soon learned that the governor was beholden to the same special interests that got Davis dumped. His cause wasn't helped by his refusal to answer questions from the press or his Hollywood-like inclination to make pronouncements from sets assembled at great expense by state workers.

Now with poll numbers that are worse than Davis', Schwarzenegger has discovered that being governor of the world's sixth (or seventh) largest economy requires more moxie than an ability to read lines. Up for re-election in 2006, it promises to be a fascinating campaign. Word that his opponents could include the likes of Warren Beatty, Rob Reiner or even Robin Williams have only added to the speculation and chatter around the next election. Of course any potential candidacies of those three might suffer from a downturn in support for actors-cum-politicians.

Meanwhile, politics isn't the only topic of the moment in the Golden State. Talk of the $500,000 'handyman special' long ago went from apocryphal to everyday reality. Despite frequent predictions that the ever-surging property prices are little more than a bubble and that financial ruin could happen at any moment, real-estate prices show no signs of abating. California's supposed love of freeways is now something more like a forced marriage as people move to 'affordable' new subdivisions two or more hours from their work (median price for a small home on former farmland: $350,000).

Culturally, the turmoil in the state's political and economic life has sparked the opposite in California's cultural life. The next big trend has yet to emerge and recent enthusiasms for everything from raw food to pint-sized motorcycles have proved to be mere diversions. In many ways California diverges from the rest of the USA; in some cases it's because the state is an early adopter of trends that others take up later (eg organic food), in others it's because the state just isn't like the rest of the country (eg gay rights). Right now there's much concern over the Bush Administration's gutting of environmental regulations and the right of the sick to use marijuana to ease their symptoms (see p255). Whether these become national trends remains to be seen.

Fast Facts

Population: 35 million

Value of gold mined in 2000: $155 million

Highest point: Mt Whitney (14,497ft, highest in 48 states)

Lowest point: Death Valley (-282ft, lowest in 48 states)

Length of coast: 880 miles

Length of coast free from any future development and with guaranteed public access: 880 miles

State slogan: Eureka! (Greek for 'I have found it!')

Percentage of vote for George Bush in 2004: 44% (51% nationally)

Number of Hollywood movies made annually: 250

Number of heads of lettuce grown annually in Salinas: over 200 million

History

THE BEGINNINGS

People have been migrating to California for thousands of years. Archeological sites indicate the state was inhabited soon after people came across the long-gone land bridge from Asia during an ice age as long as 25,000 years ago. Stone tools found in the Bakersfield area have been dated to around 8000 to 12,000 years ago. Many other sites across the state have yielded evidence, from large middens of sea shells along the coast to campfire sites in the mountains, of people from around 4000 to 8000 years ago.

The most spectacular artifact left behind by California's early inhabitants is their rock art, dating from 500 to 3000 years ago. It gives some idea of the cultural diversity of the indigenous populations, with five identifiable styles of pictographs (designs painted on rock with one or more colors) and five styles of petroglyphs (designs pecked, chipped or abraded onto the rock). Accessible sites include the Indian Grinding Rock State Historic Park in the Gold Country and the Chumash Painted Cave State Historic Park, near Santa Barbara.

California was named after a mythical island in a Spanish novel in the 17th century. The precise etymology and meaning of 'California' is not certain, but there is consensus that it's a derivation of 'Calafia,' the novel's heroine queen who ruled a race of gold-rich black Amazons.

CALIFORNIA'S INDIANS

The archeological evidence, combined with accounts from early European visitors and later ethnographic research, gives quite a clear picture of the Native Americans at the time of European contact. The indigenous peoples of California belonged to more than 20 language groups with around 100 dialects. Their total population ranged somewhere between 150,000 and 300,000, though some estimates run considerably higher. Native Americans lived in small groups and villages, often migrating with the seasons from the valleys and the coast up to the mountains.

California Indians used earthenware pots, fish nets, bows, arrows and spears with chipped stone points, but their most developed craft was basket-making. They wove baskets with local grasses and plant fibers and decorated them with attractive geometric designs.

There was some trade between the groups, especially between coastal and inland people, but generally they did not interact much, partly because even neighboring villages spoke different languages. Conflict among the groups was almost nonexistent. California Indians did not have a class of warriors or a tradition of warfare.

Several museums have good exhibits on Native American archeology and anthropology, such as the Phoebe Hearst Museum of Anthropology at the University of California (UC) Berkeley, the Museum of Man in San Diego and the Southwest Museum of the American Indian in Los Angeles.

EUROPEAN DISCOVERY

Following the conquest of Mexico in the early 16th century, the Spanish turned their attention toward exploring the edges of their new empire. Interest was spurred by tales of a fanciful golden island to the west.

In 1542 the Spanish crown engaged Juan Rodríguez Cabrillo, a Portuguese explorer and retired conquistador, to lead an expedition up the

TIMELINE

6000-10,000 BC	AD 1543
Native Californians have thriving communities across the state	Spanish explorer Juan Rodríguez Cabrillo investigates the California coast

West Coast to find the fabled land. He was also charged with finding the equally mythical Strait of Anián, an imagined sea route between the Pacific and the Atlantic.

When Cabrillo's ships sailed into San Diego harbor (which Cabrillo named San Miguel), he and his crew became the first Europeans to see mainland California. The ships sat out a storm in the harbor, then sailed north. They made a stop in the Channel Islands where, in 1543, Cabrillo fell ill, died and was buried. The expedition continued north as far as Oregon, but returned with no evidence of a sea route to the Atlantic, no cities of gold and no islands of spice. The Spanish authorities were unimpressed and showed no further interest in California for the next 50 years.

Around 1565, Spanish ships began plying the Pacific, carrying Mexican silver to the Philippines to trade for the exotic goods of Asia. These 'Manila galleons' often took a northerly route back to the Americas to catch the westerly winds, and they sometimes landed along the California coast. The galleons were harassed by English pirates, including noted booty plunderer Sir Francis Drake, who sailed up the California coast in 1579. Like many others, he missed the entrance to San Francisco Bay, but pulled in near Point Reyes (at what is now Drakes Bay) to repair his ship, which was literally bursting with the weight of Spanish silver. He claimed the land for his 'buddy' Queen Elizabeth, named it Nova Albion (New England), then left for other adventures.

In 1596 the Spanish decided they needed to secure some ports on the Pacific coast, and sent Sebastián Vizcaíno to find them. Vizcaíno's first expedition was a disaster that didn't get past Baja California, but on his second attempt, in 1602, he rediscovered the harbor at San Diego and gave it its present name. Contrary to his orders, he renamed many of the features of the coast and made glowing reports of the value of his 'discoveries,' in particular Monterey Bay, which he described as a protected harbor. Bureaucrats back home however were unimpressed by the reports and they were pigeonholed for 160 years.

> California is about 156,000 sq miles in area and is larger than Italy or Great Britain.

THE MISSION PERIOD

Around the 1760s, as Russian ships came to California's coast in search of sea otter pelts, and British trappers and explorers were spreading throughout the West, the Spanish king finally took notice. In order to protect the claim and promote the Catholic Church among the indigenous population, a combination of Catholic missions and military forts (presidios) was established in the new territory. Native American converts would live in the missions, learn trade and agricultural skills and ultimately establish pueblos that would be like little Spanish towns. Or so the plan went.

The first Spanish colonizing expedition, called the 'Sacred Expedition,' was a major undertaking, with land-based parties and supply ships converging on San Diego in 1769. On July 1 that year, a sorry lot of about 100 missionaries and soldiers, led by the Franciscan priest Junípero Serra and the military commander Gaspar de Portolá, struggled ashore at San Diego Bay. They had just spent several weeks at sea sailing from Baja California; about half of their cohorts had died en route, and many of the survivors were sick or near death. It was an inauspicious beginning for Mission San Diego de Alcalá (p600), the first of the chain of 21 California missions.

1769	1821
Padre Junípero Serra leads an expedition to set up the mission system	Mexican independence ends Spanish colonization of California

While Serra stayed in San Diego, Gaspar de Portolá continued north on land with instructions to establish a second Spanish outpost at Monterey. In a move replicated by fog-blinded tourists even today, Portolá went right past Monterey, continuing until they arrived at today's San Francisco Bay. Returning to San Diego, Portolá found Serra's party desperately awaiting an overdue supply ship and without a single Native American convert after eight months of recruitment. But just in the nick of time, a supply ship appeared over the horizon and newly fortified, Serra and Portolá returned north, actually found Monterey and established a presidio there. This is now the site of the excellent Monterey State Historic Park (p443).

Over time, three more presidios were founded, in San Diego (1769), Santa Barbara (1782) and San Francisco (1776). Ostensibly, the purpose of the presidios was to protect the missions and deter foreign intruders. In fact, these garrisons were little more than the fraternity boys from *Animal House* of their day, with resident soldiers spending their time raping and pillaging and doing little to protect Spanish claims.

Meanwhile, efforts to spread the word of God were hampered by the spread of disease. Native American populations on the missions were decimated by European illnesses, so the Spanish attempted to build up the pueblos in California with the families of soldiers and with civilians from Mexico. Sadly for the colonizers, these efforts also met with limited success as the new arrivals were much like the extras populating the town of an old western: they had no identifiable skills to benefit the community.

The missions did achieve modest success at farming, managing to just barely become self-sufficient, an essential achievement during the 1810–21 Mexican war for independence from Spain when supplies from Mexico were cut off completely.

As a way of colonizing California and converting the natives to Christianity, the mission period was an abject failure. The Spanish population remained small, the missions achieved little better than mere survival, foreign intruders were not greatly deterred and more Native Americans died than were converted.

THE RANCHO PERIOD

Upon Mexican independence in 1821, many of the new nation's people looked to California to satisfy their thirst for private land. By the mid-1830s the missions had been secularized, with a series of governors doling out hundreds of free land grants. This process gave birth to the rancho system. The new landowners were called rancheros or Californios; they prospered quickly and became the social, cultural and political fulcrums of California. The average rancho was 16,000 acres in size and largely given over to livestock to supply the trade in hide and tallow.

When intrepid explorer Jedediah Smith turned up in San Diego in 1827, the Mexican authorities were alarmed that the route from the east was not impassable. Frontiersman Kit Carson helped forge the Santa Fe Trail to Los Angeles in 1832. Yet the trails remained filled with peril as the Donner Party found on the Truckee Trail over the Sierra in 1846 (see p348).

American explorers, trappers, traders, whalers, settlers and opportunists increasingly showed interest in California, seizing on many of the prospects for profit that the Californios ignored in favor of ranching.

Richard Henry Dana records his impressions of 1835 California in *Two Years Before the Mast,* an excellent read about the rancho era.

1832	1846
Kit Carson helps blaze the Santa Fe Trail to Los Angeles	Blizzards cause the Donner Party of settlers to eat their own

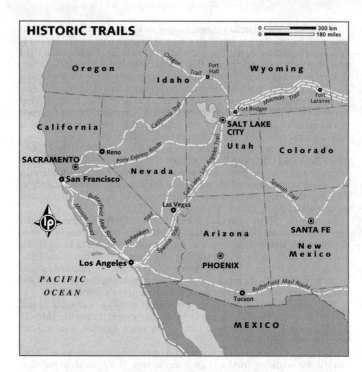

Some of the Americans who started businesses married locals, and assimilated into Californio society.

THE BEAR FLAG REPUBLIC & STATEHOOD

California Coast Trails is the delightful description of J Smeaton Chase's horseback ride along the length of California's coast in 1910 – a time when the state was on the cusp between its colonial past and the go-go days of its future.

Impressed by California's potential wealth and imbued with Manifest Destiny (the doctrine to extend the US border from coast to coast), US President Andrew Jackson sent an emissary to offer the financially strapped Mexican government $500,000 for California. Though American settlers were showing up by the hundreds, especially in Northern California, Jackson's emissary was tersely rejected. A political storm was brewing.

In 1836, Texas had seceded from Mexico and declared itself an independent republic. When the USA annexed Texas in 1845, Mexico broke off diplomatic relations and ordered all foreigners without proper papers to be deported from California. Outraged Northern California settlers revolted, captured the nearest Mexican official and, supported by US soldiers led by Captain John C Frémont, declared California's independence from Mexico in June 1846 by raising their 'Bear Flag' over the town of Sonoma (see p195). The Bear Flag Republic existed for all of one month. (The banner lives on, however, as the California state flag.)

Meanwhile, the USA had declared war on Mexico after the two countries clashed over the disputed Texas territory and the USA invaded

1848	1850
Gold is discovered near Auburn, setting off the great rush	California becomes the 31st state

---

RANCHO THIS & RANCHO THAT

Though it only lasted a couple of generations, the rancho period left a lasting mark on California. The vast landholdings often remained intact well into the 20th century – even after ranching operations had ceased – and proved a convenient purchase for developers. Thus, as you travel through the state, you will frequently see developments, towns and shopping centers with the word rancho in the name. Examples include Rancho Cucamonga near San Bernardino with a population over 150,000.

Where semiliterate rancheros once lived in crude dwellings and tended cattle there are now scads of chain restaurants whose diners live in a plethora of cookie-cutter tract homes with all the latest amenities.

Mexico. By July, US naval units occupied every port on the California coast, including the capital, Monterey. But militarily, California was a side show, as the war was mostly fought in Mexico.

When US troops captured Mexico City in September 1847, putting an end to the war, the Mexican government had little choice but to cede much of its northern territory to the USA. The Treaty of Guadalupe Hidalgo, signed on February 2, 1848, turned over California, Arizona and New Mexico to the USA. Only two years later, California was admitted as the 31st state of the United States.

THE GOLD RUSH

By an amazing coincidence, gold was accidentally discovered in Northern California within days of the signing of the treaty with Mexico. The discovery quickly transformed the future state. The population surged from about 14,000 at the time Mexican rule ended to more than 90,000 by 1849, as people from across the USA and other countries flooded into California.

The growth and wealth stimulated every aspect of life, from agriculture and banking to construction and journalism. As a result of mining, hills were stripped bare, erosion wiped out vegetation, streams silted up and mercury washed down to San Francisco Bay. San Francisco became a hotbed of gambling, prostitution, drink and chicanery, a situation that continues in some neighborhoods today.

Ostensibly under military rule, California had little effective government at all. The currency was a mixture of debased coinage, gold slugs and foreign cash; the main law was 'miners law,' an arbitrary and often deadly way of dealing with crimes – real or imagined. It was a free-wheeling time that rewarded those with the wiles to take advantage of it.

California experienced a second boom with the discovery of the Comstock silver lode in 1860, though the lode was actually over the border in what would soon become Nevada. Exploiting it required deep-mining techniques, which meant companies, stocks, trading and speculation. San Francisco made more money out of stocks than Nevada did out of mining: huge mansions sprouted on Nob Hill, and Californian businessmen became renowned for their audacity and earned the sobriquet 'robber-barons.'

THE TRANSCONTINENTAL RAILROAD

The transcontinental railroad was simple in conception, vast in scale and revolutionary in impact. It shortened the trip from New York to San

Cadillac Desert: The American West and Its Disappearing Water, by Marc Reisner, is a thorough examination of how the exploding populations of Western states have exploited and argued over every drop of available water.

1869	1906
The transcontinental railroad is completed linking California to the rest of the USA	Earthquake levels San Francisco; the city rebuilds in a few short years

Francisco from two months to four or five days and opened up markets on both coasts. Tracks were built simultaneously from Omaha in the east and Sacramento in the west, eventually converging in Utah in 1869. The track going east from Sacramento was financed by the Central Pacific Railroad, which hired thousands of Chinese laborers to get the job done. One of its principals, Leland Stanford, became state governor in 1863.

The American Civil War (1861–65) slowed down the import of goods from the East Coast to California, thus spurring local industry to pick up the slack. Agriculture diversified, with new crops (especially oranges) being grown for export. As California oranges found their way onto New York grocery shelves, coupled with a hard-sell advertising campaign, more and more easterners heeded the advice of crusading magazine and newspaper publisher Horace Greeley to 'Go west, young man.' California's population increased by 47% during the 1860s and by another 54% in the 1870s.

Inevitably the boom was followed by a bust in the late 1870s. Speculation had raised land prices to levels no farmer or immigrant could afford, the railroad brought in products that undersold the goods made in California, and some 15,000 Chinese workers, no longer needed for rail construction, flooded the labor market. A period of labor unrest ensued, which culminated in anti-Chinese laws and a reformed state constitution in 1879.

> Fresno is the self-proclaimed raisin capital of the world. Others: Gilroy and garlic, Castroville and artichokes, Half Moon Bay and pumpkins, Salinas and head lettuce

INDUSTRY & AGRICULTURE

Los Angeles was connected to the transcontinental railroad in 1876, when the Southern Pacific Railroad (SP) laid tracks from San Francisco to the fledgling city. The SP monopoly was broken in 1887, when the Atchinson, Topeka & Santa Fe Railroad Company laid tracks linking LA across the Arizona desert to the East Coast. The competition greatly reduced the cost of transport and led to more diverse development across the state, particularly in Southern California and the San Joaquin Valley. The lower fares spurred the so-called 'boom of the '80s,' a major real-estate boom lasting from 1886 to 1888. More than 120,000 migrants, mostly from the Midwest, came to Southern California in those years, many settling into areas developed from the former Spanish ranchos (see p31).

Farms tended to be developed by large companies, who had the necessary financial wealth to bring in irrigation and political clout to gain title to the huge tracts of land. Because of this, California never had the same level of family-farm traditions found in the Midwest. Among the outgrowths of this situation that still resonate today was the need of these huge 'agribusinesses' to get cheap labor by bringing in poor immigrants.

In the absence of coal, iron ore or abundant water, heavy industry developed slowly, something that left the state without the same aging industrial legacy that plagued much of the rest of the US in recent decades.

THE 20TH CENTURY

The population, wealth and importance of California grew dramatically throughout the 20th century. The big San Francisco earthquake and fire of 1906 destroyed most of the city, but it was barely a hiccup in the state's development – the population increased by 60% in the decade to 1910, reaching 2,378,000. The revolutionary years in Mexico, from 1910 to 1921, brought a huge influx of migrants from south of the border,

1928	1941
The *Jazz Singer*, the first 'talkie' movie, accelerates the worldwide demand for films, an industry centered in Hollywood	WWII transforms the state with military bases and rich defense contracts

re-establishing the Latino heritage that had been largely smothered by American dominance. The Panama Canal, completed in 1914, made bulk shipping feasible between the East Coast and West Coast.

During the 1920s, California's population grew by 2.25 million people to 5.7 million: a mammoth 66% increase, the highest growth rate since the gold rush. The Great Depression saw another wave of migrants, this time from the impoverished prairie states of the Dust Bowl, a phenomenon so movingly chronicled in John Steinbeck's *The Grapes of Wrath*.

WWII had a major impact on California, and not just from the influx of military and defense workers and the development of new industries. Women were co-opted into war work and proved themselves in a range of traditionally male jobs. Anti-Asian sentiments resurfaced at this time, many Japanese Americans were interned, and more Mexicans crossed the border to fill labor shortages. Many of the service people who passed through California actually liked the place so much that they returned to settle after the war.

Throughout the 20th century, a number of aspects of California life emerged as recurring themes.

Growth, Migration & Minorities

California's population has grown exponentially since it was admitted to the union in 1850, and most of the growth has come from immigration. This has resulted in a richly multicultural society, but also one in which race relations have often been strained.

Immigrants are typically welcomed in times of rapid growth, only to be rejected when times get tough. Chinese railroad workers, for instance, were in great demand in the 1860s but were victimized in the 1870s. The Webb Alien Land Law of 1913 prevented some Asian minorities from owning land. During WWII, upwards of 120,000 people of Japanese heritage – many of them American citizens – were forcibly placed in internment camps. African Americans came in large numbers to take jobs in the postwar boom, but often became unemployed when the economy took a downturn.

Mexican and Latin American workers still do most of the farm labor and domestic work, but in 1994, in the face of increasing unemployment and state government deficits, Californians voted in favor of Proposition 187, which denied illegal immigrants access to state-government services, including schools and hospitals. It is estimated more than 2.5 million illegal immigrants are currently in California, despite ongoing efforts to seal the notoriously porous border. Illegal immigration remains a volatile political

Chinatown (1974) is the fictionalized yet basically true account of the brutal water wars that were waged to build both Los Angeles and San Francisco.

California may produce almost 20 million gallons of wine a year but tomatoes bring in the most revenue.

EXPLOSIVE GROWTH

A classic cartoon shows Bugs Bunny arriving by mistake in postwar Los Angeles after he took a wrong turn at Albuquerque. Popping out of his hole and munching a carrot, Bugs is rapidly caught up in a nightmare world of houses popping up like weeds and new highways zipping across the land. It was a pretty accurate scene, as the state's population grew by 50% in the 1950s and continued at this clip until today (there are 37 million people). Granted, space is getting scarce, house prices have soared and as your car will know, the governor has cut highway funding to the lowest per capita of the 50 states, but people still keep coming.

1966	1968
Ronald Reagan is elected governor, setting a career precedent for fading film stars	The 'Summer of Love' heats up as hippies flock to San Francisco

topic, especially among conservatives who often ironically employ these people to tend their yards cheaply while also calling for their ouster.

The Military

During and after WWI, Douglas and the Lockheed brothers in Los Angeles, and Curtiss in San Diego, established aircraft industries. Two decades later, with another world war brewing, the aviation industry helped lift California out of the Great Depression. By the end of WWII, billions of federal dollars had been poured into Californian military contracts.

Good weather and the now alien concept of cheap land spurred the creation of huge military bases across the state as well as the accompanying military-industrial complex. California, more than any other place, was enriched by the Cold War and throughout the 1950s, '60s and '70s, California defense contractors helped spur the state's continuing growth. Many of the companies working on the space program were also based in California.

But the end of the Cold War in 1990 meant that the glory days of this business were over. Huge military bases, such as those that once dotted the San Francisco Bay Area, were closed and defense contractors moved or diversified. But other parts of the state's economy were surging and ultimately these changes mattered little.

The Film Industry

Few industries have symbolized California, and especially Los Angeles, more than movie-making. Independent producers were attracted here beginning in 1908 for numerous reasons. Southern California's sunny climate allowed indoor scenes to be shot outdoors – essential given the unsophisticated film technology of the day. Any location, from ocean to desert to alpine forest, could be realized nearby.

The industry has done a lot to promote California's image throughout the country and the world. As film, and later TV, became the dominant entertainment medium of the 20th century, California moved to center stage in the world of popular culture. TV viewers have largely watched a world based on Southern California, as most shows were produced close to the studios in Hollywood. And such dubious concepts as the 'Valley Girl' and 'Mall Rat' stem from this idealized lifestyle.

Social Change

Unconstrained by the burden of traditions, bankrolled by affluence and promoted by film and TV, California has always been a leader in new attitudes and social movements.

With 1950s affluence, the 'Beat' movement in San Francisco reacted against the banality and conformism of suburban life, turning to coffeehouses for jazz, philosophy, poetry and pot. When the postwar baby boomers hit their late teens, many took up where the Beat generation left off, rejecting their parents' values, doing drugs, dropping out and screwing around in a mass display of adolescent rebellion that climaxed, but didn't conclude, with the San Francisco 'Summer of Love' in 1967. Though the hippie 'counterculture' was an international phenomenon, California was at the leading edge of its music, its psychedelic art and its new libertarianism. Sex, drugs and rock and roll were big on the West Coast.

The Joy Luck Club (1993), based on Amy Tan's bestselling book, explores China old and China new, anchored in San Francisco's Chinatown.

LA Confidential (1997) captures the uneasy feel amidst rapid growth and rampant corruption in the city after World War II.

Hollywood Babylon, by Kenneth Anger, is the salacious account of the tawdry goings-on of Hollywood during its golden age.

1977	Late 1990s
The Apple II personal computer launches a new California industry	Dot-com multimedia wave rises and crashes over the San Francisco Bay Area

In the late '60s and early '70s, New Left politics, the anti–Vietnam War movement and Black Liberation forced their way into the political limelight, and flower power and give-peace-a-chance politics seemed instantly naive. Still, the ethos of the era remains very much a part of the state's collective culture – especially in the north. In Santa Cruz and Berkeley there are times when you'd think the 1960s had never ended, and the state's mild climate means that large numbers of original Volkswagen Beetles and microbuses have yet to fall prey to rust.

California has spawned a number of social movements. Gay Pride exploded in San Francisco in the '70s, and San Francisco is still the most openly, exuberantly gay city in the world.

In the late 1980s and '90s, California catapulted right to the forefront of the healthy lifestyle, with a mood-altering array of aerobics classes and self-actualization workshops on offer. Leisure activities, such as in-line skating, snowboarding and mountain biking, were industries spawned by California. Be careful what you laugh at. From pet rocks to hybrid cars, California's flavor of the month will probably be next year's world trend.

The Hollywood Walk of Fame, started in 1960, celebrates the city's film-making industry. It has more than 2000 stars.

Much of the radical and counterculture activity that is synonymous with the 1960s really took place in the early 1970s.

Technology

California has always been at the forefront of the technology revolution. In the 1950s, Stanford University in Palo Alto began leasing space to high-tech companies that might in some way benefit the university. Hewlett-Packard was an early tenant and this is now considered the germ cell of Silicon Valley (the term itself didn't achieve widespread use until the 1980s). Major Silicon Valley milestones were the inventions of the microchip by Intel in 1971 and the first widely popular personal computer (PC) by Apple in 1977.

In 1969 a UCLA computer science professor named Len Kleinrock first succeeded at sending data from a computer in Los Angeles to another at Stanford, 360 miles away. He typed in 'L' and, sure enough, the letter appeared on the screen in Palo Alto. He typed the letter 'O.' Same thing. Then he typed 'G' – and as billions of users since will empathize – the system crashed. But the Internet was born.

Silicon Valley and the rest of the state rode the first wave of the digital revolution with the development of the PC during the 1980s. Eventually this boom reached the end of its cycle and hundreds of businesses went bust. However, the state had become a hotbed of innovation and creativity and it was only a matter of time before another boom occurred. This time it was the World Wide Web on the Internet and it soon became the greatest investment bubble of all time. By the late 1990s unemployment in Silicon Valley had fallen to a near-mythical 0% and thousands of entrepreneurs were able to collectively secure billions in financing from lenders hoping to cash in on the next big thing. It was not unlike the Gold Rush 150 years before, only this time you could make millions with a business plan that said in essence: 'details to come.' Inevitably this boom crashed as well and as the state crossed the millennium, businesses (often with little more than a catchy name and snappy logo) closed by the score. With energy shortages bedeviling California there was something of a statewide funk.

Luckily, deep in the heart of the Golden State is the boundless optimism that the next big thing (nanotechnology? stem cell research?) will soon provide more of the good times that have been the promise for so long.

For an insightful look at the ethos of Silicon Valley at the start of the PC revolution go to www.folklore.org, which chronicles the development of the Macintosh by Steve Jobs and a host of others.

2003	2005
Arnold Schwarzenegger (aka The Governator) elected governor of California	Record rains bring mudslides in SoCal, flooding in Yosemite and a bazillion wildflowers in Death Valley

The Culture

The state of California has a particular, and some would say peculiar, place in the national psyche. Los Angeles and San Francisco are the Golden State's most dynamic cultural hubs.

Believe everything you've ever heard about Californians – as long as you realize that the stereotypes are almost always exaggerated. Sure, surfer boys shout 'Dude!' across the beaches around Los Angeles, self-made Silicon Valley millionaires have retired before the age of 30, and many people in Marin County own hot tubs, but in all, it's still hard to peg the population. Hippies who were in San Francisco during the 'Summer of Love' in 1967 aren't likely to live in the Haight-Ashbury district, which has undergone Gapification. Hollywood, a blighted neighborhood on the brink of revitalization, isn't where A-list stars reside anymore, and even major movie and TV studios have long since moved into the San Fernando Valley. Orange County (aka 'the OC') isn't a wealthy lily-white enclave any longer, and one of its congressional representatives in Washington DC is a Latina *and* a Democrat.

While most Californians are proud to be from the Golden State, they have to endure being the punch line of a lot of jokes on late-night talk shows. Part of the motivation is jealousy – California still has the allure of the American Dream, however broken it may be – and the other part is sheer disbelief at the crazy #*%! that goes on here. An action-hero movie star as governor? Celebrity trials where guilty defendants go free? We got 'em. California is literally as far west as you can go before you hit the Pacific, but to most Americans it's simply 'out there,' in terms of being outrageous, outlandish and over-the-top. Yet that doesn't stop Americans from spending more vacation dollars here than in any other state. California is still the trend-setter on the national scene, from iPods to yoga, reality TV to space tourism.

REGIONAL IDENTITY

How do Californians perceive themselves? The myth of a cultural divide between Northern and Southern California is mostly in the heads of NoCal denizens, many of whom scorn their SoCal counterparts. Some stereotypes are true: LA's obsession with body image does make beaches look like Baywatch, and the neighboring 'Silicone Valley' supports a multibillion-dollar porn industry. San Francisco really does have a vibrant queer community, with the historic Castro District still a stronghold. Napa and Sonoma Valleys are bursting with wineries. In Berkeley, left-wing zealots with 'Give Peace a Chance' bumper stickers give the finger to passing Hummers displaying 'Bush/Cheney 2004' stickers.

Just as often, you'll find the popular conceptions turned on their heads: hippies live in Topanga Canyon between LA and Malibu, Hollywood movie moguls work in state-of-the-art studios around San Francisco, and as many of America's rich and famous live in Palm Springs and the Coachella Valley as in Beverly Hills and Bel Air. The state is as divided by racial color lines as it is by geography. East LA and West LA are worlds apart, with the former being as Latino as the latter is white, while South Central is predominantly African American.

Politically, California is both progressive and retrograde. On social issues it leads the way, but also shows the rest of the country just how bad things can get. Protests during the Vietnam era began here, as did 21st-century

---

Over 60% of Californians admit to having hugged a tree, and one in four has surfed.

Mike Davis' *City of Quartz* (1990) is an excoriating history of LA and a glimpse into its possible future; in *Ecology of Fear*, he examines natural disasters and destruction in the LA Basin.

MoveOn.org, an online movement for more direct participation on the political left by younger, Net-savvy voters. But the state also bears the mantle of disastrously stupid political moves, such as propositions passed and later declared unconstitutional, or the deregulation of public utilities.

Just two parties dominate California (and US) politics. Republicans are more conservative and opposed to big government; Democrats are more liberal and support a more active role for the federal government. Independent parties, such as Libertarians or the Green Party, are insignificant in terms of elected representation, but they do provide alternative voices and perspectives that inform policy. Traditionally, Northern California and most urban areas, especially Los Angeles, vote Democrat, while the state's rural heartland, affluent San Diego and coastal counties favor Republican candidates. California is currently helmed by Arnold Schwarzenegger, a Republican. He came to power in a 2003 recall election that ousted Democrat Gray Davis.

LIFESTYLE

California is a state of extremes – from the palm-tree-lined streets and palatial mansions of Beverly Hills to yoga-centric, politically active San Francisco; from the embattled neighborhoods of the East Bay to the rural farmlands of the San Joaquin Valley. Almost half of all Californians reside in cities, but nearly as many live out the American dream in the 'burbs. After all, SoCal is one of the birthplaces of planned communities. Just over 5% of Californians live in rural areas, including on Native American tribal reservations, which account for just 0.6% of the total land in the state.

Who exactly is the average Californian? A 34-year-old white or Latino heterosexual, female, high-school graduate living in the LA Basin who moved here from another state less than 10 years ago. She probably rents her apartment or home, works in the service industry, commutes almost 30 minutes each way, and spends one dollar out of every five on car-related expenses, either paying off a loan, maintaining a vehicle, having it insured or filling up the gas tank. She votes independently, rather than with a party. She has a child, but is less likely to be married; cohabitation here is on the rise. She can expect to live for more than 80 years, longer than the US average – if she's lucky enough to be able to afford health insurance.

California has the world's seventh-largest economy, but much of the money is concentrated in the hands of a few. Women earn just 80¢ on the male dollar. The richest counties (Marin, San Francisco and San Mateo) are all in the Bay Area, though some of America's richest individuals live in SoCal – in places like Malibu, Bel Air and Pacific Palisades. There's also a significant middle class, with the average Californian earning $33K annually, the 10th-highest rate of any US state and comfortably above the national average. The state's poorest towns are found in the inland valleys and southern deserts, as well as in the northern mountains and northern coastal areas. Unemployment usually runs higher here than elsewhere in the country. The most recent recession started in 2001 at the end of the dot-com boom, when start-up companies lost investors. It's unusual to meet someone in Silicon Valley who hasn't been unemployed sometime during the last decade.

Despite regional or political differences, in everyday life people tend to be pleasant, sometimes to a fault. There are exceptions, but often everyone is so determined to get along that it can be hard to find out what they really think. Political correctness thrives. The jargon of self-help has completely infiltrated the daily language of many Californians. Unless you've mastered the lexicon, you can't be sure what precisely the speaker is trying to

California Babylon: A Guide to Sites of Scandal, Mayhem, and Celluloid in the Golden State by Kristan Lawson and Anneli Rufus is a bizarre, off-the-wall guide to infamous spots hidden all over the state.

Surfing was not invented in California. It was the traditional sport of Hawaiian royalty.

Riptionary (www .riptionary.com), the world's most definitive online lexicon of surfer slang, will help you translate stuff like 'The big mama is fully mackin' some gnarly grinders!'

Two out of every five Californians speak a language other than English at home. Over 200 different languages in total are spoken in the state, with Tagalog, Japanese and Persian in the top 10.

convey. For example, the word 'issue' gets bandied about frequently – it's usually a polite way to refer to someone else's problems without implying that the person has…well, problems. There's also the lingering influence of 1960s hippie-speak, plus surfer slang and hip-hop terminology.

However, all of this laid-back vernacular flies out the window on the always-busy freeways; a driver's extended middle finger is often the only medium of communication. Road rage is a serious problem, especially in LA. If you plan to do any driving, before you put the key in the ignition, take a deep breath and meditate on remaining calm. Expect to encounter people who won't hesitate to cut you off without signaling and then flip you off. Factor it in, let it go and don't engage the other driver in a game of one-upmanship. Rumors of freeway shootings are not urban legends, but take heart – they're not the norm.

Homelessness is a bigger problem. Over 350,000 people have no place to live. Some on-street beggars are suburban teens who have taken a joyride, but most homeless people are more troubled, whether they've become addicted to drugs or alcohol, or suffer from mental illnesses (long-term care facilities began outpatient release programs in the 1970s). Then there are the working poor who've been bankrupted by the high cost of medical care. Remember that homeless people are more likely to be victimized than to cause you harm. Whether you give them money or not is up to you, though a donation to a local charity may help more.

California Indians: A Source Book, edited by Robert Fleming Heizer, is a wide-ranging introduction to the state's network of West Coast tribes, with essays on ecology, linguistics and history, including ghost dances.

POPULATION & MULTICULTURALISM

California is the most populous US state: one in every eight Americans lives here. It's also one of the fastest growing states, with three of America's biggest cities (Los Angeles, San Diego and San Jose) and a half million new residents each year. Almost half of these nouveau Californians land in LA, Orange or San Diego Counties, which are the most densely populated areas. The statewide population density is over 200 people per sq mile – almost triple the national average. Over half of native-born Americans who live here came from another state, and most likely not that long ago.

Ever since California gained statehood in 1850, most of the state's growth has come from immigration. This has resulted in a richly multicultural society, as the state's racial makeup continues to shift. Hispanic, Latino and Asian populations are steadily increasing, while the number of whites is declining. The 2000 US Census found whites made up just 47% of California's population, and Hispanics and Latinos weren't far behind, accounting for just over 32%. In contrast, African Americans comprised less than 7% of the population, Asians and Pacific Islanders about 11% and Native Americans at most 1%. Nearly one in four California residents is foreign-born – including the state's celebrity governor, Arnold Schwarzenegger – and most have arrived within the past decade. Most immigrants live in cities and bring their cultures and languages with them, creating textured neighborhoods and districts, particularly in LA, where most of California's 'just-off-the-boat' immigrants live.

The Alliance of California Tribes (www.alliance ofcatribes.org) is a coalition of Native Californians with online news, historical background and myriad links.

In fact, one of every four immigrants to the USA lands in California; Mexicans are the largest group. From radio and TV stations to Spanish-language billboards, you'll see and hear Latino culture everywhere. Despite upward mobility, Mexican and Latin American workers still do most of the farm labor and domestic work, and some are without proper papers. An estimated two million illegal immigrants (always a politically hot topic) currently live in California. In 1994, in the face of increasing unemployment and state government deficits, Californians voted in favor of Proposition 187, which denied illegal immigrants access to state government services,

THE STATE OF SPANGLISH

California, where Spanish is spoken by about 5.5 million people, often seems like a bilingual state. The most contested issue is bilingual education, with strong opinions on both sides about the effects of Proposition 227 which, after 1987, curtailed bilingual education in favor of 'mainstreaming' students into English. Some educators argue that it would benefit all children in California to be fluent in two languages and it's hard not to agree, given the state's demographic trends.

Prevalent among a younger Latino generation is 'Spanglish,' which linguists label 'code switching' and purists like Octavio Paz call 'abominable.' Spanglish blurs the lingual boundaries across California (and Miami, New York, Texas and Puerto Rico), all in the same thought. Speakers speed up sentences with the shortest words available in either language and adopt hybrid terms; for example, *lonche* instead of *almuerzo*.

Geographical features and towns up and down the California coast that have Spanish names more often reflect early colonial history rather than the current state of the population. The many Spanish names of suburban streets reflect the desire of developers to come up with something exotic. Wouldn't you rather live on Via de la Valle than Valley Rd?

including schools and hospitals. (One state senator called it 'the last gasp of white America in California.') Legal challenges blocked Proposition 187 from becoming law, but knee-jerk anti-immigration sentiment remains, especially in pockets of white supremacists and neo-Nazis.

Nearly 40% of the USA's Asian Americans live in California.

California's astonishingly diverse population is both its weakness and its strength. Race-related incidents receive high-profile exposure, as with the 1992 Los Angeles riots following the acquittal of four white police officers charged with beating Rodney King. Yet you rarely hear of the day-to-day civility between races. The arrival of people from every corner of the globe makes California one of the most tolerant, cosmopolitan and open-minded societies on the planet. It also creates plenty of diversity in language, religion and every other element of culture, especially in the urban areas where most immigrants live. Still, Anglo-English predominates.

RELIGION

Like much of the West, California is less churchgoing than the American mainstream. One in five Californians professes no religion at all; about a third are Catholic due, at least in part, to a large Latino population; and another third are Protestants. Right-wing Christian fundamentalists are rare – this is California, after all, not the Bible Belt. California has sizable numbers of Muslims, Hindus, Sikhs, Baha'is and members of every other faith you can think of, thanks to immigration. Mosques, temples, synagogues and other religious centers abound. As many as 40% of all Buddhists living in the US reside around LA and there are more Jews here than in Tel Aviv.

LA has thousands of believers in Santeria, a fusion of Catholicism and Yoruba (Nigerian) beliefs first practiced by West African slaves in the Caribbean and South America. Drop by one of the city's hundreds of *botanica* shops for a lucky charm.

As a famously tolerant and laid-back kind of place, California is also home to a number of unusual religious persuasions, from satanic churches to faith healers. Aimee Semple McPherson popularized one of Christianity's first Pentecostal sects, the International Church of the Foursquare Gospel, in 1920s Los Angeles. Today it has over 3.5 million adherents worldwide. Meanwhile, Wicca has been forecast to become the third-largest religion in the US within a decade, a fact that California obviously has much to do with. From its earliest days, the state has had utopian religious communities tucked away in isolated places as well.

Modern 'Cultifornia' has made national headlines, starting with South Asian swamis and Charles Manson in the 1960s, Jim Jones and est in the 1970s and Heaven's Gate just before the turn of the 21st century. The Church of Scientology, which has been around since the 1950s,

Mind-control cult, trendy fad or true religion? You be the judge of all those wacky Californian belief systems after getting all the background at FACTNet (www.factnet.org).

forcibly insists it's a religion (with IRS tax-exempt status to 'prove' it), often silencing its critics with lawsuits and harassment. It has made major inroads into Hollywood – one of the most outspoken apostles of this belief system, which was instigated by sci-fi writer L Ron Hubbard, is Tom Cruise.

SPORTS

California boasts more professional sports teams than any other state. If you're in Los Angeles, San Francisco, Oakland or San Diego, depending on the season, you'll have your pick of NFL football, NBA basketball or major-league baseball action. Pro games can be sold out – especially 49ers, Raiders and San Diego Chargers football, LA Lakers basketball and LA Kings hockey matches – so buy tickets early. You probably won't have to sell your firstborn child to score a ticket to pro men's or women's (WNBA) basketball in Sacramento, pro hockey in Anaheim and San Jose, or pro soccer and arena football action in San Jose or LA.

Intercity and intracity rivalries can be intense, so when football's San Francisco 49ers play the Oakland Raiders, basketball's LA Lakers play the LA Clippers or baseball's San Francisco Giants play the LA Dodgers or the Oakland A's take on Anaheim's Angels, you best just stand back. Patrons of college sports rivalries, like UC Berkeley's Cal Bears vs the Stanford Cardinals or the USC Trojans vs the UCLA Bruins, are even more insane. In 2005, there was SoCal outrage over the Anaheim Angels renaming themselves the Los Angeles Angels of Anaheim, which is stretching the point geographically. Anaheim's civic leaders, who had custom-built the team their own stadium back in the 1960s, decided to sue and at press time a trial was pending.

Beach volleyball, now an Olympic sport, started in Santa Monica in the 1920s.

Excepting championship play-offs, the regular season for major-league baseball runs from April to September, major-league soccer from April to mid-October, WNBA basketball from late May to August, NFL football from September to early January, NHL ice hockey from October to March and NBA basketball from November to April. Professional beach volleyball (www.avp.com) holds major tournaments every summer at Hermosa and Manhattan Beaches near LA. Motor sports are an obsession, especially inland at Bakersfield.

ARTS

Throughout the 20th century and into the 21st, LA has been a mecca for artistic talent, quite the opposite of the cultural black hole many expect. And thanks to the movie industry, no other city can claim the pop-cultural influence that LA exerts worldwide. Southern California in particular has proved to be fertile ground for new architectural styles. Meanwhile, San Francisco's liberalism and humanistic tradition have long established the Bay Area as a center for the arts – modern writers and musicians have been seeking inspiration there for decades.

During the 1940s, F Scott Fitzgerald, Ernest Hemingway and Tennessee Williams all did stints as Hollywood screenwriters.

Film & TV

California's primary art forms – film and TV – are also major exports. They've got a powerful presence in the lives of not only Americans, but people around the world. Images of California are distributed far beyond its borders, ultimately reflecting back upon the state itself. Few tourists arrive without some cinematic reference to the place – nearly every street corner has been or will be a movie set. With increasing regularity, Hollywood films feature California not only as a setting but as a topic and, in

TOP 10 FILMS ABOUT CALIFORNIA

■ *Maltese Falcon* (1941) – Humphrey Bogart plays Sam Spade, the classic San Francisco private eye, in this murder mystery directed by John Huston.

■ *Sunset Boulevard* (1950) – Billy Wilder's classic, starring Gloria Swanson and William Holden, is a dramatic study of how Hollywood discards its aging stars.

■ *Vertigo* (1958) – Alfred Hitchcock's movies often used California locales, like this San Francisco psychological thriller with star-crossed lovers Jimmy Stewart and Kim Novak.

■ *The Graduate* (1967) – In status-hungry middle-class California, Dustin Hoffman finds true love after crossing the Bay Bridge to Berkeley (in the wrong direction). Here's to you, Mrs Robinson!

■ *American Graffiti* (1973) – For a taste of life in a small Central Valley town on a summer night in '62, check out George Lucas' tribute to cruising.

■ *Chinatown* (1974) – The greatest film ever made about LA is Roman Polanski's story of early-20th-century water wars.

■ *Blade Runner* (1982) – Ridley Scott's sci-fi thriller, featuring Harrison Ford, projects Los Angeles far into the 21st century, with high-rise corporate fortresses set starkly against chaotic, neglected streets.

■ *LA Story* (1991) – Steve Martin lovingly wrote this hilarious, though dated, parody of nearly every aspect of LA life, from enemas to earthquakes.

■ *The Player* (1992) – Directed by Robert Altman and starring Tim Robbins, the film is a satire on the Industry, featuring dozens of cameos by the very actors being spoofed.

■ *Sideways* (2004) – An Oscar-winning, but bizarre bachelors' romp through the Santa Barbara Wine Country.

some cases, almost as a character. Los Angeles especially loves to turn the camera on itself, often with a dark film-noir angle.

'The Industry,' as it's called, grew out of the humble orchards of Hollywoodland. The silent-movie era gave way to 'talkies' after 1927's *The Jazz Singer* premiered in downtown LA, ushering in Hollywood's glamorous Golden Age. Today, Hollywood is no longer the focus. The high cost of filming in Los Angeles has sent location scouts beyond the San Fernando Valley (where most movie and TV studios are found) and north of the border to Canada, where they're welcomed with open arms in 'Hollywood North,' particularly in Vancouver, Toronto and Montréal. A few production companies are still based in the Bay Area, including Francis Ford Coppola's Zoetrope and George Lucas's Industrial Light & Magic, made up of high-tech gurus who produce computer-generated special effects for Hollywood blockbusters. Pixar Animation Studios is in Emeryville, near Berkeley.

The first TV station began broadcasting in Los Angeles in 1931. Ever since then, TV producers have loved fabricating 'facts' about SoCal in shows like *Baywatch* and *Melrose Place*. In the 1990s, *Beverly Hills 90210* made the zip code of one of SoCal's ritziest neighborhoods famous. Now it's *The OC*, set in Newport Beach, that glamorizes teenage angst. *Six Feet Under* shows modern LA through the eyes of a bizarre family running a funeral home. More biting social satire is the fare of *Curb Your Enthusiasm*, by *Seinfeld* co-creator Larry David. Watch any TV program you want at LA's Museum of Television and Radio (p516) or join a live studio audience yourself (p529).

In *The Other Hollywood: The Uncensored Oral History of the Porn Film Industry*, Legs McNeil, Jennifer Osborne and Peter Pavia interview an encyclopedia's worth of XXX stars and trace the rise of porno chic.

Literature

CaliforniaAuthors (www
.californiaauthors.com)
gives the inside scoop on
West Coast publishing,
with online excerpts
from new works, blogged
author readings, lists of
literary awards and links
to indie bookstores.

The West Coast has always attracted artists and writers, and today the California resident literary community is stronger than ever including talent such as: Alice Walker, Pulitzer Prize-winning author of *The Color Purple*; Chilean novelist Isabel Allende; Dorothy Allison, author of *Bastard Out of Carolina*; Amy Tan, who writes popular fiction like *The Joy Luck Club*; Maxine Hong Kingston, co-editor of the landmark anthology *The Literature of California*; Dave Eggers, the hipster behind *McSweeney's* quarterly literary journal; Michael Chabon, author of the Pulitzer Prize-winning *The Amazing Adventures of Kavalier and Clay*; and Adrienne Rich, a progressive feminist poet. Many of these contemporary voices contributed to *My California: Journeys by Great Writers* (p17).

Few writers nail California culture as well as Joan Didion. In *Where I Was From* (2003), the author contrasts the mythology of California with the actuality of life in the Golden State. She's best known for her collection of essays, *Slouching Towards Bethlehem* (1968), which takes a caustic look at flower power and Haight-Ashbury. Tom Wolfe also put '60s San Francisco in perspective with *The Electric Kool-Aid Acid Test* (1968), which follows Ken Kesey's band of Merry Pranksters, who began their acid-laced 'magic bus' journey in Santa Cruz. Hunter S Thompson chronicled the death throes of hippiedom in *Fear and Loathing in Las Vegas* (1971). Charles Bukowski's semi-autobiographical novel *Post Office* (1971) captured down-and-out downtown LA. Richard Vasquez's *Chicano* (1970) took a dramatic look at LA's Latino barrio.

The El Chupacabra craze
took hold in Los Angeles
in 1996, when Mexican
folktales about a notori-
ous goat-sucking vampire
spread like wildfire, even
leading people to keep
their children home from
school.

Arguably the most influential author to ever emerge from California was John Steinbeck, who was born in Salinas in 1902. Steinbeck focused attention on the farms of the Central Valley. His first California novel, *Tortilla Flat* (1935), takes place in Monterey's Mexican American community, while his masterpiece, *The Grapes of Wrath* (1939), tells of the struggles of migrant farm workers. Eugene O'Neill took his 1936 Nobel prize money and transplanted himself near San Francisco, where he wrote the autographical play *Long Day's Journey into Night*.

After the chaos of WWII, the Beat Generation brought about a new style of writing: short, sharp, spontaneous and alive. Based in San Francisco, the scene revolved around Jack Kerouac, Allen Ginsberg and Lawrence Ferlinghetti, the Beats' patron and publisher. Poet-painter-playwright Kenneth Rexroth, considered the father of the San Francisco Renaissance, was instrumental in advancing the careers of several Bay Area writers and artists, including the Beats. He shared an interest in Japanese traditions with Buddhist Gary Snyder, a Beat poet of deep ecology, whose first book *Riprap* meditates on Yosemite.

California Poetry: From
the Gold Rush to the
Present, edited by Dana
Giola, Chryss Yost and
Jack Hicks, is a ground-
breaking anthology with
enlightening introduc-
tions that give each poet
their deserved context.

Back in the 1930s, San Francisco and Los Angeles became the capitals of the pulp detective novel, which were often made into noir films. Dashiell Hammett *(The Maltese Falcon)* made San Francisco's fog a sinister character. The king of hard-boiled crime writers was Raymond Chandler, who thinly disguised his hometown of Santa Monica as Bay City. A 1990s African American renaissance of crime fiction was masterminded by James Ellroy *(LA Confidential)*, Elmore Leonard *(Jackie Brown)* and Walter Mosley *(Devil in a Blue Dress)*.

Oakland was famously scorned by Gertrude Stein (who lived there briefly) when she quipped, 'There is no there there,' although, to be fair, she was really only saying that she couldn't find her old house when she returned from Europe. Professional hell-raiser Jack London also grew up in Oakland. He turned out a massive volume of writings, including tales of the late-19th-century Klondike Gold Rush. Zooming into the modern

---

TOP FIVE LITERARY DETOURS IN CALIFORNIA

To connect with the landscapes that inspired some of California's greatest writers:

- Stay at a **mountaintop fire lookout** (p562) like Jack Kerouac did in the summer of 1956. The **USDA Forest Service** (☎ 877-444-6777; www.fs.fed.us/r5/rwhr/rentals.html) handles some rentals.

- Soak up the atmosphere at San Francisco's **City Lights Bookstore** (p77), co-founded by Beat poet Lawrence Ferlinghetti.

- Drop by Heinold's historic **First & Last Chance Saloon** on Oakland's Embarcadero (p159), where Jack London used to knock back a few drinks; the writer's Yukon cabin stands nearby.

- Wander in downtown **Salinas** (p474), where time has stood still since Steinbeck's early days, then take a *Grapes of Wrath*–style drive into the Mojave Desert on **Route 66** (p664).

- Make a literary pilgrimage: into the wilderness of **Jack London State Historic Park** (p200); to poet Robinson Jeffers' beachside **Tor House** (p452) in Carmel; or to the **Eugene O'Neill National Historic Site** (p171) near Danville.

---

age, UC Berkeley grad Philip K Dick is chiefly remembered for his science fiction, notably *Do Androids Dream of Electric Sheep?* (1968). Ursula K Le Guin, a lauded fantasy writer, feminist and essayist, was born in Berkeley. Back in SoCal, Ray Bradbury wrote the 1950s dystopian classic *Fahrenheit 451* in Venice Beach.

Music

From smoky jazz clubs that once filled the streets of San Francisco's North Beach to hard-edged West Coast rap and hip-hop born in South Central LA, California has rocked the world.

In the 1930s and '40s, big swing bands toured in LA. After WWII, the West Oakland blues sound developed up north, while the bebop of Charlie Parker and Charlie Mingus made LA swing, especially on Central Ave in the African American community. LA's *Swingers*-style revival of the 1990s is over, but swing fans are still drawn to the sassy, bluesy belting of Lavay Smith and Her Red Hot Skillet Lickers in San Francisco. The cool West Coast Jazz of Chet Baker and Dave Brubeck evolved in the 1950s in San Francisco's North Beach, Hollywood and Hermosa Beach near LA. It was pioneered by the stylings of legendary trumpeter Miles Davis.

At the same time, doo-wop, rhythm and blues, and soul music grew strong in South Central LA's nightclubs, which rivaled New York's Harlem. At the hub of a thriving Watts musical scene was Johnny Otis, who can be heard on his Saturday-morning radio show on Berkeley's KPFA 94.1FM. In the 1960s, Sam Cooke performed hit after hit and ran his own record label, attracting soul and gospel talent to Los Angeles. By that time, the hard-edged, honky-tonk 'Bakersfield Sound' had already emerged inland. Legendary Buck Owens and his Buckaroos still play most weekends at the Crystal Palace (p430).

Rock and roll found a revolutionary home in California from its natal years. The first homegrown talent to make it big in the '50s was Richie Valens, whose 'La Bamba' was a rockified version of a Mexican folk song. In the '60s, Jim Morrison and the Doors busted onto the Sunset Strip. Meanwhile, San Francisco had launched the psychedelic revolution with big-name acts like the Grateful Dead and Janis Joplin.

The late '70s and early '80s saw the emergence of California's brand of punk, which grew up around skateboard culture. In LA, the rockabilly-edged band X stood out, while Black Flag led the hard-core way with

Taste a real slice of the state's heartland by reading *Highway 99: A Literary Journey Through California's Central Valley*, edited by Oakland-based writer Stan Yogi. It's full of multicultural perspectives, from early European settlers to 20th-century Mexican and Asian immigrant farmers.

Acclaimed writers, from John Muir to Gary Snyder, have written about California's awe-inspiring scenery. Look for their work in two outstanding anthologies, *Natural State: A Literary Anthology of California Nature Writing* and *Unfolding Beauty: Celebrating California's Landscapes*.

TOP FIVE UNIQUE CALIFORNIAN SOUNDS

■ Beck – LA-born Beck Hansen is the absurd lyricist of electronica, mixing sampled sounds with beatnik stylings to create postmodern pop rock. His most recent album, *Guero* (2004), bends genres.

■ Tom Waits – With a voice rusted over from bottom-shelf bourbon and filterless cigarettes, Pomona-born Tom Waits was influenced by the varied likes of Louis Armstrong to Charles Bukowski. *Mule Variations* (1999) is a bluesy Southern riff.

■ Frank Zappa – In revolt against the love-bead status quo, the singular Zappa launched an experimental career with the Mothers of Invention and the album *Freak Out!* in the mid-1960s.

■ Dick Dale – The 'King of Surf Guitar,' whose recording of 'Miserlou' featured in the movie *Pulp Fiction*, started experimenting with reverb effects in the 1950s, then topped the charts with his band the Del-Tones in the early '60s, influencing the Beach Boys, Jimi Hendrix and Eddie Van Halen.

■ Harry Partch – An iconoclastic avant-garde American composer, Oakland-born Partch (1901–74) built his own instruments to play odd tunings and scales, often using overheard speech from his years wandering as a hobo around California, especially Barstow. Listen at www.corporeal.com.

singer Henry Rollins. San Francisco produced the Dead Kennedys and the Avengers, who opened for the Sex Pistols at their final show in 1978 at the now-defunct Winterland Ballroom. Jello Biafra, the lead singer of the DKs, became a social activist. The Red Hot Chili Peppers exploded out of LA in the late '80s with a highly charged, funk-punk sound, while the early '90s generated pop punksters blink-182 in San Diego and Green Day, some of whose members started out playing at Berkeley's 924 Gilman Street club.

LA today is the hotbed for West Coast rap and hip-hop. What began as a grassroots art form has become one of the city's money-making cultural exports, from baggy jeans to multimillion-dollar movie deals. Eazy E, Ice Cube and Dr Dre released the seminal NWA (Niggaz With Attitude) album *Straight Outta Compton* in 1989. Death Row Records, co-founded by Dr Dre, has since launched such artists as Long Beach bad-boy Snoop Dog and the late Tupac Shakur, who grew up in Marin. Oakland is the place to look for 'hyphy' (hyperactive) New Bay hip-hop, while SoCal is still riding the 'crunk' (crazy-drunk) drum and bass beats with dance-hall stylings.

Waiting for the Sun: Strange Days, Weird Scenes and the Sound of Los Angeles, by British rock historian Barney Hoskyns, follows the twists and turns of the late-20th-century SoCal music scene, including soul, folk, punk, metal and rap.

Architecture

California's architecture, a fruitful jumble of styles, is as diverse as the state's population.

The first Spanish missions were built around courtyards with what Native Californians and the *padres* found on hand: adobe, limestone and grass. The missions themselves crumbled into disrepair as the church's influence waned, but the style remained practical for the climate. Later, Californians adapted the original Spanish Mission style to create the rancho adobe style, as seen at El Pueblo de Los Angeles (p521) and in San Diego's Old Town (p601).

During the late 19th century, California's upper class built grand mansions to keep up with East Coast fashion, which reflected popular design worldwide during the reign of the UK's Queen Victoria. Victorian architecture, including the Queen Anne style, is most prevalent in Northern California towns such as San Francisco, Ferndale (p263) and

KCRW (www.kcrw.com), Santa Monica's NPR affiliate, offers podcasting of its arts, culture and news programs on demand, or listen online to its award-winning music shows for a slice of the California soundscape.

Eureka (p265), yet one of the finest examples of Victorian whimsy is San Diego's Hotel del Coronado (p603).

With its more simple, classical lines, Spanish Colonial architecture – also called Mission revival – was a rejection of frilly Victorian styles and a nostalgic hearkening back to simpler times. Hallmarks are arched doors and windows, long covered porches, fountains, courtyards, solid walls and red-tile roofs. The train depots in LA and San Diego showcase this style, as do some buildings in San Diego's Balboa Park (p595), a legacy of the Panama-California Exposition in 1915.

Charles and Henry Greene and Julia Morgan ushered in the arts and crafts (Craftsman) movement. Simplicity and harmony were key design principles, blending Asian, European and American influences. The movement's defining building is a one-story bungalow. Overhanging eaves, terraces and sleeping porches are transitions between, and extensions of, the house into its natural environment. Pasadena's Gamble House (p527) is one of the most beautiful examples.

By the early 1920s, it had become fashionable to copy earlier architectural periods, achieving a remarkably popular aesthetic. No style was off limits: neoclassical, baroque, Moorish, Mayan, Aztec or Egyptian. Various revival styles turn up in California's public buildings, such as San Francisco's Palace of Fine Arts (p99) and downtown LA's Richard Riordan Central Library (p523). Hearst Castle (p461) – a mixture of Moorish, Spanish and Mediterranean revival styles – is the grandest example.

Art deco took off during the 1920s and '30s, with vertical lines and symmetry creating a soaring effect, often mitigated by a stepped pattern toward the top. Heavy ornamentation, especially above doors and windows, featured floral motifs, sunbursts and zigzags. Downtown Oakland (p156) has a wealth of art deco buildings. Streamline Moderne also sought to incorporate the machine aesthetic, in particular the aerodynamic look of airplanes and ocean liners. Take a walk by San Francisco's Maritime Museum (p96) to see what we mean.

Also called the 'International Style,' modernism was initiated in Europe by Bauhaus architects Walter Gropius, Ludwig Mies van der Rohe and Le Corbusier. Its characteristics include box-like building shapes, open floor plans, plain facades and abundant glass. Austrian-born Rudolph Schindler and Richard Neutra brought early modernism to LA and Palm Springs, where Swiss-born Albert Frey also worked. Both Neutra and Schindler were influenced by Frank Lloyd Wright, who designed LA's Hollyhock House (p512) in a style he fancifully called 'California Romanza.'

Postmodernism was partly a response to the starkness of the International Style, and sought to re-emphasize the structural form of the building and the space around it. Richard Meier perfected and transcended the postmodernist vision at West LA's Getty Center (p518). Canadian-born Frank Gehry, who has made his home in Santa Monica, is known for his deconstructivist buildings with almost sculptural forms and distinctive facade materials, such as at the high-profile Walt Disney Concert Hall (p523) in downtown LA.

Jim Heimann's *California Crazy & Beyond: Roadside Vernacular Architecture* is a romp through the zany, whimsical world of mimetic design where lemonade stands look like giant lemons and motels are shaped like tepees – all of which goes a long way toward explaining Las Vegas.

Visual Arts

The earliest California artists were Native Americans who used pigment to make pictographs on rocks and caves, often as part of shamanistic rituals intended to ensure successful hunts. The Chumash, who used whimsical designs and bright colors, are considered the most accomplished. In LA, the Autry National Center's Southwest Museum of the American Indian (p528) and the Museum of the American West (p514) have important collections of contemporary and traditional works by Native Californian tribal artists including baskets, carvings, pottery and painting.

The earliest European artists were trained cartographers accompanying Spanish explorers to record images of California. The Gold Rush era drew artists out West in the 1850s. The completion of the Transcontinental Railroad in 1869 lured even more painters, many of whom favored the Sierra Nevadas, especially Yosemite. Many settled in San Francisco.

By the early 20th century, the influx of landscape painters was in full swing. Often working outdoors on location – or 'plein air' – they presented a vision of California as a paradise as yet unspoiled by industrialization. Artists colonies formed along the coast in Monterey, Carmel, Pasadena, Laguna Beach and on Santa Catalina Island. The California Regionalist painters of the 1930s turned to watercolor. Today, many of California's prototypical landscape paintings hang in the Oakland Museum (p157) and Long Beach Museum of Art (p521).

The Depression-era Works Progress Administration (WPA) sponsored federal art projects statewide. Photographer Dorothea Lange, who maintained a studio in Berkeley, and her husband Paul Taylor documented Dust Bowl migrant workers. The Oakland Museum (p157) owns the most comprehensive collection of her work. The influence of early Mexican muralists such as Diego Rivera is reflected in the interior of San Francisco's Coit Tower (p96) and can be seen today in much of California's public art, for example, the LA murals of Judith Baca.

In 1940 Man Ray brought surrealism and dadaism to the West Coast, and both suited California's off-the-wall, rebellious lifestyle. Salvador Dali designed a few film sets for Alfred Hitchcock and even worked for Walt Disney. Although California art came to reflect the strong abstract expressionist movement of New York, some artists began to reject it and invented new styles in the '50s, such as the Bay Area's figurative art movement.

In the '60s, amidst the nation's growing chaos and confusion, California's romantic landscapes turned to smoggy 'freeway-scapes' that alluded to the lost American dream. During the Civil Rights era, Asian, Latino and African American artistic voices grew stronger. With Haight-Ashbury as a focal point, San Francisco saw a huge output of psychedelic poster and album cover art, as well as irreverent and idiosyncratic funk art, notably in clay. Meanwhile, pop artists, such as Wayne Thiebaud, became obsessed by advertising, consumerism and technology, especially in Southern California.

The same themes are still explored by California artists today, notably British émigré David Hockney. In LA, the Museum of Contemporary Art (p523) puts on provocative and avant-garde shows. The San Francisco Museum of Modern Art (p100) has a substantial, if more conservative, collection. San Diego's Museum of Contemporary Art (p609) specializes in post-1950s pop and conceptual art. Post-WWII works in all media hang at Long Beach's Museum of Latin American Art (p521).

Theater
Supplied by about 25% of the nation's professional actors, with more hopefuls arriving every day, LA is the second most influential city in America for theater, behind only NYC. Struggling young actors play alongside major film and TV stars returning to their stage roots. Cutting-edge contemporary playwrights launch new works in LA, such as Tony Kushner's *Angels in America*.

Spaces to watch for plays in LA include the Geffen Playhouse close to UCLA, the Mark Taper Forum (p550) and the Actors' Gang Theatre (p550), cofounded by actor Tim Robbins. Small theaters flourish in West

To find museums, galleries, fine art exhibition spaces and calendars of upcoming shows throughout SoCal, check out ArtScene (www.artscenecal.com).

With timeless, often rare, Ansel Adams photographs beside excerpts from canonical writers such as Jack Kerouac and Joan Didion, *California: With Classic California Writings*, edited by Andrea G Stillman, is an art book par excellence.

Hollywood (WeHo) and North Hollywood (NoHo), West Coast's answers to off- and off-off-Broadway, respectively. Influential multicultural theaters include Little Tokyo's East West Players (p551), while among the most critically acclaimed outlying companies are the innovative Long Beach Opera and Costa Mesa's South Coast Repertory (p580).

In San Francisco, downtown theaters blossomed before the 1906 earthquake, after which they were quickly rebuilt. The Geary Theater (p129), home to the repertory American Conservatory Theater, and the Lorraine Hansberry Theatre, an important African American company, are both downtown. EXIT Theatre is ground zero for the city's fringe-theater festival in September. The Yerba Buena Center for the Arts (p100), built in the 1990s, lures performing-arts groups from around the world and provides space for local theater troupes. Finally, the esteemed Berkeley Repertory Theatre (p169) justifies any trip across the bay.

'the esteemed Berkeley Repertory Theatre justifies any trip across the bay'

Dance

In LA, the dance trend has always been toward the experimental and the avant-garde. Martha Graham, Alvin Ailey and Bella Lewitzky were among those who were pioneers here. The American Repertory Dance Company is dedicated to keeping alive the legacy of early-20th-century modern dances, including those by Isadora Duncan. Another modern dance company is Loretta Livingston & Dancers, whose lead dancer and choreographer previously danced with Lewitzky. Lula Washington Dance Theatre is one of the premier African American dance companies in the West, known for its unique blend of African, modern and jazz techniques. Fascinating, if slightly bizarre, is Diavolo Dance Theater, which practices surreal 'hyperdance' in custom-built spaces.

The internationally renowned San Francisco Ballet (p130) is America's oldest resident professional ballet company, founded in the 1930s. It still draws dancers and commissions works from all over the globe. Among the city's modern dance troupes are the Smuin Ballet, ODC/San Francisco, Alonzo King's Lines Ballet and Joe Goode Performance Group. The East Bay has a lively experimental and ethnic dance scene.

Environment

Deserts, forests, high alpine zones, river deltas, coastal wetlands and valleys – California is home to almost every type of ecosystem and enjoys tremendously varied flora and fauna. Wherever you go, you'll have a chance to encounter wildlife on its home turf – from tiny starfish in tide pools and mighty coastal redwoods to an ancient desert tortoise resting in the shade of a Joshua tree.

California experiences over 15,000 minor earthquakes each year. Visit http://quake.wr.usgs.gov /recenteqs/latest.htm to see what's shakin' today.

THE LAND

The third-largest state after Alaska and Texas, California covers more than 160,000 sq miles and is larger than the UK. It's bordered by Oregon to the north, Mexico to the south, Nevada and Arizona to the east, and by 840 miles of glorious Pacific coastline to the west. Its cool northern border stands at the same latitude as Rome, while the arid southern border is at the same latitude as Tel Aviv.

There isn't a day without at least one earthquake here, although most of the tremors are too small or too remote to be felt by humans. California sits on one of the world's major earthquake fault zones on the edge of the Pacific Plate, which consists of the Pacific ocean floor and coastline, and the North American Plate, which covers that continent and part of the Atlantic Ocean floor. This very shaky plate boundary forms the infamous San Andreas Fault, which runs almost the entire length of the state and has spawned innumerable smaller branch faults.

The passionate writings of naturalist John Muir would be reading for half a lifetime. Dip into his canon with the Yosemite Association's rustically illustrated *The Wild Muir: 22 of John Muir's Greatest Adventures,* compiled by Lee Stetson.

But it's not faults that are to blame for California's many geographical divides; its mountain ranges and water, or the lack thereof, determine the state's most prominent regions. The Coast Mountains (part of the Coast Range) run along the entire length of the coastline, plunging straight into the Pacific on their west and rolling gently toward the Central Valley on their eastern side. Created by tectonic and volcanic activity, this coastal range is continually eroded by winds and heavy rain, which creates dunes and intertidal pools and also cause dramatic flooding and landslides. San Francisco Bay divides the Coast Range roughly in half: the foggy North Coast remains sparsely populated, while the Central Coast has a balmy climate, sandy beaches and lots of people.

The prominent Sierra Nevada mountains stretch 400 miles along California's eastern border and claim Mt Whitney (14,497ft), the highest peak in the contiguous USA. Just north of Lake Tahoe, the Sierra joins the southern end of the Cascade Range. Although these ranges appear to form an almost unbroken line, they are very different, geologically speaking: the Sierra is a westward-tilted granite fault block with glacier-carved valleys like Yosemite, while the Cascades are a chain of volcanic peaks dominated by Mt Lassen (10,457ft) and Mt Shasta (14,162ft). East of the Cascades, on the Oregon border, sits the remote Modoc Plateau. West of the Cascades, the rugged Klamath Mountains rise above the unruly Klamath and Trinity Rivers.

Take a virtual field trip courtesy of the myriad links put together by the California Geological Survey at www .conservation.ca.gov/cgs /geotour.

Between the Sierra Nevada and the Coast Range lies California's fertile Central Valley, an agricultural powerhouse. The Golden State produces over half of America's fruits, nuts and vegetables, and most of it is grown in this irrigated valley. In fact, California corners the market on almonds, kiwi fruit, olives, dates and strawberries, to name just a few of its famous exports. The Central Valley is a bit of a misnomer, though, as it's composed of two river systems: the Sacramento Valley in the north and the

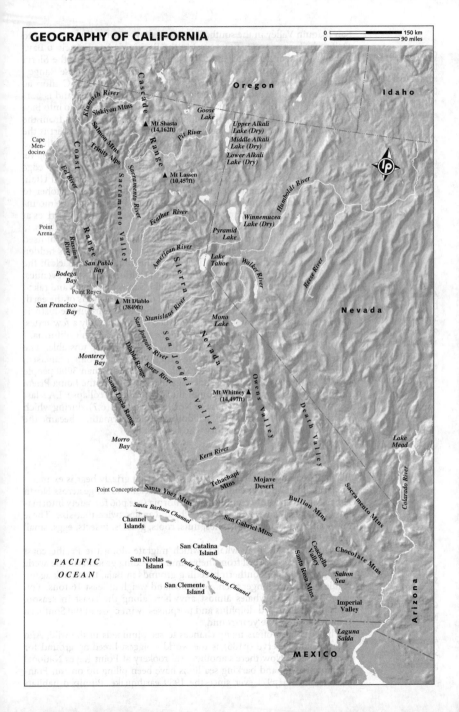

GEOGRAPHY OF CALIFORNIA

0 — 150 km
0 — 90 miles

Oregon
Idaho

Klamath River
Siskiyou Mtns
Cascade Range
Goose Lake
▲ Mt Shasta (14,162ft)
Pit River
Upper Alkali Lake (Dry)
Middle Alkali Lake (Dry)
Lower Alkali Lake (Dry)
Salmon Mtns
Cape Mendocino
Trinity Alps
Coast Range
Eel River
Sacramento Mtns
Sacramento River
Sacramento Valley
▲ Mt Lassen (10,457ft)
Feather River
Winnemucea Lake (Dry)
Humboldt River
Point Arena
Russian River
American River
Pyramid Lake
Lake Tahoe
Walker River
Reese River
San Pablo Bay
Sierra
Bodega Bay
Point Reyes
San Francisco Bay
▲ Mt Diablo (3849ft)
Stanislaus River
Nevada
Mono Lake
Nevada
Monterey Bay
Diablo Range
San Joaquin River
Kings River
San Joaquin Valley
Santa Lucia Range
▲ Mt Whitney (14,497ft)
Owens Valley
Death Valley
Lake Mead
Morro Bay
Kern River
Colorado River
Point Conception
Santa Ynez Mtns
Tchachapi Mtns
Mojave Desert
Bullion Mtns
Sacramento Mtns
Santa Barbara Channel
Channel Islands
San Gabriel Mtns
PACIFIC OCEAN
San Nicolas Island
San Catalina Island
Outer Santa Barbara Channel
San Clemente Island
Coachella Valley
Chocolate Mtns
Santa Rosa Mtns
Salton Sea
Imperial Valley
Arizona
Laguna Salda
MEXICO

San Joaquin Valley in the south. The twin valleys meet at the Sacramento Delta where river water flows west to the Pacific via San Francisco Bay.

Further down the state, the Coast Range is linked back to the Sierra by a series of unusual east–west mountains called the Transverse Ranges, which form the dividing line between Northern and Southern California. To the south, the Los Angeles Basin directly fronts the ocean and is bordered by a series of Peninsular Ranges that extend past San Diego into Baja California in Mexico. These mountains divide the coastal cities from the enormous Mojave and Sonoran Deserts to the east. The low desert is the Sonoran, commonly called the Colorado Desert, which heads south into Mexico and contains the artificial Salton Sea. The high desert, the Mojave, takes off east of Los Angeles. Death Valley is in the Mojave at the edge of the Great Basin, which extends over state lines into Nevada and Utah. When the desert experiences its cool season (roughly from October to March), warm air is pushed west from the Great Basin through the mountain barriers of channels and canyons, picking up speed until it arrives at the coast as the forceful Santa Ana winds, causing disastrous wildfires.

Putting all of the panoramic scenery aside for a moment, the promised land of California historically has been better known for what's hidden deep below ground. Gold fever first struck the Golden State back in the mid-19th century and California still leads the nation in mining revenues. In 2004, miners here accounted for 8% of all US mining activity and raked in $3.6 billion. Today, gold is being hauled out of the bowels of the earth from over a dozen active mines, around half of which are in the historic Gold Country, at the rate of almost 90,000oz per year. Only a few states, such as Nevada, Alaska and Utah, produce more gold than California.

California's soil may be mineral-rich, but it's pretty unstable. The state's most famous earthquake was the 1906 one in San Francisco, which measured 7.8 on the Richter scale and left more than 3000 people dead. The Bay Area made headlines again in 1989 when the Loma Prieta earthquake (7.1) caused a section of the Bay Bridge to collapse. LA's last 'big one' occurred in 1994 with the Northridge quake (6.7), during which parts of the Santa Monica Fwy fell down; in the aftermath, it became the most costly quake in US history – so far, that is.

WILDLIFE
Animals

It's depicted on the state flag, but the California grizzly bear is extinct – the last golden one was shot in the 1920s. Black bears range across North America and are quite common in California (see p66 for safety information). Females can weigh up to 400lb, and males twice that size. These burly omnivores feed on berries, nuts, roots, grasses, insects, eggs, small mammals and fish.

Even bigger are gray whales, which migrate along the Pacific coast from December to April from their summer feeding grounds in the arctic Bering Sea to their southern breeding grounds in Baja, then back again. Adult whales are longer then a city bus and weigh at least 16 tons. You can observe gray whales almost anywhere along the coast in season. Pods of bottle-nosed dolphins and porpoises swim close to the Southern California shoreline year-round.

The coast also offers many chances to see pinnipeds in the wild. Año Nuevo State Reserve (p186) is the world's biggest breeding ground for elephant seals. Now there's another seal rookery at Point Reyes National Seashore (p152) and barking sea lions have been piling up on San Francisco's Pier 39 (p97) ever since the 1989 earthquake. Pinniped habitats

---

California can claim both the highest point in the continental USA (Mt Whitney summit at 14,497ft) and the lowest elevation in the western hemisphere (Badwater, 282ft below sea level, in Death Valley) – plus they're only 90 miles apart, as the condor flies.

A Natural History of California, by Allan A Schoenherr, is a comprehensive, readable armchair guide to the forces of geology and ecology that have shaped every region of the state.

The National Audubon Society's portable, full-color *Field Guide to California* ranges from butterflies to giant sequoias, with bonus overviews of the Sunshine State's natural history, parks and starry skies.

scattered along the Central Coast include Point Lobos State Reserve (p454) near Carmel, San Simeon's Piedras Blancas (p460) and some of the Channel Islands (p492) off Santa Barbara.

The posterbird of conservation efforts is the endangered California condor, a black vulture with a bald pink head (the better to eat carrion with, my dear) and a wingspan longer than an NBA player is tall. Bald eagles are regaining a foothold on the Channel Islands, however, the California spotted owl, which lives in both the Sierra and coastal forests, continues to be a species of concern. Common coastal birds include brown pelicans, gulls, terns, cormorants, sandpipers and sanderlings, which look like wind-up toys as they chase waves to catch their invertebrate prey. California is an essential stop on the migratory Pacific Flyway and almost half of the bird species in North America use the state's coastal and inland refuges for rest and refueling. Monarch butterflies, beautiful orange creatures that follow remarkable migration patterns, spend the winter hibernating on California's Central Coast at places like Pismo Beach (p470), San Simeon State Park (p462), Big Sur and Santa Cruz.

If you find yourself in any open country, whether above the timberline in the Sierra or in the deserts, look up to see if you can spy a golden eagle.

Where animals live in the Sierra mountains varies according to available food and water supply. Some creatures survive the winter by migrating to lower latitudes; these include mule deer, bighorn sheep and hummingbirds. Yellow-bellied marmots, which are seen everywhere in summer, comfortably hibernate from September to May. Throughout the mountain forests are feline predators such as cougars and lynx. Coyotes can also be found in valleys and even deserts, while bobcats (so named for their truncated, white-tipped tails) have the biggest range of any feline.

Two kingly types of elk roam the valleys near the coast. The smaller, white-rumped tule elk, which gold miners once slaughtered to the brink of extinction, lives at Point Reyes and Tule Elk State Reserve (p428) near Stockton. The darker Roosevelt Elk, the largest living species of North American elk, ranges from Prairie Creek Redwoods State Park (p276) in Northern California all the way up to British Columbia.

Most desert wildlife is rarely visible during the day. Roadrunners, those mottled black-and-white ground cuckoos with long tails and a poof of feathers atop their heads, can often be spotted on the side of the road. They're fast enough to catch rattlesnakes. A rarer sight is the state reptile, the desert tortoise. Rarer still are desert pupfish, which have adapted so that they can survive only in a single stream, pool or marsh. Other desert inhabitants are burrowing kit foxes, tree-climbing gray foxes, jackrabbits, kangaroo rats and a variety of snakes, lizards and spiders, some of which are venomous. Desert bighorn sheep and birds flock to watering holes in palm oases.

Plants

Everywhere except the deserts and high mountain ranges, the hills of California turn green in winter, not summer. As soon as the autumn and winter rains arrive, the dried-out brown grasses spring to life. Wildflowers pop up as early as February. The most conspicuous and familiar is the bright orange California poppy, the state flower, which blooms in the high desert from late February to early April. But don't pick one, or you face a $500 fine. Other wildflowers like the red Indian paintbrush and purple lupine bloom in alpine meadows between April and early June, and later in summer at higher elevations such as Yosemite's Tuolumne Meadows.

California boasts three record-breaking arboreal species: some of the world's tallest (coast redwood), heaviest (sequoia) and oldest (bristlecone

The California condor is the largest flying bird in North America. In 1982, there were only two dozen or so left in the wild. Today, thanks to captive breeding programs, there are about 200.

The National Geographic Society's *Field Guide to the Birds of California* is one of the most detailed guides available, with 150 full-color photographs, state-wide range maps, field notes and identification aids.

The University of California at Berkeley's searchable digital-photo library (http://elib.cs .berkeley.edu/photos) has thousands of images of California landscapes, flora and fauna.

California Wildflowers
(www.calacademy.org
/research/botany/wild
flow) is a colorful floral
encyclopedia, profiling
species from deserts to
alpine ranges.

The oldest living trees
on earth are California's
ancient bristlecone pines
(p403), which can live for
over 40 centuries – more
than a millennia longer
than the more-famous
giant sequoias on the
coast.

The University of
California Press' popular
*California Natural History
Guides* series is recom-
mended for its weighty
wildflower tomes,
notably Philip A Munz's
*Introduction to Desert
Wildflowers*, a classic for
over 40 years that has
been recently revised.

pine) trees. The northern Coast Range has the most redwoods. There the lush forest floor supports sword ferns, redwood sorrel and other plants. Meanwhile, the Sierra Nevada has three distinct ecozones: the dry western foothills covered with oak and chaparral, conifer forests starting from about 2000ft, and a high-alpine zone above 8000ft. The giant sequoia, which is unique to California, stands in isolated groves in the Sierra, primarily in Yosemite and Sequoia National Parks. Its red shaggy bark is similar to that of the incense cedar, which incidentally also grows there, as do lodgepole and ponderosa pines, and red and white fir. Ancient gnarled bristlecone pines grow on dolomite rock in the White Mountains, northeast of Bishop.

Deciduous trees include the shimmery quaking aspen, whose large rounded leaves turn butter-yellow in fall, and the beautiful Pacific dogwood, whose greenish-white flowers bloom in spring and early summer. Along the Central Coast, Monterey cypress and pine have thick, rough, grayish bark; far-reaching branches clustered at their tops; and long needles. Species that thrive in more arid Southern California include the aromatic California laurel, which has long, slender leaves and purple fruit, and the manzanita, treelike shrubs with smooth red bark and small, sticky berries. The Torrey pine, a species adapted to sparse rainfall and sandy, stony soils, is rarer.

In the deserts, plants have adapted to the arid climate by developing thin, spiny leaves that resist moisture loss (and deter grazing animals) and seed and flowering mechanisms that kick into full gear during brief rains. Cholla cactus appear so furry that one variety, which produces a greenish-yellow flower in spring, is nicknamed the 'teddy bear cactus.' But do resist giving it a hug: the 'fur' actually consists of extremely sharp, barbed spines that can bury themselves in skin at the slightest touch. Almost as widespread are prickly pears, a flat cacti that produces showy flowers in shades of red, yellow and purple, and whose juice is still used medicinally in Mexico. Like something out of a Dr Seuss book, Joshua trees are the largest type of yucca and are related to the lily. The smoke tree, a small, fine-leafed tree with a bluish color and dark purple flowers, is said to indicate the presence of underground water. The cactus-like creosote is a small bush with a distinctive smell; Native Americans used its hard leaves to make healing teas. The ocotillo has canelike branches that produce blood-red flowers and can grow up to 20ft tall. The only palm tree native to the state is the California fan palm, which is found in desert oases. Its nickname is the petticoat palm, a reference to the way dead leaves hang down around the trunk.

NATIONAL & STATE PARKS

Almost half of California is owned by the federal government, yet less than a third of public lands are set aside as wilderness, while the vast remainder is open for logging, military exercises, dam projects, off-highway vehicles (OHVs) and other non-natural, often destructive, uses.

The majority of Californians rank outdoor recreation as vital to their quality of life. By both popular propositions and direct acts of state government, the amount of preserved land has increased thanks to several important pieces of legislation passed since the 1960s, including the landmark 1976 California Coastal Act, which saved the coastline from further development, and the controversial 1994 California Desert Protection Act, which angered many ranchers, miners and off-roaders. Still, it's in the state's economic best interests to protect its wilderness, as recreational tourism is outpacing the competing 'resource extraction' industries, such as mining.

Unfortunately, many of California's national parks are being loved to death. Overcrowding severely impacts the environment, and it's increasingly difficult to balance access with keeping parks in their natural state.

CALIFORNIA'S TOP 15 NATIONAL & STATE PARKS

Park	Features	Activities	Best Time to Visit
Anza-Borrego Desert State Park (p649)	badlands, canyons, fan-palm oases, caves, hot springs, bighorn sheep, birds	hiking, 4WD roads, stargazing, horseback riding	Nov-Mar
Calaveras Big Trees State Park (p327)	grove of giant sequoias in the mid-Sierra	hiking, bird-watching, cross-country skiing	May-Oct
Channel Islands National Park (p492)	rocky islands with steep cliffs, elephant seals, sea lions, otters, foxes	snorkeling, diving, kayaking, hiking, bird-watching	year-round
Death Valley National Park (p666)	unique geology, sand dunes, canyons, volcanic craters, ghost towns, wild horses	hiking, 4WD roads, horseback riding	Oct-Apr
Joshua Tree National Park (p654)	rocky desert, fan-palm oases, spiky Joshua trees, cactus gardens, golden eagles	rock climbing, hiking, 4WD roads, mountain biking, bird-watching	Sep-May
Lassen Volcanic National Park (p288)	volcanic peak and terrain, geothermal activity	hiking, snowshoeing	Jun-Sep
Lava Beds National Monument (p304)	lava tube caves, pit craters, cinder cones, petroglyphs, antelope, bobcats, bald eagles	spelunking, hiking, bird-watching	May-Sep
Mendocino Headlands State Park (p242)	jutting coastal bluffs, rugged beaches, wildflowers, migrating whales	nature walks, hiking, beachcombing, surfing	year-round
Mojave National Preserve (p662)	volcanic cinder cones, sand dunes, cliffside canyons, caverns, Joshua trees, desert tortoise	hiking, 4WD roads	Oct-Apr
Morro Bay State Park (p465)	saltwater marsh, lagoon, coastal dunes, volcanic rock, peregrine falcons, migratory birds	sailing, surfing, hiking, bird-watching	year-round
Muir Woods National Monument (p149)	towering stands of old-growth redwood trees, banana slug, northern spotted owl	nature walks, hiking	Apr-Nov
Point Reyes National Seashore (p152)	windswept beaches, lagoons, forested cliffs, tule elk, northern elephant seals, migrating whales	hiking, bird-watching	Apr-Nov
Redwood National & State Parks (p274)	virgin redwood groves, fern forests, pristine beaches; Roosevelt elk, great blue heron	hiking, scenic drives, kayaking	May-Sep
Sequoia & Kings Canyon National Parks (p373)	giant sequoias, deep canyons, montane forests, high-alpine wilderness, black bears	hiking, backpacking	Jun-Oct
Yosemite National Park (p359)	sheer granite-walled valley, waterfalls, alpine meadows, black bear, mule deer, bighorn sheep	hiking, backpacking, rock climbing, rafting, skiing, snowshoeing	Jun-Sep

Try visiting in the shoulder seasons (ie *not* summer) and flee the paved roads and parking lots for rugged backcountry. Lesser-known parks, especially in the Northern Mountains and SoCal deserts, may go relatively untouched for most of the year, which means you won't have to reserve permits, campsites or accommodations months in advance (see p699 for general information on camping).

During and after WWII, the US Army used the accidental Salton Sea (p649) for target practice by dropping dummy bombs into it.

Yosemite and Sequoia, created in 1890, were California's first national parks. Today there are five more, plus more than two dozen other areas protected by the **National Park Service** (NPS; ☎ 888-467-2757; www.nps.gov; annual pass $50). National preserves, such as those in the Mojave Desert, tend to be more isolated. National monuments, such as Devils Postpile in the eastern Sierra near Mammoth Lakes, are smaller but just as spectacular. National recreation areas (NRA) are poised for urban escapes, such as Golden Gate NRA (outside San Francisco) and Santa Monica Mountains NRA (LA). National historic sites (NHS) examine California's diverse history, from old-timey San Francisco Maritime NHS to the heart-breaking WWII-era internment camp at Manzanar NHS. Several cross-country historic trails end in California at the coast. There are also national forests run by the **US Forest Service** (USFS; ☎ 202-205-8333; www.fs.fed.us), which protect Mt Whitney, Mt Shasta and Big Bear Lake. National wildlife refuges (NWR), favored by birders, are managed by the **US Fish & Wildlife Service** (USFWS; ☎ 800-344-9453; www.fws.gov/refuges) and wilderness tracts are overseen by the **Bureau of Land Management** (BLM; ☎ 202-452-5125; www.blm.gov).

Visit the Nature Conservancy (http://nature .org/wherewework /northamerica/states /california) for environmental news and photos of gorgeous wilderness areas not normally open to the public.

Lest you give the feds too much credit, **California State Parks** (☎ 800-777-0369; www.parks.ca.gov; day-use fee $2-14, annual pass $125) are arguably the nation's most diverse. From underwater marine preserves to giant redwood forests, the state-park system protects nearly a third of the coastline and maintains over 3000 miles of trails. Even better, many state parks, reserves, beaches, historic sites and recreation areas are more easily accessible and less crowded than national parks. More unusual state park offerings include coastal light-houses, mission churches, historic ranches and wildflower preserves. The state parks system will soon expand into the Central Valley to better preserve its forests, grasslands, riparian habitats and historic Hwy 99 whistle-stops. Each county in California also has its own parallel system of parks.

ENVIRONMENTAL ISSUES

California is a success story in many ways, but development and growth have often come at environmental expense. The Gold Rush battered hills and valleys, and hydraulic mining clogged up streams and rivers. The creation of the Hetch Hetchy Dam and the Los Angeles Aqueduct nurtured the evolution of San Francisco and LA, respectively, but also spelled doom to the Hetch Hetchy Valley in Yosemite and the Owens Valley and Mono Lake (see p393). The pollution and destruction of wetlands in the Central Valley and on the coast has threatened migratory birds on the Pacific Flyway and salmon. Each year, motor vehicles cause unhealthy levels of air pollution, mostly smog. Plus, there's overgrazing, logging, overfishing and the occasional oil spill.

Despite these grim realities, California has blazed a path in environmental awareness. In 1864 the incomparable beauty of Yosemite was first given protection under a grant. It was John Muir, a Scottish-born naturalist who traveled all over the Sierra Nevadas, who lobbied successfully for the creation of Yosemite National Park in 1890. Muir went on to found the **Sierra Club** (☎ 916-557-1100; www.sierraclub.org/ca; annual membership from $25), now one of the most active and influential environmental groups in the nation. He later lobbied against the Hetch Hetchy Dam, which the Sierra Club is still fighting today. Coalitions of Californians have worked for the recovery of Mono Lake and to stop logging of old-growth forests in Northern California, which causes floods, mud-slides and loss of eco-habitat.

The odds are nearly two to one in favor of there being a magnitude 6.7 or greater earthquake in the San Francisco Bay area sometime in the next 25 years.

Although air quality in California has markedly improved over the past two decades, it's lamentably the worst in the country. Auto exhaust, generated by the travels of more than 23 million registered drivers, and industrial emission are the chief culprits. An even greater health hazard is ozone, the principal ingredient in smog, which makes sunny days in LA look hazy. Ozone levels peak during summer, which also brings the greatest number of inversion days, when a layer of warm air traps the noxious fumes. But there's hope: even Los Angeles, the state's infamous 'smog capital,' only exceeded federal ozone-level standards on 27 days in 2004, compared with 200 days back in the '70s. You'll see ever more low-emissions vehicles on the road, too, as Californians account for one out of every five new hybrid car owners nationally. Governor Schwarzenegger has been driving an experimental hydrogen-powered Hummer SUV to publicly promote alternative fuels.

Water has always been at the heart of conflict between agricultural, urban and environmental interests in California, which is no stranger to drought. About half of California's annual precipitation falls between December and February, so if it's a dry winter, it'll be a seriously parched summer. Between 1987 and 1992, when precipitation levels plunged 30% below normal, the state took steps to cut back on water usage: utilities offered consumers rebates on low-flush toilets; water banks facilitated transfers and sales of water between communities; cities began recycling waste water; and a few coastal towns developed desalination systems to harvest ocean water. But severe shortages are always just around the corner.

It was the energy crisis of 2000–01 that made national headlines. It came about after deregulation legislation passed in 1996 under then-governor Pete Wilson, which was supposed to lower energy costs to consumers by opening up the state's electricity industry to competition. It had the opposite effect. The state's two largest utilities – PG&E and SoCal Edison – were brought to the brink of bankruptcy. To avert a collapse, the state government had to intervene and buy extra electricity, thus depleting its own coffers. Meanwhile, Californians experienced outages and rolling blackouts, introduced to keep the state's power grid from disintegrating. PG&E went bankrupt, while power suppliers such as the corrupt Enron Corporation filled their coffers.

California is almost the country's biggest consumer of energy, but per-person consumption is laudably low. The state is a massive user of petroleum and natural gas, of which over half of the supplies are imported from other states and Canada. But California has established full-scale, alternative energy projects, such as wind farms and solar collectors. The deserts offer not only abundant sunshine, but much wind and tremendous geothermal heat. There are thousands of windmills lined up at locations such as the San Gorgonio Pass north of Palm Springs and the Tehachapi Pass southeast of Bakersfield. To get up to speed on solar-power technology, drop by Hopland's Real Goods Solar Living Center (p249).

By the author of the Pulitzer Prize–winning *Cadillac Desert: The American West and Its Disappearing Water*, Marc Reisner's *A Dangerous Place: California's Unsettling Fate* is a nightmare vision of California's impending 'big one' (earthquake).

California Outdoors

California lives up to its reputation as a splendid outdoor playground. There's plenty to do year-round, with each season offering its own special delights, be it hiking among spring wildflowers, swimming in the Pacific warmed by the summer sun, biking among a kaleidoscope of fall foliage or celebrating winter by schussing through deep powder.

If you're planning a winter vacation, log on to www.californiasnow.com for lots of useful tips and background information.

CYCLING & MOUNTAIN-BIKING

Strap on your helmet! California is superb cycling territory, whether you're off on a leisurely spin along the beach, an adrenaline-fueled mountain exploration or a multiday bike-touring adventure. The season runs pretty much year-round in the coastal areas, especially in Southern California. Avoid the mountains in winter and the desert in summer; also be aware of your skill and fitness level, and plan accordingly.

California's cities are not terribly bike-friendly, although there are exceptions, most notably Santa Barbara (p488), Davis (p417), Palo Alto, Chico, Santa Cruz (p436) and Berkeley. But even Los Angeles has some good cycling turf in the Santa Monica Mountains (p530) and along the beach on the South Bay Trail (p530). The Wine Country (p188) is ideal for bike touring.

Mountain-biking burst onto the scene in the 1970s in Marin County where Mt Tamalpais (p148) lays claim to being the sport's birthplace. Just across the Golden Gate Bridge from San Francisco, the Marin Headlands (p139) offers a bonanza of biking trails for fat-tire fans (although weekend warriors make things more frenzied than a three-legged dog on ice skates).

Information on freeway access for bicyclists, a guide to bicycle touring in California and links to free downloadable maps are available on www.cabobike.org, a site maintained by the California Association of Bicycling Organizations (CABO).

Classic, top-rated single-track rides include Mr Toads Wild Ride (p340) and the Flume Trail (p351) at Lake Tahoe, and the Downieville Downhill (p312) in the Gold Country. Other good places to barrel through include the Chicapudi Trail around Shasta Lake (p287) and Prairie Creek Redwoods State Park (p276) on the North Coast.

Speed freaks also sing the praises of Mammoth Mountain (p398), whose mountain-bike park beckons with a slalom course, an obstacle area and a kick-ass 14-mile downhill stretch. Other ski areas that open trails and chairlifts to cyclists in the summer include Big Bear Lake (p561), east of Los Angeles, and Mt Shasta (p299).

Bikes are usually not allowed in designated wilderness areas at all and are limited to paved roads in national parks. An exception is Titus Canyon (p670) in Death Valley National Park, an exciting off-road adventure that'll take you past Native American petroglyphs and a ghost town. Do not attempt in summer! Redwood National Park (p274), where you'll be cycling among the giant trees, is another bike-friendly national park, as is Joshua Tree National Park (p657), with miles of backcountry road.

State parks are a little more relaxed. Good 'chain-gang' destinations include Montaña de Oro State Park (p466) on the Central Coast and Anza-Borrego Desert State Park (p652), east of San Diego. Most of the national forests and Bureau of Land Management (BLM) lands are also open to mountain-bikers. Just be sure to stay on the tracks and not to create new ones.

For online reviews of dozens of mountain-bike trails, check out www.mtbr.com or www.dirtworld.com.

Most towns have at least one bike-rental place; many are listed throughout this book. Prices range from about $5 to $8 per hour or $10 to $30 per day (more for high-tech mountain bikes), depending on the type of bike and the rental location. For short tours, staff at the local tourist offices can supply you with ideas, maps and advice. To get the inside scoop on the local scene, you'll probably get better information from the folks in rental shops.

The website of the **Adventure Cycling Association** (☎ 416-721-1776, 800-775-2453; www.adventurecycling.org) contains useful trip-planning resources such as the *Cyclist's Yellow Pages*, an online store and excerpts from its *Adventure Cyclist* magazine.

For more information about cycling, especially how to transport your bike, see p720.

If you're serious about cycling around California, grab a copy of Lonely Planet's *Cycling USA: West Coast*. It contains detailed descriptions of 42 rides, from quick and easy day-long hops in the saddle to butt-blistering long-distance adventures.

HIKING & BACKPACKING

With its unparalleled scenery, California is perfect for exploring on foot. This is true whether you've got your heart set on peak-bagging in the Sierra Nevada, trekking through cacti groves, climbing sand dunes, rambling among the world's tallest trees or simply heading for a coastal walk accompanied by booming surf. Wherever you go, expect encounters with an entire cast of furry, feathered and flippered friends. Keep an eye out for lizards darting among the rocks, bears foraging for berries, porpoises jumping for joy or eagles plummeting for prey. In spring and early summer, a painter's palette worth of wildflowers decorates leafy meadows, shaggy hillsides and damp forest floors. The first cold snap of fall cloaks aspen and cottonwoods in a fireworks of golden hues. Even winter hiking is a delight as you scamper through frosty forest among snow-draped trees while strapped into a pair of high-tech snowshoes.

The best trails are generally found among the jaw-dropping scenery in national and state parks, national forests, wilderness areas and other public lands. You can usually choose from lots of routes, from easy, interpretive strolls negotiable by wheelchairs and baby strollers to multiday backpacking routes through rugged wilderness. The most popular trails have quotas and require permits (see Wilderness Permits p60).

Parks and forests almost always have a visitors center or ranger station with clued-in staff happy to offer route suggestions and trail-specific tips. They also hand out or sell trail maps, which may be necessary depending on the length and difficulty of your hike. Look for contact information in the destination chapters throughout this book.

Hiking aficionados should have a look at Lonely Planet's *Hiking in the Sierra Nevada*, which contains detailed descriptions of several dozen hikes in California's largest and most spectacular mountain range.

Hikes

No matter where you find yourself in California, you're never far from a trail, even in the metropolitan areas. The Marin Headlands (p139), Mt Tamalpais (p148) and the magical Muir Woods (p149) are all within an hour's drive of San Francisco and are crisscrossed by dozens of superb trails. South of the city, Big Basin Redwoods State Park (p439) is great for a ramble among the giant trees. Even in LA, you can ditch the car and head for the outdoors in the Santa Monica Mountains National Recreation Area (p530), where many movies were filmed, or Big Bear Lake (p560) in the San Bernardino National Forest, one of the nation's most popular national forests.

Of course, hiking is simply awesome in the national parks, even though trails can get crowded. In Yosemite National Park (p366) you can steer toward waterfalls, frolic among wildflowers on high desert meadows or tackle mighty Half Dome, the park's spiritual centerpiece. Sequoia National Park (p386) awes you with the world's biggest living things – the giant sequoia trees – while Lassen Volcanic National Park (p288) welcomes you into a bizarre world of hissing fumaroles, cinder cones and craters.

Back on the coast, there's excellent hiking in Big Sur, where the Ventana Wilderness (p456) combines coastal redwoods and hot springs with cool ocean views. Feel the wind in your face on a stroll around Point Reyes National Seashore (p152) or embark on a prehistoric time-warp at Prairie Creek Redwoods State Park (p276) on the North Coast.

Hiking in the deserts is at its peak in winter, when other regions may be too cold or wet. Even then, trails are rarely crowded in Joshua Tree National Park (p657), where you can explore canyon oases or walk between boulders the size of houses. In the remote Mojave National Preserve the serene Kelso Dunes (p663) are a surprisingly challenging clamber.

Altitude junkies will feel the magnetic pull of Mt Whitney (p405), the tallest mountain in the lower US, and the equally breathtaking, if slightly shorter, Mt Shasta (p299). Standing on the summit of either is a truly uplifting experience, but getting there is a serious challenge requiring top form and good prep work.

Fees

California state parks don't charge admission but most levy a parking fee ranging from $4 to $14. There is no charge if you walk or bike into these parks. The entrance fee to national parks varies from $5 to $20 per vehicle and is good for unlimited entries over seven consecutive days. If you're going to visit many national parks, in California or elsewhere, consider getting a National Parks Pass. For details, see the boxed text, p63.

Wilderness areas and most national forests are free, with the exception of the San Bernardino, Cleveland, Angeles and Los Padres forests in Southern California. For these you will need to obtain a **National Forest Adventure Pass** (www.fsadventurepass.org; day/year $5/30) unless you're just driving through, stopping at a ranger station or visitors center, are already paying another forest-use fee (eg camping or cabin fees) or have a Golden Eagle or Golden Age Pass. The annual passes are good for one year from the month of purchase and are transferable. US Forest Service (USFS) ranger stations, sporting-goods stores and other vendors sell passes, or you can order one over the phone (☎ 909-382-2622). The website has a full list of vendors by city.

Wilderness Permits

Most national parks and some forests and wilderness areas require overnight hikers (and occasionally day-hikers) to carry wilderness permits (also called backcountry permits), which are issued by ranger stations and some visitors centers. To prevent them from being loved to death, the most popular trails are subject to a quota system that limits the number of hikers and/or backpackers who start out daily from each trailhead. This system prevents overcrowding and reduces environmental impact. Quotas are only in effect during peak periods, usually from late spring to early fall.

A certain percentage of permits may usually be reserved ahead of time, while the rest are issued on a first-come, first-serve basis. Permits are usually free, although reservations may cost a few dollars. Some less-impacted trails have self-issuing permits available at the trailhead or outside ranger stations. Details about how to obtain wilderness permits for specific areas are provided throughout this book.

Safety Issues

Hiking and backpacking carry inherent risks, especially in mountain areas. To help make your trek a safe one, plan to be self-sufficient. For longer hikes especially, obtain the best available maps. Weather can be

The summit of Mt Whitney was first reached on August 18, 1873 by Charles Begole, Albert Johnson and John Lucas via the West Slope. In October of the same year, John Muir got to the top via the Mountaineers Route.

John Muir (1838–1914), one of the earliest and most influential California conservationists, founded the Sierra Club in 1892, two years after his lobbying efforts had led to the establishment of Yosemite and Sequoia National Parks.

If you were to hike the entire Pacific Crest Trail, you'd climb 60 major mountains, plummet into enormous canyons 19 times and skirt more than 1000 lakes.

LONG-DISTANCE HIKES

Several long-distance trails wind through California, including the Pacific Crest Trail that will take you from Mexico to Canada almost without leaving national park or national forest lands.

Pacific Crest Trail

California is traversed by part of perhaps the most ambitious long-distance route ever conceived, the Pacific Crest Trail (PCT). This epic footpath zigzags along the ridgelines of spectacular mountain ranges for 2638 miles from Mexico to Canada, passing through 24 national forests, seven national parks, 33 wilderness areas and five state parks at an average elevation of 5000ft.

To hike the entire trail, moving at a good clip of 15 miles a day, would take nearly six months – four of them in California. But you don't have to commit to such an ambitious cross-state trek to get a taste of the PCT. Day or weekend hikers can plan short trips on accessible segments of the trail as it wends its way through Anza-Borrego Desert State Park, Sequoia & Kings Canyon National Parks, Yosemite National Park, past Lake Tahoe and Lassen Volcanic National Park.

The website of the Pacific Crest Trail Association at www.pcta.org is an excellent planning tool.

John Muir Trail

The 212-mile John Muir Trail, which links Yosemite Valley and Mt Whitney, parallels the PCT for long stretches, veering from it only in the Devils Postpile area near Mammoth Lakes and at the Mt Whitney summit.

Tahoe Rim Trail

North of Yosemite, the Tahoe Rim Trail wraps around the Lake Tahoe Basin, along lofty ridges and mountaintops, for 150 miles. Hikers, equestrians and – in some sections – mountain-bikers can enjoy inspirational views of the lake and the snowcapped Sierra Nevada while tracing the footsteps of early pioneers, Basque shepherds and the Washoe people. For more information, contact the **Tahoe Rim Association** (☎ 775-573-0686; www.tahoerimtrail.org).

---

unpredictable, so carry adequate clothing and equipment. Afternoon summer thunderstorms, for instance, are very common in the Sierra Nevada and the deserts. Backpackers should have a pack liner (heavy-duty garbage bags work well), a full set of rain gear and food that does not require cooking.

There's nothing wrong with pushing yourself a little, but be careful not to overdo it. Pick a hike that matches your time frame and the physical ability of the least-fit member in your group. Before heading out, seek local advice on trails, equipment and weather by calling or stopping by a ranger station, visitors center or local sports shop. Pay attention on the trail and be aware of potential dangers. A minor injury, a twisted ankle or a fall down a hillside can be life-threatening if you're alone. Always let someone know where you're going and how long you plan to be gone. Use sign-in boards at trailheads or ranger stations. Carry a cell phone, but don't rely on it: service is spotty or nonexistent in many areas.

Mosquitoes are the creatures most likely to torture you while you're out in the woods. They are at their peskiest around sundown; if you're camping, building a fire will help keep them away. Besides being a major nuisance, a bite can potentially – though very rarely – transmit the West Nile virus. See p730 for advice on how to protect yourself.

Encountering animals on the trail can be a delight, but they can also represent serious danger if you invade their turf. For information on bears, see p66. Other animals, including mountain lions, rattlesnakes and spiders, are briefly discussed on p704.

Since its introduction in 1997 the National Forest Adventure Pass has raised almost $21 million. The funds are used to improve facilities, trails and signs; increase public safety; and clean up graffiti and litter. About 20% goes toward administrative costs.

Maps

For short, well-established hikes in national or state parks, the free and basic sketch maps handed out at ranger stations and visitors centers are usually sufficient. If you're headed into the rugged backcountry, though, especially on multiday trips, you shouldn't venture out on the trail without a good topographic map. The best are the series of 1:24,000 scale maps published by the **US Geological Survey** (USGS; http://store.usgs.gov; maps $6). They can be ordered through the website or purchased at local ranger stations, outfitters and visitors centers.

Consummate explorers might find it worth investing in the California edition of the *Topo! State Series* ($100) published by **National Geographic** (☎ 800-962-1643; www.maps.nationalgeographic.com). This downloadable topographic mapping software offers five levels of mapping detail (including USGS's 1:24,000 and 1:100,000 scale maps), generates elevation profiles and lets you customize and print whatever map you need. The software is also compatible with most handheld GPS units (such as those made by Garmin or Magellan), letting you upload waypoints and routes.

SKIING & SNOWBOARDING

Modern lifts, trails from 'Sesame Street' to 'Death Wish,' breathtaking scenery, cozy mountain cabins, steaming mulled wine, hearty dinners by a crackling fireplace – all these are the hallmarks of a California vacation in the snow.

The Sierra Nevada offers the best slopes and trails as well as the most reliable conditions. For sheer variety, the 14 downhill and eight cross-country resorts surrounding Lake Tahoe (p335) are unbeatable. Alongside such world-famous places as Squaw Valley USA, host of the 1960 Winter Olympic Games, and Heavenly, you'll find scores of smaller operations, many of them with lower ticket prices, smaller crowds and great runs for beginners and families. Royal Gorge, near Truckee west of Lake Tahoe, is North America's largest cross-country ski resort.

About a two-hour drive south, in the Eastern Sierra, Mammoth Mountain (p396) is another darling of downhill devotees and usually has the longest season. There are enough runs to keep you busy for a week, and not one, not two but three constantly evolving terrain parks. It has a rollicking après-ski scene where people party as hard as they ski. If you want something quieter, consider neighboring June Mountain (p395). Yosemite's Badger Pass (p348) is another low-key place that's ideal for

The often hilarious but also very informative *How to Shit in the Woods: An Environmentally Sound Approach to a Lost Art* by Kathleen Meyer is still the 'bible' on the subject and a must-read for backcountry novices.

For a big bag of tips and tricks on how to minimize your impact on the environment while traipsing through the wilderness, visit the Leave No Trace Center for Outdoor Ethics website at www.lnt.org.

TREADING LIGHTLY

If you're planning a hike or backcountry adventure in California, it's essential that you do so responsibly. One thoughtless gesture – hiking off-trail through fragile soil or building an illegal fire – can cause damage that takes years for nature to repair. The cumulative effect of millions of boots crunching along the trails every year is taking its toll on many areas.

Once in the wild, do everything possible to minimize your impact. Stick to established trails and campsites. Be particularly sensitive to areas around lakes, rivers and the like: don't wash yourself or your dishes in streams or rivers, and camp and poop at least 250ft from waterways. Use a gas stove for cooking or make fires in established fire rings only. When you leave, take out everything you packed in and remove every trace of your visit.

Conduct yourself as if you were a guest in someone's house – which, in fact, you are. Observe wildlife from a distance, but do not approach or feed it. If you find cultural or historic artifacts, leave them untouched. Finally, be aware and respectful of other visitors. Human noise travels far and is the fastest way to spoil a whole valley's worth of solitude.

NATIONAL PARKS PASSES

If you'll be visiting several national parks or are planning multiple trips within a one-year period, consider buying a National Parks Pass for $50. It entitles holders and anyone else traveling with them in the same vehicle to unlimited admission to any national park for one year from the month of purchase. You can buy it at park entrances or in advance by calling ☎ 888-467-2757 or online at www.nationalparks.org.

For an additional $15, you can upgrade to a **Golden Eagle Pass**, which is good for admission to sites managed by the US Fish and Wildlife Service, the US Forest Service and the Bureau of Land Management as well as all national parks.

The **Golden Age Passport** is a variation on the theme but only available to US citizens and permanent residents aged over 62. It costs $10 and is a lifetime entrance pass to all sites also covered by the Golden Eagle Pass. You also get 50% discount on camping, parking, tours and other fees. The pass is only available in person at any entrance station and you must show proof of age.

There's the **Golden Access Passport**, available to citizens or permanent US residents who are blind or permanently disabled. It works the same way as the Golden Age Passport, except that there is no age restriction and it is free.

The US Department of the Interior is planning to replace the various National Parks Passes with the **America the Beautiful Pass** by 2007. The single new pass will be valid for entry at all federal recreation sites that charge entrance fees. Stay tuned.

---

beginners and families. Cross-country skiing is especially wonderful in this national park as well as in Sequoia & Kings Canyon, where you can glissade among the giant trees.

In Northern California, Mt Shasta Board & Ski Park (p299) is the most popular ski area, although there's also skiing at Cedar Pass Snow Park (p306) in the Modoc National Forest and at the brand-new Dyer Mountain Resort (p291) on Lake Almanor.

Even sunny Southern California gets in on the action with two ski mountains in Big Bear Lake (p560). While these can't compete in size and variety with the Sierra resorts, they're only a 2½-hour drive from Los Angeles. Yes, you could ski in the morning and surf in the afternoon.

The skiing season generally runs from late November/early December to early April, although this of course depends on specific elevations and weather conditions. Efficient snowmaking equipment ensures winter fun even in years when nature doesn't play along. All resorts have ski schools and equipment-rental facilities as well as plenty of lodgings, restaurants, shops, entertainment venues and day-care facilities. A variety of lift tickets are available, including half-day, all-day and multi-day versions. Prices vary tremendously and can be as low as $25 or as high as $65 for adults; discounts for children, teens, students and seniors are always available. 'Ski & stay' packages may offer the best value.

Many resorts offer free or low-cost shuttle buses to area hotels.

Even if you don't surf, you'll get an adrenaline kick from the exhilarating cinematography of the surfing documentary *Riding Giants* (Stacy Peralta, 2004). For a retro take on the sport, check out the classic *The Endless Summer* (Bruce Brown, 1966).

SURFING

Surfing is California's signature sport. Invented by Pacific Islanders, it first landed here in 1907 when railroad tycoon Henry Huntington invited Hawaiian hunk George Freeth to Los Angeles to help promote a new shoreside development with his surfing demonstrations. Since then, surfing has imbued a look, language and lifestyle perceived as laid-back, easy-going and totally dedicated to sun and sea.

California has lots of easily accessible world-class surf spots up and down the coast. Famous spots include Steamers Lane (p436) in Santa Cruz, Mavericks (p184) near Half Moon Bay, Surfrider (p531) in Malibu

For the complete lowdown on surfing, pick up a copy of *Surfing California: A Complete Guide to the Best Breaks on the California Coast* by Raul Guisado and Jeff Klaas.

MORE TO DO? SURE!

If none of the activities outlined in this chapter appeal, rest assured that there's plenty of other stuff going on in the Golden State. Rock hounds can test their mettle on world-class **climbs** in places such as Yosemite National Park (p367), Joshua Tree National Park (p657), Donner Summit (p348) near Lake Tahoe, and Bishop (p402) in the Eastern Sierra. **Golfers** can tee off at more than 100 courses in Palm Springs and the Coachella Valley (p644) alone, or at the famed Pebble Beach and Spyglass Hill (p451).

Rock reefs, shipwrecks and kelp beds teem with fish ready for their close-up, especially in the warmer waters of Southern California where the San Diego–La Jolla Underwater Park Ecological Reserve (p612) and Catalina Island (p558) are major **diving and snorkeling** destinations.

Kayaking is also great around Catalina as well as in the Channel Islands National Park (p492) further north and off such Central Coast towns as Morro Bay (p465) and Monterey (p446). Other kayaking spots are scattered throughout this book.

---

and Rincón in Ventura. All are point breaks (where swells peak into steep waves as they encounter a shelf-like point), known for their consistently clean, glassy, big waves. The most powerful swells arrive in winter, while May and June are generally the flattest months, although they do bring warmer water.

Crowds are a problem in many places. Some surfers can be aggressively territorial, notably at San Diego's Windansea (p611) and Huntington Beach (p576) in Orange County. It's best to befriend a local surfer for an introduction.

Mavericks, near Half Moon Bay, is one of the world's most famous destinations for big-wave surfing, with breakers that can top out at over 50ft. The first person to surf the spot was Jeff Clark in 1975. He remained Mavericks' sole rider for 15 years.

The best places to learn surfing are at beach breaks or long, shallow bays where waves are small and rolling. Mission Beach and Tourmaline (p611), both in San Diego, and Seal Beach (p575) in Orange County are good beginner spots. South of the latter, Huntington Beach wears its 'Surf City USA' moniker with pride. It has a surfing walk of fame, a pro-am surf series championship each September and an interesting surfing museum. Other museums are in Santa Cruz and Oceanside (p628), which holds its own pair of surfing competitions every June.

You'll find surfboard rental stands on just about every beach where surfing is possible. Expect to pay about $10 per hour; group lessons start at $40 per person.

Safety issues to watch out for include riptides, which are powerful currents of water that draws you away from the shore (see p704). Sharks do inhabit California waters but attacks are extremely rare. Since 1950 there have been 106 shark attacks in this state, including 10 fatal ones. Most took place in the so-called Red Triangle between Monterey on the Central Coast, Tomales Bay just north of San Francisco and the offshore Farallon Islands.

George Freeth, the father of California surf culture, was also the state's first lifeguard and earned a Congressional Medal of Honor for rescuing a boatload of stranded fishermen. He died in the great influenza epidemic of 1919 at the age of 36.

RAFTING

California has scads of kick-ass rivers and feeling their surging power is like taking a thrilling ride on nature's rollercoaster. Sure, there are some serene floats suitable for picnics with grandpa and the kiddies, but then there are the others. White-water giants swelled by the snowmelt that rip through sheer canyons. Roaring cataracts that hurtle you through chutes where gushing water compresses through a 10ft gap between menacing boulders. Pour-overs, voracious hydraulics, endless Class III-IV standing waves wrenching at your shoulders as you scream and punch on through to the next onslaught. The thinking process is reduced to two simple words: 'survive' and 'enjoy.' Too much for you? Fortunately, between these two extremes run myriad other rivers suited to the tastes and abilities of any river rat.

Commercial outfitters run a variety of trips, from short, inexpensive morning or afternoon outings to overnight and multiday expeditions. For details see the destination chapters.

Nearest to Sacramento are the awesome American and Stanislaus Rivers. If you're a rafting virgin, a good place to get your feet and the rest of you wet is the South Fork American (p319; Class II–III, May to mid-October), which is also ideal for families. The North Fork American (Class IV, April to June) and Middle Fork American (Class IV, June to September) are quite a bit more challenging as they carve through deep gorges in the Sierra foothills.

Two rivers cascade down from Yosemite National Park. The Merced River (p367; Class III–IV, April to July), which runs past abandoned gold mines and water flumes, is the Sierra's best one-day intermediate trip. More-experienced types might prefer the more ferocious Tuolumne River (p367; Class IV, March to October). A run on 'the T,' a federally designated Wild and Scenic River, is considered the best all-around white-water trip in California.

From the highest reaches of the Kings-Kern Divide flows the Kern River (p431), which cuts a steep canyon through Sequoia National Park. Trips on the Lower Kern (Class II–IV, April to September) and the Upper Kern (Class III–IV, April to July), both staged near Bakersfield, have the best white water in the southern Sierra. There's also rafting on the Truckee River (p348; Class III, June to September), north of Lake Tahoe.

You'll be hurtling along either in large rafts for a dozen or more people, or smaller ones seating half a dozen; the latter tend to be more exhilarating because they can tackle rougher rapids and everyone participates in the paddling. Most outfitters also rent white-water kayaks and canoes, which require more skill and maneuvering. Instruction is usually provided.

White-water trips are not without danger, and it's not unusual for participants to fall out of the raft in rough conditions. Serious injuries, though, are rare and most trips are without incident. No prior experience is needed for guided trips up to Class III, but for Class IV and up you want to be healthy, active, in good shape and an excellent swimmer. Rafters must wear life jackets. All trips have at least one river guide trained in lifesaving techniques.

Rivers and rapids are ranked on the international six-point scale:

Class I (easy) Flat water to occasional series of mild rapids.

Class II (medium) Frequent stretches of rapids with waves up to 3ft high and easy chutes, ledges and falls. The best route is easy to identify, the entire river can be run in open canoes and no great skill or maneuvering is required.

Class III (difficult) Numerous rapids with high, irregular waves and difficult chutes and falls that often require scouting. These rivers are for experienced paddlers who either use kayaks or rafts or have spray covers for their canoes.

Class IV (very difficult) Long stretches of high, irregular waves, powerful back eddies and even constricted canyons. Scouting is mandatory, and rescues can be difficult in many places. Rafts or white-water kayaks in which paddlers are equipped with helmets are suitable for these rivers.

Class V (extremely difficult) Continuous violent rapids, large drops, powerful rollers and high, extreme hydraulics and holes, unavoidable waves and haystacks. These rivers are only for professional rafters and white-water kayakers who are proficient in the Eskimo roll.

Class VI (highest level of difficulty) Rarely run except by highly experienced kayakers under ideal conditions. The likelihood of serious injury or worse is high.

The last-known California grizzly bear was killed near Sequoia National Park in 1922. All bears roaming the state today are black bears.

Yosemite National Park reported 721 bear incidents in 2004, where bears damaged property, stole food or (rarely) caused injuries.

BEAR NECESSITIES

California's forests swarm with an estimated 16,000 to 24,000 black bears, which actually range in color from black to cinnamon and grow to about 3.5ft tall (standing on all four feet). Their main turf is below 8000ft in the forest and shrublands of Northern California and the Sierra Nevada, but some fellows also hang out in the wooded areas of the Central Coast and Southern California. Observing a bear can be a thrilling experience that'll etch its way into your memory forever. However, there are a few basic rules to ensure a smooth encounter.

In the Wild

If you spot a bear foraging in the woods…

- Stay together and keep your children especially close.
- Don't get too close to the animal(s); at least 50yd is a good distance.
- Stand still and watch but don't linger too long.
- Never, ever, get between a cub and momma bear.
- Avoid surprising a bear by talking, singing or otherwise making noise to alert it that you're coming.

At Campgrounds & Cabins

Bears are intelligent opportunists who quickly learn that humans come with food and tasty garbage. Some of them visit campgrounds and even work their way into locked cars if they sniff a snack inside. Unfortunately, once this association is learned, a bear has to be 'managed' by park rangers, sometimes even resulting in the need to kill it. Remember: a fed bear is (potentially) a dead bear. Here's what to do:

- Store all food products, toiletries and other smelly things in bear-resistant lockers provided at all developed campsites in bear country. Keep your campground clean and tidy.
- On many backcountry hikes, storing your food in bear-resistant canisters is mandatory. Containers may be rented for a few dollars at ranger stations, visitors centers and other places. Hanging your food in a tree (the counter-balancing method) no longer works reliably as many bears figured out that trick years ago.
- When staying in cabins or motels in high-impact areas (such as Yosemite), remove everything that looks even remotely like food from your vehicle. This includes lipstick and candy wrappers. Some parking lots near trailheads also have bear boxes; use them or risk a fine.
- If a bear wanders into your campground, don't approach it. Get everyone together and yell, clap your hands, throw stones or sticks, bang pots and try looking big and more intimidating. Always leave the bear an escape route.

If Attacked

In the extremely unlikely event that you are attacked by a bear, do the following:

- Drop to the ground, crouch face down in a ball and play dead, covering the back of your neck with your hands, and your chest and stomach with your knees. As scary as it is, try not to resist the bear's inquisitive pawing – it may get bored and go away.
- If the attack persists, fighting back by any means available like throwing rocks, hitting it with your gear or a big stick can be effective.
- Never run from a bear, as this only triggers its instinct to chase, and you cannot outrun a bear.

Food & Drink

Start with the finest, freshest ingredients on the planet. Distribute among hundreds of distinct immigrant communities, leaving just enough room for cross-fertilization. Let rise. Fold in a burgeoning foodie culture that has raised eating to cult-like status. Work up appetite hiking, swimming, strolling, surfing, getting lost, checking map, finding way again. Locate venue. Take load off feet. Eat extremely well. Repeat thrice daily.

Everything grows in California, and in abundance, which explains why 'California Cuisine' eschews complex processes and heavy sauces in favor of the magical notion that ingredients should speak for themselves. Meat is kissed with fresh herbs, dusted with salt and pepper, and then grilled on an open flame. Vegetables, bathed more than boiled, retain the satisfying crunch of rawness. It's a culinary revolution that, like so many other ideas incubated in the Golden State, has helped transform the way the world thinks about fine dining.

But in a state that attracts large numbers of immigrants from around the world, California Cuisine is just one of the ways California eats. For a fraction of the price of dinner at Chez Panisse, you can gorge on dim sum or sushi, Salvadoran tamales or a bowl of Thai noodle soup. The burrito is California's hamburger – actually, Mexican food is so ubiquitous (and delicious and cheap) that it can hardly be considered 'ethnic.' At the same time, there are plenty of all-American diners slinging bacon and eggs in the morning and turkey and gravy at night. In a rush? There's always Mickey D's. We don't recommend it, but at least you can tell yourself you're in the state where McDonald's got its start.

STAPLES & SPECIALTIES

For raw ingredients, California has no rival. From April to October, the sun shines uninterruptedly on the Central Valley, while melting Sierra snows, carefully channeled, water its deep, alluvial soil. Nearly everything grows under such conditions. Where the land turns hilly, wild grasses provide ideal pasture for cows, sheep and their hoofed cousins. And with a thousand miles of coastline, and many times that in lakes, rivers and streams, the state could go a year without repeating the fish of the day.

Much of the state's farmland is dominated by agribusiness, whose profits depend not so much on a delicious tomato but on one that packs easily, ripens en route to market and looks tomato-like on the supermarket shelf. But these days, as foodies clamor for the finest raw ingredients, Californian farmers are obliging them with heirloom fruits and vegetables, artisanal cheeses, free-range chicken and grass-fed beef.

Sometimes it can all get a little precious – who cares if tortilla chips are 'hand cut'? Still, the quality and variety of ingredients are dazzling, as is the sheer number of ways the state's chefs deploy them. Any list of California's staples and specialties must be partial.

Artichokes

At first glance the thorny artichoke hardly seems worth the effort, but Californians prize the delicate flesh at the base of the plant's leaves. You can steam the artichoke, then simply tear off one leaf at a time, dip into mayonnaise, and scrape off that precious bit of meat with your teeth. You can eat baby artichokes whole – just slice them and sauté with garlic and

Read anything by MFK Fisher (1908–92). A Whittier native, she is categorized as a 'food writer,' though her work avoids food fetishism to embrace more elemental hungers.

She sounded English and cooked French food, but Julia Childs (1912–2004) was a Pasadena native. Her classic *Mastering the Art of French Cooking*, together with her wildly popular TV shows, are credited with transforming the way Americans eat, ushering in the current 'foodie' revolution.

If you're staying in San Francisco and have access to a kitchen, get Charles Lemos' *Everybody's San Francisco Cookbook*. He demystifies the city's myriad ethnic cuisines with straightforward recipes, explanations of 'exotic' ingredients and a practical guide for the best – and freshest – ingredients.

olive oil. Or quarter the adult 'heart,' then deep-fry. That's how it's done in Castroville, the source of virtually all of America's artichokes.

Artisanal Breads & Cheeses

Dusted with ash or wrapped in stinging nettles, ripened almost to soup or pressed into savory blocks, artisanal cheeses in California have come to rival those of France for both quality and variety. Likewise, independent bakers have imported Old World techniques that put Wonder Bread to shame.

Avocado

With origins in southern Mexico, the 'alligator pear' has flourished under the California sun. Eat its buttery green flesh straight up, drizzled with salt and olive oil, or perhaps tossed in a salad. Or dress it with shrimp and a creamy sauce. And of course there's guacamole (avocado, onion and lemon), the quintessential California garnish.

Burrito

With three basic ingredients and thousands of variations, the burrito (Spanish for 'little donkey') is California's comfort food. It begins with a large flour tortilla followed by a ladle of beans (black, pinto or refried), and a dose of salsa (tomatoes, onions, cilantro and chili peppers). To this you may add any or all of the following: rice, diced meat (grilled or stewed with tomatoes and spices), grilled vegetables, cheese, guacamole, sour cream or lettuce. Cheap, ubiquitous and hard to ruin, the burrito is a great travel solution.

Dim Sum

Legend has it that Cantonese cooks invented dim sum to feed hungry travelers on the Silk Road. Kept warm in bamboo baskets set above a steam table, dim sum consists of bite-size morsels, including shrimp dumplings, pork buns, and fat rice noodles infused with scallions and salt pork. It is taken with tea and served nonstop from breakfast until the late afternoon.

Dungeness Crab

Winter means crabs for Frisco foodies. Just boil the Dungeness crab in salted water, and its claws and fat body – about the size of two cupped palms – will reward you with sweet, flaky morsels that need at most melted butter. The Dungeness forms the basis of Crab Louie, a San Francisco classic. Its meat is laid on a bed of lettuce, garnished with tomatoes and chopped egg, and dressed with a combo of mayonnaise and chili sauce.

Fish Tacos

Quintessential surfer fare, the fish taco arrived in California by way of Mexico's Baja peninsula and remains most popular in SoCal beach towns. You just can't beat this brilliant combination: small corn or flour tortilla, chunks of meaty white fish dipped in batter and lightly fried, creamy sauce and shredded iceberg lettuce.

Noodle Soup

For five or six bucks, Thai and Laotian eateries throughout the state will serve you a huge bowl of fat rice noodles in chicken broth, featuring either fish balls or shredded chicken or beef, dressed cilantro, spinach, golden bits garlic and pepper flakes. There's also a version with a spicier, thicker broth. Both are heavenly. The Vietnamese version is called *pho* –

Alice Waters' *Chez Panisse Vegetables* could be called the bible of California cuisine. Its artful engravings and simple but lovely prose teach you not just how to select, store and cook vegetables, but to admire them as aesthetic objects in their own right.

With annual sales topping $25 billion, agriculture means big money in California. The state produces almost all the nation's grapes, almonds and artichokes, 75% of its strawberries and lettuce, and half its tomatoes. Dairy products are the real cash cow, bringing in $4 billion annually.

As relief from the burdens of working on California's railroads in the mid-19th century, Chinese bakers invented the fortune cookie, a New World take on the ancient tradition of inserting messages of luck and good wishes into baked sweets.

HOMEGROWN

Californians have always mixed morals and pleasure. During the 1960s, sex and drugs made you a better person. In more conservative times, it's fine dining that'll save your soul.

California has taught the rest of America a neat trick: if you buy organic, locally grown produce, your dinner will taste better, and you'll save the environment, too. Alice Waters, founder of Chez Panisse, pioneered the idea back in the early 1970s, and for years encouraged customers to bring her the fruits of their own backyard gardens.

The difference in taste can be astounding – a vine-ripened tomato makes the ones sprayed with red-inducing chemicals appear laughable. Yet supermarkets simply cannot carry many of the tastiest fruits and vegetables – they'd never survive packing and storage. These days, the best restaurants insist on organic, locally grown products, preferably picked within the previous 24 hours. At the same time, farmers markets have sprung up around the state, bringing sustainable agriculture directly to the consumer – and often resulting in a personal relationship between grower and gourmand. Learn more about the movement at www.ferryplazafarmersmarket.com.

---

thinner noodles in broth served with a heaping plate of greens (mint, sprouts and basil) which you add yourself.

Salad

A 12-month growing season gives California salads their year-round crunch. Since the foodie revolution, a green salad usually implies 'mesclun,' which adds to lettuce the bitter and sweet tangs of kale, endive, beet greens, spinach, sorrel, radicchio, cress and mustard. Californians have taught the world to make a meal out of a salad, too. Consider the Cobb (lettuce, tomato, egg, chicken, bacon and roquefort), with origins in 1920s Hollywood.

Sourdough Bread

Its most classic form is a round loaf with a thick, golden crust surrounding a dense, white and distinctly tangy interior. Served warm from the oven with fresh butter, it has proven addictive since the Gold Rush days when, by chance, a baker in San Francisco accidentally infected his dough with the lactobacillus bug.

DRINKS

From designer water to world-class wine, Californians drink at least as well as they eat. In fact, California's entry into the USA can be traced to an excess of grape. In 1846, a group of ragtag adventurers were whooping it up in Sonoma when, under the influence of the local wine, they decided to seize the state government from Mexican authorities (p32). The war that ensued vindicated this drunken bravado. Welcome to California. Drink up.

Wine

California never saw a grape until the latter part of the 18th century, when the state's first missionaries planted them to produce communion wine. In the 1830s, secular drinkers, sick of plonk, imported the first premium varietals, and by the end of the century California was quietly winning medals at Paris expositions. But it was only in 1976 that the upstart state finally earned its international credibility. That's when Stag's Leap cabernet sauvignon and Chateau Montelena chardonnay – both from Napa Valley – beat all rivals at the Paris Tasting, aka the 'World Cup of Wine.'

These days, history has come full circle as California oenophiles raise tippling to a sacramental act. During the Internet bubble of the late

---

Lacking traditional ingredients, Chinese immigrants settled for 'chopped suey,' a bland concoction based on onions, celery and thin noodles, perhaps with seasonal vegetables and leftover meat. The name is said to originate from the phrase 'tsa sui' – 'a bit of this and that.'

In 1924, a group of hungry revelers arrived at Caesar Cardini's Tijuana restaurant after closing time. Cardini had only romaine lettuce, a few eggs, anchovies and stale bread. The revelers grew belligerent. And so was born the Caesar Salad. That's the story, anyway.

WINE FOR THOUGHT

What should you drink with roast chicken? If you came up with pinot noir, pinot blanc, Bordeaux and Champagne, you'd still only get partial credit. 'Pairing' – the art of matching the right wine with the right food – is the final frontier for California foodies. The possibilities are endless, especially in a state with such diversity in wines, raw ingredients and cooking styles.

Top restaurants have sommeliers, or at least well-informed waiters, who will gladly take the pressure off. And to make things even easier, more and more restaurants offer 'pairing menus' that include a different half-glass of wine with each course. In the end, they can be a bargain as well as an education, since you don't have to order multiple bottles.

For a quick interactive guide to matching food and wine, check out the informative website www.wineanswers.com/food_categories.asp.

Head to www.west coastwine.com for insider insight into wine from California and beyond. The interactive site includes message boards, wine notes and live chats.

'90s, oenophilia became a mark of social status, and to own a vineyard was Silicon Valley's version of knighthood. But with a 200-year history, California wines transcend trends.

Sonoma (p191), Mendocino (p255), and above all Napa counties (p217) continue to produce the state's most illustrious vintages. Napa's combination of coastal hills, sunny valley floor and proximity to cold ocean currents produce microclimates that can mean huge variations in temperature and moisture levels within even a few miles. The result: the valley mimics in just 30 narrow miles nearly all the wine-growing regions of France. Cabernet sauvignon and chardonnay vines dominate, though everything grows here. Like Napa, neighboring Sonoma and Mendocino boast complex microclimates and a wide array of grapes. Sonoma's Carneros pinot noirs are particularly prized. See p190 for more on the topic.

But in California, excellent wine isn't limited to 'Wine Country.' The 2004 film *Sideways* (p482), a paean to Central Coast pinot noirs, has woken up NoCal wine snobs to the rest of the state. A combination of sun and cooling ocean breezes, often accompanied by morning and evening fog, define the region's output, including prized Soledad pinot noirs.

The foothills of the Sierra (p322) favor the hearty zinfandel. Santa Clara County produces fine chardonnay and cabernet sauvignon. In the Central Valley, vineyards stretch out like Kansas wheat fields, generating 75% of the state's wine. Much is plonk, but smaller growers successfully defy the hot, dry climate by planting grenache, barbera and chenin blanc.

Beer

The hilarious 2004 film *Sideways* captures both the passion and folly of California's wine scene. Pinot noir, a highly sensitive grape that prospers only under very rare climatic conditions, becomes a metaphor for the main character, played brilliantly by Paul Giamatti.

San Francisco brought the world 'steam' beer, whose amber color and malty aromas put it somewhere between lager and porter. San Francisco's Anchor Steam remains among the state's most popular native brands, along with Sierra Nevada and Yard House. If you like your beer handcrafted, seek out any of the microbreweries listed in the destination chapters. Just about every city and large town has one.

Spirits

Some claim the martini was invented at San Francisco's Occidental Hotel. True or not, it's a fitting myth for a town with a long history of hard drinking. The late '90s produced a huge comeback of 1950s-style martini bars, but gin has now taken a back seat to vodka, with deviations like lemon- and chocolate-flavored martinis. Irish coffee (coffee, cream, sugar and Irish whiskey) is another California tradition, while margaritas (made with tequila, lime, Cointreau, ice and salt) are beloved throughout the state.

Coffee

In California, espresso was ubiquitous long before Starbucks. These days you can get a double cap at a gas station, so don't be ashamed to wrinkle your nose at pale brown water. However, diners and greasy spoons still usually serve only weak brews.

Juices

With its fruitful valleys and health-conscious populace, fresh juice is a California natural. Pioneering Odwalla, and now numerous imitators, deliver farm-fresh juices to supermarkets and convenience stores. Juice bars like the Jamba Juice chain specialize in smoothies: fruit blended with ice and yogurt, sorbet, 'vitamin boosters,' and other goodies.

CELEBRATIONS

Fair-weather holidays are always an excuse for barbecues, though iconoclastic Californians grill salmon and portobello mushrooms next to burgers and hot dogs. At Thanksgiving and Christmas, roast turkey takes center stage. The latest craze is to brine the fowl (soak it in saltwater) before roasting, producing a particularly succulent bird.

The state celebrates its tremendous bounty with countless festivals that typically include tastings and cooking demonstrations as well as parades, music and carnival games. The largest include Indio's date festival in February (p644), Castroville's artichoke festival in May, Gilroy's garlic festival in July (p473), Carmel's tomato festival in September and Carpinteria's avocado festival in October. Wine fans should note that the Riverside County town of Temecula celebrates all four seasons, with wine fetes in January, May, August and November.

WHERE TO EAT & DRINK

For breakfast, many urban Northern Californians rely on neighborhood cafés and bakeries for strong coffee and freshly baked bread and pastries. Nearly everywhere, diners and greasy spoons will serve eggs and bacon or pancakes for $5 or less, or you can pay twice that for gussied-up versions of the same at yuppie brunch spots.

Some Mexican joints open in the morning, serving eggs with beans, salsa and cheese wrapped in a tortilla. It's called a breakfast burrito, and it's a beautiful thing. You can always head to your local strip mall or urban blight zone, where for a buck or so you can get a good doughnut and bad coffee. Dim sum is another option if you're near a Chinese neighborhood.

The lunch hour often lasts only 30 minutes for work-happy Americans, who generally eat light, then pause for a snack in the afternoon. The soup/sandwich/salad places get packed at lunchtimes. *Taquerías* also do a swift business, serving burritos and tacos in generally humble but festive digs. Ethnic restaurants often serve buffet-style lunches (Indian places in particular) or have a special that includes appetizer or soup, main course and perhaps dessert for under $10. Expect varying levels of decor, from fluorescent lights and easy-to-clean tile to cozy booths and walls hung with relevant handicrafts. Diners as well as self-consciously retro burger joints are another option. Except in business districts, the above-mentioned lunch places usually serve dinner as well, though you may pay a few more dollars per dish.

Many upscale bistros and finer dining establishments are open at lunch too, often offering steep midday discounts. Foodies on fixed budgets, take note. This can also be a workaround when you can't get a reservation at night.

Unable to re-create the cold temperatures necessary to brew lagers, Gold Rush brewers came up with a novel idea: they stuck with the lager recipe but brewed it according to ale methods. The result is America's only indigenous brew, the 'steam.'

The origins of the margarita are lost in the fog of time, though some say a Hollywood bartender came up with the concoction to win the business of '40s starlet Rita Hayworth (full name: Margarita).

The *SF Chronicle*'s food and wine sections are nationally renowned. For insight into the zeitgeist, as well as recipes and reviews, check out the encyclopedic (and user-friendly) sections at www.sfgate.com/food.

Find out how Berkeley schools are planting – and dining off – their own organic gardens at www.edibleschoolyard.org.

The holy temples of gastronomy concentrate their energies on dinner only. Reservations are recommended at any highly rated restaurant; on weekends, they're practically mandatory, unless you want to eat before 6pm or after 10pm. And at world-famous places like the French Laundry (p224) and Chez Panisse (p168) you will need to plan literally months in advance.

Lunch is generally served between 11:30am and 2:30pm, and dinner between 5:30pm and 10pm, though some restaurants close earlier.

Quick Eats

In some countries, it's not cool to be in a rush, but in California it implies personal status and/or virtuous hard work. As a result, most grocery stores sell to-go food, including sandwiches as well as roasted chickens, pastas, sushi and salads. Keep an eye out for farmers' markets and independent grocery stores listed throughout the book, both great places to grab food on the fly. Convenience stores, especially in upscale neighborhoods, can also offer surprisingly gourmet snacks.

In traditional Chinese neighborhoods, keep an eye peeled for dim sum joints. Or look for the distinctive silver trucks that serve tacos and other Mexican fast food – California's version of the New York hotdog vendor. The quality varies but price and convenience are first-rate.

VEGETARIANS & VEGANS

Welcome to the 'land of fruits and nuts,' where even steak houses have vegetarian mains. Metropolitan areas are replete with sure-fire veggie and vegan options. In suburban or rural areas, you'll find that most proper sit-down restaurants have vegetarian (though not always vegan) options, including quiches and omelettes, pasta, pilafs and pies, salads, grilled seasonal vegetables, baked squashes and eggplant (aubergine). When in doubt, Chinese and Indian restaurants almost always feature extensive veggie options. Even many Mexican restaurants offer vegetarian dishes – just make sure they don't use lard in the beans.

In 1948, the McDonald brothers opened a self-serve burger joint in San Bernardino, appealing to a car-loving populace that, in the post-WWII boom, was too busy to cook. Today the chain feeds 50 million people a day in more than 119 countries.

EATING WITH KIDS

If you've got kids in tow, most restaurants will be happy for your business. Mexican and Asian restaurants are particularly good options; both cultures tend to take their kids pretty much everywhere, and yours will be welcome too. Chain sit-down restaurants are also generally accommodating, even providing children's menus; it's sometimes printed on a take-home coloring book or placemat.

High-end restaurants are another matter. Meals can last two hours or more, too long to expect little ones to keep from squirming. Unless they're exceptionally well behaved, properly dressed and old enough to appreciate the meal, don't bring children without first calling to inquire.

HABITS & CUSTOMS

In California, as throughout the US, the main meal of the day is eaten in the evening. Breakfasts are traditionally hearty, though busy lifestyles have cut into the eggs-and-bacon tradition. Lunch tends to be a light affair – typically a sandwich, perhaps soup or salad, and a cookie or piece of fruit. For better or worse, Americans are also big snackers.

Founded by Alice Waters, the Edible Schoolyard teaches kids both ecological principles as well as the art of eating well.

If you're looking for huge, American-style portions, California may disappoint, at least at the higher-end places, where the idea is to savor, not gorge. Considering they're gourmands, Californians eat relatively early. In fine restaurants, the peak hour is 8pm to 9pm. Arrive earlier or later for a more serene dining experience.

DOS & DON'TS

Like all things Californian, restaurant etiquette tends toward the informal. Only a handful of restaurants require more than a dressy shirt, slacks and a decent pair of shoes; most places require far less than this. Here are some other things to keep in mind:

- Tipping is expected anywhere you receive table service. Unless the service is poor, leave 15% to 20% of the total.

- Smoking is illegal indoors, and is also not done in most private homes; restaurants sometimes have outdoor smoking sections, but check with the waiter and fellow guests before lighting up.

- Business lunches rarely include booze these days, though a glass of wine, while uncommon, is generally acceptable.

- It's perfectly fine in California to taste your neighbor's dish. You can also ask the waiter to divide a main course between two (or more) people, even in finer establishments.

- If you are vegetarian, suffer food allergies or are just plain picky, you're in luck – waiters are usually good about catering to specific food needs.

- You can bring your own wine to most restaurants, but expect to pay a 'corkage' fee of $10 to $30.

Meals tend to be quicker than in Europe, and don't feel you need to order every course every time. Unfortunately, you may feel rushed by your waiter at peak hours, even at midrange places, since they're working for tips and have a vested interest in 'turning the table.'

COOKING COURSES

Balboa Park Food and Wine School (p598)
California Culinary Academy Weekend Gourmet (Map pp80-1; ☎ 415-354-9198; www.baychef.com; 625 Polk St, San Francisco; classes $175; ☑ Sat morning)
Chronicle Cooking School (Map pp80-1; ☎ 415-777-7759; Ferry Bldg, 1 Market St, San Francisco; classes $60; ☑ 7-9pm Thu)
Laguna Culinary Arts (p582)
New School of Cooking (Map pp498-9; ☎ 310-842-9702; www.newschoolofcooking.com; 8690 Washington Blvd, Culver City, Los Angeles)
Ramekins Sonoma Valley Culinary School (p196)
Relish Culinary School (p212)

EAT YOUR WORDS

Here's a quick guide to items that regularly appear on California menus. See also Staples & Specialties (p67).

al dente – way of cooking pasta or veggies to preserve chewiness or crunch
carne asada – grilled beef
carnitas – shredded, well-browned pork
cioppino – soupy dish of tomato, Dungeness crab and other seafood
dulce de leche – South American version of caramel, made with milk and sugar
hangtown fry – Placerville specialty of eggs, bacon and oysters
heirloom – uncommon, rare or rediscovered breeds of fruits or vegetables
mesclun – gourmet salad mix
Meyer lemon – foodies' favorite with soft skin and sweet flesh
Mission fig – dark, sweet fig first cultivated in California missions
mole – rich, brown sauce, originally Mexican, made with chilies and chocolate
Monterey Jack cheese – sharp white cheese similar to cheddar
sun-dried tomatoes – chewy, intensely flavored tomatoes dried and stored in oil
tamale – corn dough stuffed with meat or cheese, wrapped in a corn husk and steamed
wheatgrass – vitamin-rich grass that makes a biting juice

San Francisco

San Francisco has collected more than its share of heartfelt compliments, along with a steady stream of overwrought attempts to avoid the platitudes. But there's little point in taking issue with the praise-singers. This is one gorgeous little city by the bay. A climb to the top of one of the city's 40-odd hills yields a unique panorama of Victorian houses, immense bridges, skyscrapers and stairway gardens sweeping up and down all those other hills. Behind everything the quiet, motherly bay. The notorious fog enters the frame here and there as if awaiting an invitation to pour into the urban corridors and obliterate the view altogether.

However, San Francisco's true appeal is its panoply of diverse cultures and lifestyles, of people earning a living and seeking ways to make their lives count. It's above all a city of individuals who, whether making a fortune or a statement, are clearly in the right place.

If you really want to know what Tony Bennett was on about, explore the neighborhoods. There's Chinatown, where Asian immigrants buy and sell bok choy, roast pigs and clay pots. There's the Mission District, with its *taquerías* and hip dive bars. North Beach retains its Italian heritage while transforming from beatnik HQ to yuppie lounge-lizard destination. In SoMa, bayfront condo developments, urban live–work lofts and a museum district blend with old warehouses and nightclubs. Sample the mind-boggling array of cuisines, some traditional, some hybrids, some seemingly made up on the way home from the farmers market.

Become a part of it, and take a little home with you. But don't leave your heart in San Francisco. Squishy little pumpers keep turning up and nobody knows what to do with them.

HIGHLIGHTS

- Riding or walking over the **Golden Gate Bridge** (p92)
- Exploring the city's colorful **neighborhoods** (p91)
- Supping in world-class **restaurants** (p114)
- Spending a little time behind bars at **Alcatraz** (p92)
- Drinking in **bars** (p124), preferably old dives

- POPULATION: 801,400
- AVERAGE TEMPS: JAN 46/57°F, JUL 54/65°F

HISTORY

San Francisco has existed for just over two centuries, but the city has managed to pack a lot of action into its short history. Soon after the establishment of the Spanish Mission and Presidio in 1776 came the demise and dispersion of the native Ohlone people. As the Spanish settled, trading posts, houses, grocery stores and grog shops gave some semblance of a town to the slopes that rose from the bay. It was at that time called Yerba Buena.

In 1821, at the end of Mexico's War of Independence, California became part of Mexico but, after the 1846 Mexican War resulted in US victory, was soon claimed by the USA. It turned out to be fortuitous timing for the Americans, because gold was discovered in 1848 in the nearby Sierra Nevada foothills. Almost overnight the sleepy village, newly renamed San Francisco, grew into a full-fledged city. By 1850, the year California was admitted as the 31st state in the Union, San Francisco's population had exploded from just 800 to 25,000. The newcomers, called '49ers, were mostly men under the age of 40. To keep them entertained, some 500 saloons and 20 theaters opened in the space of five years, not to mention casinos, bordellos, opium dens and distilleries. Certain sin-loving streets in the vicinity of the port (now Jackson Sq and the eastern edge of Chinatown) were well on their way to earning the sobriquet 'Barbary Coast,' a reference to the pirate-plagued coast of North Africa.

San Francisco remained a world-class hotbed of murder and mayhem until April 18, 1906, when the 'Big One' – an earthquake estimated at 8.3 on the yet-to-be-invented Richter scale – leveled more than half the city and is believed to have killed more than 3000 people. The hastily rebuilt city rapidly developed into a bustling metropolis.

San Francisco suffered through the Great Depression, but the city also benefited from gigantic public-works projects initiated by the federal government. The Bay Bridge was built in 1936, and the Golden Gate Bridge was completed the following year; both remain vital, beautiful symbols of the city. During WWII, the Bay Area became a major launching pad for military operations in the Pacific and huge shipyards soon sprang up around the bay.

The postwar years were marked by the prominence of colorful subcultures: the Beats spearheaded the '50s counterculture, and the hippies followed in the '60s. Marijuana and LSD were the drugs of choice, accompanied by guitar-driven rock music, long hair and 'flower power.' In January 1967 an estimated 20,000 'hippies' congregated in Golden Gate Park for a free concert, kicking off the 'Summer of Love.'

Across the bay, however, peace and love were not the order of the day. While hippies in the Haight were tripping, grooving and wearing flowers in their hair, Berkeley revolutionaries were leading the worldwide student upheavals of the late '60s, slugging it out with the cops and the university administration over the free speech issue. In Oakland, Bobby Seale and Huey Newton founded the Black Panther Party for Self-Defense, the most militant of the groups involved in the black-power movement of that era.

The hippies had led a sexual revolution but it was a predominantly heterosexual one; a homosexual revolution followed in the '70s, as San Francisco's gays stepped decisively out of the closet. Gay Pride became a rallying call, and the previously underground homosexual community 'came out' in all its glory. The same decade ended on a turbulent note, as Mayor George Moscone and city Supervisor Harvey Milk were assassinated by former supervisor Dan White. Milk had been openly gay, and when White's lenient sentence was announced gays rioted at City Hall, destroying millions of dollars worth of city property on what came to be called White Night.

San Francisco did not fare well in the 1980s. The first cases of AIDS – at the time known as GRID or Gay-Related Immune Deficiency – were reported in 1981. By the end of the 1980s, AIDS had claimed thousands of lives. The late 1980s witnessed yet another startling catastrophe – the Loma Prieta earthquake, which struck on October 17, 1989. It measured 7.1 on the Richter scale, and its damage was far-reaching. A section of the Bay Bridge was damaged, parts of the Marina District crumpled and burned and, in the quake's worst disaster, a double-decker section of I-880 in Oakland collapsed, killing 42 people.

The 1990s ushered in one of the city's periods of explosive economic growth, driven

THE WEDDING PARTY

When Gavin Newsom was elected mayor of San Francisco in late 2003, he was widely expected to push forward a moderate, business-as-usual agenda. Top dogs in Washington regarded the young and ambitious Newsom as a potential future face of the Democratic Party. But the new mayor surprised the nation in February 2004 by opening the doors of City Hall to same-sex couples wishing to be married. Thousands of couples soon lined up along the streets of the Civic Center, awaiting their turn to be legally hitched. Newsom personally presided over some of the civil unions, and took the heat for defying state laws that prohibited such marriages. So much for his being a moderate.

And so much for Gavin's prospects for higher office. The national press pounced on the gay marriage story, and some Democrats across the land later blamed Newsom for inadvertently handing George W Bush his reelection in 2004. The concept of gay marriage, shrewdly questioned in Bush's 'moral issues' campaign, turned out to be a little too scary for swing voters in the nation's heartland. Republican Governor Arnold Schwarzenegger, himself fairly open-minded on the gay marriage issue, stood by the letter of the law and ordered a halt to the Frisco frolics. Some 4000 same-sex marriages were soon declared null and void by the California State Supreme Court.

by an onslaught of successful start-up Web businesses materializing from the wispiest of ideas. The get-rich-quick delirium helped boost the city's restaurant and nightclub industry too, and older neighborhoods – the Mission being a prime example – were soon inundated with new businesses and young professionals with cash to burn. This remarkable growth trend didn't last; by the late 1990s, most of the dot-coms went bust and unemployment levels skyrocketed. Although the city still hasn't fully recovered from the recession that followed, declining interest rates helped spark a startling real-estate boom that lasted through the first five years of the new millennium. The buying frenzy saw many San Franciscans cashing out and leaving the city, while others left in search of more affordable homes. Property values went up to unprecedented levels, and the price of two-bedroom houses in formerly so-so neighborhoods approached $1 million.

ORIENTATION

San Francisco is one of the most compact cities in the USA, encompassing an area of approximately 46 sq miles covering the tip of a 30-mile-long peninsula, with the Pacific Ocean on one side and San Francisco Bay on the other. The city can be neatly divided into three sections. The central part resembles a slice of pie, with Van Ness Ave and Market St marking the two sides and the Embarcadero marking the rounded edge of the pie. Squeezed into this compact

slice are the Union Sq area, the Financial District, the Civic Center area, Chinatown, North Beach, Nob Hill, Russian Hill and Fisherman's Wharf.

To the south of Market St lies the South of Market (SoMa) area, an upwardly mobile warehouse zone. SoMa fades into the Mission, the city's Latino quarter, and then the Castro, the city's gay quarter.

The third and final part of the city is physically the largest – the long sweep from Van Ness Ave all the way to the Pacific Ocean. It's a varied area encompassing upscale neighborhoods such as the Marina and Pacific Heights, suburban zones such as the Richmond and Sunset districts and areas with flavors all of their own, such as Japantown, the Fillmore and the Haight. The city's three great parks – the Presidio, Lincoln Park and Golden Gate Park – are also here.

Maps

Quality maps of San Francisco are available from bookstores, but giveaway maps available from a variety of sources are generally adequate for most visitors.

The best of the free maps is the *San Francisco Street Map & Visitor Guide*, available at many of the city's hotels. If you're going to explore the city by public transportation, the MUNI (San Francisco Municipal Railway) *Street & Transit Map* is a smart $3 investment. Get a copy at the Visitors Information Center or any large bookstore. MUNI maps are also available online at www.sfmuni.com.

SAN FRANCISCO IN THREE DAYS

Three days is enough time to get into the swing of the city. If following a plan like the one we're laying out here, be flexible and improvise – the best travel moments are the completely unexpected ones.

Stay near **Union Square** (p93), from where you can get oriented quickly, get to major sights on foot and have instant access to the city's public-transit system. Spend your first morning strolling the downtown area, making your way down toward the foot of Market St. Take a peek at the bay and swing by the **Ferry Plaza Farmers Market** (p131). Here you'll instantly understand just how much the city loves food. Have lunch at one of the fantastic eateries inside the **Ferry Building Marketplace** (p114). After lunch, catch a cab to **San Francisco Museum of Modern Art** (SFMoma) (p100) for some art, then have a coffee at the museum café. Plan to spend your first evening in the Mission District or the Castro. Slum it with a delicious burrito at **La Taquería** (p119) and some Mission St barhopping. Or try to snag a table at trendy **Delfina** (p120) and hit some snazzy clubs along Upper Market St. In this part of town you can also catch live music in **12 Galaxies** (p128) or **Café du Nord** (p128), two of the city's best small venues.

Day two, head out on foot through **Chinatown** (p95) poking into shops along Grant Ave and Stockton St. Pick a spot for a bowl of noodles or dim sum. Continue through **North Beach** (p95), where atmospheric cafés and the **City Lights Bookstore** (below) will lure you off the sidewalk. Rent a bike at **Blazing Saddles** (p104) and wheel along the bay, checking out **Fisherman's Wharf** (p96) at a leisurely 10mph pace. Cross the **Golden Gate Bridge** (p92) to Sausalito, where you can catch a ferry back to the city. Have dinner and drinks in North Beach.

Day three, slow down a bit. Take a leisurely stroll along **Haight St** (p102), do a little shopping at **Amoeba Records** (p132) and have a hefty breakfast at the **Pork Store Cafe** (p121). Continue on into **Golden Gate Park** (p103) to hike through gorgeous gardens. You might even check out the new **MH de Young Memorial Museum** (p103) or gawk at the park's herd of buffalo. Spend the afternoon on the rock, **Alcatraz** (p92). In the evening, treat yourself to a world-class meal at **Zuni** (p116) or **Farallon** (p115), or indulge in Frisco classics at **Tadich Grill** (p115). Have an Anchor Steam at **C Bobby's Owl Tree** (p124).

For convenience and durability, Lonely Planet publishes a laminated San Francisco street map.

INFORMATION
Bookstores

Many city bookstores are open late, and several hold excellent readings.

A Clean Well-Lighted Place for Books (Map pp80-1; ☎ 415-441-6670; 601 Van Ness Ave) A popular bookstore in the Opera Plaza near the Civic Center.

A Different Light Bookstore (Map pp88-9; ☎ 415-431-0891; 489 Castro St) In the Castro, this is the city's largest gay and lesbian bookstore.

Borders Books & Music (Map pp80-1; ☎ 415-399-1633; cnr Post & Powell Sts) Downtown store of the big chain.

City Lights Bookstore (Map pp84-5; ☎ 415-362-8193; 261 Columbus Ave, North Beach) The city's most famous bookstore was the center of the Beat scene in the '50s and is still owned by its founder, poet Lawrence Ferlinghetti.

Get Lost (Map pp88-9; ☎ 415-437-0529; 1825 Market St) Specializes in travel books and maps.

Green Apple Books (Map p83; ☎ 415-387-2272; cnr Clement St & 6th Ave) In the Richmond District, Green Apple has loads of used titles and is among the city's best bookstores.

Emergency & Medical Services

Check the *Yellow Pages* under 'Physicians & Surgeons' or 'Clinics' to find a doctor, or under 'Dentist Referral Services' to find a dentist.

Call ☎ 911 for an ambulance.

Haight Ashbury Free Clinic (Map pp88-9; ☎ 415-487-5632; 558 Clayton St; 🕑 1-9pm Mon, 9am-9pm Tue-Thu, 1-5pm Fri) Just off Haight St. For nonemergency situations. Appointments are required, but once you're in, a doctor will see you free of charge.

Planned Parenthood (☎ 800-967-7526; 815 Eddy St) For women's health issues.

St Luke's Women's Center (☎ 415-285-7788; 1650 Valencia St)

San Francisco General Hospital (Map pp78-9; ☎ 415-206-8000; 1001 Potrero Ave; 🕑 24hr) Be aware that fees *start* between $100 and $500 for an emergency-room visit.

(Continued on page 90)

0 —————————— 2 km
0 —————————— 1 mile

Treasure
Island

To Oakland
(4mi)

Yerba Buena
Island

Ferries to Tiburon & Angel Island
Ferries to Tiburon & Vallejo
Ferries to Larkspur
Ferries to Alcatraz
Ferries to Sausalito

80

Bay Bridge

Ferries to Oakland-Alameda

Aquatic
Park

Fort
Mason

Fisherman's
Wharf

See Chinatown & North Beach Map
(pp84–5)

The Embarcadero

Russian
Hill

North
Beach

Lombard St

Union St

Van Ness Ave

Pacific Heights
& Japantown

Nob
Hill

Chinatown

Financial
District

LP

Expwy

The Tenderloin

Union
Square

80

Lower
Haight

Hayes
Valley

Civic
Center

South of
Market
(SoMa)

Caltrain
Depot

Mission
Creek
Marina

Pier
50

80

See Downtown San Francisco & South
of Market (SoMa) Map (p80–1)

Market St

Central Fwy

280

SAN
FRANCISCO
BAY

The
Mission

BART Line

Potrero
Hill

3rd St

The
Castro

Church St

San Francisco
General Hospital

Pier
80

Noe
Valley

See The Haight, the Castro
& the Mission Map (pp88–9)

Glen
Park

Bernal
Hill

101

280

United States Hwy

Oakdale Ave

Pier
96

Mission St

Bay Shore Blvd

3rd St

Crisp Rd

McLaren
Park

To San Francisco
International
Airport (9mi),
Palo Alto (25mi),
San Jose (48mi)

Monster
Park

Candlestick
Park

Allyne Park

Lafayette Park

Pacific Heights & Japantown

Jefferson Square

Hayes Valley

Lower Haight

The Castro

Mini Park

Nob Hill

Huntington Park

Chinatown

Portsmouth Square

Chinese Playground

St Mary's Square

California St Cable Car Turnaround

California St Cable Car Line

Powell-Hyde St Cable Car Line

Powell-Mason & Powell-Hyde St Cable Car Lines

Union Square

The Tenderloin

Geary Expwy

Peter Yorke Way

Starr King Way

Hallidie Plaza

Powell St BART & MUNI Station

Powell St Cable Car Turnaround

Opera Plaza

Federal Building

State Building

City Hall

Civic Center Plaza

Civic Center

UN Plaza

Civic Center BART & MUNI Station

Van Ness MUNI Station

Hayward Playground

Broadway Tunnel

Broadway

Maiden

To Mighty (0.3mi)

Central Fwy

Street labels:
Franklin St, Vallejo St, Polk St, Van Ness Ave, Broadway, Pacific Ave, Jackson St, Washington St, Clay St, Sacramento St, California St, Pine St, Bush St, Sutter St, Post St, Geary St, O'Farrell St, Ellis St, Eddy St, Turk St, Golden Gate Ave, McAllister St, Fulton St, Grove St, Hayes St, Fell St, Oak St, Page St, Rose St, Haight St, Hermann St, Duboce Ave, Clinton Park

Octavia St, Gough St, Laguna St, Buchanan St, Webster St

Powell/Hyde St Cable Car Line, Glover St, Leavenworth St, Jackson St, John St, Pacific Ave, Washington St, Auburn St, Trenton St, Ross Al, Waverly Pl, Grant Ave, Columbus Ave, Stockton St, Powell St, Mason St, Taylor St, Jones St, Leavenworth St, Hyde St, Larkin St, Polk St, Van Ness Ave

Morrell St, Priest St, Austin St, Fern St, Hemlock St, Cedar St, Myrtle St, Olive St, Willow St, Larch St, Elm St, Cosmo Pl, Shannon St, Maiden, Geary St, Cyril Magnin St, Market St, Stevenson St, Jessie St, Mary St, Minna St, Natoma St, Howard St, Tehama St, Clementina St, Folsom St, Harrison St, Brannan St, 4th St, 5th St, 6th St, 7th St, 8th St, 9th St, 10th St, 11th St, 12th St, 13th St, Columbia Sq, Sherman St, Moss St, Rausch St, Sumner St, Langton St, Hallam St, Heron St, Gordon St, Ringold St, Sheridan St, Juniper St, Dore Al, Norfolk St, Sheridan St, McLea Ct, Bryant St, Converse St, Kate St, Decatur St

Laskie St, Mission St, Grace St, Lafayette St, Hickory St, Linden St, Lily St, Ivy St, Birch St, Ash St, Turk Blvd, Jefferson Square, Jessie St, Otis St, S Van Ness Ave, McCoppin St, Stevenson St, Elgin Park, Pearl St, Valencia St, Guerrero St, Erie St, Central Fwy

80

0 / 400 m
0 / 0.2 miles

Jackson Square E
Jackson St
Sansome St
Battery St
Sacramento St

Walton Park
Bostonship Plaza
Whaleship Plaza
Maritime Plaza
Embarcadero Plaza

Redwood Park
31
Clay St
Commercial St
Front St
Davis St
59
32
16
Halleck St
88

Embarcadero Center
Financial District
F
86
132
Pier 1/2
20
19
123
122
53

Ferry Terminal Plaza

G Ferries to Oakland-Alameda
H

SAN FRANCISCO BAY

Bay Bridge

California St Cable Car Turnaround
California St
Pine St
15
82
28
71
Bush St
27
95
6
23
Market St
La
24
3
60
101
11
Mission St
Annie St
New Montgomery St
121
104
18
33
29

Montgomery BART & MUNI Station
90
Ecker Pl
Fremont St
1st St
Minna St
Natoma St
Tehama St
Clementina St
102
139
Howard St
Beale St
Main St
Spear St
Steuart St

Embarcadero BART & MUNI Station
70
91
50
Rincon Center

Folsom St MUNI Station
Pier 22 1/2
Pier 24
Pier 26
Pier 28

80
84
Pier 30
Pier 32

Yerba Buena Gardens
26
34
South Of Market (SoMa)
130
4th St
77
Rizal St
Folsom St
Shipley St
Clara St
Merlin St
Oak-Cove St
109
Morris St

2nd St
Hawthorne St
Essex St
Lansing St
Harrison St
Bryant St

Federal St
Delancey St
Brannan St

Brannan St MUNI Station
Pier 34
Pier 36
Pier 38
Pier 40
30

Perry St
Stillman St
125
68
Taber Pl
87
S Park Ave
Varney Pl
Stanford St
South Park

Boom
Delancy St
Zoe St

South Beach Harbor Park
Breakwater

Bryant St
Welsh St
Freelon St
Ritch St
3rd St
Clarence Pl
Lusk St
Townsend St
Clyde St

2nd & King St MUNI Station
SBC Park

Mission Creek Marina

5th St
Brannan St
Bluxome St
King St
Berry St
4th St

CalTrain Depot
4th & King St MUNI Station

Pier 46B
Pier 48
Pier 48
Pier 50

Harriet St
96
Lucerne St
Gilbert St
Boardman Pl
6th St
7th St
Townsend St
Division St

Channel St
6th St
3rd St
Mission Rock St
Illinois St
Terry Francois St
Michigan St

Mission Bay Golf Center
280
Owens St

Pier 52
Pier 54

1
2
3
4
5
6

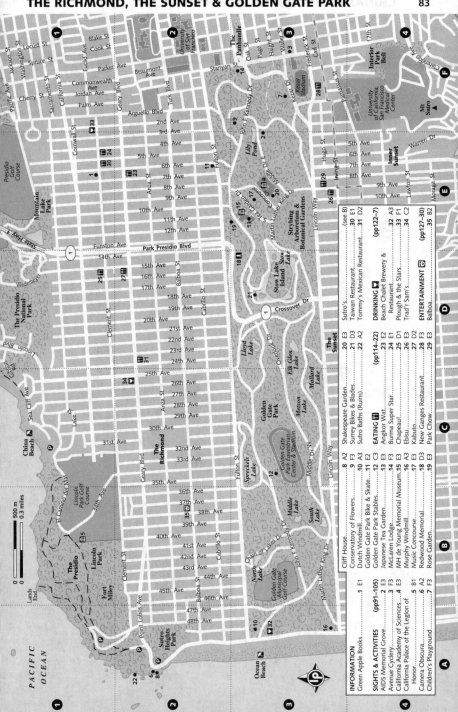

INFORMATION
Green Apple Books..............................1 E1

SIGHTS & ACTIVITIES   (pp91–105)
AIDS Memorial Grove...........................2 E3
Avenue Cyclery...................................3 F3
California Academy of Sciences............4 E3
California Palace of the Legion of
    Honor...5 B1
Camera Obscura.................................6 A2
Children's Playground..........................7 F3

Cliff House..8 A2
Conservatory of Flowers.......................9 F3
Dutch Windmill.................................10 A3
Golden Gate Park Bike & Skate..........11 E2
Golden Gate Park Stables...................12 C3
Japanese Tea Garden.........................13 E2
McLaren Lodge.................................14 F3
MH de Young Memorial Museum.........15 E2
Murphy Windmill...............................16 A3
Music Concourse...............................17 E2
New Ganges Restaurant......................18 D3
Redwood Memorial............................19 E3

Shakespeare Garden..........................20 E3
Surrey Bikes & Blades.........................21 F3
Sutro Baths (Ruins)............................22 A2

EATING   (pp114–22)
Angkor Wat......................................23 E2
Burma Super Star...............................24 E1
Chapeau...25 D1
Ebisu...26 E2
Kabuto...27 D2
Park Chow...29 E3

Sutro's...20 E3
Taiwan Restaurant..............................30 E1
Tommy's Mexican Restaurant..............31 D2

DRINKING   (pp122–7)
Beach Chalet Brewery &
    Restaurant....................................32 A3
Plough & the Stars.............................33 F1
Trad'r Sam's.....................................34 C2

ENTERTAINMENT   (pp127–30)
Balboa...35 B2

Sutro's...(see 8)

0   500 m
0   0.3 miles

PACIFIC OCEAN

Lands End

Fort Miley

The Presidio
The Presidio National Park

Presidio Golf Course

Mountain Lake Park

Lincoln Park

Lincoln Park Golf Course

China Beach

Sutro Heights Park

Ocean Beach

Golden Gate Municipal Golf Course

North Lake
Middle Lake
South Lake

Chain of Lakes Dr

Golden Gate Park

Golden Gate Park Equestrian Center & Stadium

Spreckels Lake

Elk Glen Lake
Mallard Lake
Metson Lake
Lloyd Lake

Stow Lake
Strawberry Island
Snow Lake

Lily Pond

Strybing Arboretum & Botanical Gardens

The Sunset

The Richmond

University of California, San Francisco Medical Center

University of San Francisco

The Panhandle

Kezar Stadium

Inner Sunset

Mt Sutro

Interior Park Belt

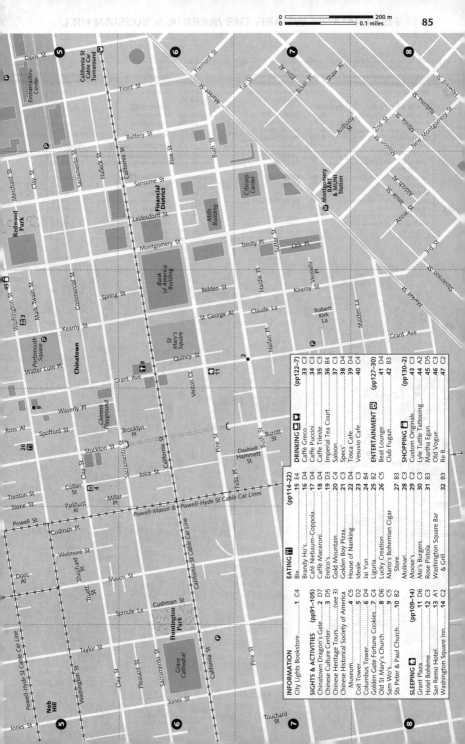

0 — 200 m
0 — 0.1 miles

INFORMATION
City Lights Bookstore.................1 C4

SIGHTS & ACTIVITIES   (pp91–105)
Chinatown Dragon's Gate.............2 D7
Chinese Culture Center...............3 D5
Chinese Heritage Tours...........(see 3)
Chinese Historical Society of America
Museum.................................4 C5
Colt Tower.................................5 D2
Columbus Tower........................6 D4
Golden Gate Fortune Cookies.....7 C4
Old St Mary's Church.................8 D6
Sam Wo's..................................9 C5
Sts Peter & Paul Church............10 B2

EATING   (pp114–22)
Bix...15 E4
Brandy Ho's..............................16 D4
Caffè Niebaum-Coppola...........17 D4
Caffè Macaroni.........................18 D4
Enrico's....................................19 D3
Gold Mountain.........................20 C4
Golden Boy Pizza......................21 C3
House of Nanking.....................22 D4
Ideale.......................................23 C3
Jai Yun....................................24 B4
Liguria.....................................25 B2
Lucky Creation.........................26 C5
Mario's Bohemian Cigar
Store.....................................27 B3
Molinari....................................28 C3
Moose's....................................29 C3
Mo's Burgers............................30 C3
Rose Pistola.............................31 B3
Washington Square Bar
& Grill...................................32 B3

DRINKING   (pp122–7)
Caffe Greco..............................33 C3
Caffe Puccini............................34 C3
Caffe Trieste.............................35 C3
Imperial Tea Court....................36 B4
Saloon.....................................37 C3
Specs'.......................................38 D4
Tosca Cafe...............................39 D4
Vesuvio Cafe...........................40 C4

ENTERTAINMENT   (pp127–30)
Beat Lounge.............................41 D4
Club Fugazi..............................42 B3

SHOPPING   (pp130–2)
Custom Originals.......................43 C3
Lyle Tuttle Tattooing.................44 A2
Martha Egan.............................45 D5
Old Vogue................................46 C3
Re B..47 C2

SLEEPING   (pp109–14)
Grant Plaza..............................11 D6
Hotel Bohème...........................12 C3
San Remo Hotel........................13 A1
Washington Square Inn.............14 C2

A · **B** · **C** · **D**

INFORMATION
California Welcome Center.............1 G2
German Consulate..........................2 E6
Italian Consulate...........................3 D5

SIGHTS & ACTIVITIES (pp91–105)
Basic Brown Bear Factory................4 F3
Blazing Saddles..............................5 F3
Cable Car Barn & Museum..............6 G5
Exploratorium.................................7 A3
GoCar Rentals.................................8 F3
Grace Cathedral..............................9 G6
Haas-Lilienthal House....................10 E5
Hyde St Pier.................................11 E2
Letterman Digital Arts Center........12 A4
Maritime Museum.....................(see 17)
Musée Mécanique.........................13 F2
Oceanic Society Expeditions..........14 D3
Palace of Fine Arts.......................15 A4
San Francisco Art Institute............16 F3
San Francisco National Maritime
    Museum...................................17 E3

Spreckels Mansion........................18 D6
SS Jeremiah O'Brien.....................19 F2
USS Pampanito.............................20 F2
Venetian Carousel........................21 G2
Wave Organ................................22 B2

SLEEPING (pp109–14)
HI Fisherman's Wharf....................23 D3
Marina Motel...............................24 B4
Motel Capri..................................25 D4
Radisson Fisherman's Wharf..........26 G2
Travelodge by the Bay..................27 E4
Wharf Inn....................................28 G2

EATING (pp114–22)
Betelnut......................................29 D5
Bistro Aix....................................30 C4
Buena Vista Café.........................31 F3
Frascati.......................................32 F4
Gary Danko.................................33 F3
Greens..34 D3
Hyde Street Bistro........................35 F5

I Fratelli......................................36 F4
Jackson Fillmore..........................37 C6
Mel's Drive-In.............................38 C4
Rainforest Café............................39 G2

DRINKING (pp122–7)
Liverpool Lil's...............................40 A4
MatrixFillmore..............................41 C4
Perry's...42 D5

ENTERTAINMENT (pp127–30)
Bimbo's 365 Club.........................43 F3
Magic Theatre..............................44 D3

SHOPPING (pp130–2)
Boudin Bakery.............................45 G2
Crosswalk...................................46 C6
Ghirardelli Chocolate Shop & Caffè.47 F3
Patagonia....................................48 F3
PlumpJack Wines.........................49 C4
Trader Joe's.................................50 G3
Uko..51 D5

0 — 500 m
0 — 0.3 miles

E **F** **G** **H**

1

SAN
FRANCISCO
BAY

Ferries to Tiburon & Angel Island

Ferries to Sausalito

Ferries to Alcatraz

2

Pier
45

19

Fisherman's Wharf

20

Pier
43½

Pier
43

Pier
41

21

Pier
39

Pier
35

11

Pier
47

13

The Embarcadero

53

52

1

Pier
33

San Francisco
Maritime National
Historic Park

Aquatic
Park

Powell-Hyde
Cable Car
Turnaround

Fisherman's
Wharf

Jefferson St

Taylor St

45

39

28

26

The Embarcadero (Herb Caen Way)

Pier
31

3

McDowell Ave

Pope Rd

17

Ghirardelli
Square

47

Victoria
Park

31

8

33

The
Cannery

4

48

Beach St

Columbus Ave

North Point St

Stockton St

Midway St

Francisco St

Ave

Russian
Hill
Park

Van Ness Ave

Polk St

Powell-Mason
Cable Car
Turnaround

Bay St

50

Vandewater

Chestnut St

Pioneer
Park/
Telegraph
Hill

Greenwich Steps

Franklin St

27

Powell-Hyde St Cable Car Line

Chestnut St

Russian
Hill

5

16

Houston
St

43

Water St

Mason St

Venard
Al

Powell St

Lombard St

Child
St

Telegraph Hill Blvd

Filbert Steps

Lombard St

Leavenworth St

Alice Marble
Tennis
Courts

Greenwich St

Greenwich
Steps

North
Beach
Playground

Greenwich St

Kearny St

Filbert St

Larkin St

Hyde St

Filbert St

Havens
St

Union St

Jones St

Taylor St

Valparaiso
St

Via
Buffano

North
Beach

Washington
Square

Filbert St

Jasper
Pl

Grant Ave

Green St

4

Russell
St

32

36

Macondray La

Vallejo St

Ina
Coolbrith
Park

Turk-
Murphy
La

Columbus Ave

Broadway

Montgomery St

Broadway

Broadway Tunnel

Lynch St

Pacific Ave

John St

Chinatown

Stockton St

Trenton St

Portsmouth
Square

5

35

Powell-Hyde St Cable Car Line

6

Washington St

Clay St

Commercial St

Jackson St

Mini
Park

Nob
Hill

Priest St

Powell St

Powell-Mason & Powell-Hyde St Cable Car Lines

Joice St

Financial
District

St
Mary's
Square

Kearny St

10

2

Franklin St

Clay St

Sacramento St

9

Huntington
Park

Pine St

Grant Ave

Sacramento St

California St Cable Car Line

California St

6

California St
Cable Car
Turnaround

Pine St

Larkin St

Hyde St

Leavenworth St

Jones St

Union
Square

Bush St

To Majestic Hotel (0.2mi);
Queen Anne Hotel (0.2mi)

Taylor St

Mason St

Powell-Hyde & Powell-Mason St Cable Car Lines

Pine St

Bush St

Sutter St

Octavia St

Gough St

Post St

INFORMATION

A Different Light Bookstore	1	D4
Get Lost Bookstore	2	F1
Haight Ashbury Free Clinic	3	B2

SIGHTS & ACTIVITIES (pp91–105)

710 Ashbury St	4	B2
Avenue Cyclery	5	A2
Harvey Milk Plaza	6	D3
Mission Dolores	7	F3
Mission Dolores Basilica	8	F3
Precita Eyes Mural Arts & Visitors Center	9	H6
Randall Museum	10	D3
Women's Building	11	F4

SLEEPING (pp109–14)

24 Henry	12	E2
Beck's Motor Lodge	13	E3
Inn on Castro	14	D3
Inn San Francisco	15	G4
Metro Hotel	16	D1
Parker Guest House	17	E3
Red Victorian B&B	18	B2
San Francisco Elements	19	G5
Village House	20	D4

EATING (pp114–22)

2223 Market	21	E3
Bagdad Cafe	22	E3
Bruno's	23	G4
Burger Joint	24	G4
California Harvest Ranch Market	25	E3
Cha Cha Cha	26	A2
Chava's	27	G6
Chow	28	E2
Delfina	29	F4
Eos	30	B3
Foreign Cinema	31	G5
Herbivore	32	G4
Kan Zaman	33	A2
Kate's Kitchen	34	E1

La Taquería	35	G6
Magnolia Pub Brewery	36	B2
Mecca	37	E2
Pancho Villa	38	G3
Pork Store Café	39	B2
Puerto Alegre	40	F3
Squat & Gobble Cafe	41	E1
Tallula	42	D4
Taquería Can-Cun	43	G4
Thep Phanom	44	E1
Truly Mediterranean	45	F3

DRINKING (pp122–7)

Amber	46	E2
Cafe Flore	47	E3
Casanova Lounge	48	G3
Club Deluxe	49	B2
Doc's Clock	50	G5
Harvey's	51	E3
Latin American Club	52	G5
Lexington Club	53	G4
Lone Palm	54	F5
Mad Dog in the Fog	55	E1
Make-Out Room	56	G5
Midnight Sun	57	D4
Mint	58	F2
Noc Noc	59	E1
Orbit Room Cafe	60	F2
People's Cafe	61	B2
Rockin' Java	62	A2
Samovar Tea Lounge	63	E4
Tartine	64	F4
Toronado	65	E1
Twin Peaks Tavern	66	D3
Uptown	67	G3
Zam Zam	68	B2
Zeitgeist	69	F2

ENTERTAINMENT (pp127–30)

12 Galaxies	70	G5
26Mix	71	G6
Cafe du Nord	72	E2
Café	73	D3
Castro Theatre	74	D3
Detour	75	D3
Elbo Room	76	G3
Intersection for the Arts	77	F3
Marsh	78	G5
Nickie's	79	E1
ODC Theater	80	G3
Red Vic Movie House	81	A2
Ritespot Café	82	H3
Roxie Cinema	83	F3
Theater Artaud	84	H3
Theatre Rhinoceros	85	F3

SHOPPING (pp130–2)

826 Valencia	86	G4
ADS Hats	87	G4
American Apparel	88	B2
Amoeba Records	89	A2
Aquarius Records	90	G5
Black & Blue Tattoo	91	F3
Cold Steel America	(see 81)	
Dema	92	G5
FTC Skateboarding	(see 81)	
Image Leather	93	E3
La Rosa Vintage	94	A2
Laku	95	G5
Piedmont Boutique	96	B2
Rabat	97	E6
Rolo on Market	98	D3
SFO Snowboarding	99	A2
Streetlight Records	100	E6
Sunhee Moon	101	F3

0   500 m
0   0.3 miles

E   **F**   **G**   **H**

To Archbishop's
Mansion
(0.2mi)

Steiner St
Fillmore St
Oak St

**Hayes
Valley**

Page St
Rose St
Octavia St

Van Ness
MUNI
Station

Mission St
11th St
Howard St
Kissling St
10th St
Dore Al
9th St
Sheridan St

Lafayette St
Lily St
Laguna St
Buchanan St

**South of
Market
(SoMa)**

Folsom St
Juniper St

Haight St
Laussat St

55
79
34
59 65 41
44

Market St
Elgin Park
Pearl St

McCoppin St
Stevenson St

Colton St
Gough St
Otis St

12th St
Norfolk St
Isis St
Harrison St

Waller St

Hermann St
60
58
2

Duboce Ave

Woodward St

5th Van Ness Ave

Central Fwy
13th St

**Duboce
Park**

Duboce Ave
Belcher St
Walter St

69

Clinton Park
Rosemont Pl
Ramona Ave

Minna St
Natoma St

14th St

Alameda St

Florida St

Reservoir
St

Brosnan St

46
37

**The
Mission**

15th St

Shotwell St

To Bottom
of the Hill
(0.8mi)

Church
St MUNI
Station
28

Landers St
Guerrero St
Valencia St

Julian St

Treat Ave

12
72

Sharon St

Alert
Al

91
77

Caledonia St
Wiese St

16th St

85

S Van Ness Ave

13
47
22
21
25
93

16th St
Chula La

8
7

Albion St

101
Gaiser
Ct
40

83 45
48

Rondel Pl
Hoff St
38

16th St
Mission
BART
Station

82
84

17
17th St

Dorland St

Lapidge St

Clarion Al
Sycamore St

67
80

17th St

Prosper St
Sanchez St
Pond St

Dearborn St

76

18th St

**The
Castro**

Hancock St
Noe St

63
Church St

18th St
Oakwood St

29 64

11

87
53
24
86

Lexington St
San Carlos St

43

18th St
19th St

Mistral
St

**Mission
Dolores
Park**

Dolores St

Linda St

Capp St

Folsom St

Cumberland St

Guerrero St
Valencia St

23

To Atlas Cafe
(50yd)

Rayburn
St

21st St

Liberty St

15

20th St

Alabama St

21st St

Hill St

Quane St
Ames St

Hill St
78
92
54
52

90
95

19
31

70
50
56

Mission St

21st St

22nd St

Harrison St

To El Metate
(0.1 mi)

Hill St

Vicksburg St
Nellie St

22nd St

Chattanooga St

Church St

Alvarado St

Capp St

S Van Ness Ave

Shotwell St
Folsom St
Treat Ave

22nd St
23rd St

23rd St
Fair Oaks St
Dolores St
San Jose Ave

To St Francis Fountain
(0.1mi)

**Noe
Valley**

97
100

Sanchez St

24th St

Jersey St

24th Mission
BART Station

24th St

27
35

Guerrero St
Poplar St
Orange Al
Bartlett St
Osage St
Lilac St
Cypress St
Balmy St
Lucky St
Harrison St
Virgil St
Horace St

9

**Garfield
Square**

25th St

Clipper St

To Mitchell's
(0.4mi)

71

To El Rio (0.2mi);
Blue Plate (0.3mi)

26th St

(Continued from page 77)

Internet Access

There are various Internet cafés scattered around town. If you're traveling with a laptop, many of the city's café's as well as some business-friendly hotels are wi-fi equipped. Access in Internet cafés costs around $8 per hour.

CompUSA (Map pp80-1; ☎ 415-391-9778; 750 Market St) For free Web access.

Main Library (Map pp80-1; ☎ 415-557-4400; cnr Larkin & Grove Sts) Near the Civic Center BART/MUNI station. There are six 'express' terminals on the 1st floor available for 15 minutes free access on a first-come, first-served basis. Library staff also can provide information on Internet access throughout the city, as can the folks at the Visitors Information Center.

Laundry

Self-service laundries are easy to find in most residential neighborhoods. Typical costs are $1.75 for washing and 50¢ per 15-minute drying cycle. Be warned that clothing theft does happen – keep an eye on your dryers.

Brain Wash (Map pp80-1; ☎ 415-861-3663; 1122 Folsom St; per wash from $2; ⏲ 7:30am-11pm Sun-Thu, 7:30am-midnight Fri & Sat) A place to jazz up the drudgery. This is a laundry café where you can sip beer or coffee, order food and even listen to live music while waiting for your washing.

Media

Northern California's largest daily, the *San Francisco Chronicle* is the best source for general news coverage. On Sundays the *Chronicle* publishes the useful 'Datebook,' an entertainment supplement also known as the 'Pink Section' for its pale-pink pages. The *Chronicle*'s website at www.sfgate.com is helpful too.

Two free weekly papers, the *San Francisco Bay Guardian* and the *SF Weekly*, have intelligent left-leaning coverage of local events and politics (often delving deeply into arcane issues that probably won't interest the casual visitor), plus reliable arts and entertainment reviews and loads of restaurant, film, music and other event listings. Both are published Wednesday.

The *Bay Area Reporter* and *Bay Times* are free gay and lesbian papers distributed in the Castro and nearby neighborhoods.

Pick up a copy of the local paper at either of the following:

SAN FRANCISCO CITYPASS

The **San Francisco CityPass** (http://citypass.com/city/sanfrancisco.html) gives you access to five major attractions, unlimited rides on the cable cars and includes a suggested itinerary for seeing the best of the city. The cost is $42/34 for an adult/child, and saves you about 50% on regular admission costs. You can buy online or at any of the attractions. It is valid for nine days from the day of first use.

Café de la Presse (Map pp80-1; ☎ 415-398-2680; 352 Grant Ave at Bush St; ⏲ 7am-10pm) Opposite the Chinatown gate and downstairs from the Hotel Triton. For European newspapers and magazines.

Harold's International Newsstand (Map pp80-1; ☎ 415- 441-2665; 454 Geary St; ⏲ 8am-11pm Tue-Sat, 8am-8pm Sun & Mon) Near Union Sq. There's a good selection of out-of-town and international newspapers.

Money

Banks are ubiquitous in San Francisco and usually offer the best rates for currency exchange. At San Francisco International Airport, there are currency-exchange offices on the 3rd level of the international terminal run by **Travelex** (☎ 650-821-0900; ⏲ 6:30am-10pm).

Post

Civic Center post office (Map pp80-1; ☎ 415-563-7284, 800-725-2161; 101 Hyde St) Mail can be sent to you here. It should be marked c/o General Delivery, Civic Center Post Office, 101 Hyde St, San Francisco, CA 94142, USA.

Union Square post office (Map pp80-1; ⏲ 10am-5:30pm Mon-Sat, 11am-5pm Sun) In the basement of Macy's department store.

Telephone

Public phones usually cost between 35¢ and 50¢ for local calls, more if you're calling to Marin County, the East Bay or the Peninsula. The cheapest and most convenient method is to use a phonecard, available from most grocery and drug stores.

Area codes in the Bay Area

East Bay (including Berkeley and Oakland)	☎ 510
Marin County	☎ 415
Palo Alto	☎ 650
Peninsula	☎ 650
San Francisco	☎ 415
San Jose	☎ 408

Tourist Information

California Welcome Center (Map pp86-7; ☎ 415-981-1280; Pier 39, Bldg P, ste 241-B; ⏰ 10am-5pm) Has travel information, brochures, maps and can help with accommodations booking.

San Francisco Visitors Information Center (Map pp80-1; ☎ 415-391-2000; www.sfvisitor.org; lower level, Hallidie Plaza, cnr Market & Powell Sts; ⏰ 8:30am-5pm Mon-Fri, 9am-3pm Sat & Sun) In the heart of the city, below the street level besides the Powell St BART station. Here you can get maps, guidebooks, brochures and phonecards.

DANGERS & ANNOYANCES

Like most big US cities, San Francisco has its share of crime, but prudent travelers are not at any undue risk. Certain neighborhoods are seedier than others and considered relatively 'unsafe,' especially at night and for those walking alone. These include the Tenderloin, parts of the Mission, the Western Addition and 6th and 7th Sts South of Market. However, these areas are not always sharply defined, and travelers should be aware of their surroundings wherever they walk in the city.

After dark, some of the city's parks, including Mission Dolores Park and Buena Vista Park, become havens for drug dealing and sleazy sex. Bayview-Hunters Point, a poor and largely African American neighborhood north of 3Com (Candlestick) Park, where the 49ers play, is not a place for wandering tourists.

The city's homeless population is unnaturally high (we won't get into who's to blame). Most people asking for spare change are harmless, some even friendly; a smile of acknowledgment, or a few coins if you can, and they'll be on their way. Some earn money selling the *Street Sheet,* a locally published newspaper on homeless issues. For aggressive panhandlers, the best strategy is to simply say 'I'm sorry' and keep walking.

If you find yourself somewhere you would rather not be, act confident and sure of yourself; then go into a store and call a taxi.

SIGHTS
The Bay & the Embarcadero

San Francisco Bay, a sizeable inlet connected to the Pacific by the narrowest of openings, is indeed a dramatic piece of geography. It is the largest bay on the California coast, stretching about 60 miles in length and up to 12 miles in width. It's fed by the Sacramento and San Joaquin Rivers, mingling with the sea through the Golden Gate. Most of the bay is surprisingly shallow, and overall averages only 6ft to 10ft deep at low tide.

The Embarcadero, after many years of slow revival, has finally re-emerged as an integral part of San Francisco. Streetcars run down the thoroughfare's wide median, there's a Major League Ballpark right on the edge of the bay, and the Ferry Building has been repurposed as a foodie paradise, with a concentration of fine restaurants and food vendors operating a few paces from the waterfront.

Long stretches of the Embarcadero are used chiefly by joggers, walkers and skateboarders. If you are looking for an undemanding place to stroll, this is it. You can head down to SBC Park (p100) to see a

(DON'T) CALL IT FRISCO

Way back in the 1860s, a well-known San Francisco kook declared himself Emperor of the United States. The people of San Francisco generally enjoyed this old character, and some bars and restaurants honored the homemade currency he carried with him. Of the absurd laws declared by Emperor Norton, one continues to resonate: his injunction against the use of the word 'Frisco.'

San Francisco was always too long a name for some people, whether they were gold panners, con artists, saxophone players or Beat poets, and Norton's law was rarely observed. Until, that is, former *Chronicle* columnist Herb Caen dug it up nearly a century later and reminded everyone that saying 'Frisco' is taboo. Evidently the people of the city nodded in agreement. Today, say 'Frisco' among local company and you're sure to be corrected by someone who has no idea who Emperor Norton was, or even that Caen is responsible for reinforcing this particular protocol.

Now, undoubtedly Emperor Norton was among the coolest cats to grace the streets of San Francisco. But Caen hasn't dated all that well and the pomposity with which San Franciscans continue to observe the 'no-to-Frisco' credo can be a bit grating. Frisco is cool, man. Fumbling with 'Shan Fran-shish-co' after a few drinks isn't.

baseball game, have lunch at Red's Java House (p115) or catch a ferry to Oakland (p134) or Marin County (p134)

GOLDEN GATE BRIDGE

Commenced in January 1933 and opened in May 1937, the beautiful Golden Gate Bridge (Map pp78–9) links San Francisco with Marin County and remains the symbol of the city. The bridge, designed by Joseph B Strauss, is nearly 2 miles long, with a main span of 4200ft. When the bridge was completed, it was the longest suspension bridge in the world. Its name comes from the entrance to the harbor, the Golden Gate. The bridge's color is 'international orange.' Painting the bridge is a never-ending job – a team of 25 painters adds 1000 golden gallons every week.

A prime starting point for bridge appreciation is the **Fort Point Lookout** at the southern end of the bridge. The lookout offers excellent views and has a gift center, a statue of Strauss and a sample of the 3ft-thick suspension cable. MUNI buses 28 and 29 run to the toll plaza. There are even better views from the lookout at **Vista Point**, on the north side of the bridge.

On weekends, pedestrians can walk across the bridge on the east side, while bicyclists can zoom along on the ocean side (see the boxed text, p143). During the week they share the east side. The bridge toll (southbound only) is $5 per car.

FERRY BUILDING

The Ferry Building (Map pp80–1) is one of San Francisco's most recognized and beloved landmarks. The tower is modeled on the Moorish Giralda tower in Seville, Spain, and at 240ft it was for some time the tallest building in San Francisco. Completed in 1898, the Ferry Building soon became one of the world's busiest transport interchanges, with dozens of ferry boats arriving and departing daily. Ferry traffic subsided considerably in the late 1930s, after the completion of the Bay and the Golden Gate Bridges, and by the late '50s the Ferry Building had been unsentimentally obscured by an elevated freeway. When the freeway turned out not to be quake proof, San Franciscans came to the realization that their cherished landmark was in dire need of an integral purpose.

Now called the Ferry Building Marketplace, it is once again bustling with action. The excellent **farmers market** (p131) operates out the front, on the Embarcadero, and several fine restaurants and purveyors of high-end foodstuffs have opened shops here. For an introduction to San Francisco's culinary culture, you need only swing by on a Saturday morning to see what sorts of seasonal produce the local chefs are most excited about and then choose where to have lunch.

You can still catch a ferry here (p134). It's the easiest way to get out on the bay. Ferries go to Jack London Sq (p156) in Oakland and to Sausalito (p142) and Tiburon (p144) in Marin County.

BAY BRIDGE

Considerably longer than the Golden Gate Bridge is the vehicle-only Bay Bridge (Map pp80–1), which carries far more traffic and predates it by six months, but it has never enjoyed the same iconic fame. The Bay Bridge actually consists of three separate parts: a double suspension bridge that leads from San Francisco to the mid-bay **Yerba Buena Island** (Map pp78–9), a tunnel that cuts straight through the rocky island, and a series of latticework spans that connect Yerba Buena Island to Oakland. There's a $3 toll westbound.

The 1989 earthquake caused a 50ft section of the Yerba Buena–Oakland span to collapse. Though repaired, it served as a wake-up call. For years, state transportation authorities deliberated over the new bridge's design and in mid-1998 a single-tower suspension design was selected. Construction quickly went over budget and Governor Arnold Schwarzenegger ordered a work stoppage. The governor proposed a simpler – and very drab – design that had no suspension pillar. After a year's hiatus, the two sides finally agreed to move ahead with the suspension design.

ALCATRAZ

You know you have had a fun vacation when part of it is spent in jail. From 1933 to 1963 the rocky island in the middle of San Francisco Bay was home of the most notorious prison in the USA. The 12-acre Alcatraz (Map pp80–1) became the prison of choice for serious offenders for a simple reason – 'the Rock' was believed to be escape-proof, until the Anglin brothers and co-conspirator Frank Morris floated away in a self-made raft in 1962 and were never seen again. That enigmatic escape was made famous by the 1979 movie *Escape from Alcatraz*, starring Clint Eastwood. Though Alcatraz is only 1.5 miles from the mainland, they are 1.5 very cold miles swept by the bay's often ferocious currents, not to mention the occasional shark.

After the prison's closure in 1963, the island was more or less forgotten for six years, when it was taken over by Native Americans, who claimed Indian peoples' ownership of the land and conducted a 19-month protest sit-in to bring national attention to their causes. The event sparked a wave of Native American activism in the USA.

Blue & Gold Fleet (☎ information 415-773-1188, reservations 415-705-5555; www.blueandgoldfleet.com; adult/child under 5/child/senior $16/free/11/14.25) runs ferries to the island from Pier 41 at Fisherman's Wharf (Map pp86–7). It's wise to book or pick up tickets well in advance, especially in summer. Departures to the island are from 9:30am to 2:15pm daily (until 4:15pm in summer). The fare includes admission to the park and an excellent audio tour featuring first-hand narratives by former guards and inmates. Guided 'Alcatraz After Dark' tours are also given twice daily from Thursday to Sunday (adult/child $23.50/20.75). The **park ranger station** (☎ 415-705-1042) on the island has information about the island and its history.

Union Square

If there is a beating heart of the city it is the area around Union Sq (Map pp80–1). Other zones, outlying neighborhoods and ethnic enclaves may feel unique and self-contained, but all of San Francisco owns Union Sq. All the main train and bus lines pass through this part of town.

This is also where most visitors are likely to stay. The city's grandest hotels and restaurants are here, as well as its best hostels and *hof braus*. Entertainment ranges from street theater to the lyric stage. Enough art galleries open to the streets that you'll not want for museums.

The blocks around Union Sq comprise San Francisco's prestigious shopping and theater districts. You can shop for diamonds or just a pair of jeans. The theaters on and around Geary St, and restaurants throughout the

neighborhood, draw people from all over the Bay Area. The hubbub typical of a thriving city center defines the area.

The actual plaza in the middle of it all gets its name from the pro-Union rallies that took place there during the Civil War. Its centerpiece is the 97ft-high **Dewey Monument**, constructed in 1903 to commemorate Admiral George Dewey's 1898 defeat of the Spanish fleet at Manila Bay, which paved the way for the Philippines to become a US territory. Among the buildings flanking the square is the 1904 **Westin St Francis Hotel** (335 Powell St), a truly grand hotel that has a past that's equally glamorous and sordid. Comedy actor Fatty Arbuckle was accused of killing a woman here with an empty booze bottle, and President Gerald Ford was shot at on the hotel's front steps.

The 1949 **Folk Art International Building** (140 Maiden Lane) is the city's only Frank Lloyd Wright building. Have a look at its interior – the spiral walkway marks it as Wright's practice run for the Guggenheim Museum in New York City.

The city's famous **cable cars** groan along Powell St, on the western side of Union Sq, to and from the Hallidie Plaza terminus, named after the cable car's inventor. This is the most popular spot to catch a cable car.

San Francisco's dense **theater district** lies immediately to the southwest of Union Sq, crumbling directly into neighboring dismal Tenderloin.

Financial District

San Francisco's Manhattanized skyscraper zone is tightly concentrated between Union Sq and the bay. This is the city's banking center, San Francisco's core business since banks started to appear in the 1850s to handle the state's Gold Rush fortunes. It's a frantically busy area during the day, with taxis, power-dressed business people and suicidal bike messengers all competing for street space. Come dark it's a different animal; apart from a handful of restaurants, the district is nearly deserted.

Visiting the city's Financial District (Map pp80–1) of the city is essentially an architectural experience. The completion of the **Bank of America Building** (555 California St) in 1969 ushered in a new era for San Francisco's previously low-rise skyline. Not only was the 52-story, 779ft building much higher than any earlier structure, but the use of red South Dakota granite in its construction made it look very different from the city's consistent pale coloring.

Probably the most recognizable building in San Francisco is the 853ft **Transamerica Pyramid** (600 Montgomery St), which supplanted the Bank of America Building as the tallest in town. It was completed in 1972 and though initially reviled, today it's accepted as a modern symbol of the city. Adjacent to the Pyramid is a half-acre stand of redwood trees known as **Redwood Park**.

The Gothic 1928 **Russ Building** (253 Montgomery St) was the tallest in the city until 1964.

Other buildings of note in the district include the **Pacific Stock Exchange** (301 Pine St), which was built in 1915 and remodeled in 1930, the 1916 **Hobart Building** (582 Market St) and the 1908 **Bank of California Building** (400 California St), fronted by Corinthian columns.

The small but interesting **Wells Fargo History Museum** (☎ 415-396-2619; 420 Montgomery St; admission free; ✆ 9am-5pm Mon-Fri) tells the story of Wells Fargo Bank, the company founded in 1852 to provide banking and stagecoach delivery services to miners and businesses throughout the West Coast.

The odd-looking **Lotta's Fountain** (cnr Geary & Market Sts), recently restored to its gilded glory, was donated to the city in 1875 by the vaudeville entertainer Lotta Crabtree. A popular gathering point after the 1906 earthquake, a dwindling handful of survivors still gather here at 5am each April 18.

The luxurious **Palace Hotel** (☎ 415-512-1111; cnr Market & New Montgomery Sts) opened in 1875 as the most opulent hotel in the city. Along the way, it contributed to the death of its creator, William Ralston, who was driven to bankruptcy and a heart attack by financial pressures. Take afternoon tea in the leafy Garden Court – a truly regal environment that's open to the hoi polloi.

Four skyscrapers mark the huge **Embarcadero Center**, between Sacramento and Clay Sts, starting on Embarcadero at the Justin Herman Plaza, a popular lunch spot for Financial District workers. At the base of the buildings (Embarcadero 1 to 4) are restaurants, shops, a movie theater and post office.

Civic Center & Tenderloin

The crown jewel of San Francisco's stately Civic Center (Map pp80–1) complex is the impressive **City Hall** (☎ 415-554-4000; cnr Van Ness Ave & Grove St). The Beaux Arts–style structure, modeled after St Peter's Basilica in Vatican City, was built in 1915. You can enter (after passing airportlike security) to admire the curved staircases and the inner rotunda.

Facing City Hall is the **Asian Art Museum** (☎ 415-379-8800; www.asianart.org; cnr Larkin & McAllister Sts; adult/child $10/6; ✆ 10am-5pm Tue-Sun, 10am-9pm Thu). The museum is home to superb art from the Middle East, the Indian subcontinent, Southeast Asia, Tibet, Korea and Japan. But the collection is most impressive in the Chinese selection, where a glass frame mounts a collage of illuminated jade and an impressive assembly of Chinese bronzes. In fact, Chinese art accounts for about a third of the permanent collection. Down the street is the **Main Library** (☎ 415-557-4400), which opened in 1996 and cost $134 million. Even if you have no library card, the library is worth visiting for its architecture – five stories built around a naturally lit, semicircular atrium – and its newspaper and magazine reading room (free and stocked with many international titles).

Across Hyde St beyond the two library buildings is UN Plaza, built to commemorate the signing of the UN Charter in San Francisco in 1945. A farmers market is held at the plaza every Wednesday and Sunday.

Squeezed between the bureaucratic Civic Center and burgeoning Union Sq, the Tenderloin (Map pp80–1) is the downtown bruise that never seems to heal. It's an entire neighborhood of skid rows, each one lined with near identical apartment buildings inhabited by the downtrodden and nearly homeless. Prostitutes and drug dealers walk some of the streets, deranged souls wander into oncoming traffic and soup kitchens draw long lines for lunch. But the 'Loin' – or the 'TL,' as some in the neighborhood call it – is an immensely interesting part of town. Its centrality has always ensured that San Franciscans never complacently ignore the area, and increasingly a younger, more solvent crowd has been moving into the Tenderloin's modest digs. The appeal, apart from location, surely must be the honest inner-city grit that's so strongly evidenced here. New businesses, too, have moved in – mostly hipster bars and clubs. Some of the depressing old dives, having made minimal cosmetic improvements, now attract a relatively optimistic crowd. The TL is also home to immigrants from Southeast Asia, and this is where you'll find the highest concentration of Vietnamese and Cambodian restaurants in the city, as well as small grocery stores and cafés that are worth snooping around in. On Sunday, people from all around come to the electrifying gospel services at **Glide Memorial United Methodist Church** (☎ 415-771-6300; 330 Ellis St).

Chinatown

Chinatown (Map pp84–5) is the most densely packed pocket of the city, and perhaps the most colorful. There are no essential sights, but it's a great place for casual wandering, soaking up the hectic atmosphere and stumbling across interesting little corners and alleys.

Packed with shops and restaurants, **Grant Ave** has had a colorful history from its inception as Calle de la Fundación, the main street of the Mexican village of Yerba Buena. Renamed Dupont St, or Du Pon Gai to the Chinese, the street became known for its brothels, gambling dives, opium dens and brawling *tongs* (Chinese gangs). Dupont St was renamed after former-president and Civil War general Ulysses S Grant when he died in 1885.

Chinatown visits usually begin at the dragon-studded **Dragon's Gate** at the Bush St entrance to Grant Ave. At California St is **Old St Mary's Church** (☎ 415-986-4388); its 90ft tower made it the tallest building in the city when it was completed in 1854. **St Mary's Square**, off California St, is one of few large open spaces in Chinatown. When Chinatown was cleaned up in the late 19th century, the brothels, gambling dens and bars from all over the area were concentrated here, only to burn down in the aftermath of the 1906 earthquake.

Get off touristy Grant Ave for a more authentic Chinatown experience. For a feel of off-the-main-street Chinatown, duck into colorful **Waverly Place**, between Grant Ave and Stockton St, with its many open balconies and upstairs temples. Just to the right, when you emerge onto Washington St, is **Sam Wo's** (813 Washington St), a hole-in-the-wall Chinese restaurant where Jack Kerouac supposedly learned how to use chopsticks.

A few steps in the opposite direction along Washington St away from Waverly Pl, take

a right turn into narrow **Ross Alley**, another dark and mysterious-looking lane. Known at one time as 'Old Spanish Alley,' this small street was wall-to-wall gambling dens and brothels in the late 1870s. A favorite location for filmmakers, it has featured in films such as *Big Trouble in Little China*. Here **Golden Gate Fortune Cookie Company** (☎ 415-781-3956; 56 Ross Alley) turns out crispy treats, which, incidentally, originated in San Francisco (they were dreamed up for the Japanese Tea Garden in Golden Gate Park).

Portsmouth Square (Kearny & Washington Sts) almost always has a crowd of young and old people talking or playing checkers, chess or mah-jongg. It was originally the plaza for the Mexican settlement of Yerba Buena, and its name comes from John B Montgomery's sloop, the *Portsmouth*. Montgomery arrived in 1846 to claim the city for the USA, and a plaque commemorates the spot where the Stars and Stripes was first raised in San Francisco.

The **Chinese Historical Society of America Museum** (☎ 415-391-1188; www.chsa.org; 965 Clay St; adult/child $3/1, 1st Thu of month free; ⏰ noon-5pm Tue-Fri, noon-4pm Sat & Sun) has an impressive collection of photos and historical artifacts – including mining tools and an 1880 Buddhist altar – that help bring home the point that the Chinese played a significant part in California's history. The museum is in a one-time YMCA building designed by Julia Morgan.

North Beach

North Beach (Map pp84–5) was the city's original Italian quarter, and its Italian heritage lives on in the area's restaurants, neighborhood bars and cafés. The Beats took over in the '50s and added jazz clubs and the City Lights Bookstore to the mix. Today, despite gentrification and an onslaught of tourists, North Beach is one of the liveliest parts of the city and a great place for a cheap meal, a cold beer and the best cappuccino in town.

The 1905 **Columbus Tower** (cnr Kearny St & Columbus Ave), with its green copper cupola, has been the property of filmmaker Francis Ford Coppola since 1970. The offices of Coppola's film company, Zoetrope, are in the building.

The block of Columbus Ave from Pacific Ave to Broadway can lay claim to being the

THE BEAT GENERATION

From the days of the Gold Rush, San Francisco has been a freewheeling city. Artists, musicians and writers often sang its praises in their works, but it wasn't until the mid-1950s that national attention was first focused on 'the City' as the birthplace of a scene of its own. When Jack Kerouac and Allen Ginsberg, upstart students at Columbia University, fled the indifference of New York City and joined forces with the San Francisco Renaissance, a poets' movement begun by poet and literary critic Kenneth Rexroth, the Beat Generation was given a voice.

They engaged in a new style of writing – short, sharp and alive. Their bible was Kerouac's *On the Road* (1957); Ginsberg's 'Howl' (1956) was their angry anthem. A writer himself, Lawrence Ferlinghetti became the Beats' patron and publisher, and today their era lives on at his City Lights Bookstore in North Beach, still churning out the hipsters after 40 years.

The Beats spoke of a life unbound by social conventions and motivated by spontaneous creativity rather than greed and ambition. Kerouac is widely credited with creating the term 'Beat Generation' after hearing poet Herbert Huncke say, 'Man, I'm beat.' The phrase echoed Hemingway's 'Lost Generation' and alluded to the supreme happiness preached in the Beatitudes of Jesus. The term 'beatnik' came along later, created, it is claimed, by *San Francisco Chronicle* columnist Herb Caen, fusing the 'far out' Beats with the just-launched Sputnik satellite.

literary heart of the city. A drink at **Vesuvio Cafe**, where Dylan Thomas and Jack Kerouac are known to have pissed away a few evenings, is a fine segue to a visit to **City Lights Bookstore** (☎ 415-362-8193), just across Jack Kerouac Alley. City Lights Publishers, with offices above the bookstore, became famous in 1957 when it published Ginsberg's poem 'Howl,' which was promptly banned for obscenity. A highly publicized court ruling finally allowed distribution of the poem.

The 1924 **Sts Peter & Paul Church** (666 Filbert St) overlooks **Washington Square**, North Beach's cultural focal point and its only open public space. The church is the largest Catholic church in San Francisco; every October the Santa Maria del Lume (patron saint of fishermen) procession makes its way down Columbus Ave to Fisherman's Wharf to bless the fishing fleet.

A short but strenuous hike to the top of Telegraph Hill will get you to the 210ft **Coit Tower** (☎ 415-362-0808; ❂ 10am-6pm), one of San Francisco's more unusual landmarks. Built in 1934, it was financed by San Francisco eccentric Lillie Hitchcock Coit, who often dressed as a man to gamble in North Beach, wore short skirts to go ice-skating and famously enjoyed chasing the fire company to fires. In 1863, the 15-year-old Lillie was adopted as the mascot of the Knickerbocker Hose Company No 5, and it's said she 'rarely missed a blaze.'

Inside Coit Tower is a superb series of Diego Rivera–style murals of San Franciscans

at work, painted by 25 local artists as part of a '30s Work Projects Administration (WPA) project. The ride to the top of the tower costs $3. Avoid driving here, as parking is limited. Those who make the hike can then trek down through the lush gardens that flank the **Filbert St Steps**, which lead down past the picturesque cottages of Darrell Pl and Napier Lane to Levi's Plaza and the Embarcadero.

Fisherman's Wharf

Most San Franciscans regard Fisherman's Wharf (Map pp86–7) with the sort of disdain that cats have for water. But visitors are inexplicably drawn to the area's tourist traps and diluted carnival atmosphere. This is a holiday land, to be sure, and if you show up at a down time, when the streets are lifeless and disheveled, the area's charmlessness is all too apparent. That said, there are legitimate excuses for spending an afternoon or even an entire day in this part of town.

Remarkably, in a city set on an attractive bay, the spit of sand at **Aquatic Park** is one of the few waterfront areas to offer pleasant and picturesque public access to the bay. The distinguished **San Francisco Maritime National Historic Park** (☎ 415-561-7100) includes the **National Maritime Museum** (300 Beach St; admission free; ❂ 10am-5pm), which overlooks Aquatic Park and recounts the Bay Area's nautical history. Five classic ships are moored at **Hyde St Pier** (2905 Hyde St; adult/child under 17 $5/free; ❂ 9:30am-5:30pm), including the *Balclutha*, an iron-hull square-rigger from 1886.

Two more historic watercraft await at Pier 45. The **USS Pampanito** (☎ 415-775-1943; adult/child $8/4; ☺ 9am-8pm Thu-Tue, 9am-6pm Wed) is a WWII US Navy submarine that made six Pacific patrols during the last years of the war and sank six Japanese ships (tragically including two carrying British and Australian POWs). The **SS Jeremiah O'Brien** (☎ 415-544-0100; Pier 45; adult/child $8/4; ☺ 10am-4pm) is the sole surviving WWII Liberty ship in complete working order. It has an illustrious history, including 11 voyages as part of the D-Day landings at Normandy.

Pier 39, mostly a schlocky shopping mall that preys upon unsuspecting tourists, is worth a visit just to view the colony of sea lions that makes its home on the old docks. A **Venetian carousel** (tickets $2) looks out of place here, but is a fun spin. Some of the panhandlers and street entertainers in this part of town have perfected highly amusing approaches to their work.

Russian Hill & Nob Hill

West of North Beach are the roller-coaster streets of Russian Hill (Map pp86–7), with some of the city's prime real estate and the famous **Lombard Street** switchback. This steep block of Lombard, touted as 'the world's crookedest street,' sashays down the hillside, notching up 10 turns. Originally, the block was as straight as any other, but its 27%

BURLY BACHELORS OF PIER 39

With all the effort and expense put into luring tourists to Pier 39, it's amusing that the pier's biggest draw simply showed up, uninvited. In the early 1990s, California sea lions began to haul out onto a section of the walkways at the marina beside Pier 39. Within a few years their takeover was complete. The boats that once docked along the walks are gone and dozens of sea lions bask in the sun, woofing noisily to the amusement of onlookers. The population varies during the year, from a peak of several hundred in January and February to just a smattering in June and July, when most of the sea lions head south for the breeding season.

Pier 39's sea lions are almost all male. They are big creatures – an adult male can be 7ft long and weigh over 800lb. By contrast, a female may reach only 6ft and 300lb.

downhill grade was a challenge for some cars' brakes. The curves were added in 1922.

The top of Russian Hill is so steep that not all the roads manage to surmount it, making way for pocket-size patches of green – and affording some incredible views of the city below. Picturesque stairways make their way through **Ina Coolbrith Park** (Vallejo St) and up densely shaded **Macondray Lane** (btwn Leavenworth & Taylor Sts). The latter was the model for 'Barbary Lane' in Armistead Maupin's *Tales of the City*. Another lane of literary interest is Russell St, where, at No 29, Jack Kerouac drafted *On the Road* and several other works in 1952 while crashing on his pal Neal Cassady's couch (and enjoying an affair with Mrs Cassady).

The **San Francisco Art Institute** (☎ 415-771-7020; 800 Chestnut St), founded during the 1870s, was ground zero for the Bay Area's figurative art scene of the 1940s and '50s, and now has public exhibitions in its **Walter and McBean Gallery** (☺ Mon-Sat 11am-6pm). Also on campus, the **Diego Rivera Gallery** (☺ 8am-9pm Mon-Sat) features a huge mural painted by Rivera. The institute's cloisters and courtyards date from 1926, with a 1970 addition. The school has a surprisingly good café and excellent views over the bay.

The next hilltop neighborhood to the south, Nob Hill (Map pp86–7) is just what its name suggests: an enclave of privilege. It has been that way ever since the installation of the California St cable car tracks in the 1870s made the 338ft summit accessible to people not given to hiking. The mansions went up, the robber barons moved in, and the 1906 quake and fire brought the lot down. Eventually several of the burned-out mansions were replaced with hotels, which remain some of the most select and expensive establishments in the city. It's worth scaling these heights to wander through the elegant marble lobby of the **Fairmont** and perhaps enjoy a drink in an opulent hotel bar.

Grace Cathedral (☎ 415-749-6300; 1100 California St) overlooks tidy Huntington Park. The cathedral's bronze doors are casts of Ghiberti's Gates of Paradise in the Cathedral Baptistry of St John in Florence, Italy, and the magnificent rose window was made in Chartres, France, in 1964.

The **Cable Car Barn & Museum** (☎ 415-474-1887; 1201 Mason St; admission free; ☺ 10am-5pm, 10am-6pm summer) dates from 1910 and is the site of the

TOP FIVE VIEWS

As you reach the top of each of San Francisco's hilly thoroughfares, another fantastic view opens up before your eyes. The undulating streets, the bay and the landmark bridges are the subjects of a lovely picture that can be composed countless ways. If you're huffing and puffing from the walk up, consider the scenery payment for your efforts. Here are the best vantage points:

- Halfway across the **Golden Gate Bridge** (Map pp78-9)
- On Russian Hill in **Ina Coolbrith Park** (Map pp86-7)
- Top of 18th St on **Potrero Hill** (Map pp78-9)
- Facing the Mission on **Bernal Hill** (Map pp88-9)
- Looking to the east from **Twin Peaks** (Map pp88-9)

power plant that tows all the cable cars, the garage where the cable cars park at night and a museum displaying, among other things, inventor Andrew Hallidie's original Clay St cable car.

For Russian and Nob Hill cafés and stores, head to **Polk Street**, which slopes down to Ghirardelli Sq.

Pacific Heights & Japantown

The wealthy hilltop Pacific Heights (Map pp86-7) area has many of the city's finest old houses, which were spared in 1906 because the fires that consumed most of downtown San Francisco stopped at Van Ness Ave. **Fillmore Street**, climbing uphill from Union St and sloping down to Japantown, is the main drag. The Pacific Heights section (roughly Jackson to Sutter Sts) is chock full of good but pricey restaurants and upscale clothing boutiques.

Most houses are not open to the public. The exception is **Haas-Lilienthal House** (☎ 415-441-3004; 2007 Franklin St; adult/child $5/3; ☺ noon-3pm Wed & Sat, 11am-4pm Sun), built in Queen Anne style between 1882 and 1886. The house is full of period furniture, but the exterior is the highlight and the hour-long tour can be slow.

Another standout is the impressive baroque **Spreckels Mansion** (2080 Washington St), built in 1912 by George Applegarth (who also created the Palace of the Legion of Honor) for sugar magnate Adolph Spreckels. It was bought by novelist Danielle Steele in 1990.

Japanese people have made San Francisco their home since the 1860s, and today only a tiny percentage of them live in the compact Japantown area, just to the south of Pacific Heights in the vicinity of Fillmore

St. Known as Nihonmachi in Japanese, this area was populated by Japanese after the 1906 earthquake. The WWII internment of Japanese and Japanese Americans devastated the community, and many of the former residents were unable to reclaim their homes after the war.

In the late 1960s, the development of the **Japan Center** once again gave the Japanese a visible presence in the city. Japantown is primarily a commercial district – it isn't a neighborhood in the sense that Chinatown is. Nevertheless, the center, with an ersatz atmosphere that feels like a public kabuki stage set, succeeds in drawing huge crowds of Asian shoppers and diners.

Japantown is strangely quiet much of the time, but comes alive during the two-weekend Cherry Blossom Festival every April, and during the two-day Nihonmachi Street Fair on the first weekend in August.

For a communal bath, try **Kabuki Springs & Spa** (☎ 415-922-6000; www.kabukisprings.com; 1750 Geary Blvd; spa $16-20; ☺ 10am-9:45pm). Nights for women are Sunday, Wednesday and Friday; men's nights are Monday, Thursday and Saturday. Tuesday is co-ed and swimsuits are required. Massage and other treatments are also available by appointment.

The Marina & Cow Hollow

The Marina (Map pp86-7), with all its 'breeder' bars and high-priced rental units, is where grown-up frat boys and sorority girls live after they've landed high-paying jobs downtown. The neighborhood exudes cash and hormones. Chestnut St is the main commercial strip of the Marina. A few blocks south, Union St is the spine of the Cow Hollow neighborhood, named after a local dairy farm that once occupied the area. In between the Marina and Cow Hollow is motel-lined Lombard St, which connects the Golden Gate Bridge with Van Ness Ave.

The land that is now the Marina materialized when waterfront marshland was filled in (mainly with rubble created by the quake of 1906) to create the grounds for the 1915 Panama-Pacific International Exposition. That expo commemorated the completion of the Panama Canal and San Francisco's phoenixlike rebirth after the earthquake and fire. When the expo was over, the displays came down, and lucrative real-estate deals began. One of the few surviving structures from the exposition is the stunning **Palace of Fine Arts** (www.palaceoffinearts.org; Palace Dr off Lyon St), bordering the Presidio. Bernard Maybeck's artificial classical ruin was so popular that it was spared from its intended demolition when the exhibition closed. In the early '60s, the decaying stucco building was resurrected in durable concrete.

Behind the ruin is the **Exploratorium** (☎ 415-561-0360; www.exploratorium.edu; 3601 Lyon St; adult/child $12/8, 1st Wed of month free; ☑ 10am-5pm Tue-Sun, extended hours in summer), founded in 1969 by physicist Frank Oppenheimer (brother of Manhattan Project director, Robert Oppenheimer) as a museum blending art, science and human perception. It's an excellent experience, popular with curious people of all ages. A highlight is the **Tactile Dome**, a pitch-black dome that you can crawl, climb and slide through (separate admission $15; advance reservations required).

Cyclists, in-line skaters, joggers and kite fliers all enjoy the waterfront strip of **Marina Green**, a great place for lounging when the weather's decent.

At the tip of the breakwater, past the Golden Gate Yacht Club, is the curious **Wave Organ**, developed by artist Peter Richards and installed (with help from the Exploratorium) in 1986. Incoming and outgoing tides running through the 'organ' produce sounds that resemble the final gurgle made by a flushed toilet – don't expect to hear Beethoven's Ninth.

Between Aquatic Park and the Marina lies **Fort Mason Center** (☎ 415-441-3400; www.fortmason.org), first a Spanish and then a US military fort. The buildings and surrounding acreage were handed to the Golden Gate National Recreation Area in the 1970s. The cultural complex now houses theaters, galleries and museums. The very popular HI Fisherman's Wharf (p112) is just up the hill.

The Presidio

The northwest corner of the San Francisco peninsula was for many decades occupied by a rather low-key army base (Jerry Garcia was stationed here briefly before he formed the Grateful Dead). As a result the area has not been developed, and most of it remains green, despite the fact that Hwys 1 and 101 meet in the middle of the Presidio and lead to the Golden Gate Bridge.

The Presidio was established in 1776 by the Spanish as the site of their first fort, or *presidio*. The Presidio's military role ended in 1994, when the 1480-acre plot became part of the Golden Gate National Recreation Area. Since that time, debates have raged over how best to utilise the valuable land, and to make the park financially sustainable.

One new tenant is filmmaker George Lucas, who opened the **Letterman Digital Arts Center** (Map pp86–7) here in June 2005. The campus is near the Lombard Gate at the park's southern extent, and is home to Lucas' Industrial Light and Magic – one of the biggest and most successful digital effects companies in the world. LucasArts, a video-game company, is also based there. Some 1500 people work in the complex. Visitors can roam the grounds, picnic or lunch at the awesome **Lucas Cafeteria**.

The **Presidio Visitors Center** (☎ 415-561-4323; cnr Montgomery St & Lincoln Blvd) has exhibits and information on the park's facilities.

Facing the bay is **Crissy Field**, a recently restored tidal marsh that features beautiful hiking and biking trails and a grassy former airstrip where unleashed dogs romp most days. The **Crissy Field Center** (Map pp86-7; ☎ 415-561-7690; cnr Mason & Halleck Sts; ☑ 9am-5pm Wed-Sun) has a café and bookstore.

Under American rule, **Fort Point** (Map pp78–9) was built at the start of the Civil War (1861–65) to guard the entrance to the bay, but not so much as a single cannon ball was fired from its battlements and the fort was abandoned in 1900. Today, Fort Point offers some of the most spectacular views of the Golden Gate Bridge, which arches over it. The view was all the more alluring in Alfred Hitchcock's 1958 film *Vertigo*, when Kim Novak plopped fully clothed into the bay from this spot. The triple-tiered brick fortress is off Marine Dr.

Along the ocean side of the peninsula is **Baker Beach** (Map pp78–9), the most picturesque of the city's beaches, with craggy rock formations backed up against cliffs. With cold water and nasty currents, it's not much of a swimming beach, but it is popular with sunbathers and a clothing-optional crowd.

South of Market

South of Market (or SoMa; Map pp80–1) is an interesting agglomeration of office buildings spilling over from the Financial District, fancy condominiums along the Embarcadero near the Bay Bridge, a busy and still-expanding museum and convention area around the **Yerba Buena Gardens**, and a well-dispersed late-night entertainment scene. Be warned that parking here is often in short supply and that long blocks can make walking any distance around the district arduous; public transportation is easily accessed nearby and is highly recommended.

Yerba Buena Gardens is the open-air public center of SoMa, a pleasant urban oasis begging a lunchtime picnic. The excellent **San Francisco Museum of Modern Art** (SFMoma; ☎ 415-357-4000; www.sfmoma.org; 151 3rd St; adult/child/student $12.50/free/7; ☯ 10am-5:45pm Fri-Tue, 10am-8:45pm Thu) is directly across from the Yerba Buena Gardens in a fetching piece of architectural eye-candy designed by Swiss architect Mario Botta. The permanent collection is particularly strong in American abstract expressionism, with major works by Clyfford Still, Jackson Pollock and Philip Guston. The SFMoma's photography collection is also world renowned. Note that admission is free the first Tuesday of the month, half price on Thursday evening.

The delightful **Cartoon Art Museum** (☎ 415-227-8666; www.cartoonart.org; 655 Mission St; adult/child/student $6/2/4; ☯ 11am-5pm Tue-Sun) exhibits cartoon art from around the world, but is particularly strong on the greats who have had Bay Area ties over the years. The work of R Crumb (a former Haight-Ashbury denizen) features prominently. 'Zippy the Pinhead' creator Bill Griffith, 'Eightball' scribe/penman Daniel Clowes, and 'Chuckling Whatsit' artist Richard Sala have also shown here.

The galleries at the **Yerba Buena Center for the Arts** (☎ 415-978-2787; www.ybca.org; cnr Mission & 3rd Sts; adult/student $6/3; ☯ 11am-5pm Tue-Sun, 11am-8pm Thu), show rotating contemporary art exhibits that are among the city's most exciting.

Across Howard St from the Metreon, on the roof of Moscone Convention Center, **Zeum Art & Technology Center** (☎ 415-777-2800; www.zeum.org; adult/child $7/5; ☯ 11am-5pm Wed-Sun) is a hands-on art and technology museum that encourages young people to create and produce their own works with audio, video, computer animation and more. Zeum also has a restored **Looff carousel** (two rides $2).

Close to the waterfront, the historic **Rincon Center** occupies the block bounded by Mission, Howard, Steuart and Spear Sts. Modern shops and offices aside, the main building is itself a treasure, a WPA (Works Progress Administration) project and former post office designed by Gilbert Stanley Underwood, who also designed Yosemite's Ahwahnee Hotel. The main reason to visit is to admire the dolphin friezes on the facade and the massive interior murals depicting California's history. The latter were completed in 1948 by Anton Refregier.

South Park, between Bryant, Brannan, 2nd and 3rd Sts, is a picturesque oval of green in the midst of the city's once-burgeoning 'Multimedia Gulch.' Built in 1852 to mimic a London city square, it's surrounded by offices and cafés.

Southeast of South Park is **SBC Park**, home of the San Francisco Giants (see p129).

The Mission

The always lively and colorful Mission District (Map pp88–9) is one of San Francisco's most vital and diverse zones. It's ethnically mixed, artistically inclined, and gritty and neighborly all at the same time. Spanish-speaking families coexist here with punky hipsters, junkie prostitutes and professionals attracetd by the neighborhood's escalating property values. The Mission is a hotspot for nightlife, with a healthy selection of cutting-edge restaurants, cheap eats, atmospheric bars and intimate live music venues. It's also San Francisco's sunbelt – the rest of the city might be blanketed by fog, but they'll be squinting on their stoops in the Mission.

Most of the action here is on Mission and Valencia Sts. Between these two thoroughfares, 16th, 18th and 22nd Sts also have concentrations of bars and restaurants.

HABITUAL DRAG QUEENS

Describing themselves as an 'order of gay male nuns,' the Sisters of Perpetual Indulgence have been a fixture in San Francisco since 1979. They got their first habits from a stage production of the *Sound of Music*. Individually they have colorful names, such as Sister Missionary Position, Sister Florence Nightmare and Sister Dana Van Iniquity. Stirring controversy everywhere they go, they also have managed to do a lot of really positive things for the gay community along the way.

During Pope John Paul II's 1987 visit to San Francisco, he took the time to add them to the Papal List of Heretics. Although the sisters were obviously delighted with this unexpected notoriety, they have at times shown a genuinely nunlike benevolence towards their fellow gay men. They proved their spiritual mettle during the direst years of the AIDS crisis, organizing the first AIDS fundraiser in 1982, and helping to educate youths about safe sex. Outrageous as they are, not all of their acts have been of the headline-grabbing variety. The sisters quietly raise funds for homebound HIV patients and organize events for gay youths on a regular basis. They've even organized regular bingo nights – just like real church ladies do.

You're most likely to see the sisters at special events in the Castro (or on Folsom St). They also make a habit of appearing on Halloween.

The Mission District is San Francisco's oldest enclave, and it takes its name from the oldest building in the city, **Mission Dolores** (☎ 415-621-8203; Dolores & 16th Sts; adult/child $3/2; ☉ 9am-4pm). Originally Misión San Francisco de Asís, it was the sixth mission founded by Father Junípero Serra for the Spanish. Its site was consecrated on June 29, 1776, but a more sturdy structure was built in 1782 by Franciscan monks, with Native American labor. Today, the modest adobe mission is overshadowed by the adjoining **basilica**, built in 1913.

A few blocks south, **Mission Dolores Park** is a popular spot on sunny days with both sunbathers and Latino families holding family barbecues. After dark the park remains a seedy enclave best avoided.

One prime Mission attraction is its hundreds of colorful **murals**, depicting everything from San Francisco's labor history to Central American independence struggles, the women's movement and local streetlife. One of the most amazing examples of mural art is on the **Women's Building** (3543 18th St), between Valencia and Guerrero Sts to the southeast. Narrow **Balmy Alley**, between Folsom and Harrison Sts and 24th and 25th Sts, is lined end-to-end with murals that reflect the neighborhood's Hispanic culture.

Public art reflecting the Mission's countercultural artistic leanings can be seen aplenty along **Clarion Alley** and nearby **Sycamore St**, just south of 16th St Mission BART station, where murals exhibit the influence of comic books, graffiti art and other forms.

If you're especially interested in murals, stop by the **Precita Eyes Mural Arts and Visitors Center** (☎ 415-285-2287; www.precitaeyes.org; 2981 24th St). The center sells postcards, books, art supplies and a mural walking-tour map ($4). It also conducts walking tours (see p108).

The Castro

As the epicenter of the city's sizable and influential gay community, the Castro (Map pp88–9) is definitely worth strolling. The neighborhood has an air of upper-middle-class urbanity colored by often outrageous sensibilities. You might notice that there has been an influx of straight folk, some with children, spilling out from Noe Valley into the Castro. But with a street scene that seems to buzz at all hours, the Castro is still one of San Francisco's best neighborhoods for people-watching, indulging in a leisurely lunch, browsing for books and clothes, or grabbing a beer.

The magnificent **Castro Theatre** (p129) is the highlight of Castro St and the center for the annual Gay and Lesbian Film Festival. **Harvey Milk Plaza** (cnr Market & Castro Sts), at the MUNI station, is dedicated to the unofficial 'mayor of Castro St,' and the first openly gay man elected to public office in San Francisco. He was murdered along with Mayor George Moscone in 1978.

Continue south along Castro or Noe Sts, and you'll come to **Noe Valley**, another of San Francisco's colorful small neighborhoods. The mix of Victorian homes, restaurants and eclectic shops gives it a villagey feel; the

SAN FRANCISCO

WHAT HAPPENED, MAN

In the mid-1960s, hippies began gravitating to the somewhat tired Victorian Haight-Ashbury. They were drawn by low rents, proximity to the park and a pre-existing bohemian community that had grown out of the Beat scene. The two or three years preceding the 'Summer of Love' were the most romantic and idealistic period of the decade. Outdoor rock concerts were free, LSD and marijuana proliferated, public nudity and free love were pretty much going on all the time, and political dialectics emanated from hangouts like the Psychedelic Shop and Mnasidika boutique. The local economy revolved around what many aptly called the 'Psychedelic Revolution.'

By the time the national media caught on to what was going on in the Haight, thousands of kids from around the country had gravitated to the neighborhood. The media attention attracted more people wanting to 'turn on' in San Francisco, and the scene quickly began to sour. By late '67, towards the end of the year-long Summer of Love, the Haight had turned into too much of a good thing. Drug overdoses and incidences of violence were increasing among the throngs of hippies, gawkers, media, and police. By the early '70s, Haight St was skid row for burnt-out hippies and winos.

---

main drag is the stretch of 24th St between Church and Castro Sts, full of clothing and gift boutiques, book and record stores, and lots of baby strollers.

The Haight

The intersection of Haight and Ashbury Sts is San Francisco's most famous crossroads (Map pp88–9) for one reason only: it was ground zero of the 'Summer of Love'. Although you'll see just a few remnants of the idealistic '60s on Haight St, this is still one of the more active and interesting neighborhoods in San Francisco. The majority of people come here to hang out in funky cafés, people-watch, shop for nostalgic curios or retro clothing and nose through leftist bookstores. For '60s buffs, a short walk will take you past many places where the famous resided and some of the decade's definitive events occurred. At night, Haight St is somewhat edgy but worth coming to for its handful of idiosyncratic bars.

Deadheads should pass by **710 Ashbury St**, the one-time communal home of the Grateful Dead (now a private residence). The **Upper Haight**, centered on Haight and Ashbury, is just east of Golden Gate Park. To the east **Lower Haight** is a colorful few blocks of grungy clubs and bars from Scott St east to Webster St. Quiet **Cole Valley**, an upscale residential area just south of the Haight, has a smattering of cafés and shops along Carl and Cole Sts.

The Richmond

Bordered by the Presidio to the north and Golden Gate Park to the south, the uniform rectangular blocks of the Richmond District (Map p83) stretch from Arguello Ave all the way to the ocean. Restaurants and shops are along Geary and Clement St, with Clement serving as the heart of New Chinatown.

Cliff House (☎ 415-386-3330; www.cliffhouse.com; 1090 Point Lobos Ave) overlooks the Pacific from the north end of Ocean Beach and was originally built in 1863 as an escape from the crowds. After the first was destroyed by fire, the second Cliff House was an impressive, elegant eight-story gingerbread resort built by Adolph Sutro in 1896, which contained art galleries, dining rooms and an observation deck. It survived the 1906 earthquake but was destroyed by fire the following year. The 1909 replacement was nowhere near as grand, but in 2004 a $19 million facelift was completed, adding walls of windows to take advantage of the ocean views and a two-story dining room and bar.

On the deck below the restaurant is a giant **Camera Obscura** (☎ 415-750-0415; admission $2; ☒ 11am-sunset), an invention that projects the view from outside the building onto a parabolic screen inside. It was built in 1946 by a local engineer, based on diagrams originally drawn by Leonardo da Vinci. After some debate about its future, it was added to the National Register of Historic Places in 2001. It's definitely worth seeing.

The ruins in the cove just north of the Cliff House are all that remain of the **Sutro Baths**, the magnificent six-pool, 3-acre indoor swimming-pool palace Sutro built in 1896. The baths never made money, however, and the building burned down in 1966 amid rumors of insurance fraud.

There's a fine walking path along this surprisingly rugged stretch of coast from Cliff House to **Lands End**, where there are terrific views across the Golden Gate. It starts by the remains of Sutro Baths and passes through **Lincoln Park**, which was established by Golden Gate park keeper John McLaren.

Off 34th Ave, within Lincoln Park, is the **California Palace of the Legion of Honor** (☎ 415-863-3330; www.legionofhonor.org; adult/child under 12/student $10/free/6, Tue free; ⏰ 9:30am-5pm Tue-Sun), one of San Francisco's premier art museums, with a world-class collection of medieval to 20th-century European art. A MUNI bus transfer gets you $2 off adult admission; from downtown, take bus 1, 2 or 38.

Golden Gate Park

San Francisco's biggest park (Map pp78–9) stretches almost halfway across the peninsula. An 1870 competition to design the park was won by 24-year-old William Hammond Hall, who a year later began to turn 1017 acres of dunes into the largest developed park in the world. By the 1880s the park had become the city's most popular attraction. John Laren took over the park's management in 1887 and stayed on as administrator for the next 56 years, until his death at age 97.

Apart from gardens, lakes, sporting facilities and trails, the park also hosts museums and other indoor attractions. Park information is available from **McLaren Lodge** (☎ 415-831-2700; park entrance, cnr Fell & Stanyan Sts).

The **Conservatory of Flowers** (☎ 415-666-7001; adult/child $5/3; ⏰ 9am-4:30pm Tue-Sun), the oldest building in the park, was brought from Ireland for millionaire James Lick's estate, but he died before it could be rebuilt and it went up instead in Golden Gate Park in 1878. Entering its tropical climes on a cold, foggy day can be surreal. The conservatory is home to thousands of exotic species, including one giant 'corpse flower' *(Amorphophallus titanum)*, the world's largest and foulest-smelling bloom.

MH de Young Memorial Museum (☎ 415-863-3330; www.thinker.org/deyoung; 50 Hagiwara Tea Garden Dr; adult/child under 12/student $10/free/7; ⏰ 10am-4:45pm Tue-Sat) opened its modern, brand-new home in 2005. It has a fine collection of pre-20th century American art, and the museum has been actively building on its already solid collections of African and Pacific Island art. The de Young has also started to exhibit

rotating selections from SFMOMA's deep photographic collection.

The popular **Japanese Tea Garden** (☎ 415-831-2700; adult/child $2/1; ⏰ 9am-6:30pm Mar-Oct, 8:30am-6pm Nov-Feb) was originally the Japanese Village exhibit at the 1894 Midwinter Fair, held in Golden Gate Park. Today it features a pagoda, gates, bridges, statues and a pleasant teahouse where you can enjoy green tea and fortune cookies for $2. Fortune cookies were actually invented here, back in 1909.

The **Strybing Arboretum & Botanical Gardens** (☎ 415-661-1316) encompasses a number of smaller gardens within its 70 acres, including the Garden of Fragrance, the California Collection of Native Plants and the Japanese Moon-Viewing Garden. Free tours take place daily; stop by the bookstore just inside the arboretum entrance for details.

The park is packed with sporting facilities, including 7.5 miles of bicycle trails, untold miles of jogging trails, 12 miles of equestrian trails, an archery range, baseball and softball diamonds, fly-casting pools, a challenging nine-hole golf course, lawn bowling greens, *pétanque* courts (a French game similar to lawn bowls), four soccer fields and 21 tennis courts. Rowing boats and pedal boats can be rented from the **Stow Lake boathouse** (☎ 415-752-0347; boat rental per hr $11-18; ⏰ 10am-4pm).

On Sunday some roads in the park are closed to traffic, allowing hordes of in-line skaters, bicyclists and street-hockey players to buzz around free from obstructing autos. There are places in the park to rent bicycles (p104) and in-line skates (p104).

The Sunset & Twin Peaks

South of Golden Gate Park, the city's hilly terrain makes two final skyward lunges at Twin Peaks (Map pp88–9) and Mt Sutro (Map p83), then rolls westward in block after uniform block to the ocean. Originally known as El Pecho de la Chola (the Breasts of the Indian Girl), the two summits of the appropriately named Twin Peaks (922ft and 904ft) offer a superb view of the Bay Area, especially at night. To drive to Twin Peaks head southwest on Market St as it climbs steeply uphill (it becomes Portola Ave) and then turn right on Twin Peaks Blvd.

The area south of Golden Gate Park down to Sloat Blvd and from about 16th Ave to the ocean is known as the Sunset District (Map p83), a mostly residential area filled with pastel-colored stucco homes built between the 1930s and 1950s. The Inner Sunset, centered on 9th Ave at Irving and Judah Sts, has a collection of decent restaurants, bars and shops only a block or two from Golden Gate Park.

Ocean Beach (Map p83) stretches for miles along the coast, from Cliff House to the cliffs of Fort Funston. On sunny days, you'll find a classic California beach scene: sunbathers, surfers and picnickers. Unfortunately, sunny days are few and far between.

San Francisco Zoo (Map pp78-9; ☎ 415-753-7080; www.sfzoo.org; Sloat Blvd & 45th Ave; adult/child 3-11/senior & youth 12-17 $11/5/8; ☼ 10am-5pm) is transforming into a more conservation-friendly outfit. Recent additions, including the Lemur Forest, a large African savanna and the ever-popular ape jungle have greatly increased the old zoo's appeal.

One mile south, **Fort Funston** is a beautiful windswept area of cliffs, trails and beach; a great place to spend an afternoon watching the hang gliders float above the cliffs.

ACTIVITIES
Cycling

Despite the hilly challenges of many San Francisco streets, cycling is actually a lot of fun and popular here. The classic ride takes you from Fisherman's Wharf along the periphery of the Bay, through Crissy Field and the Presidio and across the Golden Gate Bridge to Sausalito or the Marin Headlands. Further afield, in Marin County, **Mt Tam** is the Bay Area's supreme mountain-biking challenge (see p148). Good places in town for cycling are Golden Gate Park and the Presidio (though in the Presidio, take note that park police frequently ticket cyclists for not stopping at stop signs and other traffic violations).

If you're under 18, California law says you must wear a helmet, and every cyclist must have a light when pedaling at night. And of course, always carry a good lock; bike theft is all too common in the city. The website for the **San Francisco Bicycle Coalition** (☎ 415-431-2453; www.sfbike.org) contains all kinds of useful information about safe bicycling in San Francisco.

Blazing Saddles (Map pp86-7; ☎ 415-202-8888; 1095 Columbus Ave; bike rental per hr $7-11, per day $28-48) has its main store in North Beach, near Fisherman's Wharf, and also has a tent on Pier 41, which is super convenient if you're planning to bike across the bridge and return via ferry (maps are provided for this route too).

Avenue Cyclery (Map p83; ☎ 415-387-3155; 756 Stanyan St; bike rentals per hr/day $5/2) is just outside Golden Gate Park in the Upper Haight.

Running & Skating

Marina Green has a 2.5-mile jogging track and fitness course, and there are many running paths through Golden Gate Park. The Presidio is another great park for running, with plenty of routes from the Marina right past the Golden Gate Bridge to Baker Beach.

Surrey Bikes & Blades (Map p83; ☎ 415-668-6699; 50 Stow Lake Dr; skate rental per hr/day $6/20, bike rental $8/25), right in the heart of Golden Gate Park, rents skates and mountain bikes. Cheaper cruiser bikes are also available (same price as skate rental).

Golden Gate Park Bike & Skate (Map p83; ☎ 415-668-1117; 3038 Fulton St; skate rental per hr/day $6/24, bike rental $5/25), just outside the park, also rents out bikes and blades. If traditional, less-expensive quad skates more your style, this place has a limited supply.

Sailing & Windsurfing

A view of the bay, dotted with sails, shows that this is prime sailing country. The bay is tricky territory, though, and only for experienced sailors. If you are already a sailor, you can rent a boat from **Spinnaker Sailing** (Map pp80-1; ☎ 415-543-7333; www.spinnaker-sailing.com; Pier 40). You can also rent a skippered boat or take a two-day introductory class ($295).

The bay is also great for windsurfing, but it is not kind to beginners. For more experienced board sailors, the beach off Crissy Field, in the shadow of the Golden Gate Bridge, is a world-class spot. A good place to watch sailboarders is Fort Point, right under the Golden Gate Bridge.

Surfing

Ocean Beach is one of the most challenging and exhausting places to surf in California, especially in winter when the powerful, cold swells can reach 12ft or more. There are no lifeguards; never surf alone or without at least a 3mm full-length wetsuit. For a recorded message on the latest surfing conditions at Ocean Beach, telephone **Wise**

Surfboards (☎ 415-273-1618) or **SF Surfshop** (☎ 415-437-6683), or check www.surfpulse.com.

Tennis
There are free public tennis courts all over San Francisco. The well-maintained courts at Mission Dolores Park are popular. The 21 courts in Golden Gate Park charge a fee.

Golf
San Francisco has three 18-hole public golf courses: **Harding Park** (Map pp78-9; ☎ 415-664-4690; Harding & Skyline Blvds), near Lake Merced; **Lincoln Park** (Map p83; ☎ 415-750-4653; 34th Ave & Clement St); and, nearby the Presidio's Arguello Gate, the stunning **Presidio Golf Course** (Map pp78-9; ☎ 415-561-4653). There is also a challenging nine-hole course in **Golden Gate Park** (Map p83; ☎ 415-751-8987), near the beach.

WALKING TOUR
This walk meanders through the heart of Chinatown and North Beach before ascending Russian Hill for jaw-dropping views of the city by the bay. Much of the walk follows a flat course through busy neighborhoods.

The Russian Hill climb is a bit strenuous, but it's through peacefully quiet parks with benches. Take it slowly and soak it all in.

Begin at the **Dragon's Gate (1)** at Grant Ave and Bush St. The green, tile-topped gate with its triple portals makes a fine spot to snap a picture of your party as you 'enter the dragon.' Follow Grant Ave, a destination in itself, past sellers of tourist junk and fine arts and crafts. The street is lined with colorful buildings and lampposts resembling an amusement park version of Chinese pagodas. Most of the buildings here went after the 1906 earthquake, and time has graced them with their own authenticity.

At California St walk around **Old St Mary's Church (2)** which was built in 1854 by Chinese masons as a cathedral, and enter **St Mary's Square (3)**. Presiding over the churcch square like a wise old tin man is the serene, stainless-steel statue of Sun Yat-sen, first president of China. It's one of local sculptor Beniamino Bufano's best works.

Return to Grant and, at Clay St, head right downhill toward **Portsmouth Square (4; p95)**. Under Spanish rule, this was the city's central

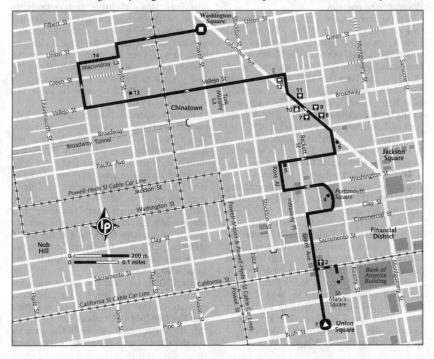

plaza, and it remained the heart of the city during the Gold Rush years. The square is often called Chinatown's 'Living Room,' for many of the neighborhood's residents who lack couch space in their own apartments spend their free time on the benches here. Cut through the square in the direction of Washington St and you'll see men gambling, women chatting and children burning off steam on the jungle gyms.

Head up Washington St, with its noodle parlors and neon signs, past Grant Ave to dark, narrow Ross Alley, the quintessential Chinatown backstreet. It's lined with mysterious shops and back entries. Drop by the **Golden Gate Fortune Cookie Company** (5; p95) and buy a bag of 'French' fortune cookies (with adult-themed fortunes) and hang a right down Jackson St.

At Kearny, turn left towards Columbus Ave. The terracotta siding and green copper bays of **Columbus Tower** (6; p95) are eye-catching, but it's the cupola that makes this one of North Beach's signature buildings. It's owned by filmmaker Francis Ford Coppola, and offices for his company American Zoetrope are upstairs.

Up the street, have a drink at the **Vesuvio Cafe** (7; p125), where Dylan Thomas and Jack Kerouac indulged in a drink or two (separately). Two other classic North Beach bars stand within spitting distance – **Specs'** (8; p124) and **Tosca** (9; p125) – so if it's your time to howl you might make an evening of it here. From Vesuvio's make your way to **City Lights Bookstore** (10; p77). The densely packed bookshop was founded in 1953 by poet Lawrence Ferlinghetti, who still owns it. Go up to the Poetry Room, where works of the Beats and others fill the shelves.

At the neon-lit corner of Columbus and Broadway, pause to read the plaque at the **Condor Club** (11), were Carol Doda danced in her birthday suit.

Continue on Columbus to Grant Ave. At the corner of Vallejo, **Caffe Trieste** (12; p122) is ample reward for the strenuous walking we've already done. Step into the North Beach landmark for an espresso or a beer. The place probably looks pretty much as it did when it opened in 1956. Francis Ford Coppola drafted parts of his screen adaptation for *The Godfather* at a table beneath the back wall mural depicting a quaint Sicilian fishing village.

Follow Vallejo St towards Russian Hill (to the west). After crossing Mason St, you begin to ascend the inviting steps that course through **Ina Coolbrith Park** (13). Named after a former California poet laureate, this is one of several stairway parks in the city. The Coolbrith stairs climb past gardens, decks and picturesque apartment buildings. As you ascend, the view changes from a quaint neighborhood outlook of North Beach and Telegraph Hill to a wide panorama taking in all the downtown area, from the high rises of the Financial District to the neon fishes of Fisherman's Wharf, with the sweeping curve of the bay and Alcatraz Island as backdrop.

Follow the steps all the way up to Jones St, turn right, and head back down the narrow wooden stairway of **Macondray Lane** (14). This shaded and atmospheric enclave was the model for Armistead Maupin's 'Barbary Lane,' from his *Tales of the City* serial. Make your way back to North Beach and find a suitable recovery room, be it a bar or an Italian restaurant.

SAN FRANCISCO FOR CHILDREN

San Francisco's nightlife and restaurants are so heavily hyped, it might seem like the city offers nothing for the under-21 set. But families visit the city all the time. As long as your idea of a fun vacation doesn't involve spending hours shopping, museum-hopping and getting to know all the bartenders in town, you ought to be able to show the kiddies a good time.

Hotel location can be critical, as some kids require frequent stops at the hotel room. Fisherman's Wharf and the Marina are full of nonfussy, family-friendly hotels and motels with sizeable rooms and extra cots. Many of these also have parking, if you're traveling by minivan. But many kids these days are well-traveled, well-mannered and, well, much more cosmopolitan than your average kid 20 years ago. For the worldly type of tyke, a large hotel such as the **Westin St Francis** (p111) in Union Sq can be fun in the same way taking a cruise is fun. Just be sure to get a large room.

Breakfast is typically the easiest meal for traveling tykes. Take 'em for pancakes and eggs and all that good finger food at **Dottie's True Blue Cafe** (p116). Or check out an Italian café in North Beach, where Italian pastries are usually on offer. Contemporary diners like **Mel's Drive-In** (p118) and **Max's Opera Deli** (Map pp80-1; ☎ 415-771-7301; 601 Van Ness Ave; dishes $5-22) can take care of all your meals and have locations around downtown SF. There are brewpubs all over town offering kid menus and a chance for Mom and Dad to try some unique local beers. The **Rainforest Cafe** (p118) in Fisherman's Wharf makes a clear pitch to families. For the adventurous little eater, ethnic eateries in Chinatown, Japantown and the Mission District attract local families so the addition of your own small ones won't make much of an impact. Take the kids for dim sum at bustling **Gold Mountain** (p117). For a snack, be sure to drop by Chinatown's **Golden Gate Fortune Cookie Factory** (p95) or grab some chocolate at **Ghirardelli Square** (p132).

There are ample sightseeing options and activities to keep a curious child busy for days. On the top of the list are **Alcatraz** (p92), which throws a boat ride into the deal; the **Exploratorium** (p99), where restless kids get to grab and touch everything in sight; the **sea lions** and **Venetian carousel** (p97) at Pier 39; the **Cartoon Art Museum** (p100), a funhouse of zany and weird drawings; **Basic Brown Bear Factory** (Map pp86-7; ☎ 415-409-2806, 800-554-1910; www.basicbrownbear.com; The Cannery, South Bldg, 2nd Level; admission from $12; ☑ 10am-6pm Mon-Sat, 11am-5pm Sun), where kids can make their own teddy bears; the **Randall Museum** (Map pp88-9; ☎ 415-554-9600; www.randallmuseum.org; 199 Museum Way; admission by donation); ☑ 10am-5pm Tue-Sat), where kids can get familiar with animals in the petting zoo; **Hyde St Pier** (p96), with its fleet of old schooners and tugs (fun for Grandpa, too); and **Zeum** (p100), a hands-on science and technology center that appeals to young 'uns from eight to 18.

For the kid with walking shoes, get out to **Golden Gate Park** (p103) and pass an entire day exploring the trails, exotic gardens, boat rides, museums and playgrounds. You will find playgrounds can be found all around town. Chinatown's **Portsmouth Square** (p95) is a unique setting for a romp, right in the heart of the city's most crowded and busy residential zone. North Beach has a few jungle gyms and swing sets, including at Washington Sq. If your kid's a video-game junkie, you'll find a state of the art arcade at the **Metreon** (Map pp80-1; ☎ 800-638-7366; www .metreon.com; 101 4th St; admission free, fees for individual attractions; ☑ 10am-10pm Sun & Mon-Thu, 10am-11pm Fri & Sat).

BABYSITTING

Some of the major hotels in San Francisco offer nannies and sitters; they rely on well-recommended providers. Prices range from $12 to $25 an hour. You can also try **American ChildCare Services, Inc** (Map pp80-1; ☎ 415-285-2300; www.americanchildcare.com; 580 California St, Suite 500, San Francisco, CA 94104).

Getting around town is just another adventure, with **cable cars** (p93) ascending the city's steep streets like slow-moving rollercoasters. Or catch a **ferry** (p134) from Pier 41 or Pier 1 and traverse the bay.

QUIRKY SAN FRANCISCO

The superb and unique **Musée Mécanique** (Map pp86-7; ☎ 415-346-2000; www.museemechanique .org; Pier 45, end of Taylor St; admission free; ☑ 11am-7pm Mon-Fri, 10am-8pm Sat & Sun) is a one-of-a-kind museum. The collection, assembled and restored by Edward Galland Zelinsky and Daniel Galland Zelinsky, spotlights early-20th-century arcade games, self-playing pianos and risqué Mutoscope motion pictures ('See what the belly dancer does on her day off!'). Odd, ingenious coin-operated 'automata' displays – mechanical folk art, really – include a spinning Ferris wheel built of toothpicks and a fully operational miniature opium den in which thumb-size hopheads loll on their floor mats while a dragon peeks from behind a curtain. By pumping quarters into the machines, you'll get more amusement than you bargained for.

Frank Chu is a man who walks the streets of the Financial District with protest signs. For years, Chu's signs called for the impeachment of President Bill Clinton, even as Clinton's final term neared its end. Chu's signs also typically contain cryptic messages, such as '12 Galaxies' and 'Zikrorhetical.' If you like head-scratchers, look for the man with the sign on weekdays. A nightclub in the Mission District was inspired by his '12 Galaxies' sign, and Chu reportedly drinks free beer in the club some nights.

Image Leather (Map pp88-9; ☎ 415-621-7551; 2199 Market St) is a hard-core leather and fetish gear shop in the Castro. Descend into the 'dungeon' to see the dildo museum.

Vivian & Marian Brown are a pair of twins who appear to be approaching 90 years of age. They are always impeccably attired in identical Queen Mother outfits, and as they walk the streets around Union Sq they seem to have smiles permanently fixed on their faces. They don't even seem to object to their unofficial title as 'mascots' of San Francisco.

TOURS
Walking Tours
San Francisco lays out a rich feast for those keen on doing their sightseeing on foot. The San Francisco Visitors Information Center caters to walkers with an excellent line of walking-tour leaflets for Chinatown, Fisherman's Wharf, North Beach, Pacific Heights and Union Sq. As for guided tours, they're often a great way to get grounded in the city during a longer visit, or to catch a quick but informed glimpse of the city and its famous neighborhoods.

Chinese Heritage Tours (Map pp84-5; ☎ 415-986-1822; www.c-c-c.org; 750 Kearny St, 3rd fl; adult/child $17/8) are run by the Chinese Culture Center, based in the Holiday Inn across from Portsmouth Sq. The tours wander through Chinatown, with stops in a Buddhist temple, an herb shop and other places of historical and architectural interest.

The **Victorian Home Walk** (☎ 415-252-9485; www .victorianwalk.com; per person $20) is a good way for budding architecture buffs to learn more about the city's famous Victorian houses. Tours leave daily at 11am from the lobby of the St Francis Hotel in Union Sq and last about 2½ hours.

The **Haight-Ashbury Flower Power Walking Tour** (☎ 415-863-1621; 2hr tour $15) points out the sites of the Human Be-In and the Grateful Dead's former house. The two-hour walk is on Tuesday and Saturday mornings.

For the inside line on San Francisco's gay history – from the Gold Rush days to modern times – and a detailed tour of the Castro District, reserve a spot with **Cruisin' the Castro** (☎ 415-550-8110; www.webcastro.com/castrotour; 4hr tour $45). The four-hour walk, beginning at 10am from Tuesday to Saturday, includes lunch at a local restaurant.

The Mission is great for walking, especially for seeking out the district's many superb murals. **Precita Eyes Mural Arts and Visitors Center** (Map pp88-9; ☎ 415-285-2287; 2981 Harrison St) conducts a two-hour Mission District Mural Walk (adult/student $12/8) at 1:30pm on Saturday and Sunday.

Go-Carts
A fun and novel way to tour the city is in a three-wheel, two-seat racing car that moves at 35mph. **GoCar Rentals** (Map pp86-7; ☎ 800-914-6227; www.gocarsf.com; 2715 Hyde St; 1/2/3hr tours $40/70/90) has a fleet of smart little yellow cars, all equipped with a GPS-triggered voice that provides commentary on sights as you pass them. You must be 18 years or older and have a valid driver's license to rent one.

Whale-Watching
Mid-October through December is the peak season for whale-watching in the Bay Area, as gray whales make their annual migration south from the Bering Sea to Baja California (see the boxed text, p153). The **Oceanic Society** (Map pp86-7; ☎ 415-474-3385; www.oceanic-society.org; tours $61-63) leads whale-watching expeditions from the Yacht Harbor near Marina Green; trips run for about eight hours.

FESTIVALS & EVENTS
January & February
Chinese New Year (☎ 415-391-9680; www.chinese parade.com) The Golden Dragon Parade is the highlight of the festivities in late January and early February.

April & May
San Francisco International Film Festival (☎ 415-929-5000; www.sfiff.org) The country's oldest film festival specializes in a wide spectrum of international titles, some of which you'd be hard-pressed to find anywhere else. The two-week festival happens every April and/or May, with screenings at the Kabuki in Japantown, the Castro Theatre and other Bay Area cinemas.

Bay to Breakers (☎ 415-359-2800; www.baytobreakers .com) On the third Sunday in May, more than 100,000 joggers make their way from the Embarcadero to the ocean. Many are in crazy costumes, some in the buff and a few come to engage in a serious footrace.

Carnaval (☎ 415-826-1401; www.carnavalsf.com) Held on the Memorial Day weekend at the end of May, Carnaval is celebrated with music, a huge parade and dancing (samba, belly dancing and more) in the streets of the Mission.

June
June is **Pride Month**, a celebratory month for San Francisco's gay community

Gay and Lesbian Film Festival (☎ 415-703-8650; www.frameline.org)

Pink Saturday Party (☎ 415-864-3733; www.sfpride .org) Held on the last Saturday in June on Castro St, this event kicks off festivities the evening before the Pride Parade. Call for information.

GAY SAN FRANCISCO *Heather Harrison*

In the early 1950s, a chapter of the Mattachine Society, the first serious homosexual rights organization in the US, sprang up in San Francisco, and in 1955 the Daughters of Bilitis (DOB), the nation's first lesbian organization, was founded in San Francisco.

During the 1959 mayoral campaign, challenger Russell Wolden accused incumbent mayor George Christopher of turning San Francisco into 'the national headquarters of the organized homosexuals in the United States.' Christopher was re-elected, but was not about to be accused of being soft on queers. He responded with a massive police crackdown on gay male cruising areas, raids which resulted in a public blacklist of gay citizens.

Resistance to this persecution did not come out of the homophile movement but out of bars, and one in particular: the Black Cat, dubbed by Allen Ginsberg 'the greatest gay bar in America.' (José Sarria, a drag performer at the Black Cat, ran for city supervisor in 1961, becoming the first openly gay person to run for public office in the USA.)

The age of tolerance had not yet arrived, however. In 1965 a dance sponsored by the Council on Religion and the Homosexual was raided by the police, and everyone in attendance was arrested and photographed. The city was outraged and even the media denounced the police behavior. This event helped turn the tide in the city's perception of the gay community. The crackdown on gay bars stopped, and a gay person was appointed to sit on the police community-relations board.

With the 1977 election of gay activist Harvey Milk to the Board of Supervisors, recognition of the gay rights movement reached a new peak, but the euphoria was to be short-lived. The following year, Milk and Mayor George Moscone were assassinated by Dan White, an avowedly antigay former police officer.

Their deaths marked the beginning of the end of the heyday, the opulence of which further faded when the first cases of AIDS – at the time known as GRID (Gay-Related Immune Deficiency) – were reported in San Francisco in 1981.

Lesbian, Gay, Bisexual and Transgender Pride Parade (☎ 415-864-3733; www.sfpride.org) The last Sunday in June, the lively and outrageous parade attracts hundreds of thousands of people.

September
Shakespeare Festival (☎ 415-422-2221; www.sf shakes.org) Starting on the Labor Day weekend. There are performances of a different play each year in Golden Gate Park and other Bay Area parks.
Blues Festival (☎ 415-979-5588; www.sfblues.com) For two days in late September, bands, blues legends and R&B artists jam outdoors on Fort Mason's Great Meadow.

October & November
Jazz Festival (☎ 415-788-7353; www.sfjazz.org) From mid- to late October and into November, you can catch performances featuring legendary and up-and-coming artists throughout the city.
Halloween With hundreds of thousands of costumed revelers taking to the streets – particularly Castro St and around Civic Center – October 31 is the city's craziest night of the year.

Pretty much every neighborhood in San Francisco hosts an annual street fair. Two of the most popular are the **Folsom St Fair**

in late September (loaded with leather accouterments and naked strutting), and the massive **Castro St Fair** in early October. North Beach is hosts to a **Columbus Day Fair**, and the popular **Haight St Fair** goes all out in early June. For more fairs, phone the Visitors Information Center.

The city also hosts a number of film festivals throughout the year including the **Asian American Film Festival** (☎ 415-863-0814) in March at Japantown's **Kabuki 8 Theater** (1881 Post St); the popular **San Francisco International Film Festival** (for information, see opposite) in April and May (mainly at the Kabuki and the Castro); the **Gay and Lesbian Film Festival** (see opposite) in June (mainly at the Castro Theatre); and the **Jewish Film Festival** (☎ 925-866-9559) in July and August (at the Castro).

SLEEPING
Deciding on a place to stay in San Francisco requires two decisions: where do you want to stay and what do you want to stay in? The decisions are interrelated; if you want a romantic B&B, you might have to stay beyond the central Union Sq area, and if you want a luxury hotel, you'll probably wind up on

---

LOOKING FOR HOTEL DEALS?

Accommodations in San Francisco are more expensive than elsewhere in California, but travelers on a tight budget needn't despair. We've included many decent economical choices in our listings below, with rooms starting at around $60 per night. Among the city's hostels are some gems – including the HI Fisherman's Wharf, with its peaceful park surroundings, and San Francisco Elements, in the Mission District. Travelers wanting something higher class should try booking through an online clearance house, like **Priceline** (www.priceline.com), where doubles for three-star hotels (and sometimes better) can drop as low as $75 a night.

Nob Hill or around Union Sq. The Visitors Information Center has a reservation line (☎ 888-782-9673), or check its website at www.sfvisitor.org.

Hostelling International (HI) has three San Francisco locations (Union Sq, City Center and Fisherman's Wharf) and there are many good independents in the city.

No matter where you stay, reservations are a good idea on summer weekends, over holiday periods (for example, Christmas to New Year) and during the city's bigger festivals (Halloween and the weekend of the Gay Pride Parade, for instance).

Union Square

Within a few blocks of Union Sq you'll find a heavy concentration of accommodations, with hostels, inns and five-star hotels sharing the same sidewalks. The area's centrality puts you in the heart of town, with all forms of transit readily available.

BUDGET

HI San Francisco Downtown (Map pp80-1; ☎ 415-788-5604, 800-909-4776; www.norcalhostels.org; 312 Mason St; dm $24-29, r $55-69) This large, well-equipped hostel is a stone's throw from Union Sq and has over 280 beds, a few dozen private rooms and 24-hour access. The closest BART station is Powell St.

Adelaide Hostel (Map pp80-1; ☎ 415-359-1915, 877-359-1915; www.adelaidehostel.com; 5 Isadora Duncan Lane; dm from $20, r $55-80; 🖳) Off Taylor St, between Post and Geary Sts, is this small

inn with free Internet access, breakfast and laundry facilities.

USA Hostels (Map pp80-1; ☎ 415-440-5600, 877-483-2950; www.usahostels.com; 749 Taylor St; dm $23, r $48-62; 🖳) Built in 1909, this old hotel has been converted into a spiffy hostel that draws an international crowd. The private rooms sleep three or four people, and you can usually save a few bucks by reserving through the website.

Dakota Hotel (Map pp80-1; ☎ 415-931-7475; 606 Post St at Taylor St; r $55-99) A snug 42-room property. All rooms have private bathroom and some afford impressive city views.

MIDRANGE

Hotel Rex (Map pp80-1; ☎ 415-433-4434, 800-433-4434; www.jdvhospitality.com; 562 Sutter St; r $159-279) The Rex is a cool property with a swanky lobby and a lounge reminiscent of New York's Algonquin in the 1920s. Each guest room is uniquely decorated, with antique rotary telephones, custom wall coverings, fresh fabrics, hand-painted light shades and the work of local artisans. Services are completely up to date.

Beresford Arms (Map pp80-1; ☎ 415-673-2600, 800-533-6533; www.beresford.com; 701 Post St; r $99-165; 🖳) This is a well-kept older hotel with a few spacious rooms, many with kitchens. It's great value, with 96 rooms.

Hotel Beresford (Map pp80-1; ☎ 415-673-9900; 635 Sutter St; r $89-165; 🖳) The 114-room sister hotel to the Beresford Arms is a few blocks away.

Commodore Hotel (Map pp80-1; ☎ 415-923-6800; www.thecommodorehotel.com; 825 Sutter St; r $129-149; 🖳) A strikingly hip property that plays on the theme of steamship travel. The rooms have private bathroom and are custom furnished and comfortable.

York Hotel (Map pp80-1; ☎ 415-885-6800, 800-808-9675; www.yorkhotel.com; 940 Sutter St; r $149-169;

AUTHOR'S CHOICE

Hotel Des Arts (Map pp80-1; ☎ 415-956-3232, 800-956-4322; www.sfhoteldesarts.com; 447 Bush St; r $59-99, ste $129-159) Arty yet unpretentious, this hotel is right between Chinatown and Union Sq. Rooms are clean and comfortable but on the small side; the cheaper rooms have shared bathrooms. The place also has a respectable art gallery off the lobby.

🖵) This is an elegant hotel with a cabaret lounge off the lobby. Scenes from Alfred Hitchcock's *Vertigo* were shot at the hotel.

Maxwell Hotel (Map pp80-1; ☎ 415-986-2000, 888-734-6299; www.maxwellhotel.com; 386 Geary St; r $129-179; P 🔀 🖵) The Maxwell is a smartly restored 1908 hotel, part of the hip Joie de Vivre chain. Prices include limited parking and breakfast.

White Swan Inn (Map pp80-1; ☎ 415-775-1755, 800-999-9570; www.jdvhospitality.com; 845 Bush St; r $159-239; 🔀 🖵) This hotel is somewhere between hotel and B&B, with traditional charm, quaint comfort and over-the-top romantic decor.

Petite Auberge (Map pp80-1; ☎ 415-928-6000, 800-365-3004; 863 Bush St; r $139-199; 🔀) The White Swan's sister shares the same characteristics and style.

Hotel Triton (Map pp80-1; ☎ 415-394-0500, 800-433-6611; www.hoteltriton.com; 342 Grant Ave; r $109-239; 🔀 🖵) This place is notable for its 140 exotically designed guest rooms, including the Carlos Santana and Jerry Garcia suites. Decor ranges from mod to groovy but in any case is always tasteful and interesting.

Inn at Union Square (Map pp80-1; ☎ 415-397-3510, 800-288-4346; www.unionsquare.com; 440 Post St; r from $119; 🔀) This inn, just a few steps from Union Sq, has 30 elegantly old-fashioned rooms and suites, all nonsmoking.

Andrews Hotel (Map pp80-1; ☎ 415-563-6877, 800-926-3739; www.andrewshotel.com; 624 Post St; r $89-179; 🔀) Just two blocks west of Union Sq, this hotel has small but comfortable rooms. The services are equivalent to hotels that are much, much bigger. Wi-fi available.

Sir Francis Drake Hotel (Map pp80-1; ☎ 415-392-7755, 800-795-7129; www.sirfrancisdrake.com; 450 Powell St; r $119-259) An old soldier near Union Sq, the Drake outdoes many of its more expensive neighbors with its authentic 1920s flair. Guest rooms are a bit small but the Drake is worth it if you can score a special rate. The hotel's swinging Starlight Room (p127) is on the top-floor.

TOP END

Adagio Hotel (Map pp80-1; ☎ 415-775-5000, 800-228-8830; www.thehoteladagio.com; 550 Geary St; r $179-239) One of the hottest addresses in town, the Adagio Hotel opened its doors in 2003. With art on the walls and the trendy Cortez restaurant downstairs, the Adagio oozes sophistication, and has become a place to

---

AUTHOR'S CHOICE

Phoenix Motel (Map pp80-1; ☎ 415-776-1380, 800-248-9466; www.jdvhospitality.com; 601 Eddy St; r $99-139; P 🔁) Long after it became well known that this is *the* rocker crash pad in the city, the rock stars continue to check in, along with their groupies. It's a recycled '50s motor lodge with mid-century basic rooms dressed up with tropical decor. The ultrahip bar Bambuddha (p124) occupies the adjacent former coffee shop. Free parking and the edgy Tenderloin environs add to the Phoenix's cache.

---

see and be seen. Service is top-notch and rooms have wi-fi.

Westin St Francis Hotel (Map pp80-1; ☎ 415-397-7000, 800-937-8461; www.westin.com; 335 Powell St; r $179-249; 🔀 P) One of the city's most famous hotels, the St Francis presides over the western edge of Union Sq. The beds are top notch here.

Clift Hotel (Map pp80-1; ☎ 415-775-4700, 800-652-5438; www.clifthotel.com; 495 Geary St; r $205-235) The Clift is an old San Francisco classic owned by Ian Schraeger, and featuring an upscale, contemporary Phillipe Starck redesign.

Financial District

Four Seasons Hotel San Francisco (Map pp80-1; ☎ 415-633-3000; www.fourseasons.com; 757 Market St; r $469-600; P 🔁) The Four Seasons is among San Francisco's poshest hotels. It's huge, confident and very corporate. Rooms are impeccably designed, many with plate-glass views of the city and bay, and the full range of services and amenities includes one of the city's best gyms.

Hyatt Regency (Map pp80-1; ☎ 415-788-1234, 800-233-1234; www.hyatt.com; 5 Embarcadero Center; r $199-315; P 🖵) The backward-leaning 17-story atrium here gave Mel Brooks vertigo in the film *High Anxiety*. If you don't suffer from vertigo, there are 805 rooms to choose from.

Pacific Tradewinds Guest House (Map pp80-1; ☎ 415-433-7970, 888-734-6783; www.san-francisco-hostel .com; 680 Sacramento St; dm $24; 🖵) This is a well-maintained, friendly 4th-floor hostel with free DSL Internet access, a fully equipped kitchen and no curfew or chore requirements. It's a great place to meet other travelers. The nearest BART station is Embarcadero.

SAN FRANCISCO

Civic Center & Tenderloin

HI San Francisco City Center (Map pp80–1; ☎ 415-474-5721; www.sfhostels.com; 685 Ellis St; dm $24-29, r $55-69; 🖳) This HI facility is right in town, with 262 beds and 11 private rooms in an old seven-story Tenderloin hotel. Guests have their choice of venturing into the Tenderloin's cheap restaurants and cool clubs or Civic Center's high-brow arts institutions.

Aida Hotel (Map pp80–1; ☎ 415-863-4141, 800-863-2432; 1087 Market St; r $44-71) The hotel is a neat and tidy flophouse with 174 rooms. If you don't mind the odd cigarette burn on the carpet, it's good value.

Chinatown & North Beach

Hotel Bohème (Map pp84–5; ☎ 415-433-9111; www.hotelboheme.com; 444 Columbus Ave; r $148-169) This small, stylish hotel has an updated gangster-era look that makes subtle reference to the neighborhood's Beat history. All rooms have wi-fi, and half of them overlook North Beach's bustling Columbus Ave.

Grant Plaza (Map pp84–5; ☎ 415-434-3883, 800-472-6899; www.grantplaza.com; 465 Grant Ave; r $59-99) Rooms here are spotless in that nondescript, easy-to-clean, Chinese-restaurant style. But guests are right in the heart of one of the USA's more fascinating ethnic enclaves at a bargain price.

Washington Square Inn (Map pp84–5; ☎ 415-981-4220, 800-388-0220; www.wsisf.com; 1660 Stockton St; r $145-265; ✗) This hospitable inn overlooks Washington Sq Park, right in the heart of the neighborhood. Its 15 rooms are perhaps a bit overwrought in terms of decor but comfy.

Fisherman's Wharf

HI Fisherman's Wharf (Map pp86–7; ☎ 415-771-7277, www.norcalhostels.org; Fort Mason, Bldg 240; dm $22-29, q $68-74; P 🖳) On a hill just west of Aquatic Park, this hostel trades downtown convenience for a quiet setting with kitchen and laundry facilities. To get there, take MUNI bus 42 from the Transbay Terminal to the stop at Bay St and Van Ness Ave. Buses 30 and 47 also stop there.

Wharf Inn (Map pp86–7; ☎ 415-673-7411, 800-548-9918; www.wharfinn.com; 2601 Mason St; r $109-185; P) This basic hotel is not a bad choice for those traveling with children. The rates fluctuate wildly with the tourist tide. Parking is free.

Radisson Fisherman's Wharf (Map pp86–7; ☎ 415-392-6700, 800-333-3333; www.radisson.com; 250 Beach St; r $165-259; P) This is a solid choice on one of the streets close to Fisherman's Wharf, which are overrun with chains and standard tourist motels.

Nob Hill

Nob Hill Hotel (Map pp80–1; ☎ 415-885-2987; www.nobhillhotel.com; 835 Hyde St; r $129-199; P) The guest rooms in this 1906 hotel have been lavishly dressed up in neo-Victorian attire. If you're prone to sleepwalking, you might wake to find yourself wrapped in flowing purple drapes. The hotel's website sometimes features rates as low as $79.

Fairmont (Map pp80–1; ☎ 415-772-5000, 800-441-1414; www.fairmont.com; 950 Mason St; r $259-439) Perched atop Nob Hill, the Fairmont is grand excess, with its swirling columns, marbled lobby, tiki bar and the ring of flags over the entry. A more modern wing has rooms with stunning views.

Mark Hopkins InterContinental Hotel (Map pp80–1; ☎ 415-392-3434, 800-327-0200; www.markhopkins.net; 999 California St; r $165-359; P) You get what you pay for at this extravagant hotel – outrageously beautiful rooms with furniture that smells like old money. Upstairs, the Top of the Mark (p125) cocktail lounge is renowned for its superb views over the bay.

Pacific Heights & Japantown

Majestic Hotel (☎ 415-441-1100, 800-869-8966; www.thehotelmajestic.com; 1500 Sutter St; r $99-125, ste $179-199) Not far from Japantown, this hotel survived the 1906 earthquake and, despite lavish restorations, retains its antique feel. The lobby is a jaw-dropper and guestrooms are flat-out gorgeous.

Queen Anne Hotel (☎ 415-441-2828, 800-227-3970; www.queenanne.com; 1590 Sutter St; r $95-179, ste $179-350) The Queen Anne occupies a fine 1890 Victorian building. All rooms, while not spectacular in decor, have private bathrooms and antiques, and some are furnished with romantic wood-burning fireplaces and bay windows.

Radisson Miyako Hotel (☎ 415-922-3200, 800-333-3333; www.radisson.com; 1625 Post St; r $95-129, ste $149-159; 🅿 🖳) This deluxe, businesslike hotel was designed with *shoji* (rice-paper) screens on its windows and deep Japanese bathtubs in the bathrooms (with instructions on how to use them).

The Marina & Cow Hollow

This is the real motel quarter of San Francisco. South of Golden Gate Bridge, Lombard St (Hwy 101) is almost wall-to-wall with older, neon-emblazoned motels and midrange chains. It's a good spot to troll for a room if you arrive by car without a reservation. The neighboring streets are brimming with shops, restaurants and the city's biggest assemblage of pick-up bars.

Marina Motel (Map pp86-7; ☎ 415-921-9406, 800-346-6118; www.marinamotel.com; 2576 Lombard St; r $79-129, ste $89-179; 🅿) The standout on Lombard St, this pleasant, family-owned motel has loads of vintage 1930s charm and a secluded courtyard

Travelodge by the Bay (Map pp86-7; ☎ 415-673-0691; www.travelodge.com; 1450 Lombard St; r $59-79; 🅿) True to its chain's aims, this motel offers predictable rooms at a reasonable rate.

Motel Capri (Map pp86-7; ☎ 415-346-4667; 2015 Greenwich St; r $75-95, with kitchenette $129-155; 🅿) This well-preserved '50s motor lodge has a subtle vintage swank factor. Some of the rooms have little kitchens, and there's ample parking.

South of Market

Mosser Victorian Hotel (Map pp80-1; ☎ 415-986-4400, 800-227-3804; www.victorianhotel.com; 54 4th St; r $69-79, with private bathroom $129-189; ⌧ 🖳) This option has simple rooms that cost much more if there's a convention in town.

Hotel Griffon (Map pp80-1; ☎ 415-495-2100, 800-321-2201; www.hotelgriffon.com; 155 Steuart St; r $245-285, ste $395-435; 🅿) The Griffon is in a great location at the waterfront, close to the Embarcadero Center and the Ferry Building. The 59 rooms are modern and comfortable, and rates include a continental breakfast. Rooms with a view cost more.

Globe Hostel (Map pp80-1; ☎ 415-431-0540; 10 Hallam St; dm $18) Set in a surprisingly quiet location off Folsom St, the Globe is well run and friendly. US citizens need a passport to

stay. Dorm rooms sleep five, and each room has a private bathroom. Private doubles are available only in the off-season. The hostel has a laundry, TV room and microwave, but no kitchen.

The Mission

Considering the Mission's become such a popular destination, it's surprisingly lacking in cheap accommodations beyond fleabags and flophouses.

San Francisco Elements (Map pp88-9; ☎ 415-647-4100, 866-327-8407; www.elementssf.com; 2524 Mission St; dm $25, d $60; 🖳) The Mission District is the place to hang out at night, particularly if you're in the age 21 to 30 demographic, so this cheapie right in the heart of the action makes sense. It is part hostel, part budget hotel, with stylish minimalist rooms and efficient service. Movie nights and rooftop barbecues make this a fun place to hang out.

Inn San Francisco (Map pp88-9; ☎ 415-641-0188, 800-359-0913; www.innsf.com; 943 S Van Ness Ave; r $105-120, with private bathroom $120-255; 🅿) This Victorian beauty has been lovingly restored and furnished with antiques and Persian rugs. The more expensive deluxe rooms offer a redwood hot tub, spa or fireplace.

The Castro

24 Henry (Map pp88-9; ☎ 415-864-5686, 800-900-5686; www.24henry.com; 24 Henry St; s $65, d $80-110, tr $100-120) A five-room Victorian in the quiet Duboce Triangle neighborhood, just a few blocks from the Castro.

Village House (Map pp88-9; 4080 18th St; r $80-129; 🖳) Run by the same folks who run 24 Henry, the Village House is right in the thick of the Castro District action.

Parker Guest House (Map pp88-9; ☎ 415-621-3222; 888-520-7275; www.parkerguesthouse.com; 520 Church St; r $119-199) This restored Edwardian mansion has homey guestrooms and immaculate parlors. The cheapest rooms in the house share a bathroom. Continental breakfast is included.

Inn on Castro (Map pp88-9; ☎ 415-861-0321; http://innoncastro.com; 321 Castro St; r $85-185) Guestrooms in this restored B&B are design-conscious, the living room has a fireplace and a full breakfast is included. The Inn has a peaceful atmosphere, where guests can unwind, but there's plenty of partying going on down the street.

Beck's Motor Lodge (Map pp88-9; ☎ 415-621-8212, 800-227-4360; 2222 Market St; r $99-149; P) This is a bland 57-room motel that gets pretty cruisey during festival times.

The Haight

Red Victorian B&B (Map pp88-9; ☎ 415-864-1978; www.redvic.com; 1665 Haight St; d $86-200; ✗) The trippy digs of choice for the modern Haight are to be found in this B&B. After a night amidst the outrageous trimmings of the Flower Child Room, the Sunshine Room or the Summer of Love Room you'll waken with your brains sufficiently scrambled.

Metro Hotel (Map pp88-9; ☎ 415-861-5364; 319 Divisadero St; r $66-77; P) The Metro Hotel faces a very busy street on the edge of the scruffy Lower Haight. It has cheap, clean rooms, all with private bathroom, plus a garden patio.

Archbishop's Mansion (☎ 415-563-7872, 800-738-7477; www.thearchbishopsmansion.com; 1000 Fulton St; r $149-199, ste $279-399; ✗) This magnificent French chateau was indeed built for the city's archbishop back in 1904. It is now one of the pearls of the local hospitality industry. All rooms have toilets and gorgeous antiques.

Airport Area

There are lots of hotels around the airport, many with free direct-dial phones at the airport's baggage-claim area and free shuttle buses that pick up and drop off guests outside the terminals.

There are numerous chains in Millbrae and Burlingame, just south of the airport along Hwy 101. Still more are to the north in South San Francisco.

Clarion Hotel (☎ 650-692-6363, 800-391-9644; www.clarionhotel.com; 401 E Millbrae Ave; r $79-135; P ♨) Just a mile from San Francisco International Airport (SFO), and on the edge of the bay, this hotel offers a modern and convenient last-night's stay before an early flight. The free 24-hour airport shuttle simplifies getting away.

EATING

You might be chowing down a burrito, or you might be having what is commonly referred to as a 'dining experience,' but either way, in San Francisco, there's no excuse for having a bad meal. This city takes its food seriously, whether it's served on a brown Formica table under florescent lighting or on a white tablecloth by the warm light of a candle.

Eating out in San Francisco is venturing into a remarkably diverse culinary landscape. Head to North Beach for Italian food (where you might instead opt for Afghani), Chinatown for the Peking duck (where you could end up eating a vegetarian 'duck' stew) or the Mission for a taco (where you'll be equally tempted by Cal-Italian and Spanish tapas).

At most midrange and top end restaurants, reservations are recommended on weekdays and are nearly mandatory on Friday and Saturday nights.

The Embarcadero

The Ferry Building Marketplace puts several winning options all under one roof, and throws in high-class takeout and a bustling farmers market. The broad Embarcadero offers steakhouses and little shacks that still

---

TOP 10 EATS

- Shaking with joy over the shaking beef at **Slanted Door** (opposite), Embarcadero
- Taste of Old Frisco at **Tadich Grill** (opposite), Financial District
- Extravagant haremlike dining room at **Fleur de Lys** (opposite), Union Sq
- Classy dim sum at **Yank Sing** (p119), South of Market
- Dinner jazz at big ol' loveable **Moose's** (p117), North Beach
- Perfection by the forkful at **Gary Danko** (p117), Fisherman's Wharf
- Going veg at **Greens** (p118), Marina
- Lively Italian at **Delfina** (p120), Mission
- Impeccable *carnitas* (pork) at **El Metate** (p119), Mission
- Those dazzling *pommes frites* (french fries) at **Tallula** (p120), Castro

serve the same cheap grub favored by old salts of the past.

Slanted Door (Map pp80-1; ☎ 415-861-8032; 1 Ferry Bldg; lunch $9-19, dinner mains $15-27) This is the hardest table to get in San Francisco, and eating here is something to write home about. Chef Charles Phan's creations, like crab with cellophane noodles and *banh xeo* (Vietnamese crepes), may have food-stall origins, but reach celestial levels here. If you can't get a reservation, snag a seat at the bustling bar.

Taylor's Automatic Refresher (Map pp80-1; ☎ 866-328-3663; 1 Ferry Plaza; mains $4-13) Some mighty fine burgers are flipped at this Ferry Building favorite. Perfect fries, fine wines and microbrews round out the offerings. The modern-utilitarian dining hall is always packed with festive ferry-hoppers, farmers market shoppers and the Financial District lunchtime crowd.

Union Square

BUDGET & MIDRANGE

Sears Fine Foods (Map pp80-1; 439 Powell St; breakfast from $6; ✆ 6:30am-2:30pm) The eternally popular Sears is an old-school breakfast joint right off the square, famous since 1938 for its silver-dollar (Swedish) pancakes.

Café Claude (Map pp80-1; ☎ 415-392-3505; 7 Claude Ln; dinner mains $12-17; ✆ lunch Mon-Sat, dinner Tue-Sat) A zinc-topped bar, live jazz and classic bistro fare all conspire to put you in that Montparnasse frame of mind. Start with a bowl of the best French onion soup in the city, then tuck into a savory coq au vin. Claude is romantic and affordable – a very classy cheap date.

Grand Café (Map pp80-1; ☎ 415-292-0101; 501 Geary St; dinner mains $16-29) At the Hotel Monaco. This old ballroom is truly dazzling to look at, and the bold bistro fare more than capably justifies being lured in.

Millennium (Map pp80-1; ☎ 415-345-3900; 580 Geary St; starters & small plates $5-10, mains $19-22; ✆ dinner) Millennium is the city's top vegan choice. The plantain torte is the signature dish, and the breaded pan-sautéed *seitan* medallions and rosemary polenta may convert hard-core carnivores.

TOP END

Fleur de Lys (Map pp80-1; ☎ 415-673-7779; 777 Sutter St) The internationally renowned Fleur de Lys entertains opulent fantasies with a

---

AUTHOR'S CHOICE

Red's Java House (Map pp80-1; Embarcadero; breakfast $1-3, lunch $2-3; ✆ 6am-4pm Mon-Fri) A beloved relic of the old port, Red's serves the cheapest lunch around. The longshoremen are long gone, but the humble white shack still specializes in coffee-and-donut breakfasts, greasy double cheeseburgers and Bud in a bottle for lunch.

---

luscious interior, classic French cuisine and impeccable service. One of the city's very best dining experiences.

Masa's (Map pp80-1; ☎ 415-989-7154; 648 Bush St; tasting menus $65-110) Dining here is a special event, where every detail seems to have been attended to by capable hands, so prepare yourself for a rare treat. This is *haute* to the core.

Farallon (Map pp80-1; ☎ 415-956-6969; 450 Post St; dinner mains $29-37; ✆ lunch Tue-Sat, dinner nightly) Farallon makes a big splash with its outrageous underwater decor and exquisite seafood. Late lunchers are treated to a more affordable bistro menu. Put on your glad rags for this one.

Postrio (Map pp80-1; ☎ 415-776-7825; 545 Post St; bar menu $11-19, dinner mains $29-39) Postrio has been among the city's prime exponents of California cuisine since celebrity chef Wolfgang Puck opened the place in 1989. Puck's famous pizza ($12 to $16) is available at the bar until midnight.

Restaurant Michael Mina (Map pp80-1; ☎ 415-397-9222; 335 Powell St; three-course dinner $78; ✆ dinner) Superchef Michael Mina's home base is this opulent establishment off the lobby of the Westin St Francis Hotel. The setting is formal but upbeat, the food inventive and complex, with the chef riffing off flavors and toying with the palate in a precise, painterly manner. You'll drop the big bills, but you won't regret it.

Financial District

Tadich Grill (Map pp80-1; ☎ 415-391-1849; 240 California St; mains $12-42; ✆ lunch & dinner Mon-Sat) The oldest restaurant in the city, Tadich was established in 1849. The joint oozes that uniquely San Francisco brand of unfussy class: a long counter for solitary diners, tables in the window, hat and coat hangers, and a veteran, pleasantly gruff waitstaff.

Frisco classics like sand dabs and seafood cioppino are a good bet.

Plouf (Map pp80-1; ☎ 415-986-6491; 40 Belden Pl; lunch $13-17, mains $14-24; ☑ lunch Mon-Fri, dinner Mon-Sat) Plouf is a popular and reliable French bistro, famous for its excellent mussels and *pommes frites* (french fries), not to mention tasty wines, sandwiches and seafood mains.

Café Bastille (Map pp80-1; ☎ 415-986-5673; 22 Belden Pl; lunch $8-11, dinner mains $13-18) Bastille is the most popular spot on hip, restaurant-jammed Belden Pl (aka the French Ghetto). Standard bistro fare, such as steak with chips, along with savory crepes and live jazz, keep Bastille lively all week.

Civic Center & Tenderloin

Zuni Cafe (Map pp80-1; ☎ 415-552-2522; 1658 Market St; mains $15-25) Zuni has been around a couple decades already, but it remains an attractive, reliable spot for mesquite-grilled meats, brick-oven pizzas and people-watching from the bar.

Original Joe's (Map pp80-1; ☎ 415-775-4877; 144 Taylor St; meals $8-22) You might be leery about wandering into this part of the Tenderloin, but beyond Joe's neon-lit entry is a bustling sanctuary of Old Frisco. Joe's is Italian-American in the truest sense: steaming pastas and greasy calamari piled up on plates while juicy steaks, impeccable chops and char-broiled burgers sizzle in an open kitchen. The burger, a fat slab patted by hand and cooked over mesquite, is one of the city's best.

Dottie's True Blue Cafe (Map pp80-1; 522 Jones St; breakfast under $10; ☑ breakfast & lunch) The Tenderloin's best place for breakfast is this place. On weekends there's a line out the door for solid standards such as eggs, pancakes and chicken sausages.

Chinatown

Jai Yun (Map pp84-5; ☎ 415-981-7438; 923 Pacific Ave; multicourse banquets from $35; ☑ lunch & dinner Fri-Wed) It's tiny and poorly decorated but the food is exceptional. At Jai Yun you and the server agree on a price (starting at $35) and chef-owner Nei Chia-Ji sets out to give you your money's worth. Daily offerings are determined by Chef Nei's morning shopping, but the endless stream of dishes never falls back on the usual greasy clichés. Cash only.

House of Nanking (Map pp84-5; ☎ 415-421-1429; 919 Kearny St; starters $5-8, mains $5-12; ☑ lunch Mon-Sat, dinner nightly) The line stretching outside (reservations are not accepted) is a genuine reflection of the good food coming out of the busy kitchen. Popular with tourists and locals alike.

Brandy Ho's (Map pp84-5; ☎ 415-788-7527; 217 Columbus Ave; dishes $8-12) Somewhere there must be a stripper or a prostitute who shares this name, but rest assured, Brandy Ho's is a respectable restaurant dishing out authentic Hunan cuisine. The snazzy decor and the pyrotechnics in the open kitchen make for a colorful and festive break from nearby North Beach bars.

DIM SUM

San Francisco rivals Hong Kong in the popularity and quality of its dim sum restaurants. In China's Canton province, where dim sum originated, the act of eating dim sum is called yum cha, or 'drink tea,' because the little snacklike dishes first appeared in teahouses. Chinese businessmen used to spend so many hours in teahouses that the restaurants served as virtual extensions of their offices, so the teahouses began serving snacks for them to graze on. Though dim sum continues to be served during business hours (usually from 10am to 3pm), it is no longer just for businessmen.

Typically, dim sum consists of bite-size pastrylike items filled with pork, shrimp, taro root, or vegetables, which have been steamed, fried or baked. Steamed vegetables and hearty congee soup (rice porridge with ingredients such as shrimp, fish, peanuts, or pork giblets) are commonly offered as well. Two or three items are served on small plates for $2 to $4. The best way to enjoy as many different dishes as possible is to eat with a group of people.

In a typical dim sum parlor, waiters roll carts between crowded tables that are crammed from wall to wall in a cavernous dining room. Patrons simply select the plates they'd like from the passing carts. A running tab is kept at your table.

There are good dim sum restaurants in many parts of San Francisco, but for an authentic experience, go to Chinatown. Dim sum is popular every day, but on weekends the crowds and the excitement level reach their peak.

Gold Mountain (Map pp84-5; ☎ 415-296-7733; 644 Broadway; dim sum $2-4) This place is an enormous multilevel dining hall where convoys of fresh dim sum carts file through the aisles during the day. A quintessential Chinatown experience.

Lucky Creation (Map pp84-5; ☎ 415-989-0818; 854 Washington St; mains $4-7; ⊙ 11am-9:30pm Thu-Tue) An excellent Chinese vegetarian restaurant, serving tasty rice and noodle dishes.

North Beach

BUDGET

Mario's Bohemian Cigar Store (Map pp84-5; ☎ 415-362-0536; 566 Columbus Ave; dishes $7-12) No longer sells cigars! Instead this relaxed café-bar, a classic North Beach spot, serves tasty focaccia sandwiches, strong espresso and rich tiramisu.

Molinari (Map pp84-5; 373 Columbus Ave; sandwiches $5-7) A traditional neighborhood delicatessen, Molinari turns out some of the best sandwiches in North Beach. It has few tables, but Washington Sq is just a few blocks away.

Mo's Burgers (Map pp84-5; ☎ 415-788-3779; 1322 Grant Ave; meals $5-10) Mo's makes a legitimate claim to the city's best burger by preparing freshly ground beef patties over a revolving grill and serving 'em up with homemade mayonnaise.

Golden Boy Pizza (Map pp84-5; 542 Green St; pizza slices $2-3) A grungy joint with a punkish attitude, serving thick slabs of excellent pizza. A slice or two and a draft beer makes a quick, filling meal.

Liguria (Map pp84-5; 1700 Stockton St; focaccia $3) This is a no-frills bakery that produces one thing and one thing only: focaccia (with tomato sauce or without). Get there for an early lunch.

MIDRANGE

Moose's (Map pp84-5; ☎ 415-989-7800; 1652 Stockton St; lunch $11-17, dinner mains $11-36; ⊙ brunch Sun, lunch Thu-Sat, dinner nightly) Big ol' lovable Moose's is one of the friendliest restaurants in town, and a good spot for nightly jazz. It draws a diverse crowd. While the Mooseburger always garners praise, the signature dish is seafood cioppino, a San Francisco classic.

Washington Square Bar & Grill (Map pp84-5; ☎ 415-982-8123; 1707 Powell St; lunch $9-20, dinner mains $14-27; ⊙ lunch Mon-Fri, brunch Sat & Sun, dinner nightly) The neo–Gold Rush atmosphere, the jazz pianist and the constant musical shaking of martinis make for a venerable San Francisco establishment. Traditional Italian and American dishes anchor a solid menu.

Caffè Macaroni (Map pp84-5; ☎ 415-956-9737; 59 Columbus Ave; mains $9-16) It may not look like much, but this tiny café with sidewalk tables is a lively spot that churns out some of the neighborhood's finest Italian food. Credit cards and reservations are not accepted.

Ideale (Map pp84-5; ☎ 415-391-4129; 1309 Grant Ave; starters $4.50-9, mains $9-18; ⊙ dinner Tue-Sun) Few restaurants in North Beach can beat Ideale's sumptuous ravioli or unforgettable tiramisu. It's an inviting, modern space with an exemplary waitstaff. Large portions make most mains suitable for sharing.

Café Niebaum-Coppola (Map pp84-5; ☎ 415-291-1700; 916 Kearny St; dishes $9-15) Filmmaker Francis Ford Coppola owns this atmospheric little place, but he doesn't welcome diners at the door. Doesn't matter. You'll enjoy the pizzas (including the Sophia, named for Francis' Oscar-winning daughter), and the Caesar salad is tops.

TOP END

Bix (Map pp84-5; ☎ 415-433-6300; 56 Gold St; lunch $14-22, dinner mains $19-29) Bix serves excellent American fare in a room with high ceilings and a swanky, old-world ambience. Jazz combos lend an air of supper-club cool, and the bustling bar serves up superb martinis of the sort favored by guys like FDR and Winston Churchill. It's hidden on a tiny street near the Transamerica Pyramid.

Enrico's (Map pp84-5; ☎ 415-982-6223; 504 Broadway; small plates $5-13, dinner mains $15-27) The city's oldest sidewalk café remains a stalwart of North Beach's lively social scene. It offers delicate pizzas, unique antipasti and traditional seafood and meat dishes. Evening combos always jazz the dining.

Rose Pistola (Map pp84-5; ☎ 415-399-0499; 532 Columbus Ave; mains $9-24) The ever-popular Rose Pistola fuses updated Beat-pop style (jazz combos play in the evening) with creative regional Italian dishes. Dinner reservations are recommended.

Fisherman's Wharf

Gary Danko (Map pp86-7; ☎ 415-749-2060; 800 North Point St; tasting menu $59-79; ⊙ dinner) Gary Danko, near Ghirardelli Sq, is among the city's (if not the nation's) top restaurants. Danko's French,

Mediterranean and American influences mix to create a serious culinary experience (and splurge). The cheese cart is legendary.

Rainforest Cafe (Map pp86-7; ☎ 415-440-5610; 145 Jefferson St; mains $6-17) This family-friendly restaurant is an entertaining equatorial theme park that throws food into the bargain – think of the *Mighty Joe Young* film set, complete with a mechanical gorilla and large tropical fish tanks. Pizzas, pastas, sandwiches, fish platters and an enviroconscious message are on the menu.

Buena Vista Café (Map pp84-5; ☎ 415-474-5044; 2765 Hyde St; dishes $5-12) This is a historic eatery, near the Hyde St cable car turnaround, is primarily a classic bar with a few tables and a menu offering breakfast and burgers. This establishment introduced Irish coffee to the USA, so naturally it would be wise to partake of that tradition while you're there.

Russian Hill & Nob Hill

Hyde Street Bistro (Map pp86-7; ☎ 415-441-7778; 1521 Hyde St; mains $12-16 ☙ dinner Tue-Sun) A neighborhood spot in the heart of Nob Hill, with a cozy atmosphere and a menu featuring simple French bistro fare.

I Fratelli (Map pp86-7; ☎ 415-474-8240; 1896 Hyde St at Green St; mains $11-20) This place offers wonderful Italian fare and glasses of Chianti in a friendly, inviting atmosphere.

Frascati (Map pp86-7; ☎ 415-928-1406; 1901 Hyde St; mains $17-24; ☙ dinner) Frascati exudes neighborhood charm, making it a perfect dinner-for-two kind of spot. Mediterranean dishes like paella and coq au vin are prepared with local finely seasoned, fresh ingredients. The mere sight of Frascati's thick, savory pork chops makes mouths water.

Pacific Heights & Japantown

The restaurant stretch of Fillmore St between Sutter and Jackson Sts, just north of Japantown, blends Japanese restaurants with other cuisines.

Jackson Fillmore (Map pp86-7; ☎ 415-346-5288; 2506 Fillmore St; mains $10-18) This is a popular eatery set in an old-fashioned room that's always bustling. It has superb southern Italian food at reasonable prices. Reservations are only required for three or more people.

Elite Cafe (☎ 415-346-8668; 2049 Fillmore St; mains $18-28; ☙ dinner) A remarkably well-preserved 1920s restaurant. The Cajun and Creole seafood is good but expensive.

Isobune (☎ 415-563-1030; 1737 Post St; dishes $2-5; Ⓟ) Isobune, in the Kintetsu Mall, is a floating sushi bar. The sushi chef stands in the center of the bar, and selections float past the patrons on wooden boats. It's fun, cheap, and the sushi is delicious.

Mifune (☎ 415-922-0337; Kintetsu Mall, 1737 Post St; noodle soup $4-8, main meals $10-17; Ⓟ) Also in the Kintetsu Mall, Mifune is popular for its big, tasty bowls of noodles at moderate prices.

The Marina & Cow Hollow

The Marina area has an exciting variety of dining options, from world class vegetarian to your basic '50s diner. There are also some excellent and intimate neighborhood spots. A few blocks south, up the hill, is the Cow Hollow neighborhood, with dozens of restaurants along Union St, from Fillmore St east to Laguna St.

Greens (Map pp86-7; ☎ 415-771-6222; Fort Mason, Bldg A; lunch $9-12, dinner mains $16-20; ☙ lunch Tue-Sat, dinner Mon-Sat; Ⓟ) Greens ranks among the USA's best and most famous vegetarian restaurants. There's real imagination at play in the dishes, and the results are generally terrific. In addition to the formal restaurant there's also a bakery and takeaway counter, so you can enjoy a picnic on the waterfront.

Bistro Aix (Map pp86-7; ☎ 415-202-0100; 3340 Steiner St; dinner $15) Warm atmosphere and heartening bistro fare (crispy roast chicken and buttery mashed potatoes) make Aix a popular neighborhood place. This eatery has a reasonable fixed-price dinner available on weeknights.

Betelnut (Map pp86-7; ☎ 415-929-8855; 2030 Union St; small plates $5-10, mains $13-20) The Marina beautiful-people scene can sometimes be a distraction, but the heady mix of flavors from Southeast Asia and Japan will ultimately command your attention. Start off with a home-brewed beer and some 'little plates' – miniservings of such things as green papaya salad and chili-crusted calamari.

Mel's Drive-In (Map pp86-7; 2165 Lombard St; dishes $5-14; ☙ 6-2am Sun-Thu, 24hr Fri & Sat; Ⓟ) Mel's is an old San Francisco standby. The old diner featured in the film *American Graffiti*, and is always a big draw at breakfast time.

South of Market

Boulevard (Map pp80-1; ☎ 415-543-6084; 1 Mission St; lunch $17-25, dinner mains $29-39; ☙ lunch Mon-Fri, dinner nightly) Housed in the prequake Audiffred

Building, Boulevard was designed by Pat Kuleto to look like a belle époque Parisian salon. Chef Nancy Oakes has a fine way with pork loins, buttery mashed potatoes and crab cakes. Last-minute diners can eat at the excellent bar.

South Park Cafe (Map pp80–1; ☎ 415-495-7275; 108 S Park Ave; mains $13-21; ☒ lunch Mon-Fri, dinner Mon-Sat) This Parisian refuge has many long-time devotees. The lure is a romantic atmosphere and traditional French fare. For toppers, there's a nice selection of reasonably priced wines and delicious desserts.

21st Amendment (Map pp80–1; ☎ 415-369-0900; 563 2nd St; dishes $8-20) Near South Park and the ballpark, 21st Amendment knocks out pizzas and surf-and-turf specials that go down easy when you're swilling the house pale ale. It's a big place that gets busy during the after-work rush and especially before and after ball games.

Basil (Map pp80–1; ☎ 415-552-8999; 1175 Folsom St; dishes $4-14; ☒ lunch Mon-Fri, dinner nightly) The scent of fish sauce gently confronts you on entering Basil, assuring you that this sleekly designed Thai restaurant has the right idea. The kitchen sets itself apart with the subtle flavors of dishes like honey-roasted duck with pineapple curry. It's near dance clubs and youth hostels.

Yank Sing Rincon Center (Map pp80–1; ☎ 415-781-1111; 201 Spear St; ☒ 11am-3pm Mon-Fri, 10am-4pm Sat & Sun); Stevenson St (Map pp80–1; ☎ 415-541-4949; 49 Stevenson St; dim sum $3-5; ☒ 11am-3pm) Yank Sing serves dim sum that many San Franciscans feel is the best this side of Hong Kong. The Rincon Center location is the better place, in terms of atmosphere, but both have the same food and are very good.

LuLu (Map pp80–1; ☎ 415-495-5775; 816 Folsom St; small plates $7-15, mains $15-30) Lulu is a stylish converted auto-repair shop that's frequently loud and busy. It has an open kitchen with several flaming ovens for rotisserie meats and pizzas. If you're looking for a good time, Lulu is a doozy.

Tu Lan (Map pp80–1; ☎ 415-626-0927; 8 6th St; meals under $10) There are two things San Franciscans go to skid row for – to buy crack and to eat Vietnamese food at Tu Lan. Some real treats await beyond the grimy facade, including a whole pompano, deep-fried and drenched in a ginger sauce. The stir-fries and imperial rolls can be a wee bit greasy, but they're damn tasty. Cash only.

The Mission
BUDGET
El Metate (☎ 415-641-7209; 2406 Bryant St; dishes $1.75-5.25) To be sure, this *taquería* is as humble and tiny as they come, and its location is inconvenient to anyone clinging to busy Mission St. But the meat is beautiful, the tortillas fresh and customers are not subjected to the assembly-line service typical in the Mission St establishments. (That's not really a complaint.) You can order tacos, burritos and dinner platters loaded with *chilies rellenos* (stuffed peppers), enchiladas, Spanish rice and the like. Worth the trek. Cash only.

La Taquería (Map pp88–9; ☎ 415-285-7117; 2889 Mission St) Just south of the 24th St BART station, La Taquería serves absolutely amazing *carne asada* (steak) and *carnitas* (roast pork) burritos and tacos. The burritos are riceless (more meat, fewer carbs), and they're a little pricier than average, but they are well worth the extra.

Chava's (Map pp88–9; ☎ 415-282-0283; 2839 Mission St; dishes $4-9.50; ☒ 6am-6pm) If you're fanatical about *menudo* (beef tripe soup), stroll on down to this convivial Mexican eatery. Chava's homemade tortillas also rate among the city's best, and they go great with the city's best chili colorado, which you can get here. Cash only.

Taquería Can-Cun (Map pp88–9; ☎ 415-252-9560; 2288 Mission St at 19th St; burritos $4-5) This is one of the most popular purveyors of big, bold burritos in the city, and it's open after midnight. Both the beef and the vegetarian burritos are justifiably lauded.

HOW TO EAT A MISSION BURRITO

The classic Mission burrito is nearly as big as a newborn baby and wrapped in tin foil. If you're dining in, this cute little bundle is served on a platter. Some novices remove the tin foil entirely and dig in with knife and fork. Perhaps these people eat pizza with knife and fork as well. But the proper way to eat a Mission burrito is with your hands. If you only peel down an inch or so of foil at a time, the foil keeps the burrito together and you can lift the hefty sucker for a bite. Careful to pull down enough foil, or else you'll give your dental work a jolt. Add a little more salsa before each bite and you'll look like a seasoned veteran.

Pancho Villa (Map pp88-9; ☎ 415-864-8840; 3071 16th St; burritos $4-5) A burrito lover's staple, and the constant line out the door means the ingredients stay fresh.

Puerto Alegre (Map pp88-9; ☎ 415-255-8201; 546 Valencia St; dishes $4-6.50) Happy hour (3pm to 6pm Monday and Wednesday to Friday) is a festive time to drop by this popular joint. Order a pitcher of margaritas for you and your friends, then select from an array of rather ordinary tacos, burritos and combo platters. The food starts to taste awfully good once you've got some of that booze under your belt.

Truly Mediterranean (Map pp88-9; ☎ 415-252-7482; 3109 16th St; meals $4-6) This tiny spot serves excellent take-out falafel and *shwarma*.

Herbivore (Map pp88-9; ☎ 415-826-5657; 983 Valencia St; mains $6-14) The efficient and sleek interior of this popular vegan restaurant is mirrored in its clean and tasty meatless dishes and rich, dairyless desserts.

St Francis Fountain (☎ 415-826-4200; 2801 24th St) East along 24th St is this magnificent authentic soda fountain and candy counter dating from 1918.

Mitchell's (☎ 415-648-2300; www.mitchellsicecream .com; 688 San Jose Ave) Excellent homemade ice cream can be found south of Cesar Chavez Blvd at Mitchell's, family-owned since 1953. Mango and avocado(!) are among the top flavors.

Burger Joint (Map pp88-9; ☎ 415-824-3494; 807 Valencia St; meals $5-8) Great burgers – made out of turkey, veggies or hormone-free Niman Ranch beef – are turned out at this Mission favorite.

MIDRANGE & TOP END

Blue Plate (☎ 415-282-6777; 3218 Mission St; mains $12-18) Enjoy American comfort food done to near-perfection in a homey and friendly atmosphere. The meatloaf and thick-cut pork chops are a chow hound's dream.

Foreign Cinema (Map pp88-9; ☎ 415-648-7600; 2534 Mission St; starters $7-11, mains $16-30; dinner nightly, brunch Sat & Sun) For dinner and a movie in a single stop, head to Foreign Cinema. Foreign films are screened in the stylish and boisterous courtyard while diners feast on wonderful French cuisine. The movies are really just active wallpaper.

Bruno's (Map pp88-9; ☎ 415-550-7455; 2389 Mission St; meals $10-20) Once a standard-issue 1940s Italian joint, Bruno's is now a hip and swank

bar-restaurant-nightclub sporting snazzy vinyl booths and alluring exotica-inspired decor. The venue's ownership, and its menu, seem to change frequently, but whatever it serves, this martini-perfect place always seems to jump.

The Castro

Tallula (Map pp88-9; ☎ 415-437-6722; 4230 18th St; starters $6-14, mains $17-20; dinner) Tallula is modern but down to earth, colorful but easy on the eyes, Indian but with an unusual French bias. The menu is unlike any other, with tea-smoked cornish game hens sidling *pomme frites* drizzled with pickled mango aioli. A search for Indian classics proves futile – the vindaloo contains buffalo meat, tandoori firing is applied to skirt steaks – but the place always wins people over.

Chow (Map pp88-9; ☎ 415-552-2469; 215 Church St; mains $6-12) A few doors off Market St, Chow is a remarkably affordable place that serves tasty pizzas, pastas and grilled and roasted meats. It also offers a smattering of Asian noodle dishes. Chow is a popular late-night hangout.

Mecca (Map pp88-9; ☎ 415-621-7000; 2029 Market St; starters $9-20, mains $18-29; dinner Tue-Sun) This is as much a nightclub as it is a restaurant, and it exudes a cool, sophisticated vibe, with a DJ who spins soulful, mid-tempo grooves. The kitchen turns out respectable mains, with a menu that ranges from fish to quail to grilled pork, all served in classic California style, with plenty of exotic greens and fresh veggies. Reservations are recommended.

2223 Market (Map pp88-9; ☎ 415-431-0692; 2223 Market St; mains $10-25) This place sits in the lap of the Castro District, loved and cherished, but nameless. The ever-changing menu is small but interesting. Dress is casual and reservations are recommended.

Bagdad Cafe (Map pp88-9; ☎ 415-621-4434; 2295 Market St; meals $5-10; ☉ 24hr) Open round the clock, Bagdad has been around longer than George W. It's a good place to head to if you crave a hot turkey sandwich or pancakes in the wee small hours.

California Harvest Ranch Market (Map pp88-9; 2285 Market St; lunch $4-8) A gourmet and organic grocery store with a large, excellent salad bar and deli. It doesn't have tables inside, but outdoor benches provide a perfect spot to take a break and to dig into your healthy purchases.

The Haight

Pork Store Cafe (Map pp88-9; ☎ 415-864-6981; 1451 Haight St; breakfast $5-10) For standard hash-house truck stop fare, drop by this shambling little joint.

Magnolia Pub Brewery (Map pp88-9; ☎ 415-864-7468; 1398 Haight St; sandwiches $8-10, mains $9-15) In a historic Victorian building (the former 'Drogstore Cafe'), Magnolia is a friendly brewpub with a Grateful Dead–inspired decor that you can either absorb or ignore. It dishes out sandwiches, fries, dinner plates and great craft-brewed ales, many naturally carbonated and served via a British-style hand pump (its specialty).

New Ganges Restaurant (Map p83; ☎ 415-661-7290; 775 Frederick St; mains $3-8, prix fixe $14) You'll find excellent Indian food – all meatless – here. Soothing lighting and soft raga music create an ambience that may induce you to go with the pillow-seating option (tables and chairs are also available). The garbanzo and mushroom curry is a highlight. Reservations are recommended.

Kan Zaman (Map pp88-9; ☎ 415-751-9656; 1793 Haight St; mains $8-13; ☉ 5pm-midnight Sun-Thu, 5pm-2am Fri, noon-2am Sat) Kan Zaman's offerings feature good and reasonably priced Middle Eastern food, funky Arabian Nights decor and the opportunity to smoke from a hookah. On some weekend nights there's a belly-dancing performance.

Cha Cha Cha (Map pp88-9; ☎ 415-386-5758; 1801 Haight St; lunch $8-10, dinner mains $14-20) Lively, loud and extremely popular Cha Cha Cha offers spicy Caribbean tapas and main dishes. It does not take reservations, so most nights you'll have to wait up to an hour for a table.

Thep Phanom (Map pp88-9; ☎ 415-431-2526; 400 Waller St; mains $8-14; ☉ dinner) Near Haight St in the Lower Haight is this reliable and worthwhile Thai restaurant. Order from the list of nightly specials for the freshest and best selections.

Eos (Map pp88-9; ☎ 415-566-3063; 901 Cole St; mains $22-28; ☉ dinner) Eos, in Cole Valley, is one of the city's most highly regarded East–West fusion restaurants. Impressively designed starters get the palate warmed up for Eric Arnold Wong's inventive main courses. It runs a nice wine bar next door too.

In the Lower Haight, worthwhile brunch and lunch spots include **Kate's Kitchen** (Map pp88-9; ☎ 415-626-3984; 471 Haight St; meals $5-10) and the **Squat & Gobble Cafe** (Map pp88-9; ☎ 415-487-0551; 237 Fillmore St; meals $5-10), the latter serves cheap and tasty crepes.

The Richmond

When you're looking for great food in San Francisco, do not overlook the Richmond. The neighborhood's easy to reach without a car, as bus 38 runs up and down Geary St all night long.

On Clement St, one block north of Geary St, between Arguello and Park Presidio Blvds is 'New Chinatown,' lined with a slew of shops and Chinese, Thai, Korean, Vietnamese, Indonesian and other Asian restaurants.

Taiwan Restaurant (Map p83; ☎ 415-387-1789; 445 Clement St; meals under $15) This place has some very cheap lunch specials, along with handcrafted noodles and dumplings made in the restaurant's glassed-in kitchen.

Chapeau! (Map p83; ☎ 415-750-9787; 1408 Clement St; starters $7-11, mains $14-19; ☉ dinner Tue-Sun, brunch Sun) This is a family-run restaurant

---

AUTHOR'S CHOICE

Cliff House (Map p83; ☎ 415-386-3330; 1090 Point Lobos; mains at Sutro's $18-32; Bistro breakfast $8-17, lunch $12-17; ☉ Sutro's lunch & dinner, Bistro breakfast, lunch & dinner; Ⓟ) No longer is the Cliff House a faded tourist trap. A 2004 overhaul of the historic seaside restaurant incorporated a snazzy new wing and some badly needed updating in the kitchen. Dine formally in the contemporary stylings of Sutro's, or more casually in the Bistro or simply sidle up to the sleek Zinc Bar for appetizers and Bloody Marys.

with nonstop charm and a genuine passion for its food.

Burma Super Star (Map p83; ☎ 415-387-2147; 309 Clement St; mains $5-10) The Burmese cuisine served here shares similarities with that of India, China and Thailand. Rich curries and crunchy samosas are worthwhile and, while the interior's nondescript, the meals are cheap and satisfying.

Angkor Wat (Map p83; ☎ 415-221-7887; 4217 Geary Blvd; mains $9-14) This restaurant serves up terrific Cambodian food at inexpensive prices.

Kabuto (Map p83; ☎ 415-752-5652; 5116 Geary Blvd; sushi $2-7, mains $9-13; ⏲ dinner Tue-Sat) Kabuto, near 15th Ave, has inspired more than a few sushi enthusiasts to proclaim that it has the best sushi bar in the city. There's a good vegetarian selection too.

Tommy's Mexican Restaurant (Map p83; ☎ 415-387-4747; 5929 Geary Blvd; dishes $7-15) Between 23rd and 24th Aves, Tommy's specializes in Yucatán cuisine. Its fresh-squeezed lime margaritas are among the best in town and the tequila selection at the bar is truly unbeatable.

The Sunset

The Sunset District, south of Golden Gate Park, has a large collection of budget ethnic restaurants, particularly along Irving St from 5th Ave all the way to 25th Ave. The Inner Sunset, concentrated around the intersection of 9th Ave and Irving St, has a healthy mix of traditional neighborhood establishments and some fashionable new eateries.

Park Chow (Map p83; ☎ 415-665-9912; 1240 9th Ave; mains $6-12) Park Chow, offering tasty pastas and other comfort dishes, is just as easygoing and satisfying as its sister restaurant near the Castro District.

Ebisu (Map p83; ☎ 415-566-1770; 1283 9th Ave; lunch $6-14, mains $9-17; ⏲ lunch Mon-Fri, dinner Mon-Sat) A highly regarded Japanese restaurant and sushi bar that usually has long lines of eager eaters waiting to get in.

DRINKING

San Francisco is indeed one bibulous burg, with bars, coffeehouses, cafés and lounges in every part of town. You're never more than a few blocks away from a comfortable spot in which to kick back with a beer or an espresso shot.

Cafés

San Francisco was a coffee-achieving town long before Seattle started making noise about the caffeinated monkey on its back. In North Beach, the old Italian cafès come in twos or threes per block. Of late, tea parlors with overwhelming selections of exotic blends have been opening around town.

DOWNTOWN AREA

Café de la Presse (Map pp80-1; ☎ 415-398-2680; 352 Grant Ave) Here is a popular, European-style café with an international selection of newspapers and magazines.

Cafe Bianco (Map pp80-1; ☎ 410-421-2091; 39 Sutter St) Cafe Bianco's back patio is a retreat from the Financial District hustle. It serves a top-notch cuppa joe in an honest-to-gosh cup and saucer (no paper cup chintz here). You can also nibble on sandwiches, pizzas and lasagna.

Caffe Espresso (Map pp80-1; ☎ 415-395-8585; 462 Powell St) On the ground floor of the Sir Francis Drake Hotel, the window tables are superb for people-watching. As ersatz 1920s Parisian cafés go, this one's not bad. In addition to good, strong coffee, wines and aperitifs are also available.

CHINATOWN

Imperial Tea Court Chinatown (Map pp84-5; ☎ 415-788-6080; 1411 Powell St); Embarcadero (☎ 415-544-9830; Ferry Building) A tea break at the serene Imperial Tea Court, where birdcages hang above antique tables, is meant to be a relaxed, cultured experience. The helpful staff, whose knowledge and appreciation of tea rivals that of your above-average wine snob, will help you to select from an amazing variety of aromatic green and black leaves. If you're taking your tea on the premises, they will prepare your brew and answer any questions you might have.

NORTH BEACH

Caffe Trieste (Map pp84-5; ☎ 415-392-6739; 601 Vallejo St) Family-owned since 1956, Trieste harks back to the Beat days and over the years has become a comfortable old gathering place that has no need to prove itself. The real crowds show up on Saturday afternoon, when the singing proprietors break out bel canto standards, with accordion and brass accompaniment.

Caffè Greco (Map pp84-5; ☎ 415-397-6261; 423 Columbus Ave) Greco's friendly crew prepare fine espressos, but only if you're lucky will you snag one of the sidewalk tables on a warm Saturday afternoon. The place has some of North Beach's most devoted regulars, and you'll feel like an outsider for not knowing your server's name.

Caffe Puccini (Map pp84-5; ☎ 415-989-7033; 411 Columbus Ave) Puccini's sidewalk tables collide with nearby Greco's. Inside the tiny café recorded arias create an operatic atmosphere. It's one of North Beach's most charmed rooms, and you'll get a sterling coffee here.

THE MISSION
Tartine (Map pp88-9; ☎ 415-487-2600; 600 Guerrero St) Lines out the door of a pastry shop are always indicative of good things within, and the queue leading to Tartine is no exception. Most customers come fixated on something to go with coffee or tea, which are of course available here. The nonpareil tarts are kings of the oven, but superb sandwiches, cakes and croissants ($2 to $8) all have their devotees. Tables are few, but the line moves quickly.

Atlas Cafe (☎ 410-648-1047; 3049 20th St) A most artsy and bohemian place, haunted by local struggling artists of all media. Some of their works hang on the walls, and there is a bluegrass jam on Thursday (8pm to 10pm). The menu sports exemplary coffees, full breakfasts, sandwiches, soups and small pizzas.

THE CASTRO
Cafe Flore (Map pp88-9; ☎ 415-621-8579; 2298 Market St) Looking much like a prefab shed from a botanical garden, airy Cafe Flore attracts a rotating cast of flexible-schedule types – from espresso-driven gay activists to cappuccino-sipping mommies. Weekends draw the Castro scenesters.

Orbit Room Cafe (Map pp88-9; ☎ 415-252-9525; 1900 Market St) A fashionable mixed crowd is attracted to the Orbit Room, a postindustrial art deco café. It stays open late, boasts a good jukebox and panoramic windows, and its sidewalk tables make it well suited to lingering over coffee, draught beer or a very light meal. Bartender Alberta Straub, a truly gifted and creative mixer, works her magic on Tuesday night.

Samovar Tea Lounge (Map pp88-9; ☎ 415-626-4700; 498 Sanchez St; pot of tea $4-8) This smart teahouse

is popular for light breakfasts and Asian-inflected dishes. Or you can just choose from dozens of teas, varying from peppermint to aged *pu-ehr*. If you want to expand your knowledge of tea – just how good does the stuff really get, anyway? – the Tuesday night tasting is an eye-opening experience ($10 to $15, open 7pm to 9pm). Weekends are busy.

THE HAIGHT
People's Cafe (Map pp88-9; ☎ 415-553-8842; 1419 Haight St) People's Cafe is a nice enough spot for breakfast, a sandwich or light vegetarian meal. Or just get a coffee and a table by a window, great for people-watching.

Rockin' Java (Map pp88-9; ☎ 410-831-8842; www.joerizzo.com/rockinjava.htm; 1821 Haight St) One of the city's best open mike nights is held not at a bar, but in this coffee house – every Tuesday (7pm to 9pm). Check out the website for information. Non-musicians will appreciate the casual atmosphere during the day.

Bars
The global lounge trend is creeping into all of San Francisco's neighborhoods, including those that already had healthy bar scenes. Some old dives, once habituated by drunks, have been stripped, spiffed and repopulated with 20-somethings with cash to burn. In these sorts of places your basic martini has become something involving vodka and kiwi fruit and will cost you a tenner or more. Other old dives, with decades of character, have been left alone or simply dusted off, and these suddenly are cherished by the diverse crowd that yawns at the lounge thing.

The best parts of town in which to tie one on are North Beach, the Mission, SoMa, Union Sq and the Tenderloin. Polk St, running along the western edge of the Tenderloin and Nob Hill, is picking up. In any of these parts of town you'll have your choice of slick, seedy or somewhere in between.

Smoking is banned inside all bars, clubs, coffeehouses and restaurants. Some bars have smoking patios, but in most cases, smokers tend to congregate right outside the door.

UNION SQUARE & FINANCIAL DISTRICT
Gold Dust Lounge (Map pp80-1; 247 Powell St) The good old Gold Dust Lounge has been serving Irish coffee and cheap booze since Prohibition ended. For a good time, pass

---

THREE GREAT DIVES

An old boozer gets its character from time, stories and smoke. A dive's commendable virtues are many, but include comfortable furniture that doesn't aim to impress, laid-back clientele (a few characters among them), a lack of fruity martini concoctions and reasonable prices. San Francisco has dozens of great dives, but the following three standouts are especially worth seeking out.

C Bobby's Owl Tree (Map pp80-1; ☎ 415-776-9344; 601 Post St) Old C Bobby, near Union Sq, has a single-minded fascination with owls. The walls of this dive are covered with photos of owls, display cases of owl statuettes and there are a few stuffed specimens hanging from the ceiling as well. The clientele consists mostly of well-behaved, silver-haired men, but there's always a smattering of curious younger folk swiveling in their Naugahyde chairs to admire the sundry examples of Bobby's favorite bird.

Specs' (Map pp84-5; ☎ 415-421-4112; 12 William Saroyan Pl) Hidden away on a tiny pedestrian alley in North Beach, Specs' is a dark, cavelike dive enjoyed by barflies in the afternoon and a mix of hipsters and loosened-tie types in the evening. With its hodgepodge of intriguing memorabilia culled from ports around the globe, the place feels like a merchant marine's basement. The taps are limited to Budweiser, but better brews are served in bottles.

Uptown (Map pp88-9; ☎ 415-861-8231; 200 Capp St) Great dives in the Mission District are plentiful, but this unassuming tavern is particularly sweet. The street is rife with prostitutes and drug addicts, and the bar doesn't look especially welcoming from the outside. Inside, though, it's all warmth and seductive atmosphere. Pool, pinball, tap beers, a refreshingly local and down-to-earth crowd, the occasional dog and well-worn couches earn this place an unabashed thumbs-up.

---

through the swinging doors into a faded fake Gold Rush interior, where inauthentic Dixieland jazz is performed here every night.

Voda (Map pp80-1; ☎ 415-677-9242; 56 Belden Pl) The coolest after-work crowd enters Voda's cool, blue-lit environs to cool off and look cool. Vodka mixes are a specialty and prices are fair. DJs spin cool jazz, house and hip hop and often start in the early evening.

Redwood Room (Map pp80-1; ☎ 415-929-2372; 496 Geary St) Thanks to a Phillipe Starck makeover, this once-classic art deco lounge in the Clift Hotel is now an übertrendy hangout for well-heeled professionals. It is striking to behold but a bit hoity-toity.

Red Room (Map pp80-1; ☎ 415-346-7666; 827 Sutter St) A tiny, trendy spot at the Commodore Hotel that is an extravagant study in reds – red vinyl, red bottles, red lights and red martinis.

CIVIC CENTER & TENDERLOIN

Bambuddha Lounge (Map pp80-1; ☎ 415-885-5088; 601 Eddy St) This poolside spread adjacent to the Phoenix Hotel has a sleek Asian-tinged design and a huge reclining Buddha. It's exotic-kooky, space-age sophistication – updated just a little. Follow the leggy supermodel barflies who frequent the joint and order a coco-tini or a lychee-tini and

maybe some small plates (pan-Asian) for nibbling.

Hemlock Tavern (Map pp80-1; ☎ 415-923-0923; 1131 Polk St) On the Polk Gulch strip, the nonlethal Hemlock is a dark but congenial space with groovy ceiling lamps and a long oval bar in the middle. A key draw for smokers is the closed-in, heated smoking section – no sidewalk puffing here. In the intimate back room respected rock bands play several nights a week ($5 cover to go back there).

222 Club (Map pp80-1; ☎ 415-440-0222; 222 Hyde St; admission $5; ☾ Tue-Sun) On a fairly seedy block of the Tenderloin, 222 Club is a dive gussied up just a tad to welcome a younger crowd. Upstairs you can order pizzas and other light Italian dishes, while in the downstairs lounge DJs cook up a sonic gruel for the dancing masses. Drinks are inexpensive and the bartenders certainly know how to mix 'em.

Edinburgh Castle (Map pp80-1; ☎ 415-885-4074; 950 Geary St) This enormous Scottish pub has an array of British ales on tap, greasy fish and chips and a pub quiz every Tuesday. You can shoot pool in the back or head upstairs to hear live rock music or maybe see a play.

Martuni's (Map pp80-1; ☎ 415-241-0205; cnr Market & Valencia Sts) Up Market St in the direction of the Castro, this swank and gay-friendly cocktail lounge specializes in fabulous martinis. Thanks to the frequent piano playing and singing, it feels like a cabaret.

NORTH BEACH

Tosca Cafe (Map pp84-5; ☎ 415-391-1244; 242 Columbus Ave) A classic spot dating from 1919 and loaded with old-world character, not to mention a famous jukebox loaded with opera records.

Vesuvio Cafe (Map pp84-5; ☎ 415-362-3370; 255 Columbus Ave) Vesuvio's history as a Beat hangout may make it a tourist attraction, but it continues to be a popular neighborhood bar. It has the dense, timeworn character of a great old pub, but with a decidedly Left Coast quirkiness.

Saloon (Map pp84-5; ☎ 415-989-7666; 1232 Grant Ave) Founded in 1861, the Saloon is the city's oldest bar. The landmark venue is truly a dive and feels like a dimly lit garage. It has a regular roster of local blues stalwarts including the unstoppable Johnny Nitro.

FISHERMAN'S WHARF

Buena Vista Café (Map pp86-7; ☎ 415-474-5044; 2765 Hyde St) This place, near the cable car turnaround, is so popular for food and drink you may have to wait in line to get in.

NOB HILL

Top of the Mark (Map pp80-1; ☎ 415-392-3434; 999 California St) Atop the Mark Hopkins Hotel is

---

> **WHERE THE BAR BANDS ARE**
>
> Grumbling locals sometimes complain you can't see live music anywhere in the city today, but don't listen to 'em. You can still see really good bands perform live in Frisco bars. Usually a nominal admission charge is levied, but sometimes the entertainment is gratis. In addition to the following bars, check out the Live Music section, where bars that function more like clubs are listed.
>
> - Hemlock Tavern (opposite), Tenderloin
> - Make-Out Room (p126), Mission
> - Catalyst Cocktails (right), South of Market
> - Doc's Clock (p126), Tuesday nights, Mission
> - Plough & the Stars (p126), Richmond District

---

this upscale bar and dance floor. The view is among the finest in town.

Tonga Room (Map pp80-1; ☎ 415-772-5278; cnr Mason & California Sts) Tonga Room, downstairs at the Fairmont hotel, is a kooky tourist-friendly tiki lounge where rainstorms blow through twice an hour and cheesy bands play on a raft in the artificial lagoon. Some drinks are served in fake coconut shells, and of course mai tais are in order.

THE MARINA

Perry's (Map pp86-7; ☎ 415-922-9022; 1944 Union St) Perry's is a bona fide cruising spot, as it was when Armistead Maupin wrote it into his *Tales of the City* novels.

MatrixFillmore (Map pp86-7; ☎ 415-563-4180; 3138 Fillmore St) Another famous breeder bar where the atmosphere is effervescent with hormones. A well-dressed crowd comes here for cocktails and microbrews and hopefully a hook-up. A bar menu of charcuterie will satisfy other appetites.

Liverpool Lil's (Map pp86-7; 2942 Lyon St) For more relaxed drinking and talking, slide into this neighborhood stalwart, near the Presidio. It's an old pub.

SOUTH OF MARKET

Catalyst Cocktails (Map pp80-1; ☎ 415-621-1722; 312 Harriet St) This little hideaway is worth finding, and not just because it's a hideaway. Live bands play sometimes in the early evening (no cover charge) and trendy martini drinks are heavily featured – especially on Tuesday nights, when they're half price. Food is also served.

House of Shields (Map pp80-1; ☎ 415-392-7732; 39 New Montgomery St) Tourists, locals and students from the nearby Academy of Art whet their whistles in this jumpin' little joint just across from the Palace Hotel. It looks and feels like a hunting lodge, complete with decorative taxidermy and dark mahogany booths, but it's classy enough to qualify as a historic treasure – it opened in 1908. Lunch and dinner are available off the grill. It closes absurdly early – at 10pm.

Kate O'Brien's (Map pp80-1; ☎ 415-882-7240; 579 Howard St) A comfortable Irish pub that frequently gets crowded with Guinness swillers and clubbers teetering to techno on the upstairs dance floor each weekend.

Eagle (Map pp80-1; ☎ 415-626-0880; cnr 12th & Harrison Sts) This is a quintessential gay leather bar, with an excellent, heated outdoor patio, friendly staff and occasional live bands.

THE MISSION

Make-Out Room (Map pp88-9; ☎ 415-647-2888; 3225 22nd St) Here's a spacious venue with high ceilings, cheap drinks and rotating art on the walls. DJs spin several nights a week and, usually on Sunday and Monday, the stage hosts an eclectic selection of live bands, from indie-rock to jazz to honky-tonk.

Doc's Clock (Map pp88-9; 2575 Mission St) The dazzling sign over the entrance to Doc's Clock is a bona fide attention grabber, even on neon-happy Mission St. This is one of the district's more relaxed dives and is never a bad place to duck into for a few pints. Generally, it's quiet enough for conversation.

Casanova Lounge (Map pp88-9; ☎ 415-863-9328; 527 Valencia St) This venue is grungy and cool with an excellent jukebox. Like most Valencia St bars, it can get mighty crowded and noisy, especially on weekends.

Zeitgeist (Map pp88-9; ☎ 415-255-7505; cnr Valencia & Duboce Sts) Three blocks north of 16th St, Zeitgeist is a popular spot for San Francisco's urban biker scene, from bike messengers to motorcyclists. The beer selection's good, and the back patio is huge and a great place to spend a warm evening.

Lexington Club (Map pp88-9; ☎ 415-863-2052; 3464 19th St) This club is a small, friendly and always-busy corner dive, and the only full-time lesbian bar in the city.

Lone Palm (Map pp88-9; ☎ 415-648-0109; 3394 22nd St) With a seductive desert oasis vibe, Lone Palm could pass for a secluded corner of Rick's Cafe Americain in the film *Casablanca*. It attracts a smartly dressed crowd, and smoking is tolerated here.

Latin American Club (Map pp88-9; ☎ 415-647-2732; 3286 22nd St) Just east of Valencia St, this is a low-key, funky and fun local hangout.

THE CASTRO & UPPER MARKET ST

Amber (Map pp88-9; ☎ 415-626-7827; 718 14th St) Smokers are free to light up and puff away on one of the sleek, early-1960s couches or right at the bar itself. Nonsmokers seem to flock here, too, no doubt simply because it's a good lookin' spot that's been claimed by a friendly, mixed crowd.

Harvey's (Map pp88-9; ☎ 415-431-4278; 500 Castro St) The peachy, suburban exterior and the gay memorabilia on the walls of Harvey's are

clear indications that this is a theme-oriented, tourist-friendly place. Windows overlook the 18th and Castro crossroads, affording great people-watching opportunities. Standard bar food is available.

Midnight Sun (Map pp88-9; ☎ 415-861-4186; 4067 18th St) This video bar, featuring screenings of *Will and Grace* and other gay-friendly programs, has cordial bartenders and cheap drinks. The dressed-down after-work crowd is pretension-free, but don't expect to make friends easily – people are generally gawking at the boob tubes.

Mint (Map pp88-9; ☎ 415-626-4726; 1942 Market St) Mint attracts a diverse karaoke-loving crowd. It's open all day, but things only get interesting after 9pm, when the microphone is plugged in. It's by turns outrageous and, occasionally, impressive.

Twin Peaks Tavern (Map pp88-9; ☎ 415-864-9470; 401 Castro St) This was allegedly the city's first gay bar to have windows. Today it's a sedate spot for a postmovie cocktail alongside an older gay crowd.

THE HAIGHT

Zam Zam (Map pp88-9; ☎ 415-861-2545; 1633 Haight St) If Zam Zam's seductive Moroccan portal strikes your fancy, follow that impulse to this very hospitable and swanky den of dissolution. The retro atmo and jukebox spinning Sinatra tunes surely call for a mixed bev of some sort.

Toronado (Map pp88-9; ☎ 415-863-2276; 547 Haight St) This is the Holy Mother Church of All Things Craft Brewed, thanks to its broad and ever-changing draft selection, always the biggest and best in town.

Mad Dog in the Fog (Map pp88-9; ☎ 415-863-2276; 530 Haight St) A popular English pub with dartboards, good beer, soccer on TV and tasty pub grub.

Club Deluxe (Map pp88-9; ☎ 415-552-6949; 1509 Haight St) A retro venue where snazzily dressed Sinatra fans still come to worship. Live bands, from swing to rockabilly, keep the place hopping many nights.

Noc Noc (Map pp88-9; ☎ 415-861-5811; 557 Haight St) Noc Noc has a wacky cavelike interior that often draws comparisons to the Bedrock home of the Flintstones.

THE RICHMOND

Plough & Stars (Map p83; ☎ 415-751-1122; 116 Clement St) You're likely to be treated to a memorable and distinctly Irish experience at the Plough and Stars, where blue-collar Irish expats come to knock a few back after work. Most nights, musicians perform Irish music, and a few people in the crowd even know how to jig to it.

Beach Chalet Brewery & Restaurant (Map p83; ☎ 415-386-8439; 1000 Great Hwy; P) At the western end of Golden Gate Park, across from Ocean Beach, is this bustling bistro in a historic building. The food is overpriced, but the house-brewed beers are quite good, as are the evening sunsets.

Trad'r Sams (Map p83; ☎ 415-221-0773; 6150 Geary Blvd) For fake-tiki exotica, c 1940, head way out into the foggy avenues to Trad'r Sam's. The old bamboo canopies and bamboo telephone booth that are crammed into this tiny bar leave hardly enough room for the young drunkards who hang out here on Saturday night. Tip well – making fruity drinks is hard work.

ENTERTAINMENT

San Francisco's nightlife doesn't hinge on huge and hyperfashionable nightclubs but rather on its eclectic bars, dance clubs and cutting-edge concert spaces. The city also has a number of theater venues, a renowned opera house, a symphony, a ballet company and numerous modern-dance companies.

The city's most extensive rundown of entertainment possibilities is found in the free weeklies, the *San Francisco Bay Guardian* and the *SF Weekly*.

TIX Bay Area (Map pp80-1; ☎ 415-433-7827; 251 Stockton St; ☺ ticket booth 11am-6pm Tue-Thu, 11am-7pm Fri & Sat) In Union Sq, Tix Bay Area sells half-price tickets to select musical performances, opera, dance and theater, on the day of the performance. It accepts cash only and charges a small service fee.

For tickets to theater shows and big-name concerts, call **Ticketmaster** (☎ 415-421-8497) or **BASS** (☎ 415-478-2277).

Nightclubs

Mighty (☎ 415-626-7001; www.mighty119.com; 119 Utah St; admission $10; ☺ 10pm-4am Fri-Sun) In a huge former warehouse, sequestered in a no-man's land between SoMa, the Mission and Potrero Hill, Mighty packs a wallop. It has three long bars, a balcony and an expansive dance floor. Better still the club books high-calibre DJs (touring and local) and maintains a fun,

attitude-free vibe. Weekly house parties are among SF's most popular.

Harry Denton's Starlight Room (Map pp80-1; ☎ 415-395-8595; 450 Powell St) On the 21st floor of the Sir Francis Drake Hotel in Union Sq, this place has amazing views. It tends to attract a cheesy middle-aged crowd, but everyone has fun and you'll never feel self-conscious.

1015 Folsom (Map pp80-1; ☎ 415-431-1200; www .1015.com; 1015 Folsom St; admission from $10; ☺ 10pm-6am Thu-Sun) Here's the city's foremost dance club, generally featuring the best in local and visiting DJ talent and hosting a rotating roster of popular club nights.

Endup (Map pp80-1; ☎ 415-646-0999; 401 6th St; cover from $10; ☺ 10pm-4:30am Thu, 10pm-6am Fri, 6am-4pm & 10pm-4am Sat, 6am-8pm & 10pm-4am Sun) A SoMa institution that attracts gays and straights alike for its throbbing house music and lively crowds. Fag Fridays and the all-day Sunday 'T' dances are legendary. Things often run past 4am.

111 Minna (Map pp80-1; ☎ 415-431-1200; www .111minnagallery.com; 111 Minna St; ☺ Tue-Sun) This is a gallery by day and trendy nightclub come darkness. It's a cool space that draws a smart SoMa crowd.

Stud (Map pp80-1; ☎ 415-252-7883; www.studsf .com; 399 9th St; admission $5-7; ☺ 5pm-3am) This is the elder statesman of SoMa dance clubs, having been around close to 40 years. Straights do frequent it, but it remains first and foremost a gay hot spot.

Nickie's (Map pp88-9; ☎ 415-621-6508; www.nick ies.com; 460 Haight St; admission $3-5; ☺ 9pm-2am) One of the city's more eclectic and down-to-earth DJ bars, featuring reggae, funk, Grateful Dead, disco and ambient music on different nights. This is no place to look suave with a martini – only beer is served. It's usually packed with a party crowd from all over town. Tuesday is usually a big night.

Beat Lounge (Map pp84-5; ☎ 415-982-5299; 501 Broadway; admission $5; ☺ 9pm-2am) In a North Beach basement, beneath a restaurant, the Beat trades on the neighborhood's jazzy past. It's cool, it's small, it's underground, and jazz and Latin combos take the small stage some nights. The rest of the time, DJs quietly spin savvy sets for a mellow crowd.

Club Six (Map pp80-1; ☎ 415-982-5299; www.club six1.com; 60 6th St; admission $5-15; ☺ 9am-late Wed-Sun) Bilevel Club Six defines casual cool with lumpy sofas and worn out hardwood floors. Weekly parties delve into dancehall reggae, and hip-hop and draw a mixed crowd with an urban, up-for-anything sensibility. You can hang in the street-level lounge or dive into the thick of it on the basement dance floor.

Café (Map pp88-9; ☎ 415-861-3846; 2367 Market St) This venue attracts a young, ethnically mixed population of gays, lesbians and straights. This may be the only dance floor in the Castro, and the long deck overlooking Market St is a good place to cool off – or eyeball passing fancies in the street below.

Detour (Map pp88-9; ☎ 415-861-6053; 2348 Market St) Detour has the Castro's longest happy hour (2pm to 8pm), a superior sound system, chain-link urban playground decor, male go-go dancers and a gay crowd out for a good time.

26Mix (Map pp88-9; ☎ 415-826-7378; www.26mix .com; admission $5-10; 3024 Mission St; ❥ Tue-Sun) It looks like an ordinary dive, but 26Mix is clearly all about DJs and dancing. A little ways beyond the 24th St BART station, 26Mix showcases the talents of local DJs every night of the week. The sound system pops and the crowd is pretty low key. The club tends to get cranking later in the evening, and when it's packed it gets downright steamy. Early weeknights can be slow.

El Rio (☎ 415-282-3325; www.elriosf.com; 3158 Mission St; admission $3-8; ❥ 5pm-2am Mon-Thu, 3pm-2am Fri-Sun) Near Cesar Chavez Blvd, El Rio is an upbeat club that draws a diverse (gay and straight), down-to-earth crowd to its two indoor rooms and large backyard. Live bands play on Saturday, there's world beat dancing on Friday, and the Sunday afternoon salsa parties are always happening affairs (get here by 3:30pm).

Live Music

Fillmore (☎ 415-346-6000; www.thefillmore.com; cnr Geary & Fillmore Sts) North from Haight St in Japantown is the famous Fillmore, still a superb concert venue, with a big stage and a world-famous pedigree dating back to the city's psychedelic heyday.

Warfield (Map pp80-1; ☎ 415-775-7722; www.the fillmore.com/warfield.asp; 982 Market St) The old War-field was originally a vaudeville theater. It is now managed by Bill Graham Presents, which often books accomplished artists looking for a medium-sized concert venue.

Great American Music Hall (Map pp80-1; ☎ 415-885-0750; 859 O'Farrell St) Previously a bordello

and a dance hall, this well-loved venue now hosts an excellent roster of rock, jazz, country and blues artists. The over-the-top baroque interior adds to the character and experience.

12 Galaxies (Map pp88-9; ☎ 415-970-9777; www .12galaxies.com; 2565 Mission St; admission $8-20) 12 Galaxies has a superb track record for booking touring talent with growing followings. If you keep tabs on those smart songwriters who get some press but haven't broken through to the mainstream, this is where you'll find them in SF. The club is right on Mission St, amongst half a dozen great dive bars and cheap eateries.

Bottom of the Hill (☎ 415-621-4455; www.bottom ofthehill.com; 1233 17th St; admission $5-12) East of the Mission in Potrero Hill is this live music venue bringing a steady stream of top-notch indie-rock acts to its small but vibrant room.

Slim's (Map pp80-1; ☎ 415-621-3330; www.slims -sf.com; 333 11th St; admission $13-35; ❥ from 8pm) Slim's is a boxy SoMa club with a crisp sound system. An impressive string of rock, blues, country and R&B artists pass through.

Café du Nord (Map pp88-9; ☎ 415-861-5016; www .cafedunord.com; 2170 Market St; admission $7-15) This is a below-the-street-level, '30s-style former speakeasy that features live jazz, rockabilly, West Coast blues and salsa acts. It's on Upper Market St, near the Castro.

Bruno's (Map pp88-9; ☎ 415-643-5200; www .brunoslive.com; 2389 Mission St; admission $5-10) A swank bar-restaurant, Bruno's hosts a regular schedule of jazz, indie-rock and other interesting performers.

Elbo Room (Map pp88-9; ☎ 415-552-7788; www .elbo.com; 647 Valencia St; admission $5-8) The Elbo Room has a swank curved bar that's always packed with Mission District scenesters. DJs and live musicians perform upstairs, playing anything from Latin jazz to hip-hop.

Rickshaw Stop (Map pp80-1; ☎ 415-861-2011; www.rickshawstop.com; 155 Fell St; admission $3-8) The Rickshaw, near Civic Center, is a friendly joint with an East-meets-West aesthetic that spills over into the nightly entertainment. There are DJs on hand a lot of the time, but eccentric rockers and noise-poppers from both sides of the Pacific often take the stage.

Ritespot Café (Map pp88-9; ☎ 415-552-6066; www .ritespotcafe.net; 2099 Folsom St) The Ritespot is a dive that serves up food, but has staked its reputation on nurturing the talents of some of San Francisco's more interesting and experimental musicians. Local combos playing anything from Honolulu swing to experimental Moog synthesizer compositions crowd into a corner just out of reach of the dining tables.

Bimbo's 365 Club (Map pp86-7; ☎ 415-474-0365; 1025 Columbus Ave) Bimbo's, which is in North Beach, is one of the city's swankiest nightclubs, featuring everything from live swing and rockabilly to alternative rock, country and soul.

Theater

San Francisco is not a cutting-edge place for theater, but it has one major company, the **American Conservatory Theater** (ACT; ☎ 415-749-2228), which puts on performances at a number of theaters in the Union Sq area.

Geary Theater (Map pp80-1; ☎ 415-749-2228; 450 Geary St) Home to the American Conservatory Theater, San Francisco's landmark theater was built in 1909. Its fruit-adorned terracotta columns and classical form make it a sight in itself.

Magic Theatre (Map pp86-7; ☎ 415-441-8822; Bldg D, Fort Mason Center; P) This is probably the city's most adventurous large theater.

Club Fugazi (Map pp84-5; ☎ 415-421-4222; 678 Green St; tickets $25-62) Club Fugazi, located in North Beach, features Beach Blanket Babylon, San Francisco's longest-running comedy extravaganza, now into its third decade and still packing them in.

The big spectacular shows – such as the Andrew Lloyd-Webber musicals – play at a number of theaters. Call ☎ 415-512-7770 for tickets for all the following.

Curran Theatre (Map pp80-1; 445 Geary St) Between Mason & Taylor Sts.

Golden Gate Theatre (Map pp80-1; 1 Taylor St at Golden Gate Ave & Market St)

Orpheum Theatre (Map pp80-1; cnr Market & Hyde Sts)

San Francisco also has many small theater spaces that host solo and experimental shows. Check listings in the city's newspapers.

Intersection for the Arts (Map pp88-9; ☎ 415-626-3311; 446 Valencia St)

Marsh (Map pp88-9; ☎ 415- 826-5750; 1062 Valencia St)

Theater Artaud (Map pp88-9; ☎ 415-621-7797; 450 Florida St)

Theatre Rhinoceros (Map pp88-9; ☎ 415-861-5079; 2926 16th St)

Cinemas

Forget those slick multiscreen theaters because San Francisco boasts some excellent rep houses and lovingly restored, vintage single-screen theaters loaded with cinematic charm. Ticket prices range between $6 and $10 for evening shows.

Castro Theatre (Map pp88-9; ☎ 415-621-6120; 429 Castro St) The Castro undoubtedly tops the list for cinemas. The building is as interesting and beautiful as the mix of independent, foreign and classic films. A magnificent Wurlitzer organ is played before evening screenings.

Roxie Cinema (Map pp88-9; ☎ 415-863-1087; 3117 16th St) In the Mission, Roxie, with its eclectic and adventurous programming of new independent, art and classic genre films – including many impressive and rare film noir pictures – is another local treasure.

Balboa (Map p83; ☎ 415-221-8184; 3630 Balboa St) A renovated art deco gem in the outer Richmond District, Balboa has been operating since 1926 and screens thoughtfully paired double features.

Red Vic Movie House (Map pp88-9; ☎ 415-668-3994; 1727 Haight St) This repertory venue in the Upper Haight screens popular cult films and other interesting oldies and re-releases.

San Francisco Cinematheque (☎ 415-822-2885) This is a world-class avant-garde and experimental film organization that screens a challenging mix of shorts and features at different venues, including Yerba Buena Center for the Arts (p100) and the San Francisco Art Institute (p97). There's no program in summer.

Sports

San Francisco 49ers (☎ 415-656-4900) San Francisco's National Football League team, the 49ers, is one of the most successful teams in the NFL's history, having brought home no fewer than five Super Bowl championships. Home for the 49ers is the cold and windy Candlestick Park (currently dubbed Monster Park; Map pp78–9), off Hwy 101 in the southern part of the city.

San Francisco Giants (☎ 415-972-2000) The city's National League baseball team draws big crowds to beautiful SBC Park (p100).

Performing Arts

CLASSICAL MUSIC & OPERA

Davies Symphony Hall (Map pp80-1; ☎ 415-864-6000; cnr Grove St & Van Ness Ave) The San Francisco

Symphony, whose musical director is the popular Michael Tilson Thomas, performs from September to May in this hall. Tickets typically cost from about $25 to over $50.

Herbst Theatre (Map pp80-1; ☎ 415-392-4400; 401 Van Ness Ave) This theatre, in the Veterans Building, hosts some classical performances as well as lectures.

War Memorial Opera House Map pp80-1; ☎ 415-864-3330; 301 Van Ness Ave) This place hosts performances of the acclaimed San Francisco Opera from early September through to mid-December. For only $20, students with a valid ID can sit in the $100 orchestra section; these tickets go on sale two hours before curtain up. Standing-room tickets, available for some shows, are $10 and also go on sale two hours before performances.

DANCE

San Francisco Ballet (☎ 415-865-2000) This company performs at the opera house and the Yerba Buena Center for the Arts (p100).

San Francisco also has a large and diverse modern dance scene. **ODC Theater** (Map pp88-9; ☎ 415-863-9834; 3153 17th St) has modern dance nearly every weekend. The Yerba Buena Center and Theater Artaud (p129) also frequently have dance performances.

SHOPPING

San Francisco's shopping, like its nightlife, is best when the words 'small,' 'odd' and 'eccentric' come into play. Sure, there are big department stores and international name-brand boutiques, but the quirky and cool places lining the streets of the Haight, the Castro, Hayes Valley and the Mission are much more fun.

Union Sq (Map pp80-1) is where you will find the city's biggest stores, such as **Macy's** (☎ 415-397-3333; 170 O'Farrell St) and **Neiman-Marcus** (☎ 415-362-3900; 150 Stockton St), as well as its largest concentration of brand-name, high-fashion boutiques. Nearby on Market St, **Nordstrom** (☎ 415-243-8500) occupies the top several floors of the stylish **San Francisco Shopping Centre** (cnr Market & 5th Sts), and a huge new addition, including Bloomingdale's, is due to open next door in the next year or two.

The section of Hayes St between Franklin and Laguna Sts, near the Civic Center, is a trendy little enclave known as Hayes Valley (Map pp80-1). The boutiques and stores are smaller and more cutting edge than

ones you'll find downtown, often featuring local designers.

Haight St (Map pp88-9) tries hard to sustain its role as a youth-culture mecca. While tie-dye just won't die, the overall trends these days are more about punk chic and platform shoes than hippie beads and sandals. Shopping here is particularly good for vintage clothing and music, especially secondhand CDs and vinyl.

Union St in Cow Hollow (Map pp86-7) is dotted with designer boutiques and upscale gift shops. Only a few blocks north toward the bay is Chestnut St in the Marina, with a host of chain stores. Both neighborhoods cater to a yuppie crowd.

Fisherman's Wharf (Map pp86-7), of course, is saturated with junkie souvenir and garish 'gift' shops, most notably in and around claustrophobic Pier 39. The Cannery and Ghirardelli Sq offer a slightly less frenetic experience. More tourist trinkets can be found throughout Chinatown (Map pp84-5), though adventurous types can explore Chinatown's back streets and alleys for bargain-priced cookware and unusual herbal pharmaceuticals.

The Castro (Map pp88-9) has men's clothing stores, good bookstores and fun novelty stores, all aimed to one degree or another at an affluent gay crowd. Come as much for the vibe and the people-watching as for what's in the stores.

South of the Castro, over a high hill, lies Noe Valley (Map pp88-9). The main drag is 24th St, between Diamond and Church Sts, and it's easily reached via MUNI's J-Church streetcar. The area's packed with young parents pushing baby strollers, and who seem to be constantly browsing the numerous good clothing boutiques, bookstores, gourmet food and wine shops, and kids' stores.

In the Mission District (Map pp88-9), Valencia St continues to be a hot spot for vintage shops, locally designed clothing, secondhand furniture and Mexican folk art. Dave Eggers' kooky store **826 Valencia** (826 Valencia St), sells strange pirate supplies and items relating to his journal *McSweeney's*, and also holds free writing workshops for local kids.

The Richmond (Map p83) shouldn't be overlooked for its wealth of curious shops along busy Clement St, including numerous

Asian gift and grocery emporiums, and the city's biggest and best used bookstore, Green Apple Books (p77).

Clothing

San Francisco is a stylish city, but the great thing is that the style spectrum is far-ranging and diverse. In San Francisco, anything goes, from sharp tailored suits to vintage dresses to drag extravagance.

Custom Originals (Al's Attire; Map pp84-5; ☎ 415-693-9900; 1314 Grant Ave) Al's is all about beautiful, hand-tailored clothes; with an impeccable eye for retro style and serious attention to detail.

Martha Egan (Map pp84-5; ☎ 415-397-5451; 1 Columbus Ave) This local designer fashions contemporary clothes for women and men with vintage fabrics.

Old Vogue (Map pp84-5; ☎ 415-392-1522; 1412 Grant Ave) A classic vintage shop offering Hawaiian shirts, gorgeous Chinese silk pajamas (with matching robe, naturally), cashmere sweaters, a large selection of men's hats and more.

Re B (Map pp84-5; ☎ 415-362-4826; 1612 Stockton St) In this eclectic shop you'll find choice vintage clothing for women (last season's Michael Kors skirt for $75!), great handbags and accessories.

Jeremy's (Map pp80-1; ☎ 415-882-4929; 2 South Park Ave) This shop sells last season's big-name designer duds (for men and women) and select second-hand threads are all at jaw-dropping bargain prices.

Sunhee Moon (Map pp88-9; ☎ 415-355-1800; 3167 16th St) Many of Sunhee's designs, using stretch denims and silky satins in vibrant prints, are geared toward petites who have a hard time finding pants that fit. She also sells groovy Dita sunglasses and jewelry by local designers.

Laku (Map pp88-9; ☎ 415-695-1462; 1069 Valencia St) Owner and designer Yaeko Yamashita creates whimsical delights in her quaint Mission storefront. Beautifully unique pieces like her trademark elfin slippers are made from Japanese kimono fabric, French velvets and vintage materials.

Dema (Map pp88-9; ☎ 415-206-0500; 1038 Valencia St) Youthful prints and patterns abound in this fun boutique. Vintage-inspired designs mix with higher-end knits and tees.

Rabat (Map pp88-9; ☎ 415-282-7861; 4001 24th St) Rabat offers some sophisticated choices for

women including items by Betsey Johnson, Nanette Lepore and Cop-Copine, but the European shoes for men and women are the real stars of this show.

Rolo on Market (Map pp88-9; ☎ 415-431-4545; 2351 Market St) Rolo carries top-brand names like Comme des Garcons, G-Star, Paul Smith and their ilk.

ADS Hats (Map pp88-9; ☎ 415-255-2787; 758 Valencia St) Spiffy fedoras for the men, charming cocktail hats for the ladies and even tiny knitted caps for the little ones – there is something here for everyone.

American Apparel (Map pp88-9; ☎ 415-431-4038; 1615 Haight St) This LA-based company offers brand-free, sweatshop-free clothing for men and women at affordable prices.

La Rosa Vintage (Map pp88-9; ☎ 415-668-3744; 1171 Haight St) La Rosa features very select, high-class merchandise of Old Hollywood caliber (no bargains here).

Piedmont Boutique (Map pp88-9; ☎ 415-864-8075; 1452 Haight St) Come here for totally outrageous glam attire – feather boas in every rainbow color, Travolta disco suits, mile-high wigs, imaginative undergarments – and all the chintzy accessories you'll need to customize your get-up.

Crosswalk (Map pp86-7; ☎ 415-921-0292; 2122 Fillmore St) Crosswalk sells shoes for men and women by comfy brands like Born, Earth Vegan, Dansko and Camper.

Uko (Map pp86-7; ☎ 415-563-0330; 2070 Union St) Uko has garments for men and women, made from lovely fabrics, and an accessory range.

Wine & Food

Ferry Plaza Farmers Market (Map pp80-1; ✆ 10am-2pm Tue & Sun, 4-8pm Thu, 8am-2pm Sat) On the waterfront, the farmers market makes for a great morning excursion for its fresh, organic produce, good coffee and pastries, and bustling atmosphere. The market takes place opposite the Ferry Building, and is easily spotted if you're walking towards it on Market St.

Other farmers markets are held Wednesday and Sunday on UN Plaza, in the Civic Center, though they're not as exciting.

Ferry Plaza Wine Merchant (Map pp80-1; ☎ 415-391-9400; 1 Ferry Plaza) Here's a convenient place to stock up on California wines after you've tasted a few. Staff are friendly and knowledgeable, and the wine list is written in a colloquial way to make non-snobs feel welcome.

Trader Joe's (Map pp86-7; ☎ 415-351-1013; 401 Bay St) This chain carries excellent deals on wines and is also a great place for snacks and groceries.

PlumpJack Wines (Map pp86-7; ☎ 415-346-9870, 888-415-9463; 3201 Fillmore St) PlumpJack has a great selection from all over the world, and staff can make excellent recommendations.

Boudin Bakery (Map pp86-7; 156 Jefferson St) In Fisherman's Wharf, this is a good place to find classic sourdough bread. Other branches are scattered throughout the city, including inside Macy's and at Ghirardelli Sq.

Ghirardelli Chocolate Shop & Caffè (Map pp86-7; ☎ 415-474-1414; www.ghirardelli.com; Ghirardelli Sq) Ghirardelli is the big name in chocolate in this town. Packaged Ghirardelli treats are available throughout the city, but this place sells them on the site of the company's old factory.

Cameras

Adolph Gasser (Map pp80-1; ☎ 415-495-3852; 181 2nd St) In SoMa, between Mission and Howard Sts, this store has a huge range of new and used photographic and video equipment and also processes film.

Music

Amoeba Records (Map pp88-9; ☎ 415-831-1200; 1855 Haight St) This store, near Stanyan St, is the best place for interesting new and used records in all genres. This huge emporium, formerly a bowling alley, will keep you occupied for hours.

Streetlight Records (Map pp88-9; ☎ 415-282-3550; 3979 24th St) In Noe Valley, Streetlight, is yet another place to look for used records, CDs and tapes.

Aquarius Records (Map pp88-9; ☎ 415-647-2272; 1055 Valencia St) In the Mission, this is a friendly, helpful neighborhood store specializing in hard-to-find indie-rock, electronica, metal, experimental and other unique sounds.

Outdoor Gear

Many of these stores sell not only clothing but the necessary equipment for outdoor adventure, including travel guides. They can give good advice, and they have bulletin boards full of information. There are also some great outdoor stores in Berkeley (see p169).

North Face factory outlet store (Map pp80-1; ☎ 415-626-6444; 1325 Howard St) North Face makes high-quality outdoor and adventure gear, some of which is discounted at its outlet store between 9th and 10th Sts in SoMa.

Patagonia (Map pp86-7; ☎ 415-771-2050; 770 North Point St) In the Fisherman's Wharf area, Patagonia is another respected name in outdoor gear.

G&M Sales (Map pp80-1; ☎ 415-863-2855; 1667 Market St) This is a large, generalized store with camping, hiking and other outdoor gear.

SFO Snowboarding (Map pp88-9; ☎ 415-386-1666; 618 Shrader St), in the Upper Haight, has state-of-the-art snowboards; **FTC Skateboarding** (☎ 415-386-6693), its sister shop, is next door.

Piercings & Tattoos

Numerous body-piercing professionals will pierce parts of your body nowhere near your ears. Nipples, navels and tongues are all popular, and the genitals are certainly not off limits for many discerning gentlemen and women. Don't worry, these shops are clean, sterile and generally quite friendly.

Cold Steel America (Map pp88-9; ☎ 415-933-7233; 1783 Haight St) In the Haight, this is an upscale homage to body art. It has the look and feel of a museum-cum-boutique.

Black & Blue Tattoo (Map pp88-9; ☎ 415-626-0770; www.blackandbluetattoo.com; 381 Guerrero St) At 16th St, his tattoo parlor is women-owned and operated.

Lyle Tuttle Tattooing (Map pp84-5; ☎ 415-775-4991; 841 Columbus Ave) In North Beach, Lyle Tuttle is probably the city's best-known and longest-running tattoo studio. It also has a small museum.

GETTING THERE & AWAY
Air

The Bay Area has three major airports: **San Francisco International Airport** (SFO; ☎ 650-821-8211), on the west side of the bay; Oakland International Airport, only just a few miles across the bay on the east side; and San Jose International Airport, at the southern end of the bay. The majority of international flights use SFO. All three airports are important domestic gateways, but travelers from other US cities (particularly West Coast ones) may find cheaper flights into Oakland, a hub for discount airlines such as Southwest.

SFO is on the Peninsula, 14 miles south of downtown San Francisco, off Hwy 101. It has undergone massive renovations, with the addition of a new international terminal and a BART extension directly to the airport.

The airport is structured like a semicircle, and it's a long walk from one end to the other. Short-term parking is in the center. The international terminal is a separate building, home to all international flights except those to Canada.

All three terminals have ATMs and information booths on the lower level, complete with computer consoles to help if the booth is not staffed. **Travelers' Aid information booths** (✆ 9am-8pm) are on the upper level. If you need further assistance, the airport paging and information line is staffed 24 hours; call from any white courtesy phone.

Bus

All bus services arrive at and depart from the **Transbay Terminal** (Map pp80-1; 425 Mission St at 1st St), two blocks south of Market St. You can take **AC Transit** (☎ 510-839-2882) buses to East Bay, **Golden Gate Transit** (☎ 415-932-2000) buses north to Marin and Sonoma counties, and **SamTrans** (☎ 800-660-4287) buses south to Palo Alto and along the coast.

Greyhound (☎ 415-495-1575, 800-231-2222; www .greyhound.com) also leaves from the Transbay Terminal, with multiple buses daily to Los Angeles ($45.50, eight to 12 hours) and other destinations.

Train

CalTrain (☎ 800-660-4287) operates down the Peninsula, linking San Francisco with Palo Alto (Stanford University) and San Jose. The CalTrain terminal (Map pp80–1) is south of Market St at the corner of 4th and Townsend Sts. MUNI's N-Judah streetcar line runs to and from the CalTrain station.

The nearest **Amtrak** (☎ 800-872-7245) terminals are in Emeryville (see p170) and Oakland (see p161). From these stations Amtrak provides a bus service to the Ferry Building in San Francisco.

GETTING AROUND
To/From the Airport
Bay Area Rapid Transit (BART; ☎ 415-989-2278) provides direct train service to San Francisco airport ($5.15). It is the easiest, most efficient way to reach the airport.

SamTrans (☎ 800-660-4287) also serves the airport. Express bus KX ($4) takes about 30 minutes to reach San Francisco's Transbay Terminal, running 6am and 1am Monday to Friday. Bus 292 takes 50 minutes, but costs only $1.50.

Door-to-door shuttle vans are cheaper than cabs if you are traveling alone or as a couple, and they'll pick you up from any San Francisco location. Call for a reservation. From the airport, reservations are not necessary, and vans leave from the departures level outside all terminals. Fares are generally $17 to $20 each way, although it's cheaper ($15) to get dropped off or picked up at any hotel.
American Airporter Shuttle (☎ 415-202-0733, 800-282-7758)
Lorrie's (☎ 415-334-9000)
Quake City (☎ 415-255-4899)
SuperShuttle (☎ 415-558-8500)

Bicycle

For most visitors, bikes will not be an ideal way of getting around the city, because of the traffic and hills, but the Bay Area is a great place for recreational bike riding. Bicycles are allowed on BART, but there are restrictions. During morning commute hours (about 7am to 9am), bikes are allowed in the Embarcadero Station only for trips to the East Bay. During evening commute hours (about 4:30pm to 6:45pm), bicyclists are not allowed on trains to the East Bay; bicyclists traveling from the East Bay into San Francisco in commute hours must exit at the Embarcadero Station (see the *BART Trip Planner* and the *All About BART* brochures).

Car & Motorcycle

A car is the last thing you want in downtown San Francisco – it's a nightmare negotiating the hills and battling for parking spaces, not to mention the traffic. Remember, on hill streets (with a grade as little as 3%) you must curb your wheels so that they ride up against the curb – toward the street when facing uphill, toward the curb on a downhill. Failure to do so can result in daunting fines. **AAA** (☎ 415-565-2012, emergency road service & towing 800-222-4357; 150 Van Ness Ave) can help members with roadside service.

Some of the cheaper downtown parking garages are the downtown **Sutter-Stockton Garage** (☎ 415-982-7275; cnr Sutter & Stockton Sts), **Ellis-O'Farrell Garage** (123 O'Farrell St; ☎ 415-986-4800) and **Fifth & Mission Garage** (☎ 415-982-8522;

833 Mission St), near Yerba Buena Gardens. The parking garage under Portsmouth Sq in Chinatown is reasonably priced for shorter stops; ditto for the **St Mary's Square Garage** (California St) near Grant Ave, under the square. Daily rates range between $18 and $28.

Parking restrictions in San Francisco are strictly enforced. Parking in bus stops and blue wheelchair spots can leave you with fines of $250 or more. Blocking a rush-hour lane, a downtown loading zone (yellow) or a driveway can result in a costly tow.

Beware also of street-cleaning days and signs in residential neighborhoods indicating a residential permit system (tickets $35). If you suspect your car has been towed, call **AutoReturn** (☎ 415-558-7411; 850 Bryant St, Rm 145).

All major car-rental operators are represented at the airports, and many have downtown offices (Map pp80–1).

Alamo (☎ 415-882-9440, 800-327-9633; 687 Folsom St)
Avis (☎ 415-885-5011, 800-331-1212; 675 Post St)
Budget (☎ 415-928-7864, 800-527-0700; 321 Mason St)
Dollar (☎ 866-434-2226, 800-800-4000; 364 O'Farrell St)
Hertz (☎ 415-771-2200, 800-654-3131; 433 Mason St)
Thrifty (☎ 415- 788-8111, 800-367-2277; 520 Mason St)

Ferry

The opening of the Bay Bridge (in 1936) and the Golden Gate Bridge (in 1937) virtually killed the city's ferries, although in recent years they have enjoyed a modest revival for both commuters and tourists.

The main operator is the Blue & Gold Fleet, which runs the **Alameda-Oakland Ferry** (Map pp80-1; ☎ 510-522-3300) from the Ferry Building at the foot of Market St, and for some services from Pier 41 at Fisherman's Wharf, to Alameda and Oakland. Transfers are available to and from MUNI and AC Transit buses. Blue & Gold's popular ferries to Alcatraz and **Angel Island** (Map pp86-7; ☎ 415-705-5555, 415-773-1188) leave from Pier 41 at Fisherman's Wharf.

To take the ferry to Sausalito or Tiburon in Marin County, board at Pier 41. (During commute hours, there are a few ferries between Tiburon and the Ferry Building in San Francisco.) Blue & Gold also operates the **Vallejo Ferry** (☎ 415-773-1188), which goes to Vallejo from the Ferry Building on weekdays and from Pier 39 at Fisherman's Wharf on weekends and holidays. It also has a variety of bay cruises and connections to the Six Flags Marine World theme park in Vallejo.

Golden Gate Ferries (☎ 415-923-2000), part of Golden Gate Transit, has regular services from the Ferry Building in San Francisco to Larkspur and Sausalito in Marin County. Transfers are available to MUNI buses, and bicycles are permitted.

Public Transportation

BART

The **Bay Area Rapid Transit system** (BART; ☎ 415-989-2278) is a subway system linking San Francisco with the East Bay. BART opened in 1972 and is convenient, economical and generally quite safe to use, although caution is required around some BART stations at night and the system shuts down around midnight. Four of the five lines pass through the city.

Downtown, the route runs beneath Market St. The Powell St station is the most convenient to Union Sq. From downtown, it's a quick 10-minute ride to the Mission District; take any train heading south.

One-way fares start at $1.25 within San Francisco, and range between $2 and $5 from downtown to various outlying areas. From San Francisco BART stations, half-price transfers ($1 for a round-trip ride) are available for MUNI bus and streetcar services. You can buy them (with quarters) from the white MUNI ticket machines before you exit the BART paid area.

MUNI

San Francisco's principal public-transportation system is the **San Francisco Municipal Railway** (MUNI; ☎ 415-673-6864; www.sfmuni.com), which operates nearly a hundred bus lines (many of them electric trolley buses), Metro streetcars, historic streetcars and the famous cable cars. The detailed *Street & Transit Map* costs $3 and is available at newspaper stands around Union Sq. A free timetable, worth having if you're riding a line with irregular service, is available at Metro stations and displayed at some bus stops. Don't expect your bus necessarily to be on time.

Standard MUNI fares are $1.50 for buses or streetcars and $5 for cable cars. Transfer tickets are available at the start of your journey, and you can then use them for two connecting trips within about 90 minutes or so. However, they are *not* transferable to cable cars.

A MUNI Pass, available in one-day ($11), three-day ($18) or seven-day ($24) versions, allows unlimited travel on all MUNI transportation (including cable cars). Passes are available from the Visitors Information Center at Hallidie Plaza, which is the half-price tickets kiosk on Union Sq, and some hotels and businesses displaying the MUNI Pass sign in their window. A cheaper Weekly Pass (valid from Monday to Sunday) is $15 and allows unlimited bus and MUNI railway travel and discounts on cable car rides.

Taxi

Taxi fares start at $2.85 for the first mile and cost 45¢ per fifth of a mile thereafter. Some of the major companies:

De Soto Cab (☎ 415-970-1300)
Luxor Cab (☎ 415-282-4141)
Yellow Cab (☎ 415-626-2345)

San Francisco Bay Area

A huge, densely populated metropolitan area surrounds San Francisco, but the Bay Area is not your typical complex of suburbs and bedroom communities. Many of the cities and towns around the bay draw inventive and creative people from around the world. The area is also rich in beautiful undeveloped lands with their own microclimates, making it possible to get out of San Francisco and into the sunny outdoors in a matter of minutes.

The Bay Area's prime outdoor playgrounds are in Marin County, north of San Francisco via the Golden Gate Bridge. Within an hour's drive of the city, Marin offers some of Northern California's superior coastal hiking and biking excursions. Many of the small towns in the county are quaint refuges with highly refined tastes. A strenuous day of outdoor activities can always be rewarded with a fine meal or a night in an exquisite B&B.

The Bay Area's reputation for political activism comes not so much from San Francisco as from Berkeley, the college town across the bay. California cuisine originated just blocks from the UC Berkeley campus, and travelers head to the East Bay to eat in the fine restaurants.

In many ways, the South Bay is an independent entity. Tech industries set up shop in Silicon Valley towns from San Jose to Palo Alto and launched an economy that often outshines any industry in San Francisco. Stanford University gives the area an intellectual cache, and the Palo Alto community around it enjoys a relaxed prosperity. San Jose, actually greater in area and population than San Francisco, is nevertheless a cultural satellite. But the area puts its own modest spin on things while offering an array of museums and attractions.

HIGHLIGHTS

- Motoring south along beautiful Hwy 1 past **Half Moon Bay** (p184)
- Hiking, biking and camping in the dramatic **Marin Headlands** (p138)
- Delving into Berkeley's **Gourmet Ghetto** (p166) for California cuisine
- Clubbing in San Jose's hopping **SOFA district** (p182)
- Strolling among downtown Oakland's **historic buildings** (p156) and around salty **Lake Merritt** (p157)
- Trekking across windswept **Point Reyes National Seashore** (p152)
- Discovering the secretive coastal town of **Bolinas** (p150)

- AVERAGE TEMPS IN BERKELEY: JAN 43/56°F, JUL 54/70°F

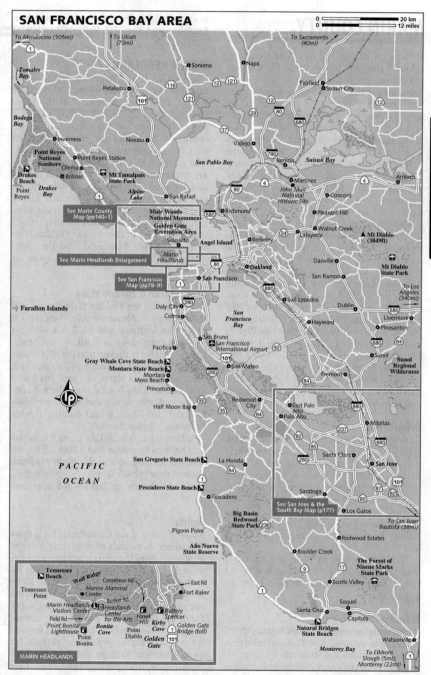

SAN FRANCISCO BAY AREA

0 _____ 20 km
0 _____ 12 miles

To Mendocino (105mi)
To Ukiah (70mi)
To Sacramento (40mi)

Tomales Bay

Sonoma

Napa

Fairfield

Suisun City

Petaluma

Bodega Bay

Inverness

Novato

Vallejo

Benicia

Suisun Bay

Point Reyes National Seashore

Olema

Point Reyes Station

San Pablo Bay

Martinez

Antioch

Drakes Beach

Bolinas

Mt Tamalpais State Park

John Muir National Historic Site

Concord

Point Reyes

Drakes Bay

Alpine Lake

San Rafael

Richmond

Pleasant Hill

Walnut Creek

Mt Diablo (3849ft)

See Marin County Map (pp140–1)

Muir Woods National Monument

Golden Gate Recreation Area

Sausalito

Angel Island

Berkeley

Lafayette

Danville

Mt Diablo State Park

See Marin Headlands Enlargement

Marin Headlands

Oakland

San Ramon

To Los Angeles (340mi)

See San Francisco Map (pp78–9)

San Francisco

San Leandro

Dublin

Livermore

Farallon Islands

Daly City

Colma

San Francisco Bay

Hayward

Pleasanton

Pacifica

San Bruno

San Francisco International Airport

Sunol

Sunol Regional Wilderness

Gray Whale Cove State Beach

Montara State Beach

Montara

Moss Beach

Princeton

San Mateo

Fremont

Half Moon Bay

Redwood City

East Palo Alto

Palo Alto

Milpitas

PACIFIC OCEAN

San Gregorio State Beach

La Honda

Santa Clara

San Jose

Pescadero State Beach

Saratoga

Pescadero

See San Jose & the South Bay Map (p177)

Los Gatos

To San Juan Bautista (38mi)

Big Basin Redwood State Park

Pigeon Point

Redwood Estates

Año Nuevo State Reserve

Boulder Creek

The Forest of Nisene Marks State Park

Scotts Valley

Soquel

Santa Cruz

Capitola

Natural Bridges State Beach

Watsonville

Monterey Bay

To Elkhorn Slough (5mi); Monterey (22mi)

MARIN HEADLANDS

Tennessee Beach

Wolf Ridge

Conzelman Rd

East Rd

Tennessee Point

Marine Mammal Center

Bunker Rd

Fort Baker

Marin Headlands Visitors Center

Headlands Center for the Arts

Hawk Hill

Battery Spencer

Field Rd

Point Bonita Lighthouse

Bonita Cove

Kirby Cove

Golden Gate Bridge (toll)

Point Bonita

Point Diablo

Golden Gate

MARIN COUNTY

If there's a part of the Bay Area that consciously attempts to live up to the California dream, it's Marin County. Just a short drive across the Golden Gate Bridge from San Francisco, the region is populated by wealthy people who cultivate a seemingly laid-back lifestyle. Sprawling homes cluster along densely forested roads. Towns may look like idyllic rural hamlets but the shops cater to cosmopolitan and expensive tastes. Escapees from Beverly Hills have colonized some of the towns. The 'common' folk here eat organic, vote Democrat and drive sports utility vehicles (SUVs).

Geographically, Marin County is a near mirror image of San Francisco. It's a south-pointing peninsula (that nearly touches the north-pointing tip of the city), and it's surrounded to the west and east by ocean and bay. But Marin is wilder, greener and more mountainous. Redwoods grow on the coast side of the hills, the surf crashes against cliffs, and hiking and biking trails crisscross the blessed scenery of Point Reyes, Muir Woods and Mt Tamalpais. Nature is what makes Marin County such an excellent day trip from San Francisco. Of course, after you've exerted yourself on the trails, it doesn't hurt that the area is rife with excellent restaurants and homey B&Bs.

Orientation

Busy Hwy 101 heads north from the Golden Gate Bridge ($5 toll when heading back into San Francisco), spearing through Marin's middle; quiet Hwy 1 winds its way along the sparsely populated coast. In San Rafael, Sir Francis Drake Blvd cuts across west Marin from Hwy 101 to the ocean. Tank up before heading toward the coast – from Mill Valley, the closest gas stations are in Olema and Point Reyes Station.

Hwy 580 comes in from the East Bay over the Richmond–San Rafael bridge ($3 toll for westbound traffic) to meet Hwy 101 at Larkspur.

Information

Marin County Convention & Visitors Bureau (☎ 415-499-5000; www.visitmarin.org; 1013 Larkspur Landing Circle, Larkspur; ☼ 9am-5pm Mon-Fri) handles tourist information for the entire county. Information

is also available from the visitors center in Sausalito and the Mill Valley Chamber of Commerce.

MARIN HEADLANDS

The headlands rise majestically out of the water at the north end of the Golden Gate Bridge, their rugged beauty all the more striking given the fact that they're only a few miles from San Francisco's urban intensity. A few forts and bunkers are left over from a century of US military occupation – which is, ironically, the reason they are protected parklands today and free of development. It's no mystery why this is one of the Bay Area's most popular hiking and biking destinations. As the trails wind through the scenic headlands, they afford stunning views of the sea, the Golden Gate Bridge and San Francisco, and they lead to isolated beaches and secluded spots for picnics.

Orientation & Information

After crossing the Golden Gate Bridge, exit immediately at Alexander Ave, then dip left under the highway and head out west for the expansive views and hiking trailheads. Conzelman Rd snakes up into the hills, where it eventually forks. Conzelman Rd continues west, becoming a steep, one-lane road as it descends to Point Bonita, from there it continues to Rodeo Beach and Fort Barry. McCullough Rd heads inland, joining Bunker Rd toward Rodeo Beach.

Information is available from the **Golden Gate National Recreation Area** (GGNRA; ☎ 415-561-4700; www.nps.gov/goga) and the **Marin Headlands Visitors Center** (☎ 415-331-1540; ☼ 9:30am-4:30pm), in an old church off Bunker Rd near Fort Barry.

Sights

About 2 miles along Conzelman Rd is **Hawk Hill**, where thousands of migrating birds of prey soar along the cliffs from late summer to early fall. At the end of Conzelman Rd is the **Point Bonita Lighthouse** (☼ 12:30-3:30pm Sat-Mon), a breathtaking half-mile walk from the parking area (which has limited spaces). From the tip of Point Bonita, you can see the distant Golden Gate Bridge and beyond it the tips of the San Francisco skyline. It's an uncommon vantage point of the bay-centric city, and photographs from here can look like they've been snapped from an ocean-bound steamer.

On the hill above Rodeo Lagoon is the **Marine Mammal Center** (☎ 415-289-7325; admission free; ☽ 10am-4pm), a 'hospital' that rehabilitates injured, sick and orphaned sea mammals before returning them to the wild. During the spring pupping season the center can have up to several dozen orphaned seal pups on site. The poor little guys are awfully cute, which naturally helps engender sympathy for the center's cause.

In Fort Barry, you will find the **Headlands Center for the Arts** (☎ 415-331-2787; www.headlands .org). It's a refurbished barracks converted into artists' work spaces and conference facilities. The center hosts open studios with its artists-in-residence three times a year, and two or three times a month there are talks, performances and other events.

Activities

HIKING

At the end of Bunker Rd sits **Rodeo Beach**, protected from wind by high cliffs. From here the **Coastal Trail** meanders 3.5 miles inland, past abandoned military bunkers, to the **Tennessee Valley Trail**. It then continues 6 miles along the blustery headlands all the way to Muir Beach.

MOUNTAIN-BIKING

The Marin Headlands have some excellent mountain-biking routes, and there is no more exhilarating ride than the trip across the Golden Gate Bridge to reach them (see the boxed text, p143).

For a good 12-mile dirt loop, choose the **Coastal Trail** west from the fork of Conzelman and McCullough Rds, bumping and winding down to Bunker Rd where it meets **Bobcat Trail** which joins **Marincello Trail** and descends steeply into the Tennessee Valley parking area. The **Old Springs Trail** and the **Miwok Trail** take you back to Bunker Rd a bit more gently than the Bobcat Trail, though any attempt to avoid at least a couple of hefty climbs on this ride is futile.

Sleeping

HI Marin Headlands Hostel (☎ 415-331-2777; www .norcalhostels.org/marin/index.html; Fort Barry, Bldg 941, Marin Headlands; dm/private r $18/54) Located in a spartan 1907 military compound in a sweet spot amidst woods. It has comfortable beds and fresh, line-dried linen for rent ($1). Guests can gather round a fireplace in the common room, shoot pool or play ping-pong. Most importantly, the hostel affords ready access to trails.

There are four small campgrounds in the headlands, and all involve hiking in at least 1 mile from the nearest parking lot. **Kirby Cove** (☎ 800-365-2267; sites $25) is in a spectacular shady nook near the entry to the bay. There's a small beach with the Golden Gate Bridge arching over the rocks nearby. At night you can watch the phantom shadows of cargo ships passing by (and sometimes be lulled to sleep by the dirgelike tones of a fog horn); reserve far ahead. **Hawk, Bicentennial** and **Haypress** campgrounds are inland, and camping is free but must be reserved through the Marin Headlands Visitors Center.

WHY IS IT SO FOGGY?

When the summer sun's rays warm the air over the chilly Pacific, fog forms and hovers offshore; to grasp how it moves inland requires an understanding of California's geography. The vast agricultural region in the state's interior, the Central Valley, is ringed by mountains. Think of it as a giant bathtub. The only substantial sea-level break in these mountains occurs at the Golden Gate, to the west, which happens to be the direction from which prevailing winds blow. As the inland valley heats up and the warm air rises, it creates a deficit of air at surface level, generating wind that gets sucked through the only opening it can find: the Golden Gate. It happens fast and it's unpredictable. Gusty wind is the only indication that the fog is about to roll in. But it's inconsistent: there can be fog at the beaches south of the Golden Gate and sun a mile to the north. Hills block fog – especially at times of high atmospheric pressure, as often happens in summer. Because of this, weather forecasters speak of the Bay Area's 'microclimates.' In July it's not uncommon for inland areas to reach 100°F, while the mercury at the coast barely reaches 70°F. But as the locals say, if you don't like the weather, just wait a minute.

SAN FRANCISCO BAY AREA

MARIN COUNTY

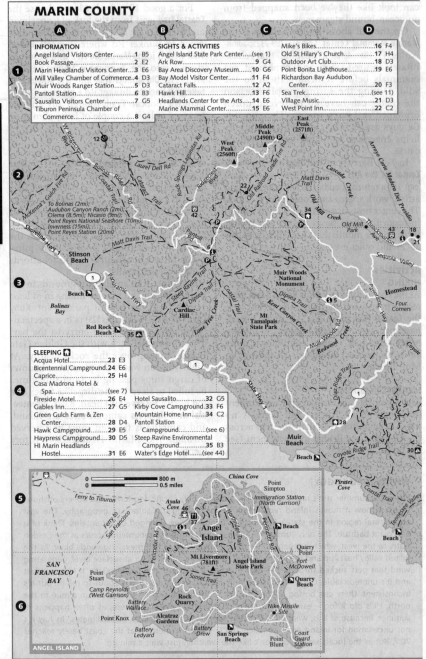

INFORMATION
Angel Island Visitors Center............1 B5
Book Passage.........................2 E2
Marin Headlands Visitors Center....3 E6
Mill Valley Chamber of Commerce..4 D3
Muir Woods Ranger Station............5 D3
Pantoll Station..........................6 B3
Sausalito Visitors Center...............7 G5
Tiburon Peninsula Chamber of
    Commerce.............................8 G4

SIGHTS & ACTIVITIES
Angel Island State Park Center.....(see 1)
Ark Row.................................9 G4
Bay Area Discovery Museum.......10 G6
Bay Model Visitor Center............11 F4
Cataract Falls.........................12 A2
Hawk Hill..............................13 F6
Headlands Center for the Arts.....14 E6
Marine Mammal Center..............15 E6

Mike's Bikes...........................16 F4
Old St Hilary's Church...............17 H4
Outdoor Art Club.....................18 D3
Point Bonita Lighthouse..............19 E6
Richardson Bay Audubon
    Center..............................20 F3
Sea Trek..............................(see 11)
Village Music..........................21 D3
West Point Inn........................22 C2

SLEEPING
Acqua Hotel..........................23 E3
Bicentennial Campground.24 E6
Caprice................................25 H4
Casa Madrona Hotel &
    Spa................................(see 7)
Fireside Motel.........................26 E4
Gables Inn............................27 G5
Green Gulch Farm & Zen
    Center.............................28 D4
Hawk Campground.........29 E5
Haypress Campground......30 D5
HI Marin Headlands
    Hostel..............................31 E6

Hotel Sausalito.................32 G5
Kirby Cove Campground.33 F6
Mountain Home Inn.......34 C2
Pantoll Station
    Campground...............(see 6)
Steep Ravine Environmental
    Campground.............35 B3
Water's Edge Hotel.......(see 44)

ANGEL ISLAND

0   800 m
0   0.5 miles

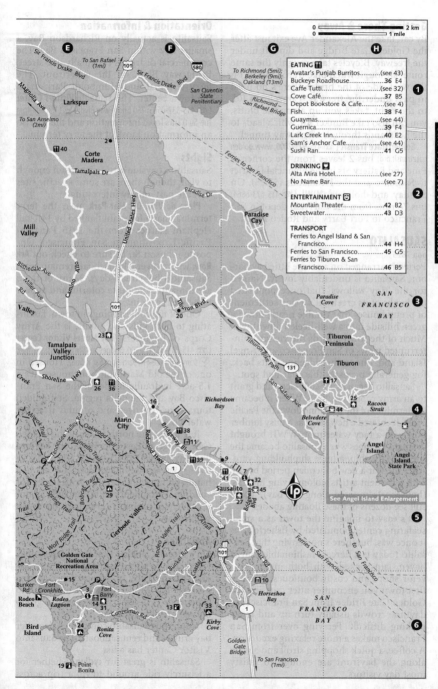

EATING 🍴
Avatar's Punjab Burritos..........(see 43)
Buckeye Roadhouse.................**36** E4
Caffe Tutti..............................(see 32)
Cove Café..............................**37** B5
Depot Bookstore & Cafe..........(see 4)
Fish.......................................**38** F4
Guaymas................................(see 44)
Guernica.................................**39** F4
Lark Creek Inn.......................**40** E2
Sam's Anchor Cafe..................(see 44)
Sushi Ran...............................**41** G5

DRINKING 🍷
Alta Mira Hotel.......................(see 27)
No Name Bar..........................(see 7)

ENTERTAINMENT 🎭
Mountain Theater.....................**42** B2
Sweetwater..............................**43** D3

TRANSPORT
Ferries to Angel Island & San
  Francisco...............................**44** H4
Ferries to San Francisco...........**45** G5
Ferries to Tiburon & San
  Francisco...............................**46** B5

Getting There & Away

By car, take the Alexander Ave exit just after the Golden Gate Bridge and dip left under the freeway. Bicycles take roughly the same route, although when bike traffic moves on the west side of the bridge there's no need to pass under the freeway. Conzelman Rd, to the right, takes you up along the bluffs; you can also take Bunker Rd, which leads to the headlands through a one-way tunnel.

Golden Gate Transit (☎ 415-923-2000; www.golden gatetransit.org) bus 2 leaves from the corner of Pine and Battery Sts in the Financial District to Sausalito and the Headlands ($3.25). On Sunday and holidays **MUNI** (☎ 415-673-6864) bus 76 runs from the CalTrain depot in San Francisco to Fort Barry and Rodeo Beach.

SAUSALITO

pop 7825

Perfectly arranged on a secure little bay harbor, Sausalito is undeniably lovely. Named for the 'tiny willows' that once populated the banks of its creeks, it's a tiny settlement of pretty houses that tumble neatly down a green hillside into a well-heeled downtown. Much of the town affords the visitor uninterrupted views of San Francisco and Angel Island and, due to the ridgeline at its back, fog generally bypasses this charmed spot.

Sausalito began as a 19,000-acre land grant to an army captain in 1838. When it became the terminus of the train line down the Pacific coast, it entered a new stage as a busy lumber port with a racy waterfront. WWII brought dramatic changes when Sausalito became the site of Marinship, a huge shipbuilding yard. After the war a new bohemian period began, with a resident artists' colony living in 'arks' (houseboats moored along the bay). You'll still see dozens of these floating abodes.

It's easy to imagine the town as a small seafaring center populated by fisherfolk, as it once was, but there's no denying that Sausalito today is a fiercely fashionable tourist haven, jam-packed with both junkie souvenir shops and costly boutiques. It is the first town you encounter after crossing the Golden Gate Bridge from San Francisco, so daytime crowds usually turn up and make parking difficult. Ferrying over from San Francisco makes a more relaxing excursion. A coffee, a quick shopping stroll and a walk along the bayfront are enough to satisfy most day visitors.

Orientation & Information

Sausalito is actually on Richardson Bay, a smaller bay within San Francisco Bay. The commercial district is essentially one street, Bridgeway Blvd, on the waterfront. The ferry terminal and Humboldt Park mark the town center. The **Sausalito Visitors Center** (☎ 415-332-0505; 780 Bridgeway Blvd; ☯ 11:30am-4pm Tue-Sun) has local information and there's also an information kiosk at the ferry terminal.

Sights

Sausalito's bayside setting is reason enough to visit, though there are some specific sites that are particularly interesting.

Plaza de Viña Del Mar Park, near the ferry terminal, has a fountain flanked by 14ft-tall elephant statues from the 1915 Panama-Pacific Exposition in San Francisco. Opposite Johnson St, be sure to check out **Ark Row**, where several houseboats remain from Sausalito's bohemian days. Many of them are romantic and quite colorful and appear to be well lived in.

One of the coolest things in town, fascinating to both kids and adults, is the Army Corps of Engineers' **Bay Model Visitor Center** (☎ 415-332-3871; 2100 Bridgeway Blvd; admission free; ☯ 9am-4pm Tue-Fri, 9am-5pm Sat & Sun). Housed in one of the old Marinship warehouses, it's a 1.5-acre hydraulic model of the San Francisco Bay and the delta region. Self-guided tours take you over and around it as the water flows.

Just under the north tower of the Golden Gate Bridge, at East Fort Baker, the **Bay Area Discovery Museum** (☎ 415-487-4398; adult/child $8.50/ 7.50; ☯ 9am-4pm Tue-Fri, 10am-5pm Sat & Sun) is a hands-on museum specifically designed for children. Permanent exhibits include an underwater sea tunnel, a ceramic studio and a science lab.

Activities

On a nice day, Richardson Bay is irresistible. Kayaks can be rented from **Sea Trek** (☎ 415-488-1000; kayaks per hr $15), in Schoonmaker Marina near the Bay Model Visitor Center, and no experience is necessary. Lessons and group outings are also available.

Numerous Sausalito companies also offer bay cruises and rent sailboats. The Sausalito Visitor Center has a list.

Sausalito is great for **cycling**, whether for a leisurely ride around town, a trip across

HIKING & BIKING THE BRIDGE

Walking or cycling across the Golden Gate Bridge to Sausalito is a fun way to avoid traffic, get some great ocean views and bask in that refreshing Marin County air as you work a few muscles. It's a fairly easy journey, mostly flat or downhill when heading north from San Francisco (biking back to the city involves one big climb out of Sausalito). You can also simply hop on a ferry back to SF (see p144).

The trip is about 4 miles from the south end of the bridge and takes less than an hour. Pedestrians have access to the bridge's east walkway between 5am and 9pm daily. Cyclists generally use the west side, except on weekdays between 5am and 3:30pm, when they must share the east side with pedestrians (who have the right of way). After 9pm, cyclists can still cross the bridge on the east side through a security gate.

For more information on rules and rides, contact the **San Francisco Bicycle Coalition** (☎ 415-431-2453; www.sfbike.org).

the Golden Gate Bridge (see the boxed text), a coastal jaunt or a tour of other Marin County towns. From the ferry terminal, an easy option is to head south on Bridgeway Blvd, veering left onto East Rd toward the Bay Area Discovery Museum. Another nice route heads north along Bridgeway Blvd, then crosses under Hwy 101 to Mill Valley. At Blithedale Ave, you can veer east to Tiburon; a bike path parallels parts of Tiburon Blvd.

For information on routes, regulations and group rides, contact the **Marin County Bike Coalition** (☎ 415-456-3469; www.marinbike.org), publisher of the *Marin Bicycle Map*.

Mike's Bikes (☎ 415-332-3200; 1 Gate 6 Rd; bikes for 24hr $30), at the north end of Bridgeway Blvd near Hwy 101, rents out road and mountain bikes. Supplies are limited and reservations are not accepted.

Sleeping

Gables Inn (☎ 415-289-1100, 800-966-1554; www.gablesinnsausalito.com; 62 Princess St; r $135-325; P) In a historic home with nine guest rooms, Gables offers quietude and proximity to the water. The more expensive rooms have Jacuzzi baths, fireplaces and balconies with spectacular views. But even the smaller, cheaper rooms are stylish and tranquil. Breakfast and evening wine are included.

Hotel Sausalito (☎ 415-332-4155; www.hotelsausalito.com; 16 El Portal; r $145-190, ste $270-290; ☒) The grand old hotel right downtown was built in 1915. Each guestroom has been decorated in Mediterranean hues and even the bathrooms are sumptuously appointed.

Casa Madrona Hotel & Spa (☎ 415-332-0502, 800-288-0502; http://casamadrona.com; 801 Bridgeway

Blvd; r $149-379; P ☒) Uphill from Sausalito town, the Casa Madrona is a compound of contemporary cottages around an original Victorian mansion. Accommodations are luxurious indeed. Smaller mansion rooms are cheaper than the more private cottages. There's also an excellent Italian restaurant, Poggio.

Eating

Bridgeway Blvd is packed with both moderately priced cafés as well as more costly restaurants.

Sushi Ran (☎ 415-332-3620; 107 Caledonia St; items $4-15) Many Bay Area residents claim this place is the best sushi spot around. A wine and sake bar next door eases the pain of the long wait for a table.

Fish (☎ 415-331-3474; 350 Harbor Dr; mains $10-19; ☽ Wed-Sun) Fish looks down home, with its redwood picnic tables and chalkboard menu. Items like tuna melts, chowders and the day's catch clearly don't aim to impress, but everything is fresh (whether sustainably fished from the ocean or responsibly farmed), the preparation is superior and the atmosphere is perfect.

Guernica (☎ 415-332-1512; 2009 Bridgeway Blvd; mains $11-15) This restaurant has been serving Basque meals in a comfortable, lived-in atmosphere for more than a quarter of a century. Paella's the way to go here.

Caffe Tutti (12 El Portal Dr) This café has strong cappuccinos, excellent French pastries and sit-down meals.

Drinking

Alta Mira Hotel (125 Bulkley Ave) A cocktail on the heated terrace of this hotel, the entire bay stretched out in front of you, is almost obligatory.

No Name Bar (757 Bridgeway) It's worth dropping by this old bohemian tavern, where a laid-back crowd is occasionally treated to live bands.

Getting There & Away

Driving to Sausalito from San Francisco, take the Alexander Ave exit (the first exit after the Golden Gate Bridge) and follow the signs into Sausalito. There are five municipal parking lots in town, which are worth using as street parking restrictions are strictly enforced.

Golden Gate Transit (☎ 415-923-2000; www.golden gatetransit.org) buses 10 and 50 run daily to Sausalito from San Francisco (one-way $3.25). Catch them at 1st and Mission Sts outside the Transbay Terminal.

The ferry is a fun and easy method for getting to Sausalito. **Golden Gate Ferries** (☎ 415-923-2000; one-way fare $6.45) operates to and from the San Francisco Ferry Building. The ferries operate nine times daily and the trip takes 30 minutes. The **Blue & Gold Fleet** (☎ 415-773-1188; Pier 41, Fisherman's Wharf; one-way fare $7.50) sails to Sausalito year-round and you can transport bicycles for free.

TIBURON

pop 8900

At the end of a small peninsula pointing out into the center of the bay, Tiburon is blessed with gorgeous views, much like Sausalito. It's a small community, but has a handful of fine restaurants that constitute destinations in themselves. The name comes from the Spanish Punta de Tiburon (Shark Point). Take the ferry from San Francisco, browse the shops on Main St, grab a bite to eat and you've seen Tiburon. The town is also the jumping-off point for nearby Angel Island (see opposite).

Orientation & Information

The central part of town is comprised of Tiburon Blvd, with Juanita Lane and charming Main St arcing off. Main St, which is also known as Ark Row, is where the old houseboats have taken root on dry land and metamorphosed into classy shops and boutiques.

The **Tiburon Peninsula Chamber of Commerce** (☎ 415-435-5633; www.tiburonchamber.org; 96B Main

St; ⏰ 8am-4pm Mon-Fri) can provide information about the area.

Sights & Activities

There are great views from the lovely hillside surrounding **Old St Hilary's Church** (☎ 415-435-1853; 201 Esperanza; ⏰ 1-4pm Wed-Sun Apr-Oct), a fine 19th-century example of Carpenter Gothic.

The Angel Island–Tiburon Ferry offers **sunset cruises** (☎ 415-435-2131; adult/child $12/7) on Friday and Saturday evenings from May to October. Reservations are recommended.

Back toward Hwy 101 the **Richardson Bay Audubon Center** (☎ 415-388-2524; 376 Greenwood Beach Rd; ⏰ 9am-5pm Sun-Fri), off Tiburon Blvd, is home to a huge variety of waterbirds.

Sleeping & Eating

Water's Edge Hotel (☎ 415-789-5999; 25 Main St; r $185-255) This hotel, with its deck extending out over the bay, is exemplary for its tasteful modernity. Rooms have an elegant minimalism that combines comfort and style, and all afford an immediate view of the bay and have a fireplace. The rooms with rustic wood ceilings are quite romantic.

Caprice (☎ 415-435-3400; 2000 Paradise Dr; mains $23-32) Here's an intimate waterfront spot. The views are spectacular, especially at sunset, and the food (steaks and chops served with a Continental flair) is nearly equal.

Sam's Anchor Cafe (☎ 415-435-4527; 27 Main St; mains $11-24) Even shambling little shacks like this one have unbeatable views. Sam's has been slinging seafood and burgers since 1920. You might also have a cocktail on the deck, as many local professionals do.

Guaymas (☎ 415-435-6300; 5 Main St; mains $10-18) Noisy Guaymas, also on the waterfront, packs in a fun, boisterous crowd. Margaritas energize the place, and solid Mexican seafood dishes help keep people upright.

Getting There & Away

Golden Gate Transit (☎ 415-923-2000; www.goldengate transit.org) bus 10 travels from San Francisco (one-way $3.95) and Sausalito (one-way $2) via Mill Valley to Tiburon. During the week, commute bus 8 runs direct between San Francisco and Tiburon.

On Hwy 101, look for the off-ramp for Tiburon Blvd, E Blithedale Ave and Hwy 131; driving east, it leads into town and intersects with Juanita Lane and Main St.

DETOUR: ANGEL ISLAND

Angel Island (☎ 415-435-1915; www.angelisland.org), in San Francisco Bay, has a mild climate with fresh bay breezes that make the island pleasant for hiking and biking. For a unique treat, spread out a picnic in a protected cove overlooking the close but immeasurably distant urban surroundings. You can camp on the island, and at night the shadowy cargo ships passing nearby are eerie and cool. The island's varied history – it was a hunting and fishing ground for the Miwok people, served as a military base, an immigration station, a WWII Japanese internment camp and a Nike missile site – has left it with some interesting and thought-provoking old forts and bunkers to poke around in. Most recently it was the site of a native-plant restoration project.

There are 12 miles of roads and trails around the island, including a hike to the summit of 781ft **Mt Livermore** (no bikes) and a 5-mile perimeter trail. On weekends and holidays, the **Immigration Station**, which operated 1910-40, is open and staffed with docents. **Camp Reynolds**, the **East Garrison Chapel**, and the **Guard House** at Fort McDowell offer guided tours. At 1pm and 2pm, a Civil War cannon is fired from the shore near Camp Reynolds.

On Sunday between May and October, **Sea Trek Ocean Kayaking** (☎ 415-488-1000, www.sea trekkayak.com; tours per person 2½hr/day $75/130) offers guided kayaking excursions around Angel Island. Tours include equipment and instructions, and the day-long trip includes lunch.

The island has nine hike-in **campsites** (☎ 800-444-7275; www.reserveamerica.com; sites $20). You need to reserve months in advance. For meals, bring a picnic. A snack bar, called the **Cove Cafe** (☎ 415-897-0715; Ayala Cove; ☑ Sat & Sun Apr-Nov), is near the ferry dock and purveys very basic, packaged meals (for cash only).

From San Francisco, take a **Blue & Gold Fleet** (☎ 415-773-1188) ferry from Pier 41. From May to September, there are three ferries a day on weekends and two on weekdays; the rest of the year the schedule is reduced. Round-trip tickets cost $13.50 for adults and $8 for children.

From Tiburon, take the **Angel Island–Tiburon Ferry** (☎ 415-435-2131; www.angelislandferry.com), which costs $10 for the round-trip; add $1 for bicycles.

You can rent bicycles at Ayala Cove for $10/30 per hour/day, and there are **tram tours** (☎ 415-897-0715; tours #13.75) around the island. Schedules vary seasonally; go to www.angelisland.com for more information.

Blue & Gold Fleet (☎ 415-773-1188; Pier 41, Fisherman's Wharf; one-way $7.50) sails daily from San Francisco to Tiburon; ferries dock right in front of the Guaymas restaurant on Main St. You can transport bicycles for free. From Tiburon, ferries also connect regularly to nearby Angel Island.

MILL VALLEY
pop 13,300

Nestled under the redwoods at the base of Mt Tamalpais, tiny Mill Valley is one of the Bay Area's most picturesque hamlets. It was originally a logging town, the name stemming from an 1830s sawmill that was the first in the Bay Area to provide lumber. Though the 1892 Mill Valley Lumber Company still greets motorists on Miller Ave, the town's a vastly different place today, packed with wildly expensive homes, fancy cars and pricey boutiques.

Mill Valley also served as the starting point for the scenic railway that carried visitors up Mt Tam (see p147). The tracks were removed in 1940, and today the Depot Bookstore & Cafe occupies the space of the former station.

Mill Valley visitor information is available from the **chamber of commerce** (☎ 415-388-9700; www.millvalley.org; 85 Throckmorton Ave; ☑ 10am-4pm Mon-Fri).

Sights & Activities

Several blocks west of downtown along Throckmorton Ave is **Old Mill Park**, perfect for a picnic. Here you'll also find a replica of the town's namesake sawmill. Just past the bridge at Old Mill Creek, the **Dipsea Steps** mark the start of the Dipsea Trail.

Said to have been founded by 35 Mill Valley ladies determined to preserve the local environment, the private **Outdoor Art Club** (☎ 415-388-9886; www.outdoorartclub.org; cnr W Blithedale & Throckmorton Aves) is housed in a landmark 1904 building designed by Bernard Maybeck.

Amidst the antiques and bath-products shops downtown is the long-standing record store **Village Music** (☎ 415-388-7400; www.village music.com; 9 E Blithedale Ave). The walls plastered with memorabilia give it a museum feeling.

Each October the **Mill Valley Film Festival** (☎ 415-383-5256) presents an innovative, internationally regarded program of independent films.

Tennessee Valley Trail, in the Marin Headlands, offers beautiful views of the rugged coastline and is one of the most popular hikes in Marin (expect crowds on weekends). It has easy, level access to the beach and ocean and is a short 3.8 miles, though it can get windy. From Hwy 101, take the Mill Valley–Stinson Beach–Hwy 1 exit and turn left onto Tennessee Valley Rd from the Shoreline Hwy; follow it to the parking lot and trailhead.

A more demanding option is the 7-mile **Dipsea Trail**, which climbs over the coastal range and down to Stinson Beach, cutting through a corner of Muir Woods. The trail starts at Old Mill Park with a climb up 676 steps in three separate flights, and includes a few more steep ups and downs before reaching the ocean.

Sleeping

Mountain Home Inn (☎ 415-381-9000; www.mtnhome inn.com; 810 Panoramic Hwy; r $175-325; **P**) Set amidst redwood, spruce and pine tress on a ridge of Mt Tam, this retreat is both modern and rustic. The larger (more expensive) rooms are rugged beauties, with unfinished timbers forming columns from floor to ceiling as though the forest is shooting up through the floor. Smaller rooms are cozy dens for two. Rooms have fireplaces and high-speed Internet but no TVs.

Acqua Hotel (☎ 415-380-0400, 888-662-9555; www .marinhotels.com/acqua_guestrooms.html; 555 Redwood Hwy; r $129-169; **P** **X** **🔅**) With views of the bay and Mt Tam, the Acqua strives to soothe its guests. Rooms are sleekly designed with subtle exotic touches here and there for very modern sensibilities.

Fireside Motel (☎ 415-332-6906; 115 Shoreline Hwy; s/d $55/75) A decent older property with tons of roadside character. Just off Hwy 101, you can't miss the big signs.

Eating

Buckeye Roadhouse (☎ 415-331-2600; 15 Shoreline Hwy; mains $12-19) A classic from the days when roadhouses were a common stop along the highway, the Buckeye is a Marin County gem. The food, American to the core, far surpasses traditional truck stop fare. Seared *ahi* (tuna) salad, fresh sole and Mongolian spiced pork chops appeal to contemporary taste buds and won't leave anyone hungry.

Avatar's Punjab Burritos (15 Madrona St; burritos from $5) For a quick bite, try the tasty lamb and curry burritos.

Depot Bookstore & Cafe (87 Throckmorton Ave; meals under $10) Smack in the town center, Depot serves cappuccinos, sandwiches and light meals. The bookstore sells lots of local publications, including trail guides.

Entertainment

Sweetwater (☎ 415-388-2820; www.sweetwatersaloon .com; 153 Throckmorton Ave) A most intimate music venue, the Sweetwater regularly books renowned folk, blues and world music talents. When there's no music it's still a comfortable pub.

Getting There & Away

From San Francisco or Sausalito, take Hwy 101 north to the Mill Valley–Stinson Beach–Hwy 1 exit. Follow Hwy 1 (also called the Shoreline Hwy) to Almonte Blvd (which becomes Miller Ave), then follow Miller Ave into downtown Mill Valley.

From the north, take the E Blithedale Ave exit from Hwy 101, then head west into downtown Mill Valley.

Golden Gate Transit (☎ 415-923-2000; www.golden gatetranist.org) bus 4 runs from San Francisco to Mill Valley ($3.25) on weekdays; on weekends take bus 10, which also stops in Sausalito and Tiburon.

LARKSPUR, SAN ANSELMO & CORTE MADERA

The inland towns of Larkspur, Kentfield, Corte Madera, Ross, San Anselmo and Fairfax evoke charmed small-town life, even though all are clustered around busy Hwy 101 and Sir Francis Drake Blvd. Some very fine restaurants here await hungry hikers.

In **Larkspur**, window-shop along Magnolia Ave or explore the redwoods in nearby Baltimore Canyon. On the east side of the freeway is the hulking mass of **San Quentin State Penitentiary**, California's oldest and most notorious prison, founded in 1852. Johnny Cash recorded an album here in

1969 after scoring a big hit with his live *Folsom Prison* album a few years earlier.

San Anselmo has a cute, small downtown area, including several antique shops, along San Anselmo Ave. **Corte Madera** is home to one of the Bay Area's best bookstores, **Book Passage** (☎ 415-927-0960; 51 Tamal Vista Blvd), in the Market Place shopping center. It has a strong travel section, plus frequent author appearances.

Lark Creek Inn (☎ 415-924-7766; 234 Magnolia Ave, Larkspur; mains $18-35) is in a lovely spot and is a fine-dining experience. It's housed in an old Victorian building tucked away in a redwood canyon, and the farm-fresh American food (roast veal, seared scallops, roasted chestnut ravioli) is gratifying. The main dining room has a Sunday dinner formality, but you can also dine in the adjacent bar.

Fork (☎ 415-453-9898; 198 Sir Francis Drake Blvd, San Anselmo; small plates $5-9, mains $15-17; ⏲ lunch & dinner Tue-Sat) is an unassuming little spot that is as relaxed as it looks, and its French-Californian inflected menu is very inviting. You can construct a meal of small plates or, if really famished, go for lamb loins or fish and potatoes.

Golden Gate Transit (☎ 415-923-2000; www.golden gatetransit.org) offers a daily ferry service from the Ferry Building in San Francisco to Larkspur Landing on E Sir Francis Drake Blvd, directly east of Hwy 101. The trip takes 50 minutes and costs $6.45. You can take bicycles on the ferry.

SAN RAFAEL
pop 54,800

San Rafael, the oldest and largest town in Marin, is slightly less upscale than most of its neighbors but doesn't lack atmosphere. It's a common stop for travelers on their way to Point Reyes. Just north of San Rafael, Lucas Valley Rd heads west to Point Reyes Station, passing George Lucas' Skywalker Ranch. Fourth St, San Rafael's main drag, is lined with cafés and shops. If you follow it west out of downtown San Rafael, it meets Sir Francis Drake Blvd and continues west to the coast.

Sights & Activities

The town began with **Mission San Rafael Arcángel** (☎ 415-454-8141; 1104 5th Ave; ⏲ museum 11am-4pm), founded in 1817 which served as a sanitarium for Native Americans suffering

from European diseases. The present building is a replica dating from 1949.

Designed by Frank Lloyd Wright, the **Marin County Civic Center** (☎ 415-472-3500) is a long, beautiful structure blending into the hills directly east of Hwy 101; exit on N San Pedro Rd, 2 miles north of San Rafael. Tours begin here Wednesday at 10:30am; reserve by calling ☎ 415-499-6646. The center hosts regular concerts and events, including the **Marin County Fair** each July and a **farmers market** every Thursday and Sunday morning.

China Camp State Park (☎ 415-456-0766), about 4 miles east of San Rafael is a pleasant place to stop for a picnic or short hike. From Hwy 101, take the N San Pedro Rd exit and continue 3 miles east. The name comes from the remains of a Chinese fishing village here, one of many Chinese shrimp-fishing encampments once prevalent around San Francisco Bay.

Rafael Film Center (☎ 415-454-1222; 1118 4th St), a restored downtown cinema run by the Film Institute of Northern California, offers innovative art house programming in state of the art surroundings.

Sleeping & Eating

Panama Hotel (☎ 415-457-3993; www.panamahotel .com; 4 Bayview St; r $100-160) This is a 16-room B&B dating from 1910, with charm, history and style. The hotel restaurant has an inviting patio. If traveling solo, the hotel has cozy singles with shared bathrooms for $75.

China Camp State Park (☎ 415-456-0766, reservations 800-444-7275; sites $12) This park has 30 walkin campsites.

Las Camelias (912 Lincoln Ave; meals $12-20) Las Camelias is a favorite for homemade Mexican meals that go beyond tacos and enchiladas. Good margaritas, too.

Getting There & Away

Numerous **Golden Gate Transit** (☎ 415-923-2000; www.goldengatetransit.org) buses operate between San Francisco and the San Rafael Transit Center at 3rd and Hetherton Sts. Bus 40 is the only service that takes bicycles across the Golden Gate Bridge.

MT TAMALPAIS STATE PARK

Standing guard over Marin County, majestic Mt Tamalpais (Mt Tam) has breathtaking 360-degree views of ocean, bay and hills rolling into the distance. The rich, natural beauty of 2571ft Mt Tam and the surrounding area is inspiring – especially considering that it lies within an hour's drive from one of the state's largest metropolitan areas.

Mt Tamalpais State Park was formed in 1930, partly from land donated by Congressman and naturalist William Kent (who also donated the land that became Muir Woods National Monument in 1907). Its 6300 acres are home to deer, foxes, bobcats and many miles of hiking and biking trails.

Mt Tam was a sacred place to the coastal Miwok people for thousands of years before the arrival of European and American settlers. By the late 19th century, San Franciscans were escaping the bustle of the city with all-day outings on the mountain, and in 1896 the 'world's crookedest railroad' (281 turns) was completed from Mill Valley to the summit. Though the railroad was closed in 1930, Old Railroad Grade is today one of Mt Tam's most popular and scenic hiking and biking paths.

Orientation & Information
Panoramic Hwy climbs from Mill Valley through the park to Stinson Beach. **Pantoll Station** (☎ 415-388-2070; 801 Panoramic Hwy) is the park headquarters. Detailed park maps are sold here.

Sights
From Pantoll Station, it's 4.2 miles by car to **East Peak Summit**; take Pantoll Rd and then panoramic Ridgecrest Blvd to the top. Parking is $6 and a 10-minute hike leads to the very top and the best views.

The park's natural-stone, 4000-seat **Mountain Theater** (☎ 415-383-1100) hosts the annual 'Mountain Play' series on six Sundays between mid-May and late June. Free shuttles are provided from Mill Valley. Free **astronomy programs** (☎ 415-455-5370) also take place here each summer around the new moon.

Activities
HIKING
The park map is a smart investment, as there are a dozen worthwhile hiking trails in the area. From Pantoll Station, the **Steep Ravine Trail** follows a wooded creek on to the coast (about 2.1 miles each way). For a longer hike, veer right (northwest) after 1.5 miles onto the **Dipsea Trail**, which meanders through trees for 1 mile before ending at Stinson Beach.

Grab some lunch, then walk north through town and follow signs for the **Matt Davis Trail**, which leads 2.7 miles back to Pantoll Station, making a good loop. The Matt Davis Trail continues on beyond Pantoll Station, wrapping gently around the mountain with superb views.

Another worthy option is **Cataract Trail**, which runs along Cataract Creek from the end of Pantoll Rd; it's approximately 3 miles to Alpine Lake. The last mile is a spectacular rooty staircase as the trail descends alongside Cataract Falls.

MOUNTAIN-BIKING
Bikers must stay on fire roads (and off the single-track trails) and keep speeds under 15mph. The rangers take these rules seriously, and a ticket can result in a steep fine.

The most popular ride is the **Old Railroad Grade**. For a sweaty, 6-mile, 2280ft climb, start in Mill Valley at the end of W Blithedale Ave and bike up to East Peak. It takes about an hour to reach the **West Point Inn** from Mill Valley. For an easier start, begin partway up at the Mountain Home Inn (see p146) and follow the **Gravity Car Grade** to the Old Railroad Grade and the West Point Inn. From the Inn, it's an easy half-hour ride to the summit.

From just west of Pantoll Station, bikers can either take the **Deer Park fire road**, which runs close to the Dipsea Trail, through giant redwoods to the main entrance of Muir Woods, or the southeastern extension of the **Coastal Trail**, which has breathtaking views of the coast before joining Hwy 1 about 2 miles north of Muir Beach. Either option requires a return to Mill Valley via Frank Valley/Muir Woods Rd, which climbs steadily (800ft) to Panoramic Hwy and then becomes Sequoia Valley Rd as it drops toward Mill Valley. A left turn on Wildomar and two right turns at Mill Creek Park lead to the center of Mill Valley at the Depot Bookstore & Cafe.

For further information on bike routes and rules, contact the **Marin County Bike Coalition** (☎ 415-456-3469; www.marinbike.org).

Sleeping & Eating
Pantoll Station (☎ 415-388-2070; sites $15) From the parking lot it's a 100yd walk to the campground, with 16 tent sites but no showers.

Steep Ravine Environmental Campground (☎ reservations 800-444-7275; campsites/cabins $15/60) Just off Hwy 1 about 1 mile south of Stinson Beach, this place has six beachfront campsites and several rustic five-person cabins overlooking the ocean. Both options are booked out months in advance and reservations can be made up to seven months ahead.

West Point Inn (☎ 415-388-9955) Hosts monthly pancake breakfasts during the summer, a hearty reward for all those switchbacks.

Getting There & Away
To reach Pantoll Station, take Hwy 1 to the Panoramic Hwy and look for the Pantoll signs. On weekends and holidays you can take **Golden Gate Transit** (☎ 415-923-2000; www .goldengatetransit.org) bus 63 from the Marin City transfer station to Pantoll Station and the Mountain Home Inn.

MUIR WOODS NATIONAL MONUMENT
Walking through an awesome stand of the world's tallest trees is an experience to be had only in Northern California and a small part of southern Oregon. The old-growth redwoods at **Muir Woods** (☎ 415-388-2595; admission $3; ⏰ 8am-sunset, 8am-5pm in winter), just 12 miles north of the Golden Gate Bridge, is the closest redwood stand to San Francisco. The trees, of course, were initially eyed by loggers, and Redwood Creek, as the area was known, seemed ideal for a dam. Those plans were halted when Congressman and naturalist William Kent bought a section of Redwood Creek and, in 1907, donated 295 acres to the federal government. President Theodore Roosevelt made the site a national monument in 1908, the name honoring John Muir, naturalist and founder of environmental organization the Sierra Club.

Muir Woods can become quite crowded, especially on weekends. Try to come midweek, early in the morning or late in the afternoon, when tour buses are less of a problem. Even at busy times, a short hike will get you out of the densest crowds and onto trails with huge trees and stunning vistas.

Hiking
An gentle walk is the 1-mile **Main Trail Loop** alongside Redwood Creek to the 1000-year-old trees at **Cathedral Grove**; it returns via **Bohemian Grove**, where the tallest tree in the park stands 254ft high. The **Dipsea Trail** is a good 2-mile hike up to the top of aptly named **Cardiac Hill**.

You can also walk down into Muir Woods by taking trails from the Panoramic Hwy, such as the **Bootjack Trail** from the Bootjack picnic area, or from Mt Tamalpais' Pantoll Station campground, along the **Ben Johnson Trail**.

Getting There & Away
Muir Woods is just 12 miles north of the Golden Gate Bridge. Driving north on Hwy 101, exit at Hwy 1 and continue north along Hwy 1/Shoreline Hwy to the Panoramic Hwy (a right-hand fork). Follow that for about 1 mile to Four Corners, where you turn left onto Muir Woods Rd (there are plenty of signs). There are no direct buses to Muir Woods – a fact that's seriously silly since parking and traffic are real problems. However, at the time of writing, there was a summer shuttle bus in the works. Check www.nps.gov/muwo for more information.

THE COAST
Muir Beach
The turnoff to Muir Beach from Hwy 1 is marked by the longest row of mailboxes on the North Coast. Muir Beach is a quiet little town with a nice beach, but it has no direct bus service. Just north of Muir Beach there are superb views up and down the coast from the **Muir Beach Overlook**; during WWII, watch was kept from the surrounding concrete lookouts for invading Japanese ships.

Pelican Inn (☎ 415-383-6000; www.pelicaninn.com; 10 Pacific Way; r from $200) is the only commercial establishment in Muir Beach. The downstairs restaurant and pub is an anglophile's dream and perfect for pre- or post-hike nourishment (meals $9 to $25).

Green Gulch Farm & Zen Center (☎ 415-383-3134; www.sfzc.com; 1601 Shoreline Hwy) is a Buddhist retreat in the hills above Muir Beach. The center's **Lindisfarne Guest House** (r $75-155, cottage $200) is elegant, restful, modern and Japanese in style. Buffet-style vegetarian meals are offered. The Center's Hope Cottage is a hilltop retreat 25 minutes away by foot.

Stinson Beach
The town of Stinson Beach, 5 miles north of Muir Beach, flanks Hwy 1 for about three blocks and is densely packed with galleries, shops, eateries and B&Bs. The beach itself is often blanketed with fog and when the sun's shining, it's blanketed with surfers, families

and gawkers. Nevertheless it's nice, with views of Point Reyes and San Francisco on clear days, and the beach is long enough for a vigorous stroll. From San Francisco it's nearly an hour's drive, though on weekends plan for long traffic delays.

Three-mile-long **Stinson Beach** is a popular surf spot, but swimming is advised from late May to mid-September only; for updated weather and surf conditions call ☎ 415-868-1922. The beach is one block west of Hwy 1.

Around 1 mile south of Stinson Beach is Red Rock Beach. It's a clothing-optional beach that attracts smaller crowds, probably because it's accessed by a steep trail from Hwy 1.

About 3.5 miles north of town on Hwy 1, in the hills above the Bolinas Lagoon, the **Audubon Canyon Ranch** (☎ 415-868-9244; www.egret .org; donations requested; ☉ 10am-4pm Sat, Sun & holidays mid-Mar–mid-Jul) is a major nesting ground for great blue herons and great egrets.

Stinson Beach Motel (☎ 415-868-1712; www.stinsonbeachmotel.com; 3416 Hwy 1; r $85-200) is managed by a muscle man named Frodo. This 70-year-old motel is a collection of remodeled beach cottages surrounded by gardens. Nothing fancy, but it's only two blocks from the beach.

Parkside Cafe (☎ 415-868-1272; 43 Arenal Ave; mains $9-19) is famous for its hearty breakfasts and lunches, and noted far and wide for its excellent coastal cuisine. For dinner, reservations are recommended.

Golden Gate Transit (☎ 415-923-2000; www.goldengatetransit.org) bus 63 runs to Stinson Beach, on weekends only, from the Marin City transfer center.

Bolinas

For a town that is so famously unexcited about tourism, Bolinas offers some fairly tempting attractions for the visitor. Known as Jugville during the Gold Rush days, the sleepy beachside community of Bolinas is home to writers, musicians and fisherfolk, and it is deliberately hard to find. The highway department used to put up signs at the turnoff from Hwy 1, and locals kept taking them down so the highway department finally gave up.

The free monthly *Pacific Coastal Post* gives an interesting perspective on local and world events.

SIGHTS & ACTIVITIES
Bolinas Museum (☎ 415-868-0330; www.bolinasmuseum.org; 48 Wharf Rd; ☉ 1-5pm Fri, noon-5pm Sat & Sun) has exhibits showcasing local artists as well as highlighting the region's history.

There are tide pools along some 2 miles of coastline at **Agate Beach**, around the end of Duxbury Point. The **Point Reyes Bird Observatory** (☎ 415-868-1221; ☉ 9am-5pm), off Mesa Rd west of downtown, has bird-banding and netting demonstrations, monthly guided walks, a visitors center and nature trail. Banding demonstrations are in the morning every Tuesday to Sunday from May to late November and on Wednesday, Saturday and Sunday the rest of the year.

Beyond the observatory is the Palomarin parking lot and access to various **walking trails**, including the easy (and popular) 2-mile trail to lovely **Bass Lake** and, beyond it, **Alamere Falls** and **Wildcat Beach**.

SLEEPING & EATING
Smiley's Schooner Saloon & Hotel (☎ 415-868-1311; www.coastalpost.com/smileys; 41 Wharf Rd; r $74-84) This is a crusty old place dating back to 1851, with simple but decent rooms. The bar has live bands on weekends and is frequented by plenty of salty dogs and grizzled deadheads.

Blue Heron Inn (☎ 415-868-1102; www.blueheron-bolinas.com; 11 Wharf Rd; r incl breakfast $125) This inn has two rooms tastefully decorated with antiques and a small restaurant, open for dinner Thursday through Monday. Meals ($16 to $21) are made with local ingredients, including organic free-range meats from nearby Niman Ranch.

GETTING THERE & AWAY
By car, follow Hwy 1 north from Stinson Beach. The turnoff for Bolinas is the first past Audubon Canyon Ranch, on the left. Parking in town is scarce.

Olema & Nicasio
About 10 miles north of Stinson Beach near the junction of Hwy 1 and Sir Francis Drake Blvd, Olema was the main settlement in West Marin in the 1860s. Back then, there was a stagecoach service to San Rafael and there were *six* saloons. In 1875, when the railroad was built through Point Reyes Station instead of Olema, the town's importance began to fade. In 1906, it gained distinction again as the epicenter of the Great Quake.

The **Bolinas Ridge Trail**, a 12-mile series of ups and downs for hikers or bikers, starts about 1 mile west of Olema, on Sir Francis Drake Blvd. It has great views.

About a 15-minute drive inland from Olema, at the geographic center of Marin County, is Nicasio, a tiny town with a low-key rural flavor and a cool saloon and music venue. It's at the west end of Lucas Valley Rd 10 miles from Hwy 101.

Olema Inn (☎ 415-663-9559; www.theolemainn.com; 1000 Sir Francis Drake Blvd; r $145-185) This six-room inn and restaurant is a very stylish and peaceful country retreat. Rooms retain some of the building's antiquated charm, but are up to modern standards of comfort. The Cal-Med restaurant delivers with finely prepared, heartwarming meals ($16 to $28) for lunch on the weekends and dinner nightly except Tuesday.

Six miles east of Olema on Sir Francis Drake Blvd, **Samuel P Taylor State Park** (☎ 415-488-9897; sites $15) has beautiful, secluded campsites in redwood groves.

In the town center, **Rancho Nicasio** (☎ 415-662-2219; mains $13-25; ☽ dinner daily, brunch Sat & Sun) is the local fun spot. It's a rustic saloon which regularly attracts local and national blues, rock and country performers.

On weekends and holidays, **Golden Gate Transit** (☎ 415-923-2000; www.goldengatetransit.org) bus 65 runs to Olema and Samuel P Taylor State Park from the San Rafael Transit Center.

Point Reyes Station

Though the railroad stopped coming through in 1933 and the town is small, Point Reyes Station is nevertheless the hub of West Marin. Dominated by dairies and ranches, the region was invaded by artists in the '60s. Today it's an interesting blend of art galleries and tourist shops. The town has a rowdy saloon and the occasional smell of cattle on the afternoon breeze.

The weekly *Point Reyes Light* has local news and helpful listings of events, restaurants and lodgings.

Cute little cottages, cabins and B&Bs are plentiful in and around Point Reyes. The **West Marin Chamber of Commerce** (☎ 415-663-9232; www.pointreyes.org) has numerous listings. The only budget choice is the **Point Reyes Hostel** (☎ 415-663-8811; dm/r $16/54) at the nearby Point Reyes National Seashore (see p152).

Holly Tree Inn (☎ 415-663-1554; www.hollytreeinn.com; Silverhills Rd; r $130-180, cottages $190-265), off Bear Valley Rd, has four rooms and three private cottages in a beautiful country setting. Its Sea Star Cottage is a romantic refuge at the end of a small pier on Tamales Bay.

Station House Cafe (☎ 415-663-1515; 11180 Shoreline Hwy; dinner mains $10-20) needs help with the decor, but the kitchen observes California standards of preparation and the food is quite good, with organic local meats and many vegetarian options.

Bovine Bakery (Shoreline Hwy) has great coffee and even better homemade pastries.

Tomales Bay Foods and Cowgirl Creamery (80 4th St) is a local market in an old barn. Picnic items, including gourmet cheeses and organic produce, are available.

Dance Palace (☎ 415-663-1075; 503 B St) has weekend events, movies and live music.

Western Hotel (cnr Shoreline Hwy & 2nd St) is a rustic 1906 saloon with occasional live bands.

Hwy 1 becomes Main St in town, running right through the center. On weekends and holidays, **Golden Gate Transit** (☎ 415-923-2000; www.goldengatetransit.org) bus 65 runs to Point Reyes Station from the San Rafael Transit Center ($5).

Inverness

This tiny town, the last outpost on your journey westward, is spread along the west side of Tomales Bay. It's got good places to eat and, among the surrounding hills and picturesque shoreline, multiple rental cottages and quaint B&Bs. Several great beaches are only a short drive north.

Blue Waters Kayaking Tours & Rentals (☎ 415-669-2600; www.bwkayak.com; 12938 Sir Francis Drake Blvd; kayak rental 2/4 hrs $30/45), at the Golden Hinde Inn, offers various Tomales Bay cruises, or you can rent a kayak and paddle around secluded beaches and rocky crevices on your own; no experience necessary.

Manka's Inverness Lodge (☎ 415-669-1034; www.mankas.com; r $195-245) was originally built as a hunting lodge in 1917, but has shrewdly updated the rugged mountain-retreat concept. The rooms are comfortable and have a masculine elegance with leather sofas, rough-cut timbers and river-rock fireplaces. The 'indulgent' baths, however, clearly have a woman's sensibility in mind. The restaurant serves fabulous prix fixe meals ($58) focusing on wild, local ingredients and meats roasted on

SIR FRANCIS DRAKE

Sir Francis Drake was an extraordinary character: a self-made man, fearless, resourceful, clever, ruthless and very lucky. In 1577 he set off from England in a fleet of five small ships. His mission was exploration and adventure, to be financed by what could best be described as piracy, with the hated Spanish the intended victims.

In 1579 the *Golden Hind* was alone off the California coast. Two of the ships, brought only to carry supplies, had been abandoned. The third ship had sunk with all hands during the rounding of Cape Horn, and the fourth had lost contact and turned back to England. Drake and his crew had found rich pickings at the expense of the Spanish, but the *Golden Hind* was in sorry shape. Somewhere along the Marin County coast, possibly at Drakes Beach near Point Reyes, Drake put in to a sheltered bay, ran his ship aground at high tide and tipped it on its side to repair the ravaged hull. He stayed there for five weeks, trading with the local Native Americans and exploring inland, with one of his crew noting that the land was much more welcoming than it appeared from the sea.

Eventually Drake sailed off on a trip that would carry him right around the world and bring him back to England as a phenomenally wealthy and famous explorer. He cemented his fame by helping defeat the Spanish Armada in 1588.

an open fire. It's tucked up the hill on Argyle St, which is just north of town (look for signs off Sir Francis Drake Blvd).

Inverness Valley Inn (☎ 415-669-7250; www.inver nessvalleyinn.com; 13275 Sir Francis Drake Blvd; r $110-130; 🐾) is hidden away in the woods, just a mile from town. It offers clean, modern rooms in A-frame structures, is family friendly and has tennis courts, horseshoe pitches and barbecue pits. It's past the town, on the way down the Pt Reyes Peninsula.

From Hwy 1, Sir Francis Drake Blvd leads straight into Inverness. On weekends and holidays, **Golden Gate Transit** (☎ 415-923-2000; www.goldengatetransit.org) bus 65 makes its final stop here from San Rafael.

Point Reyes National Seashore

The windswept peninsula Point Reyes is a rough-hewn beauty that has always lured marine mammals and migratory birds as well as scores of shipwrecks. It was here in 1579 that Sir Francis Drake landed to repair his ship the *Golden Hind*. During his five-week stay he mounted a brass plaque near the shore claiming this land for England. Historians believe this occurred at Drakes Beach and there is a marker there today. In 1595 the first of scores of ships lost in these waters, the *San Augustine*, went down. She was a Spanish treasure ship out of Manila laden with luxury goods such as porcelain, and to this day bits of her cargo wash up on the shore. Despite modern navigation, the dangerous waters here continue to claim the odd boat.

Point Reyes National Seashore has 110 sq miles of pristine ocean beaches, and the peninsula offers excellent hiking and camping opportunities. Be sure to bring warm clothing, as even the sunniest days can quickly turn cold and foggy.

INFORMATION

The park headquarters, **Bear Valley Visitor Center** (☎ 415-663-1092; Bear Valley Rd; 🕙 9am-5pm Mon-Fri, 8am-5pm Sat & Sun), is near Olema and has information and maps. You can also get information at the Point Reyes Lighthouse and the **Ken Patrick Center** (☎ 415-669-1250; 🕙 10am-5pm Sat, Sun & holidays) at Drakes Beach.

SIGHTS & ACTIVITIES

For an awe-inspiring view, follow the **Earthquake Trail** from the park headquarters at Bear Valley. The trail reaches a 16ft gap between the two halves of a once-connected fence line, a lasting testimonial to the power of the 1906 earthquake that was centered in this area. Another trail leads from the visitors center a short way to **Kule Loklo**, a reproduction of a Miwok village.

Limantour Rd, off Bear Valley Rd about 1 mile north of Bear Valley Visitor Center, leads to the Point Reyes Hostel and to **Limantour Beach**. At the beach there's a trail that runs along Limantour Spit, with Estero de Limantour on one side and Drakes Bay on the other. The **Inverness Ridge Trail** heads from Limantour Rd up to 1282ft Mt Vision, from where there are spectacular views of the entire national seashore. You can drive almost to the top of Mt Vision from the other side.

About 2 miles past Inverness, Pierce Point Rd splits off to the right from Sir Francis Drake Blvd. From here you can get to two nice swimming beaches on the bay: Marshall Beach requires a mile-long hike from the parking area, while Hearts Desire, in **Tomales Bay State Park**, is directly accessible by car.

Pierce Point Rd continues to the huge windswept sand dunes at **Abbotts Lagoon**, full of peeping killdeer and other shorebirds. At the end of the road is Pierce Point Ranch, the trailhead for the 3.5-mile Tomales Point Trail through the **Tule Elk Reserve**. The elk are an amazing sight, standing with their big horns against the backdrop of Tomales Point, with Bodega Bay to the north, Tomales Bay to the east, and the Pacific Ocean to the west.

The **Point Reyes Lighthouse** (☎ 415-669-1534; ☺ 10am-4:30pm Thu-Mon) is at the very end of Sir Francis Drake Blvd. This spot, with its wild terrain and ferocious winds, feels like the end of the earth and offers the best **whale-watching** along the coast. The lighthouse sits below the headlands; to reach it requires descending (then ascending) over 300 stairs. Nearby **Chimney Rock** is an fine short hike, especially in spring when the wildflowers are blossoming. A nearby viewing area allows you to spy on the park's **elephant seal colony**.

On weekends during good weather, from late December through mid-April, the road to Chimney Rock and the lighthouse is closed to private vehicles. Instead you must take a shuttle ($2.50; children under 12 free) from **Drakes Beach**, a safe place to wade or swim.

If you're intrigued by the surf crashing onto the exposed North Beach and South Beach, make sure you keep back from the water's edge, as people have been dragged in and drowned by frequent rogue waves.

SLEEPING & EATING
Point Reyes Hostel (☎ 415-663-8811; dm/r $16/54) Just off Limantour Rd is this rustic HI property in a beautiful, secluded valley 2 miles from the ocean and surrounded by lovely hiking trails.

Point Reyes has four hike-in **campgrounds** (☎ 415-663-1092; sites $15) with pit toilets, untreated water and tables (no wood fires). Permits are required; reserve at the Bear Valley Visitor Center or by calling ☎ 415-663-8054. Reaching the campgrounds requires a 2- to 6-mile hike.

Drake's Bay and nearby Tamales Bay are famous for excellent oysters.

Johnson Oyster Company (☎ 415-669-1149; 17171 Sir Francis Drake Blvd, Inverness; 1 dozen oysters $5-7) This is a great place to stop for a snack to slurp a dozen on the half-shell.

GRAY WHALES
Gray whales may be seen at various points along the California coast, and the Point Reyes lighthouse is a superb viewpoint for observing these huge creatures on their annual 6000-mile migration. During summer, the whales feed in the Arctic waters between Alaska and Siberia. Around October, they start to move south down the Pacific coast of Canada and the USA to sheltered lagoons in the Gulf of California, by the Mexican state of Baja California.

The whales, led by the pregnant cows, pass Point Reyes in December and January. They're followed by pods of females and courting males, usually in groups of three to five, and then by the younger whales. The whales spend about two months around Baja California, during which time the pregnant whales give birth to calves 15ft or 16ft long and weighing 2000lb to 2500lb. The newborn whales put on 200lb a day, and in February the reverse trip begins.

Gray whales live up to 50 years, grow to 50ft in length and weigh up to 45 tons. Spotting whales is a simple combination of patience and timing. Spouting, the exhalation of moist warm air, is usually the first sign that a whale is about. A series of spouts, about 15 seconds apart, may be followed by a sight of the creature's tail as the whale dives. If you're lucky, you may see whales spy-hopping (sticking their heads out of the water to look around) or even breaching (leaping clear out of the water). Bring binoculars as whales are typically a quarter- to a half-mile out to sea, though they're closer to shore on the southbound leg of the journey.

SF Bay Whale Watching (☎ 415-331-6267; www.sfbayadventures.com; tours per person $85-100) leads whale-watching expeditions during migration seasons. Trips run from San Francisco's City Yacht Harbor (10 Marina Blvd) out to the Farallon Islands. Reservations are required.

GETTING THERE & AWAY

By car you can get to Point Reyes a few different ways. The curviest is along Hwy 1, through Stinson Beach and Olema. More direct is to exit Hwy 101 in San Rafael and follow Sir Francis Drake Blvd all the way to the tip of Point Reyes. For the latter route, take the Central San Rafael exit and head west on 4th St, which turns into Sir Francis Drake Blvd. By either route, it's about 1½ hours to Olema from San Francisco.

Just north of Olema, where Hwy 1 and Sir Francis Drake Blvd come together, is Bear Valley Rd; turn left to reach the Bear Valley Visitor Center. If you're heading to the further reaches of Point Reyes, follow Sir Francis Drake Blvd through Point Reyes Station and out onto the peninsula, about an hour's drive.

On weekends and holidays, **Golden Gate Transit** (☎ 415-923-2000; www.goldengatetransit.org) bus 65 makes stops at the Bear Valley Visitor Center, Olema, Point Reyes Station and Inverness ($5).

EAST BAY

By 'East Bay,' most San Franciscans simply mean Oakland and Berkeley, although the area includes numerous other suburbs that swoop up from the bayside flats into exclusive enclaves in the hills. While many residents of the big city would like to think they needn't ever cross the Bay Bridge or take a BART train under water, it is undeniable that the city would be incomplete if it didn't have its East Bay. Museums, celebrity restaurants, universities, woodsy parklands and better weather are just some ways the East Bay lures travelers from San Francisco.

OAKLAND

pop 402,100

Oakland, having suffered every mid-20th-century ailment, has slowly come back to life. It has always been an important African American cultural center, with music, literature and art flowing through the city's tough veins. Oakland, with less than half San Francisco's population, has more urban grit and moxie than its bigger neighbor. It also has a lovely old downtown, with many architectural gems surviving from the early

---

> **SAY WHAT, GERTRUDE?**
>
> The writer Gertrude Stein, who lived in Oakland during her school years, returned to her old neighborhood as an adult in 1934 and was distraught over its dissolution. Her famous line, 'There is no *there* there,' is frequently misapplied by Oakland's detractors, as though Stein meant to say that Oakland was nowheresville. In fact, Stein was expressing her disappointment on discovering the loss of her old home.

20th century, and a sweet little saltwater lake in the heart of town. It is a city of neighborhood joints, local groceries, small clusters of clubs and restaurants.

Orientation

The two main freeways through Oakland are I-880 and I-580, which parallel each other. Adding to the city's maze of freeways, the short Hwy 980 runs right through downtown. Both split off from I-80 at the east end of the Bay Bridge and head south. The Bay Bridge lets you off in West Oakland, a heavily industrial area with residential pockets and housing projects. Downtown and Lake Merritt are southeast of there.

Broadway is the backbone of downtown Oakland, running from Jack London Sq at the waterfront all the way north to Piedmont and Rockridge. Telegraph Ave branches off Broadway at 15th St and heads straight to Berkeley. Running east from Broadway is Grand Ave, leading to the Lake Merritt commercial district. San Pablo Ave heads north from downtown into Berkeley. Large regional parks rise into the hills along the city's eastern border. East Oakland spreads southeast toward San Leandro and Fremont; generally speaking it's best avoided, unless you're heading to the Oakland Coliseum or the airport.

Downtown BART stations are on Broadway at both 12th and 19th Sts; other stations are near Lake Merritt and in Rockridge.

Information

Oakland's daily newspaper is the *Oakland Tribune*. The free weekly *East Bay Express* has good Oakland and Berkeley listings.
Diesel (☎ 510-653-9965; 5433 College Ave) One of Oakland's many fine new and used bookstores.

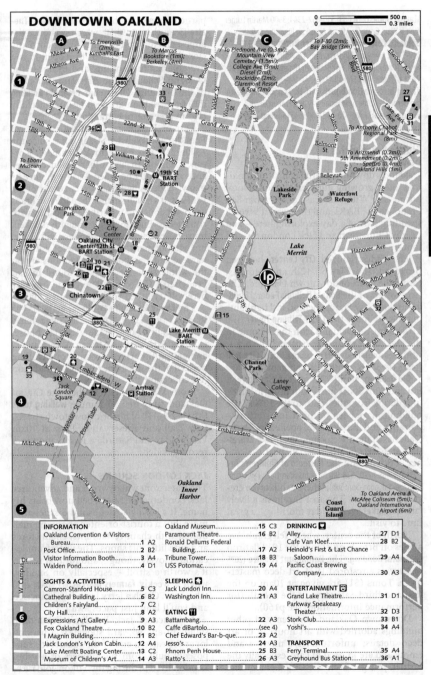

DOWNTOWN OAKLAND

SAN FRANCISCO BAY AREA

INFORMATION
Oakland Convention & Visitors
  Bureau.................................**1** A2
Post Office...............................**2** B2
Visitor Information Booth..........**3** A4
Walden Pond...........................**4** D1

SIGHTS & ACTIVITIES
Camron-Stanford House............**5** C3
Cathedral Building....................**6** B2
Children's Fairyland..................**7** C2
City Hall..................................**8** A2
Expressions Art Gallery.............**9** A3
Fox Oakland Theatre...............**10** B2
I Magnin Building....................**11** B2
Jack London's Yukon Cabin......**12** A4
Lake Merritt Boating Center.....**13** C2
Museum of Children's Art........**14** A3

Oakland Museum....................**15** C3
Paramount Theatre.................**16** B2
Ronald Dellums Federal
  Building...............................**17** A2
Tribune Tower........................**18** B3
USS Potomac..........................**19** A4

SLEEPING
Jack London Inn.....................**20** A4
Washington Inn......................**21** A3

EATING
Battambang............................**22** A3
Caffe diBartolo....................(see 4)
Chef Edward's Bar-b-que........**23** A2
Jesso's...................................**24** A3
Phnom Penh House.................**25** B3
Ratto's...................................**26** A3

DRINKING
Alley.....................................**27** D1
Cafe Van Kleef.......................**28** B2
Heinold's First & Last Chance
  Saloon...............................**29** A4
Pacific Coast Brewing
  Company............................**30** A3

ENTERTAINMENT
Grand Lake Theatre.................**31** D1
Parkway Speakeasy
  Theater...............................**32** D3
Stork Club.............................**33** B1
Yoshi's..................................**34** A4

TRANSPORT
Ferry Terminal.......................**35** A4
Greyhound Bus Station............**36** A1

Marcus Bookstore (☎ 510-652-2344; 3900 Martin Luther King Jr Way) Great for African American literature or history.
Oakland Convention & Visitors Bureau (☎ 510-839-9000; www.oaklandcvb.com; 475 14th St, Suite 120; ⊗ 8:30am-5pm Mon-Fri) Between Broadway and Clay St.
Post office (1446 Franklin St)
Visitor information booth (Jack London Sq) Underneath the Barnes & Noble near Broadway and Embarcadero.
Walden Pond (☎ 510-832-4438; 3316 Grand Ave) Another fine bookstore.

Sights & Activities
DOWNTOWN
Oakland's downtown is full of historic buildings and a growing number of colorful local businesses. With such easy access from San Francisco via BART and the ferry, it's worth spending part of a day exploring here – and nearby Chinatown and Jack London Sq – on foot.

The pedestrianized **City Center**, between Broadway and Clay St, 12th and 14th Sts, forms the heart of downtown Oakland. The twin towers of the **Ronald Dellums Federal Building** are on Clay St, just behind it. Highlighting the skyline is the 1923 **Tribune Tower** (13th & Franklin Sts), an Oakland icon that's home to the *Oakland Tribune* newspaper. The beautiful, refurbished 1914 beaux arts **City Hall** (14th & Clay Sts) is another urban gem.

Old Oakland, along Washington St between 8th and 10th Sts, is lined with historic buildings dating from the 1860s to the 1880s. The buildings have been restored and some restaurants and hotels have opened up here. Galleries in the area include the funky **Expressions Art Gallery** (815 Washington St), near the corner of 8th St, and the **Museum of Children's Art** (☎ 510-465-8770; 538 9th St; admission free; ⊗ 10am-5pm Tue-Sat, noon-5pm Sun), where exhibits are created by children. The area also hosts a lively **farmers market** every Friday morning – a great time to visit.

North of the center, where Telegraph Ave angles off Broadway, stands the 1913 flatiron **Cathedral Building**. The **Paramount Theatre** (2025 Broadway) is a restored 1931 art deco masterpiece. Tours ($1) are given at 10am on the first and third Saturdays of the month (for performance information, see p160).

Downtown Oakland has plenty of other buildings adorned with art nouveau or art deco details; unfortunately, many stand empty and are in need of care, especially the further you get from the City Center. One particular jewel is the 1928 **Fox Oakland Theatre** (Telegraph Ave & 19th St), which was once the largest cinema west of Chicago; it's currently closed but plans are afoot to reopen it as a live entertainment venue and to house the Oakland School of the Arts on other parts of the building. The stellar **I Magnin Building** (2001 Broadway) is an art deco beaut, gracefully clad in green terra cotta tiling.

East of Broadway, **Chinatown** centers on Franklin and Webster Sts, as it has since the 1870s. It's also home to Vietnamese, Korean, Cambodian and other Asian cultures and might better be called Asiatown, since its many residents hail from every corner of the Far East. It's much smaller than the San Francisco version but nevertheless bustles with commerce. English is infrequently spoken, tourists are few, and Oaklanders will argue, not without merit, that its Chinese (and Vietnamese and Cambodian) restaurants are on the whole superior to those found in San Francisco's C-Town. At any rate, nobody here will try to sell you cheap tourist junk.

The **Ebony Museum** (☎ 510-763-0141; 1034 14th St; admission from $3; ⊗ 11am-6pm Tue-Sat), a dense collection in a ramshackle Victorian house, exhibits African and African American art and antiquities. Head upstairs for a chilling perusal of the museum's Black Degradation Art collection.

From May through October, the City of Oakland runs free 90-minute **walking tours** (☎ 510-238-3234) of historic downtown streets, City Hall and Preservation Park at 10am Wednesday and Saturday. Reservations are recommended.

JACK LONDON SQUARE
The waterfront where writer and adventurer Jack London once raised hell now bears his name. It's hardly a roughshod district anymore, but a tourist-oriented shopping mall dotted with chain restaurants, chain stores and cute little gift shops. The waterfront location is lovely, though, and for that reason it's worth a stroll – especially on Sunday, when a weekly **farmers market** (⊗ 10am-2pm) takes over. Catch a ferry from San Francisco and you'll land just paces away.

A replica of Jack London's **Yukon cabin** stands in an awkward spot near a parking lot at the eastern end of the square. It's supposedly built from the timbers of a cabin London lived in during the Yukon gold rush,

OAKLAND'S IMPERIAL WALKERS

The huge container cranes hovering threateningly above the Oakland docks are said to have inspired the Imperial Walkers that George Lucas dreamed up for *The Empire Strikes Back*.

though many of the original materials had to be replaced during reconstruction. Another worthwhile stop, adjacent to the old cabin, is **Heinhold's First & Last Chance Saloon** (p159).

The 165ft **USS Potomac** (☎ 510-627-1215; www.usspotomac.org; admission $7; 10:30am-3:30pm Wed, noon-3:30pm Fri & Sun), Franklin D Roosevelt's 'floating White House,' is moored at Clay and Water Sts by the ferry dock, and is open for dock-side tours. Two-hour history **cruises** (adult/child $40/20) are also held several times a month from April to October; call for reservations. They leave from Jack London Sq.

LAKE MERRITT
Lake Merritt is an urban jewel and a popular place to stroll or go running (a 3.5-mile track circles the lake). Once a tidal marsh teeming with waterfowl, it became a lake in 1869 with the damming of an arm of the Oakland Estuary. The following year, the state legislature designated Lake Merritt a wildlife refuge, the first in the USA. The lake still supports migratory waterfowl, and it's still connected to the estuary via a culvert, so its 155 acres are saltwater. Like many other Bay Area parks, Lake Merritt is fine during the day, but be cautious at night.

Near the southern end of the lake is the **Oakland Museum** (☎ 510-238-2200; 1000 Oak St; adult/child/student $8/free/5, 2nd Sun of month free; 10am-5pm Wed-Sat, noon-5pm Sun, 10am-9pm 1st Fri of month), which has rotating exhibitions on artistic as well as scientific themes, not to mention three worthwhile permanent galleries. These are dedicated to the state's diverse ecology; its history, from its native past to the suburban present; and California art, from lavish 19th-century landscapes to edgy contemporary works. The Lake Merritt BART station is a block away.

Lakeside Park, at the northern end of the lake, includes **Children's Fairyland** (☎ 510-452-2259; admission $6; 10am-4pm daily summer, Wed-Sun spring & fall, Fri-Sun winter), which dates from 1950 and has charming fairy tale–themed rides

and displays that'll delight kids and parents alike. For a jaunt on the lake, the **Lake Merritt Boating Center** (☎ 510-238-2196; 10.30am-4pm) rents canoes, rowboats, kayaks, pedal boats and sailboats. Hourly charges are $8 to $15.

In the late 19th century, Lake Merritt was lined with fine homes, only one of which remains: the 1876 **Camron-Stanford House** (☎ 510-444-1876; 1418 Lakeside Dr; tours $5). There are tours on the second and third Wednesday (11am to 4pm) and on the third Sunday (1pm to 5pm) each month. But the best aspect of the house is really its wonderful lakeside setting and the hint it gives of how Oakland looked in its Victorian heyday, which can be admired from the sidewalk.

The two main commercial streets skirting Lake Merritt are **Lakeshore Ave** on the eastern edge of the lake and **Grand Ave**, running along the north shore. Both have some nice spots for meals (see p159), cocktails and coffee (see p159).

PIEDMONT AVE & ROCKRIDGE
North of downtown Oakland, Broadway becomes a lengthy strip of car dealerships called Broadway Auto Row. Just past that is Piedmont Ave, wall-to-wall antique stores, coffeehouses, fine restaurants and an art cinema. At the end of Piedmont Ave, **Mountain View Cemetery** (☎ 510-658-2588; 5000 Piedmont Ave) is perhaps the most serene and lovely man-made landscape in all the East Bay. Designed by Frederic Law Olmstead, the man who designed New York City's Central Park, it's great for walking and the views are stupendous.

Another popular shopping area is **Rockridge**, a lively, upscale neighborhood. It is centered on College Ave, which runs from Broadway all the way to the UC Berkeley Campus. College Ave is lined with clothing boutiques, good bookstores, a vintage record shop, several pubs and cafés, and quite a few upscale restaurants – maybe the largest concentration in the Bay Area. You could easily spend a satisfying afternoon or evening browsing, eating and drinking here. Exiting BART at the Rockridge station puts you in the thick of things.

THE OAKLAND HILLS
East of downtown and the I-580, the streets become convoluted, winding through exclusive communities such as Montclair before

reaching the ridgeline, where a series of parks edge the hills.

Opened in 2000, the **Chabot Space & Science Center** (☎ 510-336-7300; www.chabotspace.org; 10000 Skyline Blvd, Oakland; adult/child $13/9; ☺ 10am-5pm Wed & Thu, 10am-10pm Fri & Sat, 11am-5pm Sun) is a science and technology center in the Oakland Hills, with loads of exhibits on subjects such as space travel and eclipses. The center's open Friday and Saturday evenings for **planetarium shows** and – check it out – free viewing through a 20in refractor telescope (weather permitting).

The large parks of the Oakland Hills are ideal for day hiking. Information is available from the **East Bay Regional Parks District** (☎ 510-562-7275; 2950 Peralta Oaks Ct). The district manages 59 regional parks, preserves and recreation areas in the Alameda and Contra Costa counties, which contain some 1000 miles of trails.

Off Hwy 24, **Robert Sibley Volcanic Regional Preserve** is the northernmost of the Oakland Hills parks. It has great views of the Bay Area from its Round Top Peak (1761ft), an old volcano cone. From Sibley, Skyline Blvd runs south past **Redwood Regional Park** and adjacent **Joaquin Miller Park** to **Anthony Chabot Regional Park**. A hike or mountain-bike ride through the groves and along the hilltops of any of these sizable parks will make you forget you're in an urban area. At the southern end of Chabot Park is the enormous **Lake Chabot**, with an easy trail along its shore and canoes, kayaks and other boats for rent from the **Lake Chabot marina** (☎ 510-582-2198).

AC Transit bus 53 runs daily from the Fruitvale BART station to the Chabot Center and Joaquin Miller Park. Bus 46 runs from the Coliseum BART along Skyline Blvd, during weekday commute hours.

INTERNATIONAL BOULEVARD

Formerly known as E 14th St and once a neglected part of town, International Blvd is now a great place to stroll on a Sunday afternoon. Latino and Asian immigrants have turned it into a 3-mile carnival of food and festivities. You'll find an impressive fleet of excellent taco trucks parked along Fruitvale Ave or at the corner of High St and International Blvd. The Bay Area's best *pho* (Vietnamese noodle soup) joints are just blocks away. Mexican and Central American restaurants rub elbows with Vietnamese. Dive

bars selling cheap beer and margaritas open their doors here and there. Families out for the paseo, squads of young men, bevies of young women, strolling musicians and pushcart sellers of tamales and ice cream jam the boulevard and bring it to life every week.

Sleeping

Oakland has a few nice hotels downtown and in the hills, but budget choices – at least clean ones in safe secure neighborhoods – are less plentiful. You're better off looking in San Francisco or Berkeley.

A good option to consider is a B&B. The **Berkeley and Oakland Bed & Breakfast Network** (☎ 510-547-6380; www.bbonline.com/ca/berkeley-oakland) has listings of 20 private homes that rent rooms, suites and cottages; prices start from $90 or so per night. Reservations a week or two in advance are recommended. Most homes are nonsmoking.

Washington Inn (☎ 510-452-1776; www.thewashingtoninn.com; 495 10th St, Oakland; r $118-158; ☒) This historic downtown hostelry offers updated comfort and character, with a lobby and guest rooms that project snazz and efficient sophistication. The carved lobby bar is perfect for a pre-dinner cocktail, and you're surrounded by several fine restaurants.

Claremont Resort and Spa (☎ 510-843-3000, 800-551-7266; www.claremontresort.com; 41 Tunnel Rd; r $165-420; ☒ ☐ ☒) Near Rockridge, the Claremont is top of the heap if you're looking to indulge. Inside this glamorous, white 1915 building are classy restaurants, a fitness center, swimming pools, tennis courts and a full-service spa (room/spa packages are available).

Jack London Inn (☎ 510-444-2032, 800-549-8780; www.jacklondoninn.com; 444 Embarcadero W; r $95-130; ☒ ☐ ☒) An affordable 1950s-style motor lodge in Jack London Sq, with clean, simple rooms.

There are 75 campsites in **Anthony Chabot Regional Park** (☎ 510-639-4751; sites $18), a few miles south of Oakland off I-580. Reservations ($7 service charge) can be arranged by calling ☎ 510-562-7275.

Eating
DOWNTOWN

Ratto's (821 Washington St; sandwiches from $5) If you want to eat outside on a sunny day, grab a sandwich from Ratto's, a vintage Oakland grocery (since 1897) with a deli counter that attracts a devoted lunch crowd.

Jesso's (☎ 510-451-1561; 901 Washington St; mains $9-15; ☽ lunch & dinner Wed-Mon) Jesso's is a simple charmer with indoor and outdoor seating and a full bar. Heavy on Cajun dishes, but also serving good, reliable fish and chips, poor boy sandwiches, okra, collards, beans and rice, it's very family friendly.

Chef Edward's Bar-b-que (1998 San Pablo Ave; mains from $5) The Piggly Wiggly sandwich at this tiny place is a fabulous treat, and the service is equally sweet.

Phnom Penh House (251 8th St; mains under $10) and **Battambang** (850 Broadway; mains under $10) are excellent Cambodian restaurants.

LAKE MERRITT
Arizmendi (3265 Lakeshore Ave; pizza slices $3) On a commercial strip just north of MacArthur Blvd is Arizmendi, a bakery co-op selling gourmet pizza by the slice, along with hearty pastries and breads.

Spettro (3355 Lakeshore Ave; mains $10-16; ☽ dinner) Spettro has a quirky decor and friendly attitude that keeps fans coming back for its homespun, culturally mixed cuisine. Pizzas, stir fries and chili Colorado give an idea of the unusual mix offered. Very family friendly.

Caffe diBartolo (3310 Grand Ave; sandwiches $6-8) Grab a sidewalk table or head for the back courtyard at this smart café. You can enjoy hot panini sandwiches or just wake up with a strong coffee.

PIEDMONT AVE & ROCKRIDGE
Some of the East Bay's finest restaurants are in these two hopping shopping areas along College and Piedmont Aves. Reservations are recommended for the first four placed noted below.

Bay Wolf (☎ 510-655-6004; 3853 Piedmont Ave; mains lunch $12-18, dinner $17-25) At this deservedly famous eatery the menu changes each fortnight, but the emphasis is always Mediterranean. It attracts a well-to-do crowd, but dining on the plant-shrouded, heated front porch is a charming, relaxed experience.

Oliveto Cafe & Restaurant (☎ 510-547-5356; 5655 College Ave; mains $16-27; ☽ café 7am-10pm Mon-Sat, 8am-9pm Sun, restaurant lunch Mon-Fri, dinner Thu-Tue) Oliveto is one of the finest restaurants in Oakland. The specialties are house-cured meats and handmade pastas. You can have a cocktail or a pizza in the downstairs café, where the sidewalk tables are nice on a warm day.

À Côté (☎ 510-655-6469; 5478 College Ave; dishes $4-14; ☽ dinner Tue-Sun) It's one of the best restaurants along College Ave, because À Côté appeals to locals with fine taste. Small plates are the specialty, so while they are priced quite low you might have a lot of them. What the menu calls 'flatbread' is actually pizza for the gods. Mussels with Pernod is a signature dish.

Red Tractor Cafe (☎ 510-595-3500; 5634 College Ave; meals $6-8) More family friendly and downhome is this cheery and aromatic eatery serving affordable comfort food such as roast turkey and meatloaf (a meatless version is also available).

Zachary's Pizza (☎ 510-655-6385; 5801 College Ave; pizzas $12-16) Heavy-duty Chicago-style pizzas are the specialty here, though the thin-crust pizzas are just as good, if not better. Expect a long wait for a table.

Drinking
Cafe Van Kleef (☎ 510-763-7711; 1621 Telegraph Ave) On an otherwise quiet block, this artsy bar is trying to start something downtown. The owner and his staff are quite cordial, and bands play many nights to a usually full house. It's a real fun spot.

Alley (☎ 510-444-8505; 3325 Grand Ave) The Alley has a staged shore-leave feel to it, but it's so old and worn out the place has become a genuine article of its own unique category. Injecting a nightly shot of subdued life is the bar's hard-living piano player, Rod Dibble, and his troupe of regular fans, who pass a microphone around.

Heinold's First & Last Chance Saloon (☎ 510-839-6761; 56 Jack London Sq) You'll have to hold onto your beer here. The floor and bar at Heinhold's have had a 20% slant since the 1906 earthquake tried to set the tiny tavern on its end. Watch that first step. It's a doozy. But Heinhold's real claim to fame is that author Jack London was a regular patron.

Pacific Coast Brewing Company (906 Washington St) Right in the heart of Old Oakland, this place serves full meals alongside its own tasty brews (try the Gray Whale Ale).

For beer fans, there are a couple of bustling spots with large selections of microbrews, plus pub food: **Ben & Nick's** (562 College Ave), located in Rockridge, and **Cato's Alehouse** (3891 Piedmont Ave), which is a few blocks off Broadway.

Entertainment

LIVE MUSIC

Yoshi's (☎ 510-238-9200; 510 Embarcadero W; shows $15-30) Yoshi's has a solid jazz calendar, with jazz talent from around the world passing through on a near-nightly basis. Often, touring artists will stop in for a stand of two or three nights. It's also a Japanese restaurant, so you might enjoy a sushi plate before the show.

Kimball's East (☎ 510-658-2555; 5800 Shellmound St) In Emeryville, northwest of Oakland, this huge jazz supper club books big-name musicians and the occasional comedy act. The club's in the Emerybay Public Market; from I-80 take the Powell St exit.

Stork Club (2330 Telegraph Ave) The Stork is a funky dive catering to the East Bay's indie-rock scene with an eclectic lineup of punk, experimental, lo-fi, spoken word, country and other performers.

5th Amendment (3255 Lakeshore Ave) A lively Lake Merritt venue that's popular with African American professionals. The bar books local jazz and blues bands and has a friendly, flirty atmosphere.

THEATERS & CINEMAS

Paramount Theatre (☎ 510-465-6400; www.paramounttheatre.com; 2025 Broadway) This massive art deco theater shows classic films a few times each month – an amazing experience. The theater is also home to the Oakland East Bay Symphony (☎ 510-446-1992) and the Oakland Ballet (☎ 510-465-6400) and periodically books big-name concerts.

Grand Lake Theatre (☎ 510-452-3556; 3200 Grand Ave) This place, in Lake Merritt, is another beauty, and it has one of the hugest screens around (avoid the dinky screening room).

Parkway Speakeasy Theater (☎ 510-814-2400; 1834 Park Blvd) Two blocks east of Lakeshore Ave is this great, laid-back movie-going experience. It shows quality second-run films in a comfy setting and serves beer, wine, sandwiches and pizza.

SPORTS

BASS (☎ 510-762-2277) You can book for game tickets through BASS but expect a heavy booking charge (euphemistically called a 'convenience' fee). A's tickets start at $8 for bleacher seats and $22 for infield seats. For most baseball games, it's no problem to just turn up and save the booking fee. Tickets to Warriors and Raiders games, however, often sell out well in advance.

Golden State Warriors (☎ 888-479-4667) The Bay Area's only NBA basketball team plays at the Oakland Arena.

Oakland A's (☎ 510-638-4900) The Bay Area's American League baseball team plays at McAfee Coliseum, off I-880 (Oakland Coliseum BART).

Raiders (☎ 510-864-5000) Also playing at the McAfee Coliseum are Oakland's NFL team, attracting a particularly rabid brand of fan.

Getting There & Away

AIR

Oakland International Airport (☎ 510-563-3300; www.flyoakland.com) is directly across the bay from San Francisco International Airport. Arriving in or departing from the Bay Area through smaller Oakland can make good sense, as it's usually less crowded. Note that Southwest Airlines flies into Oakland, not San Francisco.

BART

Within the Bay Area, the most convenient way to get to Oakland and back is by **BART** (☎ 415-989-2278, 510-465-2278). Trains run on a set schedule from 4am to midnight on weekdays, 6am to midnight on Saturday, and 8am to midnight Sunday. There are five different routes, operating at 15- or 20-minute intervals on average.

To downtown Oakland, catch a Richmond or Pittsburg/Bay Point train. Fares to the 12th or 19th St stations from downtown San Francisco are $2.55.

For Lake Merritt ($2.55) or the Oakland Coliseum/Airport station ($3.15), catch a BART train that is heading for Fremont or Dublin/Pleasanton. Rockridge ($2.90) is on the Pittsburg/Bay Point line.

Between Oakland and downtown Berkeley you can also catch a Fremont–Richmond train ($1.25).

A BART-to-Bus transfer ticket, available from white AC Transit machines near BART station exits, costs $1.25.

BUS

Regional company **AC Transit** (☎ 510-839-2882) runs convenient buses from San Francisco's Transbay Terminal, at Mission and 1st Sts, to downtown Oakland and Berkeley and between the two East Bay cities. A score of buses go to Oakland from San Francisco during commute hours (fares $3.50), but only the 'O' line runs both ways all day and on weekends; you can catch the 'O' line at the corner of 5th and Washington Sts in downtown Oakland.

If you are out late at night and want to get between San Francisco and Oakland, the 'A' line runs hourly between the Transbay Terminal and the corner of 14th St and Broadway.

Between Berkeley and downtown Oakland (fares $1.50) take bus 15, which runs via Martin Luther King Jr Blvd, or bus 40, which travels along Telegraph Ave between the two city centers. Bus 51, which runs along Broadway in Oakland and then along College Ave in Berkeley, is less direct but has some handy stops, including Rockridge, the UC Berkeley campus and the Berkeley Marina.

Greyhound (☎ 510-834-3213; 2103 San Pablo Ave) operates direct buses from Oakland to Vallejo, San Francisco, San Jose, Santa Rosa and Sacramento (the San Francisco terminal has many more direct-service options). The station is pretty seedy.

CAR & MOTORCYCLE
From San Francisco by car, cross the Bay Bridge and enter Oakland via one of two ways: I-580, which leads to I-980 and drops you near the City Center; or I-880, which curves through West Oakland and lets you off near the south end of Broadway. I-880 then continues to the coliseum, the Oakland International Airport and, eventually, San Jose.

FERRY
Ferries are the slowest and most expensive, but undoubtedly the most enjoyable, way of traveling between San Francisco and Oakland. From San Francisco's Ferry Building, the **Alameda-Oakland ferry** (☎ 510-522-3300) sails to Jack London Sq about 12 times a day on weekdays and six to nine times a day on weekends. The trip takes about 30 minutes, and the one-way fare is $5.50; buy tickets onboard. Ferry tickets include a free transfer, which you can use on AC Transit buses from Jack London Sq.

TRAIN
Oakland is a regular stop for Amtrak trains operating up and down the coast. From Oak-

land's **Amtrak station** (☎ 510-238-4306; 245 2nd St) in Jack London Sq, you can catch AC Transit bus 58, 72 or 73 to downtown Oakland, or take a ferry across the bay to San Francisco.

Amtrak passengers with reservations on to San Francisco need to disembark at the **Emeryville Amtrak station** (☎ 510-450-1081; 5885 Landregan St), one stop prior to Oakland. From there, an Amtrak bus will shuttle you to San Francisco's Transbay Terminal.

Getting Around
A taxi from Oakland International Airport to downtown Oakland costs about $30, to downtown San Francisco about $45. **Super-Shuttle** (☎ 800-258-3826) is one of many door-to-door shuttle services operating out of Oakland International Airport. One-way service to San Francisco destinations costs about $30 for the first person and $8 for the second. East Bay service destinations are also served. Call to reserve.

A cheap, easy transportation option is BART. Air-BART buses run between the airport and the Coliseum BART Station every 10 minutes. Tickets cost $2 and can be purchased from machines at the BART station or in airport terminals. AC Transit Bus 58 also travels between Oakland International Airport and Jack London Sq (stopping at the Coliseum BART Station); the local fare is $1.35.

AC Transit (☎ 510-839-2882) has a comprehensive bus network within Oakland. Bus 13 will take you from 14th St downtown to Lake Merritt and Lakeshore Ave. From Broadway downtown, bus 58 goes to Grand Ave; bus 59 runs from Jack London Sq to the Piedmont district; and bus 51 heads to Rockridge and UC Berkeley. Fares are $1.75 and exact change is required.

Weekdays between 11am and 2pm, the Broadway Shuttle provides free transportation along Broadway between the Kaiser Center (Webster and 20th Sts) and Jack London Sq.

BERKELEY
pop 102,750
With more than 30,000 students and enough Nobel Prize winners to give the Swedish Academy its reason for being, the University of California is clearly what makes Berkeley something more than a picturesque bedroom community. The student body is not

SAN FRANCISCO BAY AREA

BERKELEY

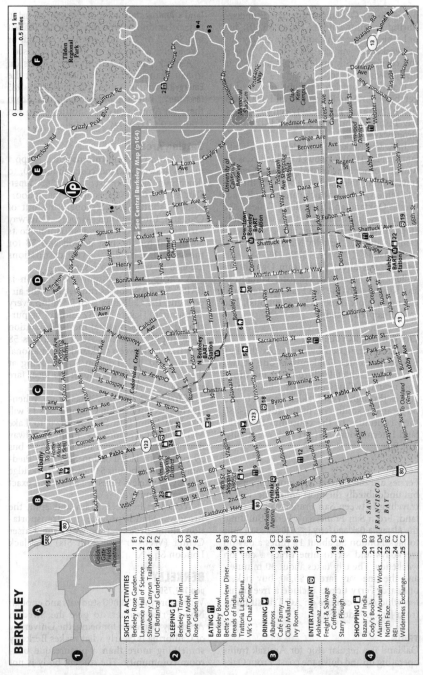

0　　1 km
0　　0.5 miles

SIGHTS & ACTIVITIES
Berkeley Rose Garden	1	E1
Lawrence Hall of Science	2	F2
Strawberry Canyon Trailhead	3	F2
UC Botanical Garden	4	F2

SLEEPING
Berkeley Travel Inn	5	C3
Campus Motel	6	D3
Rose Garden Inn	7	E4

EATING
Berkeley Bowl	8	D4
Bette's Oceanview Diner	9	B3
Breads of India	10	E4
Trattoria La Siciliana	11	E4
Vik's Chaat Corner	12	B3

DRINKING
Albatross	13	C3
Cafe Fanny	14	C4
Club Mallard	15	B1
Ivy Room	16	B1

ENTERTAINMENT
Ashkenaz	17	C2
Freight & Salvage Coffeehouse	18	C3
Starry Plough	19	E4

SHOPPING
Bazaar of India	20	D3
Cody's Books	21	B3
Marmot Mountain Works	22	D4
North Face	23	B2
REI	24	C2
Wilderness Exchange	25	C2

stirring things up the way it did during the free speech movement of the 1960s, but the city at large still seems to fire-breathe its politics. The town is thick with intellectual inquiry, discourse and creativity. For an idea of what Berkeley stands for, get stuck in the town's maddening traffic and catch up on your reading – of bumper stickers. Alongside 'Lick Bush in '04' (which you can rely on seeing until at least 2010), you can ponder complex-inducing mottoes such as 'Don't Believe Everything You Think!'

Much of Berkeley's youthful, radical culture concentrates on a few intense blocks of Telegraph Ave, immediately south of the University campus. It's a good shopping zone if you're after books and music, and the cafés here twitch with student energy. But probably the number one reason to visit Berkeley is to eat a fine meal at the northern end of Shattuck Ave. Chez Panisse and many of its offshoots operate along this drag through the town's 'hood of haute cuisine.

Orientation

Approximately 13 miles east of San Francisco, Berkeley is bordered by the bay to the west, the hills to the east and Oakland to the south. I-80 runs along the town's western edge, next to the marina; from here University Ave heads east to downtown and the campus.

Shattuck Ave crosses University Ave one block west of campus, forming the main crossroads of the downtown area. Immediately to the south is the downtown shopping strip and the Berkeley BART station. In North Berkeley, Shattuck becomes the Gourmet Ghetto.

San Pablo Ave is another major thoroughfare, crossing University Ave several blocks east of I-80. Heading north, San Pablo leads to Albany, El Cerrito, Richmond and other towns. To the south it takes you straight into downtown Oakland (about 5 miles).

If driving, the biggest navigational difficulties are the numerous barriers set up to prevent traffic from clogging residential streets. Traversing these areas often leads to backtracking and frustration. Parking isn't easy, either, especially near the campus or downtown. Try the city garages on Durant Ave near Telegraph Ave, or on Center St just west of Shattuck Ave (Map p164).

Information

Berkeley Convention & Visitors Bureau (Map p164; ☎ 510-549-7040, 800-847-4823, 24hr recorded info 510-549-8710; www.visitberkeley.com; 2015 Center St; ⏱ 9am-5pm Mon-Fri) This helpful bureau has free visitors packets and also sells the useful book *41 Walking Tours of Berkeley*.

Berkeley Historical Society (Map p164; ☎ 510-848-0181; 1931 Center St; tours $10) Offers excellent walking tours several times monthly, each exploring very specific themes.

UC Berkeley Visitor Services Center (Map p164; ☎ 510-642-5215; www.berkeley.edu; 101 University Hall, 2200 University Ave) Campus maps and information are available. Free 90-minute campus tours are given at 10am Monday to Saturday and 1pm Sunday.

Sights & Activities

UNIVERSITY OF CALIFORNIA, BERKELEY

The Berkeley campus of the University of California (called 'Cal' by both students and locals; Map p164) is the oldest university in the state. The decision to found the college was made in 1866, and the first students arrived in 1873. Today UCB has over 30,000 students, more than 1000 professors and more Nobel laureates than you could point a particle accelerator at.

From Telegraph Ave, enter the campus via Sproul Plaza and Sather Gate, a center for people-watching, soapbox oration and pseudotribal drumming. Or you can enter from Center and Oxford Sts, near the downtown BART station.

The **Campanile** (elevator rides $2; ⏱ 10am-4pm Mon-Fri, 10am-5pm Sat, 10am-1:30pm & 3-5pm Sun), which is officially called Sather Tower, was modeled on St Mark's Basilica in Venice. The 328ft spire offers fine views of the Bay Area, and at the top you can stare up into the carillon of 61 bells, ranging from the size of a cereal bowl to that of a Volkswagen. Recitals take place daily at 7:50am, noon and 6pm, with a longer piece performed at 2pm on Sunday.

UC Berkeley Art Museum (☎ 510-642-0808; 2626 Bancroft Way; adult/student $8/5, Thu free; ⏱ 11am-5pm Wed-Sun, 11am-7pm Thu) has 11 galleries showcasing a huge range of works from ancient Chinese to cutting-edge contemporary. The complex also houses a bookstore, café and sculpture garden, and the much-loved Pacific Film Archive (see p169).

Bancroft Library (☎ 510-642-3781; http://bancroft.berkeley.edu/; ⏱ 9am-5pm Mon-Fri) houses, among other gems, a copy of Shakespeare's First

Folio and the records of the Donner Party (see the boxed text, p348). Its small public exhibits of historical Californiana include the surprisingly small gold nugget that sparked the 1849 Gold Rush. You must register to use the library and, to do so, you need to be 18 (or to have graduated from high school) and present two forms of iden-

tification (one with a photo). Stop by the registration desk on your way in.

The **Museum of Paleontology** (☎ 510-642-1821; www.ucmp.berkeley.edu; admission free; ☼ atrium 8am-9pm Mon-Fri, 8am-5pm Sat & Sun), in the ornate Valley Life Sciences Building, is a research museum. It's mostly closed to the public, but you can see a few exhibits in

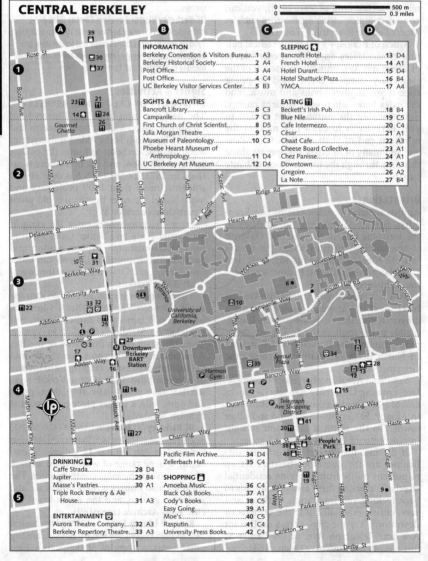

CENTRAL BERKELEY

0 _____ 500 m
0 _____ 0.3 miles

INFORMATION
Berkeley Convention & Visitors Bureau...**1** A3
Berkeley Historical Society..................**2** A4
Post Office.....................................**3** A4
Post Office.....................................**4** C4
UC Berkeley Visitor Services Center.....**5** B3

SIGHTS & ACTIVITIES
Bancroft Library..............................**6** C3
Campanile.....................................**7** C3
First Church of Christ Scientist...........**8** D5
Julia Morgan Theatre.......................**9** D5
Museum of Paleontology..................**10** C3
Phoebe Hearst Museum of
    Anthropology............................**11** D4
UC Berkeley Art Museum..................**12** D4

SLEEPING 🛏
Bancroft Hotel...............................**13** D4
French Hotel..................................**14** A1
Hotel Durant.................................**15** D4
Hotel Shattuck Plaza.......................**16** B4
YMCA..**17** A4

EATING 🍴
Beckett's Irish Pub..........................**18** B4
Blue Nile......................................**19** C5
Cafe Intermezzo.............................**20** C4
César...**21** A1
Chaat Cafe...................................**22** A3
Cheese Board Collective...................**23** A1
Chez Panisse.................................**24** A1
Downtown....................................**25** A3
Gregoire......................................**26** A2
La Note.......................................**27** B4

DRINKING 🍷
Caffe Strada.................................**28** D4
Jupiter...**29** B4
Masse's Pastries.............................**30** A1
Triple Rock Brewery & Ale
    House......................................**31** A3

ENTERTAINMENT 🎭
Aurora Theatre Company......**32** A3
Berkeley Repertory Theatre...**33** A3

Pacific Film Archive..........................**34** D4
Zellerbach Hall...............................**35** C4

SHOPPING 🛍
Amoeba Music................................**36** C5
Black Oak Books.............................**37** A1
Cody's Books.................................**38** C5
Easy Going....................................**39** A1
Moe's..**40** C5
Rasputin.......................................**41** C4
University Press Books......................**42** C4

the atrium, including a *Tyrannosaurus rex* skeleton.

South of the Campanile in Kroeber Hall, the **Phoebe Hearst Museum of Anthropology** (☎ 510-643-7648; adult/student $4/1, Thu free; ✆ 10am-4:30pm Wed-Sat, noon-4pm Sun) includes exhibits from indigenous cultures around the world, including ancient Peruvian, Egyptian and African items. There's also a large collection highlighting native Californian cultures.

SOUTH OF CAMPUS
Telegraph Ave (Map p164) is undeniably the throbbing heart of studentville in Berkeley, pumping out a sidewalk-flow of students and shoppers, vagrants and vendors, brisk walkers and sluggish strollers, those trying to squeeze their way out and those who never seem to leave.

The frenetic energy buzzing from the university's Sather Gate on any given day is a mixture of youthful post-hippies reminiscing about days before their time and young hipsters who sneer at tie-dyed nostalgia. Ponytailed panhandlers press you for change, and street stalls hawk everything from crystals to bumper stickers to self-published books. It's all very interesting, but the street is also immensely useful to anyone who loves browsing for books, and music. Cody's is arguably the best bookstore in the Bay Area, and Moe's is a three-level emporium of new and used titles. Across the street from both, Amoeba and Rasputin can help relieve music lovers of any excess savings they might have.

Just east of Telegraph, between Haste St and Dwight Way, is the site of **People's Park** (Map p164), a marker in local history as a political battleground between residents and city government in the late '60s. The park has since served mostly as an unofficial residence for Berkeley's homeless. A publicly funded restoration spruced it up a bit, and occasional festivals do still happen here, but on the surface it's still just a mangy patch of trampled grass.

On the park's southeast end stands Bernard Maybeck's impressive 1910 **First Church of Christ Scientist** (☎ 510-845-7199; 2619 Dwight Way; ✆ services Sun), which uses concrete and wood in its blend of Craftsman, Asian and Gothic influences. Maybeck was a professor of architecture at UC Berkeley and designed San Francisco's Palace of Fine Arts,

plus many landmark homes in the Berkeley Hills. Free tours are given the first Sunday of every month at 12:15pm.

To the southeast of the park is the beautifully understated, redwood-infused 1910 **Julia Morgan Theatre** (☎ 510-845-8542; 2640 College Ave), a performance space (formerly a church) created by Bay Area architect Julia Morgan, who designed numerous Bay Area buildings and, most famously, the Hearst Castle. South along College Ave is the **Elmwood District** (Map p162), a charming nook of shops and restaurants that offers a calming alternative to the frenetic buzz around Telegraph Ave. Continue further south and you'll be in Rockridge.

DOWNTOWN
Berkeley's downtown, which is centered on Shattuck Ave between University Ave and Dwight Way, has far fewer traces of the city's tie-dyed reputation. The area has emerged as a bustling neighborhood with numerous shops and restaurants, restored public buildings and a burgeoning arts district. At the center of that district are the acclaimed thespian stomping grounds of the Berkeley Repertory Theatre (see p169) and the **Aurora Theatre Company** (Map p164; 2081 Addison St); nearby are several good movie houses.

BOWLING FOR GROCERIES

A Berkeley institution since 1977, **Berkeley Bowl** (Map p162; ☎ 510-843-6929; 2020 Oregon St; ✆ 9am-8pm Mon-Sat, 10am-6pm Sun) got its name from its original location in a former bowling alley. Its narrow aisles offer the absolute best and worst of Berkeley: produce, deli goods, wines and organic dry goods of the highest quality threaten to topple off the shelves, while incredibly cranky and arrogant shoppers try to navigate oversize carts through the gridlock. The self-centered rudeness amidst piles of celery and bulk granola bins can be exasperating and at times is downright laughable. (Yoga, so popular in Berkeley, doesn't seem to put people in a positive mindset for the Bowl.) Get a picnic lunch here (weekdays, well ahead of the dinner rush, are relatively sane) and escape with it to Tilden Regional Park (p166) or the Berkeley Marina (p166).

NORTH BERKELEY

Just north of campus is a neighborhood filled with lovely homes, parks and some of the best restaurants in California. The popular **Gourmet Ghetto** (Map p164) stretches along Shattuck Ave north of University Ave for several blocks, anchored by Chez Panisse. Northwest of here, **Solano Ave** (Map p162), which crosses from Berkeley into Albany, is lined with lots of funky shops, more good restaurants and a couple of movie theaters.

North Berkeley, heading up into the hills, is also chock-full of magnificent homes. You can see numerous examples of Bernard Maybeck's superb architecture, including 1515 La Loma Ave and at 2704, 2711, 2733, 2751, 2754 and 2780 Buena Vista Way (Map p164). Wander these and other streets to examine the elaborate gardens and Asian-influenced front gates that are a feature of this neighborhood.

On Euclid Ave just south of Eunice St is the **Berkeley Rose Garden** (Map p162) and its eight terraces of Technicolor explosions. Here you'll find quiet benches and a plethora of almost perpetually blooming roses. Across the street is a picturesque park with a children's playground (including a fun concrete slide about 100ft long).

THE BERKELEY HILLS

In the hills east of town is Berkeley's crown jewel, **Tilden Regional Park** (Map p162; ☎ 510-562-7275). The 2077 acre park has more than 30 miles of trails of varying difficulty, from paved paths to hilly scrambles, including part of the magnificent Bay Area Ridge Trail. Other attractions include a miniature steam train ($1.75), children's farm, a wonderfully wild-looking botanical garden, 18-hole **golf course** (☎ 510-848-7373) and environmental education center. **Lake Anza** is a favorite area for picnics. From spring through late fall you can swim in Lake Anza for $3.50 (children $2.50). AC Transit bus 67 runs to the park from the downtown BART station.

The **Lawrence Hall of Science** (Map p162; ☎ 510-642-5132; Centennial Dr; adult/child $8.50/6.50; ☺ 10am-5pm daily), near Grizzly Peak Blvd, is named after Ernest Lawrence, who won the Nobel Prize for his invention of the cyclotron particle accelerator. He was a key member of the WWII Manhattan Project, and he's also the name behind Lawrence Berkeley and Lawrence Livermore laboratories. As for the Hall of Science, it has a huge collection of exhibits on subjects ranging from lasers to earthquakes and, outside, a 60ft model of a DNA molecule. AC Transit buses 8 and 65 run to the hall from the downtown BART station. You can also catch the university's Bear Transit shuttle (H line) from the Hearst Mining Circle.

Another great find in the hills is the **UC Botanical Garden** (Map p162; ☎ 510-643-2755; 200 Centennial Dr; adult/student $5/2, Thu free; ☺ 9am-5pm), in Strawberry Canyon, below the Hall of Science. With 34 acres and more than 13,000 species of plants, the garden is one of the most varied collections in the USA. It can be reached via the Bear Transit shuttle H line.

The nearby fire trail is a woodsy walking loop around Strawberry Canyon that has great views of town and of the off-limits Lawrence Berkeley National Laboratory. Enter at the trailhead at the parking lot on Centennial Dr just southwest of the Botanical Garden; you'll emerge near the Lawrence Hall of Science.

WEST BERKELEY

Hidden within an industrial area near I-80 lies a three-block area known as the **4th St Shopping District** (Map p162), offering shaded sidewalks for upscale shopping, or just strolling, and a few good restaurants too. Take heed, it's often very hard to park in this area, especially on weekends.

At the west end of University Ave is the **Berkeley Marina** (Map p162), frequented by squawking seagulls, silent types fishing from the pier, unleashed dogs and, especially on windy weekends, lots of colorful kites. Construction of the marina began in 1936, though the pier has much older origins. It was originally built in the 1870s, then replaced by a 3 mile–long ferry pier in 1920 (its length was dictated by the extreme shallowness of the bay). Part of the original pier is now rebuilt, affording visitors sweeping bay views.

San Pablo Ave was formerly US Rte 40, the main thoroughfare from the east before I-80 came along. The area north of University Ave is still lined with a few older motels, diners and atmospheric dive bars with neon signs. South of University Ave are pockets of trendiness, such as the short stretch of gift shops and cafés around Dwight Way.

Sleeping

The Berkeley Convention & Visitors Bureau can recommend local hotels. The **Berkeley & Oakland Bed & Breakfast Network** (☎ 510-547-6380; www.bbonline.com/ca/berkeley-oakland) has listings of private homes offering lodging, from rooms to secluded garden cottages.

AROUND CAMPUS & DOWNTOWN

Bancroft Hotel (Map p164; ☎ 510-549-1000, 800-549-1002; www.bancrofthotel.com; 2680 Bancroft Way; r $105-139) Here's traditional Berkeley at its best. Across from campus and near Telegraph Ave, the Bancroft is in a gorgeous 1928 Craftsman building that was originally a women's club. It has 22 comfortable, beautifully furnished rooms.

Hotel Durant (Map p164; ☎ 510-845-8981, 800-238-7268; www.hoteldurant.com; 2600 Durant Ave; r $120-160) The Durant, which is a block from campus and Telegraph Ave, is a classy 1928 establishment with 140 nice rooms and the popular Henry's Publick House and Grille downstairs.

YMCA (Map p164; ☎ 510-848-6800; 2001 Allston Way; s $39-46, d $50-60; 🏊) The best budget option, and compensation for the fact Berkeley doesn't have an official hostel, is the YMCA, in the heart of downtown. Rates for the small rooms (all with shared bathroom) include use of the sauna and pool. Advance bookings are recommended.

Hotel Shattuck Plaza (Map p164; ☎ 510-845-7300; www.hotelshattuckplaza.com; 2086 Allston Way; r $79-125) Also downtown and close to the BART station is this stately 174-room facility. Renovated by the Howard Johnson chain, it dates from 1910.

French Hotel (Map p164; ☎ 510-548-9930; 1538 Shattuck Ave; r $95-105) Right in the Gourmet Ghetto. The modern brick building has 18 very straightforward rooms. Downstairs is a popular café.

Rose Garden Inn (Map p162; ☎ 510-549-2145, 800-922-9005; www.rosegardeninn.com; 2740 Telegraph Ave, Berkeley; r $139-199) This charmer is quaint and just a few blocks down from the Telegraph Ave action. Two old houses are surrounded by pretty gardens. Breakfast and afternoon tea are included in the rates.

WEST BERKELEY

University Ave is dotted with budget motels. It's not the tidiest part of Berkeley, but many accommodations have been remodeled and are perfectly adequate and safe for overnighters.

Campus Motel (Map p162; ☎ 510-841-3844; 1619 University Ave; r $70-90) A small, simple, well-kept establishment with genuine 1950s character, near California St.

Berkeley Travel Inn (Map p162; ☎ 510-848-3840; 1461 University Ave; r $70-100) Near the Campus Motel is this equally acceptable option, another simple, 1950s-era place with a neat and clean appearance.

Eating

Telegraph Ave is packed with cafés, pizza counters and cheap restaurants. Many more restaurants can be found downtown along Shattuck Ave near the BART station. The section of Shattuck Ave north of University Ave is the 'Gourmet Ghetto,' home to a whole other batch of eating establishments, including California cuisine landmark Chez Panisse.

AROUND CAMPUS

Cafe Intermezzo (Map p164; 2442 Telegraph Ave; mains $5) Great for quick, filling meals, Intermezzo holds the title for the biggest and best sandwiches and salads; the bread's homemade as well.

Blue Nile (Map p164; 2525 Telegraph Ave; mains under $10) Serves great Ethiopian food in a peaceful, pleasant setting.

Trattoria La Siciliana (Map p162; 2993 College Ave; mains $8-16) An Italian hotspot south of campus among the restaurants of the charming Elmwood District.

NORTH BERKELEY

César (Map p164; ☎ 510-883-0222; 1515 Shattuck Ave; tapas $4-13) This airy tapas bar recalls a rustic Andalucían taverna with its heavy wooden benches and tables and open hearth. It turns out simple and delicious small dishes that change with the season. It's jammed at mealtimes, but is a perfect spot for an impromptu snack or a lazy afternoon beer.

Cheese Board Collective (Map p164; 1504 Shattuck Ave) This place offers a vast selection of gourmet cheeses and homemade breads, enabling you to put together a fantastic lunch. Head next door for a take-out slice of pizza that'll knock your socks off.

Gregoire (Map p164; ☎ 510-883-1893; 2109 Cedar St; lunch $4-8, dinner mains $11-16; 🕒 lunch & dinner Mon-Sat) The best takeaway by the bay offers

AUTHOR'S CHOICE

Chez Panisse (Map p164; ☎ 510-548-5525; 1517 Shattuck Ave; café mains $18-25, restaurant prix fixe $50-75; ⓨ café lunch & dinner Mon-Sat, restaurant dinner Mon-Sat) Chez Panisse is the Church of Alice Waters, inventor of California cuisine. The restaurant is as good and popular as it ever was, and despite its fame the place has retained a welcoming atmosphere. It's in a lovely Arts and Crafts house and you can chose to pull all the stops with a prix fixe meal downstairs, or go less expensive and less formal in the café upstairs. Reserve weeks ahead.

classic French fare. The weekly menu features what's in season locally, which may be grilled artichoke with aioli, impeccably fresh salad, steak in a wine reduction and, always, the ethereal potato puffs. Located just a few blocks from the park-like UC campus or the Berkeley Rose Garden (on Euclid at Rose), this is the perfect place to outfit a picnic.

DOWNTOWN & WEST BERKELEY

Downtown (Map p162; ☎ 510-649-3810; 2102 Shattuck Ave; lunch $11-16, dinner mains $17-28; ⓨ lunch Tue-Fri, dinner Tue-Sun) This venue is the cool spot downtown. The long bar is great for schmoozing, the open brick oven fends off the Berkeley/SF chill, and the fine French-Californian cuisine will warm any heart. Most nights live jazz or blues is featured after 8pm. It's easy to find – only just a few steps from BART.

La Note (Map p164; ☎ 510-843-1535; 2377 Shattuck Ave; meals $5-16; ⓨ breakfast & lunch daily, dinner Thu-Sat) Also downtown, La Note is a rustic country-French bistro serving superb ham-and-Gruyère omelettes, rich French toast and other fabulous dishes.

Beckett's Irish Pub (Map p164; 2271 Shattuck Ave; meals $7-16) The cozy but spacious and beautifully restored French-provincial building that houses Beckett's puts it way above your average fake-Irish pub. It serves hearty Irish meals and a decent Guinness.

Bette's Oceanview Diner (Map p162; 1807 4th St; mains from $5) The diner food is fresh and well-prepared at this hugely popular spot. Table waits can be long, but you can opt to take out from the adjacent deli counter.

Drinking

CAFES

Cafe Fanny (Map p162; 1603 San Pablo Ave; breakfast & lunch $4-8) North of University Ave is this café owned by Alice Waters. As you'd expect, it serves excellent cafés au lait, homemade pastries and poached-egg dishes.

Caffe Strada (Map p164; 2300 College Ave) A popular, student-saturated hangout with an inviting shaded patio and strong espressos.

Masse's Pastries (Map p164; 1469 Shattuck Ave) Makes excellent, inventive cakes and buns and you can enjoy a coffee at sidewalk tables at the edge of the bustling Gourmet Ghetto.

BARS

Berkeley isn't a wild party school, and there are very few drinking establishments near the university or downtown. But there are a few gems scattered around town. Further north on San Pablo Ave, Albany has several popular dives that attract hip crowds.

Albatross (Map p162; 1822 San Pablo Ave) A block north of University Ave, Albatross is one of the most inviting and friendly pubs in the entire Bay Area. Some serious darts are played here, and poker games and Trivial Pursuit will be going on around many of the worn out tables.

Jupiter (Map p164; 2180 Shattuck Ave) This downtown pub has loads of regional microbrews, a beer garden, good pizza and occasional live bands. It's popular with students and professionals.

Triple Rock Brewery & Ale House (Map p164; 1920 Shattuck Ave) Opened in 1986, Triple Rock was one of the country's first brewpubs. The house beers are quite good and there's pub food too.

Club Mallard (Map p162; 752 San Pablo Ave, Albany) This place has outdoor seating, tiki torches and hourly pool tables.

Ivy Room (Map p162; 860 San Pablo Ave, Albany) The Ivy Room boasts live country, blues and rockabilly bands and an excellent jukebox of classic 45s.

Entertainment

LIVE MUSIC

Berkeley has a lot of intimate live music venues. Cover charges range from $5 to $20, depending on who's playing.

Freight & Salvage Coffeehouse (Map p162; ☎ 510-548-1761; 1111 Addison St) Just off San Pablo Ave, this legendary club has great traditional folk and bluegrass bands but, be warned, no alcohol.

Ashkenaz (Map p162; ☎ 510-525-5054; 1317 San Pablo Ave) Ashkenaz is a 'music and dance community center' attracting activists, hippies and fans of folk, swing and world music who love to dance (lessons offered).

Starry Plough (Map p162; ☎ 510-841-2082; 3101 Shattuck Ave) This comfy Irish pub is more of a neighborhood dive (no fake decor) with a varied lineup of local and touring rock, jazz, country and blues bands.

CINEMAS
Pacific Film Archive (Map p164; ☎ 510-642-1124; 2575 Bancroft Way; admission $8) Cineastes should seek this place out. It's a world-renowned film center with an ever-changing schedule of international and classic films, many near-impossible to see anywhere else.

THEATER & DANCE
Berkeley Repertory Theatre (Map p164; ☎ 510-647-2949; 2025 Addison St) Downtown is home to this highly respected company that has produced bold versions of classical and modern plays since 1968.

Zellerbach Hall (Map p164; ☎ 510-642-9988) On the south end of campus near Bancroft Way and Dana St, Zellerbach Hall features dance events, concerts and performances of all types by national and international groups. Call for tickets or check the adjoining Cal Performances Ticket Office.

SPORTS
Memorial Stadium (Map p162), which dates from 1923, is the university's 76,000-seat sporting venue. This is the site (in alternating years) of the famous football frenzy between the UC Berkeley and Stanford teams.

Cal Athletic Ticket Office (☎ 800-462-3277) Call for ticket information on all UC Berkeley sports events, and keep in mind that some sell out weeks in advance.

Shopping
Telegraph Ave offers everything for the urban hippie, from handmade sidewalk-vendor jewelry to head-shop paraphernalia. Most appealing are, irrefutably, its terrific book and music stores.

Another strip of shops is along College Ave in the Elmwood District. On 4th St, north of University Ave, you'll find upscale clothing, kitchen supply, book and gift stores.

BOOKS
Cody's Books (☎ 800-995-1180) Downtown (Map p164; ☎ 510-845-7852; 2454 Telegraph Ave); 4th St Shopping District (Map p162; ☎ 510-559-950; 1730 4th St) This venerable store stocks a huge selection of new books and hosts almost daily appearances by top authors. There's a great magazine rack too.

Moe's (Map p164; ☎ 510-849-2087; 2476 Telegraph Ave) A longstanding local favorite, offering four floors of new, used and remaindered books for hours of browsing.

University Press Books (Map p164; ☎ 510-548-0585; 2430 Bancroft Way) This option stocks works by UC Berkeley professors and from other academic and museum publishers.

Black Oak Books (Map p164; ☎ 510-486-0698; 1491 Shattuck Ave) A fine store in North Berkeley with new and used selections and a full calendar of author appearances.

Easy Going (Map p164; ☎ 510-843-3533; 1385 Shattuck Ave) An excellent travel bookstore that also hosts readings.

MUSIC
Amoeba Music (Map p164; ☎ 510-549-1125; 2455 Telegraph Ave) If you're a music junkie you might plan on spending a few hours at the original Berkeley branch of Amoeba Music, packed with massive quantities of new and used CDs, DVDs, tapes and records (yes, lots of vinyl).

Rasputin (Map p164; ☎ 510-848-9004; 2401 Telegraph Ave) Nearby Rasputin is another large store full of new and used releases.

Down Home Music (☎ 510-525-2129; 10341 San Pablo Ave, El Cerrito) North of Berkeley in El Cerrito is this world-class store for roots, blues, folk, Latin and world music. It's affiliated with the Arhoolie record label, which has been issuing landmark recordings since the early 1960s.

OUTDOOR GEAR
At the intersection of San Pablo Ave and Gilman St are several outdoor stores.

Marmot Mountain Works (Map p162; ☎ 510-849-0735; 3049 Adeline St) Has climbing, ski and backpacking equipment.

North Face (Map p162; ☎ 510-526-3530; cnr 5th & Gilman Sts) A well-respected Berkeley-based brand of outdoor gear a few blocks west of San Pablo Ave.

SAN FRANCISCO BAY AREA

REI (Map p162; ☎ 510-527-4140; 1338 San Pablo Ave) Large and busy.

Wilderness Exchange (Map p162; ☎ 510-525-1255; 1407 San Pablo Ave) Selling new and used gear.

Getting There & Away

BART

The easiest way to travel between San Francisco, Berkeley, Oakland and other East Bay points is on **BART** (☎ 510-465-2278). Trains run approximately every 10 minutes from 4am to midnight on weekdays, with limited service from 6am on Saturday and from 8am on Sunday.

To get to Berkeley, catch a Richmond-bound train to one of three BART stations: Ashby (Adeline St and Ashby Ave), downtown Berkeley (Shattuck Ave and Center St) or North Berkeley (Sacramento and Delaware Sts). The fare ranges from $2.90 to $3.10 between Berkeley and San Francisco and is $1.25 between Berkeley and downtown Oakland. After 8pm on weekdays, 7pm on Saturday and all day Sunday, there is no direct service operating from San Francisco to Berkeley; instead, catch a Pittsburg/Bay Point train and transfer at 12th St station in Oakland.

A BART-to-Bus transfer ticket, available from white AC Transit machines near BART station exits, reduces the connecting bus fare to $1.25.

BUS

The regional company **AC Transit** (☎ 510-839-2882) operates a number of buses from San Francisco's **Transbay Terminal** (Mission & 1st Sts) to the East Bay. The F line leaves from the Transbay Terminal to the corner of University and Shattuck Aves approximately every half-hour (fare $3, 30 minutes).

Between Berkeley and downtown Oakland, take AC Transit bus 15, which runs along Martin Luther King Jr Way, or bus 40, which travels up and down Telegraph Ave ($1.50). Bus 51 travels along Broadway in Oakland and then along College Ave in Berkeley, past the UCB campus and down to the Berkeley Marina.

CAR & MOTORCYCLE

With your own wheels you can approach Berkeley from San Francisco by taking the Bay Bridge and then following either I-80 (for University Ave, downtown Berkeley

and the UCB campus) or Hwy 24 (for College Ave and the Berkeley Hills).

The city runs two parking garages (see p163), and UCB runs one on Bancroft Way between Telegraph Ave and Dana St (Map p164). The situation improves in the evenings and on weekends, when the other university lots open to the public (check times carefully; fees vary).

TRAIN

Though **Amtrak** (☎ 800-872-7245) does stop in Berkeley, the shelter (University Ave and 3rd St) is not staffed and direct connections are few. More convenient is the nearby **Emeryville Amtrak station** (☎ 510-450-1081; 5885 Landregan St), a few miles south of the Berkeley stop.

To reach Emeryville station from downtown Berkeley, take BART to the MacArthur station and from there take AC Transit bus 57 to the train station.

Getting Around

Public transport and your feet are the best options for getting around crowded central Berkeley. For instance, walking from the downtown Berkeley BART station to Telegraph Ave takes about 10 minutes.

AC Transit operates public buses in and around Berkeley. UC Berkeley's **Bear Transit** (☎ 510-642-5149) runs a shuttle from the downtown BART station to various points on campus (50¢). From its stop at the Hearst Mining Circle, the H Line runs along Centennial Dr to the higher parts of the campus ($1).

MT DIABLO STATE PARK

Mt Diablo at 3849ft is more than 1000ft higher than Mt Tamalpais in Marin County. On a clear day (early on a winter morning is a good bet) the views from Diablo's summit are huge and sweeping. To the west you can see over the bay and out to the Farallon Islands; to the east you can see over the Central Valley to the Sierra Nevada. The **state park** (☎ 925-837-2525; www.mdia.org; per vehicle $6; ☉ 8am-sunset) has 50 miles of hiking trails (beware of poison oak), and can be reached from Walnut Creek or Danville. You can also drive to the top if you wish, where there's a **visitors center** (☉ Wed-Sun 10am-4pm). The park office is at the junction of the two entry roads. Simple campsites cost $14 to $19 per night (registration only at Southgate Check-In Station, at the southern entrance

EAST BAY GLOBE TROT

The 'I' in I-80 and I-880, the East Bay's north–south arteries, may as well stand for 'International.' Many immigrant communities have sprouted up in the cities on this side of the bay, from Berkeley down to San Jose. All are worth visiting for a taste of immigrant life in the US as well as a taste of some great international cuisine.

Little India

Berkeley's Little India runs along the University Ave corridor. It's interspersed with non-Indian businesses, but the concentration of Indian restaurants, sari stores and shops selling Bollywood DVD releases makes the street worth investigating. Try the **Chaat Cafe** (Map p164; 1902 University Ave; dishes $4-10) for the small plates of *chaat* (small savory snacks) and tasty naan wraps. Within a few blocks of University Ave, **Breads of India** (Map p162; 2448 Sacramento St; mains $10-14) is famous for its inventive curries and fine naan, while **Vik's Chaat Corner** (Map p162; 724 Allston Way; dishes $4-6) is a very popular *chaat* house in a large, stark warehouse space. The aisles of **Bazaar of India** (Map p162; 1810 University Ave) are loaded with spices, clothing, musical instruments and movies.

Little Kabul

Roughly midway between Oakland and San Jose, the city of Fremont is a fairly bland 1950s suburb, but the area has attracted the USA's largest concentration of Afghans. Head straight to Fremont Blvd and you'll find interesting shops and restaurants. **Salang Pass** (37426 Fremont Blvd; dishes $5-12) is a colorful little spot for wonderful flatbreads, lamb dishes, *aushak* (leek-filled ravioli) and a variety of small plates. Next door, the **Pamir Food Mart** (37422 Fremont Blvd) is an excellent place to buy fresh flatbreads and peruse shelves stocked with intriguing Afghani foods.

Vietnamese Shopping Mall

San Jose has one of the largest Vietnamese communities in the USA and many immigrants arrived immediately after the fall of Saigon in 1975. The community is well established, fairly affluent and has clearly taken to mainstream American culture. The **Grand Century Shopping Mall** (Map p177; 1001 Story Rd) is a case in point – it's a huge American shopping mall that's as ordinary as they come, except for the fact that the mall's stores cater specifically to the Vietnamese community. Most of the shops here sell jewelry, music, DVDs, Vietnamese-language books and clothing. The real attraction, of course, is the food court, where you can order noodle soups, rice plates, baguette sandwiches, spring rolls and sweet bean puddings. The experience is an Americanized version of dining at food stalls in the markets of Saigon. Particularly good are the *banh xeo* sold at Dinh Cong Trang. *Banh xeo* are thin yellow pancakes filled with pork, bean sprouts and peppers. They're served piping hot and are crispy around the edges, and they taste heavenly when wrapped in lettuce and dipped in fish sauce. Be sure to have a strong Vietnamese coffee with syrupy condensed milk before you go.

to the park); reserve by calling ☎ 800-444-7275.

DANVILLE
pop 42,600

Set in the shadow of Mt Diablo, Danville is the archetype of the perfect upper-middle-class Californian suburb. But the only real reason to come here is to check out the surprisingly impressive automobile collection in the **Blackhawk Museum** (☎ 925-736-2277; 3700 Blackhawk Plaza Circle; adult/student $8/5; ☉ 10am-5pm Wed-Sun). The museum includes six different galleries, two of which are devoted to cars –

about 100 of them all told, including many one-of-a-kind models. There are also galleries devoted to science and natural history, a 'Discovery Room' for kids and an ongoing series of rotating exhibits curated by the Smithsonian Institution.

The museum is adjacent to **The Shops at Blackhawk**, an upscale retail center, situated at the corner of Crow Canyon Rd and Camino Tassajara, 5 miles from the Sycamore Valley Rd exit on I-680.

Eugene O'Neill National Historic Site (☎ 925-838-0249; admission free; ☉ tours 10am & 12.30pm Wed-Sun) is an interesting stop too. The famed playwright built Tao House with his 1936 Nobel Prize money and wrote *The Iceman Cometh, Long Day's Journey into Night* and *Moon for the Misbegotten* while living here between 1937 and 1944. You must book in advance, because you have to be picked up by a shuttle from downtown Danville. Apparently the residents don't want tourists parking in their neighborhood.

JOHN MUIR NATIONAL HISTORIC SITE

Less than 15 miles north of Walnut Creek, sleepy Martinez (population 37,050) was the birthplace of Hall of Fame baseball slugger 'Joltin' Joe DiMaggio. The town is also indirectly honored in the name of the martini cocktail. Some local bartenders even insist the martini was invented here, although the town lacks that worldly martini vibe and seems more like a fine spot for a cold beer.

John Muir residence (☎ 925-228-8860; 4202 Alhambra Ave; admission $3; ☼ 10am-5pm in summer, Wed-Sun rest of year) is the house where the pioneering conservationist and Sierra Club founder lived from 1890 until 1914. The property, built by his father-in-law in 1882, reflects Muir's in-laws' tastes and lifestyle more than his own. Still, the Muir history, lovely countryside and view inside his study are worthwhile. The grounds include the 1849 **Martinez Adobe**, part of the rancho on which the house was built. The park is just north of Hwy 4.

VALLEJO

pop 116,800

For one week in 1852 Vallejo was officially the California state capital – but the fickle legislature changed its mind. It tried Vallejo a second time in 1853, but after a month moved on again (to Benicia). That same year, Vallejo became the site of the first US naval installation on the West Coast (Mare Island Naval Shipyard, now closed). **Vallejo Naval & Historical Museum** (☎ 707-643-0077; 734 Marin St; admission $2; ☼ 10am-4:30pm Tue-Sat) tells the story.

The town's biggest tourist draw, though, is **Six Flags Marine World** (☎ 707-643-6722; www.six flags.com/parks/marineworld; adult/child under 4ft $48/26; ☼ 10am-8pm Fri-Sun spring & fall, 10am-10pm daily summer), a modern theme park offering mighty coasters and other rides alongside animal shows featuring sharks, killer whales, dolphins, seals and sea lions. Good discounts (more than $10 off) are frequently available on the park's website. Exit I-80 at Marine

World Parkway, 5 miles north of down-town Vallejo. Parking is available for $10.

Blue & Gold Fleet (☎ 415-773-1188, 707-643-3779; one-way adult/child $10/5) runs ferries from San Francisco's Pier 41 at Fisherman's Wharf to Vallejo.

THE PENINSULA

South of San Francisco, squeezed tightly between the bay and the coastal foothills, a vast swath of suburbia continues to San Jose and beyond. Dotted within this area are Palo Alto, Stanford University and Silicon Valley, the center of the Bay Area's immense tech industry. West of the foothills, Hwy 1 runs down the Pacific coast via Half Moon Bay and a string of beaches to Santa Cruz. Hwy 101 and I-280 both run to San Jose, where they connect with Hwy 17, the quickest route to Santa Cruz. Any of these routes can be combined into an interesting loop or extended to the Monterey Peninsula.

SAN FRANCISCO TO PALO ALTO

South of the San Francisco peninsula, I-280 is the dividing line between the densely populated South Bay area and the rugged and lightly populated Pacific coast. With its sweeping bends, I-280 is a more scenic choice than gritty, crowded Hwy 101. Unfortunately, these parallel north–south arteries are both clogged with traffic during the weekday commute.

Daly City (population 102,000) is for the most part an ordinary residential suburb, but its Westlake subdivision is an interesting enclave of kooky looking, post-WWII, single-family homes. Designed by Henry Doelger and Ed Hageman, many of the district's houses have that crazy atomic-age geometry, with slanted roofs and tilted plate-glass windows turning 90-degree corners. If the neighborhood looks eerily well kept, it's because there's a strict city ordinance requiring front lawns be neatly trimmed. Immediately south is **Colma** (population 1570), where the living are a small minority. Most of Colma has been covered by graveyards since San Francisco banned cemeteries within the city limits, and more than a million stiffs reside here. The dead outnumber the living by a ratio greater than 630:1.

SILICON VALLEY

Don't look for Silicon Valley on the map – it doesn't exist. Silicon is the element used to make the silicon chips that form the basis of modern microcomputers. Since the Santa Clara Valley – stretching from Palo Alto down through Mountain View, Sunnyvale, Cupertino and Santa Clara to San Jose – is thought of as the birthplace of the microcomputer, it's been dubbed 'Silicon Valley.' Not only does the valley not exist on the map, it's pretty hard to define even at ground level. The Santa Clara Valley is wide and flat, and its towns are essentially a string of shopping centers and industrial parks linked by a maze of freeways. It's hard to imagine that even after WWII this was still a wide expanse of orchards and farms.

There's very little to see in Silicon Valley; the cutting-edge computer companies are secretive and not keen on factory tours. Their anonymous-looking buildings – expanses of black glass are an architectural favorite – are bland and uninviting. The Tech Museum (p178) gives an idea of some of the valley's technological flavor, as does Santa Clara's Intel Museum (p183). Since the computer business is famed for its garage start-ups, enthusiasts may also want to drive by 367 Addison Ave, just five blocks south of University Ave in downtown Palo Alto. This is the garage where William Hewlett and David Packard started computer giant Hewlett-Packard.

Right on the bay at the northern edge of San Mateo, 4 miles south of San Francisco International Airport, is **Coyote Point Park** (per vehicle $5). The main attraction is the **Coyote Point Museum** (☎ 650-342-7755; www.coyoteptmuseum .org; adult/child $6/2; 🕙 10am-5pm Tue-Sat, noon-5pm Sun), with innovative exhibits for kids and adults concentrating on ecological and environmental issues. Exit Hwy 101 at Coyote Point Dr.

PALO ALTO
pop 57,540

Palo Alto is home to Stanford University. If it doesn't feel like your average college town, that'd be because this is also the northern extent of Silicon Valley. In fact, it can be said that Silicon Valley started here, just before WWII, when Stanford recruited several esteemed professors from MIT. Hewlett-Packard and Sun Microsystems are headquartered in Palo Alto. The quaint town exudes that relaxed California affluence characterized by BMW convertibles and expensive sandals.

Orientation

Palo Alto is bordered by Hwy-101 on its northeast edge and I-280 to the southwest. In between it's bisected by El Camino Real, which also divides the town from the campus. University Ave is Palo Alto's main street and continues, with a name change to Palm Dr, straight into the heart of the Stanford campus. The extensive Stanford Shopping Center is on El Camino Real just north of campus. East Palo Alto, on the east side of Hwy 101, is best avoided.

Information

Chamber of Commerce (☎ 650-324-3121; www .paloaltochamber.com; 325 Forest Ave; 🕙 9am-5pm Mon-Fri) Dispenses information. For entertainment listings get a copy of the free *Palo Alto Weekly* newspaper or check the website at www.paloaltoonline.com.

Kepler's Bookshop (☎ 650-324-4321; 1010 El Camino Real; 🕙 9am-11pm Sun-Thu, 9am-midnight Fri & Sat) A bright, modern store with a popular adjacent café; in nearby Menlo Park.

Sights & Activities
STANFORD UNIVERSITY

Sprawled over 8200 leafy acres, **Stanford University** (www.stanford.edu) was founded by Leland Stanford, one of Central Pacific Railroad's 'Big Four' founders and a former governor of California. When the Stanfords' only child died of typhoid during a European tour in 1884, they decided to build a university in his memory. Stanford University was opened in 1891, just two years before Leland Stanford's death, but the university grew to become a prestigious and wealthy institution. The campus was built on the site of the Stanfords' horse-breeding farm, and as a result, Stanford is still known as 'The Farm.'

The main booth for Stanford's **Visitor Information Services** (VIS; ☎ 650-723-2560; 🕙 8am-5pm Mon-Fri, 9am-5pm Sat & Sun) is in the lobby of Memorial Auditorium. Free one-hour walking tours of the campus depart from Memorial Auditorium daily at 11am and

SAN FRANCISCO BAY AREA

3:15pm, except during the winter break (mid-December through early January) and some holidays. Parking can be a real pain. Meters are $1.50 per hour, and if carrying that much change sounds unwieldy, buy an all-day parking permit ($12) from VIS.

Auguste Rodin's *Burghers of Calais* bronze sculpture marks the entrance to the **Main Quad**, an open plaza where the original 12 campus buildings, a mix of Romanesque and Mission revival styles, were joined by the **Memorial Church** in 1903. The church is noted for its beautiful mosaic-tiled frontage, stained-glass windows and organ with 7777 pipes.

East of the Main Quad, the 285ft-high **Hoover Tower** (ⓧ 8am-5pm Mon-Fri, 10am-5pm Sat, closed during final exams, breaks btwn sessions & some holidays) offers superb views of the campus. The tower houses the university library, offices and part of the right-wing Hoover Institution on War, Revolution & Peace. At the entrance level there are exhibits on President Herbert Hoover, who was among the first class of students to attend Stanford in 1891. The ride to the top costs $2/1 per adult/child.

The **Cantor Center for Visual Arts** (☎ 650-723-4177; 328 Lomita Dr; admission free; ⓧ 11am-5pm Wed & Fri-Sun, 11am-8pm Thu) is a large museum originally dating from 1894. Its collection spans works from ancient civilizations to contemporary art, sculpture and photography.

Immediately south is the open-air **Rodin Sculpture Garden**, with a large collection of sculpture by Auguste Rodin, including reproductions of his towering *Gates of Hell*. Dotted around the campus is more sculpture, all detailed in the free *Guide to Outdoor Sculpture* leaflet, available at the museum or at www.stanford.edu/dept/ccva.

The **Red Barn**, part of Leland Stanford's original farm, stands just west of campus. It's here that Eadweard Muybridge, under patronage of Leland Stanford, photographed moving horses in a study that led to the development of motion pictures. Hiking and biking trails lead from the barn into the foothills west of campus.

STANFORD LINEAR ACCELERATOR CENTER
Few drivers speeding along I-280 realize that things are speeding by beneath them at far higher velocities. The **Stanford Linear Accelerator Center** (SLAC; ☎ 650-926-2204; www.slac.stanford .edu; 2575 Sand Hill Rd), run by the university for the US Department of Energy, goes right under the freeway. Positrons (positively charged subatomic particles) hurtle down a straight 2-mile path in a 4in diameter linac (an accelerator beam tube), on their way to high-speed impacts at the other end of the tube. Experiments at SLAC have resulted in the discovery of the existence of further subatomic particles, including quarks, and have gained the facility three Nobel Prizes so far. At 2 miles long, SLAC's Klystron Gallery is the world's longest building. Visitors (must be over the age of 12) can have a look inside during the free two-hour tours conducted several times a month. Advance reservations are required. SLAC is about 2 miles west of campus, east of I-280.

NASA-AMES EXPLORATION CENTER
A few miles southeast of Palo Alto, the **NASA-Ames Exploration Center** (Map p177; ☎ 650-604-6274; www.nasa.gov/centers/ames; admission free; ⓧ 8am-4:30pm Mon-Fri) sits at the north side of Moffett Field. The research center here has contributed to discoveries in hyper-velocity flight, and its gigantic wind tunnel is still used for advanced aerospace research. A one-third scale model of a space shuttle is out front. Inside is a Mercury capsule, a moon rock, astronaut suits and the Immersive Theater with a circular screen that shows awesome footage from the ongoing Mars mission. Turn off Hwy 101 at the Moffett Field exit and turn left immediately in front of the main gate to reach the visitors center.

Sleeping
Cardinal Hotel (☎ 650-323-5101; www.cardinalhotel .com; 235 Hamilton Ave; r $70-90, with bathroom $135-165; ▣) In the downtown area, this restored 1924 hotel oozes historic California character with its pristine Mission-style lobby. Guest rooms are small but elegantly appointed.

Cowper Inn B&B (☎ 650-327-4475; www.cowper inn.com; 705 Cowper St; r incl breakfast $150; ⊠ ▣) The Craftsman details have been lovingly preserved at this large B&B. It has two homey (but unfrilly) rooms and is on a shady street two blocks from University Ave. The two rooms with shared bathroom cost $80 to $100.

Hotel California (☎ 650-322-7666; www.hotelcali fornia.com; 2431 Ash St; r $83-115; ℗ ⊠ ▣) Two blocks from the California Ave train station, this hotel has 20 rooms and free DSL.

Garden Court Hotel (☎ 650-322-9000, 800-824-9028; www.gardencourt.com; 520 Cowper St; r $299-379; ℗ ❷)

Modern and exceedingly cheery, the Garden Court offers a bit of downtown luxury. Rooms have balconies overlooking a Spanish courtyard and are wi-fi equipped.

Coronet Motel (☎ 650-326-1081; 2455 El Camino Real; r $75; **P**) Just north of Page Mill Rd, this motel is fairly close to the campus' south side. It can be a bit noisy, but is good value. There are loads of similar motels along El Camino Real north and south of Palo Alto.

Hidden Villa (☎ 650-949-8648; www.hiddenvilla.org; 26870 Moody Rd; dm $19-22; ☒ Oct-May) This is a HI hostel tucked away in a calm, pastoral setting in Los Altos Hills, 2 miles west of I-280. It is the country's oldest hostel (it opened in 1937), and is part of an organic farm and environmental educational center. The modern dormitory was completely rebuilt in 2001, but the private cabins are more rustic (and are heated) and also more romantic. The location is stellar, with many hiking trails, but there's no public transport nearby.

Eating

There are dozens of good restaurants, from cheap eats to elegant bistros, in the compact blocks of downtown Palo Alto – mainly on University Ave between Cowper and Emerson Sts.

Tamarine (☎ 650-325-8500; 546 University Ave; dishes $8-22) Palo Alto's most beautiful restaurant is this contemporary Vietnamese place. The dishes have a slight seafood bias and are finely prepared in the style of California cuisine. Most mains are suitable for sharing, and this is one of the Bay Area's best destinations for exotic cocktails.

Spago (☎ 650-833-1000; 265 Lytton Ave; mains lunch $10-18, dinner $16-38) Spago, owned by celebrity chef Wolfgang Puck (and presided over by Chef Aram Mardigian), attempts to dazzle at every turn, and mostly succeeds. This is California cuisine with the occasional Puckish Austrian twist (try the spicy beef goulash). Dress to the nines for this one.

Bistro Elan (☎ 650-327-0284; 448 California Ave; mains $15-24; ☒ lunch & dinner Tue-Sat) Among Palo Alto's best restaurants for over a decade, Bistro Elan's excellent country French cuisine attracts power lunchers during the day and romantic couples in the evening. For the best atmosphere, head to the garden patio when the weather's nice.

Osteria (☎ 650-328-5700; 247 Hamilton Ave; mains $16-26) For excellent Northern Italian, a loyal fan base crowds into intimate little Osteria. The service is very friendly, but you'll often have to wait for your table (even if you have made reservations).

Peninsula Fountain and Grill (☎ 650-323-3131; 566 Emerson St; mains $8-12) A lively beauty, the Peninsula Fountain was founded in 1923 but still has that opening day buzz and sparkle. It's famous for its frothy milkshakes ($5) and for hefty American breakfasts.

University Cafe (☎ 650-322-5301; 271 University Ave; mains $8-12) Step inside this relaxed space for coffee or a light meal. High ceilings and potted palms make it an airy spot for tasty sandwiches.

Evvia (☎ 650-326-0983; 420 Emerson St; mains lunch $11-22, dinner $18-35; ☒ lunch Mon-Fri, dinner daily) If you like lamb, here's your spot. Evvia is a high-end Greek restaurant with a rustic taverna interior. It's food for the gods.

Empire Grill & Tap Room (☎ 650-321-3030; 661 Emerson; mains $10-16) The local yuppies favor this lively hangout that got play in Po Bronson's novel *The First 20 Million is Always the Hardest*. You can get pizza, sandwiches and sturdy meat-and-potato platters on the shady patio and wash it down with something from the 25 taps.

Drinking

Gordon Biersch (640 Emerson St) Palo Alto is home to the original link in the Gordon Biersch chain of brewpubs. The German-style lagers are good, while the thick crowds are more stockbroker-geek than hipster-chic.

Antonio's Nut House (321 S California Ave) The Nut House stands out in orderly, gentrified Palo Alto. It's a down-to-earth, beer-and-peanuts sort of place. Said nuts are dispensed from a huge mechanical gorilla, so watch out.

Rose and Crown (547 Emerson St) Hidden away behind Emerson St is this tiny ale house. It's a friendly spot for a pint, or to watch soccer on TV. Pub food and live music several nights a week also draw in the regulars.

Entertainment

Palo Alto Bowl (☎ 650-948-1031; 4329 El Camino Real) This is the real deal if you hanker to knock a few back (meaning pins). Adding a trendy twist, on Friday and Saturday nights students and singles take over the lanes until 1am.

Stanford Theatre (☎ 650-324-3700; 221 University Ave) This recently restored movie house screens some vintage Hollywood gems and

SAN FRANCISCO BAY AREA

international classics, accompanied by a 'mighty' Wurlitzer organ.

Getting There & Around

Palo Alto is about 35 miles south of San Francisco and 15 miles north of San Jose. The easiest way to get here from either end of the Peninsula is via **CalTrain** (☎ 800-660-4287, 650-817-1717), which stops in Menlo Park, Palo Alto and Stanford. Departures are every 30 or 60 minutes on weekdays, hourly on Saturday and every two hours on Sunday. San Francisco to Palo Alto takes about an hour and costs $5. Palo Alto to San Jose takes half an hour and costs $3.50. Palo Alto's Cal-Train Station is beside Alma St, just north of University Ave.

Buses arrive at and depart from Palo Alto at the Transit Center, adjacent to the CalTrain station. From Palo Alto, **SamTrans** (☎ 800-660-4287, 650-817-1717; www.samtrans.com) bus 390 runs to the Daly City BART station ($1.50), and bus KX goes to San Francisco's Transbay Terminal via San Francisco International Airport ($4). Both operate about every half-hour daily.

The **Santa Clara Valley Transportation Agency** (VTA; ☎ 800-894-9908, 408-321-2300) serves Palo Alto and the Santa Clara Valley. Bus 22 runs from Palo Alto to San Jose ($1.75).

Marguerite (☎ 650-723-9362) is Stanford University's free public shuttle, providing service from CalTrain's Palo Alto and California Ave stations to the campus. Trains run about every 15 minutes during the day, and every half-hour between 8pm and midnight.

There's free two-hour car parking all over town, or you can park all day for $1.50 at CalTrain stations. See p174 for information about parking on campus.

Palo Alto Bicycles (☎ 650-328-7411; 171 University Ave) rents bicycles at its Bike Station, at the CalTrain depot.

SAN JOSE

pop 905,000

Although it's a larger city and it anchors Silicon Valley, San Jose (lazily pronounced 'sanno-*zay*' by most of the locals) has always been in San Francisco's shadow. It's an old city that has only recently prospered and its downtown is small for a city of its size. Industrial parks, high-tech computer firms and look-alike housing developments have, in the past few decades, come to domi-nate the city's landscape, taking over where farms, ranches and open spaces once spread between the bay and the surrounding hills. It sprawls over a frame of freeways and feels more like LA or Phoenix than its near neighbor to the north.

But San Jose is a culturally diverse city that's packed full of historic buildings, excellent museums and an impressive number of fine restaurants and funky old bars. The city seems to shrug its shoulders at comparisons to San Francisco, and has taken a refreshingly modest approach to establishing its own cultural niche within the greater Bay Area. San Jose's fun nightlife district is called SOFA (South of First Area), which clearly plays on SF's SoMa and gets the upper hand in terms of wit. It's on a stretch of 1st St south of San Carlos St and includes numerous nightclubs, restaurants, galleries and the historic 1927 California Theatre.

Other neighborhoods to explore include the burgeoning business district along the Alameda, home to restaurants and cafés, and Santana Row, a contemporary development that attempts to re-create the traditional Main St formula of residences, shops and restaurants. These sorts of developments are popping up around California. The wave of the future, possibly? You might want to check it out.

Founded in 1777 as El Pueblo de San José de Guadalupe, San Jose is California's oldest Spanish civilian settlement. Surviving remnants of that era include Plaza de Cesar Chavez and the Peralta Adobe. Between 1849 and 1851 the state's first capital was in San Jose, where the governing body became known as the 'Legislature of a Thousand Drinks.' 'Let's have a drink, let's have a thousand drinks,' was the alleged rallying cry at the end of the day. The capital shifted places several more times before settling in Sacramento in 1854.

Speaking of tomfoolery, at History Park stands a replica of the 1881 Electric Light Tower, a harebrained scheme to light all of downtown. And elements of the Old West are still tucked away in the city's corners, from the Almaden Feed & Fuel, a one-time stagecoach stop south of town near the former New Almaden quicksilver mine, to Waves Smokehouse & Saloon downtown on a street formerly known as El Dorado and

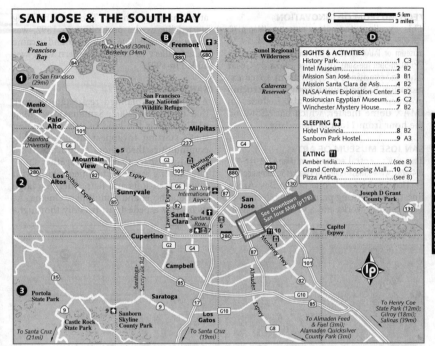

SAN JOSE & THE SOUTH BAY

SIGHTS & ACTIVITIES
History Park..............................1 C3
Intel Museum...........................2 B2
Mission San José.......................3 B1
Mission Santa Clara de Asís........4 B2
NASA-Ames Exploration Center..5 B2
Rosicrucian Egyptian Museum......6 C2
Winchester Mystery House..........7 B2

SLEEPING
Hotel Valencia..........................8 B2
Sanborn Park Hostel...................9 A3

EATING
Amber India.........................(see 8)
Grand Century Shopping Mall....10 C2
Pizza Antica........................(see 8)

which was once home to the city's red-light district.

If you see a jet flying close overhead, don't be alarmed. Those are just planes approaching a runway at San Jose International Airport, immediately north of downtown.

Orientation

Downtown San Jose is at the junction of Hwy 87 and I-280. Hwy 101 and I-880 complete the box. Running roughly north–south the length of the city, from the old port town of Alviso on the San Francisco Bay all the way downtown, is 1st St; south of I-280, its name changes to Monterey Hwy.

San Jose State University is immediately east of downtown. The San Jose International Airport is at the intersection of Hwys 87 and 101, north of the city center.

Parking is free in city-owned lots and garages downtown after 6pm midweek, and all day on weekends.

Information

The helpful **Visitor Information & Business Center** (Map p178; ☎ 408-977-0900, 888-726-5673; www.sanjose

.org; 150 W San Carlos St; ☺ 8am-5pm Mon-Fri, 11am-5pm Sat & Sun) is inside the San Jose Convention Center. Ask for the useful *Historical Walking Tour* leaflet.

To find out what's happening and where, try the **Event Information Hotline** (☎ 408-277-3900), the free weekly **Metro newspaper** (www.metroactive .com), biweekly the *Wave* or the Friday 'Eye' section of the daily *San Jose Mercury News*.

Sights & Activities
PLAZA DE CESAR CHAVEZ

This leafy square in the center of downtown, part of the original plaza of El Pueblo de San José de Guadalupe (Map p178), is the oldest public space in the city. It's named after Cesar Chavez – founder of the United Farm Workers, who lived part of his life in San Jose – and is surrounded by museums, theaters and hotels.

At the top of the plaza is the **Cathedral Basilica of St Joseph** (80 S Market St), the pueblo's first church. Originally constructed of adobe brick in 1803, it was replaced three times due to earthquakes and fire; the present building dates from 1877.

TECH MUSEUM OF INNOVATION

This excellent **technology museum** (Map p178; ☎ 408-294-8324; www.thetech.org; 201 S Market St; museum or IMAX theater $10, combination ticket $16; ☑ 10am-5pm Tue-Sun), opposite Plaza de Cesar Chavez, examines subjects from space exploration to the human body to microchip production. The museum also includes an IMAX dome theater, which has shows on the hour from 11am to 4pm daily.

SAN JOSE MUSEUM OF ART

The city's central **art museum** (Map p178; ☎ 408-294-2787; www.sjmusart.org; 110 S Market St; admission free; ☑ 11am-5pm Tue-Sun) is one of the Bay Area's finest, with a strong permanent collection of 20th-century works and a variety of imaginative changing exhibits. The main building started life as the post office in 1892, was damaged by the 1906 earthquake and became an art gallery in 1933. A modern wing was added in 1991.

SANTANA ROW

A completely planned real-estate venture that opened in 2002, Santana Row (Map p177) reflects the kind of urban planning that's starting to appear in fast-growing communities throughout California. It's a mixed-use space that brings together shopping, dining and entertainment along with townhouses, lofts and flats. There's a large boutique hotel and a multiplex cinema. At its heart is a pedestrian-friendly thorough-

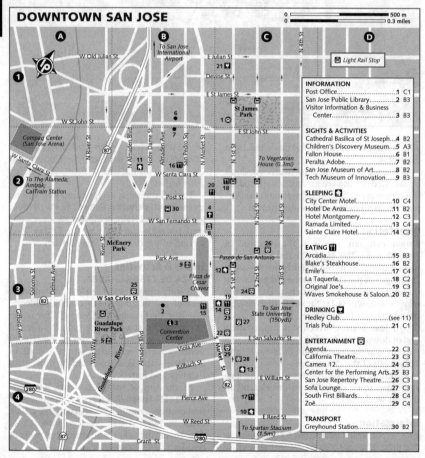

DOWNTOWN SAN JOSE

0 ————— 500 m
0 ————— 0.3 miles

🚈 Light Rail Stop

INFORMATION
Post Office......................................1 C1
San Jose Public Library..................2 B3
Visitor Information & Business
Center......................................3 B3

SIGHTS & ACTIVITIES
Cathedral Basilica of St Joseph....4 B2
Children's Discovery Museum......5 A3
Fallon House....................................6 B1
Peralta Adobe.................................7 B2
San Jose Museum of Art...............8 B2
Tech Museum of Innovation.......9 B3

SLEEPING 🛏
City Center Motel.........................10 C4
Hotel De Anza..............................11 B2
Hotel Montgomery.......................12 C3
Ramada Limited............................13 C4
Sainte Claire Hotel.......................14 C3

EATING 🍴
Arcadia...15 B3
Blake's Steakhouse.......................16 B2
Emile's..17 C4
La Taqueria...................................18 C2
Original Joe's................................19 C3
Waves Smokehouse & Saloon....20 B2

DRINKING 🍷
Hedley Club.............................(see 11)
Trials Pub.....................................21 C1

ENTERTAINMENT 🎭
Agenda...22 C3
California Theatre.........................23 C3
Camera 12....................................24 C3
Center for the Performing Arts....25 B3
San Jose Repertory Theatre.......26 C3
Sofa Lounge.................................27 C3
South First Billiards......................28 C4
Zoë...29 C4

TRANSPORT
Greyhound Station.......................30 B2

fare that calls to mind 'Main St' ideals of traditional American small-town life, but the style of architecture and overall effect is Mediterranean. The restaurants spill out onto sidewalk terraces, and public spaces have been designed to invite loitering and promenading. The idea is a popular one, and on warm evenings, the area is swarming with an energetic crowd. There are some excellent restaurants here, so it might behoove the traveler to join the fun.

Santana Row is interesting even if the thought of ersatz European spaces doesn't smell quite right. Proponents of this type of development call Santana Row a 'model for smart growth.' Detractors complain that the project simply draws shoppers away from San Jose's real downtown. Of course, over the centuries, some of the most vital urban areas were similarly calculated, so perhaps in time Santana Row will attain its own authenticity.

Intriguingly, in August 2002, just weeks before Santana Row's opening, a fire burned down the largest building on the block. The 11-alarm fire was the largest in San Jose's history.

PERALTA ADOBE & FALLON HOUSE

These historic San Jose **houses** (Map p178; admission free; ☉ noon-5pm Sat & Sun) represent two very different early architectural styles, sitting across the road from each other near San Pedro Sq. To see the houses, drop by the **visitors center** (☎ 408-993-8182; 175 W St John St).

The Peralta Adobe, the city's oldest building, dates from 1797 and is the last survivor from the original Spanish pueblo. The building is very basic, and the two rooms have been furnished as they might have been during their occupation by the Gonzales and Peralta families. Luis Maria Peralta came to the Bay Area at age 16 and died an American citizen and a millionaire, the owner of a large chunk of the East Bay.

Thomas Fallon married the daughter of an important Mexican landowner, built the fine Victorian Fallon house in 1854–55 and went on to become mayor of San Jose. There are 15 furnished rooms.

HISTORY PARK

Historic buildings from all over San Jose have been brought together in this open-air history **museum** (Map p177; ☎ 408-287-2290; www.historysanjose.org; 1650 Senter Rd; admission free; ☉ noon-5pm Tue-Sun), southeast of the city center in Kelley Park. The centerpiece is a half-scale replica of the 237ft-high 1881 **Electric Light Tower**. The original tower was a pioneering attempt at street lighting, intended to illuminate the entire town center. It was a complete failure but, lights or not, was left standing as a central landmark until it toppled over in 1915 because of rust and wind. Other buildings include an 1888 **Chinese temple** and the **Pacific Hotel**, which has rotating exhibits inside. The **Trolley Restoration Barn** restores historic trolley cars to operate on San Jose's light-rail line. The trolleys are also run along the park's own short line.

Tours are offered on weekends between 12:30pm and 2:30pm, and many of the buildings are closed during the week.

ROSICRUCIAN EGYPTIAN MUSEUM

One of San Jose's more interesting attractions is the unusual and educational **Egyptian Museum** (Map p177; ☎ 408-947-3636; www.egyptianmuseum.org; adult/child/student $9/5/7; ☉ 10am-5pm Mon-Fri, 11am-6pm Sat & Sun), which has an extensive collection that includes statues, household items and mummies. There's even a two-room, walk-through reproduction of an ancient subterranean tomb. The museum is the centerpiece of **Rosicrucian Park** (cnr Naglee & Park Aves), west of downtown San Jose.

Even more intriguing than the museum is the Rosicrucian Order itself. Headquartered in Rosicrucian Park, the order is a nonreligious fraternity whose members seek to achieve spiritual enlightenment and material success through the study of mysticism and metaphysics. As the order's own website slyly says: 'Rosicrucians are normal men and women. Perhaps some of your friends or relatives are Rosicrucians and you are not aware of it.'

CHILDREN'S DISCOVERY MUSEUM

This downtown tech **museum** (☎ 408-298-5437; www.cdm.org; 180 Woz Way; admission $7; ☉ 10am-5pm Tue-Sat, noon-5pm Sun) for kids has hands-on science and space displays, plenty of nifty toys and some pretty cool play-and-learn areas such as the kooky 'Alice's Wonderland.' The museum is on Woz Way, which is named after Steve Wozniak, the co-founder of Apple and now a fifth-grade teacher.

WINCHESTER MYSTERY HOUSE

The billboards up and down every highway in California may have set off your tourist-trap alarm, but **Winchester Mystery House** (Map p177; ☎ 408-247-2101; www.winchestermysteryhouse.com; 525 S Winchester Blvd) is a bona fide curiosity. It's a ridiculous Victorian mansion with 160 rooms of various sizes (many of them utterly useless), dead-end hallways and a staircase that runs up to a ceiling all jammed together like a child's build-a-house game. The woman responsible for it is Sarah Winchester, heir of the Winchester rifle fortune, who, beginning in 1884, spent 38 years building this sprawling mansion because the spirits of those killed by her husband's guns told her to do so. Apparently no expense was spared in the construction and the extreme results sprawl over the 4 acre grounds. You'll have to decide whether it's enough to have heard the story, or if it's worth shelling out the overpriced admission fees to see the house for yourself.

The house is west of central San Jose, just north of I-280. Most people shell out $19.95/13.95 (adult/child) for the 65-minute guided mansion tour, which includes a self-guided romp through the gardens as well as entry to an exhibition of guns and rifles. The 50-minute 'Behind the Scenes' tour is for diehards willing to pay an extra $16.95/15.95 to see the house's basement, plumbing facilities and several other underwhelming features. A combined tour costs $24.95/21.95. All tours are offered every 30 minutes or so from 9:30am to 5pm daily, until 7pm in summer.

HIKING & BICYCLING

There are several parks in the hills around San Jose, each laced with a network of hiking and biking trails.

Almaden Quicksilver County Park (☎ 408-268-8220) is south of town at the site of the old New Almaden mercury mine. Don't eat fish from the reservoirs, but do check out the trails, spring wildflower displays and mining museum, open Friday to Sunday. From San Jose, head south via the Almaden Expressway.

West of San Jose lies **Castle Rock State Park** (Map p177; ☎ 408-867-2952), where hiking trails are alternately lush and sun-drenched, providing beautiful ocean vistas. The park is on Hwy 35 in the Santa Cruz mountains,

just south of the intersection with Hwy 9. Parking is available ($2).

Sleeping

The hotels downtown are busy year-round, thanks to conventions and trade shows. Because the city is a hotbed of business travelers, midweek rates are often higher than weekends (generally considered Friday to Sunday). The cheapest lodging options are the HI hostel near Saratoga and camping in Henry Coe State Park, each requiring a long drive out of town. There's a string of older motels south of downtown on Monterey Hwy though the motels along the Alameda are generally in better shape. More are found on N 1st St near the airport.

Hotel Montgomery (Map p178; ☎ 408-282-8800, 866-823-0530; 211 S 1st St; r $159-189; Ⓟ 🅧 🖵) Built in 1911 and recently restored, the Montgomery combines the stately grandeur of a traditional downtown hotel with cutting-edge exuberance of contemporary design concepts. A beautiful property, the rooms are sizable and comfortable. In addition to amenities such as bathrobes and high-speed Internet, there's a fitness room and the fine Paragon Restaurant off the lobby.

Hotel Valencia (Map p177; ☎ 408-551-0010, 866-842-0100; www.hotelvalencia.com; 355 Santana Row; r $189-319; Ⓟ 🖵 🐾) In the busy confines of the Santana Row development, this fully modern hotel evokes European luxury with 211 stylish rooms that have leather chairs and marble baths. Some rooms have balconies overlooking the dining and entertainment strip.

Sainte Claire Hotel (Map p178; ☎ 408-295-2000; www.thesainteclaire.com; 302 S Market St; r weekend/midweek from $99/159; Ⓟ 🅧 🖵) This landmark hotel was built in 1926 overlooking Plaza de Cesar Chavez. It was renovated in 1992 and the lobby is a beauty. Guest rooms, while smallish, are modern and smartly designed.

Hotel De Anza (Map p178; ☎ 408-286-1000, 800-843-3700; www.hoteldeanza.com; 233 W Santa Clara St; r $129-179; Ⓟ 🅧) This downtown hotel is a restored art deco beauty, although contemporary stylings overwhelm the place's history. Guest rooms offer plush comforts and full concierge service is available.

Ramada Limited (Map p178; ☎ 408-298-3500; www.ramada.com; 455 S 2nd St; r $74-109; Ⓟ 🅧 🐾) This basic chain is at the edge of the busy SOFA nightlife district and, unlike most hotels of its type, has a fitness center.

City Center Motel (Map p178; ☎ 408-998-5990; cnr 2nd & E Reed Sts; s/d $59/69; [P] [🐾]) Within stumbling distance of the SOFA district is this slightly run-down choice. The rooms are acceptable for the price.

Sanborn Park Hostel (Map p177; ☎ 408-741-0166; www.sanbornparkhostel.org; 15808 Sanborn Rd; dm $14-16) This is a HI hostel in an amazingly beautiful 1908 log building among dense redwoods in 3600-acre Sanborn County Park, 12 miles west of San Jose. The setting is incredible, and few locals even know it exists. Bring all your food and supplies, as the nearest shops and restaurants are 4 miles away in Saratoga. From Saratoga, drive west on Hwy 9 and look for signs to Sanborn County Park. If you don't have a car, the hostel will pick you up from downtown Saratoga; call before 9pm. With a car, from downtown San Jose, follow N 1st St north for approximately 2 miles. It's on the north side of I-880 but west of Hwy 17.

Henry Coe State Park (☎ 408-779-2728, reservations 800-444-7275; www.coepark.org; sites $11) Southeast of San Jose near Morgan Hill, this huge state park has 20 drive-in campsites at the top of an open ridge overlooking the hills and canyons of the park's back country. There are no showers. To reserve call at least two days in advance.

Eating

There are plenty of places to choose from along S 1st St and on San Pedro St by San Pedro Sq. Vietnamese restaurants are gathered along E Santa Clara St from 4th to 12th Sts (also see East Bay Globe Trot, p171). Santana Row has several good restaurants.

Arcadia (Map p178; ☎ 408-278-4555; 100 W San Carlos St; mains lunch $14-18, dinner $25-37) Chef Michael Minna, San Francisco's biggest celebrity chef, opened this fine New American restaurant in the Marriott Hotel. It's not the daring, cutting-edge style Minna is known for, but it's slick, expensive and, of course, very good.

Amber India (Map p177; ☎ 408-248-5400; 1140 Olsen Dr; dinner mains $12-29) Just off Santana Row, Amber is an upscale Indian restaurant offering a full complement of kebabs, curries and tandooris. The cooking here is superb and the presentation highly styled, with artsy china and groovy paintings on the walls. Whet your whistle with an exotic cocktail.

Original Joe's (Map p178; ☎ 408-292-7030; 301 S 1st St; mains from $12) This is a San Jose land-

mark serving standard Italian dishes in a chrome-and-glass dining room loaded with boisterous 1950s charm. Expect a wait.

Pizza Antica (Map p177; ☎ 408-557-8373; 334 Santana Row; mains $8-15) Artisan pizzas baked the old-fashioned way, in stone ovens, are the specialty here. Grab a sidewalk table on Santana Row and enjoy a cold tap beer while San Jose's best pizza is crafted to order.

La Taquería (Map p178; 15 S 1st St; mains $3-5; [☺] Mon-Sat) Excellent burritos and tacos are assembled in this wonderful little taquería.

Waves Smokehouse & Saloon (Map p178; ☎ 415-885-9283; 65 Post St; mains $7-23) Waves serves up barbecue platters and burgers in an Old West–style saloon and former brothel dating from 1873. If you're not hungry, a drink in the historic bar, where stained glass and dark wood prevail, will take you back to a time when Post St bustled with all manner of sin and commerce. At night there's music, dancing and karaoke.

Vegetarian House (☎ 408-292-3798; 520 E Santa Clara Ave; mains $6-10) Prepares an international assortment of vegetarian dishes, from Asian noodles to lasagna. The airy dining room has an excellent juice bar and homages to spiritual master Ching Hai.

Emile's (Map p178; ☎ 408-289-1960; 545 S 2nd St; mains $27-32; [☺] dinner Tue-Sat) Emile's, run by Swiss-born chef Emile Mooser since 1973, is San Jose's longstanding standard-bearer. The setting is romantic, if slightly dated, and the California-European cuisine fabulous.

Blake's Steakhouse (Map p178; ☎ 408-298-9221; 17 N San Pedro St; mains $20-30) Blake's serves seafood, chops, prime rib and classic cuts of top-shelf steak.

Drinking

Trials Pub (Map p178; 265 N 1st St) If you seek a well-poured pint in a supremely comfortable atmosphere, Trials Pub, north of San Pedro Sq, has many excellent ales on tap (try a Fat Lip), all served in a warm and friendly room with no TVs. There's good pub food too.

Hedley Club (Map p178; 233 W Santa Clara St) Also downtown, inside the elegant 1931 Hotel De Anza, Hedley Club is a good place for a quiet drink in art deco surroundings. Jazz combos play Friday and Saturday night.

Almaden Feed & Fuel (18950 Almaden Rd) If you've been hiking all day in Almaden Quicksilver County Park, stop for a bite and a beer at this funky, century-old joint that was once a stagecoach stop. It's about 10 miles south of San Jose, just off the Almaden Expressway.

Entertainment

CLUBS

The biggest conglomeration of clubs is on S 1st St, aka SOFA.

Agenda (Map p178; 399 S 1st St) Agenda is a bar and restaurant that also serves up live jazz and cocktail music upstairs and house music in the cellar. A happy-hour cocktail in the lovely upstairs bar makes a pleasant start to the evening.

Zoë (Map p178; 417 S 1st St) The young and stylish shake it up in this ultra lounge. Hip-hop rules the weekend. Admission is free Thursday.

Sofa Lounge (Map p178; 372 S 1st St) In a cool loft space above the Eulipia Restaurant, Sofa is a relaxed club that puts on live music and DJs. The space has anchored the 1st St scene and attracts a savvy, mixed crowd.

South First Billiards (Map p178; 420 S 1st St) It's a great place to shoot some stick, and a welcoming club to boot. Sunday's free rock shows always draw a fun crowd.

THEATER & CINEMA

San Jose Repertory Theatre (Map p178; ☎ 408-367-7255; www.sjrep.com; 101 Paseo de San Antonio; tickets $20-44) Now in its third decade, this company offers a full season of top-rated productions in a new, 525-seat venue downtown.

California Theatre (Map p178; 345 S 1st St) This entertainment landmark venue has undergone a thorough renovation and its absolutely stunning Spanish interior is cathedral worthy. It is home to Opera San Jose, Symphony Silicon Valley and an ongoing classic film series. This is one venue for the city's annual film festival, Cinequest (☎ 408-995-5033; www.cinequest.org), held in late February or early March.

Camera 12 (Map p178; ☎ 408-998-3300; 201 S 2nd St; admission $9) A multiplex with a state-of-the- art sound system, and featuring independent and foreign films along with the better Hollywood releases.

SPORTS

HP Pavilion (Compaq Center, cnr Santa Clara & Autumn Sts; tickets $17-117) The San Jose Sharks, the city's NHL team, plays at the HP Pavilion, a massive glass-and-metal stadium. The NHL season runs from September to April.

Spartan Stadium (cnr 7th & Alma Sts; tickets $13-45) Major League soccer team the San Jose Earthquakes (formerly the Clash) plays at the Spartan Stadium from late March to mid-October.

Tickets for either team are available from the **Compaq Center box office** (☎ 408-999-5721) or, for a surcharge, book through **Ticketmaster** (☎ 408-998-8497).

Getting There & Away

The quickest and most convenient connection between San Jose and San Francisco is with CalTrain, a commuter rail service that operates daily up and down the Peninsula.

AIR

Two miles north of downtown, between Hwy 101 and I-880, is the **San Jose International Airport** (Map p177; ☎ 408-277-4759). The airport has grown busier as the South Bay gets more crowded, with numerous domestic flights at two terminals and a new Interim International Arrivals Facility. Expansion is in the works.

BUS & BART

Greyhound buses to San Francisco ($6, 90 minutes) and to Los Angeles ($39 to $58, seven to nine hours) leave from the **Greyhound station** (Map p178; ☎ 408-295-4151; 70 Almaden Ave).

To access the BART system in the East Bay, bus 180, operated by the **Santa Clara Valley Transportation Agency** (VTA; ☎ 408-321-2300, 800-894-9908), runs daily between the Fremont BART station and downtown ($3.50).

CAR & MOTORCYCLE

San Jose is right at the bottom end of the San Francisco Bay, about 40 miles from Oakland (via I-880) or San Francisco (via Hwy 101 or I-280). Expect lots of traffic at all times of day on Hwy 101. Although I-280 is slightly longer, it's much prettier and usually less congested. On the East Bay side, I-880 – another ugly, hugely congested highway – runs between Oakland and San Jose. Hwy 17 leads over the hill to Santa Cruz.

TRAIN

Between San Jose and San Francisco, **CalTrain** (☎ 800-660-4287) makes over three dozen trips daily (fewer on weekends); the 90-minute journey costs $6.50 each way. San Jose's main **CalTrain station** (65 Cahill St) is just south of the Alameda.

The Cahill St CalTrain station doubles as the **Amtrak** (☎ 800-872-7245) station, serving Seattle, Los Angeles and Sacramento.

VTA runs a weekday shuttle from the station to downtown (known as the Downtown Area Shuttle or DASH; Rte 804).

Getting Around

Every 10 minutes, a free shuttle runs from both terminals to the Metro/Airport Light Rail station, where you can catch the San Jose light rail to downtown San Jose ($1.75).

SuperShuttle (☎ 408-225-4444) offers door-to-door bus service to most Silicon Valley destinations; fares start at $19.

The main San Jose light-rail line runs 20 miles north–south from the city center. Heading south gets you as far as Almaden and Santa Teresa. The northern route runs to the Civic Center, the airport and Baypointe, where it connects with another line that heads west past Great America to downtown Mountain View.

VTA buses run all over Silicon Valley. Fares for buses (except express lines) and light-rail trains are $1.75 for a single ride and $5.25 for a day pass. For information and schedules phone ☎ 408-321-2300 or ☎ 800-894-9908.

San Jose's historic trolley cars, dating from 1903 to 1928, operate on a 1.5-mile loop through downtown San Jose. These vintage vehicles operate on weekends from April to September, and also during the Christmas season.

AROUND SAN JOSE
Mission Santa Clara de Asís

The eighth mission in California, Mission Santa Clara de Asís (Map p177) is located on the Santa Clara University campus, west of downtown San Jose. The mission started life in 1777, on the Guadalupe River. Floods forced the first move; the second site was only temporary; the third church burned; while the fourth church, a substantial adobe construction, was finished in 1784, but an earthquake in 1818 forced the move to the present site. That church, the fifth, was completed in 1822, but in 1926 it burned down, so the present church – an enlarged version of the 1822 church, completed in 1928 – is the sixth church on the fifth site.

Many of the roof tiles came from the earlier buildings, and the church is fronted by a wooden cross from the original mission of 1777. The only remains from the 1822 mission are a nearby adobe wall and an adobe building. The first college in California was opened at the mission in 1851. The college grew to become Santa Clara University, and the mission church is now the college chapel. Santa Clara University is within walking distance of the Santa Clara CalTrain station.

Mission San José

This **mission** (Map p177; ☎ 510-657-1797; 43300 Mission Blvd; ☉ museum & church 10am-5pm daily, mass 8am Mon-Fri) is not in the city of San Jose, but in Fremont. Founded in 1797, the Mission San José was the 14th California mission. Its large Native American population and fertile agricultural lands made it one of the most successful, until a major earthquake struck in 1868, virtually leveling the mission's original 1809 church, which was then replaced by a wooden one. In 1979, the wooden church was sold and moved to San Mateo. The adobe church seen today is a reasonably faithful reconstruction of the 1809 structure. A statue of St Bonaventure, in a side altar, dates from around 1808. The adjacent living quarters, now housing a small mission museum, are original.

The mission is at the foot of Mission Peak Regional Preserve. From I-880 or I-680, take the Mission Blvd exit to Washington Blvd.

Intel Museum

Check out the **Intel Museum** (Map p177; ☎ 408-765-0503; www.intelmuseum.com; 2200 Mission College Blvd; admission free; ☉ 9am-6pm Mon-Fri, 10am-5pm Sat), which has displays on the birth and growth of the computer industry with special emphasis, not surprisingly, on Intel's involvement. Call ahead if you want to schedule a guided tour.

SAN FRANCISCO TO HALF MOON BAY

One of the real surprises of the Bay Area is how fast the urban landscape disappears along the rugged and largely undeveloped coast. The 70-mile stretch of coastal Hwy 1 from San Francisco to Santa Cruz is one of the most beautiful motorways anywhere. For the most part a winding two-lane blacktop, it passes beach after beach, many of them little sandy coves hidden from the highway. Most beaches along Hwy 1 are buffeted by wild and unpredictable surf, making them more suitable for sunbathing (weather permitting) than swimming. The state beaches along the coast don't charge an access fee, but parking can cost a few dollars.

A cluster of isolated and supremely scenic HI hostels, at Point Montara (22 miles south of San Francisco) and Pigeon Point (36 miles), make this an interesting route for cyclists, though narrow Hwy 1 itself can be stressful, if not downright dangerous, for inexperienced cyclists.

Pacifica & Devil's Slide

Pacifica and Point San Pedro, 15 miles from downtown San Francisco, signal the end of the urban sprawl. South of Pacifica is Devil's Slide, an unstable cliff area through which Hwy 1 winds and curves. Drive carefully, especially at night and when it is raining, as rock and mud slides are frequent. Heavy winter storms often lead to the road's temporary closure. A tunnel will soon bypass this dramatic stretch of the highway.

Collecting a suntan or catching a wave are the attractions at **Rockaway Beach** in Pacifica and the more popular **Pacifica State Beach**.

Gray Whale Cove to Mavericks

Just south of Point San Pedro is **Gray Whale Cove State Beach** (☎ 415-330-6300), one of the coast's popular 'clothing-optional' beaches. There are steps down to the beach from a parking lot ($5). **Montara State Beach** is just a half-mile south. From the town of Montara, 22 miles from San Francisco, trails climb up from the Martini Creek parking lot into **McNee Ranch State Park**, which has hiking trails aplenty.

Point Montara Lighthouse HI Hostel (☎ 650-728-7177; www.norcalhostels.org/montara; cnr Hwy 1 & 16th St; dm $18-21, private r $51-78) started life as a fog station in 1875. The hostel is adjacent to the current lighthouse, which dates from 1928. This very popular hostel has a living room, kitchen facilities, an outdoor hot tub and an international clientele. There are a few private rooms for couples or families. Reservations are a good idea anytime, but especially on weekends during summer. SamTrans bus 294 will let you off at the hostel if you ask nicely. Montara has a number of B&Bs too, including the **Goose & Turrets** (☎ 650-728-5451; http://goose.montara.com; 835 George St; r $145-190) and the **Farallone Inn**

(☎ 650-728-8200; www.faralloneinn.com; 1410 Main St; r $95-195; ✖).

South of the lighthouse, **Fitzgerald Marine Reserve** (☎ 650-363-4020) at Moss Beach is an extensive area of natural tidal pools. Feel free to walk out and explore the pools at low tide, though be careful, as it's slippery. Also, it's illegal to remove any creatures, shells or even rocks – this is a marine reserve, after all. From Hwy 1 in Moss Beach, turn west onto California Ave and drive to the end. SamTrans bus 294 stops along Hwy 1.

Moss Beach Distillery (☎ 650-728-5595; cnr Beach Way & Ocean Blvd; mains from $15) is a 1927 landmark overlooking the ocean. In fair weather the deck here is the best place for miles around to have a leisurely cocktail or glass of vino.

South of here is a stretch of coast called Pillar Point. Fishing boats bring in their catch at the Pillar Point Harbor, some of which gets cooked up in seafront restaurants at Princeton such as **Barbara's Fishtrap** (281 Capistrano Rd), off Hwy 1, a true old-time fisherman's rest.

At the western end of Pillar Point is **Mavericks**, a serious surf break that attracts the world's top big-wave riders to battle its huge, steep and very dangerous waves. The annual Quiksilver/Mavericks surf contest is held between December and March, depending on conditions.

HALF MOON BAY
pop 11,300

Half Moon Bay is the main coastal town between San Francisco (28 miles north) and Santa Cruz (40 miles south). It developed as a beach resort back in the Victorian era, and its long stretches of beach still attract weekenders and hearty surfers.

Orientation & Information

Half Moon Bay spreads out along Hwy 1 (called Cabrillo Hwy in town), but despite the development it's still relatively small. The main drag is a five-block stretch called Main St lined with shops, cafés, restaurants and a few upscale B&Bs.

Visitor information is available from the **Half Moon Bay Coastside Chamber of Commerce** (☎ 650-726-8380; www.halfmoonbaychamber.org; 520 Kelly Ave; ◷ 9am-4pm Mon-Fri).

Sights & Activities

Inland **Purisima Creek Preserve** has a small but worthwhile set of trails for cyclists and hikers; follow Higgins–Purisma Rd from Hwy 1.

Seahorse (☎ 650-726-9903), around 1 mile north of the Hwy 92 junction, offers daily horseback rides along the beach. A two-hour ride is $60; early-bird specials start between 8am and 9am and cost just $35.

Pumpkins are a major crop around Half Moon Bay, and the pre-Halloween harvest is celebrated in the annual **Art & Pumpkin Festival** (☎ 650-726-9652). The mid-October event kicks off with the World Championship Pumpkin Weigh-Off, where the bulbous orange beasts can bust the scales at over 1000lb.

Sleeping & Eating

San Benito House (☎ 650-726-3425; www.sanbenito house.com; 356 Main St; r $80-176) Popular for honeymooning, San Benito House is a traditional inn that retains much of its simple Victorian elegance. It has 12 neatly antiquated rooms.

Half Moon Bay State Beach (☎ 650-726-8820; sites $12) Just west of town on Kelly Ave is this cheap overnight option, with spartan campsites available on a first-come, first-served basis.

Flying Fish Grill (cnr Hwy 92 & Main St; items from $3) This place has excellent fresh cod or salmon tacos, along with other seafood plates, which you can take out or eat in.

M Coffee (522 Main St; lunch $5-7) This café has espresso drinks, ice-cream cones and lunchtime sandwiches and salads.

Cameron's Restaurant & Inn (☎ 650-726-5705; 1410 S Cabrillo Hwy; r from $99) A couple miles south of the Hwy 92 junction, Cameron's is an English-style pub in a century-old building, with a large selection of beer and food (mains from $8). If you don't mind bar-room noise there are three large, comfortable rooms over the pub.

Getting There & Away

SamTrans (☎ 800-660-4287) bus 294 operates from the Hillsdale CalTrain station to Half Moon Bay, and up the coast to Moss Beach and Pacifica, daily until about 6pm ($1.50).

HALF MOON BAY TO SANTA CRUZ

More beaches lie south of Half Moon Bay, starting with **San Gregorio State Beach**, 10 miles to the south. It has a clothing-optional stretch to the north, but the beach can get so chilly that only polar bears would find the idea appealing.

> **DETOUR: LA HONDA & HIGHWAY 84**
>
> Inland, large stretches of the hills are protected in a patchwork of parks that, just like the coast, remain remarkably untouched despite the huge urban populations only a short drive to the north and east. Heading east toward Palo Alto, Hwy 84 winds its way through thick stands of redwood trees. Along the way is the tiny township of **La Honda**, 9 miles east of San Gregorio State Beach, and several local parks with mountain-biking and hiking opportunities. La Honda's **Apple Jack's Inn** (☎ 650-747-0331), housed in an old blacksmith's shop, is a rustic, down-home bar offering live music on weekends and lots of local color.

Pomponio and Pescadero State Beaches are further down the coast. Bird-watchers enjoy **Pescadero Marsh Reserve**, across the highway from Pescadero State Beach, where numerous species feed year-round. **Butano State Park**, about 5 miles south of Pescadero, is good for day hikes.

Originally an old farm village, **Pescadero** (www.pescaderovillage.com) is now a little getaway for those in the know. Three miles east of Hwy 1 it's a small crossroads on the way to the interior and a collection of mountainous parks and forest preserves. The hamlet is also well supplied with antiques, curiosity shops, a fine bakery, handmade-furniture studio, historic church and the perfect isolation needed to feel away from it all. It is accessible from Hwy 1, south of San Gregorio State Beach on Pescadero Creek Rd.

Pescadero Creekside Barn (☎ 650-879-0868; www.pescaderolodging.com; 248 Stage Rd; r $125; ✗) is just that, a barn by the creek. But its loft has been converted into a cozy and romantic hideaway lodging for two, and two only, with a two-night minimum on weekends.

Pigeon Point Lighthouse Hostel (☎ 650-879-0633; www.norcalhostels.org/lighthouses.html; 210 Pigeon Point Rd, Pescadero; dm $18-26, r $46-59), an HI facility at Pigeon Point, 5 miles south of Pescadero along Hwy 1, is based in the old lighthouse-keeper's quarters. The 115ft lighthouse, one of the tallest in America, was constructed in 1872. The hostel is such a pleasant place that, especially on weekends and throughout the summer season, advance reservations are essential.

ELEPHANT SEALS

Elephant seals follow a precise calendar: between September and November young seals and the yearlings, who left the beach earlier in the year, return and take up residence. In November and December, the adult males return and start the ritual struggles to assert superiority; only the largest, strongest and most aggressive 'alpha' males gather a harem. From December through February, the adult females arrive, pregnant from last year's beach activities, give birth to their pups and, about a month later, mate with the dominant males.

At birth an elephant seal pup weighs about 80lb and, while being fed by its mother, puts on about 7lb a day. A month's solid feeding will bring the pup's weight up to about 300lb, but around March, the females depart, abandoning their offspring on the beach. For the next two to three months the young seals, now known as 'weaners,' lounge around in groups known as 'pods,' gradually learning to swim, first in the rivers and tidal pools, then in the sea. In April, the young seals depart, having lost 20% to 30% of their weight during this prolonged fast.

Duarte's Tavern (☎ 650-879-0464; www.duartestavern.com; 202 Stage Rd; mains $16-23) is like going home for dinner. It has been run by the same family for three generations. The menu is basic roadhouse fare: chops, steaks, deep-fried seafood, French dip sandwich, burgers and fries. There is a salad on the menu somewhere, but you'll have to look closely.

Big Basin Redwoods State Park (p439) is further down the coast, with the easiest access from Santa Cruz.

Año Nuevo State Reserve

A visit to the elephant seal colony on Año Nuevo Beach is a wonderful experience, but in the midwinter peak season, you must plan well ahead. The beach is 5 miles south of Pigeon Point and 27 miles north of Santa Cruz.

Elephant seals were just as fearless two centuries ago as they are today, but unfortunately, club-toting seal trappers were not in the same seal-friendly category as camera-toting tourists. Between 1800 and 1850, the elephant seal was driven to the edge of extinction. Only a handful survived around the Guadalupe Islands off the Mexican state of Baja California. With the availability of substitutes for seal oil and the conservationist attitudes of more recent times, the elephant seal has made a comeback, reappearing on the Southern California coast from around 1920. In 1955, they returned to Año Nuevo Beach, and today the reserve is home to thousands in the peak season.

The peak season is during the mating and birthing time, December 15 to the end of March, when visitors are only permitted access through heavily booked guided tours. For the busiest period, mid-January to mid-February, it's recommended you book eight weeks ahead. Although the **park office** (☎ 650-879-0227; www.anonuevo.org) can advise on your chances of getting a place, bookings can only be made by calling ☎ 800-444-7275. Tours cost $5, plus $6 for parking. From the ranger station it's a 3- to 5-mile round-trip hike to the beach, and the visit takes two to three hours. If you haven't booked, bad weather can sometimes lead to last-minute cancellations. The rest of the year, advance reservations aren't necessary, but visitor permits from the entrance station are required; arrive before 3pm.

Wine Country

A patchwork of vineyards, orchards and gnarled oak trees covers toast-colored hills in pastoral Wine Country. Extending from the cool, foggy Pacific coast to the parallel hot, inland Sonoma and Napa Valleys, Wine Country is mesmerizing and idyllic. It's also one of the world's premier viticulture regions and goes tête-à-tête with some of France's greatest *terroirs*.

The Wine Country's tradition of high-quality batch production dates to 1857, when Hungarian Count Ágoston Haraszthy established the state's first commercial winery, Buena Vista, in rural Sonoma Valley. But it wasn't until the mid-1970s that the region's wineries first won worldwide acclaim. The turning point was a blind wine-tasting competition in France in 1976, when two Napa Valley entries – Chateau Montelena's 1973 chardonnay and a 1973 cabernet sauvignon from Stag's Leap – outscored a venerable collection of French Bordeaux. Today there are over 450 wineries in Napa and Sonoma Counties. Though a quarter of California's 1300 commercial wineries are located here, Napa and Sonoma make only 10% of the state's total production. Quality, not quantity, sets the region apart.

Food is a big deal: Napa Valley fancies itself an extension of San Francisco's high-end culinary scene. You'll eat well here – really well, if you want to – but you don't necessarily have to spend a fortune doing so. Remember, Wine Country is an agricultural region. Despite all the hype about 'Wine Country style,' the area is basically farmland. You'll find fabulous fresh fruit, lip-smacking jams, brick-oven bread and wonderful cheeses, especially in Sonoma County. Plan to picnic. And pack a corkscrew. You're gonna need it.

WINE COUNTRY

HIGHLIGHTS

- Exploring Sonoma's fabulous back roads near **Occidental** (p206)
- Succumbing to your senses at **Copia** (p220)
- Eating your way through **Healdsburg** (p212)
- Sipping sauvignon blanc at **Frog's Leap** (p219)
- Indulging in a **mud bath** (p227) in Calistoga
- Canoeing the Russian River from **Guerneville** (p207) or **Healdsburg** (p212)
- Getting tattooed at **Roshambo Winery** (p201)

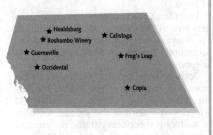

★ Healdsburg
★ Roshambo Winery   ★ Calistoga
★ Guerneville
★ Frog's Leap
★ Occidental
★ Copia

■ AVERAGE TEMPS IN NAPA: JAN 37/54°F, JUL 54/82°F

Wine Tasting

The wineries in this chapter are family-owned boutique wineries, which produce fewer than 20,000 cases annually. You can't easily find these wines elsewhere, except at a few restaurants and in some specialty shops in San Francisco, Los Angeles and New York.

Tastings are called 'flights' and include four to six different wines. Napa Valley wineries charge $5 to $30 per flight. In Sonoma Valley, tastings cost $5 to $10, refundable with purchase. In Sonoma County, tastings are usually free. You must be 21 to taste.

It's not wise to drink and drive. The narrow, curvy roads can be dangerous, and police monitor traffic intently, especially on Hwy 29 in Napa.

Aim to visit about three wineries in one day. Most offer tastings daily from 10am or 11am to 4:30pm or 5pm, but call ahead if you don't want to miss a tasting, or if you absolutely want a tour, especially in Napa, where local regulations require that some wineries accept visitors only by appointment. If you're buying wine, ask if the winery has a wine club, which is usually free to join and provides discounts and benefits.

Regarding picnics, zoning laws in Napa prohibit picnicking at most wineries. But in Sonoma, every place allows it. Just remember to buy a bottle of your host's wine.

Getting There & Around

Napa and Sonoma counties each has a city and valley of the same name. So, the town of Sonoma is located in Sonoma County, at the southern end of Sonoma Valley. The same goes for the city, county and valley of Napa.

From San Francisco, public transportation gets you to the valleys, but it's insufficient for vineyard-hopping. For public-transit information, dial ☎ 511 from any Bay Area telephone.

Both of the valleys are 90 minutes by car from San Francisco. Napa Valley, the further inland of the two, has more than 230 wineries and attracts the greatest number of visitors (expect heavy traffic on summer weekends). Sonoma County has 240 wineries, 60 in Sonoma Valley, which is less commercial and marginally less congested than Napa. Greater Sonoma County has an additional 180 wineries. If you have time to visit only one valley, see Sonoma.

BICYCLE

Touring Wine Country by bicycle is unforgettable. Stick to the back roads. Through Sonoma Valley, take Arnold Dr instead of Hwy 12; through Napa Valley, take the Silverado Trail instead of Hwy 29.

Both valleys are fairly flat and cycle-friendly. Pedaling between wineries isn't too demanding. Crossing from one valley to the other is challenging, particularly via steep Oakville Grade and Trinity Rd (between Oakville and Glen Ellen).

Bicycles, in boxes, can be checked on Greyhound buses for $15 (for details, see p720). You can also transport bicycles on Golden Gate Transit buses, which usually have bike racks available free (first-come, first-served). For rentals, see Tours opposite.

CAR

From San Francisco, take Hwy 101 north then Hwy 37 east then Hwy 121 north; continue to the junction of Hwys 12 and 121. For Sonoma Valley, take Hwy 12 north; for Napa Valley, take Hwy 12/121 east. Plan 70 minutes in light traffic, two hours during weekday commute times.

Highway 12/121 splits just south of Napa: Hwy 121 turns north and joins with Hwy 29 (aka St Helena Hwy); Hwy 12 merges with the southbound extension of Hwy 29. Highway 29 backs up weekdays 4pm to 7pm, which slows return trips to San Francisco.

From the East Bay (or from downtown San Francisco), take I-80 east to Hwy 37 west (just north of Vallejo), and turn north on Hwy 29.

From Santa Rosa, take Hwy 12 east to access the northern end of Sonoma Valley. From Petaluma and Hwy 101, take Hwy 116 east toward Sonoma.

PUBLIC TRANSPORTATION

Sonoma Airporter (☎ 707-938-4246, 800-611-4246; www.sonomaairporter.com) operates a door-to-door shuttle service ($40) between San Francisco Airport (SFO) and Sonoma Valley.

Greyhound (☎ 800-231-2222; www.greyhound.com) operates from San Francisco to Santa Rosa and Vallejo for $16; transfer for local buses.

Golden Gate Transit (☎ 415-923-2000; www.golden gate.org) operates bus 70/80 from San Francisco to Petaluma ($6.90) and to Santa Rosa ($7.60); catch it at 1st and Mission Sts, across from the Transbay Terminal.

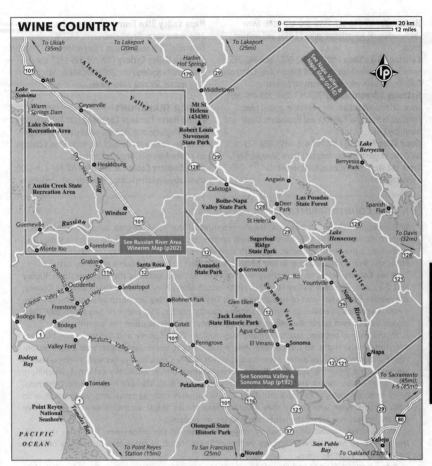

WINE COUNTRY

See Napa Valley & Napa Map (p216)
See Russian River Area Wineries Map (p202)
See Sonoma Valley & Sonoma Map (p192)

WINE COUNTRY

Napa Valley Vine (☎ 800-696-6443, 707-251-2800; www.nctpa.net) operates bus 10 from the Vallejo Ferry Terminal and Vallejo Transit bus station, through Napa to Calistoga ($2.50); it also runs local trolley services in Napa ($1).

Sonoma County Transit (☎ 707-576-7433, 800-345-7433; www.sctransit.com) runs the bus service from Santa Rosa to Petaluma (70 minutes), Sonoma (1¼ hours) and western Sonoma County, including the Russian River Valley towns (30 minutes).

Downtown Napa Trolley (☎ 800-696-6443, 707-251-2800; www.nctpa.net) operates without charge and makes a loop around downtown, every 20 minutes, 11am to 6pm Monday through Wednesday, 11am to 8pm Thursday and Sunday and 11am to 11pm Saturday.

Amtrak (☎ 800-872-7245; www.amtrak.com) trains travel to Martinez (south of Vallejo), with connecting buses on to Napa (40 minutes), Santa Rosa (1½ hours) and Healdsburg (1¾ hours).

BART trains (☎ 415 989-2278, www.bart.gov) run from San Francisco to El Cerrito (40 minutes), where you need to transfer to **Vallejo Transit** (☎ 707-648-4666; www.vallejotransit.com) for Vallejo (30 minutes); then you take Napa Valley Vine buses to Napa and Calistoga.

Tours
BICYCLE

Guided bike tours start at about $90 per day including bikes, tasting fees and lunch. Daily rentals cost $25 to $40; make reservations.

Backroads (☎ 510-527-1555, 800-462-2848; www .backroads.com) All-inclusive guided biking and walking tours.

Calistoga Bike Shop (☎ 707-942-9687, 866-942-2453; www.calistogabikeshop.com; 1318 Lincoln Ave, Calistoga) Daily rentals with wine bottle-carrying baskets!

Getaway Adventures (☎ 707-763-3040, 800-499-2453; www.getawayadventures.com) Fabulous guided tours. Locations in Petaluma, Calistoga and Healdsburg. Single- and multi-day trips.

Good Time Touring (☎ 707-938-0453, 888-525-0453; www.goodtimetouring.com) Tours Sonoma, Dry Creek and West County; bikes transported via Volkswagen van.

Napa Valley Bike Tours (☎ 707-944-2953, 800-707-2453; www.napavalleybiketours.com; 6488 Washington St, Yountville) Daily rentals; Napa Valley guides.

Sonoma Valley Cyclery (☎ 707-935-3377; www .sonomavalleycyclery.com; 20093 Broadway, Sonoma) Daily rentals; Sonoma Valley guides.

OTHER TRANSPORT

Flying Horse Carriage Company (☎ 707-849-8989; www.flyinghorse.org; 3hr tours per person $95) See the Alexander Valley from the back of a horse-drawn carriage on a three-hour tour. Bring a picnic lunch.

Wine Country Cable Car Shuttle (☎ 707-838-3200; www.cablecarcharters.com; per person $30; ⊗ Fri-Sun

---

A WINE COUNTRY PRIMER

When people talk about Sonoma, they're referring to the *whole* county, which unlike Napa is huge. It extends all the way from the coast, up the Russian River Valley, into Sonoma Valley and eastward to the Napa Valley; in the south it stretches from San Pablo Bay (an extension of San Francisco Bay) to Healdsburg in the north. It's essential to break Sonoma down by district.

West County refers to everything west of Hwy 101 and includes the **Russian River Valley** and the coast. **Sonoma Valley** stretches north–south along Hwy 12. In northern Sonoma County, **Alexander Valley** lies east of Healdsburg, and **Dry Creek Valley** lies north of Healdsburg. In the south, **Carneros** straddles the Sonoma–Napa county border, just north of San Pablo Bay. Each region has its own particular wines; what grows where depends upon the weather.

Inland valleys get hot; coastal regions stay cool. In West County and Carneros, fog blankets the vineyards at night, so Burgundian-style wines do best, particularly pinot noir and chardonnay. Further inland, Alexander, Sonoma and much of Dry Creek Valleys (as well as Napa Valley) are protected from the fog; here Bordeaux-style wines thrive, especially cabernet sauvignon, sauvignon blanc, merlot and other heat-loving varieties. For California's most famous cabernets, head to Napa Valley. Zinfandel and Rhône-style varieties such as syrah and viognier grow in both regions, warm and cool: if they grow in cooler climes, the resultant wines are lighter, more elegant; in warmer areas, the wines are heavier, more rustic.

As you drive around Wine Country, notice the bases of the grapevines. The fatter they are, the older they are. 'Old vine' grapes yield a richness, depth of color and complexity of flavor not found in younger vines.

A few basics: wineries and vineyards are not the same thing. Grapes grow in a vineyard, then get fermented into wine at a winery. Wineries that grow their own grapes are called estates, as in 'estate grown' or 'estate bottled,' but estates, too, often ferment grapes from other vineyards as well as their own. When vintners speak of 'single-vineyard' or 'vineyard-designate' wines, they mean that the grapes all came from the same vineyard, which allows for tighter quality control. 'Single varietal' means that all the grapes are the same variety (such as 100% merlot), but might come from different vineyards. Reserve wines are the vintner's special wines, of which only a few are made; they're usually only available at the winery.

But it all comes down to personal taste. If you don't like cabernet, who cares how well it grows in Napa? And if you're a neophyte, uncertain of what to try, don't be afraid to ask questions. Vintners love to share their knowledge with interested visitors. And if you don't know how to taste wine or what to look for, ask the person behind the tasting-room counter to help you discover what you like. Just remember to spit out the wine once you've tasted it; even the slightest buzz will diminish your capacity to distinguish one wine from another.

The hands-down best place for a crash course is Copia, the American Center for Wine, Food, and the Arts (p220), in Napa. For a handy-dandy reference on the road, pick up a paperback copy of Jancis Robinson's *Concise Wine Companion* (2001, Oxford University Press) to carry in the car.

May-Oct) Open-sided trolley cars make a continuous loop from the Healdsburg Plaza through the Alexander and Dry Creek Valleys, stopping at 12 wineries along the way; riders hop on and off the shuttles as they like. The first car leaves at 9:45am, the last at 4:45pm.

Wine Country Jeep Tours (☎ 707-546-1822, 800-539-5337; www.jeeptours.com; 3hr tour $75) Tour Wine Country's back roads and boutique wineries by Jeep. Tours depart year-round at 10am and 1pm. They also operate tours of the Sonoma Coast.

LIMOUSINE
Antique Tours Limousine (☎ 707-226-9227; www .antiquetours.net; 2205 Loma Heights Rd) Fancy a drive in a 1947 Packard convertible limousine? Antique Tours leads Napa Valley tours and charters for $100 per hour (minimum five).

Beau Wine Tours (☎ 707-257-0887, 800-387-2328; www.beauwinetours.com) For winery tours in sedans and stretch limos, Beau charges $50 to $80 per hour (minimum four); gourmet picnics cost $25 per person.

TRAIN
A cushy, touristy way to see Wine Country, the **Napa Valley Wine Train** (☎ 707-253-2111, 800-427-4124; www.winetrain.com; adult/child under 12 $48/24, add lunch adult/child $30-43/23 or dinner adult/child $48-68/23) offers three-hour daily trips in vintage Pullman dining cars, from Napa to St Helena and back. Trains depart from McKinstry St near 1st St.

SONOMA VALLEY

Locals call it 'Slow-noma.' Indeed, the kick-back vibe is infectious. If you aren't one of those destination-driven travelers, you'll love Sonoma. Anchoring the 17-mile-long valley, the town of Sonoma makes a good jumping-off point and has important California-historical sights and the state's largest town square. If that's still too fast, head to itty-bitty Glen Ellen, a town right out of a Norman Rockwell painting. At the valley's north end, Santa Rosa is the workaday urban center known mostly for its traffic. If you've more than one day, explore the quieter, rustic side of Sonoma County, which extends along the Russian River Valley (p201) from Healdsburg to the sea.

Sonoma Hwy/Hwy 12 is lined with wineries and runs from Sonoma to Santa Rosa, then to western Sonoma County; Arnold Dr has less traffic (but fewer wineries) and runs parallel, up the valley's western side, to Glen Ellen.

SONOMA VALLEY WINERIES
Sonoma Valley's 60 wineries get less attention than Napa's, but many are equally as good. The 17-mile by 7-mile valley is one of the most romantic places in California. If you love zinfandel and syrah, you're in for a treat.

Picnicking is allowed at Sonoma wineries. Get maps and discount coupons in the town of Sonoma (p195) or, if you're approaching from the south, the **Sonoma Valley Visitors Bureau** (☎ 707-935-4747; www.sonomavalley.com; ☯ 9am-4pm), off Hwy 121 on the grounds of Viansa winery (skip the winery).

The following are in south–north order. Plan at least five hours to visit the valley from bottom to top. For more on other Sonoma County wineries, see p201.

HOMEWOOD
'Da redder, da better' at **Homewood** (☎ 707-996-6353; www.homewoodwinery.com; 23120 Burndale Rd at Hwy 121/12; tastings free), a tiny Carneros District winery that makes fruit-forward, vineyard-designate wines. The tasting room is essentially a garage, but you'll get a warm welcome from Bo, the chocolate lab who sleeps underfoot. Ask about 'vertical tastings,' in which you sample the same wines from the same vineyards, but different years; also ask about chocolate pairings. Bottles cost $15 to $25; annual production 3000 cases.

ROBLEDO
Sonoma Valley's feel-good winery, **Robledo** (☎ 707-939-6903; www.robledofamilywinery.com; 21901 Bonness Rd, off Hwy 116; tastings $5-10) was founded by a former grape-picker from Mexico who worked his way up to vineyard manager, then landowner, now vintner. His nine kids run the place. The wine is excellent, including a crisp, no-oak sauvignon blanc; jammy, inky syrah; bold, spicy, lingering cabernet; and bright-fruit pinot noir. The windowless tasting room has hand-carved Mexican furniture, but ugly fluorescents. Bottles cost $15 to $40; annual production 5000 cases.

GUNDLACH-BUNDSCHU
One of Sonoma Valley's oldest and prettiest wineries, **Gundlach-Bundschu** (☎ 707-938-5277;

WINE COUNTRY

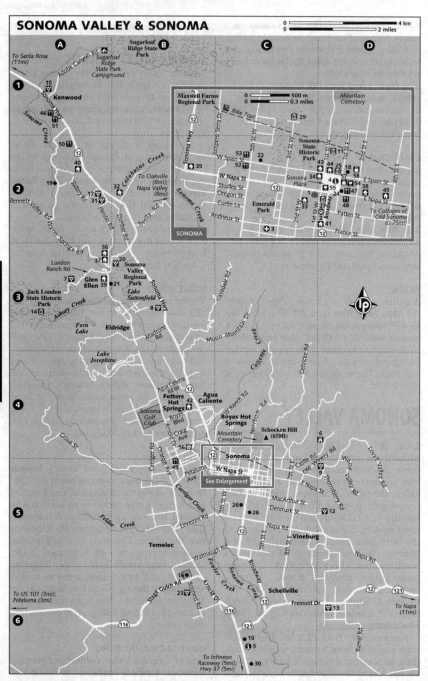

SONOMA VALLEY & SONOMA

www.gunbun.com; 2000 Denmark St; tastings $5-10) was founded in 1858 by Bavarian immigrant Jacob Gundlach. Rieslings and gewürzttraminers are the signatures, but 'Gun-Bun' was the first winery in America to produce 100% merlot. Tours of the 2000-barrel cave are available weekends noon to 3pm, by appointment weekdays. There's good picnicking, hiking trails and a small lake. Since it's up a winding road, it's a good bike-to winery. Bottles cost $20 to $35; annual production 38-55,000 cases.

BENZIGER
West of Glen Ellen, this educational **winery** (☎ 707-935-3000, 888-490-2739; www.benziger.com; 1883 London Ranch Rd, Glen Ellen; tastings $5-10) give Sonoma's best crash course in winemaking. If you know nothing of wine production, come straight here. The worthwhile, nonreservable tour ($10) includes an open-air tram ride through the vineyards, and a four-wine tasting. There's a peacock aviary too. Benziger specializes in cabernets; they're OK, but head for the reserves. The tour's the thing. Bottles cost $20 to $45; annual production 170,000 cases.

BR COHN
The winemaker manages the Doobie Brothers, and gold records hang on the wall at **BR Cohn** (☎ 707-938-4064; www.brcohn.com; 15000 Sonoma Hwy; tastings $5-10). Cabernet is what's best, and it's all 100% estate grown. Also sample wonderfully complex picholine olive oil, also estate grown. Picnic in the olive grove. The winery hosts summer concerts, sometimes including the Doobies. Bottles cost $20 to $40; annual production 25,000 cases.

LOXTON
Say g'day to Chris the Aussie winemaker at **Loxton** (☎ 707-935-7221; www.loxtonwines.com; 11466 Dunbar Rd, Glen Ellen; tastings free), a no-frills winery with a million-dollar view. The 'tasting room' is actually a small warehouse, where you can taste wonderful syrah. There's also terrific port; nonoaky, fruit-forward chardonnay; and good zinfandel. Bottles cost $15 to $25; annual production 1700 cases.

WELLINGTON
Known for port (including a white) and meaty, chewy reds, **Wellington** (☎ 707-939-0708; www.wellingtonvineyards.com; 11600 Dunbar Rd, Glen Ellen;

WINE COUNTRY

NAPA OR SONOMA?

Napa and Sonoma valleys run parallel to each other, only a few miles apart, separated by the narrow but imposing Mayacamas Mountains. The two couldn't be more different in character. It's easy to make fun of aggressively sophisticated Napa, with its trophy homes and trophy wives, $1000-a-night inns, $30 tastings and wine-snob visitors like the character Miles in the movie *Sideways*, but Napa makes some of the world's best wines. Constrained by its geography, it stretches along a single valley, so it's easy to visit. The drawbacks are high prices and heavy traffic, but there are 200 nearly side-by-side wineries. And the valley is gorgeous.

Sonoma County is much more folksy, down to earth and politically left leaning. You'll see a lot more unmown grass. Though it's becoming gentrified, Sonoma lacks Napa's chic factor, and the locals like it that way. The wines tend to be more approachable, but the county's 240 wineries are spread out (see A Wine Country Primer, p190). If you're here on a weekend, head to Sonoma (County or Valley), which gets less traffic, but if you're visiting on a weekday, see Napa, too. Ideally schedule two to four days: one for each valley, and one or two additional days for western Sonoma County.

Spring and fall are the best times to visit. Summers are hot, dusty and crowded. Fall brings fine weather, harvest time and the 'crush,' the pressing of the grapes.

---

tastings $5) makes damn good zinfandel, one from vines planted 1892 – wow, what color! The *noir de noir* is a cult favorite. The tasting room is inside out, though: the servers have vineyard views, while you face the warehouse. Bottles cost $15 to $30; annual production 8000 cases.

KAZ

It's about blends at supercool **Kaz** (☎ 707-833-2536; www.kazwinery.com; 233 Adobe Canyon Rd, Kenwood; tastings $2; ⏰ 11am-5pm Fri-Mon), Sonoma's cult favorite. Whatever is in the vineyard goes into the wine (but they're blended at crushing time, not during fermentation). Expect lesser-known varieties like alicante bouchet and lenoir, as well as a worthwhile cabernet-merlot blend. Kids can sample grape juice and mold Playdoh while you taste. Dogs welcome. Bottles cost $10 to $40; annual production 1000 cases.

SONOMA & AROUND
pop 9350
Built around a giant central square, Sonoma has an easy-going small-town feeling in spite of ongoing gentrification. But its charms are no secret. Downtown gets packed summer weekends, when traffic clogs the streets around the leafy, green plaza – where you can drink openly, a rarity in California parks. Sonoma loves a party and hosts celebrations, cook-offs, concerts and events year-round.

Sonoma was the site of a second American revolution, this time against Mexico. In 1846 General Mariano Guadalupe Vallejo deported all foreigners from California, which prompted outraged American frontiersmen to occupy the lightly guarded Sonoma presidio and declare independence (see p32). They dubbed California the Bear Flag Republic, after the battle flag they had fashioned. The unfortunate Vallejo was thereafter bundled off to imprisonment in Sacramento.

The republic was short-lived. One month later the Mexican-American War broke out and California was taken over by the US government. The abortive revolt did, however, give California its state flag, which features a bear and still proclaims 'California Republic.' Vallejo, whose name pops up all over town, was soon back in Sonoma and continued to play a major role in the development of the region. He was elected to the first state senate in 1850 and was mayor of Sonoma from 1852 to 1860.

Orientation & Information
Sonoma Hwy (Hwy 12) runs through town. Sonoma Plaza, laid out by General Vallejo in 1834, is the heart of downtown Sonoma, lined with hotels, restaurants and shops. Pick up a walking tour brochure from the visitors bureau. North of downtown along Hwy 12, expect a suburban landscape.

BOOKSTORES
Chanticleer Books & Prints (☎ 707-996-7613; 127 E Napa St; ⏰ Wed-Mon) Antiquarian, 1st editions and California history.

Readers' Books (☎ 707-939-1779; 130 E Napa St) Independent bookseller.

EMERGENCY & MEDICAL SERVICES
Police, fire, ambulance (☎ 911) Emergencies.
Sonoma Valley Hospital (☎ 707-935-5000; 347 Andrieux St; ✆ 24hr) Emergency room.

INTERNET ACCESS
Adobe Net Cafe (☎ 707-935-0390; www.adobenetcafe .com; 135 W Napa St)

MEDIA
KRSH 95.5 and 95.9 FM Eclectic music, locally programmed.
KSVY 91.3 FM Community radio; world music to local politics.

POST
Sonoma post office (☎ 800-275-8777; 617 Broadway; ✆ Mon-Fri)

TOURIST INFORMATION
Sonoma Valley Visitors Bureau (☎ 707-996-1090; www.sonomavalley.com; 453 1st St E; ✆ 9am-6pm Jul-Sep, 9am-5pm Oct-Jun) Arranges accommodations (no fee); has a good walking-tour pamphlet and information on festivals and events.

Sights
SONOMA PLAZA & AROUND
Right in the middle of the plaza, the Mission revival-style **City Hall** (1906–08) has identical facades on all four sides, supposedly because plaza businesses all demanded City Hall face their direction. At the plaza's northeast corner, the **Bear Flag Monument** marks Sonoma's moment of revolutionary glory.

Other noteworthy buildings include the **Sebastiani Theatre** (476 1st St E), a 1934 Mission revival cinema that still screens films. Just off the plaza, **Blue Wing Inn** (139 E Spain St) was apparently built by General Vallejo around 1840 to house visiting soldiers and travelers. It later served as a hotel, saloon and stage-coach depot.

On the plaza's north side, next to the Sonoma Barracks, the **Toscano Hotel** (20 E Spain St) opened as a store and library in the 1850s, then became a hotel in 1886. Peek into the lobby from 10am to 5pm; except for the traffic noise outside, you'd swear you'd stepped back in time. Free tours are given 1pm through 4pm, weekends and Mondays.

Vallejo's first Sonoma home, **La Casa Grande**, was built around 1835 along this side of the plaza, but burned down in 1867. It had a variety of uses after the Vallejo family moved out. Today, the only remains are the servants' quarters, where the general's Native American servants lived.

SONOMA STATE HISTORIC PARK
The mission, Sonoma Barracks and Vallejo Home are part of **Sonoma State Historic Park** (☎ 707-938-1519; www.parks.ca.gov; adult/child under 17 $2/free; ✆ 10am-5pm).

The **Mission San Francisco Solano de Sonoma** (E Spain St), at the northeast corner of the plaza, was built in 1823, in part to forestall the Russian coastal colony at Fort Ross from moving inland. The mission was the 21st and final California mission and the only one built during the Mexican period (the rest were founded by the Spanish; p30). It marks the northernmost point on El Camino Real. Five of the mission's original rooms remain. The not-to-be-missed chapel dates from 1841.

The adobe **Sonoma Barracks** (E Spain St) were built by Vallejo between 1836 and 1840 to house Mexican troops. The barracks later became American military quarters. Now a museum, the barracks houses displays on life during the Mexican and American periods.

A half-mile northwest, the **Vallejo Home**, otherwise known as *Lachryma Montis* (Latin for 'Tears of the Mountain'), was built in 1851–52 for General Vallejo. It's named for the spring on the property; the Vallejo family later made a handy income piping water to the town. The property remained in the Vallejo family until 1933, when the state of California purchased it, retaining most of its original furniture. A bike path leads to the house from downtown.

Admission here includes admission to the **Petaluma Adobe**, a historic ranch 15 miles away in suburban Petaluma; ask for directions when you buy your ticket.

DEPOT PARK MUSEUM
Hidden two blocks north of the plaza, the **Depot Park Museum** (☎ 707-938-1762; www.vom.com /depot; 270 1st St W; admission free; ✆ 1-4:30pm Wed-Sun) has art and historical exhibits. The adjacent park hosts a farmers market Fridays from 9am to noon.

TRAINTOWN
Little kids love **Traintown** (☎ 707-938-3912; www .traintown.com; 20264 Broadway; ✆ 10am-5pm daily in

WINE COUNTRY

summer, Fri-Sun only mid-Sep–late May), 1 mile south of the plaza. A miniature steam engine makes 20-minute loops ($3.75). There are also vintage amusement-park rides, including a carousel and Ferris wheel; each ride costs $1.75.

BARTHOLOMEW PARK

Though it's also a winery, hiking, picnicking and history are the draws at **Bartholomew Park** (☎ 707-935-9511; www.bartholomewparkwinery.com; 1000 Vineyard Lane off Castle Rd). The wine's nothing great, but the winery houses a free Sonoma Valley history museum. The Palladian Villa at the park's entrance is a turn-of-the-20th-century replica of Count Haraszthy's original residence, open between 10am and 4pm on Wednesdays and weekends. For information, call the **Bartholomew Park Foundation** (☎ 707-938-2244).

CORNERSTONE FESTIVAL OF GARDENS

Twenty-five world-famous landscape designers designed 25 avant-garde garden plots at **Cornerstone Gardens** (☎ 707-933-9474, 707-933-3010; www.corenerstonegardens.com; 23570 Hwy 121; adult/child/student/senior $9/4/6.50/7.50; ☜ 10am-5pm Wed-Mon, 10am-4pm Tue), where ever-changing installations include a children's garden and giant sculptures. There's also a garden-design shop and good deli.

SONOMA VALLEY MUSEUM OF ART

New in 1999, this 8000-sq-ft **museum** (☎ 707-939-7862; www.svma.org; 551 Broadway; adult/family $5/8, Sun free; ☜ 11am-5pm Thu-Sun) shows local and national artists, has a sculpture gallery and a fantastic annual *Dio de la Muerta* exhibition in October. Call about the live-music series.

WILDWOOD FARM NURSERY SCULPTURE GARDEN

Tripped-out, funky abstract sculptures, large and small, fill flowering gardens at **Wildwood** (☎ 707-833-1161, 888-833-4181; www.wildwoodmaples .com; 10300 Sonoma Hwy, Kenwood; ☜ 9am-4pm Wed-Sun, 9am-2pm Tue), a nursery for exotic plants and Japanese maples.

Activities

Sonoma is great for biking. Get maps and advice at **Sonoma Valley Cyclery** (☎ 707-935-3377; 20093 Broadway), which rents bicycles for $6 per hour, $25 per day.

If you like horseback riding, call **Triple Creek Horse Outfit** (☎ 707-996-8566; www.triplecreek horseoutfit.com), April through October. One- and two-hour rides through Jack London State Historic Park or Sugarloaf Ridge State Park cost $60/70. Reservations required.

Doctor your swing at the public, nine-hole **Los Arroyos Golf Course** (☎ 707-938-8835; 5000 Stage Gulch Rd), $14 on weekends. Tennis fans can play at **Sonoma Valley High School** (☎ 707-933-4010; 20000 Broadway) weekends and after 5pm weekdays.

Dudes who dig cars love **Infineon Raceway** (☎ 800-870-7223; www.infineonraceway.com), at the Hwy 37/121 intersection. There are events year-round – from the Nascar Cup to the American Le Mans and Superbike tours. At the resident **Jim Russell Racing School** (☎ 800-733-0345; www.jimrussellusa.com), you can learn racing techniques using your own vehicle.

Festivals & Events

For up-to-date event listings, see the website www.sonoma county.com.
Sonoma Valley Olive Festival December through February
Cinema Epicuria Sonoma Valley Film Festival Mid-April
Sonoma Lavender Festival Mid-June
Sonoma Valley Harvest Wine Auction Labor Day weekend

Courses

Ramekins Sonoma Valley Culinary School (☎ 707-933-0450; www.ramekins.com; 450 W Spain St, Sonoma) offers demonstrations and hands-on classes for home chefs. Ask about the winemaker dinners.

Sleeping

Rates are for summer. Off-season rates plummet. Reserve in advance. Also consider Glen Ellen (p199) and, if you're watching pennies, Santa Rosa (p211).

B&BS & COTTAGES

Victorian Garden Inn (☎ 707-996-5339; www.victorian gardeninn.com; 316 E Napa St; r incl breakfast $149-229, cottage $269; ☒ ☒ ☒) Mature trees surround this inviting 1870 farmhouse, set back from the street. Victorian furnishings fill the parlor. The rooms are simple, but homey and functional.

Hidden Oak Inn (☎ 707-996-9863, 877-996-9863; www.hiddenoakinn.com; 214 E Napa St; r incl breakfast

$175-195; ⊠ ⊠ ⊠) Cascading wisteria climbs this 1914, four-room B&B. The comfy rooms are decorated with country-Americana furnishings. The inn provides bicycles to ride around town.

Magliulo's Rose Garden Inn (☎ 707-996-1031, 707-738-9293; www.sonomarose.net; 681 Broadway; r incl breakfast midweek/weekends with bath $125/150, without bath $110/125; ⊠ ⊠) This four-room, single-story B&B is good for simple accommodations with basic rooms, just like in someone's home.

Cottages of Old Sonoma (☎ 707-933-0340, 800-291-8962; www.cottagesofoldsonoma.com; 1190 E Napa St; cottages $148-248; ⊠ ⊠) A mile east of the plaza, these four small cottages have a bedroom, living room, kitchen and gas barbecue, with extras like stereos, DVDs and bicycles to rent. Not all have bedroom air-conditioning; ask when you book.

MOTELS & HOTELS

Sonoma Creek Inn (☎ 707-939-9463, 888-712-1289; www.sonomacreekinn.com; 239 Boyes Blvd; r $119-159; ⊠ ⊠) This unexpectedly cute-as-a-button motel has cheery, retro-Americana rooms, with primary colors and country quilts. It's not downtown, but there's easy access to valley wineries.

El Pueblo Inn (☎ 707-996-3651, 800-900-8844; www .elpuebloinn.com; 896 W Napa St; r old midweek/weekend $110/150 new $165/185; ⊠ ⊠ ⊠) One mile west of downtown, El Pueblo has comfortable older rooms with adobe-like brick walls, and fresher-looking new ones with semiprivate patios.

Best Western Sonoma Valley Inn (☎ 707-938-9200, 800-334-5784; www.sonomavalleyinn.com; 550 2nd St W; r $179-225; ⊠ ⊠ ⊠) All the rooms have patios facing a central courtyard with pool and hot tub. They're comfortable and functional, with above-average solid-wood furniture. For maximum privacy, book upstairs. There are some stylish older hotels on the plaza. Ask about parking.

Sonoma Hotel (☎ 707-996-2996; www.sonomahotel .com; 110 W Spain St; r $145-195; ⊠ ⊠) Occupying a grand 1880s building which anchors the plaza's northwest corner, this spiffy hotel is decked with Spanish-colonial and American-country-crafts furnishings. The street outside is noisy in the daytime, but quiet at night. There's no elevator.

El Dorado Hotel (☎ 707-996-3030, 800-289-3031; www.hoteleldorado.com; 405 1st St W; r midweek/weekends

$170/190; ⊠ ⊠ ⊠) Most of the rooms at this 27-room hotel have a private balcony with French doors, looking out over the plaza or a central courtyard. There are lots of swanky touches like high-end linens, DVD and CD players, and flat-panel TVs.

Swiss Hotel (☎ 707-938-2884; www.swisshotelsonoma .com; 18 W Spain St; r midweek/weekend $140-160/160-220; ⊠ ⊠) It opened in 1905, so you'll forgive the wavy floors in its five rooms. Think knotty pine and wicker. In the morning sip coffee on the shared plaza-view balcony. Downstairs there's a popular bar and restaurant.

CAMPING

Sugarloaf Ridge State Park (☎ 707-833-5712, reservations 800-444-7275; www.reserveamerica.com; 2605 Adobe Canyon Rd; sites $20-25) Sonoma's nearest campground is this 50-site park, north of Kenwood.

Eating

Also see the Glen Ellen section, p199.

Pearl's Homestyle Cooking (☎ 707-996-1783; 561 5th St W; mains $5-9; ◷ 7am-2:30pm) In a strip mall across from Safeway's west-facing wall, Pearl's dishes up giant American breakfasts. Look for the namesake kitty-cat out front.

Juanita Juanita (☎ 707-935-3981; 19114 Arnold Dr; mains ◷ 11am-8pm) This funky and festive roadside Mexican – the local favorite – makes winning tostadas, garlic-garlic burritos and dee-lish enchiladas. The patio is dog-friendly. Beer and wine.

Jesus Taco Truck (Hwy 12) For Mexican late at night, find the truck among the mobile *taquerías* (Mexican fast-food restaurants) on Hwy 12's east side, between Boyes Blvd and Agua Caliente. Look to the Lord for the best tacos; He's painted on the back of the truck.

599 Thai Cafe (☎ 707-938-8477; 599 Broadway; mains $7-10; ◷ 11am-9pm Mon-Sat) There are eight tables at this bright, fresh Thai café in a sunny store front near the plaza. Expect a wait at peak periods, or order take-out.

Taste of the Himalayas (☎ 707-996-1161; www .himalayanexp.com; 464 1st St E; mains $9-17; ◷ Tue-Sun) Down an alley next to the Sebastiani Theatre, sample fiery curries and savory tandoori meats. 11am to 3:30pm, there's a garbanzo-bean-heavy all-you-eat buffet for $8.

Della Santina's (☎ 707-935-0576; www.dellasantinas .com; 135 E Napa St; mains $11-17) The waiters have been at Della Santina's forever, and its 'specials' never change (*penne con funghili* and

WINE COUNTRY

veal parmigiania), but the food is consistent ($12 plates of pasta pesto, $15 rotisserie chickens) and the brick courtyard is charming, especially on warm evenings. Try the '*delizia*' for dessert.

Café la Haye (☎ 707-935-5994; www.cafelahaye.com; 140 E Napa St; mains $15-23; ☒ dinner Tue-Sat) Scrawled on a chalkboard, the six nightly New American specials at this 35-seat café are driven by availability of local ingredients – wild salmon, quail and lamb – all from within 60 miles of the restaurant. One of Sonoma County's best. If you're a foodie, don't miss it.

girl & the fig (☎ 707-938-3634; www.thegirlandthefig .com; 110 W Spain St; lunch mains $10-15, dinner 19-24) At Sondra Bernstein's big, soulful, überfun bistro, every dish reveals her love for earthy, French-provincial-inspired cooking. Small plates ($10 to $14) include steamed mussels with matchstick fries, and duck confit with lentils. Sunday through Thursday, there's a three-course prix-fixe menu for $28; add $7 for wine. Make reservations; sit outside on warm nights. Check out the cheese bar, too.

Sonoma Market (☎ 707-996-3411; 500 W Napa St) For the Sonoma's best groceries and picnic sandwiches.

Cheesemaker's Daughter (☎ 707-996-4060; 127 E Napa St; ☒ Tue-Sun) Skip the Cheese Shop on the plaza; this deli has better European, domestic and local cheeses.

The farmers market meets Fridays 9am to noon at Depot Park and, in summer, Tuesdays 5pm to 8pm on the plaza.

Drinking

There are several bars on the plaza.

Steiner's (☎ 707-996-3812; 456 1st St) Open since 1927, Steiner's is Sonoma's oldest bar, popular with bicyclists and motorcyclists on Sunday afternoons. Check out the taxidermy mountain lions.

Swiss Hotel (☎ 707-938-2884; 18 W Spain St) For drinks, history and a lively crowd, the 1909 Swiss Hotel is perfect for afternoon cocktails. (There's OK food, but the bar's better.)

Murphy's Irish Pub (☎ 707-935-0660; 464 1st St E) Don't ask for Bud, as they don't have any – only *real* brews here. Good hand-cut fries and shepherd's pie too. There's live music Thursday through Sunday evenings.

Entertainment

There are free jazz concerts every second Tuesday of the month, June to September at

the plaza, from 6pm to 8pm; arrive early and bring a picnic. The Sonoma Valley Museum of Art (p196) sometimes hosts live-music events.

Little Switzerland (☎ 707-938-9990; www.lilswiss .com; 401 Grove St; ☒ Fri-Sun) Long before Sonoma became 'Wine Country,' people drank at this old-fashioned beer garden. Live bands play Latin music Friday evenings, jazz, swing or zydeco on Saturdays and – the great tradition – polka on Sunday afternoons, when you can bring the family. It sometimes serves barbecue; call ahead.

Shopping

La Haye Art Center (☎ 707-996-9665; 148 E Napa St; ☒ Fri-Mon) See the work of five local artists – a bronze sculptor, potter and three painters – inside a former foundry.

Artifax (☎ 707-996-9494; 450-C 1st St E) Peruse unusual Asian artifacts, rare beads and spiritual objects at this small shop.

Sign of the Bear (☎ 707-996-3722; 435 1st St W) Kitchen-gadget freaks: make a beeline to this indie cookware store.

Earthworks (☎ 707-935-0290; 403 1st St W) Jewelry hounds like Earthworks' consignment pieces and art glass.

Wine Exchange of Sonoma (☎ 800-938-1794; 452 1st St E, Suite C; ☒ 10am-6pm) If you can't make it to the wineries, sample local vintages for $1 per ounce at this wine shop, which also has international beers too.

Vella Cheese Co (☎ 707-928-3232; 315 2nd St E) Inside a 1904 stone building, Vella has been making cheese since 1931. The dry jack is especially good; staff will vacuum-pack for shipping.

GLEN ELLEN
pop 992

Tucked on the western edge of Sonoma Valley, along a poplar- and oak-lined creek, Glen Ellen is a leafy hamlet of white picket fences, cute cottages and 19th-century brick buildings. It's great for a stroll or to overnight. While throngs of tourists fight for parking at Sonoma Plaza, you can meander through Glen Ellen and feel far from civilization. At night, the skies twinkle with a million stars.

Arnold Drive is the main drag and the valley's back-way route. Kenwood is just north, along Hwy 12, but has no town center like Glen Ellen does. For services, drive 8 miles to Sonoma.

Glen Ellen's biggest draws are Jack London Historic State Park (p200) and Benziger winery (p193); several interesting shops line Arnold Drive.

Sample award-winning chardonnay at **Navillus Birney** (☎ 707-933-8514; www.navillusbirney .com; 13647 Arnold Dr) Just south of the tiny downtown area, in Jack London Village, and inside a former 19th-century mill, the **Olive Press** (☎ 707-939-8900; www.theolivepress.com; 14301 Arnold Dr) presses olive oil on site; sample varieties from mild to pungent to peppery. Next door, **Avalon Glass Studio** (☎ 866-296-9793; www.avalon -glassstudio.com; ◷ Thu-Sun) is a working art-glass-maker's studio. Behind the mill are creekside picnic tables.

On hot days, families cool off in mineral-spring-fed swimming pools at **Morton's Warm Springs Resort** (☎ 707-833-5511, 800-551-2177; www .mortonswarmsprings.com; 1651 Warm Springs Rd; adult/ child 2-13 $8/7; ◷ 10am-6pm Tue-Sun, May-Oct), in Kenwood. Take Sonoma Hwy to Warm Springs Rd, and turn west.

Sleeping

Beltane Ranch (☎ 707-996-6501; www.beltaneranch .com; 11775 Sonoma Highway; r incl breakfast $140-170, ste $180-220; ☒) One of Wine Country's best country inns, Beltane's cheerful, lemon-yellow-painted 1890s ranch house occupies 100 acres and has double porches lined with swinging chairs and white wicker furniture. Though technically a B&B, each unfussy, country-Americana-style room has a private entrance – and you can have breakfast in bed. There are no phones or TVs (or air-con) to distract from the pastoral bliss.

Jack London Lodge (☎ 707-938-8510; http://jacklon donlodge.com; 13740 Arnold Dr; r midweek/weekend $120/ 170; ☒ ☒ ☒) A two-story whitewashed-wood motel, the lodge has friendly service and well-cared-for rooms decorated with some antiques. There's also a Jacuzzi, and the saloon is a happening spot for billiards and booze.

Glen Ellen Cottages (☎ 707-996-1174; www.glen elleninn.com; 13670 Arnold Dr; cottage weekday/weekend $135/225; ☒ ☒) In the shade of giant oaks, at the edge of Sonoma creek, all five hidden cottages have queen-size beds, oversized jetted tubs, steam showers and gas fireplaces. In-room fruit and cookies greet you on your arrival.

For a splurge, skip the corporate-fancy Fairmont Sonoma Mission Inn. Instead pick one of these two fabulous, top-of-the-line inns. Leave the kids home.

Gaige House Inn (☎ 707-935-0237, 800-935-0237; www.gaige.com; 13540 Arnold Dr; r incl breakfast $275-325, ste $475; ☒ ☒ ☒ ☒) For a romantic hideaway, it's hard to beat the Gaige House. An 1890 house contains five of the 22 rooms, decked out in Asian style with some European-antique accents such as oak-wood armoires. Breakfast is lavish. Outside, an expansive deck has rattan furniture, perfect for dozing with a book. Japanese-style spa suites have all the latest bells and whistles including free-standing hollowed-out granite-boulder tubs.

Kenwood Inn & Spa (☎ 707-833-1293, 800-353-6966; www.kenwoodinn.com; 10400 Sonoma Hwy, Kenwood; r incl breakfast $375-550, ste $550-700; ☒ ☒ ☒ ☒) Lush garden paths connect ivy-covered bungalows and hidden terraces at this very special inn, which feels like a Mediterranean château. Rooms are impeccably styled with sumptuous fabrics, one-of-a-kind art and wood-burning fireplaces. Spend $25 extra for an upstairs balcony room. There's an on-site spa (nonguests welcome), two hot tubs (one with a waterfall), and a guests-only dining room (dinner Friday and Saturday, mains $22 to $30).

Eating

Buy groceries and picnic supplies at **Glen Ellen Village Market** (☎ 707-996-6728; 13751 Arnold Dr; ◷ 6am-9pm).

fig café (☎ 707-938-2130; www.thefigcafe.com; mains $11-17; ◷ brunch Fri-Sun, dinner nightly) Make a special trip to Glen Ellen for flavor-packed California-Provençale comfort food such as flash-fried calamari with spicy-lemon aioli, chopped salad, *moules et frites* (mussels and French fries) lamb stew and pot roast; all wines cost $7 a glass; bottles cost under $38.

Cafe Citti (☎ 707-833-2690; 9049 Sonoma Hwy; mains $8-15) Locals flock to this mom-and-pop Italian-American deli-trattoria, where you order at the counter then feast on rotisserie-roasted chicken or the homemade gnocchi and ravioli. At lunch there are housebaked focaccia-bread sandwiches and pizzas with homemade marinara, just like Mama made.

Mayo Winery Reserve Room (☎ 707-833-5544; 9200 Sonoma Hwy, Kenwood; ◷ 10:30am-6:30pm Thu-Mon) If you're budgeting but want to try a seven-course menu paired with wine, here's your chance – for $20. Granted, portions are small and the place is a tasting room, but the food

TASTING ROOM ETIQUETTE

If you've never gone wine tasting, here are some things to help you avoid awkward moments and dirty looks.

■ Don't smoke. Not in the gardens either. Wait till you're far from the tasting room and off property to light up.

■ Wear no perfume and avoid scented soaps. Nothing annoys winemakers so much as someone who arrives in a cloud of cologne. Remember, wine tasting requires there be no olfactory distractions.

■ Avoid getting shit-faced. If you're serious about tasting or worried about drinking too much, use the spit buckets on tasting-room bars. Besides, a buzz gets in the way of properly assessing a wine's essence. It's okay to get giggly, of course.

■ Embrace sensuality. Linger over the wine's aroma and color before you sip it. There's no need to rush. This is Wine Country, after all.

■ Don't chew gum. 'Nuf said.

■ Check your criticism. You might be standing in front of the winemaker!

■ Be open to unfamiliar wines. You may think you only like, say, merlot, but allow your host to show you other varieties as well. In Anderson Valley (p252) for example, there are fantastic Alsatian-style wines like gewürztztraminer, which most people wrongly assume are sweet. These aren't. Let yourself be surprised.

■ Don't be afraid to ask questions. There's nothing wrong with not knowing what you're doing. Starry-eyed enthusiasm is charming, and most winemakers love helping visitors understand what they're tasting. But if you don't get the assistance you want, or if you find the place snooty, then leave. There are hundreds of others who'd love to help you.

■ If you picnic at a winery, buy a bottle of your host's wine.

■ Take wine tasting lightly. Don't be intimidated by snobs who insist it takes years to appreciate the esoteric art of oenology. Maybe it does, but who cares?

is fantastic – wild boar, duck pâté, prawns and other richly flavored foods – and paired with rockin' zins and fat cabs.

Wolf House (☎ 707-996-4401; 13740 Arnold Dr; mains $17-28; ◷ Tue-Sun) Big steaks and chops are staples on the American-Cal menu at this creekside dining room, great for carnivores (think Texas meets California). In nice weather, sit outside and watch ducks float by below.

Also recommended:

Garden Court Cafe (☎ 707-935-1565; 13647 Arnold Dr; mains $6-11; ◷ 7:30am-2:30pm Wed-Mon) Basic breakfasts, sandwiches and salads.

Glen Ellen Inn (☎ 707-996-6409; www.glenelleninn .com; 13670 Arnold Dr; lunch mains $10-13, dinner $18-22; ◷ lunch Fri-Tue, dinner nightly) Heavy-handed cooking (think brie-topped steak), but the garden is one of Sonoma's prettiest.

Kenwood Restaurant & Bar (☎ 707-833-6326; 9900 Sonoma Hwy, Kenwood; mains $14-24; ◷ 11:30am-9pm Wed-Sun) A skirt-and-sweater favorite for French-California, vineyard-view lunches.

JACK LONDON STATE HISTORIC PARK

Napa has Robert Louis Stevenson, but Sonoma's got Jack London. This 1400-acre **park** (☎ 707-938-5216; www.parks.ca.gov; off Hwy 12, Glen Ellen; parking $6; ◷ 10am-5pm) traces the last years of the author's short life (1876–1916).

Shifting occupations from Oakland fisherman to Alaska gold prospector to Pacific yachtsman – and as novelist on the side – London finished by taking up farming. He bought Beauty Ranch in 1905 and moved there in 1910. With his second wife, Charmian, he lived and wrote in a small cottage while his huge mansion, Wolf House, was being built. On the eve of its completion in 1913, it burned down. The disaster devastated London, and although he toyed with the idea of rebuilding, he died before construction got under way. After her husband's death, Charmian built the House of Happy Walls, which is now preserved as a Jack London **museum**. It's a half-mile walk from there to the remains of Wolf House, passing London's **grave** along the way. Other paths wind around the farm to the cottage where he lived and worked. The hiking is gorgeous. Ten miles of trails (some open to mountain bikes) weave through oak-dotted woodlands, between 600ft and 2300ft elevation. Watch out for poison oak (shiny red or green leaves that release a poisonous oil, causing a severe rash and itching).

RUSSIAN RIVER VALLEY

Meandering through a hilly landscape dotted with vineyards, small towns and redwood forests, the Russian River is named for 19th-century settlers and sea-otter hunters. Only two hours from San Francisco, towns here serve as summer camp for urbanites, who come to taste wine, canoe downstream, wander country lanes and take life at a lazy pace. In winter the river often floods its banks, and nobody's here.

Though the Russian River begins in the mountains north of Ukiah, in Mendocino County, the valley's most famous sections lie in Sonoma County, southwest of Healdsburg, where it cuts a serpentine course toward the sea. Just north of Santa Rosa, River Rd, the lower valley's main artery, connects Hwy 101 with Hwy 1 on the coast at Jenner. Another principal route, Hwy 116 heads northwest from Cotati through Sebastopol and on to Guerneville. Westside Rd connects Guerneville and Healdsburg. Unlike in Napa and Sonoma valleys, which stretch along one main artery, West County's winding roads can be confusing; carry a map.

RUSSIAN RIVER AREA WINERIES

Outside Sonoma Valley, Sonoma County's wine-growing regions encompass several diverse areas, each famous for different reasons (see A Wine Country Primer, p190). Pick up the free, useful *Russian River Wine Road* map (www.wineroad.com) in tourist-brochure racks.

Russian River Valley

Nighttime coastal fog drifts up the Russian River Valley, then clears by midday. Pinot noir does beautifully, as does chardonnay, which also grows in hotter regions, but prefers the longer 'hang time' of cooler climes.

The highest concentration of wineries is along Westside Rd, between Guerneville and Healdsburg. Some are photogenic and historic, but corporately owned, such as **Hop Kiln Winery** (☎ 707-433-6491; www.hopkilnwinery .com; 6050 Westside Rd). Several are downright unfriendly; trust your instincts. Skip Rocchioli. The following are laid out west–east, from south of Guerneville toward Healdsburg.

IRON HORSE

Atop a hill with drop-dead views over Sonoma County, **Iron Horse Vineyards** (☎ 707-887-1507; www.ironhorsevineyards.com; 9786 Ross Station Rd, off Hwy 116, Sebastopol; tastings free) is known for sparkling wines and pinot noir, which the White House often pours. The outdoor tasting room is refreshingly unfussy: when you're done with your wine, you pour it in the grass! Bottles cost $15 to $30; annual case production 36,000.

HARTFORD FAMILY WINERY

In a quiet valley surrounded by redwood-forested hills on one of the Russian River's prettiest roads, **Hartford Family Winery** (☎ 707-887-1756; www.hartfordwines.com; 8075 Martinelli Rd, Forestville; tastings free) specializes in producing single-vineyard pinot, chardonnay and zinfandel, some from old-vine fruit. The tasting room is upscale (think khakis, not denim), but not stuffy. The gardens have umbrella tables for picnicking. Bottles cost $23 to $65; annual case production 15,000.

PORTER CREEK

Porter Creek (☎ 707-433-6321; www.portercreekvine yards.com; 8735 Westside Rd; tastings free) is classic old-school Northern California. Inside a vintage-1920s garage, the tasting bar is a former bowling-alley lane plunked atop two barrels. The grapes are organically grown, and equipment runs on biodiesel. The high-acid, food-friendly pinot noir and chardonnay are the specialties, but there's a silky zinfandel and other Burgundian and Rhône-style wines too. Check out the aviary and yurt. Bottles cost $18 to $36; annual case production 3300.

ROSHAMBO

If you're self-conscious about your piercings and tats, head for **Roshambo** (☎ 707-431-2051; 888-525-9463; www.roshambowinery.com; 3000 Westside Rd; tastings free), where you will fit right in. 'Roshambo' refers to the game Rock, Paper,

Scissors, which embodies the aggressively playful tone of this way-cool winery. A concrete, glass and steel tasting room doubles as a sometimes controversial pop-art gallery. The picnic area has entrancing valley views. The wines are affordable, designed to consume now, including crisp chardonnay and easy-to-drink zinfandel. Oh, and if you don't have a tattoo, fret not: they'll give you a temporary one. All bottles under $20; annual case production 16,500.

DE LA MONTANYA

Be prepared for the occasional practical joke at this tiny **winery** (☎ 707-433-3711; www.dlmwine .com; 2651 Westside Rd, at Foreman Lane; tastings free), where you can meet the winemaker on week-

ends. He makes small batches of 17 different varieties, using estate-grown fruit. Viognier is the signature white, Portivo the red. The 'summer white' blend and gewürztraminer are great 'back porch' wines, infinitely drinkable. Bottles cost $18 to $38; annual case production 3500.

ARMIDA WINERY

Taste inside a geodesic dome at **Armida** (☎ 707-433-2222; www.armida.com; 2201 Westside Rd; tastings free, reserves $2). Head directly to the zinfandel – the 'Poizin: the Wine to Die For' is top of the line. Before you keel over, play boccie, then picnic on the deck beneath moss-covered oaks, and take in the views. Bottles cost $12 to $50; annual production 10,000 cases.

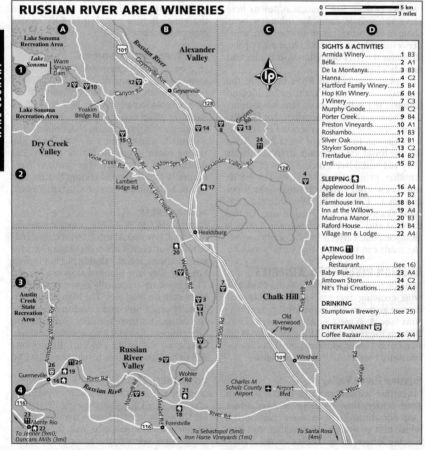

RUSSIAN RIVER AREA WINERIES

SIGHTS & ACTIVITIES	
Armida Winery	1 B3
Bella	2 A1
De la Montanya	3 B3
Hanna	4 C2
Hartford Family Winery	5 B4
Hop Kiln Winery	6 B4
J Winery	7 C3
Murphy Goode	8 C2
Porter Creek	9 B4
Preston Vineyards	10 A1
Roshambo	11 B3
Silver Oak	12 B1
Stryker Sonoma	13 C2
Trentadue	14 B2
Unti	15 B2

SLEEPING	
Applewood Inn	16 A4
Belle de Jour Inn	17 B2
Farmhouse Inn	18 B4
Inn at the Willows	19 A4
Madrona Manor	20 B3
Raford House	21 B4
Village Inn & Lodge	22 A4

EATING	
Applewood Inn Restaurant	(see 16)
Baby Blue	23 A4
Jimtown Store	24 C2
Nit's Thai Creations	25 A4

DRINKING	
Stumptown Brewery	(see 25)

ENTERTAINMENT	
Coffee Bazaar	26 A4

J WINERY

South of Healdsburg, J (☎ 707-431-3646; www .jwine.com; 11447 Old Redwood Highway; tastings free) is known for lip-smackingly crisp sparkling wines and also makes terrific pinot noir and a pinot gris with lush tropical-fruit overtones. Inside its fancy concrete-and-glass visitor center, J has excellent food-and-wine pairings ($12; no reservations), featuring four wines and eight hors d'oeuvres, great for sharpening your senses. Weekends you can reserve a sit-down pairing in the swanky Bubble Room ($25 to $35), which two people can share. Bottles range from $28 to $40; annual case production 70,000 cases.

Dry Creek Valley

Nighttime fog doesn't usually ascend the 2000ft-high mountains west of Dry Creek. The warmer weather is ideal for sauvignon blanc, zinfandel, and cabernet sauvignon. The valley lies west of Hwy 101, between Healdsburg and Lake Sonoma. Dry Creek Rd is the main thoroughfare. Running parallel, West Dry Creek Rd is an undulating, winding country lane with no center stripe. It's one of Sonoma's great back roads, ideal for bicycling. The following are in north–south order.

BELLA VINEYARDS

Up a hill at the valley's north end, always-fun Bella (☎ 707-473-9171, 866-572-3552; www.bella winery.com; 9711 W Dry Creek Rd; tasting free) has caves built into the hillside. The estate-grown grapes include 110-year-old vines from the Alexander Valley. The focus is on big reds – zin and syrah – but there's terrific rosé, an ideal barbecue wine, and late-harvest zin that goes fabulously with brownies. The wonderful vibe and dynamic staff make Bella a special place indeed. Bottles cost $15 to $34; annual case production 3000.

PRESTON VINEYARDS

Preston Vineyards (☎ 707-433-3327, 800-305-9707; www.prestonvineyards.com; 9282 W Dry Creek Rd; tastings $3, refundable with purchase) is a 19th-century organic farm. A weathered picket fence frames the farmhouse's tasting room, where candy-colored walls and tongue-in-groove ceilings set an inviting country mood. The signature is citrusy sauvignon blanc, but try the Rhône varietals and small-lot wines: mourvèdre, viognier, cinsault and the cult favorite, bar-

bera. Lou Preston is known for his bread: picnic in the shade of the walnut tree, then play boccie. Bottles cost $16 to $25; annual case production 8000.

UNTI VINEYARDS

Inside a windowless garage with fluorescent lighting, Unti (☎ 707-433-5590; www.untivineyards .com; 4202 Dry Creek Rd; ◷ Sat & Sun, by appointment Mon-Fri) makes all estate-grown wines, including a Châteauneuf-du-Pape-style grenache, a slutty syrah – big, powerful and compelling – and a 100% sangiovese, favored by oenophiles. If you love wine, don't miss Unti. Bottles cost $16 to $30; annual case production 5000.

Alexander Valley

East of Hwy 101, Alexander Valley abuts the Mayacamas Mountains – cross the ridgeline and you're in Napa. Summers are hot. Consequently you'll find cabernet sauvignon, merlot and warm-weather chardonnay, but there's fine sauvignon blanc and zinfandel too. Plan to take pictures in the valley's southern reaches, where the rolling hills and wide-open vineyards are postcard perfect. For events info, including First Weekend happenings, visit www.alexandervalley.org. The following are in north–south order.

SIZE MATTERS

There are three categories of winery: boutique, medium-sized, and large-scale or factory. Boutiques produce under 20,000 cases annually, medium-sized wineries between 20,000 and 100,000, and factory wineries over 100,000. So why does it matter? Well, think of a dinner party. If you throw two parties, one for 12 people and one for 100, which meal will be better?

Boutique wineries are able to exert much tighter control over production. Take grape growing. Boutique-vineyard managers select the trellises to best accommodate photosynthesis, taking into account variables such as rainfall, sunlight, temperature and the sugar content the vintner desires of the final fruit. At factory vineyards, managers set trellises to accommodate the grape-picking machines. Still, even factory wineries make a thousand or two cases of reserve wines, so don't write them off entirely – even if there are a million cases of junk behind the reserves.

WINE COUNTRY

SILVER OAK

One of Napa Valley's most famous cabernets is **Silver Oak** (☎ 800-273-8809; www.silveroak.com; 24625 Chianti Rd; tastings $10); the Alexander Valley appellation is similarly luxurious (though more fruit-forward) and lingers long, but instead of costing $30 to taste and $100 a bottle as in Napa, the Sonoma variety costs $10 to taste with $60 bottles. Pricey, yes, but Silver Oak is legendary. Annual case production 60,000.

TRENTADUE

Named for its 32 founding Italian families, **Trentadue** (☎ 707-433-3104, 888-332-3032; www.trentadue.com; 19170 Geyserville Ave; port tastings $5) specializes in ports (ruby, not tawny) that are crisp, light and clean, not syrupy. The chocolate port is a crowd-pleaser and great gift. Don't be surprised if you see a bus outside. Bottles cost $12 to $30; annual case production 22,000.

MURPHY GOODE

The gift shop-like tasting room lacks style, but wines are consistently good at **Murphy Goode** (☎ 707-431-7644; www.murphygoodewinery.com; 4001 Hwy 128; tastings free), which is known for *fumé blanc* (aka sauvignon blanc) and oaky chardonnay. The zinfandel – Liar's Dice – is worth tasting too. Bottles cost $18 to $30; annual case production 140,000.

STRYKER SONOMA

Wow! Check out the view from **Stryker Sonoma** (☎ 707-433-1944; www.strykersonoma.com; 5110 Hwy 128; tastings free), whose modern concrete-and-glass hilltop tasting room overlooks the valley. Plan to picnic. The standouts are fruit-forward zinfandel and sangiovese, neither of which you'll find anywhere else. Bottles cost $18 to $48; annual case production 7000.

HANNA

Abutting oak-studded hills, **Hanna** (☎ 707-431-4310, 800-854-3987; http://hannawinery.com; 9280 Hwy 128; tastings free) looks like a Tuscan-style train depot outside and also has stellar views and good picnicking. At the bar, look for estate-grown merlot and cabernet, and big-fruit zins and syrah. Friday through Sunday there's an appointment-only sit-down reserve wine–and–cheese tasting ($10). Bottles cost $20 to $40; annual case production 37,000.

SEBASTOPOL

pop 8100

Surrounded by orchards and rolling hills, Sebastopol is known for antiques and Gravenstein apples – though grapes are the new cash crop.

Orientation & Information

Highways 116 and 12 form Sebastopol's major intersection. Hwy 116 becomes Main St through town; southbound traffic uses Main St, northbound traffic Petaluma Ave, one block east. At Main St's northern end, the road turns 90 degrees and becomes Healdsburg Ave, continuing north out of town, where it's then called Gravenstein Hwy N, toward Forestville and Guerneville. At the south end of town, Main St becomes Gravenstein Hwy S and heads southeast toward Hwy 101.

The **Sebastopol Area Chamber of Commerce & Visitors Center** (☎ 707-823-3032, 877-828-4748; www.sebastopol.org; 265 S Main St; ◷ 9am-5pm Mon-Fri) provides maps and information and has historical exhibits next door. Events include the following:

Apple Blossom Festival April
Gravenstein Apple Fair August
Celtic Festival Late September

Sights & Activities

East of the plaza, **Sebastopol Center for the Arts** (☎ 707-829-4797; www.sebarts.org; 6780 Depot St; admission free; ◷ 10am-5pm Mon-Fri, 1-4pm Sat & Sun) hosts exhibitions by California artists, and free art walks, the first Thursday of each month.

Surrounding Sebastopol, look for farms, gardens, animal sanctuaries and agricultural sights open to the public. For a countywide list, pick up the free **Sonoma County Farm Trails Guide** (www.farmtrails.org).

In Sebastopol, check out **Hallberg Butterfly Gardens** (☎ 707-823-3420; 8687 Oak Grove Rd; suggested donation $5 ◷ by appointment Wed-Sun, Apr-Oct), a nonprofit butterfly garden, and **Kozlowski Farms** (☎ 707-887-1587; 800-473-2767; www.kozlowskifarms.com 5566 Gravenstein Hwy N; ◷ 9am-5pm Mon-Fri, 8am-5pm Sat & Sun), which makes jams and preserves.

Ace Cider (☎ 707-829-1223; cnr Hwy 116 & Graton Rd) brews fruit ciders and imports beers for its little **Ace-in-the-Hole Pub** (◷ 11am-7pm Sun-Wed, 10am-9pm Thu-Sat), which hosts live music on weekends.

Sleeping

Sebastopol is good for get-up-and-go travelers exploring the Russian River Valley and the coast.

Sebastopol Inn (☎ 707-829-2500, 800-653-1082; www.sebastopolinn.com; 6751 Sebastopol Ave; r $148-178 ⊗ ⊗ ⊠) Rooms are quiet and well kept at this independent, *non*-cookie-cutter motel, with solid pine furniture, Americana furnishings and hot tub. Weekday rates sometimes drop to $85.

Holiday Inn Express (☎ 707-829-6677, 800-465-4329; www.lokhotels.com; 1101 Gravenstein Hwy S; r $99-159; ⊗ ⊠) This modern hotel has business-class-like rooms, with extras including in-room refrigerators, cordless phones, coffee makers and a hot tub.

Vine Hill Inn (☎ 707-823-8832; www.vine-hill-inn .com; 3949 Vine Hill Rd; r incl breakfast $150; ⊗ ⊗ ⊠) Mature landscaping surrounds this four-room 1897 Victorian farmhouse, with gorgeous vineyard views, just north of town off Hwy 116. Breakfast is made with fresh eggs from the barn's chickens. Two rooms have Jacuzzis.

Raccoon Cottage (☎ 707-545-5466; 2685 Elizabeth Court; cottage $105-120; ⊗) Stay in a private cottage, off Vine Hill Rd, amid oaks, fruit trees and English gardens.

Eating

Mom's Apple Pie (☎ 707-823-8330; 4550 Gravenstein Hwy N; whole pies $6-14; ☾ 10am-6pm) There are OK sandwiches, but pie's the thing at Mom's. Apple is predictably good, but wild blueberry is worth trying. Yum, that flaky crust!

Slice of Life (☎ 707-829-6627; 6970 McKinley St; meals under $10; ☾ 11am-9pm Tue-Sun) This terrific vegetarian kitchen doubles as an all-natural pizzeria and serves breakfast all day. Great smoothies and date shakes.

East West Cafe (☎ 707-829-2822; 128 N Main St; meals $7-11; ☾ 8am-9pm) At this unpretentious café there's everything from grass-fed burgers to macrobiotic wraps, from stir-fries to *huevos rancheos* (corn tortilla with fried egg and chili tomato sauce). Try the blue-corn pancakes.

Viva Mexicana (☎ 707-823-5555, 707-829-5555; 841 Gravenstein Hwy S; mains $5-8; ☾ 11am-8pm) This tiny roadside *taquería* has five outdoor tables, and veggie-heavy burritos with minimal oil and homemade salsa.

K&L Bistro (☎ 707-823-6614; www.klbistro.com; 119 S Main St; lunch $9-18, dinner $15-25; ☾ lunch & dinner

Tue-Sat) The provincial Cal-French cooking is fabulous at this hole-in-the-wall bistro, Sebastopol's best – by far. K&L is significantly cheaper than comparable Napa and Sonoma restaurants, and worth a drive from neighboring towns. Make reservations. Tables are tight, but the crowd is friendly and fun.

Stella's Cafe (☎ 707-823-6637; www.stellascafe .net; 4550 Gravenstein Hwy N; lunch mains $9-13, dinner $16-22; ☾ lunch Mon & Wed-Sat, dinner Wed-Mon) This roadhouse's eclectic menu includes lunchtime salmon sandwiches, and halibut, paella and pork ribs at dinner. No corkage fee if you reserve Monday, Wednesday and Thursday.

Lucy's (☎ 707-829-9713; www.lucysrestaurant.com; 6948 Sebastopol Ave; mains $20-30; ☾ dinner) Sebastopol's biggest, loudest eatery has giant wood-fired ovens to make thin-crust pizzas and roasted meats. The food's OK, but over-priced. Full bar. Make reservations.

Farmers market (cnr Petaluma & McKinley Aves; ☾ 10am-1:30pm Sun Apr–mid-Dec) is held at the downtown plaza.

Goodbye Ben & Jerry, hello **Screamin' Mimi** (☎ 707-823-5902; 6902 Sebastopol Ave; ☾ 11am-10pm) for rich homemade ice cream. There's also **Sebastopol Cookie Co** (☎ 707-824-4040; 168 N Main St).

Drinking

Jasper O'Farrell's (☎ 707-823-1389; 6957 Sebastopol Ave) There's pub grub and nightly entertainment at this Irish-style bar. Tuesday is open-mic night.

Hardcore Espresso (☎ 707-823-7588; 1798 Gravenstein Hwy S; ☾ 6am-7pm) Meet the local art freaks, over coffee and smoothies, at this classic No-Cal, off-the-grid, indoor-outdoor coffeehouse that's essentially a corrugated metal-roofed shack surrounded by umbrella tables. The organic coffee is the best in town.

Entertainment

Main Street Theatre (☎ 707-823-0177; www.the-rep .com; 104 N Main St) Presents repertory and new drama.

Coffee Catz (☎ 707-829-6600; 6761 Sebastopol Ave; ☾ 7am-10pm Fri & Sat, 7am-6pm Sun-Thu) This roast-ery and café, east of downtown inside historic Gravenstein Station, hosts live acoustic music most weekends.

Shopping

Antique shops line Gravenstein Hwy S toward Hwy 101.

DETOUR: GRATON

If you like teeny-tiny towns and great food, take a detour to Graton (*Gray*-ton), a block-long hamlet, 4 miles north of Sebastopol, a half-mile west of Hwy 116 via Graton Rd.

Far Fetched Jewelry Outlet (☎ 707-829-1867; www.farfetched.com; 3140 N Edison; ☷ noon-4:30pm Mon-Fri) carries locally designed jewelry and has a trippy spaceship sculpture out front. Contemporary California artists show at **Graton Gallery** (☎ 707-829-8912; 9050 Graton Rd). **Mr Ryder & Co Art & Antiques** (☎ 707-824-8221; 9040 Graton Rd; ☷ Thu-Mon) carries Asian home furnishings and has an inviting tea bar with imported loose-leaf teas.

Part general store, part café, **Wildwood Market** (☎ 707-823-0233; 9020 Graton Rd; mains $8-17; ☷ 8am-9pm Mon-Sat, 9am-3pm Sun) serves damn good California comfort food such as pan-roasted salmon, polenta with goat cheese, and roasted chicken; sit in the garden if it's warm. Cosmopolitan **Underwood Bar & Bistro** (☎ 707-823-7023; 9113 Graton Rd; tapas $5-11, mains $11-16; ☷ lunch & dinner Tue-Sat) draws accolades for its Mediterranean-style small plates; bon vivants pack the swingin' bar.

Sebastopol Antique Mall (☎ 707-823-1936; 755 Petaluma Ave) Asian importers and antique dealers share space here.

Midgley's Country Flea Market (☎ 707-823-7874; 2200 Gravenstein Hwy S; ☷ 6:30am-4:30pm Sat & Sun) The region's largest flea market.

Downtown there's **Copperfield's Books** (☎ 707-823-2618; www.copperfields.net; 138 N Main St), which hosts literary events, and legendary **Incredible Records** (☎ 707-824-8099; 112 N Main St).

OCCIDENTAL
pop 500

One of Sonoma County's picture-perfect villages, Occidental was originally a 19th-century logging center. Today, artisans' shops, historic buildings and restaurants line the single main drag, making it a good place to stop for lunch, if not the night, and soak up the small-town vibe. The country roads around Occidental – some of the prettiest in Northern California – pass through second-growth redwoods and over open, rolling hills. For the best drive on a clear day, take **Coleman Valley Road**, which winds through pastoral valleys and over hills to Bodega Bay (p234).

At Christmastime, Bay Area families flock to Occidental to buy Christmas trees. The town decorates up to the nines, and there's weekend cookie decorating and caroling at the Union Hotel's Bocce Ballroom. (Locals whisper that many Christmas-tree farms are actually tax write-offs.)

All the cool stuff at **Renga Arts** (☎ 707-874-9407; 3605 Main St; ☷ Fri-Mon) is made from reclaimed materials, including arts and crafts, handbags, jewelry, birdhouses and benches.

Three miles south in Freestone, a Zen-like tranquillity prevails at **Osmosis Enzyme**

Bath & Massage (☎ 707-823-8231; www.osmosis.com; 209 Bohemian Hwy; ☷ 9am-9pm), which indulges patrons with dry enzyme baths using aromatic cedar fibers (bath-and-blanket wrap $80 to $85), gorgeous tea and meditation gardens, plus outdoor massages in a pagoda. Make reservations.

Rooms at the **Occidental Hotel** (☎ 707-874-3623, 877-867-6084; www.occidentalhotel.com; 3610 Bohemian Hwy; r $70-115, 2-bedroom ste with kitchen weekday/weekend $90/140; ☒ ☒ ☒) haven't been redecorated in 20 years, but they're clean.

Rooms at the **Inn at Occidental** (☎ 707-874-1047, 800-522-6324; www.innatoccidental.com; 3657 Church St; r incl breakfast $229-339; ☒ ☒ ☒) are full of collectible antiques. All the rooms at this beautifully restored 1876 Victorian inn – one of Sonoma's finest – have gas fireplaces, feather beds and rich color schemes.

Foodies: head to Graton Gallery for dinner (above). A farmers market meets Friday, June to October, on Main St. In Freestone, **Wild Flour Bakery** (☎ 707-874-3928; 140 Bohemian Hwy; ☷ 8am-6pm Fri-Mon) makes organic brick-oven breads, biscotti, scones and coffee.

Panini, crepes and slowly braised meats are specialties at **Pignoili** (☎ 707-874-9012; 3668 Bohemian Hwy; mains $12-22; ☷ dinner Thu-Mon, Sat & Sun brunch), a sunny 19th-century former home.

Come for big plates of comfort food at **Howard Caffe & Espresso Bar** (☎ 707-874-2838; 75 Main St; meals under $10; ☷ breakfast & lunch); there's also a juice bar and terrific breakfast.

At **Naked Lady Woodfire Café** (☎ 707-874-2408; 3728 Bohemian Hwy; mains $11-23; ☷ dinner Wed-Sun, brunch Sat & Sun), most dishes are wood-fired, including pizzas, roasted chicken and seafood.

Negri's (☎ 707-823-5301; 3700 Bohemian Hwy; meals $9-18) and the **Union Hotel** (☎ 707-874-3555; meals

$9-20), opposite one another, serve six-course family-style dinners. The Union is slightly better (neither is great) and has a hard-to-beat lunch special – whole pizza, salad and soda for $8 – in its 1869 saloon; at dinner, sit in the Bocce Ballroom. Both are kid-friendly. There's live music on weekends.

GUERNEVILLE & AROUND
Pop 7000

Of Russian River's old-fashioned vacation-resort towns west of Hwy 101, honky-tonk Guerneville is the largest by far and gets jammed in summer with party-scene gay men, sun-worshipping lesbians and long-hair Harley-Davidson riders wearing black-leather chaps, generating the nickname 'Groin-ville.' Four miles downriver, tiny Monte Rio's has a sign over Hwy 166 declaring it 'Vacation Wonderland,' an overstatement, at least the 'wonder' part, but it gets packed. Its real claim to fame is a public, dog-friendly beach, popular with minivan-driving hausfraus with passels of kids and wet canines. Further west, past the throngs, idyllic Duncans Mills is home to only a few dozen souls, but it has charming historic buildings. Upriver, and east of Guerneville, Forestville feels more like Wine Country.

Orientation & Information
Get information and lodging referrals from the following:

Russian River Chamber of Commerce & Visitor Center (☎ 707-869-9000, 877-644-9001; www.russianriver.com; 16209 1st St, Guerneville; ☽ 10am-5pm Mon-Sat, 10am-4pm Sun)

Russian River Visitor Information Center (☎ 707-869-4096; ☽ 10am-3:45pm) At Korbel Cellars.

Sights & Activities
Two miles north of Guerneville, the 805-acre **Armstrong Redwoods State Reserve** (☎ 707-869-2015; www.parks.ca.gov; 17000 Armstrong Woods Rd; day use per vehicle $6) shelters magnificent virgin redwoods, set aside by Colonel Armstrong, a 19th-century lumber magnate. Walk or cycle in for free; pay only to drive in. Short interpretive trails lead further into magical forest, where miles of backcountry trails and campgrounds await. **Armstrong Woods Pack Station** (☎ 707-887-2939; www.redwoodhorses.com) leads year-round 2½-hour trail rides ($60), full-day rides and overnight treks. Reservations required.

Look for sandy beaches and swimming holes along the river. There's year-round fishing. Outfitters operate mid-May to early October, after which winter rains dangerously swell the river.

Burke's Canoe Trips (☎ 707-887-1222; www.burkescanoetrips.com; 8600 River Rd, cnr Mirabel Rd, Forestville) operates self-guided canoe trips and shuttles you back to your starting point for $55 (per canoe, not person), plus $9 per person to camp in its riverside redwood grove. Make reservations.

Johnson's Beach (☎ 707-869-2022; end of Church St, Guerneville) rents inner tubes, canoes, paddle-boats and other watercraft at some reasonable rates.

King's Sport & Tackle (☎ 707-869-2156; 16258 Main St, Guerneville) is *the* local source for fishing and river-condition information; it rents kayaks ($30 to $45) and canoes ($50) too.

The **Northwood Golf Course** (☎ 707-865-1116; www.northwoodgolf.com; 19400 Hwy 116, Monte Rio) is a 1920s-vintage Alistair MacKenzie–designed par-36, nine-hole course.

Pee Wee Golf & Arcade (☎ 707-869-9321; 16155 Drake Rd at Hwy 116; games $6; ☽ 11am-11pm Memorial Day–Labor Day, weekends Easter–Memorial Day), just south of the Hwy 116 bridge, is a kitschy, retro-1950s miniature-golf course. It also rents bicycles ($30).

Festivals & Events
Women's Weekends (www.russianriverwomensweekends.com) Lesbians and liberal-minded grrrls come for these in late spring and early autumn.
Stumptown Days Parade, Rodeo & BBQ June
Russian River Blues Festival June
Lazy Bear Weekend Read: heavy, hirsute gay men; happens mid-July.
Jazz on the River September
Russian River Food & Wine Fest September

Sleeping
Russian River has few budget sleeps; prices drop midweek. Weekends and holidays, book ahead: there are more visitors than rooms. Many places don't have TVs. Because the river sometimes floods, some lodgings have cold linoleum or tile floors; pack slippers!

B&BS
Inn at the Willows (☎ 707-869-2824, 800-953-2828; www.innatthewillows.com; 15905 River Rd; r $89-159; ✗ ✗) Perhaps the prettiest gay resort, the Willows occupies riverfront land just east

of downtown. Rooms (some with air-con) are in an early 1940s lodge with library and grand piano, as well as hot tub and on-site spa, open to nonguests.

Raford House (☎ 707-887-9573, 800-887-9503; www .rafordhouse.com; 10630 Wohler Rd; r $125-185; ✗ ✗) Off River Rd, this 1880 Victorian summer-house sits alone on a vineyard-view hill. The rooms have lace curtains and antiques; some have fireplaces. From the front porch, the sunset views are mesmerizing. Some rooms have air-con.

Farmhouse Inn (☎ 707-887-3300, 800-464-6642; www .farmhouseinn.com; 7871 River Rd; cottages $175-299; ✗ ✗ ▣ ♨) The top spot to kiss and make up (or just kiss), the Farmhouse's eight cushy rooms have saunas, waterfall showers and wood-burning fireplaces. The beds have too many pillows, but they're so deliciously comfortable, who cares? There's a small spa too.

Applewood Inn (☎ 707-869-9093, 800-555-8509; www.applewoodinn.com; 13555 Hwy 116; r $185-345; ✗ ✗ ♨) Luxurious, romantic Applewood's rooms sport Frette linens, gas fireplaces, Jacuzzis and couples' showers. There's also a library, solarium with a forest view, fountain courtyard and an excellent restaurant. Some rooms have air-con.

Tea House Inn (☎ 707-865-2763; www.teahouseinn .com; 22746 Sylvan Way; teahouse incl breakfast $150, apt $80; ✗) Details are exquisite at this Japanese teahouse, from the shoji screens and kimonos to the altar space with a madrone trunk rising to the ceiling. The private hot tub and garden are perfect for lovers. Next door, there's a bargain studio apartment with kitchen.

MOTELS, COTTAGES & RESORTS

Fern Grove Cottages (☎ 707-869-8105; www.ferngrove .com; 16650 River Rd, Guerneville; cabins incl breakfast $89-219; ✗ ▣ ♨) The quality is in the details at lovely Fern Grove, which has 1920s vintage cabins in the redwoods, right downtown, some with Jacuzzis and fireplaces. Some cabins are small, but the warm service and wonderful homebaked goodies more than compensate.

Creekside Inn & Resort (☎ 707-869-3623, 800-776-6586; www.creeksideinn.com; 16180 Neeley Rd, Guerneville; B&B r $90-175, cottages $105-165; ✗ ✗ ♨) Across the river from downtown, quiet and secluded-feeling Creekside has cottages with kitchens (some with fireplaces), and simple B&B rooms in the main house. There's a

hot tub and pool beneath redwoods. Some rooms have air-con.

Village Inn & Lodge (☎ 707-865-2304; www.village inn-ca.com; 20822 River Blvd, Monte Rio; r $105-195; ✗ ▣) This charming, old-fashioned 11-room resort hotel sits beneath towering trees, right on the river's grassy bank. Some rooms have full river views. All have a refrigerator and microwave.

Rio Villa Beach Resort (☎ 707-865-1143, 877-746-8455; www.riovilla.com; 20292 Hwy 116, Monte Rio; r with kitchen $120-170, without kitchen $100-130; ✗ ▣) Landscaping is lush at this small riverside resort with excellent sun exposure (you see redwoods, but you're not under them). Rooms are well kept, but simple; the emphasis is on the outdoors, evident by the large riverside terrace, giant outdoor fireplace and barbecue grills.

Far Reaches (☎ 415-864-4554; www.russianriver cottage.com; Monte Rio; cottage $200; ✗) Surrounded by lush gardens and wrap-around deck, this hillside cottage up the hill above the river sleeps two to six and has Balinese furnishings, kitchen, stereo, sauna, meditation garden and outdoor shower. Directions given with reservations.

Highlands Resort (☎ 707-869-0333; www.highlands resort.com; 14000 Woodland Dr, Guerneville; cottages weekday $105-45, weekend $125-165, r $80/90, without bathroom $50/60, camping $20/25; ♨) Guerneville's mellowest all-gay resort sits on a wooded hillside, walkable to town, and has simply furnished rooms and little cottages with front porches. Best of all: the large, rectangular, clothing-optional pool and hot tub (weekday/weekend day use $5/10). You can also camp.

Fifes Guest Ranch (☎ 707-869-0656, 800-734-3371; www.fifes.com; 16467 River Rd, Guerneville; cabins $70-109, 2-r ste $159-189; ✗ ♨) On 15 in-town riverfront acres, Fifes has side-by-side cabins under the redwoods, a restaurant and bar. Despite efforts to re-brand itself as 'mixed,' Fifes is decidedly a gay men's party destination, especially poolside, where Speedo-clad circuit queens lie packed like oiled sardines (day use $10).

Riverlane Resort (☎ 707-869-2323, 800-201-2324; www.riverlaneresort.com; 16320 1st, Guerneville; cabins $80-125; ♨) In the downtown area, Riverlane has cabins with kitchens, dated furniture, and futons, best for no-frills travelers or campers wanting an upgrade. Service is friendly, the pool heated, and there's a private beach and hot tub.

CAMPING

Casini Ranch (☎ 707-865-2255, 800-451-8400; www
.casiniranch.com; 22855 Moscow Rd; tent sites $26, RV sites
$31-34) In quiet Duncans Mills, beautifully
set on riverside ranchlands, Casini is popular
with families. Amenities include hot showers
and watercraft.

Johnson's Beach Resort (☎ 707-869-2022; 16241
1st St; tent/RV sites from $10/20-30, rustic cabins $45-50,
per week $225-250) On the river in Guerneville,
Johnson's has little to boast about (think
weeds and trailers) other than location.

Inn at the Willows (sites $25-62) and **Fifes Guest
Ranch** (csites $29-59) also offer camping.

Reached via a steep mountain road out of
Armstrong Redwoods, **Bullfrog Pond** (sites $15)
has forested campsites with cold water, and
primitive hike-in and equestrian **backcountry
campsites** (sites $15). All sites are first-come,
first-served, open year-round.

Lastly there's the **Schoolhouse Canyon Campground** (☎ 707-869-2311; 12600 River Rd) or gay-
friendly **Faerie Ring Campground** (☎ 707-869-
2746; 16747 Armstrong Woods Rd; sites $27), outside
Guerneville.

Eating

GUERNEVILLE

Nit's Thai Creations (☎ 707-869-3576; mains $7-10;
15025 Old River Rd; ❨ Tue-Sun) Flavors sparkle at
this Thai-owned restaurant, but spiciness is
tailored to Americans; ask them to amp it up!
The food is prettier than the room – except
outside overlooking the river. (NB: The sign
says Rios, not Nit's.)

Coffee Bazaar (☎ 707-869-9706; 14045 Armstrong
Woods Rd; dishes $3-6; ❨ 6am-8pm) This happenin'
hangout has salads, sandwiches and pastries; it's attached to a bookstore.

Stumptown Brewery (☎ 707-869-0705; 15045
River Rd; meals $6-14; ❨ 4-9pm Wed, 4-10pm Fri &
Sat) Mostly a bar, Stumptown has fish and
chips, house-smoked meats and ribs.

Main Street Station (☎ 707-869-0501; 16280 Main
St; meals $8-15; ❨ breakfast, lunch & dinner) A family-
friendly Italian pizzeria has evening jazz.
Expect iceberg-lettuce salads. There's also
breakfast.

Applewood Inn Restaurant (☎ 707-869-9093, 800-
555-8509; www.applewoodinn.com; 13555 Hwy 116; mains
$20-28; ❨ dinner) The Applewood's earthy
cooking is big and bold, rich with color and
texture, as in the coriander-marinated pork
chops with cherry chutney, blue cheese and
spinach, or roasted quail with black chan-

terelles and fava bean-sage vinaigrette. The
rustic tone is repeated in vaulted wood ceilings and forest views. Make reservations.

There's usually a taco truck outside Safeway grocery on Main St. A farmers market
meets downtown Wednesdays, June through
September, 4pm to 7pm; Saturdays in summer, there's one at Monte Rio Beach, 11am
to 2pm.

FORESTVILLE

Farmhouse Inn (☎ 707-887-3300; www.farmhouseinn
.com; 7871 River Rd; mains $25-32; ❨ dinner Thu-Sun)
One of Wine Country's best, the Farmhouse
changes its seasonal Euro-Cal menu daily,
using locally raised, organic ingredients such
as Sonoma lamb, wild salmon and rabbit.
Details are perfect, from aperitifs in the
garden to the tableside cheese course. Make
reservations.

MONTE RIO

Village Inn (☎ 707-865-2304; 20822 River Blvd; mains
$15-21; ❨ dinner Wed-Sun) The straightforward
steaks-and-seafood menu doesn't distract
from the gorgeous river view. Sit inside or
out. There's a good list of local wines, too.

Baby Blue (☎ 707-865-9184; 20391 Hwy 116; mains
$8-13; ❨ breakfast & lunch) The knotty-pine walls
and ceiling lend a woodsy feel to this otherwise standard American diner, which has
good, albeit pricey, coffeeshop cooking.

DUNCANS MILLS

Cape Fear Cafe (☎ 707-865-9246; 25191 Hwy 116; breakfast & lunch $8-14, dinner $16-24). This window-lined
roadhouse has pastel walls and butcher-paper
tablecloths, and serves big salads, house-
smoked salmon, prime rib and Southern-
inspired cooking like shrimp grits. It's one of
the best midrange spots along the river. Make
reservations. There's breakfast, too.

Wine & Cheese Tasting of Sonoma County
(☎ 707-865-0565; 25179 Hwy 116; wine tastings $6-12;
❨ 11am-5:30pm Wed-Mon) Try vino, breads and
cheeses alfresco at this little wine bar-shop.

Blue Heron Restaurant (☎ 707-865-9135; 25300
Steelhead Blvd; lunch $5-15, dinner $10-20; Tue-Sun) This
casual bar and grill makes OK grilled seafood
and pub grub, but the bar's really the thing.

Drinking

Stumptown Brewery (☎ 707-869-0705; 15045 River
Rd) Guerneville's best straight bar is also gay-
friendly and has a foot-stompin' jukebox,

pool table, riverside beer garden (great for smokers), and nine beers on tap, three made on-site.

Rainbow Cattle Company (☎ 707-869-0206; 16220 Main St) Santa Rosa's popular gay watering hole.

Fifes Roadhouse Bar (☎ 707-869-0656; 16467 River Rd) Fifes' mostly gay bar sometimes has two-step dancing.

Entertainment
Most nightlife happens in Guerneville.

Rio Theater (☎ 707-865-0913; cnr Bohemian Hwy & Hwy 116, Monte Rio) Inside an old riverside Quonset hut, the Rio shows first-run movies and has great hot dogs!

Main Street Station (☎ 707-869-0501; 16280 Main; cover $2-6) There's live jazz, blues, and cabaret nightly in summer, weekends winter.

Coffee Bazaar (☎ 707-869-9706; 14045 Armstrong Woods Rd) This coffeehouse occasionally hosts live music, but closes at 9pm.

Club FAB (☎ 707-869-5708; 16135 Main St; cover free-$10) The biggest gay club north of San Francisco, FAB has DJs and live music, drag shows and occasionally drag bingo!

SANTA ROSA
pop 147,595

More suburban than agricultural, sprawling Santa Rosa is Wine Country's biggest city – and it has the traffic to prove it. Santa Rosa lacks the charm of smaller towns, but has reasonably priced accommodations providing easy access to Sonoma County and Valley.

Santa Rosa can claim two famous native sons – a world-renowned cartoonist and a celebrated horticulturalist – and you'll find plenty of museums, gardens and shopping to keep you busy for an afternoon. Otherwise, there's not much to do, unless you're here in July during the **Sonoma County Fair** (☎ 707-545-4200; www.sonomacountyfair.com), at the fairgrounds on Bennett Valley Rd.

Orientation & Information
The main shopping stretch is 4th St, which abruptly ends at Hwy 101 but reemerges on the other side at historic Railroad Square. Downtown parking lots are free for the first 1½ hours. East of town, 4th St turns into Hwy 12 to Sonoma Valley.

Aroma Roasters (☎ 707-576-7765; 95 5th St (Railroad Square); ☽ 6am-11pm Mon-Thu, 7am-midnight Fri & Sat;

7am-10pm Sun) Check email and sip coffee with art freaks; free wi-fi.

California Welcome Center & Santa Rosa Visitors Bureau (☎ 707-577-8674, 800-404-7673; www.visit santarosa.com; 9 4th St; ☽ 9am-5pm Mon-Sat, 10am-5pm Sun) At Railroad Sq, west of Hwy 101; take the downtown Santa Rosa exit off Hwy 12 or Hwy 101.

Sights & Activities
LUTHER BURBANK HOME & GARDENS
Luther Burbank (1849–1926), a pioneering horticulturist, developed many hybrid plant and tree species at his 19th-century Greek-revival home, at the corner of Santa Rosa and Sonoma Aves. The extensive **gardens** (☎ 707-524-5445; admission free; ☽ 8am-5pm) are lovely for lingering. The house and adjacent **Carriage Museum** (guided tour adult/child/senior $4/ free/3, self-guided audio tour $3; ☽ 10am-3:30pm Tue-Sun Apr-Oct) have displays on Burbank's life and work.

Across the street from Burbank's home, Julliard Park has a **playground**.

CHARLES M SCHULZ MUSEUM
Charles Schulz, creator of the *Peanuts* cartoon strip, was a long-term Santa Rosa resident. Born in 1922, he published his first drawing in 1937, introduced the world to Snoopy and Charlie Brown in 1950, and produced Peanuts cartoons until just before his death in 2000.

At the **museum** (☎ 707-579-4452; www.schulz museum.org; 2301 Hardies Lane; adult/child/senior $8/5/5; ☽ noon-5pm Mon & Wed-Fri, 10am-5pm Sat & Sun) there is a glass wall overlooking a courtyard, where's there's a Snoopy labyrinth. Exhibits include Peanuts-related art and Schulz's actual studio. Skip Snoopy's Gallery; the museum has the good stuff.

SNOOPY'S GALLERY & REDWOOD EMPIRE ICE ARENA
Close to the museum, this so-called **'gallery'** (☎ 707-546-3385; 1667 W Steele Lane; admission free; ☽ 10am-6pm) is in fact a gift shop replete with stuffed animals strategically positioned at children's eye level.

But if you ice-skate, make sure that you do not miss the adjacent **Redwood Empire Ice Arena** (☎ 707-546-7147; adult/child incl skates weekdays $9/11, weekends $12/10), formerly owned and deeply loved by Charles Schulz. It's open most afternoons (call for schedules). Bring a sweater!

Sleeping

MOTELS & HOTELS

Most of the motels are along Cleveland Ave, fronting Hwy 101's western side, between the Steele Lane and Bicentennial Lane exits.

Hillside Inn (☎ 707-546-9353; www.hillside-inn .com; 2901 Fourth St; s/d/q $73/76/88; ✕ ☒) Santa Rosa's best-kept motel is closest to Sonoma Valley; add $4 for kitchens. Some furnishings are dated, but everything is scrupulously maintained, with nary a cock-eyed lampshade.

Best Western Garden Inn (☎ 707-546-4031; www .thegardeninn.com; 1500 Santa Rosa Ave; r $95-120; ✕ ☒) Rooms in back are quieter, rooms in front have more privacy at this well-kept motel, just south of downtown. The street is kinda seedy at night, but the motel is secure, clean and comfortable.

Sandman Hotel (☎ 707-544-8570; 3421 Cleveland Ave; s/d $82/94; ✕ ☒) This is Cleveland Ave's reliable budget choice.

Hotel La Rose (☎ 707-579-3200; www.hotellarose .com; 308 Wilson St; r $129-179; ✕ ☒ ☐) At Railroad Square, this charming 1907 hotel has rooms with marble baths, sitting areas with thick carpeting and wing chairs, and super-comfy mattresses with feather beds. Great for a moderate splurge. There's a rooftop hot tub too.

Flamingo Resort Hotel (☎ 707-545-8530, 800-848-8300; www.flamingoresort.com; 2777 4th St; r $99-179; ✕ ☒ ☐) This 1950s vintage 150-room resort extends over 11 acres and doubles as a conference center. Kids *love* its gigantic, 82°-year-round swimming pool. There's an on-site health club and day spa too. Rooms are comfortable, but more like a motel than hotel.

Stone House Inn (☎ 707-526-1666, 800-526-1602; www.historicstonehouseinn.com; 3555 Sonoma Hwy/Hwy 12); r incl breakfast $150-175; ✕ ☒ ☒) Wood trim complements the grey rock walls at this 1912 château-like inn, where antiques lend an easy gentility to the decor. The location east of downtown is convenient to Sonoma Valley.

Vintners Inn (☎ 707-575-7350, 800-421-2584; www .vintnersinn.com; 4350 Barnes Rd, near River Rd; r $225-305; ✕ ☒ ☐) North of town, surrounded by vineyards, Santa Rosa's 1980s-era luxury inn has private garden-view patios, king beds and high-thread-count sheets. Last-minute specials sometimes lower rates to a range from $180 to $200.

CAMPING

Spring Lake Regional Park (☎ 707-539-8092, reservations 707-565-2267; www.sonoma-county.org/parks; 5585 Newanga Ave; sites $15) There are 29 campsites 4 miles from downtown; make reservations ($7 fee) between 10am and 3pm weekdays. The regional park is open year-round; the campground is open daily May to September, weekends only October to April. Take 4th St eastbound, turn right on Farmer's Lane, pass the first Hoen St and turn left on the *second* Hoen St, continue straight, then left on Newanga Ave.

Eating

Pho Vietnam (☎ 707-571-7687; 711 Stony Point Rd, #8; dishes $5-6; ⏱ 10am-8:30pm Mon-Sat, 10am-7:30pm Sun) Noodle bowls, rice plates, char-grilled meats and piping-hot soups are the specialties at this hole-in-the-wall shopping-center restaurant, just off Hwy 12, west of downtown.

Taqueria Las Palmas (☎ 707-546-3091; 415 Santa Rosa Ave; dishes $3-6; ⏱ 9am-9pm) If you like Mexican, this place is the real deal, with the usual combos – enchiladas, *rellenos* (stuffed peppers) – all properly spiced. The barbecued pork and homemade salsa are dee-lish. There's also brown rice.

Mac's Delicatessen (☎ 707-545-3785; 630 4th St; dishes under $10; ⏱ breakfast & lunch Mon-Sat) Mac's serves bagels and lox, kosher-deli sandwiches and chicken-noodle soup.

Zazu (☎ 707-523-4814; www.zazurestaurant.com; 3535 Guerneville Rd; mains $19-26; ⏱ dinner Wed-Mon) In a raucous roadhouse only 10 minutes west of downtown, chef-owner John Stewart's Cal-Ital cooking packs a wallop, with invigorating, clean flavors and a sure-handed dynamic style. There's nothing fussy about it, but every dish sings, from the hand-thrown pizzas to slow-roasted balsamic pork shoulder. His competition isn't Sonoma chefs, but Tuscan grandmothers. Bring earplugs.

La Gare (☎ 707-528-4355; 208 Wilson St; mains $14-20; ⏱ dinner Weds-Sun) La Gare serves straight-forward classical French cooking, such as *boeuf à la bourguignonne* and escargots, at Railroad Sq.

John Ash & Co (☎ 707-527-7687; www.johnashres taurant.com; lunch mains $13-18, dinner $28-32; ⏱ lunch Mon-Fri, brunch Sun, dinner nightly). At the Vintners Inn, John Ash is popular with the over-45 set for swanky, contemporary Euro-Cal meals. Wear heels or a tie.

WINE COUNTRY

A farmers market meets at 4th and B Sts, 4:30pm to 8pm, Wednesday, Memorial Day to Labor Day.

Drinking

Last Day Saloon (☎ 707-545-2343; www.lastdaysaloon .com; 120 5th St; ❍ Tue-Sun) Live bands play most nights; cover ranges $3 to $15.

Aroma Roasters (☎ 707-576-7765; 95 5th St (Railroad Sq); ❍ 6am-11pm Mon-Thu, 6am-midnight Fri & Sat; 7am-10pm Sun) Town's hippest café serves no booze, but tattooed and pierced art freaks flock here.

Russian River Brewing Co (☎ 707-545-2337; 729 4th St) Drink locally crafted brews in an industrial space or outside on the sidewalk with the dudes.

Third Street Aleworks (☎ 707-523-3060; 610 3rd St) There are half a dozen pool tables and a big smokers' patio at this giant brew pub that gets packed weekends and game days. Good garlic fries.

HEALDSBURG

pop 11,468

The heart of north Sonoma County's wine country, Healdsburg has emerged as the region's hot, new destination. Chic boutiques, tasting rooms and foodie-scenester restaurants abound around Healdsburg Plaza, the town's picturesque central square, bordered by Healdsburg Ave and Center, Matheson and Plaza Sts. Locals aren't entirely happy with the influx of new money to their oncesleepy town, but they've protected the historic look and color, despite the Volvos and Land Rovers jamming the streets summer weekends. Bourgeoisie or no, Healdsburg is a must-visit if you're in the area, if only to stroll the pretty streets, sample great food, and soak up the No-Cal-now flavor.

Information

Healdsburg Chamber of Commerce & Visitors Bureau (☎ 707-433-6935, 800-648-9922; www.healds burg.org; 217 Healdsburg Ave; ❍ 9am-5pm Mon-Fri, 10am-2pm Sat & Sun) A block south of the plaza, it has winery maps and information on hot-air ballooning, golf and tennis, spas, and nearby farms (get the *Farm Trails* brochure).
Toyon Books (☎ 707-433-9270; 104 Matheson St) Sells guidebooks and maps.

Sights

East of the plaza, **Healdsburg Museum** (☎ 707-431-3325; www.healdsburgmuseum.org; 221 Matheson

St; donation requested; ❍ 11am-4pm Tue-Sun) stocks Native American baskets from the local Pomo and Wappo, and excellent exhibits on northern Sonoma County history. Pick up a historic-homes walking tour pamphlet from the museum bookshop.

The **Sonoma Country Wine Library** (☎ 707-433-3772; www.sonoma.lib.ca.us; cnr Piper & Center Sts; ❍ 9:30am-6pm), inside Healdsburg's public library, is one of the best oenology reference libraries in California. Free summer concerts are held Tuesday afternoons on the plaza. **Levin & Company** (☎ 707-433-1118; 306 Center St) has fiction, CDs and a co-op art gallery. The community-driven **Plaza Arts Center** (☎ 707-431-1970; www.healdsburgarts.org; 130 Plaza St; ❍ 11am-5pm) spotlights California artists.

Activities

WC 'Bob' Trowbridge Canoe Trips (☎ 707-433-7247, 800-640-1386; www.trowbridgecanoe.com; 20 Healdsburg Ave; ❍ Thu-Mon) has canoe and kayak rentals, April to September, for $65/100 (half/full day) including transportation.

Getaway Adventures (☎ 707-763-3040, 800-499-2453; www.getawayadventures.com) offers morning vineyard cycling in Alexander Valley, followed by lunch and canoeing or kayaking on Russian River ($155). **Healdsburg Spoke Folk Cyclery** (☎ 707-433-7171; www.spokefolk.com; 201 Center St) rents touring, racing and tandem bicycles.

Relish Culinary School (☎ 707-431-9999, 877-759-1004; www.relishculinary.com) teaches courses for home chefs, from cake decorating to teen-pizza workshops, and operates out of local kitchens.

Festivals & Events

Russian River Wine Road Barrel Tasting March
Healdsburg Jazz Festival Memorial Day
Healdsburg Harvest Century Bicycle Tour Mid-July
Wine & Food Affair November

Sleeping

The cost of accommodation plummets in autumn, winter and spring.

B&BS

Most of Healdsburg's Victorian B&Bs are within walking distance of the plaza. There are two noteworthy B&Bs in the surrounding countryside.

Healdsburg Inn on the Plaza (☎ 707-433-6991, 800-431-8663; www.healdsburginn.com; 110 Matheson St;

weekday $200-250, weekend $220-275; (X) (B)) Renovated in 2005 with a nod to Tuscany, the fresh-looking rooms have fine linens and gas fireplaces; some have jetted tubs for two. There's a solarium and afternoon wine and hors d'oeuvres. Free bicycles too.

Madrona Manor (☎ 707-433-4231, 800-258-4003; www.madronamanor.com; 1001 Westside Rd; r & ste $195-445; (X) (B) (R)) If you love country inns and stately manor houses, the regal 1881 Madrona Manor exudes Victorian elegance. Surrounded by eight acres of woods and gardens, the hilltop mansion is decked out with many original furnishings. There are also rooms in a separate carriage house, cottage and former schoolhouse. A mile west of Hwy 101, it's convenient to Westside Rd's wineries.

Belle de Jour Inn (☎ 707-431-9777; www.belle dejourinn.com; 16276 Healdsburg Ave; r $195-275, ste $335; (X) (B)) Across from Simi Winery, Belle de Jour's spiffy rooms have American-country furnishings, with extra touches like sun-dried sheets, hammocks and CD players. The manicured gardens are perfect for a lovers' tryst.

Also within walking distance of the plaza:

Camellia Inn (☎ 707-433-8182, 800-727-8182; www .camelliainn.com; 211 North St; r $119-229; (X) (B) (R)) 1869 Italianate house; one room accommodates families.

George Alexander House (☎ 707-433-1358, 800-310-1358; fax 707-433-1367; www.georgealexanderhouse.com; 423 Matheson St; r $145-235; (X) (B)) Single-story 1905 Queen Anne with Victorian and Asian antiques; also a sauna.

Piper Street Inn (☎ 707-433-8721, 877-703-0370; www.piperstreetinn.com; 402 Piper St; r $175-195; (X) (B)) Two rooms: one a homey bedroom, one a garden cottage.

Haydon Street Inn (☎ 707-433-5228, 800-528-3703; fax 707-433-6637; www.haydon.com; 321 Haydon St; r $130-220; (X) (B)) Two-story Queen Anne Victorian with big front porch and cottage out back.

MOTELS & HOTELS

Two older motels lie south of the plaza; two more are to the north, at Hwy 101's Dry Creek exit.

Best Western Dry Creek Inn (☎ 707-433-0300, 800-222-5784; 198 Dry Creek Rd; r $129-139; (X) (B)) Healdsburg's nicest motel, the Best Western has good service, free laundry and outdoor hot tub; look for weekday discounts, sometimes as low as $89.

L&M Motel (☎ 707-433-6528; www.landmmotel .com; 70 Healdsburg Ave; r $100-120; (X) (B) (R)) A simple, single-story motel, the L&M has grassy picnicking lawns, mature trees and barbecues.

Best Value Inn (☎ 707-433-5548; www.bestvalue inn.com; 74 Healdsburg Ave; r midweek $79-89, weekend $118-128; (B) (R)) Budgeteers: try this one if the L&M is booked.

Healdsburg Travelodge (☎ 707-433-0101, 800-499-0103; www.travelodge.com; 178 Dry Creek Rd; r $109-169; (B) (R)) Make this your last choice.

Hotel Healdsburg (☎ 707-431-2800, 800-889-7188; www.hotelhealdsburg.com; 25 Matheson St; r incl breakfast $260-490; (X) (B) (B) (R)) Smack on the plaza, the chic HH has a coolly minimalist style and all the requisite bells and whistles of a top-end hotel. Wear Armani and blend right in. The ultracushy, muted earth-toned rooms have deliciously comfy beds and bathrooms with extra deep soaking tubs. Downstairs there's a full-service spa.

CAMPING

Also see Lake Sonoma, p249.

Cloverdale Wine Country KOA (☎ 707-894-3337, 800-368-4558; www.winecountrykoa.com; 26460 River Rd, Cloverdale; tent/RV sites from $34/38, 1-/2-bedroom cabins $58/68; (R)) Six miles from the Central Cloverdale exit off Hwy 101, amenities here include hot showers, swimming pool and hot tub, nature trails, laundry, paddleboats and bicycles.

Alexander Valley RV Park (☎ 707-431-1453, 800-640-1386; http://alexandervalleyrvpark.com; 2411 Alexander Valley Rd; tent sites per person $10; (Y) Mar-Nov) Four miles northeast of Healdsburg, this campground has mixed-use sites with hookups for RVs. Some have no shade.

Eating

Foodies may think they've died and gone to heaven. Reservations are essential weekends and many weekdays.

RESTAURANTS

Bovolo (☎ 707-431-2962; 106 Matheson St; (Y) 11am-9pm Thu-Tue, 9am-9pm Sat & Sun) Inside Plaza Farms, Bovolo serves 'slow food fast,' including deelish housemade antipasti and salami, savory hot sandwiches, hand-thrown pizzas and hand-turned gelato. Order at the counter and sit outside or in. There's breakfast on the weekends.

Santi (☎ 707-857-1790; www.tavernasanti.com; 21047 Geyserville Ave, Geyserville; lunch $9-14, dinner $15-25; (Y) lunch Thu-Mon, dinner nightly) Among the region's best, never-fussy and always-wonderful Santi cooks *bellissima* rustic northern-Italian cooking, like spaghetti calabrese and osso buco,

WINE COUNTRY

worth the 10-minute drive north. On balmy evenings, hold hands by candlelight on the big wooden deck out back.

Manzanita Restaurant (☎ 707-433-8111; 336 Healdsburg Ave; mains $12-24; ☙ Wed-Sun dinner) Concrete floors, zinc-topped tables and stacked manzanita logs decorate the stark dining room at Manzanita, where the simple, rustic, wood-fired Mediterranean-style cooking capitalizes on local ingredients. You can eat well without spending a bundle (but it's decidedly midrange, not budget). There's also a cool little bar for wine and appetizers.

Willi's Seafood & Raw Bar (☎ 707-433-9191; www .williswinebar.net; 403 Healdsburg Ave; small plates $8-13; ☙ 11:30am-9pm Wed-Mon) Sit at the palm-wood bar, on the sunny patio or at a semiprivate booth at this stylin' spot for fresh-off-the-boat seafood, oysters and small plates like roasted shrimp, lobster rolls, and skewered scallops. There are 30 wines by the glass. NB: however cheap they seem, these are *small* plates; prices add up.

Madrona Manor (☎ 707-433-4231, 800-258-4003; www.madronamanor.com; 1001 Westside Rd; mains $17-29; ☙ dinner) You'd be hard-pressed to find a lovelier place to pop the question than at Madrona Manor, where in warm weather you can sit outside on the mansion's garden-view veranda and dine on the sophisticated Euro-Cal cooking.

Barndiva (☎ 707-431-0100; www.barndiva.com; 231 Center St; lunch mains $11-16, dinner $18-24; ☙ noon-11pm Wed-Sun) The face of the new Healdsburg, Barndiva's hip-and-happening dining room and giant bar have a sexy lounge feel. The nontraditional menu is 'flavor profiled,' with food to fit your mood: from light to spicy to comfort cooking. Despite the aggressive style, there's passion and substance behind the New American cooking, all made with sustainably farmed ingredients. On Sunday there's brunch in the garden.

Also consider the following:

Bistro Ralph (☎ 707-433-1380; 109 Plaza St; lunch mains $10-15, dinner $17-27; ☙ Mon-Sat) Long-standing favorite for down-to-earth bistro fare; great martinis too.

Ravenous Cafe (☎ 707-431-1302; 420 Center St; lunch mains $10-15, dinner $17-24; ☙ Wed-Sun) Bon vivants come for seasonal California cooking. Good burgers at lunchtime.

Zin (☎ 707-473-0946; www.zinrestaurant.com; 344 Center St; lunch mains $8-14, dinner $16-25; ☙ lunch Mon-Fri, dinner nightly) Big portions of Cal-American comfort food; fun wine bar.

AUTHOR'S CHOICE

Cyrus (☎ 707-433-3311; www.cyrusrestaurant .com; fixed-price menus $52-85; ☙ dinner Wed-Mon) Napa's venerable French Laundry (p224) has stiff competition in swanky Cyrus, an ultrachic dining room in the great tradition of the French-country auberge. The emphasis is on luxury foods – foie gras, caviar, lobster – expertly prepared with a French sensibility and flavored with global spices, as in the signature Thai-marinated lobster. The staff moves as if in a ballet, ever intuitive of your pace and tastes. From the caviar cart to the cheese course, this is one meal to remember. If you're a serious foodie, don't miss Cyrus.

QUICK EATS & GROCERIES

During the warmer months, **farmers markets** (☎ 707-431-1956; www.healdsburgfarmersmarket.org) are held at **Healdsburg Plaza** (☙ 4pm-6:30pm Tue Jun-Oct) and the **municipal parking lot** (cnr Vine & North Sts; ☙ 9am-noon Sat May-Nov).

Plaza Farms (☎ 707-433-2345; 106 Matheson St; ☙ Thu-Tue) This fantastic collective of food and wine shops showcases some of the best local names on the Northern California food scene: Sharffen Berger Chocolate, DeVera-Sonoma Olive Oil, Bellwether Farms Creamery, and Coffaro Winery.

Jimtown Store (☎ 707-433-1212; www.jimtown .com; 6706 Hwy 128) If you're heading to Alexander Valley, don't miss Jimtown, famous for its picnic supplies and sandwiches made using housemade flavor-packed spreads (eg artichoke, olive and caper; fig and olive).

Oakville Grocery (☎ 707-433-3200; 124 Matheson St; sandwiches around $5; ☙ 9am-7pm Sun-Thu, 9am-8:30pm Fri & Sat summer) The definitive Wine Country market, Oakville Grocery anchors the plaza's southeast corner and sells top-of-the-line smoked fish and gourmet sandwiches as well as salads, caviar and picnics. It serves wine on its plaza-view terrace.

Downtown Bakery & Creamery (☎ 707-431-2719; www.downtownbakery.net; 308A Center St; ☙ 7am-5:30pm) Healdsburg's finest bakery crafts scrumptious pastries.

Costeaux French Bakery & Cafe (☎ 707-433-1913; 417 Healdsburg Ave; ☙ 6:30am-6pm Tue-Sat, 6am-5pm Sun) Costeaux makes good boxed lunches.

Anstead's Marketplace & Deli (☎ 707-431-0530; 428 Center St) An indie alternative for groceries, organic produce, picnic supplies and sandwiches, Anstead's is more reasonably priced than the Oakville Grocery (although not as fancy).

Flaky Cream Coffee Shop (☎ 707-433-3895; Healdsburg Shopping Center, 441 Center St; dishes $3-7; ⏰ breakfast & lunch) For bacon, eggs and hash browns, visit this greasy spoon.

Drinking

Flying Goat Coffee (☎ 707-433-9081; www.flyinggoatcoffee.com; 324 Center St; ⏰ 7am-6pm) Refuel on the town's best coffee while reading the *New York Times*.

Bear Republic Brewing Company (☎ 707- 433-2337; 345 Healdsburg Ave; ⏰ 11:30am-late) Bear Republic features fine handcrafted award-winning ales, a pub-style menu and live music weekends.

Barndiva (☎ 707-431-0100; www.barndiva.com; 231 Center St; ⏰ Wed-Sun) For swanky cocktails, like blood-orange margaritas, you can't beat Barndiva. NB: drinks cost over $10.

Entertainment

Raven Theater & Film Center (☎ 707-433-5448; www.raventheater.com; 115 N Main St) The Raven hosts concerts, events and first-run art-house screenings.

Madrona Manor (☎ 707-433-4231, 800-258-4003; www.madronamanor.com; 1001 Westside Rd) There's jazz on the veranda on either Friday or Saturday evenings in summer (phone ahead); wear nice shoes.

Shopping

Lucky Star (☎ 707-433-0191; 105 Plaza St) For super-cute women's clothing, visit this boutique on the plaza's north side. The clothes are reasonably priced

---

DETOUR: GEYSERVILLE

Eight miles north of Healdsburg, tiny Geyserville (population 2370) centers around a one-block-long main street, Geyserville Ave (aka Hwy 128). The turn-of-the-20th-century Old West-style buildings make a wonderful backdrop for pictures. Stop by the **Locals Tasting Room** (☎ 707-857-4900; www.tastelocalwines.com), which represents seven small wineries that have no tasting room of their own. After you've downed your fill, head next door for an earthy Italian meal at the adjoining Santi (see p213).

Fideaux (☎ 707-433-9935; 43 North St) For dog- and cat-fetishist items, here's a storeful of them.

Jimtown Store (☎ 707-433-1212; www.jimtown.com; 6706 Hwy 128) Behind the deli and café, browse carefully chosen antique bric-a-brac, candles and Mexican oilcloths at this roadside store near Alexander Valley.

Gardener (☎ 707-431-1063; www.thegardener.com; 516 Dry Creek Rd) If you love garden stores, this one's a beauty, with fab furniture and imported terra-cotta.

NAPA VALLEY

Mention Wine Country and most people think immediately of Napa Valley. Famous for regal, elegant cabernets and château-like wineries, Napa is the true birthplace of modern-day Wine Country and all its attendant trends, from cuisine to style.

In 1968, Napa County was declared the 'Napa Valley Agricultural Preserve,' effectively blocking all future valley development for nonagricultural purposes. The law stipulates that nobody can buy a plot of land smaller than 40 acres. This succeeded in preserving the valley's natural beauty, but sent land values through the roof. Only the very rich can afford to buy and build here. This is why you'll see so many architecturally stunning wineries: people build monuments. Major corporations are the other big players in Napa, and as they did in California's Central Valley, they're eating up the land. It's not like folksy Sonoma, where land values have traditionally been lower (though they skyrocketed there too in the 1990s). Still Napa is gorgeous, and if you have the time, you should come.

Orientation

Napa Valley is 30 miles long and five miles wide at its widest point (the city of Napa), one mile at its narrowest (around Calistoga). Two roads run north–south along the valley: Hwy 29 (the St Helena Hwy) and the more scenic Silverado Trail, a mile or two east. Ideally, plan to drive up one, down the other.

In 2005, an American Automobile Association study determined that Napa Valley is the eighth most congested rural vacation destination in America. The traffic can be unbearable on weekends in summer and

WINE COUNTRY

WINE COUNTRY

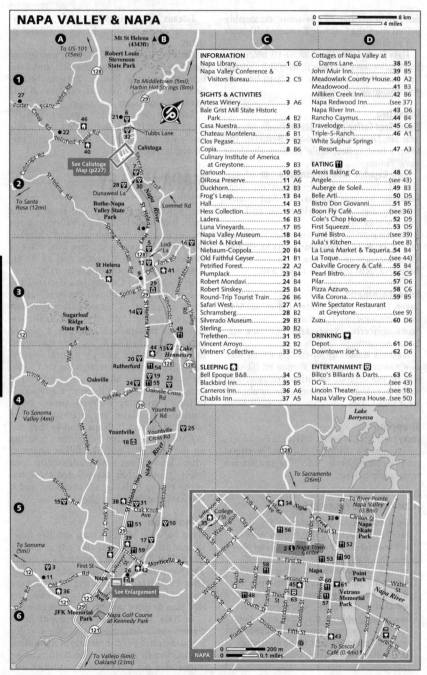

NAPA VALLEY & NAPA

0 —— 8 km
0 —— 4 miles

INFORMATION
Napa Library..........................1 C6
Napa Valley Conference &
    Visitors Bureau..................2 C5

SIGHTS & ACTIVITIES
Artesa Winery.......................3 A6
Bale Grist Mill State Historic
    Park................................4 B2
Casa Nuestra.......................5 B3
Chateau Montelena...............6 B1
Clos Pegase.........................7 B2
Copia...................................8 B6
Culinary Institute of America
    at Greystone....................9 B3
Darioush.............................10 B5
DiRosa Preserve...................11 A6
Duckhorn............................12 B3
Frog's Leap..........................13 B4
Hall....................................14 B3
Hess Collection....................15 A5
Ladera................................16 B3
Luna Vineyards....................17 B5
Napa Valley Museum............18 B4
Nickel & Nickel....................19 B4
Niebaum-Coppola................20 A4
Old Faithful Geyser..............21 B1
Petrified Forest....................22 A2
PlumpJack..........................23 B4
Robert Mondavi...................24 B4
Robert Sinskey....................25 B4
Round-Trip Tourist Train......26 B6
Safari West..........................27 A1
Schramsberg.......................28 B2
Silverado Museum................29 B3
Sterling..............................30 B2
Trefethen............................31 B5
Vincent Arroyo....................32 B2
Vintners' Collective..............33 D5

SLEEPING
Bell Epoque B&B.................34 C5
Blackbird Inn......................35 B5
Carneros Inn.......................36 A6
Chablis Inn.........................37 A5

Cottages of Napa Valley at
    Darms Lane.....................38 B5
John Muir Inn.....................39 B5
Meadowlark Country House..40 A2
Meadowood.........................41 B3
Milliken Creek Inn................42 B6
Napa Redwood Inn..........(see 37)
Napa River Inn....................43 D6
Rancho Caymus...................44 B4
Travelodge..........................45 C6
Triple-S-Ranch....................46 A1
White Sulphur Springs
    Resort.............................47 A3

EATING
Alexis Baking Co..................48 C6
Angele..........................(see 43)
Auberge de Soleil................49 B3
Belle Arti............................50 D5
Bistro Don Giovanni.............51 B5
Boon Fly Café................(see 36)
Cole's Chop House...............52 D5
First Squeeze......................53 D5
Fumé Bistro..................(see 39)
Julia's Kitchen.................(see 8)
La Luna Market & Taqueria..54 B4
La Toque.......................(see 44)
Oakville Grocery & Café.......55 B4
Pearl Bistro........................56 C5
Pilar..................................57 D6
Pizza Azzuro.......................58 C6
Villa Corona.......................59 B5
Wine Spectator Restaurant
    at Greystone................(see 9)
Zuzu.................................60 D6

DRINKING
Depot.................................61 D6
Downtown Joe's...................62 D6

ENTERTAINMENT
Billco's Billiards & Darts........63 C6
DG's............................(see 43)
Lincoln Theater..............(see 18)
Napa Valley Opera House..(see 50)

fall, especially on Hwy 29 between Napa and St Helena. Plan accordingly.

Roads across the valley that link the Silverado Trail with Hwy 29 – including the Yountville, Oakville and Rutherford crossroads – are bucolic and see less traffic. If you want scenery, the Oakville Grade and rural Trinity Rd (which leads southwest to Hwy 12 in Sonoma Valley) are narrow, curvy and beautiful – but treacherous in the rain. Mt Veeder Rd leads through pristine countryside west of Yountville.

Note that the cops watch out like hawks for traffic violators (especially if your skin is brown, so say locals). Don't drink and drive.

The city of Napa anchors the valley – though the real work happens 'up valley.' Napa isn't nearly as pretty as other towns, but it has a few noteworthy sights, among them Copia (p220). More scenic towns include St Helena and Yountville and, at the northern end of the valley, Calistoga – a name more famous for mineral water than wine.

NAPA VALLEY WINERIES

Cab is king in Napa – cabernet sauvignon, that is – not only because it grows so well here, but because it fetches a high price in the marketplace. Other hot-weather-loving varieties, such as Sangiovese and merlot, also thrive here, but cabernet – whose French equivalent is Bordeaux – captures imaginations like no other wine.

Napa's wines merit their reputation as some of the world's finest. If you like deep-red wines with complex noses and luxurious finishes, you're gonna freak out in Napa. (Though in Napa, you don't 'freak out' per se, you get *excited* or *luxuriate,* but you definitely don't freak out. Dude, where do you think you are, Sonoma?)

Napa wineries sell a lot of 'buy-and-hold' wines (versus the 'drink-now' varieties common in Sonoma). With the odd exception, they're pricey. To defray costs, look for free tasting coupons at hotels, concierge desks and visitors centers. Many of the valley's 230 wineries are small operations, and because of strict county zoning laws, some legally cannot receive drop-in visitors; unless you've come strictly to buy, not taste, you'll have to call first. This is *not* the case with all wineries, only some. Also because of zoning,

picnicking is forbidden at many wineries (see the boxed text, above).

The following are listed in south–north order. Unless otherwise stated, they do not require appointments.

ARTESA WINERY

Begin or end the day with a glass of bubbly or pinot at **Artesa** (☎ 707-224-1668; www.artesawinery.com; 1345 Henry Rd; nonreserve/reserve tastings $10/15), high up on a hill in Carneros, southwest of Napa. Built into the side of a mountain, the ultramodern Barcelona-style architecture is stunning, and you can't beat the top-of-the-world vistas over San Pablo Bay. Free tours leave 11am and 2pm. Bottles cost $15 to $60; annual case production 70,000.

HESS COLLECTION

Art lovers should not miss the modern **Hess Collection** (☎ 707-255-1144; www.hesscollection.com; 4411 Redwood Rd; nonreserve/reserve tastings $5/10), whose galleries display mixed-media and large-canvas works over three floors, including works by Francis Bacon and Louis Soutter. In the cave-like tasting room, cabernet and chardonnay are the best known, but also try the viognier. Hess overlooks the valley from a mountainside; be prepared to drive a winding road. (NB: don't confuse Hess Collection with Hess Select. The former is the good stuff, the latter the grocery-store variety.) Bottles cost $13 to $40; annual case production 8000 (not counting Hess Select).

LUNA VINEYARDS

For earthy Sangiovese, fruit-forward pinot grigio, and other Italian varietals, head for **Luna Vineyards** (☎ 707-255-2474; www.lunavineyards.com; 2921 Silverado Trail; nonreserve/reserve tastings $5/10). There's a mellow vibe about this understated winery, especially in the wood-ceilinged tasting room, which is supposed to look Italian but appears more Spanish Mission. Have your last glass upstairs in the romantic lookout tower with lovely valley views. Bottles cost $18 to $50; annual case production 45,000.

DARIOUSH

Like a modern-day Persian palace, **Darioush** (☎ 707-257-2345; www.darioush.com; 4240 Silverado Trail; nonreserve/reserve tastings $5/15) ranks high on the fabulosity scale, with towering columns, Le Corbusier furniture, Persian rugs, travertine walls, and a shattered-glass tasting bar lit by pyramidal skylights and halogen pin-spot lights. Though known for cabernet, Darioush bottles chardonnay, merlot and shiraz, made using 100% of their respective varietals. Call about wine-and-cheese pairings. Bottles cost $34 to $68; annual case production 11,000.

TREFETHEN

One of Napa's longest established wineries, **Trefethen** (☎ 707-255-7700; www.trefethen.com; 1160 Oak Knoll Ave; nonreserve/reserve tastings $10/20) occupies a whopping 850 acres and is listed on the National Register of Historic Places for its 1886 gravity-flow winery barn, the last in the valley; call for tours. Trefethen grows many different grape varieties. Head directly to the reserves; there's also good dry riesling, one of the only ones produced in Napa. Bottles cost $13 to $45; annual case production 60,000 cases.

ROBERT SINSKEY

For hilltop wines and food-friendly wines, visit the chef-owned **Robert Sinskey** (☎ 707-944-9090; www.robertsinskey.com; 6320 Silverado Trail; tastings $15), whose discreetly dramatic stone, redwood and teak tasting room resembles a small cathedral. Best known for organically grown pinot, merlot and cabernet, Sinskey also makes great Alsatian varietals, vin gris, cabernet franc and dry rosé. There's food to taste with the wines. Tasting fees are refunded with purchase, a rarity in Napa. Call about cave and culinary-garden tours ($25), with wine-and-cheese pairings. Bottles cost $18 to $46; annual case production 25,000.

ROBERT MONDAVI

This huge, corporately owned **winery** (☎ 888-766-6328; www.robertmondavi.com; 7801 Hwy 29, Oakville;

tour $20) draws huge, oppressive crowds, but if you know nothing about wine and plan *not* to visit Copia (p220), learn about winemaking here on a $20 tour. Otherwise skip it, unless you're here for one of the wonderful summer concerts, ranging from classical and jazz to R&B and Latin; call for schedules. Bottles cost $17 to $25; annual case production 300,000.

PLUMPJACK

Founded by San Francisco's Mayor Gavin Newsom, **PlumpJack** (☎ 707-945-1220; www.plumpjack.com; 621 Oakville Cross Rd, Oakville; tastings $5) is one of Napa's sexiest, least pretentious boutique wineries, whose whimsical, fashion-forward design sets a superfun mood. The smoky, caramel-y, estate-grown cabernet is the stellar standout, but there's also a big, fat syrah. The $5 tasting fee is a bargain. Oh, and the bottles have screw tops, even the $165 reserve cab! The burgeoning PlumpJack empire includes top-flight restaurants in San Francisco and Lake Tahoe's Squaw Valley. Bottles cost $36 to $62; annual case production 10,000.

NICKEL & NICKEL

An offshoot of famous Far Niente across the road, **Nickel & Nickel** (☎ 707-967-9600; www.nickelandnickel.com; 8164 St Helena Hwy, Oakville; tour $30) occupies a 19th-century farmstead, including a weathered, red barn dating to 1775 and 1884 farmhouse, where you can taste elegant single-vineyard, single-varietal wines, all from the same plot of earth (called a 'terroir tasting'). The tour and six-wine flight are expensive, but these are great wines. Reservations essential. Bottles cost $38 to $125; annual case production 17,000.

NIEBAUM-COPPOLA

The former Inglenook **estate** (☎ 707-968-1100; 1991 St Helena Hwy, Rutherford; tastings $15, optional tour $25) is owned by the filmmaker Francis Ford Coppola and has a free movie 'museum,' which displays a Tucker car and Coppola's *Godfather* Oscars. The optional tour ($25) focuses on the striking château, built in 1887. There's no charge to wander into the château and roam the park-like grounds. The wines are so-so (head for the Rubicon); the setting is what's great here. Borrow a sailboat to float in the fountain. Bottles cost $16 to $65; estimated annual case production 60,000.

WINE COUNTRY

FROG'S LEAP

If you see only one Napa winery, make it **Frog's Leap** (☎ 707-963-4704, 800-959-4704; www.frogs leap.com; 8815 Conn Creek Rd; tours & tastings free, by appointment only), where meandering paths wind through magical gardens and fruit-bearing orchards surrounding an 1884 barn and farmstead. But more than anything, it's the vibe that's so wonderful here – casual and down to earth, with a major emphasis on *fun*. The sauvignon blanc is the best-known wine, but the merlot is also good. All grapes are organically grown. NB: you *must* make an appointment to visit (which includes a *free* tour and tasting), so call ahead, dammit. Bottles cost $14 to $49; annual case production 55,000.

HALL

One of Napa's hot new wineries, **Hall** (☎ 707-967-2620; www.hallwines.com; 401 St Helena Hwy, St Helena; tasting $10) specializes in cabernet franc, sauvignon blanc, merlot and cabernet sauvignon. There's a cool abstract-sculpture garden and lovely picnic area shaded by mulberry trees (with wines by the glass). In 2006 construction was scheduled to begin on a Frank Gehry-designed visitors center. You don't need an appointment for standard tastings, but call ahead for $20 barrel tastings, in which wine is drawn right from the barrel before it's even bottled. Bottles average $20 to $38; annual case production 8000.

DUCKHORN

Famous for luscious merlot, **Duckhorn** (☎ 707-963-7108, 888-354-8885; www.duckhorn.com; 1000 Lodi Lane, St Helena; tasting $10-15) caters to the skirt-and-sweater bourgeoisie, but the wines are dee-lish. And you can sit down while you taste. It also offers $25 food-and-wine pairings (call ahead), led by an educator who provides insight into food, wine and the valley. If you like merlot, comb your hair and drop by Duckhorn. Bottles cost $28 to $68; annual case production 70,000.

CASA NUESTRA

A peace flag and picture of Elvis greet your arrival in the tasting barn at old-school, '70s-vintage, mom-and-pop **Casa Nuestra** (☎ 707-963-5783; www.casanuestra.com; 3451 Silverado Trail, St Helena; tastings $5, refundable with purchase), which produces unusual blends and interesting varietals, including good chenin blanc, and

100% cabernet franc. Best of all, you can picnic free (call ahead) beneath weeping willows, next to two goats named Nava and Cross. (Buy a bottle.) Bottles cost $15 to $45; annual case production 1500.

LADERA

High on the flanks of Howell Mountain, above the valley's east side, **Ladera** (☎ 707-965-2445, 866-523-3728; www.laderavineyards.com; 150 White Cottage Rd S, Angwin; tastings free; ☺ by appointment) makes wonderful, little-known, estate-grown cabernet sauvignon. Make an appointment to visit this well-off-the-beaten-path 19th-century winery. There's only one group at a time: yours. Bottles cost $35 to $65; annual case production 3000.

SCHRAMSBERG

Up a wooded lane off Hwy 29, **Schramsberg** (☎ 707-942-2414; www.schramsberg.com; 1400 Schramsberg Rd, off Peterson Dr; tastings $25) makes some of California's best brut sparkling wines and was the first domestic wine served at the White House (in 1972). Blanc de blancs is the signature. The appointment-only tasting and tour is expensive, but you'll sample all the *tête de cuvées*, not just the low-end wines, making it worth the investment – if you're into sparkling wine. Tours include a walk through the caves; bring a sweater. Bottles cost $35 to $80; annual case production 50,000.

STERLING

The reason to stop in at **Sterling** (☎ 707-942-3344; www.sterlingvineyards.com; 1111 Dunaweal Lane, Calistoga; gondola ride $15) is to ride a gondola to the hilltop winery for superb views down valley. Modeled after a Greek villa, the winery is architecturally interesting, but the wine is nothing special. Come for the gondola, not the grapes. The website has two-for-one coupons. Bottles cost $15 to $45; annual case production 80,000.

CLOS PEGASE

Clos Pegase (☎ 707-942-4981; www.clospegase.com; 1060 Dunaweal Lane; tastings $5-15) has a $65 million modern-art collection with works by Jean Dubuffet and Henry Moore – though there may be a rack of sweatshirts obscuring the Francis Bacon hanging in the gift shop. On the tasting bar, look for food-friendly chardonnay, pinot noir, merlot and cabernet sauvignon. Free tours leave at 11am and

WINE COUNTRY

2pm. Bottles cost $19 to $36; annual case production 40,000.

VINCENT ARROYO

The tasting room is in a garage at **Vincent Arroyo** (☎ 707-942-6995; www.vincentarroyo.com; 2361 Greenwood Ave, Calistoga; tastings free), where you may even meet Mr Arroyo, who's known for making great petite syrah and cabernet sauvignon. All are estate grown, and they're not distributed anywhere else. They're so consistently good that 75% of total production is sold before it's even bottled, so you have to buy the production year in which you visit. Tastings are free, but you *must* make an appointment. Bottles cost $15 to $50; annual case production 8000.

CHATEAU MONTELENA

Housed in an 1882 stone château, with a beautiful lake and Chinese-style bridges outside, **Chateau Montelena** (☎ 707-942-5105; www.montelena.com; 1429 Tubbs Lane, Calistoga; tastings $10-25) makes wine that stands on its own merit. Montelena produced the chardonnay that won the now-famous Paris tasting of 1976. The chardonnay undergoes no malolactic fermentation, so there's no oak or butter to it, only a crisp, austere flavor showcasing the original fruit. Also noteworthy are the estate-grown zinfandel and cabernet sauvignon. You can also book a sit-down reserve tasting for $25. Call for tours. Bottles cost $18 to $125, average is $38; annual case production 40,000.

NAPA

pop 71,412

Napa is the valley's population center. The city has undergone a transformation in recent years. The cost of living in smaller, more northerly towns has risen so high that few can afford them. Newcomers have turned to Napa instead. The downtown is booming. Where once there were warehouses, now there are happening restaurants and a burgeoning arts scene. Napa is home to Copia – reason enough to visit – and the terminus of the Napa Valley Wine Train.

Orientation & Information

Napa's main drag, 1st St, is lined with shops and restaurants.

Napa is sandwiched between Silverado Trail and St Helena Hwy/Hwy 29. Coming

from San Francisco on Hwy 12/121, go past the turnoff for Sonoma Valley and turn left (north) onto Hwy 29 (labeled Hwy 121/29 within city limits). For downtown, exit at 1st St and head east.

Napa Library (☎ 707-253-4241; www.co.napa.ca.us; 580 Coombs St; ⏰ 10am-9pm Mon-Thu, 10am-5:30pm Fri, 10am-5pm Sat, 2-9pm Sun) For email connections.

Napa Valley Conference & Visitors Bureau (☎ 707-226-7459; www.napavalley.org; 1310 Napa Town Center; ⏰ 9am-5pm) Hidden in a mall between 1st and Pearl Sts, two blocks west of Main St. This is the biggest information center. Pick up the free *Inside Napa Valley*, with its almost-comprehensive winery guide. The staff will help make same-day room reservations, but not advance.

Sights & Activities

Named for the Roman god of abundance, **Copia: The American Center for Wine, Food & the Arts** (☎ 707-259-1600; www.copia.org; 500 1st St; adult/child 13-20/under 12 $13/5/free; ⏰ 10am-5pm Wed-Mon) is a $50 million cultural center, bringing together all things Wine Country in one smart package. Interactive exhibits include a wine-tasting station that demystifies the experience, preparing you to visit wineries unafraid. Fascinating installations tackle the question, 'What is American food?' Every ticket includes free tastings and a cooking demonstration. The outside extensive gardens include one for children (with roosters and a beanstalk teepee) and a 'wine garden' planted with things people use to describe wine, from lemon to tobacco. The café serves lovely salads and sandwiches (under $10); Julia's Kitchen (see p222) provides whitetablecloth service. There are outdoor concerts, forums, barbecues and films; check the website. If you see only one thing in Napa, make it Copia. Budget three to four hours.

At supercool **Vintners' Collective** (☎ 707-255-7150; www.vintnerscollective.com; 1245 Main St; ⏰ Wed-Mon 11am-6pm), sample tiny-scale-production cult wines from 18 wineries that area too small to have their own tasting rooms.

In Carneros, see fabulous modern art in 217-acre **DiRosa Preserve** (☎ 707-226-5991; www.dirosapreserve.org; 5200 Carneros Hwy; admission $3; ⏰ Tue-Fri 9:30am-3pm, tours by appointment Tue-Sat), where there's an outdoor sculpture garden, 35-acre lake and indoor galleries.

Sleeping

Supply is stretched in summer, so weekend rates skyrocket. Also try Calistoga (p228).

FLYING & BALLOONING

Wine Country is every bit as stunning from the air as on the ground. The rolling hills, deep valleys, and proximity to San Francisco Bay and the Pacific Ocean make it ideal for sightseeing by air. Make reservations.

The **Vintage Aircraft Company** (☎ 707-938-2444; www.vintageaircraft.com; 23982 Arnold Dr, Sonoma; 20min tours 1/2 adults $130/190, 'intensely aerobatic' flights $220/280) flies over Sonoma in a vintage biplane with an awesome pilot, who'll even do loop-de-loops if you want.

For glider rides, contact **Crazy Creek Soaring** (☎ 707-987-9112; www.crazycreekgliders.com; 20-40min flights 1 person $140-215, 2 people $190-290), which operates from the glider port in Middletown, off Hwy 29 about 10 miles north of Calistoga.

Napa Valley's signature hot-air balloon flights take off early in the morning, around 6am or 7am, when the air is coolest; they usually include a sparkling wine breakfast on landing. Adults pay about $190 to $210, kids $100 to $150. Phone **Balloons above the Valley** (☎ 707-253-2222, 800-464-6824; www.balloonrides.com) or **Napa Valley Balloons** (☎ 707-944-0228, 800-253-2224; www .napavalleyballoons.com), both in Yountville.

Chablis Inn (☎ 707-257-1944; 800-443-3490; www .chablisinn.com; 3360 Solano Ave; r weekday $99-109, weekend $149-159; ✗ ❄ 🖭) It may seem pricey, but this well-kept two-story motel has one of the best quality-to-value ratios in Napa. There's also a hot tub.

Napa Redwood Inn (☎ 707-257-6111, 877-872-6272; www.napavalleyredwoodinn.com; 3380 Solano Ave; r weekday $83-95, weekend $127-139; ❄ 🖭) You'll have seen this motel a thousand times beside other freeways. This one is next door to the Chablis Inn, and though it's a good value, it's a step down in comfort.

John Muir Inn (☎ 707-257-7220, 800-522-8999; www .johnmuirinn.com; 1998 Trower Ave; r incl breakfast weekday $135-150, weekend $155-165; ✗ ❄ 🖭) Of the cookie-cutter hotels lining Hwy 29 north of downtown, this one's the best – comparable to the Marriott, but less expensive. The very-clean rooms have marble baths and good mattresses, and include breakfast at Marie Callender's coffee shop.

RiverPointe Napa Valley (☎ 707-252-4200, 877-258-2282; www.riverpointenapa.com; 500 Lincoln Ave; studios $115, 1-bedroom r $187-250; ✗ ❄ 🖭) The website calls this place a five-star resort. It's not. What it really is: a beautifully landscaped, cleverly disguised, upmarket trailer park with 100 spotless units on 11 acres riverfront acres. Once you get over the mobile-home thing, they're quite nice, if boxy. All have kitchenettes. Oddly, they're timeshares and book up on weekends.

Napa River Inn (☎ 707-251-8500, 877-251-8500; www.napariverinn.com; 500 Main St; r weekday $179-199, weekend $199-249; ✗ ❄) On the river in the historic 1884 Hatt Building, the inn has super-comfy, upper-midrange rooms with extras like triple-sheeted beds, good fabrics and bathrobes; for $25 extra, get a doggie bed, cookies and chardonnay doggie biscuits.

Cottages of Napa Valley at Darms Lane (☎ 707-252-7810; www.napacottages.com; q $275-375; ✗ ❄ 🖳) Formerly called Darms Lane Inn, eight one-bedroom 1940s vacation cottages nestle beneath 200ft-tall trees. They were gutted in 2005 and rebuilt with high-end amenities. They sleep four and have kitchenettes, two-person Jacuzzi tubs, pull-out sofas and gas fireplaces.

Milliken Creek Inn (☎ 707-255-1197, 888-622-5775; www.millikencreekinn.com; 1815 Silverado Trail; r incl breakfast $395-650; ✗ ❄) Understatedly elegant Milliken Creek combines the charm of a small inn, service of a fine hotel, and intimacy of a B&B hideaway. The impeccably styled, English-Colonial rooms have top-flight amenities – flat-panel televisions, DVDs, stereos, fireplaces, plush towels, ultrahigh-thread-count linens – but the beauty is in the details like evening candles in your room and breakfast in bed. Call 24 hours ahead for occasional last-minute, one-night-only rates of $195.

Carneros Inn (☎ 707-299-4900; www.thecarneros inn.com; 4048 Sonoma Hwy (Hwy 121/12); r weekday $435-595, weekend $475-655; ✗ ❄ 🖳 🖭) The pinnacle of chic for the under-50 set, Carneros Inn's snappy design-aesthetic and retro-small-town-agricultural theme shatters the predictable Wine Country mold – no lace curtains here! The semidetached, corrugated metal units look like itinerant housing, but inside they're überchic, with cherry-wood floors,

WINE COUNTRY

ultrasuede headboards, bright white duvets, chocolate leather club chairs, wood-burning fireplaces, heated-tile bathroom floors, giant soaking tubs and indoor-outdoor showers. For a serious splurge, this is the coolest place, especially the vineyard-view rooms.

Also recommended:

Blackbird Inn (☎ 707-226-2450, 888-567-9811; www .blackbirdinnnapa.com; r incl breakfast weekday $145-200, weekend $185-275; ☒ ☒) Gorgeous, eight-room Craftsman-style house.

Belle Epoque B&B (☎ 707-257-2161, 800-238-8070; www.labelleepoque.com; 1386 Calistoga Ave; r incl breakfast $255-295; ☒ ☒) Fancy 1893 Victorian with high-thread-count sheets.

Travelodge (☎ 707-226-1871; www.travelodge.com; 853 Coombs St at 2nd St; r midweek/weekends $110/150; ☒ ☒ ☒) Thin-walled, budget option; 3rd-floor rooms are quietest.

Eating

If you're here in spring, look for the strawberry stand on Silverado Trail's east side (*not* the one on the west), a mile north of Trancas St; the berries are incredible. (Skip the cherry stand a quarter-mile further north.)

Pizza Azzuro (☎ 707-255-5552; 1401 2nd St; mains $10-12) Apart from inventive pizzas with tender crusts, Azzuro makes good pastas – try the 'little ear' with spinach and garlic – and one of the county's best Caesar salads. Good veggie sandwiches too.

Alexis Baking Co (☎ 707-258-1827; www.alexis bakingcompany.com; 1517 3rd St; dishes $5-9; ☒ breakfast &lunch) This is the spot for scrambles, granola, focaccia-bread sandwiches, big cups of joe and boxed lunches to go.

Villa Corona (☎ 707-447-7683; 3614 Bel Air Plaza; dishes $5-9; ☒ 9am-9pm Mon-Sat, 9am-8pm Sun) For fat burritos and awesome chimichangas, come to this hole-in-the-wall Mexican behind the Lamplighter Lounge on Trancas St, just east of Hwy 29.

First Squeeze (☎ 707-224-6762; 1126 1st St; dishes $5-7; ☒ breakfast & lunch) Come for the freshly squeezed juices, salads, smoothies and sandwiches with homemade mustard. There's breakfast till 2pm.

Soscol Café (☎ 707-252-0651; 632 Soscol Av; dishes $5-8; ☒ 6am-2pm Mon-Sat, 7am-1pm Sun) For the ultimate American greasy-spoon-style plate – massive and overflowing – Soscol makes great huevos rancheros, and chicken-fried steak and eggs. There's not a high heel in sight.

Boon Fly Cafe (☎ 707-299-4870; www.thecarneros inn.com; 4048 Sonoma Hwy; mains $9-19; ☒ 7am-10pm) For New American comfort food done well, make a beeline to Boon Fly. At breakfast, everything's under $10 (try the homemade doughnuts or brioche French toast); at lunch and dinner the diverse menu features grilled Reuben sandwiches, cracker-crust pizzas, roasted chicken with mashers and tangy-sweet spinach salads. Save room for warm chocolate-chip cookies.

Bistro Don Giovanni (☎ 707-224-3300; www.bistro dongiovanni.com; 4110 Howard Lane, at Hwy 29; mains $16-21) A long-running favorite, this always-jammin' trattoria-style roadhouse cooks up modern-Italian pastas, crispy pizzas and wood-roasted meats. Make reservations. The weekends get packed – and loud. For vineyard-view seats, request tables 50 to 59 or 70 to 79.

Pearl Bistro (☎ 707-224-9161; www.therestaurant pearl.com; 1339 Pearl St; mains $12-18; ☒ Tue-Sat) Meet locals at this dog-friendly bistro with red-painted concrete floors, pinewood tables and open-rafter ceiling. Expect straightforward, flavor-rich cooking such as double-cut pork chops, chicken verde with polenta, steak tacos and the specialty, oysters.

There are a number of other interesting dining options:

Angele (☎ 707-252-8115; www.angele.us; 540 Main St; mains $18-23) Perfect provincial-French cooking on a river-view patio. Beautiful *boeuf à la bourguignonne*; great burgers too.

Cole's Chop House (☎ 707-224-6328; www.coles chophouse.com; 1122 Main St; mains $25-32; ☒ dinner) For the best steaks, visit this classic American steakhouse.

Julia's Kitchen (☎ 707-265-5700; www.copia.org; 500 First St, at Copia; mains $16-25, 4-course lunch $40, 6-course dinner $60; ☒ lunch Wed-Mon, dinner Thu-Sun) Swank Cal-French white-tablecloth dining; Thursday evening's three-course prix-fixe costs $29 – with no corkage!

Belle Arti (☎ 707-255-0720; www.bellearti-napa.com; 1040 Main St; mains $12-21; ☒ lunch Mon-Fri, dinner nightly) Sicilian cooking in a hidden creekside garden; Sundays are Italian-movie night.

Fumé Bistro (☎ 707-257-1999; www.fumebistro.com; 4050 Byway E at Hwy 29; mains $18-21) Lively roadhouse for New American cooking. Good happy hour. Monday nights: $5 burgers.

Pilar (☎ 707-252-4474; www. 807 Main St; lunch mains $11-16, dinner $22-26; ☒ lunch Tue-Sat, dinner Mon-Sat) Small, sexy Cal-French bistro with Spanish overtones. Rearmost tables are quietest.

Zuzu (☎ 707-224-8555; www.zuzunapa.com; 829 Main St; small plates $6-9; ☽ lunch Mon-Fri, dinner nightly) Small plates, big waits.

Drinking & Entertainment

Downtown Joe's (☎ 707-258-2337; 902 Main St at 2nd St) Live music plays Thursday to Sunday, while DJs spin Tuesday and Wednesday at this microbrewery-restaurant, which gets packed after dinner.

Depot (☎ 707-252-4477; 806 4th St, off Soscol Av; ☽ Tue-Thu 3pm-midnight, Fri & Sat 3pm-2am, 3-9pm Sun) Napa's gay bar is tricky to find; it's behind Greenberg's used-car lot inside an Italian restaurant.

DG's (☎ 707-253-8474; www.dgsjazz.com; 530 Main St; ☽ Wed-Sun) A gallery by day, jazz bar at night, DG's hosts salsa-dancing Thursdays, blues Friday, jazz Saturdays and open-mic Sundays.

Napa Valley Opera House (☎ 707-226-7372; www .nvoh.org; 1030 Main St) This vintage-1880s opera house was restored during 2003 and stages straight plays, comedy and live musicians like Ravi Shankar.

Billco's Billiards & Darts (☎ 707-226-7506; 1234 3rd St; ☽ noon-1am) The crowd is mostly beer-swilling men wearing khakis. Eleven pool tables, two dart boards.

YOUNTVILLE
pop 2916

Yountville (pronounced *yawnt*-vill), one of the valley's larger towns, is nine miles north of Napa, 21 miles south of Calistoga. It straddles Hwy 29 (the St Helena Hwy), though most restaurants and shops are on Washington St, parallel to and just east of the highway.

Yountville has banks, markets, several places to stay and famous top-end restaurants, but otherwise St Helena and Calistoga make better bases.

Yountville's modernist 40,000-sq-ft **Napa Valley Museum** (☎ 707-944-0500; www.napavalley museum.org; 55 Presidents Circle, off California Dr; adult/ child $4.50/2.50; ☽ 10am-5pm Wed-Mon) chronicles cultural history and showcases local paintings. You can picnic outside.

Skip the 1870 vintage shops, unless you're shopping for your grandmother in Kansas.

Sleeping

Maison Fleurie (☎ 707-944-2056, 800-788-0369; www .maisonfleurienapa.com; 6529 Yount St; r incl breakfast $130-285; ☒ ☒ ☒) The rooms at this country inn

are inside a turn-of-the-20th-century, ivy-covered home and former carriage house, decorated in unfussy French-provincial style. There's a big breakfast and afternoon wine and hors d'oeuvres. Outside there's a hot tub.

Burgundy House (☎ 707-944-0889; www.burgundy houseinn.com; 6711 Washington St; r incl breakfast weekday/ weekend $135/175; ☒ ☒ ☐) Built in 1890, this five-room French-country inn has 20in-thick stone walls and smallish, simply furnished rooms, long on charm.

Napa Valley Lodge (☎ 707-944-2468; www.napa valleylodge.com; 2230 Madison St at Washington St; r $252-362; ☒ ☒ ☒) It looks like a condo complex on the outside, but the rooms are spacious and modern, with comfortable beds with pillow-top mattresses; some have fireplaces. Extras include a hot tub, sauna and exercise room.

Petit Logis (☎ 707-944-2332, 877-944-2332; www .petitlogis.com; 6527 Yount St; r $160-205; ☒ ☒) Next door to Maison Fleurie, this cedar-sided inn has five individually decorated rooms. Think white wicker furniture and dusty-rose fabric. Add $20 for breakfast for two.

Napa Valley Railway Inn (☎ 707-944-2000; www .napavalleyrailwayinn.com; 6523 Washington St; r midweek $90-160, weekend $110-175; ☒ ☒) Sleep in a converted railroad car, part of two short trains parked at a central platform. They don't have much privacy, but they're moderately priced, and kids love 'em.

Eating
Make reservations whenever possible.

Bouchon Bakery (☎ 707-944-2253; 6528 Washington St; dishes $3-6; ☽ 7am-7pm) For glorious pastries, croissants, ham sandwiches and strong, flavorful coffee, visit this *trés* French carry-out bakery and café, and sit outside at tiny tables.

Gordon's Cafe & Wine Bar (☎ 707-944-8246; 6770 Washington St, Yountville; dishes $9-12; ☽ breakfast & lunch) Hang with the locals at the community table of this down-to-earth café, where everything is made from scratch. At breakfast, there's baby organic oatmeal, at lunch crispy-buttermilk chicken salad. Yum!

Bistro Jeanty (☎ 707-944-0103; www.bistrojeanty .com; 6510 Washington St; mains $16-29) In a land of fussy French cuisine, chef-owner Philippe Jeanty's earthy, bistro-style cooking is a refreshing reminder that French food is more than foie gras. Expect cassoulet, coq au vin,

WINE COUNTRY

steak frites, braised pork with lentils and scrumptious tomato soup.

Wine Garden (☎ 707-945-1002; www.napawinegarden.com; 6476 Washington St; small plates $7-11, mains $10-17) Stylish, but never overbearing, the Wine Garden makes a variety of small plates, finger foods, salads, steaks and chops, that won't break the bank. The outdoor picnic garden is great for kids who can't sit still. Grown-ups love the wine bar.

Bouchon (☎ 707-944-8037; www.frenchlaundry.com; 6534 Washington St; mains $16-28) At celeb chef Thomas Keller's French brasserie, everything from food to decor is so authentic, from the zinc bar to the white-aproned waiters, you'd swear you were in Paris – even the Bermuda shorts–clad Americans look out of place. On the menu: giant platters of oysters, onion soup, roasted chicken, leg of lamb, trout with almonds, runny cheeses and profiteroles for desert, all perfectly prepared. The fries are some of the best anywhere. Yum!

Mustards Grill (☎ 707-944-2424; www.mustardsgrill.com; 7399 St Helena Hwy; mains $15-23) The valley's long-standing roadhouse – an archetype in the genre – attracts crowds of tourists for California comfort food: wood-fire meats, lamb shank, pork chops, hearty salads and sandwiches.

French Laundry (☎ 707-944-2380; www.frenchlaundry.com; 6640 Washington St, Yountville; prix fixe menu $175; dinner nightly, lunch Fri-Sun) The pinnacle of California dining, the French Laundry is epic, a high-wattage culinary experience on par with the world's best. Book two months ahead at 10am sharp. Avoid booking a table before 7pm; service during the first seating moves along faster than during the second – sometimes too fast.

Drinking & Entertainment

Pancha's (☎ 707-944-2125; 6764 Washington St) Swill tequila with locals at this dive bar. Vineyard workers come early, waiters from chic restaurants late.

Lincoln Theater (☎ 707-944-1300, 866-944-9199; www.lincolntheater.org) Various artists play this 1200-seat theater, including the Napa Valley Symphony.

OAKVILLE & RUTHERFORD

Tiny Oakville (pop 300) lies five miles north of Yountville. It has no sights to speak of, but is well endowed with wineries. Rutherford (pop 525) is likewise neither town nor village, but a loose-knit collection of wineries, homes, important restaurants, and roadside antique and gift shops.

There is no budget lodging.

Sleeping

Rancho Caymus (☎ 707-963-1777, 800-845-1777; www.ranchocaymus.com; 1140 Rutherford Rd, Rutherford; r $250-320;) Long on atmosphere, this ever-so-charming hacienda-style inn is reminiscent of California's Mission period, with rooms surrounding a tiled fountain courtyard. All have wood-beamed ceilings and wood floors. Winter rates drop by over $100.

Eating

Oakville Grocery & Cafe (☎ 707-944-8802; www.oakvillegrocery.com; 7856 Hwy 29, Oakville; 8am-5:30pm) The definitive Wine Country deli sells stinky cheeses, charcuterie meats, freshly baked bread, olives, wine and lunch boxes ($15), which you can order in advance. There are three tables outside, but ask where to picnic nearby.

La Luna Market & Taqueria (☎ 707-963-3211, 707-967-3497; 1153 Rutherford Rd, Rutherford; dishes $4-6; 8am-7:30pm) If you're wondering where Mexican laborers get burritos, look no further. The hot sauce is homemade.

Auberge du Soleil (☎ 707-963-1211; www.aubergedusoleil.com; 180 Rutherford Hill Rd, Rutherford; mains breakfast $16-18, lunch $19-25; 4-/6-course prix fixe dinner $79/105) You won't find more mesmerizing valley views than from Auberge's hillside terrace. The Euro-Cal menu is expertly prepared with an easy, elegant style. Though pricey, this is one of the valley's best for a swanky breakfast, lazy lunch, or a will-you-wear-my-ring dinner. Make reservations; arrive before sunset. Auberge also rents rooms from $725.

La Toque (☎ 707-963-9770; www.latoque.com; 1140 Rutherford Rd, Rutherford; 5-course menu $98; Wed-Sun) Napa's unsung hero of Gallic cooking, chef Ken Frank exquisitely crafts haute-contemporary French cuisine, eking out the complexity and subtlety of all his ingredients, especially evident in his foie gras and use of truffles. The artistry is mirrored in the wine director's five accompanying selections ($62 supplement). Service is refreshingly unpretentious. La Toque isn't for everyone, but if you're a foodie, this might be your trip's best meal. Men: wear a jacket. Reservations essential.

ST HELENA
pop 6000

The Rodeo Drive of Napa, St Helena's (pronounced ha-*lee*-na) boutique-lined Main St is also Hwy 29, which guarantees traffic tie-ups as you approach downtown from the south. Interesting old buildings, shops and restaurants make it perfect for strolling, but the town gets packed on busy summer weekends.

The **chamber of commerce** (☎ 707-963-4556, 800-799-6456; www.sthelena.com; 1010 Main St, Suite A; 🕑 10am-5pm Mon-Fri, 11am-3pm Sat) has information and in-person-only lodging assistance.

Sights & Activities

Silverado Museum (☎ 707-963-3757; www.silverado museum.org; 1490 Library Lane; admission free; 🕑 noon-4pm Tue-Sun) contains a fascinating collection of Robert Louis Stevenson memorabilia. In 1880 the author – at that time sick, penniless and unknown – stayed in an abandoned bunkhouse at the old Silverado Mine with his new wife, Fanny Osbourne. His novel *The Silverado Squatters* is based on his time there. To reach Library Lane, turn east off Hwy 29 at the Adams St traffic lights and cross the railroad tracks.

The **Culinary Institute of America at Greystone** (☎ 707-967-2320; www.ciachef.edu/california; 2555 Main St; cooking demonstration $12.50; 🕑 10am-5pm), a continuing-education campus for food-and-wine professionals, occupies the Christian Brothers' 1889 château and offers public cooking demonstrations, Friday through Monday.

Sleeping

El Bonita Motel (☎ 707-963-3216, 800-541-3284; www .elbonita.com; 195 Main St; r $135-249; ✗ 🐾 🖥 🏊) Book in advance to secure a room at this sought-after motel, with up-to-date rooms (quietest are in back), attractive grounds, hot tub and sauna.

Hotel St Helena (☎ 707-963-4388; www.hotelst helena.com; 1309 Main St; r $95-155, with bathroom $125-225; ✗ 🐾) Decorated with period furnishing, this 1881 hotel sits right on Main St. Rooms are small, but a good bargain, especially those with a shared bathroom.

White Sulphur Springs Resort (☎ 707-963-8588; 3100 White Sulphur Springs Rd; r $95-200; ✗ 🐾 🏊) A year-round creek runs through the property, beneath 100-year-old oaks and towering redwoods, at California's oldest resort, two miles

west of town. Accommodations are simple and basic (some have a shared bathroom), but there's a delightful retro-rustic vibe. There's also a hot spring, Jacuzzi, swimming pool and full-service spa.

Also consider the following:

Eagle & Rose Inn (☎ 707-963-1532; www.eagleand roseinn.com; 1431 Railroad Ave; hotel r with kitchenette $189-229, motel r $129-149; ✗ 🐾) Operates a 12-room in-town hotel (with kitchenettes), and five-room motel, one mile north.

Inn at Southbridge (☎ 707-967-9400, 800-520-6800; innatsouthbridge.com; 1020 Main St; r $350-425; ✗ 🐾 🏊) Luxury rooms on Main St.

Meadowood (☎ 707-963-3646, 800-458-8080; www .meadowood.com; 900 Meadowood Lane; r from $625; ✗ 🐾 🖥 🏊) Napa's grandest resort has luxury cottages and a wooded, country-club setting.

Eating

RESTAURANTS

Cindy's Backstreet Kitchen (☎ 707-963-1200; www .cindysbackstreetkitchen.com; 1327 Railroad Ave; mains $14-19) The inviting retro-homey decor complements the menu's Cal-American comfort food, such as avocado-and-papaya salad, wood-fired duck, steak and French fries, and the simple grilled burger. There's a small patio, where you will meet local cognoscenti.

Cook St Helena (☎ 707-963-7088; 1310 Main St; lunch mains $9-18, dinner $13-22; 🕑 Tue-Sat) Locals also love this storefront bistro, with counter seats and tables in back. Half the mains are pasta; the others are dishes like braised short ribs, spicy-tomato mussels, clams and sausages, and a terrific BLT at lunch. Bring earplugs at dinner.

Terra (☎ 707-963-8931; www.terrarestaurant.com; 1345 Railroad Ave; mains $20-30; 🕑 dinner Wed-Mon) Inside an 1884 stone building, Terra wows diners with its seamlessly blended Japanese, French and Italian cooking. This is one of Wine Country's best; it's pricey, but you won't soon forget what you ate.

Martini House (☎ 707-963-2233; www.martini house.com; 1245 Spring St; lunch mains $13-24, dinner $22-38; 🕑 lunch Fri-Mon, dinner nightly) One of Wine Country's handsomest dining rooms, Martini House occupies a 1923 California Craftsman–style house, with food as fine as the room is gorgeous. Celeb chef-owner Todd Humphries ensures the seasonal-regional menu is always up to snuff. Book a table in the grand main dining room or

WINE COUNTRY

the romantic, sun-dappled garden. Drinkers: see the supercool downstairs bar.

Cafe 29 (☎ 707-963-9919; www.cafe29.com; 3000 Hwy 29; breakfast & lunch mains $8-13, dinner $9-13; ☺ breakfast & lunch Tue-Sun, dinner Thu-Sat) Just north of town, Cafe 29 makes good omelettes and pancakes at breakfast, and sandwiches, burgers and pot pies at lunch.

Wine Spectator Greystone Restaurant (☎ 707-967-1010; www.ciachef.edu; 2555 Main St; mains $17-29) Inside the renowned Culinary Institute of America, head directly to the gorgeous patio bar for cocktails or garden-view lunch. The menu is pure California, with a broad selection of local wines and microbrews.

GROCERIES & QUICK EATS

A **farmers market** (Railroad Ave at Pine St; ☺ 7:30am-11:30am Fri, May-Nov) meets in warmer months.

Taylor's Auto Refresher (☎ 707-963-3486; 933 Main St; dishes $6-10; ☺ 10:30am-9pm) Taylor's roadside hamburger stand draws huge crowds for Cobb salads, calamari and burgers, which you can eat barefoot sitting at tables in the grass.

Model Bakery (☎ 707-963-9731; 1357 Main St; ☺ Tue-Sun) Serves great scones, muffins, salads, gelato, pizzas, sandwiches and strong coffee.

Sunshine Foods (☎ 707-963-7070; 1115 Main St) Carries the best groceries in town.

Napa Valley Olive Oil Mfg Co (☎ 707-963-4173; 835 Charter Oak St; ☺ 8am-5:30pm) This is an old-fashioned Italian grocery with no deli, but you'll find great salamis, prosciutto, olives, biscotti, bread, and of course olive oil. It'll lend you a knife and board to make your picnic, which you can eat outside.

Armadillo's (☎ 707-963-8082; 1304 Main St; mains $7-12) This is a bright Mexican restaurant with reasonable prices.

Shopping

Main St is lined with high-end boutiques (think $100 socks), but there remain some mom-and-pop shops like the barber and hardware store.

Diva Perfumes (☎ 707-963-4507; 1309 Main St) If you can't get to Paris, come here for hard-to-find perfumes.

Campus Store (☎ 707-967-2309; 2555 Main St) Inside the Culinary Institute, the campus store carries fantastic cookbooks as well as kitchen gadgets.

Woodhouse Chocolates (☎ 800-966-3468; 1367 Main St) Woodhouse looks more like Tiffany than a candy shop, and the chocolates are priced accordingly: $56 per pound. Welcome to St Helena.

St Helena Premier Outlets (☎ 707-963-7282; www .sthelenapremieroutlets.com; 3111 N St Helena Hwy) Eight outlet shops include Brooks Brothers, Tumi, Coach and Jones New York.

Main Street Books (☎ 707-963-1338; 1315 Main St; ☺ Mon-Sat) Sells good used books.

CALISTOGA

pop 5190

Thank goodness the hordes stay south of St Helena and rarely make it to Calistoga, Wine Country's least-gentrified town. Storefronts line the main drag, but they're *shops*, not *boutiques*, and you'll see a diverse mix of folks on the sidewalks – some with tattoos, some with bad hair – a refreshing change from the bleached-and-scrubbed, Cadillac-driving bourgeoisie of the midvalley towns.

Robert Louis Stevenson said, '…the whole neighborhood of Mount St Helena is full of sulfur and boiling springs…Calistoga itself seems to repose on a mere film above a boiling, subterranean lake.' Indeed, it does. Calistoga is synonymous with the mineral water bearing its name – Guiseppe Musante began bottling it here in 1924 – and these natural hot springs and geysers earned the town the nickname the 'hot springs of the west.' Plan to visit one of the many spas, where you can indulge in the local specialty, a hot mud bath.

Some believe the town's curious name comes from tongue-tied Sam Brannan, who in 1859 founded the town, believing it would develop like the New York spa town of Saratoga, as the 'Cali-stoga' of 'Sara-fornia.'

Orientation & Information

Calistoga's shops and restaurants line Lincoln Ave.

Hwy 128 and Hwy 29 run together as one road between Rutherford and St Helena. In Calistoga, they split. Hwy 29 turns east and becomes Lincoln Ave, continuing across the Silverado Trail and on to Clear Lake. Hwy 128 continues north as Foothill Blvd (not St Helena Hwy).

Calistoga Bookshop (☎ 707-942-4123; 1343 Lincoln Ave) A local independent bookseller.

Chamber of Commerce & Visitors Center (☎ 707-942-6333, 866-306-5588; www.calistogachamber.com; 1458 Lincoln Ave; ☺ 10am-4pm) Right downtown.

Sights & Activities

The small **City Hall**, on Washington St, was built in 1902 as the Bedlam Opera House. Today it houses offices.

Across the street, and created by an ex-Disney animator, **Sharpsteen Museum** (☎ 707-942-5911; www.sharpsteen-museum.org; 1311 Washington St; admission free; 🕐 11am-4pm) has exhibits from the town's colorful history, and features a restored cottage from Brannan's original Calistoga resort. (The only Brannan cottage still at its original site is at 106 Wapoo Ave, near the Brannan Cottage Inn.)

Calistoga has lots of **hot-spring spas** and **mud-bath emporiums**, where you can be buried in hot mud and emerge feeling supple, detoxified and enlivened. (The mud is made with volcanic ash and peat; the higher the ash content, the better the bath.)

Packages take 60 to 90 minutes and cost $70 to $85. You start semisubmerged in hot mud, then shower and soak in hot mineral water. An optional steam bath, shower and blanket-wrap follow. The treatment can be extended to include a massage, increasing the cost to $120 or more.

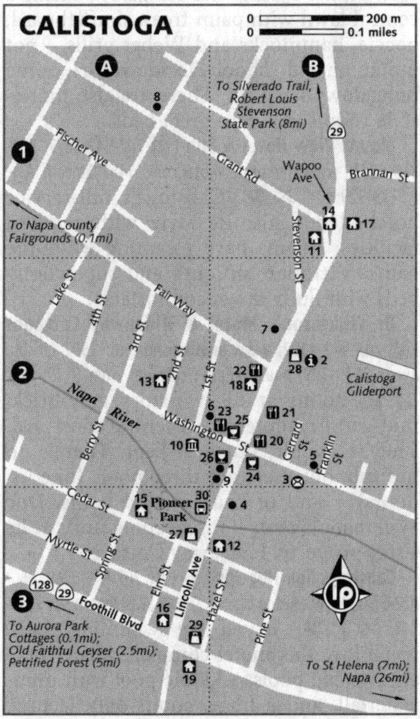

Baths can be taken solo or, at some spas, as couples. Variations include thin, painted-on clay-mud wraps (called 'fango' baths, good for those uncomfortable sitting in mud), herbal wraps, seaweed baths and all sorts of massages. Discount coupons are sometimes available from the visitor center. Book ahead, especially on summer weekends.

The following spas in downtown Calistoga offer one-day packages. Some also offer discounted spa-lodging packages (see p228).

Indian Springs (☎ 707-942-4913; www.indianspringscalistoga.com; 1712 Lincoln Ave) The longest

INFORMATION
Calistoga Bookshop....1 B2
Chamber of Commerce & Visitors Center....2 B2
Post Office....3 B2

SIGHTS & ACTIVITIES
Calistoga Bike Shop....4 B3
Calistoga Spa Hot Springs....5 B2
City Hall....6 A2
Dr Wilkinson's Hot Springs....7 B2
Golden Haven Hot Springs....8 A1
Indian Springs....(see 17)
Lavender Hill Spa....(see 19)
Lincoln Avenue Spa....9 B2
Mount View Spa....(see 18)
Sharpsteen Museum....10 A2

SLEEPING
Brannan Cottage Inn....11 B1
Calistoga Inn & Brewery....12 B3
Calistoga Spa Hot Springs (SLEEPING)....(see 5)
Chelsea Garden Inn....13 A2
Cottage Grove Inn....14 B1
Dr Wilkinson's Motel & Hideaway Cottages....(see 7)
Elms B&B....15 A3
Garnett Creek Inn....16 A3
Golden Haven....(see 8)
Hotel d'Amici....(see 21)
Indian Springs Resort....17 B1
Mount View Hotel & Spa....18 B2
Wine Way Inn....19 A3

EATING
All Seasons Bistro....20 B2
Checkers....(see 20)
Flat Iron Grill....21 B2
Puerto Vallarta....22 B2
Wappo Bar & Bistro....23 B2

DRINKING
Brannan's Grill....24 B2
Hydro Grill....25 B2
Susie's Bar....26 B2

SHOPPING
Calistoga Pottery....(see 19)
Ca'toga Galleria d'Arte....27 A3
Rendezvous....28 B2
Wine Garage....29 A3

TRANSPORT
Bus Depot....30 A3

continually operating spa in town has concrete mud tubs for the classic Calistoga experience. Great cucumber body lotion. Outside there's a huge, hot-spring-fed pool and palm-tree-lined lawn.

Dr Wilkinson's Hot Springs (☎ 707-942-4102; www .drwilkinson.com; 1507 Lincoln Ave) Fifty years running; 'the doc' uses high-ash-content mud in a mid-century-modern spa.

Mount View Spa (☎ 707-942-6877, 800-816-6877; www.mountviewhotel.com; 1457 Lincoln Ave) Contemporary, full-service, 12-room spa on the pricey side, but good for the skirt-and-sweater crowd or those who prefer painted-on mud to submersion.

Golden Haven Hot Springs (☎ 707-942-6793; www .goldenhaven.com; 1713 Lake St) Old-school and unfussy; offers couples' mud baths and couples' massage.

Calistoga Spa Hot Springs (☎ 707-942-6269, 866-822-5772; www.calistogaspa.com; 1006 Washington St) Traditional mud baths and massage at a motel complex with two huge swimming pools where the kids can play while you soak (pool passes $25).

Lavender Hill Spa (☎ 707-942-4495; www.lavender hillspa.com; 1015 Foothill Blvd) Small, cute two-room spa; good for couples' massages.

Lincoln Avenue Spa (☎ 707-942-5296; www.lincoln avenuespa.com; 1339 Lincoln Ave) Has paint-it-yourself mud-clay treatments for couples and singles, but no couples' massages.

Hardcore mountain bikers can tackle the **Oat Hill Mine Trail**, one of Northern California's most technically challenging trails, just outside town. Find information and rentals at **Calistoga Bike Shop** (☎ 707-942-9687, 866-942-2453; www.calistogabikeshop.com; 1318 Lincoln Ave), which rents full-suspension mountain bikes (per hour/day $18/60), one-speed beach cruisers (per hour/day $7/25) and 'wine-touring bikes' with custom-made wine carriers (per day $35); it'll even pick up your vino for you if you don't want to carry it!

Sleeping

Also see Safari West (p231) for a safari-like adventure.

B&BS

Meadowlark Country House (☎ 707-942-5651, 800-942-5651; www.meadowlarkinn.com; 601 Petrified Forest Rd; r incl breakfast $195-210, ste $235-265; ☒ ☒ ☒) On 20 acres west of town, Meadowlark has luxury rooms decorated in contemporary style. All have decks and Jacuzzis. Outside there's a hot tub, sauna and clothing-optional pool. The truth-telling innkeeper lives in another house; he offers helpful advice, then vanishes when you want privacy. There's a superfabulous cottage for $425.

Brannan Cottage Inn (☎ 707-942-4200; www .brannancottageinn.com; 109 Wapoo Ave; r incl breakfast $145-175, ste $165-185; ☒ ☒ ☒) Sam Brannan built this 1860 cottage, which is listed on the National Register of Historic Places. Long on charm, it's decorated with floral-print fabrics and simple country furnishings. Suites sleep four. Guests use the pool at nearby Golden Haven motel.

Elms B&B (☎ 707-942-9476, 888-399-3567; www.the elms.com; 1300 Cedar St; r incl breakfast weekdays $120-155, weekends $165-245; ☒ ☒) Next to Pioneer Park, shaded by mature trees, this 1871 Victorian B&B looks like a whitewashed haunted house and has seven simple rooms, plus a front porch for leisurely summer afternoons. There's a hot tub out back.

SPA HOTELS

Indian Springs Resort (☎ 707-942-4913; www.indian springscalistoga.com; 1712 Lincoln Ave; motel r $195-225, studio $205-255, 1-bedroom bungalow $225-305; ☒ ☒ ☒ ☒) The definitive Calistoga resort, Indian Springs has bungalows facing a central lawn with palm trees, shuffleboard, boccie, hammocks and Weber grills – not unlike an old-school Florida resort. Some bungalows sleep six. There are also motel-style rooms. All have great beds.

Mount View Hotel & Spa (☎ 707-942-6877, 800-816-6877; www.mountviewhotel.com; 1457 Lincoln Ave; r $179-329; ☒ ☒ ☒) Calistoga's full-service hotel blends historic style with modern facilities. Rooms have gleaming white-tile baths, Victorian antiques and supercomfy beds with fluffy down comforters.

Dr Wilkinson's Motel & Hideaway Cottages (☎ 707-942-4102; www.drwilkinson.com; 1507 Lincoln Ave; r $139-199, housekeeping cottages from $119; ☒ ☒ ☒) Rooms at this two-story, grey-brick, mid-century motel face a central courtyard. They're simple, but well kept. There's no hot tub, but there are three pools (one indoors) – and of course, mud baths. Doc Wilkinson's rents housekeeping units at its sister property, Hideaway Cottages.

Calistoga Spa Hot Springs (☎ 707-942-6269, 866-822-5772; www.calistogaspa.com; 1006 Washington St; r $128-144; ☒ ☒ ☒) If you like swimming pools, you'll love this motel complex, where there are two big pools, a kiddie pool with mini-waterfall, and a huge, adults-only Jacuzzi.

The place is packed with kids on weekends. The clean, motel-style rooms have a kitchenette, great for an easy weekend getaway. Outside are barbecues and a snack bar.

Golden Haven Hot Springs (☎ 707-942-6793; www .goldenhaven.com; 1713 Lake St; r $79-99, with kitchenette $119-149; ☒ ☒ ☒) The plain motel rooms are nothing special – at all – but if you're on a budget, they're appropriately priced – unlike the chain motels on Lincoln Ave.

Also consider these options:

Cottage Grove Inn (☎ 707-942-8400, 800-799-2284; www.cottagegrove.com; 1711 Lincoln Ave; cottages $250-325; ☒ ☒) Romantic, cute-as-a-button cottages with wood-burning fireplaces, two-person tubs, DVDs and front porches with rocking chairs. Top pick for a honeymoon.

Chelsea Garden Inn (☎ 707-942-0948; www.chelsea gardeninn.com; 1443 2nd St; r incl breakfast $195-225; ☒ ☒ ☒ ☒) On a quiet side street, five B&B rooms with private entrances and lovely, meandering gardens.

Garnett Creek Inn (☎ 707-942-9797; www.garnett creekinn.com; r 1139 Lincoln Ave; r midweek $155-225, weekend $185-295; ☒ ☒) Rooms are small and frilly (think Laura Ashley), but there's a big veranda and in-room breakfast.

Wine Way Inn (☎ 707-942-0680, 800-572-0679; www .winewayinn.com; 1019 Foothill Blvd; r $130-190; ☒ ☒) Small B&B in 1910 house, owned by a lovely English couple.

HOTELS & COTTAGES

Calistoga Inn & Brewery (☎ 707-942-4101; 1250 Lincoln Ave; r midweek $75, weekend $110-125) A steal in pricey Napa, this historic hotel within the town center has 18 small, simple rooms with shared bathroom. Surprise, surprise: they're nicely kept too. No TVs.

Hotel d'Amici (☎ 707-942-1007; www.hoteldamici .com; 1436 Lincoln Ave; r $185-230; ☒ ☒) All four rooms at this 2nd-floor hotel have crisp linens, sunny paint jobs, and lots of sunlight. In the morning, there's continental breakfast. NB: There's no on-site staff and no elevator.

Aurora Park Cottages (☎ 707-942-6733, 877-942-7700; www.aurorapark.com; 1807 Foothill Blvd; cottages incl breakfast $225-245; ☒ ☒) All six sunny-yellow cottages were built in 1948 and remodeled in 2001. They're inviting and spacious, and have down comforters and feather beds, but they are near a busy road. The innkeeper couldn't be nicer.

Triple-S Ranch (☎ 707-942-6730; 4600 Mt Home Ranch Rd; cottages $85; ☒ Apr-Dec; ☒) Off Petrified Forest Rd, 3 miles northwest of town, the scene couldn't be more pastoral – and cottages couldn't be more rustic. They feel like summer-camp cabins for kids, and they're great for backpackers or budgeteers. The lodge restaurant serves simple steak dinners and continental breakfast. No air-con.

CAMPING

Bothe-Napa Valley State Park (☎ 707-942-4575, reservations 800-444-7275; www.reserveamerica.com; sites $15-20; ☒) Three miles south, Bothe has good camping and gorgeous hiking.

Napa County Fairgrounds & RV Park (☎ 707-942-5111, 707-942-5221; 1435 Oak St; tent sites $10, RV sites $22-25) This dusty RV park is northwest of downtown.

Eating

Puerto Vallarta (☎ 707-942-6563; 1473 Lincoln Ave; dishes $7-9) Behind a fence next to Cal-Mart grocery's parking, this hole-in-the-wall joint makes good burritos.

Calistoga Inn & Brewery (☎ 707-942-4101; www .calistogainn.com; 1250 Lincoln Ave; dishes $7-20) Meet locals while you munch on simple home-style American cooking like pastas and steaks; there's also pub grub at the bar. You won't remember what you ate, but you will remember the big garden patio, the micro-brews, and games of horseshoes. There's live music summer weekends.

All Seasons Bistro (☎ 707-942-9111; www.all seasonsnapavalley.net; 1400 Lincoln Ave; lunch mains $9-11, dinner $19-28; ☒ lunch Fri-Sun, dinner nightly) Winemakers and local gourmands come to All Seasons for the eclectic, always-good, Euro-Cal bistro fare. The sparsely decorated room gets noisy, but it's also fun. The wine list is fantastic.

Wappo Bar & Bistro (☎ 707-942-4712; www.wappo bar.com; 1226-B Washington St; mains $8-19; ☒ Wed-Mon) Dine on an open-air patio in a beautiful garden, perfect on warm evenings. The bistro bills its cooking as 'global cuisine' and draws inspiration from Indian, Italian, Thai, French, Spanish and Central American traditions. Despite the name, there's no bar (but there's wine).

Checkers (☎ 707-942-9300; 1414 Lincoln Ave; pizzas $8-14, mains $10-15) Checkers serves simple food and draft beer for hungry folks – big salads, fried chicken, soups, pasta and pizzas.

Flat Iron Grill (☎ 707-942-1220; www.flatirongrill .com; 1440 Lincoln Ave; mains $11-20) Flat Iron caters to carnivores, with brisket and ribs to burgers and steaks; the fish and chips have home-made tartar sauce.

WINE COUNTRY

Drinking

Hydro Grill (☎ 707-942-9777; 1403 Lincoln Ave) There's live music weekends at this hoppin' corner bar that's a reasonably priced American restaurant by day. Music starts at 9pm Saturday and 7pm Sundays.

Brannan's Grill (☎ 707-942-2233; www.brannansgrill .com; 1374 Lincoln Ave) Calistoga's handsomest restaurant is primarily a steak house, but the mahogany bar is a great spot for martinis, especially on weekends, when jazz combos play.

Susie's Bar (☎ 707-942-6710; 1365 Lincoln Ave) Turn your baseball cap front to back, do shots and shoot pool while the juke box blares classic rock and country and western.

Shopping

Wine Garage (☎ 707-942-5332; www.winegarage.net; 1020 Foothill Blvd) Every bottle costs under $25 at this cool wine store, where you can blend wines right from the barrels.

Rendezvous (☎ 707-942-6384; 1458 Lincoln) In a rail car at Calistoga Depot shops, Rendezvous carries fine linens, women's hats, jewelry, aromatherapy paraphernalia and hemp clothing.

Calistoga Pottery (☎ 707-942-0216; www.calistoga pottery.com; 1001 Foothill Blvd) Winemakers aren't the only artisans in Napa. Watch a potter throw vases, bowls and plates, all for sale.

Ca'toga Galleria d'Arte (☎ 707-942-3900; www .catoga.com; 1206 Cedar St) This gallery specializes in trompe l'oeil painting; on weekends you can tour the artist's over-the-top villa (call ahead).

AROUND CALISTOGA
Bale Grist Mill & Bothe-Napa Valley State Parks

There's good picnicking at the small **Bale Grist Mill State Historic Park** (☎ 707-963-2236; adult/child under 16 $4/free; ☼ 10am-5pm daily Jun-Sep, 10am-5pm Sat & Sun Oct-May), which features a 36ft water-powered mill wheel, dating from 1846, the largest still operating in North America. You can watch it grind corn and wheat into flour on Saturday and Sunday; call for times. In early October, look for the living-history festival, Old Mill Days.

There's a mile-long trail leading to adjacent **Bothe-Napa Valley State Park** (☎ 707-942-4575; per car $6; ☼ 8am-sunset) where there's a **swimming pool** (adult/child $3/1, ☼ summer only), fantastic hiking and horseback riding through redwood

groves. **Triple Creek Horse Outfit** (☎ 707-996-8566; www.triplecreekhorseoutfit.com) guides 60- and 90-minute rides, April through October, for $60/65; reservations required.

Admission to one park includes the other. If you're not traveling solo, go to Bothe park first, and pay only $6 instead of paying $4 multiplied by the number of people in your party.

The mill and both park are on Hwy 29/128, midway between St Helena and Calistoga.

Old Faithful Geyser

Calistoga's slightly smaller version of Yellowstone's Old Faithful spouts off on a 45-minute cycle, shooting boiling water 60ft to 100ft into the air.

The **geyser** (☎ 707-942-6463; 1299 Tubbs Lane; adult/child/senior $8/3/7; ☼ 9am-6pm summer, 9am-5pm winter) is 2 miles north of town, off Silverado Trail. The attraction is overpriced, but it's cool to see the geyser blow. Look for discount coupons around town.

Petrified Forest

Three million years ago, a volcanic eruption at nearby Mt St Helena blew down a stand of redwood trees between Calistoga and Santa Rosa. The trees fell in the same direction, away from the center of the blast, and were covered in ash and mud. Over the millennia, the trunks of these mighty trees turned to stone; gradually the overlay eroded and exposed them. The first stumps were discovered in 1870, and a monument marks the Robert Louis Stevenson's 1880 visit. He describes it in *The Silverado Squatters*.

The **petrified forest** (☎ 707-942-6667; 4100 Petrified Forest Rd; adult/child/senior $6/3/5; ☼ 9am-7pm summer, 9am-5pm winter) is 5 miles northwest of town off Hwy 128.

Robert Louis Stevenson State Park

The volcanic cone of Mt St Helena, which is long extinct, closes off the end of the valley 8 miles north of Calistoga, in this undeveloped **state park** (☎ 707-942-4575; www.parks.ca.gov; admission free) on Hwy 29 that often gets snow in winter.

It's a strenuous 5-mile climb to the peak's 4343ft summit, but what a view – 200 miles on a clear day! Check conditions before you set out. The park includes the site of the Silverado Mine where Stevenson and his wife, Fanny, honeymooned in 1880.

Safari West

Giraffes in Wine Country? You bet! This wild **animal preserve** (☎ 707-579-2551, 800-616-2695; www.safariwest.com; 3115 Porter Creek Rd; adult/child $60/28) covers 400 acres and protects zebras, cheetahs, giraffes and other exotic animals, which mostly roam free. You can see them on a guided three-hour safari in an open-sided jeep; reservations required. You'll also walk thorough an aviary and a lemur condo. You can eat lunch and dinner in the café (also by reservation only). Best of all – especially for families with kids – you can stay overnight in nifty canvas-sided **tent cabins** (cabins incl breakfast $225; ✕), right in the preserve.

North Coast

Craggy cliffs tower over timber-strewn beaches and hidden rocky coves along California's North Coast. Land of spotted owls, timber wars, flannel shirts and Christian rock, this is the antithesis of Southern California in almost every way. Think Hitchcock, not *Baywatch*. You don't go north to get a tan, not even in July – *especially* not in July, when you're lucky if you see the sun at all. Why? The fog. Once you get over its icy chill (carry a sweater), you'll come to appreciate the fog's brooding beauty and graceful, ghost-like swirls.

As you head northward through Sonoma and Mendocino counties, luxury sedans with babies on board give way to pickup trucks with gun racks. Welcome to the Redwood Empire, where Hwy 1 ends its long trek from Southern California and cuts inland to join Hwy 101. The land along the Pacific – called the Lost Coast – is too steep and rugged to support a major highway. Working your way northbound through Humboldt County, you'll wind beneath towering redwoods, the tallest trees in the world, as you approach the small harbor-side Victorian cities of Eureka and Arcata, where 'heavy traffic' means a five-minute delay. Lagoons and marshes yield to giant trees and roaming elk, and you're back in the woods, twisting and turning your way toward Del Norte County, the beginning of the Pacific Northwest and the northernmost end of California. Disneyland couldn't feel further away.

HIGHLIGHTS

- Meandering beneath the world's tallest trees at **Redwood National Park** (p274)
- Soaking up the vibe at soothing hot springs at **Vichy** (p255), **Orr** (p256) and **Harbin** (p251)
- Exploring the picture-perfect New England-style village of **Mendocino** (p240)
- Oohing and aahing over tiny marine creatures in tidepools at **Salt Point State Park** (p237) or **Patrick's Point State Park** (p274)
- Whale-watching atop bluffs at **Mendocino Headlands State Park** (p242)
- Driving beneath soaring redwoods along the **Avenue of the Giants** (p260)
- Trekking the windswept **Lost Coast** (p261)
- Hiking the *Jurassic Park* landscape of **Fern Canyon** (p276) at Prairie Creek Redwoods State Park
- Climbing to the top of **Point Arena Lighthouse** (p239)

★ Fern Canyon
★ Redwood National Park
★ Patrick's Point State Park
★ Avenue of the Giants
Lost Coast ★
Mendocino
Mendocino Headlands ★ Orr
State Park ★ ★ Vichy
Point Arena Lighthouse ★
★ Harbin
Salt Point State Park ★

■ AVERAGE TEMPS IN MENDOCINO: JAN 47/567°F, JUL 50/71°F

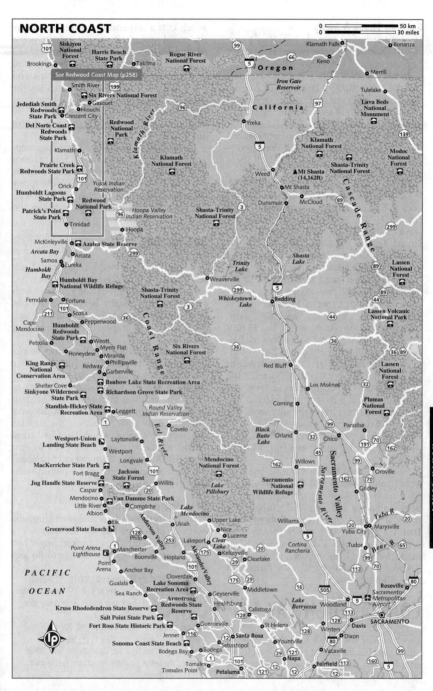

NORTH COAST

0 — 50 km
0 — 30 miles

See Redwood Coast Map (p258)

Oregon

California

PACIFIC OCEAN

NORTH COAST

Getting There & Away

Hwy 101 is the fast, inland route; Hwy 1 runs along the coast, then cuts inland and ends at Leggett, where it joins Hwy 101.

Amtrak (☎ 800-872-7245; www.amtrak.com) operates the *Coast Starlight* between Los Angeles and Seattle, with connecting bus services to several North Coast towns including Leggett and Garberville.

Greyhound (☎ 800-231-2222; www.greyhound.com) operates bus services from San Francisco to Santa Rosa, Ukiah, Willits, Rio Dell (near Fortuna), Eureka and Arcata.

In Santa Rosa, **Golden Gate Transit** (☎ 707-541-2000, 415-923-2000; www.goldengate.org) bus 80 goes to San Francisco, **Sonoma County Transit** (☎ 707-576-7433, 800-345-7433; www.sctransit.com) serves Sonoma County and **Sonoma County Airport Express** (☎ 707-837-8700, 800-327-2024; www.airportexpressinc.com) operates buses to San Francisco and Oakland airports.

The **Mendocino Transit Authority** (MTA; ☎ 707-462-1422, 800-696-4682; www.4mta.org) operates bus 65, which travels between Mendocino, Fort Bragg, Willits, Ukiah and Santa Rosa daily, with an afternoon return service. Bus 95 runs between Point Arena and Santa Rosa, via Jenner, Bodega Bay and Sebastopol. Bus 54 connects Ukiah and Hopland on weekdays. Bus 75 heads north every weekday from Gualala to the Navarro River junction at Hwy 128, then runs inland through the Anderson Valley to Ukiah, returning in the afternoon. The North Coast route also heads out of Navarro River junction, passing through Albion, Little River, Mendocino and Fort Bragg, Monday to Friday.

North of Mendocino County, the **Redwood Transit System** (☎ 707-443-0826; www.hta.org) operates buses Monday through Saturday between Scotia and Trinidad, stopping en route at Eureka and Arcata. **Redwood Coast Transit** (☎ 707-464-9314; www.redwoodcoasttransit .org) runs two buses a day, Monday to Saturday, between Crescent City, Klamath and Redwood National Park, with numerous stops along the way.

COASTAL HIGHWAY 1

Down south it's called the 'PCH,' or Pacific Coast Highway, but North Coast locals simply call it 'Highway One.' However you label it, say hello to the fabulous coast road, which cuts a serpentine course high above the crashing surf. (If you get carsick, pop a motion sickness pill, such as Dramamine.) Stop along the way to comb fog-shrouded beaches, gaze at churning whitecaps and listen for the braying of sea lions on the wind. From December to April, keep your eyes peeled for migrating gray whales; you should be able to spot them from almost any headland.

Coastal accommodations (including campgrounds) fill up from Memorial Day to Labor Day and on autumn weekends, so reservations are essential. Try to visit during spring or autumn, especially September and October when the fog lifts, the ocean sparkles and most other visitors have gone home.

BODEGA BAY
pop 950

Sonoma County's Bodega Bay could not feel further from Wine Country. Perched on coastal bluffs, the bayside village attracts visitors for its nearby beaches, tidepools, whale-watching, fishing, surfing and seafood – fish, not grapes, is the big industry here.

Originally inhabited by the Pomo people, the bay takes its name from Juan Francisco de la Bodega y Quadra, captain of the Spanish sloop *Sonora*, which entered the bay in 1775. The area was then settled by Russians in the early 19th century, and farms were established to grow wheat for the Russian fur-trapping empire, which stretched from Alaska all the way down the coast to Fort Ross. The Russians pulled out in 1842, abandoning fort and farms, and American settlers moved in.

Orientation & Information

Hwy 1 runs through the town and along the east side of Bodega Bay. On the west side, a peninsula resembling a crooked finger juts out to sea, forming the entrance to Bodega Harbor.

Business Services Unlimited (☎ 707-875-2183; 1400 Hwy 1, Pelican Plaza; per hr $12; ☺ 9am-5pm Mon-Fri, 10am-2pm Sat) Check your emails while doing your laundry at the launderette next door.

Sonoma Coast Visitors Center (☎ 707-875-3866; www.bodegabay.com; 850 Hwy 1; ☺ 10am-6pm Sun-Thu, 9am-7pm Fri & Sat) Opposite the Tides Wharf complex, the center provides information for the area north to Sea Ranch.

HITCHCOCK'S BODEGA BAY

An otherwise unremarkable stop on a remarkable stretch of Hwy 1, Bodega Bay has the enduring claim to fame as the setting for Alfred Hitchcock's *The Birds*. Although special effects radically altered the actual layout of the town, you can still get a good feel for the bay and its western shore, the supposed site of the farm owned by Mitch Brenner (played by Rod Taylor). The Tides Restaurant, where much avian-caused havoc occurs in the movie, is still there but since 1962 it has been transmogrified into a vast tourist-processing plant, and is no longer the charming seaside restaurant the movie portrays. But venture 5 miles inland of Bodega Bay to the tiny town of Bodega, and you'll find two icons from the film: the schoolhouse and the church. Both stand just as they did in the film – see a crow overhead, and you may feel the hair raise on your neck.

Coincidentally, right after production of *The Birds* began, a real-life bird attack occurred in Capitola, the sleepy seaside town south of Santa Cruz. Thousands of seagulls ran amuck, destroying property, attacking people and making a stinking mess.

Sights & Activities

Bodega Bay's activities are mostly outdoors, but for Japanese and California art head to the **Ren Brown Collection Gallery** (☎ 707-875-2922; 1781 Hwy 1; ☻ 10am-5pm Wed-Sun).

Landlubbers enjoy **hiking** above the surf at Bodega Head, where several good trails include a 3.75-mile trek to Bodega Dunes Campground and a 2.2-mile walk to Salmon Creek Ranch. They don't call it 'Blow-dega Head' for nothing: bring a kite. **Candy & Kites** (☎ 707-875-3777; 1415 Hwy 1) sells single-line and dual-line varieties. At the peninsula's tip, Bodega Head rises 265ft above sea level. To get there (and to see the open ocean), head west from Hwy 1 onto Eastshore Rd, then turn right at the stop sign onto Bay Flat Rd. It's a great place for whale-watching.

Chanslor Riding Stables (☎ 707-875-3333; www .chanslor.com; 2660 Hwy 1) offers horseback riding on the beach and along Salmon Creek ($30 to $60). On the oceanfront, **Bodega Harbour Golf Links** (☎ 707-875-3538; www.bodegaharbourgolf .com; green fees $45-90) is an 18-hole Scottish-style course designed by Robert Trent Jones Jr.

Bodega Bay Surf Shack (☎ 707-875-3944; www .bodegabaysurf.com) rents boards ($13 per day), windsurfing gear, bicycles ($5 per hour) and wet suits, and offers surfing lessons. **Bodega Bay Kayak** (☎ 707-875-8899; www.bodega baykayak.com; 1580 Eastshore Rd) rents kayaks ($45 for four hours) and provides guided tours. **Bodega Bay Pro Dive** (☎ 707-875-3054; www.bbpro dive.com; 1275 Hwy 1) offers diving instruction, rentals and expeditions.

Make reservations for sportfishing charters and, from December to April, whale-watching cruises, as they're very popular. **Bodega Bay Sportfishing Center** (☎ 707-875-3344; www.usafishing.com; 1410 Bay Flat Rd), beside the Sandpiper Cafe, organizes harbor cruises ($15), full-day fishing trips ($70) and whale-watching excursions (adult/child $30/25); it also sells bait, tackle and fishing licenses. The **Boathouse** (☎ 707-875-3495; 1445 Hwy 1) and **Will's Bait & Tackle** (☎ 707-875-2323; www.bodega bayfishing.com; 1580 Eastshore Rd) also run scheduled trips.

Festivals & Events

The **Bodega Bay Fishermen's Festival** in April is the big annual event and includes the blessing of the fleet, a flamboyant parade of vessels, an arts-and-crafts fair, kite-flying and feasting. The great **crab feed** takes place in February or March.

Sleeping

Bodega Bay Lodge & Spa (☎ 707-875-3525, 800-368-2468; www.bodegabaylodge.com; 103 Hwy 1; r $210-290; ☒ ☐ ☒) Bodega's best, this small resort has indulgent amenities such as evening wine tastings, ocean-view swimming pool, whirlpool spa and fitness club. Many of the luxurious rooms have fireplaces and overlook marshland and dunes to the sea beyond. Ask about spa and golf packages.

Branscomb's Bodega Bay Inn (☎ 707-875-3388, 888-875-8733; www.bodegabayinn.com; 1588 Eastshore Rd; r incl breakfast $90-180; ☒) Local art fills this converted house, where there's no uniformity to the folksy decor, but the rates are reasonable, especially midweek. Outside there's a big garden courtyard. Wi-fi, too.

Bodega Harbor Inn (☎ 707-875-3594; www.bodega harborinn.com; 1345 Bodega Ave; r $60-95, cottages $125-195; ☒) Half a block past Hwy 1, this modest blue-and-white shingled motel is the town's

NORTH COAST

most economical option. It's furnished with both real and faux antiques.

Campgrounds fill up early in the day. **Sonoma County Regional Park** (☎ information 707-875-3540, reservations 707-565-2267; sites $17) operates **Doran Park** (201 Doran Beach Rd), which is best for tents, and **Westside Regional Park** (2400 Westshore Rd), best for RVs. Both parks have windy exposures, beaches, hot showers, fishing and boat ramps.

Eating

Seaweed Cafe (☎ 707-875-2700; www.seaweedcafe .com; 1580 Eastshore Dr; brunch mains $10-18, dinner $18-27; ☺ brunch Sat & Sun, dinner Thu-Sun) The top spot for brunch and dinner is a colorful little café adorned with local paintings, and filled with food-savvy art-heads and bon vivants. The dynamic Slow Food–style (dedicated to preserving traditional food-preparation ways and educating people about food) uses farm-fresh greens, seafood and poultry, most from within 30 miles of the restaurant – including the wine. When there's red meat, it's an unusual cut like elk or beef cheeks. The menu's pricey, but you're paying for craftsmanship and supporting local farmers.

Duck Club (☎ 707-875-3525; 103 Hwy 1; breakfast $9-12, dinner mains $20-28; ☺ breakfast & dinner) The Bodega Bay Lodge's smart-looking Duck Club is the town's fanciest restaurant, serving a loosely Cal-French menu. It's the kind of place you could take your in-laws – safe and predictable.

Gourmet Au Bay (☎ 707-875-9875; 913 Hwy 1; ☺ 11am-6pm Thu-Tue) Sit on the back deck of this wine bar and sniff salt air with your pre- or post-dinner zinfandel.

Sandpiper Dockside Cafe & Restaurant (☎ 707-875-2278; 1410 Bay Flat Rd; mains $11-20; ☺ 8am-8pm) Popular with the locals, Sandpiper serves straightforward seafood (think tartar sauce) with a water-level view of the bay. There's also breakfast. To get there, turn seaward from Hwy 1 onto Eastshore Rd and then go straight at the stop sign to the marina.

Dog House (☎ 707-875-2441; 573 Hwy 1; dishes $5-9; ☺ 11am-6pm) For hot dogs and shakes, Dog House has Vienna beef dogs, hand-cut fries and *real* shakes made with hand-scooped ice cream. There's even a view.

For dockside seafood, **Tides Wharf & Restaurant** (☎ 707-875-3652; 835 Hwy 1; breakfast mains $6-12, lunch $11-22, dinner $16-25) and **Lucas Wharf Restaurant & Bar** (☎ 707-875-3522; 595 Hwy 1; mains

$15-25) both have views, clam chowder, fried fish and coleslaw. Although Tides brags a great fish market, Lucas Wharf feels less like a factory and has a take-out deli.

SONOMA COAST STATE BEACH

Stretching 17 miles north from Bodega Head to Vista Trail, **Sonoma Coast State Beach** (☎ 707-875-3483) is actually a series of beaches separated by rocky headlands. Some are tiny, hidden in little coves, while others stretch far and wide.

These are not swimming beaches, however; the surf is so treacherous that it's often unsafe to even wade. Never turn your back on the ocean, always stay above the high-tide line and keep an eye on children.

Heading north along the coast, notable beaches include **Bodega Dunes**; 2-mile **Salmon Creek Beach**; sandy **Portuguese** and **Schoolhouse Beaches**; **Duncan's Landing**, where small boats unload; **Shell Beach**, for tide-pooling and beachcombing; and scenic **Goat Rock**, with its harbor-seal colony at the mouth of the Russian River. Most of the beaches are connected by coastal hiking trails.

A mile north of Bodega Bay, **Bodega Dunes Campground** (☎ 800-444-7275; www.reserveamerica .com; sites $25) has high dunes and hot showers. Another 5 miles north, year-round **Wright's Beach Campground** (☎ 800-444-7275; www.reserve america.com; sites $25-35) has popular beachside sites but they lack privacy.

On Willow Creek Rd, inland from Hwy 1 on the southern side of the Russian River Bridge, are two first-come, first-served environmental **campgrounds**, Willow Creek and Pomo Canyon (sites $15). Willow Creek has no water; Pomo Canyon has cold-water faucets. Both are usually open April to November.

JENNER

pop 170

Perched on the hills above the mouth of the Russian River, tiny Jenner offers convenient access to the coast and the Russian River wine region (see p201). Hwy 1 to the north provides views of the **harbor-seal colony** at the river's mouth; pups are born from March to August. This is one of the most beautiful, difficult-to-drive stretches of California highway. Stay focused, and use turnouts to allow non-sightseers to pass you.

There are seaside cottages to river-view guestrooms to choose from at **Jenner Inn &**

Cottages (☎ 707-865-2377, 800-732-2377; www.jenner inn.com; 10400 Hwy 1; creekside r $98-178, ocean-view r $158-278, cottages $178-278; ✕ 🖵). Rates include breakfast and afternoon tea. Most rooms have no TV; some are pet friendly.

There are ocean-view cottages and comfortable rooms, with no TVs or phones, at **River's End** (☎ 707-865-2484; www.rivers-end.com; 11048 Hwy 1; r & cabins $115-185; ✕), which has a good, but overpriced, restaurant (lunch mains $13 to $26, dinner $25 to $39; open daily in summer and Thursday to Monday fall through spring). Come for drinks instead.

FORT ROSS STATE HISTORIC PARK

In March 1812, a group of 25 Russians and 80 Alaskans (including members of the Kodiak and Aleutian tribes) built a wooden fort here, near a Kashaya Pomo village. The southernmost outpost of the 19th-century Russian fur trade on America's Pacific coast, Fort Ross was established as a base for sea-otter hunting operations and trade with Alta California, and for growing crops for Russian settlements in Alaska. The Russians dedicated the fort in August 1812 and occupied it until 1842, when it was abandoned because the sea otter population had been decimated and agricultural production had never taken off.

Today, 11 miles north of Jenner, **Fort Ross State Historic Park** (☎ 707-847-3286; 19005 Hwy 1; per car $6; ☺ 10am-4:30pm) presents an accurate reconstruction of the fort. The original buildings were sold, dismantled and carried off to Sutter's Fort (see p411) during the Gold Rush. The **visitors center** (☎ 707-847-3437) has historical displays and an excellent bookshop on Californian and Russian history and nature. Ask about hikes to the Russian cemetery.

On Fort Ross Heritage Day, the last Saturday in July, costumed volunteers bring the fort's history to life; check the website or call for other special events.

Timber Cove Inn (☎ 707-847-3231, 800-987-8319; www.timbercoveinn.com; 21780 N Hwy 1; r midweek/weekend from $78/110, ocean-view r from $178/222), a dramatic and quirky '60s-modern seaside inn, was once a top-of-the-line luxury lodge but today it needs work – lots of it. The grounds are overrun with raccoons, and the koi pond needs a good scrubbing, but the architectural shell is still stunning. You'll either love it or hate it. If you're not a risk-taker, keep heading north and choose Sea Ranch Lodge instead.

Reef Campground (☎ 707-847-3286; sites $15; ☺ Apr-Oct), 2 miles south of the park, has first-come, first-served campsites (cold water, no showers) in a sheltered seaside gully.

Stillwater Cove Regional Park (☎ information 707-847-3245, reservations 707-565-2267; www.sonoma -county.org/parks; 22455 N Hwy 1; sites $16), 2 miles north of Timber Cove, has campsites, hot showers and hiking under Monterey pines.

SALT POINT STATE PARK

Sandstone cliffs drop dramatically down to the sea at the 6000-acre **Salt Point State Park** (☎ 707-847-3221; per car $6). Hiking trails head inland to crisscross grasslands and wooded hills, connecting pygmy forests and coastal coves rich with tidepools. The park is bisected by the San Andreas fault – the rock on the east side of the park is vastly different from that on the west. The notable geology includes *tafonis*, honeycombed-sandstone formations, near Gerstle Cove.

For views of the pristine coastline, walk to the platform overlooking **Sentinel Rock**; it's just a short stroll from the Fisk Cove parking lot, at the park's north end. Just south, **Stump Beach** has picnic areas with firepits and beach access. Further south, look for seals lazing at **Gerstle Cove Marine Reserve**, one of California's first underwater parks; tread lightly around tidepools, and don't lift the rocks: even a glimpse of sunlight can kill some small critters.

If you're here in spring, a visit to **Kruse Rhododendron State Reserve** is a must. Growing abundantly in the forest's filtered light, the rhododendrons reach heights of over 30ft, with a magnificent display of pink blossoms; turn east from Hwy 1 onto Kruse Ranch Rd, then follow the signs.

The **Salt Point Lodge** (☎ 707-847-3234, 800-956-3437; www.saltpointlodgebarandgrill.com; 23255 Hwy 1, Jenner; r $90-140; ✕) has motel rooms and a restaurant.

Two campgrounds, **Woodside** and **Gerstle Cove** (☎ 800-444-7275; www.reserveamerica.com; sites $25), both signposted off Hwy 1, have campsites with cold water. Woodside is protected by Monterey pines; Gerstle Cove's trees burned a decade ago, so it's more exposed. Walk-in **environmental campsites** (sites $10) are half a mile from the parking area, on Woodside campground's east side.

NORTH COAST

SEA RANCH

The upmarket subdivision of Sea Ranch sprawls along the coast for 10 miles, and except for a lodge and small store, is almost entirely residential. There's no commercial area, so for gasoline you'll need to go to Gualala. Strict zoning laws require that houses are constructed of weathered wood only. According to *The Sea Ranch Design Manual*: 'This is not a place for the grand architectural statement; it's a place to explore the subtle nuances of fitting in…'

After years of litigation, public throughways onto private beaches have been legally mandated. Hiking trails lead from roadside parking lots to the sea and along the bluffs (don't trespass on adjacent lands though). **Stengel Beach** (Hwy 1 mileage marker 53.96) has a beach-access staircase, **Walk-On Beach** (mileage marker 56.53) provides wheelchair access and **Shell Beach** (mileage marker 55.24) also has beach-access stairs; parking costs $4. For hiking details, including maps, contact the **Sea Ranch Association** (☎ 707-785-2444; www.tsra.org).

Sea Ranch Lodge (☎ 707-785-2371, 800-732-7262; www.searanchlodge.com; 60 Sea Walk Dr; r incl breakfast $205-395; ⊠), a marvel of '60s-modern California architecture, has spacious, luxurious rooms, many with dramatic views to the sea; some have hot tubs and fireplaces. The fine contemporary restaurant serves meals throughout the day; there's also a bar. Golf packages are available. North of the lodge you'll see Sea Ranch's iconic nondenominational chapel; it's on the inland side of Hwy 1, mileage marker 55.66.

Depending on the season, it can be surprisingly affordable to rent a house in Sea Ranch; contact **Rams Head Realty** (☎ 707-785-2427, 800-785-3455; www.ramshead-realty.com), **Sea Ranch Rentals** (☎ 707-884-4235; www.searanchrentals.com), **Sea Ranch Vacation Rentals** (☎ 800-643-8899; www.searanchgetaway.com) or **Sea Ranch Escape** (☎ 888-732-7262; www.888searanch.com).

For crusty artisanal breads and delicious pastries, visit **Two Fish Baking Co** (☎ 707-785-2443; 355090 Verdant View Dr, off Annapolis Rd; 🕑 7am-2pm Wed-Sun).

GUALALA

pop 1912

Founded as a lumber-mill town during the 1860s, Gualala is the region's commercial center. **Redwood Coast Chamber of Commerce** (☎ 707-884-1080, 800-778-5252; www.redwoodcoastchamber.com) has local business information. The **Dolphin Arts Gallery** (☎ 707-884-3896; 39225 Hwy 1; 🕑 10am-5pm Wed-Mon, noon-4pm Tue), behind the Gualala Hotel, has maps and limited information.

Inland along Old State Rd, at the south end of town, **Gualala Arts Center** (☎ 707-884-1138; www.gualalaarts.org; 🕑 9am-4pm Mon-Fri, noon-4pm Sat & Sun) has changing exhibitions and organizes the Art in the Redwoods Festival in late August.

At the 195-acre **Gualala Point Regional Park** (☎ 707-785-2377, reservations 707-565-2267; www.sonoma-county.org/parks; 42401 Hwy 1; day use $4, sites $16), a mile south of town, there are good camping facilities and wooded hiking trails up the Gualala River.

In summer a sand spit forms at the mouth of the Gualala River, cutting it off from the ocean and turning it into a warm-water lake. **Adventure Rents** (☎ 707-884-4386, 888-881-4386; www.adventurerents.com) rents canoes and kayaks and provides instruction.

Ocean-view inns line the main drag. Most are overpriced, with one exception: the century-old **Gualala Hotel** (☎ 707-884-3441, 888-482-5252; www.gualalahotel.com; 39301 S Hwy 1; r $50-55, with bathroom $85-105; ⊠) has simple accommodations and mushy mattresses, but rates are reasonable, especially above the saloon (light sleepers beware). There's a pretty good restaurant downstairs.

There's no place like **St Orres Inn** (☎ 707-884-3303; www.saintorres.com; 36601 Hwy 1; B&B $90-105, cottages from $135; ⊠), which is famous for its unusual Russian-inspired architecture. The main hotel has dramatic rough-hewn timbers and copper domes. On the property's 90 acres, hand-built cottages range from rustic to luxurious. The inn's fine dining room (☎ 707-884-3335; open for dinner only, mains $40) serves inspired California cuisine in one of the coast's most romantic rooms.

Inland along Old State Rd you can camp (and hike) at **Gualala River Redwood Park** (☎ 707-884-3533; www.gualalapark.com; day use $6, sites $22-42; 🕑 Memorial Day-Labor Day).

Everybody loves to eat at **Pangaea** (☎ 707-884-9669; www.pangaeacafe.com; 39165 S Hwy 1; mains $22-35; 🕑 dinner Wed-Sun), where the eclectic, soulful menu features such hearty dishes as brined pork loin with polenta and bacon, and halibut with corn succotash. Be sure to make reservations.

ANCHOR BAY

pop 500

Quiet Anchor Bay has several inns, a tiny shopping center and, heading north, a string of secluded, hard-to-find beaches. It makes an excellent jumping-off point for exploring the area.

Seven miles north of town, pull off at mileage marker 11.41 for **Schooner Gulch** (☎ 707-937-5804). A trail into the forest leads down cliffs to a sandy beach with tidepools. Bear right at the fork in the trail to reach **Bowling Ball Beach**, the next beach north, where at low tide rows of big, round rocks resemble bowling balls – but only at low tide. Consult tide tables for Arena Cove. The forecast low tide must be lower than +1.5ft on the tide chart; otherwise the rocks remain covered with water.

Perched on a hillside beneath towering trees, surrounded by lovely gardens, **North Coast Country Inn** (☎ 707-884-4537, 800-959-4537; www.northcoastcountryinn.com; 34591 S Hwy 1; r incl breakfast $185-225; ✕) has six spacious country-style rooms with fireplaces, books, board games and private entrances. Hot tub.

Stock up at **Anchor Bay Store** (☎ 707-884-4245; Hwy 1; ☯ 8am-8pm, 8am-7pm Sun). There are two so-so eateries next door.

POINT ARENA

pop 400

The name of this former fishing village derives from the windswept point where a lighthouse has stood since 1908. **Point Arena Lighthouse** (☎ 707-882-2777; www.pointarenalighthouse .com; adult/child $5/1; ☯ 10am-4:30pm summer, 10am-3:30pm winter) stands 10 stories high and is 2 miles

---

AUTHOR'S CHOICE

Mar Vista Cottages (☎ 707-884-3522, 877-855-3522; www.marvistamendocino.com; 35101 S Hwy 1; 1-bedroom cottages $140-205, 2-bedroom cottages $200-230; ✕) is one of the most charming spots on the entire California coast. Really. All 12 simple, cozy, spotlessly clean 1930s vacation cottages have old-fashioned kitchens and sumptuously comfy beds. In the 9-acre grounds there are barbecues, a redwood soaking tub, goats and an organic vegetable garden (grazing encouraged). Across the road is a great beach. Families and dogs welcome. If you're looking for a retro-cozy hideaway cottage, this is the place.

---

north of town. It's the only lighthouse in California you can ascend. Check in at the museum, then climb the 145 steps to the top and see the Fresnel lens and the jaw-dropping view.

One mile down Lighthouse Rd from Hwy 1, look for the Bureau of Land Management (BLM) signs on the left indicating the 1132-acre **Stornetta Public Lands** (☎ 707-468-4000; www .blm.gov), which has fabulous bird-watching, hiking on terraced rock past sea caves, and access to hidden coves.

You can rent one of the three-bedroom former Coast Guard homes (think tract houses) next to the lighthouse. Prices range from $185 to $210; contact the lighthouse keepers for more details.

A mile west of town at Arena Cove, there's a tourist restaurant, an ugly pier and the **Wharf Master's Inn** (☎ 707-882-3171, 800-932-4031; www .wharfmasters.com; 785 Port Rd; r $85-195), a cluster of small, modern inn buildings overlooking the cove.

Rollerville Junction (☎ 707-882-2440; www.camp ingfriend.com/RollervilleJunction; 22900 Shoreline Hwy; tent/ RV sites $28/328, cabins/cottages $55/100), at the turnoff from Hwy 1, has hot showers, a convenience store, laundry and hot tub.

Downtown there's a good burrito shop, several cafés and a nothing-special motel. **Carlini's Cafe** (☎ 707-882-2942; 206 Main St; dishes $5-8; ☯ breakfast & lunch Thu-Tue) serves the best food in town. Refuel on all-organic burritos at **El Burrito** (☎ 707-882-2910; 165 Main St; ☯ 11am-7pm) or pick up sandwiches, coffee and organic groceries at the **Record** (☎ 707-882-3663; 265 Main St; ☯ 7am-8pm Mon-Sat, 8am-6pm Sun), which has Internet access.

Arena Cinema (☎ 707-882-3456; 214 Main St) shows mainstream, foreign and art films in a beautifully restored movie house. Sue, the ticket seller, has been in that booth for 40 years. Got a question about Point Arena? Ask Sue.

MANCHESTER STATE BEACH

Seven miles north of Point Arena, a turnoff leads from Hwy 1 to Manchester Beach, a long, wild stretch of sand.

Ross Ranch (☎ 707-877-1834; www.elkcoast.com/ross ranch) at Irish Beach, another 5 miles to the north, arranges two-hour horseback beach ($60) and mountain ($50) rides; reservations are recommended.

Mendocino Coast KOA (☎ 707-882-2375, 800-562-4188; www.manchesterbeachkoa.com; tent/RV sites from

$33/43, cabins $61-77; ⚑) has campsites beneath Monterey pines plus a cooking pavilion, hot showers, hot tub, pool, hiking and bicycles.

A half-mile north, **Manchester State Park** (☎ 707-882-2463; sites $15) has a grassy campground with cold water. Ten nonreservable **environmental campsites** (sites $15) are hidden in the dunes, and are a 1.5-mile walk from the parking area; these have untreated creek water.

ELK
pop 250

Blink-and-miss-it Elk sits atop a bluff overlooking mesmerizing rock formations jutting out of the Pacific. Elk's **visitors center** (5980 Hwy 1; ☉ 11am-1pm Sat & Sun mid-Mar–Oct) has exhibits on the town's logging past. At the southern end of town, **Greenwood State Beach** (☎ 707-877-3458) has a path to the beach where Greenwood Creek meets the sea. **Force 10** (☎ 707-877-3505; www.force10tours.com) guides ocean-kayaking tours ($115).

Sleeping & Eating

Several upmarket B&Bs take advantage of the views.

Harbor House Inn (☎ 707-877-3203, 800-720-7474; www.theharborhouseinn.com; 5600 S Hwy 1; r & cottages incl breakfast $295-470; ✗) The finest of Elk's inns, this 1915 Craftsman-style mansion has gorgeous cliff-top gardens; rates include a superb four-course dinner for two.

Elk Cove Inn (☎ 707-877-3321, 800-275-2967; www .elkcoveinn.com; 6300 S Hwy 1; r $135-250, ocean-view r $295-395; ✗) This lovely inn has fine linens, a spa and California-cuisine restaurant (dinner Thursday to Sunday, mains $18 to $25).

Greenwood Pier Inn (☎ 707-877-9997; www.green woodpierinn.com; 5928 S Hwy 1; r $140-300; ✗) This New Age retreat has adequate cottages and a café (open for lunch Saturday to Wednesday and for dinner Wednesday to Saturday).

Griffin House (☎ 707-877-3422; www.griffinn.com; 5910 S Hwy 1; cottages $118-158, ocean-view cottages $198-238; ✗ ▣) Griffin House doesn't pretend to be more than it is – an unpretentious cluster of simple beachside cottages with wood-burning stoves.

Victorian Gardens (☎ 707-882-3606; www.innat victoriangardens.com; 14409 S Hwy 1, Manchester; r $190-250) Hidden on 92 acres with ocean-views, exquisite Victorian Gardens has four beautifully appointed guestrooms. From Thursday to Sunday the Italian-born innkeeper pre-pares a five-course classical-Italian menu, paired with superb wines and served by his gracious wife (dinner for two $150); reservations essential.

Queenie's Roadhouse Cafe (☎ 707-877-3285; 6061 S Hwy 1; dishes $6-10; ☉ 8am-3pm Thu-Mon) Make Queenie's your first choice for breakfast or lunch for great omelettes, scrambles, salads and sandwiches.

Bridget Dolan's (☎ 707-877-1820; 5910 S Hwy 1; dishes $10-15; ☉ dinner Fri-Tue) This dressed-down pub serves straight-forward cookin' like pot pies, and bangers and mash.

VAN DAMME STATE PARK

Three miles south of Mendocino, this state **park** (☎ 707-937-5804, 707-937-5397; www.parks .ca.gov; per car $6) is known for its **pygmy forest**, where the acidic soil and an impenetrable layer of hardpan just below the surface create a bonsai forest with decades-old trees growing only several feet high. There is a wheelchair-accessible boardwalk that provides access to the forest. To get there, turn east off Hwy 1 onto Little River Airport Rd, a half-mile south of Van Damme State Park, and drive for 3 miles. Alternatively, hike or bike up from the campground on the 3.5-mile **Fern Canyon Scenic Trail**, which crosses back and forth over Little River.

The **visitors center** (☎ 707-937-4016; ☉ 10am-4pm summer, 10am-4pm Sat & Sun fall-spring) has nature exhibits, videos and interpretive programs; a half-hour marsh loop trail starts nearby.

For sea-cave kayaking tours ($50), contact **Lost Coast Kayaking** (☎ 707-937-2434; www .lostcoastkayaking.com).

There are two **campgrounds** (☎ 800-444-7275; www.reserveamerica.com; sites $20-25) with hot showers, one is just off Hwy 1, the other is in a highland meadow. Ten **environmental campsites** (sites $15) lie just under a 2-mile hike up Fern Canyon; there's untreated creek water.

MENDOCINO
pop 1000

Picture-perfect Mendocino sits perched on a rocky headland jutting out to sea. Built by transplanted New Englanders in the 1850s, Mendocino thrived late into the 19th century, with ships transporting redwood timber from here to San Francisco. The mills shut down in the 1930s, and the town fell into disrepair until it was rediscovered in the 1950s by artists and bohemians. Today the culturally savvy, politically aware, well-traveled citizens welcome visitors, but eschew corporate interlopers – don't look for a Big Mac or try to use your cell phone.

The whole of Mendocino is listed on the National Register of Historic Places. With New England-style water towers and Victorian architecture, the town has served as the backdrop for over 50 films, including *East of Eden* (1954) and *The Majestic* (2001).

So many tourists come here for the galleries, restaurants and B&Bs that, at times, Mendocino seems like a parody of itself, earning it the nickname 'Spendocino.' To avoid crowds, come midweek or off-season, when the vibe is pure – and prices more reasonable.

Information

Ford House Visitors center & Museum (☎ 707-937-5397; www.gomendo.com; 735 Main St; suggested donation $1; ☺ 11am-4pm) Maps, books, information and exhibits including a scale model of 1890 Mendocino. There's also hot cider, picnic tables and restrooms.

Gallery Books (☎ 707-937-2665; 319 Kasten St) History, nature, travel and children's books.

Mendocino Coast Clinics (☎ 707-964-1251; 205 South St; ☺ 9am-6pm Mon-Fri, 9am-1pm Sat) Nonemergencies.

Mendocino Coast District Hospital (☎ 707-961-1234; 700 River Dr, Fort Bragg) Emergency room (24hr).

Moody's Coffee Bar (☎ 707-933-4843; www.moodys coffeebar.com; per minute 10¢; ☺ 5:30am-9pm) Internet access, good coffee and the *New York Times*.

Moore Used Books (☎ 707-937-1537; 990 Main St)

Post office (☎ 707-937-1650; 10500 Ford St)

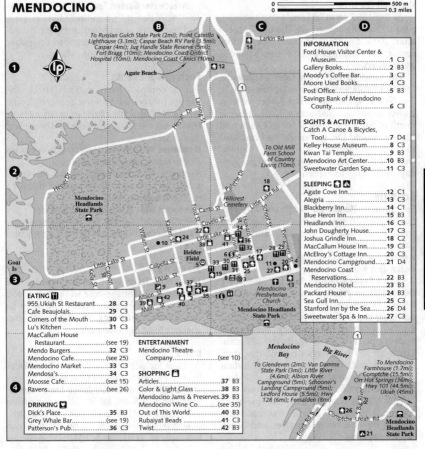

MENDOCINO

0 —————— 500 m
0 —————— 0.3 miles

NORTH COAST

Sights

The **Mendocino Art Center** (☎ 707-937-5818, 800-
653-3328; www.mendocinoartcenter.org; 45200 Little Lake
St; ☯ 10am-5pm Apr-Oct, 10am-4pm Tue-Sat rest of
year) hosts exhibitions, arts-and-crafts fairs,
theater and a nationally recognized program
of over 200 art classes. Art galleries around
town hold events on the second Saturday of
each month from 5pm to 8pm.

The 1861 **Kelley House Museum** (☎ 707-937-
5791; www.mendocinohistory.org; 45007 Albion St; $2;
☯ 11am-3pm Thu-Tue Jun-Sep, Fri-Mon rest of year) has
a research library and changing exhibits on
early California and Mendocino. In summer the museum hosts **walking tours** ($10; Fri-
Mon); call for times.

At the 1852 **Kwan Tai Temple** (45160 Albion St),
peer in the window to see the old Chinese
altar. Back on Main St, near the visitors
center, you can see one of the town's famous
water towers.

The restored 1909 **Point Cabrillo Lighthouse**
(☎ 707-937-0816; www.pointcabrillo.org; Point Cabrillo Dr;
free; ☯ 11am-4pm Mar-Oct, Fri-Mon Nov-Dec, Sat & Sun
Jan-Feb) stands on a 300-acre wildlife preserve
north of town, between Russian Gulch and
Caspar Beach. On weekends you can visit
the old lightkeeper's home, too. Guided
walks of the preserve leave at 11am on Sundays from May to September.

Activities

Spectacular **Mendocino Headlands State Park**
(☎ 707-837-5804) surrounds the village, with
trails crisscrossing the bluffs and rocky
coves. Ask at the visitors center about guided
weekend walks, including spring wildflower
walks and whale-watching walks.

Catch A Canoe & Bicycles, Too! (☎ 707-937-0273,
800-331-8884; www.stanfordinn.com; Comptche-Ukiah Rd
& Hwy 1; ☯ 9am-5pm) rents bikes, kayaks and
outrigger canoes for self-guided trips up the
8-mile Big River tidal estuary, the longest
undeveloped estuary in Northern California.
There are no highways or buildings, only
beaches, forests, marshes, streams, abundant
wildlife and historic logging sites, including
century-old train trestles and log dams.

Tiny Albion, hugging the north side of the
Albion River mouth, 5 miles south of Mendocino, offers a navigable river and ocean
bay for **kayaking**.

STAR OF THE SILVER SCREEN

Over 50 films for TV and the silver screen
have been shot around tiny Mendocino village, starting with *The Promise*, a 1916 silent film about a train wreck. Some of the
best-known movies made here include *East
of Eden* (1954) and *Rebel Without a Cause*
(1955), both starring James Dean; *The Island
of the Blue Dolphins* (1964), filmed on the
southern Mendocino coast; and the *Murder, She Wrote* TV series (1984–96), starring
Angela Lansbury. Most recently, *The Majestic* (2001) with Jim Carrey included scenes
shot at Point Cabrillo Lighthouse and Fort
Bragg's Skunk Train depot.

Sweetwater Garden Spa (☎ 707-937-4140, 800-
300-4140; 955 Ukiah St; ☯ noon-10pm) offers massage
and bodywork. A one-hour private tub-and-
sauna session costs $16; entry to the public
tub costs $10 ($7.50 Wednesdays).

Festivals & Events

For the complete list of festivals, check with
the visitors center or www.gomendo.com.
Mendocino Crab & Wine Days Late January and early
February, with wine tasting, cooking classes, whale-watching
and crab cruises.
Mendocino Whale Festival Early March, with wine and
chowder tastings, whale-watching and music.
Mendocino Music Festival Mid-July, with orchestral
and chamber music concerts on the headlands, children's
matinees and open rehearsals.
Mendocino Wine & Mushroom Festival Early
November, guided mushroom tours and symposia.
Mendocino Coast Christmas Festival Candlelight inn
tours and music.

Sleeping

Most inns have white picket fences, lace
curtains and cabbage-rose wallpaper. If you
don't fancy Victorian B&Bs, you may be
out of luck. Fort Bragg, 10 miles north, has
cheaper lodgings (see p246).

B&BS

All rates include breakfast; only a few places
have TVs. For a range of vacation cottages
and B&Bs, contact **Mendocino Coast Reservations** (☎ 707-937-5033, 800-262-7801; www.mendocino
vacations.com; 45084 Little Lake St; Main St; ☯ 9am-5pm).
Alegria (☎ 707-937-5150, 800-780-7905; www.ocean
frontmagic.com; 44781 Main St; r $129-159, ocean-view

r $209-249, cottages $199; ⊠) Perfect for a romantic hideaway, Alegria's rooms have ocean-view decks and wood-burning fireplaces; outside there's private beach access, a rarity in Mendo. The ever-so-friendly innkeepers also rent housekeeping cottages.

McElroy's Cottage Inn (☎ 800-780-7905; www.mc elroysinn.com; 998 Main St; r $90-159) Across the street, and run by Alegria, these simpler, reasonably priced rooms are in a 1900s Craftsman-style house.

Stanford Inn by the Sea (☎ 707-937-5615, 800-331-8884; www.stanfordinn.com; Comptche-Ukiah Rd; r $240-295; ⊠ ⬛ 🐾) A masterpiece of a lodge standing on 10 acres, Mendo's best inn has wood-burning fireplaces, fine art, stereos and top-quality mattresses with fine linens in every room – and *no* Victoriana. The organic gardens provide produce for the dining room. The solarium-enclosed pool and hot tub are open 24 hours, and there's an on-site spa. Pets welcome.

Sweetwater Spa & Inn (☎ 707-937-4076, 800-300-4140; www.sweetwaterspa.com; 44840 Main St; r & cottages $110-2205) Sweetwater owns a variety of accommodations, both in and near town. Rates for B&B rooms, ocean-view cottages and fanciful water-tower units include spa privileges.

Joshua Grindle Inn (☎ 707-937-4143, 800-474-6353; www.joshgrin.com; 44800 Little Lake Rd; r $179-259; ⊠) Mendocino's oldest B&B has bright, airy, uncluttered rooms in an 1869 house, a weathered saltbox cottage and water tower. There are afternoon goodies, warm hospitality and gorgeous gardens.

MacCallum House Inn (☎ 707-937-0289, 800-609-0492; www.maccallumhouse.com; 45020 Albion St; r/ste $135-325/265-375; ⊠ ⬛) Stay in an 1882 refurbished barn, a cottage or 20th-century luxury home; all have cushy extras like robes, DVD players, stereos, plush linens and spa services. Pets welcome. There's also a hoppin' bar and terrific restaurant.

Packard House (☎ 707-937-2677, 888-453-2677; www.packardhouse.com; 45170 Little Lake St; r $225; ⊠) Decked out in contemporary style, this place is Mendocino's chic B&B choice – sleek and elegant, with beautiful fabrics and limestone bathrooms.

Also recommended:

Agate Cove Inn (☎ 707-937-0551, 800-527-3111; www .agatecove.com; 11201 Lansing St; r $140-210, ocean-view r & cottages $270-310; ⊠) On a spectacular bluff overlooking the sea.

Blue Heron Inn (☎ 707-937-4323; 390 Kasten St; www.theblueheron.com; r $95-115; ⊠) Spartan rooms above a restaurant; crisp linens; some shared bathrooms.

Fensalden (☎ 707-937-4042, 800-959-3850; www .fensalden.com; 33810 Navarro Ridge Rd, Albion; r $129-198, bungalow $239; ⊠) An 1880s stagecoach stop, 8 miles south of town. Super-cool bungalow sleeps four.

Glendeven (☎ 707-937-0083, 800-822-4536; www.glen deven.com; 8205 N Hwy 1; r $135-235; ⊠) Elegant estate with contemporary-art gallery, 2 miles south of town.

Headlands Inn (☎ 707-937-4431; www.headlandsinn .com; cnr Albion & Howard Sts; r $129-209; ⊠) Cozy saltbox with featherbeds and fireplaces.

John Dougherty House (☎ 707-937-5266; 800-486-2104; www.jdhouse.com; 571 Ukiah St; r $135-240; ⊠)

Mendocino Farmhouse (☎ 707-937-0241, 800-475-1536; www.mendocinofarmhouse.com; Comptche-Ukiah Rd; r $139-159; ⊠) Just outside town, beneath redwoods.

Old Mill Farm School of Country Living (☎ 707-937-0244, 707-937-3047; www.oldmillfarm.org; rustic cabin $80; ⊠) Self-sustaining organic farm with rustic cabin. Call ahead. Check the website for info on farm events and workshops.

Sea Gull Inn (☎ 707-937-5204, 888-937-5204; www .seagullbb.com; 44960 Albion St; r $65-135, barn $165; ⊠) A cozy bargain!

MOTELS & HOTELS

Blackberry Inn (☎ 707-937-5281, 800-950-7806; www .mendocinomotel.com; 44951 Larkin Rd; r $140-200; ⊠) Above town on a hill, the Blackberry looks like a row of Old West storefronts. Many of the Americana-style rooms have distant ocean views and fireplaces.

Mendocino Hotel (☎ 707-937-0511, 800-548-0513; www.mendocinohotel.com; 45080 Main St; r $95, with bathroom $120-235, ste $295; ⊠) Built in 1878 as the town's first hotel. Many of the Victorian guestrooms share bathrooms. For thicker walls, book a modern garden suite.

CAMPING

Russian Gulch State Park (☎ reservations 800-444-7275; www.reserveamerica.com; sites $20-25) Russian Gulch, 2 miles north of town, has shady camping with hot showers, a sandy beach, small waterfall and Devil's Punch Bowl, a collapsed sea arch.

Mendocino Campground (☎ 707-937-3130; www .mendocino-campground.com; Comptche-Ukiah Rd; sites $20-22; ☯ Apr-Oct) Uphill from Hwy 1, this rustic option has 60 sites, hot showers and forested trails.

Caspar Beach RV Park (☎ 707-964-3306; www.cas parbeachrvpark.com; 14441 Cabrillo Dr; tent sites $25, RV sites $30-35) This park occupies a sheltered gully beside Caspar Beach, 3.5 miles north of Mendocino.

About 5 miles south of town, Albion has riverside camping: **Schooner's Landing Campground** (☎ 707-937-5707; sites $30-35) and **Albion River Campground** (☎ 707-937-0606; www.albion rivercampground.com; 34500 Hwy 1; tent/RV sites $20/30).

Eating

Mendocino's restaurants are popular so reservations are recommended.

RESTAURANTS

Cafe Beaujolais (☎ 707-937-5614; www.cafebeaujolais .com; 961 Ukiah St; mains $23-28; ⊗ dinner) In a refurbished house built in 1896, Mendocino's iconic California-cuisine restaurant serves innovative, refined and inspired cooking, using organic meats and produce.

MacCallum House Restaurant (☎ 707-937-0289; www.maccallumhouse.com; 45020 Albion St; café dishes $6-12, mains $20-32; ⊗ dinner) Sit on the veranda or fireside for a romantic dinner of duck, gnocchi, lamb, steak or fish. The chef-owner uses all-organic ingredients. The bar menu is one of Mendocino's few bargains. Great breakfasts.

Ledford House (☎ 707-937-0282; www.ledfordhouse .com; 3000 N Hwy 1, Albion; bistro meals $15-18; mains $22-28) For ocean-view dining, head 8 miles south to this Cal-Med roadhouse, which has a better-priced 'bistro menu' in addition to regular mains – try the cassoulet. Come before sunset. There's live jazz most nights.

Moosse Cafe (☎ 707-937-4323; www.theblueheron .com; 390 Kasten St; lunch mains $9-14, dinner $17-20) The blond-wood floors and paper tablecloths set a relaxed tone for the Cal-French cooking. Try the cioppino or pork chops at dinner; at lunch there are salads, toasted-cheese sandwiches and great burgers.

955 Ukiah St Restaurant (☎ 707-937-1955; www .955restaurant.com; 955 Ukiah St; mains $20-25; ⊗ dinner Wed-Sun) A throwback to the 1970s (think macramé), 955 prepares consistently good steaks, seafood, stews and pastas.

Ravens (☎ 707-937-5615; www.stanfordinn.com; Stanford Inn, Comptche-Ukiah Rd; breakfast $8-13, mains $14-28; ⊗ breakfast & dinner) Haute-contemporary cuisine meets vegetarianism at Ravens, where the produce comes from the inn's own organic gardens. Omnivores may foreswear meat after dining here, as there's everything from sea-palm strudel to pizza. It also serves

Mendo's best breakfasts – and has a good view, too.

Mendocino Cafe (☎ 707-937-6141; 10451 Lansing St; lunch mains $9-14, dinner $11-20) One of Mendocino's few midpriced dinner spots also serves lovely alfresco lunches, blending American cooking with Asian and Mexican. Try the fish tacos or Thai burrito. At dinner there's grilled steak and seafood.

GROCERIES & QUICK EATS

Harvest Market in Fort Bragg has the best groceries (p247).

Corners of the Mouth (☎ 707-937-5345; 45016 Ukiah St; ⊗ 9am-7pm) Carries natural foods.

Mendosa's (☎ 707-937-5879; 10501 Lansing St; ⊗ 8am-9pm) Sells basics and good meat.

Mendocino Market (☎ 707-937-3474; 45051 Ukiah St; sandwiches $6-9; ⊗ 10am-6:30pm) Pick up deli sandwiches and picnics. There's a small meat counter.

Mendo Burgers (☎ 707-937-1111; 10483 Lansing St; meals $6-9; ⊗ 11am-4:30pm Thu-Tue) Behind Mendocino Bakery, this old-fashioned lunch counter makes great burgers and hand-cut fries; veggie burgers too.

Lu's Kitchen (☎ 707-937-4939; 45013 Ukiah St; dishes $7-10; ⊗ 11:30am-5:30pm) Lu makes fab organic-veggie burritos in a tiny shack; outdoor-only tables.

Drinking

Have cocktails at the **Mendocino Hotel** or the **Grey Whale Bar** at the MacCallum House Inn (p243).

Patterson's Pub (☎ 707-937-4782; 10485 Lansing St) An inviting Irish-style bar, Patterson's has an appealing pub menu of sandwiches, seafood and salads ($8-13) before 9:30pm.

Dick's Place (☎ 707-937-5643; 45080 Main St) Do shots with rowdy locals.

Entertainment

Mendocino Theatre Company (☎ 707-937-4477; www.1mtc.org; 45200 Little Lake St) The company performs contemporary plays.

Shopping

Color & Light Glass (☎ 707-937-1003; 10525 Ford St; ⊗ Fri-Tue) Inside an artist's studio, see original fused and stained-glass works.

Out of This World (☎ 707-937-3335; 45100 Main St) Birders, astronomy buffs and science geeks: head directly to this telescope, binocular and science-toy shop.

Articles (☎ 707-937-3891; 611 Albion St; ☻ Thu-Tue) Check out cool crafts inside an old water tower you can ascend.

Rubaiyat Beads (☎ 707-937-1217; 10550 Lansing St) For beaded jewelry and imported silver, visit this little shop.

Twist (☎ 707-937-1717; 45140 Main St) Twist carries eco-friendly, natural-fiber clothing and trippy hand-blown 'tobacco-smoking accessories' (Dude: that means bongs).

Mendocino Jams & Preserves (☎ 707-937-1037; 440 Main St) Mendo Jams offers tastes of its goodies. Try the ketchup.

Mendocino Wine Co (☎ 800-860-3347; 45070 Main St) Sample zinfandel, syrah and cabernet ($4).

JUG HANDLE STATE RESERVE

Between Mendocino and Fort Bragg, Jug Handle preserves an **ecological staircase** that you can view on a 5-mile (round-trip) self-guided nature trail. Five wave-cut terraces ascend in steps from the seashore, each 100ft and 100,000 years removed from the previous one, and each with its own distinct geology and vegetation. One of the terraces has a pygmy forest, similar to the better-known example at Van Damme State Park (p240). Pick up a printed guide detailing the area's geology, flora and fauna from the parking lot. The reserve is also a good spot to stroll the headlands, whale-watch or lounge on the beach. It's easy to miss the entrance to the reserve – watch for the turnoff, just north of Caspar.

Opposite the state reserve, **Annie's Jughandle Beach B&B** (☎ 707-964-1415, 800-964-9957; www.jug handle.com; Hwy 1, mileage marker 55; r incl breakfast $120-220) is an 1880s farmhouse with cheery rooms, some with Jacuzzis and gas fireplaces.

Jug Handle Creek Farm and Nature Center (☎ 707-964-4630; http://jughandle.creek.org; sites $11, r & cabins adult $27-35, child $11, student $21-30) is a nonprofit 39-acre farm with rustic cabins and hostel rooms in a 19th-century farmhouse. Call ahead about work-stay discounts.

FORT BRAGG

pop 7025

Although it's less charming than Mendocino, Fort Bragg makes an excellent base for exploring the coast, and serves as a jumping-off point for whale-watching and deep-sea fishing excursions. The fort established here in 1857 was named for Colonel Braxton Bragg, a veteran of the Mexican

War. Ostensibly used to 'supervise' the local Pomo, it was abandoned a decade later. A lumber company was established in 1885, and the California Western Railroad (later nicknamed the 'Skunk Train') was built to haul giant redwoods from forest to coast. The last of the mills closed in 2002, and the town relies increasingly on tourism.

Orientation & Information

Twisting, nausea-inducing Hwy 20 provides the main access to Fort Bragg, and most facilities are near Main St, a 2-mile stretch of Hwy 1. Shops, a movie theater and the post office are on Franklin St, which runs parallel, one block east. Fort Bragg's wharf, with its fishing-boat docks and seafood restaurants, lies at Noyo Harbor – the mouth of the Noyo River – south of downtown.

Fort Bragg-Mendocino Coast Chamber of Commerce (☎ 707-961-6300, 800-726-2780; www.fortbragg.com, www.mendocinocoast.com; 332 N Main St; ☻ 9am-5pm Mon-Fri, 9am-3pm Sat) Information about Fort Bragg, Mendocino and the surrounding area.

Sage's Computer (☎ 707-964-9955; Depot Shopping Center, 401 N Main St; per 10min $1.25) For Internet access visit Sage's Computer, which uses Macs.

Seal of Approval (☎ 707-964-7099; 260 N Main St; per 10min $1.50; ☻ 8am-8pm Mon-Fri, 10am-6pm Sat)

Sights & Activities

Fort Bragg's pride and joy is the vintage **Skunk Train** (☎ 707-964-6371, 866-457-5865; www.skunktrain .com; adult/child 3-11 $35/20). The train got its nickname in 1925 for its stinky gas-powered steam engines but today the historic steam and diesel locomotives are odorless. Passing through redwood-forested mountains, along rivers, over bridges and through deep mountain tunnels, the trains run from both Fort Bragg and Willits (p256) to the midway point of Northspur, where they turn around (if you want to go to Willits, plan to spend the night). The depot is downtown at the foot of Laurel St, one block west of Main St.

The **Guest House Museum** (☎ 707-964-4251; 343 N Main St; $2; ☻ 10am-4pm Tue-Sun summer, 11am-3pm Thu-Sun winter), a majestic Victorian structure built in 1892, displays historical photos and relics of Fort Bragg's history. Literally and figuratively on the other side of the street, the **Triangle Tattoo & Museum** (☎ 707-964-8814; www.triangletattoo.com; 356B N Main St; ☻ noon-7pm) is flanked by galleries that unveil new shows and stay open till 8pm on the second

NORTH COAST

Saturday of each month. **Northcoast Artists** (☎ 707-964-8266; http://northcoastartists.org; 362 N Main St) is a co-op gallery. Antique and book shops line Franklin St, one block east.

Once the city dump, **Glass Beach** is named for the sea-polished glass lying on the sands. Take the headlands trail from Elm St, off Main St, but don't walk barefoot. Nearby **North Coast Brewing Co** (☎ 707-964-2739; 455 N Main St) offers brewery tours Monday to Saturday; call ahead.

Small boats at Noyo Harbor offer coastal and whale-watching cruises and deep-sea fishing trips. Try **Noyo Fishing Center** (☎ 707-964-3000; www.fortbraggfishing.com; 32440 N Harbor Dr).

A Northern California's hidden gem, **Mendocino Coast Botanical Gardens** (☎ 707-964-4352; www.gardenbythesea.org; 18220 N Hwy 1; adult/child/teen/senior $7.50/1/3/6; ⏱ 9am-5pm Mar-Oct, 9am-4pm rest of year) displays native flora along serpentine paths on 47 seafront acres south of town. Primary trails are wheelchair-accessible.

Festivals & Events

Fort Bragg Whale Festival Held on the 3rd weekend in March with microbrew tastings, crafts fairs and whale-watching trips.

Rhododendron Show Takes place in late April or early May.

World's Largest Salmon BBQ Held at Noyo Harbor on the Saturday nearest 4th of July.

Paul Bunyan Days Held on the Labor Day weekend in September, the festival celebrates California's logging history with a logging show, square dancing, parade and fair.

Sleeping

Fort Bragg's lodging is cheaper than Mendocino's, but most of the motels along noisy Hwy 1 don't have air-conditioning so you'll hear traffic through your open windows. The places listed below do not have noise problems.

B&BS & INNS

Most B&Bs do not have TVs and they all include breakfast in their rates.

Weller House Inn (☎ 707-964-4415, 877-893-5537; www.wellerhouse.com; 524 Stewart St; r $115-180; ✕) Rooms in this beautifully restored 1886 Victorian have down comforters, good mattresses and fine linens. The water tower is the tallest structure in town – and it has a hot tub at the top! Breakfast is in the massive redwood ballroom.

Grey Whale Inn (☎ 707-964-0640, 800-382-7244; www.greywhaleinn.com; 615 N Main St; r $90-180, ste 193; ✕) Fort Bragg's original hospital has huge rooms and big windows. The penthouse suites have sweeping views.

Rendezvous Inn (☎ 707-964-8142, 800-491-8142; www.rendezvousinn.com; 647 N Main St; r $110; ✕) The rooms are spartan, but Fort Bragg's best chef cooks breakfast.

Lodge at Noyo River (☎ 707-964-8045, 800-628-1126; www.noyolodge.com; 500 Casa del Norte Dr; r $95-175; ✕) Overlooking Noyo Harbor, the lodge has spacious rooms inside a 19th-century lumber-baron's house, and modern suites with oversized tubs.

MOTELS

Colombi Motel (☎ 707-964-5773; www.colombimotel.com; 647 Oak St; 1-/2-bedroom units $45-70) All units have two rooms – a bedroom and kitchen or two bedrooms – at this sparkling-clean motel, the best bargain on the Mendocino Coast; check in at the Colombi Market cum deli on the corner of Oak and Harold Sts. There's a launderette adjacent.

Hi-Sea Inn (☎ 707-964-5929, 800-990-7327; www.hiseainn.com; 1201 N Main St; r $79-109) Of the oceanfront motels north of downtown, this is the best (and cheapest) because it doesn't pretend to be more than a straightforward motel with spectacular views.

Beachcomber Motel (☎ 707-964-2402, 800-400-7873; www.thebeachcombermotel.com; 1111 N Main St; r $79-129, ocean-view r $109-139, r with kitchen $159) Next to the Hi-Sea Inn, the Beachcomber has more amenities and better furniture; book upstairs for privacy.

Super 8 (☎ 707-964-4003, 800-206-9833; www.super8.com; 888 S Main St; r $75-92; ✕) Of the motels near the bridge, this one is appropriately priced, clean and has air-conditioning, microwaves and refrigerators.

Anchor Lodge (☎ 707-964-4283; www.wharf-restaurant.com; 32260 N Harbor Dr; r $55, ocean-view r $90, r with kitchen $95) At Noyo Harbor, the Wharf Restaurant rents basic rooms. Those under the restaurant have water views; some have kitchens.

Also consider:

Beach House Inn (☎ 707-961-1700, 888-559-9992; www.beachinn.com; 100 Pudding Creek Rd; r $90-150; ✕) Five condo-like buildings north of town; some have creek views.

Holiday Inn Express (☎ 707-964-1100, 800-465-4329; www.holidayinnexpress.com; 250 Hwy 20; r $119-139; ✕ 🛁) Predictable comfort and modern amenities – indoor pool, hot tub and fitness center.

Pine Beach Inn (☎ 707-964-5603, 800-987-8388; www.pinebeachinn.com; 16801 N Hwy 1; r $89-129; ☒) Between Mendocino and Fort Bragg, this 12-acre motel complex needs upgrading; cheapest rooms are near the highway; quieter 'garden-view' rooms offer the best value.

CAMPING
California Department of Forestry (☎ 707-964-5674; www.fire.ca.gov/php/rsrc-mgt_jackson.php; 802 N Main St; ☒ Mon-Fri) has maps, permits and camping information for the Jackson Demonstration Forest, east of Fort Bragg.

Pomo RV Park & Campground (☎ 707-964-3373; www.infortbragg.com/pomorvpark; 17999 Tregoning Lane; tent/RV sites $24/35) A mile south of town, this wooded campground is back from Hwy 1. Gates close at 11pm.

Eating
Rendezvous Inn (☎ 707-964-8142; www.rendezvousinn .com; 647 N Main St; mains $18-24; ☒ dinner Wed-Sun) Rustic charm meets big-city cooking at Fort Bragg's best restaurant, which serves expertly prepared, down-to-earth, French-provincial cooking in a redwood-paneled, Craftsman-style house. If you're a foodie, don't miss it. Make reservations.

Nit's Cafe (☎ 707-964-7187; 322 N Main; lunch $8-15, dinner $18-22; ☒ Tue-Sat) There are eight tables at this tiny storefront café, where the Thai-born chef-owner wows with imaginative, wonderfully spiced French-Thai cooking. Vegans and vegetarians welcome. Reserve.

Mendo Bistro (☎ 707-964-4974; www.mendobistro .com; 301 N Main St; dishes $11-20; ☒ dinner) Upstairs in the Company Store building, lively Mendo Bistro serves good crab cakes, steaks, roasted chicken and housemade pasta. Great for groups with diverse tastes. Request a window table.

Chapter & Moon (☎ 707-962-1643; 32150 N Harbor Dr; mains $8-15; ☒ 8am-8pm) Overlooking Noyo Harbor, this small café serves blue-plate American cooking: chicken and dumplings, meatloaf with mashers, and fish with yam chips. Save room for the fruit cobbler.

Piaci Pub & Pizzeria (☎ 707-961-1133; 120 W Redwood Ave; pizza $8-12; ☒ Mon-Fri lunch, dinner nightly) For thin-crust pizzas, focaccia sandwiches, local wines and microbrews, this is the place.

North Coast Brewing Co (☎ 707-964-3400; 444 N Main St; mains $8-17; ☒ 11:30am-9pm) Down a pint of microbrew and munch on garlic fries, sandwiches or steaks.

Headlands Coffeehouse (☎ 707-964-1987; 120 E Laurel St; dishes $4-8; ☒ 7am-10pm) The town's best café has Belgian waffles at breakfast; at lunch and dinner try homemade soups, veggie-friendly salads, paninis and lasagna.

Eggheads (☎ 707-964-5005; 326 N Main St; meals $8-13; ☒ 7am-2pm Thu-Tue) For breakfast, Eggheads makes 50 varieties of omelettes, some with local Dungeness crab. They also have good sandwiches.

Laurel Deli (☎ 707-964-7812; Depot Shopping Center, 401 N Main St; mains $6-8) Locals come for fat sandwiches and homemade pies. Kids love the giant locomotive.

Unless you're with your grandparents, skip the overpriced Wharf Restaurant (aka Silver's), and head next door to unpretentious **Cap'n Flint's** (☎ 707-964-9447; 32250 N Harbor Dr; ☒ 11am-9pm) to eat the same fried fish for less. **Sharon's by the Sea** (☎ 707-962-0680; 32096 N Harbor Dr; lunch $6-17, dinner $11-24) is one of the Wharf's best options for seafood.

For the best groceries, visit **Harvest Market** (☎ 707-964-7000; cnr Hwys 1 & 20; ☒ 5am-11pm). A **farmers market** (☎ 707-937-4330; cnr Laurel & Franklin Sts; ☒ 3:30-6pm Wed, May-Oct) meets downtown, near **Cowlick's Ice Cream** (☎ 962-9271; 250B Main St) and the **Mendocino Cookie Company** (☎ 964-0282; 303 N Main St).

Drinking & Entertainment
Locals cherish their indie cafés. When Starbucks arrived in 2005, the townspeople started wearing T-shirts emblazoned with a Starbucks-like logo reading 'Corporate Coffee Sucks!' (to get one, visit the website www.corporatecoffeesucks.com).

Headlands Coffeehouse (☎ 707-964-1987; www .headlandscoffeehouse.com; 120 E Laurel St) This not-to-be-missed café features live music every evening – jazz, folk and classical – and jazz jams on Sunday afternoons. Free wi-fi.

Caspar Inn (☎ 707-964-5565; 14957 Caspar Rd; live entertainment cover, Tue-Sat, $3-25) Five miles south of Fort Bragg, off Hwy 1, Caspar Inn has live reggae, hip-hop, rockabilly, R&B, world beat and open-mic Sundays. It's worth the drive.

Opera Fresca (☎ 707-937-3646, 888-826-7372; www .operafresca.com) This ambitious company performs fully staged operas year-round.

Gloriana Opera Company (☎ 707-964-7469; www .gloriana.org; 721 N Franklin St) Gloriana stages musical theater and operettas.

Footlighters Little Theater (☎ 707-964-3806; 248 E Laurel St) Footlighters presents 1890s-style musicals, comedy and melodrama on Wednesday and Saturday in summer.

Sample some of the microbrews at **North Coast Brewing Company** (☎ 707-9 64-3400; 444 N Main St) or do shots at **Old Coast Hotel** (☎ 707-961-4488; 101 N Franklin St).

Getting Around
Mendocino Transit Authority (MTA; ☎ 707-462-1422, 800-696-4682; www.4mta.org) runs local route 5 'BraggAbout' buses between Noyo Harbor and Elm St, north of downtown; the route doesn't always parallel Main St (Hwy 1).

Fort Bragg Cyclery (☎ 707-964-3509; www.fort braggcyclery.com; 221-A N Main St) rents bicycles.

MACKERRICHER STATE PARK
Three miles north of Fort Bragg, the **Mac-Kerricher State Park** (☎ 707-964-9112; www.parks .ca.gov) preserves 9 miles of pristine rocky headlands, sandy beaches, dunes and tide pools.

The **visitors center** (☼ 10am-6pm Sat & Sun summer, 11am-3pm Sat & Sun rest of year) sits next to the whale skeleton at the park entrance. Hike the **Coastal Trail** along dark-sand beaches and see rare and endangered plant species (tread lightly). **Lake Cleone** is a 30-acre freshwater lake stocked with trout. At nearby **Laguna Point** an interpretive boardwalk overlooks seals and, from December to April, migrating whales. **Ricochet Ridge Ranch** (☎ 707-964-7669; www.horse-vacation.com; 24201 N Hwy 1) offers horseback-riding trips through redwoods or along the beach ($45 for 90 minutes). Guides are great, the horses top quality.

Popular **campgrounds** (☎ 800-444-2725; www.re serveamerica.com; sites $20-25), nestled in pine forest, have hot showers and water. Ten semi-secluded walk-in sites (sites $25), 50yd from the parking area, are first-come, first-served.

WESTPORT
pop 200
The last hamlet before the Lost Coast (p261), Westport feels like a frontier settlement. A turn-of-the-20th-century shipping port, it once had the longest logging chute in California. Today there's little here except for romantic beaches and abundant peace. It's a twisting 15-mile drive from Fort Bragg to Westport, and another 22 miles to Hwy 1's terminus at Hwy 101 in Leggett.

Head north of town for 1.5 miles for the **Westport-Union Landing State Beach** (☎ 707-937-

5804; sites $14), which extends for 3 miles on coastal bluffs. It's mostly a primitive campground, but a rough hiking trail passes by tidepools and streams, accessible at low tide, arriving at **Westport Beach RV & Camping** (☎ 707-964-2964; www.westportbeachrv.com; 37700 N Hwy 1; tent sites $22, RV sites $32-36), which has showers and beachside tent camping.

Simple accommodations in town include the sleepy, four-room **Lost Coast Inn** (☎ 707-964-5584; www.lostcoastinn.com; 38921 N Hwy 1; r $70-100; ☒) and the plastic-flower-festooned **Westport Inn** (☎ 707-964-5135; 37040 N Hwy 1; r $66; ☒) motel.

Further north lie two wonderful rural retreats. **Howard Creek Ranch** (☎ 707-964-6725; www .howardcreekranch.com; 40501 N Hwy 1; r $75-125, ste $145-185; ☒), on 60 stunning acres of forest and farmland abutting the wilderness, has accommodations in the 1880s farmhouse or the carriage barn, whose way-cool redwood rooms have been expertly handcrafted by the owner. Rates include full breakfast. Bring hiking boots, not high heels.

DeHaven Valley Farm (☎ 707-961-1660, 877-334-2836, www.dehaven-valley-farm.com; 39247 N Hwy 1; r $94-150, cottages $140-150) is a secluded 1875 house on 20 acres with comfy B&B rooms – one with a fireplace – and gorgeous mountain views. Dinner is served Wednesday to Sunday.

Want to rent a house? Consider the two-bedroom 1832 **Westport House** (☎ 707-937-4007; www.vrbo.com/61409; $200 per night, 2-night minimum; ☒), overlooking pounding surf, or the four-bedroom **Seagate Vacation Rental** (☎ 530-873-6793; www.vrbo.com/30340; 36875 N Hwy 1; $200 per night; ☒).

INLAND HIGHWAY 101

North of Santa Rosa, Hwy 101 heads through a series of fertile valleys along the Russian River, intersecting with Hwy 1 in Leggett. Although Hwy 101 may not look as enticing as the coastal route, it's faster and less winding, leaving you time along the way to detour into Sonoma and Mendocino counties' wine regions, explore pastoral Anderson Valley, splash about Clear Lake or soak at hot-springs resorts outside Ukiah – time well spent indeed!

LAKE SONOMA
Formed by Warm Springs Dam in 1983, Lake Sonoma has two major arms, 4 miles and

8 miles long, and many smaller coves. The 319ft-high, 3000ft-long dam is at the lake's east end. To get there from Hwy 101, take the Dry Creek Rd exit north of Healdsburg and head northwest for 11 miles through the gorgeous valley's vineyards (see the Russian River Valley on p201).

The **visitors center** (☎ 707-433-9483; www.parks .sonoma.net/laktrls.html; ☒ 8am-4pm Mon-Fri) has historical exhibits, maps and information on fishing, boating, camping and hiking over 40 miles of trails. Behind the center is a fish hatchery and 2 miles further along the **marina** (☎ 707-433-2200) rents everything from canoes to houseboats.

Liberty Glen Campground has 190 unreserved sites, hot showers and panoramic vistas. Primitive boat-in and hike-in campsites are dotted around the lake; contact the park for reservations.

HOPLAND
pop 818

Cute Hopland is the gateway to Mendocino County's wine country. Hops were first grown here in 1866, but Prohibition brought the industry temporarily to a halt. In 1983, the Mendocino Brewing Company opened up the first brewpub licensed in California since Prohibition and put Hopland back on the map. Now wine-tasting rooms are the primary draw.

Sights & Activities

Don't miss **Fetzer Vineyards Organic Gardens** (☎ 800-846-8637; www.fetzer.com; 13601 Eastside Rd; ☒ 9am-5pm), overseen by Kate Frey, goldmedal winner at England's 2005 Chelsea Flower Show.

Graziano Family of Wines (☎ 707-744-8466; www .grazianofamilyofwines.com; 13251 S Hwy 101; ☒ 10am-5pm) specializes in 'Cal-Ital' wines – nebbiolo, dolcetto, barbera and sangiovese – at some great prices. **McDowell Valley Vineyards** (☎ 707-744-1053; www.mcdowellsyrah.com; 13380 S Hwy 101; ☒ 11am-5pm) is famous for Rhône varietals and makes luscious, jammy reds and a lovely rosé. Two miles north, the fun-to-visit **Jepson Vineyards** (☎ 800-516-7342; www.jepsonwine .com; 10400 S Hwy 101; ☒ 10am-5pm) makes chardonnay and brandy in its giant alembic still; tours by appointment.

Brutocao Schoolhouse Plaza (☎ 800-433-3689; Schoolhouse Plaza, 13500 S Hwy 101; ☒ bocce 11am-8pm) has pizza, so-so wine and six bocce courts.

Drop by **Real Goods Solar Living Center** (☎ 707-744-2100; www.solarliving.org; 13771 S Hwy 101; suggested donation $1-5; ☒ 10am-7pm) to learn about alternative energy on a self-guided tour of this 12-acre site, just south of town; guided tours leave at 11am and 3pm, Friday to Sunday. Kids' areas include a solar-powered miniature **carousel** ($1; ☒ noon-4pm).

Festivals & Events

SolFest Energy Fair Features music, speakers and workshops on sustainable living, solar and wind power, and organic gardening. Held in June.

Hopland Women's Festival Takes place on Memorial Day (last Monday in June).

Sleeping & Eating

Fetzer Valley Oaks Inn (☎ 707-744-7413, 800-846-8637; www.fetzer.com; 13601 Eastside Rd; r $149, cottage $200, ste $175-250; ☒ ☒ ☒) Once a 19th-century carriage house, this inn on the Fetzer Vineyards' grounds has ever-so-charming rooms with redwood paneling, super-comfy beds and mesmerizing vineyard views from private terraces – the perfect spot for morning coffee.

Munchies (☎ 707-744-1600; 13275 S Hwy 101; sandwiches $5; ☒ 8am-2pm Mon-Thu, 9am-5pm Fri-Sun) Munchies has juice, gelato, pastries, espresso, picnic baskets, and bicycles for rent.

Bluebird Cafe (☎ 707-744-1633; 13340 S Hwy 101; breakfast & lunch $5-10, dinner $10-15; ☒ 7am-2pm Mon-Thu, 8am-8pm Fri-Sun) This classic American diner serves heavy breakfasts, giant burgers and homemade pie.

Shotgun Restaurant at Lawson's Station (☎ 707-744-1947; 13441 S Hwy 101; lunch $8-10, dinner $18-22; ☒ Tue-Sat) The Shotgun serves good steaks but is unnecessarily fancy for round here.

Mendocino Brewing Company (☎ 707-744-1015; 13351 S Hwy 101; meals around $12; ☒ noon-7pm Thu-Mon) One of Northern California's best-known brewpubs is moribund: the beer is made in Ukiah now, the kitchen closed down, and the bar shuts at seven friggin' o'clock. Still, if you love beer, get some take-out food from the Bluebird or Munchies, bring it to the garden, order a pint and listen to the crickets.

At the time of research, the 1890 **Hopland Inn** (13401 S Hwy 101) had closed, but check to see if it's back in business.

CLEAR LAKE

With over 100 miles of shoreline, Clear Lake is the largest, naturally occurring freshwater lake in California (Tahoe is bigger, but straddles the state line with Nevada). In summer the warm water thrives with algae, giving it a murky-green appearance and creating a fabulous habitat for fish – especially bass – and tens of thousands of birds. Mt Konocti, a 4200ft-tall dormant volcano, lords it over the scene. Alas, the human settlements don't always live up to the grandeur. Clear Lake is 18 miles east of Hwy 101.

Orientation & Information

Locals refer to 'upper lake' (the northwest portion) and 'lower lake' (the southeast portion). Lakeport (population 4800) sits on the northwest shore, a 45-minute drive east of Hopland along Hwy 175 (off Hwy 101); Kelseyville (population 2928) is 7 miles south. Clearlake (population 13,200), off the southeastern shore, is the biggest (and ugliest) town. It's best avoided as it's more famous for methamphetamine busts than outdoor recreation.

The town is presently undergoing redevelopment, but for now skip it. ('Clear Lake' is the lake; 'Clearlake' is the city.) Highway 20 links the north-shore hamlets of Nice (the northernmost town) and Lucerne, 4 miles southeast. Middletown, an average suburb, lies 20 miles south of Clearlake at the junction of Hwys 175 and 129, 40 minutes north of Calistoga.

Lake County Visitor Information Center (☎ 707-263-9544, 800-525-3743; www.lakecounty.com; 6110 E Hwy 120, Lucerne; ⏰ 8:30am-5:30pm Mon-Fri, 10am-4pm Sat, noon-4pm Sun summer, shorter hours in winter) has complete information.

Sights & Activities

In Lakeport, the **Old County Courthouse** (255 N Main St) is a state historic landmark from 1871. Inside, so-so **Lake County Museum** (☎ 707-263-4555; ⏰ 10am-4pm Wed-Sat, noon-4pm Sun) has Pomo artifacts and historical exhibits.

Six miles from Lakeport, **Clear Lake State Park** (☎ 707-279-4293; 5300 Soda Bay Rd, Kelseyville; per car $6), on the lake's west shore, is all that a state park should be – idyllic and gorgeous – with hiking trails, fishing, boating and camping. The **bird-watching** is extraordinary. The **visitors center** has geological and historical exhibits. **Taylor Planetarium & Observatory** (☎ 707-279-8372 after 3pm; 5727 Oak Hills Lane, Kelseyville; adult/child $3/1) offers stargazing programs; call for times.

In Lower Lake there's the conservation group **Redbud Audubon Society** (☎ 707-994-1545; www.redbudaudubon.org), but birding is better at Clear Lake State Park. The **Lower Lake Historical Schoolhouse Museum** (☎ 707-995-3565; 16435 Morgan Valley Rd; ⏰ 11am-4pm Wed-Sat) is infested with bats, but the restored 19th-century classroom is worth checking out.

Clear Lake Queen (☎ 707-994-5432; www.paddlewheel.com; 2hr cruise $16-25, 3hr cruise $18-33), docked in Lucerne on the north shore, is an elegant, three-story paddlewheel steamboat offering sightseeing cruises, with pretty good dining, a bar and live music. Reservations essential.

Many outfits rent boats, including **On the Waterfront** (☎ 707-263-6789; 60 3rd St, Lakeport) and Konocti Harbor Resort & Spa in Kelseyville.

From north to south, the following four wineries are the best; some offer tours by appointment.

Ceago Vinegarden (☎ 707-274-1462; www.ceago.com; 5115 E Hwy 20, Nice; ⏰ 10am-6pm) Ceago (cee-*ay*-go) occupies a spectacular spot on the north shore, and pours bio-dynamic, fruit-forward wines.

Wildhurst Vineyards (☎ 800-595-9463; 3855 Main St, Kelseyville; ⏰ 10am-5pm) Wildhurst makes the best wine on the lake – try the sauvignon blanc – but lacks atmosphere.

Ployez Winery (☎ 707-994-2106; 1171 S Hwy 29, Lower Lake; ⏰ 11am-5pm) Ployez makes above-average *méthode champenoise* sparkling wines and is surrounded by farmland.

Guenoc & Langtry Estate Vineyards (☎ 707-987-2385 ext 200; 21000 Butts Canyon Rd, Middletown; ⏰ 11:30am-5pm) These are the most beautiful vineyards; port is what's best to drink.

Sleeping & Eating

Make reservations on weekends and during summer.

LAKEPORT & KELSEYVILLE

Lakeport English Inn (☎ 707-263-4317; www.lakeportenglishinn.com; 675 N Main St, Lakeport; r $145-175, cottages $190; ⊠ ❋) The finest B&B at Clear Lake is an 1875 Carpenter Gothic with 10 impeccably furnished rooms, styled with a nod to the English countryside. Saturday and Sunday, there's high tea (public welcome by reservation) – with real Devonshire cream.

Arbor House Inn (☎ 707-263-6444; www.arborhousebnb.com; 150 Clear Lake Ave, Lakeport; r $89-119, ste $139-155; ⊠ ❋) Decorated with dried flowers, this straightforward B&B feels like someone's house. Rooms are dark, but the innkeeper is friendly; there's a garden hot tub.

NORTH COAST

Konocti Harbor Resort & Spa (☎ 707-279-4281, 800-660-5253; www.konoctiharbor.com; 8727 Soda Bay Rd; r $79-139, apt & beach cottages $169-229, ste $219-349; ⊠ ✷ ⊠) On Konocti Bay, 4 miles from Kelseyville, the lake's biggest resort is famous for huge concerts. The gargantuan grounds include four pools, a fitness center, tennis, golf, marina and spa. Rates spike on concert nights.

Waterfront motels with boat slips include well-kept **Skylark Shores Motel** (☎ 707-263-6151, 800-675-6151; www.skylarkshores.com; 1120 N Main St, Lakeport r $91-96, r with kitchen $91-139; ⊠ ✷ ⊠) and cottage-style **Mallard House** (☎ 707-262-1601; www.mallardhouse.com; 970 N Main St; r $59-99; r with kitchen $69-139 ⊠ ✷).

Clear Lake State Park has four **campgrounds** (☎ 800-444-7275; www.reserveamerica.com; sites $15-30) with showers.

Sawshop Bistro (☎ 707-278-0129; www.sawshop bistro.com; 3825 Main St, Kelseyville; small plates $10-12, mains $16-22; ✷ dinner Tue-Sat) You'd be hard-pressed to find any better in Lake County. As well as the regular California-cuisine menu of wild salmon and rack of lamb, there's a small-plates menu of sushi, lobster tacos, Kobe-beef burgers, fish and chips, and flatbread pizzas, all available at the small wine bar.

Park Place (☎ 707-263-0444; 50 3rd St, Lakeport; dinner mains $10-22; ✷ 11am-9pm) Everything is made in-house at this cheerful café, where the consistently good cooking includes lunchtime soups and sandwiches, and pastas, steak, duck and seafood at dinner.

For meatloaf and BLTs, visit **Ashley's** (☎ 707-263-1399; 155 N Main St, Lakeport; mains $8-16; ✷ 11am-8:30pm). The Mexican food at **TNT on the Lake** (☎ 707-263-4868; 1 1st St; mains $8-11; ✷ 11am-9pm) is nothing special, but the views are.

Kelseyville hosts a **farmers market** (☎ 707-928-4685; Hwy 29 & Thomas Rd; ✷ 8am-noon Sat May-Oct).

NORTH SHORE
Sea Breeze Resort (☎ 707-998-3327; www.seabreeze resort.net; 9595 Harbor Dr, Glenhaven; cottages $95, cottages with kitchen $120-140; ⊠ ✷) Just south of Lucerne on a small peninsula, these seven spotless lakeside cottages are surrounded by gardens. All have barbecues.

Gingerbread Cottage (☎ 707-274-0200, 888-880-5253; www.gingerbreadcottages.com; cottages $140-210; 4057 E Hwy 20, Nice; ⊠ ✷ ☐ ⊠) Cottages on a hill face the lake, with good mattresses and extras like in-room sherry and bathrobes. Kayaks are available for rent.

Featherbed Railroad Co (☎ 707-274-8378, 800-966-6322; www.featherbedrailroad.com; 2870 Lakeshore Blvd, Nice; cabooses incl breakfast $102-180; ⊠ ✷ ⊠) A treat for train buffs and kids, Featherbed has 10 comfy, real cabooses on a grassy lawn. Some of the cabooses straddle the border between kitschy and tacky (the 'Easy Rider' has a mirrored ceiling), but they're great fun if you keep a sense of humor. There's a tiny beach across the road.

Scotty's Garden Cafe (☎ 707-274-0134; 6034 E Hwy 20, Lucerne; dishes under $10; ✷ 7am-7pm Sun & Mon, 7am-9pm Tue-Sat) Scotty's makes breakfasts, sandwiches, soups, salads and pastas.

MIDDLETOWN
Harbin Hot Springs (☎ 707-987-2377, 800-622-2477; www.harbin.org; Harbin Hot Springs Rd, Middletown; camping midweek/weekend $25/30, dm $35/50, s midweek $60-75, weekend $90-115, d midweek $90-180, weekend $130-250) Harbin is classic Northern California. Originally a 19th-century health spa and resort, it now has a retreat-center vibe and people come to unwind in silent, clothing-optional hot- and cold-spring pools. This is the birthplace of Watsu (floating massage) and there are wonderful body therapies as well as yoga, holistic-health workshops and 1160 acres of hiking. Accommodations are in Victorian buildings (which could use sprucing up) and share a common vegetarian-only kitchen. Food is available at the market, café and restaurant. Day-trippers are welcome; day rates cost $20/25 (weekday/weekend).

The springs are 3 miles off Hwy 175. From Middletown, take Barnes St, which becomes Big Canyon Rd, and head left at the fork.

Drinking
Mount St Helena Brewing Co (☎ 707-987-3361; 21167 Calistoga Rd, Middletown) This microbrewery has decent pub grub.

Carlos & Vinny's (☎ 707-263-6493; 370 S Main St) There's live music on Friday and Saturday, and food nightly.

Entertainment
Konocti Harbor Resort & Spa (☎ 707-279-4281; 800-225-2277; www.konoctiharbor.com; 8727 Soda Bay Rd) presents headliners like Lyle Lovett in an outdoor amphitheater and indoor concert hall.

Library Park, in Lakeport, has free lakeside Friday-evening summer concerts, from blues to rockabilly.

Harbin Hot Springs (www.harbin.org; Harbin Hot Springs Rd, Middletown) presents a surprising line-up of world music and dances.

Getting There & Around

From San Francisco to Clear Lake takes 2½ to three hours to drive. Highway 175 from Hopland is winding and slow; Hwy 101 to Hwy 20 is easier and takes as long.

Greyhound no longer serves Clear Lake. **Lake Transit** (☎ 707-263-3334, 707-994-3334; www.laketransit.org) operates weekday routes. Buses between Middletown and Calistoga run on Monday and Wednesday; on Thursday they connect through to Santa Rosa. Buses serve Ukiah, from Clearlake via Lakeport, Monday through Saturday.

ANDERSON VALLEY

Rolling hills lord it above pastoral Anderson Valley, famous for apple orchards, vineyards, pastures and quiet. Visitors come primarily to winery-hop, but there's good hiking and bicycling in the surrounding hills, and the chance to escape civilization – just like the locals have.

Orientation & Information

Boonville (population 700) and Philo (population 400) are the valley's principal towns. From Ukiah, winding Hwy 253 heads 20 miles south to Boonville. Equally scenic Hwy 128 twists and turns 60 miles between Cloverdale on Hwy 101, south of Hopland, and Albion on coastal Hwy 1. This is the route to Mendocino from San Francisco.

Anderson Valley Chamber of Commerce (☎ 707-895-2379; www.andersonvalleychamber.com) For tourist information.

KZYX FM Tune to 88.3, 90.7 or 91.5 for community radio.

Sights & Activities

The **Anderson Valley Historical Society Museum** (☎ 707-895-3207; www.andersonvalleymuseum.org; 12340 Hwy 128; ☽ 1-4pm Fri-Sun Mar-Nov), in a little red schoolhouse west of Boonville, displays historical artifacts. **Anderson Valley Brewing Co** (☎ 707-895-2337; www.avbc.com; 17700 Hwy 153; tours $5), east of the Hwy 128 crossroads, crafts award-winning beers in a Bavarian-style brewhouse. Tours leave at 1:30pm and 4pm daily; call ahead.

The valley's cool nights yield high-acid, fruit-forward, food-friendly wines. Pinot noir, chardonnay and dry gewürztraminer

flourish. Most **wineries** (www.avwines.com) are outside Philo. Many are family-owned and offer tastings; some give tours:

Navarro (☎ 707-895-3686; 5601 Hwy 128; ☽ 10am-6pm) This is the best option, and picnicking is encouraged.

Lazy Creek (☎ 707-895-3623; 4741 Hwy 128) Surrounded by lovely gardens, romantic and tiny Lazy Creek is up a half-mile dirt road; it's open when the gate is (call ahead).

Handley (☎ 707-895-3876, 800-733-3151; www.handleycellars.com; 3151 Hwy 128; ☽ 10am-6pm) The tasting room at Handley has cool tribal art.

Husch (☎ 800-554-8724; 4400 Hwy 128; ☽ 10am-5pm) Husch serves tastings inside a rose-covered cottage.

Esterlina (☎ 707-895-2920; www.esterlinavineyards.com) For big reds, pack a picnic and head high up the rolling hills to Esterlina; call ahead.

For the best fruit, skip the obvious roadside stands and instead head to **Apple Farm** (☎ 707-895-2333; www.philoapplefarm.com; 18501 Greenwood Rd, Philo) for organic preserves, chutneys, heirloom apples and pears; open daylight hours. The farm also rents spiffy orchard cottages for $175 to $200, and hosts **cooking classes** with some of the Wine Country's best chefs.

Festivals & Events

Annual celebrations include the **Boonville Beer Festival**, **California Wool & Fiber Festival** and **Pinot Noir Festival**, all in May, followed by the **Wild Iris Folk Festival** in June. Mid-September brings the **Mendocino County Fair**.

Sleeping

Accommodations fill on weekends.

Philo Pottery Inn (☎ 707-895-3069; www.philopotteryinn.com; 8550 Hwy 128, Philo; r $110-165) Made from unfinished redwood, this cozy 1888 B&B has comfy rooms and flower gardens. The house is the oldest structure in the entire valley and has a wonderful historic vibe.

Boonville Hotel (☎ 707-895-2210; www.boonvillehotel.com; 14040 Hwy 128; r $100-175, ste $200-250; ✗) Decked out in a contemporary American-country style with sea-grass flooring, pastel colors and fine linens that would make Martha Stewart proud, this historic hotel's rooms are safe for urbanites who refuse to abandon style just because they've gone to the country.

Anderson Valley Inn (☎ 707-895-3325; www.avinn.com; 8480 Hwy 128, Philo; r $65-85, r with kitchen $85-95; ✗) This small motel has fresh-looking, good-value rooms.

Other Place (☎ 707-895-3979; www.sheepdung.com; cottages $175-250) Outside of town, the Other Place has secluded, private hilltop cottages surrounded by 500 acres ranch lands. Dogs welcome.

Hendy Woods State Park (☎ 707-937-5804, reservations 800-444-7275; www.reserveamerica.com; sites $20-25; cabins $50) Bordered by the Navarro River on Hwy 128, west of Philo, the park has hiking, picnicking and a forested campground with hot showers.

Wellspring Retreat Center (☎ 707-895-3893; www.wellspringrenewal.org; Ray's Rd, Philo; sites $20, cabins from $30) Wellspring has rustic cottages without bathrooms; bring bedding and towels. Reservations essential.

Eating & Drinking

Boonville Hotel (www.boonvillehotel.com; 14040 Hwy 128; mains $13-25; ☷ dinner Thu-Mon) The Boonville serves perfect roadhouse cooking for food-savvy travelers. The New American menu features simple dishes done well, like roasted chicken and strawberry shortcake. Thursdays there's a three-course prix-fixe deal ($28) with no corkage.

Libby's (☎ 707-895-2646; 8651 Hwy 128, Philo; mains $6-12; ☷ Tue-Sun) Miss Libby makes good Mexican. There's no tequila but there's beer.

Lauren's (☎ 707-895-3869; 14211 Hwy 128, Boonville; mains $9-14; ☷ dinner Tue-Sat) Locals pack Lauren's for homemade Cal-American cookin'. Musicians sometimes jam.

Boonville General Store (☎ 707-895-9477; 17810 Farrer Lane; dishes $5-8; ☷ 9am-3pm Thu-Mon) Opposite the Boonville Hotel, the general store is perfect for picnics – sandwiches on homemade bread, thin-crust pizzas and organic cheeses.

A **farmers market** (☷ 9:45am-noon Sat Jun-Oct) is held at the Boonville Hotel. **Boont Berry Farm** (☎ 707-895-3576; 13981 Hwy 128) has a small deli.

UKIAH

pop 15,500

Ringed by 4000ft-high peaks, in the fertile Yokayo Valley, Ukiah means 'deep valley' in the Pomo language. During autumn, orchards and vineyards explode with fruit. Although it's Mendocino's county seat, there's not a lot here, but there are numerous affordable lodgings and great hiking nearby, making Ukiah a good base for hopping between outlying wineries, hot springs and nature reserves.

> **BOONTLING**
>
> Boonville is famous for its unique language, 'Boontling,' which developed about the turn of the 20th century when Boonville was very remote. Locals developed the language to *shark* (stump) outsiders and amuse themselves. You may hear *codgie kimmies* (old men) asking for a horn of *zeese* (a cup of coffee) or some *bahl gorms* (good food). If you are really lucky, you'll spot the tow truck called Boont Region De-arkin' Moshe (literally, Anderson Valley Un-wrecking Machine).

Orientation & Information

Running north–south, west of Hwy 101, State St is Ukiah's main drag, the location of most motels and restaurants. School St, near Perkins St, is good for strolling.

Bureau of Land Management (☎ 707-468-4000; 2550 N State St) Maps and information on backcountry camping, hiking and biking in wilderness areas.

Greater Ukiah Chamber of Commerce (☎ 707-462-4705; www.gomendo.com; 200 S School St; ☷ 9am-5pm Mon-Fri) One block west of State St, come here for information on Ukiah, Hopland and Anderson Valley.

Sights

Don't miss **Sun House-Grace Hudson Museum** (☎ 707-467-2836; www.gracehudsonmuseum.org; 431 S Main St; donation $2; ☷ 10am-4:30pm Wed-Sat, noon-4:30pm Sun), one block east of State St. The collection's mainstays are paintings by Grace Hudson (1865–1937), whose sensitive depictions of Pomo people complement the ethnological work and Native American baskets collected by her husband, John Hudson. Guided tours of their 1911 Craftsman-style redwood bungalow depart on demand.

North of downtown, check out the **Redwood Tree Service Station** (859 N State St), a former gas station carved out of a redwood tree.

Festivals & Events

Special events include the **Redwood Empire Fair**, on the second weekend of August, and the **Ukiah Country PumpkinFest** in late October, with an arts and crafts fair, children's carnival and fiddle contest.

Sleeping

Chains include Motel 6, Days Inn and Best Western, and there are resorts and campgrounds around Ukiah (see p255).

NORTH COAST

Robinson Creek Inn (☎ 707-468-9039; www.robin soncreek.com; 1901 Boonville Rd; r $120-140; ✗ ⊠ ☐) Gorgeous gardens lead from the 1878 farmhouse to a swimming hole behind this country-casual, peaceful, two-room B&B-cum-flower farm. Breakfast includes eggs from the inn's own chickens.

Holiday Inn Express (☎ 707-462-5745, 800-465-4329; www.hiexpress.com/ukiahca; 1720 N State St; r $89-99; ✗ ☐ ☒) Of Ukiah's cookie-cutter chains, this is the newest and best, and provides an expanded continental breakfast, laundry machines and wi-fi.

Sunrise Inn (☎ 707-462-6601; www.sunriseinn.net; 650 S State St; r $48-68; ✗) Ukiah's best budget motel is clean and well kept, with microwave and refrigerator in every room. Request a remodeled room.

Also consider:

Discovery Inn Motel (☎ 707-462-8873; www.5motels .com; 1340 N State St; r $82-89; ✗ ☒) Clean, but dated; facilities include a 75ft pool and four Jacuzzis.

Sanford House B&B (☎ 707-462-1653; www.sanford house.com; 306 S Pine St; s $75-125, d $150; ✗ ✗)

Eating

Patrona (☎ 707-462-9181; www.patronarestaurant .com; 130 W Standley St; lunch mains $9-15, dinner $16-22; ✗ lunch Mon-Fri, dinner Tue-Sat) Foodies flock to Patrona for earthy, flavor-packed, seasonal-regional organic cooking. The unfussy menu includes dishes like roasted chicken with pan jus, brined-and-roasted pork chops, housemade pasta, flat-bread pizzas and local wines. Make reservations and be sure to arrive early for the three-course, $16 prix fixe.

Oco Time (☎ 707-462-2422; 111 W Church St; lunch mains $7-10, dinner $8-16; ✗ lunch Tue-Fri, dinner Mon-Sat) Always-busy Oco Time makes Ukiah's best sushi, teriyaki, noodle bowls and *oco* – grilled cabbage, egg and noodles. Yum.

Ruen Tong (☎ 707-462-0238; 801 N State St; mains $8-12; ✗ 11am-9pm) This little Thai spot is decked out with glittering decorations; try the pumpkin curry, spicy eggplant or barbecued salmon.

Schat's Courthouse Bakery & Cafe (☎ 707-462-1670; 113 W Perkins St; lunch $3-7, dinner $8-14; ✗ 6am-8:30pm Mon-Sat) Schat's makes chewy, dense breads, great sandwiches, wraps, big salads, dee-lish hot mains and homemade pastries.

Himalayan Cafe (☎ 707-467-9900; 1639 S State St; lunch buffet $7, dinner $8-12) South of downtown Ukiah, the Himalayan serves up delicately spiced Nepalese cooking – tandoori breads, curries and veggie dishes.

Angelo's Italian (☎ 707-462-0448; 920 N State St; lunch $9-11, dinner $12-16; ✗ lunch Mon-Fri, dinner Mon-Sat) If you have any screaming kids, feed 'em spaghetti.

Coffee Critic (☎ 707-462-6333; 476 N State St; snacks $3-6; ✗ 7am-7pm) Espresso, ice cream and occasional live music.

Ukiah farmers market (cnr School & Clay Sts; ✗ 8:30am-noon Sat, 3-6pm Tue Jun-Oct) has farm-fresh produce, crafts and entertainment.

Moore's Flour Mill & Bakery (☎ 707-462-6550; 1550 S State St; ✗ 7:30am-6pm Mon-Sat) grinds flour for its homebaked soft-style bread used on its deli sandwiches; great cookies, too. For order-at-the-counter, so-so vegetarian, try **Ellie's Mutt Hut** (☎ 707-468-5376; 732 S State St; dishes under $10; ✗ 6:30am-8pm Mon-Sat).

Drinking & Entertainment

Dive bars, scruffy cocktail lounges and saloons line State St downtown. Ask at the chamber of commerce about the cultural events, including Sunday summer concerts at Todd Grove Park and local square dances.

Ukiah Brewing Co (☎ 707-468-5898; 102 S State St) This local brewpub makes organic beer and draws weekend crowds for live music.

Mendocino College (☎ 707-468-3063, 707-468-3172, 707-468-3012; www.mendocinocollege.edu; 1000 Hensley Creek Rd, Ukiah) Students present theater, dance and music concerts.

Shopping

Ukiah's best shopping is along School St, near the courthouse.

Nomad's World (☎ 707-462-4060; 111 S School St; ✗ Mon-Sat) Step inside for cool jewelry and home furnishings.

POETIC LANDSCAPE

Hippie-dippie locals point out that Ukiah written backwards spells haiku. For a fun car game, write relevant verse about the landscape in the classic five-seven-five form. Here's one to get you started:

Apples, wine and cheese
The bounty of the season
Ukiah autumn.

NORTH COAST

> ## MEDICAL MARIJUANA: CULTIVATING CONFLICT
>
> In 1996 California voters approved Proposition 215, which legalized the medicinal use of marijuana. With a doctor's note, patients could now legally grow pot or buy it at 'cannabis clubs' without fear of legal reprisal.
>
> The North Coast has the ideal pot-growing climate. In Mendocino County, you might even spot Mary Jane growing in people's *front* yards. In Ukiah in August, the pungent, sweet smell of skunk-weed fills the air. But growers risk theft. The law allows people to plant a 10ft-by-10ft plot. You can fit 20 plants in a plot that size. Each can yield $4000 on the black market, so one plot alone can bring in $80,000. Interestingly enough, the number of pot permits in Mendocino County coincides with the number of concealed-weapons permits: about 1300.
>
> Legal conflicts abound. California's law directly contradicts federal drug laws, and in America federal law trumps state law – theoretically. In June 2005, the US Supreme Court ruled that federal agents could indeed enforce federal law and pursue medical-marijuana users. However, the justices did *not* specifically overturn Prop 215. In Gonzales v. Raich, Justice Stevens wrote in the Opinion of the Court: '…despite a congressional finding to the contrary, marijuana does have valid therapeutic purposes.'
>
> Local conflicts have also arisen. In the 1980s, while Nancy Reagan told America's kids to 'just say no,' Ronnie sprayed California's marijuana fields with the toxic herbicide paraquat. Young botanists retaliated by just saying no, thank you, and quietly began formulating new strains of genetically modified pot that grew well indoors – and they were *far* more potent than outdoor pot had ever been. Fast-forward to Mendocino, March 2004, when voters approved a new law banning the propagation of genetically modified organisms (GMOs) anywhere in the county. If this law is enforced, then technically Mendo's pot crops are illegal – under local law – in a county that overwhelmingly supported Prop 215. Go figure.
>
> For the latest updates while you're in Mendo and Humboldt counties, tune in to community FM-radio stations. In June, you might even hear 'fly-over warnings' broadcasted to alert locals about federal officials running pot-spotting training missions.

Ukiah Antique Mall (☎ 707-462-5559; 116 N School St; ⊗ Mon-Sat) Browse around the mall for a mishmash of antiques.

Ruby Slippers (☎ 707-462-7829; 110 N School St; ⊗ Mon-Sat) Ruby Slippers has super-fun vintage drag.

Mendocino Book Co (☎ 707-468-5940; 102 S School St; ⊗ Mon-Sat) The best bookstore in town.

AROUND UKIAH
Wineries
Pick up a wineries map from the **Ukiah Chamber of Commerce** (200 S School St).

Fruit-forward reds from **Fife** (☎ 707-485-0323; www.fifevineyards.com; 3621 Ricetti Lane, Redwood Valley; ⊗ 10am-5pm) winery include a peppery zinfandel and petite sirah, both affordable and food-friendly. And oh! the hilltop views; bring a picnic.

Germain-Robin (☎ 707-462-0314; www.caddellwilliams.com; 3001 S State St, Unit #35; ⊗ 10am-4pm Mon-Sat) makes some of the world's best brandy, which is handcrafted by a fifth-generation brandy-maker from the Cognac region of France. Really. It's just a freeway-side warehouse, but if you're into cognac, you gotta come. Call ahead.

Lolonis (☎ 925-938-8066, 707-485-7544; www.lolonis.com; 1905 Rd D; Redwood Valley) is known for big reds – cabernet, merlot and petite sirah – and for its signature Ladybug Red, some made with estate-grown old-vine grapes. Appointments required.

Vichy Hot Springs Resort
Opened in 1854, Vichy is the oldest continuously operating mineral-springs spa in California. The water's composition perfectly matches that of its famous namesake in Vichy, France. A century ago, Mark Twain, Jack London and Robert Louis Stevenson traveled here for the water's restorative properties, which ameliorate everything from arthritis to poison oak.

Today, the beautifully maintained historic **resort** (☎ 707-462-9515; www.vichysprings.com; 2605 Vichy Springs Rd; RV sites $25, lodge s/d $115/155, creek-side r $165/205, cottages $285; ☒ ☒ ☒) has the only warm-water, naturally carbonated mineral baths in North America. Unlike others, Vichy requires swimsuits (rentals $1.50). Day use costs $25 for two hours, $38 for a full day.

Facilities include a swimming pool, outdoor mineral hot tub, 10 indoor and outdoor tubs with natural 100°F waters, and a grotto for sipping the effervescent waters. Massages and facials are also available. Entry includes use of the 700-acre grounds, abutting BLM lands; hiking trails lead to a 40ft waterfall, an old cinnabar mine and 1100ft peaks – great for sunset views.

The resort's suite and two cottages, built in 1854, are Mendocino County's three oldest structures. The cozy rooms have wooden floors, top-quality beds, breakfast and spa privileges but no TVs. RV parking doesn't include breakfast or spa entry; there's no tent camping.

From Hwy 101, exit at Vichy Springs Rd and follow the state-landmark signs east for 3 miles. Ukiah is five minutes, but a world, away.

Orr Hot Springs

A clothing-optional resort that's beloved by locals, back-to-the-land hipsters, backpackers and liberal-minded tourists, **Orr Hot Springs** (☎ 707-462-6277; hotwater@pacific.net; sites $40-45, dm $55-65, s $92-100, d $115-135, cottages $160-185 ☷ 10am-10pm) has a communal redwood hot tub, private porcelain tubs, outdoor tile-and-rock heated pools, sauna, springfed rock-bottom swimming pool, steam, massage and magical gardens. Day use cost is $22.

Accommodation includes use of the spa and communal kitchen (carnivores are welcome). Reservations are essential.

To get there from Hwy 101, take N State St exit, go north a quarter of a mile to Orr Springs Rd, then 9 miles west. The steep, winding mountain road takes 30 minutes to drive.

Montgomery Woods State Reserve

Two miles west of Orr, this 1140-acre **reserve** (☎ 707-937-5804) protects five old-growth redwood groves. A 2-mile loop trail crosses the creek, winding through the groves, starting near the picnic tables and toilets. Day use only; no camping.

Lake Mendocino

Amid rolling hills, only just 5 miles northeast of Ukiah, this 1822-acre artificial lake fills a valley, once the ancestral home of the Pomo people. On the lake's north side, **Pomo Visitors Center** (☎ 707-485-8285; Marina Dr; ☷ 9am-5pm Wed-Sun summer) is modeled after a Pomo roundhouse, with exhibits on tribal culture and the dam.

Coyote Dam, 3500ft long and 160ft high, marks the lake's southwest corner; the lake's eastern part is a 689-acre protected wildlife habitat. The **Army Corps of Engineers** (☎ 707-462-7581; www.spn.usace.army.mil/mendocino; 1160 Lake Mendocino Dr; ☷ Mon-Fri) built the dam, manages the lake, and provides recreation information. Its office is inconveniently located on the Lower Lake.

There are 300 **campsites** (☎ 877-444-6777; www.reserveusa.com; sites $16-22), most with hot showers. Some are reservable, others first-come, first-served. There are also primitive boat-in sites ($8).

For Upper Lake, turn east from Hwy 101 onto Hwy 20, north of Ukiah. You'll see the lake on your right. Follow the signs to the visitors center and campgrounds.

City of Ten Thousand Buddhas

Three miles east of Ukiah, via Talmage Rd, the **City of Ten Thousand Buddhas** (☎ 707-462-0939; www.advite.com/sf; 2001 Talmage Rd; ☷ 8am-6pm) used to be a state mental hospital. Now it's a 488-acre Chinese-Buddhist community. Don't miss the temple hall, which really does have 10,000 Buddhas! Be discreet. Stay for lunch in the vegetarian-Chinese **restaurant** (4951 Bodhi Way; dishes $6-9; ☷ 11am-3pm Mon, Wed & Thu, 11am-6pm Fri-Sun).

WILLITS
pop 5000

Twenty miles north of Ukiah, Willits has a NoCal boho vibe. Ranching, timber and manufacturing may be its mainstays but tie-dye is de rigueur. For visitors, Willits' greatest claim to fame is as the eastern terminus of the Skunk Train. Fort Bragg is 35 miles away on the coast; allow an hour to navigate the improperly graded, winding Hwy 20 (bring Dramamine).

Just south of downtown, the Willits Arch proclaims: 'Gateway to the Redwoods' and 'Heart of Mendocino County' – a bit of a stretch. The arch originally towered over Reno, from 1964 to 1987, until it was re-erected here in the 1990s. Still, it's good for pictures.

NORTH COAST

Orientation & Information

To the north, Hwy 101 becomes Main St.
Sugar Magnolia (☎ 707-459-0396; 212 S Main St; Internet access free; ⏱ 11am-10pm Mon-Sat, noon-8pm Sun) Check your email over an ice cream.
Willits Chamber of Commerce (☎ 707-459-7910; www.willits.org; 239 S Main St; ⏱ 10am-4pm Mon-Fri) Oodles of information.

Sights & Activities

The depot for the **Skunk Train** (☎ 707-459-5248, 866-457-5865; www.skunktrain.com) is on E Commercial St, three blocks east of Hwy 101. Trains run between Willits and Fort Bragg (for details, see p245).

The not-to-be-missed **Mendocino County Museum** (☎ 707-459-2736; 400 E Commercial St; by donation individual/family $2/5; ⏱ 10am-4:30pm Wed-Sun) has an entire 1920s soda fountain and barber shop inside. You could spend an hour perusing Pomo and Yuki basketry and artifacts, or reading about local scandals and counter-cultural movements. Outside, the **Roots of Motive Power** (www.rootsofmotivepower.com) exhibit has occasional demonstrations of steam logging and machinery, plus lumberjack handcar races in September.

Willits' most famous resident was the horse Seabiscuit, which grew up on **Ridgewood Ranch** (☎ 707-459-5992, reservations 707-459-7910; www.seabiscuitheritage.com; 16200 N Hwy 101; tours $15-25). There are 90-minute tours on Monday, Wednesday and Friday from June to September; Saturday once a month there's a three-hour tour by reservation.

Set among giant redwoods, **Brooktrails Golf Course** (☎ 707-459-6761; 24860 Birch St), off Sherwood Rd, 2 miles north of downtown, is one of Northern California's most picturesque nine-hole public courses. Greens fees cost $12/18 (nine/18 holes).

Jackson Demonstration State Forest, 15 miles west of Willits on Hwy 20, offers day-use recreational activities, including educational hiking trails and mountain-biking (the Department of Forestry in Fort Bragg has maps and information; see p247).

Festivals & Events

Celtic Renaissance Faire Held in May, the event features Highland Scottish games, food, music, dancing, jugglers, arts and crafts.
Willits Frontier Days & Rodeo Held on the first week in July, and dating from 1926, Willits' is 'the oldest continuous rodeo in California.'

Sleeping

Beside Still Waters Farm (☎ 707-984-6130, 877-230-2171; www.besidestillwatersfarm.com; 30901 Sherwood Rd; 1-bedroom cottages $229-249, 2-bedroom cottages $269; ✗) For a romantic splurge, stay in a luxurious B&B cottage on 21 acres.

Willits Creek Cabin (☎ 707-456-0201; willitscreekcabin@sbcglobal.net; 190 Bittenbender Lane; s/d $85/100) A 1930s mill-worker's cottage walkable to downtown, this vacation rental has a loft, gas fireplace and barbecue, and sleeps six.

Some of the in-town motels are dumps, so choose carefully. Ask about Skunk Train packages.

Upmarket motels include the top-choice **Baechtel Creek Inn & Spa** (☎ 707-459-9063, 800-459-9911; www.baechtelcreekinn.com; 101 Gregory Lane; r $70-100; ✗ 😺 🖥 🐾) and second-choice **Super 8 Motel** (☎ 707-459-3388, 800-800-8000; www.super8.com; 1119 S Main St; r $69-89; ✗ 😺 🐾).

Cheaper options include **Best Value Inn Holiday Lodge** (☎ 707-459-5361, 800-835-3972; www.bestvalueinn.com; 1540 S Main St; r $69-99; 😺 🖥 🐾); the quiet, Old West-themed **Old West Inn** (☎ 707-459-4201, 800-700-7659; fax 707-459-3009; 1221 S Main St; r $69-89; ✗ 😺 🐾); or the dated but clean **Edgewood Motel** (☎ 707-459-5914; fax 707-459-4875; 1521 S Main St; r $45-55; 😺).

Creekside Cabins & RV Resort (☎ 707-459-2521; www.creeksidecabinsandrvresort.com; 29801 N Hwy 101; tent sites $22, RV sites $27-33, cabins $155) Seven miles north of Willits, camp or stay in a six-person housekeeping cabin.

Willits KOA Resort (☎ 707-459-6179, 800-562-8542; Hwy 20; tent sites $20-36, RV sites $31-45, cabins $38-64; 🐾) Two miles west of downtown, KOA has hiking and family-oriented activities.

Jackson Demonstration State Forest (☎ 707-964-5674; www.fire.ca.gov/php/rsrc-mgt_jackson.php; sites free) This forest has campsites with barbecue pits and pit toilets, but no water. Get a permit from the on-site host.

Eating

Purple Thistle (☎ 707-459-4750; 50 S Main St; mains $13-19; ⏱ dinner) Willits' best cooks up Cajun- and Japanese-inspired 'Mendonesian' cuisine, using fresh organic ingredients. Make reservations.

Anna's Asian House (☎ 707-459-6086; 47 Mendocino Ave; mains $6-10; ⏱ 11am-9pm) Skip the Chinese joint on Main St and come here for Szechuan cooking, made with no MSG and little oil.

Phoenix Bread Co (☎ 707-456-9970; www.phoenixbreadcompany.com; 861 S Main St; dishes under $10;

8am-8pm Wed-Mon) Next door to Safeway, Phoenix makes fantastic cheese-and-meat-stuffed country-style bread and finger-lickin' barbecue.

There are good quick eats in Willits. Tiny **Ardella's Kitchen** (☎ 707-459-6577; 35 E Commercial St; meals $5-8; 6am-noon Tue-Sat) is tops for breakfast – and *the* place for gossip. For soup and sandwiches, visit **Loose Caboose** (☎ 707-459-1434; 10 Woods St; dishes under $10; breakfast & lunch). **Gribaldo's Cafe** (☎ 707-459-2256; 1551 S Main St; dishes $6-10; 6am-10pm) has $2.99 breakfasts and $7 weekday breakfast-and-lunch buffets. For healthful Mexican, try **Burrito Exquisito** (☎ 707-459-5421; 42 S Hain St; dishes $6; 11am-9pm).

A **farmers market** (cnr Humboldt & State Sts; 3-6pm Thu, May-Oct) meets one block off Hwy 101. Pick up natural foods at the **Mariposa Market** (☎ 707-459-9630; 600 S Main St).

Drinking & Entertainment

Shanaghie Pub (☎ 707-459-9194; 50B S Main St; Mon-Sat) and **Sugar Magnolia** (☎ 707-456-0396; 212 S Main) have live entertainment on Wednesday and Friday.

Willits Community Theatre (☎ 707-459-0895; www.allaboutwct.org; 212 S Main St) stages award-winning plays, poetry readings and comedy year-round.

THE REDWOOD COAST

Few visitors venture beyond the 'redwood curtain,' so you will have room to roam and won't see many people. But you will see trees. Lots of them. So much of the coastal drive passes through forested areas that you can lose perspective and forget that you're by the ocean. Though it's magical beneath the canopy of trees, stop at pullouts for an overview of the rocky coast, the wildflower-studded prairie lands and dense woods through which you're driving. You'll marvel at the scale.

LEGGETT

pop 200

Leggett marks the redwood country's beginning and Hwy 1's end. There ain't much but an expensive gas station, lunch counter, pizza joint and two markets.

The 1000-acre **Standish-Hickey State Recreation Area** (☎ 707-925-6482; 69350 Hwy 101; per car $6), 1.5 miles to the north, has picnicking, swim-

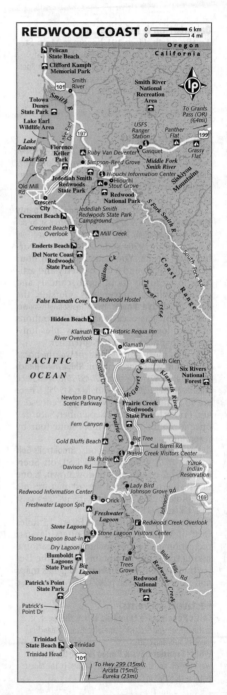

ming and fishing in the Eel River and hiking trails among virgin and second-growth redwoods. Year-round **campgrounds** (☎ 800-444-7275; www.reserveamerica.com; sites $15-20) with hot showers book up in summer. Avoid highway-side sites.

Chandelier Drive-Thru Tree Park (☎ 707-925-6363; www.drivethrutree.com; Drive-Thru Tree Rd; per car $3; ☺ 8am-dusk) has 200 private acres of virgin redwoods with picnicking and nature walks. And yes, there's a redwood with a square hole carved out, which cars can drive through. Only in America.

Across from the Confusion Hill tourist trap, **Redwoods River Resort** (☎ 707-925-6249; www.redwoodriverresort.com; 75000 Hwy 101; tent sites $22-28, RV sites $31-33, cabins $80-115, lodge r $75-125) has a range of lodgings, good for families.

For basic supplies, groceries, sandwiches and brownies, visit **Price's Peg House** (☎ 707-925-6444; 69501 Hwy 101; ☺ 8am-9pm).

RICHARDSON GROVE STATE PARK

Fifteen miles to the north, and bisected by the Eel River, **Richardson Grove** (☎ 707-247-3318; Hwy 101; per car $6) occupies 1400 acres of virgin forest. Many trees are over 1000 years old and 300ft tall. The **visitors center** (☎ 707-247-3318; ☺ 9am-2pm) sells books and gifts inside a 1930s lodge, which often has a roaring fire going in cool weather.

The park has three **campgrounds** (☎ reservations 800-444-7275; www.reserveamerica.com; sites $15-20) with hot showers, some remain open year-round.

BENBOW LAKE

On the Eel River, 2 miles south of Garberville, the 1200-acre **Benbow Lake State Recreation Area** (☎ in summer 707-923-3238, in winter 707-923-3318; per car $6) holds a dam that forms 26-acre Benbow Lake, mid-June to mid-September. Events include summer jazz and Shakespeare festivals, and holiday celebrations from Thanksgiving to New Year's Day.

A monument to 1920s rustic elegance, **Benbow Inn** (☎ 707-923-2124, 800-355-3301; www.benbowinn.com; 445 Lake Benbow Dr; r $130-305, cottage $375; ☒ ☒ ☒) is a national historic landmark and the Redwood Empire's first luxury resort. Hollywood's elite once frolicked in the Tudor-style resort's lobby, where you can play chess by the crackling fire, and enjoy a complimentary afternoon tea

and evening hors d'oeuvres. Rooms have top-quality beds and antique furniture. The window-lined dining room (breakfast and lunch $10 to $15, dinner mains $22 to $32) serves excellent Euro-Cal cuisine and Sunday brunch. There's an adjoining golf course and smart-looking RV resort.

Across Hwy 101, the year-round riverside **campground** (☎ reservations 800-444-7275; www.reserveamerica.com; sites $23-28) is subject to bridge closures due to flooding. There's one shower; sites endure highway noise.

GARBERVILLE
pop 1800

Garberville and its ragtag sister Redway (2 miles west) became famous in the 1970s for sinsemilla (potent, seedless marijuana), grown in the surrounding hills after feds chased growers out of Santa Cruz County. Aging hippies and pot-farmer-wannabes roam Redwood Dr, the main drag. Garberville is the primary commercial center.

Information
Garberville-Redway Area Chamber of Commerce (☎ 707-923-2613, 800-923-2613; www.garberville.org; 784 Redwood Dr; ☺ 8am-4pm Mon-Fri, 10am-4pm Sat & Sun summer) Inside the Redwood Dr Center, on the corner of Church St, come here for tourist information.
KMUD FM91 Find out what's really happening by tuning in to community radio.
Treats (☎ 707-923-3554; 764 Redwood Dr; per min 10¢; ☺ 10am-6pm) Internet access and wi-fi.

Festivals & Events
Reggae on the River (☎ 707-923-4583; www.reggaeon theriver.com) in early August draws huge crowds for reggae, world music, arts-and-craft fairs, camping and swimming in the river. Three-day passes ($175) go on sale March 1 and sell out; no single tickets.

Other annual events:
Avenue of the Giants Marathon This race is held in May.
Harley-Davidson Redwood Run Held in June.
Garberville Rodeo June rodeo.
Hemp Fest Celebrate all things hemp in November.
Winter Arts Fair A mid-December fair.

Sleeping
Best Western Humboldt House Inn (☎ 707-923-2771, 800-528-1234; 701 Redwood Dr; r $112-129; ☒ ☒) The best place in town with good beds, upgraded furnishings and refrigerators.

NORTH COAST

For cheaper lodging, first try **Sherwood Forest** (☎ 707-923-2721; www.sherwoodforestmotel.com; 814 Redwood Dr; r $60-76; 🐾 🎵), then **Garberville Motel** (☎ 707-923-2422; fax 707-923-2599; 948 Redwood Dr; r $70-79; 🐾) or **Humboldt Redwoods Inn** (☎ 707-923-2451; www.humboldtredwoodsinn.com; 987 Redwood Dr; r $55-90; 🐾 🎵).

There's camping and lodging at Benbow Lake and the Ave of the Giants.

Eating

Woodrose Cafe (☎ 707-923-3191; 911 Redwood Dr; meals $7-11; ☾ breakfast & lunch) Garberville's best-loved restaurant cooks delicious breakfasts and lunches of tasty sandwiches and organic salads. Vegan dishes, too.

Calico's Deli & Pasta (☎ 707-923-2253; 808 Redwood Dr, Garberville; dishes $6-13; ☾ 11am-9pm) Calico's has housemade pasta and sandwiches.

Mateel Cafe (☎ 707-923-2030; 3342-44 Redwood Dr, Redway; lunch $8-12, dinner $16-24; ☾ 11:30am-9pm Mon-Sat) In Redway, Mateel prepares steaks and chops, stone-baked pizzas, and organic salads.

Cecil's (☎ 707-923-7007; www.cecilsrestaurant.com; 773 Redwood Dr; mains $18-27; ☾ dinner Thu-Mon) Cajun cooking is Cecil's specialty – crawfish *étoufée*, pecan catfish and pork chops with sweet-potato mashers.

Nacho Mama (☎ 707-923-4060; 375 Sprowel Creek Rd; meals under $6; ☾ 11am-7pm Mon-Sat) This tiny shack on the corner of Redwood Dr has organic fast-food Mexican.

Eel River Cafe (☎ 707-923-3783; 801 Redwood Dr; dishes under $10; ☾ 6am-2pm Thu-Mon) This is the place for blueberry-pancake breakfasts.

Chautauqua Natural Foods (☎ 707-923-2452; 436 Church St; ☾ Mon-Sat) Sells natural groceries.

Drinking & Entertainment

Sicilito's (☎ 707-923-2814; 445 Conger St; meals $6-14; ☾ 11:30am-10pm) Behind the Best Western, Sicilito's serves microbrews and frat-boy food.

Benbow Inn (☎ 707-923-2124, 800-355-3301; www.benbowinn.com; 445 Lake Benbow Dr) Sip cocktails in an elegant 1920s Tudor-style inn.

Garberville Theatre (☎ 707-923-3580; 766 Redwood Dr) For first-run movies.

HUMBOLDT REDWOODS STATE PARK & AVENUE OF THE GIANTS

Don't miss this magical drive through California's largest redwood park, **Humboldt Redwoods State Park** (☎ 707-946-2409), which covers 53,000 acres – 17,000 of which are old-growth – and

contains some of the world's most magnificent trees. Exit Hwy 101 when you see the 'Avenue of the Giants' road sign, and travel parallel along this incredible 32-mile, two-lane stretch. You'll find free driving guides at roadside signboards at both the avenue's southern entrance, 6 miles north of Garberville, near Phillipsville, and at the northern entrance, south of Scotia, at Pepperwood; there are access points off Hwy 101.

South of Weott, a volunteer-staffed **visitors center** (☎ 707-946-2263; ☾ 9am-5pm summer, 10am-4pm winter) shows videos and sells field guides, maps and books. Don't bypass its small, excellent **museum** housing the historic 1917 'Travel Log.'

Primeval **Rockefeller Forest**, 4.5 miles west of the avenue via Mattole Rd, appears as it did a century ago. Today it's the world's largest contiguous old-growth redwood forest. In Founders Grove, north of the visitors center, the **Dyerville Giant** was knocked over in 1991 by another falling tree. A walk along its gargantuan 370ft length, with its wide trunk towering above, helps you appreciate how huge these ancient trees are.

The park has over 100 miles of trails for hiking, mountain-biking and horseback riding. Easy walks include short nature trails in Founders Grove and Rockefeller Forest and **Drury-Chaney Loop Trail** (with berry picking in summer). Challenging treks include popular **Grasshopper Peak Trail**, south of the visitors center, which climbs to the 3379ft fire lookout.

For a break from hiking, taste wine at **Riverbend Cellars** (☎ 707-943-9907; www.riverbendcellars.com; 12990 Ave of the Giants, Myers Flat; ☾ 11am-6pm).

Several towns along the avenue have simple lodgings; some are creepy, some run by bigots. The best is the family-friendly **Miranda Gardens Resort** (☎ 707-943-3011; www.mirandagardens.com; 6766 Ave of the Giants, Miranda; cottages $105-135, cottages with kitchen $145-185; 🎵). The cozy, slightly rustic cottages have redwood paneling, and some have fireplaces. Across the street there's a family restaurant.

The park runs three **campgrounds** (☎ reservations 800-444-7275; www.reserveamerica.com; sites $15-20) with hot showers, two environmental camps, five trail camps, a hike/bike camp and an equestrian camp. Of the developed spots, Burlington Campground is open year-round beside the visitors center and near a number of trailheads. Hidden Springs Campground,

5 miles south, and Albee Creek Campground, on Mattole Rd past Rockefeller Forest, are open mid-May to early autumn.

If the park's campsites are full, **Giant Redwoods RV & Campground** (☎ 707-943-3198; www .giantredwoodsrvcamp.com; 455 Boy Scout Camp Rd, Myers Flat; tent/RV sites $24/35) has showers, riverside sites, beaches and activities.

Harley riders pack **Riverwood Inn** (☎ 707-943-3333; www.riverwoodinn.info; 2828 Ave of the Giants, Phillipsville; ⊗ lunch Sat & Sun, dinner Wed-Mon), a haunted roadhouse near Garberville, that hosts blues, folk and rock bands, mixes up strong drinks, and serves OK Mexican cooking. It also rents rooms (r $55-75).

Knights Restaurant (☎ 707-943-1525; 12866 Ave of the Giants, Myers Flat; mains $8-12; ⊗ 8am-3:30pm) is good for breakfast and lunch, with pancakes and benedicts, hot sandwiches and meal-sized salads.

For burgers worth breaking your trip, **Chimney Tree** (☎ 707-923-2265; 1111 Ave of the Giants, Phillipsville; ⊗ 10am-7pm May-Sep) raises its own grass-fed beef. Alas, the fries are frozen, but those burgers…mmm-mmm!

SCOTIA
pop 1000

Scotia is a rarity in modern times: it's one of the last 'company towns' in California, entirely owned and operated by the Pacific Lumber Company (Palco), which runs the world's largest redwood lumber mill. The **Scotia Museum & Visitors Center** (☎ 707-764-2222; www.palco.com; cnr Main & Bridge Sts; ⊗ 8am-4:30pm Mon-Fri summer) is at the town's south end. Free self-guided mill tours are available Monday to Friday. In summer, go to the museum for information; otherwise head to the guardhouse at the mill's entrance.

As you drive along Hwy 101 and see what appears to be a never-ending redwood forest, understand that this 'forest' sometimes consists of trees only a few rows deep, a carefully crafted illusion for tourists. Most of the old-growth trees have been cut. Once you've grasped Palco's party line about 'forestry stewardship,' log on to the website www.headwaterspreserve.org to learn about clear-cutting and the politics of the timber wars. Also tune in to community-radio station KMUD FM 90.3 and 91.1.

But keep your mouth shut. For Scotia's official 'Code of Conduct,' consult placards posted around town. There's one at Hoby's Market, directly opposite the Scotia Inn's front door. You may neither yell, scream nor sing loud enough for anyone else to hear; in other words, no protesting or you'll get arrested.

Scotia is downright creepy, like a set from the *Twilight Zone*. If you're under 50, need a haircut, and forgot to carry your American flag, you'll get suspicious looks. Watch your back: if you feel like you're being followed, you *are*.

There's no compelling reason to linger in Scotia. At this writing, the **Scotia Inn** (☎ 707-764-5683, 707-764-2222, 888-764-2248; www.scotiainn.com; 100 Main St) had closed, but may reopen.

Hoby's Market (☎ 707-764-5331; 105 Main St) sells sandwiches and groceries. There are some nothing-special motels and diners in Rio Dell, across the river.

LOST COAST

California's 'Lost Coast' extends from where Hwy 1 cuts inland, north of Westport, to its northern border near Ferndale. It became 'lost' when the state's highway system bypassed the region early in the 20th century. The steep, rugged King Range rises over 4000ft, less than 3 miles from the coast, with near-vertical cliffs plunging to the sea. High rainfall (over 100 inches annually) causes frequent landslides.

The Lost Coast is one of California's most pristine coastal areas. The central and southern stretches fall respectively within the King Range National Conservation Area and the Sinkyone Wilderness State Park. The area north of the King Range is more accessible, but the scenery less dramatic.

In autumn the weather is clear, if cool. Wildlowers bloom from April through May, and gray whales migrate from December through April. The warmest, driest months are June to August, but days are foggy. The weather can quickly change.

Information

Although there are several one-horse rural settlements (Petrolia and Honeydew, for example), the only sizable community is Shelter Cove, an isolated unincorporated town 25 long miles west of Garberville. The area is a patchwork of government-owned land and private property. Take it easy while driving, especially in fog, and pull over to let people pass. Check for ticks; Lyme disease

NORTH COAST

is common. Don't jump fences or trespass, especially in October at harvest time; this is pot-growing country, and some locals won't hesitate to fire a shotgun in your direction. Locals claim that nearby Cape Mendocino is the westernmost point in the contiguous US. It's not. That honor belongs to Cape Alava, Washington.

Shelter Cove

Surrounded by King Range National Conservation Area, remote Shelter Cove lies on a large south-facing cove. It's a tiny seaside subdivision with an airstrip in the middle – indeed, many visitors are private pilots. Fifty years ago, southern California swindlers subdivided the land, built the airstrip, and flew potential investors into here, fast-talking them into buying seaside plots of land for retirement houses. But they didn't tell buyers that a steep, winding, one-lane dirt road provided the *only* access, and that the seaside plots were eroding into the sea.

Today, there's still only one route, but it is now paved. Cell phones don't work here, so if you want to disappear this is a good place. For a complete list of lodgings, log on to www.sojourner2000.com.

The best place to stay hands down is the sparkling oceanfront **Shelter Cove Bed & Breakfast** (☎ 707-986-7161; www.sheltercovebandb.com; 148 Dolphin Dr; r $145-195; ✗), managed by super-cool, design-savvy owners. Think love nest, and leave the kids at home.

The tidy, modern rooms at **Oceanfront Inn & Lighthouse** (☎ 707-986-7002; www.oceanfrontinn ca.com; 10 Seal Court; r $125-145, ste $145; ✗) have microwaves, refrigerators, and balconies overlooking the sea; kitchen suites are a bargain.

Other recommendations:

Cliff House at Shelter Cove (☎ 707-986-7344; www .cliffhousesheltercove.com; 141 Wave Dr; ste $139-149; ✗) The kitchens in the suites look prefabricated but they're by the ocean.

Inn of the Lost Coast (☎ 707-986-7521, 888-570-9676; www.sheltercovemotorinn.com; 205 Wave Dr; r $125-250; ✗) This motel has clean, albeit charmless, rooms; downstairs there's the Lost Coast Coffee Company.

Marina Motel (☎ 707-986-7595; www.mariosof sheltercove.com; 533 Machi Rd; r $90).

Northern California Properties (☎ 707-986-7346; 101 Lower Pacific Dr) Rents vacation properties.

Shelter Cove Beachcomber Inn (☎ 707-986-7551, 800-718-4789; 412 Machi Rd; r $65-105; ✗) Slightly inland, lodgings here include apartments.

Shelter Cove RV Park, Campground & Deli (☎ 707-986-7474; 492 Machi Rd; tent/RV sites $25/35) has hot showers and outdoor tables; fish and chips is the deli's specialty.

The first-choice **Cove Restaurant** (☎ 707-986-1197; 10 Seal Court; dishes $6-19; ⏰ Thu-Sun) has everything from veggie stir-fries to New York steaks. For straightforward American, there is **Mario's** (☎ 707-986-1401; 533 Machi Rd; breakfast & lunch $6-11, dinner $10-20), which has a **bar**.

Get groceries and gasoline at **Shelter Cove General Store** (☎ 707-986-7733; 7272 Shelter Cove Rd), 2 miles beyond town.

King Range National Conservation Area

Stretching over 35 miles of virgin coastline, with ridge after ridge of mountainous terrain plunging down to the surf, the 60,000-acre wilderness tops out at namesake King's Peak (4087ft).

Nine miles east of Shelter Cove in Whitethorn, the **BLM** (☎ 707-986-5400, 707-825-2300; 768 Shelter Cove Rd; ⏰ 8am-4:30pm Memorial Day-Labor Day, Mon-Fri 8am-4:30 Sep-May) has maps and directions for trails and campsites; they're posted outside after-hours. Information is also available from the BLM in Arcata (p269).

The best way to see the Lost Coast is to hike. **Lost Coast Trail** follows 24 miles of coastline from Mattole Campground in the north, near Petrolia, to Black Sands Beach at Shelter Cove in the south. The prevailing northerly winds make it best to hike from north to south; plan three or four days. For information on backpacker shuttles, call the BLM or contact **Lost Coast Trail Transport Services** (☎ 707-986-9909; www.lostcoasttrail.com).

Highlights include an abandoned lighthouse at Punta Gorda, remnants of early shipwrecks, tidepools and abundant wildlife including sea lions, seals and more than 300 bird species. The trail is mostly level, passing beaches and over rocky outcrops. Consult tide tables, as some outcroppings are passable only at low tide.

A good day hike starts at the Mattole Campground trailhead and travels 3 miles south along the coast to the Punta Gorda lighthouse (return against the wind). Mattole Campground is at the ocean end of Lighthouse Rd, 4 miles from Mattole Rd, southeast of Petrolia.

Both Wailaki and Nadelos have developed **campgrounds** (sites $8). There are another four campgrounds scattered around the range, plus multiple primitive walk-in sites. For camping outside developed campgrounds, you'll need a bear canister and free fire permit, both available from BLM offices.

Sinkyone Wilderness State Park

Named for the Sinkyone people who once lived here, this 7367-acre wilderness extends south of Shelter Cove along pristine coastline. The **Lost Coast Trail** continues along here for another 22 miles, from Whale Gulch south to Usal Beach Campground, taking at least three days. Near the park's northern end, **Needle Rock Ranch** (☎ 707-986-7711) serves as a remote visitors center; register for campsites and get information. (It's the only source of potable water.)

To get here, drive west from Garberville and Redway, on Briceland–Thorn Rd, 21 miles through Whitethorn to Four Corners. Turn left (south) and continue for 3.5 miles down a very rugged road to the ranch house; it takes 1½ hours. There's also access to Usal Beach Campground at the south end of the park from Hwy 1: north of Westport, unpaved County Rd 431 begins from Hwy 1's milepost 90.88 and travels 6 miles up the coast to the campground. These roads are *not* maintained autumn through spring and quickly become impassable. To get through you'll need a 4x4 and chainsaw. Seriously.

North of the King Range

You can reach the Lost Coast's northern section year-round via paved, narrow Mattole Rd. Plan three hours to navigate the winding 68 miles from Ferndale in the north, to the coast at Cape Mendocino, then inland to Humboldt Redwoods State Park and Hwy 101. Don't expect redwoods: the vegetation is grassland and pasture. It's beautiful in spots, but there are few places to stop.

You'll pass two tiny settlements. **Petrolia** is the site of California's first oil well, capped-off on private property. Locals dislike outsiders. Visit the cemetery instead. There's a **store** (☎ 707-629-3345; ☼ 9am-5pm) with bear-canister rentals and post office, but no gasoline. At **Honeydew** there's a semireliable gas station at the **post office** (☎ 707-629-3310; ☼ 9am-5pm). Locals are friendly, but there's nothing to do but hang out on the front porch. The drive is enjoyable, but the Lost Coast's wild, spectacular scenery lies further south in the more remote regions.

There's camping at **AW Way County Park** (☎ 707-445-7651; Mattole Rd; per vehicle $15), 6 miles southeast of Petrolia, on the road toward Honeydew.

FERNDALE

pop 1400

Twenty miles south of Eureka, Ferndale has so well preserved its Victorian architecture that the entire town is listed as a state and federal historical landmark. Stroll along Main St and visit galleries, antiquarian bookshops, quaint emporiums and soda fountains. Although Ferndale relies on tourism, the town has refreshingly avoided becoming a tourist trap. It's a lovely place to spend the night.

Information

Computer Assistance (☎ 707-786-1016; 524b Main St). Check your email.
Ferndale Chamber of Commerce (☎ 707-786-4477; www.victorianferndale.org/chamber) Prints a visitors guide, which is available around town.

Sights & Activities

As Ferndale's settlers became wealthy from dairy farming, some built ornate mansions called 'butterfat palaces.' The **Gingerbread Mansion** (400 Berding St), an 1898 Queen Anne–Eastlake, is the town's most photographed building. **Shaw House** (703 Main St) was the first permanent structure in Ferndale. The town's founder, Seth Shaw, started constructing the gabled Carpenter Gothic in 1854; it wasn't completed until 1866. Called 'Fern Dale' for the 6ft-tall ferns that grew here, it housed the first post office, of which Shaw was the postmaster – hence the town's name. The 1866 **Fern Cottage** (☎ 707-786-4835; Centerville Rd), west of town, is only open by appointment.

The **Ferndale Museum** (☎ 707-786-4466; www .ferndale-museum.org; cnr Shaw & 3rd Sts; admission by donation) is jam-packed with artifacts. Call for opening times.

The **Kinetic Sculpture Museum** (www.kinetic sculpturerace.org; 580 Main St; ☼ 10am-5pm Mon-Sat, noon-4pm Sun) houses fanciful, astounding kinetic sculptures used in the town's annual Kinetic Sculpture Race.

Half a mile from downtown via Bluff St, enjoy short tramps through fields of wildflowers, beside ponds, redwood groves and eucalyptus trees at 110-acre **Russ Park**.

Festivals & Events

Contact the Chamber of Commerce for details of the town's many festivals.

Kinetic Sculpture Race The famous race is held in May.

Tour of the Unknown Coast This bicycle race takes place in May.

Scandinavian Mid-Summer Festival Folk dancing and feasting in June.

Humboldt County Fair Held in mid-August.

Victorian Village Oktoberfest & Harvest Day An Oktoberfest in October.

Christmas celebrations Ferndale is famous for its elaborate Christmas festivities.

Sleeping

B&BS

Shaw House (☎ 707-786-9958, 800-557-7429; www.shaw house.com; 703 Main St; r $115-175, ste $245-275; ✕) California's oldest B&B is also Ferndale's first grand home. Original details remain, including painted wooden ceilings. If you like B&Bs, this one's a charmer.

Gingerbread Mansion Inn (☎ 707-786-4000, 800-952-4136; www.gingerbread-mansion.com; 400 Berding St; r $160-400; ✕) Ferndale's iconic B&B drips with gingerbread trim. The 11 exquisitely detailed rooms are decked out with high-end 1890s Victorian furnishings. Rates include high-tea service, evening wine and three-course breakfast. No kids under 12.

Collingwood Inn B&B (☎ 707-786-9219, 800-469-1632; www.collingwoodinn.com; 831 Main St, r $99-203, cottages $230; ✕ ▣) This 1885 Hart House has four rooms with extras like featherbeds, bathrobes, coffee delivered to your door and breakfast at your convenience. It's gay friendly too.

HOTELS & MOTELS

Victorian Inn (☎ 707-786-4949, 888-589-1808; www .a-victorian-inn.com; 400 Ocean Ave; r $95-225; ✕) The bright, sunny rooms inside this 1890 two-story, former bank building are comfortably furnished with thick carpeting, good linens and antiques.

Hotel Ivanhoe (☎ 707-786-9000; www.hotel-ivan hoe.com; 315 Main St; r $95-145; ✕) Ferndale's oldest hostelry opened in 1875. It has four antique-laden rooms and an Old West-style second-floor porch, perfect for morning coffee.

Francis Creek Inn (☎ 707-786-9611; 577 Main St; r $68-78; ✕) This motel has four plain rooms.

Ferndale Laundromat & Motel (☎ 707-786-9471; 632 Main St; r $60; ✕) Attached to the launder-ette, the motel has two, two-bedroom units, each with kitchen.

CAMPING

Humboldt County Fairgrounds (☎ 707-786-9511; www .humboldtcountyfair.org; 1250 5th St; tent & RV sites $15) The fairgrounds provide lawn camping and showers; turn west onto Van Ness St, and go a few blocks.

Eating

Bakeries, cafés, a pizzeria and old-fashioned lunch counters line Main St.

Hotel Ivanhoe (☎ 707-786-9000; 315 Main St; mains $10-20; ✸ dinner Wed-Sun) For Italian-American food and prime rib, the Ivanhoe has a quiet dining room and a small-portions menu ($10 to $14), which you can also have while at the bar.

Curley's Grill (☎ 707-786-9696; 400 Ocean Ave; dishes $8-21) Curley's bar and grill serves everything from steak sandwiches and meatloaf to braised lamb shank and Niçoise salads, served on brightly colored Fiestaware. Good cocktails.

Ferndale Meat Co (☎ 707-786-4501; 376 Main St; sandwiches $5; ✸ 8am-5pm) Makes sandwiches heavy with cheeses and smoked meats. Good pastrami.

Entertainment

Ferndale Repertory Theatre (☎ 707-786-5483; www .ferndale-rep.org; 447 Main St) This terrific company produces shows year-round. Do not miss it.

Angelina Inn (☎ 707-725-3153; 281 Fernbridge St, Fernbridge; ✸ Fri-Tue) Near the Ferndale turnoff from Hwy 101, this Italian restaurant sometimes has dancing and live music; call for details.

Shopping

Golden Gait Mercantile (☎ 707-786-4891; 421 Main St) You could spend hours browsing the shelves of yesteryear's goods.

Hobart Gallery (☎ 707-786-9259; 393 Main St) Check out the mixed-media art here; some is for sale.

Silva's (☎ 707-786-4425; Victorian Inn, 400 Ocean Ave) Silva's has gorgeous jewelry.

Blacksmith Shop & Gallery (☎ 707-786-4216; www .ferndaleblacksmith.com; 455 & 491 Main St) From wrought-iron art to hand-forged furniture, this is the largest collection of contemporary blacksmithing in America.

NORTH COAST

HUMBOLDT BAY NATIONAL WILDLIFE REFUGE

This **wildlife refuge** (☎ 707-733-5406; ☼ sunrise-sunset) protects wetlands habitats for more than 200 species of birds migrating annually along the Pacific Flyway. In one single day in 2004, there were a whopping 26,000 Aleutian cackling geese counted outside the visitors center!

The peak season for waterbirds and raptors runs September to March, for black brant geese and migratory shorebirds mid-March to late April. Gulls, terns, cormorants, pelicans, egrets and herons come year-round. Look for harbor seals offshore; bring binoculars. If it's open, drive out South Jetty Rd to the mouth of Humboldt Bay for a stunning perspective.

Pick up a map from the **visitors center** (1020 Ranch Rd; ☼ 8am-5pm). It highlights two 30-minute interpretive walks. Exit Hwy 101 at Hookton Rd, 11 miles south of Eureka, turn north along the frontage road, on the freeway's west side. In April, look for the Godwit Days festival (www.godwitdays.com).

EUREKA

pop 25,600

Eureka hugs the shores of Humboldt Bay, the state's largest bay north of San Francisco. As you drive into the town along Hwy 101, Eureka's suburban strip is unimpressive. But venture into Old Town, a couple of blocks away, and there are colorful Victorians, impressive museums and a refurbished waterfront. There are lots of artists here: you'll see photographs, paintings and sculpture in restaurants, bars and public spaces. Unfortunately, it's an early-to-bed town; sidewalks roll up by 9pm.

Orientation & Information

The streets lie on a grid; numbered streets cross lettered streets. For the best window-shopping, head to the 300, 400 and 500 blocks of 2nd St, between D and G Sts.

Eureka Chamber of Commerce (☎ 707-442-3738, 800-356-6381; 2112 Broadway; ☼ Mon-Sat) The main visitor information center is on Hwy 101.

Eureka-Humboldt County Convention and Visitors Bureau (☎ 707-443-5097, 800-346-3482; 1034 2nd St; ☼ Mon-Fri) Has maps and brochures.

Going Places (☎ 707-443-4145; 328 2nd St) Travel-oriented bookstore. One of several excellent bookstores in Old Town.

Has Beans (☎ 707-442-1535; 738 2nd St; per hr $8) On the corner of I St, Has Beans has Internet access and homemade pastries.

Pride Enterprises Tours (☎ 707-445-2117, 800-400-1849) Local historian leads outstanding tours. Licensed to guide in the national parks.

Six Rivers National Forest Headquarters (☎ 707-442-1721; 1330 Bayshore Way; ☼ Mon-Fri) Has maps and information.

Sights

Eureka has some fine Victorian buildings and the most famous of them is the ornate **Carson Mansion** (134 M St), the 1880s home of lumber baron William Carson. It took 100 men a full year to build. Today it's a private men's club. The pink house opposite, at 202 M St, is an 1884 Queen Anne Victorian designed by the same architects and built as a wedding gift for Carson's son.

The free *Eureka Visitors Map*, available at tourist offices, details walking tours and scenic drives, focusing on architecture and history. **Old Town**, along 2nd and 3rd Sts from C St to M St, was once Eureka's down-and-out area, but has been refurbished into a pleasant pedestrian district of galleries, shops,

NORTH COAST

cafés and restaurants. The F Street Plaza and Boardwalk run along the waterfront at the foot of F St.

One of only seven of its kind in America, the incredible **Blue Ox Millworks & Historic Park** (707-444-3437, 800-248-4259; www.blueoxmill.com; adult/child $7.50/3.50; 9am-4pm Mon-Sat) uses antique tools and mills to produce authentic gingerbread trim and decoration for Victorian buildings; one-hour self-guided tours take you through the mill and historical buildings, including a blacksmith shop and 19th-century skid camp. Kids love the oxen. At the time of publication, there were plans to move in 2007; call for current address.

A relic of Eureka's recent past, the **Romano Gabriel Wooden Sculpture Garden** (315 2nd St) is enclosed by glass, between D and E Sts. For 30 years the brightly painted folk art in Gabriel's front yard delighted locals. After he died in 1977, the city moved the collection here.

The **Clarke Memorial Museum** (707-443-1947; 240 E St; admission by donation; 11am-4pm Tue-Sat), in the former 1912 Bank of Eureka building, has Native American artifacts and thousands of pieces on Humboldt County history.

Also in Old Town, there's **Humboldt Bay Maritime Museum** (707-444-9440; www.humboldt baymaritimemuseum.com; 423 1st St; free; noon-4pm most days) and **Discovery Museum** (707-443-9694; 517 3rd St; admission $4; 10am-4pm Tue-Sat, noon-4pm Sun), a hands-on kids' museum.

Across Hwy 101, the **Morris Graves Museum of Art** (707-442-0278, events 442-9054; www.humboldt arts.org; 636 F St; admission by donation; noon-5pm Wed-Sun) has rotating exhibitions of California artists inside a three-story, 1904 Carnegie library, the state's first public library. It hosts weekend jazz, dance and spoken-word performances (September to May).

Fort Humboldt State Historic Park (707-445-6567; 3431 Fort Ave; free; 8am-5pm) lies off Broadway, south of downtown; turn inland onto Highland Ave. The fort was established in 1853 on a bluff overlooking Humboldt Bay. Outdoor exhibits show how giant redwoods were felled. Take a steam engine ride the 3rd Saturday of the month, May through September.

Sequoia Park (707-442-6552; 3414 W St; admission by donation; 10am-7pm Tue-Sun May-Sep, 10am-5pm rest of year), a 77-acre old-growth redwood grove, has biking and hiking trails, children's playground and picnic areas, as well as a small zoo.

Activities

Board the 1910 *Madaket*, America's oldest continuously operating passenger vessel, for a **harbor cruise** (707-445-1910; www.humboldtbay maritimemuseum.com; foot of C St; adult/child/teen/senior $15/7.50/13/13; May-Oct), and learn the history of Humboldt Bay. The *Madaket* originally ferried mill workers and passengers until the Samoa Bridge was built in 1972.

Hum-Boats Sail, Canoe & Kayak Center (707-443-5157; www.humboats.com; Startare Dr), at Woodley Island Marina, rents kayaks and sailboats. They also have lessons and tours, ecotours, a water taxi, sailboat charters, sunset sails and full-moon paddles.

Northern Mountain Supply (707-445-1711; 125 W 5th St) sells canoes and kayaks, as well as renting camping and backpacking gear. **Pro Sport Center** (707-443-6328; 508 Myrtle Ave) has a full-service bike shop (no rentals) and sells camping gear; they also rent and sell kayaks and scuba, diving and skiing gear.

Festivals & Events

On the first Saturday of every month, there is a progressive tour of the town's galleries. Summer concerts are held at the F Street Pier. Contact the visitors bureau for details of the town's festivals.

Redwood Coast Dixieland Jazz Festival Dixieland jazz comes to town in April.

Rhododendron Festival An April flower festival.

Blues by the Bay Waterfront concerts are held in July.

Kinetic Sculpture Race The race passes through Eureka on the Memorial Day weekend in September, when folks on self-propelled contraptions travel 38 miles from Arcata to Ferndale.

Sleeping

Room rates run high midsummer; you can sometimes find cheaper in Arcata.

B&BS

Cornelius Daly Inn (707-445-3638, 800-321-9656; www.dalyinn.com; 1125 H St; r with/without bathroom $165/125;) This impeccably maintained 1905 Colonial Revival mansion has individually decorated rooms with turn-of-the-20th-century European and American antiques. Guest parlors are trimmed with rare woods; outside are century-old flowering trees.

Abigail's Elegant Victorian Mansion (707-444-3144; www.eureka-california.com; 1406 C St; r $115-155, r with breakfast $155-195;) Inside this National Historic Landmark that's practically a Victorian living-history museum, the sweet-as-could-be innkeepers lavish guests with warm hospitality, including a ride around Eureka in 1920s automobiles.

Carter House Victorians (☎ 707-444-8067, 800-404-1390; www.carterhouse.com; r $190-275, ste $350-450, cottage $595; ⊠) Stay in one of three sumptuously decorated houses: a single-level 1900 house, a honeymoon-hideaway cottage or a replica of an 1880s San Francisco mansion, which the owner built himself, entirely by hand (the craftsmanship is astounding). Unlike elsewhere, you won't see the innkeeper unless you want to. Guests can have an in-room breakfast or eat at the adjacent hotel's understatedly elegant restaurant.

Also consider:

Old Town B&B Inn (☎ 707-443-5235, 888-508-5235; www.oldtownbnb.com; 1521 3rd St; r $130-150; ⊠) Built 1871; cozy rooms at Old Town's edge.

Ship's Inn (☎ 707-443-7583, 877-443-7583; www.shipsinn.net; 821 D St; r $100-150; ⊠) Three spacious rooms with modern furnishings.

Upstairs at the Waterfront (☎ 707-444-1301, 888-817-5840; www.upstairsatthewaterfront.com; 102 F St; r $125, ste $175; ⊠) Victorian apartment above Café Waterfront.

MOTELS & HOTELS

Hotel Carter (☎ 707-444-8067, 800-404-1390; www.carterhouse.com; 301 L St; r incl breakfast $155-205, ste $275-350; ⊠ ⚑) Hotel Carter bears the standard for North Coast luxury. Recently constructed in period style, it's a Victorian lookalike without drafty windows. Rooms have top-quality linens and modern amenities; suites have in-room whirlpools and marble fireplaces. Rates include made-to-order breakfast, plus evening wine and hors d'oeuvres.

Dozens of motels line Hwy 101. Most cost $55 to $95 and have no air-conditioning; choose places set back from the road for less noise. The cheapest are south of downtown on the suburban strip. At this writing, the venerable old Eureka Inn had closed.

Best Western Humboldt Bay Inn (☎ 707-443-2234, 800-521-6996; www.humboldtbayinn.com; 232 W 5th St; r $115-135; ⊠ ⚑) This high-end motel has firm mattresses and thick carpeting; upgraded rooms have DVDs, robes, microwaves and refrigerators. Request a quiet room.

Bayview Motel (☎ 707-442-1673, 866-725-6813; www.bayviewmotel.com; 2844 Fairfield St; r $85; ⊠) South of the town, the upscale Bayview has spotless rooms with extras including refrig-

erators and patios overlooking Humboldt Bay. Jacuzzi suites have fireplaces.

CAMPING

Eureka KOA (☎ 707-822-4243, 800-562-3136; www.koakampgrounds.com; 4050 N Hwy 101; tent sites $25-29, RV sites $30-37, cabins $50-60; ⚑) About halfway to Arcata, Eureka KOA has a heated pool, convenience store, laundry, playground and bicycle rentals.

There's also camping on Samoa Peninsula (p269).

Eating

La Chapala (☎ 707-443-9514; 201 2nd St; dishes $6-14; ⏰ 11am-9pm) For Mexican, family-owned La Chapala makes strong margaritas and homemade flan.

Waterfront Cafe Oyster Bar & Grill (☎ 707-443-9190; 102 F St; lunch $8-13, dinner $13-20; ⏰ 9am-9pm) Eureka's best lunch spot, the Waterfront serves mostly seafood – steamed clams, chowder, fish and chips and oysters. Good fish burgers too.

Hurricane Kate's (☎ 707-444-1405; www.hurricanekates.com; 511 2nd St; lunch mains $9-14, dinner $16-24; ⏰ Tue-Sat) Loud and bustling Kate's pumps out eclectic, tapas-style dishes, roast meats and wood-fired pizzas. Full bar. There's a party atmosphere.

Cafe Marina & Woodley's Bar (☎ 707-443-2233; 601 Startare Dr; dishes $10-16; ⏰ 11am-10pm) Across the water in Woodley Island Marina, this harborside bar and grill makes great Bloody Marys and pretty good American food, served on a deck overlooking the small-craft harbor. Perfect on a sunny day.

Ritz (☎ 707-443-7489; 240 F St; sushi $4-6, lunch mains $8-10, dinner $10-17; ⏰ lunch Mon-Fri, dinner nightly) It looks like an Italian joint, but the food is pure Japanese. There's good sushi and teppanyaki tables in back, where chefs throw knives in the air while cooking your dinner (make reservations).

O.H.'s Townhouse (☎ 707-443-4652; 206 W 6th St; mains $15-21; ⏰ dinner Tue-Sun) Carnivores: if you're hungry for steak, pick your own meat from the display case at this 1970s throwback with wood-veneer-paneled walls. The veggies suck; the steak's great.

Roy's (☎ 707-442-4574; 218 D St; dishes $13-20; ⏰ dinner Tue-Sat) If Eureka had a Mafia, they'd eat pasta at Roy's. The five-cheese ravioli and balsamic vinaigrette are delicious, but avoid complicated dishes.

NORTH COAST

Restaurant 301 (☎ 707-444-8062; www.carterhouse
.com; 301 L St; breakfast $11, dinner $23-29, 4-course
menu $45; ☺ breakfast & dinner) Eureka's most
refined dining room offers a contemporary
California menu using produce from its
organic gardens (tours available). Try the
four-course prix-fixe menu. The wine list
is stunning.

Avalon (☎ 707-445-0500; 3rd & G Sts; mains $21-28;
☺ dinner Tue-Sat) Sophisticated Avalon's diverse
California menu features everything from
foie gras to fried calamari. Leave room for
chocolate soufflé.

Ramone's (☎ 707-445-2923; 209 E St; dishes under
$10; ☺ 7am-6pm Mon-Sat, 8am-4pm Sun) For grab-
and-go sandwiches, Ramone's makes good
soups and wraps.

Pick up groceries at **Eureka Natural Foods**
(☎ 707-442-6325; 1626 Broadway) or **Eureka Co-op**
(☎ 443-6027; cnr 5th & L Sts). There's also a **farmers market** (☎ 707-441-9999; Old Town Gazebo, cnr 2nd
& F Sts; ☺ 10am-1pm Tue Jun-Oct) and cafés and
sandwich shops in Old Town.

Drinking
Shanty (☎ 707-444-2053; 213 2nd St; ☺ noon-2am)
The coolest spot in town is grungy and fun.
Play pool, Donkey Kong, Ms Pac Man or
Ping Pong, or kick it on the back patio with
local 20- and 30-something hipsters. Shanty
is gay friendly, but not gay per se. Sunday
there's a bloody Mary bar open from 10am
to 2pm.

Lost Coast Brewery (☎ 707-445-4480; 617 4th St)
Lost Coast makes good beer – try the Downtown Brown Ale. There's also tasty fried
pub grub, 11am until midnight.

Casa Blanca (☎ 707-443-6190; 1436 2nd St, at P St;
☺ 4-9pm) Drink margaritas with a bay view;
arrive before sunset.

321 Coffee (☎ 707-444-9371; 321 3rd St; ☺ 8am-
9pm) Students sip French-press coffee and
play chess at this living-room-like coffeehouse. Good soup.

Entertainment
Morris Graves Museum of Art hosts performing-
arts events between September and May,
usually on Saturday evenings and Sunday
afternoons.

Broadway Cinema (☎ 707-444-3456; Broadway,
near 14th St) Broadway has first-run movies.

Club Triangle at Club West (☎ 444-2582; 535 5th
St) Sunday nights, this becomes the North
Coast's big gay dance club.

Getting There & Around
Horizon Air (☎ 800-547-9308; horizonair.alaskaair.com)
and **United Express** (☎ 800-241-6522; www.united
.com) serve Arcata-Eureka Airport, 20 miles
north.

Eureka Transit Service (☎ 707-443-0826; www
.hta.org/ets) operates local buses, Monday to
Saturday.

SAMOA PENINSULA
A windswept beauty, 7 miles long and half
a mile wide, Samoa Peninsula is the north
spit of Humboldt Bay, which supposedly
resembles Pago Pago Harbor, Samoa (never
mind the lumber mill). The shoreline road
(Hwy 255) is a backdoor route between Eureka and Arcata. Reach the beach by walking
west through the dunes.

At the south end of the peninsula, **Samoa
Dunes Recreation Area** (☎ 707-825-2300; ☺ sunrise-
sunset) is popular for picnicking and fishing.
For wildlife, head to **Mad River Slough & Dunes**;
from Arcata, take Samoa Blvd west 3 miles,
then turn right at Young St, the Manila turnoff. Continue to the community center parking lot, from where a trail passes mudflats,
salt marsh and tidal channels. There are over
200 species of birds: migrating waterfowl
in spring and fall, songbirds in spring and
summer, shorebirds in fall and winter, and
abundant waders year-round.

The 475-acre **Lanphere Dunes Preserve** protects one of the finest examples of dune suc-
cession on the entire Pacific coast. These
undisturbed dunes reach heights exceeding
80ft. Because of the environment's fragil-
ity, access is by guided tour only. **Friends of
the Dunes** (☎ 707-444-1397; www.friendsofthedunes
.org) leads 2½-hour rain-or-shine Saturday
guided walks at 10am through Lanphere
Dunes and Manila Dunes. The first and
third Saturdays of the month, walks depart
from the Pacific Union School parking lot
at 3001 Janes Rd, Arcata. On the second
and fourth Saturdays, meet at Manila Dunes
Community Center. Bring a jacket and soft-
soled shoes. Volunteer restoration workdays
are scheduled on alternate Saturdays. Call
or check the website.

A couple of miles south from Lanphere
Dunes, the 100-acre **Manila Dunes Recreation
Area** (☎ 707-445-3309) is open to the public,
with access from Peninsula Dr.

The West's last surviving lumber-camp
cookhouse, the **Samoa Cookhouse** (☎ 707-442-

1659; www.humboldtdining.com/cookhouse; off Samoa Blvd; breakfast/lunch/dinner $9/10/14) serves all-you-can-eat family meals, course by course, at long tables with checkered tablecloths. Kids eat half-price. Stop by the little museum. The cookhouse is five minutes northwest of Eureka, across the Samoa Bridge; follow the signs. From Arcata, take Samoa Blvd (Hwy 255).

There's camping available at **Samoa Boat Ramp County Park** (☎ 707-445-7651; sites $14), on the peninsula's bay side, 4 miles south of Samoa Bridge. There's limited tent camping (it's mostly RVs) and few facilities, just some picnic tables, toilet and parking lot – but it has lovely views and an on-site host.

ARCATA
pop 16,500

On a hill overlooking Humboldt Bay, Arcata was founded in 1850 by the Union Timber Company. Originally called Union Town, it was a base for nearby lumber camps. In the late 1850s when Bret Harte worked here as a journalist, the town became the setting for some of his Gold Rush-era stories. Today, Humboldt State University (HSU) has redefined Arcata as a college town.

The aesthetic is decidedly scruffy, and posses of fun-loving carousing students roam downtown on weekend evenings. On the plaza keep your distance from the ragtag junkie punks. Arcata prides itself on its go-it-alone far-left politics. Indeed, the City Council passed an ordinance in April 2003, not only condemning the USA Patriot Act, but *outlawing* voluntary compliance with it. If you like to argue politics, you're gonna love it here.

Orientation

Roads run on a grid, with numbered streets traveling east–west and the lettered streets going north–south. G and H Sts run north and south (respectively) to HSU and Hwy 101. The plaza is bordered by G and H and 8th and 9th Sts. Eureka is 5 miles south on Hwy 101. Or, take Samoa Blvd to Hwy 255 for a scenic route around Arcata Bay.

Information

Bureau of Land Management (BLM; ☎ 707-825-2300; 1695 Heindon Rd) Has information on the Lost Coast.
California Welcome Center (☎ 707-822-3619; www.arcatachamber.com; 1635 Heindon Rd; ☺ 9am-5pm)

Two miles north of town, off Giuntoli Lane, Hwy 101's west side. Operated by Arcata Chamber of Commerce, the center provides local and statewide information. Get the free *Official Map Guide to Arcata*.
Humboldt Internet (☎ 707-825-4638; 750 16th St; per hr $3; ☺ 10am-5pm Mon-Fri) PC Internet access.
Kinko's (☎ 707-822-8712; 1618 G St; per min 20¢; ☺ 7am-10pm Mon-Fri, 9am-5pm Sat & Sun) Uses Macs and PCs.
Northtown Books (☎ 707-822-2384; 957 H St) New books, periodicals, travel maps and guides.
Tin Can Mailman (☎ 707-822-1307; 1000 H St) Used volumes on two floors; excellent for hard-to-find books.

Sights

Some notable buildings cluster around the **Arcata Plaza**, including two National Historic Landmarks: the 1857 **Jacoby's Storehouse** (cnr H & 8th Sts) and the 1915 **Hotel Arcata** (cnr G & 9th Sts). Others are the vintage 1914 **Minor Theatre** (1013 10th St) and the 1854 **Phillips House Museum** (☎ 707-822-4722; www.arcatahistory.org; cnr 7th & Union Sts; admission by donation; ☺ 2-4pm Sun & by appointment), which has historical exhibits and runs tours.

On the northeastern side of town, **Humboldt State University** (HSU; ☎ 707-826-3011; www.humboldt.edu) is Arcata's *raison d'être*. The **HSU Natural History Museum** (☎ 707-866-4479; www.humboldt.edu/~natmus; 1315 G St; adult/child $3/2; ☺ 10am-5pm Tue-Sat) has kid-friendly interactive exhibits of fossils, live animals, a beehive, tide-pool tank, and cool tsunami and seismic displays.

On the shores of Humboldt Bay, **Arcata Marsh & Wildlife Sanctuary** has 5 miles of walking trails and outstanding birding. The **Redwood Region Audubon Society** (☎ 707-826-7031; www.rras.org; donation welcome) offers guided walks Saturdays at 8:30am, rain or shine, from the parking lot at I Street's south end. Friends of Arcata Marsh guide tours Saturdays at 2pm from the **Arcata Marsh Interpretive Center** (☎ 707-826-2359; 600 South G St; tours free; ☺ 9am-5pm).

At the east end of 11th and 14th Sts, **Redwood Park** has beautiful redwoods and picnic areas. Adjoining the park is the **Arcata Community Forest**, a 575-acre old-growth forest crisscrossed by 10 miles of trails, with dirt paths and paved roads good for hikers and mountain-bikers.

Northeast of Arcata, 2 miles east of Hwy 101, **Azalea State Reserve** (☎ 707-488-2041; Hwy 200) explodes with color from late April to late May; otherwise skip it.

NORTH COAST

Activities

If you're at all bohemian, you must visit **Finnish Country Sauna & Tubs** (☎ 707-822-2228; cnr 5th & J Sts; ☖ noon-10pm Sun-Thu, noon-12:30am Fri & Sat), where you can sip chai fireside or in meditative outdoor gardens, then rent a private open-air redwood hot tub ($8 per half-hour) or sweat in one of two saunas. Reserve in advance, especially on weekends.

HSU Center Activities (☎ 707-826-3357), on the 2nd floor of the University Center, beside the campus clock tower, sponsors myriad activities, workshops, outings, sporting-gear rentals and consignment sales; nonstudents welcome.

Take a drop-in class at the **Community Yoga Center** (☎ 707-440-2111; www.innerfreedomyoga.com; 890 G St; classes $10). **Arcata Community Pool** (☎ 707-822-6801; 1150 16th St; adult/child/senior $5/3/4) has a coed hot tub, sauna and exercise room.

Adventure's Edge (☎ 707-822-4673; www.adventuresedge.com; 650 10th St; ☖ 10am-6pm Mon-Sat, 11am-5pm Sun) rents, sells and services outdoor equipment. The **Outdoor Store** (☎ 707-822-0321; 876 G St; ☖ 10am-6pm Mon-Sat, noon-5pm Sun) also sells outdoor gear, and rents snowboards and kayaks.

Festivals & Events

Arcata's most famous event is the **Kinetic Sculpture Race**, which is held Memorial Day weekend, when people on self-propelled contraptions travel 38 miles from Arcata to Ferndale. The **Arcata Bay Oyster Festival** and

ARCATA

0 — 500 m
0 — 0.3 miles

INFORMATION
Humboldt Internet...................1 B2
Kinko's.............................(see 23)
Post Office.........................2 B3

SIGHTS & ACTIVITIES
Arcata Community Pool...........3 B2
Community Yoga Center...........4 B3
Finnish Country Sauna & Tubs..5 B3
HSU Center Activities.............6 C1
HSU Natural History Museum..7 B2
Humboldt State University......8 C2
Jacoby's Storehouse..............9 B3
Northtown Books..................10 B3
Phillips House Museum..........11 C4
Tin Can Mailman..................12 B3

SLEEPING
Fairwinds Motel....................13 C2
Hotel Arcata.......................14 B3
Lady Anne Inn.....................15 B2

EATING
Arcata Co-op.......................16 B3
Arcata Pizza & Deli..............(see 27)
Big Blue Cafe......................17 B3
Bon Boniere.......................(see 9)
Don's Donuts.....................(see 10)
Folie Douce........................18 B2
Golden Harvest Cafe.............19 B3
Hey Juan! Burritos..............(see 23)
Los Bagels.........................20 B3
Pacific Rim Noodle House......(see 20)
Philly Cheese Steak Shoppe....21 C2
Tomo Japanese Restaurant...(see 14)
Wildberries Marketplace.......22 B2
Wildflower Cafe & Bakery.....23 C2

DRINKING
Cafe Mokka.......................(see 5)
Humboldt Brewing Company..24 B3
Muddy Waters Coffee Co.....(see 1)
Plaza Grill.........................(see 9)

ENTERTAINMENT
Arcata Theatre....................25 B3
Jamabalaya........................26 B3
Minor Theatre.....................27 B3

TRANSPORT
Arcata Transit Center............28 B3
Library Bike........................29 B3
Life Cycle Bike Shop............(see 18)
Revolution Bicycle...............30 B2

To Pacific Union School (1mi)

To Hwy 299 (1.6mi); Giuntoli Ln (1.8mi); California Welcome Center (1.9mi); Bureau of Land Management (1.9mi); North Coast Inn (2.4mi); Best Western Arcata Inn (2.6mi); Motel 6 (2.6mi); Azalea State Reserve (6mi); Trinidad (15mi)

Sunset Ave

Jolly Giant Ck

Greenwood Cemetery

Plaza Ave

Arcata High School

18th St

Humboldt State University

17th St

Laurel Dr

16th St

Harpst Dr

Stewart Park

15th St

HSU Visitor Information

14th St

13th St

12th St

11th St

10th St

9th St

Arcata Plaza

8th St

7th St

6th St

5th St

To Mad River Slough & Dunes (3mi); Samoa Peninsula (8mi); Eureka (8mi)

Samoa Blvd

To Arcata Community Forest (0.2mi)

Gunnon Slough

7th St

3rd St

2nd St

1st St

Samoa Blvd

Arcata Marsh & Wildlife Sanctuary

To Arcata Marsh Interpretive Center (0.1mi)

To Eureka KOA (4mi); Eureka (8mi)

NORTH COAST

Bebop and Brew happen in June. September brings the **North Country Fair**.

Sleeping

Arcata has affordable but limited lodgings; it's a good base for exploring the redwoods further north.

Arcata Stay (☎ 707-822-0935, 877-822-0935; www .arcatastay.com; apt $130-175; ✗) Live like a local in a beautifully furnished apartment or cozy cottage hideaway; all are walkable to the plaza and have kitchens, and lots of privacy. Two-night minimum.

Lady Anne Inn (☎ 707-822-2797; www.humboldt1 .com/ladyanne; 902 14th St; r $90-115; ✗) Rooms at this 1888 mansion are full of Victorian bric-a-brac. No breakfast, but lovely (inedible) gardens.

Hotel Arcata (☎ 707-826-0217, 800-344-1221; www .hotelarcata.com; 708 9th St; r $79-105, ste $130-150) Anchoring the plaza, the renovated 1915 brick Hotel Arcata has high ceilings and comfortable, small rooms. Quietest rooms face the air shaft.

Fairwinds Motel (☎ 707-822-4824; www.fairwinds motelarcata.com; 1674 G St; r $65-79) This standard-issue motel has OK rooms, but noise from Hwy 101, right behind, is loud.

Other motels lie 2 miles north off Hwy 101's Giuntoli Lane exit.

Best Western Arcata Inn (☎ 707-826-0313, 800-528-1234; r $99; ✗ ⌨) This is the best motel choice.

North Coast Inn (☎ 707-822-4861, 800-406-0046; 4975 Valley West Blvd; r $80-85; ✗ ✗ ⌨) A satisfactory option, with an on-site restaurant and airport transfers.

Motel 6 (☎ 707-822-7061, 800-466-8356; s $44-49, $50-56; ✗ ⌨)

The nearest camping is Eureka KOA (p267). Also see Trinidad (p273) and Patrick's Point (p274).

Eating

Folie Douce (☎ 707-822-1042; 1551 G St; brunch mains $8-14, dinner $22-31; ✗ Tue-Sat dinner, Sun brunch) Arcata's best dining option, Folie Douce presents a short but inventive menu of seasonally inspired bistro cooking, from Asian to Mediterranean, with an emphasis on local organics. Wood-fired pizzas ($12-18) are a specialty. There's Sunday brunch too. Reservations essential.

Tomo Japanese Restaurant (☎ 707-822-1414; 708 9th St; lunch $8-11, dinner $14-17; ✗ lunch Mon-Sat, dinner nightly) Tomo, in the Hotel Arcata, packs 'em in for the town's best sushi and tasty sake cocktails. There's good stuff for veggies and vegans too.

Pacific Rim Noodle House (☎ 707-826-7604; 1021 I St; dishes $4-7; ✗ 11am-7pm Mon-Sat) Super-duper noodles, rice bowls, potstickers and sushi rolls are mainstays at this take-out, order-at-the-counter favorite, with tables outside.

Wildflower Cafe & Bakery (☎ 707-822-0360; 1604 G St; dishes $5-8; ✗ 8am-8pm Mon-Sat, 9am-1pm Sun) Tops for vegetarians, the Wildflower serves fab frittatas and pancakes, and big crunchy salads and crepes.

Golden Harvest Cafe (☎ 707-822-8962; 1062 G St; breakfast $4-8; ✗ breakfast & lunch) Arguably here is Arcata's best breakfast. Golden Harvest serves classic benedicts, four-egg omelettes, and pancakes with *real* maple syrup. Too bad the coffee sucks.

Big Blue Cafe (☎ 707-826-7578; 846 G St; dishes $4-7; ✗ breakfast & lunch) Big Blue has good coffee, pretty-good breakfasts and tasty lunches with hot sandwiches and big salads.

Hey Juan! Burritos (☎ 707-822-8433; 1642 1/2 G St; ✗ 11am-11pm) and **Philly Cheese Steak Shoppe** (☎ 707-825-7400; cnr 18th & G Sts; ✗ 11am-9pm) are ever-popular with hungry, cash-strapped students. Inside Jacoby's Storehouse, get sundaes at **Bon Boniere** (☎ 707-822-6388; 791 8th St; ✗ 11am-10pm), an old-fashioned ice-cream parlor. Everyone stops in at **Los Bagels** (☎ 707-822-3150; 1061 I St; dishes $2.50-6; ✗ Wed-Mon) sooner or later.

After bar-hopping, there's **Arcata Pizza & Deli** (☎ 707-822-4650; 1057 H St; ✗ 11-1am, 11-3am Fri & Sat) or get a Southeast-Asian sandwich at **Don's Donuts** (☎ 707-822-6465; 933 H St; ✗ 24hr).

There are **farmers markets** (☎ 707-441-9999; Arcata Plaza ✗ 9am-2pm Sat Apr-Nov; Wildberries ✗ 3:30-6:30pm Tue Jun-Oct) on Arcata Plaza and outside **Wildberries Marketplace** (☎ 707-822-0095; 747 13th St; ✗ 7am-11pm), which is Arcata's best grocery, with natural foods, a good deli, bakery and juice bar. **Arcata Co-op** (☎ 707-822-5947; cnr 8th & I Sts; ✗ 6am-10pm) carries natural foods and has a good butcher with grass-fed beef.

Drinking

Humboldt Brewing Company (☎ 707-826-2739; 856 10th St; pub grub $5-10; ✗ Mon-Sat) Humboldt has 13 brews on tap, fab fish tacos and bitchin' buffalo wings. There's live music Thursday to Saturday nights.

Plaza Grill (☎ 707-826-0860; 791 8th St; ✗ 5-11pm) Upstairs in Jacoby's Storehouse, this is the handsomest bar in town. The pork chops are good too.

Dive bars and cocktail lounges line the plaza's northern side. Arcata is awash in coffeehouses.

Muddy Waters Coffee Co (☎ 707-826-2233; 1603 G St) This is a happenin' indie joint, with live music weekends. Beer and wine too.

Cafe Mokka (☎ 707-822-2228; cnr 5th & J Sts) At Finnish Country Sauna & Tubs, Mokka is worth checking out. On weekend evenings, there's hearthside mellow acoustic music (usually European folk); other nights, read international newspapers and join multilingual conversations. The vibe is pure boho.

Entertainment

Center Arts (☎ 707-826-4411; tickets 707-826-3928; www.humboldt.edu/~carts) An HSU division, Center Arts sponsors performances, headline concerts and international music.

Arcata Theatre (☎ 707-822-1220; www.arcatatheater .com; 1036 G St) Undergoing renovations at this writing, the theatre is slated to host concerts, foreign films and dance parties.

Minor Theatre (☎ 707-822-3456; 1013 H St) The historic Minor Theatre shows first-run and classic films.

Jambalaya (☎ 707-822-4766; 915 H St) Jambalaya hosts jazz, blues and other genres Saturday nights. At the time of writing, it had changed ownership; check to see if it has expanded the calendar.

Getting There & Around

See p268 for airport information. **Redwood Transit System** (☎ 707-443-0826; www.hta.org), Greyhound (☎ 800-231-2222; www.greyhound.com) and Arcata city buses (☎ 707-822-3775; ☻ Mon-Sat) stop at the **Arcata Transit Center** (☎ 707-825-8934; 925 E St at 9th St).

Revolution Bicycle (☎ 707-822-2562; 1360 G St) and **Life Cycle Bike Shop** (☎ 707-822-7755; 1593 G St; ☻ Mon-Sat) rent, service and sell bicycles.

Only in Arcata: borrow a bike from **Library Bike** (☎ 707-822-1122; www.arcata.com/greenbikes; 865 8th St) for a $20 deposit, which gets refunded when you return the bike – up to six months later! They're beaters, but they ride. And hello – they're basically free.

TRINIDAD

pop 400

Fifteen miles north of Arcata, spiffy Trinidad gained its name when Spanish sea cap-

tains arrived on Trinity Sunday in 1775 and named the area La Santisima Trinidad (the Holy Trinity). Trinidad didn't boom, though, until the 1850s, when it became an important port for miners. Schooners from San Francisco brought supplies for inland gold fields, and carried back lumber from the North Coast. Today, tourism and fishing keep the economy going.

Orientation & Information

Trinidad is small, so it's easy to get your bearings. Approach via Hwy 101 (exit at Trinidad) or from the north via Patrick's Point Dr (which becomes Scenic Dr further south); to reach town, take Main St.

Beachcomber Café (☎ 707-677-0106; 363 Trinity St; per hr $5; ☻ 7am-4pm Mon-Thu, 7am-9pm Fri, 9am-4pm Sat & Sun) Internet access.

Information kiosk (cnr Patrick's Point Dr & Main St) Just west of the freeway, pick up the pamphlet *Discover Trinidad*, which has an excellent map.

Trinidad Chamber of Commerce (☎ 707-667-1610; www.trinidadcalif.com) Provides tourist information on the web, but it doesn't have a visitors center.

Sights & Activities

Trinidad Memorial Lighthouse (cnr Trinity & Edwards Sts), a replica of an 1871 lighthouse, sits on a bluff at the end of the commercial district, overlooking the bay. The annual Trinidad Fish Festival is celebrated in June; it's one of the few times the lighthouse opens to visitors.

Half a block inland, **Trinidad Museum** (☎ 707-677-3883; 529b Trinity St; ☻ noon-3pm Fri-Sun May-Sep) has exhibits on the area's natural and human history.

HSU Telonicher Marine Laboratory (☎ 707-826-3671; www.humboldt.edu/~marinelb; Ewing St; admission free; ☻ 9am-5pm Mon-Fri, 10am-5pm Sat & Sun Sep–mid-May), near Edwards St, has a touch tank, several aquariums (look for the giant Pacific octopus), an enormous whale jaw and a cool three-dimensional map of the ocean floor.

The free town map available from the information kiosk shows several fantastic hiking trails, most notably the **Trinidad Head Trail**, which affords superb coastal views. It's also excellent for whale-watching (December to April). Stroll along an exceptionally beautiful cove at **Trinidad State Beach**; take Main St and bear right at Stagecoach, then take the second turn left (the first is a picnic area) into the small lot.

Scenic Dr twists south along coastal bluffs, passing tiny coves with views back toward the bay. After 2 miles, it leads to the broad expanses of **Luffenholtz Beach** (accessible via the staircase) and to **Moonstone Beach**, one of the few white-sand beaches along the North Coast not littered with giant driftwood. Further south it becomes Clam Beach County Park, but Scenic Dr ends sooner, forcing you onto Hwy 101 to reach the county park.

Trinidad is famous for its fishing. Arrange a trip through **Salty's Surf 'n' Tackle Tours** (☎ 707-677-0300; 332 Main St) or **Trinidad Bay Charters** (☎ 707-839-4743, 800-839-4744; www.trinidadbaycharters .net). The harbor is at the bottom of Edwards St, at the foot of Trinidad Head. A five-hour trip costs about $65.

Surfing is good year-round, but potentially dangerous: unless you know how to judge conditions and get yourself out of trouble – there are no lifeguards here – surf in better-protected Crescent City (see p279).

North Coast Adventures (☎ 707-677-3124; www .northcoastadventures.com; 2hr/day $50/90) gives sea- and river-kayaking lessons and guided eco-trips (including tide-pool tours) around the North Coast.

Sleeping

Trinidad Bay B&B (☎ 707-677-0840; www.trinidadbay bnb.com; 560 Edwards St; r $165-195; ✗) Right in the town, opposite the lighthouse, this four-room Cape Cod–style house overlooks the harbor and Trinidad Head. Breakfast is delivered to your room.

Lost Whale Inn (☎ 707-677-3425; www.lostwhaleinn .com; 3452 Patrick's Point Dr; r incl breakfast $200-230, ste $300; ✗) Perched atop a grassy cliff, high above crashing waves and braying sea lions, this spacious, modern, light-filled B&B has jaw-dropping views out to the sea. Outside are lovely gardens and a 24-hour hot tub. Rooms have knotty-pine trimmings, red-wood floors and homey touches like country quilts. Kids welcome.

Turtle Rocks Oceanfront Inn (☎ 707-677-3707; www.turtlerocksinn.com; 3392 Patrick's Point Dr; r incl break-fast $200-240; ✗) Next door to the Lost Whale, Turtle Rocks has stark, modern rooms with glass-paneled decks and ocean views.

Trinidad Inn (☎ 707-677-3349; www.trinidadinn .com; 1170 Patrick's Point Dr; r $65-90; ✗) Rooms are sparklingly clean and attractively decorated at this up-market, gray-shingled motel under tall trees. Most rooms have kitchens.

Bishop Pine Lodge (☎ 707-677-3314; www.bishop pinelodge.com; 1481 Patrick's Point Dr; cottages $80-110, cot-tages with kitchen $90-120; ✗) It feels like summer camp at super-cute Bishop Pine, where you can rent free-standing redwood cottages in a grassy meadow. Expect woodsy charm and unintentionally retro-funky furniture.

View Crest Lodge (☎ 707-677-3393; www.viewcrest lodge.com; 3415 Patrick's Point Dr; tent/RV sites $16/24, 1-bedroom cottages $95-125; ✗) On a hill above the ocean on the inland side, some of the well-maintained, modern cottages have views and Jacuzzis; most have kitchens. There's also a good campground. Good bargain.

Emerald Forest (☎ 707-677-3554; www.cabinsinthe redwoods.com; 753 Patrick's Point Dr; tent sites $24, RV sites $34-36, cottages with kitchen $100-135; ✗) Has shady campsites and friendly proprietors, but the cottages are nothing special. There's a market on-site.

Trinidad Retreats (☎ 707-677-1606; www.trinidad retreats.com; daily/weekly rates from $90/540; ✗) Want to rent a house? Trinidad Retreats handles local properties.

Clam Beach (☎ 707-445-7491; sites per vehicle $10) South of town off Hwy 101, Clam Beach has excellent camping. Pitch your tent where you want to in the dunes (look for natural windbreaks). Facilities include pit toilets, cold water, picnic tables and fire rings.

Eating

Larrupin' Cafe (☎ 707-677-0230; 1658 Patrick's Point Dr; mains $20-30; ☺ dinner Thu-Tue) Trinidad's best-known, best-loved restaurant serves consistently great mesquite-grilled seafood and meat in a sophisticated, unpretentious country house; make reservations.

Catch Café (☎ 707-677-0390; 355 Main St; ☺ 11am-7pm Tue-Sun) For mostly organic, good food fast, head to Catch for pizettas, burgers, brown rice and veggies, homemade soups and vegan falafel. Order at the counter and sit outside.

Seascape Restaurant (☎ 707-677-3762; Trinidad Harbor; breakfast & lunch $8-10, dinner $11-22; ☺ 7am-10pm, shorter hours in winter) Sit in a vinyl booth and watch the fishermen from this harbor-side diner which serves good breakfasts and standard-American seafood dishes.

Trinidad Bay Eatery (☎ 707-677-3777; cnr Parker & Trinity Sts; breakfast & lunch $6-12, dinner $14-20; ☺ 7am-3pm Sun-Thu, 7am-8pm Fri & Sat) The Eatery makes OK diner food; dinners are pricey.

Katy's Smokehouse & Fishmarket (☎ 707-677-0151; www.katyssmokehouse.com; 740 Edwards St;

$\circ$ 9am-6pm) Katy's makes its own chemical-free smoked and canned fish, using line-caught sushi-grade seafood. Some of it is vacuum-packed for convenient transport.

Drinking

Beachcomber Café ($\textcircled{a}$ 707-677-0106; 363 Trinity St)
For the best homemade cookies and to meet hella-fun locals, head straight here. Good sandwiches and bagels too. Friday night there's live music.

Moonstone Grill ($\textcircled{a}$ 707-677-1616; Moonstone Beach; $\circ$ Wed-Sun) For drop-dead sunset views over a picture-perfect beach, have a cocktail at Moonstone. Comb your hair.

PATRICK'S POINT STATE PARK

Five miles north of Trinidad, coastal bluffs jut out to sea at 640-acre **Patrick's Point** ($\textcircled{a}$ 707-677-3570; 4150 Patrick's Point Dr; day use $6), where forests yield to meadows and sandy beaches abut the rocky headlands. Stroll scenic overlooks, climb giant rock formations, watch whales breach, gaze into tidepools or listen to barking sea lions and singing birds from this manicured park.

Sumêg is an authentic reproduction of a Yurok village, with hand-hewn redwood buildings where Native Americans gather for traditional ceremonies. In the native plant garden you'll find species for making traditional baskets and medicines.

On **Agate Beach** look for stray bits of jade and sea-polished agate. Follow the signs to tidepools, but tread lightly and obey regulations. The 2-mile **Rim Trail**, a former Yurok trail around the bluffs, circles the point with access to huge rocky outcroppings. Don't miss **Wedding Rock**, one of the park's most romantic spots. Other trails lead around unusual formations like **Ceremonial Rock** and **Lookout Rock**.

The park's three well-tended **campgrounds** ($\textcircled{a}$ reservations 800-444-7275; www.reserveamerica.com; sites $15-20) have coin-operated hot showers. Penn Creek and Abalone campgrounds are more sheltered than Agate Beach.

HUMBOLDT LAGOONS STATE PARK

Stretching out for miles along the coast, this **park** ($\textcircled{a}$ 707-488-2041) has long sandy beaches and two large coastal lagoons – Big Lagoon and Stone Lagoon – both excellent for bird-watching. The **Stone Lagoon Visitors Center** (Hwy 101; $\circ$ 10am-3pm Jun-Sep) opens when there are

volunteers. About a mile north of the visitors center, Freshwater Lagoon is also great for birding. Picnic at Stone Lagoon's north end.

All state campsites are first-come, first-served. The state park runs two **environmental campgrounds** (sites $12), open April to October; bring water. Stone Lagoon has six boat-in environmental campsites; Dry Lagoon, off Hwy 101, has six walk-in campsites. Check in at Patrick's Point State Park, at least 30 minutes before sunset. **Humboldt County Parks** ($\textcircled{a}$ 707-445-7651; sites $12) operates a lovely cypress-grove picnic area and campground beside Big Lagoon, a mile off Hwy 101, with flush toilets and cold water, but no showers.

Redwood Trails RV & Campground ($\textcircled{a}$ 707-488-2061; rv4fun.com/redwood.html; Hwy 101; tent/RV sites $15/25), opposite the turnoff to Dry Lagoon, has a general store, bakery, arcade, horse-back rides and, if you're lucky, elk lazing in the meadow outside.

REDWOOD NATIONAL PARK

A patchwork of public lands jointly administered by the state and federal governments, Redwood National and State Parks are actually a string of parks, starting in the north at Jedediah Smith Redwoods (p280) and continuing southward until Del Norte Coast Redwoods (p278), Prairie Creek Redwoods (p276) and Redwood National Park. Together, these parks have been declared an International Biosphere Reserve and World Heritage Site.

Redwood National Park is where you'll find some of the world's tallest trees and the Redwood Creek watershed, a place of great controversy in the years preceding the park's establishment in 1968.

The small town of **Orick** (population 650), at the southern tip of the park, is barely more than a few storefronts, among them a pretty good Mexican joint. (At the time of writing, Orick's much-beloved, überdelicious German restaurant, Rolf's Park Café, had been forced to move after three decades in the park, but promised to reopen. Ask the locals where it's gone, and seek it out!)

Orientation & Information

Unlike most national parks, there are no fees and no highway entrance stations at Redwood National Park, so it's imperative to pick up the free official map either at the park headquarters (p278) in Crescent City or

COAST REDWOODS: THE TALLEST TREES ON EARTH

Though they covered much of the northern hemisphere millions of years ago, redwood trees now grow only in China and two areas of California (and a small grove in Oregon). Coast redwoods *(Sequoia sempervirens)* are found in a narrow, 450-mile-long strip along California's Pacific coast between Big Sur and southern Oregon. They can live for 2200 years, grow to 370ft tall (the tallest tree ever recorded) and achieve a diameter of 22ft at the base, with bark up to 12in thick.

There's disagreement between the people who measure trees. Some say the tallest is the 370ft-high Stratosphere Giant in Rockefeller Forest (p260), others claim it's the Mendocino Tree in Montgomery Woods State Reserve (p256), but all concur that the second tallest redwood tree in the world is the National Geographic Tree, which is located here in Redwood National Park's Tall Trees Grove. But the 369ft-tall tree bears no sign, so you won't be able to find it. No matter, though, because you wouldn't be able to distinguish it from others in the grove anyway. The tallest trees reach their maximum height some time between 300 and 700 years of age. Because they're narrow at their bases, they generally aren't the ones you notice as you walk through the forest. The dramatic, fat-trunked giants, which make such a visually stunning impact from the ground, are ancient, as much as 2000 years old. But they're not as tall as the younger ones because their tops have been blown off in intense storms that have occurred over the centuries.

The structure of coast redwoods has been compared to a nail standing on its head. Unlike most trees, coast redwoods have no deep taproot and their root system is shallow in relation to their height – only 10ft to 13ft deep and spreading out 60ft to 80ft around the tree. The trees sometimes fall due to wind, but they are very flexible and usually sway in the wind as if they're dancing.

What gives these majestic giants their namesake color? It's the redwoods' high tannin content. It also makes their wood and bark resistant to insects and disease. The thick, spongy bark also has a high moisture content, enabling the ancient trees to survive many naturally occurring forest fires.

Coast redwoods are the only conifers in the world that can reproduce not only by seed cones, which grow to about the size of an olive at the ends of branches, but also by sprouting from their parents' roots and stumps, using the established root systems. Often you'll see a circle of redwoods standing in a forest, sometimes around a wide crater; this 'fairy ring' is made up of offspring that sprouted from one parent tree, which may have deteriorated into humus long ago. Burls, the large bumpy tissue growths on trunks and fallen logs, are a third method of reproduction.

Today only 4% of the North Coast's original two million acres of ancient redwood forests remain standing. Almost half of these old-growth forests are protected in Redwood National and State Parks.

at the **Redwood Information Center** (aka Kuchel Visitors center; ☎ 707-464-6101, ext 5265; www.nps.gov/redw; Hwy 101; ۞ 9am-5pm) in Orick, where there's a 12-minute introductory video. Rangers issue permits here to visit Tall Trees Grove. For in-depth redwood ecology, buy the excellent official park's handbook ($7.50).

Reserve park campgrounds in advance, lest you be relegated to the less-attractive nearby private RV parks.

Sights & Activities

Just north of the visitors center, turn east on Bald Hills Rd 2 miles to **Lady Bird Johnson Grove**, one of the park's most beautiful groves, accessible via a gentle 1-mile loop trail. Look for the signed turnoff. Continue for another 5 miles up Bald Hills to **Redwood Creek Overlook**. On the top of the ridgeline at 2100ft

elevation, you'll see over the trees and the entire watershed – provided it's not foggy. Just past the overlook lies the gated turnoff for the **Tall Trees Grove**, location of several of the world's tallest trees. Rangers issue only 50 vehicle permits per day, but they rarely run out. Pick one up, along with the gate-lock combination, from the Redwood Information Center or the park headquarters in Crescent City (p278). Allow four hours for the round trip, which includes a 6-mile drive down a rough dirt road (speed limit 15mph) and a steep 1.3-mile one-way hike, which descends 800ft to the grove.

Several longer trails include the awe-inspiring **Redwood Creek Trail**, which also reaches Tall Trees Grove. You'll need a free backcountry permit to hike and camp, accessible only from Memorial Day to Labor

TEDDY ROOSEVELT'S ELK

Roosevelt elk are the largest of their kind, with males weighing up to 1000lb and carrying massive antlers. They are named in honor of US President Teddy Roosevelt, who established the national wildlife refuge system in the early 1900s, and made Washington's Olympic National Park a protected habitat for the endangered elk. By 1925, there were only 25 left; today, the population stands at over 1000 animals. The elks' biggest threats are now from poachers and reckless drivers.

The best places to view these beasts in their velvety glory are all near Orick: along Davison Rd, west of Hwy 101; in Elk Prairie, on the Newton B Drury Scenic Parkway; and at Gold Bluffs Beach, near Fern Canyon. Try to visit in the early morning and late evening, when the herds feed.

Although the elk are visible year-round, their most active period is during the autumn 'rut' (late August to early October), when mature bulls aggressively challenge each other for the right to a harem. Late May and early June, when calves are born, is another busy time, but newborns are kept well hidden in the tall grasslands until they're ready to keep up with the herd. The elk can be especially unpredictable and dangerous at these times – keep at a safe distance!

Day, when summer footbridges are up. Otherwise, there's no way across the creek.

You can also come on horseback; phone **Redwood Trails** (☎ 707-488-3895). There's primitive camping in the park; inquire at visitors centers.

PRAIRIE CREEK REDWOODS STATE PARK
Famous for virgin redwood forests and unspoiled coastline, this 14,000-acre section of Redwood National and State Parks has 70 miles of hiking trails and spectacular scenic drives. Pick up maps and information and sit by the river-rock fireplace at **Prairie Creek Visitors Center** (☎ 707-464-6101, ext 5300; 9am-5pm Mar-Oct, 10am-4pm rest of year). Kids will love the taxidermy dioramas with their push-button, light-up displays. Outside, elk roam grassy flats.

Sights & Activities
The 8-mile **Newton B Drury Scenic Parkway** runs parallel to Hwy 101, passing through untouched ancient redwood forests. It's worth the short detour off the freeway to view the magnificence of these trees from your car. Numerous trails branch off from roadside pullouts. Intersecting scenic drives include the 3-mile-long **Cal Barrel Rd**, which intersects the parkway just north of the visitors center.

There are 28 mountain-biking and hiking trails through the park, from simple to strenuous. If you're tight on time or have mobility impairments, stop at **Big Tree**, an easy 100yd walk from the car park. Several other short nature trails start near the visitors center, including the Revelation Trail, Five-Minute Trail, Elk Prairie Trail and

Nature Trail. If you're depressed by the overall destruction of redwood forests, stop in at the **Ah-Pah Interpretive Trail** at the park's north end and stroll the recently reforested logging road: you will be surprised at how quickly the forest recovers and be inspired by humankind's ingenuity. Other fine treks include the 11.5-mile **Coastal Trail** and the 3.5-mile **South Fork–Rhododendron–Brown Creek Loop**, particularly beautiful in spring when rhododendrons and wildflowers bloom. Approach from the Brown Creek to South Fork direction – unless you like tramping uphill.

The **Coastal Drive** follows Davison Rd to Gold Bluffs. Go west 3 miles north of Orick and doubleback north along a sometimes-rough gravel road for 3.5 miles over the coastal hills to the **fee station** (per vehicle $6), then head up the coast to **Gold Bluffs Beach**, where you can picnic or camp. One mile ahead, take an easy half-mile trail to prehistoric-looking **Fern Canyon**, whose 60ft fern-covered sheer-rock walls can be seen in Steven Spielberg's *Jurassic Park 2: The Lost World*.

Sleeping & Eating
There are no motels or cabins. Pitch a tent in the campgrounds at the southern end of the park.

Elk Prairie Campground (☎ reservations 800-444-7275; www.reserveamerica.com; sites $15-20) Elk roam this popular campground, where you can sleep under redwoods or at the prairie's edge. The site has hot showers and some hike-in sites.

Gold Bluffs Beach (no reservations; sites $15) This campground sits between 100ft cliffs and wide-open ocean, but there are some windbreaks and solar-heated showers. Look for sites up the cliff under the trees.

The park also has three backcountry **campsites** (per person $3), as well as one **environmental campsite** (per person $12).

KLAMATH
pop 1420

It's easy to miss tiny Klamath, the southernmost unincorporated town in Del Norte County. The most noticeable landmark from the highway is the Klamath River Bridge at the southern end of town, where golden California bears stand sentry. Pull off Hwy 101 onto Klamath Rd, the main street.

There's not much here except water and trees, making it an excellent base for outdoor adventurers. For information or to learn about August's Salmon Festival, contact the **Klamath Chamber of Commerce** (☎ 800-200-2335; www.klamathcc.org). For hiking maps, stop by the Redwood National and State Parks Headquarters in Crescent City (p278) or the Redwood Information Center in Orick (p275).

Sights & Activities

The mouth of the **Klamath River** is a dramatic sight. Marine, riparian, forest and meadow ecological zones all converge: the birding is exceptional! For the best views, head north of town to Requa Rd and the **Klamath River Overlook**, and picnic on high bluffs above driftwood-strewn beaches. On a clear day, this is one of the most spectacular viewpoints on the North Coast, and one of the best whale-watching spots in California. For a good hike, head north along the Coastal Trail. You'll have the sand to yourself at **Hidden Beach**; access the trail at the northern end of Motel Trees.

Just south of the river, on Hwy 101, follow signs for the scenic **Coastal Drive**, a narrow, winding country road (unsuitable for RVs and trailers) atop extremely high cliffs over the ocean. Come when it's not foggy, and mind your driving. Though technically in Redwood National Park, it's much closer to Klamath.

It's hard to miss the giant statues of Paul Bunyan and Babe the Blue Ox towering over the parking lot at **Trees of Mystery** (☎ 707-482-2251, 800-638-3389; www.treesofmystery.net; 15500 Hwy 101; adult/child/senior $13.50/6.50/10; ☺ 8am-7pm Jun-Aug, 9am-4pm rest of year), a shameless tourist trap with a gondola running through the redwood

canopy, hardly worth the cost of admission. However, the **End of the Trail Museum**, hidden behind the gift shop, has an outstanding collection of Native American arts and artifacts, and it's free.

Sleeping & Eating

Woodsy Klamath is cheaper than nearby Crescent City, but there aren't as many places to eat or buy groceries, and there's nothing to do at night but play cards. You'll find a market and simple diner on the main street.

Historic Requa Inn (☎ 707-482-1425, 866-800-8777; www.requainn.com; 451 Requa Rd; r incl breakfast $85-135; ☒) By far the best option in Klamath (if not the entire county), this 1914 inn sits atop the riverbank at the edge of the national park; many of the charming country-style rooms have mesmerizing views, as does the dining room, where guests have breakfast and dinner. After a day hiking, play Scrabble by a roaring fire in the lodge-like common area. The restaurant is sometimes open to the public; call 24 hours ahead.

Ravenwood Motel (☎ 707-482-5911, 866-520-9875; www.ravenwoodmotel.com; 131 Klamath Blvd; r/ste with kitchen $58/105; ☒) The spotlessly clean rooms are better than anything in Crescent City and individually decorated with furnishings you'd expect in a city hotel, not a small-town motel. Mattresses are good, and sheets have fairly high thread counts. Outside there are barbecues.

Woodland Villa Cabins (☎ 707-482-2081, 888-866-2466; www.klamathusa.com; 15870 Hwy 101; d cottage $65-70, cottage with kitchen $84-88; ☒ 💻) Rent modest, cozy, lovingly tended cottages here. There's a picnic area and small market on-site.

Motel Trees (☎ 707-482-3152, 800-848-2982; www.treesofmystery.com; 15495 Hwy 101 S; d/q $60/82) Opposite Trees of Mystery, Motel Trees has standard-issue rooms and some theme rooms. The on-site family-style restaurant (open 8am to 8pm in summer; closed on Tuesday and Wednesday in winter) serves plain old American cooking.

Steelhead Lodge (☎ 707-482-8145; Hwy 169; mains $16-25; ☺ Fri-Sun dinner) Three miles upriver in Klamath Glen, this Western-style lodge grills big, juicy steaks. It also rents clean, basic motel rooms with kitchens ($65). Full bar.

Kamp Klamath (☎ 707-482-0227, 866-552-6284; www.kampklamath.com; tent/RV sites $18/22) If park campgrounds are full, pitch a tent at this 33-acre campground on the river's south shore.

DEL NORTE COAST REDWOODS STATE PARK

Marked by steep canyons and dense woods, half the 6400 acres of this **park** (vehicle day-use fee $6) are virgin redwood forest, crisscrossed by 15 miles of hiking trails. Pick up maps and inquire about guided walks at the Redwood National and State Parks Headquarters in Crescent City (right) or the Redwood Information Center in Orick (p275).

At the park's north end, watch the surf pound at **Crescent Beach**, just south of Crescent City via Enderts Beach Rd. Continue uphill to **Crescent Beach Overlook** and picnic area for wintertime whale-watching. Hike via the Crescent Beach Trail (or along the Coastal Trail from the south) to **Enderts Beach** for magnificent tidepools at low tide (tread lightly and obey posted regulations).

Tall trees cling precipitously to canyon walls that drop to the rocky, timber-strewn coastline, and it's almost impossible to get to the water, except via gorgeous but steep Damnation Trail or Footsteps Rock Trail. If you don't want to hike, head south to **False Klamath Cove**, where you can picnic and stretch your legs on the sand.

HI Redwood Hostel (☎ 707-482-8265, 800-909-4776; www.norcalhostels.org; 14480 Hwy 101; dm/r $16/42; ☘ closed Dec-Feb except for groups) is a rambling 1908 farmhouse on a bluff overlooking False Klamath Cove. It's quite special, so reserve well in advance.

Mill Creek Campground (☎ 800-444-7275; www .reserveamerica.com; sites $15-20) has hot showers and 145 sites in a redwood grove, 2 miles east of Hwy 101, 7 miles south of Crescent City.

CRESCENT CITY

pop 8800

On a crescent-shaped bay, Crescent City is California's last big town north of Arcata. Though founded in 1853 as a seaport and supply center for inland gold mines, Crescent City retains few old buildings: half the town was destroyed by a tsunami in 1964 (see the boxed text, opposite), a defining event that has oddly become a point of civic pride, as evidenced by the tsunami-logo flags decorating downtown lampposts. Completely rebuilt, it lacks 19th-century charm, but has a certain '60s-kitsch appeal, with many structures of utilitarian design, colored avocado, pink and white. The local economy depends heavily on shrimp and

crab fishing, and on the Pelican Bay maximum-security prison, just north of town.

Orientation & Information

Hwy 101 splits into two parallel one-way streets, with the southbound traffic on L St, northbound on M St. To see the major sights, turn west on Front St toward the lighthouse. Crescent City's tiny downtown is centered along 3rd St.

Crescent City–Del Norte Chamber of Commerce
(☎ 707-464-3174, 800-343-8300; www.northerncalifornia .net; 1001 Front St; ☘ 9am-5pm summer, Mon-Fri rest of year) Pick up local information.

Redwood National & State Parks Headquarters
(☎ 707-464-6101; 1111 2nd St; ☘ 9am-5pm) On-staff rangers and information about all four parks under its jurisdiction. The park's HQ is on the corner of K St.

Sights & Activities

The 1856 **Battery Point Lighthouse** (☎ 707-464-3089; www.delnortehistory.org/lighthouse), at the south end of A St, still operates on a tiny, rocky island that you can easily reach at low tide. From April to September, tour the **museum** (adult/child $3/1; ☘ 10am-4pm Mon-Sat Sep-May); hours vary with tides and weather. Phone for schedules, or check the bulletin board in the parking lot.

Six miles offshore near the California–Oregon border, the **St George Reef Lighthouse** (☎ 707-464-8299; www.stgeorgereeflighthouse.us; ☘ Oct-May) is visible from the mainland on clear days. The only way there is by monthly helicopter ($170), which includes a one-hour tour.

Inside a 1926 jailhouse on the corner of 6th St, the **Del Norte Historical Society Museum** (☎ 464-3922; 577 H St; adult/child $3/1; ☘ 10am-4pm Mon-Sat May-Sep) has collections of local Native American artifacts and minor historical exhibits on Del Norte's pioneer past, the 1964 tsunami and a giant Fresnel lens from the St George Reef Lighthouse. Free harborside **walking tours** leave the Crescent Harbor Gallery at 140 Marine Way on Wednesdays and Saturdays at 10am.

North Coast Marine Mammal Center (☎ 707-465-6265; www.nothcoastmarinemammal.org; 424 Howe Dr; by donation; ☘ 10am-5pm), just east of Battery Point, is where injured seals, sea lions and dolphins recuperate after being rescued.

Beachfront Park (Howe Dr), between B & H Sts, has a great harborside beach for little ones, with no big waves. There are picnic tables and a bicycle trail. Further east on

---

CRESCENT CITY'S GREAT TSUNAMI

On March 28, 1964, most of downtown Crescent City was destroyed by a great tsunami (tidal wave). At 3:36am, a giant earthquake occurred on the north shore of Prince William Sound in Alaska. Measuring 9.2 on the Richter scale, the quake was the most severe ever recorded in North America. The first of the ensuing giant ocean swells reached Crescent City only a few hours later.

Officials warned the sheriff's office, and at 7:08am evacuation of the waterfront began. The waves arrived an hour later. The first two were small, only about 13ft above the tide line, and many rejoiced, thinking the worst had passed. Then the water receded until the bay was emptied, leaving boats that had been anchored offshore sitting in the mud. Frigid water surged in, rising all the way up to 5th St, knocking buildings off their foundations, carrying away cars, trucks and anything else in its path. By the time the fourth and final wave receded, 29 blocks of town were destroyed, with more than 300 buildings displaced. Five gasoline storage tanks exploded. Eleven people died, three of whom were never found.

Many old-timers are still remembered for their heroic acts during and after the waves, helping to save their neighbors and later rebuild the town. Today the contemporary little downtown shopping center that replaced many of the destroyed buildings bears an unusual but appropriate name – Tsunami Landing.

Howe Dr, near J St, you'll come to **Kidtown**, with slides and swings and a make-believe castle for the kids. For a scenic drive, head north on Pebble Beach Dr, which ends at **Point St George**, where you can walk through grassy dunes.

Rent a board from **Rhyn Noll Surf & Skate** (☎ 707-465-4400; 275 L St). **Bikes & Trikes** (☎ 707-954-5078; 400 Front St) rents (and delivers) bikes. Go whale-watching or deep-sea fishing aboard the **Tally Ho II** (☎ 707-464 1236; Crescent City Harbor). There's weekend glow-in-the-dark bowling at **Tsunami Lanes** (☎ 707-464-4323; 760 L St).

The Del Norte County Fair takes place in August.

Sleeping

Most people stop here for only one night while traveling between San Francisco and Portland, so the motels are overpriced. For other accommodations, see under Pelican State Beach (p281).

Castle Island Getaway (☎ 707-465-5102; www .castleislandgetaway.com; 1830 Murphy Ave; r $100-150; ✗) Two blocks from the ocean, this B&B has three rooms (reservations required) in a home owned by a charming, sophisticated innkeeper; the upstairs suite has the most space.

Hampton Inn (☎ 707-465-5400; www.hamptoninn .com; 100 A St; r $139-179; ✗ ❄ 🖳 🖧) Crescent City's best corporate-style option has ocean-view rooms.

Cottage by the Sea (☎ 707-464-9068, 877-642-2254; www.waterfrontvacationrental.com; 205 South A St;

r with kitchen $145; ✗) Near the lighthouse, this sparkling-clean cottage is decorated with too many pillows on the bed. It's by the sea but has no view.

Curly Redwood Lodge (☎ 707-464-2137; www.curly redwoodlodge.com; 701 Hwy 101 S; r $62-67; ✗) Aficionados of 50s-modern love this motel, whose rooms are paneled with the lumber of just a single giant curly redwood, but the place needs upgrades such as thicker carpeting and door seals.

Anchor Beach Inn (☎ 707-464-2600; www.anchor beachinn.com; 880 Hwy 101 S; r $79-89; ✗) If you want amenities like microwave, DSL and sound-proof walls, this personality-free motel has up-to-date rooms.

Crescent Beach Motel (☎ 707-464-5436; www.cres centbeachmotel.com; 1455 Hwy 101 S; s $81-90, d $86-96) Just south of town, this basic motel has no phones, but does have some stunning un-obstructed ocean views.

Bayview Motel (☎ 707-465-2050, 800-446-0583; 310 Hwy 101 S; r $64-79; ✗) The nonsmoking rooms at this nondescript motel are nicer than the smoking rooms; they also have air-conditioning (nonsmoking rooms don't). On-site diner.

The county operates two reservable **campgrounds** (☎ 707-464-7230; sites $10) just outside town. **Florence Keller Park** (3400 Cunningham Lane) has 50 sites in a beautiful redwood grove (take Hwy 101 north to Elk Valley Cross Rd and follow the signs). **Ruby Van Deventer Park** (4705 N Bank Rd) has 18 sites along the Smith River, off Hwy 197.

NORTH COAST

Eating & Drinking

Beachcomber Restaurant (☎ 707-464-2205; 1400 Hwy 101 S; meals $13-19; ❍ dinner, closed Wed) For fish dinners, the Beachcomber has full ocean views (arrive before sunset), vinyl booths and straightforward preparations of seafood and meat. It's a salad-bar kind of place, but it's better than the harborside tourist joints. 'Small dinners' cost $7 to $11.

Thai House (☎ 707-464-2427; 105 N St; dishes $8-11; ❍ lunch & dinner) Behind Safeway, the Thai House serves surprisingly good Thai and Vietnamese cooking, with a few Chinese dishes as well.

Good Harvest Cafe (☎ 707-465-6028; 700 Northcrest Dr; dishes $4-8; ❍ breakfast & lunch) On the corner of Hwy 101, the Good Harvest serves Crescent City's best breakfast and lunch, with homemade soups, smoothies, sandwiches and great salads, with lots for vegetarians. Too bad it's closed at dinner.

Glen's Restaurant and Bakery (☎ 707-464-2914; 722 3rd St; dishes under $10; ❍ 5am-6:30pm Tue-Fri, 5am-2pm Sat) An old-school diner, Glen's serves all the standards, plus fresh baked goods. The atmosphere is better than the food.

Surfside Grill & Brewery (☎ 707-464-7962; 400 Front St; dishes $7-11; ❍ 11am-10pm) The cavernous Surfside goes in and out business, but when it's open it has good microbrews and pub grub.

Java Hut (☎ 707-465-4439; 437 Hwy 101 N; ❍ 5am-10pm) It's almost impossible to find strong coffee on the North Coast, but you'll find it here.

Getting There & Around

United Express (☎ 800-241-6522) flies into tiny **Crescent City airport** (CEC; ☎ 707-464-5750), north of town. Rent a vehicle, by reservation only, at **Hertz** (☎ 707-464-5750, 800-654-3131). **Redwood Coast Transit** (☎ 707-464-9314; www.redwoodcoast transit.org) serves Crescent City. Greyhound no longer comes here.

TOLOWA DUNES STATE PARK & LAKE EARL WILDLIFE AREA

Two miles north of Crescent City, this **state park and wildlife area** (☎ 707-464-6101, ext 5112; ❍ sunrise-sunset) encompasses 10,000 acres of wetlands, dunes, meadows and two lakes, **Lake Earl** and **Lake Tolowa**. This area is a major stopover on the Pacific Flyway route and there are birds everywhere, over 250 species (see p287). Listen for the whistling, warbling

chorus. On land, look for coyotes and deer; at sea, spot whales, seals and sea lions. Anglers fish for trout, and there are 20 miles of hiking and horseback trails. Tread lightly. In summer ask about guided walks. The best wetlands trails lie at the northern portion of the park, where a delicate balance exists between freshwater and marine habitats. Pick up information from the Crescent City–Del Norte County Chamber of Commerce or the Redwood National and State Parks office in Crescent City (p278). All is green and lush in spring and early summer; in winter it's wet; and in summer and fall it's dry.

The park and wildlife area is a patchwork of lands administered by California State Parks and the Department of Fish and Game (DFG). The DFG focuses on single-species management, hunting and fishing; the California State Parks' focus is on ecodiversity and recreation. You might be hiking a vast expanse of pristine dunes, then suddenly hear a shotgun or whining all-terrain vehicle. Strict regulations limit where and when you can hunt and drive; trails are clearly marked.

There are two primitive, nonreservable **campgrounds** (sites $10): a walk-in environmental campground (no water) and an equestrian campsite (nonpotable well water). Register at the Jedediah Smith or Del Norte Coast Redwoods State Park campgrounds. Bring firewood and mosquito repellent in spring and early summer.

JEDEDIAH SMITH REDWOODS STATE PARK

California's northernmost redwood park, **Jedediah Smith** (day-use fee $6) sits 10 miles northeast of Crescent City (via Hwy 101 east to Hwy 197). The redwood stands are so dense that there are few trails through the park, but the outstanding 11-mile **Howland Hill scenic drive** cuts through otherwise inaccessible areas (take Hwy 199 to South Fork Rd; turn right after crossing two bridges). It's a rough road, impassable for RVs, but if you can't hike, it's the best way to see the forest.

As you drive along Hwy 199, you will see brown wooden signs with yellow lettering announcing the names of the groves. Pull over. There's rarely a trail, but overlooks give glimpses of the forest's lush diversity.

Stop for a stroll through the **Simpson-Reed Grove**. If it's foggy at the coast it may be sunny

---

DETOUR: SMITH RIVER NATIONAL RECREATION AREA

West of Jedediah Smith Redwoods, the Smith River, the state's last remaining undammed water-way, runs right beside Hwy 199. Originating high in the Siskiyou Mountains, its serpentine course cuts through deep canyons beneath thick forests. Chinook salmon and steelhead trout annually migrate up its clear waters. Camp, hike, raft and kayak; check regulations if you want to fish. Stop by the **Six Rivers National Forest Headquarters** (☎ 707-457-3131; www.fs.fed.us/r5/sixrivers; 10600 Hwy 199, Gasquet; ☙ 8am-4:30 summer, Mon-Fri fall-spring) to get your bearings. Pick up pamphlets for the **Darlingtonia Trail** and **Myrtle Creek Botanical Area**, both easy jaunts into the woods where you can see rare plants and learn about the area's geology.

Patrick Creek Lodge (☎ 707-457-3323; www.patrickcreeklodge.com; r $90-130), a 1926 log-cabin-style roadhouse, has simple accommodations and serves three surprisingly good meals a day (lunch $6-11, dinner $15-22).

---

here. There's a **swimming hole** and picnic area near the park entrance, off Hwy 199, 5 miles east of Hwy 101. An easy half-mile trail, departing from the far side of the campground, crosses the Smith River via a summer-only footbridge, leading to **Stout Grove**, the park's most famous grove. The **visitors center** (☎ 707-464-6101, ext 5113; ☙ 10am-4pm summer, Sat & Sun fall & spring) sells hiking maps and nature guides. If you wade in the river, be careful in spring when currents are swift and the water is cold.

The popular **campground** (☎ reservations 800-444-7275; www.reserveamerica.com; sites $20) has hot showers and sits beneath redwoods beside the Smith River.

Just east, **Hiouchi Information Center** (☎ 707-464-6101, ext 5064; ☙ 9am-5pm, mid-Jun–mid-Sep) stocks maps and books. Families are able to borrow free activity backpacks with projects for kids. When the visitors centers are closed, go to the Redwood National and State Parks Headquarters in Crescent City (p278).

A mile east of the park in Hiouchi, rent inner tubes, inflatable kayaks and mountain bikes at **Lunker Fish Trips** (☎ 707-458-4704, 800-248-4704; 2590 Hwy 199), one of the North Coast's finest steelhead-fishing guides (fishing is best September to April).

Hiouchi Motel (☎ 707-458-3041, 866-446-8244; www.hiouchimotel.com; 2097 Hwy 199; s $36, d $55-60; ▣) has straightforward motel rooms. Over

the street, **Hiouchi Hamlet RV Resort** (☎ 707-458-3321, 800-722-9468; tent sites $15, RV sites $22-27) also has a small market where you can pick up supplies and fishing licenses.

PELICAN BEACH STATE PARK

Never-crowded **Pelican State Beach** (☎ 707-464-6101, ext 5151) occupies five coastal acres on the Oregon border. From the south, pull off Hwy 101 immediately before the state agricultural inspection station. There are no facilities. It's a great beach for kite flying; pick one up at the shop just over the border in Oregon.

The best reason to visit here is to stay at secluded, charming **Casa Rubio** (☎ 707-487-4313; 17285 Crissey Rd; www.casarubio.com; r $78-158; ✖), where three of the four ocean-view inn rooms have kitchens. Next door, the **Nautical** (☎ 707-487-5006; 16850 Hwy 101 N; mains $19-29; ☙ dinner Wed-Sun) has spectacular sunset views and stylized Cal-French cooking, the best for miles around. **White Rock Resort** (☎ 707-487-1021, 888-487-4659; www.whiterockresort.com; 16800 Hwy 101 N; r $150-175; ✖) has 'cottages' (converted mobile homes); pay the extra $25 for ocean-front views. **Sea Escape** (☎ 707-487-7333; www.seaescape.us; 15370 Hwy 101 N; r $95-135; ✖) has clean motel-style suites, some with ocean views and kitchens.

Pitch a tent by the ocean (no windbreaks) at **Clifford Kamph Memorial Park** (☎ 707-464-7230; 15100 Hwy 101; sites $5); no RVs.

Northern Mountains

When visitors envision Northern California – even when Californians picture Northern California – their mental images are of cable cars, redwoods, foggy wharfs, grapevines, wild coasts and a tall orange bridge…all beautiful and accurate. But there is another Northern California, a northern Northern California that has yet to fill the pages of the imagination.

Nearly 37 million people live in the Golden State, more than any other, and it's the country's number one tourist destination. Yet in this most populous, most visited state in the Union there remains a hidden corner of untouched wonder, where few live and few venture.

Vast expanses of untamed wilderness cover the Northern Mountains region. The terrain courses with rivers and streams, and cobalt lakes grace alpine peaks. The region is lightly populated and the intimate towns beckon with charm and lore. Here you'll encounter all the natural splendor of Yosemite and all the '49er romance of the Gold Country. There is only one thing the Sierra has that this counterpart lacks…crowds. Even in peak summer the region's biggest draws, Mt Shasta and Lassen Volcanic National Park, are accessible and calm.

What has safeguarded the beauty thus far is this: of the approximately 24,000 sq miles that comprise the region, roughly 65% is protected national forest. Still, where growth is possible it is flourishing, and recently public land has been exposed to private development. Ex-urbanites are drawn here in the hope of mining this era's gold – space and tranquillity. For now, however, the Northern Mountains remain California's most innocent and wild frontier.

HIGHLIGHTS

- Climbing stunning **Mt Shasta** (p297)
- Camping near, hiking around, boating on and swimming in **Manzanita Lake** (p289) in Lassen Volcanic National Park
- Dancing to Latin hip-hop at **Sengthongs** (p296) in Dunsmuir
- Exploring lightless caves all day and sleeping under starlit skies all night at **Lava Beds National Monument** (p304)
- Watching magnificent bald eagles swoop down and lift up huge salmon from **Trinity Lake** (p308)

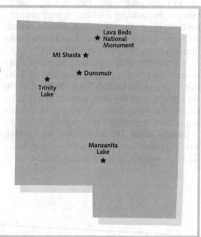

- AVERAGE TEMPS IN REDDING: JAN 35/55°F, JUL 64/98°F

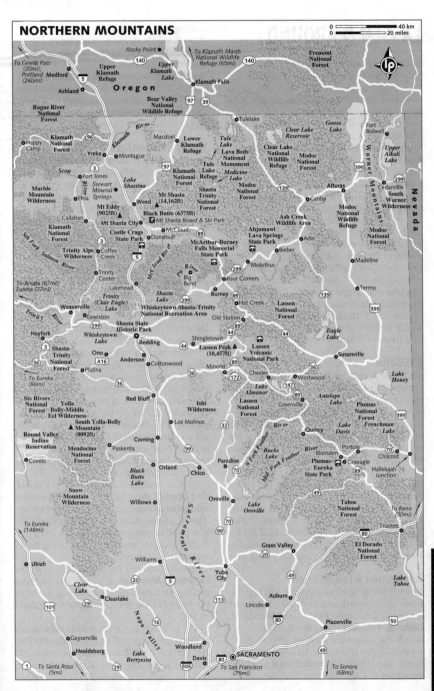

LASSEN & AROUND

Lassen Volcanic National Park and Shasta Lake are the Lassen area's most popular destinations, however, there are many other treasured spots in the region to explore. Redding is the region's gateway city, and the last sizable town in this northern part of the state. The city is not a tourist destination (though it promotes itself as such), but it does make a fine base from which to venture out into the surrounding scenic wilderness. Lovely forest-framed Whiskeytown Lake is a short jaunt to the west on Hwy 299, and vast Shasta Lake is easily accessible 15 minutes north along I-5. Lassen Volcanic National Park is only 50 miles from Redding, close enough to be enjoyed on a daytrip. However, to really do justice to the park and to yourself, you'll want to invest a few days exploring that area.

From Lassen Volcanic National Park you can take one of two very scenic routes: Hwy 36, which heads east past Chester, Lake Almanor and historic Susanville; or Hwy 89, which heads southeast to the cozy mountain town of Quincy.

REDDING

pop 88,500 / elevation 557ft

Originally called Poverty Flats during the gold rush for its lack of wealth, Redding now thrives. Travelers used to dismiss Redding as no more than a pit stop at the north end of the Sacramento Valley, but in the last decade Redding has transformed itself into one of the fastest growing, most desirable residential areas (and pit stops) in the country. (Amazingly, it currently has *the* fastest percentage growth in median housing prices in the USA.) A tourist destination it is not, though it is eagerly trying to become one. Recent constructions like the Sundial Bridge and Turtle Bay Exploration Park are enticing lures and worth a visit…but not a long one.

Orientation & Information

Downtown is bordered by the Sacramento River on the north and east, with the major thoroughfares being Pine St and Market St. **California Welcome Center** (☎ 530-365-1180, 800-474-2782; www.shastacascade.org; 1699 Hwy 273, Anderson; ☷ 9am-6pm Mon-Sat, 10am-6pm Sun) About 10 miles south of Redding, at the south end of Anderson's Prime Outlets Mall.

Redding Convention & Visitors Bureau (☎ 530-225-4100, 800-874-7562; www.visitredding.org; 777 Auditorium Dr; ☷ 9am-6pm Mon-Fri, 10am-5pm Sat) Near Turtle Bay Exploration Park.

Shasta-Trinity National Forest Headquarters (☎ 530-226-2500; 3644 Avtech Parkway; ☷ 8am-4:30pm Mon-Fri) Has maps and free camping permits for all seven national forests in Northern California. South of town in the USDA Service Center near the airport.

Sights & Activities

Situated on 300 acres, **Turtle Bay Exploration Park** (☎ 530-243-8850, 800-887-8532; www.turtlebay.org; 800 Auditorium Dr; adult/child $11/6; ☷ 9am-5pm, closed Tue Nov-Feb) is an artistic, cultural and scientific center for visitors of all ages, with an emphasis on the Sacramento River watershed. The complex houses art and natural science museums, interactive exhibits for kids focusing on forest ecology, extensive arboretum gardens, a butterfly house and 22,000-gallon, walk-through river aquarium full of regional aquatic life, including namesake turtles. The **Café at Turtle Bay** (☎ 530-242-3181; meals $10; ☷ 8am-7pm Sun-Thu, 8am-10pm Fri & Sat) serves excellent gourmet coffee and great light meals.

Resembling a run-aground (and wildly off-course) cruise ship, shimmering-white **Sundial Bridge** spans the river vista. Completed in 2004, this impressive glass-deck pedestrian overpass connects the Turtle Bay Exploration Park to the north bank of the Sacramento. Designed by renowned Spanish architect Santiago Calatrava, the bridge/sundial now attracts visitors from around the world who come to marvel at this unique feat of engineering artistry.

Further west in Caldwell Park is the **Redding Aquatic Center** (☎ 530-245-7247; www.redding aquaticcenter.com; adult/child $3.50/3; ☷ 1-5pm summer). This hugely popular center has an Olympic-size pool, another vast recreation pool and a 160ft-long water slide. The opening hours are subject to change.

Also in Caldwell Park you can pick up the **Sacramento River Trail**, a paved walking and cycling path that meanders along the river for miles (13 for now, with plans to extend to 20).

Try to catch some live music downtown at the refurbished 1935 art deco **Cascade Theater** (☎ 530-243-8877; www.cascadetheater.org; 1731 Market St). If nothing else, take a peek inside; this is a neon-lit gem.

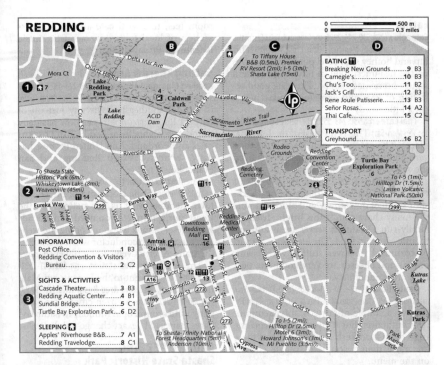

REDDING

0 ————————————— 500 m
0 ————————————— 0.3 miles

EATING 🍴
Breaking New Grounds..........9 B3
Carnegie's..........................10 B3
Chu's Too...........................11 B2
Jack's Grill.........................12 B3
Rene Joule Patisserie...........13 B3
Señor Rosas.......................14 A2
Thai Cafe..........................15 C2

TRANSPORT
Greyhound........................16 B2

INFORMATION
Post Office.........................1 B3
Redding Convention & Visitors
  Bureau............................2 C2

SIGHTS & ACTIVITIES
Cascade Theater..................3 B3
Redding Aquatic Center........4 B1
Sundial Bridge....................5 C1
Turtle Bay Exploration Park....6 D2

SLEEPING 🛏
Apples' Riverhouse B&B.........7 A1
Redding Travelodge..............8 C1

Sleeping

Redding's many motels and hotels huddle around extremely noisy thoroughfares, though a few rooms can be found on less busy N Market. B&Bs offer a quiet alternative.

Tiffany House B&B Inn (☎ 530-244-3225; www.tiffanyhousebb.com; 1510 Barbara Rd; r/cottage $100/150; 🌐) On a quiet cul-de-sac a mile north of the river. Full of antiques, rosebuds and ruffles, this Victorian property has an expansive garden with sweeping views. The hosts are extremely hospitable and make a big yummy to-do over breakfast. The rooms are cozy, the cottage especially.

Apples' Riverhouse B&B (☎ 530-243-8440; www.applesriverhouse.com; 201 Mora Court; r $105; ✖) Literally steps from the Sacramento River Trail, this modern, suburban ranch-style home has three comfortable upstairs rooms, two with decks. In the evening the sociable hosts invite you for cheese and wine. Bikes are yours to borrow.

O'Brien Mountain Inn (see p287) For another B&B option in the area try this sweet place located just 15 minutes north off I-5 near Shasta Lake.

Redding Travelodge (☎ 530-243-5291, 800-243-1106; www.reddingtravelodge.com; 540 N Market; d $80; ✖ 🌐) The best of the four motels at the north end of N Market. The rooms are particularly tidy and the staff friendly. There's wireless access, and a full breakfast at the adjoining restaurant is included.

There are a couple of 'motel rows' that are located close to I-5 at the southern end of town. On the east side of the freeway, Hilltop Dr has a number of larger, more upmarket (but not quieter) chain hotels and motels. The following two places are on Bechelli Lane, just west of the freeway close to the Cypress Ave exit.

Motel 6 (☎ 530-221-0562, 800-466-8356; www.motel6.com; 2385 Bechelli Lane; d $65) Relatively quiet rooms facing away from the highway.

Howard Johnson's (☎ 530-223-1935, 800-446-4656; www.hojo.com; 2731 Bechelli Lane; d $90; ✖ 🌐)

There are plenty of RV parks on the outskirts of town, including Premier RV Resort to the north. For good options in tent camping visit Whiskeytown Lake (p287) or Shasta Lake (p288).

NORTHERN MOUNTAINS

Eating

Carnegie's (☎ 530-246-2926; cnr Oregon & Yuba Sts; mains $10; ✆ 10am-3pm Mon-Tue, 10am-11pm Wed-Fri) This hip and homey split-level pubby place serves up the healthiest food in town (eg big fresh salads, homemade soup). There's a good selection of beer and wine too. Friday nights get a little rowdy.

Thai Cafe (☎ 530-243-5523; 820 Butte St; meals $10-15; ✆ Mon-Sat) This is the best of the few Thai places. The menu is extensive and the food very good. The seafood mains (so far from the sea) are surprisingly fresh.

Mi Pueblito (☎ 530-224-9888; 916 E Cypress #100; meals $10; ✆ 11am-9pm) At the corner of Larkspur south of downtown, and hidden among the many chain giants, this bright, friendly, family-run restaurant serves fresh and authentic Mexican food. The *huarraches* (a sort of cornmeal turnover stuffed with beans, onions and cheese) are very good; the burritos are fat and juicy.

Señor Rosas (☎ 530-241-8226; 2056 Eureka Way; meals $10; ✆ 11am-3pm Mon-Thu & Sat, 11am-8pm Fri) Run by a couple of gringos, this taco joint isn't authentic, but it's genuinely *delicioso*. Ingredients are fresh and organic and there are more than a couple of veggie choices on the menu.

Chu's Too (☎ 530-244-2987; 1135 Pine St; mains $10-25; ✆ lunch & dinner Mon-Fri, dinner Sat) Though billed as Chinese, more than half the menu is Japanese. Along with all the sweet-and-sour standards there's an impressive fresh-caught array of sushi offerings.

Jack's Grill (☎ 530-241-9705; 1743 California St; mains $10-25; ✆ 5-11pm Mon-Sat) This funky little old-time place is popular with locals (and curious visitors who wonder what all the fuss is about). All the fuss is about steak – big, thick, charbroiled chunks of it. Regulars start lining up for dinner at 4pm, when cocktail hour begins. There are no reservations, so it easily takes an hour for seating…hey, no wait at the bar.

Rene Joule Patisserie (☎ 530-241-6750; 1720 Market St; breakfast $8; ✆ 6am-2pm Mon-Fri, 7am-2pm Sat & Sun) Across from the Cascade Theater, this laidback little café is an excellent choice for breakfast, whether it be gourmet coffee and an oven-fresh muffin or the featured morning egg dish.

Breaking New Grounds (☎ 530-246-4563; 1320 Yuba St; ✆ 6am-7pm Mon-Thu, 6am-10pm Fri, 7am-4pm Sat) With a sort of relaxed yet formal living-room feel, this wi-fi café attracts a cross-section of local folks. Live acoustic music is featured Friday nights.

Getting There & Around

Redding Municipal Airport (☎ 530-224-4321; www.ci .redding.ca.us/airports/rma/rma.htm; 6751 Woodrum Circle) is 4 miles southeast of the city just off of Airport Rd. Horizon Airlines now has daily round-trip flights from Redding to Los Angeles and Portland. And United Express has daily services between Redding and San Francisco.

The **Amtrak station** (☎ 800-872-7245; www.amtrak .com; 1620 Yuba St), one block west of the Downtown Redding Mall, is not staffed. For the *Coast Starlight* (p726) you need to make advance reservations by phone or via the website, then pay the conductor when you board the train. Alternatively, visit a travel agency.

The **Greyhound bus station** (☎ 530-241-2531; 1321 Butte St), adjacent to the Downtown Mall, never closes. **Redding Area Bus Authority** (RABA; ☎ 530-241-2877) has a dozen city routes operating until around 6pm Monday to Saturday. Fares start at $1 (exact change only).

AROUND REDDING

Shasta State Historic Park

On Hwy 299, 6 miles west of Redding, this **state historic park** (✆ sunrise-sunset) preserves the ruins of an 1850s Gold Rush mining town called Shasta – not to be confused with Mt Shasta City (p299). When the Gold Rush was at its heady heights, everything and everyone had to pass through Shasta. But when the railroad bypassed it to set up in Poverty Flats (present-day Redding), poor Shasta lost its reason for being.

An 1861 courthouse houses an excellent **museum** (☎ 530-243-8194; admission $2; ✆ 10am-5pm Wed-Sun), with a mighty fine gun collection and a gallows out back. Pick up walking-tour pamphlets from the visitor information desk here. Trails pass by the Catholic cemetery, brewery ruins and many other historic sites. The Masonic lodge, two stores and a bakery are still functioning buildings.

Whiskeytown Lake

Two miles further west on Hwy 299, **Whiskeytown Lake** (☎ 530-242-3400; www.nps.gov/whis; day-use per vehicle $5) takes its name from an old mining camp. When the lake was created in the 1960s by the construction of a 263ft

NORTHERN MOUNTAINS

dam, designed for power generation and Central Valley irrigation, the few remaining buildings of old Whiskeytown were moved and the site was submerged. Today, people descend upon the lake's 36 miles of forested shoreline to engage in a range of activities, including camping, swimming, sailing, gold panning, hiking and mountain biking.

The **visitors center** (☎ 530-246-1225; ⏲ 9am-6pm summer, 10am-4pm winter), on the northeast point of the lake just off Hwy 299, offers free maps and information relating to Whiskeytown and Whiskeytown-Shasta-Trinity National Recreation Area. Look for the schedules of ranger-led interpretive programs and guided walks.

On the southern shore of the lake, **Brandy Creek** is good for swimming and has lifeguards on duty during summer. Just off Hwy 299, on the northern edge of the lake, **Oak Bottom Marina** (☎ 530-359-2269) has boats for rent. The **Tower House Historic District** is at the west end side of the lake, with the El Dorado mine ruins and the pioneer Camden House open for summer tours.

Oak Bottom Campground (☎ 800-365-2267; tent/RV sites $12/25) is a privately run place with RV and tent camping. Most attractive are the walk-in sites right on the shore. **Primitive campsites** (sites summer/winter $10/5) surround the lake.

SHASTA LAKE

About 15 minutes north of Redding, Shasta Lake (www.shastalake.com) is the largest reservoir in California and home to the state's biggest population of nesting bald eagles. It is surrounded on its several arms by hiking trails and campgrounds, and teeming with just about anything that will float – it's popular.

The **ranger station** (☎ 530-275-1589; 14250 Holiday Rd; ⏲ 8am-5pm Mon-Sat, 8am-4:30pm Sun summer, 8am-4:30pm Mon-Fri rest of year) offers free maps and information about fishing, boating and hiking. To get here, take the Mountaingate Wonderland Blvd exit off I-5, about 9 miles north of Redding, and turn right.

Sights & Activities

At the south end of Shasta Lake on Shasta Dam Blvd (Hwy 151), is the colossal **Shasta Dam**, a 15-million-ton dam second only in size to Hoover Dam in Nevada. Its 487ft spillway is as high as a 60-story building – three times higher than Niagara Falls. The dam

---

THE AVIAN SUPERHIGHWAY

California is on the Pacific Flyway, a migratory route for hundreds of species of birds heading south in winter and north in summer. There are birds to see year-round, but the best viewing opportunities are during the spring and fall migrations. Flyway regulars feature everything from tiny finches, hummingbirds, swallows and woodpeckers to eagles, hawks, swans, geese, ducks, cranes and herons. Much of the flyway route corresponds with I-5 (or fly-5 in the birds' case), so a drive up the interstate in spring or fall is a show: great Vs of geese undulate in the sky and noble hawks stare from roadside perches.

In Northern California, established wildlife refuges safeguard wetlands used by migrating waterfowl. Klamath Basin National Wildlife Refuges (p305) near Tule Lake offer extraordinary year-round bird-watching.

---

was built from 1938 to 1945; Woody Guthrie wrote 'This Land Is Your Land' while he was here working on the dam. The **Shasta Dam Visitors Center** (☎ 530-275-4463; ⏲ 8:30am-4:30pm) offers fascinating free guided tours of the structure's rumbling interior.

High in the limestone megaliths at the north end of the lake hide the prehistoric **Lake Shasta Caverns** (☎ 530-238-2341, 800-795-2283; www.lakeshastacaverns.com; adult/child $20/12). Tours of the crystalline caves operate daily and include a boat ride across Lake Shasta. Bring a sweater, as the temperature inside is 58°F year-round. Take the Shasta Caverns Rd exit from I-5, about 15 miles north of Redding, and follow the signs for 1.5 miles.

Sleeping & Eating

O'Brien Mountain Inn (☎ 530-238-8026, 888-799-8026; www.obrienmtn.com; Shasta Caverns Rd; r $135-250, tree house $275; ✗) As a tribute to their love of music (both were involved in the LA music biz in prior lives) the owners have tastefully decked out each room with a musical-genre theme (ie jazz, world beat, classical). There's also a phenomenal (and very romantic) tree house with cherry-wood floors, skylights, hot tub, kitchen and fireplaces. Breakfast is an orchestrated symphony.

Holiday Harbor Resort (☎ 530-238-2383, 800-776-2628; www.lakeshasta.com; Holiday Harbor Rd; sites

NORTHERN MOUNTAINS

$32) This resort has tent and RV camping (mostly RV), houseboat rentals and a busy marina offering parasailing and fishing-boat rentals. There is also a little **café** (8am-3pm) with lakefront deck tables. It's off the Shasta Caverns Rd next to the lake.

Lakeshore Inn & RV (530-238-2003, 888-238-2003; 20483 Lakeshore Dr; tent/RV sites $25-35, cabins from $90;) On the western side of I-5, this vacation spot has a restaurant and tavern.

Houseboats (www.shastalake.com; per week winter/summer from $1200/1700) These are a wildly popular lodging option. Most of them sleep six to 10 people and require a two-night minimum stay. If you want to rent one – especially in the summer months – make reservations as far in advance as possible.

Antlers RV Park & Campground (530-238-2322, 800-642-6849; www.shastalakevacations.com; 20679 Antlers Rd; tent/RV sites $15-33, cabins from $97;) East of I-5 in Lakehead, at the north end of the lake, this family-oriented campground has a country store and marina renting watercraft and houseboats.

US Forest Service (USFS) campgrounds (877-444-6777; www.reserveusa.com; sites $6-26) About half of the USFS campgrounds around the lake are open year-round. Free boat-in sites are first-come, first-served. Camping outside organized campgrounds requires a campfire permit from May to October, available free from any national forest service office.

LASSEN VOLCANIC NATIONAL PARK

The dry, smoldering, treeless terrain within this 106,000-acre national park stands in stunning contrast to the cool, green conifer forest that surrounds it. Entering the park (especially from the southern entrance), is to suddenly step into another world – onto another planet. The Venusian scape here offers a fascinating glimpse into the earth's fiery core. In a fuming display, the terrain is marked by roiling hot springs, steamy mud pots, noxious sulfur vents, fumaroles, lava flows, cinder cones, craters and crater lakes.

In earlier times, the region was a summer encampment and meeting point for Native American tribes – namely the Atsugewi, Yana, Yahi and Maidu. They hunted deer and gathered plants for basket-making here. Some indigenous people still live near and work closely with the park to help educate visitors on their ancient history and contemporary culture.

Information

Wherever you enter the park, you'll be given a free map with general information.

Kom Yah-mah-nee Visitor Facility (9am-6pm Jun-Sep, hours vary rest of year) About a mile north of the park's southwest entrance station. A handsome new center with educational exhibits, bookstore, auditorium, gift shop and restaurant. Visitor information and maps are also available.

Manzanita Lake Visitors center & Loomis Museum (530-595-4444, ext 5180; 9am-5pm Jun-Sep) Just past the entrance-fee station inside the park's northern boundary. Holds more specialized publications about the park's history and natural features and topographic maps. There are exhibits and an orientation video inside the museum; during summer, rangers and volunteers lead interpretive programs dealing with geology, wildlife, astronomy and cultural topics.

Park headquarters (530-595-4444; www.nps.gov /lavo; 38050 Hwy 36; 8am-4:30pm, Mon-Fri Oct-May) About a mile west of the tiny town of Mineral, it's the nearest stop for refueling and supplies.

Sights & Activities

Lassen Peak, the world's largest plug-dome volcano, rises 2000ft over the surrounding landscape to 10,457ft above sea level. Classified as an active volcano, its most recent eruption took place in 1915 when it blew a giant cloud of smoke, steam and ash 7 miles into the atmosphere. The national park was created the following year to protect the newly formed landscape. Some areas destroyed by the blast, including the aptly named **Devastated Area**, northeast of the peak, are recovering impressively.

Hwy 89, the road through the park, wraps around Lassen Peak on three sides and provides access to the geothermal areas, lakes, picnic areas and hiking trails. It's only possible to drive through the park in summer, usually around June to October. There have been times when the road has been closed due to snow (as much as 40ft of it) well into July.

In total, the park has 150 miles of **hiking trails**, including a 17-mile section of the popular Pacific Crest Trail. Experienced hikers can attack the Lassen Peak Trail, if you have at least 4½ hours to make the 5-mile round trip. Early in the season you'll need snow and ice-climbing equipment to reach the summit. Near Lassen Chalet, a gentler 2.3-mile trail leads through meadows and forest to **Mill Creek Falls**. Further north on Hwy 89, the roadside **Sulfur Works** have bubbling

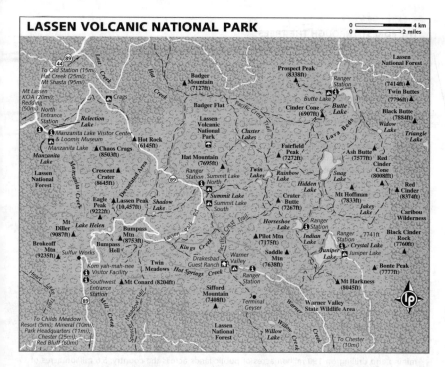

mud pots, a hissing steam vent, fountains and fumaroles. At **Bumpass Hell**, a moderate 1.5-mile trail and boardwalk leads to an active geothermal area, with weirdly colored pools and billowing clouds of steam. You can go fishing and boating on **Manzanita Lake**.

Sleeping

Drakesbad Guest Ranch (☎ 530-520-1512, ext 120; www.drakesbad.com; Warner Valley Rd; rooms per person $135-185; ❧ Jun-early Oct; ▣) Seventeen miles northwest of Chester, this is a fabulously secluded place inside the park's southern boundary. Guests, many of whom are faithful repeat visitors, use the hot springs–fed swimming pool or go horseback riding. Except in the main lodge, there's no electricity here (think kerosene lamps and campfires). Rates include country-style meals (vegetarian cuisine available) and campfire barbecues every Wednesday; ask about weekly discounts.

Childs Meadow Resort (☎ 530-595-3383, 888-595-3383; www.childsmeadowresort.com; 41500 Hwy 36E, Mill Creek; d/cabins $60/175) This old-fashioned resort is around 9 miles outside the park's southwest entrance. The rustic cabins sit at the edge of a spectacularly lush mountain meadow.

Mt Lassen KOA (☎ 530-474-3133, 800-562-3403; 7749 KOA Rd; tent sites $20-25, cabins $45-70; ❧ mid-Mar–Nov; ▣) Off Hwy 44, in Shingletown almost 20 miles west of the park. This place has all the KOA amenities: a children's playground, deli and laundry facilities.

The park has eight developed **campgrounds** (sites $10-14) with many more in the surrounding Lassen National Forest. Campgrounds in the park are open from late May to late October, depending on snow conditions. Manzanita Lake is the only one with hot showers, but both Summit Lake campgrounds, in the middle of the park, are also popular. All sites are first-come, first-served.

Getting There & Away

The park has two entrances. The northern entrance, at Manzanita Lake, is 50 miles east of Redding via Hwy 44. The southwest entrance is on Hwy 89 about 5 miles north of the junction with Hwy 36. From this junction it is 5 miles west on Hwy 36 to Mineral and 48 miles west to Red Bluff. Heading east

THE FOREST THROUGH THE TREES

The wonder is that we can see these trees and not wonder more.

Ralph Waldo Emerson

What characterizes, unites and defines the Northern Mountains region are, of course, mountains – great, densely green, richly forested mountains. The Northern Mountains cover an area roughly the size of West Virginia and approximately 65% of that total landmass is thickly treed national forest. The most wild and delicate wilderness regions in California are found here. And the region is home to some of the world's richest biodiversity. The Klamath-Siskiyou eco-region, for example, protects one of the four most diverse temperate coniferous forests on the globe.

Over the years, the wooded Northern Mountains territory – at least the part that's accessible to humans – has been the source of contentious struggles between loggers and environmentalists; however, until recently the area's most remote habitats have continued to thrive in pristine seclusion. Within the inner, roadless reaches of the area's five national forests, old-growth groves survive untouched, rivers and streams run clear, and wildlife remain mostly out of hunters' range.

In 2005 the National Forest Service celebrated its centennial anniversary. A little over 100 years ago President Theodore Roosevelt initiated the agency with the visionary objective of preserving and protecting, for perpetuity, the nation's richest treasure – its wild lakes, rivers and forests and the myriad creatures that inhabit them. 'Leave it as it is,' he said of the land. 'The ages have been at work on it and man can only mar it.'

Subsequent leaders have championed and furthered Roosevelt's cause. During his last term, President Clinton introduced the Roadless Area Conservation Rule, the most ecology-centric statute instated since the inception of the forest service a century ago. This rule was to permanently protect 58.5 million roadless acres of national forests from potential future road building, logging, drilling and mining.

In late 2003, however, President Bush revoked the Roadless Rule and established instead the controversial 'Healthy Forest Initiative.' This initiative promotes road development, logging, mining and drilling on 190 million acres of public lands across the country; 5.6 million acres of Northern California's national forest lands – including the unique and fragile Klamath-Siskiyou habitat – could be opened to road building and the subsequent logging those roads allow.

Many feel the Healthy Forest Initiative promotes the wealth of the timber industry and not the health of the forests. Currently, environmentalists and concerned citizens nationwide are working to counteract this legislation and its potential effects. Their goal is to defend the wisdom of the national forests' original steward, Teddy Roosevelt, who recognized that 'To waste, to destroy our natural resources, to skin and exhaust the land…will result in undermining in the days of our children the very prosperity which we ought by right to hand down to them…'

on Hwy 36 Chester is 25 miles away and Susanville 60. Quincy is 65 miles south from the junction on Hwy 89.

Mt Lassen Transit (☎ 530-529-2722) buses between Red Bluff and Susanville run by Mineral, which is the stop closest to the park. There's no public transport within the park or on the 5 miles between Hwy 36 and the park entrance.

LASSEN NATIONAL FOREST

This vast **national forest** (www.r5.fs.fed.us/lassen) surrounds Lassen Volcanic National Park and covers 1.2 million acres (1875 sq miles) of wilderness in an area called 'The Crossroads,' where the granite Sierra, volcanic

Cascades, Modoc Plateau and Central Valley meet.

The forest contains 460 miles of **hiking trails**, including 120 miles of the Pacific Crest Trail, the 12-mile Spencer Meadows National Recreation Trail and the 3.5-mile Heart Lake National Recreation Trail. Special points of interest: a 600yd walk through the **Subway Cave** lava tube; the 1.5-mile volcanic **Spattercone Crest Trail**; **Willow Lake** and **Crater Lake**; 7684ft **Antelope Peak**; and the 900ft-high, 14-mile-long **Hat Creek Rim** escarpment.

The forest also contains three wilderness areas. The **Caribou Wilderness** and **Thousand Lakes Wilderness** are best visited from mid-June to mid-October; the **Ishi Wilderness**, at a much lower elevation in the Central Valley foothills east of Red Bluff, is more comfortable in spring and fall, as summer temperatures often climb to over 100°F.

The **Lassen National Forest Supervisor's Office** (p292) is in Susanville. Other ranger offices include **Eagle Lake Ranger District** (☎ 530-257-4188), **Hat Creek Ranger District** (☎ 530-336-5521; Fall River Mills), and **Almanor Ranger District** (☎ 530-258-2141; Hwy 36), about a mile west of Chester.

MCARTHUR-BURNEY FALLS

Six miles northwest of Four Corners, the crossroads where Hwy 89 from the Lassen Volcanic National Park intersects Hwy 299 from Redding, is **McArthur-Burney Falls Memorial State Park** (☎ 530-335-2777; www.parks.ca.gov; day-use per vehicle $6). Fed by a spring, the 129ft falls run with the same amount of water and at the same temperature, 42°F, year-round. Clear, lava-filtered water comes surging not only over the top but also from springs in the rocks right across the waterfall's face, adding up to some 100 million gallons flowing over the falls each day.

There's a lookout point beside the parking lot, with trails going up and down the creek from the falls. A nature trail heading downstream leads you on to Lake Britton. Other hiking trails include a portion of the Pacific Crest Trail. The park's **campgrounds** (☎ summer reservations 800-444-7275; www.reserveamerica.com; drive-in sites $15) have hot showers and are open year-round, even when there's snow on the ground.

About 10 miles northeast of McArthur-Burney Falls, the 6000-acre **Ahjumawi Lava Springs State Park** is known for its abundant springs, aquamarine bays and islets, and jagged flows of black basalt lava. It can only be reached by boats that are launched at Rat Farm, 3 miles north of the town of McArthur along a graded dirt road. Arrangements for primitive camping can be made by calling McArthur-Burney Memorial State Park.

LAKE ALMANOR AREA

Lake Almanor is south of Lassen Volcanic National Park via Hwys 89 and 36. Manmade, this calm turquoise lake surrounded by lush meadows and tall pines may not be natural, but it is a wonder. Once little-visited, Lake Almanor is now a burgeoning mini–Lake Tahoe. Properties are being snapped up, exclusive country clubs are mushroom-

---

NORTHERN BITES

Northern California was propelled into culinary stardom by the Bay Area and Wine Country's fine restaurants, not by the mountain region's greasy spoons. Still, the area doesn't suffer from foodie famine. You will not encounter concentrations of fine cafés here, but you will enjoy the sprinkling (like a fine dusting of cocoa powder over tiramisu) of exceptional restaurants you do find.

Try the area's top five recommended eateries:

- Cynthia's Homemade Bakery & Café (p292), Chester
- Café Le Coq (p294), Quincy
- Café Maddalena's (p296), Dunsmuir
- Trinity Café (p301), Mt Shasta City
- La Grange Café (p307), Weaverville

---

ing and, by the time you read this, a 3000-acre ski area, Dyer Mountain Resort, will be the area's new winter polestar.

Chester (population 2500, elevation 4528ft) is the main town near the lake. You could whiz right by Chester and dismiss it as a few blocks of nondescript roadside storefronts. Don't – it's not. This robust little community has a fledgling art scene, very good restaurants and some attractive places to stay.

Information

Boats and water-sports equipment can be rented at many places around the lake.
B&B Booksellers (☎ 530-258-2150; 140 Main St, Chester) A bookstore and gallery with free wi-fi access.
Bodfish Bicycles & Quiet Mountain Sports (☎ 530-258-2338; 152 Main St, Chester) Rents bicycles, cross-country skis and snowshoes and sells canoes and kayaks. It's a great source of mountain-biking and bicycle-touring advice.
Chester-Lake Almanor Chamber of Commerce (☎ 530-258-2426, 800-350-4838; www.chester-lake almanor.com; 529 Main St; 9am-4pm Mon-Fri) Has the same type of information as Almanor ranger station.
Lassen National Forest Almanor Ranger Station (☎ 530-258-2141; Hwy 36; 8am-4:30pm Mon-Fri) About a mile west of town. There is information here about every type of lodging and recreation in, on and around the lake, in the surrounding Lassen National Forest and in nearby Lassen Volcanic National Park.

Sleeping & Eating

AROUND THE LAKE

Knotty Pine Resort & Marina (☎ 530-596-3348; www.knottypine.net; 430 Peninsula Dr; weekly RV sites $150, 2-bedroom cabins with kitchen day/week $140/840) Seven miles east of Chester, Knotty Pine Resort & Marina rents out boats, kayaks and canoes.

Little Norway Resort (☎ 530-596-3225; www.little norway.net; 432 Peninsula Dr; cabins day/week from $100/600) At Big Cove on Country Rd, Little Norway Resort also rents boats, kayaks and canoes.

North Shore campground (☎ 530-258-3376; www .northshorecampground.com; tent/RV sites $29/27, weekly $180/165) Two miles east of Chester on Hwy 36, these expansive shoreside grounds have sites right near the water.

Federal campgrounds (☎ reservations 877-444-6777; www.reserveusa.com) These campgrounds are available within the surrounding Lassen and Plumas National Forests on the lake's southwest shore. Their camping sites tend to be more tranquil than the RV-centric private campgrounds.

CHESTER

Bidwell House B&B (☎ 530-258-3338; www.bidwell house.com; 1 Main St; r $100-155, cottage $170) Set back from the street, this is the historic summer home of pioneers John and Annie Bidwell. Antique inside and out, the Bidwell House offers classic accommodations with modern amenities (spa in some rooms). Breakfast is served to guests, and nonguests with reservations.

Cinnamon Teal Inn (☎ 530-258-3993; 227 Feather River Dr; r $70-110) This is a shady B&B a half-block back from Main St. There's river access from the green grounds. Each quaint room features a big feather bed.

Timber House Lodge (☎ 530-258-2729; 501 Main St at First St; r from $70) This place has small but decent rooms. The adjoining family-style restaurant/bar is known for its steak, prime ribs and seafood.

St Bernard Lodge (☎ 530-258-3382; www.stbernard lodge.com; d $60) St Bernard is located 10 miles west of Chester at Mill Creek. This old-world charmer has seven B&B rooms with shared bathrooms. The tavern serves breakfast, lunch and dinner.

Cynthia's Homemade Bakery & Café (☎ 530-258-1966; 278 Main St; lunch $8-12, dinner $12-20; ❨ lunch & dinner, Mon, Tue, Thu-Sat) Here, Chef Cynthia

---

> **DETOUR: WESTWOOD & THE BIZZ JOHNSON TRAIL**
>
> A few miles east of Chester is Westwood, a tiny speck of a town that marks the beginning of the **Bizz Johnson Trail**, an extremely scenic trail that runs for 25.5 miles between Westwood and Susanville. Once part of the old Southern Pacific right-of-way, the trail can now be traveled by foot, mountain bike, horseback or cross-country skis (no motorized vehicles are permitted). It's easiest to do the trail in the Westwood–Susanville direction, as it's mostly downhill that way. Trail guides are available at the chamber of commerce in Chester (p291) and at the Susanville Railroad Depot (opposite).

Ware excels in artisan cuisine. Handmade pizzas, smoked vegetables and grilled meat are all served hearth-side during winter, creek-side in summer.

Knotbumper Restaurant (☎ 530-258-2301; 274 Main St; meals $6-8; ❨ 11am-8pm Mon-Sat) Next door to Cynthia's, this cozy café has a generous deli menu, including tamale pies, shrimp salad sandwiches and other eclectic selections. The front porch scene is lively on summer days.

Mt Fusion (☎ 530-258-3310; 605 Main St; mains $10-15; ❨ lunch & dinner) While its name and appearance don't suggest it, this bright forest-green house at the western end of town is a restaurant specializing in Mexican food.

SUSANVILLE

pop 18,300 / elevation 4258ft

At the junction of Hwy 36 and Hwy 139 (4 miles off Hwy 395 to Alturas), Susanville is just 35 miles east of Lake Almanor and 85 miles northwest of Reno. This high desert plateau town is the Lassen County seat and is not a tourist destination in itself but a fascinating place full of Wild West history and exceptionally friendly folk. There are lots of basic services here for the many travelers passing through.

Lassen County Chamber of Commerce (☎ 530-257-4323; www.lassencountychamber.org; 84 N Lassen St; ❨ 9am-5pm Mon-Fri) For tourist information.

Lassen National Forest Supervisor's Office (☎ 530-257-2151; 55 S Sacramento St at Main St; ❨ 8am-4:30pm Mon-Fri) Has maps and outdoors recreation information.

Sights & Activities

The restored **Susanville Railroad Depot**, south of Main St off Weatherlow St, has a **visitors center** (☎ 530-257-3252; 601 Richmond Rd; ☺ May-Oct) and rents bicycles at good rates. It's beside the terminus of the Bizz Johnson Trail (see the boxed text, opposite); there are brochures on other **mountain-biking trails** in the area.

The town's oldest building is named after Susanville's founder, Isaac Roop (namesake Susan was his daughter). **Roop's Fort**, built in 1853, was a trading post on the Nobles Trail, a California emigrant route. Beside the fort is the tame **Lassen Historical Museum** (☎ 530-257-3292; 75 N Weatherlow St; by donation; ☺ 10am-4pm Mon-Fri May-Oct).

Sleeping

Roseberry House B&B (☎ 530-257-5675; www.rose berryhouse.com; 609 N St; r/ste $95/120; ☒) This sweet 1902 Victorian house is two blocks north of Main St. The wallpaper and linens are standard rosebuds and frill, but the big dark-wood antique headboards and armoires are strikingly nonstandard. Children welcome.

Motels along Main St, none of them exceptional, average $50 to $75 per night:
River Inn Motel (☎ 530-257-6051; 1710 Main St)
Susanville Inn (☎ 530-257-4522; 2705 Main St)
Super 8 Motel (☎ 530-257-2782, 800-800-8000; 2975 Johnstonville Rd)

Eating

Grand Café (☎ 530-257-4713; 730 Main St; mains $8; ☺ 7am-2pm Mon-Sat) Step through the door and back in time. Established in 1909, this art deco café is a time capsule. The wooden booths, green and black floor tiles, table lamps, jukebox...they're all original. The menu hasn't changed much over time either – pancakes, soup, homemade bread and malts.

Pioneer Café (☎ 530-257-2311; 724 Main St) The Pioneer is older still. One saloon or another has been operating on this site since 1862, or so states the plaque outside that claims this to be the oldest established business in northeastern California. Today it's a combination bar, billiards room and inexpensive café.

EAGLE LAKE

About 15 miles northwest of Susanville, this is California's second largest natural lake. From late spring until fall this lovely lake attracts visitors who come to swim, fish, boat and camp.

On the south shore, you'll find a 5-mile **recreational trail** and several **campgrounds** (sites $15-30; ☺ May-Oct, some sites year-round) administered by **Lassen National Forest** (☎ camping reservations 877-444-6777; www.reserveusa.com) and the **Bureau of Land Management** (BLM; ☎ 530-257-5381). Nearby **Eagle Lake Marina** (☎ 530-825-3454) offers hot showers, laundry and boat rentals.

Eagle Lake RV Park (☎ 530-825-3133; www.eagle lakeandrv.com; 687-125 Palmetto Way; tent/RV sites $25/30; cabins $75-145) and **Mariners Resort** (☎ 530-825-3333; Stones Landing; RV sites $30-35, cabins $90-135), on the quieter shore, both rent boats.

QUINCY

pop 5000 / elevation 3432ft
Idyllic Quincy, the Plumas County seat, is nestled in a high valley in the northern Sierra, southeast of both Lassen Volcanic National Park and Lake Almanor via Hwy 89. Students from small, local Feather River College give this laid-back mountain town just enough of an edge to keep the atmosphere lively.

Orientation & Information

Once in town, Hwy 70/89 splits into two oneway streets, with traffic on Main St heading east, and traffic on Lawrence St heading west. Jackson St, runs parallel to (and one block south of) Main St and is another main artery. Just about everything you need is on, near, or between these three streets, making up Quincy's low-key commercial district.

Mt Hough Ranger District Office (☎ 530-283-0555; 39696 Hwy 70; ☺ 8am-4:30pm Mon-Fri) Five miles west of town. Has maps and outdoor information.

Plumas County Visitors Bureau (☎ 530-283-6345; 800-326-2247; www.plumascounty.org; 550 Crescent St; ☺ 8am-5pm Mon-Sat) Half a mile west of town.

Plumas National Forest headquarters (☎ 530-283-2050; 159 Lawrence St; ☺ 8am-4:30pm Mon-Fri) For maps and outdoors recreational information.

Sights & Activities

The large 1921 **Plumas County Courthouse** at the west end of Main St has huge interior marble posts and staircases and a 1-ton bronze-and-glass chandelier in the lobby.

In the block behind the courthouse, the **Plumas County Museum** (☎ 530-283-6320; 500 Jackson St at Coburn St; adult/child $1/50c; ☺ 8am-5pm Mon-Fri, also 10am-4pm Sat, Sun & holidays May-Sep) has flowering gardens and exhibits of hundreds of historical photos and relics from the county's pioneer and Maidu days, its early mining

NORTHERN MOUNTAINS

and timber industries and construction of the Western Pacific Railroad.

The first weekend in July, quiet Quincy is host to the **High Sierra Music Festival** (www.high sierramusic.com) or what some locals not-so-affectionately refer to as the 'hippie fest.' The four-day event presents a five-stage smorgasbord of music: rock, blues, folk, jazz. And contrary to local billing, the audience is not all that crunchy, women don't go topless and not everyone is stoned. Festival-goers come from different walks of life, even different parts of the globe. If you plan to attend, reserve a room or campsite a couple of months in advance.

Ask at the very helpful visitors bureau for free walking and driving tour pamphlets if you're keen on seeing more historical buildings or the surrounding **American Valley**. In summer, the icy waters of the county namesake, the **Feather River** (*plumas* is Spanish for feathers), are popular spots for swimming, kayaking, fishing and floating about in old inner tubes. There are also lots of winter activities in the area, especially at Bucks Lake. Cross-country ski gear and snowshoes can be rented at **Sierra Mountain Sports** (☎ 530-283-2323; 501 W Main St) across from the courthouse.

Sleeping

Feather Bed B&B (☎ 530-283-0102, 800-696-8624; www.featherbed-inn.com; 542 Jackson St at Court St; r & cottages $100-150) This 1893 Queen Anne home is just behind the courthouse. The rooms are full of antiques and cuteness – a teddy bear adorns every quilted bed. The gracious hosts make afternoon tea with cookies and guests can borrow bikes.

Ada's Place (☎ 530-283-1954; www.adasplace.com; 562 Jackson St; cottages $110-140; ✗) Not a B&B, just a B. You're responsible for your own breakfast here – no problem, each of the three cottage units has a full kitchen. Very cozy, quiet and private.

Pine Hill Motel (☎ 530-283-1670, 866-342-2891; www.pinehillmotel.com; 42075 Hwy 70; d/cabin $75/80; ✗) A mile west of downtown Quincy, a cooling emerald lawn surrounds this homey place. All units are equipped with a microwave, coffeemaker and refrigerator. Some cabins have full kitchens.

Greenhorn Guest Ranch (☎ 800-334-6939; www.greenhornranch.com; 2116 Greenhorn Ranch Rd; adult/child/junior $255/90/165; ✗ May-Oct; ✗) No bull, this is a working dude ranch and there's all kinds of horsing around: mountain trail rides, riding lessons, even rodeo practice. Other scheduled activities include fishing, hiking, square dancing, evening bonfires, cookouts and frog races. Meals included. Weekly discounts available.

Eating

Café Le Coq (☎ 530-283-0114; 189 Main St; prix fixe menu lunch/dinner $12/25; ✗ Mon-Sat) The French owner and chef here makes this enchanted-gardened little house feel like *your own* enchanted-gardened little house. Delicious gourmet French meals served inside or out.

Pangaea Café & Pub (☎ 530-283-0426; 461 W Main St; mains $10; ✗ 11am-9pm Mon-Fri, 4-9pm Sat) Like a stranger you feel you've met before, this earthy spot feels warmly familiar. The specialty is *panino* (hot Italian pressed sandwich) with a zillion flavorful (mostly veggie) combos. The microbrew choices are just as tempting. There's a cozy little nook in the back with a computer ($2 per hour). There's wireless connection throughout and live music most weekends.

Sweet Lorraine's (☎ 530-283-5300; cnr Main & Harrison Sts; meals $10-17; ✗ lunch & dinner Mon-Fri, dinner Sat) Aptly named. On a warm day – or better yet – evening, the patio here is especially sweet. The menu features light California cuisine: fish, poultry, soups and salads.

Morning Thunder Café (☎ 530-283-1310; 557 Lawrence St; meals $5-8; ✗ 6am-2pm) Homey. Hip. Best place for breakfast; lunch is good too. The menu is mainly, though not exclusively, vegetarian. There's an espresso bar; beer and wine are also available.

Moon's (☎ 530-283-0765; 497 Lawrence St; mains $9-20; ✗ dinner Tue-Sun) A welcoming little chalet with tempting aromas and a charming ambience that fires up some choice steaks and Italian-American fare, including great pizza and rich lasagna.

Ten-Two Dinner House (☎ 530-283-1366; 8270 Bucks Lake Rd; dinner mains $12-15; ✗ dinner Thu-Mon) A small, moderately priced place in Meadow Valley on the road to Bucks Lake, an 8-mile drive from Quincy. It serves superb food with all-natural ingredients and has a changing menu with great specials. In summer you can sit outside by the creek. Reservations are recommended. Winter hours vary.

Farmers market (cnr Church & Main Sts, ✗ 5-8pm Thu mid-Jul–mid-Sep) Stock up on fresh organic produce at this lively market and help support local sustainable agriculture.

BUCKS LAKE

About 17 miles southwest of Quincy, via Bucks Lake Rd (Hwy 119), this clear mountain lake surrounded by pine forests is popular for fishing and boating. There are good **hiking trails**, including the Pacific Crest Trail passing through the adjoining 21,000-acre Bucks Lake Wilderness in the northwestern part of Plumas National Forest. **Bucks Lake Stables** (☎ 530-283-1147) offers trail rides ($25 to $60) and overnight pack trips. In winter, the last 3 miles of Bucks Lake Rd are closed by snow, making it ideal for cross-country skiers.

Haskins Valley Inn (☎ 530-283-9667; www.haskins valleyinn.com; r from $140) offers rustic but formal antique-furnished rooms, some with Jacuzzi, fireplace and deck. **Bucks Lakeshore Resort** (☎ 530-283-6900; www.lakeshoreresortbuckslake.com; 1100 Bucks Lake Rd, Meadow Valley; cabins from $110) is a full-service lakeshore lodge with a restaurant, bar and country store. In summer it operates a campground, cabins and boating marina; in winter, it's a cross-country skiing resort. There is a minimum two night say; ask about special packages. **Bucks Lake Lodge** (☎ 530-283-2262, 800-481-2825; 16525 Bucks Lake Rd; r/cabins from $75/90) rents boats and fishing tackle in summer and cross-country skiing in winter. The restaurant at the lodge serves three meals a day and is known for good food; locals often drive out from Quincy for dinner.

Most campgrounds and services are open from June to September. Ask at the Plumas National Forest Headquarters (p293) or the ranger station in Quincy for details on public campgrounds with basic facilities

MOUNT SHASTA & AROUND

At Mt Shasta's base sit three must-see towns: Dunsmuir, Mt Shasta City and McCloud. Each community has a distinct personality but all share a wild-mountain sensibility (plus great restaurants and places to stay). Then of course there is the mountain itself, which you'll need no urging to visit. One hypnotic glimpse and you'll find it hard to stay away. In the same dramatic vicinity are the snaggle-toothed peaks of Castle Crags, just 6 miles west of Dunsmuir.

Northeast of Mt Shasta, a long drive and a world away, is remote, eerily beautiful Lava Beds National Monument, a blistered badland of petrified fire. The contrasting cool wetlands of Klamath Basin Wildlife Refuges are just west of Lava Beds near Tule Lake.

Further east, high desert plateaus give way to the mountains of the northern Sierra. Folks in this remote area are genuinely happy to greet a traveler, even if they're a bit uncertain why you've come.

DUNSMUIR

pop 2000 / elevation 2289ft

If for no other reason, stop here to quench your thirst at the public fountain. This could easily be – as locals claim – 'the best water on earth.' And while you're at it, stay and eat. Surprisingly, tiny Dunsmuir has a better selection of restaurants than anywhere else in the region.

Built by Central Pacific Railroad, Dunsmuir was originally named Pusher, for the auxiliary 'pusher' engines that muscled the heavy steam engines up the steep mountain grade. In 1886 Canadian coal baron Alexander Dunsmuir came to Pusher and was so enchanted that he promised the people a fountain if they would name the town after him. The fountain stands in the park today.

A more apt name for the town may have been Phoenix however. Rising from the ashes (sometimes literally), this town has survived and triumphed over mythic-sized woes. Over the past century Dunsmuir has been subjected to avalanche, fire and flood; and in 1991, a toxic railroad spill damaged the river's aquatic life and people's morale. Long since cleaned up, the river has been restored to pristine levels and the community now prospers like never before.

Today artists, naturalists, urban refugees and native Dunsmuirians make up a thriving community. In its bawdy Gold Rush heyday five saloons and three brothels crowded downtown. Today shops, cafés, restaurants and galleries line Dunsmuir and Sacramento Aves.

The **Dunsmuir Chamber of Commerce** (☎ 530-235-2177, 800-386-7684; www.dunsmuir.com; 4118 Pine St; ✆ 10am-4pm Mon-Sat, noon-4pm Sun) has free maps, walking-guide pamphlets and excellent information on outdoors recreation.

Sights & Activities

On Dunsmuir Ave at downtown's north end stands what was once, and soon-to-be-again, the town's pride: the **California Theater** (☎ 530-235-9934). In a grassroots community effort this long-defunct, once-glamorous venue is being carefully restored to its original glory. First opened in 1926, the theater hosted stars like Clark Gable, Carol Lombard, and the Marx Brothers. Today the lineup features musical performances, theater groups and comedians, as well as films.

The most notable and original gallery in town is Jayne Bruck-Fryer's **Ruddle Cottage** (☎ 530-235-2022; 5815 Sacramento Ave). The artist makes each and every ingenious creation here – sculptures to jewelry – from recycled materials. The pretty fish hanging in the window?…Dryer lint!

As you follow winding Dunsmuir Ave north over the freeway, look for the **vintage steam engine** in front of tame Dunsmuir City Park & Botanical Gardens. There's a small waterfall up a forest path from the riverside gardens, but **Mossbrae Falls** is the larger and more spectacular of Dunsmuir's waterfalls. To get there from Dunsmuir Ave, turn west onto Scarlett Way, passing under an archway marked 'Shasta Retreat.' Park by the railroad tracks (there's no sign), then walk north along the right-hand side of the tracks for a half-hour until you reach a railroad bridge built in 1901. Backtracking slightly from the bridge, you'll find a little path going down through the trees to the river and the falls. Be *extremely careful* of trains as you walk by the tracks – the river's sound can make it impossible to hear them coming.

Sleeping

Cave Springs Resort (☎ 530-235-2721; www.cavesprings.com; 4727 Dunsmuir Ave; RV sites/cabins/r $22/72/87; 🞨 🐾) Location. Location. Location. These very rustic cabins are nestled into a piney crag above the Sacramento River. Though mostly frequented by anglers, this place has high funky romance appeal. At night: nothing but the sound of rushing water and the haunting whistle of trains. The motel rooms have more amenities, less character.

Railroad Park Resort (☎ 800-974-7245; www.rrpark .com; 100 Railroad Park Rd; tent/RV sites $16/24, caboose & boxcar ste $75-100) About a mile south of town off I-5, this spot offers unique accommodation inside vintage railroad cars. The deluxe

boxcars are furnished with antiques and claw-foot tubs; the cabooses are simpler. The view of Castle Crags is tremendous and the creekside setting peaceful. Tall pines shade the adjoining campground.

Dunsmuir Lodge (☎ 530-235-2884, 877-235-2884; 6604 Dunsmuir Ave; r $65-135; 🞨) Toward the south entrance of town, the simple but tastefully renovated rooms have hardwood floors, big chunky blond-wood bed frames and tiled baths. There's wi-fi throughout and a grassy communal picnic area overlooking a grassy canyon slope.

Cedar Lodge (☎ 530-235-4331; www.cedarlodgedunsmuir.com; 4201 Dunsmuir Ave; r from $65; 🐾) At the far north end of town, this large, welcoming, woodsy property has accommodations on both sides of Dunsmuir Ave. Some of the rooms have kitchens; all have microwave ovens and small refrigerators.

Dunsmuir Inn B&B (☎ 530-235-4543; 5423 Dunsmuir Ave; r $120) At the time of research, this long-time backpackers' favorite was under new ownership and being drastically refurbished. Plans are to deck out rooms with Hollywood themes (eg Marilyn Monroe suite).

Eating & Drinking

Café Maddalena (☎ 530-235-2725; 5801 Sacramento Ave; mains $17-22; 🕑 5-10pm Thu-Sun) This café put Dunsmuir on the foodie map. Though original owner, Maddalena Sera, no longer runs the café (rumor has it she is now Francis Ford Coppola's personal chef), Bret LaMott (of Mt Shasta Trinity Café fame, p301) maintains the restaurant's stellar reputation. The menu features southern European and North African specialties and the wine bar is stocked with rare Mediterranean labels.

Sengthongs Restaurant & Blue Sky Room (☎ 530-235-4770; 5843 Dunsmuir Ave; mains $11-20; 🕑 lunch & dinner) This very attractive place specializes in Thai, Lao and Vietnamese food; the menu is long but not that varied. Most dishes translate to a heaping bowl of noodleiciousness. First-rate – and often danceable – musical acts (jazz, reggae, salsa, blues) play most nights. (Check out www.positiveproductions.net for the performance schedule.)

Cornerstone Bakery & Café (☎ 530-235-4677; 5759 Dunsmuir Ave; mains $10-15; 🕑 breakfast & lunch Tue-Sun) Serves smooth, strong coffee, espresso and chai. All the baked goods – including thick, gooey cinnamon rolls – are warm from the oven. There's an array of veggie (as well as

NORTHERN MOUNTAINS

non-veggie) dishes to choose from including creative omelettes (like cactus), soups and salads; the wine list is extensive as is the dessert selection.

Brown Trout Café & Gallery (☎ 530-235-4677; 5841 Sacramento Ave; mains $10; ✆ 6am-2pm) This is a casual, high-ceilinged, brick-walled, wi-fi hangout with a light satisfying menu. Enjoy excellent espresso drinks including Mexican mocha. Lunch highlights include specialty sandwiches (eg veggie with pesto or Jamaican jerk chicken) and salads (pear and blue cheese…yum). There's also a short wine and microbrew list.

Salt H20 Café (☎ 530-235-4988; 5740 Dunsmuir Ave; prix fixe menu $25; ✆ dinner Thu-Sun) Dinner here is…different. The menu, like the decor (walls smothered in fishing nets, paintings, posters, snapshots, sea creature cutouts…), discombobulates. Parts of the seven-course offering are superb (cedar-plank salmon); others are lily-gilding confusions (sweet coconut covered oysters). Edible orchids (not gilded) are part of the meal, as are rich desserts.

Railroad Park Dinner House (Railroad Park Resort; mains $11-17; ✆ dinner Thu-Sun) Set inside a vintage railroad car, this popular restaurant-bar offers trainloads of dining-car ambience and California cuisine.

Getting There & Away

Dunsmuir is right off I-5, 8 miles south of Mt Shasta City and 6 miles north of Castle Crags. The **Amtrak station** (☎ 800-872-7245; www .amtrak.com; 5750 Sacramento Ave) is the only train stop in Siskiyou County and is not staffed. You can buy tickets for the north–south *Coast Starlight* on board the train, but only after making reservations by phone or via the website.

CASTLE CRAGS STATE PARK

Abour a 20-minute drive from Mt Shasta, this glorious state park inside Castle Crags Wilderness Area features soaring spires of ancient granite formed some 225 million years ago, with elevations ranging from 2000ft along the Sacramento River to more than 6500ft at the top of the Crags. The crags are similar to the granite formations of the eastern Sierra, and Castle Dome here resembles Yosemite's famous Half Dome.

Rangers at the **park entrance station** (☎ 530-235-2684; day-use per vehicle $6) have information and maps covering nearly 28 miles of **hiking**

DETOUR: STEWART MINERAL SPRINGS

Stewart Mineral Springs (☎ 530-938-2222; www.stewartmineralsprings.com; 4617 Stewart Springs Rd; sauna & mineral baths $15-20, sauna $10, tent & RV sites $15, teepees $25, r $45-80; ✆ 10am-10pm Thu-Sat May-Sep; 10am-6pm Oct-Apr; ✗) This popular alternative hangout attracts locals who come for the day and visitors from afar who come and stay for weeks. Henry Stewart founded these springs in 1875 after Native Americans revived him from a near-death experience here. He attributed his recovery to the healthful properties of the mineral waters, said to draw toxins out of the body.

Today you can soak in a private claw-foot tub or steam in the sauna. Other amenities include massage, body wraps, meditation, a Native American sweat lodge, and riverside sunbathing deck. Dining and accommodations are available. To reach the springs, go 10 miles north of Mt Shasta City on I-5, past Weed to the Edgewood exit, then turn left at Stewart Springs Rd and follow the signs.

---

trails. There's also **fishing** in the Sacramento River at the picnic area on the opposite side of I-5.

If you drive past the campground you'll reach **Vista Point**, near the start of the strenuous 2.7-mile **Crags Trail**, which rises through the forest past the Indian Springs spur trail, then clambers up to the base of **Castle Dome**, rewarding you with unsurpassed views of Mt Shasta, especially if you scramble the last hundred yards or so up into the rocky saddle gap. The park also has gentle **nature trails** and 8 miles of the **Pacific Crest Trail**, which passes through the park at the base of the Crags.

The **campground** (☎ summer reservations 800-444-7275; www.reserveamerica.com; sites $15), has running water and hot showers; sites are shady, but suffer from traffic noise. You can camp anywhere in the Shasta-Trinity National Forest surrounding the park if you get a free campfire permit, issued at park offices

MOUNT SHASTA

'When I first caught sight of it I was 50 miles away and afoot, alone and weary. Yet all my blood turned to wine, and I have not been weary since,' wrote naturalist John Muir in

1874. Mt Shasta's beauty is intoxicating; and the closer you get to her the headier you begin to feel.

When the European fur trappers arrived in the area in the 1820s they encountered several Native American tribes, including the Shasta, Karuk, Klamath, Modoc, Wintu and Pit River. By 1851 hordes of Gold Rush miners had arrived, completely disrupting the tribes' traditional life. Later the newly completed railroad began to swiftly import workers and export timber for the booming lumber industry. And since Mt Shasta City (called Sison at the time) was the only non-dry town around, it became *the* bawdy, good-time hangout for lumberjacks.

The lumberjacks have now been replaced by New Agers. Today Mt Shasta is a mecca for mystics; seekers are attracted to the peak's reported cosmic properties. In 1987 about 5000 believers from around the world convened here for the Harmonic Convergence, a communal meditation for peace. Reverence for the mountain is nothing new; for centuries Native Americans have honored the mountain as sacred, considering it to be no less than the Great Spirit's wigwam.

With its abundant appeal, Mt Shasta City makes the perfect base for exploring the area's natural wonders. Outdoor recreational possibilities include camping, hiking, river rafting, skiing, mountain biking and boating. Peak tourist season is from Memorial Day through Labor Day and also weekends during ski season (late November to mid-April).

Orientation & Information

Orienting yourself is easy, with Mt Shasta looming over the east side of town. The downtown area is a few blocks east of I-5. Take the Central Mt Shasta exit, then drive east on Lake St past the visitors bureau up to the town's main intersection at Mt Shasta Blvd, the principal drag.

Mt Shasta Ranger Station (☎ 530-926-4511; 204 W Alma St; ☽ 8am-4:30pm) One block west of Mt Shasta Blvd. Issues wilderness and mountain-climbing permits, good advice, weather reports and everything else you need for exploring the area. It also sells topographic maps.

Mt Shasta Visitors Bureau (☎ 530-926-4865, 800-397-1519; www.mtshastachamber.com; 300 Pine St at Lake St; ☽ 9am-5pm Mon-Sat, 9am-3pm Sun summer, 10am-4:30pm Mon-Sat, 9am-4pm Sun winter) Has detailed handouts on outdoors recreation and lodging

across Siskiyou County. It also sells a map ($3) to sacred wilderness sites.

The Mountain

Dominating the landscape, Mt Shasta is visible for more than 100 miles from many parts of Northern California and southern Oregon. Though not California's highest peak (at 14,162ft it ranks fifth), Mt Shasta is especially magnificent because it rises alone on the horizon, unrivaled by other mountains.

Mt Shasta is part of the vast volcanic Cascade chain that includes Lassen Peak to the south and Mt St Helens and Mt Rainier to the north in Washington state. The presence of thermal hot springs indicates that Mt Shasta is dormant, not extinct. Smoke was seen puffing out of the crater on the summit in the 1850s, though the last eruption is believed to have been about 200 years ago. The mountain has two cones: the main cone has a crater about 200 yards across, and the younger, shorter cone on the western flank, called Shastina, has a crater about half a mile wide.

Fifth Season Sports (☎ 530-926-3606; 300 N Mt Shasta Blvd at Lake St) in Shasta City rents camping, mountain-climbing and backpacking gear, mountain bikes, skis, snowshoes and snowboards. Ski and snowboard rentals are also available at **Sportsmen's Den Snowboard & Ski Shop** (☎ 530- 926-2295; 402 N Mt Shasta Blvd) and **House of Ski & Board** (☎ 530-926-2359; 316 Chestnut St), which rents bicycles as well. Ski and snowboard packages run about $20 a day. Bike rentals are $26 for a full day.

DRIVING

You can drive almost the whole way up the mountain via the Everitt Memorial Hwy (Hwy A10), and there are fine views along the route at any time of year. Simply head east on Lake St from downtown, then left onto Washington Dr and keep going. **Bunny Flat** (6860ft), which has a trailhead for Horse Camp and the Avalanche Gulch summit route, is a busy place with parking spaces, information signboards and a toilet. The section of highway beyond Bunny Flat is only open from about mid-June to October, depending on snows. Trails from **Lower Panther Meadow** connect the campground there to a Wintu sacred spring, in the upper meadows near the **Old Ski Bowl** (7800ft) parking area. Shortly thereafter is the highlight of the drive,

Everitt Vista Point (7900ft), where a short inter-pretive walk from the parking lot leads to a stone-walled outcropping affording excep-tional views of Lassen Peak to the south, the Mt Eddy and Marble Mountains to the west and the whole Strawberry Valley below.

CLIMBING

Reaching the summit is best done between May and September, preferably in spring and early summer, when there's still enough soft snow on the southern flank to make footholds easier on the nontechnical route. Though the round-trip could conceivably be done in one day with 12 or more hours of solid hiking, it's best to allow at least two days and spend a night on the moun-tain. How long it actually takes to climb up and back depends on the route selected, the physical condition of the climbers and weather conditions (for weather informa-tion call ☎ 530-926-9613).

Although the hike to the summit from Bunny Flat is only about 7 miles, it is a verti-cal climb of more than 7000ft, so acclima-tizing to the elevation is important. You'll need crampons, an ice axe and a helmet, all of which can be rented locally. Rock slides and unpredictable weather can be hazard-ous, so novices should contact the Mt Shasta Ranger Station for a list of available guides.

There's a charge to climb the mountain: a three-day summit pass costs $15, an annual pass is $25. Contact the ranger station for details. You must obtain a free wilderness permit any time you go into the wilderness, whether on the mountain or in the surround-ing area.

MOUNT SHASTA BOARD & SKI PARK

On the south slope of Mt Shasta, off Hwy 89 heading toward McCloud, this winter **sports park** (☎ snow reports 530-926-8686; www.skipark.com; ☯ 9am-10pm Wed-Sat, 9am-4pm Sun-Tue winter, 10am-4pm Wed-Thu & Sun, 10am-9pm Fri & Sat late Jun-early Sep) provides skiing and snowboarding options; opening dates depend on snowfall. The park has a 1390ft vertical drop, over two dozen alpine runs and 18 miles of cross-country trails; rentals, instruction and weekly spe-cials are available. It's Northern California's largest night-skiing operation.

In summer, the park offers scenic chair-lift rides, paragliding flights, a 24ft climbing tower and Frisbee golf. Mountain bikers can take the chairlift up and come whooshing back down. Special events, including out-door concerts, are regularly scheduled.

The Lakes

There are a number of pristine mountain lakes near Mt Shasta. Some of them are ac-cessible only by dirt roads or hiking trails and are great for getting away from it all.

The closest lake to Mt Shasta City is **Lake Siskiyou** (also the largest), 2.5 miles southwest on Old Stage Rd, where you can peer into **Box Canyon Dam**, a 200ft-deep chasm. Another 7 miles up in the mountains, southwest of Lake Siskiyou on Castle Lake Rd is **Castle Lake**, an unspoiled place surrounded by granite formations and pine forest. Swim-ming, fishing, picnicking and free camp-ing are popular here in summer; in winter, people ice-skate on the lake. **Lake Shastina**, about 15 miles northwest of town off Hwy 97, is another beauty, favored by short-board windsurfers.

Mount Shasta City

pop 3600 / elevation 3554ft

No town, no matter how lovely – and Mt Shasta City is lovely – could compete with the surrounding natural beauty here. Un-derstandably most visitors don't make a pilgrimage here to visit the fish hatchery; they come to meet the mountain. Still, there are a few attractions around town (the fish hatchery among them!) worth checking out. Downtown itself is charming; you can spend hours there poking around bookstores, gal-leries and boutiques.

Sisson Museum (☎ 530-926-5508; 1 Old Stage Rd; admission free; ☯ 10am-4pm Jun-Sep, 1-4pm Oct-May) is a half-mile west of the freeway. The museum is full of curious mountaineering artifacts and old pictures. The changing exhibitions highlight history – geological and human – but also occasionally showcase local artists. Right next door to the museum is the **Mt Shasta Fish Hatchery** (☎ 530-926-2215; ☯ 7am-sunset), the oldest operating hatchery in the west. The outdoor ponds hold thousands of rainbow trout that will eventually be released into lakes and rivers.

At **Mt Shasta City Park** (Nixon Rd), off Mt Shasta Blvd about a mile north of down-town, the headwaters of the Sacramento River gurgle up from the ground in a large, cool spring. The park also has walking trails,

picnic spots, sports fields and courts, and a
children's playground. East of downtown,
in **Shastice Park** (☎ 530-926-2494; cnr Rockfellow &
Adams Drs), is an immense outdoor skating
rink, open to ice skaters in winter and roll-
erbladers in summer.

Activities

River Dancers (☎ 530-926-3517, 800-926-5002; www
.riverdancers.com; 302 Terry Lynn Ave) is a very good
outfit run by concerned environmentalists;
they guide one- to five-day white-water rafting excursions down the area's rivers (the
Klamath, Sacramento, Salmon, Trinity and
Scott). **Osprey Outdoors Kayak School** (☎ 530-926-
6310; www.ospreykayak.com; 2925 Cantara Loop Rd) has
a reputation for quality classes. Expect to
pay around $100 per adult per day for either
River Dancers or Osprey.

Mt Shasta Resort (☎ 530-926-3052; www.mount
shastaresort.com; 1000 Siskiyou Lake Blvd; green fees $35-50)
has a rolling, tree-lined, 18-hole golf course
with expansive views. The green fees are discounted for twilight play.

Shasta Mountain Guides (☎ 530-926-3117; www
.shastaguides.com) offers two-day guided climbs
of Mt Shasta, all gear and meals included,
for around $500. **Mt Shasta Mountaineering
School** (☎ 530-926-6003; www.swsmtns.com; 210-A
East Castle) conducts clinics and courses for
serious climbers, or those who want to get
serious.

For a uniquely Mt Shasta outdoor experience try **Shasta Vortex Adventures** (☎ 530-926-
4326; www.shastavortex.com; 400 Chestnut St). Their
trips accent the spiritual quest as much as
the outward journey.

To head out on your own, first stop by
the Mt Shasta ranger station or the visitors
bureau for excellent free trail guides including several access points along the **Pacific
Crest Trail**. Highly recommended (although
not on a hot summer day) is **Black Butte**, a
striking treeless, black volcanic cone rising
almost 3000ft. A 2.5-mile hiking trail to the
top takes at least 2½ hours for the round-
trip. It's steep and rocky in many places,
and there is neither shade nor water, so heat
can be a problem. Wear good hiking shoes
and bring plenty of water. Or try the 9-mile
Sisson-Callahan National Recreation Trail, a historic route established in the mid-1800s by
prospectors, trappers and cattle ranchers to
connect the mining town of Callahan with
the town of Sisson, now called Mt Shasta.

Sleeping

Make reservations well in advance, especially on weekends or holidays and during
ski season.

B&BS

Shasta MountInn (☎ 530-926-1810; www.shastamount
inn.com; 203 Birch St; r with/without fireplace $175/125)
Only antique on the outside. Inside, this Victorian farmhouse is relaxed minimalism.
Each airy room has a private bathroom and
scrumptious designer mattress. There's an
expansive garden and wrap-around deck
with outdoor sauna. Best of all (better than
the beds) are the views; whether in the house
or on the grounds, the luminous mountain
is as present as an honored guest.

ShasTao (☎ 530-926-4154; www.shastao.com; 3609
N Old Stage Rd; d $125; ✕) A pair of very mel-
low and likable philosophy professors runs
ShasTao. You won't find your granny's wallpaper here…or her library; they've got book-
shelves stacked with titles from Aesthete to
Zen, with Tantric in between. The wooded
setting and peaceful vibe make for a pretty
idyllic retreat. Vegetarian/vegan breakfast
included.

Dream Inn (☎ 530-926-1536, 877-375-4744; 326
Chestnut St; r with shared bath $60-70, ste $90-100)
Dream Inn has two houses (a sort of a his
and hers set) on its premises – one a meticulously kept Victorian home stuffed with
fussy knickknacks; the other a Spanish-style
two-story with chunky raw-wood furniture
and no clutter. A rose garden with koi pond
joins the two properties. A hefty breakfast
is included.

Alpenrose Cottage Guest House (☎ 530-926-
6724; www.snowcrest.net/alpenrose; 204 E Hinckley St;
dm/s/d/cottage $40/60/80/120; ✕) You'll find
this homey spot a few long blocks north of
downtown. A hostel in its former life, this
roomy two-bedroom house retains a communal feel. There's a mountain-view deck,
wood-burning stoves, enchanting gardens
and shared kitchen.

Mt Shasta Ranch B&B (☎ 530-926-3870; www.stay
inshasta.com; 1008 WA Barr Rd at Ream Ave; carriage house
d with shared bathroom & kitchen from $60, main house
d with private bathroom $110, cottage $115-160; ✕) The
main house and everything in this stately
country property is supersized – the rooms,
the baths, the fireplace, the views. There's a
games room plus a hot spring spa. Breakfast
(also big) included.

MOTELS

Many motels offer discount ski packages in winter and lower midweek rates year-round.

Strawberry Valley Inn (☎ 530-926-2052; 1142 S Mt Shasta Blvd; d from $75; ✗) The serenely understated rooms surround a garden courtyard. This place has all the intimate feel of a B&B without the have-to-chat-with-the-newlyweds-in–the-hall social pressure. A full, vegetarian breakfast is included; in the evenings there's complimentary wine.

Strawberry Valley Court (☎ 530-926-2052; 305 Old McCloud Rd; cabins from $75) The Inn's equally cute sister property has a white picket fence and shady brick cabins with private garages.

Finlandia Motel (☎ 530-926-5596; www.finlandia motel.com; 1612 S Mt Shasta Blvd; r $55-100) This place is an excellent deal. The standard rooms are…standard – clean and simple. The suites get a little chalet flair from vaulted pinewood ceilings and mountain views. There's an outdoor hot tub and the Finnish sauna is available by appointment.

Several nice modest motels stretch along S Mt Shasta Blvd. All have hot tubs and are between $60 and $140 in peak season:

Swiss Holiday Lodge (☎ 530-926-3446; www.snowcrest .net/swissholidaylge; 2400 S Mt Shasta Blvd; ✗ 🖳) Quiet.

Evergreen Lodge (☎ 530-926-2143; www.snowcrest.net /evergreenlodge; 1312 S Mt Shasta Blvd; ✗ 🖳) Friendly.

Mountain Air Lodge & Ski House (☎ 530-926-3411; 1121 S Mt Shasta Blvd) Old-fashioned with a recreation room and complimentary breakfast.

RESORTS

Mt Shasta Resort (☎ 530-926-3052; www.mountshasta resort.com; 1000 Siskiyou Lake Blvd; 1-/2-bedroom chalets $170/220) Divinely situated, this upscale golf resort and spa has Craftsman-style chalets nestled in the woods around the shores of Lake Siskiyou. Each has a kitchen and gas fireplace. Lodge rooms near the golf course are not such a good deal. The restaurant here offers California cuisine and excellent views.

CAMPING

The visitors bureau has details on over two dozen campgrounds around Mt Shasta. Check with the Mt Shasta and McCloud ranger stations about USFS campgrounds in the area. Of course, the best are on Mt Shasta itself.

Lake Siskiyou Camp-Resort (☎ 530-926-2618; www .lakesis.com; 4239 WA Barr Rd; tent/RV sites from $18/25,

cabins $85-140) This is a great camping destination on the shore of Lake Siskiyou. It has a swimming beach and offers kayak, canoe, fishing boat and paddle boat rentals.

McBride Springs (sites $10) Easily accessible from the Everitt Memorial Hwy, this site has running water, no showers and pit toilets; it's near mile-marker 4 at an elevation of 5000ft. Arrive early in the morning to secure a spot (no reservations).

Panther Meadows (sites free) Seven miles further up the mountain at 7000ft, these sites are also accessible from Everitt Memorial Hwy. Mystic Panther Meadows has 10 walk-in tent sites at the timberline. No reservations here either; arrive early to secure a site.

Horse Camp (per person with/without tent $5/3) This 1923 alpine lodge run by the Sierra Club is a 2-mile hike uphill from Bunny Flat at 8000ft. Caretakers staff the hut from May to September only.

As long as you set up your camp at least 200ft from the water and get a free campfire permit from the ranger stations, you can camp beside many mountain lakes. Castle Lake has six free tent sites, but no drinking water and it's closed in winter. Gumboot Lake, 15 miles southwest of Mt Shasta, also has free tent camping (purify your own drinking water). Toad Lake, 18 miles from Mt Shasta City, is lovely; it's not a designated camping area, but you may camp there if you follow the regulations. To get there, go down the 11-mile gravel road (4WD advised) and walk the last quarter-mile.

Eating

Trendy restaurants and cafés here come and go with the snowmelt. Most of the following are tried and true establishments favored by locals as well as visitors.

Trinity Café (☎ 530-926-6200; 622 N Mt Shasta Blvd; mains $15-22; ☺ dinner Tue-Sat) Trinity has long rivaled any big-city 'haute' spot. The former chef has moved on to Café Maddalena's in Dunsmuir (p296), but the new owners, who hail from Napa, have added a wine-country touch (and a lot of California wine) to the organic menu. The warm, mellow mood makes for an overall delicious experience.

Ken Zen (☎ 530-926-2345; 315 N Mt Shasta Blvd; meals $25; ☺ lunch & dinner Wed-Sun) New squid on the block, Ken Zen is a first-rate sushi bar. Don't be put off by the drab exterior, inside is all sleek mahogany and calm. The owner

JOAQUIN MILLER

'Lonely as God, white as a winter moon…' wrote Joaquin Miller about Mt Shasta in his introduction to *Life Amongst the Modoc*. This line is quoted by locals and cited in every (reputable) guidebook around. As poetic as his prose may have been, however, Miller was as much a famed charlatan as celebrated scribe in his time. Cincinnatus Hiner Miller (he later christened himself 'Joaquin' in honor of infamous bandit Joaquin Murietta) was born in Indiana in 1837, though he claimed to have been born in a covered wagon in 1842.

The author took his entitlement to poetic license literally; his name, age and birthplace were only the beginning of his fabrications. The flamboyant character (he often wore a flaming red shirt, sombrero and polka-dot bandana) insisted he was shot in the face by an arrow while fighting against Native Americans in the Battle of Castle Crags… There is no record of his having fought there. And he liked to recall his exploits as a soldier in Nicaragua too, though he never traveled to the Central American country.

In reality Miller's actual history was as fascinating as anything he could contrive. At 17 he left Oregon, where his family was living, and came to Mt Shasta in search of gold and adventure – he found the latter. He did indeed live among the Modoc at this time; in fact, he had a long-term relationship and a daughter with a Modoc woman. And he did fight in Indian wars, only it was not on the side of the whites as he later claimed. The young Miller even tried to organize an autonomous Native American state called Shasta Republic.

At age 24 Miller left Mt Shasta and returned to Oregon (though he eventually settled in California). In his later life he became a newspaper owner, lawyer, judge, teacher, philanthropist (and philanderer) and, of course, writer and poet. Though generally considered a drunk, womanizer and all around poseur (contemporary Ambrose Bierce called him 'the greatest liar this country has ever produced'), Joaquin Miller had a strong streak of righteous integrity. He was an ardent environmentalist, antiwar (Civil) activist and lifelong defender of Native American rights.

As for Miller's writing, it has drawn as many fans as critics. First published as an autobiography, *Life Amongst the Modoc* is now catalogued as fiction, and his poetry considered ornate. Regardless, lovers of Mt Shasta – guidebook writers among them – are ever grateful for a certain, perfect description…'Lonely as God…'

flies in just-caught, grade-A fish daily. The quality is excellent, though the import cost is reflected in the prices.

Lily's (☎ 530-926-3372; 1013 S Mt Shasta Blvd; breakfast & lunch $8-11, dinner mains $14-20; ⏰ breakfast, lunch & dinner Mon-Fri, brunch & dinner Sat & Sun) Delivers more ambience than quality California cuisine. Still, the food is passable and outdoor tables overhung by flowering trellises are almost always full, especially for breakfast.

Michael's Restaurant (☎ 530-926-5288; 313 N Mt Shasta Blvd; mains $22; ⏰ lunch & dinner Tue-Fri, dinner Sat) There are a few Italian places in town – all overpriced. Michael's is no exception, but the food here is comparably exceptional. The pasta is fresh – a rarity in these parts, and the desserts are homemade. There are a lot of non-Italian options (like jambalaya) on the menu too.

Berryvale Grocery & Deli (☎ 530-926-1576; 305 S Mt Shasta Blvd; mains $8) Sells health-conscious groceries and organic produce. The deli café here is excellent. It serves good coffee and an array of tasty – mostly, but not all, veggie – salads, sandwiches and burritos.

Poncho & Lefkowitz (☎ 530-926-1102; cnr Mt Shasta Blvd and Water St; meals under $10) A classy, wood-sided food-cart – sort of a café on wheels. From juicy polish sausage to veggie burritos, this combo Mexican food/gourmet hot dog stand serves yummy little meals.

There are a couple of kitschy, breakfast-served-all-day options:

The Skillet (☎ 530-926-4047; 610 S Mt Shasta Blvd; mains $8; ⏰ breakfast, lunch & dinner) Mexican-leaning and serving good *huevos rancheros* (corn tortilla with fried egg and chili tomato sauce); known for its huge portions.

Black Bear Diner (☎ 530-926-4669; 401 W Lake St; mains $8; ⏰ breakfast, lunch & dinner) Part of a cute bear-themed chain; this link's got a view, though.

Drinking & Entertainment

Has Beans Coffeehouse (☎ 530-926-3602; 1011 S Mt Shasta Blvd; ⏰ 5:30am-7pm; 💻) This is a snug little hangout serving organic, locally roasted coffee. There's one computer tucked away in the back corner ($2 per hour) and wi-fi throughout. There's live acoustic music some evenings.

Laurie's Mt View Cafe (☎ 530-918-9019; 401 N Mt Shasta Blvd) A small friendly place with a mountain-view patio. It serves espresso, beer, wine and light snacks. (Very popular are the Friday night fish-and-chip fests.)

Stage Door Coffeehouse & Cabaret (☎ 530-926-1050; www.stagedoorcabaret.com; 414 Mt Shasta Blvd; 🕑 7am-10pm) A big venue: part café-bar and part theater. The menu features espresso, microbrews, wine and lots of veggie dishes. On Wednesday nights they play indie films; on weekends there's usually live music – anything from blues to bluegrass.

Vet's Club Bar (☎ 530-926-3565; 406 N Mt Shasta Blvd) Live music (mostly rock and roll) and dancing, usually on weekends.

Mt Shasta Cinemas (☎ 530-926-1116; Mt Shasta Shopping Center, 118 Morgan Way) Shows first-run films.

Shopping

Both **Village Books** (☎ 530-926-1678; 320 N Mt Shasta Blvd) and **Golden Bough Books** (☎ 530-926-3228; 219 N Mt Shasta Blvd) carry fascinating volumes about Mt Shasta on topics from geology and hiking to folklore and mysticism; as does the **Sisson Museum shop** (p299).

The **Visions Gallery** (☎ 530-926-1189; 201 N Mt Shasta Blvd) in the Black Bear Building has skylight exhibition spaces and quality crafts.

Getting There & Around

Greyhound (☎ 800-231-2222; www.greyhound.com) buses heading north and south on I-5 stop opposite the Vet's Club and at the **depot** (☎ 530-938-4454; 628 S Weed Blvd) in Weed.

The **STAGE bus** (☎ 530-842-8295, 800-247-8243) includes the town of Mt Shasta in its local I-5 corridor route, which also serves McCloud, Dunsmuir, Weed and Yreka several times daily on weekdays only. Other buses connect at Yreka (see p309).

The **California Highway Patrol** (CHP; ☎ 530-842-4438) recorded report gives weather and road conditions for all Siskiyou County roads.

MCCLOUD

pop 1600 / elevation 3254ft
The historic mill town of McCloud sits on the north side of Hwy 89, some 10 miles east of the I-5, at the foot of the south slope of Mt Shasta. McCloud is the closest settle-

ment to Mt Shasta Board & Ski Park. This tiny town is enchanting in its own right but rendered even more so by the abundant natural beauty that surrounds it.

McCloud Chamber of Commerce (☎ 530-964-3113; www.mccloudchamber.com; 205 Quincy Ave; 🕑 10am-4pm Mon-Fri)

McCloud Ranger District Office (☎ 530-964-2184; Hwy 89; 🕑 8am-4:30pm Mon-Fri, Mon-Sat summer) A quarter-mile east of town. Has detailed information handouts on camping, hiking and all kinds of recreation.

Sights & Activities

The **Shasta Sunset Dinner Train** (☎ 530-964-2142, 800-733-2141; www.shastasunset.com; adult/child $12/8; 🕑 Thu-Sat summer only) offers one-hour, super-scenic, open-air train rides through Mt Shasta's forested southern slopes, departing at 4pm. Opposite the depot, there's a tiny **historical museum** (🕑 11am-3pm Mon-Sat, 1-3pm Sun).

The **McCloud River Loop**, a 6-mile, partially paved road along the Upper McCloud River, begins at Fowlers Camp, 5.5 miles east of town, and emerges onto Hwy 89 about 11 miles east of McCloud. Along the way you'll pass turnoffs to Three Falls, a lovely trail that passes…yup, three falls, and a riparian habitat for bird-watching in the Bigelow Meadow. The loop can easily be done by car, bicycle or on foot.

Other good hiking trails include the **Squaw Valley Creek Trail** (not to be confused with the ski area near Lake Tahoe), an easy 5-mile loop trail south of town, with options for swimming, fishing and picnicking. Sections of the Pacific Crest Trail are accessible from Ah-Di-Na campground, off Squaw Valley Rd, and also up near Bartle Gap, offering head-spinning views.

Fishing and swimming are popular on remote **Lake McCloud** reservoir, 9 miles south of town on Squaw Valley Rd, which is signposted as Southern Ave in town off Hwy 89. You can also go fishing on the Upper McCloud River (stocked with trout) and at the Squaw Valley Creek. **Friday's RV Retreat** (☎ 530-964-2878; Squaw Valley Rd), 6 miles south of McCloud near Squaw Valley Creek, has a fly-fishing school.

Sleeping

There are two types of accommodations in McCloud: rough or fluff. Other than camping, the only lodging option in town is a room in one of the cushy B&Bs.

B&BS

McCloud B&B Hotel (☎ 530-964-2822, 800-964-2823; www.mccloudhotel.com; 408 Main St; r $75-115, ste with Jacuzzi $125-165; ✗) This regal block-long, butter-yellow, grand hotel first opened in 1916. The elegant historic landmark has been lovingly restored to a luxurious standard where breakfast is taken very seriously.

McCloud River Inn (☎ 530-964-2130, 800-261-7831; www.riverinn.com; 325 Lawndale Court; r $70-145; ✗ ✗) This not as large (but even more yellow) Victorian is also on the National Register of Historic Places. The rooms here are fabulously big – the bathrooms alone could sleep two. The atmosphere is relaxed and familial.

Stoney Brook Inn (☎ 530-964-2300, 800-369-6118; www.stoneybrookinn.com; 309 W Colombero Dr; s/d from $49/74; ✗) Dating from 1922, this was once the Park Hotel. It is now an alternative B&B that sponsors group retreats but is open to individuals as well. Amenities include a hot tub, sauna, Native American sweat lodge and massage by appointment. There are a variety of rooms (downstairs ones are nicest), some with kitchenettes. Vegetarian breakfast available.

McCloud Century House Inn (☎ 530-964-2206; www.mccloudcenturyhouse.com; 433 Lawnsdale Ct; ste $100-150) This is a cozy getaway at the west end of town, offering suites with full kitchens. It's a very private place and reservations are recommended. Kids warmly welcome.

CAMPING

McCloud Dance Country RV Park (☎ 530-964-2252, 530-964-2083; 480 Hwy 89 at Southern Ave; tent sites $14, RV sites $18-22) This place is green and quiet but chock-full of RVs.

The USFS maintains about a half-dozen campgrounds nearby; Fowler's Camp is the most popular. Campgrounds have a range of facilities and charge fees of up to $15 per site, while others are free but more primitive (no running water). Ask the rangers for details.

Eating

McCloud's eating options are good but few. For more variety, you may want to make the 10-mile trip over to Mt Shasta City.

McCloud Restaurant (☎ 530-964-2099; 424 Main St; dinner $15-25; ✓ Thu-Sat, dinner Wed-Sun) In this long-running Italian dining room, you can get homemade gnocchi and other country house specialties.

McCloud B&B Hotel (☎ 530-964-2822, 800-964-2823; www.mccloudhotel.com; 408 Main St; breakfast/dinner mains $8/17; ✓ breakfast & dinner) Enjoy gourmet meals in the elegant dining room here or on the flower-shrouded garden patio.

McCloud Soda Shoppe (☎ 530-964-2747; 245 Main St) Located in the Old Mercantile Building, this old-fashioned little soda fountain serves burgers and shakes.

Shasta Sunset Dinner Train (☎ 800-733-2141; www .shastasunset.com; Main St; 3hr ride with multicourse dinner $80) A superscenic dinner opportunity aboard 1916-vintage restored dining cars. In summer, the train departs at 5:30pm Thursday to Saturday, with several routes going west and east from McCloud; trips are scaled back the rest of the year.

Entertainment

McCloud Dance Country (☎ 530-964-2578; cnr Broadway & Pine Sts; admission per couple $15; ✓ 7pm Fri & Sat) You can do-si-do your way down here for some square dancing. This big dance hall was built in 1906 and is a central community gathering spot.

LAVA BEDS NATIONAL MONUMENT

Off Hwy 139 immediately south of Tule Lake National Wildlife Refuge, **Lava Beds National Monument** (www.nps.gov/labe; 7-day entry per vehicle/hiker/biker $5/3/3) is a truly remarkable 72-sq-mile landscape of volcanic features – lava flows, craters, cinder cones, spatter cones, shield volcanoes and remarkable lava tubes.

Lava tubes are formed when hot, spreading lava cools and hardens on the surfaces exposed to the cold air. The lava inside is thus insulated and stays molten, flowing away to leave an empty tube of solidified lava. Nearly 400 such tubular caves have been found in the monument, and many more are expected to be discovered. About two dozen or so are currently open for exploration by visitors.

On the south side of the park, the **visitors center** (☎ 530-667-2282, ext 230; ✓ 8am-6pm summer, 8am-5pm rest of year) has free maps, activity books for kids and information about the monument and its volcanic features and history. Rangers lead summer interpretive programs, including campfire talks and guided cave walks. Near the visitors center, a short one-way loop drive provides access to many lava tube caves with names like Labyrinth, Hercules Leg, Golden Dome and Blue Grotto. In **Mushpot Cave**, the one nearest the visitors center, lighting and informative signs have been installed. The visitors center provides free flashlights for cave explorations; you can buy a special caver's 'bump hat' for a nominal price. It's essential you use a high-powered flashlight, wear good shoes (lava is sharp) and not go exploring alone.

Other notable features of the Lava Beds area include the tall black cone of **Schonchin Butte** (5253ft), which has a magnificent outlook accessed via a steep 1-mile hiking trail (once you reach the top, you can visit the fire-lookout staff between June and September); **Mammoth Crater**, the source of most of the area's lava flows; and ancient, faded **petroglyphs** at the base of a high cliff at the far northeastern end of the monument. A leaflet explaining the origin of the petroglyphs and their probable meaning is available in the visitors center, and it's really not worth visiting without it. Look for the hundreds of birds' nests in holes high up in the cliff face, which provide shelter for birds that can be seen at the wildlife refuges nearby.

Also at the north end of the monument, **Captain Jack's Stronghold** is a must-see. A brochure will guide you through the Stronghold trail; allow plenty of time to be halted in your tracks, meditating on the history of the labyrinthine landscape. The brochure and other books about the Modoc War are available at the visitors center.

Indian Wells Campground (sites $10), near the visitors center at the south end of the park, has water and flush toilets, but no showers. A couple of motels are on Hwy 139 in the nearby town of Tulelake.

KLAMATH BASIN NATIONAL WILDLIFE REFUGES

Of the six national wildlife refuges in this group, Tule Lake and Clear Lake refuges are wholly within California, Lower Klamath refuge straddles the California–Oregon border, and the Upper Klamath, Klamath Marsh and Bear Valley refuges are across the border in Oregon. Bear Valley and Clear Lake (not to be confused with the Clear Lake just east of Ukiah) are closed to the public to protect their delicate habitats, but the rest are open during daylight hours.

These refuges provide habitats for birds migrating along the Pacific Flyway (see the boxed text, p287); some stop over only briefly, others stay longer to mate, make nests and raise their young. There are always birds here and during the spring and fall migrations, there can be hundreds of thousands of waterfowl.

The **Klamath Basin National Wildlife Refuges Visitors center** (☎ 530-667-2231; http://klamathbasin refuges.fws.gov; 4009 Hill Rd, Tulelake; ⊙ 8am-4:30pm Mon-Fri, 10am-4pm Sat & Sun) is on the west side of the Tule Lake refuge, about 5 miles west of Hwy 139 near the town of Tulelake. Follow the signs from Hwy 139 or from Lava Beds National Monument. The center has a non-profit bookstore and interesting video program about the birds and the refuges, as well as maps, books, information on recent bird sightings and updates on road conditions.

The spring migration peaks during March, and in some years more than a million birds fill the skies. In April and May, the songbirds, waterfowl and shorebirds arrive, some to stay and nest, others to build up their energy before they continue north. In summer, ducks, Canada geese and many other waterbirds are raised here. The fall migration begins in early September and by late October peak numbers of birds have departed. In cold weather, the area hosts the largest wintering concentration of bald eagles in the lower 48 states, with sometimes more than 1000 in residence from December to February; Tule Lake and Lower Klamath refuges are the best places to see eagles, as well as other raptors.

The Lower Klamath and Tule Lake and refuges attract the largest numbers of birds year-round, and **auto trails** (per vehicle $3) have been set up; a free pamphlet from the visitors center shows the routes. Self-guided **canoe trails** have been established in three of the refuges. Those in Tule Lake and Klamath Marsh refuges are usually open July 1 to September 30; no canoe rentals are available. Canoe trails in Upper Klamath refuge are open year-round; canoes can be rented at **Rocky Point Resort** (☎ 541-356-2287), on the west side of Upper Klamath Lake in Oregon.

There's camping nearby at Lava Beds National Monument. A couple of RV parks and budget motels are on Hwy 139 near the tiny town of **Tulelake**, including the friendly **Ellis Motel** (☎ 530-667-5242; 2238 Hwy 139; d with/without kitchen $55/50). **Fe's B&B** (☎ 877-478-0184; www.fes bandb.com; 660 Main St; r $65) is simple and comfortable. There are four rooms with shared bathroom; a big breakfast's included.

NORTHERN MOUNTAINS

MODOC NATIONAL FOREST

This **national forest** (www.r5.fs.fed.us/modoc) covers almost two million acres of California's northeastern corner. Fourteen miles south of Lava Beds National Monument on the western edge of the forest, **Medicine Lake** is a stunning crater lake in a caldera (collapsed volcano) surrounded by pine forest, campgrounds and volcanic formations. Several flows of obsidian (shiny, black volcanic glass) came out of the volcano that formed Medicine Lake. Pumice eruptions were followed by flows of obsidian, as at **Little Glass Mountain**, east of the lake.

Roads are closed by snow from around mid-November to mid-June, but the area is still popular for winter sports, and accessible by cross-country skiing and snowshoeing. Other notable geologic features of the area, such as lava caves and tubes, are part of a self-guided **roadside geology driving tour**, best done in summer or early fall. You can pick up detailed tour pamphlets from the Mc-Cloud ranger station (p303).

The **Warner Mountains**, on the east side of the forest, are a spur of the Cascade Range. The weather on the Warners is extremely changeable and there've been snowstorms here in every season of the year, so always be prepared. The range divides into the North Warners and South Warners at Cedar Pass (elevation 6305ft), east of Alturas. **Cedar Pass Snow Park** (☎ 530-233-3323; http://cedarpasssnowpark .com; ☺ 10am-4pm Sat, Sun & holidays during ski season) offers downhill and cross-country skiing. The **South Warner Wilderness** contains 77 miles of hiking and riding trails; the best time to use them is from July to mid-October.

Maps, campfire permits and information are all available at the **Modoc National Forest Supervisor's Headquarters** (☎ 530-233-5811; 800 W 12th St; ☺ 8am-5pm Mon-Fri) in Alturas, a small town that provides basic services, motels, coffee shops and family-style restaurants.

WEST OF I-5

West of I-5 you'll find some of the the mountain area's most rugged towns and seductive wilderness. The Gold Rush past of Weaverville is palpable even today. The town's current community – a multi-generational mix of artists, naturalists, young, old, white, Chinese and city trans-

plant – is, wittingly or not, nurtured by the town's Wild West roots.

Heavenly Hwy 3 (a highly recommended – although slower and windier – alternative route to I-5) begins in Weaverville. This mountain byway will transport you through the Trinity Alps – a stunning range of azure-laked peaks, past the shores of Lewiston and Trinity Lakes, over the Scott Mountains, and finally into emerald, mountain-rimmed Scott Valley. Rough and ready Yreka awaits you at the end of the line.

WEAVERVILLE

pop 3300 / elevation 2011ft

Weaverville is the seat of Trinity County, a mountain and forest area that's 75% federally owned. With its almost 3300 sq miles, the county is roughly the size of Delaware and Rhode Island together, yet has a total population of only 13,000, and not one traffic light or parking meter.

In 1941 a reporter interviewed James Hilton, British author of *Lost Horizon*. 'In all your wanderings,' the journalist asked the writer, 'what's the closest you've found to a real-life Shangri-La?' Sighing wistfully (one imagines) Hilton responded, 'A little town in northern California…a little town called Weaverville.'

Weaverville is a small gem of a town (a veritable Shangri-La) on the National Register of Historic Places. You can easily spend a day here just strolling around, visiting art galleries, museums and other historic structures.

Information

Trinity County Chamber of Commerce (☎ 530-623-6101, 800-487-4648; www.trinitycounty.com; 215 Main St; ☺ 9am-noon & 1-4pm Mon-Fri, Mon-Sat in summer) Has lots of useful information.

Weaverville Ranger Station (☎ 530-623-2121; 210 N Main St; ☺ 8am-4:30pm Mon-Fri) Able to help with maps, information and permits for all the lakes, national forests and wilderness areas in and near Trinity County, with specifics on hiking trails, camping areas and recreation sites.

Sights & Activities

Joss House State Historic Park (☎ 530-623-5284; cnr Hwy 299 & Oregon St; admission $2; ☺ 10am-5pm Sat in winter, Wed-Sun rest of year), in the center of town, holds the oldest continuously used Chinese temple in California – it dates back to the 1870s. Its Taoist shrine features an ornate altar, more than 3000 years old, which was brought here from China. Tours depart from 10am until 4pm on the hour. Next door, the **JJ Jackson Memorial Museum & Trinity County Historical Park** (☎ 530-623-5211; www.trinitymuseum.org; 508 Main St; donation requested; ⏰ 10am-5pm May-Oct, noon-4pm Apr & Nov-Dec 24, noon-4pm Tue & Sat Dec 26-Mar) has gold-mining and cultural exhibits, plus vintage machinery, amazing memorabilia and an old miner's cabin outside.

Six Pack Packers (☎ 530-623-4656) leads fishing and scenic horse pack trips into the Trinity Alps Wilderness. There's **river rafting** at Willow Creek, 55 miles west of Weaverville. **Big Foot Rafting Company** (☎ 530-629-2263, 800-722-2223; www.bigfootrafting.com) leads guided trips and also rents rafts and kayaks (from $32 per day).

Sleeping

Weaverville Hotel (☎ 800-750-8957; www.weavervillehotel.com; 203 Main St; r $100-260; ⊠) This upscale hotel and historic landmark has been refurbished in grand Victorian style. It's luxurious but not stuffy and the very gracious owners take great care in looking after you. As a guest you're entitled to use the local gym, and breakfast at a neighboring café is on the house.

Red Hill Motel & Cabins (☎ 530-623-4331; www.redhillresorts.com; Red Hill Rd; motel d/duplex $38/48, cabins with/without kitchen $53/43) This is a very sweet, very quiet place at the west end of town, just off Main St, next to the library.

Carrville Inn B&B (p308) This B&B is well out of town but it is worth the effort to get to.

The ranger station has information on many USFS campgrounds in the area, especially around Trinity Lake. Commercial RV parks, some with tent sites, are dotted along Hwy 299.

Eating & Drinking

La Grange Café (☎ 530-623-5325; 315 N Main St; mains $12-25; ⏰ lunch & dinner daily, breakfast Sun) Spacious, yet intimate, this celebrated multistar restaurant serves exceptional light, fresh and satisfying fare (fish, poultry, pasta and big fresh salads). There's a very friendly atmosphere in both the pub and dining room.

Noelle's Garden Café (☎ 530-623-2058; 252 Main St; mains $8; ⏰ breakfast & lunch) The best (and pretty much only) place for breakfast. There's seating inside the cheery house as well as on the adjoining vine-trellised deck. It has many lunch choices – soups, sandwiches, salads – with lots of veggie options. The breakfast burrito is especially good.

La Casita (☎ 530-623-2058; 254 Main St; mains $8; ⏰ lunch & dinner) Crouched down right next door to Noelle's, low-ceilinged little La Casita serves really good, authentic Mexican dishes.

Mamma Llama (☎ 530-623-6363; 208 N Main St; ⏰ 7am-6pm Mon-Sat, 8:30am-3pm Sun) Excellent chill spot. Roomy and relaxed. You can get espresso, browse through the selection of books and CDs or make yourself at home on the couch. There's wi-fi throughout and occasional live music.

Trinideli (☎ 530-623-5856; 201 Trinity Lakes Blvd at Center St; sandwiches $5-7; ⏰ 6:30am-5:30pm) This happy place prepares decadent sandwiches, stuffed with all kinds of fresh goodness, with good vibes all around.

The Red House (☎ 530-6231635; 218 S Miner St; ⏰ 7am-6pm Mon-Sat, 8:30am-3pm Sun) Airy, bambooey, light – definitely well feng shuied. This inviting spot serves light snacks, coffee, espresso and a wide selection of teas. If you're in a hurry (rare in Weaverville), there's a drive-thru window.

Mountain Marketplace (☎ 530-623-2656; 222 S Main St; ⏰ 9am-6pm Mon-Fri, 10am-5pm Sat) A natural foods grocery store with a juice bar and vegetarian deli.

Farmers market (⏰ 4:30-7:30pm Wed May-Oct) The lively organic market is open on Main St in the warmer months.

DETOUR: ALPEN CELLARS

A highly recommended side trip if you're in the Weaverville area is to small, little-known, utterly picturesque **Alpen Cellars** (☎ 530-266-9513; www.alpencellars.com; ⏰ 10am-4pm summer, by appointment Oct-May). Specializing in white riesling, gewürztraminer, chardonnay and pinot noir, the vineyard is open for tours, tasting and picnicking on the idyllic riverside grounds. To get there from Weaverville take Hwy 3 for about 45 miles to the north end of Trinity Lake (5 miles past Trinity Center), turn right on East Side Rd, 8 miles further head left on East Fork Rd, continue 2 miles.

Getting There & Away

From Monday to Friday, a local bus makes a Weaverville–Lewiston loop via Hwy 299 and Hwy 3. Another local bus runs between

Weaverville and Hayfork, a small town about 30 miles to the southeast on Hwy 3. **Trinity Transit** (☎ 530-623-5438) can provide details.

THE LAKES
Lewiston Lake

Twenty-six miles west of Redding, around 5 miles off Hwy 299 on Trinity Dam Blvd, **Lewiston** (population 1300) makes a pleasant rest stop. It's right beside the Trinity River, where there's good fishing below the dam. About 1.5 miles north, tiny Lewiston Lake is a peaceful alternative to the other area lakes because of its 10mph boat speed limit. The water is kept at a constant level, providing a nurturing habitat for fish and waterfowl. It is a stopover for a number of migrating bird species – early in the evening you may see ospreys and bald eagles diving for fish.

An 1875 house in the middle of the old town on the river, The **Old Lewiston Inn B&B** (☎ 530-778-3385, 800-286-4441; www.theoldlewistoninn .com; Deadwood Rd; s/d $85/130; 🞩), serves country-style breakfasts. Enjoy the hot tub, or ask about all-inclusive, fly fishing and romantic getaway packages. Another pleasant facility 5 miles north of Lewiston is **Lakeview Terrace Resort** (☎ 530-778-3803; www.lakeviewterraceresort.com; RV sites $18-21, trailers/cabins from $50/60) which also has boat rentals and weekly discounts.

The only marina on the lake, **Pine Cove Marina & RV Park** (☎ 530-778-3770, 800-778-3838; 9435 Trinity Dam Blvd), provides free information about the lake and its wildlife. There are also boat and canoe rentals, potluck dinners and guided off-road tours.

Lewiston Valley Motel (☎ 530-778-3942; 4789 Trinity Dam Blvd; RV sites $20, motel s/d $45/55; 🞩) is a tidy place with swimming pool and RV park, all next to a gas station and convenience store.

Several of the commercial campgrounds are spaced around the lake. For information on USFS campgrounds, contact the ranger station (p306) in Weaverville. Near town there are a few quiet places such as **Old Lewiston Bridge RV Resort** (☎ 530-778-3894, 800-922-1924; Rush Creek Rd at Turnpike Rd; tent/RV sites $14/24), with campsites beside the river bridge.

In the center of town, the **Lewiston Hotel** (☎ 530-778-6800; Deadwood Rd; 🕐 bar from 4pm, restaurant 5pm-9pm Wed-Sat) was built in 1862. Although it is no longer a functioning hotel, this is a hangout with a lot of character, serving excellent drinks and dinners. If you're lucky, there may be live music and dancing.

Trinity (Clair Engle) Lake

North of Lewiston Lake, Trinity Lake is California's third-largest reservoir. It attracts multitudes who come for swimming, fishing and other water sports. The west side of the lake has most of the campgrounds, RV parks, motels, boat rentals and restaurants.

Carrville Inn B&B (☎ 530-266-3511; www.carrvilleinn .com; Carrville Loop Rd; r from $125; cabin $175; 🞩) This beautiful B&B is located north of the lake. It offers elegant accommodations in a huge Victorian home surrounded by expansive green grounds. There's a charming barnyard populated with the usual residents plus exotic extras: an emu, llama and potbellied pig. This place makes for a romantic getaway or a family retreat. Kids welcome. To get here take Hwy 3 6 miles past Trinity Center, turn left on Carrville Loop Rd.

Cozy **Pinewood Cove Resort** (☎ 530-286-2201, 800-988-5253; www.pinewoodcove.com; 45110 Hwy 3; tent/RV sites $25/34, A-frame/loft cabins $95/135; 🕐 campground Apr-Oct), on the waterfront, is a popular place to stay.

Trinity Alps Marina (☎ 530-286-2282, 800-824-0083; www.trinityalpsmarina.com; houseboats per week from $1500) rents fishing boats as well as houseboats. Low-season rates are considerably lower.

The east side is quieter, with more secluded campgrounds, some accessible only by boat. The Weaverville ranger station (p306) has information on USFS campgrounds.

SCOTT VALLEY

North of Trinity Lake, Hwy 3 climbs to the Scott Mountain Summit (5401ft) and then drops gracefully down into verdant Scott Valley, a bucolic agricultural area nestled between towering mountains.

Etna, toward the north end of the valley, is known for its tiny **Etna Brewing Company** (☎ 530-467-5277; 131 Callahan St; brewery tours free; 🕐 pub 11am-6pm Wed-Sun, tours by appointment). If you're sticking around, try the **Motel Etna** (☎ 530-467-5338; 317 Collier Way; s/d $35/40). If you are hungry, there's food at the Etna Brewing Company pub, and old-fashioned ice-cream sodas at **Scott Valley Drug** (☎ 530-467-5335; 511 Main St; 🕐 Mon-Sat).

Beyond Etna is **Fort Jones**, which is just 18 miles from Yreka. There is a **visitors center** (☎ 530-468-5442; 11943 Main St; 🕐 10am-5pm Tue-Sat, noon-4pm Sun) at the back of the Guild Shop mercantile, and a small **museum** (☎ 530-468-5568; 11913 Main St; donation requested; 🕐 Mon-Sat summer) of Native American artifacts down the street.

YREKA

pop 7400 / elevation 2625ft

Inland California's northernmost city, Yreka (pronounced wy-ree-kah) was once a booming Gold Rush town. Although most travelers only pass by en route to Oregon, Yreka – especially the quaint historic downtown – makes a good spot to stretch, eat and refuel before heading out into the hinterlands of the Scott Valley or the northeastern California wilderness.

AAA office (☎ 530-842-4416; 1876 Fort Jones Rd)

Klamath National Forest Supervisor's office (☎ 530-842-6131; 1312 Fairlane Rd at Oberlin Rd; ⊙ 8am-4:30pm Mon-Fri) At the south edge of town, with the lowdown on outdoor recreation and camping in the National Forest.

Yreka Chamber of Commerce (☎ 530-842-1649, 800-669-7352; www.yrekachamber.com; 117 W Miner St; ⊙ 9am-5pm summer, hrs vary winter) For information.

Sights & Activities

The **Siskiyou County Courthouse** (311 4th St) downtown was built in 1857 and has a collection of gold nuggets in the foyer. Many blocks further to the south, the exceptionally well-curated **Siskiyou County Museum** (☎ 530-842-3836; 910 S Main St; admission $1; ⊙ 9am-5pm Tue-Sat) brings together pioneer and Native American history. An outdoor section has several historic buildings brought from around the county. Behind the museum is the **Yreka Creek Greenway**, where walking paths wind through the trees.

About 25 miles north of Yreka on I-5, just across the Oregon border, **Siskiyou Summit** (elevation 4310ft) closes often in winter – even when the weather is just fine on either side. Call ☎ 530-842-4438 to check.

Sleeping

Best Western Miner's Inn (☎ 530-842-4355; 122 E Miner St; s/d $49/54) At the Central Yreka exit, this hotel offers a bit more luxury than the rest in town.

Klamath Motor Lodge (☎ 530-842-2751; 1111 S Main St; d from $60; 🐾) This tidy lodge is especially friendly.

Klamath National Forest operates several area campgrounds; the supervisor's office has information. There are several RV parks on the outskirts of town.

Eating

Nature's Kitchen (☎ 530-842-1136; 412 S Main St; dishes $7; ⊙ 8am-3pm Mon-Sat) This friendly natural foods store and bakery serves healthy and tasty vegetarian dishes, fresh juices and good espresso.

Village Grind (☎ 530-842-4607; 400 W Miner; dishes $7; ⊙ 7:30am-7pm Mon-Fri, 8am-7pm Sat, 8:30am-5pm Sun) This attractive wooden-floor, local-art-on-the-walls espresso bar and café adds a little urbane dash. Nice light meals – omelettes, salads, pizzas. Wi-fi friendly.

Klander's Deli (☎ 530-842-3806; 211 S Oregon St; sandwiches $6; ⊙ 9am-4pm Mon-Fri) This fun little deli is where locals go for lunch. There's a long list of yummy hot and cold sandwiches, or you can create your own.

Grandma's House (☎ 530-842-5300; 123 E Center St; breakfast & lunch $5-7, dinner $8-15; ⊙ 6am-10pm) Grandma's is popular for its home-style cooking. It's east of downtown Yreka between Main St and I-5. Look for the cutesy gingerbread house.

Angelini's Italian Restaurant (☎ 530-842-5000; 322 W Miner St; lunch/dinner $15/25; ⊙ lunch & dinner) At the time of research this upscale new eatery had yet to open but the last bricks were being laid on the back patio's wood-fire oven. The proposed menu promised fresh pasta, steaks, pizza, seafood and a short but varied wine selection.

Getting There & Away

Greyhound (☎ 800-231-222; www.greyhound.com) buses northbound and southbound along I-5 stop at the **Greyhound depot** (☎ 530-842-3145; 115 Miner St).

STAGE (☎ 530-842-8295, 800-247-8243) buses run throughout the region from a few different stops in Yreka, several times daily on weekdays along the I-5 corridor to Weed, Mt Shasta, McCloud and Dunsmuir. Other buses depart daily for Fort Jones, Greenview and Etna in the Scott Valley and, on Monday and Friday only, out to Klamath River and Happy Camp.

NORTHERN MOUNTAINS

Gold Country

You may think that California's Gold Country gets its name from the tawny tones of the rolling foothills of the Sierra mountains, but, although fitting, this is not the case. For there really was (and is) gold in them thar hills and this was where the modern California was born.

Fortunately for us, the incalculable wealth that flowed out of the hills was spent developing the state elsewhere and for many decades after the 1849 Gold Rush subsided, the Gold Country returned to a kind of peaceful repose. Today, towns redolent with a feel more than a century old are strung out like vintage pearls along Hwy 49.

Although Nevada City and its slightly larger companion Grass Valley seem clipped from a history book, the towns share a vibrant culture that's not dependent on tourism. Auburn and thriving Placerville are close to the quiet and moody place where it all began at the Marshall Gold Discovery State Historic Park. Sutter Creek is at the heart of a grouping of towns such as Volcano that are right off the beaten track. Finally, Sonora and its surrounds (including such storied names as Jamestown and Angels Camp) exudes frontier legacy.

The Gold Country is one of the Golden State's highlights, and if you are going to Yosemite, Lake Tahoe or Nevada then towns such as Sonora, Placerville or Nevada City should definitely figure into your itinerary. Better yet, make Hwy 49 part of a grand circle tour that includes the coast in one direction and this evocative and compelling region in the other.

HIGHLIGHTS

- Searching out the alternative charms of **Nevada City** (p315)
- Panning for gold at the **Marshall Gold Discovery State Historic Park** (p320)
- Strutting down Placerville's **Main St** (p320)
- Tasting liquid gold at Amador County's seductive **vineyards** (p322)
- Rediscovering forgotten **Volcano** (p323)
- Detouring through serene **Calaveras Big Trees State Park** (p327)
- Hopping your way along **Angels Camp** (p325)
- Re-creating the past at **Columbia State Historic Park** (p327)
- Hitching a ride on Jamestown's **choo-choos** (p329)

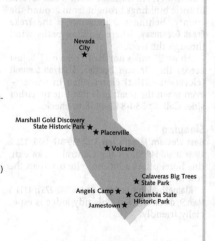

- AVERAGE TEMPS IN GRASS VALLEY: JAN 31/53/F, JUL 55/87°F

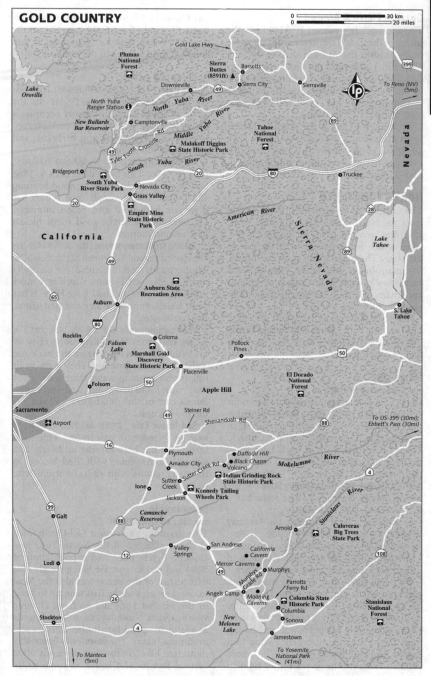

GOLD COUNTRY

0 ———— 30 km
0 ———— 20 miles

Gold Lake Hwy

Plumas National Forest

Sierra Buttes (8591ft)

Bassetts

Sierra City

Downieville

Sierraville

To Reno (NV) (5mi)

395

89

Lake Oroville

North Yuba Ranger Station

North Yuba River

Camptonville

New Bullards Bar Reservoir

Middle Yuba River

Tahoe National Forest

Tyler Foote Crossing Rd

Malakoff Diggins State Historic Park

South Yuba River

Bridgeport

20

South Yuba River State Park

Nevada City

Grass Valley

Empire Mine State Historic Park

80

Truckee

California

49

American River

Sierra Nevada

28

Lake Tahoe

89

Auburn State Recreation Area

65

Auburn

80

Rocklin

Folsom Lake

Coloma

Marshall Gold Discovery State Historic Park

Pollock Pines

50

S. Lake Tahoe

Folsom

50

Placerville

Apple Hill

El Dorado National Forest

Sacramento

Airport

49

Steiner Rd

Shenandoah Rd

88

To US-395 (30mi); Ebbett's Pass (30mi)

16

Plymouth

Amador City

Sutter Creek Rd

Daffodil Hill

Black Chasm

Volcano

Mokelumne River

4

Ione

Sutter Creek

Indian Grinding Rock State Historic Park

Jackson

Kennedy Tailing Wheels Park

99

Galt

88

Camanche Reservoir

Stanislaus River

Arnold

Calaveras Big Trees State Park

108

Valley Springs

San Andreas

California Cavern

Lodi

12

Mercer Caverns

Murphys

Parrotts Ferry Rd

Angels Camp

49

Murphys Grade Rd

Moaning Caverns

Columbia State Historic Park

Columbia

Sonora

Stanislaus National Forest

26

Stockton

4

New Melones Lake

Jamestown

To Manteca (5mi)

To Yosemite National Park (41mi)

Nevada

GOLD CO

Getting There & Around

The appropriately named Hwy 49 links the towns of the Gold Country. Except for some buses around the Auburn district, Nevada City and Placerville, the Gold Country is definitely car country. To fully enjoy one of the state's most scenic roads – let alone to simply get around – you will need your own wheels.

From Sierra City in the north to Jamestown in the south is over 200 miles on Hwy 49. It's a good, mostly two-lane road. To even begin to appreciate everything along it, plan a minimum of a five-day journey.

NORTH YUBA RIVER

The northernmost segment of Hwy 49 follows the North Yuba River through some stunning, remote parts of the Sierra Nevada, which feel removed from the rest of the state. There are many trails for hikers, mountain-bikers and skiers. Even in summer, snow is likely at the highest elevations and many places have roaring fireplaces year-round.

The best source of trail and camping information is the **North Yuba Ranger Station** (☎ 530-288-3231; 15924 Hwy 49; ☾ 8am-4:30pm Mon-Fri) in Camptonville.

Sierra City

pop 300 / elevation 4187ft

Sierra City is the primary supply station for people headed to the **Sierra Buttes**, probably the closest thing to the Alps you'll find in California without hoisting a backpack. There's a vast network of trails here, ideal for backpacking as well as casual hikes. Get the *Lakes Basin, Downieville – Sierra City* map ($2) from the **Sierra Country Store** (☎ 530-862-1181; Hwy 49; ☾ 9am-7pm). The town has a useful website (www.sierracity.com).

Sierra City's local museum, the **Kentucky Mine** (☎ 530-862-1310; adult/child $7/3.50; ☾ 10am-4pm Wed-Sun Jun-Aug), has tours of a gold mine and stamp mill plus very nicely organized historical displays. It's just north of town.

To reach the Buttes, and the many lakes and streams nearby, take Gold Lake Hwy north from Hwy 49 at Bassetts, 9 miles northeast of Sierra City. There are signs indicating numerous campgrounds and hiking trails in the area. An excellent hiking trail leads 1.5 miles to **Haskell Peak** (8107ft), where you can see from the Sierra Buttes right to

Mt Shasta and beyond. To reach the trailhead, turn right from Gold Lake Hwy at the sign to Haskell Peak Rd (Forest Rd 9) and follow it for 8.5 miles to the trailhead.

SLEEPING & EATING

Buttes Resort (☎ 530-862-1170, 800-991-1170; www.sierracity.com; 230 Main St; cabins $55-145) In the heart of Sierra City, this resort occupies a lovely spot overlooking the river. Most cabins have a private deck and barbecue, and some have full kitchens.

Old Sierra City Hotel (☎ 530-862-1300; 212 Main St; r $55; ☾ Jun-Oct) This hotel dates back to 1862 and has a good bar with a wood-burning stove. Each of the simple four rooms has a private bathroom and nice trimmings. On weekends it serves good fried-chicken lunches and dinners.

Salmon Creek campground (☎ 530-993-1410; sites $18) One of several US Forest Service (USFS) campgrounds recommended for camping north of Hwy 49, Salmon Creek is 2 miles north of Bassetts on Gold Lake Hwy. It has vault toilets, running water and first-come, first-serve sites.

USFS campgrounds (☎ 530-993-1410; sites $18) Going east from Sierra City along Hwy 49 are Wild Plum, Sierra, Chapman Creek and Yuba Pass campgrounds. They have vault toilets and running water (Sierra has river water only), and first-come, first-serve sites. Locals concur that Wild Plum (47 sites) is the most scenic.

Red Moose Cafe (☎ 530-862-1502; 224 Main St; meals $6; ☾ breakfast & lunch Tue-Sun) This local institution has been serving up hearty fare since 1940. Anything with 'Red Moose' in the name comes with chili, be it omelette or burger.

Downieville

pop 350 / elevation 2899ft

This charming and remote Gold Rush town at the confluence of the North Yuba and Downie Rivers once had a population of 5000 and was known for being rough – its first justice of the peace was also the local saloon keeper, and the first woman to hang in the Mother Lode did so from Downieville's gallows. Nowadays the town is known as a launching pad for climbers, hikers and mountain-bikers. The **Downieville Downhill**, a mountain-bike course that descends 5000 vertical feet in 12.4 miles, is consistently

GOING FOR THE GOLD

California's Gold Rush started in 1848 when James Marshall was inspecting the both fatefully and poorly sited lumber mill he was building for John Sutter near present-day Coloma (p319). He saw a fleck of gold in the mill's tailrace water and pulled out a gold nugget 'roughly half the size of a pea.' Marshall consulted Sutter, who tested the gold by methods described in an encyclopedia, and the two men found the piece to be of high quality. Sutter, however, wanted to finish his mill and thus made an agreement with his laborers that they could keep all the gold they found in their spare time if they kept working. Before long, word of the find leaked out.

Sam Brannan, for example, went to Coloma to investigate the rumors just a few months after Marshall found his nugget. After finding 6oz of gold in one afternoon, the riches clearly went to his head as he returned to San Francisco and paraded through the streets proclaiming, 'There's gold in the Sierra foothills!' Convinced that there was money to be made, he bought every piece of mining equipment in the area – from handkerchiefs to shovels. When gold seekers needed equipment for their adventure, Brannan sold them goods at a 100% markup and was a rich man by the time the first folks hit the foothills.

By the time construction of the mill was finished, in the spring of 1848, gold seekers had begun to arrive, the first wave coming from San Francisco. The new miners found gold so easily that they thought nothing of blowing all they had in one night, knowing that they could find just as much again the next day. By the end of 1848, San Francisco was nearly depleted of able-bodied men, while towns near the 'diggins' – as the mines were called – swelled with thousands of people. News spread around the world, and by 1849 more than 60,000 people (often called '49ers) rushed to California to find the mother lode – the mythical big deposit that miners believed was the source of all the gold found in the streams and riverbeds.

Most prospectors didn't stick around after the initial diggings petered out. In 1859 when the Comstock Lode was found on the eastern side of the Sierra in Virginia City, Nevada, many left. Those who did stay signed on with large operations (such as the Empire Mine in Grass Valley) which were financed by businesses or private fortunes. Gold-extraction processes became increasingly complex and invasive, culminating in the practice of hydraulic mining, by which miners drained lakes and rivers to power their water cannons and blast away entire hillsides (see Malakoff Diggins State Historic Park, p314). People inundated downstream by the muck sued, and eventually the environmental cost was too great to justify staying in business.

Currently, specimen gold – gold that is still attached to a piece of quartz, making it ideal for museum display – fetches higher prices than gold ore. The largest piece of crystalline gold leaf ever found is owned by Ironstone Vineyards in Murphys (see p326). Several large-scale, open-pit mines, primarily owned by out-of-state corporations, still exist. Locals will tell you that there's still plenty of gold in the hills – most easily found in rivers and streams after a heavy rain. And there are still many part-time prospectors today.

rated among the best downhill routes in the USA by bicycle magazines.

For groceries, maps and the local scoop, stop in at **Downieville Grocery** (☎ 530-289-3596; ☻ 8am-8pm Mon-Sat, 8am-6pm Sun), housed in an 1852 building. **Yuba Expeditions** (☎ 530-289-3010; www.yubaexpeditions.com; 105 Commercial St; bike rentals $65-100; ☻ 9am-5pm Wed-Mon) is a center of the summer trail-bike scene. Like several other businesses in town, it offers shuttles to trails as well as guided tours and helps maintain trails.

Favorite hikes in the area include the Chimney Rock Trail and Empire Creek Trail. Both are a bit tricky to reach, so pick up a map or trail guide at the North Yuba Ranger Station or the USFS Headquarters (p315) in Nevada City.

SLEEPING & EATING

West of Downieville, Hwy 49 passes numerous campgrounds and trailheads in the Tahoe National Forest. Carlton Flat, Fiddle Creek, Indian Valley, Rocky Rest and Ramshorn **campgrounds** (☎ 530-993-1410; sites $18) all have vault toilets, running water and unreserved sites along the Yuba River. The town's charming streets boast several vintage bars and eateries, some with river views.

Sierra Shangri-La (☎ 530-289-3455; www.sierra shangrila.com; r $70-115, cabins $85-250) People stay for a weeks at a time at this popular flower-scented option, 3 miles east of Downieville on Hwy 49. In July and August the cabins are usually booked with standing reservations, but rooms – each with a balcony overlooking the river – are often available.

Downtown Downieville has several places to stay where the rustle of the rapids will lull you to sleep.

Riverside Inn (☎ 530-289-1000; www.downieville .us; 206 Commercial St; r $75-155) This place has 11 rooms – some with balconies that overlook the river. Rooms have TVs and bathrooms, and a screen door lets you keep the main door open and listen to the river run by.

Carriage House Inn (☎ 530-289-3573; www.downie villecarriagehouse.com; 110 Commercial St; r $55-100) This home-like option has nine rooms with country-style charm that include rockers and a great sitting area right on the river. Some have private baths and TVs.

SOUTH YUBA RIVER STATE PARK

The California State Park System owns 2000 acres of land along the South Yuba River and leases another 5000 acres from the Bureau of Land Management (BLM). Through the South Yuba River Project, the system hopes to acquire even more river access and con-nect the Malakoff Diggins and South Yuba River state parks with hiking trails. Some of these trails are already in place, including the fully accessible **Independence Trail**, which starts from the south side of the South Yuba River bridge on Hwy 49 and goes for over 2 miles.

The longest, single-span, wood-truss **cov-ered bridge** in the USA, all 251ft of it, crosses the South Yuba River at Bridgeport (not to be confused with the Eastern Sierra town of the same name, p390). The bridge – built for private commercial use in 1862 – is at the end of a curvy, 7-mile drive (westward off Hwy 49 on Pleasant Valley Rd). The park's hiking and swimming are definitely well worth the trip and can be enjoyed for at least half a day. The Buttermilk Bend trail skirts the South Yuba for 1.4 miles, offering river access and wonderful wildflower view-ing around April.

Maps and park information are available from the **state park headquarters** (☎ 530-432-2546; ☼ 11am-4pm) in Bridgeport, or from the Tahoe National Forest USFS Headquarters in Nevada City.

MALAKOFF DIGGINS STATE HISTORIC PARK

With its restored town site, interesting museum, red stratified cliffs and gigantic mounds of tailings left behind by years of hydraulic mining, Malakoff Diggins is worth a full day's exploration.

Water cannons – designed specifically for hydraulic mining – cut a 200ft can-yon through ancient bedrock during the 1850s to unearth rich veins of gold. Rubble washed down from the hillsides, and the tailings dropped back into the Yuba River. This ultimately created a problem when the often-toxic waste (filled with heavy metals) reached the flat Sacramento Valley floor: by the 1860s, 20ft mud glaciers blocked riv-ers and caused severe flooding each spring during the Sierra snowmelt. After a year of heated courtroom (and bar-room) debate between farmers and miners, most of the hydraulic mining practices were prohibited. North Bloomfield, the small mining com-munity at the center of Malakoff's opera-tion, went bankrupt and fell dormant.

Malakoff Diggins State Historic Park Head-quarters and Museum (☎ 530-265-2740; admission per vehicle $6; ☼ 9am-5pm) shows an interesting video. There are tours (1:30pm) of North Bloomfield's many buildings, which have been restored to their original condition, albeit with rather twee white picket fences. The one-mile **Digging Loop Trail** is one of sev-eral and is a good introduction to the deeply scarred moonscape.

The park has primitive campsites, three developed **campgrounds** (☎ 800-444-7275; www .parks.ca.gov; sites $15) and four converted old miners' cabins ($35), as well as many picnic areas and a network of hiking trails. There are no RV hookups and no food for sale.

Tyler Foote Crossing Rd, the turnoff for the park, is 10 miles northwest of Nevada City on Hwy 49. Follow the signs 15 miles to the park entrance.

Three miles down Tyler Foote Crossing Rd at Oak Tree Rd you'll find **Mother Truckers** (☎ 530-292-3250; ☼ 8am-7pm) where locals chat about their alternative lifestyles, buy or-ganic groceries and snacks, catch up on the local news and peruse the anarchic bulletin board.

NEVADA CITY

pop 3000 / elevation 2525ft

Nevada City manages to be popular with tourists while maintaining an edgy local vibe. Like many of the Gold Rush towns, people looking for someplace far from the hustle of the cities discovered its inherent charms several decades ago and today it is home to a delightful mix of crusty old-timers, artists, folks bent on preserving a hippie lifestyle and well-off urban refugees.

The town's liberal roots go far back to Aaron Sargent, a transplanted New England journalist who served in Congress and the Senate. He helped author the 19th Amendment granting women the right to vote (with input from his friend Susan B Anthony, pioneer crusader for women's rights). Today, arts are a big part of life here – there are theater companies, alternative film houses, bookstores and live music performances almost every night. The downtown area is well preserved and has a quaint yet authentic feel that makes it one of the most intriguing places in the Gold Country to spend a few days.

Nevada City's streets, often jammed with pedestrians, are best navigated on foot. Broad St is the main thoroughfare, reached by the Broad St exit off Hwy 49/20. In December the whole town gets decked out in Christmas garb and there are special events every weekend.

Information

Harmony Books (☎ 530-265-9564; 231 Broad St) For maps and travel guides, history books, bestsellers and magazines. The town is blessed with several other bookstores selling used and rare books.

Nevada City Chamber of Commerce (☎ 530-265-2692, 800-655-6569; www.nevadacitychamber.com; 132 Main St; ☽ 9am-5pm Mon-Sat, 11am-4pm Sun) At the east end of Commercial St. Has an immaculate public toilet and much local information.

Tahoe National Forest USFS Headquarters (☎ 530-265-4531; 631 Coyote St; ☽ 8am-5pm Mon-Sat) A useful and friendly resource for trail and campground information, covering the area from here to Lake Tahoe. It sells topographical maps.

Sights & Activities

Much of the fun of Nevada City is simply wandering the streets and sampling the antique shops, galleries and libation-sellers. But there's also no shortage of history.

The town's 1856 foundry produced the first Pelton waterwheel in 1879, which revolutionized hydraulic mining. After WWII, the foundry was a metaphor for the town as it made Health Master juicers, which became popular with health gurus. Now it's the **Miners Foundry Cultural Center** (☎ 530-265-5040; 325 Spring St), one block off Broad St, and is used for performance art and private parties. You can view the foundry's original equipment on a self-guided tour, which starts at the foundry's entrance. In May the center hosts a jazz jubilee that attracts musicians from around the USA.

Housed in Nevada City's original 1861 firehouse, the **Nevada County Historical Society Museum** (☎ 530-265-5468; 214 Main St; admission by donation; ☽ call for hours) has an extensive collection from the Chinese laborers who provided so much of mining's back-breaking work.

The **Nevada City Winery** (☎ 530-265-9463; 321 Spring St; ☽ 11am-5pm Mon-Sat, noon-5pm Sun) offers tastes of its tasty syrah and zinfandel.

Sleeping

During weekends, Nevada City fills up with urban refugees who inevitably weigh themselves down with real-estate brochures.

US Hotel B&B (☎ 530-265-7999, 800-525-4525; www.ushotelbb.com; 233 Broad St; r $139-189; ☒ ▢) Right in the thick of the action, this 1856 B&B has seven elegantly restored and luxurious rooms (CD players etc); rates include a waffle breakfast and wine in the evening.

Emma Nevada House (☎ 530-265-4415, 800-916-3662; www.emmanevadahouse.com; 528 E Broad St; r $150-230; ☒) At the top of town, this B&B is in the childhood home of 1890s opera star Emma Nevada. It has large and luminous sitting areas and nicely appointed rooms that feel light and airy. Porches make good spots to unwind, as do whirlpool baths.

National Hotel (☎ 530-265-4551; www.thenational hotel.com; 211 Broad St; r $75-119; ☒ ▢ ☲) This historic hotel in the heart of the downtown area claims to be the oldest continuously operating hotel west of the Rocky Mountains and its unreconstructed charm supports this. The building was constructed in the 1850s; the 39 rooms are rather basic.

Outside Inn (☎ 530-265-2233; www.outsideinn.com; 575 E Broad St; r $69-150; ☒ ▢ ☲) This is an exceptionally friendly and fun motel, with 14 individually named and decorated rooms and a staff that loves the outdoors. Some rooms have a patio overlooking a small creek. It's a 10-minute walk from downtown.

Northern Queen Inn (☎ 530-265-5824; www.northernqueeninn.com; 400 Railroad Ave; r $80-125; 🗶 🝋) This place has 86 very nice rooms and chalets. Amenities include a heated pool, spa and restaurant, though it's a bit distant from the heart of town. The inn is on the site of Nevada City's Chinese cemetery, though the grave markers, if there were any, are long gone. It's also home to a collection of historic trains.

Eating & Drinking

Ike's Quarter Cafe (☎ 530-265-6138; 401 Commercial St; meals $6-8 ⏱ breakfast & lunch Wed-Mon) The pick of many good choices in town, Ike's serves up splendid Cajun fare with a sassy charm that leaves the blue hairs pink-cheeked. The large and creative menu features treats such as banana and pecan pancakes, jambalaya and more. The outside patio with its quiet fountain is right out of the Garden District in New Orleans.

Citronee Bistro & Wine Bar (☎ 530-265-5697; 320 Broad St; mains $8-20; ⏱ lunch Mon-Fri, dinner Mon-Sat) This small restaurant has a cheery charm backed by splendid examples of local art on the walls. The menu is comfortable with highlights including pulled pork on flatbread and garlicky short ribs.

Cirino's (☎ 530-265-4204; 309 Broad St; mains $16-20; ⏱ dinner) This local institution recalls classic supper clubs with its familiar and tasty menu of Italian classics from fettuccini Alfredo to veal parmigiana. An open kitchen in back caps the inviting long wooden bar.

Café Mekka (☎ 530-478-1517; 237 Commercial St; meals $5-15; ⏱ 8am-7pm Mon-Thu, 8am-midnight Fri-Sun) Decorated in a style best described as 'whorehouse baroque,' this charmer serves up good coffees and beers through the day as well as sandwiches, pizzas and famous desserts. Keep an eye out for live folk music some nights.

Wisdom Cafe & Gallery (☎ 530-265-4204; 426 Broad St; meals $4-7; ⏱ breakfast & lunch) This café serves light meals and alluring baked goods, and has a large, tree-shaded patio.

Cooper's (☎ 530-265-0116; 235 Commercial St; ⏱ 2pm-2am Mon-Sat) This rollicking venue serves local wines by the glass, has good beers on tap and there's music from open-mic blue grass to garage-band rock most nights. Enjoy the martini specials on the patio.

Entertainment

The Arts section of the *Union* newspaper comes out on Thursday, with a listing of what's going on around the area.

Nevada Theater (☎ 530-265-6161; 401 Broad St) This is one of California's first theaters (1865) and has welcomed the likes of Jack London and Mark Twain to its stage. Now it's used for productions of the very good and prolific **Foothill Theater Company** (☎ 530-265-8587), as well as off-beat movie screenings.

Magic Theatre (☎ 530-265-8262; www.themagictheatrenc.com; 107 Argall Way) This fantastic theater screens a matchless line-up of unusual films and is about a mile south of downtown Nevada City. Enjoy bowls of fresh popcorn, coffee in real mugs and hot brownies at intermission.

Getting There & Away

The **Gold Country Stage** (☎ 530-477-0103; www.goldcountrystage.com) bus service links Nevada City with Grass Valley at least hourly from 7am to 5pm and serves the Amtrak station in Auburn several times a day ($1 to $5).

GRASS VALLEY

pop 10,900 / elevation 2420ft

Grass Valley is where area residents buy groceries, service their cars and get their pets groomed. Its historic business district, while still intact and flush with nice stores, is an island amid a sprawl of strip malls, gas stations and fast-food restaurants – it's well worth fording the abyss to soak up the feel of the center.

Grass Valley's mines – notably George Bourne's Empire Mine – were among the first shaft mines in California. They showed mine owners and investors that, with promotion of a company's stock and the use of large-scale operations, there were big bucks to be made in lode mining. The Empire Mine was the first mining company to sell stock. The hills around here were the source of some of the largest finds of gold in the state, see p313 for details.

Grass Valley's main thoroughfares of Mill St and W Main St are the heart of the historic business district, which boasts an old-time movie theater, cafés, bars and more. E Main St goes north to the shopping centers and mini-malls, continuing north into Nevada City, while S Auburn St divides E and W Main St.

TOP 10 GOLD-PRODUCING COUNTIES

Following is a list of the top gold-producing counties (and notable city or town) in California, with an estimate of the value of gold mined since the Gold Rush – well, at least that reported for taxes.

Rank	County	Value
1	Nevada (Grass Valley)	$440 million
2	Amador (Jackson)	$200 million
3	Tuolumne (Sonora)	$190 million
4	Butte (Chico)	$150 million
5	Calavaras (Angel's Camp)	$150 million
6	Sierra (Downieville)	$150 million
7	Yuba (Yuba City)	$145 million
8	Sacramento (Sacramento)	$135 million
9	Placer (Auburn)	$120 million
10	El Dorado (Placerville)	$110 million

On Friday nights in July and August, Mill St is closed to car traffic while farmstead food, arts and crafts, and music entertain people in the street.

Information

Booktown Books (☎ 530-272-4655; 107 Bank St) Hosts several used-book dealers under one roof.
Book Seller (☎ 530-272-2131; 107 Mill St) Carries local publications, history books, travel guides and bestsellers.
Grass Valley/Nevada County Chamber of Commerce (☎ 530-272-8315; www.grassvalleychamber.com; 248 Mill St; ☾ 9am-5pm Mon-Fri) In the former Mill St home of enchantress Lola Montez. It has some very good maps and brochures. Be sure to pick up a copy of the historic walking-tour brochure.

Sights & Activities

The downtown area brims with atmosphere. Star of the historic buildings is the **Nevada County Bank** (131 Mill St), a site which dates from 1917, a time when bank buildings needed to reassure you that your money was safe.

Situated atop 367 miles of mine shafts, which from 1850 to 1956 produced six million ounces of gold (or about two billion modern dollars' worth), **Empire Mine State Historic Park** (☎ 530-273-8522; 10791 E Empire St; admission $2; ☾ 9am-6pm Jun-Sep, 10am-5pm Oct-May) is the Gold Country's best-preserved gold quartz-mining operation – worth at least a half-day's exploration. The large mine yard contains head frames, waterwheels, stamp

mills and pulleys, and is surrounded by the company offices, in buildings made of waste rock (left over after quartz mining).

The visitors center and museum shows a worthwhile movie and offers ranger-led tours (call for hours). If there's no tour, be sure to see the color-coded mine system model in the room adjacent to the visitor center. Next to the largest head frame in the mine yard is a stairway that leads 40ft down into the main mine shaft.

On the other side of the visitor center you'll find stately buildings that belonged to the Bourne family, under whose ownership the Empire Mine prospered. You can visit the elegant country club, English manor home, gardener's house and rose garden on a docent-led tour; check the visitors center for the day's schedule.

Hiking trails begin near the old stamp mill in the mine yard and pass abandoned mines and equipment. A trail map is available at the visitors center. The park is 2 miles east of Grass Valley via the Empire St exit off Hwy 49.

Grass Valley's **North Star Mine** used the largest Pelton waterwheel ever made. The mine's 1895 stone powerhouse on the west bank of Wolf Creek, at Mill St's southern end, is now a **museum** (☎ 530-273-4255; donation requested; ☾ 10am-5pm May-Oct) with a small collection of Pelton waterwheels (and their prototypes), mining equipment and artifacts. A few shady, creek-side tables behind the museum make nice picnic spots.

Sleeping & Eating

There are several good eateries and bars around downtown and one especially fine hotel. Chains lurk among the strip malls.

Holbrooke Hotel (☎ 530-273-1353, 800-933-7077; www.holbrooke.com; 212 W Main St; r $75-175; 🗶 🖳) This 1862 hotel has Mark Twain's signature in the hotel register and well-appointed rooms named after the presidents who slept there (Garfield et al). The Holbrooke's bistro (mains $7 to $20) serves good casual fare in the ornate dining room or on the shady patio. The locally popular bar has tables over-looking the Main St action.

Grass Valley Courtyard Suites (☎ 530-272-7696; www.gvcourtyardsuites.com; 210 N Auburn St; r $100-240; 🗶 🖳) A modern and luxurious place with rooms featuring balconies and patios, this is a good choice for extended stays as many rooms have full kitchens. Downtown is a one-block walk.

Tofanelli's (☎ 530-272-1468; 302 W Main St; meals $8-20) Hugely popular with those locals in the know, this creative restaurant has everything from salads to hearty steaks with seasonal accents like summer squash ravioli. Portions are large, prices are small and you can't beat the patio.

Dorado Chocolates (☎ 530-272-6715; 104 E Main St; snacks $3; �),10am-5pm Tue-Sat) Ken Kossoudji creates incredible handmade chocolates at this temple of indulgence. There's amazing coffee drinks and, yes, hot chocolate.

Getting There & Away

Gold Country Stage (☎ 530-477-0103; www.gold countrystage.com) links Grass Valley with Nevada City at least hourly from 7am to 5pm and serves the Amtrak station in Auburn several times a day (fares $1 to $5). The stop is near the post office on E Main St.

AUBURN

pop 13,600 / elevation 1255ft

Auburn was a major stop on the Central Pacific's transcontinental route and is still busy with trains on the Union Pacific's main line to the east. Interstate 80 follows this route between the Bay Area and Lake Tahoe, and is a commuter passage for people who live in Auburn and work in Sacramento. Auburn's place astride I-80 makes it one of the most visited places in the Gold Country, though it's not as interesting as some of the other towns.

The historic part of town (called Old Town) is touristy and hoovers up people right off the interstate. But venture a little further into town along Lincoln Way and you'll be rewarded with a thriving center and several good places for respite.

On Sunday, the Old Town hosts a huge traffic-jamming flea market, complete with live music and food vendors.

Information

Auburn Area Chamber of Commerce (☎ 530-885-5616; www.auburnchamber.net; 601 Lincoln Way; �),9am-5pm Mon-Fri) Housed in the old Southern Pacific railroad depot at the north end of Lincoln Way, it has lots of useful local info. There's a nearby monument to the first transcontinental railroad.

California Welcome Center (☎ 530-887-2111; www .visitplacer.com; 13411 Lincoln Way; �),9am-3pm) Right

off I-80 at the Foresthill exit, there is oodles of information for those entering the state from the east (as well as anyone else).

Sights & Activities

Placer County Museum (☎ 530-889-6500; 101 Maple St; admission free; �),11am-4pm Tue-Sun), on the 1st floor of the monumental 1898 **Placer County Courthouse** (�),8am-5pm), has Native American artifacts and displays of Auburn's transportation heritage.

In the Old Town, **Shanghai Bar** (☎ 530-8446; 291 Washington St) has been in operation since 1912, right through the Depression and Prohibition. It's a worthy place that wears its past like a fine patina and there's much to ponder.

Those who want to delve into local lore can head to the **Gold Country Museum** (☎ 530-889-6500; 1273 High St; admission free; �),11am-4pm Tue-Sun), toward the back of the fairgrounds. The **Bernhard Museum Complex** (☎ 530-888-6891; 291 Auburn-Folsom Rd; donation requested; �),11am-4pm Tue-Sun), at the south end of High St, was built in 1851 as the Traveler's Rest Hotel. The museum has displays depicting the typical life of a 19th-century farm family and at times volunteers in period garb ham it up.

Sleeping & Eating

Upper Lincoln Way toward the Chamber of Commerce has several restaurants popular with locals.

Power's Mansion (☎ 530-885-1166; www.vfr.net /~powerinn; 164 Cleveland St; r $160-250; ☒) Built with a gold fortune in 1898, this B&B exudes the rich opulence of the era. All 10 rooms are antique-filled and luxuries abound.

Foothills Motel (☎ 530-885-8444; 13431 Bowman Rd; s/d $60/65; ☒ ☒) Alongside I-80 not far from Old Town are a few motels, including this 62-room option, which has a hot tub and friendly owners. Rooms are comfortable.

Latitudes (☎ 530-885-9535; 130 Maple St; meals $15-25; �),Wed-Sun) One of the best restaurants in the Sierra foothills, Latitudes serves up carefully prepared seasonal fare in a dining room where the entrance is framed by jasmine. It's right across from the courthouse. Excellent wine list.

Monkey Cat Restaurant (☎ 530-888-8492; 805 Lincoln Way; meals $10-28) The smart decor accented by local artworks is the right setting for creative casual fare that ranges from unusual salads and huge burgers at lunch to steaks and seafood with fusion accents at dinner. It has a quiet patio.

Sweet Spot (☎ 530-888-8678; 802 Lincoln Way; treats $3-5; ☺ noon-8pm Tue-Sat, noon-5pm Sun, closes earlier in winter) The name says it all at this classic ice-cream store run by the ebullient Hawaiian shirt–wearing Jim Paskel (there's 10% off if you are wearing a Hawaiian shirt). Coffee drinks complement shakes and sundaes.

Ikedas (☎ 530-885-4243; 13500 Lincoln Way; meals $7-15; ☺ 8am-9pm) For many Californians, an I-80 journey is not complete without a stop at this small empire near Old Town. The menu groans with pleasure from its offerings of top-notch burgers, sandwiches and more. The store area is a produce wonderland of treats grown in the region.

Getting There & Away

Amtrak's *California Zephyr* stops in Auburn on its daily runs between the Bay Area and Chicago via Reno and Denver. **Amtrak** (☎ 800-872-7245; www.capitolcorridor.org) also runs several buses a day west linking Auburn with Sacramento ($11; one hour) where you can connect to Bay Area and Central Valley trains. There are usually two buses daily east to Reno (2½ hours).

The **Gold Country Stage** (☎ 530-477-0103; www .goldcountrystage.com) links Auburn with Grass Valley and Nevada City several times a day (fares $3 to $5).

AUBURN STATE RECREATION AREA

The North and Middle Forks of the American River converge below a bridge on Hwy 49, about 4 miles south of Auburn. In summer this is a popular **park** (☎ 530-885-4527) for sunning and swimming, though the current can be dangerous. Numerous trails in the area are shared by hikers, mountain-bikers and horses. Boaters have an entire campground and boating trail exclusively for them.

One of the most popular trails is the **Western States Trail**, which connects Auburn State Recreation Area to Folsom Lake State Recreation Area and Folsom Lake. It is the site of the annual '100 Miles in One Day' horseback ride, which starts in Soda Springs, near Truckee (visit www.foothill.net/tevis for more information) and ends in Auburn.

The **Quarry Trail** takes a level path from Hwy 49, just south of the bridge, along the Middle Fork of the American. Several side trails go down to the river.

COLOMA
pop 1100 / elevation 750ft

Originally known for its proximity to Sutter's Mill (the site of California's first gold discovery), Coloma is now renowned for its world-class white-water **rafting**. On the **South Fork American River**, around 11 miles north of Placerville, the town itself is a not terribly salubrious collection of businesses north of Marshall Gold Discovery State Historic Park (p320). Almost every establishment fronts for one or more rafting outfits.

Half-day rafting trips usually begin upstream at Chile Bar sand bar and end close to the state park. Full-day trips put in at the Coloma Bridge and take out at Salmon Falls, near Folsom Lake. The half-day options start in Class III water and are action-packed to the end (full-day trips start out slowly, then build up to Class III as a climax). The full-day trips include a lavish lunch. Some companies also organize and lead trips lasting two or more days. The season usually runs from May to mid-October, depending on how much winter snow there was and when it starts melting. Prices are generally lower weekdays.

Typical of the area's rafting companies is **Whitewater Connection** (☎ 530-622-6446, 800-336-7238; www.whitewaterconnection.com; half-day trips $89-109, full-day trips $109-129), which has knowledgeable guides and excellent food.

Another good outfit with similar offerings is **American Whitewater Expeditions** (☎ 800-825-3205; www.americanwhitewater.com). It is located close to the state park.

Don't want to get wet? Watch people navigate the **Trouble Maker Rapids**, upstream from the bridge next to Sutter's Mill in the state park.

Sleeping & Eating

Most rafting companies own private campgrounds for their guests who do overnight trips. If the campgrounds are not full, however, they often let day-trippers camp for around $15.

American River Resort (☎ 530-622-6700; www .americanriverresort.com; 6019 New River Rd; tent & RV sites $25-35, cabins $115-130; ☒) This place is only a quarter of a mile off Hwy 49, just south of the state park, and has a restaurant and bar, a playground, a pond and farm animals. The campsites are basic, but they are shady and have excellent river access.

Coloma Resort (☎ 530-621-2267; www.colomaresort .com; 6921 Mt Murphy Rd; tent & RV sites $33-35, tent cabins $45; 🖭) Another long-established riverside campground, this one comes with a full range of activities, playgrounds and the like.

Coloma Club Cafe & Saloon (☎ 530-626-6390; 7171 Hwy 49; 🕑 restaurant 6:30am-9pm, bar 10am-2am) Just north of Marshall Gold, this popular hangout comes alive with guides and river rats when the water is high.

MARSHALL GOLD DISCOVERY STATE HISTORIC PARK

California was a backwater in 1848, albeit a rather pleasant one. It was an all but ignored far corner of North America, but this all changed when farmer John Sutter and his lumber-business partner James Marshall built a mill on the swift-flowing American River and found gold.

The rest of the California Gold Rush (see p313) is the stuff of lore, but the site of the first find has been carefully preserved at the **Marshall Gold Discovery State Historic Park** (admission per car $5; 🕑 8am-sunset). Eschewing development and sensation, the park is a pastoral and low-key affair where you can follow a simple dirt path to the place along the bank where Marshall made his discovery on January 24, 1848. The effect is sublime.

The **State Park Visitors Information Center & Museum** (☎ 530-622-3470; Bridge St; 🕑 10am-3pm), just off Hwy 49 which passes through the heart of the park, has exhibits in a near-permanent state of reconstruction (blame budget cuts by the governor). Several nearby period buildings – including a reconstruction of the dubious mill – are open for inspection. The official park brochure is excellent.

The entire area is quite bucolic. On a hill overlooking the park is the **James Marshall Monument**, where he was buried in 1885 after a life that was notable for how little he profited from his discovery (he died a ward of the state). You can drive a circuit or, much better, follow some of the many trails around the park. Some pass old mining artifacts and pioneer cemeteries.

Panning for gold is popular – you can pay $3.50 to pan at Beckeart's Gun Shop (across from the visitors center), and there is a decent café and plenty of places for picnics.

Although the park does not usually get crowded, you can really soak up the atmosphere by spending the night at the **Coloma**

Country Inn (☎ 530-622-6919; www.colomacountryinn .com; r $110-135). Built by a prospecting family in 1852, the old farmhouse offers cute little rooms, excellent food (the berries that grow locally in profusion are used) and utter peace.

PLACERVILLE
pop 9800 / elevation 1866ft

'Old Hangtown' (as Placerville is fondly known, because five men were hung here in 1849) has always relied on travelers passing through for its livelihood. Originally it was a destination for gold seekers who reached California by following the South Fork of the American River. In 1857 the first stagecoach to cross the Sierra Nevada linked Placerville to Nevada's Carson Valley – a route that eventually became part of the nation's first transcontinental stagecoach route. Today, Placerville is a gas and food stop for people traveling between Sacramento and South Lake Tahoe on Hwy 50. Also the El Dorado County seat, the town has a thriving and well-preserved downtown with antique shops, outdoor activity stores, galleries and character-filled bars.

Orientation & Information

Main St, the heart of downtown Placerville, runs parallel to Hwy 50 between Canal St and Cedar Ravine Rd. Hwy 49 meets Main St at the west edge of downtown.

Bookery (☎ 530-626-6454; 326 Main St) A good used-book store.

El Dorado County Chamber of Commerce (☎ 530-621-5885, 800-457-6279; www.visiteldorado.com; 542 Main St; 🕑 9am-5pm Mon-Fri) Has decent maps and local information.

Placerville News Co (☎ 530-622-4510; 409 Main St) Wooden-floored, with a wealth of maps, history and local interest books, newspapers and magazines.

Sights & Activities

Most buildings along Main St date back to the 1850s, and many places stock the good, free walking-tour brochure. One delightful stop is the still-authentic 1852 **Placerville Hardware** (☎ 530-622-1151; 441 Main St), the oldest continuously operating hardware store west of the Mississippi River. One area is devoted to gift items but much of the store is just the place to go if you want an unusual screw.

Placerville Historical Museum (☎ 530-626-0773; 524 Main St; admission free; 🕑 noon-4pm Fri-Sun), inside the Fountain & Tallman Soda Works Building, has a small collection of soda factory relics and old Placerville photographs.

Prominent on Main St is the **Bell Tower**, a relic from 1856 that was used to summon volunteer firemen.

One mile north of town on Bedford Ave, **Gold Bug Park** (☎ 530-642-5207; www.goldbugpark.org; ☽ 8:30am-5pm) is on the site of four mining claims that yielded gold from 1849 to 1888. You can visit the Gold Bug Mine and Stamp Mill (adult/child $4/2), do some gold panning ($2) and explore the grounds and picnic area for free.

El Dorado County Historical Museum (☎ 530-621-5865; 104 Placerville Dr; admission free; ☽ 10am-4pm Wed-Sat, noon-4pm Sun), on the El Dorado County Fairgrounds west of downtown (exit north on Placerville Drive from Hwy 50), is an extensive complex of restored buildings, mining equipment and re-created businesses.

For something entirely different, you may wish to join the annual **Highway 50 Association Wagon Train** (www.hwy50wagontrain.com), which, as the name implies, sees a caravan of vintage Connestogas make the seven-day trip from Carson City, Nevada, to Placerville.

Sleeping & Eating

Chain motels and fast-food places can be found at either end of the historic center of Placerville along Hwy 50.

Cary House Hotel (☎ 530-622-4271; www.caryhouse .com; 300 Main St; r from $80; ✗ ✗ ▣) This historic hotel in downtown Placerville has modern rooms with period decor that belies its bordello history. Ask for a room at the back of the hotel, overlooking the courtyard, to avoid street noise.

Chichester-McKee House B&B (☎ 530-626-1882, 800-831-4008; www.innlover.com; 800 Spring St; r $110-130; ✗ ✗) This house was built in 1892 by the head of the local lumber company and features wonderful wood insets, stained-glass windows and four elegant rooms. Brownies are served in the evening and a full breakfast is provided in the morning.

Combellack-Blair House B&B (☎ 530-622-3764; www.combeblair.com; 3059 Cedar Ravine Rd; r $115-150) This large place is on the National Register of Historic Places. It's two blocks south of Main St and has three Victorian-style rooms and a small garden.

Placerville KOA (☎ 530-676-2267; www.koa-placer ville.com; 4655 Rock Barn Rd; tent sites $24-30, cabins

$50-65; ▣) This park, 6 miles west of Placerville on Hwy 50 (exit north onto Shingle Springs Dr), sits on 18 acres of land. Tent sites are shaded. RV hookups also available.

Tomei's (☎ 530-626-9766; 384 Main St; mains $8-25; ☽ Tue-Sat) This brightly decorated restaurant has an attractive menu that matches the crisp decor. Local patrons are so loyal they run into the street urging you to try the Italian-accented cuisine.

Cozmic Cafe (☎ 530-642-8481; 594 Main St; meals $6-10; ☽ breakfast, lunch & dinner) Expect to see patrons sitting in the lotus position at this funky place in an 1859 building. The menu is organic and boasts vegetarian and healthy fare plus treats like fresh smoothies. There's a good selection of microbrews and live music on weekends, when it is often open late.

Gelato D'Oro Cafe (☎ 530-626-8097; 311 Main St; meals $6-10; ☽ lunch) This place serves crepes, sandwiches and creamy Italian ice cream. The hearty Sunday brunches are popular.

Drinking

Placerville's bars are akin to the neighborhood watering holes in the Midwest: they open around 6am, get an annual cleaning at Christmas and are great for people who want to soak up local color. Marked by vintage signs, the **Hangman Tree** (☎ 530-622-3878; 305 Main St) is built over the stump of the eponymous tree, while the **Liars' Bench** (☎ 530-622-0494; 255 Main St) has a classic old martini sign beckoning like a neon siren.

Getting There & Away

Amtrak (☎ 800-872-7245; www.capitolcorridor.org) runs three buses daily to Sacramento ($14; 1hr 20min) and South Lake Tahoe ($14; 1hr). The **Placerville Transit Station** (2984 Mosquito Rd) is a charming covered bus stop with benches and restrooms; it's about half a mile from downtown, on the north side of Hwy 50.

AROUND PLACERVILLE
Apple Hill

In 1860 a miner planted a Rhode Island Greening apple tree on what is the present-day property of a family named Larsen, and thus began what is now the prolific Apple Hill, a 20-sq-mile area east of Placerville and north of Hwy 50 where there are more than 60 orchards. The miner's Rhode Island Greening tree still stands (a major gimmick for the Larsens, who operate a museum) and is flanked by Granny Smiths, pippins, red and yellow delicious, Fujis from Japan and Braeburns from New Zealand. Apple growers sell directly to the public, usually from August to December, and some let you pick your own. At other times other fruits are in season and at Christmas several places let you cut your own tree.

A decent map of Apple Hill is available at the **Apple Hill Visitors Center** (☎ 530-644-7692; www.applehill.com) in the Camino Hotel, near the Camino exit off Hwy 50. To take a condensed Apple Hill tour, follow the Camino exit north onto Barkley Rd until it becomes Larsen Drive. Follow Larsen Drive (which will become Cable and then Mace Rd) until it meets the Pony Express Trail back beside Hwy 50. White signs emblazoned with bright red apples mark connecting side roads and byways.

Wineries

The El Dorado County wines are becoming popular and frequently appear on California menus. Area wineries have invested a great deal in their properties, and most offer free tastings on weekends. You can pick up a good map at the El Dorado County Chamber of Commerce (p320) or from the **El Dorado Winery Association** (☎ 800-306-3956; www.eldoradowines.org).

Some noteworthy wineries, all north of Hwy 50, include **Lava Cap Winery** (☎ 530-621-0175; www.lavacap.com; 2221 Fruitridge Rd; ❤ 11am-5pm) and **Boeger Winery** (☎ 530-622-8094; www.boeger winery.com; 1709 Carson Rd; ❤ 10am-5pm). The latter makes a fine viognier.

AMADOR COUNTY WINERIES

The Swiss-born Uhlingers began the wine industry in Amador County by planting the first vines in 1856. The region wasn't really developed until the 1960s, however, when grapes that were traditionally sold to large winemakers for blending started yielding juice and skin of high enough quality to be made into wine on their own.

Amador County is best known for its zinfandel, a peppery wine with hints of berries and black currants. Italian varietals also do well here, so barberas, sangioveses and nebbiolos are common. Tastings at the small, family-run wineries are very laid-back, almost always free and can be extremely educational since folks here are willing to

discuss just about any aspect of the wine business you're interested in.

Maps are available at the wineries and from the **Amador Vintners Association** (☎ 209-267-2297; www.amadorwine.com). To set off, head east from Plymouth on Shenandoah Rd, which eventually links up with Steiner Rd. Signs indicate where the wineries are and which ones are open (some are closed weekdays).

Recommended wineries:

Karly (☎ 209-245-3922; www.karlywines.com; 11076 Bell Rd; ❤ noon-4pm) Off Shenandoah Rd.

Shenandoah Vineyards (☎ 209-245-4455; www.shen andoahvineyards.com; 12300 Steiner Rd; ❤ 10am-5pm)

Sobon Estate (☎ 209-245-6554; www.sobonwine.com; 14430 Shenandoah Rd; ❤ 10am-5pm) Founded in 1856 and home to the Shenandoah Valley Museum with wine-related memorabilia.

Story Winery (☎ 209-245-6208; www.zin.com; 10525 Bell Rd; ❤ noon-4pm) Off Shenandoah Rd.

Vino Noceto (☎ 209-245-6556; www.noceto.com; 11011 Dickson Rd; ❤ 11am-4pm)

AMADOR CITY

pop 270 / elevation 620ft

This quiet little village some 30 miles south of Placerville is going to get a lot quieter when a new bypass opens on Hwy 49 in late 2006. This should only increase the charm of this delightful bend in the road. Once home to the Keystone Mine – one of the most prolific gold producers in California – the town lay deserted from 1942 (when the mine closed) until the 1950s, when a family from Sacramento bought the dilapidated buildings and converted them into antique shops. Now the town has half a dozen shops and cafés along its shady streets. The **Amador Whitney Museum** (☎ 209-267-0928; Main St; admission free; ❤ noon-4pm Fri-Sun) has changing exhibits of local artworks in a vintage building.

Behind Amador City's old firehouse (the building with a bright red garage door and bell tower in front) is a stone arastra (a round, shallow pool with a turnstile in the middle used to crush rocks into gravel), once used here to grind gold-laced quartz. The arastra still works and is put to use during the Jose Amador Fiesta in late April.

The **Imperial Hotel** (☎ 209-267-9172, 800-242-5594; www.imperialamador.com; 14202 Main St; r $100-140; dinner $20-30; ❂), built in 1879, serves inventive dinners in an elegant dining room. The bar is a genteel hangout. The rooms combine local art with antiques.

SUTTER CREEK

pop 2350 / elevation 1198ft

Many travelers consider Sutter Creek their favorite Gold Country town. Its residential areas and the raised, arcaded sidewalks and high-balconied buildings along Main St are excellent examples of 19th-century architecture. The one off-note in this preserved gem has been the traffic on Hwy 49, but that will change when the bypass opens in 2006.

Stop at the **Sutter Creek Visitor Center** (☎ 209-267-1344; www.suttercreek.org; 25 Eureka St; ☟ hours vary) to collect a walking-tour map of the town. Also well worth obtaining is an excellent free driving tour to local gold mines.

Sights & Activities

Next door to the visitor center, **Monteverde General Store** (☎ 209-267-5155; admission free; ☟ 10am-3pm) has been restored to look just as tidy as it was in 1898.

In its prime Sutter Creek was the Gold Country's main supply center. Three foundries operating in 1873 made pans and rock crushers. The **Knight Foundry** (☎ 209-267-0201; 81 Eureka St) operated until 1996 as the last water-powered foundry and machine shop in the US. You can still see the workings of the foundry, and on some days volunteers can explain how everything worked while they toil to put the foundry back into production.

Nearby, **Seabreeze Sculpture Studio** (☎ 209-267-5883; 10 Eureka St; ☟ 9am-7pm) displays the mystical carved stone works of Thomas Baugh in a moody garden.

One of several excellent Gold Country arts groups, the **Sutter Creek Theatre** (☎ 877-547-6518; www.suttercreektheater.com; 44 Main St) has a nearly 100-year-long history of presenting live drama, films and other cultural events.

Sleeping & Eating

Eureka Street Inn (☎ 209-267-5500; www.eurekastreet inn.com; 55 Eureka St; r $110-130; ☒) Each of the four rooms in this 1914 home has a different decor. Once the home of a wealthy stagecoach operator, the inn is on a quiet street close to everything and serves a good breakfast.

Sutter Creek Inn (☎ 209-267-5606; www.suttercreek inn.com; 75 Main St; r $90-195; ☒) The 17 rooms and cottages here vary in decor and amenities (antiques, fireplaces, patios) but all have private bathrooms. Guests can enjoy the lush gardens and the large lawn which is dotted

with comfy chairs for curling up in with a book.

Foxes Inn (☎ 209-267-5882; www.foxesinn.com; 77 Main St; r $160-210; ☒ ☒) Next door to Sutter Creek Inn, Foxes has seven plush rooms with TVs, VCRs, refrigerators and bathrobes. Breakfasts are inspired and there are free beverages throughout the day.

Corner Cafe (☎ 209-267-0500; 40 Hanford St; meals $5-9; ☟ breakfast & lunch, dinner Fri & Sat; ☐) A real star in a galaxy of them, this eponymous place serves classic fare ranging from eggs Benedict to prime rib dinners. There's a sunny little patio. It's one of several fine cafés in Sutter Creek.

Sutter Creek Coffee Roasting Co (☎ 209-267-5550; 20 Eureka St; meals $4-7; ☟ breakfast & lunch) This café's patio is a local social hub.

Chatter Box Café (☎ 209-267-5935; 39 Main St; meals $6-9; ☟ breakfast & lunch Wed-Sun) This place makes all its own bread, buns and pies. Dishes show real flair: that isn't bacon and eggs, it's *pancetta* and eggs.

Zinfandel's (☎ 209-267-5008; cnr Main & Hanford Sts; mains $18-22; ☟ dinner Thu-Sun) This refined restaurant is well known for its eclectic California menu. The menu reflects what's fresh in the markets; expect numerous elaborate vegetarian options as well as steaks and seafood. Diners are encouraged to bring along any prime bottles of wine they've scored during the day's travels.

The **Saturday Farmers Market** (☟ 8-11am Jun-Oct) is a good place to sample the bounteous delights of this fertile region.

VOLCANO

pop 100 / elevation 2053ft

Volcano spewed forth gold in such quantities that in 1848 the average miner was making $100 a day. It shot its wad early though, and by 1865 the mines were played out and the town was tapped out. Today it is a rural aerie which slumbers away in lovely solitude, especially on weekdays.

Hand-painted signs outside the buildings give amusing insights into Volcano's colorful past. The town lays claim to the first astronomical observation site, the first private law school and the first library in California. Large sandstone rocks line Sutter Creek, which runs through the center of town. The rocks, now flanked by picnic tables, were blasted from surrounding hills by hydraulic processes, then scraped clean of gold-bearing dirt. Nearby monuments attest to Volcano's boastful past.

The 12-mile drive from Sutter Creek is along lovely Sutter Creek Rd.

Sights & Activities

Between mid-March and mid-April, **Daffodil Hill**, 2 miles northeast of Volcano, is blanketed with more than 300,000 daffodils. The McLaughlin and Ryan families have operated the hilltop farm since 1887 and keep hyacinths, tulips, violets, lilacs and the occasional peacock among the daffodils. The hill is open daily when the flowers are in bloom. There's no fee, but donations toward next year's planting are appreciated.

Indian Grinding Rock State Historic Park (☎ 209-296-7488; Pine Grove-Volcano Rd; admission per vehicle $6), 2 miles southwest of Volcano, is a sacred area for the local Miwok people. There's a limestone outcrop that's covered with petroglyphs – 363 originals and a few modern additions – and over 1000 mortar holes called *chaw'ses* used for grinding acorns into meal.

Near the rock are several impressive replica Miwok structures and the **Regional Indian Museum** (☼ 11am-3pm Mon-Fri, 10am-4pm Sat & Sun), which has interesting displays about northern Miwok culture and organizes tours of the park on weekends.

Black Chasm (☎ 888-762-2837; www.caverntours.com; 15701 Pioneer Volcano Rd; adult/child $12/6; ☼ 9am-4pm), a quarter of a mile east of Volcano, is known for its helictite crystals – rare, sparkling white formations that look like an enlarged snowflake. For extra loot you can try your hand at gemstone mining.

Entertainment

On weekends between April and November, the highly regarded **Volcano Theatre Company** (☎ 209-223-4663; www.volcanotheatre.org; adult/child $14/9) produces live dramas in the restored Cobblestone Theater.

Sleeping & Eating

St George Hotel (☎ 209-296-4458; www.stgeorgehotel .com; 16104 Main St; r $80-190) This hotel has 20 rooms which vary in size and amenity. However, all share a look that is refreshingly free from excessive froufrou. Some open directly onto the balcony from where you can observe not much going on. The restaurant (open for brunch on Sundays and for dinner from Thursday to Sunday) wins raves for its

creative use of herbs and produce grown in the hotel's garden. The steaks really shine.

Volcano Union Inn (☎ 209-296-7711; www.volcano unioninn.com; 21375 Consolation St; r $90-170; ☐) The four elegant and contemporary rooms here have large bathrooms and numerous conveniences such as wi-fi access and cable TV. Enjoy the fruits of the breakfast buffet in your room or on the large balcony overlooking the town. The bar is folksy inside and refreshing outside.

The beautiful **campground** (sites $15-20) at Indian Grinding Rock State Historic Park has fresh water, plumbing and 23 unreserved sites set among the trees.

Getting There & Away

Reach Volcano by traveling 9 miles northeast from Jackson on Hwy 88 and turning north at Pine Grove, or by the scenic 12 miles of curves along Sutter Creek Rd from Sutter Creek.

JACKSON

pop 4000 / elevation 1200ft

Between 1860 and 1920 when the Kennedy and Eureka mines were in full swing, Jackson was the area's primary entertainment center, known for its saloons, gambling halls and bordellos. Nowadays Jackson – the Amador County seat – is more of a commercial center than a charming historic village and/ or center of pleasure.

Hwy 88 turns east from Hwy 49 here and heads over the Sierra near the Kirkwood ski resort (see p336). The **Amador County Chamber of Commerce** (☎ 209-223-0350; 125 Peek St; ☼ 9am-4pm Mon-Fri), on the corner of Hwys 49 and 88, has a range of brochures, all watched over by models in photos for the adjoining beauty shop.

You can get to know Jackson's small historic center by taking a **tour** (☎ 209-223-5192; $7.50) with local historian and author Larry Cenotto. Call for times.

Sights & Activities

Perched on a hill overlooking downtown, the **Amador County Museum** (☎ 209-223-6386; 225 Church St; donation requested; ☼ 10am-4pm Wed-Sun), two blocks north of Main St, celebrates Gold Country history and has some cool models of working mines.

One mile from downtown Jackson via interesting North Main St, **Kennedy Tailing Wheels**

Park doesn't look like much at first glance, but it's worth closer inspection. It contains four iron and wood wheels, 58ft in diameter (they look like fallen carnival rides), that transported tailings from the Eureka Mine over two low hills into an impounding dam by way of gravity flumes. The wheels aren't very old – they were built in 1914 – but they are marvelous examples of engineering and craftsmanship. Be sure to climb to the top of the hill behind the wheels to see the impounding dam.

Somewhat undiscovered **Mokelumne Hill**, which lies 7 miles south of Jackson just off Hwy 49, was settled by French trappers in the early 1840s. It's a good place to see historic buildings without the common glut of antique stores and gift shops.

Sleeping & Eating

Jackson's cheap and chain motels are on the outskirts of town along Hwys 49 and 88.

National Hotel (☎ 209-223-0500; fax 223-4845; 2 Water St; r $75-195) Downtown is this historic building with 23 old rooms that are decorated with various icons: John Wayne, Elvis Presley etc (you'll have to decide whether you want the Duke or the King watching over your sleep). The rooms have access to a balcony that overlooks the town. Plenty of noise is provided by the lively bar where locals gather on the balcony to smoke and carouse.

Best Western Amador Inn (☎ 209-223-0211; www .bestwestern.com; 200 S Hwy 49; r $75-105; ✖ ☐ ☎) This large motel is close to downtown and has 118 spacious and comfortable rooms. However, the pool is rather small.

Amador Inn (☎ 209-223-0970; 12408 Kennedy Flat Rd; r midweek/weekend $45/55; ✖ ✖ ☎) A low-key place with a small garden and 10 decent rooms with barbecue facilities.

Hotel Leger (☎ 209-286-1401; www.hotelleger.com; 8304 Main St; r $65-155; ✖ ☎) In Mokelumne Hill, this quite comfortable hotel has a classic bar (established in 1851) and a restaurant (open Thursday to Monday) that serves burgers, steaks and a variety of sandwiches.

Mel's and Faye's Diner (☎ 209-223-0853; 205 N Hwy 49; meals $5-12; ✖ breakfast, lunch & dinner) *Not* affiliated with the chain of the similar name, this local institution near Hwy 88 serves up excellent diner fare that includes vast breakfasts, classic burgers in baskets and even a decent salad bar. Go nuts and

suck down a thick, smooth banana shake on the patio.

Teresa's Place (☎ 209-223-1786; 1235 Jackson Gate Rd; meals $12-18; ✖ Fri-Tue) One mile out of town past Kennedy Park, Teresa's is as thoroughly a classic as its meals are complete. The Italian standards come with soup, salad, pasta and ice cream. Three generations of Teresa's offspring yuck it up with regulars in the convivial bar.

SAN ANDREAS
pop 2300 / elevation 1008ft

San Andreas, the seat of Calaveras County, has utilitarian businesses concentrated on Hwy 49. The old town along N Main St is noteworthy for its county courthouse housing an art gallery, restored jail and jail yard where notorious stagecoach robber Black Bart awaited trial. Also here is the **Calaveras County Historical Museum Complex** (☎ 209-754-1058; 30 N Main St; adult/child $3/1; ✖ 10am-4pm), which has one of the area's most-engaging history displays and a native plant garden.

In Cave City, 8 miles east of San Andreas (take Mountain Ranch Rd to Cave City Rd), is the intricate **California Cavern** (☎ 209-736-2708; www.caverntours.com; adult/child $12/6; ✖ 10am-5pm Jun-Sep, 10am-4pm Sat & Sun Oct-May), which John Muir described as 'graceful flowing folds deeply placketed like stiff silken drapery.' Regular tours take 60 to 90 minutes. For $130 you can try a Middle Earth Expedition, which lasts five hours and includes some serious spelunking.

ANGELS CAMP
pop 2900 / elevation 1379ft

Famous as the spot where Mark Twain gathered notes for his short story *The Celebrated Jumping Frog of Calaveras County, and Other Sketches*, Angels Camp makes the most of this historic tie. The International Frog Jump Competition is held the third weekend in May and Mark Twain Days are celebrated on the Fourth of July weekend. Dozens of bronze frogs, which are imbedded along the sidewalk of Main St, commemorate the International Frog Jumping champions for nearly the past 80 years. See if you can find the ultimate record-holder (hint: the year was 1986). The winner for 2005 (19ft, 4in) had residents jumping for joy as it was the first local frog to win the competition in almost 50 years.

Angel's Camp was established by George Angel in 1849 as a service center for surrounding mines. Hard-rock mining peaked in the 1890s, when 200 stamp mills worked around the clock. Remains of the last mine are visible in Utica Park at the west end of Main St. Today the town is an attractive mix of buildings from the Gold Rush to art-deco periods.

The **Angels Camp Museum** (☎ 209-736-2963; 753 S Main St; ☽ 10am-3pm Mar-Dec) is but a hop, skip and a jump from the center. Documents, photographs, relics and 3 acres of old equipment tell of the area's mining heyday.

Calaveras County Visitors Bureau (☎ 209-736-0049; www.gocalaveras.com; 1192 S Main St; ☽ 9am-5pm Mon-Sat, 11am-3pm Sun) has a walking and driving tour of Angels Camp, history books and lots more information for your trip.

Sleeping & Eating

Jumping Frog Motel (☎ 209-736-2191; www.jumping frogmotel.com; 330 Murphys Grade Rd; r $60-100; ☒) A block off Main St, toward the center of town, this motel has friendly owners and basic rooms around a courtyard featuring the requisite frog sculpture.

Gold Country Inn (☎ 209-736-4611, 800-851-4944; www.goldcountryinnangelscamp.com; 720 S Main St; r $50-120; ☒) Across from the museum, this is such a good deal that you might just croak when you see the price. There are 40 modern, comfy rooms, many with refrigerators.

Pickle Barrel (☎ 209-736-4704; 1225 S Main St; meals $6-18; ☽ lunch Mon-Sat, dinner Fri & Sat) The ambitious owners of this local institution have expanded the menu to include savory barbecued fare on weekends. The deli counter is home to such a fandango of fixin's that you might get a frog in your throat trying to pronounce them all.

Crusco's (☎ 209-736-1440; 1240 S Main St; mains $14-17) The simple decor belies a serious Italian menu at this local favorite. Each year the owners travel to Italy in search of new recipes and bring home treats like polenta Castellana (creamy corn meal with garlic and parsley).

MURPHYS

pop 3400 / elevation 2171ft

Murphys, which is 8 miles east of Hwy 49 on Murphys Grade Rd, is named for Daniel and John Murphy, who founded a trading post and mining operation on Murphy Creek in 1848, in conjunction with the local Maidu

people. John was apparently very friendly with the tribe and eventually married the chief's daughter. The town's Main St is shady and refined with boutiques and galleries. But fear not, at least one shop sells that sundrenched Gold Country staple: ice cream.

Sights & Activities

Wine has become such a big deal that the most visited place in Calaveras County has nothing to do with frogs, it's the **Ironstone Vineyards** (☎ 209-728-1251; www.ironstonevineyards .com; 1894 Six Mile Rd; ☽ 10am-5pm). This large winery has fun for the whole family, with beautiful grounds, a deli and a museum which displays the world's largest crystalline gold leaf specimen. It weighs 44lb and was found in Jamestown in 1992. While crowds are frequent, the wine-tasting room is spacious. Ironstone is 1 mile south of town via Six Mile Rd, and other wineries cluster nearby.

In town you'll find the free tasting rooms for several much smaller wineries. These include the **Zucca Mountain** (☎ 209-736-2949; 425 E Main St; ☽ noon-5pm) underground grotto and **Milliaire Winery** (☎ 209-728-1658; 276 Main St; ☽ 11am-5pm).

Stevenot Winery (☎ 209-728-0638; 2690 San Domingo Rd; ☽ 10am-5pm) comes a close second to Ironstone in popularity. Its amphitheatre hosts **Theatre Under the Stars** (☎ 866-463-8659; www.sierratickets.com; ☽ Thu-Sat Jun-Sep), a well-regarded drama series. The winery is 2 miles west of Murphys, off Sheep Ranch Rd.

Nearby is the **Murphys Old Timers Museum** (☎ 209-728-1160; donation requested; ☽ 11am-4pm Fri-Sun). It has an interesting photograph collection housed in an 1856 building. The 'Wall of Relative Ovation' was dedicated by the mostly silly Gold Rush–era organization called E Clampus Vitus, a men's social organization that still exists today. **Sasha's Reading Room** (☎ 209-728-2200; 416 Main St) is a good source of new and used books, maps and local history guides.

Mercer Caverns (☎ 209-728-2101; adult/child $11/6.50; ☽ 10am-5pm Jun-Aug, 10am-4:30 Sep-May) were discovered in 1885 by Walter Mercer, who, after a long day of gold prospecting, tried to find some water to quench his thirst but found a cool stream of air coming out of the ground instead. A 45-minute guided tour takes you past enormous stalactites, stalagmites and vaulted chambers with names such as 'Chinese Meat Market' and 'Organ

---

DETOUR: CALAVERAS BIG TREES STATE PARK

From Angel's Camp, Hwy 4 ascends into the High Sierra, eventually cresting at Ebbetts Pass (8730ft) and then descending to junctions with Hwys 89 and 395. Along the way the road passes through the workmanlike town of Arnold, which has a few cafés and motels strung along the roadside. But the real reason for taking Hwy 4 is 2 miles east of Arnold and 20 miles east of Murphys: a chance to commune with the largest living things on the planet.

Calaveras Big Trees State Park (☎ 209-795-2334; admission per vehicle $6) is home to giant sequoia redwood trees. Reaching as high as 325ft and with trunk diameters up to 33ft, these leftovers from the Mesozoic era are thought to weigh upwards of 3000 tons, or close to 20 blue whales. That gets the gold for the sequoias in the size department (some naysayers argue that a monster fungus growing underground in the Midwest is larger but, come on, we're talking about a fungus).

The redwood giants are distributed in two large groves, one of which is easily seen from the **North Grove Big Trees Trail**, a 1.5-mile self-guided loop, near the entrance. There is an immediate calm that descends over you as you enter this living cathedral. A 4-mile trail that branches off from the self-guided loop climbs out of the North Grove, crosses a ridge and descends 1500ft to the Stanislaus River.

It's possible to find giant trees throughout the park's 6000 acres, though the largest are in fairly remote locations. The **visitors center** (⏰ 9am-4pm) can offer maps and lots of good advice on the miles of trails. It also has good exhibits about the trees and how a few dedicated individuals fought for decades to save them from becoming so many thousands of picnic tables.

Camping is popular and **reservations** (☎ 800-444-7275; www.parks.ca.gov; sites $15-25) are essential. North Grove Campground is near the park entrance; less crowded is Oak Hollow Campground, 4 miles further on the park's main road. Most atmospheric are the hike-in environmental sites.

Loft.' This black hole is 1.5 miles north from downtown on Sheep Ranch Rd.

Sleeping & Eating

Most accommodations in Murphys are expensive B&Bs. Check nearby Angels Camp or Arnold for cheaper alternatives.

Murphys Historic Hotel & Lodge (☎ 209-728-3444, 800-532-7684; www.murphyshotel.com; 457 Main St; r $69-125) Dating back to either 1855 or 1856 (you have your pick of plaques out front), Murphys anchors Main St. The original building is a little rough (it is 150 years old) and has a locally popular bar and all-day restaurant (meals $8 to $20). Outside there are gardens and a patio. Motel units off to the side have modern features like air-con and TVs.

Victoria Inn (☎ 209-728-8933; www.victoriainn-murphys.com; 402 Main St; r $115-310) This B&B is actually newly built but has an eccentric design to offer some of the charm implied by the name. Rooms vary widely; only some have air-con while others have whirlpools. There's a long veranda where you can enjoy good tapas food and wines from the long list at the bar (dishes $6 to $12; open noon to 10pm Wednesday to Sunday).

Murphys Inn Motel (☎ 209-728-1818, 888-796-1800; www.centralsierralodging.com; 76 Main St; r $75-105;

✖ ▢ ▣) Just off Hwy 4, half a mile from the center of town, this option has very clean and modern motel rooms with a small pool.

Grounds (☎ 209-728-8663; 402 Main St; meals $8-24; ⏰ breakfast & lunch, dinner Wed-Sun) Big and bustling, Grounds is popular with locals who appreciate its long and varied menu that runs from omelettes to salads to steaks. You can relive *Blazing Saddles* and order the 'Pinto Bean Cowboy Lunch.'

Alchemy Market & Wine Bar (☎ 209-728-0700; 191 Main St; meals $7-15; ⏰ 11am-7pm Sun-Thu, 7am-8pm Fri & Sat) Arrange a fancy picnic and this upscale food store and deli will make you an excellent sandwich. The adjoining wine bar has a small fusion menu you can enjoy on the patio.

COLUMBIA STATE HISTORIC PARK

Historically called the 'Gem of the Southern Mines,' Columbia is a compelling meeting of commercial and historic interests. Four blocks of the town are preserved as a State Historic Park, where the fudge and candle shops are restrained and at times volunteers perambulate in vintage costumes. This is a popular place most times and especially on July 4.

Among the highlights are a blacksmith's shop, a theater, two old hotels, one authentic bar, a place to pan for gold ($3) and shady places to picnic. On the fringe of these blocks are regular homes and businesses that blend in so well that it's hard to tell what's park and what's not.

Limestone and granite boulders (they look like whale vertebrae or dinosaur bones) are noticeable around town. These were washed out of the surrounding hills by hydraulic mining and scraped clean by prospectors. There's a fascinating explanation of this kind of mining at the renovated **Columbia Museum** (☎ 209-532-4301; cnr Main & State Sts; admission free; ⏱ 10am-4:30pm). For information and snacks, stop in at the friendly **Columbia Mercantile** (☎ 209-532-7511; cnr Main & Jackson Sts; ⏱ 9am-6pm) which also has a wide variety of groceries.

After most shops and attractions close around 5pm, you can have the town to its atmospheric self which makes staying there an attractive option.

Run by students of Columbia College's Culinary Arts Program, **City Hotel** (☎ 209-532-1479; www.cityhotel.com; r $110-130; ⛌) is eager to please. Rooms overlook a deeply shaded stretch of street. The dining room (mains $12-25; ⏱ dinner Wed-Sun) serves excellent burgers, steaks and seasonal items.

Fallon Hotel (☎ 209-532-1470; cnr Washington St & Broadway; r $75-130; ⛌ ⛌) is one of the venues used by the excellent **Sierra Repertory Theatre** (☎ 209-532-3120; www.sierrarep.org). The hotel's 14 rooms have been refurbished and are comfortable.

SONORA
pop 5500 / elevation 1796ft
Settled in 1848 by miners from Sonora, Mexico, this town was, in its heyday, a cosmopolitan center. It had shady parks, elaborate saloons and the Southern Mines' largest concentration of gamblers, drunkards and gold. The Big Bonanza Mine, at the north end of Washington St where Sonora High School now stands, yielded 12 tons of gold in two years (including a 28lb nugget). It's the county seat of Tuolumne County and its obvious foothill charms are attracting many newcomers. A Wal-Mart and chain restaurants like Applebee's on the fringe attest to the growth. Fortunately, the historic center is changing with the times (antique stores abound) and it stays lively even after the sun goes down.

Orientation & Information
Two highways cross the Sierra Nevada east of Sonora and connect with Hwy 395 in the Eastern Sierra: Hwy 108 via Sonora Pass and Hwy 120 via Tioga Pass. Note that the section of Hwy 120 traveling through Yosemite National Park is only open in summer (see the boxed text, p333).

The center of downtown Sonora is the T-shaped intersection of Washington and Stockton Sts, with Washington the main thoroughfare. There are boutiques, shops, cafés, bars and more.

Sierra Nevada Adventure Company (☎ 209-532-5621; 173 S Washington St) For maps, equipment and friendly advice on where to climb, hike and fish.

Tuolumne County Visitors Center (☎ 209-533-4420; www.tcvb.com; 542 Stockton St; ⏱ 9am-6pm Jun-Sep, 9am-6pm Mon-Sat Oct-May) Helpful and has information on recreation, winter road conditions and lodging. It also covers Yosemite National Park and Stanislaus National Forest up in the Sierras on Hwy 108.

Sights & Activities
In the former 1857 Tuolumne County Jail, the **Tuolumne County Museum** (☎ 209-532-1317; 158 W Bradford St; admission free; ⏱ 10am-4pm), two blocks west of Washington St, is an interesting museum with $100,000 worth of gold on display.

Among the historic structures is the wood and adobe **Snugg House** (cnr S Stewart & Theall Sts), which was built in 1857 by a freed slave and is now under renovation. Residential neighborhoods, off the north end of Washington St, are lined with restored Victorian houses, and the spooky old **cemetery** at the west end of Jackson St has many graves from that era. **St James Episcopal Church** (N Washington St), a local landmark north of Elkin St, has been in continuous use since it was built in 1860 and is now simply called the 'Red Church.'

Sonora is also a base for white-water rafting: the Tuolumne River is known for its Class IV rapids and its population of golden eagles and red-tailed hawks, while the Stanislaus River is more accessible and better for novices. **Sierra Mac River Trips** (☎ 209-532-1327; www.sierramac.com; trips from $195) has a good reputation and runs trips of one or more days.

Sleeping & Eating
Bradford Place Inn (☎ 209-532-2400; www.bradford placeinn.com; 56 W Bradford St; r $150-200; ⛌ ⛌ ⛁) Gorgeous gardens and welcoming porches

signify the comfort you'll find inside this four-room B&B. Breakfasts are elaborate and you can't get any closer to town.

Sonora Days Inn (☎ 209-532-2400; www.sonoradays inn.com; 160 S Washington St; r $70-100; 🖳 🖳) This is Sonora's oldest (1896) and most central hotel. It has atmospheric Spanish arches along the street. There is a rooftop pool and a modern motel addition behind the original hotel. Rooms have been refreshed and are comfortable.

Gunn House Hotel (☎ 209-532-3421; www.gunn househotel.com; 286 S Washington St; r $69-106; 🖳 🖳) Also central, this family-run place has a nice veranda, shady trees and little fountains. Rooms are simple but quite nice.

Diamondback Grill (☎ 209-532-6661; 110 S Washington St; meals $6-10) Fittingly pie-shaped, this wonderful little café serves up extraordinary food at superb prices. Sandwiches come with creative ingredients like pesto and the burgers are simply fantastic. Everything is homemade, including the addictive buttermilk parsley salad dressing. Daily specials feature steaks and seafood.

Banny's Café (☎ 209-209-533-4709; 83 S Stewart St; mains $12-18) This charming café has clean lines and a seasonal eclectic Mediterranean menu. The wine list is reasonable and highlights many of the area's best vintages.

Heart Rock (☎ 209-533-1221; 1 S Washington St; meals $5-7; 🕐 breakfast & lunch Mon-Thu, breakfast, lunch & dinner Fri & Sat; 🖳) We won't tell the copyright police about this excellent coffee café with free wireless and a serene back patio. On some weekend nights there's live rock.

The downtown **Saturday farmers market** (🕐 8am-noon May-Oct) is renowned for its rich selection of regional bounty.

Entertainment

The free and widely available weekend supplement of the *Union Democrat* comes out on Friday and lists movies, music, performance art and events for Tuolumne County.

Iron Horse Lounge (☎ 209-532-4482; 97 S Washington St) The most elaborate of the traditional old taverns in the center; bottles glitter like gold on the backlit bar. The Sonora Days Inn bar is a local institution.

Stage 3 Theater (☎ 209-536-1778; www.stage3.org; 208 S Green St; tickets $10-15) This troupe is right out of *Waiting for Guffman* and performs a highly regarded range of off-Broadway and original modern dramas.

Sierra Repertory Theatre (☎ 209-532-3120; www .sierrarep.com; 13891 Hwy 108; tickets $15-22) In East Sonora, close to the Junction Shopping Center, is the same critically acclaimed company that performs in the Fallon Hotel in Columbia.

Getting There & Away

Bus service to Sonora, the major town in the region, ended in 2005. Hwy 108 is the main access road and it links up with I-5, 55 miles west near Stockton. An entrance to Yosemite National Park (p361) is 60 scenic miles south on Hwy 120. Many Yosemite visitors stay in the Sonora area.

JAMESTOWN

pop 600 / elevation 1405ft

Three miles south of Sonora, just south of the Hwy 49/108 junction, Jamestown is affectionately called 'Jimtown' by area residents. Its history developed in waves: the first with Tuolumne County's first gold strike in 1848; the second when the railroad struck in 1897; and, lastly, in the 1920s, when Jamestown became construction headquarters for dams on the Stanislaus and Tuolumne Rivers. Today it is a classic slice of Americana, with charming houses surrounding a downtown of stores as diverse as an old-time grocery and a trendy olive oil boutique.

Sights & Activities

A renumbering scheme for Main St has only partially caught on, thus the mixture of two- and five-digit numbers. It's really only a few blocks long.

Railtown 1897 State Historic Park (☎ 209-984-3953; 5th Ave; admission per person $2; 🕐 9:30am-4:30pm), five blocks south of Main St, has a 26-acre collection of trains and railroad equipment and has been the backdrop for countless films and TV shows including *High Noon*. On weekends and holidays you can ride the narrow-gauge railroad once used to transport ore, lumber and miners to and from the mines. You can really smell the creosote here and this delightful park includes a restored station, engine house and good bookstore.

Gold Prospecting Adventures (☎ 209-984-4653; www.goldprospecting.com; 18170 Main St) has a range of gold-finding outings involving pans, sluices and more that start at $30. It even offers a three-day college-accredited gold-prospecting course ($595).

The **Emporium** (☎ 209-9840262; 18180 Main St) is typical of many Main St stores and has an exceptionally wide selection of vintage bric-a-brac at reasonable prices.

Sleeping & Eating

Jamestown has some historic hotels on Main St. On weekends book in advance.

National Hotel (☎ 209-984-3446; www.national -hotel.com; 77 Main St; r $95-160; ✗ ✗) The seven rooms in this 1859 place feature period pieces such as brass beds. Some of them have access to the shady balcony and you can enjoy dinner (mains $8 to $20) on the lovely veranda.

Jamestown Hotel (☎ 209-984-3902, 800-205-4901; www.jamestownhotel.com; r $85-205; ✗ ✗) There are 11 spacious and restored rooms here. Some have whirlpools and others come off the charming balcony. The hotel's restaurant (mains $12 to $25) celebrates local wines.

Jamestown Coffee Emporium (☎ 209-984-0138; 18202 Main St; meals $6; ✗ breakfast & lunch) Enjoy your sandwich and a smoothie at the shady benches fronting this friendly, simple place.

Willow Steakhouse (☎ 209-984-3998; cnr Main & Willow Sts; mains $13-22) This place is a popular old watering hole with a refined saloon and a dining room that features cheese fondue with all of its hearty meals.

Sierra Nevada

If you've done coastal, cultural, creative and culinary California, it might be time to shake off all those civilizing influences and discover another side of the state altogether. This would be, of course, the nature, adventure, blue skies and sheer wildness of its dominant mountain range, the majestic Sierra Nevada. This is where you come to shed all the stresses nibbling at your psyche and to get back to some elemental discoveries about yourself and where you fit into Nature's grand design.

The Sierra is possibly the most accessible range of its size anywhere in the world and it's certainly among the most beautiful. Classic Western towns harkening back to the Gold Rush days are its handmaidens and the portals through which an endless stream of seekers pursue their dreams: artists, fishers, trekkers, hedonists, deep-powder crowds and those who are only truly alive when belayed 1000ft above the ground on naked granite. Each group approaches with its distinct visions of perfection and the Sierra disappoints none of them.

John Muir called it the 'Range of Light' and the 400-mile-long phalanx of craggy peaks and awesome landscapes still tugs mightily at the hearts of visionaries, wanderers and those hungry for adventure – or peace. Cradling three of the nation's most dazzling national parks (Yosemite, Sequoia and Kings Canyon), the Sierra is quite literally a wonderland of superlatives. It's home to the contiguous USA's highest mountain, North America's tallest waterfall and the world's biggest tree. It's all there for the taking, demanding only that you bring a sense of wonderment and respect.

HIGHLIGHTS

- Trying to grasp the grandeur of **Yosemite National Park** (p359)
- Finding a favorite ski slope among the nearly 200 surrounding **Lake Tahoe** (p335)
- Imagining the grime, greed and bawdiness of the Gold Rush in **Bodie** (p392)
- Lake-hopping in the high country of **Mammoth Lakes** (p396)
- Feeling like an ant under the dense canopy of giant trees in **Sequoia National Park** (p386)
- Experiencing the rush of barreling downhill into **Kings Canyon** (p375)
- Kayaking among the whimsical tufa towers on **Mono Lake** (p394)

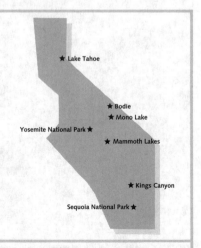

- AVERAGE TEMPS IN SOUTH LAKE TAHOE: JAN 17/37°F, JUL 43/79°F

SIERRA NEVADA

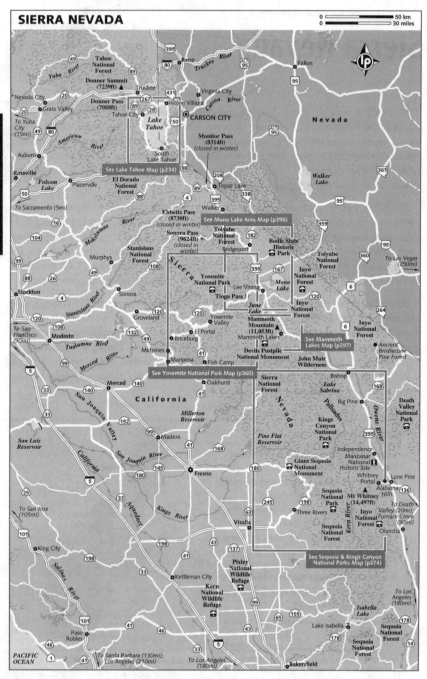

IMPASSABLE TIOGA PASS

Hwy 120, the main route into Yosemite National Park from the Eastern Sierra, climbs through Tioga Pass, the highest pass in the Sierra at 9945ft. On most maps of California, you'll find a parenthetical remark – 'closed in winter' – printed on the map near the pass. While true, this statement is also misleading. Tiga Rd is usually closed from the first heavy snowfall in October to May, June or even July! If you're planning a trip through Tioga Pass in spring, you're likely to be out of luck. According to official park policy, the earliest date the road will be plowed is 15 April, yet the pass has been open in April only once since 1980. Other mountain roads further north, such as Hwys 108, 4 and 88/89, may also be closed for heavy snow, albeit only temporarily. Call ☎ 800-427-7623 for road and weather conditions.

LAKE TAHOE

Shimmering softly in myriad shades of blue and green, Lake Tahoe, which straddles the California–Nevada state line, is one of the most beautiful lakes in the USA and also its second deepest with an average depth of 1000ft. Driving around the lakeshore's 72 miles would give you quite a workout behind the wheel, but also reward you with spellbinding scenery. Generally speaking, the north shore is quiet and upscale, the west shore rugged and old-timey, the east shore undeveloped and the south shore busy and a tad tacky with aging motels and gaudy casinos.

The sun shines on Tahoe three out of four days in the year, making it ideal for outdoor pursuits of all stripes. Swimming, boating, kayaking, windsurfing and other water-based activities are all popular, as are hiking and camping among the horned peaks around the lake. Winter brings bundles of snow, perfect for hitting the slopes at more than a dozen ski resorts.

Unfortunately, the news isn't all good: the lake is gradually losing its famous clarity. Development, erosion, runoff and air pollution reduce visibility by about 1.5ft every year. Steps are underway to stop this decline, but the challenge is enormous and the future remains murky.

Accommodations

Lake Tahoe has beds for all budgets, but it gets packed in summer, around holidays and on winter weekends when prices soar and reservations are essential. If you're traveling as a group or staying a week or longer, renting a condo may work out cheaper than ponying up for individual rooms.

Motels and big casinos cluster in South Lake Tahoe, where rates are generally lowest. The less developed western and northern shores teem with B&Bs, inns and smaller hotels. The nicest campgrounds are on the western shore. In winter, many properties, including the casinos, offer ski packages.

Tahoe reservation agencies include the following:

Lake Tahoe Central Reservations (☎ 530-583-3494, 888-434-1262; www.mytahoevacation.com)
South Lake Tahoe Visitor's Authority (☎ 800-210-3459; www.virtualtahoe.com)
Squaw Valley Central Reservations (☎ 800-403-0206; www.squawvacations.com)

Getting There & Around

The closest airport is Reno/Tahoe International (p358). Greyhound and Amtrak have services to Truckee and Reno, where you can catch local buses to most Lake Tahoe towns. For details, see Tahoe City (p345), Truckee (p347) and South Lake Tahoe (p337).

If you're driving, you might need snow chains any time between late fall and early

TOP FIVE LAKE TAHOE TRIVIA

- Lake Tahoe is 22 miles long and 12 miles wide, making it the largest alpine lake in North America.
- It contains enough water to submerge California to a depth of 14.5in.
- It could supply every person in the USA with 50 gallons of water for five years.
- The water evaporating from its surface annually is equivalent to LA's water consumption for five years.
- At 6225ft, it is one of the highest lakes in the USA.

Source: US Geographical Survey

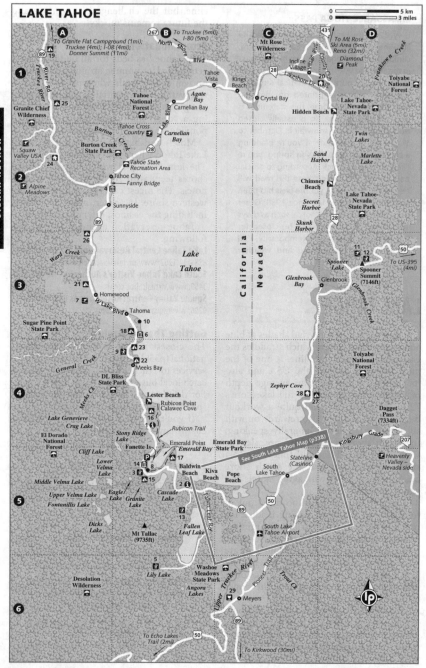

LAKE TAHOE

SIERRA NEVADA

0 — 5 km
0 — 3 miles

A To Granite Flat Campground (1mi); Truckee (4mi); I-08 (4mi); Donner Summit (11mi)

B To Truckee (5mi) I-80 (5mi)
North Shore Blvd

C Mt Rose Wilderness

D To Mt Rose Ski Area (5mi); Reno (32mi) Diamond Peak

Tahoe Vista
Kings Beach
Incline Village
Lakeshore Dr

Agate Bay
Carnelian Bay
Crystal Bay

Tahoe National Forest

Lake Tahoe-Nevada State Park

Hidden Beach

Toiyabe National Forest

Granite Chief Wilderness

Truckee River
River Rd

Tahoe Cross Country
Carnelian Bay

Twin Lakes
Marlette Lake

Squaw Valley USA

Burton Creek
Burton Creek State Park

Sand Harbor

Alpine Meadows

Tahoe State Recreation Area
Tahoe City
Fanny Bridge

Chimney Beach

Lake Tahoe-Nevada State Park

Sunnyside

Secret Harbor

Lake Tahoe

California | Nevada

Skunk Harbor

Ward Creek

Spooner Lake

Homewood

Glenbrook Bay
Glenbrook

Spooner Summit (7146ft)

To US-395 (4mi)

Sugar Pine Point State Park

W Lake Blvd
Tahoma

Glenbrook Creek

General Creek

Meeks Bay

Toiyabe National Forest

DL Bliss State Park

Meeks Ck

Zephyr Cove

Lester Beach
Rubicon Point
Calawee Cove

Dagget Pass (7334ft)

Lake Genevieve
Crag Lake

Rubicon Trail

El Dorado National Forest
Cliff Lake

Stony Ridge Lake
Fannette Is.

Emerald Point
Emerald Bay

Emerald Bay State Park

See South Lake Tahoe Map (p338)

Kingsbury Grade

Heavenly Valley – Nevada side

Lower Velma Lake

Baldwin Beach
Kiva Beach
Pope Beach

Stateline (Casinos)
South Lake Tahoe

Middle Velma Lake

Eagle Lake
Granite Lake
Cascade Lake

Upper Velma Lake
Fontanillis Lake

Fallen Leaf Lake

South Lake Tahoe Airport

Falling Leaf Rd

Dicks Lake

Mt Tallac (9735ft)

Lily Lake

Washoe Meadows State Park

Desolation Wilderness

Angora Lakes
Meyers

Upper Truckee River
Pioneer Trail
Trout Ck

To Echo Lakes Trail (2mi)

To Kirkwood (30mi)

spring if you're heading for Tahoe and the Sierra. For road conditions in California call ☎ 800-427-7623; for Nevada ☎ 877-687-6287.

TAHOE SKI AREAS

Lake Tahoe has awesome skiing, with thousands of acres of the white stuff beckoning at more than a dozen resorts. These complexes range from the giant, jet-set slopes of Squaw Valley and Heavenly to no less enticing insider playgrounds such as Sugar Bowl and Homewood. Tahoe's simply got a hill for everybody, kids to kamikazes. Ski season generally runs November to April, although it can start as early as October with the last storm whipping through in June.

All resorts have ski schools, equipment rental, lodges and other facilities as well as websites with updated snow conditions and weather reports. Many also operate shuttle buses.

Downhill Skiing
TRUCKEE & DONNER SUMMIT

Sugar Bowl (☎ 530-426-9000; www.sugarbowl.com; Soda Springs/Norden exit off I-80; adult/teen $59/44; 😊 9am-4pm) Cofounded by Walt Disney in 1939, this is one of the oldest ski resorts in the Sierra and a miniature Squaw Valley in terms of variety of terrain, including plenty of exhilarating gullies and chutes. Views are stellar on sunny days, but conditions go downhill pretty quickly, so to speak, during stormy weather. Stats: 12 lifts, 1500 vertical feet, 84 runs. Three miles east on Hwy 40.

Northstar-at-Tahoe (☎ 530-562-1010, 800-466-6784; www.northstarattahoe.com; Hwy 267; adult/child/teen $61/21/51; 😊 8:30am-4pm) This hugely popular resort, 6 miles south of I-80, has great intermediate terrain, although the advanced and expert skier can look for challenges on the back of the mountain. Recent additions include the slick Village Plaza and a kids' terrain park. Its relatively sheltered location makes it the second-best choice after Homewood (p336) when it's snowing. Weekends get superbusy. Stats: 17 lifts, 2280 vertical feet, 70 runs.

Boreal (☎ 530-426-3666; www.borealski.com; Boreal /Castle off I-80; adult/child day $36/10, night $22/15; 😊 9am-9pm) Boreal is fun for newbies and intermediate skiers, and is traditionally the first resort to open in the Tahoe area. Boarders have eight terrain parks (the most among Tahoe resorts) and a competition-level superpipe to play with. This is also the only area resort besides Squaw offering night skiing. Stats: nine lifts, 500 vertical feet, 41 runs.

Soda Springs (☎ 530-426-3666; www.sodasprings .com; Soda Springs/Norden exit off I-80; adult/child/teen $25/10/16, tubing $15; 😊 9am-4:30pm) This cute little resort is a winner with kids. They can snow-tube, ride around in pint-sized snowmobiles or try the Kids X Park. Stats: two lifts, 650 vertical feet, 16 runs.

Donner Ski Ranch (☎ 530-426-3635; www.donner skiranch.com; Soda Springs/Norden exit off I-80; adult/child/teen $29/5/25; 😊 9am-4pm) Generations of skiers have enjoyed this itty-bitty mom-and-pop resort. It's a great place to teach your kids how to ski or for beginners to build their skills. Stats: six lifts, 750 vertical feet, 52 runs. It's 3.5 miles east on Donner Pass Rd.

Tahoe Donner (☎ 530-587-9444; www.skitahoedon ner.com; Donner State Park exit off I-80; adult/child $34/13; 😊 9am-4pm) Small, low-key and low-tech,

Tahoe Donner is a darling resort with family-friendly beginner and intermediate runs only. Stats: three lifts, 600 vertical feet, 14 runs.

TAHOE CITY

Squaw Valley USA (☎ 530-583-6985; www.squaw.com; off Hwy 89; adult/child/teen $62/5/31; ⊙ 9am-9pm Mon-Fri, 8:30am-9pm Sat & Sun) Few ski hounds can resist the siren call of this mega-sized, world-class, see-and-be-seen resort – nicknamed Squawlywood – that hosted the 1960 Winter Olympic Games. Hardcore skiers thrill to white-knuckle cornices, chutes and bowls, while beginners can practice their turns in a separate area on the upper mountain. On weekends, the place is a zoo. Stats: 33 lifts, 2850 vertical feet, over 100 runs. Squaw Valley is 5 miles northwest of Tahoe City.

Alpine Meadows (☎ 530-583-4232, 800-441-4423; www.skialpine.com; off Hwy 89; adult/child/teen $39/15/39; ⊙ 9am-4pm) Alpine is a no-nonsense resort without the fancy village, attitude or crowds. It gets more snow than neighboring Squaw and its open-boundary policy makes it the most backcountry-friendly around. Boarders can jib down the mountain in a terrain park designed by Eric Rosenwald. Also look for the adorable – and supersmart – ski patrol dogs. Stats: 13 lifts, 1802 vertical feet, 100 runs. It's 6 miles northwest of Tahoe City.

Homewood (☎ 530-525-2992; www.skihomewood .com; Hwy 89; adult/child/teen Fri-Sun $44/free/30, Mon-Thu $25/free/25; ⊙ 9am-4pm) This gem, 5 miles south of Tahoe City, proves that bigger isn't always better. Locals and in-the-know visitors cherish the awesome lake views, laid-back ambience, smaller crowds, tree-lined slopes and open bowls (including the excellent but expert 'Quail Face'). Families love the wide, gentle slopes and free kids' tickets. This is also the best place to ski during stormy weather. Stats: 8 lifts, 1650 vertical feet, 60 runs.

SOUTH LAKE TAHOE

Heavenly (☎ 775-586-7000, 800-4328-3659; www.ski heavenly.com; Cnr Wildwood & Saddle, South Lake Tahoe; adult/child $65/29; ⊙ 9am-4pm Mon-Fri, 8:30am-4pm Sat & Sun) The 'mother' of all Tahoe mountains boasts the most acreage, the longest run and the biggest vertical drop in the western USA. Follow the sun by skiing on the Nevada side in the morning, moving to the California side in the afternoon. Views of the lake and the high desert are heavenly indeed. Stats: 29 lifts, 3500 vertical feet, 91 runs.

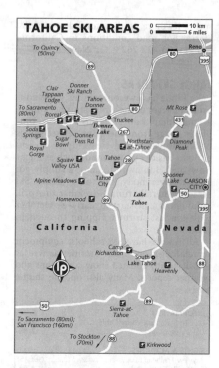

Kirkwood (☎ 209-258-6000, 877-547-5966; www.kirk wood.com; Hwy 88; adult/child/teen $59/13/47; ⊙ 9am-4pm) Off-the-beaten-path Kirkwood, set in a high-elevation valley, gets great snow and holds it longer than any other Tahoe resort. It has stellar tree-skiing, gullies and chutes. Novice out-of-bounds skiers should check out the backcountry safety-skills clinics. Stats: 12 lifts, 2000 vertical feet, 68 runs. It's 35 miles southwest of South Lake Tahoe via Hwy 89.

Sierra-at-Tahoe (☎ 530-659-7453; www.sierraattahoe .com; Hwy 50; adult/child/teen $57/14/47; ⊙ 9am-4pm Mon-Fri, 8:30am-4pm Sat & Sun) Sierra, 12 miles west of South Lake Tahoe, is snowboarding central with five raging terrain parks and a 17ft superpipe. A great beginners' run meanders gently for 2.5 miles from the summit, but there are also gnarly steeps and chutes for speed demons. Stats: 12 lifts, 2212 vertical feet, 46 runs.

NEVADA

Diamond Peak (☎ 775-832-1177; www.diamondpeak .com; 1210 Ski Way, Incline Village; adult/child/teen $44/16/35; ⊙ 9am-4pm) This midsize mountain is

SIERRA NEVADA

a good place to learn, but experts might get bored quickly. Boarders can romp around the new and improved Snowbomb Super-Park. From the top you'll have a 360-degree panorama of desert, peaks and lake. Stats: six lifts, 1840 vertical feet, 30 runs.

Mt Rose (☎ 775-849-0704; www.skirose.com; 22222 Mt Rose Hwy/Hwy 431; adult/child/teen $52/12/38; ☻ 9am-4pm) Mt Rose has Tahoe's highest base elevation (8260ft) and offers good snow conditions well into spring. The newly opened expert terrain (the Chutes) delivers some screamers along its 15 north-facing steeps. Crowds aren't too bad, but the mountain's exposure means it gets hammered in a storm. Stats: six lifts, 1440 vertical feet, 43 runs.

Cross-Country Skiing

Royal Gorge (☎ 530-426-3871; www.royalgorge.com; Soda Springs/Norden exit off I-80; adult/child weekend $28/15, midweek $24/14; ☻ 9am-5pm Mon-Fri, 8:30am-5pm Sat & Sun) Cross-country aficionados won't want to pass up a spin around North America's largest resort with its mind-boggling 330km of groomed track crisscrossing some 9000 acres of terrain on 90 trails. It has great skating lanes and diagonal stride tracks and also welcomes telemark skiers and snowshoeing fans. Consider overnighting at one of its two cozy lodges.

Spooner Lake (☎ 775-749-5349; www.spoonerlake.com; adult/child/teen $16.50/free/9; ☻ 9am-5pm) This area, near junction of Hwys 28 & 50, offers some of the prettiest trails – some around the lake, some through aspen and pine forest and some through high country with fabulous views. Altogether there are 80km for all levels of expertise and fitness.

Camp Richardson Resort (☎ 530-542-6584; www.camprichardson.com; 1900 Jameson Beach Rd; adult/child $18/11) At this woodsy resort with 35km of groomed track you can ski lakeside or head for the solitude of the Desolation Wilderness (p342). Locals turn out in droves for the Full Moon Ski & Snowshoe Parties, which kick off at the Beacon Bar & Grill (p341).

Tahoe Donner (☎ 530-587-9484; www.tdxc.com; 11509 Northwoods Blvd; adult/child $19/14; ☻ 8:30am-5pm, night skiing 5-7pm usually Wed) Occupying 4800 acres of forest north of Truckee, this is lovely and varied terrain with 113km of groomed tracks covering three track systems and 48 trails. The most beautiful area is the secluded Euer Valley, where a warm-

ing hut serves foods on weekends. A 2.5km loop stays open for night skiing.

Clair Tappaan Lodge (☎ 530-426-3632; 19940 Donner Pass Rd; lodge guest/visitor free/$7; ☻ 9am-5pm) You can ski right out the door if you're staying at this rustic mountain lodge (p348) on Donner Summit, near Truckee. Its 12km of groomed and tracked trails are great for beginners and intermediate skiers and connect to miles of backcountry skiing.

Tahoe Cross Country (☎ 530-583-5475; www.tahoexc.org; adult/child $20/15; 925 Country Club Dr; ☻ 8:30am-5pm) Run by the nonprofit Tahoe Cross Country Ski Education Association, this center, 3 miles north of Tahoe City, has 65km of groomed tracks (17 trails) winding through lovely forest. Dogs are allowed on two trails. Ask about the free skate clinics.

Northstar-at-Tahoe (☎ 530-562-1010; www.northstarattahoe.com; adult/child $27/15; Hwy 267; ☻ 8:30am-5pm) This resort, 6 miles south of I-80, has a highly regarded Nordic and telemark school, making it a great choice for novices. A package including the trail fee, ski rental and a group lesson is $65. Afterwards you can explore the 50km of groomed trails.

SOUTH LAKE TAHOE & STATELINE
pop 34,000 / elevation 6254ft

With dozens of motels, eateries and mini-malls lining busy Hwy 50, South Lake Tahoe projects an urban vibe that contrasts sharply with the natural charisma of other lake towns. It has the liveliest nightlife on the lake, as well as gambling in Stateline, just across the Nevada border, and world-class skiing at Heavenly.

Orientation

The main east–west thoroughfare is a 5-mile stretch of Hwy 50 called Lake Tahoe Blvd. Most hotels and businesses cluster around the California–Nevada state line and Heavenly Village. Casinos are located in Stateline, which is officially a separate city. West of town, Hwy 50 runs into Hwy 89 at the 'Y' junction. Heavy snowfall sometimes closes Hwy 89 north of the Tallac Historic Site. The section of Hwy 89 between South Lake Tahoe and Emerald Bay is also known as Emerald Bay Rd.

Traffic along Hwy 50 gets jammed around noon and 5pm Monday to Friday but winter Sunday afternoons (when skiers head back down the mountain) are the worst.

SOUTH LAKE TAHOE

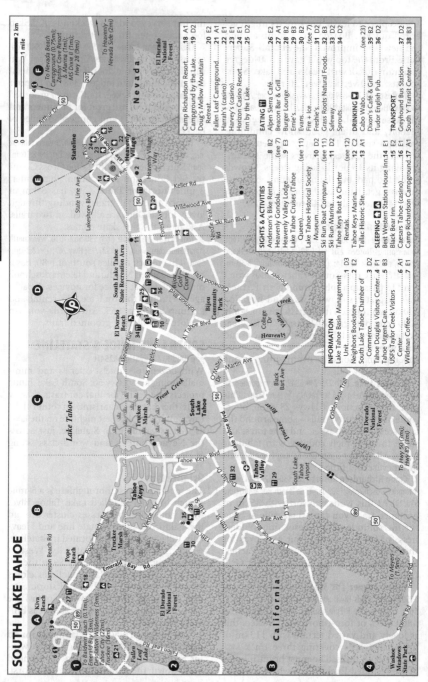

0   1 mile
0   2 km

INFORMATION	
Lake Tahoe Basin Management	
Unit...	1 D3
Neighbors Bookstore........................	2 E2
South Lake Tahoe Chamber of	
Commerce...................................	3 D2
Tahoe Douglas Visitors Center........	4 F1
Tahoe Urgent Care..........................	5 B3
USFS Taylor Creek Visitors	
Center..	6 A1
Wildman Coffee...............................	7 E1

SIGHTS & ACTIVITIES	
Anderson's Bike Rental.....................	8 B2
Heavenly Gondola........................	(see 7)
Heavenly Valley Lodge.....................	9 E3
Lake Tahoe Cruises (Tahoe	
Queen)......................................	(see 11)
Lake Tahoe Historical Society	
Museum....................................	10 D2
Ski Run Boat Company..................	(see 11)
Ski Run Marina...............................	11 D2
Tahoe Keys Boat & Charter	
Rentals......................................	(see 12)
Tahoe Keys Marina........................	12 C2
Tallac Historic Site.........................	13 A1

SLEEPING	
Best Western Station House Inn...	14 E1
Black Bear Inn..............................	15 E2
Caesars Tahoe (casino)..................	16 E1
Camp Richardson Campground.....	17 E1

Camp Richardson Resort...............	18 A1
Campground by the Lake.............	19 D2
Doug's Mellow Mountain	
Retreat.......................................	20 E2
Fallen Leaf Campground................	21 A1
Harrah's (casino)............................	22 E1
Harvey's (casino)...........................	23 E1
Horizon Casino Resort....................	24 E1
Inn by the Lake..............................	25 D2

EATING	
Alpen Sierra Café............................	26 E2
Beacon Bar & Grill..........................	27 A1
Burger Lounge................................	28 B2
Ernie's..	29 B3
Evans..	30 B2
Fire + Ice.....................................	(see 7)
Freshie's..	31 D2
Grass Roots Natural Foods.............	32 B3
Safeway..	33 D2
Sprouts...	34 D2

DRINKING	
Cabo Wabo...................................	(see 23)
Dixon's Café & Grill.......................	35 B2
Tudor English Pub.........................	36 D2

TRANSPORT	
Greyhound Bus Station..................	37 D2
South Y Transit Center..................	38 B3

SIERRA NEVADA

An alternate route through town is Pioneer Trail, which branches east off the Hwy 89/50 junction (south of the 'Y') and reconnects with Hwy 50 at Stateline.

Information

BOOKSTORES

Neighbors Bookstore (☎ 530-541-6296; 4000 Lake Tahoe Blvd; ⊙ 9am-9pm)

INTERNET ACCESS

Wildman Coffee (☎ 530-543-1200; 1001 Heavenly Village; per min 25¢) Internet kiosk and free wi-fi.

MEDICAL SERVICES

Tahoe Urgent Care (☎ 530-541-3277; 2130 Lake Tahoe Blvd; ⊙ 24hr)

TOURIST INFORMATION

Lake Tahoe Basin Management Unit (☎ 530-543-2600; 35 College Dr; ⊙ 8am-4:30pm Mon-Fri) Wilderness permits.

South Lake Tahoe Chamber of Commerce (☎ 530-541-5255; www.tahoeinfo.com; 3066 Lake Tahoe Blvd; ⊙ 9am-5pm Mon-Sat)

Tahoe Douglas Visitors Center (☎ 775-588-4591; www.tahoechamber.org; 195 Hwy 50, Stateline; ⊙ 9am-5pm or 6pm) At the Round Hill Square shopping center in Nevada, about 2 miles north of Stateline.

USFS Taylor Creek Visitors Center (☎ 530-543-2674; Hwy 89, 3 miles north of 'Y'; ⊙ 8am-5:30pm mid-Jun–Sep) Outdoor information and wilderness permits.

Sights

HEAVENLY GONDOLA

Feel on top of the world after a ride aboard this **gondola** (☎ 775-586-7000; www.skiheavenly.com; Heavenly Village; adult/child/teen/senior $22/14/20/20), which sweeps you from Heavenly Village some 2.4 miles up the mountain in 12 minutes for panoramic views of the entire Tahoe Basin, the Desolation Wilderness and Carson Valley.

TALLAC HISTORIC SITE

Three miles north of 'Y', tucked within a pine grove bordering a wide, sandy beach, the **Tallac Historic Site** (☎ 530-541-5227; Hwy 89) sits on the grounds of the former Tallac Resort, a superswish vacation retreat for California high society around the turn of the 20th century.

The **Tallac Museum** (donation requested; ⊙ 10am-4pm Jun-Sep), inside the Baldwin Estate, has exhibits on the history of the resort and its founder, Elias 'Lucky' Baldwin. There's also the 1894 **Pope Estate**, now used for art exhibits and open for guided tours ($5). The boathouse of the grand **Valhalla Estate** now functions as a theater and concert venue. Other buildings contain a cultural arts store and an art gallery.

The forested grounds serve as a community arts hub and, in summer, host concerts and other events, most notably the **Valhalla Festival of Arts & Music** (☎ 530-541-4975; www.valhalla-tallac.com; ⊙ Jun-Sep).

CASINOS

Las Vegas it ain't, but there's still plenty of blackjack and slot machines here to help you part with your hard-earned cash. The main casinos are **Caesars Tahoe**, **Harrah's**, **Horizon** and **Harvey's**, each with live entertainment, multiple restaurants and bars. See p341 for details.

LAKE TAHOE HISTORICAL SOCIETY MUSEUM

This well-meaning **museum** (☎ 530-541-5458; 3058 Lake Tahoe Blvd; adult/discount $2/1; ⊙ 10am-5pm Tue-Sat Jun-Aug) offers a glimpse into Tahoe's pioneer past. The modest exhibits include some fine early photographs, Washoe Indian baskets and a 150-year-old pipe organ.

Activities

For an overview of ski resorts in and around South Lake Tahoe, see p335.

HIKING

Three major trailheads provide easy access to the Desolation Wilderness (p342): Echo Lakes south of town, Glen Alpine near Lily Lake south of Fallen Leaf Lake and Tallac near the northwestern end of Fallen Leaf Lake. The latter two lead to the peak of Mt Tallac (9735ft), a strenuous 10- to 12-mile day hike. Wilderness permits are required.

SWIMMING

El Dorado Beach is a free public beach in town, just off Lake Tahoe Blvd. The nicest beaches, though, are Pope, Kiva and Baldwin along Emerald Bay Rd (Hwy 89), west and east of the Tallac Historic Site, each with picnic tables and barbecues. Fallen Leaf Lake, where scenes from *The Bodyguard* with Kevin Costner were filmed, is also good for swimming.

BOATING

Ski Run Boat Company (☎ 530-544-0200; 900 Ski Run Blvd) at the Ski Run Marina and **Tahoe Keys Boat & Charter Rentals** (☎ 530-544-8888; 2435 Venice Dr) at the Tahoe Keys Marina both rent powerboats, pontoons and sailboats (from $75 per hour) as well as kayaks, canoes and paddleboats (from $15 per hour). Boat rentals are also available at Camp Richardson and Zephyr Cove Resort & Marina.

CYCLING & MOUNTAIN-BIKING

For an easy spin, take the **South Lake Tahoe Bike Path**. It heads west from El Dorado Beach (p339), eventually connecting with the **Pope-Baldwin Bike Path** to Camp Richardson and the Tallac Historic Site.

For expert mountain-bikers, the classic **Mr Toads Wild Ride**, with its steep downhill sections and banked turns, should prove sufficiently challenging. Intermediate riders should steer towards the mostly single-track **Powerline Trail**, which traverses ravines and creeks. Anyone with good lungs might try the **Angora Lakes Trail**, which is steep but technically easy and rewards you with sweeping views of Mt Tallac and Fallen Leaf Lake.

Anderson's Bike Rental (☎ 530-541-0500; 645 Emerald Bay Rd/Hwy 89), about 1.5 miles north of the 'Y,' rents bikes and inline skates.

The USFS Taylor Creek Visitor Center has a list of Lake Tahoe trails and good maps.

Tours

Two paddle wheelers operated by **Lake Tahoe Cruises** (☎ 530-541-3364, 800-238-2463; www.laketahoe cruises.com) ply the 'big blue' year-round with a variety of food and sightseeing cruises, including a narrated two-hour trip to Emerald Bay (p343; adult/child/senior $29/9/26). The *Tahoe Queen* leaves from the Ski Run Marina, right in South Lake Tahoe, while the MS *Dixie II* is based at the Zephyr Cove Resort & Marina.

A popular winter option is the ski shuttle to Squaw Valley ($99), which includes a coach trip to the slopes, an all-day lift ticket and a leisurely après-ski party cruise, with live music, back to South Lake Tahoe.

Sleeping

HOSTELS

Doug's Mellow Mountain Retreat (☎ 530-544-8065; hostelguy@hotmail.com; 3787 Forest Ave; dm $15) This funky 15-bed private hostel is a fun place to

chill and meet fellow travelers, even though it could be cleaner. Guests can whip up simple meals in the kitchen.

HOTELS, MOTELS & RESORTS

South Lake Tahoe has lodging options for all wallet sizes. Places line Lake Tahoe Blvd (Hwy 50) between Stateline and Ski Run Blvd. Further west, closer to the 'Y,' are various budget motels ranging from barely adequate to grotty. Prices listed below are for peak season. Some properties may impose minimum rental periods.

Black Bear Inn (☎ 530-544-4451, 877-232-7466; www.tahoeblackbear.com; 1202 Ski Run Blvd; r incl breakfast $215-255, cabins $275-450; ✕ ✕) This is a mannered, moneyed and masculine B&B, warmly furnished with stylish Western antiques and immaculately kept and run. Sleep in the lodge or a cabin with kitchenette.

Best Western Station House Inn (☎ 775-586-7050, 800-822-5953; www.stationhouseinn.com; 901 Park Ave; r incl breakfast $100-158; ✕ ▢ ▣) This central property looks dated but the mostly decent-sized rooms have just been given a makeover. The cooked breakfast is delicious. The poolside lunch barbecues in summer are fun too.

Inn by the Lake (☎ 530-542-0330, 800-877-1466; www.innbythelake.com; 3300 Lake Tahoe Blvd; r incl breakfast $130-230; ▣) The rooms won't elicit gushing reviews, but are well kept, comfortable and have all main amenities. Those in back are cheaper and quieter, but you'll miss the lake views. Repeat visitors praise the caring staff, modern gym, bilevel outdoor hot tub and free bicycle and snowshoe rentals.

Camp Richardson Resort (☎ 530-541-1801, 800-544-1801; www.camprichardson.com; 1900 Jameson Beach Rd; tent sites from $23, r $95-165, cabins $95-200; ✕) This sprawling resort is a world removed from the downtown strip mall aesthetic. It's a busy place with lodging options – from camping to beachside hotel rooms – to match most comfort needs, plus a full-service marina and popular restaurant, the Beacon Bar & Grill. A paved bike trail runs by the resort (rentals available) and in winter you can cross-country ski right out the door.

Zephyr Cove Resort & Marina (☎ 775-588-4906, 800-238-2463; www.zephyrcove.com; 760 Hwy 50; tent sites $27-33, cabins $140-470; ✕) On the Nevada side, about 4 miles north of Stateline, this is another family-oriented lakeside resort with historic cabins scattered among the pines and similar facilities as Camp Richardson. The MS *Dixie II* cruise departs from here.

CASINOS

Prices at these multilevel 'coin collectors' fluctuate heavily by season, day of the week and type of room. In winter ask about special ski and stay packages.

Harrah's (☎ 775-588-6611, 800-427-7247; www .harrahs.com/our_casinos/tah; 15 Hwy 50; r $70-200; 🔀 ▯ 🕭) Clad in an oddly tasteful forest-green facade, this is a glitzy contender. Even the standard rooms are spacious and have two (!) bathrooms, each featuring small TVs and telephone. If you snag a window table, the top-floor buffet restaurant provides some memorable views.

Harvey's (☎ 775-586-6719, 800-745-4320; www .harrahs.com/our_casinos/hlt; 18 Hwy 50; r $70-200; 🔀 ▯ 🕭) Harvey's was South Lake Tahoe's first casino and, with 740 rooms, it's also the biggest. Rooms in the Mountain Tower are pretty small, so get one in the Lake Tower for extra space and fancy marble bathrooms.

Caesars Tahoe (☎ 775-588-3515, 800-648-3353; www.caesars.com/Caesars/Tahoe; r $120-180; 🔀 🕭) The decor may be on the kitschy side, but the extra-large Roman tubs are definitely a fun factor, as is the lavish indoor pool accented by a rockscape and waterfalls. Catch top-flight entertainers in the Circus Maximus or book a cruise on the casino's own yacht.

Horizon Casino Resort (☎ 775-588-6211, 800-648-3322; www.horizoncasino.com; 50 Hwy 50; r midweek $60-200, weekend $160-250; 🔀 ▯ 🕭) Diehard Elvis fans can stay in the special suite where the star once boozed and snoozed at this otherwise fairly generic property. Distinctive touches include Tahoe's largest outdoor pool, a huge game arcade and a multiplex movie theater.

CAMPING

Fallen Leaf Campground (☎ 877-444-6777; www .reserveusa.com; Fallen Leaf Lake; sites $20; 🕓 mid-May–mid-Oct) One of the biggest and most popular campgrounds with 200 sites near the name-sake lake's north shore.

Nevada Beach (☎ 877-444-6777; www.reserveusa .com; off Hwy 50; sites $22-24; 🕓 mid-May–mid-Oct) Pleasant beachfront campground that packs 54 sites into a stand of Jeffrey pine.

Campground by the Lake (☎ 530-542-6096; www .recreationintahoe.com/campground.htm; 1150 Rufus Allen Blvd; sites with/without hookups $30.50/22.50; 🕓 Apr-Oct) Woodsy in-town campground where highway noise is the main detriment.

There's also camping available at Camp Richardson and the Zephyr Cove Resort & Marina.

Eating

Freshie's (☎ 530-542-3630; 3330 Lake Tahoe Blvd; mains $8-20) From vegans to steak-lovers, nobody should have a problem finding a favorite on the extensive menu of this local mainstay with its exotic Hawaiian looks. Most of the produce is local and organic, and the fish tacos are the best in town.

Evans (☎ 530-542-1990; 536 Emerald Bay Rd; mains $19-29; 🕓 dinner) This intimate and elegant dining room inside a little Tahoe cabin has been a highlight on the local foodie map for quite some time. It scores big for its exquisitely prepared and flavor-intensive Cal-French cuisine, subtle but attentive service and expertly put-together wine list. Reservations advised.

Beacon Bar & Grill (☎ 530-541-0630; Camp Richardson Resort, 1900 Jameson Beach Rd; mains lunch $9-13, dinner $16-28) This charismatic player possesses just the right mix of assets to ensure it'll never go out of style: Lake Tahoe as a front yard, tasty meals and a big wooden deck where bands rock in summer. Its Rum Runner signature drink is only $3 during happy hour (4pm to 7pm).

Sprouts (☎ 530-541-6969; 3123 Harrison Ave; mains under $10; 🕓 8am-9pm) The lively chatter of friendly folks greets you at this energetic natural-foods café that gets extra kudos for its smoothies. The eclectic menu will have you noshing happily on healthy, satisfying soups, rice bowls and sandwiches.

Ernie's (☎ 530-541-2161; 1207 Emerald Bay Rd; mains under $10; 🕓 6am-2pm) This Tahoe breakfast legend just moved into a sparkling new log cabin south of the 'Y' but still makes the same, no-nonsense, all-American breakfasts. Portions are big, prices are not.

Also recommended:

Alpen Sierra Café (☎ 530-544-7740; 3940 Lake Tahoe Blvd; sandwiches $7; 🕓 6am-7pm) Hand-selected gourmet coffees and teas, made-to-order gourmet sandwiches and free wi-fi.

Burger Lounge (☎ 530-542-4060; 717 Emerald Bay Rd; burgers $4-6; 🕓 11am-8pm) Soul-and-belly-sustaining half-pounders best paired with a bucket of fries gussied up with pesto, garlic or Cajun spices.

DARTING AROUND DESOLATION WILDERNESS

This compact **wilderness area** (www.fs.fed.us/r5/eldorado/wild/deso), sculpted by powerful glaciers eons ago, spreads south and west of Lake Tahoe and is the most popular in the Sierra Nevada. It's a 100-sq-mile wonderland of polished granite peaks, deep blue alpine lakes, glacier-carved valleys and pine forests that thin quickly at the higher elevations. In late spring and summer, wildflowers nudge out from between the rocks.

All this splendor makes for some exquisite backcountry exploration. Six major trailheads provide access from the Lake Tahoe side: Glen Alpine, Tallac, Echo Lakes, Bayview, Eagle Falls and Meeks Bay. Tallac and Eagle Falls get the most traffic, but solitude comes quickly once you've scampered past the day hikers. Suggestions for hiking routes are sprinkled through this chapter.

Wilderness permits are required year-round for both day and overnight explorations. Day hikers can self-register at the trailheads, but overnight permits must be picked up at the USFS Taylor Creek Visitor Center or the Lake Tahoe Basin Management Unit, both in South Lake Tahoe (p339). Permits cost $5 per person for one night and $10 per person for two or more nights.

Quotas are in effect from late May to late September. Half of the permits may be reserved for $5 by calling ☎ 530-647-5415 after the third Thursday in April; the other half are available on a first-arrival basis on the day of entry.

Bearproof canisters are compulsory. Also bring bug repellent as the mosquitoes can be merciless. Wood fires are a no-no, but portable stoves are OK.

Fire + Ice (☎ 530-542-6650; 4100 Lake Tahoe Blvd; lunch/dinner $13/19) Hip, healthful and a delicious twist on the all-you-can-eat Mongolian barbecue with views of the Heavenly gondola.

Self-caterers can stock up at **Grass Roots Natural Foods** (☎ 530-541-7788; 2040 Dunlap Dr) or at **Safeway** (☎ 530-542-7740; 1020 Johnson Blvd).

Drinking

Tudor English Pub (☎ 530-541-6603; 1041 Fremont Ave) With Boddingtons on tap, fish 'n chips on the menu and a dart board on the wall, this dark and bustling pub wouldn't look out of place in Lancashire.

Divided Sky (☎ 530-577-0775; 3200 Hwy 50) Hang with locals at this mellow bar in the hamlet of Meyers, about 4 miles south of the 'Y.' The action heats up when live bands take to the little stage.

Dixon's Café & Grill (☎ 530-542-3389; 675 Emerald Bay Rd) The freshly made food ain't bad but it's the 15 microbrews on tap that lure everyone, from ski bunnies to couch potatoes, to this convivial hangout. Happy hour is 4pm to 6pm daily.

Cabo Wabo (☎ 775-588-2411; Harvey's Casino, Stateline) Ex–Van Halen Sammy Hagar's 'church of hard rock' is a wacky, high-energy party pit where the tequila flows as freely as does the testosterone, and a shag-happy crowd sweats it out to the live music action until dawn.

Getting There & Around

South Lake Tahoe's main transportation hub is the South Y Transit Center, just south of the 'Y.' Amtrak Thruway buses to Sacramento stop here several times daily ($21, 2½ hours) but can only be boarded in conjunction with a train ticket.

Tahoe Casino Express (☎ 800-446-6128; one way/round trip $20/26) runs hourly buses (1½ hours) to the Reno/Tahoe International Airport from the Horizon Casino in Stateline from 7am to 9pm.

BlueGO (☎ 530-541-7149; www.bluego.org) local buses operate year-round from 6am to 1am daily, stopping all along Hwy 50 between the South Y Transit Center and Stateline. Rides cost $1.75.

BlueGO also operates casino shuttles ($1) and 24-hour on-demand shuttle services to anywhere within South Lake Tahoe (per person $3). Order rides by phone or from touch-screen kiosks located throughout town.

From mid-June to early September, Blue-GO's Nifty Fifty Trolley barrels along two loop routes between 11:30am and 8:30pm: from Ski Run Marina to Zephyr Cove and from the 'Y' to Camp Richardson, with onward connections to Emerald Bay. A day pass costs $3.

In winter, BlueGO provides free and frequent shuttle service to all Heavenly base operations every 20 to 30 minutes from stops along Hwy 50.

WESTERN SHORE

Lake Tahoe's densely forested western shore, between Emerald Bay and Tahoe City, is blissfully free of major development. Hwy 89 sinuously wends past gorgeous state parks with swimming beaches, easy trails, pine-shaded campgrounds and fanciful historic mansions. Several trailheads access the rugged splendor of the Desolation Wilderness. Note that campgrounds and many businesses here close between November and May.

Emerald Bay State Park

Sheer granite cliffs and a jagged shoreline hem in glacier-carved Emerald Bay, a spot of supreme natural beauty that will have you burning up the pixels in your digicam. Its most captivating aspect is the water, which changes from cloverleaf green to light jade depending on the angle of the sun. There are plenty of pullouts along Hwy 89, including one at **Inspiration Point**.

For a different perspective, explore the 3-mile-long bay by boat, which is also the only way to get to **Fanette Island**, Lake Tahoe's lone isle. It is open for exploring and swimming from 6am to 9pm daily, except from February to June 15 to protect nesting Canadian geese. The nearest boat rentals are in Meeks Bay (p344) and South Lake Tahoe (p340). From the latter you can also catch a narrated bay cruise (p340).

The focal point of the **state park** (☎ 530-541-3030; www.parks.ca.gov/?page_id=506; day-use fee $6; ☺ late May–Sep), embracing the fjordlike bay is **Vikingsholm Castle** (tours adult/child $5/3; ☺ 10am-4pm late May–Sep), a pet project of millionaire heiress Lora Knight and a rare example of ancient Scandinavian-style architecture in these parts. Completed in 1929, it has trippy design elements aplenty, including sod-covered roofs that sprout wildflowers in late spring. The mansion is reached by a steep 1-mile trail, which also leads to a visitors center.

Knight also built a teahouse on Fanette Island, but vandals have sadly reduced it to little more than a stone shell.

HIKING

Two trailheads lead from Emerald Bay into the Desolation Wilderness (see the boxed text, opposite). Starting at the Eagle Falls parking lot ($3), the **Eagle Falls Trail** travels one steep mile to Eagle Lake, crossing by Eagle Falls along the way. This scenic short hike often gets choked with visitors, but crowds thin out immediately beyond the lake as the trail continues to the Tahoe Rim Trail and Velma, Dicks and Fontanillis Lakes.

From the Bayview Trailhead at the back of the Bayview Campground, it's a steep 1-mile climb to glacial **Granite Lake** at the foot of Maggies Peaks. The less ambitious might want to opt for the easy to moderate 1.5-mile round-trip to **Cascade Falls**.

Vikingsholm Castle serves as the southern terminus of the famous Rubicon Trail (see below).

CAMPING

Eagle Point Campground (☎ 530-525-7277, 800-444-7275; www.reserveamerica.com; sites $20-25; ☺ mid-Jun–early Sep) Perched on the tip of Eagle Point, this campground has flush toilets, hot pay showers, beach access and views of the bay.

Bayview Campground (sites $11; ☺ Jun-Sep) This rustic campground has 12 first-arrival sites and vault toilets, but its potable water supplies are often exhausted in July. It's off Hwy 89 across from Inspiration Point.

DL Bliss State Park

Emerald Bay State Park spills over into **DL Bliss State Park** (☎ 530-525-7277; www.parks.ca.gov/?page_id=505; day-use fee $6; ☺ late May-Sep), which has the western shore's nicest beaches at Lester Cove and Calawee Cove. A short nature trail leads to the **Balancing Rock**, a giant chunk of granite perched on a rocky pedestal. Pick up information from the **visitors center** (☺ 8am-5pm) by the park entrance.

Near Calawee Cove is the trailhead of the scenic **Rubicon Trail**, which ribbons along the lakeshore for 4.5 mostly gentle miles to Vikingsholm Castle in Emerald Bay State Park. It leads past an old lighthouse and small coves for taking a cooling dip, treating you to great views along the way.

If you don't want to backtrack, you'll need to arrange for a vehicle to be parked at Emerald Bay as there is no public transportation between the two parks. Also note that it's another steep 1 mile up from the castle to the parking lot on Hwy 89.

The small parking lot at Calawee Cove usually fills up by 10am, in which case it's a 2-mile walk from the park entrance to the beach. Or ask at the ranger station by the entrance for closer access points to the Rubicon Trail.

The park's **campground** (☎ 800-444-7275; www.reserveamerica.com; sites $20-35; ⏰ Jun–mid-Sep) has 168 sites, including some supercoveted spots near the beach, along with flush toilets and hot pay showers.

Meeks Bay

This sleek, shallow bay with a wide sweep of shoreline has warm water by Tahoe standards and is fringed by a beautiful, but busy, sandy beach. There's a trailhead on the west side of the highway, a few hundred feet north of the fire station. From here a moderate, nicely shaded path parallels Meeks Creek on its way to swimmable Lake Genevieve (4.5 miles) and other Desolation Wilderness ponds.

Meeks Bay Campground (☎ 877-444-6777; www.reserveusa.com; sites $17; ⏰ mid-May–Oct) has 38 sites along the beach and flush toilets. For showers head to the adjacent Washoe-operated **Meeks Bay Resort** (☎ 530-525-6946, 877-326-3357; www.meeksbayresort.com; 7941 Emerald Bay Rd; tents/RV sites $25/30, 2-/6-person cabins $200/400; ⏰ May-Nov; ✗), which offers various lodging options plus kayak and boat rentals.

Sugar Pine Point State Park

This **state park** (☎ 530-525-7982; www.parks.ca.gov/?page_id=510; day-use fee $6) occupies a promontory blanketed by a fragrant mix of pine, juniper, aspen and fir. It has a swimming beach, hiking trails, abundant fishing in General Creek and, in winter, 20km of groomed cross-country trails. A paved bike path travels north to Tahoe City and Squaw Valley.

Non-natural sights include the modest 1860 **cabin** of William 'General' Phipps, an early Tahoe settler, and the considerably grander 1903 Queen Anne–style **Hellman-Ehrman Mansion** (tours adult/child $5/3; ⏰ 11am-4pm late May–Sep). Guided tours take in the richly detailed interior, including marble fireplaces, leaded-glass windows and period furnishings.

The secluded **General Creek campground** (☎ 800-444-7275; www.reserveamerica.com; sites $20-25; ⏰ year-round) has 175 fairly spacious, pine-shaded sites, plus flush toilets and hot pay showers.

Tahoma

pop 1065

Tahoma has the western shore's greatest concentration of places to stay and eat, as well as a post office and the **PDQ Market**

(☎ 530-525-7411; ⏰ 6:30am-10pm), which has groceries and a deli. In the warmer months, the tiny **gas station** (7062 W Lake Blvd) rents kayaks. DL Bliss State Park (p343) is a great spot to put in.

The darling red cabins of **Tahoma Meadows B&B Cottages** (☎ 530-525-1553, 866-525-1533; www.tahomameadows.com; 6821 W Lake Blvd; cottages $95-190, with kitchen $145-345; ✗) dotted around a pine grove are as warm and welcoming as a hug from an old friend. Each has classy country decor, thick down comforters, a small TV and bathrooms with clawfoot tubs. The homecooked gourmet breakfasts will sustain you well beyond lunchtime. Extras include free wi-fi and a big fluffy toy bear waiting on your bed.

The lakeside **Chamber's Landing** (☎ 530-525-7261; 6300 W Lake Blvd; mains $18-35; ⏰ Jul-Sep) serves up fancy Mediterranean cuisine, but the biggest crowds descend for drinks and appetizers in the all-day bar, especially during Happy Hour (5pm to 7pm). Try a 'Chamber's Punch,' the signature cocktail.

Homewood

pop 271

This place revolves around Homewood Mountain (p336) in winter and also provides good backcountry ski access to Desolation Wilderness via Black Canyon (marked from Hwy 89). **Tahoe Gear** (☎ 530-525-5233; 5095 W Lake Blvd) is a good spot for trail information and equipment rentals. **Kingfish** (☎ 530-525-5360; 5190 W Lake Blvd), operates fishing trips out of the Homewood Marina. A six-hour trip in pursuit of kokanee, mackinaw, rainbow and brown trout will set you back $80, but you *will* catch fish!

The nearest campground is the nine-site, tent-only **Kaspian Campground** (☎ 877-444-6777; www.reserveusa.com; sites $15; ⏰ late May-Sep) with flush toilets. It's around 1.5 miles north of Homewood.

Sunnyside

Sunnyside is a blink-and-you've-missed-it hamlet with two great restaurants. **Sunnyside Resort** (☎ 530-583-7200; www.sunnysideresort.com; 1850 W Lake Blvd; mains lunch $6-14, dinner $22-31; r $100-250; ✗) offers classic and innovative takes on steak and seafood in its fine dining room (reservations required). In summer you'll probably have more fun doing lunch – or drinks and appetizers – on the huge lakefront deck. The 23 rooms with lake views ooze Old Tahoe flair.

For breakfast, head to the **Fire Sign Café** (☎ 530-583-0871; 1785 W Lake Blvd; mains under $10; ⏰ 7am-3pm) for yummy omelettes, pancakes, waffles and other carbo-bombs.

To work it off, rent a bicycle or in-line skates from **Cyclepaths** (☎ 530-581-1171; 1785 W Lake Blvd). The folks working here will happily give you the scoop on all sorts of local outdoor information.

TAHOE CITY
pop 1800 / elevation 6240ft

The north shore's commercial hub, Tahoe City sits right at the junction of Hwys 89 and 28 and is great for grabbing supplies at supermarkets and information at the visitors center. It's also the closest lake town to Squaw Valley USA (p346). N Lake Blvd, the main drag, has outfitters, boutiques and restaurants, but overall, the little towns east of here tend to be more attractive.

Information

Bookshelf (☎ 530-581-1900; 760 N Lake Blvd, Boatworks Mall) Great indie bookstore.

Vicky's Cyber Café (☎ 530-581-5312; 255 N Lake Blvd; per 15min $3, wi-fi per hr $2.50; ⏰ 8am-6pm Mon-Sat)

Visitors center (☎ 530-581-1685, 800-824-6348; 380 N Lake Blvd; ⏰ 8:30am-5pm) Next to the fire station, makes free room reservations.

Sights

Just south of the Hwy 89/28 junction, the Truckee River flows through floodgates and passes beneath **Fanny Bridge**, cutely named for the most prominent feature of people leaning over the railings to look at fish – their fanny (or rear end). In a reconstructed log cabin nearby, the **Gatekeeper's Cabin Museum** (☎ 530-583-1762; 130 W Lake Blvd/Hwy 89; adult/child/senior $3/1/2; ⏰ 11am-5pm Wed-Sun May–mid-Jun & Sep, daily mid-Jun–Aug, Sat & Sun Oct) has a great collection of Tahoe memorabilia, and, in a new wing, an exquisite array of Native American baskets. A few blocks east, the 1908 **Watson Cabin Museum** (☎ 530-583-1762; 560 N Lake Tahoe Blvd; donation requested; ⏰ noon-4pm Jun-Aug), one of the town's oldest buildings, exemplifies local lifestyles in the early 20th century.

Activities

Tahoe City has no outstanding swimming beaches, although **Commons Beach** was recently

redesigned as a small, attractive park with sandy and grassy areas as well as picnic benches, barbecues, and a climbing rock and playground for kids.

Hikers should explore the fabulous trails of the **Granite Chief Wilderness** north and west of Tahoe City. For maps and trailhead directions, stop by the visitors center or the outfitters listed below. Recommended day hikes include the moderately strenuous **Five Lakes Trail** (round-trip 5 miles) and the easy trek to **Paige Meadows** (leading on to the Tahoe Rim Trail, p61). Paige Meadows is also good terrain for novice mountain-bikers and for snowshoeing. Wilderness permits are not required, not even for overnight trips.

The paved 6-mile **Truckee River Bike Trail** runs between Tahoe City and Squaw Valley. It's easy but expect crowds on summer weekends.

The Truckee River itself is gentle and wide as it flows northwest from the lake – perfect for novice rafters who like to drag a six-pack behind the boat. **Truckee River Raft Rentals** (☎ 530-583-0123; 185 River Rd; adult/child $32/27) rents rafts for the 5-mile float from Tahoe City to the River Ranch Lodge, including transportation back to town. For more challenging white-water runs, see p347.

For information about nearby **ski resorts**, see p335.

Good outfitters include the following:

Back Country (☎ 530-581-5861; www.thebackcountry .net; 690 N Lake Blvd) Mountain-biking experts; great website.

Porter's Ski & Sport (☎ 530-583-2314; 501 N Lake Blvd)

Tahoe Dave's (☎ 530-583-6415; www.tahoedaves.com; 620 N Lake Tahoe Blvd)

Sleeping

Cottage Inn (☎ 530-581-4073, 800-581-4073; www.the cottageinn.com; 1690 W Lake Blvd; r $140-330; ✖) Romantic types will be enchanted by the rooms here, each with knotty-pine paneling and other mountain-cabin frills. All have stone fireplaces and TV/VCR. Follow up a swim in frigid Lake Tahoe (private beach access) with a trip to the sauna.

Mother Nature's Inn (☎ 530-581-4278, 800-558-4278; 551 N Lake Blvd; r $70-140; ✖) Right in town, behind the Cabin Fever knickknack boutique, this good-value option offers motel-style rooms with a tidy country look, eclectic furniture and comfy pillowtop mattresses.

River Ranch Lodge (☎ 530-583-4264, 800-535-9900; www.riverranchlodge.com; Hwy 89 at Alpine Meadows Rd;

SIERRA NEVADA

r incl breakfast $90-170; ✕) Drift off to dreamland as the Truckee River tumbles right below your window at this delightful inn. Rooms bulge with character and feature either elegant antiques or classy lodgepole-pine furniture as well as all mod-cons.

For camping head north to the three USFS campgrounds off Hwy 89 (p349) or 2 miles south to **William Kent Campground** (☎ 877-444-6777; www.reserveusa.com; sites $16; ☯ mid-May–mid-Oct), where the 94 nicely shaded, but cramped, sites often fill up. Amenities include flush toilets and beach access.

Eating

Bridgetender (☎ 530-583-3342; 65 W Lake Blvd; dishes $8-10) This local institution, near Fanny Bridge, has a lively bar, wood stove, pool table and a menu stocked with oldies but goodies, from burgers to sandwiches and fingerlickin' ribs. In summer, insiders gravitate outside to the riverside tables.

River Ranch Lodge (☎ 530-583-4264; Hwy 89 at Alpine Meadows Rd; mains lunch $7-12, dinner $17-28) This place makes great barbecue lunches in summer and its patio is also a popular stop for rafters and bikers. Dinner is a meat-heavy gourmet affair, with special nods to the filet mignon and the roasted elk loin.

Jake's on the Lake (☎ 530-583-0188; Boatworks Mall; bar appetizers $4.50-10, mains lunch $9-17, dinner $16-26) There's no shortage of tummy-tantalizing choices at this breezy dining room with a big deck overlooking a small marina. The bar is great for grazing on appetizers, especially during Happy Hour (4:30pm to 6:30pm Sunday to Friday) when prices drop 50%. Finish up with a hula pie, its signature dessert.

Also recommended:

Rosie's Cafe (☎ 530-583-8504; 571 N Lake Blvd; breakfast & lunch $6-9, dinner $10-16; ☯ 6:30am-10pm) Lots of standard bearers in a quirky setting; breakfast served until 2:30pm.

Tahoe House (☎ 530-583-1377; Hwy 89; meals under $7; ☯ 6am-6pm) A half-mile south of the 'Y'. Gourmet coffees, baked goods and fresh sandwiches.

Getting There & Around

Tahoe Area Rapid Transit (TART; ☎ 530-550-1212; www.laketahoetransit.com; ☯ 6:30am-6:30pm) operates buses along the northern shore as far as Incline Village, south along the western shore to Sugar Pine Point State Park and to Truckee via Hwy 89. Tickets cost $1.50 each or $3.50 for an all-day pass.

From June to early September, TART also operates the Tahoe Trolley between Tahoe City and Squaw Valley, and Tahoe City and Crystal Bay. Rides are also $1.50 each or 3.50 for an all-day pass during the day and free between 6pm and 11pm.

SQUAW VALLEY USA

The host of the 1960 Olympic Winter Games, Squaw Valley USA still ranks among the world's top ski resorts (also see p335). The stunning setting amidst granite peaks, though, makes it a superb destination in any season. The village at the mountain base is about a 15- to 20-minute drive from Tahoe City or Truckee via Hwy 89 (turn off at Squaw Valley Rd).

Much of the action centers on 8200ft **High Camp**, reached by cable car ($19), which has an outdoor **ice-skating rink** (with/without cable car ride, incl skates $24/10) and a heated outdoor **swimming pool** (with/without cable car ride $25/10). Your cable car ticket also includes admission to the **Olympic Museum**, which relives magic moments from 1960. Discounts are available for children, teens and seniors.

Several hiking trails radiate out from High Camp, or try the lovely, moderate **Shirley Lake Trail** (round-trip 5 miles), which follows a sprightly creek to waterfalls, granite boulders and abundant wildflowers. It starts at the mountain base, near the end of Squaw Peak Rd, behind the cable car building.

Fun activities down below include a **ropes course**, a **climbing wall** and a **Sky Jump** (a bungee trampoline), all operated by the **Squaw Valley Adventure Center** (☎ 530-583-7673; www.squaw adventure.com). Tee up at the 18-hole, par 72, Scottish-style links **Resort at Squaw Creek Golf Course** (☎ 800-327-3353; greens fee $110-125) designed by Robert Trent Jones. **Squaw Valley Stables** (☎ 530-583-7433; half-/1-/2-day rides $27/50/85) operates horseback rides.

For lodging information, call **central reservations** (☎ 800-545-4350). The nicest place for our money is **PlumpJack Squaw Valley Inn** (☎ 530-583-1576, 800-323-7666; www.plumpjack.com; 1920 Squaw Valley Rd; r incl breakfast summer $160-200, winter $180-260; ✕ ⊠), an artsy boutique hotel right in the Village. Each room has mountain views and lots of comfort factors, including plush terry-cloth robes. The elegant restaurant (dinner mains $17 to $28), with its crisp linens and charcoal banquettes, serves masterful Mediterranean cuisine and great wines. Nearby, the more casual **Balboa Café** (☎ 530-583-5850; mains $11-25) has an American bistro feel and a big mountain-view terrace.

TRUCKEE & DONNER LAKE
pop 15,800 / elevation 5840ft
Cradled by mountains and the Tahoe National Forest, Truckee is a thriving town steeped in Old West history. It was put on the map by the railroad, grew rich on logging and ice harvesting and even had its brush with Hollywood during the 1924 filming of Charlie Chaplin's *The Gold Rush*. Today tourism fills much of the city's coffers, thanks to a well-preserved historical downtown and its proximity to Lake Tahoe and world-class ski resorts.

West of Truckee, 3-mile-long Donner Lake is a busy recreational hub. The Donner Party (see the boxed text, p348) camped nearby during the fateful winter of 1846. Donner Summit, further west, has six downhill and cross-country ski resorts.

Orientation
Truckee straddles the I-80 and is connected to northern Lake Tahoe via Hwy 89 to Tahoe City and Hwy 267 to Kings Beach. Hwy 267 dead-ends in Truckee's historic downtown, also known as Commercial Row. Lined by restaurants, shops and the Amtrak train depot, it is essentially one long block of the town's main drag called Donner Pass Rd. Most services, gas stations and outfitters are in the modern town about 1.5 miles west along Donner Pass Rd, near the junction with Hwy 89. Donner Memorial State Park and Donner Lake are about another 2 miles further west.

Information
Joe's Coffee (☎ 530-550-8222; 10191 Donner Pass Rd) Free wi-fi with purchase.
Tahoe Forest Hospital (☎ 530-587-6011; cnr Donner Pass Rd & Pine Ave; 🕑 24hr) Emergency room.
USFS Ranger Station (☎ 530-587-3558; 10342 Hwy 89; 🕑 8am-5pm Mon-Sat) Shorter winter hours.
Visitors center (☎ 530-587-2757, 866-443-2027; www .truckee.com; 10065 Donner Pass Rd; Internet access per 15 min $3; 🕑 9am-5:30pm) Inside the Amtrak train depot.

Sights
HISTORIC TRUCKEE
The aura of the Old West still lingers over Truckee's teensy historic downtown where

railroad workers and lumberjacks once milled about in raucous saloons, bawdy brothels and shady gambling halls. Most of the late-19th-century buildings now contain restaurants and cutesy boutiques. The **Old Jail** (☎ 530-582-0893; cnr Jiboom & Spring Sts; admission free; 🕑 11am-4pm Sat & Sun), in use until the 1960s, is filled with relics from the wild days of yore. The visitors center has free walking-tour maps.

DONNER LAKE
Warmer than Lake Tahoe, tree-lined Donner Lake is great for swimming, boating, fishing (license required), waterskiing and windsurfing. **West End Beach** (adult/child $3/2) is popular with families for its volleyball, basketball, snack stand and roped-off swimming area.

On the lake's eastern end, **Donner Memorial State Park** (☎ 530-582-7892; www.parks.ca.gov/?page _id=503; vehicle fee $6) occupies one of three sites where the Donner Party got trapped (see p348). Though its history is gruesome, the park is lovely and has a nice campground (p349), a sandy beach with picnic tables, hiking trails and, in winter, cross-country ski trails.

The vehicle fee includes admission to the excellent **Emigrant Trail Museum** (☎ 530-582-7892; 🕑 9am-4pm, longer hrs possible Jun-Aug), which has exhibits and a 25-minute film re-enacting the Donner Party's horrific plight. Outside, the **Pioneer Monument** has a 22ft pedestal – the exact depth of the snow that fateful winter. A short trail leads to a memorial at one family's cabin site.

Activities
HIKING
Truckee is a great base for outdoor explorations in the Tahoe National Forest, especially in the Donner Summit area. One popular hike is to the top of 8243ft **Mt Judah** (4.5 miles, moderate) for awesome views of Donner Lake and the surrounding peaks. A longer and more strenuous ridge-crest hike links Donner Pass and Squaw Valley (15.5 miles, moderate to difficult) skirting the base of four prominent peaks. The TART bus takes you back to the trailhead.

For maps and further route suggestions, drop by the USFS ranger station at Truckee.

OTHER ACTIVITIES
Truckee is close to eight downhill and four cross-country ski resorts (p335).

SIERRA NEVADA

THE DONNER PARTY

This is one 'party' you'd want to miss. In the 19th century, tens of thousands of people migrated west along the Overland Trail with dreams of a better life in California. Among them was the ill-fated Donner Party, whose story takes the prize for morbid intensity.

The families of George and Jacob Donner and their friend James Reed departed Springfield, Illinois, in April 1846. With six wagons and a herd of livestock, they intended to make the arduous journey as comfortable as possible. But the going was slow and, when other pioneers told them about an alternate trail that would save 200 miles, they jumped at the chance.

It soon became apparent that the 'shortcut' was anything but. There was no road for the wagons in the Wasatch Mountains, and most of the livestock succumbed under the merciless heat of the barren 80-mile Great Salt Lake Desert. Arguments and fights broke out. James Reed killed a man, was kicked out of the group and left to trundle off to California alone. By the time the party reached the eastern foot of the Sierra Nevada, near present-day Reno, morale and food supplies ran dangerously low. To restore energies and provisions, they decided to rest for a week. Bad move.

Winter struck early and with a vengeance, quickly rendering Donner Pass impassable and forcing the pioneers to build basic shelter near Donner Lake. They had food to last a month and the fervent hope that the weather would clear by then. It didn't.

Snow fell for weeks, reaching a depth of 22ft. Hunting and fishing became impossible. In mid-December, a small group of people made a desperate attempt to cross the pass. They quickly became disoriented and had to ride out a three-day storm that killed four of them. One month later, less than half of the original 15 staggered into Sutter's Fort near Sacramento, having survived on one deer and their dead friends.

By the time the first rescue party arrived at Donner Lake in late February, the trapped pioneers were still surviving – barely – on boiled ox hides. But when the second rescue party, led by the banished James Reed, made it through in March, evidence of cannibalism was everywhere. Journals and reports tell of 'half-crazed people living in absolute filth, with naked, half-eaten bodies strewn about the cabins.' Many were too weak to travel. When the last rescue party arrived in mid-April, only a sole survivor, Lewis Keseberg, was there to greet them. The rescuers found George Donner's body cleansed and wrapped in a sheet, but no sign of Tasmen Donner, George's wife. Keseberg admitted to surviving on the flesh of those who had died, but denied charges that he had killed Tasmen for fresh meat. He spent the rest of his life trying to clear his name. In the end, only 47 of the 89 members of the Donner Party survived. They settled in California, their lives forever changed by the harrowing winter at Donner Lake.

Donner Summit is a major rock-climbing mecca, with over 300 traditional and sport climbing routes. To learn the ropes, so to speak, try **Alpine Skills International** (☎ 530-582-9170; www.alpineskills.com; 11400 Donner Pass Rd).

From roughly June to September, **Tributary Whitewater Tour** (☎ 530-346-6812, 800-672-3846; www.whitewatertours.com; half-day weekday/weekend $68/78) operates a thrilling 7-mile, half-day rafting run on the Truckee River from Boca to Floriston (about 6 miles northeast of Truckee off the I-80) on Class III+ rapids.

For guided high-Sierra adventures, contact **Tahoe Adventure Company** (☎ 530-913-9212, 866-830-6125; www.tahoeadventurecompany.com; tours per person from $85). Staff members know the backcountry inside out and can customize any outing to your interest and skill level, from kayaking, hiking, mountain-biking,

rock climbing or any combination thereof. Tours also introduce you to the area's natural and human history and its geology, flora and fauna.

Local outfitters include the following:

Back Country (☎ 530-582-0909; www.thebackcountry .com; 11400 Donner Pass Rd) Good climbing section.

Porter's Ski & Sport (☎ 530-587-1500; www.porters tahoe.com; 11391 Deerfield Dr, Crossroads Center mall)

Sports Exchange (☎ 530-582-4510; 10095 W River St) Big climbing gym and deals on used equipment.

Sleeping

LODGES & INNS

Clair Tappaan Lodge (☎ 530-426-3632, 800-629-6775; www.sierraclub.org/outings/lodges/ctl; 19940 Donner Pass Rd; dm members/nonmembers Easter-late Nov $41/44, Dec-Easter $47/52) Cozy and convivial, this Sierra Club–owned rustic mountain lodge puts you near major ski resorts and has space for 140 people in dorms and family rooms. Rates include meals, but you're expected to do small chores and bring your own pillow, sleeping bag, towel and swimsuit for soaking in the hot tub. In winter you can cross-country ski right out the door.

River Street Inn (☎ 530-550-9290; www.riverstreet inntruckee.com; 10009 E River St; r midweek/weekend $100/140; ✗) This sweet 1885 inn in Truckee's historic downtown has 11 rooms that blend nostalgia (clawfoot tubs) with modern comforts (TV/VCR, down comforter). Meet fellow guests during breakfast in the loungy common room, and bring earplugs to dull the occasional train noise.

Truckee Hotel (☎ 530-587-4444, 800-659-6921; www.thetruckeehotel.com; 10007 Bridge St; r incl breakfast $50-100, with bathroom $100-140; ✗) Truckee's most historic abode has welcomed weary travelers since 1873. It's fully restored but still gives you that total Victorian immersion, made all the more authentic because only eight of the 37 rooms have private bathrooms. Expect some train noise.

Also recommended:

Inn at Truckee (☎ 530-587-8888, 888-773-6688; www .innattruckee.com; 11506 Deerfield Dr; r incl breakfast $70-135) Dependable, good-value option with nice Jacuzzi and sauna; in the newish part of town.

Donner Lake Village Resort (☎ 530-587-6081, 800-920-0994; www.donnerlakevillage.com; 15695 Donner Pass Rd; studios $90-190, kitchen ste $120-170; ☎) Condominium resort overlooking a private beach on the lake's western shore.

CAMPING
Donner Memorial State Park (☎ 530-582-7892, reservations 800-444-7275; www.reserveamerica.com; sites $20-25; ✓ Jun-Sep) This park has 154 campsites with water, flush toilets and hot pay showers.

Along Hwy 89 are three riverside **USFS campgrounds** (☎ 877-444-6777; www.reserveusa .com; sites $13-15; ✓ May-Sep); Granite Flat, Goose Meadow and Silver Creek. All have potable water and vault toilets.

Eating
Some of the best Tahoe area restaurants are in Truckee's historic downtown.

Dragonfly (☎ 530-587-0557; 10118 Donner Pass Rd; mains lunch $8-10, dinner $20-25) Cal-Asian fusion really shines at this handsome upstairs spot where Billy McCullough works his magic

with fresh produce and a potpourri of spices. At lunchtime try one of the fragrant 'dragon bowls.'

Moody's (☎ 530-587-8688; 10007 Bridge St; mains lunch $10-16, dinner $18-25) With its sophisticated supper-club looks and live jazz (Wednesday to Saturday), this gourmet restaurant in the Truckee Hotel oozes surprisingly urbane flair. Only the freshest organic ingredients make it into such perfectly pitched concoctions as pepper-encrusted halibut or rock shrimp risotto. The restaurant is a favorite of Paul McCartney, who sometimes vacations nearby.

OB's Pub & Restaurant (☎ 530-587-4164; 10046 Donner Pass Rd; mains lunch $8-11, dinner $10-20) Creaky wooden beams and Old West paraphernalia form the rough-and-tumble setting of this Truckee institution. The menu makes some gutsy departures from the burger-and-sandwich circuit with such offerings as wild mushroom strudel and Thai beef salad.

Squeeze Inn (☎ 530-587-9814; 10060 Donner Pass Rd; mains under $10; ✓ 7am-2pm) For breakfasts big enough to feed a lumberjack you can't beat this snug locals' favorite, which serves over 60 varieties of omelettes.

Getting There & Around
Greyhound has daily buses to Reno ($10.50, 50 minutes), Sacramento ($21, three hours) and San Francisco ($30, five to six hours). Buses stop at the train depot, as do Amtrak Thruway buses and the daily *California Zephyr* train to Emeryville/San Francisco ($44, 6½ hours), Reno ($15, one hour) and Sacramento ($40, four hours).

The **Truckee Trolley** (☎ 530-587-7451; one-way/all-day $1/2; ✓ 9am-5pm) connects the train depot hourly with Donner Lake. During ski season, it serves Northstar-at-Tahoe and Sugar Bowl.

For Tahoe City and the northern or western shore, hop on the TART bus (p346) at the train depot. Tickets are $1.50 or $3.50 for a day pass.

NORTHERN SHORE
Heading northeast of Tahoe City, Hwy 28 takes you to a string of twee, low-key towns, many on superb sandy beaches, with reasonably priced motels and hotels. It rolls into Nevada at Crystal Bay and continues south along the eastern shore.

Tahoe Vista

pop 1680 / elevation 6232ft

Tahoe Vista has more public beaches (six) than any other lake town, including small but pretty **Moon Dune Beach** with firepits and picnic tables across from the Rustic Cottages and the **Tahoe Vista Recreation Area** with a small grassy area and marina. **North Tahoe Regional Park**, at the northern end of National St, has hiking, biking, cross-country ski trails and nice picnic facilities.

Many of the old-timey cabins along here are being converted into condominiums, but not the **Rustic Cottages** (☎ 530-546-3523, 888-778-7842; www.rusticcottages.com; 7449 N Lake Blvd; cabins incl breakfast $60-200; ✕), a cluster of about 20 little storybook houses blending smoothly into the pines. All sport beautiful wrought-iron beds and a bevy of modern amenities. Other perks: make-your-own waffles at breakfast and free popcorn, movies and cookies. The same people also own the nearby **Tahoe Vista Lodge & Cabins** (☎ 530-546-3523; 6631 N Lake Blvd; cabins $70-160; ✕).

Mourelatos Lakeshore Resort (☎ 530-546-9500, 800-824-6381; www.mourelatosresort.com; 6834 N Lake Blvd; r $130-345) is an upscale beachfront property where most of the traditionally furnished rooms have at least partial lake views. Half also have cooking facilities. The two Jacuzzis are great for unwinding after a day on the slopes or trail.

Spindleshanks (☎ 530-546-2191; 6873 N Lake Blvd; mains $11-26; ☽ dinner) looks just like an all-American country cabin but has a chef with international inspiration. Udon noodles and lemongrass chicken share a menu with grilled ribs, filet mignon and rack of lamb.

Gar Woods Grille & Pier (☎ 530-546-3366; 5000 N Lake Blvd; mains lunch $11-17, dinner $20-25; ☽ lunch & brunch Sun summer, dinner year-round) A lakeshore hot spot is the salty Gar Woods whose dining room pays tribute to the era of classic wooden boats. Come for grilled anything and a Wet Woody cocktail, best slurped watching the sunset from the lake-view deck.

Old Post Office (☎ 530-546-3205; 5245 N Lake Blvd; mains under $10; ☽ 6:30am-2pm) For scrumptious breakfasts the place to beat is the Old Post Office, nearby Gar Woods Grille & Pier.

Kings Beach

pop 4000 / elevation 6280ft

The utilitarian character of Kings Beach belies the fact that it has some of the area's best restaurants. The town is one of the more ethnically diverse lakeshore communities with a large Latino population, many of whom work in the tourism industry around Lake Tahoe. In summer much of the action focuses on **Kings Beach State Recreation Area**, a 700ft-long beach that often gets deluged with sun-seekers and water rats. Concessions rent kayaks, jet skis and paddleboats.

Jason's Beachside Grille (☎ 530-546-3315; 8338 N Lake Blvd; mains lunch $6-10, dinner $8-19) has a fun lake-view deck and unpretentious American fare alongside an abundant salad bar. On colder days, the red velvet sofas orbiting a sunken fireplace are the coziest.

Nearby, **Las Panchitas** (☎ 530-546-4539; 8345 N Lake Blvd; mains $7-12; ☽ 11:30am-10pm) exerts a magnetic pull on fans of authentic Mexican food. Try the Panchitas special starring nicely spiced chorizo-and-egg enchiladas drenched in ranchera sauce.

Next to the Safeway supermarket is **Lanza's** (☎ 530-546-2434; 7739 N Lake Blvd; mains $10-18; ☽ dinner), a beloved Italian trattoria where a tantalizing aroma of garlic, rosemary and 'secret' spices perfumes the air. Dinners include salad and bread. Look for the owner's endearing old family photos in the entranceway.

Crystal Bay

Just past Kings Beach, Hwy 28 rolls into Nevada at Crystal Bay, where you can indulge your gambling urges at several aging casinos, including the historic **Cal-Neva Resort** (☎ 775-832-4000, 800-225-6382; www.calnevaresort.com; 2 Stateline Rd; r $60-110; 🐾). It literally straddles the California–Nevada border and has a colorful history involving ghosts, mobsters and Frank Sinatra, who once owned the joint. Ask about the tunnel tours. New owners are poised to pump millions of dollars into a top-to-bottom renovation, which might return the property to its onetime glory.

Meanwhile, a better place to ensconce yourself is the **Tahoe Biltmore Lodge & Casino** (☎ 775-831-0660, 800-245-8667; www.tahoebiltmore.com; 5 Hwy 28; r from $60; 🖳 🐾), which exudes plenty of campy, old-timey charm, even if the walls and floors are pretty thin.

EASTERN SHORE

Lake Tahoe's eastern shore lies entirely within Nevada. Much of it is relatively undeveloped thanks largely to George Whittell, an eccentric San Francisco playboy who owned much of the land, including 27 miles of shoreline. Upon his death in 1969, most of it was deeded to the US Forest Service. Whittell's massive mansion, the **Thunderbird Lodge** (☎ 775-832-8750, 800-468-2463; www.thunder birdlodge.org; tours from $20; ⊙ May-Oct, reservations required) – where he spent summers with his pet lion Bill – recently opened to the public. Tours include a trip down a 600ft tunnel to the Card House where George used to play poker with Howard Hughes and other famous recluses. The only way to get to the lodge is by shuttle bus, catamaran cruise or your own kayak. Call or check the website for full details and tour times.

The lodge is near one of Lake Tahoe's ritziest communities, **Incline Village**, the gateway to the Diamond Peak ski resort (p336) and home of the ultradeluxe **Hyatt Regency Lake Tahoe** (☎ 775-832-1234, 800-633-7313; www .hyatt.com; 111 Country Club Dr; r $320-450; ❒ ⬛ ⬛), where the spa is bigger than the casino. Decorated like a Craftsman-style mountain lodge, every room – public or private – speaks of refinement. The outdoor pool, heated to a tepid 82° year-round, is just what the doctor ordered after a day on the slopes. For dinner, treat your taste buds to a meal at the exquisite **Lone Eagle Grille** (mains $25-35), which overlooks the hotel's private beach. If it's full, sample the ambience over a drink in the bar.

A short drive north of the lake, via Hwy 431 (Mt Rose Hwy), **Mt Rose Wilderness** offers miles of unspoiled terrain. Take the Timberline Rd, Galena Creek County Park or Mt Rose Summit exits. A well-trodden trail leads to the summit of Mt Rose (10,776ft). No wilderness permits are required. The Mt Rose ski area (p337) is also nearby.

Back on the lake, one of George Whittell's legacies is **Lake Tahoe-Nevada State Park** (☎ 775-831-0494; http://parks.nv.gov/lt.htm), which has beaches, lakes and miles of trails. The highlight here is beautiful **Sand Harbor**, where two sand spits have formed a shallow bay with brilliant, warm turquoise water and white, boulder-strewn beaches. It gets busy. At the park's southern end, near the Hwy 50/Hwy 28 junction, **Spooner Lake** is popular for catch-and-release fishing, picnicking and cross-country skiing (p337).

Spooner Lake is also the start of the famous 15-mile **Flume Trail** (www.flumetrail.com), a holy grail for experienced mountain-bikers.

From trail's end near Incline Village you can either backtrack via Hwy 28 or board a shuttle bus ($12.50) at Hidden Beach. Bikes are available at the trailhead from **Flume Trail Mountain Bikes** (☎ 775-749-5349; per day from $40).

RENO

pop 194,000 / elevation 4500ft

Reno is the kind of place where you can feast your eyes on great art, your palate on tasty French food and your ears on catchy jazz. You can sip a cabernet or slurp a steamy latte in artsy cafés steps away from kayakers doing battle with rapids in the chilly Truckee River. Then you can enjoy a stress-melting massage in a classy spa before retiring to your boutique hotel room.

Wait a minute! Reno? Las Vegas' little lowbrow cousin? Yup, there's a new Reno in the making that goes far beyond the aging casinos and tacky, neon-lined streets. It's still a little rough around the edges, but there's an undeniable vibrancy in this northern Nevada town a mere half-hour's drive from Lake Tahoe. Pockets of hipness are emerging throughout the 'Arts District' with edgy galleries, bars and cafés that wouldn't look out of place in LA or San Francisco. A busy festival and events schedule and frequent A-lister concerts also contribute to this renaissance. The self-proclaimed 'biggest little city in the world' may finally be coming of age.

ORIENTATION

Downtown's N Virginia St, with most of the casinos, is wedged between the I-80 and the Truckee River. South of the river it continues as S Virginia St for several miles of motels, malls and yet more casinos. Back downtown, W 4th St is the main east–west thoroughfare. The Arts District is west of Virginia St; California Ave and 1st St are the most happening. Sparks, which is technically a separate city, is about 4 miles east of downtown Reno via I-80.

INFORMATION
Bookstores

Dharma Books (☎ 775-786-8667; 11 N Sierra St; Tue-Sun) Used and rare books.

Sundance Bookstore (☎ 775-786-1188; 1155 W 4th St) Great indie bookstore.

Emergency & Medical Services

National Council on Problem Gambling (☎ 800-522-4700; ⊙ 24hr)
Police, fire, ambulance (☎ 911) Emergencies.
Police – nonemergency (☎ 775-334-2550; 199 E Plaza St)
St Mary's Regional Medical Center (☎ 775-770-3000; 235 W 6th St)
Washoe Medical Center (☎ 775-982-4100; 77 Pringle Way; ⊙ 24hr) Emergency room.

Internet Access

Dreamer's Coffee House (☎ 775-322-8040; 17 S Virginia St; per 15 min $2; ⊙ 8am-9pm or 10pm) Loungy place with free wi-fi with purchase, great coffees, sandwiches and art produced by residents of the Riverside Artist Lofts upstairs.

Media

Reno Gazette-Journal (www.rgj.com) Daily newspaper.
Reno News & Review (www.newsreview.com) Free citywide listings magazine.

Money

Deluxe Travel Ltd (☎ 775-686-7000; 100 California Ave; ⊙ 8am-6pm Mon-Fri)

Post

Downtown post office (50 S Virginia St)

Tourist Information

For pretrip planning, look at www.visitreno tahoe.com or call ☎ 800-367-7366.
City of Reno Welcome Center (☎ 775-786-4340; Reno-Tahoe Airport; ⊙ 9am-9pm) Near baggage claim.

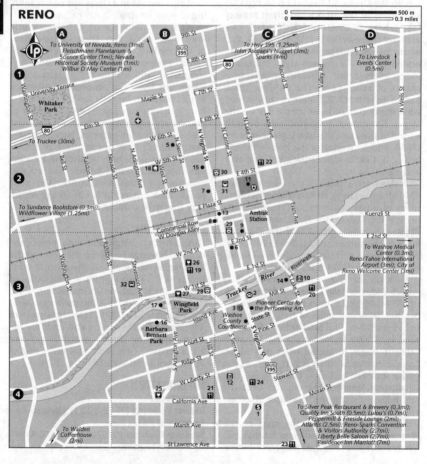

Reno-Sparks Convention & Visitors Authority
(☎ 775-827-7600; 2nd fl, Reno Town Mall, 4001 S
Virginia St; ⊙ 8am-5pm Mon-Fri)

SIGHTS
Virginia St
North Virginia St is casino central with one
neon-festooned behemoth after another.
Approaching the strip from the north, the
first big casino is **Circus Circus** (☎ 775-329-0711;
500 N Sierra St), easily the most family-friendly
of the bunch. Free circus acts entertain
kids beneath the giant, candy-striped big

top, which also harbors a gazillion carnival
games.

Next up is the **Silver Legacy** (☎ 775-325-7401;
407 N Virginia St), easily recognized by its bulbous white dome sheltering a giant mock
mining rig underneath a massive sky painting that periodically erupts into a fairly
tame sound-and-light spectacle. It's close
to the new **Reno Events Center** (p358) and the
National Bowling Stadium (☎ 775-334-2695; 300 N
Center St), which has a mind-boggling 78 lanes
but is only open during competitions.

A bit further on, the **Eldorado** (☎ 775-786-
5700; 345 N Virginia St) has a kitschy Fountain of
Fortune – featuring Neptune and nymph-
ets (OK, angels) – that probably has Italian
sculptor Bernini spinning in his grave.

South of here, across the new train trench,
you can rub a Blarney Stone for good luck
before heading inside **Fitzgerald's** (☎ 775-785-
3300; 255 N Virginia St), an older yet buzzy 351-room
property with a dopey 'lucky leprechaun'
theme and the cheapest buffet in town. It's
right next to the landmark **Reno Arch**, built
in 1926 to commemorate the completion of
the first transcontinental highway in North
America. The original has since been replaced twice (the last time in 1987) but still
proclaims Reno as being the 'Biggest Little
City in the World.'

Nearby is **Harrah's** (☎ 775-786-3232; 219 N Center
St), founded by Nevada gambling pioneer
William Harrah in 1946 and still one of the
biggest and most popular casinos in town.
From about mid-May to September, live
bands get the crowd hopping several nights
weekly at Harrah's Plaza facing Virginia St.

Closer to the Truckee River, the **Club Cal
Neva** (☎ 775-954-4540; 40 N Virginia St) has seen
better days but enjoys a reputation for having some of the loosest slots in town.

Just a block east is Reno's ritziest hotel-
casino, the Tuscan-themed **Siena** (☎ 775-337-
6260; 1 S Lake St), which has a full spa as well
as Enoteca, a comfy jazz bar. Its Sunday
brunch ($25, ⊙ 10am to 2pm) is report-
edly the best in town.

About 2 miles south of downtown are two
of Reno's biggest hotels. The **Peppermill** (☎ 775-
826-2121; 2707 S Virginia St) dazzles with fancy
neon, such over-the-top features as the
palazzo-style Million Dollar Bathroom (near
the Romanza restaurant), and the hip Fireside
Lounge. At the nearby **Atlantis** (☎ 775-825-4700;
3800 S Virginia St) you can loose your quarters in

SIERRA NEVADA

SIERRA NEVADA

a trippy tropical setting of indoor waterfalls, tiki huts and palm trees. The atrium-like Sky Terrace is a rare smoke-free gambling area.

Also in this part of town is the **Liberty Belle Saloon** (☎ 775-825-1776; 4250 S Virginia St; ⏰ 11am-9pm), a bat cave of a restaurant-bar that doubles as a slot machine museum.

National Automobile Museum

At this engaging **car museum** (☎ 775-333-9300; www.automuseum.org; 10 Lake St; adult/child/senior $8/3/7; ⏰ 9:30am-5:30pm Mon-Sat, 10am-4pm Sun) stylized street scenes illustrate a century's worth of automobile history and how it has shaped American society. Famous vintage cars include the 1949 Mercury driven by James Dean in *Rebel Without A Cause*, Elvis's 1973 Cadillac and Buckminster Fuller's experimental 1934 Dymaxion.

Nevada Museum of Art

In a sparkling new building inspired by the geologic formations of the Black Rock Desert north of town, this **art museum** (☎ 775-329-3333; www.nevadaart.org; 160 W Liberty St; adult/child/student/senior $10/1/8/8; ⏰ 10am-5pm Tue, Wed, Fri-Sun, 10am-8pm Thu) has been a major spark plug in the revitalization of downtown Reno. A floating staircase leads to galleries showcasing images related to the American West and temporary exhibits. Great café for postcultural refueling.

Wilbur D May Center

Wilbur May (1898–1982) was a rich traveler, adventurer, pilot, big-game hunter, rancher and philanthropist, who spent his latter years in Reno. This **museum** (☎ 775-785-5961; www.maycenter.com; 1595 N Sierra St, Rancho San Rafael Park; adult/child/senior $4.50/2.50/3.50; ⏰ 10am-5pm Tue-Sat, noon-5pm Sun) has exhibits on May's life and displays of the many artifacts, oddities and trophies he collected (or shot) during his travels. There's a shrunken head from South America, Eskimo scrimshaw and horse sculptures from the Chinese T'ang dynasty. The museum is surrounded by 12 acres of gardens and a children's fun park.

WHAT IS BURNING MAN? *Mark Morford*

Three thousand topless women covered in nothing but body paint, glitter and dust are riding crazily decorated bicycles around the center ring of an enormous, scorching desert campground, singing and whistling and laughing and calling themselves the Critical Tits brigade, as the crowd cheers and hopes they're all wearing lots of SPF 30 on their nipples.

And just over there, rising from the desert floor like a wicked steel flower, is the *Hand of God,* a 30ft metal appendage-sculpture that shoots colossal tongues of flame from its fingertips 300ft into the ink-black night sky, and you can feel the heat and hear the thunder and taste the smoke from a half-mile away.

There is a 25ft-high sculpture made of plaster and wire mesh and real animal bones called the *Tree of Life.* There is an intricate laser-light installation beaming unknowable messages to the cosmos. There are, well, all manner of sculpture, installation, maze, structure, light show or noisemaker, from the sacred to the deliciously profane, scattered around the desert floor like confetti tossed from the heavens.

And this is just the beginning. This is just a hint of what Burning Man is all about.

There are vehicles. There are semitrucks reimagined as floating luminescent party wagons, enormous mobile pirate galleons, motorized couches on wheels, rolling art vehicles of every shape and size and twisted metal Mad-Maxish mutation, enormous neon animated sea creatures floating slowly like Fellini dream-scraps across the desert floor at night.

There are fully functioning bars. There are huge, booming, generator-powered nightclubs. There are pagan wedding chapels, elaborate mazes and world-class sculptures. There is, maybe, a dust-choked casino. There are lounges and stages and huge dome tents filled with giant pillows for frolicking and chatting and sleeping it all off.

And there are upwards of 30,000 people, camping in a huge semicircle 2 miles across, a surprisingly organized spectacle of calmly euphoric individuals who, for one week per year, trek from all parts of the country (and world) to this same spot in the Nevada desert and use this oddly beautiful, inimitable event called Burning Man to strip away their everyday inhibitions and peel back the masks of 'normal' to discover themselves anew.

University of Nevada, Reno

UNR has attractive grounds and buildings which are best explored on a free **campus tour** (☎ 775-784-4700; ☺ 10am & 2pm Mon-Fri); reservations required. Afterwards you could pop into the flying saucer–shaped **Fleischmann Planetarium & Science Center** (☎ 775-784-4811; admission free; ☺ 8am-8pm Mon-Fri, 10:30am-8pm Sat & Sun), a pint-sized and endearingly old-fashioned facility that offers a window on the universe during star shows ($4) and feature presentations (adult/child $5/4). Call for show times. Nearby is the **Nevada Historical Society Museum** (☎ 775-688-1190; 1650 N Virginia St; adult/child/senior $3/free/2; ☺ 10am-5pm Mon-Sat).

ACTIVITIES

A major milestone in Reno's renaissance was the 2004 opening of the **Truckee River Whitewater Park** (admission free; ☺ year-round). Mere steps from the casinos, its Class II and III rapids are gentle enough for kids riding inner tubes, yet sufficiently challenging for professional freestyle kayakers. Two courses wrap around Wingfield Park, a small river island that hosts free concerts in summertime. **Tahoe Whitewater Tours** (☎ 775-787-5000; 400 Island Ave) rents kayaks.

Reno is a 30- to 60- minute drive from Tahoe ski resorts (p335). Many hotels and casinos offer special stay and ski packages. Call the visitors center or check individual websites.

FESTIVALS & EVENTS

Reno River Festival (☎ 800-367-7366; www.renoriverfestival.com) The world's top freestyle kayakers compete in a mad paddling dash through Whitewater Park in mid-May.

Reno Rodeo (☎ 775-329-3877; www.renorodeo.com) One of the West's wildest rodeos held over nine days at the Livestock Events Center (cnr of E 9th & Sutro Sts) in mid-June.

Tour de Nez (☎ 775-348-6673; www.tourdenez.com) Called the 'coolest bike race in America,' the Tour de Nez brings together pros and amateurs for three days of races and partying in mid-June.

Hot August Nights (☎ 775-356-1956; www.hotaugustnights.net) Catch the *American Graffiti* vibe during this seven-day celebration of hot rods and rock and roll in early August.

SIERRA NEVADA

Burning Man. It is that famously impossible-to-describe event that takes place every year in a sunbaked, crusted, dusted, windblown, desperately stark slab of desert (aka 'the playa') about 100 miles northeast of Reno, Nevada (500 from Vegas) during the first week of September.

It is that glittery, sexed-up, free-form, profoundly liberating, often incredibly silly week-long experience that defies all attempts to characterize it but I'll try it anyway by saying it's one part survivalist camping trip, one part top-notch art festival, one part continuous rave party, one part moneyless community experiment, and all parts freedom of expression and costume and libido and self. At the end of it all everyone gathers to watch a neon-lit, five-story wooden effigy of a man burn to the ground in a spectacular, cheering, energized roar of love and community and time. It is, I guarantee you, like nothing else happening on the planet right now.

If you go, you participate. Somehow, some way. You bring art, you decorate your camp, you dress up (or down), you share, you give. This is the only true rule. There are no spectators.

It all started way back in 1986 when a handful of friends gathered on a San Francisco beach to erect an 8ft effigy of a 'man' to burn, just because. Within a few years their little ritual was drawing hundreds, then thousands. Its current home has been christened Black Rock City, the name given the enormous functioning 'city' that springs up in the Nevada desert, out of nowhere, for this one precious week every year, then vanishes completely and leaves no trace behind.

As of this writing, tickets to attend Burning Man are $250 each. They go on sale at the beginning of the year, and are available through the second official day of the event, in September, via www.burningman.com.

Burning Man. It is, all at once, extraordinary and dirty and dangerous and hilarious and annoying and raw and smelly and hot and deeply whimsical. It is for artists and alternative types and spiritual nomads, yuppie dads and receptionists and cubicle workers and lost souls and found spirits. It is for anyone. But it's definitely not for everyone.

You supply your own everything: food, water, camping gear, transportation, a bike (mandatory to get around the playa), inebriants, costumes, SPF 30. Laughter and euphoria and awe and the deep sense that you have, upon arrival, somehow transcended time and space and self, are, of course, free.

Best in the West Nugget Rib Cook-Off (☎ 775-356-3428; www.nuggetribcookoff.com) The world's best rib-*meisters* compete for prestige and prizes in Sparks, in early September.

National Championship Air Races & Air Show (☎ 775-972-6663; www.airrace.org) Biplanes, jets, WWII fighters and other racing planes test their aerial mettle over Reno Stead Field, about 15 miles north of town, in mid-September.

SLEEPING

Lodging rates are pretty reasonable but vary widely depending on the day of the week, the season, the week's activities and the type of room. As a rule, you get the best rates Sunday through Thursday; Friday is somewhat higher and Saturday can be as much as triple the midweek rate. Prices are usually a bit lower in winter than in summer. Figures below can only serve as a loose guide.

Casinos

See p353 for additional details about many properties mentioned here.

Siena (☎ 775-337-6260, 877-743-6233; www.siena reno.com; 1 Lake St; r weekday/weekend from $90/110; ☒ ☒) The Tuscan city of Siena inspired this smooth newcomer, a sophisticated boutique hotel-casino complete with campanile (tower) overlooking the river. Instead of the usual casino frenzy, you'll find lots of stress-melting options, including a serene spa.

Peppermill (☎ 775-826-2121, 800-648-6992; www.peppermillreno.com; 2707 S Virginia St; tower r midweek/weekend from $50/200; ☒ ☐ ☒) The popular Peppermill stands out from the pack with its sparkling outdoor pool (complete with faux mountainscape and waterfall), and free access to a health club and sauna. Rooms unintentionally ride the retro wave with their turquoise-and-black color scheme.

John Ascuaga's Nugget (☎ 775-356-3300, 800-648-1177; www.janugget.com; 1100 Nugget Ave; r $70-140; ☒ ☐ ☒) This 1500-room behemoth in Sparks began as a coffee shop some 50 years ago and has been owned by the same Basque family ever since. Rooms are decked out in pleasingly subdued hues, but the Nugget's trump card is the huge atrium pool with individual whirlpools, a massage waterfall and mountain views. Big fitness center, too.

Circus Circus, Eldorado and Silver Legacy are all connected by a skywalk.

Circus Circus (☎ 775-329-0711, 800-648-5010; www.circusreno.com; 500 N Sierra St; r midweek/weekend from $40/100; ☒ ☐) Standard rooms are sheathed in garish pinks and blues at this kid-friendly property. Some are in the separate Sky Tower, reached via a short tram ride from the main casino.

Eldorado (☎ 775-786-5700, 800-648-5966; www.eldoradoreno.com; 345 N Virginia St; r midweek/weekend from $60/110; ☒ ☐ ☒) Eldorado has over 800 rooms, mostly standard affairs with little character, although the renovated ones in the Skyline Tower are really quite a step up. It has one of the best casino restaurants (Roxy's), bars (Brew Brothers) and clubs (BuBinga).

Silver Legacy (☎ 775-325-7401, 800-687-8733; www.silverlegacyreno.com; 407 N Virginia St; r $70-90; ☒ ☒) Big and flash, this giant takes up two city blocks and boasts a three-tiered tower. That aside, the 1720 Victorian-themed rooms are crisp, comfortable and quiet. Rooms with better views cost a bit more.

Atlantis (☎ 775-825-4700, 800-723-6500; www.atlantiscasino.com; 3880 S Virginia St; r midweek/weekend from $80/150; ☒ ☐ ☒) Tropical flair pervades this 1000-room property where rooms come in four levels of comfort. Those with VIP ambitions should opt for the Concierge Tower category on the upper floors where extras include great views, private butler service and a cocktail hour. Avoid the motor-lodge units unless you're on a serious budget.

Harrah's (☎ 775-786-3232, 800-427-7247; www.harrahs.com/our_casinos/ren; 219 N Center St; r midweek $55-195, weekend $85-300; ☒ ☐ ☒) Another one of the fancier places downtown, in a gold-embossed sort of way. The 950 rooms may not have hugely exciting decor, but they're still plenty nice.

Hotels & Motels

Downtown Reno brims with cheap 'no-tell' motels, but a short drive nets some quality options, including the following.

Quality Inn South (☎ 775-329-1001, 800-626-1900; www.qualityinn.com; 1885 S Virginia St; r $75-85; ☒ ☒) A good choice along S Virginia St, this place has spacious and immaculate rooms with a balcony or patio overlooking the pool or nicely landscaped grounds. Rates include a discount coupon for breakfast at the on-site restaurant.

Residence Inn Marriott (☎ 775-853-8800, 800-331-3131; www.residenceinn.com/rnori; 9845 Gateway Dr; r incl breakfast midweek/weekend $140/160; ☒ ☐ ☒) This attractive property is a long way from downtown (7 miles), but the one- and two-bedroom kitchen units give you plenty of elbow room. Welcome perks include a pretty good spread of breakfast goodies and an afternoon cocktail and appetizer hour. Free wi-fi in the lobby and high-speed access in the rooms.

Wildflower Village (☎ 775-747-8848; www.wild flowervillage.com; 4395 W 4th St; dm $25, motel units $45-85, B&B $100; ✗ ▣) If you like quirk and character, this artistic haven about 3 miles west of downtown should fit you like a glove. The four structures have been beautified by artists-in-residence whose work is displayed at the on-site gallery. Rooms are snug but each has a private bathroom, cooking facilities and eclectic decor; the motel units offer the best value.

Seasons Inn (☎ 775-322-6000, 800-322-8588; www .seasonsinn.com; 495 West St; r midweek/weekend $45/100; ✗) This place is a good choice if you'd like to be in the heart of downtown without braving the casino mazes. Rooms are at no risk of being featured in *Architectural Digest*, but they're comfortable enough to give you a good night's sleep.

EATING

Reno's dining scene goes far beyond the casinos. In fact, many of the best places are not even in downtown at all.

Silver Peak Restaurant & Brewery (☎ 775-324-1864; 124 Wonder St; mains lunch $6-9, dinner $7-21; ✹ 11am-midnight) Casual and pretense-free, this place hums with the chatter of happy locals settling in for a night of microbrews and great eats, from wild mushroom pizza to pesto salmon and nut-encrusted mahimahi. Live music on Tuesday nights.

Lulou's (☎ 775-329-9979; 1470 S Virginia St; mains $25-35; ✹ dinner Tue-Sat) This arty gourmet eatery is a surprise find on this otherwise drab strip. Bold canvases brighten brick walls, and a tantalizing mélange of aromas wafts from the open kitchen where chefs fuss over Eurasian concoctions. Reservations essential.

Beaujolais Bistro (☎ 775-323-2227; 130 West St; mains lunch $8-14, dinner $16-24) With its starched white linens, brick walls, framed posters and formal service, this place pulls off the Left Bank vibe with panache. Besides such culinary challenges as frogs legs and veal sweetbreads, the menu also features *boeuf à la bourguignonne*, braised lamb and other dishes for less adventurous gourmets.

Deux Gros Nez (☎ 775-786-9400; 249 California Ave; mains under $8; ✹ 6am-midnight) Hipster to banker, everybody's got a soft spot for Reno's oldest coffeehouse, which does a lot more than brew knock-your-socks-off espresso. Its 'dynaflows' (smoothies) are veritable vitamin bombs, while the steamed eggs, healthy sandwiches and delicious pastas all fill the belly nicely. The full liquor license keeps patrons lubed up at night. Owner Tim is a certified bike nut and the brains behind the Tour de Nez (see p355). His insistent charm inspired Lance Armstrong and other famous racers to donate their jerseys which – framed behind glass – now form part of the café's raging decor.

SIERRA NEVADA

Bertha Miranda's (☎ 775-786-9697; 336 Mill St; mains under $10) This Reno institution is beloved for its fiesta decor, roving mariachis (on weekends) and big-flavored dishes, from the excellent enchiladas to the nicely spiced chimichangas. Its margaritas pack a punch.

Roxy's (☎ 775-786-7500; 345 N Virginia St; mains 19-34; ✹ dinner) Inside the Eldorado, this is one of Reno's best casino restaurants. Snuggle into a red velvet booth or sit on the indoor patio overlooking the Fountain of Fortune. Food here is mostly of the meat-and-seafood persuasion and best preceded by one of Roxy's 100 martinis.

Luciano's (☎ 775-322-7373; 719 S Virginia St; mains $13-20; ✹ dinner Tue-Sat) This intimate feel-good trattoria is perfect if you're in the mood for deftly prepared, no-nonsense Italian food. All the classics are here – luscious lasagna to plucky penne puttanesca and tasty chicken parmigiana.

The all-you-can-eat buffets at the casinos are popular fueling-up options and can be a good bargain if you like to stuff yourself silly. Expect to pay about $8 for breakfast, $10 for lunch and $16 for dinner. Prices tend to be higher on Friday and Saturday nights when most casinos put out especially lavish spreads. Some serve Sunday brunch. Local favorites include the Eldorado's Chef's Buffet, the Silver Legacy's Victorian Buffet, Atlantis' Toucan Charlie's Buffet & Grille and nearby Peppermill's Island Buffet. See p353 for addresses.

More good eats:

Peg's Glorified Ham & Eggs (☎ 775-329-2600; 420 S Sierra St; mains under $10; ☒ 6:30am-2pm) Popular breakfast spot.

Cheese Board (☎ 775-323-3115; 247 California Ave; dishes $6-10; ☒ 10am-4pm Mon-Sat) Gourmet salads and sandwiches.

Louis' Basque Corner (☎ 775-323-7203; 301 E 4th St; dinner $18) Hearty Basque dinners served family-style.

DRINKING

Jungle Vino (☎ 775-329-4484; 248 W 1st St) This tiny, smokefree wine bar with its Technicolor mosaic floor, Parisian café tables and art-clad walls is the boozy cousin of the Jungle Java coffeehouse next door. It also serves sandwiches and light meals ($6 to $12).

Chocolate Bar (☎ 775-337-1122; 475 S Arlington Ave; ☒ from 10am Mon-Sat, 10am-5pm Sun) This sinfully delicious hot spot enjoys most-favorite status with Reno scenesters for its wicked chocolate-themed drinks (both virgin and alcohol-infused), awesome desserts and big-city-cool decor.

Fireside Lounge (☎ 775-826-2121; 2707 S Virginia St; ☒ 24hr) Dark and lurid, this lounge in the Peppermill Casino (near the coffee shop) is a great make-out spot. The choicest seats orbit a fireplace surrounded by water and small music-video screens. Free appetizers during happy hour (4pm to 8pm Monday to Friday).

Green Room (☎ 775-324-1224; 144 West St) This hole-in-the-wall inside a former fire station comes with a big performance space where you can chill with free indie movies on Tuesday and bands most nights after 10pm.

More watering holes:

Sapphire (☎ 775-786-3232; 219 N Center St; ☒ Tue-Sat) A slice of New York sophistication at Harrah's.

Brew Brothers (☎ 775-786-5700; 345 N Virginia St) Nightly bands, eight custom microbrews and tasty grub ($5 to $10) at the Eldorado.

ENTERTAINMENT

The free weekly *Reno News & Review* (www .newsreview.com) is your best source for getting a fix on Reno's what's-on scene. In summertime, bands perform for free in the Wingfield Park Amphitheatre and Harrah's Plaza.

Walden Coffeehouse (☎ 775-787-3307; 3940 Mayberry Dr) This charismatic coffeehouse comes alive with a bluegrass jam on Thursday, open-mike night on Friday and local and touring

bands on Saturday. There's free wi-fi and a small menu of sandwiches, but no booze.

BuBinga Lounge (☎ 775-786-5700; 345 N Virginia St; men/women $10/5; ☒ from 9pm Tue-Sat) At Reno's sexiest dance club, inside the Eldorado, DJs pull in the eye-candy crowd with a pulsating mix of house and hip-hop. After you've sweated it out on the crammed dance floor, you can chill in one of the two bars.

Century Riverside 12 (☎ 775-786-7469; 11 N Sierra St) Enjoy Hollywood flicks in the comfort of this state of the art 12-screen multiplex.

Reno Events Center (☎ 775-335-8800; 400 N Center St) Another installment in the downtown revitalization, this 7000-seat venue hosts former and current chart toppers, comics and the occasional championship boxing match.

The casinos put on free lounge and cabaret acts that range from the enjoyable to the ridiculous. Some also have big showrooms where you can take in rock bands, magic shows or golden-throated stalwarts such as Tony Bennett.

GETTING THERE & AWAY

Reno/Tahoe International Airport (RNO; ☎ 775-328-6870; www.renoairport.com) is about 5 miles southeast of downtown and is served by such airlines as Alaska, American, Continental, Delta, Northwest, Southwest and United.

Greyhound (☎ 775-322-2970; 155 Stevenson St) has daily nonstop services to Truckee (one way $10.50, 50 minutes), San Francisco (one way $30, five to seven hours) and Sacramento (one way $23, 2¾ to 3¾ hours).

Reno is a stop on the *California Zephyr* route operated by **Amtrak** (☎ 775-329-8638, 800-872-7245; 135 E Commercial Row). Westbound trains stop at Truckee ($15, one hour), Sacramento ($33, five hours) and Emeryville/San Francisco ($36, 7½ hours).

GETTING AROUND

A **taxi** (☎ 775-355-5555) between the airport and downtown Reno costs about $18, but many casinos offer free shuttle service for their guests. The free Sierra Spirit bus loops around all major downtown landmarks, including the casinos and the Nevada Museum of Art. For longer trips hop aboard **Citifare buses** (☎ 775-348-7433; www.citifare.com; per ride/all-day $1.50/4). Most routes converge at the CitiCenter Transit Center downtown. Useful routes include bus 1 for points along

SIERRA NEVADA

DETOUR: VIRGINIA CITY

Virginia City, about 23 miles south of Reno, was the site of the legendary Comstock Lode, a massive silver bonanza that began in 1859 and stands as one of the world's richest strikes. Some of the silver barons went on to become major players in California history, among them Leland Stanford of university fame and Bank of California founder William Ralston. Much of San Francisco was built with the treasure dug up from the soil beneath Virginia City.

At its peak, it had over 30,000 residents and, as befits a mining town, was a wild and raucous place. A young local newspaper writer named Samuel Clemens vividly captured the shenanigans in a book called *Roughing It*, published under his pen name Mark Twain. A National Historic Landmark since 1961, Virginia City draws big crowds in search of Old West icons and lore. Although it sometimes has the feel of a frontier theme park, it's still a fun place to while away a few hours.

On the main drag, 'C' St, you'll find the **visitors center** (☎ 775-847-7500; www.virginiacity-nv.com; 89 'C' St; ✆ 10am-4pm) and vintage buildings restored into wacky saloons, cheesy souvenir shops and small museums ranging from hokey to quirky to intriguing. Here's a sampling:

Julia C Bullette Red Light Museum (☎ 775-847-9394; 5 C St; admission $1; ✆ 10am-9pm) An incongruous collection of vintage erotica and antiquated medical equipment.

Fourth Ward School Cultural Center (☎ 775-847-0975; 537 C St; adult/child $5/3; ✆ 10am-5pm May-Oct) Exhibits about the history of the Comstock inside an 1876 school building.

Nevada Gambling Museum (☎ 775-847-9022; 50 C St; admission $1.50; ✆ 10am-6pm Apr-Sep, 10am-5pm Oct-Mar) Antique slot machines, ingenious cheating devices and guns.

Way it Was Museum (☎ 775-847-0766; 113 C St; admission $3; ✆ 10am-6pm) Comstock mining artifacts galore.

If you want to spend the night, the **Gold Hill Hotel** (☎ 775-847-0111; www.goldhillhotel.net; r $55-225; 🍽), 1 mile south of town on Hwy 342, is clean, full of character and claims to be Nevada's oldest hotel. Another good choice is the equally historical **Silver Queen Hotel** (☎ 775-847-0440; 28 C St; r $45-125; 🖵).

The drive to Virginia City from Reno offers great views of the mountain. Take Hwy 395 south for about 10 miles, then Hwy 341 east for 13 miles.

S Virginia St, 7 for the university, 11 for Sparks and 14 for the airport.

YOSEMITE NATIONAL PARK

Yosemite (yo-*sem*-it-tee) is the Taj Mahal of national parks and you'll first encounter it with the same mixture of reverence and awe. It's also a Unesco World Heritage Site that packs in so much jaw-dropping beauty that it makes even Switzerland look like God's practice run. As far as we can tell, America's third-oldest national park has only one downside: the impact of the astonishing four million visitors annually who wend their way here. But lift your eyes ever so slightly above the crowds and you'll feel your heart instantly moved by unrivalled splendors. The haughty profile of Half Dome, the hulking presence of El Capitan, the drenching

mists of Yosemite Falls, the gemstone lakes of the high country's subalpine wilderness, the giant sequoias of Wawona, Hetch Hetchy's pristine pathways. These and other unforgettable sights pretty much guarantee that you'll be storing memories by the gigabyte.

HISTORY

The Ahwahneechee, a group of Miwok and Paiute peoples, lived in the Yosemite area for 4000 years before a group of pioneers, most likely led by legendary explorer Joseph Rutherford Walker, came through in 1833. During the Gold-Rush era, conflict between the miners and native tribes escalated to the point where a military expedition (the Mariposa Battalion) was dispatched in 1851 to punish the Ahwahneechee, eventually forcing the capitulation of Chief Tenaya and his tribe later that year.

Tales of thunderous waterfalls and towering stone columns followed the Mariposa Battalion out of Yosemite and soon spread into

SIERRA NEVADA

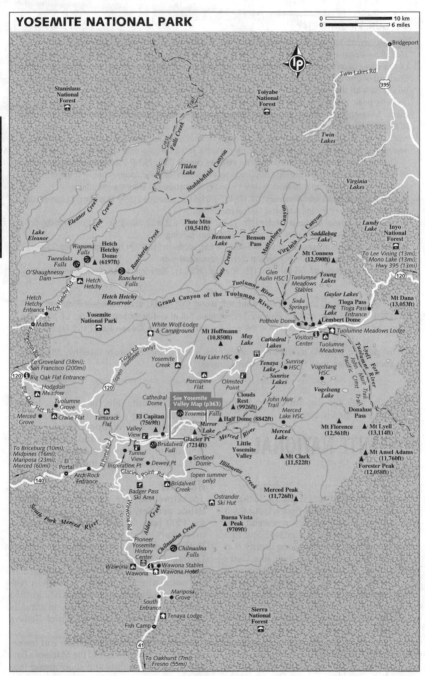

YOSEMITE NATIONAL PARK

0 — 10 km
0 — 6 miles

Bridgeport

Twin Lakes Rd
395

Stanislaus National Forest

Toiyabe National Forest

Twin Lakes

Tilden Lake

Stubblefield Canyon

Pacific Crest Falls Creek Trail

Virginia Lakes

Piute Mtn (10,541ft)

Benson Lake

Benson Pass

Matterhorn Canyon

Virginia Canyon

Saddlebag Lake

Mt Conness (12,590ft)

Lundy Lake

Inyo National Forest

To Lee Vining (13mi); Mono Lake (13mi); Hwy 395 (13mi)
120

Lake Eleanor

Eleanor Creek

Frog Creek

Wapama Falls

Hetch Hetchy Dome (6197ft)

Tueeulala Falls

O'Shaughnessy Dam

Rancheria Falls

Rancheria Creek

Piute Creek

Tuolumne River

Glen Aulin HSC

Tuolumne Meadows Stables

Young Lakes

Soda Springs

Gaylor Lakes

Tioga Pass

Dog Lake

Tioga Pass Entrance

Lembert Dome

Mt Dana (13,053ft)

Hetch Hetchy

Hetch Hetchy Reservoir

Grand Canyon of the Tuolumne River

Pothole Dome

Hetch Hetchy Entrance

Mather

Hetch Hetchy Rd

Yosemite National Park

Evergreen Rd

White Wolf Lodge & Campground

Mt Hoffmann (10,850ft)

May Lake

Cathedral Lakes

Visitors Center

Tuolumne Meadows

Tuolumne Meadows Lodge

Lyell Fork Tuolumne River

To Groveland (38mi); San Francisco (200mi)

Big Oak Flat Entrance
120

Tioga Rd (open summer only)

Yosemite Creek

May Lake HSC

Tenaya Lake

Sunrise HSC

Vogelsang HSC

John Muir Trail / Pacific Crest Trail

Hodgdon Meadow

Tuolumne Grove

Porcupine Flat

Olmsted Point

Sunrise Lakes

Vogelsang Lake

120

Big Oak Flat Rd

Merced Grove

Crane Flat

Tamarack Flat

Cathedral Dome

See Yosemite Valley Map (p363)

Yosemite Falls

Clouds Rest (9926ft)

John Muir Trail

Merced Lake HSC

Donahue Pass

El Capitan (7569ft)

Mirror Lake

Half Dome (8842ft)

Merced River

Mt Florence (12,561ft)

Mt Lyell (13,114ft)

To Briceburg (10mi); Midpines (16mi); Mariposa (23mi); Merced (60mi)

El Portal

Valley View

Bridalveil Fall

Glacier Pt (7214ft)

Little Yosemite Valley

Merced Lake

Mt Ansel Adams (11,760ft)

El Portal Rd

Tunnel View

Dewey Pt

Sentinel Dome

Mt Clark (11,522ft)

Forester Peak (12,058ft)

140

Arch Rock Entrance

Inspiration Pt

Glacier Point Rd (open summer only)

Bridalveil Creek

Illilouette Creek

Merced Peak (11,726ft)

South Fork Merced River

Badger Pass Ski Area

Ostrander Ski Hut

Wawona Rd

Alder Creek

Buena Vista Peak (9709ft)

Pioneer Yosemite History Center

Chilnualna Creek

Chilnualna Falls

Wawona

Wawona Stables

Wawona Hotel

Sierra National Forest

Mariposa Grove

South Entrance

Tenaya Lodge

Fish Camp

41

To Oakhurst (7mi); Fresno (55mi)

the public's awareness. In 1855 San Francisco entrepreneur James Hutchings organized the first tourist party to the valley. Published accounts of his trip, in which he extolled the area's untarnished beauty, prompted others to follow and it wasn't long before inns and roads began springing up. Alarmed by this development, conservationists petitioned Congress to protect the area – with success. In 1864 President Abraham Lincoln signed the Yosemite Grant, which eventually ceded Yosemite Valley and the Mariposa Grove of Giant Sequoias to California as a state park. This landmark decision paved the way for a national park system of which Yosemite became a part in 1890, thanks to efforts led by pioneering conservationist John Muir.

Yosemite's popularity as a tourist destination continued to soar throughout the 20th century and, by the mid-1970s, traffic and congestion draped the valley in a smoggy haze. The General Management Plan (GMP) developed in 1980 to alleviate this and other problems ran into numerous challenges and delays. Despite many improvements, it still hasn't been fully implemented, at least in part because of federal funding cuts. Ultimately, the powers that be must balance the needs of visitors with the preservation of the natural beauty that draws them to Yosemite in the first place.

WHEN TO GO

It's quite simple: from June to September, the entire park is accessible, all visitor facilities are open and everything from backcountry campgrounds to ice-cream stands are at maximum capacity. This is also when it's hardest – though not impossible – to evade the crush of humanity.

Crowds are smallest in winter but road closures (most notably of Tioga Rd, see p333, but also of Glacier Point Rd beyond Badger Pass Ski Area) mean that activity is concentrated in the valley and on Badger Pass. Visitor facilities are scaled down to a bare minimum and most campgrounds are closed and other lodging options limited. Note that 'winter' in Yosemite starts with the first heavy snowfall, which can be as early as October, and often lasts until May.

Many people feel that spring and fall are the nicest times to visit Yosemite. In May and June, the park's waterfalls – fed by the snowmelt – are at their most spectacular, while late August to October bring fewer people, a rainbow of fall foliage and crisp, clear weather. Waterfalls, however, have usually slowed to a trickle by that time.

ORIENTATION

There are four main entrances: South Entrance (Hwy 41), Arch Rock (Hwy 140), Big Oak Flat (Hwy 120 W) and Tioga Pass (Hwy 120 E). Hwy 120 traverses the park as Tioga Rd (see the boxed text, p333), connecting Yosemite Valley with the Eastern Sierra.

Visitor activity concentrates in Yosemite Valley, especially in Yosemite Village, which has the main visitors center, a post office, a museum, eateries and other services. Curry Village is another hub. Notably less busy, Tuolumne (too-*ahl*-uh-*mee*) Meadows, towards the eastern end of Tioga Rd, primarily draws hikers, backpackers and climbers. Wawona, the park's southern focal point, also has a good infrastructure. In the northwestern corner, Hetch Hetchy gets the smallest number of visitors and has no services whatsoever.

Gas up year-round at Wawona and Crane Flat inside the park or at El Portal on Hwy 140 just outside its boundaries. In summer, gas is also sold at Tuolumne Meadows. The stations usually close after dark but you can always pay at the pump with a credit card.

INFORMATION

Yosemite's entrance fee is $20 per vehicle or $10 for those on bicycle or foot and is valid for seven consecutive days. Upon entering the park, you'll receive an NPS map, an illustrated booklet and, most importantly, a copy of the biweekly *Yosemite Today* newspaper, which includes an activity schedule and current opening hours of all facilities.

For recorded park information, campground availability and road and weather conditions, call ☎ 209-372-0200.

Bookstores
Yosemite Association Bookstore (Map p363; ☎ 209-379-2648; www.yosemitestore.com; Yosemite Valley Visitors Center) Best selection of books about Yosemite and the Sierra.

Emergency & Medical Services
Police, fire, ambulance (☎ 911) Emergency.
Yosemite Dental Clinic (☎ 209-372-4200; Ahwahnee Dr, Yosemite Valley) 24-hour service available.

SIERRA NEVADA

Yosemite Medical Clinic (☎ 209-372-4637; Ahwahnee Dr, Yosemite Valley) 24-hour service available.

Internet Access
Public library (Map p363; ☎ 209-372-4552; Girls' Club Bldg, Yosemite Valley; access free; ☺ vary)
Yosemite Lodge at the Falls (p368; per min 25¢) Terminals are in the lobby. Wireless costs $10 per day.

Internet Resources
Yosemite National Park Service (www.nps.gov/yose) Official Yosemite National Park Service site with the most comprehensive and current information.
Yosemite Web (www.yosemite.ca.us) Excellent portal to Yosemite-related websites, including online versions of writings by John Muir and others.
Yosemite Park (www.yosemitepark.com) Online home of DNC Parks & Resorts, Yosemite's main concessionaire. Has lots of practical information and a lodging reservations function.

Laundry & Showers
Soap up year-round at Curry Village and seasonally at the Tuolumne Meadows Lodge, White Wolf Lodge and Housekeeping Camp. The latter also has a coin-op laundry.

Money
There is no bank, but the stores in Yosemite Village, Curry Village and Wawowa all have ATMs, as does the Yosemite Lodge at the Falls.

Post
The main post office is in Yosemite Village, but Wawona and the Yosemite Lodge at the Falls also have year-round services. Seasonal branches operate in Curry Village and Tuolumne Meadows. All are closed on Sunday.

Telephone
There are pay phones at every developed location throughout the park. Cell phones generally do not work.

Tourist Information
Extended summer hours may apply.
Big Oak Flat Information Station (Map p360; ☎ 209-379-1899; ☺ 9am-5pm Apr-Oct) Issues wilderness permits.
Tuolumne Meadows Visitor Center (Map p360; ☎ 209-372-0263; ☺ 9am-5pm late spring-early fall)
Tuolumne Meadows Wilderness Center (Map p363; ☺ 8am-5pm, extended hr in Jul & Aug) Issues wilderness permits.

Wawowa Information Station (Map p360; ☎ 209-375-9531; ☺ 8:30am-4:30pm late May-early Oct) Issues wilderness permits.
Yosemite Valley Visitors Center (Map p363; ☎ 209-372-0299; Yosemite Village; ☺ 9am-5pm year-round) The main office with exhibits and free film screenings of *Spirit of Yosemite*.
Yosemite Wilderness Center (☎ 209-372-0740; Yosemite Village; ☺ 8am-5pm May-Sep) Wilderness permits, maps and backcountry advice.

DANGERS & ANNOYANCES
Yosemite is prime black bear habitat. To find out how to protect the bears and yourself from each other, see the boxed text, p66. Mosquitoes are particularly pesky in summer, so stock up on bug spray. And please don't feed those squirrels. They may look cute but they've got a nasty bite.

SIGHTS
Yosemite Valley
Meadow-carpeted Yosemite Valley is 7 miles long, bisected by the rippling Merced River and hemmed in by some of the most spectacular chunks of granite Nature has wrought anywhere on earth. The most famous are, of course, the monumental **El Capitan** (El Cap; 7569ft), one of the world's largest monoliths and a magnet for rock climbers, and **Half Dome** (8842ft), the park's spiritual centerpiece, whose rounded granite pate forms an unmistakable silhouette. You'll have great views of both from **Valley View** on the valley floor, but for the classic photo op head up Hwy 41 to **Tunnel View**. With a little sweat you'll have even better postcard panoramas – sans the crowds – from the **Inspiration Point Trail** (2.6-mile round-trip), which starts at the tunnel.

TOP FIVE STRATEGIES FOR COPING WITH THE CROWDS

- Don't visit in summer
- Park your car and use the free shuttle buses (p371) or rent a bicycle (p371)
- Bring a picnic to avoid waiting in line at stores and busy eateries (p371)
- Hit the most popular sights and trails early in the morning or late afternoon
- Get out in the wild on horseback (p367)

Yosemite's waterfalls mesmerize even the most jaded traveler, especially when the spring runoff turns them into thunderous cataracts. Most are reduced to a mere trickle by late summer. **Yosemite Falls** is considered the tallest in North America, dropping 2425ft in three tiers. A slick new wheel-chair-accessible trail leads to the bottom of this cascade or, if you prefer solitude and different perspectives, you can also clamber up **Yosemite Falls Trail** that puts you atop the falls after a grueling 3.4 miles. No less impressive are nearby **Bridalveil Fall** and others scattered throughout the valley.

Any aspiring Ansel Adams should lug their camera gear along the 1-mile paved trail to **Mirror Lake** early or late in the day to catch the ever-shifting reflection of Half Dome in the still waters. The lake all but dries up by late summer.

South of here, where the Merced River courses around two small islands, lies **Happy Isles**, a popular area for picnics, swimming and strolls. It also marks the start of the John Muir Trail and Mist Trail to several waterfalls and Half Dome. The **Happy Isles Nature Center** (admission free; ✪ May-Sep) features kid-friendly hands-on exhibits.

Places of cultural interest in the valley include the **Yosemite Museum** (☎ 209-372-0200; admission free; ✪ 9am-4:30pm, closed for lunch), which has Miwok and Paiute artifacts, including woven baskets, beaded buckskin dresses and dance capes made from feathers. Renowned

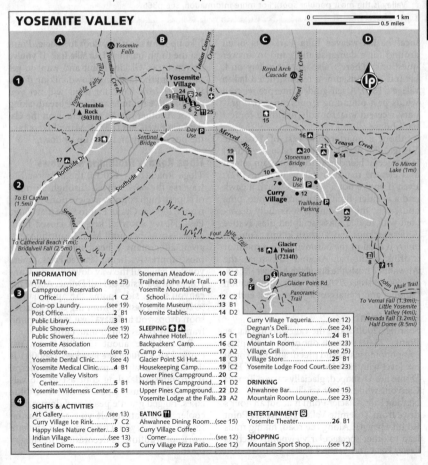

YOSEMITE VALLEY

INFORMATION		Stoneman Meadow............10 C2		Curry Village Taqueria.........(see 12)	
ATM...................................(see 25)		Trailhead John Muir Trail....11 D3		Degnan's Deli......................(see 24)	
Campground Reservation		Yosemite Mountaineering		Degnan's Loft....................24 B1	
Office..................................1 C2		School.............................12 C2		Mountain Room.................(see 23)	
Coin-op Laundry.............(see 19)		Yosemite Museum............13 B1		Village Grill.........................(see 25)	
Post Office...........................2 B1		Yosemite Stables..............14 D2		Village Store....................25 B1	
Public Library.......................3 B1				Yosemite Lodge Food Court..(see 23)	
Public Showers.................(see 19)		**SLEEPING** 🏠 🏕			
Public Showers.................(see 12)		Ahwahnee Hotel................15 C1		**DRINKING**	
Yosemite Association		Backpackers' Camp............16 C2		Ahwahnee Bar..................(see 15)	
Bookstore.........................(see 5)		Camp 4..............................17 A2		Mountain Room Lounge.....(see 23)	
Yosemite Dental Clinic.....(see 4)		Glacier Point Ski Hut.........18 C3			
Yosemite Medical Clinic.........4 B1		Housekeeping Camp.........19 C2		**ENTERTAINMENT** 🎭	
Yosemite Valley Visitors		Lower Pines Campground...20 C2		Yosemite Theater...............26 B1	
Center..................................5 B1		North Pines Campground...21 D2			
Yosemite Wilderness Center..6 B1		Upper Pines Campground...22 D2		**SHOPPING**	
		Yosemite Lodge at the Falls..23 A2		Mountain Sport Shop..........(see 12)	
SIGHTS & ACTIVITIES					
Art Gallery.......................(see 13)		**EATING** 🍴			
Curry Village Ice Rink..........7 C2		Ahwahnee Dining Room.....(see 15)			
Happy Isles Nature Center....8 D3		Curry Village Coffee			
Indian Village..................(see 13)		Corner.............................(see 12)			
Sentinel Dome......................9 C3		Curry Village Pizza Patio....(see 12)			

SIERRA NEVADA

LEGENDARY HALF DOME

According to Native American legend, one of Yosemite Valley's early inhabitants went down from the mountains to Mono Lake, where he wed a Paiute named Tesaiyac. The journey back to the valley was difficult, and by the time they reached what was to become Mirror Lake, Tesaiyac had decided that she wanted to go back down to live with her people at Mono Lake. However, her husband refused to live on such barren, arid land with no oak trees from which to get acorns. With a heart full of despair, Tesaiyac began to run toward Mono Lake, and her husband followed her. When the powerful spirits heard quarreling in Yosemite, they became angry and turned the two into stone: he became North Dome and she became Half Dome. The tears she cried made marks as they ran down her face, thus forming Mirror Lake.

Though its origins are mythical, there's no doubt that Half Dome is Yosemite's most distinctive natural monument. It is 87 million years old and has a 93% vertical grade – the sheerest cliff in North America. Climbers come from around the world to grapple with its legendary north face, but good hikers can reach its summit via a 17-mile round-trip trail from Yosemite Valley. The trail gains 4900ft in elevation and has cable handrails for the last 200yd. The hike *can* be done in one day, but is more enjoyable if you break it up by camping along the way (Little Yosemite Valley is the most popular spot). For more information, see p366.

local basket-weaver Julia Parker is often around for a demonstration and to answer questions. There's also an **art gallery** and, behind the museum, a reconstructed **Indian village** c 1870. A self-guided interpretive trail winds past pounding stones, an acorn granary, a ceremonial roundhouse and a conical bark house.

About a quarter-mile east of Yosemite Village, the **Ahwahnee Hotel** (also see p368) is a graceful blend of rustic mountain retreat and elegant mansion dating back to 1927. Even if you're not a guest, it's worth a gawk and a wander. Built from local granite, pine and cedar, the building is splendidly decorated with leaded glass, sculpted tiles, Native American rugs and Turkish kilims. You can enjoy a meal in the baronial dining room or a drink in the bar. Around Christmas, the Ahwahnee hosts the **Bracebridge Dinner** (☎ 559-253-5604; per person $330), sort of a combination banquet and Renaissance *faire*. Book early.

Glacier Point

Soaring 3200ft above the valley floor, Glacier Point (7214ft) presents one of the park's most eye-popping vistas and practically puts you at eye level with Half Dome. To the left of Half Dome lies U-shaped, glacially carved Tenaya Canyon, while below you'll see Vernal and Nevada Falls. Glacier Point is about an hour's drive from Yosemite Valley via Glacier Point Rd off Hwy 41. Along the road, hiking trails lead to other spectacular viewpoints such as **Dewey Point** and **Sentinel Dome**. You can also

hike up from the valley floor to Glacier Point via the thigh-burning **Four Mile Trail**. If you've driven up to Glacier Point and want to get away from the madding crowd, hiking down the Four Mile Trail for a bit will net you comparative solitude and more breathtaking views. Another way to get here is on the **Glacier Point Hikers' Bus** (p371). Many hikers take the bus one way and hike up or down.

Tioga Road & Tuolumne Meadows

Tioga Road (Hwy 120 E), the only road to traverse the park, travels through 56 miles of superb high country at elevations ranging from 6200ft at Crane Flat to 9945ft at Tioga Pass. Heavy snowfall keeps it closed from about November until May. Beautiful views await after many a bend in the road, the most impressive being **Olmsted Point**, where you can gawp all the way down Tenaya Canyon to the backside of Half Dome. Above the canyon's east side looms the aptly named 9926ft **Clouds Rest**. Continuing on Tioga Rd soon drops you at **Tenaya Lake**, a placid pond framed by pines and granite cliffs.

Beyond here, about 55 miles from Yosemite Valley, **Tuolumne Meadows** (8600ft) is the largest subalpine meadow in the Sierra. It provides a dazzling contrast to the valley, with its lush open fields, clear blue lakes, ragged granite peaks and domes, and cooler temperatures. If you come during July or August, you'll find a painter's palette worth of wildflowers decorating the shaggy meadows.

TOP FIVE SPOTS FOR TOTS

- Raft down the Merced River (p367)
- Meet giants at the Mariposa Grove (below)
- Get snap-happy during a children's photo walk (p371)
- Earn a Junior Ranger badge (p702)
- Learn about local Native Americans at the Yosemite Museum (p363)

Tuolumne is far less crowded than the valley, though the area around the campground, lodge store and visitors center does gets busy, especially on weekends. Some hiking trails, such as the one to Dog Lake, are also well traveled. Remember that the altitude makes breathing a lot harder than in the valley. Nights can get chilly, so pack warm clothes.

The **main meadow** is about 2.5-miles long and lies on the north side of Tioga Rd between Lembert Dome and **Pothole Dome**. The 200ft scramble to the top of the latter – preferably at sunset – gives you great views of the meadow. An interpretive trail leads from the stables to muddy **Soda Springs**, where carbonated water bubbles up in red-tinted pools. The nearby **Parsons Memorial Lodge** has a few displays. Another cabin, McCauley Cabin, is closed to the public.

Hikers and climbers will find a paradise of options around Tuolumne Meadows, which is also the gateway to the High Sierra Camps (p369). Visitors center staff can help you identify the perfect trail.

For nondrivers, the **Tuolumne Meadows Tour & Hikers' Bus** (p371) makes the trip along Tioga Rd once daily in each direction. There's also the free **Tuolumne Meadows Shuttle** (p371), which travels between the Tuolumne Meadows Lodge and Olmsted Point, including a stop at Tenaya Lake.

Wawona

Wawona, about 27 miles south of Yosemite Valley, is the park's historical center, but the main lure really is the **Mariposa Grove of Giant Sequoias**, the biggest and most impressive cluster of big trees in Yosemite. The star of the show – and what everyone comes to see – is the **Grizzly Giant**, a behemoth that sprang to life some 2700 years ago, or about the time

the ancient Greeks held the first Olympic Games. You can't miss it – it's a half-mile walk along a well-worn path starting near the parking lot. Beyond here, crowds begin to thin out a bit, although for more solitude you should arrive early in the morning or after 6pm.

The big attraction in the upper grove is the **Fallen Wawona Tunnel Tree**, the famous drive-through tree that toppled over in 1969. For scenic views, take a 1-mile (round-trip) amble from the fallen tree to **Wawona Point**. Also in the upper grove is the **Mariposa Grove Museum** (usually Sat & Sun) with displays about sequoia ecology. The full hike from the parking lot to the upper grove is about 2.5 miles.

Parking is very limited, so come early or late or take the free shuttle bus from the Wawona Store or the park entrance. The grove can also be explored on a one-hour **guided tour** (adult $16; usually May-Sep) aboard a noisy open-air tram leaving from the parking lot.

In Wawona itself, about 6 miles north of here, wander around the manicured grounds of the elegant **Wawona Hotel** (p368) and the rustic **Pioneer Yosemite History Center** (admission free; 24hr), where some of the park's oldest buildings were relocated. It also features stagecoaches that brought early tourists to Yosemite.

Hetch Hetchy

In the park's northwestern corner, Hetch Hetchy (which is Miwok for 'place of tall grass') gets the least amount of traffic yet sports waterfalls and granite cliffs that rival its famous counterparts in Yosemite Valley. The main difference is that Hetch Hetchy Valley is now filled with water, following a long political and environmental battle in the early 20th century. It's a lovely, quiet spot and well worth the 40-mile drive from Yosemite Valley, especially if you're tired of the avalanche of humanity rolling through that area.

The 8-mile long Hetch Hetchy Reservoir, its placid surface reflecting clouds and cliffs, stretches behind **O'Shaughnessy Dam**, site of a parking lot and trailheads. An easy 5.4-mile (round-trip) trail leads to the spectacular **Tueeulala** (*twee*-lala) and **Wapama Falls**, which each plummet more than 1000ft over fractured granite walls on the north shore of the reservoir. **Hetch Hetchy Dome** rises up in the distance. This hike is best in spring, when

SIERRA NEVADA

TOP FIVE VIEWS

- Glacier Point (p364)
- Olmsted Point (p364)
- O'Shaughnessy Dam (p365)
- Pothole Dome (p365)
- Tunnel View (p362)

temperatures are moderate and wildflowers poke out everywhere. Bring bug spray and keep an eye out for rattlesnakes, especially in summer.

There are no visitors services at Hetch Hetchy. The road is only open during daylight hours; specifics are posted at the Evergreen Rd turnoff. After hours the gate is locked in keeping with regulations set forth by the Department of Homeland Security, which considers O'Shaughnessy Dam a terrorist target.

ACTIVITIES
Hiking

With over 800 miles of **hiking** trails, Yosemite is a delight for trekkers of all abilities. You can take an easy half-mile stroll on the valley floor; venture out all day on a quest for viewpoints, waterfalls and lakes or go wilderness camping in the remote outer reaches of the backcountry.

Some of the park's most popular hikes start right in Yosemite Valley, including, the most famous of all, to the top of **Half Dome** (17-mile round-trip). It follows a section of the John Muir Trail and is strenuous, difficult and best tackled in two days with an overnight in Little Yosemite Valley. Reaching the top can only be done after rangers have installed fixed cables. Depending on snow conditions, this may occur as early as late May or as late as July. Cables usually come down in mid-October. The less ambitious or physically fit will still have a ball following the same trail as far as **Vernal Fall** (2.6-mile round-trip), the top of **Nevada Fall** (6.5-mile round-trip) or idyllic **Little Yosemite Valley** (8-mile round-trip). The **Four Mile Trail** to Glacier Point, which is actually 9.2-mile round-trip, is a strenuous but satisfying climb to a glorious viewpoint (also see p364).

If you've got the kids in tow, nice and easy destinations include **Mirror Lake** (2-mile

round-trip, 4.5 miles via the Tenaya Canyon Loop) in the valley as well as the trails meandering beneath the big trees of the **Mariposa Grove** in Wawona. Also in the Wawona area is one of the park's prettiest (and often overlooked) hikes to **Chilnualna Falls** (8.6-mile round-trip). Best done between April and June, it follows a cascading creek to the top of the falls, starting gently, then hitting you with some grinding switchbacks before sort of leveling out again.

The highest concentration of hikes lies in the high country of Tuolumne Meadows, which is only open in summer. A popular choice here is the hike to **Dog Lake** (2.8-mile round-trip), but it gets busy. You can also trek along a relatively flat part of the John Muir Trail into lovely **Lyell Canyon** (17.6-mile round-trip if going all the way), following the Lyell Fork of the Tuolumne River.

Additional hiking options are mentioned throughout this chapter.

Backpacking

Trekking into Yosemite's cosmic wilderness quickly gets you away from the hubbub. Start by identifying a route that matches your schedule, skill and fitness level. The next step is to secure a wilderness permit, which is free but mandatory for overnight trips. To prevent tent cities sprouting in the woods, a quota system limits the number of people leaving from each trailhead each day. For trips between mid-May and mid-September around 60% of the quota may be reserved for a $5 fee by phone (☎ 209-372-0740) or online (www.nps.gov/yose/wilderness/permits.htm) from 24 weeks to two days before your trip. The remainder are distributed (on a first-come, first-served basis no earlier than 24 hours before your planned hike) at the following places (see p362 for details of where to collect your permits): Yosemite Valley Wilderness Center, Tuolumne Meadows Wilderness Center, the information stations at Wawona and Big Oak Flat and the Hetch Hetchy Entrance. Reservations are not available from October to April, but you'll still need to get a permit.

At night you must be sure to store all scented items in bear-resistant containers, which may be rented for $5 per trip at the wilderness centers, visitors centers and some stores throughout the park. Check *Yosemite Today* for details.

If you don't have a decent backpack and tent, you can rent these and other equipment at the **Yosemite Mountaineering School** (☎ 209-372-8344; www.yosemitemountaineering.com; Curry Village Mountain Sport Shop; trips incl food & equipment per day per person 1/2/3/4 or more people $256/160/138/100; ☽ 8:30am-5pm). The school also offers two-day Learn to Backpack trips for novices and three- and four-day guided backpacking trips, which are great for inexperienced and solo travelers. The cost depends on the number of people in your group. In summer, the school operates a branch from Tuolumne Meadows.

Rock Climbing

With its sheer spires, polished domes and soaring monoliths, Yosemite is rock-climbing nirvana. The main climbing season runs from April to October. Most climbers, including some legendary stars, stay at Camp 4 (p370) near El Cap, especially in spring and fall. In summer, another base camp springs up at Tuolumne Meadows Campground (p370). Climbers looking for partners post notices on bulletin boards at either campground.

Yosemite Mountaineering School offers top-flight instruction for novice to advanced rock hounds, plus guided climbs and equipment rental. All-day beginners classes are $117 per person if the group size is at least three people, more if there are fewer.

Climbers consider any of the books written by Don Reid their bibles, especially the classic *Yosemite Free Climbs*.

The meadow across from El Capitan and the northeastern end of Tenaya Lake (off Tioga Rd) are good for watching climbers dangle from granite (binoculars are needed for a really good view). Look for the haul bags first – they're bigger, more colorful and move around more than the climbers, making them easier to spot.

Cycling

Mountain-biking is a no-no within the park, but biking along the 12 miles of paved trails is a popular and environment-friendly way explores the valley. See p371 for rental information.

Horseback Riding

Yosemite Stables (☎ in Tuolumne Meadows 209-372-8427, in Wawona 209-375-6502, in Yosemite Valley 209-372-8348; trips 2hr/half-/full-day $51/67/94) runs guided

> **TOP FIVE THINGS TO DO IN WINTER**
>
> ■ Ice-skating at Curry Village (p368)
>
> ■ Feeling like royalty at the Bracebridge Dinner (p364) in the Ahwahnee Hotel
>
> ■ Snowshoeing among the giants of Mariposa Grove (p365)
>
> ■ Taking an overnight cross-country skiing trip to Glacier Point Lodge (p368)
>
> ■ Toasting s'mores in the Mountain Room Lounge (p371)

trips to such scenic locales as Mirror Lake, the Chilnualna Falls and the Mariposa Grove of Giant Sequoias from three bases. The season runs from May to October, although this varies slightly by location. No experience is needed for the two-hour and half-day rides, but reservations are advised, especially at the Yosemite Valley stables.

Rafting

From around late May to July, floating the Merced River from Stoneman Meadow, near Curry Village, to Sentinel Bridge is a leisurely way to soak up Yosemite Valley views. **Raft rentals** (☎ 209-372-8341; per person $13.50) for the 3-mile trip are available at Curry Village and include equipment and a tram ride back to the rental kiosk. Rafting above Yosemite Stables or below Cathedral Beach Picnic Area is forbidden.

River rats are also attracted to the fierce **Tuolumne River**, a classic Class IV run that plunges and thunders through boulder gardens and cascades. Both Oars and Zephyr Whitewater Expeditions (p372) run a variety of trips.

Winter Sports

As the days shorten, the valley becomes a quiet, frosty world of snow-draped evergreens, ice-coated lakes and vivid vistas of gleaming white mountains sparkling against blue skies. Winter tends to arrive in full force by mid-November and whimper out in early April. Most of the action converges on the family-friendly **Badger Pass Ski Area** (Map p360; ☎ 209-372-1000; www.badgerpass.com; lift ticket adult/child $35/18), one of California's oldest ski resorts, whose gentle slopes are perfect for families and beginning skiers and

SIERRA NEVADA

snowboarders. It's about 22 miles from the valley on Glacier Point Rd. There are five chairlifts, 800 vertical feet and 10 runs, a full-service lodge, equipment rental (about $24 for a full set of gear) and the excellent **Yosemite Ski School** (☎ 209-372-8430) where generations of novices have learned how to get down a hill safely (lessons from $59).

Cross-country skiers can explore 350 miles of skiable trails and roads, including 90 miles of marked trails and 25 miles of machine-groomed track near Badger Pass. The scenic but grueling trail to Glacier Point – 21-mile round-trip – also starts from here. More trails are at Crane Flat and the Mariposa Grove. The nongroomed trails can also be explored with snowshoes.

The **Badger Pass Cross-Country Center & Ski School** (☎ 209-372-8444) offers beginners' packages ($31), guided tours (from $42) and equipment rentals ($17). The center also runs overnight trips to **Glacier Point Ski Hut** (Map p363) a rustic stone and log cabin. Rates, including meals, are $160/192 midweek/weekend for one night or $240/288 for two nights.

Another hut, the **Ostrander Ski Hut** (Map p360; ☎ 209-372-0740; www.ostranderhut.com), on Ostrander Lake, is operated by the Yosemite Association. It is staffed all winter and open to backcountry skiers and snowshoers for $20 per person, per night. The 10-mile trip (one way) requires experience and a high fitness level. The website has details.

One most delightful winter activity is taking a spin on Curry Village's **open-air ice rink** (Map p363; ☎ 209-372-8341; per session $6.50, rental skates $3.25; ☽ Nov-Mar) where you'll be skating under the watchful eye of Half Dome.

A free shuttle bus connects the valley and Badger Pass. Roads in the valley are plowed, and Hwys 41, 120 and 140 are usually kept open, conditions permitting. The Tioga Rd (Hwy 120 E), though, closes with the first snowfall. Be sure to bring snow chains with you, as prices for them double once you hit the foothills.

TOURS

Five of the six tours are in big tour buses and make few stops. Still, first-timers might appreciate the two-hour **Valley Floor Tour** (per person $22; ☽ year-round) which covers all the highlights. For other tour options stop at the tour and activity desks at Yosemite Lodge, Curry

Village or Yosemite Village, call ☎ 209-372-1240 or check www.yosemitepark.com.

The Yosemite Mountaineering School (p367) offers guided hikes and cross-country ski trips.

SLEEPING
Cabins & Lodges

All noncamping reservations within the park are handled by **DNC Parks & Resorts** (☎ 559-253-5635; www.yosemitepark.com) and can be made up to 366 days in advance; they are absolutely critical from May to early September. Rates – and demand – drop from October to April.

Yosemite Lodge at the Falls (Map p363; Yosemite Valley; r $113-161; 🖥 🐾) This multibuilding complex gets a thumbs up for its centrality, wide range of eateries, lively bar, big pool and other handy amenities. Rooms have been spruced up but are still fairly generic; the nicest are the upstairs units with beamed ceilings and Native American touches. All have cable TV, a telephone and, mostly, great panoramas unfolding from your patio or balcony.

Curry Village (Map p363; Yosemite Valley; canvas cabins $70, cabins with/without bathroom $108/85, r $113; 🐾) Founded in 1899 as a summer camp, Curry has hundreds of units squished tightly together beneath towering evergreens. The canvas cabins are basically glorified tents, so for more comfort and privacy get one of the cozy wood cabins, which were recently treated to new bedspreads, drapes and vintage posters. There are also 18 attractive motel-style rooms in the Stoneman House, including a loft suite sleeping up to six.

Ahwahnee Hotel (Map p363; Yosemite Valley; r $360; 🐾) The rich, royal and renowned regularly reside at this historic property. Turkish kilims line the hallways leading to sumptuous rooms with beautiful views and all the trappings, although we wish more of them had balconies. If you can't afford the price tag, soak up the ambience during afternoon tea, a drink in the bar or a gourmet meal.

Wawona Hotel (Map p360; Wawona; r with/without bathroom $170/113; ☽ mid-Mar–Nov & Dec holidays; ✗ 🐾) Filled with ghosts and character, this genteel property is a Victorian-era throwback with wide wraparound porches and manicured lawns. Repro antiques, original clawfoot tubs but no TV or telephones characterize the 104 rooms in eight white buildings, the oldest dating to 1876. About half share bathrooms.

HIGH SIERRA CAMPS

In the backcountry near Tuolumne Meadows, the exceptionally popular High Sierra Camps provide shelter and sustenance to hikers who'd rather not carry food or a tent. The camps – called Vogelsang, Merced Lake, Sunrise, May Lake and Glen Aulin – are set 6 miles to 10 miles apart along a loop trail. They consist of dormitory-style canvas tent cabins with beds, blankets or comforters, plus showers and a central dining tent. Guests bring their own sheets and towels. The rate is $126 per adult, per night, including breakfast and dinner. Organized hiking or saddle trips led by ranger naturalists are also available (from $720).

A short season (roughly late June to September) and high demand require a lottery for reservations. Applications may be requested between September 1 and November 20 (☎ 559-253-5676; www.yosemitepark.com) and must be submitted between October 15 and November 30 (dates may change). The lottery is in mid-December. If you don't have a reservation, call ☎ 559-253-5674 to check for cancellations.

Housekeeping Camp (Map p363; Yosemite Valley; units $67; Apr-Oct) This cluster of 266 cabins, each walled-in by concrete on three sides and lidded by a canvas roof, is crammed and noisy but the setting along the Merced River has its merits. Each unit sleeps up to four and has electricity, light, a table and chairs and a covered patio with picnic tables.

Tuolumne Meadows Lodge (Map p360; Tioga Rd; tent cabins $75; mid-Jun–mid-Sep) In the high country, about 55 miles from the valley, this option attracts hikers to its 69 canvas tent cabins with four beds, a wood-burning stove and candles (no electricity). It's much less crowded than Housekeeping Camp. Breakfast and dinner are available.

White Wolf Lodge (Map p360; Tioga Rd; tent cabins $71; cabin with bathroom $105; mid-Jun–mid-Sep) Also in the high country, about 33 miles from the valley, this is also primarily a tent-cabin setup, although those wanting a bit more comfort should try snagging one of the four wooden cabins with private bathroom. The rustic dining room makes breakfast and dinner.

Evergreen Lodge (☎ 209-379-2606, 800-935-6343; www.evergreenlodge.com; 33160 Evergreen Rd; cabins $80-230; Apr-Oct) While technically not inside the park, the woodsy Evergreen Lodge, near the Hetch Hetchy Entrance about 7 miles north of Hwy 120, is worth mentioning. Rustic cabins have private porches but no phones or TV. For entertainment, you can swap tales with fellow guests in the lounge, restaurant or during staff-led outdoor activities, many of them family-oriented.

Camping

Competition for campsites is fierce from May to September, when arriving without

a reservation and hoping for the best is tantamount to getting someone to pack your Barcalounger up Half Dome. Even first-come, first-served campgrounds tend to fill by noon, especially on weekends and around holidays. **Reservations** (☎ 301-722-1257, 800-436-7275; http://reservations.nps.gov) are accepted up to five months in advance, beginning the 15th of each month.

Without a booking, your only chance is to proceed to one of four campground reservation offices, preferably before they open at 8am, put your name on a waiting list and hope for a cancellation or early departure. Return when the ranger tells you (usually 3pm) and if you hear your name, consider yourself one lucky devil. There are offices in Yosemite Valley, Wawona, the Big Oak Flat Entrance and Tuolumne Meadows. The latter three are only open seasonally.

All campgrounds have flush toilets, except for Tamarack Flat, Yosemite Creek and Porcupine Flat, which have vault toilets and no potable water. Those at higher elevations get chilly at night, even in summer, so pack accordingly. The Yosemite Mountaineering School (p367) rents camping gear.

If you hold a wilderness permit, you may spend the nights before and after your trip in the backpacker campgrounds at Tuolumne Meadows, Hetch Hetchy and behind North Pines in Yosemite Valley. The cost is $5 per person, per night and reservations are not necessary.

Opening dates for seasonal campgrounds vary slightly each year.

Bridalveil Creek (Map p360; Glacier Point Rd; sites $12; Jul–early Sep) Quieter than the valley campgrounds with 110 sites at 7200ft.

Camp 4 (Map p363; Yosemite Valley; sites $5; year-round) Walk-in campground at 4000ft popular with climbers; price is per person and sites must be shared.

Crane Flat (Map p360; Big Oak Flat Rd; sites $18; Jun-Sep) Large family campground, at 6192 ft, with 166 sites; reservations required.

Hodgdon Meadow (Map p360; Big Oak Flat Rd; sites $12-18; year-round) Utilitarian and crowded 105-site campground at 4872ft; reservations required May to September.

Lower Pines (Map p363; Yosemite Valley; sites $18; Mar-Oct) Crammed and noisy with 60 sites at 4000ft; reservations required.

North Pines (Map p363; Yosemite Valley; sites $18; Apr-Sep) A bit off the beaten path (4000ft) with 81 sites near Mirror Lake; reservations required.

Porcupine Flat (Map p360; Tioga Rd; sites $8; Jul-Sep) Primitive 52-site area, at 8100ft, near the road.

Tamarack Flat (Map p360; Tioga Rd; sites $8; Jun-early Sep) Quiet, secluded, primitive at 6315ft; the 52 sites are a rough 3-mile drive off Tioga Rd.

Tuolumne Meadows (Map p360; Tioga Rd; sites $18; Jul-Sep) Biggest campground in the park (8600ft) with 304 fairly well-spaced sites.

Upper Pines (Map p363; Yosemite Valley; sites $18; year-round) Busy, busy, busy – and big (238 sites, 4000ft); reservations required.

Wawona (Map p360; Wawona; sites $12-18; year-round) Idyllic riverside setting at 4000ft with 93 spaces; reservations required May to September.

White Wolf (Map p360; Tioga Rd; sites $12; Jul-early Sep) Attractive setting at 8000ft, but the 74 sites are fairly boxed in.

Yosemite Creek (Map p360; Tioga Rd; sites $8; Jul-early Sep) Most secluded and quiet campground (7659ft), reached via a rough 4.5-mile road.

EATING

Eating options are plentiful in Yosemite Park – pizza to filet mignon – even if few would get a nod of approval from cardiologists. Hours vary seasonally and some close down in winter.

Restaurants

Mountain Room (☎ 209-372-1274; Yosemite Lodge; mains $16-24; dinner year-round) The chefs at the lodge's casual-elegant dining room produce some of the best meals in the park, but your sesame-encrusted *ahi* (tuna) or filet mignon will likely be competing for your attention with the stunning views of Yosemite Falls. Reservations recommended.

Ahwahnee Dining Room (☎ 209-372-1489; Ahwahnee Hotel; mains breakfast & lunch $10-15, dinner $24-35; year-round) The formal ambience (mind

your manners) may not be for everybody, but few would not be awed by the sumptuous decor, soaring beamed ceiling and palatial chandeliers. The menu is constantly in flux, but most dishes have perfect pitch and are beautifully presented. There's a dress code at dinner, but otherwise shorts and sneakers are OK. Sunday brunch ($32, 7am to 3pm) is amazing.

Wawona Hotel Dining Room (Wawona Hotel; breakfast & lunch $5-10, dinner $14-25; mid-Mar–Nov & Dec holidays) This venerable dining room is a great spot for a repast. Breakfast might be French toast, lunch a fresh sandwich or salad, but it's dinnertime when the chef's talents truly shine. The flatiron steak is a signature dish. On summer Saturdays, the delicious lawn barbecue is the place to be. For snacks, head to the golf shop.

Degnan's Loft (Yosemite Village; pizza $5-20; Apr-Oct) At this convivial place, with high-beamed ceilings and a fireplace, you can mingle with fresh-off-the-trail hikers kicking back over beer and pizza. Salads, pasta and appetizers are other satisfying hunger weapons.

Curry Village Dining Pavilion (Curry Village; breakfast $10, dinner $12; Apr-Nov) The all-you-can-eat breakfast and dinner buffets are great for families, gluttons and the undecided, although the cafeteria-style setting has all the charm of a train-station waiting room.

Quick Eats

Yosemite Lodge Food Court (Yosemite Lodge at the Falls; mains under $10; year-round) This self-service restaurant serves breakfast, lunch and dinner. Make your selection at several tummy-filling stations serving pastas, burgers, hot sandwiches and other fare that holds up well under heat lamps, then proceed to the cashier and find a table inside or on the patio.

Curry Village Pizza Patio (Curry Village; pizza $6-14; year-round) Enjoy views of Half Dome (OK, through the foliage) and tasty pizza at this buzzing eatery that turns into a chatty après-hike hangout in the late afternoon. Try one of its bird bath–sized margaritas – if you dare.

Other refueling stops:

Degnan's Deli (Yosemite Village; sandwiches $6) Made-to-order sandwiches and snack foods.

Village Grill (Yosemite Village; items $4-8; Apr-Oct) Burgers and fries alfresco.

Curry Village Taqueria (snacks $2.50-6; spring-fall) Shares a deck with the Pizza Patio.

Curry Village Coffee Corner (☾ midspring-fall) For that coffee jolt or sugar fix.

Groceries

Bringing in or buying your own food in the park saves money but can be a hassle because you must remove it all from your car (or backpack or bicycle) and store it overnight in a bear box or canister. The Village Store in Yosemite Village has the best selection, while stores at Curry Village, Wawona, Tuolumne Meadows, Housekeeping Camp and the Yosemite Lodge are more limited.

DRINKING

Yosemite is not exactly nightlife central, but there are some nice spots to relax with a cabernet, cocktail or cold beer. Outside the park, the Yosemite Bug Rustic Mountain Resort (p373) and the Evergreen Lodge (p373) both have lively lounges.

Mountain Room Lounge (Yosemite Lodge) Catch up on the latest sports news while knocking back draft brews at this large bar. A big hit are the s'mores kits: graham crackers, chocolate squares, and marshmallows that you roast in the open-pit fireplace before mashing everything into a delicious 'sandwich.'

Ahwahnee Bar (Ahwahnee Hotel) A drink at this cozy bar, complete with pianist, is a great way to sample this august property without dipping too deep into your pockets. Appetizers and light meals provide sustenance ($8 to $24).

ENTERTAINMENT

Yosemite Theater (Yosemite Village, West Auditorium; adult/child $8/4) The fascinating life and philosophy of John Muir is brought to the stage by actor Lee Stetson several times weekly. His wife, Connie, does a humorous yet poignant program portraying a 19th-century pioneer woman. There are also special children's shows and the occasional guest performer.

Other activities scheduled year-round include campfire programs, children's photo walks, twilight strolls, night-sky watching, ranger talks and slide shows while the tavern at the Evergreen Lodge (p373) has live bands some nights. *Yosemite Today* has full details.

GETTING THERE & AWAY

Yosemite is accessible year-round from the west (via Hwys 120 W and 140) and south

(Hwy 41) and in summer also from the east (via Hwy 120 E). Roads are plowed in winter but snow chains may be required at any time.

Yosemite is one of the few national parks that can be reached by public transportation relatively easily. Greyhound buses and Amtrak trains serve Merced west of the park, where they are met by buses operated by **Yosemite Area Regional Transportation System** (Yarts; ☎ 209-388-9589, 877-989-2787; www.yarts.com). Buses travel to Yosemite Valley along Hwy 140 several times daily year-round stopping along the way. In summer, another Yarts route runs from Mammoth Lakes (p396) along Hwy 120 East via the Tioga Pass. Tickets are $20 one-way from either Merced or Mammoth Lakes, less if boarding in between. They include the park entrance fee, making them a real bargain.

GETTING AROUND
Bicycle

Bicycling is ideal for beating traffic in Yosemite Valley. You can rent one (per hour/day $7.50/24.50) at the Yosemite Lodge at the Falls and Curry Village.

Bus

The free, air-conditioned Yosemite Valley Shuttle Bus is a comfortable and comparatively efficient way of traveling around the park. Buses operate year-round at frequent intervals and stop at 21 numbered locations, including parking lots, campgrounds, trailheads and lodges. For a route map, see *Yosemite Today.*

Free buses also operate between Wawona and the Mariposa Grove (spring to fall), Yosemite Valley and Badger Pass (winter only), and the Tuolumne Meadows Shuttle between Tuolumne Lodge and Olmsted Point in Tuolumne Meadows (usually mid-June to early September).

Two fee-based hikers' buses also travel from Yosemite Valley. For trailheads along the Tioga Rd, catch the **Tuolumne Meadows Tour & Hikers' Bus** (☎ 209-372-1240; ☾ Jul-early Sep), which runs once daily in each direction. Fares depend on distance traveled; the trip to Tuolumne Meadows costs $14.50/23 one way/round-trip. The **Glacier Point Hikers' Bus** (☎ 209-372-1240; one-way/return $20/32.50; ☾ mid-May–Oct) is good for hikers as well as for people reluctant to drive up the long, windy road themselves. Reservations are required.

Car

The speed limit is 45mph, except in Yosemite Valley, where it drops to 35mph. Truth is, traffic will make you slow down anyway. Glacier Point Rd and Tioga Rd are closed in winter.

YOSEMITE GATEWAYS
Fish Camp

Fish Camp, just south of the park on Hwy 41, is not much of a town but it does have some good lodging options as well as the endearing **Sugar Pine Railroad** (☎ 559-683-7273; www.ymsprr.com; rides adult/child $15/7.50; ☺ Mar-Oct), a historical steam train that chugs through the woods on a 4-mile loop.

At the friendly **Narrow Gauge Inn** (☎ 559-683-7720, 888-644-9050; www.narrowgaugeinn.com; 48571 Hwy 41, Fish Camp; r incl breakfast Nov-Mar $80-110, Apr-Oct $130-195; ✕ 🐾), cedar-shingled facades conceal 26 good-sized rooms, each with balcony or patio and radiating warmth and comfort. The restaurant (mains $16 to $36) is open for dinner Wednesday to Sunday, April to October, and serves inspired Continental cuisine. It's among the best around.

The hulking, modern, full-service **Tenaya Lodge** (☎ 559-683-6555, 800-635-5807; 1122 Hwy 41; r $100-190, ste $225-260; ✕ 🏖 🖳 🐾) sports luxury ski lodge looks and amenities but can't quite shake the sterile, corporate feel that comes from also having a big convention center. The two restaurants get top marks, though (mains $11 to $32).

The USFS **Summerdale Campground** (☎ 877-444-6677; sites $17-19; ☺ May-Sep) has pretty sites along Big Creek.

Oakhurst

At the junction of Hwys 41 and 49, about 15 miles south of the park entrance, Oakhurst functions primarily as a service town. This is your last chance to stock up on reasonably priced groceries, camping supplies, gasoline and bug spray. Among the chain motels, the **Shilo Inn** (☎ 559-683-3555; 40644 Hwy 41; r $60-190; 🏖 🐾) and **Best Western Yosemite Gateway Inn** (☎ 559-683-2378; 40530 Hwy 41; r $48-104; 🏖 🐾) are good choices.

For something a little more special, make a detour along a bucolic country road to these immaculate adobe-and-stone cottages

of **Homestead** (☎ 559-683-0495, 800-483-0495; www .homesteadcottages.com; r $115-400; ✕ 🐾). Each has its own eclectic decor and all the creature comforts, but no direct telephones. Call for directions.

Merced River Canyon

The approach to Yosemite via Hwy 140 is one of the most scenic, especially the section that meanders through Merced River Canyon. The springtime runoff makes this a spectacular spot for **river rafting** with many miles of class III and IV rapids. Outfitters include **Zephyr Whitewater Expeditions** (☎ 209-532-6249, 800-431-3636; www.zrafting.com) and **Oars** (☎ 800-346-6277; www.oars.com). Half-day trips cost about $100.

Mariposa

About halfway between Merced and Yosemite Valley, at the junction of Hwy 140/149, Mariposa is the largest and most interesting town near the park. Established as a mining and railroad town during the Gold Rush, it has the oldest courthouse in continuous use (since 1854) west of the Mississippi and the excellent **California State Mining & Mineral Museum** (☎ 209-742-7625; admission $3; ☺ 10am-4pm Wed-Mon Oct-Apr, 10am-6pm daily Mar-Sep), about 2 miles south of downtown. The undisputed highlight from its collection of over 13,000 minerals is the Fricot Nugget, which weighs in at nearly 13lb and is the largest crystallized gold specimen from the California Gold Rush era. Other exhibits illustrate the tough process of hard-rock mining.

Pick up information about the area and Yosemite at the **Mariposa County Chamber of Commerce** (☎ 209-966-2456; www.mariposa.org; 5158 Hwy 41; ☺ 7am-8pm Mon-Sat, 8am-5pm Sun), which has friendly staff, racks of brochures and awesome hours. It's at the north junction of Hwys 140 and 49.

The charming **River Rock Inn** (☎ 209-966-5793, 800-627-8439; www.riverrockinn.com; 4993 7th St, off Hwy 140; r incl breakfast $60-90; 🏖 ✕) should be a case study on how to turn a nondescript motel into an oasis of charm. Purple doors lead to snug rooms with hand-picked furniture and nice accessories. Rates include breakfast at the next-door Euro-style deli, which also makes great fresh sandwiches and salads.

More conventional downtown lodging options include the friendly **Mariposa Lodge** (☎ 209-966-3607, 800-966-8819; 5052 Hwy 140; r $48-

112; ⊠ ⊠), which has spacious rooms and wi-fi. Tucked into the surrounding hills are numerous B&Bs with rooms starting at $70. Check www.yosemitebnbs.com or stop by the chamber for information.

The best restaurant in town is **Savoury's** (☎ 209-966-7677; 5027 Hwy 140; mains $11-20), whose food and walled-in courtyard will mentally transport you to Italy.

Midpines

Tucked into a leafy dell about 25 miles outside the park, the folksy **Yosemite Bug Rustic Mountain Resort** (☎ 209-966-6666, 866-826-7108; www.yosemitebug.com; dm $18, tent cabins $30-50, r $55-115, cabins with shared bathroom $40-70; ⊠ ⊡ ⊡) feels more like a convivial mountain retreat than a hostel. At night, a United Nations of friendly folks of all ages share stories, music and inexpensive meals in the woodsy café-lounge before retreating to whatever bed their money can buy: a dorm bunk, a tent cabin, a private room with shared facilities or a uniquely decorated cabin with private bathroom (the website has pictures). Dorm dwellers have access to a communal kitchen. A wooden outdoor hot tub and a health spa were in the planning stages during our recent visit. The Yarts bus stops right outside.

Briceburg

Some 20 miles outside the park, right where the Merced River meets Hwy 140, Briceburg consists of a **visitors center** (☎ 209-379-9414; ⊙ 1-6pm Fri, 9am-6pm Sat & Sun May-early Sep) and three primitive first-arrival campgrounds ($10) with a to-die-for location right on the river. They're between 2 miles and 3 miles from Hwy 140 via a narrow dirt road.

El Portal

Right outside the Arch Rock Entrance, El Portal makes a very convenient Yosemite base.

The rambling, modern **Yosemite View Lodge** (☎ 209-379-2681, 800-321-5261; www.yosemiteresorts.us; 11156 Hwy 140; r Apr-Oct $140-440, Nov-Mar $85-255; ⊠ ⊡ ⊠) is more like a small village with its 335 rooms spread over several buildings, two restaurants, one bar, four pools, five spas, an ATM and other conveniences. All rooms have kitchenettes, and the nicest overlook the river.

Carved bears welcome you to **Cedar Lodge** (☎ 209-379-2612, 800-321-5261; www.yosemite-motels

.com; 9966 Hwy 40; r $96-150; ⊠ ⊡ ⊠) but that's where the cute factor ends. The 209 rooms wear that generic patina nicely and come in all kinds of sizes and configurations. Some are more amenity-laden than others, so ask if you really need that microwave.

Groveland

From the Big Oak Flat Entrance, it's 22 miles to Groveland, an adorable town with restored Gold Rush–era buildings.

New owners have poured their hearts, imagination and cash into updating the 10 rooms at the 1918 **Hotel Charlotte** (☎ 209-962-7872, 800-961-7799; www.hotelcharlotte.com; 18736 Hwy 120; r $96-120; ⊠ ⊠ ⊡) while keeping the vintage flair alive. The cute café (mains $9 to $20) does creative things with chicken. Free wi-fi, too.

Across the street from the Hotel Charlotte, the historic **Groveland Hotel** (☎ 209-962-4000, 800-273-3314; www.groveland.com; 18767 Main St; r incl breakfast $135-275; ⊠) dates from 1850 and now houses a saloon with Gold Rush flair, an upscale restaurant (mains $10 to $29) and 17 bright, lovingly decorated rooms accessed from wraparound verandas.

SEQUOIA & KINGS CANYON NATIONAL PARKS

At this celebrated twin park you'll find yourself in the company of giants. Giant sequoias, that is, which grow bigger, stronger and more abundantly here than anywhere else in the world. There are giant mountains, too, most famously Mt Whitney, at 14,497ft, the tallest in the lower 48 states. And finally there's giant Kings Canyon, gored out of granite by the powerful Kings River. These incredible creations of nature are what lure most of the 1.5 million annual visitors here. But those seeking quiet and solitude need only hit the trail to quickly find themselves in breathtaking wilderness.

In 1890 Sequoia became the second national park in the USA (after Yellowstone). A few days later, the 4 sq miles around Grant Grove were declared Grant Grove National Park and, in 1940, absorbed into the newly created Kings Canyon National Park. In

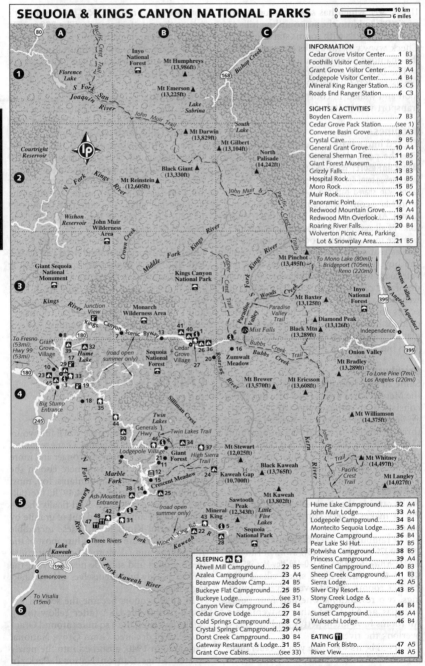

SEQUOIA & KINGS CANYON NATIONAL PARKS

0 ─────── 10 km
0 ─────── 6 miles

SIERRA NEVADA

INFORMATION
Cedar Grove Visitor Center	**1** B3
Foothills Visitor Center	**2** B5
Grant Grove Visitor Center	**3** A4
Lodgepole Visitor Center	**4** B4
Mineral King Ranger Station	**5** C5
Roads End Ranger Station	**6** C3

SIGHTS & ACTIVITIES
Boyden Cavern	**7** B3
Cedar Grove Pack Station	(see 1)
Converse Basin Grove	**8** A3
Crystal Cave	**9** B5
General Grant Grove	**10** A4
General Sherman Tree	**11** B5
Giant Forest Museum	**12** B5
Grizzly Falls	**13** B3
Hospital Rock	**14** B5
Moro Rock	**15** B5
Muir Rock	**16** C4
Panoramic Point	**17** A4
Redwood Mountain Grove	**18** A4
Redwood Mtn Overlook	**19** A4
Roaring River Falls	**20** B4
Wolverton Picnic Area, Parking Lot & Snowplay Area	**21** B5

SLEEPING
Atwell Mill Campground	**22** B5
Azalea Campground	**23** A4
Bearpaw Meadow Camp	**24** B5
Buckeye Flat Campground	**25** B5
Buckeye Lodge	(see 31)
Canyon View Campground	**26** B4
Cedar Grove Lodge	**27** B4
Cold Springs Campground	**28** C5
Crystal Springs Campground	**29** A4
Dorst Creek Campground	**30** B4
Gateway Restaurant & Lodge	**31** B5
Grant Cove Cabins	(see 33)
Hume Lake Campground	**32** A4
John Muir Lodge	**33** A4
Lodgepole Campground	**34** B4
Montecito Sequoia Lodge	**35** A4
Moraine Campground	**36** B4
Pear Lake Ski Hut	**37** B5
Potwisha Campground	**38** B5
Princess Campground	**39** A4
Sentinel Campground	**40** B4
Sheep Creek Campground	**41** B3
Sierra Lodge	**42** A5
Silver City Resort	**43** B5
Stony Creek Lodge & Campground	**44** B4
Sunset Campground	**45** A4
Wuksachi Lodge	**46** B4

EATING
Main Fork Bistro	**47** A5
River View	**48** A5

2000, to protect additional sequoia groves, vast tracts of land in the surrounding national forest became the Giant Sequoia National Monument. This status is currently under threat as the Bush administration is keen to open up the area to commercial logging. Environmental groups vehemently oppose this plan, as does the California government, which in January 2005 filed a lawsuit to block it. Stay tuned.

Information
The two parks, although distinct, are operated as one unit with a single admission (valid for seven consecutive days) of $10 per carload or $5 for individuals arriving on bicycle or foot. For 24-hour recorded information, call ☎ 559-565-3341 or visit www .nps.gov/seki, the parks' comprehensive website. At either entrance station, you'll receive an NPS map, an illustrated booklet and a useful newspaper with phone numbers, hours and descriptions of all visitor facilities, including those in the surrounding national forests and the Giant Sequoia National Monument.

Gas is available at Hume Lake and Stony Creek Lodge, both on forest land. Most cell phones do not work in this area.

Wilderness Permits
With 800 miles of marked trails, the parks are a backpacker's dream. Cedar Grove and Mineral King offer the best backcountry access. Trails are usually open by mid-May.

For overnight backcountry trips you'll need a wilderness permit ($15), which is subject to a quota system. About 75% of spaces can be reserved, the rest are available in person on a first-come, first-served basis. Reservations can be made from March 1 until three weeks before your trip. For details see www.nps.gov/seki/bcinfo.htm.

Topo maps and hiking guides are available at all ranger stations and visitors centers. For trail conditions and backcountry information call ☎ 559-565-3341. On some trails you need to store your food in bearproof canisters, which may be rented for a few dollars at markets and visitors centers.

Dangers & Annoyances
Sequoia and Kings Canyon are both often shrouded by air pollution wafting up from the Central Valley. People with respiratory problems should check with a visitors center about current pollution levels. Black bears are common and proper food storage is required. Check bulletin boards at visitors centers and parking lots for current instructions and also have a look at the boxed text, p66.

KINGS CANYON NATIONAL PARK
Kings Canyon would be deluged with visitors were it not for Yosemite, its more famous neighbor to the north. But just as well. This leaves this giant gash in the earth's crust to the true adventure-seekers who crave its endless trails, rushing streams and gargantuan rock formations. The camping, backcountry exploring and climbing here are all superb and, best of all, you'll be able to survey giant sequoias, caves and a superb driving road at your unimpacted leisure.

Orientation
Kings Canyon National Park has two developed areas with markets, lodging, showers and visitor information. Grant Grove Village is only 4 miles past the Big Stump Entrance, while Cedar Grove Village is 31 miles east at the bottom of the canyon. The two are separated by the Giant Sequoia National Monument and are linked by Kings Canyon Hwy/Hwy 180.

Information
The gift shops at Grant Grove Village and the Cedar Grove market have ATMs. The post office is in Grant Grove Village.
Cedar Grove Visitor Center (☎ 559-565-3793; ◐ 9am-5pm late May-Sep) For tourist information.
Grant Grove Visitor Center (☎ 559-565-4307; ◐ 8am-6pm mid-Jun–Sep, 9am-5pm Oct–mid-Jun) Has exhibits, maps and wilderness permits.
Roads End Ranger Station (◐ 7am-3pm) Six miles east of Cedar Grove Village. Sells wilderness permits.

Sights & Activities
GENERAL GRANT GROVE
The magnificence of this grove was recognized as early as 1890 when Congress designated it General Grant National Park. In 1940 it became part of the newly created Kings Canyon National Park. A highlight on the short, paved **Grant Grove Trail** is the **General Grant Tree**, which holds triple honors

SIERRA NEVADA

SIERRA NEVADA

as the world's third-largest living tree, a memorial to US soldiers killed in war and as the nation's Christmas tree. The nearby **Fallen Monarch**, a massive, fire-hollowed trunk, has been a cabin, hotel, saloon and stables for US Cavalry horses.

PANORAMIC POINT

For a breathtaking view, head up 2.3 miles on supersteep Panoramic Point Rd (trailers and RVs not recommended). Steep canyons and the snowcapped peaks of the rugged ridge known as the Great Western Divide unfold below you. Snow closes the road to vehicles but not to cross-country skis.

KINGS CANYON HIGHWAY (HIGHWAY 180)

The 31-mile rollercoaster road connecting Grant Grove and Cedar Grove ranks among the most dazzling in all of California. It winds past the **Converse Basin Grove**, which loggers turned into a sequoia cemetery in the 1880s. A half-mile loop trails leads to the **Chicago Stump**, the remains of the tree that was cut down, sectioned and reassembled for the 1893 World Columbian Exposition in Chicago. Skeptical Easterners, thinking it was put together from several trees, called it the 'California hoax.' North of here, a second side road goes to **Stump Meadow**, where stumps and fallen logs make good picnic platforms, and to the **Boole Tree Trail**, a 2.5-mile loop to the only 'monarch' spared the lumberman's axe.

Kings Canyon Hwy soon begins its jaw-dropping descent into the canyon, serpentining past chiseled rock walls, some tinged by green moss and red iron minerals, others decorated by waterfalls. Turnouts provide superb views, most notably at **Junction View**.

Eventually the road runs parallel with the gushing Kings River, its thunderous roar ricocheting off granite cliffs soaring as high as 8000ft, making Kings Canyon deeper than even the Grand Canyon in Arizona. Stop at **Boyden Cavern** (☎ 209-736-2708; www.caverntours.com; adult/child/senior $10/5/9; ☷ 10am-5pm Jun-Sep, 11am-4pm May & Oct) for a tour of its whimsical formations. While beautiful, they are smaller and less impressive than Crystal Cave (p386) in Sequoia National Park. About 5 miles further east, **Grizzly Falls** can be torrential or

drizzly, depending on the time of year. Further on are Cedar Grove Village and Roads End, both back in the national park.

On your return trip, consider a detour via **Hume Lake**, created in 1908 as a dam for logging operations and now offering boating, swimming and fishing. A 2.5-mile trail encircles the lake. Facilities include a small market, snack bar, coin-op laundry and gas station.

CEDAR GROVE VILLAGE & ROADS END

At Cedar Grove Village a simple lodge and snack bar provide the last outpost of civilization before the rugged grandeur of the backcountry. Pretty spots around here include **Roaring River Falls**, where water whips down a sculpted rock channel before tumbling into a churning pool, and the 1.5-mile **Zumwalt Meadow Loop**, an easy nature trail across a fragrant, fern-laced landscape. There's excellent fly-fishing here (fishing license required) and around **Muir Rock** at Roads End. The latter also has great swimming.

A popular hiking destination is **Mist Falls** (8-mile round-trip). The trail is easy to moderate but the first 2 miles are fairly exposed, so start early to avoid the midday heat. It continues past Mist Falls, eventually connecting with the John Muir/Pacific Crest Trail to form the 42-mile **Rae Lakes Loop**, the most popular long-distance trek in Kings Canyon National Park (wilderness permit required, p375).

For guided horse trips, both day and overnight, check with **Cedar Grove Pack Station** (☎ 559-565-3464).

REDWOOD CANYON

South of Grant Grove Village, more than 15,000 sequoias cluster in this secluded and pristine corner of the park, making it the world's largest such grove. Relatively inaccessible, this area lets you enjoy the majesty of the giants away from the crowds on several moderate-to-strenuous trails. The trailhead is at the end of an unsigned, 2-mile bumpy dirt road across from the Hume Lake/Quail Flat sign on Generals Hwy, about 6 miles south of the village. If you want to pitch a tent, pick up a free permit from the Grant Grove Visitor Center.

(Continued on page 385)

JOHN ELK III

San Francisco's Victorian architectural heritage (p98)

RICHARD CUMMINS

Paseo Nuevo Shopping Mall
(p491), Santa Barbara

Americana central, Swingers Diner (p541), Los Angeles

RAY LASKOWITZ

RICHARD CUMMINS

Gaslamp Quarter, downtown San Diego (p591)

Paris–Las Vegas hotel and casino (p683),
Las Vegas

RICHARD CUMMINS

RICHARD CUMMINS

Jazz and blues club Blue Guitar (p647), Palm
Springs

White-water rafting on the
American River (p319)

LEE FOSTER

LEE FOSTER

Mountain-biking, Mammoth Mountain
(p398)

Mt Whitney Trail (p405), a testing challenge in all seasons

CHEYENNE L ROUSE

WES WALK

Mono Lake (p394), Eastern Sierra

One of nature's giants, Sequoia National Park (p386)

ROBERTO SONCIN GEROMETTA

RICHARD CUMMINS

Rock formations, Anza-Borrego
Desert State Park (p651)

Trees of Mystery (p277), off
Highway 101

LEE FOSTER

RAY LASKOWITZ

The King and happy couple, Viva Las Vegas
Wedding Chapel (p686), Las Vegas

DAVID PEEVERS

Tail O' the Pup (p541) hot dog stand, West
Hollywood

1927 Dodge at the gold-mining ghost town of Bodie, Bodie State Historic Park (p392)

EDDIE BRADY

CURTIS MARTIN

A young girl in traditional costume,
Golden Dragon Parade (p108), Chinese
New Year, San Francisco

Sikh minstrel, Venice Beach (p519), Los Angeles

CHRISTIAN ASLUND

Latino dancers, Cinco de Mayo (p532) or '5th of May' celebrations, Olvera St, Los Angeles

RAY LASKOW

A colorful neon welcome to the desert fun city of Reno (p353)

RAY LASKOWITZ

CLAVER CARROLL

Old-style Route 66 Motel signs
(p664)

Big Sur coastline between Carmel and San
Luis Obispo (p454)

THOMAS WINZ

California salmon taco (p68)

Fruit served the Mexican way,
Olvera St (p521), Los Angeles

Malty Anchor steam beer (p70)

Olives, a favorite harvest from the orchards of Sonoma Valley (p191)

(Continued from page 376)

Sleeping
CABINS & LODGES
John Muir Lodge (☎ 559-335-5500, 866-522-6966; www
.sequoia-kingscanyon.com; Grant Grove Village; r $160;
⊠) Quiet, classy and modern, this woodsy
lodge is as comfortable as things get in
Kings Canyon National Park. A stone fireplace anchors the handsome lobby with a
small selection of toys, books and board
games. All the rooms have telephones and
coffeemakers.

Grant Grove Cabins (☎ 559-335-5500, 866-522-
6966; www.sequoia-kingscanyon.com; Grant Grove Village;
tent cabins $45, cabins $69-79, with private bathroom $115-
125; ⊠) Match your comfort needs to cabin
type. The nicest are the historic cabins with
private bathrooms, while the cheapest are
tent cabins with wooden walls and a canvas
roof (summer only). From spring to fall rustic cabins without plumbing or electricity
(the lamps are battery-operated) are also
available.

Cedar Grove Lodge (☎ 559-335-5500, 866-522-6966;
www.sequoia-kingscanyon.com; Cedar Grove Village;
r $109-125; ☿ May-Oct; ⊠ ☒) The 21 motel-style
rooms are frill-free but comfortable and the
only noncamping option within earshot of
the Kings River. The three downstairs units
are smaller and pricier but come with a
refrigerator, microwave, coffeemaker and
river-facing patio.

CAMPING
Unless noted, all campsites are first-come,
first-served. Showers are available at Grant
Grove Village and Cedar Grove Village.
The latter also has laundry facilities.

The following campgrounds are located
close to Grant Grove Village at an elevation
of 6500ft.

Azalea (sites $18; ☿ year-round) Flush toilets, 113 sites;
the nicest sites border a meadow.
Crystal Springs (sites $18; ☿ late May–mid-Sep) Flush
toilets, 62 sites; the least attractive in the Grant Grove area
with little ground cover and privacy.
Sunset (sites $18; ☿ late May–mid-Sep) Newly
renovated, flush toilets, 200 sites, some overlooking the
western foothills and the Central Valley.

Campgrounds within the Giant Sequoia National Monument include the following.
Princess (☎ 877-444-6777; www.reserveusa.com; sites
$15-17; ☿ May-Sep) Vault toilets, 90 sites; next to a
huge meadow about 6 miles north of Grant Grove.
Hume Lake (☎ 877-444-6777; www.reserveusa.com;
Hume Lake Rd; sites $17-19; ☿ May-Sep) Flush toilets,
74 sites; on the lake's northern shore about 10 miles
northeast of Grant Grove.

Cedar Grove's four camping areas – Sheep
Creek, Sentinel, Canyon View and Mor-
aine – are open whenever Hwy 180 is open.
They're usually the last to fill up on busy
summer weekends and are also good bets
early and late in the season thanks to their
comparatively low elevation (4600ft). All
have flush toilets and $18 sites. Other fa-
cilities in the village don't start operating
until mid-May.

Eating
Grant Grove Village Restaurant (☎ 559-335-5500;
breakfast & lunch $5-9, dinner $9-17; ☿ year-round) This
casual dining parlor is your only choice for a
sit-down meal in this park. The all-American
food – burgers, sandwiches, steaks – may not
give you fits of euphoria but should fill the
belly nicely.

Armando's Cantina (☎ 559-565-0100; Cedar Grove
Lodge; breakfast & lunch $2.50-8, dinner $10-17; ☿ May-
early Oct) This basic snack bar is all about
burgers, hot dogs, fried chicken, pork chops

GIANT SEQUOIAS: KINGS OF THE FOREST

In California you can stand under the world's oldest trees (in the Ancient Bristlecone Pine Forest, p403) and its tallest (the coastal redwoods in Redwood National Park, p274), but the record
for biggest in terms of volume belongs to the giant sequoias *(Sequoiadendron giganteum)*. They
grow only on the Sierra's western slope and are most abundant in Sequoia and Kings Canyon
and Yosemite National Parks. John Muir called them 'Nature's forest masterpiece' and anyone
who's ever craned their neck to take in their soaring vastness has done so with the awe usually
reserved for Gothic cathedrals. Trees can grow to 300ft tall and 40ft in diameter with bark over
2ft thick. The Giant Forest Museum (p386) in Sequoia National Park has excellent exhibits about
their fascinating history and ecology.

and other hot and greasy fare. Lunch is served weekends only.

The markets in Grant Grove Village and Cedar Grove Village have a limited selection of groceries.

Getting There & Around

From the west, Kings Canyon Hwy (Hwy 180) travels 53 miles east from Fresno to the Big Stump Entrance. Coming from the south, you're in for a long 46-mile drive through Sequoia National Park along sinuous Generals Hwy. Budget about two hours' driving time from the Ash Mountain Entrance to Grant Grove Village. The road to Cedar Grove Village is only open from around April or May until the first snowfall. For more on winter travel, see the boxed text, opposite.

SEQUOIA NATIONAL PARK

Picture unzipping your tent flap and crawling out into a 'front yard' of trees as high as a 20-story building and as old as the Bible. Brew some coffee as you plan your day in this extraordinary park with its soul-sustaining forests and gigantic peaks soaring above 12,000ft. Even though access to nature's highlights here is wonderfully simple, Sequoia, among national parks, is on a 'road less traveled.' You'll feel privileged by its discovery.

Orientation

Nearly all of the park's star attractions are conveniently lined up along the Generals Hwy, which starts at the Ash Mountain Entrance and continues north into Kings Canyon. Tourist activity concentrates in the Giant Forest area and in Lodgepole Village, which has the most facilities, including a visitors center and market. The road to remote Mineral King veers off Hwy 198 in the town of Three Rivers, just south of the park's Ash Mountain Entrance. It is open from about late May until September or October.

Information

Lodgepole Village has an ATM and a post office.

Foothills Visitor Center (☎ 559-565-3135; ☽ 8am-5pm Jun, 8am-6pm Jul & Aug, 8am-4:30pm Sep-May) One mile north of Ash Mountain Entrance.

Lodgepole Visitor Center (☎ 559-565-4436; ☽ 7am-5pm Jun, 7am-6pm Jul & Aug, 9am-4:30pm Sep-May) Maps, information, exhibits, Crystal Cave tickets

(sold until 3:45pm) and wilderness permits (7am to 4pm). Near the Giant Forest.

Mineral King Ranger Station (☎ 559-565-3768; ☽ 8am-4:30pm Jun-early Sep) Twenty-four miles east of Generals Hwy.

Sights & Activities

GIANT FOREST

The Giant Forest, about 2 miles south of Lodgepole Village, is a great introduction to the park. A short trail from the new Wolverton Rd parking lot leads to the **General Sherman Tree**, the largest living tree on earth in terms of volume. From here, the 2-mile **Congress Trail** loops past many other famous specimens, including the **Washington Tree**, the world's second biggest. To really lose the crowds, though, you'll need to embark on the 5-mile **Trail of the Sequoias**, which puts you into the heart of the forest.

For a primer on the intriguing ecology and history of the 'big trees', drop in at the excellent **Giant Forest Museum** (☎ 559-565-4480; admission free; ☽ 8am-5pm Jun, 8am-6pm Jul-Aug, 9am-4:30pm Sep-May), then follow up your visit with a spin around the paved 0.6-mile interpretive **Big Trees Trail**, which starts right from the museum parking lot.

Open in the warmer months, Crescent Meadow Rd heads east from the museum for 3 miles to **Crescent Meadow**, a relaxing picnic spot, especially in spring when it's ablaze with wildflowers. Several short hikes start from here, including the 1-mile trail to **Tharp's Log**, where the area's first settler spent summers in a fallen tree. The road also passes **Moro Rock**, a landmark granite dome whose top can be reached via a quarter-mile carved staircase for great Sierra views.

CRYSTAL CAVE

Discovered in 1918 by two fishermen, **Crystal Cave** (☎ 559-565-3759; www.sequoiahistory.org; Crystal Cave Rd; adult/child/senior $11/6/9; ☽ tours 11am-4pm mid-May–Oct) was carved by an underground river and has formations estimated to be 10,000 years old. It is filled with stalagmites and stalactites, all of milky white marble and curiously shaped into curtains, domes, columns and shields. The 45-minute tour covers a half-mile of chambers. Longer tours ($19) and all-day, off-trail spelunking explorations ($110) are also available.

Tickets are *only* sold at the Lodgepole and Foothills visitors center and *not* at the cave.

WINTER FUN

Winter is a special time to visit Sequoia and Kings Canyon National Parks. A thick blanket of snow drapes over trees and meadows, the pace of activity slows and a hush falls over the roads and trails.

Snowshoeing and **cross-country skiing** are both hugely popular activities with about 40 miles of marked but ungroomed trails crisscrossing the Grant Grove and Giant Forest areas. Trail maps are available at the visitors centers and on weekends rangers lead free guided tours. Trails connect with those in the Giant Sequoia National Monument and the 50 miles of groomed terrain maintained by the private Montecito Sequoia Lodge (p388; day pass including lunch $30). Equipment rentals are available at Grant Grove Village, the Wuksachi Lodge and the Montecito Sequoia Lodge. There are also **snowplay areas** near Big Stump and Wolverton Picnic Area & Parking Lot.

Note that snow often closes Generals Hwy between Grant Grove and Giant Forest and that tire chains may be required at any time. These can usually be rented near the park entrances, although you're not supposed to put them on rental cars. For up-to-date road conditions call ☎ 559-565-3341 or check www.nps.gov/seki.

Allow about one hour to get to the cave entrance, which is a half-mile walk from the parking lot at the end of a twisty 7-mile road; the turnoff is about 3 miles south of the Giant Forest. Bring a sweater or light jacket.

FOOTHILLS

From the Ash Mountain Entrance in Three Rivers, the Generals Hwy ascends steeply through this southern section of Sequoia National Park. With an average elevation of about 2000ft, the Foothills are much drier and warmer than the rest of the park. **Hiking** here is best in spring when the air is still cool and wildflowers put on a colorful show. Summers are buggy and muggy, but fall again brings moderate temperatures and lush foliage.

The Potwisha people lived in this area until the early 1900s, relying primarily on acorn meal. Pictographs and grinding holes still grace the **Hospital Rock** picnic area, once a Potwisha village site. **Swimming holes** abound along the Marble Fork of the Kaweah River, especially near Potwisha Campground (p388). Be careful, though – the currents can be deadly, especially when the river is swollen from the spring runoff.

MINERAL KING

Gorgeous and gigantic, Mineral King is a glacially sculpted valley ringed by massive mountains, including the jagged Sawtooth Peak. It is reached via a slinky, steep and narrow 25-mile road not suitable for poor drivers or the impatient.

From the 1860s to 1890s, Mineral King witnessed heavy silver mining and lumber activity. There are remnants of old shafts and stamp mills, though it takes some exploring to find them. A proposal by the Walt Disney Corporation to develop the area into a massive ski resort was thwarted when Congress annexed it to the national park in 1978.

Mineral King is Sequoia's backpacking mecca and a good place to find solitude. Hiking anywhere from here involves a steep climb out of the valley along strenuous trails. You'll be starting at 7500ft, so be aware of the altitude, even on short hikes. Enjoyable day hikes go to Crystal, Monarch, Mosquito and Eagle Lakes. For long trips, locals recommend the **Little Five Lakes** and, further along the High Sierra Trail, **Kaweah Gap**, surrounded by the sawtooth Black Kaweah, Mt Stewart and Eagle Scout Peak – all above 12,000ft.

Mineral King has tons of marmots which, mostly in spring and early summer, have the nasty habit of chewing on radiator hoses, belts and wiring of vehicles to get the salt they crave after their winter hibernation. One way to avoid damage to your vehicle is by surrounding the space beneath it with chicken wire.

Sleeping & Eating

The market at Lodgepole Village is the best stocked in either park, but basic supplies are also available at the small store in Stony Creek Lodge (closed in winter).

ALONG GENERALS HWY

Wuksachi Lodge (☎ 559-253-2199, 888-252-5757; www .visitsequoia.com; r $155-220 May-Sep, $100-150 Oct-Apr;

SIERRA NEVADA

year-round) Six miles north of Giant Forest, this elegant, modern mountain lodge offers the poshest digs in either park. Rooms, all with TV and telephone, come in three sizes and are in three buildings a short walk from the main lodge with the reception and a restaurant open for breakfast, lunch and dinner (dinner mains $18-24). It serves delicious fare with a healthy bent, including several choices for vegetarians.

Montecito Sequoia Lodge (☎ 559-565-3388, 800-227-9900; www.mslodge.com; per person incl meals $80-145; ☼ daily Sep–mid-Jun, Sat only Jun-Aug; ☒) Framed by forest and overlooking its own small lake, this is a casual, family-oriented private resort about 9 miles south of Grant Grove Village. The 36 rooms and cabins are rustic yet comfortable, but it's the many recreational opportunities offered here – from archery to tennis, kayaking to cross-country skiing – that give this place its appeal. Rates include three buffet-style meals and access to a stocked kitchen. The restaurant (breakfast/lunch/dinner $9/10/20) is open to nonguests as well. From Sunday to Friday in June, July and August, it's a family summer camp for prebooked groups.

Stony Creek Lodge (☎ 559-335-5500, 866-522-6966; www.sequoia-kingscanyon.com; r $135-145; ☼ May-Oct; ☒) About halfway between Grant Grove Village and Giant Forest, this lodge has a big river-rock fireplace in its lobby and 11 aging motel rooms with TV and telephone.

There is a handful of campgrounds lining the highway that rarely fill up, although space may get tight on holiday weekends. Those in the Foothills area are best in spring and fall when the higher elevations are still chilly, but they get hot and buggy in summer. Unless noted, sites are available on a first-come, first-served basis. Free dispersed camping is possible in the Giant Sequoia National Monument. Stop by a visitors center or ranger station for details and a fire permit. Lodgepole Village and Stony Creek Lodge have public showers.

Stony Creek (☎ 877-444-6777; www.reserveusa.com; sites $17-19; ☼ late May-Oct) USFS-operated with about 50 sites, including some right on the creek, and flush toilets.

Dorst Creek (☎ 800-365-2267; http://reservations.nps .gov; sites $20; ☼ late May-early Sep) Big and busy campground with 204 sites and flush toilets.

Lodgepole (☎ 800-365-2267; http://reservations.nps .gov; sites $20; ☼ year-round) Closest to the Giant Forest area with 214 sites and flush toilets.

Buckeye Flat (sites $18; ☼ late May-Sep) In the Foothills area, about 6 miles north of the Ash Mountain Entrance with 28 sites and flush toilets.

Potwisha (sites $18; ☼ year-round) Also in the Foothills, 3 miles from the Ash Mountain Entrance with 42 sites, flush toilets and a pay phone.

Lodgepole Deli & Snack Bar (Lodgepole Village; meals $3-7; ☼ deli 11am-6pm, snack bar 8am-8pm) Ease hunger pangs with burgers, pizza, hot dogs and sandwiches at these self-service places.

BACKCOUNTRY

Bearpaw Meadow Camp (☎ 888-252-5757; www.visit sequoia.com; adult/child $165/75; ☼ mid-Jun–early Sep; ☒) About 11.5 miles east of the Giant Forest on the High Sierra Trail, this tent hotel is ideal for exploring the backcountry without lugging your own camping gear. Rates include showers, meals, bedding and towels. Bookings start at 7am on January 2 and fill quickly, although you can always check for cancellations.

Pear Lake Ski Hut (☎ 559-565-3759; www.sequoia history.org; dm $22; ☼ mid-Dec–Apr; ☒) You'll be glad to see this 10-bunk ski hut after the strenuous 6-mile cross-country ski or snowshoe trek from Wolverton Meadow. Reservations are by lottery. Call or check the website for details.

MINERAL KING AREA

Silver City Resort (☎ 559-561-3223; www.silvercityresort .com; cabins $75-175, chalets $200-300; ☼ late May-Oct) This private cabin resort offers warm beds, full kitchens and a sense of being in the 'middle of nowhere.' Choose from basic cabins with shared facilities or comfortable knotty-pine chalets. You need to bring sheets, towels and food and there is a two-night minimum stay. From Thursday to Monday the small restaurant serves breakfast and simple fare, such as burgers and quesadillas, for lunch and dinner (meals around $7), although it's really famous for its excellent pies.

Mineral King's two campgrounds, **Atwell Mill** (sites $12; ☼ late May-Sep) and **Cold Springs** (sites $12; ☼ late May-Sep) often fill up on summer weekends.

THREE RIVERS

Just south of the Ash Mountain Entrance, Three Rivers is a relaxed, artsy community stretched out along Hwy 198 (here called Sierra Dr), which parallels the Kaweah River.

Sierra Dr is sparsely lined with motels, stores, galleries, cafés and restaurants.

Gateway Restaurant & Lodge (☎ 559-561-4133; www.gateway-sequoia.com; 45978 Sierra Dr; r midweek/ weekend $100/120, cottage $140/165, house $265/325; mains lunch $9-12, dinner $18-28; ✕ ✖) The steaks are juicy, the bar lively and the service swift and friendly, but most likely it'll be the views of the bubbling Kaweah River you'll remember long after paying the bill. Right outside the park entrance, this convivial inn also has five homey motel rooms, a small riverside cottage with private dry sauna and a large house with full kitchen and a big terrace right above the cascading stream.

Buckeye Lodge (☎ 559-561-5900; www.buckeyetree .com; 46000 Sierra Dr; r 72-127; ✖) This small motel makes another good jumping-off point for your Sequoia explorations. The 12 motel-style units overlook a lush garden fronting the Kaweah and feature a TV/VCR combination, refrigerator and coffeemaker.

Main Fork Bistro (☎ 559-561-4917; 41775 Sierra Dr; mains breakfast & lunch $5-11, dinner $10-19) Fresh ingredients, creative flavor pairings and beautiful presentation make this place a perennial winner with locals and visitors. Hunker down on the riverview patio for such treats as sesame-seared *ahi* tuna salad, cedar-planked salmon or a portobello burger.

Also recommended:

Sierra Lodge (☎ 559-561-3681, 800-367-879; www.sierra-lodge.com; 43175 Sierra Dr; r $55-100, ste $95-200; ✖) Older property with attractive, good-value rooms.

River View (☎ 559-561-2211; 42323 Sierra Dr; lunch $6-9, dinner $11-23) Colorful honky-tonk with live music from Friday to Monday.

Getting There & Around

Coming from the south, Hwy 198 runs north from Visalia through Three Rivers past Mineral King Rd to the Ash Mountain Entrance. Beyond here the road continues as the Generals Hwy, a narrow and windy road snaking all the way into Kings Canyon National Park where it joins the Kings Canyon Hwy (Hwy 180) near the western Big Stump Entrance. Vehicles over 22ft long may have trouble negotiating the steep road with its many hairpin curves, although they are not prohibited from trying. For winter travel, see the boxed text on p387. Budget about one hour to drive from the entrance to the Giant Forest/Lodgepole area and another hour from there to Grant Grove Village in Kings Canyon.

EASTERN SIERRA

Stark, startling and vast, the Eastern Sierra is where slashing peaks – many of them over 14,000ft – rush abruptly upward from the arid expanses of the Great Basin and Mojave deserts. It's a dramatic juxtaposition that makes for a potent cocktail of scenery. Pine forests, lush meadows, crystal-clear lakes, simmering hot springs and glacier-gouged canyons are only some of the fabulous wealth that Nature has bestowed upon this region.

The Eastern Sierra Scenic Byway, officially known as Hwy 395, runs the entire length of the range. Turnoffs dead-ending at the foot of the mountains deliver you to pristine wilderness and countless trails, including the famous Pacific Crest Trail, John Muir Trail and Main Mt Whitney Trail. The most important portals are the towns of Bridgeport, Mammoth Lakes and Bishop. Note that in winter, when traffic thins, many facilities are closed.

Wilderness Permits

Free wilderness permits for overnight camping are required year-round in the Ansel Adams, John Muir, Golden Trout and Hoover Wilderness areas. For the first three, trailhead quotas are in effect from May to October. About 60% of the quota may be reserved for a $5 fee by telephone, fax and mail from the **Inyo National Forest Wilderness Permit Office** (☎ 760-873-2483; fax 760-873-2484; 351 Pacu Lane, Suite 200, Bishop, CA 93514). From November to April, you can pick up permits at any ranger station mentioned in this section. If you find the station closed, look for self-issue permits outside the office. Regulations change on occasion, so call ☎ 760-873-2485 or check www .fs.fed.us/r5/inyo/passes for the latest.

Hoover Wilderness (www.fs.fed.us/r4/htnf/passes /hoover_permits.shtmlarea), in boundaries of the Humboldt-Toiyabe National Forest has similar permit requirements. Check the website for details. For information about the Main Mt Whitney Trail, see the boxed text, p405.

Getting There & Around

The Eastern Sierra is best explored under your own steam, although it is possible to access the area by public transportation. Buses operated by **Carson Ridgecrest Eastern Sierra Transit** (CREST; ☎ 760-872-1901) make round trips between Bishop and Reno on Tuesday, Thursday and Friday and between Mammoth Lakes and Ridgecrest on Monday, Wednesday and Friday, stopping at all towns in between. Fares depend on distance; one-way tickets from Reno to Mammoth cost $23, from Ridgecrest to Mammoth $21. Reservations are required.

For details on getting to Reno, see p358. Getting to Ridgecrest involves catching a **Greyhound** (☎ 800-231-2222; www.greyhound.com) bus to Mojave and then switching to a **Kern Regional Transit** (☎ 800-323-2396; fare $4) bus.

Inyo Mono Transit (☎ 760-872-1901) operates a weekday bus service three times daily between Bishop and Lone Pine (via Big Pine and Independence) and from Bishop to Mammoth Lakes twice daily. One-way fares range from $2 to $5.50.

BRIDGEPORT
pop 500 / elevation 6500ft

Sitting pretty amidst open range and lush meadows, Bridgeport flaunts classic western flair with charming old storefronts and a homey ambience. Winters can be brutal, but the rest of the year the town is a magnet for anglers, hikers, climbers and hot spring fans. Stop by the **Bridgeport Ranger Station & Visitor Center** (☎ 760-932-7070; Hwy 395; ⏰ 7:30am-5pm daily Jul & Aug, 8am-4:30pm Mon-Fri Sep-Jun) for maps, information and Hoover Wilderness permits (p389). A quota system is in effect from the last Friday in June until September 15.

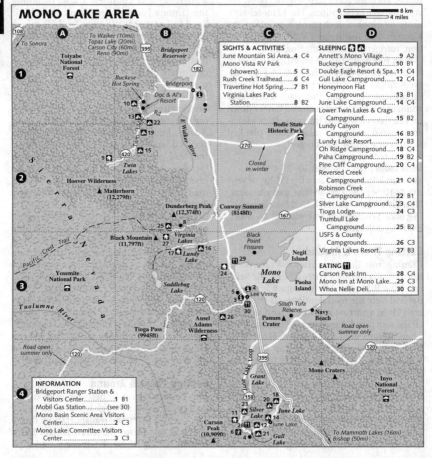

MONO LAKE AREA

0 _____ 8 km
0 _____ 4 miles

SIGHTS & ACTIVITIES
June Mountain Ski Area..4 C4
Mono Vista RV Park
(showers)........................5 C3
Rush Creek Trailhead......6 C4
Travertine Hot Spring......7 B1
Virginia Lakes Pack
Station.........................8 B2

SLEEPING
Annett's Mono Village........9 A2
Buckeye Campground......10 B1
Double Eagle Resort & Spa..11 C4
Gull Lake Campground......12 C4
Honeymoon Flat
Campground.................13 B1
June Lake Campground ...14 C4
Lower Twin Lakes & Crags
Campground.................15 B2
Lundy Canyon
Campground.................16 B3
Lundy Lake Resort............17 B3
Oh Ridge Campground.....18 C4
Paha Campground...........19 B2
Pine Cliff Campground.....20 C4
Reversed Creek
Campground.................21 C4
Robinson Creek
Campground.................22 B1
Silver Lake Campground...23 C4
Tioga Lodge.....................24 C3
Trumbull Lake
Campground.................25 B2
USFS & County
Campgrounds...............26 C3
Virginia Lakes Resort........27 B3

EATING
Carson Peak Inn...............28 C4
Mono Inn at Mono Lake....29 C3
Whoa Nellie Deli..............30 C3

INFORMATION
Bridgeport Ranger Station &
Visitors Center................1 B1
Mobil Gas Station............(see 30)
Mono Basin Scenic Area Visitors
Center............................2 C3
Mono Lake Committee Visitors
Center............................3 C3

Sights & Activities

The gavel has been dropped since 1880 at the **Mono County Courthouse** (☽ 9am-5pm Mon-Fri), an all-white Italianate structure surrounded by a gracious lawn. Two blocks away, in an old schoolhouse, the **Mono County Museum** (☎ 760-932-5281; Emigrant St; adult/child $1.50/75¢; ☽ 10am-4pm Jun-Sep) has some fine Paiute baskets.

A bit south of town, **Travertine Hot Spring** lets you soak in 105°F water amidst chiseled rock formations with awesome views of the Sierra peaks. To get there, turn east on Jack Sawyer Rd just before the ranger station, then follow the dirt road uphill for about 1 mile.

Great spots for trolling for trout include the **Bridgeport Reservoir** and especially the **East Walker River**. For information and outdoor gear, stop by **Ken's Sporting Goods** (☎ 760-932-7707; www.kenssport.com; 258 Main St).

Sleeping & Eating

Redwood Motel (☎ 760-932-7060, 888-932-3292; www.redwoodmotel.net; 425 Main St; d from $73; ☽ mid-Mar–Nov; ☒) A kicking horse, a cow in a Hawaiian shirt and other wacky farm animal sculptures provide a cheerful welcome to this little motel. Rooms are spotless and your host, a professional artist and clown, is superhelpful in dispensing local area tips. From 10am to 1pm nonguests can shower up for $10, including towel and toiletries.

Silver Maple Inn (☎ 760-932-7383; www.silvermapleinn.com; 310 Main St; r $75-105; ☽ late Apr–mid-Nov) This well-kept property wraps around a large tree-shaded lawn dotted with lounge chairs and tables. The rooms are clean and easy on the eyes, but nothing special.

Restaurant 1881 (☎ 760-932-1918; 362 Main St; mains $13-25; ☽ dinner) Gourmet food is thin on the ground along Hwy 395, which makes this place in a cute historic mansion all the more popular. Feast on local alpers trout, pistachio-encrusted rack of lamb or such imaginative meatfree creations as eggplant Wellington.

Pop's Galley (☎ 760-932-1172; 247 Main St; mains $5-8; ☽ 9am-9pm) This casual eating joint prepares finger-lickin' fish and chips and also serves breakfast. Sit inside with a view of the mountains or outside for front-row seats on Main St.

TWIN LAKES

Cradled by the fittingly named Sawtooth Ridge, Twin Lakes is famous for its fishing, especially since some lucky guy bagged the state's largest ever brown trout here in 1987 (it weighed in at a hefty 26 lbs). Lower Twin is quieter, while Upper Twin allows boating and water skiing. Other activities include mountain-biking and, of course, hiking in the Hoover Wilderness and on into the eastern, lake-riddled reaches of Yosemite National Park. The main trailhead is at the end of Twin Lakes Rd just past Annett's Mono Village; overnight parking is $7 per stay.

Twin Lakes Rd (Rte 420) runs through pastures and foothills for about 10 miles before reaching Lower Twin Lake. Honeymoon Flat, Robinson Creek, Paha, Crags, Matterhorn and Lower Twin lakes are all **USFS campgrounds** (☎ 800-444-7275; www.reserveusa.com; sites

---

HIGHWAY 395: BRIDGEPORT TO RENO

North of Bridgeport, Hwy 395 barrels on through narrow **Walker Canyon**, paralleling a 10-mile stretch of the West Walker River, a designated Wild and Scenic River, which enjoys legendary status among trout fishers. The road eventually spills out into the fertile Antelope Valley, where the little western town of Walker has a few cheap motels and eateries. **Walker Burger** (☎ 530-495-2219) and **Mountain View Barbecue** (☎ 530-495-2107), both with meals under $8, are recommended.

A few miles further north, the Walker River empties into **Topaz Lake**, which straddles the California–Nevada border. It's open for all sorts of watersports but is really best known for its exceptionally long fishing season (January to September). Overlooking the lake from the Nevada side, the old-timey **Topaz Lodge** (☎ 775-266-3338, 800-962-0732; www.topazlodge.com; r $65-85) offers gambling, grub and comfy motel rooms.

Beyond here, you can forget about scenery, although **Carson City**, the Nevada state capital, warrants a stop for a stroll around its pretty downtown with some nice old buildings and the imposing capitol building. From here it's another 30 miles to Reno.

If you're headed for Tahoe, leave Hwy 395 just south of Topaz Lake and head into the mountains on incredibly scenic Hwy 89, which eventually merges with Hwy 50.

$13-15; ☺ usually mid-May–Sep) set among Jeffrey pine and sagebrush along Robinson Creek and Lower Twin Lake. All have flush toilets except for Honeymoon Flat, which has vault toilets.

Twin Lakes Rd dead-ends at **Annett's Mono Village** (☎ 760-932-7071; www.monovillage.com; tent sites $14-22, r $55, cabins $75-160; ☺ late Apr-Oct; ☐), a huge resort on Upper Twin Lake. It has cheap but cramped lodging, a market with ATM, showers and laundry facilities, boat rentals, a greasy-spoon café and a cocktail lounge with Internet access. There's also free wi-fi throughout. Cabins sleep three to six people.

Buckeye Hot Spring

This secluded spring is lovely but can get crowded. The water emerges piping hot from atop a steep hillside but cools quickly as it trickles down into several rock pools right by the side of lively Buckeye Creek, which is handy for taking a cooling dip. One pool is in a small cave. Clothing is optional.

To get there, turn right onto the graded dirt road just past Doc & Al's Resort, cross the bridge at Buckeye Creek, then turn right at the sign for Buckeye Campground. Go up-hill until you see a flat parking area on your right. The pools are down the hillside.

West of the springs, at a bridge spanning Buckeye Creek, a road goes 2 miles to **Buckeye Campground** (sites $11; ☺ May–mid-Oct) with tables, fire grates, potable water and toilets. You can also camp for free in undeveloped spots along Buckeye Creek on both sides of the bridge.

BODIE STATE HISTORIC PARK

For a time-warp back to the Gold Rush era, swing by **Bodie** (☎ 760-647-6445; admission $3; ☺ 8am-7pm Jun-Aug, 9am-4pm Sep-May), one of the West's most authentic and best-preserved ghost towns. Gold was first discovered here in 1859, and within 20 years the place grew from a rough mining camp to an even rougher boomtown with a population of 10,000 and a reputation for unbridled lawlessness. Fights and murders took place almost daily, the violence no doubt fueled by liquor dispensed in the town's 65 saloons, some of which did double duty as brothels, gambling halls or opium dens. The hills disgorged some $35 million worth of gold and silver in the 1870s and '80s, but when production plummeted,

so did the population and eventually the town was abandoned to the elements.

About 200 weather-beaten buildings still sit frozen in time in this cold, barren and windswept valley. Peering through dusty windows you'll see stocked stores, furnished homes, a schoolhouse with desks and books, and workshops filled with tools. The jail is still there, as are the fire station, churches, a bank vault and many other buildings. The former Miners' Union Hall now houses a **museum** and **visitors center**. Rangers conduct free general tours daily at 10am. On summer weekends, they also offer stamp mill and twilight tours on Saturdays ($15; reservations required).

Bodie is about 13 miles east of Hwy 395 via Rte 270; the last 3 miles are unpaved. Although the park is open year-round, the road is usually closed in winter and early spring, so you'd have to don snowshoes or cross-country skis to get there.

VIRGINIA LAKES & LUNDY LAKE

South of Bridgeport, Hwy 395 gradually climbs to its highest point, **Conway Summit** (8148ft), where you'll be whipping out your camera for the awe-inspiring panorama of Mono Lake, backed by the Mono Craters, backed by June and Mammoth Mountains.

Also at the top is the turnout for Virginia Lakes Rd, which parallels Virginia Creek for about 6 miles to a cluster of lakes flanked by **Dunderberg Peak** (12,374ft) and **Black Mountain** (11,797ft). A trailhead at the end of the road gives access to the Hoover Wilderness and the Pacific Crest Trail, which continues down Cold Canyon to Yosemite National Park. Check with the folks at the 1923 **Virginia Lakes Resort** (☎ 760-647-6484; www.virginialakesresort.com; cabins per week $510-1730; ☺ usually mid-May–mid-Oct; ☒) for maps and tips about specific trails. The resort itself has snug cabins, a café and a general store that sells fishing tackle and licenses. Cabins sleep two to 12 people and are subject to a three- or seven-night minimum rental. Otherwise, there's camping at **Trumbull Lake Campground** (☎ 800-444-7275; www.reserveusa.com; sites $13; ☺ mid-Jun–mid-Oct) with shady sites among lodgepole pines. Nearby, **Virginia Lakes Pack Station** (☎ 760-937-0326; www.virginialakes.com) does everything from two-hour rides ($50) to multiday pack trips.

WATER FOR A THIRSTY GIANT: A TALE OF TWO LAKES

Los Angeles may be 250 miles away, but its history and fate are closely linked with that of the Eastern Sierra. When LA's population surged around the turn of the 20th century, it became clear that groundwater levels would soon be inadequate to meet the city's needs, let alone sustaining future growth. Water had to be imported, and Fred Eaton, a former LA mayor, and William Mulholland, head of the LA Department of Water & Power (LADWP), knew just how and where to get it: by aqueduct from the Owens Valley, which receives enormous runoff from the Sierra Nevada.

The fact that the Owens Valley itself was settled by farmers who needed the water for irrigation didn't bother either of the two men. Nor did it cause qualms in the least with the federal government, which actively supported the city's less-than-ethical maneuvering in acquiring land and securing water rights in the valley area. Voters gave Mulholland the $24.5 million he needed to build the aqueduct and work began in 1908. An amazing feat of engineering – crossing barren desert as well as rugged mountain terrain – the aqueduct opened to great fanfare on November 5, 1913. The Owens Valley, though, would never be the same.

With most of its inflows diverted, Owens Lake, which once had been 30ft deep and an important stopover for migrating waterfowl, quickly shriveled up. A bitter feud between local farmers and ranchers and the city grew violent when some of the opponents tried to sabotage the aqueduct by blowing up a section of it. All to no avail. By 1928 LA owned 90% of the water in Owens Valley and agriculture was effectively dead. These early water wars formed the basis for the 1974 movie *Chinatown*.

But as LA kept burgeoning, its water needs grew right along with its size. In the 1930s, the LADWP bought up water rights in the Mono Basin and extended the aqueduct by 105 miles, diverting four of the five streams feeding into Mono Lake. Not surprisingly, the lake's water volume dropped significantly, doubling its salinity and posing a major threat to its ecological balance.

In 1976 environmentalist David Gaines began to study the concerns surrounding the lake's depletion and found that, if left untouched, it would totally dry up within about 20 years. To avert this certain disaster, he formed the Mono Lake Committee in 1978 and enlisted the help of the National Audubon Society. Years of lobbying and legal action followed, but eventually the committee succeeded. In 1994, the California State Water Resources Control Board mandated the LADWP to substantially reduce its diversions and allow the lake level to rise by 20ft. In July 2005 its surface stood at 6282ft, still about 10ft short of the goal.

The Owens Lake, meanwhile, was not as lucky. It remains a barren lakebed that's often the site of alkali dust storms, which are especially harmful to people with respiratory problems. To alleviate the problem, the LADWP, in 1997, agreed to restore a 62-mile stretch of the Lower Owens River by 2003. When both this deadline and a two-year extension were ignored, a county judge swung into action in July of 2005, imposing stiff daily fines and other sanctions. If noncompliance continues, he's even threatened to cut off a second aqueduct built in 1970.

If followed through, the judge's threats would certainly hurt LA: In an average year, the city still gets about 50% of its water supply via the LA aqueducts from the Eastern Sierra. The remainder is siphoned from the Sacramento and San Joaquin Rivers via the California Aqueduct and the Colorado River via the Colorado River Aqueduct; only about 15% comes from groundwater.

After Conway Summit, Hwy 395 twists down steeply into the Mono Basin. Before reaching Mono Lake, Lundy Lake Rd meanders west of the highway for about 5 miles to **Lundy Lake**. This is a gorgeous spot, especially in spring when wildflowers carpet the canyon along Mill Creek, or in fall when it is brightened by colorful foliage. Before reaching the lake, the road skirts first-come, first-served **Lundy Canyon Campground** (sites $8; May-Oct), with vault toilets but no water.

Lundy Lake Resort (☎ 626-309-0415; tent sites $11.50, cabins $65-100; late Apr-Oct) is a funky old place on the site of an 1880s mining town. You can stay in ramshackle cabins with shared facilities, nicer ones with bathrooms and a handful of campsites. There's a small store and boat rentals.

Past the resort, a good dirt road leads into **Lundy Canyon** where it dead-ends at the trailhead for Hoover Wilderness. A moderate 1.5-mile hike follows Mill Creek to the 200ft-high

Lundy Falls. Ambitious types can continue on via Lundy Pass to Saddlebag Lake.

MONO LAKE

North America's second-oldest lake is a quiet and mysterious expanse of deep blue water whose glassy surface reflects jagged Sierra peaks, young volcanic cones and the unearthly tufa (*too*-fah) towers that make Mono Lake so distinctive. Jutting from the water like drip sand castles, the tufas form when calcium bubbles up from subterranean springs and combines with the carbonate in the alkaline lake waters.

In *Roughing It*, Mark Twain described Mono Lake as California's 'dead sea.' Hardly. The brackish water teems with buzzing alkali flies and brine shrimp, both considered delicacies by dozens of migratory bird species that return here year after year. So do about 85% of the state's nesting population of California gulls which takes over the lake's volcanic islands from April to August. Mono Lake has been at the heart of an environmental controversy (see p393).

Orientation

Hwy 395 skirts the western bank of Mono Lake, rolling into the support town of Lee Vining, where you can eat, sleep, gas up and catch Hwy 120 to Yosemite National Park (summer only; see the boxed text, p333).

Information

Mono Basin Scenic Area Visitors Center (☎ 760-647-3044; Hwy 395, ⏲ usually 9am-4pm) Half a mile north of Lee Vining. Maps, interpretive displays, wilderness permits, bear-canister rentals (per week $5), bookstore and a 20-minute movie about Mono Lake.

Mono Lake Committee Visitors Center (☎ 760-647-6595; www.monolake.org; cnr Hwy 395 & 3rd St; ⏲ 9am-5pm late Sep-Jun, 9am-10:30pm Jul–mid-Sep) Internet access (per 15 minutes $2), maps, books, free 30-minute video about Mono Lake and passionate, preservation-minded staff.

Sights & Activities

Tufa spires ring the lake, but the biggest grove is the **South Tufa Reserve** (adult/child under 18 $3/free) on the south rim with a mile-long interpretive trail. Ask about ranger-led tours at the visitors center. To get to the reserve, head south of Lee Vining on Hwy 395 for 6 miles, then east on Hwy 120 for 5 miles to the dirt road leading to a parking lot.

The best place for swimming is at **Navy Beach**, just east of the reserve. Rinse off the salt residue at the **Mono Vista RV Park** (Hwy 395; showers $2.50; ⏲ 9am-6pm) in Lee Vining, but don't forget to bring soap and a towel.

Navy Beach is also the best place to put in canoes or kayaks. From June to early September, Mono Lake Committee operates one-hour **canoe tours** (☎ 760-647-6595; adult/child $17/7; ⏲ 8am, 9:30am & 11am Sat & Sun) around the tufas. Half-day kayak tours along the shore or out to Paoha Island are also offered by **Caldera Kayaks** (☎ 760-934-1691; www.calderakayak.com; tours $65, kayaks $40; ⏲ mid-May–mid-Oct). Both companies require reservations.

Rising above the south shore, **Panum Crater** is the youngest (about 640 years old), smallest and most accessible of the craters that string south toward Mammoth Mountain. A panoramic trail circles the crater rim (about 30 to 45 minutes), and a short but steep 'plug trail' puts you at the crater's core. A dirt road leads to the trailhead from Hwy 120, about 3 miles east of the junction with Hwy 395.

On the north shore are the **Black Point Fissures**, narrow crags that opened when lava mass cooled and contracted about 13,000 years ago. Access is from three places: east of Mono Lake County Park, from the west shore off Hwy 395, or south of Hwy 167. Check at a visitors center for specific directions.

Sleeping & Eating

El Mono Motel (☎ 760-647-6310; www.elmonomotel.com; 51 Hwy 395; r $55-90; ⏲ May-Oct) This homey and friendly place attached to a café has been operating since 1927. Rooms with TV are neat, clean and decorated with unique art and outdoor themes.

Tioga Lodge (☎ 760-647-6423, 888-647-6423; www.tiogalodge.com; r $55-107; ⏲ Apr-Oct; ☒) About 2 miles north of Lee Vining is this cluster of cheery cabins with porches overlooking Mono Lake. The buildings housing the restaurant (mains breakfast $5 to $9, dinner $10 to $15) and the registration office were moved here from Bodie in 1897.

The closest campsites are the six creekside **USFS** and **county campgrounds** (☎ 760-932-5440; sites $8) along Tioga Rd (Hwy 120) in the direction of Yosemite, all with vault toilets and stream water.

Whoa Nellie Deli (☎ 760-647-1088; near junction of Hwys 120 & 395, Lee Vining; mains $7-18; ⏲ 7am-9pm late Apr-Oct) Great food in a gas station? Come on… No, really, you gotta try this amazing kitchen where chef Matt 'Tioga' Toomey feeds delicious fish tacos, wild buffalo meat-loaf and other tasty morsels to locals and clued-in passersby.

Mono Inn at Mono Lake (☎ 760-647-6581; www .monoinn.com; mains $19-26; ☺ dinner Wed-Mon Jun-Oct, Thu-Sun Nov-May) Owned by Sarah Adams, who is the granddaughter of photographer Ansel Adams, this woodsy restaurant pairs inventive California cuisine with spectac-ular lake views. You can stick to the basics (burgers, spaghetti) or choose to go gourmet with orange-glazed quail, roast venison or lamb shank with porcini jus. Reservations advised.

JUNE LAKE LOOP

Under the shadow of massive Carson Peak (10,909ft), the 14-mile June Lake Loop me-anders through a picture-perfect horseshoe canyon past the relaxed resort town of June Lake and four sparkling, fish-rich lakes: Grant, Silver, Gull and June. It's especially scenic in fall when the basin is ablaze with golden aspens. Catch the loop (Hwy 158) a few miles south of Lee Vining.

Activities

June Lake is backed by the Ansel Adams Wilderness, which runs into Yosemite Na-tional Park. Rush Creek Trailhead has a day-use parking lot, posted maps and self-registration permits. Gem and Agnew Lakes make spectacular day hikes, while Thousand Island and Emerald Lake (both on the Pacific Crest/John Muir Trail) are good overnight destinations. Overnight wilderness permits are required (p375).

You can also saddle up with **Frontier Pack Train** (☎ 760-648-7701; 888-437-6853; www.frontierpack train.com). Trips run from $25 for one hour to $85 for a full day. Multiday pack trips start at $500.

Boat and tackle rentals, as well as fishing licenses, are available at five marinas. One of the most established outfitters is **Ernie's Tackle & Ski Shop** (☎ 760-648-7756; 2604 Hwy 158) in June Lake village.

Winter fun concentrates in the **June Mountain Ski Area** (☎ 760-648-7733, 888-586-3686; www.junemountain.com; lift tickets adult/child $53/28), which is smaller and less crowded than nearby Mammoth Mountain (p396) and

perfect for beginner and intermediate ski-ers. Some 35 trails crisscross 500 acres of terrain served by eight lifts, including two high-speed quads. Boarders can get their adrenaline flowing at three terrain parks with a kick-ass superpipe.

Sleeping

Double Eagle Resort & Spa (☎ 760-648-7004; www .doubleeagleresort.com; 5587 Hwy 158; r incl breakfast $230-250, cabins $315-350; ☒ ☒) The sleek log cabins and brand-new balconied hotel rooms at this relaxing resort lack no comfort, while wrinkles and worries disappear at the swank spa (day pass $20). Ask about discounts for multiday stays.

June Lake Villager Motel (☎ 760-648-7712, 800-655-6545; www.junelakevillager.com; r $50-265; ☒) Owner Jamie and her dog Samantha pre-side over this rambling cluster of rooms and cabins that mix and match retro and mod-ern. All have TVs and VCRs, and some also have kitchens. In winter, relax in the indoor Jacuzzi. The motel is right in the village, a block from June Lake.

June Lake, Oh Ridge, Silver, Gull Lake and Reversed Creek are all **USFS campgrounds** (☎ 800-444-7275; www.reserveusa.com; sites $15; ☺ mid-Apr-Oct). Only the first two campgrounds accept reservations.

The private **Pine Cliff Resort Campground** (☎ 760-648-7558; tents $12, RV sites $17-22, camping trailers per week $185-460), next to Oh Ridge, has a store and public hot showers ($1).

Eating

Double Eagle Resort restaurant (☎ 760-648-7897; 5587 Hwy 158; mains breakfast & lunch $6-9, dinner $15-28) The restaurant at this deluxe resort exudes rustic elegance, with cozy booths and a huge fireplace.

Tiger Bar (☎ 760-648-7551; 2620 Hwy 158; dishes $6-15) After a day on slopes or trails, people gather at the long bar or around the pool table of this no-nonsense, no-attitude kind of place. The kitchen feeds all appetites with burgers, salads, tacos and other tasty grub, including homemade fries.

Carson Peak Inn (☎ 760-648-7575; Hwy 158 btwn Gull & Silver Lake; meals $13-25; ☺ dinner) In-side a cozy house with fireplace, this well-regarded restaurant is much beloved for its tasty old-time indulgences such as beef brochette, broiled pork chop and chopped sirloin steak.

SIERRA NEVADA

MAMMOTH LAKES

pop 7200 / elevation 7800ft

Mammoth Lakes, an Eastern Sierra commercial hub, is a fast-growing four-seasons resort town framed by breathtaking scenery. Summers bring sunny days, cool nights and a bonanza of outdoor activities, from hiking and backpacking to mountain-biking and fishing in the town's half-dozen lakes. In winter the action revolves around **Mammoth Mountain** (11,053ft), one of California's top ski resorts, which usually gets more snow than any other place in the Sierra.

Skiing pioneer Dave McCoy was the first to harness nature's bounty in 1941 by installing a portable rope tow powered by his jacked-up Model A Ford. After the first chairlift began operating in 1955, Mammoth soon evolved into a popular resort but managed to maintain its cozy, low-key, small-town character for decades. Things started changing in the 1990s when McCoy partnered with Canadian development company Intrawest. And so began the 'condo-fication' of Mammoth. Aside from condominium complexes, Intrawest also created the **Village at Mammoth**, a cookie-cutter insta-mall, complete with gondola to the mountain base. Efforts are under way to expand either Mammoth Airport or the one in Bishop further south to lure in the jet-set crowd. Mammoth, the town, may be changing, for better or for worse. But the mountain still stands: raw, fierce and eternal.

Orientation

Mammoth Lakes is 3 miles off Hwy 395 via Hwy 203, which turns into Main St after the first traffic light. At the second light it turns right and continues as Minaret Rd past the new Village at Mammoth to Mammoth Mountain Ski Area and shuttle bus to Reds Meadow/Devils Postpile. Continue straight at the second light for Mammoth Lakes Basin via Lake Mary Rd (closed in winter).

Information

BOOKSTORES

Booky Joint (☎ 760-934-2176; 437 Old Mammoth Rd) Inside the Minaret Village Mall; also rents movies.

EMERGENCY & MEDICAL SERVICES

Mammoth Hospital (☎ 760-934-3311; 85 Sierra Park Rd; ☾ 24hr) Emergency room.
Police, fire & medical (☎ 911) Emergency.

INTERNET ACCESS

Looney Bean (☎ 760-934-1345; Gateway Center Mall, 26 Old Mammoth Rd; per 15 min $3; ☾ 6am-8pm or 9pm) DSL and wi-fi.
Mammoth Lakes Library (☎ 760-934-4777; 960 Forest Trail; ☾ 10am-7pm Mon-Fri, 9am-5:30pm Sat) Free DSL and wi-fi.

MEDIA

Mammoth Times (www.mammothtimes.com) Free weekly tabloid.

POST

Main post office (3330 Main St) Just past the Chevron gas station.

TOURIST INFORMATION

Mammoth Lakes Visitor Center & Ranger Station (☎ 760-934-5500, 888-466-2666; www.visitmammoth .com; Hwy 203; ☾ 8am-5pm) One-stop center for information and wilderness permits.

Sights

Not only snow fans are drawn to the sparkling new **Mammoth Ski Museum** (☎ 760-934-6592; 100 College Parkway; adult/child/student $3/free/2; ☾ noon-5pm Tue-Sun), which shines an artistic light on the sport with its great collection of vintage posters, photographs, paintings and pins. The small theater presents historical films, lectures and other events and also has exhibits about local ski history.

For another walk down memory lane, stop by the little **Mammoth Museum** (☎ 760-934-6918; 5489 Sherwin Creek Rd; donations welcome; ☾ 9:30am-4:30pm Jun-Oct), inside a historic log cabin.

Activities

SKIING & SNOWBOARDING

Mammoth Mountain Ski Area (☎ information 760-934-0745, 800-626-6684, 24hr snow report 888-766-9778; www.mammothmountain.com; lift tickets adult/senior & child Mon-Fri $61/30, Sat & Sun $70/35) is still a true skiers' and snowboarders' resort, where playing hard and having fun are more important than who designed your anorak. Sunny skies, reliable snow (the season generally runs from November to June) and over 3500 acres of fantastic tree-line and open-bowl skiing prove to be a potent cocktail. At the top you'll be dealing with some gnarly, nearly vertical chutes. The other stats are just as impressive: 3100 vertical feet, 150 trails, 27 lifts (including 10 quads). Boarders, meanwhile, will find world-class

SIERRA NEVADA

MAMMOTH LAKES

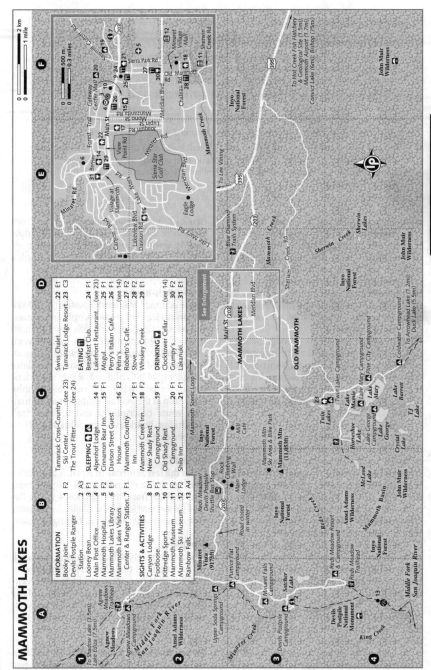

INFORMATION
Booky Joint...................................1	F2
Devils Postpile Ranger	
Station.......................................2	A3
Looney Bean...............................3	F1
Main Post Office..........................4	F1
Mammoth Hospital.......................5	F2
Mammoth Lakes Library................6	E1
Mammoth Lakes Visitors	
Center & Ranger Station..............7	F1

SIGHTS & ACTIVITIES
Canyon Lodge.............................8	D1
Footloose...................................9	F1
Kittredge Sports.........................10	F1
Mammoth Museum......................11	F2
Mammoth Ski Museum.................12	F2
Rainbow Falls.............................13	A4

Tamarack Cross-Country	
Ski Center.............................(see 23)	
The Trout Fitter.....................(see 24)	

SLEEPING
Alpenhof Lodge..........................14	E1
Cinnamon Bear Inn.....................15	F1
Davison Street Guest	
House.....................................16	E2
Mammoth Country	
Inn...17	E1
Mammoth Creek Inn....................18	F2
New Shady Rest	
Campground...........................19	F1
Old Shady Rest	
Campground...........................20	F1
Shilo Inn...................................21	F1

Swiss Chalet..............................22	E1
Tamarack Lodge Resort...............23	C3

EATING 🍴
Breakfast Club............................24	F1
Lakefront Restaurant..............(see 23)	
Mogul..25	E1
Perry's Italian Cafe.....................26	F1
Petra's.......................................27	F2
Roberto's Cafe...........................28	E1
Stove...29	E1

DRINKING 🍷
Clocktower Cellar..................(see 14)	
Grumpy's..................................30	F2
Lakanuki....................................31	E1

TOP THREE MAMMOTH HIKES

■ Duck Lake (11-mile round trip, Duck Lake trailhead, moderate to strenuous) This day hike starts at Coldwater campground near Lake Mary and climbs to intensely blue Duck Lake, skirting a necklace of smaller lakes along the way, including Arrowhead Lake (reached after 1.2 miles), which has some fine cliff-jumping. It's a great hike no matter how far you make it.

■ Shadow Lake/Lake Ediza (15-mile round trip, Agnew Meadows trailhead, moderate) This classic Sierra hike travels along a cascading creek into the Ansel Adams Wilderness from Agnew Meadows with stupendous views of the imposing Ritter Range and the glacier-draped Minarets. For a shorter hike, turn back at Shadow Lake after 3.5 miles.

■ McLeod Lake (1-mile round trip, Mammoth Pass trailhead, easy) Great for kids, this little hike takes you from Horseshoe Lake in Mammoth Basin to sparkling McLeod Lake. More ambitious types can continue for another 3.5 miles to Reds Meadow and catch the shuttle ($7) back into town.

challenges in three terrain parks with intense superpipes and urban-style jibs.

Four hubs are at the base of the mountain: Main Lodge, Canyon Lodge, Eagle Lodge and the Mill Café, each with ticket offices and parking lots. Free ski shuttles pick up throughout town. Alternatively, hop on the new Village Gondola that whisks you up to Canyon Lodge – the base of several chair lifts – in six minutes.

Main Lodge and Canyon Lodge have ski schools and state-of-the-art equipment rental (ski package $17 to $27, snowboards $22 to $30), although prices are lower at outfitters in town, including **Footloose** (☎ 760-934-2400; 3043 Main St) and **Kittredge Sports** (☎ 760-934-7566; 3218 Main St).

CROSS-COUNTRY SKIING

There's free cross-country skiing along the 30km of nongroomed trails of the Blue Diamond Trails System, which winds through several patches of scenic forest around town. Pick up a map at the visitors center.

A nicer if pricier option is the **Tamarack Cross-Country Ski Center** (☎ 760-934-5293; Lake Mary Rd; all-day trail pass adult/child/senior $22/free/17; ☺ 8am-5pm) Right at Twin Lakes, it has 45km of meticulously groomed track around Twin Lakes and the lakes basin. The terrain is also great for snowshoeing. Rentals and lessons are available.

HIKING & BACKPACKING

Mammoth Lakes rubs up against the Ansel Adams Wilderness and John Muir Wilderness, both laced with fabulous trails leading to shimmering lakes, rugged peaks and hidden canyons. Major trailheads leave from the Mammoth Lakes Basin, Reds Meadow and Agnew Meadows, the latter two are accessible only by shuttle (p400). Kittredge Sports is a good outfitter.

MOUNTAIN-BIKING

Come summer, **Mammoth Mountain** (☎ 760-934-0706; day pass $32; ☺ 8am-6pm) morphs into a massive Mountain-Bike Park with more than 80 miles of well-kept single-track trails. Several other trails traverse the surrounding forest. In general, Mammoth-style riding translates into plenty of hills and soft, sandy shoulders, which are best navigated with big knobby tires. Stop at the visitors center for a free map with route descriptions and updated trail conditions. Footloose rents bikes for $24 to $48 per day.

FISHING

From the last Saturday in April, Mammoth's lakes exert their lure to trout anglers from near and far. **Trout Fitter** (☎ 760-924-3676; cnr Hwy 203 & Old Mammoth Rd) in the Shell Mart Center rents equipment and issues fishing licenses.

Sleeping

Mammoth rarely sells out during midweek when rates tend to be lower. During ski season, reservations are a good idea on weekends and essential during holidays. Many properties offer special ski and stay packages. Check with the visitors center.

HOSTELS

Davison Street Guest House (☎ 760-924-2188, reservations 619-544-9093, 858-755-8648; www.mammoth-guest

moth, chilly Mammoth Creek blends with hot springs and continues its journey as Hot Creek. It eventually enters a small gorge and forms a series of steaming, bubbling cauldrons with water shimmering in shades of blue and green reminiscent of the tropics. It's possible to soak in the pools, but sections can be scalding. Pay attention to posted signs.

Turn off Hwy 395 about 5 miles south of town and follow signs to the Hot Creek Fish Hatchery. From here, it's another 2 miles on gravel road to the parking area, from where it's a short but steep trek down into the canyon and to the creek. The hatchery itself raises about three million trout each year for stocking the Sierra's lakes and streams, and is open for visitors.

Convict Lake
Convict Lake is one of the area's prettiest lakes, with pellucid emerald water embraced by massive peaks. A trek along the gentle trail skirting the lake, through aspen and cottonwood trees, is great if you're still adjusting to the altitude. A trailhead on the southeastern shore gives access to Genevieve, Edith, Dorothy and Mildred Lakes in the John Muir Wilderness.

In 1871 Convict Lake was the site of a bloody shoot-out between a band of escaped convicts and a posse that had given chase. Posse leader, Sheriff Robert Morrison, was killed during the gunfight and the taller peak, Mt Morrison (12,268ft), was later named in his honor. The bad guys got away only to be apprehended later near Bishop.

The **campground** (sites $15; ⊗ mid-Apr–Oct) has flush toilets and nicely terraced sites. Otherwise your only option is **Convict Lake Resort** (☎ 760-934-3800, 800-992-2260; www.convictlake.com; cabins from $120), whose 29 cabins with kitchens sleep from two to 34 and range from rustic to ritzy. Food fanciers with deep pockets flock to the stuffily elegant restaurant (mains $19-32), which many consider the best within a 100-mile radius.

BISHOP
pop 3450 / elevation 4140ft
Many people think of Bishop as a place to refuel their car and their tummy, and given the abundance of gas stations, fast-food outlets and supermarkets, who can blame them? The truth is that this little western-flavored town is surrounded by awesome

nature where you can wear yourself out with world-class rock climbing, fishing and hiking. The area is especially lovely in fall when dropping temperatures cloak aspen, willow and cottonwood in myriad glowing shades. It's no coincidence that celebrated wilderness photographer and climber Galen Rowell made Bishop his adopted home until his fatal plane crash in 2002.

Orientation
Bishop's main street is full of motels, restaurants, coffeehouses, gas stations, small malls and outfitters as well as a good bookstore, a tiny movie theater and a casino. Line St heads into the mountains as Hwy 168.

Information
Bishop Area Visitor Center (☎ 760-873-8405; www.bishopvisitor.com; 690 N Main St; ⊗ 9am-5pm Mon-Fri, 10am-4pm Sat & Sun).
Kava Coffeehouse (☎ 760-872-1010; 206 N Main St; 1st 10min $3, then per min 10¢) Internet access and free wi-fi with purchase.
Spellbinder Books (☎ 760-873-4511; 124 S Main St) Indie bookstore with attached café.
White Mountain Ranger Station (☎ 760-873-2500; 798 N Main St; ⊗ 8am-5pm late May-early Sep, shorter hours rest of year) Wilderness permits, trail and campground information for the entire area.

Sights
The rich traditions and heritage of Bishop's first inhabitants come to life at the **Paiute Shoshone Indian Cultural Center** (☎ 760-873-4478; 2300 W Line St; adult/child $4/1; ⊗ 9am-5pm Mon-Fri, 10am-5pm Sat & Sun), a few blocks west of Hwy 395. It was closed for renovation when we went to press but should have reopened by the time you're reading this. Exhibits include fanciful bead-covered baskets, leathercraft, clothing and tools, but the most interesting are the re-created traditional living spaces, including a reed shelter, sweat lodge and winter camp. Check with the Bishop Area Visitor Center for hours and admission prices.

Back on Main St, pop into the **Mountain Light Gallery** (☎ 760-873-7700; 106 S Main St; admission free; ⊗ 10am-6pm Sun-Thu, 10am-9pm Fri & Sat), which displays and sells many of Galen Rowell's most magical photos taken in the Sierra and elsewhere.

Railroad and Old West aficionados might want to make the 6-mile detour north on Hwy 6 to the **Laws Railroad Museum** (☎ 760-873-5950;

SIERRA NEVADA

www.thesierraweb.com/bishop/laws; admission by donation; ☺ 10am-4pm). It re-creates the village of Laws, an important stop on the route of the *Slim Princess*, a narrow-gauge train that hauled freight and passengers across the Owens Valley for nearly 80 years. The original 1883 train depot is here, as are a post office, a schoolhouse and other rickety old buildings. Many contain funky and eclectic displays (dolls, bottles, fire equipment, antique stoves etc) from the pioneer days.

Activities

Bishop is prime **bouldering** and **rock climbing** territory with terrain to match any level of fitness, experience and climbing style. The main areas are the granite Buttermilk Country west of town, and the stark Volcanic Tablelands and Owens River Valley to the north. For details, download free miniguides from www.rockfax.com or consult with the staff at **Wilson's Eastside Sports** (☎ 760-873-7520; 224 N Main St), which rents equipment and sells maps and guidebooks. The tablelands are also great for Native American petroglyph spotting.

Hikers will want to head to the high country by following Line St (Hwy 168) west along Bishop Creek Canyon past Buttermilk Country and on to several lakes, including Lake Sabrina and South Lake. Trailheads lead into the John Muir Wilderness and on into Kings Canyon National Park. Check with the White Mountain Ranger Station (p401) for suggestions, maps and wilderness permits for overnight stays. **Fishing** is good in all lakes but North Lake is the least crowded.

If you'd rather let horses do the walking, sign up with a pack outfitter, each offering a variety of tours. **Rainbow Pack Outfitters** (☎ 760-872-8803; 600 Main St) and **Bishop Pack Outfitters** (☎ 760-873-4785, 800-316-4252) are both based in Bishop.

About 8 miles south of Bishop is **Keough's Hot Springs** (☎ 760-872-6911; 800 Keough Hot Springs Rd; adult/concession $7/4; ☺ 11am-7pm Wed-Mon), a recently renovated historic outdoor pool (dating from 1919), filled with tepid water from local mineral springs.

Sleeping

Bishop has plenty of roadside motels with unexciting rooms from $40. For a little more style and comfort, try the following places.

Chalfant House (☎ 760-872-1790, 800-641-2996; www.chalfanthouse.com; 213 Academy St; r incl breakfast

$80-105; ✗) The doors swing open and you enter another time and world at this heroically restored B&B, the onetime home of Bishop's first newspaper publisher, Pleasant A Chalfant. Rooms are named after Chalfant family members and dripping with chintz and antiques.

Best Western Creekside Inn (☎ 760-872-3044, 800-273-3550; 725 N Main St; r incl breakfast $109-159; ✗ ◻ ✿) You'll be well taken care of at this motel where rooms offer plenty of elbow space and easy-on-the-eyes decor. The nicest are upstairs facing the garden with a little stream. Free high-speed Internet access.

The only campground in town is big, shady **Brown's Town** (☎ 760-873-8522; sites $14-19), which is popular with the RV crowd and has a store, café and small Old West museum. The closest **USFS campgrounds** (sites $16), all first-come, first served, are between 9 miles and 15 miles west of town on Bishop Creek along Hwy 168. Most are open from May to September or October. Shower at Keough's Hot Springs or in town at the **Wash Tub** (236 N Warren St; ☺ 7am-9pm), where you can also wash your smalls.

Eating

Erick Schat's Bakkerÿ (☎ 760-873-7156; 763 N Main St; sandwiches $3.50-7; ☺ 6am-6:30pm) Ignore the gift shop and hordes of bus tourists and focus on the huge selection of yummy homemade breads, cookies, pastries and other tasty treats. For more sustenance order one of the made-to-order sandwiches.

Whiskey Creek Bar & Restaurant (☎ 760-873-7174; 524 N Main St; mains $10-23; ☺ 7am-9pm) In a gabled country inn, this somewhat stuffy restaurant serves all-American fare, including juicy steaks, slow-roasted prime ribs and big salads. For a looser vibe head to the saloon with its mountain-view sundeck, appetizers and local ales on tap.

Upper Crust Pizza Co (☎ 760-872-8153; 1180 N Main St; mains lunch $5-8, dinner $11-19; ☺ 11am-9pm) The toothsome pizza pies, washed down with local brews, taste best after a day of exertion in the outdoors. Good pastas and salads too.

Other recommended eats:

Bar-B-Q Bills (☎ 760-872-5535; 187 S Main St; sandwiches $4-10, dinners $9-17; ☺ 11am-8:30pm) Smoked-meat sandwiches drenched in a zingy barbecue sauce.

Imperial Gourmet Chinese Restaurant (☎ 760-872-1144; Cottonwood Mall, 785 N Main St; mains $7-19; ☺ 11am-10pm)

BIG PINE

pop 1350 / elevation 3985ft

This blink-and-you-missed-it town has a few motels, basic eateries and two gas stations. It mainly functions as a launch pad for the Ancient Bristlecone Pine Forest (see the boxed text, below) and to the granite **Palisades** in the John Muir Wilderness, a rugged cluster of peaks including six above 14,000ft. Stretching beneath the pinnacles is **Palisades Glacier**, the southernmost in the USA and the largest in the Sierra. Stop by the **visitors center** (☎ 760-938-2114; www.bigpine.com; 126 S Main St; ☺ 10am-5:30pm Tue-Sat) for maps and information about the entire area. The closest place for wilderness permits is White Mountain Ranger Station (p401) in Bishop.

To get to the trailhead, turn onto Glacier Lodge Rd (Crocker Ave in town), which follows trout-rich Big Pine Creek up **Big Pine Canyon** 10 miles west into a bowl-shaped valley. The strenuous 9-mile hike to Palisade Glacier via the North Fork Trail skirts several lakes – turned a milky turquoise color by glacial runoff – and a stone cabin built by horror-film actor Lon Chaney in 1925. **Glacier Pack Train** (☎ 760-938-2538) offers horseback rides from $50 and pack trips from $90 per day.

Glacier Lodge Rd passes by a trio of **USFS campgrounds** (☎ 877-444-6777; www.reserveusa.com; sites $15; ☺ May–mid-Oct) – Big Pine Creek, Sage Flat and Upper Sage Flat. Showers are available for $4 at **Glacier Lodge** (☎ 760-938-2837; www.jewelofthesierra.com; cabins $80; ☺ mid-Apr–mid-Nov), a bunch of rustic cabins with kitchens and a two-night minimum stay in July and August; it was one of the earliest Sierra getaways when built in 1917. The small store has only basics, so bring groceries. With advance notice, Cathy and her crew will barbecue burgers, steaks and chicken for lunch (about $7) and dinner ($10 to $22).

INDEPENDENCE

pop 1000 / elevation 3925ft

This sleepy highway town has been a county seat since 1866 and is home to the **Eastern California Museum** (☎ 760-878-0364; 155 N Grant St; donation requested; ☺ 10am-4pm Wed-Mon). Exhibits touch on numerous chapters in Sierra history, including the pioneer days and life at the Manzanar relocation camp (see boxed text, p404). It also has a prized collection of Paiute and Shoshone baskets.

West of town via Onion Valley Rd (Market St in town), pretty **Onion Valley** harbors the trailhead for the **Kearsarge Pass** (10-mile round-trip), an old Paiute trade route. This is also the quickest eastside access to the Pacific Crest Trail and Kings Canyon National Park. Another trail goes to Golden Trout Lake, but it's strenuous and poorly marked. A herd

---

DETOUR: ANCIENT BRISTLECONE PINE FOREST

For encounters with some of the earth's oldest living things, plan at least a half-day trip to the **Ancient Bristlecone Pine Forest** (☎ 760-873-2500). These gnarled, otherworldly-looking trees thrive above 10,000ft on the slopes of the seemingly inhospitable White Mountains, a parched and stark range that once stood even higher than the Sierra. The oldest tree – called Methuselah – is estimated to be over 4700 years, beating even the Great Sphinx of Giza by about two centuries.

To reach the groves, take Hwy 168 east 13 miles from Big Pine to White Mountain Rd, then turn left (north) and climb the curvy road 10 miles to **Schulman Grove**, named for the scientist who first discovered the trees' biblical age in the 1950s. There's a **visitors center** (☎ 760-873-2500; ☺ 8am-5pm late May-Oct) and access to self-guided trails. The entire trip should take about one hour. White Mountain Rd is usually closed from November to April. It's nicest in August when wildflowers sneak out through the rough soil.

A second grove, the **Patriarch Grove**, is dramatically set within an open bowl and reached via a 13-mile graded dirt road. Four miles further on is the Barcroft High Altitude Research Station, the departure point for day hikes to the **White Mountain Peak** – at 14,246ft it's the third-highest mountain in California and only 251ft lower than Mt Whitney. The round-trip is about 15 miles via an abandoned road. Although the route is easy to find, the high elevation makes the going tough. Allow plenty of time and bring at least two quarts of water per person. For maps and details, stop at the White Mountain Ranger Station (p401) in Bishop.

To adjust to the altitude, it's a good idea to spend a night at the free but undeveloped **Grandview Campground** at 8600ft. It has awesome views, but bring your own water.

SIERRA NEVADA

CAMP OF INFAMY

On December 7, 1941, Japanese war planes bombed Pearl Harbor, a day that, according to President Roosevelt, would forever live in infamy. The sneak attack plunged the US into WWII and fanned the flames of racial prejudice that had been fomenting against Japanese Americans for decades. Amidst fears of sabotage and espionage, bigotry grew into full-blown hysteria, prompting Roosevelt to sign Executive Order 9066 in February 1942; another day that lives in infamy. The act stated that all West Coast Japanese – most of them American-born citizens – were to be rounded up and moved to relocation camps.

Manzanar was the first of 10 such camps, built among pear and apple orchards in the dusty Owens Valley near Independence. Between 1942 and 1945, up to 10,000 men, women and children lived crammed into makeshift barracks pounded by fierce winds and the blistering desert sun and enclosed by barbed wire patrolled by military police.

After the war, the camp was leveled and its dark history remained buried beneath the dust for decades. Recognition remained elusive until 1973 when the site was given landmark status; in 1992 it was designated a national historic site and in 2004 a long-awaited interpretive center opened. A full-scale reconstruction of a guard tower is in the works. Former internees and their descendants make a pilgrimage to the camp every last Saturday in April (www.manzanarcommit tee.org). For a vivid and haunting account of what life was like at the camp, read Jean Wakatsuki Houston's classic *Farewell to Manzanar*.

of California bighorn sheep lives south of Onion Valley around Shepherd Pass.

You can sample the historic ambience of the **Winnedumah Hotel** (☎ 760-878-2040; www .winnedumah.com; 211 N Edwards St; r incl breakfast $50-80; ☒), a 1927 country-style inn that was popular with Hollywood celebs when the cameras were rolling in the Alabama Hills near Lone Pine. Onion Valley also has a couple of **campgrounds** (sites $13; ☼ May-Sep) along Independence Creek.

For eats, it's mostly greasy spoons, which makes the French gourmet bistro called **Still Life Café** (☎ 760-878-2555; 135 S Edward St; mains lunch $8-14, dinner $18-30; ☼ usually lunch & dinner Wed-Sun) pop out like an orchid in a salt flat. Escargot, duck-liver mousse, steak *au poivre* and other French delectables are served with Gallic charm in this bright, artistic dining room.

MANZANAR NATIONAL HISTORIC SITE

One of the darkest chapters in US history unfolded on a barren and windy sweep of land some 5 miles south of Independence. Little remains of the infamous war relocation camp, where over 10,000 people of Japanese ancestry were corralled during WWII following the attack on Pearl Harbor. Since 2004, the camp's lone remaining building, the former high-school auditorium, houses a superb **interpretive center** (☎ 760-878-2194; www.nps .gov/manz; admission free; ☼ 9am-4:30pm, extended sum-

mer hours). A visit here is one of the historical highlights along Hwy 395 and should not be missed.

Start by watching the 20-minute documentary that will touch your heart, open your eyes and add poignancy to the state of the art exhibits that chronicle various facets of life in the camp, from living conditions to medical care and education. Afterwards, take a self-guided 3.2-mile driving tour around the grounds, which takes you past vestiges of buildings and gardens as well as the camp cemetery. Also ask about guided ranger tours.

LONE PINE
pop 2800 / elevation 3700ft

Lone Pine may be tiny but it is the gateway to big things, most notably Mt Whitney (14,497ft), the loftiest peak in the contiguous USA, and...Hollywood. In the 1920s cinematographers discovered the nearby Alabama Hills were a picture-perfect movie set for Westerns, and stars from Gary Cooper to Gregory Peck could often be spotted swaggering about town. You can see their names scratched into the walls of the **Indian Trading Post** (137 Main St) and view exhibits in the small **Movie Room** (126 Main St). A brand-new **Museum of Lone Pine Film History** (www.lonepinefilmhistorymuseum.org) was in the works at press time and should hae opened by the time you're reading this.

For updates, check the website or ask the folks at any of the visitors centers in the area.

Orientation & Information

A few basic motels, restaurants and stores flank Hwy 395 (Main St in town). Whitney Portal Rd heads west at the lone stoplight, while Hwy 136 to Death Valley veers away about 2 miles south of town.

Eastern Sierra Interagency Visitor Center (☎ 760-876-6222; ☺ 8am-5pm, extended summer hours possible) Information central for the Sierra and Death Valley; about 1.5 miles south of town at the junction of Hwys 395 and 136.

Lone Pine Chamber of Commerce (☎ 760-876-4444; www.lonepinechamber.com; 126 S Main St; ☺ 9am-5pm Mon-Sat)

Mt Whitney Ranger Station (☎ 760-876-6200; ☺ 7am-4:30pm May-Oct, later in Jul & Aug) Shares a building with the visitors center and issues wilderness permits.

Sights & Activities
MOUNT WHITNEY

West of Lone Pine, the jagged incisors of the Sierra surge skyward in all their raw and fierce glory. Cradled by scores of smaller pinnacles, Mt Whitney is a bit hard to pick out from Hwy 395, so for the best views, take a drive along Whitney Portal Rd through the Alabama Hills. As you get a fix on this majestic megalith, remember that the country's lowest point is only 80 miles (as the crow flies) east of here: Badwater (p670) in Death Valley. Climbing to Mt Whitney's summit is among the most popular hikes in the entire country (see boxed text).

ALABAMA HILLS

Just off Whitney Portal Rd, nature has wrought a wonderfully warped landscape of coyote-colored boulders piled up in bizarre formations that form a fabulous foreground to Mt Whitney and the razor-edged Sierra.

CLIMBING MOUNT WHITNEY

The mystique of Mt Whitney captures the imagination, and conquering its hulking bulk becomes a sort of obsession for many. The Main Mt Whitney Trail (the easiest and busiest one) leaves from Whitney Portal, about 13 miles west of Lone Pine via the Whitney Portal Rd (closed in winter), and climbs about 6000ft over 11 miles. It's a super-strenuous, really, *really* long walk that'll wear out even experienced mountaineers but doesn't require technical skills if attempted in summer or early fall. Earlier or later in the season, you'll likely need an ice axe and crampons.

Many people in good physical condition make it to the top, although only superbly conditioned, previously acclimatized hikers should attempt this as a day hike. Breathing becomes difficult at these elevations and altitude sickness is a common problem. Rangers recommend spending a night or two camping at the trailhead and another at one of the two camps along the route: Outpost Camp at 3.5 miles or Trail Camp at 6 miles up the trail.

When considering an ascent, do your homework. A recommended guide is *Climbing Mt Whitney* by Walt Wheelock and Wynne Benti. Before setting out, call or stop by the Mt Whitney Ranger Station in Lone Pine to get the latest scoop about weather and trail conditions.

Whitney Portal has two attractive campgrounds tucked into a pine forest along Lone Pine Creek: **Whitney Portal** (☎ 877-444-6777; www.reserveusa.com; sites $16; ☺ May–mid-Oct), about half a mile from the trailhead, with 44 lovely terraced sites, chemical flush toilets and potable water; and the 10-site first-come, first-served **Whitney Trailhead** (sites $8; ☺ May–mid-Oct), which has a one-night maximum and the same facilities. If they're full, consider the 38-site **Lone Pine Campground** (☎ 877-444-6777; www.reserveusa.com; sites $14; ☺ mid-Apr–Oct), about 7 miles east of the trailhead off Whitney Portal Rd. The **Whitney Portal Store** sells groceries and snacks, and rents bear-resistant food containers. It also has public showers and a café with hot meals.

The biggest obstacle in getting to the peak may be to obtain a wilderness permit (per person $15), which is required for all overnight trips and for day hikes past Lone Pine Lake (about 2.8 miles from the trailhead). A quota system limits daily access to 60 overnight and 100 day-hikers from May through October. Because of the huge demand, permits are distributed via a lottery. Send or fax your application to the **Wilderness Permit Office Info National Forest** (fax 760-873-2484; 351 Pacu Lane, Bishop, CA 93514) anytime in February. Check www.fs.fed.us/r5/inyo/recreation /wild/mtwhitney.shtml for full details and application forms.

The landscape has enchanted artists, climbers and Hollywood filmmakers, who used them in such Hollywood classics as *Gunga Din* and *How the West Was Won*. You can drive, walk or mountain-bike along dirt roads rambling through the boulders, and along Tuttle and Lone Pine creeks. Head west on Whitney Portal Rd and either turn left at Tuttle Creek Rd, after a half-mile, or north on Movie Rd, after about 3 miles. Pick up maps at the Lone Pine Chamber of Commerce.

Sleeping & Eating

Historical Dow Hotel & Dow Villa Motel (☎ 760-876-5521, 800-824-9317; www.dowvillamotel.com; 310 S Main St; hotel r with/without bathroom $56/42, motel r $86-120; ☒) John Wayne and Errol Flynn are among the stars who have stayed at this venerable hotel. Built in 1922, the place has been restored but retains much of its rustic charm. The rooms in the newer motel section are more comfortable but also more generic.

Best Western Frontier (☎ 760-876-5571; 1008 S Main St; r incl breakfast $60-110; ☒) South of town, this motel has pleasant, good-sized rooms, including some with a Jacuzzi tub. It's all pretty generic, but the framed movie stills and local landscapes add a local touch and the free wi-fi is a rare perk in these parts.

Mt Whitney Restaurant (☎ 760-876-5751; 227 S Main St; dishes $6-12; ☼ 6:30am-9pm) Walls covered with old-timey movie stills compete for attention with the classic and exotic burgers (made with buffalo, ostrich or venison as well as beef and turkey) at this funky institution that occupies a special spot in locals' hearts and stomachs.

High Sierra Café (☎ 760-876-5796; 446 S Main St; meals $5-12; ☼ 24hr) The food won't knock your socks off, but this coffee shop is one of the few places along Hwy 395 that feeds hungry travelers 24/7.

Central Valley

The Central Valley is the part of California that seems to belong in some other state. Travelers tend to be in a hurry to get somewhere else because the valley lies between the coast and the Sierra Nevada. These are the plains of California; a vast, flat zone given over mostly to agriculture. It's a land of Podunk towns, endless fields, truck stops, produce stands and aluminum sheds. It's home to laborers from Mexico, descendents of Dustbowl migrants, large Portuguese communities and agribusiness execs. When San Franciscans are befuddled by US politics, they need only drive an hour to the Central Valley for a dose of reality.

Truth is, this is an integral part of California, full of overlooked towns and curiosities worth seeing, even if you're moving on to bigger fish elsewhere. Sacramento, the state capital, is a friendly burg that puts forth good food and entertainment with little pretense or big city attitude. Major universities are in Chico, Davis and Merced. Bakersfield still swings the way it did when Buck Owens first made California a country music force – in fact, ole Buck still swings at his own club. Some towns in the California Delta, though inhabited, have an eerie ghost-town feel that makes you want to pull off the highway to absorb the atmosphere.

As added incentive, the Central Valley is actually a two-for-one deal: two valleys, carved by the Sacramento and San Joaquin Rivers, join to make up one big valley some 400 miles long and 50 miles wide. This chapter mostly follows Hwy 99, which leaves I-5 south of Bakersfield and meets up with I-5 again in Red Bluff, north of Sacramento. Interstate 5 is the route to take from San Francisco to LA if you want to fly through the valley without seeing anything.

CENTRAL VALLEY

HIGHLIGHTS

- Hopping freights at Sacramento's **California State Railroad Museum** (p411)
- Absorbing the ghost town atmosphere in **Locke** (p415)
- Exploring Fresno's confounding **Forestiere Underground Gardens** (p426)
- Double-taking at the amazing 19th-century artifacts in **Oroville's Chinese Temple** (p417)
- Swinging at **Buck Owens' Crystal Palace** club in Bakersfield (p430)
- Kicking the tires at the **Hedrick Ag History Center's** tractor & truck museum (p417)
- Inner tubing through the party town of **Chico** (p420)

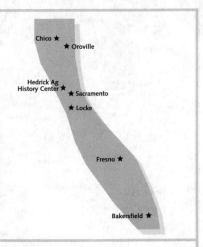

Chico ★   ★ Oroville

Hedrick Ag History Center ★   ★ Sacramento

★ Locke

Fresno ★

Bakersfield ★

- AVERAGE TEMPS IN SACRAMENTO: JAN 37/52°F, JUL 55/87°F

CENTRAL VALLEY

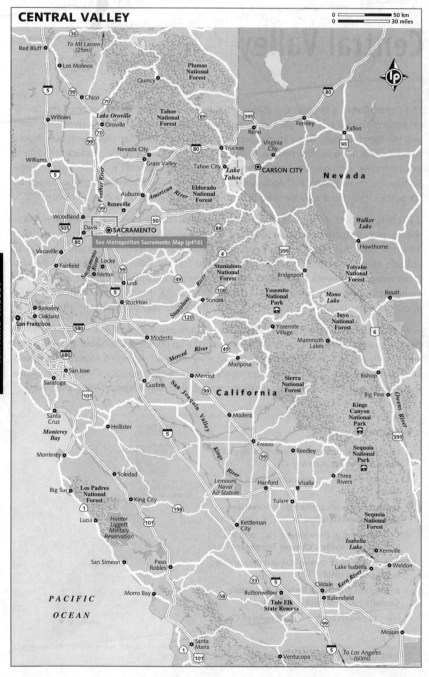

0 ——— 50 km
0 ——— 30 miles

Red Bluff
To Mt Lassen (25mi)
Los Molinos
Quincy
Plumas National Forest
Chico
Willows
Lake Oroville
Oroville
Tahoe National Forest
Williams
Nevada City
Grass Valley
Tahoe City
Lake Tahoe
Reno
Virginia City
Fernley
Fallon
CARSON CITY
Nevada
Feather River
Auburn
American River
Eldorado National Forest
Roseville
Woodland
Davis
SACRAMENTO
Walker Lake
Hawthorne
See Metropolitan Sacramento Map (p410)
Vacaville
Fairfield
Sacramento River
Locke
Isleton
Lodi
Stanialous National Forest
Bridgeport
Toiyabe National Forest
Basalt
Berkeley
Oakland
San Francisco
Stockton
Sonora
Yosemite National Park
Mono Lake
Stanislaus River
Modesto
Yosemite Village
Inyo National Forest
Merced River
Mammoth Lakes
San Jose
Mariposa
Saratoga
Gustine
Merced
California
Sierra National Forest
Bishop
Santa Cruz
Monterey Bay
Hollister
San Joaquin Valley
Madera
Kings Canyon National Park
Big Pine
Owens River
Monterey
Kings River
Fresno
Reedley
Sequoia National Park
Soledad
Big Sur
Los Padres National Forest
Lemoore Naval Air Station
Hanford
Visalia
Three Rivers
King City
Tulare
Lucia
Hunter Liggett Military Reservation
Kettleman City
Sequoia National Forest
San Simeon
Paso Robles
Isabella Lake
Kernville
Lake Isabella
Weldon
Kern River
Oildale
Bakersfield
Morro Bay
Buttonwillow
Tule Elk State Reserve
Mojave
PACIFIC OCEAN
Santa Maria
Ventucopa
To Los Angeles (60mi)

Getting There & Around

The main route through this part of California is Hwy 99. I-80 meets Hwy 99 in Sacramento, and I-5 meets Hwy 99 south of Bakersfield. Amtrak trains are a leisurely way up and down the state, but only go as far south as Bakersfield. Amtrak runs buses from there to Los Angeles. The train stops in just about every town but Visalia – travelers to that town get off at Hanford and transfer to a shuttle provided by the train company. Greyhound (☎ 800-229-9424) buses stop in all of the Central Valley towns and cities covered in this chapter.

SACRAMENTO VALLEY

The Sacramento River, California's largest, carved out the northern half of the Central Valley. The river runs down the northern mountains from Shasta Lake before hitting the valley basin above Red Bluff; from here it snakes leisurely through the state capital and fans across the delta before meeting San Francisco Bay. The valley has a subtle beauty, particularly in spring when fruit orchards are in full blossom. In fall the leaves turn gold and in early winter the sky teems with migratory birds following the path of the Pacific Flyway. In summer's oven temperatures the sky is bleached and the landscape parched, but the river flows as steadily as ever.

Most travelers on their way from the Bay Area to the Gold Country or Lake Tahoe pass through Davis and Sacramento. All of the Valley's other sights require just a minor detour.

SACRAMENTO

pop 407,000

The state's capital, Sacramento, is a city of politicians, lobbyists and a beefy governor with an odd, orange-hued tan who commutes from Los Angeles. The city has its share of stately government buildings, and long, tree-lined streets of Victorian homes. On the river's edge, the original city, Old Sacramento, evokes simpler times of river boats and wooden sidewalks.

Sacramento's better half is the city of regular people who enjoy a good time without the burden of putting on cosmopolitan airs. The Midtown club and restaurant scene is friendly, fun and attitude-free.

During rush hour, highway travel through Sacramento (or 'Sacto') can be a maddening, backed-up mess. If you're stuck passing through at such a time, cool your head at one of the city's vintage ice-cream parlors.

History

Many formative events in California's history took place in and around Sacramento.

John Sutter, the Swiss immigrant on whose sawmill the gold rush began, arrived in California in 1839 and built an outpost around the confluence of the American and Sacramento Rivers. It was the only secure fort between San Francisco and the Canadian border and quickly became a rendezvous point for white traders.

When James Marshall discovered gold in the tailrace of Sutter's lumber mill near Coloma in 1848, hundreds of thousands of people flocked to California, most traveling through Sutter's Fort. Sutter gave his fort to his son, who christened the newly sprung town 'Sacramento.' Though plagued by fires and flood, the riverfront settlement prospered and became the state capital in 1850.

The transcontinental railroad was conceived in Sacramento by a quartet of local merchants known as the 'Big Four' – Leland Stanford, Mark Hopkins, Collis P Huntington and Charles Crocker. Together they founded the Central Pacific Railroad, which began construction in Sacramento in 1863 and connected with the Union Pacific in Promontory, Utah in 1869.

Orientation

Sacramento sits at the confluence of the Sacramento and American Rivers, roughly halfway between San Francisco and Lake Tahoe. The Sacramento River runs along the western edge of downtown.

Four main highways cross through Sacramento. Hwy 99 and I-5 enter the city from the south; I-80 skirts downtown on the city's northern edge, heading west to the Bay Area and east to Reno; and Hwy 50 runs along downtown's southern edge (where it's also called Business Route 80) before heading east to Lake Tahoe.

Downtown, numbered streets run from north to south, lettered streets run east to west (Capitol Ave replaces M St). One-way J St is a main drag east from downtown to Midtown. The Tower District is south of downtown at the corner of Broadway and 16th St.

Cal Expo, the site of the California State Fair every August, is east of I-80 from the Cal Expo exit.

Information

Avid Reader (Map pp412–13; ☎ 916-443-7323; 1003 L St) A good bookstore across from the capitol.

Convention & Visitors Bureau (☎ 916-264-7777; www.sacramentocvb.org; 1303 J St; ✆ 8am-5pm Mon-Fri) Local information, including event and bus schedules.

Old Sacramento Visitor Center (Map pp412–13; ☎ 916-442-7644; 1002 2nd St; ✆ 10am-5pm) Also has local information, including event and bus schedules.

UC Davis Medical Center (Map p410; ☎ 916-734-2011; 2315 Stockton Blvd) On the east side of town, south of Hwy 50.

Sights

CALIFORNIA STATE CAPITOL

The **California State Capitol** (Map pp412–13; ☎ 916-324-0333; cnr 10th & L Sts; ✆ 9am-5pm) is Sacramento's most recognizable structure. Built in the late 19th century, it underwent major reconstruc-

tion in the 1970s. Rooms on the ground floor, called the Capitol Museum, contain furniture, portraits, photographs and documents from various periods of California history. Free tours leave hourly between 9am and 4pm from the tourist information office in the basement. Also in the basement are great murals, a free video and a **bookstore** (✆ 9:30am-4pm Mon-Fri, 10:30am-4pm Sat & Sun).

The 40 acres surrounding the capitol make up **Capitol Park**. With trees from all over the world it's a nice place to picnic or escape the summer heat. At the east end is a powerful Vietnam War memorial.

North of the Capitol is the **Governor's Mansion State Historic Park** (Map pp412–13; ☎ 916-323-3047; cnr 16th & H Sts; adult/child $4/2; ✆ 10am-5pm), built in 1877 and acquired by the state in 1903. No governor has lived in the house since Ronald Reagan moved out in the 1960s. Guided tours are given hourly from 10am to 4pm.

OLD SACRAMENTO

The old river port, adjacent to downtown Sacramento, is still largely intact, but due to poor restoration efforts looks more like

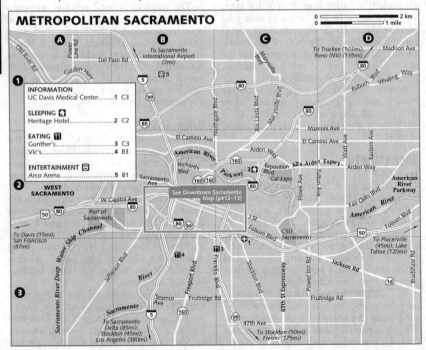

METROPOLITAN SACRAMENTO

0 ——— 2 km
0 ——— 1 mile

INFORMATION
UC Davis Medical Center........1 C3

SLEEPING
Heritage Hotel........................2 C2

EATING
Gunther's................................3 C3
Vic's......................................4 B3

ENTERTAINMENT
Arco Arena............................5 B1

a second-rate *Deadwood* set than a well-preserved remnant of the past. The pervasive scent of salt-water taffy does not help. It's worth looking past these disappointments to appreciate California's largest concentration of buildings on the National Register of Historic Places. Some of Sacramento's best attractions are in this part of town.

At Old Sac's north end is the excellent **California State Railroad Museum** (Map pp412-13; ☎ 916-445-6645; www.csrmf.org; cnr 2nd & I Sts; adult/child $6/2; ☺ 10am-5pm), near where the notorious Big Four masterminded the transcontinental railroad. The museum is the largest of its kind in the US and has an impressive collection of railcars, locomotives, toy models and memorabilia. The fully outfitted Pullman sleeper and vintage diner cars will induce a joyful palsy for railroad enthusiasts. Tickets include entrance to the restored **Central Pacific Passenger Depot**, across the plaza from the museum entrance. From the depot, on weekends from April to September, you can board a steam-powered passenger train (adult/child $6/3) for a 40-minute jaunt along the riverfront.

On your way to the depot, drop by the **Huntington & Hopkins Hardware** (Map pp412-13; ☎ 916-323-7234; I St; admission free; ☺ 11am-4pm, sometimes closed Mon-Wed), an exhibit of the business run by two of the Big Four railroad barons. The store, a rough reproduction, is stocked with the innocuous merchandise (doorknobs, lanterns, railroad spikes etc) upon which some huge fortunes, and the nation's most important railroad, were built.

Old Sac's other great feature is its riverfront setting. The **Spirit of Sacramento** (Map pp412-13; ☎ 916-552-2933, 800-433-0263; www.spiritofsacramento.com; tours $12.50), an 1842 paddle wheeler, makes one-hour sightseeing tours of the Sacramento River that are well worth the price. There are also cocktail and dinner cruises ($18 to $67). The boat leaves several times daily in summer from the L St dock.

Next door to the railroad museum, the **Discovery Museum** (Map pp412-13; ☎ 916-264-7057; 101 I St; adult/child $5/3; ☺ 10am-5pm Jun-Aug, Tue-Sun Sep-May) has hands-on exhibits and gold rush displays.

CROCKER ART MUSEUM
One of Sacramento's must-see attractions. Margaret and Judge Edwin B Crocker (tycoon Charles Crocker's brother) built two

magnificent Victorian mansions side by side, with one designed to house the Crocker personal art collection (along with a ballroom, skating rink and bowling alley). The **museum** (Map pp412-13; ☎ 916-264-5423; 216 O St; adult/student $6/3, admission free Sun morning; ☺ 10am-5pm Tue-Sun, 10am-9pm Thu) is stunning as much for its outrageous stairways and beautiful tile floors as it is for its fine collection. There are some fine early California paintings and some stellar European works purchased by the widely traveled Crockers. The curators are continually adding to the collection with a surprisingly fun sensibility for modern art.

SUTTER'S FORT STATE HISTORIC PARK
Strangely located amidst a slew of contemporary development, **Sutter's Fort State Historic Park** (Map pp412-13; ☎ 916-445-4422; cnr 27th & L Sts; adult/child $6/3; ☺ 10am-5pm), built by John Sutter, was once the only trace of white civilization for hundreds of miles. The fort has been restored to its 1850s appearance, complete with original furniture and equipment. It's not a huge thrill, but gives a comprehensive rundown of the area's European history.

CALIFORNIA STATE INDIAN MUSEUM
A necessary antidote to touring Sutter's Fort is a trip to the adjacent **State Indian Museum** (Map pp412-13; ☎ 916-324-0971; 2618 K St; adult/child $2/free; ☺ 10am-5pm). It's actually more interesting, too. The museum presents a side of the gold rush that's typically overlooked. Viewing exhibits on native lifestyles and handicrafts, you get some sense of the beautiful and complicated culture that was abruptly destroyed by the onslaught of gold miners, railroads and farmers that began in 1849.

TOWER DISTRICT
The Tower District consists of a small stretch of shops, bars, ethnic restaurants and the landmark **Tower Theatre** (Map pp412-13; ☎ 916-442-4700; 2508 Landpark Dr), a beautiful 1938 art deco movie palace. The **Tower Records** chain started here and the original sign survives on the theater (the current store is across the street).

Activities
The **American River Parkway** (Map p410), a 23-mile river system on the north bank of the American River, is surely Sacramento's most appealing geographic feature. It's one of

the most extensive riparian habitats in the continental US. The park's network of trails and picnic areas is accessible from Old Sacramento by taking Front St north until it becomes Jiboom St and crosses the river, or by taking the Jiboom St exit off I-5/Hwy 99.

The parkway includes a nice walking/running/bicycling path called the **Jedediah Smith National Recreation Trail** that's accessible from Old Sacramento at the end of J St. Rent bicycles at the waterfront from **Bike Sacramento** (Map pp412-13; ☎ 916-444-0200; 1050 Front St) for $6/20 per hour/day.

Sleeping

Delta King (Map pp412-13; ☎ 916-444-5464, 800-825-5464; www.deltaking.com; 100 Front St; r $139-164; 🔀) You can't beat the experience of sleeping aboard the *Delta King*, a 1927 paddlewheeler docked in Old Sacramento. There's a restaurant and a cocktail lounge onboard and the atmosphere is historic and fun.

Inn and Spa at Parkside (Map pp412-13; ☎ 916-658-1818, 800-995-7275; www.innatparkside.com; 2116 6th St; r $169-329; P 🔀 💻) Among Sacramento's more stylish hotels is this grand villa opposite Southside Park. Guestrooms are colorful, atmospheric and romantic, whether furnished with Victorian antiques or South Pacific rattan trimmings. Complete spa services are available.

Clarion Hotel Mansion Inn (Map pp412-13; ☎ 916-444-8000; fax 916-442-8129; 700 16th St; r $109-139; P 🔀 💻) Directly across from the Governor's Mansion (from which the hotel derives part of its name) is the Clarion, an attractive property with a shady courtyard and a restaurant. Rooms are spruced up in a fairly conservative style.

Amber House (Map pp412-13; ☎ 916-444-8085, 800-755-6526; www.amberhouse.com; 1315 22nd St; r $149-259; 🔀) This Dutch Colonial home is in the Midtown area. Guestrooms have a frilly exuberance that seems designed to match a classical composer's wardrobe (rooms have names like the Vivaldi and the Mozart). Most have Jacuzzi baths and some also have fireplaces. Breakfast is served in the rooms.

Heritage Hotel (Map p410; ☎ 916-929-7900; 1780 Tribute Rd; r $89-99; P 🔀 💻) If you have a car, this hotel close to Cal Expo is a very good budget option. It looks like a fairly bland

DOWNTOWN SACRAMENTO

dormitory but is surrounded by lush gardens. Guestrooms are clean, quiet and spacious and all have patios or balconies.

Sacramento HI Hostel (Map pp412-13; ☎ 916-443-1691; www.norcalhostels.org/sac/index.html; 925 H St; dm $20-23, private r $45-100; ⓨ office 7:30-9:30am & 5-10pm; ✂ 🖵) In a grand Victorian mansion, this hostel offers some impressive trimmings at rock-bottom prices. Dorms have at most nine beds and linens cost a nominal fee. It's within walking distance of the capitol, Old Sac and the train station. It attracts an international crowd and is a useful place to find rides to San Francisco and Lake Tahoe.

Basic but convenient are the **Vagabond Inn** (Map pp412-13; ☎ 916-446-1481; www.vagabondinn.com; 909 3rd St; r $92-99; 🅿 ✂), near Old Sacramento, and **Quality Inn** (Map pp412-13; ☎ 916-444-3980; 818 15th St; r $79-99; 🅿 ✂), a few blocks from the capitol.

Eating

Most of the tourist joints in Old Sacramento are overpriced and overrated, while Midtown and the Tower District have a

growing number of hip, creative and affordable restaurants.

Paragary's Bar & Oven (Map pp412-13; ☎ 916-457-57737; 1401 28th St; lunch $8-17, dinner mains $10-20) Randy Paragary's stylish Mediterranean eatery is well loved for its wood-fired pizzas, hand-cut pastas, great wine list and quality meat and fish dishes.

Moxie (Map pp412-13; ☎ 916-443-7585; 2028 H St; lunch $6-13, dinner mains $13-21) Moxie is darkly lit and romantic, and the service is cordial and down-to-earth. The menu applies Californian attitudes to American standards and seafood specialties, with some fusion cross-breeding. Great crab pot stickers and mashed potatoes.

Cafe Bernardo (Map pp412-13; ☎ 916-443-1189; 2726 Capitol Ave; mains $7-14) This is a Midtown favorite serving all meals. Stop by for strong coffee or have a full-on meal with pasta, a grilled skirt steak and wine. There's an outdoor seating area and an adjacent martini bar that's popular around happy hour.

Edokko (Map pp412-13; ☎ 916-448-2828; 1724 Broadway; meals $8-11) You'll find lots of good, affordable ethnic restaurants in the Tower

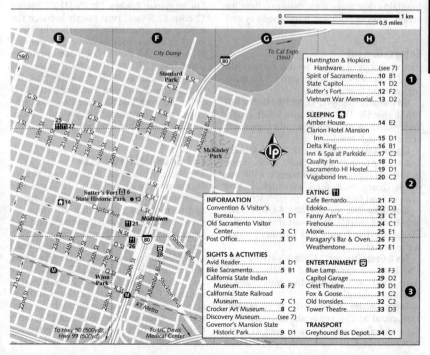

District on Broadway, including Edokko, a popular Japanese place serving sushi, tempura and lots of rice and noodle dishes.

Firehouse (Map pp412-13; ☎ 916-442-4772; 1112 2nd St; lunch $10-18, dinner mains $24-49; ☺ lunch Mon-Fri, dinner Mon-Sat) Old Sac's most refined restaurant is the historic firehouse, which still has a fire pole coming out of its ceiling and nude paintings on the brick walls. The steaks, chops and seafood are somewhat overpriced, but the atmosphere is as good as it gets. Head straight to the courtyard for lunch.

Fanny Ann's (Map pp412-13; ☎ 916-441-0505; 1023 2nd St; food from $5) At the other end of the spectrum is this ancient and colorful bar that serves decent burgers.

Weatherstone (Map pp412-13; ☎ 916-441-0222; 812 21st St) For hearty, strong coffee and great pastries, Weatherstone is a class outfit with a lovely patio.

Sacramento gets plenty hot in summer, so cooling off with a refreshing milkshake or ice-cream cone is worth driving away from downtown. Both **Vic's** (Map p410; 3199 Riverside Blvd; shakes $4) and **Gunther's** (Map p410; 2801 Franklin Blvd; shakes $4) are beautiful vintage soda fountains that make their own excellent ice cream. They're both south of Broadway and Hwy 50.

Entertainment

Pick up a copy of the free weekly *Sacramento News & Review* for a list of current happenings around town.

Old Ironsides (Map pp412-13; ☎ 916-442-3504; 1901 10th St; cover $3) This cool, somewhat crusty venue hosts some of the best indie bands that come through town.

Capitol Garage (Map pp412-13; ☎ 916-444-3633; 1500 K St) Another good indie-rock venue is this Midtown hipster magnet, with live music (blues, rock, punk etc) nightly. You can get food here as well.

Blue Lamp (Map pp412-13; ☎ 916-455-3400; 1400 Alhambra Blvd; cover $5) Check out this cool spot for bluesy bar bands and various touring indie rockers.

Fox & Goose (Map pp412-13; ☎ 916-443-8825; 1001 R St) This is a spacious old warehouse-pub with good beer on tap, live music and a fun atmosphere.

Tower Theatre (Map pp412-13; ☎ 916-442-4700; 2508 Landpark Dr) This venue shows classic, foreign and alternative films as well as some new releases. Call to confirm that your film

is showing on the main screen, rather than in a smaller side room.

Crest Theatre (Map pp412-13; ☎ 916-442-7378; www .thecrest.com; 1013 K St) Another classic old movie house that's been lovingly restored is the 1949 Crest, hosting indie and foreign films and the annual Trash Film Orgy.

Arco Arena (Map p410; ☎ information 916-928-6900, tickets 916-649-8497; 1 Sports Parkway) The Kings, Sacramento's professional basketball (NBA) team, play home games at this arena from November to May. Ringling Bros and arena rockers pass through as well.

Getting There & Away

The small but busy **Sacramento International Airport** (☎ 916-929-5411; www.sacairports.org), 15 miles north of downtown off I-5, is serviced by all major airlines and offers some indirect flights to Europe.

Greyhound (Map pp412-13; ☎ 916-444-6858; cnr 7th & L Sts) stops near the capitol. Sacramento's **Amtrak Station** (Map pp412-13; cnr 4th & I Sts) is between downtown and Old Sac.

Getting Around

The regional **Yolobus** (☎ 916-371-2877) route 42 costs $1.50 and runs hourly between the airport and downtown (take the clockwise loop) and also goes to West Sacramento, Woodland and Davis. Local **Sacramento Regional Transit** (RT; ☎ 916-321-2877) buses cost $1.50 per ticket or $3.50 for a day pass. RT also runs the Downtown Area Shuttle (DASH) trolley between Old Sacramento and downtown, and Sacramento's light-rail system, which is mostly used for commuting to outlying communities.

THE SACRAMENTO DELTA

The Sacramento Delta, directly southwest of Sacramento, is comprised of 1000 miles of waterways and historic towns. It's a sporty and picturesque region that encompasses the confluence of the Sacramento and San Joaquin Rivers. From here, the water runs to San Francisco Bay. In the 1930s the Bureau of Reclamation issued an aggressive water redirection program – the Central Valley and California State Water Projects – that dammed California's major rivers and directed 75% of their supply through the Central Valley, for agricultural use, and Southern California. The siphoning has affected the Sacramento Delta, its wetlands and estuaries, and has been a source of environmental, ecological and political debate ever since.

After WWII, agricultural production in the San Joaquin Valley grew enormously, and the use of chemical pesticides and fertilizers became commonplace. Simultaneously, dams appeared on many of the delta's tributaries, stopping the annual floods and redirecting the flow that once took all the harmful buildup out to sea. Soon afterward, the Sacramento River had to be redirected into a peripheral canal to avoid being contaminated by the delta's backflow. Water is let back into the delta from control points along the canal and further redirected to supply 40% of California's drinking water and 45% of its irrigation.

While still a major part of California's political and environmental arena, the delta is also a favorite place for boating, water skiing and duck hunting.

Hwy 160, which runs south from Sacramento to Antioch, follows the Sacramento River levee, is the delta's main drag. Along the way you'll encounter lush landscapes and curious towns. **Isleton** has an interesting main street lined with a few shops, restaurants, bars and old buildings, some hinting at the town's Chinese heritage. Isleton's Crawdad Festival, at the end of June, draws people from all over the state. The regional crawdad yield is generally of very high quality, so it's not a watered down version of the Louisiana tradition.

Locke, the delta's most fascinating town, was built by Chinese farmers after a fire wiped out Walnut Grove's Chinatown in 1912. Locke was not attached to a larger white town and was the only free-standing Chinatown in the US. However, due to California's Alien Land Act, the Chinese were not permitted to own property. The entire town was owned by a man named George Locke, who agreed to lease the land to the Chinese. Tucked below the highway and levee, Locke feels like a Western ghost town, with dilapidated buildings leaning into each other over the town's single street. Shops and galleries (some still open for business) are worn by age and proximity to the water, yet quite picturesque in their decrepitude. There's evidence here and there of construction work having been done to keep buildings from toppling altogether, but as Locke is on the National Register of Historic Places,

only preservationist work can be done – an ironic disincentive to keep properties up at all. Still more ironic is that the town is more beautiful for its lack of attention.

Keeping the town's heritage alive is the dusty but worthwhile **Dai Loy Museum** (☎ 916-776-1661; www.locketown.com; admission $1.25; ☺ 11am-5pm Sat & Sun), an old gambling hall filled with photos and relics.

Locke's unlikely centerpiece is **Al the Wop's** (☎ 916-776-1800; meals $8-20). This place is an old memorabilia-filled bar that's been in business since 1934. A rowdy but friendly crowd comes to drink heavily and eat steak meals.

DAVIS
pop 60,310
The unexciting name of this town doesn't exactly draw motorists off the highway, but Davis has some commendable qualities. It's a college town, with students comprising about 50% of the population, and a progressive outpost amid the conservative agricultural towns of Sacramento Valley. In addition to a well-educated citizenry, it boasts more bikes per capita than any other town in the US. The student population and year-round community have a mutual respect for each other and together support a vibrant café, pub and arts scene.

Downtown Davis looks like you might expect a town named Davis to look. Many of the buildings are practical-looking structures that went up in the 1970s. But the streets are shaded and the shops and businesses friendly. There's a discernable but likeable nerd factor here.

Orientation
I-80 skirts the south edge of town, with the Davis/Olive St exit giving the easiest access to downtown, via Richards Blvd and 1st St. University of California Davis (UCD) lies southwest of downtown, bordered by A St, 1st St and Russell Blvd. The campus' main entrances are accessed from I-80 via Old Davis Rd or from downtown via 3rd St. East of the campus, Hwy 113 heads north 10 miles to Woodland, where it intersects with I-5. Another 28 miles north it connects with Hwy 99.

Information
The **Davis Conference and Visitor Bureau** (☎ 530-297-1900; www.davisvisitor.com; 105 E St, Suite 300;

8:30am-4:30pm Mon-Fri) has free maps and brochures. Another useful website to peruse is www.davis411.com.

Good bookstores include the **Avid Reader** (☎ 530-758-4040; 617 2nd St) and **Bogey's Books** (☎ 530-757-6127; 223 E St).

Sights & Activities

The impressive, purpose-built **Pence Gallery** (☎ 530-758-3370; 212 D St; ☽ noon-5pm Wed-Sun) has exhibits of contemporary California art and hosts lectures. **The Artery** (☎ 530-758-8330; 207 G St; ☽ 10am-6pm Mon-Thu & Sat, 10am-9pm Fri, noon-5pm Sun) is a gallery that exhibits contemporary paintings and crafts (lots of pots).

For a short hike, there is a paved 2-mile trail through the peaceful **UC Davis Arboretum**. On summer Saturdays the **Equestrian Center** (☎ 530-752-2372; Equestrian Lane; ☽ rides 10am Sat) offers hour-long trail rides for $25; reservations required 48 hours ahead.

The **Davis farmers market** (cnr 4th & C Sts; ☽ 8am-noon Sat, 4.30-8.30pm Wed, 2-6pm Wed Oct-Mar) features food vendors, street performers and live bands.

Bicycling is popular here, probably because the only hill around is the bridge that crosses over the freeway. A favorite destination is **Lake Berryessa**, around 30 miles west. See opposite for bike rental information.

Sleeping

Like most university towns, Davis' hotel rates are generally stable, except during graduation or special campus events, when they rise high and sell out fast.

University Inn Bed and Breakfast (☎ 530-756-8648, 800-756-8648; 340 A St; r $80-85; ☒) Just a few steps from the campus, this B&B is in an attractive Spanish-style house. It offers full breakfasts and the rooms have private bathrooms, phones and cable TV. If you don't want breakfast you can arrange a cheaper rate.

Aggie Inn (☎ 530-756-0352; www.stayanight.com /aggieinn; 245 1st St; r $85-127; ☒ ☒) Across from UCD's east entrance, the Aggie is neat, modern and unassuming. The hotel has a Jacuzzi and offers free coffee and pastries.

Davis Bed & Breakfast Inn (☎ 530-753-9611, 800-211-4455; www.davisbedandbreakfast.com; 422 A St; r from $79; ☒) It's a bit like grandma's house. An old-fashioned parlor and wallpapered guestrooms make the Davis Inn a good, homey choice. Full breakfasts, private

bathrooms and proximity to campus are the place's attributes.

Eating & Drinking

Woodstocks (☎ 530-757-2525; 219 G St; slice $2, pizzas $15-20) Woodstocks has Davis' most popular pizza, also sold by the slice for lunch.

Delta of Venus Coffeehouse & Pub (☎ 530-753-8630; 122 B St; meals $5-10) This groovy converted Craftsman bungalow has a very social and shaded front patio. The chalkboard menu has breakfast items, salads, soups and sandwiches, including some vegetarian and vegan options. At dinner time you can order jerk-seasoned Caribbean dishes and wash it down with a beer or wine.

Osaka Sushi (☎ 530-758-2288; 630 G St; sushi $1.50-3.50) Here you'll find sushi to rival San Francisco's best, plus excellent sashimi, tempura and teriyaki dinners. It also has a floating sushi bar, – you serve yourself from colored plates going around on boats.

Redrum (☎ 530-756-2142; 978 Olive Dr; meals $5-10) Formerly known as Murder Burger, Redrum is popular with students and travelers alike for its fresh, made-to-order beef, turkey and ostrich burgers, thick espresso shakes and excellent curly fries.

Mishka's Café (☎ 530-759-0811; 514B 2nd St) Lap-topping students and chatty town folk gather at this busy roastery for fair-trade coffees and pastries. It's wi-fi equipped.

Entertainment

Mondavi Center for the Performing Arts (☎ 530-757-3199; www.mondaviarts.org; 1 Shields Ave) Major theater, music, dance and other performances take place at this brand-new venue on the UC Davis campus.

Varsity Theatre (☎ 530-759-8724; 616 2nd St) also stages performances. For tickets and information on shows at either the Varsity or the Mondavi Center, you can also call the **UC Davis Ticket Office** (☎ 530-752-1915, 866-823-2787).

Palm's Playhouse (www.palmsplayhouse.com) Davis' long-standing favorite live music venue moved to the town of Winters, about 12 miles west of Davis. Shows take place in the historic **Winters Opera House** (☎ 530-795-1825; 13 Main St). The old hall is an absolutely fantastic place to see a show.

Getting There & Away

Yolobus (☎ 530-666-2877; $1.50; ☽ 5am-11pm) route 42 loops between Davis and the Sacramento

> **DETOUR: TRACTOR & TRUCK MUSEUM**
>
> The Central Valley is all about agriculture, and its people are proud of their history. Well worth a side trip is the huge **Hedrick Ag History Center** (☎ 530-666-9700; 1962 Hays Ln, Woodland; adult/child $7/4; ☼ 10am-5pm Mon-Fri, 10am-6pm Sat, 10am-4pm Sun), which has the world's largest collection of antique tractors and one of the biggest collections of old trucks. Check out the Deere One-Horse Plow, a 1910 relic, or the 1917 Riker Fire Engine, plus there's hundreds of other vehicles produced by Mac Trucks, John Deere, Caterpillar, Allis Chalmers, Dodge and Pierce-Arrow from the 1890s through to the 1940s. The center is in Woodland, just a few miles north of Davis via Hwy 113.

airport. The route also connects Davis with Woodland and downtown Sacramento.

Davis' **Amtrak station** (☎ 530-758-4220; 840 2nd St) is on the southern edge of downtown.

Getting Around

When driving around – especially when you pull out from a parking space – be aware of bike traffic: it's the primary mode of transportation here. **Ken's Bike & Ski** (☎ 530-758-3223; 650 G St; from $10 per day) rents basic bikes as well as serious road and mountain bikes.

If you're not biking, student-run **Unitrans** (☎ 530-752-2877; http://unitrans.ucdavis.edu; $1; ☼ 7am-11.30pm Mon-Thu, 7am-7pm Fri, 9am-5pm Sat & Sun) shuttles people around town and campus. Many buses are red double-deckers.

OROVILLE
pop 13,100

Gold attracted the first settlers to Oroville and sawmills kept them here, but that's all over. There's now a plastic bag factory on the outskirts of town, but apart from that, this is just a damn pretty little town with half a dozen antique stores on every block. Oroville's most enduring attraction is an excellent museum left behind by a long-gone Chinese community.

Gold was discovered near here in 1848 by John Bidwell, at a site along the Feather River known as Bidwell Bar (it's now under Lake Oroville). The town boomed quickly and was originally called Ophir (Gold) City.

Oroville was where Ishi, the last surviving member of the local Yahi tribe, was 'found' back in 1911 (p418).

Lake Oroville, a popular summertime destination, sits 9 miles northeast of town behind Oroville Dam. The surrounding Lake Oroville State Recreation Area attracts boaters, campers, swimmers, bicyclists, backpackers and fishing folk. Oroville is also a gateway to the gorgeous Feather River Canyon and the rugged northern reaches of the Sierra Nevada.

Information

The **Oroville Area Chamber of Commerce** (☎ 530-538-2542, 800-655-4653; www.oroville-city.com; 1789 Montgomery St; ☼ 9am-4:30pm Mon-Fri) has information on local history and outdoor activities. The office of the US Forest Service (USFS) **Feather River Ranger District** (☎ 530-534-6500; 875 Mitchell Ave; ☼ 8am-4:30pm Mon-Fri) has maps and brochures. For road conditions phone ☎ 800-427-7623.

Sights & Activities

By the levee, the **Chinese Temple** (☎ 530-538-2496; 1500 Broderick St; adult/child $2/free; ☼ noon-4pm) is a compelling draw that really exceeds expectations. Today there is no Chinatown in Oroville, but at one time the town was bustling with more than 10,000 Chinese. A 1907 flood wiped out Chinatown and many Chinese stayed to help rebuild the levee, but their numbers rapidly dwindled afterwards. During the 19th century, traveling theater troupes from China toured a circuit of Chinatowns in California. Oroville was the end of the line, and the troupes often left their sets, costumes and puppets here before heading back to China. Consequently, Oroville has a collection of 19th-century stage finery unrivaled anywhere in California. The old temple, a beautifully preserved building, is also jam-packed with religious shrines, festival tapestries, ancient lion masks and furniture. Be sure to take advantage of docent-led tours, which can take an hour or more but really put everything into context.

From downtown, follow Oroville Dam Rd or Olive Hwy (Hwy 162) to the **Lake Oroville State Recreation Area**, home to many outdoor activities and the 770ft Oroville Dam. Completed in 1967, it's the tallest earthen dam in the US. The **Lake Oroville State Recreation Area Visitor Center** (☎ 530-538-2219; 917 Kelly Ridge

CENTRAL VALLEY

LONE YAHI FOUND IN OROVILLE

In the early morning of August 29, 1911, a frantic barking of dogs woke the butchers sleeping inside a slaughterhouse outside Oroville. When they came out, they found their dogs holding a man at bay – a Native American clad only in a loincloth, who was starving, exhausted, afraid and spoke no English.

They called the sheriff, who took the man to the jail until something could be decided. Newspapers declared a 'wild man' had been discovered and people thronged in, hoping to see him. Local people came and tried to communicate with him in Maidu and Wintu, to no avail; his language was different from those of the surrounding tribes.

Professors Alfred L Kroeber and Thomas Talbot Waterman, anthropologists from the University of California, Berkeley, read the accounts in the news. Waterman took the train to Oroville and, using lists of vocabulary words of the Yana people who once lived in this region, discovered that the man belonged to the Yahi, the southernmost tribe of the Yana, who were believed to be extinct.

Waterman took 'Ishi,' meaning 'man' in the Yahi language, to the museum at the university, where he was cared for and brought back to health. Ishi spent his remaining years there, telling the anthropologists his life story and teaching them his tribal language, lore and ways.

Ishi's tribe had been virtually exterminated by settlers before he was born. In 1870, when he was a child, there were only 12 or 15 Yahi left, hiding in remote areas in the foothills east of Red Bluff. By 1908 Ishi, his mother, sister and an old man were all who were left of the Yahi. In that year the others died and Ishi was left alone. On March 25, 1916, Ishi died of tuberculosis at the university hospital and the Yahi disappeared forever.

In Oroville, you can drive to the site where Ishi was found (east of town along Oro–Quincy Hwy at Oak Ave), though all that stands is a small monument. Part of the Lassen National Forest in the foothills east of Red Bluff, including Deer Creek and other areas where Ishi and the Yahi lived, is now called the Ishi Wilderness. If you go to Berkeley, you can also see an exhibit on Ishi at the Phoebe Hearst Museum of Anthropology.

Rd; ☻ 9am-5pm) has exhibits on the California State Water Project and local Native American history, plus a viewing tower and loads of recreational information.

The **Freeman Bicycle Trail** is a 41-mile off-road loop that takes cyclists to the top of Oroville Dam, then follows the Feather River back to the Thermalito Forebay and Afterbay storage reservoirs, west of Hwy 70. The ride is mostly flat, but the dam ascent is steep. Get a free map of the ride from the chamber of commerce. The **Forebay Aquatic Center** (☎ 530-624-6919; Garden Dr), just off Hwy 70, rents bikes for $7 per hour.

The afterbay also abuts the **Oroville Wildlife Area**, located along the Pacific Flyway and a great place for bird-watching. Serious birders might also head to the **Sacramento National Wildlife Refuge** during winter, where the migratory waterfowl are a spectacular sight. The **visitors center** (☎ 530-934-2801; 752 County Rd, Willows; ☻ 7:30am-4pm Mon-Fri) is off I-5 near Willows; driving ($3) and walking trails are open daily.

The area surrounding Lake Oroville is full of hiking trails, and a favorite is the 7-

mile round-trip walk to 640ft **Feather Falls**, which takes about four hours.

Highways 162 and 70 head northeast from Oroville into the mountains and on to Quincy (p293). Hwy 70 snakes along the magnificent **Feather River Canyon**, an especially captivating drive during the fall.

Sleeping & Eating

The chamber of commerce, USFS office and the Lake Oroville visitors center have details about campgrounds in the area, including boat-in campsites. Make reservations by calling ☎ 800-444-7275.

Several budget motels are on Feather River Blvd, which runs east of Hwy 70 and south of Montgomery St.

Bidwell Canyon Marina (☎ 530-589-3165, 800-637-1767; www.gobidwell.com; 801 Bidwell Canyon Rd; 3 night weekends in summer from $1000) Houseboats that sleep 10 to 16 people can be rented at this marina, on the south end of the lake.

Villa Court (☎ 530-533-3930; 1527 Feather River Blvd; r $50-70; P ☒ ☒) This tidy, old-fashioned motor court has a neat kidney-shaped pool.

Riverside Bed & Breakfast (☎ 530-533-1413; www.riversidebandb.com; 45 Cabana Dr; r $85-165; ▨) A real outdoorsy getaway, the Riverside's eight rooms are just a few skips and a hop from the water. Some rooms have lovely views and Jacuzzis, and all have private bathrooms. It's along the Feather River west of Hwy 70.

CL & Harry's (☎ 530-534-8797; 2053 Montgomery St; lunch $7-11, dinner $14-30; ❤ Tue-Sun) A classy sort of place with a rustic, exposed brick dining room, CL & Harry's sizzles up steaks and chops and other American fare.

Getting There & Away

Greyhound buses stop at **Tom's Sierra Chevron** (☎ 530-533-1333; cnr 5th Ave & Oro Dam Blvd), a few blocks east of Hwy 70.

CHICO

pop 64,400

With an all-American, oak-shaded downtown and a sizable university, Chico is one of Sacramento Valley's more attractive municipalities as well as a social and cultural hub. It has good restaurants, coffeehouses, nightclubs, bars and entertainment venues. Chico State University (CSU), with 16,000 students, has a reputation for being a party school, which certainly heats things up during the school year.

During the summertime Chico can be a little sleepy – temperatures that regularly surpass 90°F contribute to the lethargy. Wandering the downtown in the evening in T-shirts and short pants is truly relaxing, though. The swimming holes in shady Bidwell Park help take the edge off during the day and tubing down the Sacramento River is always fun. The fine pale ales produced at the Sierra Nevada Brewing Company, near downtown, is yet another of Chico's blessings.

Chico was established in 1860 by John Bidwell, who came to California in 1841 and proceeded to make himself one of its most illustrious early pioneers. In the late 1840s he purchased 40 sq miles here, called Rancho del Arroyo Chico. In 1868, Bidwell and his wife, Annie Ellicott Kennedy, moved to the new mansion he had built. It is now the Bidwell Mansion State Historic Park. After John died in 1900, Annie continued as a philanthropist until her death in 1918.

Orientation & Information

Downtown is west of Hwy 99, most easily reached via Hwy 32 (8th St). Main St and Broadway are the central downtown streets; from there, Park Ave stretches southward and tree-lined The Esplanade heads north.

Chico Chamber of Commerce & Visitor Center (☎ 530-891-5559, 800-852-8570; www.chicochamber.com; 300 Salem St; ❤ 9am-5pm Mon-Fri, 10am-3pm Sat) offers local information. For entertainment options, pick up the free weekly *Chico News & Review*. **The Bookstore** (118 Main St) has tons of quality used books that are reasonably priced.

Sights

Chico's most prominent landmark is **Bidwell Mansion State Historic Park** (☎ 530-895-6144; 525 The Esplanade; adult/child $2/free; ❤ noon-5pm Wed-Fri, 10am-5pm Sat & Sun), the opulent Victorian home built for Chico's founders John and Annie Bidwell. The 26-room mansion was built between 1865 and 1868. Bidwell, having served in the US Congress, was well connected, and many US presidents visited the house. You'll learn all about it by taking the tour, which starts every hour on the hour.

One of the best-known, and finest, craft breweries in the country (too big to officially qualify as a 'microbrewery') is the **Sierra Nevada Brewing Company** (☎ 530-893-3520; 1075 E 20th St), which makes many excellent brews, most notably Sierra Nevada Pale Ale. Free tours are given at 2:30pm daily, and continuously from noon to 3pm Saturday. There's also a pub and restaurant (see p420).

Chico Museum (☎ 530-891-4336; cnr Salem & W 2nd Sts; admission free; ❤ noon-4pm Wed-Sun), in the former 1904 Carnegie Library, contains a historical museum, a re-creation of an old Taoist temple altar and rotating exhibits. The Chico timeline, traces the city's history from 1837 to 2000 with photos and other artifacts and can pull you in.

Ask for a free map of the **Chico State University** campus, or ask about campus events and tours, at the **CSU Information Center** (☎ 530-898-4636; cnr Chestnut & W 2nd Sts), on the main floor of Bell Memorial Union. The attractive campus is infused with sweet floral fragrances in spring, and there's a nice rose garden at its center.

The historic 1894 **Honey Run Covered Bridge** is the sort of covered bridge you encounter in Washington Irving stories like *The Legend of Sleepy Hollow*. There are few in

CENTRAL VALLEY

California and none like this one, whose roof consists of three separate sections. Take the Skyway exit off Hwy 99 on the southern outskirts of Chico, head east about a mile, turn left onto Honey Run-Humbug Rd; the bridge is 5 miles along, in a small park.

Activities

Starting right downtown, 3670-acre **Bidwell Park** is the nation's third-largest municipal park. It stretches 10 miles northwest along Chico Creek with lush groves and miles of trails. The upper part of the park is a fairly untamed wilderness, surprising to find in the midst of an American city. Several classic movies have been shot here, including *The Adventures of Robin Hood* and parts of *Gone with the Wind*.

The park is full of hiking and mountain-biking trails and swimming spots. You'll find pools at One-Mile and Five-Mile recreation areas and swimming holes (including Bear Hole, Salmon Hole and Brown Hole) in Upper Bidwell Park, north of Manzanita Ave; expect some skinny-dipping. In the park the **Chico Creek Nature Center** (☎ 530-891-4671; suggested donation $1; ☺ showroom 11am-4pm Tue-Sun) has a living animal museum.

In summer **tubing** on the Sacramento River is extremely popular and really fun. Inner tubes can be rented at grocery stores and other shops along Nord Ave (Hwy 32) for around $6. Tubers enter at the Irvine Finch Launch Ramp on Hwy 32, a few miles west of Chico, and come out at the Wash-out off River Rd.

Festivals & Events

Chico's chock-full of community spirit and pride, which surfaces most visibly during the numerous family-friendly outdoor events held each summer. The **Thursday Night Market** takes over several blocks of Broadway every Thursday evening from April to September. At City Plaza you'll find free **Friday Night Concerts** starting in May. **Shakespeare in the Park** (☎ 530-891-1382), at Cedar Grove in lower Bidwell Park, runs from mid-July to the end of August.

Sleeping

Chico has an abundance of well-kept independent motels with clean swimming pools, some of them along the pretty Esplanade north of downtown. Since this is a campus

town, graduation and homecoming ceremonies (in May and October respectively) can fill up hotels and raise the price.

Matador Motel (☎ 530-342-7543; 1934 The Esplanade; r $47-51; P ⊠ ⊠) A pleasant courtyard motel not far from downtown. The rooms are simple but still have some old-fashioned Mission-style character. The buildings wrap around a beautiful tiled swimming pool shaded by palms.

Music Express Inn (☎ 530-891-9833; http://northvalley.net/musicexpress; 1091 El Monte Ave; r $61-125; P ⊠) Guestrooms in this B&B are slightly cheesy but huge, and some have Jacuzzi tubs. A hearty breakfast is included. It's east of Hwy 99, directly off Hwy 32.

The Grateful Bed (☎ 530-342-2464; http://northvalley.net/gratefulbed; 1462 Arcadian Ave; r $105-150; ⊠) Well, obviously you're a bedhead if you stay here. Tucked in a residential neighborhood near downtown, it's a lovely, stately 1905 Victorian home. Some of the decor is trying too hard, but overall it's very comfortable. Breakfast is included.

Johnson's Country Inn (☎ 530-345-7829; 3935 Morehead Ave; r $83-125; P ⊠) About a mile west of downtown you'll find this motel in an attractive almond orchard. It's a modern building that's meant to look 'Victorian' and the rooms have antique furnishings.

For a budget choice smack in the middle of downtown, check out the **Vagabond Inn** (☎ 530-895-1323; 630 Main St; s/d $45/55; P ⊠) and the nearby **Thunderbird Lodge** (☎ 530-343-7911; 715 Main St; r $45-60; P ⊠). Both are a tad run-down but still acceptable.

Woodson Bridge State Recreation Area (☎ 530-839-2112, 800-444-7275; sites $11-14; ⊠) This shaded campground, adjacent to a huge native riparian preserve, has 46 tent sites on the banks of the Sacramento River. It's about 25 miles north of Chico on Hwy 99, then west toward Corning.

Eating

Sierra Nevada Taproom & Restaurant (☎ 530-345-2739; 1075 E 20th St; meals $8-15; ☺ lunch & dinner Tue-Sun) At the Sierra Nevada Brewery, this place is a genuine Chico destination. It has better than average pub food; fresh, superb ales; and lagers on tap, some not available anywhere else. The apple-malt pork loin is a standout.

Broadway Heights (☎ 530-899-8075; 300 Broadway; meals $7-12.50) Upstairs overlooking a busy corner, Broadway Heights puts inexpensive pizzas, focaccia sandwiches and Cal-Med entrees on the table.

Red Tavern (☎ 530-894-3463; 1250 The Esplanade; dinner mains $15-24; ☺ dinner Mon-Sat) Just north of downtown is the swanky Red Tavern, one of Chico's more sophisticated places. The kitchen draws discriminatingly from Europe and (occasionally) Asia, leading to delicious meat, fish and pasta dishes.

Big Al's Drive-In (☎ 530-342-2722; cnr The Esplanade & E 9th Av; meals $1.35-3) If you're staying out on The Esplanade, this classic greasepit will come in handy. It's primarily a takeout burger and hot dog stand where tasty, if unhealthy, food is sold at retro prices.

Tacos de Acapulco (☎ 530-892-8176; 429 Ivy St; meals $3-6) Your best bulk-up budget option is this *taquería* (taco joint) serving huge burritos. The food's good and plenty popular with students.

Upper Crust (☎ 895-3866; 130 Main St; meals $3-7) For coffee and excellent baked goods check out this place, which also serves lunch Monday to Saturday.

Outdoor farmers market (☺ 7:30am-1pm Sat) Held year-round in the city parking lot at the corner of Wall and E 2nd Sts.

Chico Natural Foods (818 Main St; ☺ 7am-10pm) One of several natural food supermarkets.

Shubert's Ice Cream & Candy (178 E 7th St; ☺ 9.30am-10pm Mon-Fri, 11am-10pm Sat & Sun) This is a beloved Chico landmark; they've made delicious homemade ice cream and chocolates for more than 60 years.

Drinking

Naked Lounge (☎ 530-895-0676; 118 2nd St; ☺ 10am-9pm Sun-Thu, 10am-midnight Fri & Sat) Local hipsters seem to favor this groovy lounge for coffee and tea. Choose between a garish red sofa or your basic wooden coffeehouse table.

Madison Bear Garden (☎ 530-891-1639; 316 W 2nd St; ☺ noon-2am) A classic, spacious student hangout, the venerable Madison Bear Garden is a funky saloon and burger bar. It's in an interesting old building on the corner of Salem St.

Moxie's (☎ 530-345-0601; 128 Broadway; ☺ 11am-10pm) This smart-looking coffeehouse has jazz, acoustic and other low-key sounds several nights a week.

Entertainment

LaSalle's (☎ 530-893-1891; 229 Broadway) This venue is open nightly for hip-hop, Top 40 and

retro dance nights and live bands from reggae to hard rock.

Pageant Theatre (☎ 530-343-0663; 351 E 6th St) Screens international and alternative films; Monday is bargain night, with all seats just $2.50.

For theater, films, concerts, art exhibits and other cultural events at the CSU campus, contact the **CSU Box Office** (☎ 530-898-6333) or the **CSU Information Center** (☎ 530-898-4636) in the Bell Memorial Union.

Getting There & Around

Greyhound (☎ 530-343-8266) buses stop at the **Amtrak station** (cnr W 5th & Orange Sts). The train station is unattended so purchase tickets in advance from travel agents.

B-Line (☎ 530-342-0221, 800-822-8145;) handles all buses throughout Butte County, and can get you around Chico and down to Oroville (tickets $1).

Bicycles can be rented from **Campus Bicycles** (☎ 530-345-2081; 330 Main St; mountain bikes half/full day $20/35).

RED BLUFF
pop 13,500

Red Bluff is a sleepy cow town populated by ranchers and farmers. The town also boasts pleasant tree-lined neighborhoods full of restored 19th-century Victorian mansions, and a business district lined with old storefronts. Red Bluff is fairly flat, but nearby mountain peaks (including the Trinity Alps to the northwest and snow-topped Mt Lassen to the east) edge into the sky from almost every direction, adding a comforting beauty and making the little town all the more attractive. Peter Lassen laid out the town site in 1847 and it grew into a key port along the Sacramento River.

Red Bluff is notoriously hot as blazes during the summer, but it's not hard to find relief in shaded riverside picnic spots and ample water recreation opportunities.

Cowboy culture is strong here; catch it in action the third weekend of April at the **Red Bluff Round-Up** (☎ 530-527-1000; www.redbluff roundup.com; tickets $10-19), a major rodeo event dating back to 1921. It's held east of downtown at the Tehama District Fairgrounds.

Orientation & Information

Downtown Red Bluff is on the west bank of the Sacramento River, just to the west of I-5. The town's main intersection is at Antelope Blvd and Main St. The historic Victorian neighborhood is in the blocks west of Main St.

Hwy 99 is reached by taking Antelope Blvd east from downtown. Heading south from downtown Main St becomes a narrow, scenic stretch of historic Hwy 99W, which parallels I-5 and leads to the farm towns of Corning, Orland and Willows.

Restaurants and antique stores line busy Main St. A few blocks south of downtown is the small **Red Bluff-Tehama County Chamber of Commerce** (☎ 530-527-6220, 800-655-6225; 100 Main St; ☯ 8:30am-4pm Mon, 8:30am-5pm Tue-Thu, 8:30am-4:30pm Fri).

Sights & Activities

The **Kelly-Griggs House Museum** (☎ 530-527-1129; 311 Washington St; admission by donation; ☯ 1-4pm Thu-Sun) is the most impressive of Red Bluff's classical Victorian homes. It's dressed up with period exhibits. Dig the mannequins.

Set on a beautiful, shaded piece of land overlooking a languorous section of the Sacramento River, the **William B Ide Adobe State Historic Park** (☎ 530-529-8599; 21659 Adobe Rd) preserves the original adobe home and grounds of pioneer William B Ide, who 'fought' in the 1846 Bear Flag Revolt at Sonoma (p32) and was named president of the short-lived California Republic. These are humble digs for a president. To get to the park, head about a mile north on Main St, turn east onto Adobe Rd and go another mile, following the signs.

The **Red Bluff Lake Recreation Area**, on the east bank of the Sacramento River, is a spacious park full of trees, birds and meadows. It offers numerous picnicking, swimming, hiking and camping opportunities and has interpretive trails, bicycle paths, boat ramps, a wildlife-viewing area with excellent bird-watching, a fish ladder (in operation between May and September) and a 2-acre native plant garden. The visitors center, called the **Sacramento River Discovery Center** (☎ 530-527-1196; ☯ 11am-4pm Tue-Sat) has kid-friendly displays about the river, questionable propaganda on the benefits of cattle grazing and information on the Diversion Dam just outside its doors. From mid-May to mid-September, the dam diverts water into irrigation canals and in the process creates Red Bluff Lake, which is a popular swimming destination.

Sleeping

Motels are found beside I-5 and south of town along Main St.

Jeter Victorian Inn (☎ 530-527-7574; www.jetervictorianinn.com; 1107 Jefferson St; r $95-160; ☯) Just east of the business district, Jeter is a massive 1881 Victorian building surrounded by ancient trees. It has five rooms and a separate cottage.

Faulkner House (☎ 530-529-0520, 800-549-6171; 1029 Jefferson St; r $80-105; ☯) On a quiet block near downtown is this gorgeous Queen Anne Victorian. Rooms are furnished with antiques and the screened-in porch is a lovely place to pass the evening.

Cinderella Riverview Motel (☎ 530-527-5490; 600 Rio St; r $34-60; ☯ ☯ ☯) Cinderella, on the west side of the Sacramento River, is dated but charming (some rooms still have shag carpeting). It has a pool and some rooms have riverfront views.

Travel Lodge (☎ 530-527-6020; 38 Antelope Blvd; s/d $59/65; ☯ ☯ ☯) It's not just a chain, but an exemplary and well-preserved example of 1960s motorist accommodation. Rooms are large and clean and the grounds around the pool are well kept.

Sycamore Grove Camping Area (☎ 530-824-5196; sites $10; ☯) Beside the river in the Red Bluff Lake Recreation Area is this quiet, attractive USFS campground. Campsites are on a first-come, first-served basis. It also has a large group campground, Camp Discovery, where cabins are available and reservations are required.

Eating

Palomino Room (☎ 530-527-5470; 723 Main St; beef plates $8-20) Downtown, the dark and moody Palomino Room, on the site of the historic Tremont Hotel, has tasty steaks and burgers and a cool cowboy ambience.

Raging Fork Riverfront Grille (☎ 530-529-9453; 500 Riverside Way; mains $12-20) Just south of Antelope Blvd and one block east of Main St, it has a beautiful dining room, bar and deck overlooking the river.

Green Barn (☎ 530-527-3161; 5 Chestnut Ave; dinner mains $8-14) This is a long-established family restaurant serving American fare for lunch and dinner.

Hal's Eat 'Em Up (☎ 530-529-0173; 158 Main St) If the heat is raging, grab a root-beer float from Hal's, a drive-in just south of downtown.

Getting There & Away

The **Greyhound station** (☎ 530-527-0434; 22825 Antelope Blvd) is east of town at the corner of Hwy 36 E.

SAN JOAQUIN VALLEY

The southern half of California's Central Valley stretches from Stockton to the Tehachapi Mountains southeast of Bakersfield. Through elaborate irrigation systems this arid basin has been converted into one of the most agriculturally productive regions in the world. Neat and tidy rows of crops cover nearly every rural acre between the Sierra to the east and the coastal ranges to the west. Most of the people who work these fields are Mexican. While some of the tiny towns scattering the region, such as Gustine and Reedley, retain a classic Main St Americana feel, many more, like Cutler and Lamont, feel almost entirely like little Tijuanas.

Traveling Hwy 99 – a road with nearly as long a history as the famous Route 66 – is the most interesting way through this part of the state. It connects the region's most important towns, acting as a window into the valley's – and the state's – colorful history.

Keep in mind that in midsummer temperatures in the valley often hover around 100°F or more.

STOCKTON

pop 244,000

Here's an honest representation of a small American city that once had a purpose. Stockton is still a port city, linked by deep water channels to the San Francisco Bay, but it's no longer the main disembarkation point for men and goods heading to California's mines and farmlands. Many of the city's streets are lined with run-down houses, old doughnut shops, liquor stores and taco trucks. The rehabilitated downtown is bland and treeless. There's no need to linger here, but do slow down and ponder the fact that Pavement, one of the leading indie-rock bands of the 1990s, came from Stockton. Retro crooner Chris Isaak also hails from here

Maps and information are available at the **Greater Stockton Chamber of Commerce's Department of Tourism** (☎ 209-547-2770; www.visitstockton .org; 445 W Weber Ave, Suite 220; ⏰ 9am-5pm Mon-Fri).

Worth checking out are the hopping **Miracle Mile** district (a stretch of Pacific Ave north of downtown), the architecturally rich **Magnolia Historic District** and the **Haggin Museum** (☎ 209-940-6300; 1201 N Pershing Ave; adult/student $5/2.50; ⏰ 1:30-5:30pm Wed-Sun), which has an excellent collection of American landscape paintings, historical items such as Native American baskets and early Caterpillar tractors, which were developed in Stockton.

Howard Johnson Express (☎ 209-948-6151; 33 N Center St; r $60-89; Ⓟ ⌧ ⬚) is fairly practical

CENTRAL VALLEY

BLOODLESS BULLFIGHTS

Bullfighting has been illegal in the USA since 1957, but there are exceptions to the rule. When Portuguese communities in the Central Valley have religious festivals, called *festas*, they are permitted to stage bloodless bullfights. The festas are huge events, attracting as many as 25,000 Portuguese Americans, and the bullfights are generally the climax of several days of parades, food, music and beauty contests.

Portuguese fishermen and farmers, mostly from the Azores, began settling in California during the late 19th century. The communities grew, especially the Central Valley, with steady immigration continuing until very recently. Many people in the valley still speak Portuguese fluently and attend the *festas* that are held up and down the state.

Festas typically honor religious icons such as St Anthony or Our Lady of Fátima. But they are largely cultural events. Candlelight processions, folk dancing, blessing of the cows, performances of *pezinho* songs (sad melodies with a lilting violin accompaniment) and eating till you feel like a plump sausage are all part of the experience. The *festa* queen contests are taken very seriously by the contestants.

Festas are held throughout the summer, with major events in Hanford, Gustine (along Hwy 33, north of the junction of I-5 and Hwy 152) and Stevinson (east of Gustine). They're not well publicized and the relevant websites that go up are often temporary. The only reliable thing to do is search 'festas california' and see what comes up in English.

and central. Its kidney-shaped pool gets more attractive as the mercury rises.

A modern hotel south of the river, the **Radisson Hotel Stockton** (☎ 209-957-9090; 2323 Grand Canal Blvd; r $89-119; P ⊠ ⊠) offers comfort to the road weary.

On the outskirts of town, near Hwy 99, is this likeable classic. Opened in 1946, **Ye Olde Hoosier Inn** (☎ 209-463-0271; 1537 N Wilson Way; meals $5-13) still has those comfy red booths and has accumulated lots of folksy antiques over the years. Country breakfasts to satisfy a king are the specialty. Chicken-fried steak'll do you for lunch or dinner.

MODESTO
pop 207,600

Cruising was banned in Modesto in 1993, but the town still touts itself as the 'cruising capital of the world.' That notoriety stems mostly from hometown boy George Lucas' 1973 film *American Graffiti*. You'll still see hot rods and flashy wheels around town, but they won't be clogging thoroughfares on Friday night. At its heart, Modesto is simply a fairly prosperous city where people are more urbane than rural despite the town's largely agricultural economy. The Ernest & Julio Gallo Winery, makers of America's best-selling jug wines, is among the town's biggest businesses. Old oaks arch over the city's attractive streets and you can eat well in the compact downtown. This is a good spot for getting off the dusty old highway. You may recognize Modesto from the news: murder victims Chandra Levy and Laci Peterson lived here.

Downtown sits just east of Hwy 99 (avoid the area west of the freeway), centering on 10th and J Sts. From downtown, Yosemite

---

GOT NO GOAT

The old arch that made Modesto famous tells a traveler what the four main tenets of the town are. The slogan, 'Water Wealth Contentment Health,' resulted from a local contest held prior to the construction of the arch. It is a pithy little poem and is as true today as it was when the arch went up in 1912. Interestingly, the slogan gracing the arch didn't actually win the contest. Judges chose the folksy, if less eloquent, slogan 'Nobody's Got Modesto's Goat' but were overruled by the city government.

Blvd (Hwy 132) runs east toward Yosemite National Park.

Sights & Activities

The spacious **McHenry Museum** (☎ 209-577-5366; cnr 14th & I Sts; admission free; ☿ noon-4pm Tue-Sun) offers local history, photographs and displays that are well worth a quick look. One block away, the lovely Victorian Italianate **McHenry Mansion** (☎ 209-577-5344; cnr I & 15th Sts; admission free; ☿ 1-4pm Sun-Thu, noon-3pm Fri), built in 1883, is the former home of prominent local rancher and banker Robert McHenry.

Many historic buildings have survived revitalization efforts, including the 1934 **State Theatre** (☎ 209-527-4697; 1307 J St), which hosts films and live music, and the old SP depot, a Mission-style beauty. The famous **Modesto Arch** (cnr 9th & I Sts), erected in 1912, stands at what was once the city's main entry point. Classic car shows are held in 'Graffiti Month' (June); for details, call the **chamber of commerce** (☎ 209-577-5757; 1114 J St).

Sleeping & Eating

Doubletree Hotel Modesto (☎ 209-526-6000; www .doubletree.com; 1150 9th St; r $109-189; P ⊠ ⊠) This large, modern property is Modesto's best choice for comfort and service. Amenities include a fitness room, a pool and a barber shop.

Best Western Town House Lodge (☎ 209-524-7261; 909 16th St; r $65; P ⊠ ⊠) Near downtown, this is a nice choice.

A&W Drive-In (☎ 209-522-7700; cnr 14th & G Sts) A relic from the city's cruising heyday, this vintage burger stand (part of a chain founded in nearby Lodi) still offers roller-skating carhops and frosty, frothy mugs of refreshing root beer. On Friday nights in summer, classic cars flood into the parking and the place really jumps.

Tresetti's World Caffe (☎ 209-572-2990; 927 11th St; lunch $6-11, dinner mains $15-27) Modesto's most sophisticated eatery, Tresetti's is a lovely spot. Its enticing menu reflects the kitchen's Cal-Med leanings, and the wine list is impressive.

MERCED
pop 69,800

Yosemite's primary gateway town has a certain all-American appeal, with its tree-lined streets, historic Victorian homes and magnificent 1875 courthouse. The downtown

TULE FOG

Radiation or tule (**too**-lee) fog causes dozens of collisions each year on San Joaquin Valley roads, including Hwy 99 and I-5. As thick as the proverbial pea soup, the fog limits visibility to about 10ft, making driving nearly impossible. The fog is thickest from November to February, when cold mountain air settles on the warm valley floor and condenses into fog as the ground cools at night. The fog often lifts for a few hours during the afternoon, just long enough for the ground to warm back up and thus perpetuate the cycle.

Call **Caltrans** (☎ 800-427-7623) to check road conditions before traveling. If you end up on a fog-covered road, drive with your low beams on, keep a good distance from the car in front of you, stay at a constant speed, avoid sudden stops and never try to pass other cars.

business district, centered along classic Main St, has 1930s movie theaters, antique stores and a few casual eateries.

The University of California campus opened in the fall of 2005, a year late and with most of the construction still not completed. UC Merced's first freshman class numbered just 1000 students, but as the school grows to its planned student body of 10,000 to 15,000, it will surely have a huge impact on the town.

Orientation & Information

Downtown Merced is east of Hwy 99 along Main St, between R St and Martin Luther King Jr Way. The **California Welcome Center** (☎ 209-384-2791, 800-446-5353; 710 W 16th St), adjacent to the bus depot, has local maps and information on Merced and Yosemite.

Sights & Activities

The big attraction is the **Castle Air Museum** (☎ 209-723- 2178; 5050 Santa Fe Dr; adult/child $8/6; ⏰ 10am-4pm), in Atwater, about 6 miles northwest of Merced. Arranged across a huge field is a vast collection of restored military aircraft from WWII, the Korean War and the Vietnam War. Even if you're a conscientious objector you'll be impressed by the designs of some of these old streamlined beauties.

Surrounded by a green, serene square, the 1875 **Merced County Courthouse** is Merced's architectural patriarch, the last still standing of eight county courthouses designed by Albert A Bennett. Inside is the excellent **Courthouse Museum** (☎ 209-723-2401; admission free; ⏰ 1-4pm Wed-Sun), well worth a quick peek.

Sleeping & Eating

Hooper House Bear Creek Inn (☎ 209-723-3991; www .hooperhouse.com; 575 W North Bear Creek Dr; r $95-135; P 🐾) In a grand old Colonial-style man-

sion, the Hooper House is a leisurely retreat. Rooms are large, beautifully furnished and have private bathrooms. A full breakfast is included.

HI Merced Home Hostel (☎ 209-725-0407; dm $15-18; ⏰ evenings; P) This eight-bed, family-style hostel is in the home of longtime Merced residents who know tons about Yosemite. The hostel fills quickly, especially during summer weekends. Beds must be reserved in advance; call between 5:30pm and 10pm. The hostel doesn't give out its address but it will pick up and drop off guests at the bus and train stations.

Slumber Motel (☎ 209-722-5783; 1315 W 16th St; r $35-50; P 🐾 🔧) Merced has no shortage of budget motels. Among the older, independent establishments close to downtown, the Slumber Motel is kept up and well run. Look for the snazzy sign if you're entering town on 16th St.

Branding Iron (☎ 209-722-1822; 640 W 16th St; lunch $9-11, dinner mains $17-25; ⏰ lunch Mon-Fri, dinner nightly) This old roadhouse has been spruced up a bit for the tour buses, but folks still love the place for its hearty steak platters and Western atmosphere. Presiding over the dining room is 'Old Blue,' a massive stuffed bull's head from a local dairy farm.

For breakfast, it's hard to resist the chatty, small-town-diner scene at **Cinema Cafe** (☎ 209-722-2811; 661 W Main St; meals $4-6), next door to the **Mainzer** (☎ 209-722-4042), a stately old movie house.

Getting There & Away

Yarts (☎ 209-388-9589, 877-989-2787; www.yarts.com) buses depart four times daily for Yosemite Valley from several Merced locations, including the **Merced Transpo Center** (cnr 16th & N Sts) and the **Amtrak station** (cnr 24th & K Sts). The trip takes about 2½ hours and stops include Mariposa,

Midpines and the Yosemite Bug Lodge & Hostel in Midpines. Round-trip adult/child tickets cost $20/14 and include the park entrance fee (quite a bargain!). Greyhound also operates from the Transpo Center.

FRESNO
pop 445,200

Bulging like a blister in the hot, dry center of the state, Fresno is by far the biggest city in the San Joaquin Valley. The old brick warehouses lining the Santa Fe railroad tracks are an impressive sight, as are the many historic downtown buildings such as the 1894 Fresno Water Tower and the 1928 Pantages (Warnors) Theatre. These compete for attention with newer structures such as the sprawling Convention Center and the modern ballpark for Fresno's Triple A baseball team, the Grizzlies.

The biggest surprise Fresno throws a traveler's way is the Tower District, which boasts the only active alternative-culture neighborhood between Sacramento and Los Angeles. North of downtown, the Tower District has book and record stores, music clubs and a handful of stylish, highly regarded restaurants.

Like many valley towns, Fresno's surprisingly diverse. Mexican, Basque and Chinese communities have been here for decades, and, more recently, thousands of Hmong have put down roots in the area. The longstanding Armenian community is most famously represented by author and playwright William Saroyan, who was born, lived and died in this city he loved dearly.

Orientation & Information

Downtown lies between Divisadero St, Hwy 41 and Hwy 99. Two miles north, the Tower District sits around the corner of E Olive Ave and N Fulton Ave.

Fresno Convention & Visitors Bureau (☎ 559-237-0988, 800-788-0836; cnr Fresno & 0 Sts; ☯ 10am-4pm Mon-Fri, 11am-3pm Sat) is inside the Fresno Water Tower.

Sights & Activities

If you see only one thing in Fresno, make it the **Forestiere Underground Gardens** (☎ 559-271-0734; www.undergroundgardens.com; 5021 W Shaw Ave; adult/child $10/7; ☯ tours 10am & noon Wed-Fri, 10am, noon, 2pm & 6pm Sat, 10am noon & 2pm Sun), one block east of Hwy 99. The gardens are the singular

result of Sicilian immigrant Baldasare Forestiere's creative obsession. Beginning in 1906, Forestiere – whose plans for citrus groves were foiled by the hardness of the soil – dug out some 70 acres beneath the hardpan soil, and, with a unique skylight system, created a beautiful subterranean space for commercial crops and his own living quarters. The tunnel system includes bedrooms, a library, patios, grottos and a fish pond, and is now a historic landmark. This utterly fantastical accomplishment took Forestiere some 40 years to complete. He died in 1946.

Fresno's **Tower District** began as a shopping mecca during the 1920s, gaining its name after the **Tower Theatre** (☎ 559-485-9050; 815 E Olive Ave), a beautiful art deco movie house that opened in 1939. The theater is now used as a center for the performing arts. Surrounding it are bookstores, shops, high-end restaurants and coffeehouses that cater to Fresno's gay and alternative communities. This is the city's best neighborhood for browsing and kicking back with an iced latte – even if the hipster quotient is tiny by comparison to that of, say, San Francisco's Mission District.

The **Fresno Art Museum** (☎ 559-441-4221; www.fresnoartmuseum.org; 2233 N 1st St; adult/student $4/2, Tue admission free; ☯ 11am-5pm Tue-Sun, 11am-8pm Thu), in Radio Park, has rotating exhibits of contemporary art – including work by local artists – that are among the most intriguing in the valley.

A favorite with children, the **Fresno Metropolitan Museum** (☎ 559-441-1444; www.fresnomet.org; 1515 Van Ness Ave; adult/student $8/5; ☯ 11am-5pm Tue-Sun, 11am-8pm Thu) has hands-on science exhibits, Native American crafts, a large collection of antique puzzles and a William Saroyan gallery. The museum's holdings also include a large collection of Ansel Adams photographs.

On Olive Ave just east of Hwy 99, large and shady **Roeding Park** ($1 per car) is home to the small **Chaffee Zoological Gardens** (☎ 559-498-2671; adult/child $7/3.50; 9am-4pm Mar-Oct, 10am-3pm Nov-Feb). Adjacent to it are **Storyland** (☎ 559-264-2235; adult/child $4/3; 11am-4pm Mon-Fri May-Sep, 10am-5:30pm Sat & Sun), a kitschy children's fairy-tale world dating from 1962, and **Playland**, which has kiddie rides and games.

Sleeping

Garden Inn & Suites (☎ 559-277-3888, 800-335-1868; www.gardeninnandsuites.com; 4949 N Forestiere Ave; r $89-349; P) This modern, Spanish-style compound surrounds a swimming pool and looks like a condominium complex, but it has large, comfortable rooms and is near Forestiere Gardens. Some rooms have Jacuzzis.

Days Inn (☎ 559-268-6211; 1101 N Parkway Dr; r $50-90; P) Among the inexpensive options around N Parkway and Olive Sts this Days Inn stands out. It's set slightly back from the road, has well maintained grounds, a palm-shaded pool and sizable, clean rooms.

Water Tree Inn (☎ 800-762-9071, 559-222-4445; www.bviwatertree.com; 4141 N Blackstone Ave; r $59-79; P) About 3 miles north of downtown, among numerous comparable choices, the Water Tree Inn has large, clean, comfortable rooms.

Eating

Believe it or not, Fresno has quite a few upscale eateries with inventive menus and inviting interiors.

Echo (☎ 559-442-3246; 609 E Olive Ave; mains $24-31; dinner Tue-Sat) This lovely restaurant in the Tower District, serves dishes made with local, seasonal and often organic ingredients. The aqua-colored chairs, designed by Frank Lloyd Wright, were salvaged from a funeral home in Delano.

Irene's Cafe (☎ 559-237-9919; 47 E Olive Ave; lunch $5-9, dinner $9-13) In the hip Tower District, Irene's is popular for its chicken-fried steaks (made with Angus beef), whopping 9oz burgers and veggie burgers. Its trendy atmosphere comes off as friendly rather than hip and the place does three meals a day.

Grand Marie's Chicken Pie Shop (☎ 559-237-5042; 2861 E Olive Ave; meals $5-12) You can get tasty chicken potpies here, or you can order heaping breakfasts and other all-American

fare. This Tower District haunt does three meals daily.

Entertainment

In addition to the glorious Tower Theatre, the Tower District has several favorite haunts. Among them are indie-rock hangout **Club Fred** (1426 N Van Ness Ave), where live performances often begin during happy hour; divey blues bar **Zapp's Park** (1105 N Blackstone Ave); and **Butterfield Brewing Company** (777 E Olive Ave), which serves its own beer and has occasional live music.

Downtown, **Warnors Theatre** (☎ 559-264-6863; 1412 Fulton St) is home to several more classic old theaters, including the stunning 1928 Warnors, which hosts concerts, musicals and other events.

Getting There & Around

Greyhound (☎ 559-268-1829; 1033 Broadway) stops downtown near the new ballpark.

The local **Fresno Area Express** (FAX; ☎ 559-488-1122; $1) has daily bus services to the Tower District (bus 22 or 26) and Forestiere Underground Gardens (bus 20, transfer to bus 9) from the downtown transit center at Van Ness Ave and Fresno St.

HANFORD

pop 44,400

Hanford, less than 10 miles west of Hwy 99, is a picture-perfect small American town, looking like a heartland community from the mid-20th century. It has a compact, restored downtown that centers around a shaded square and the 1896 **Kings County Courthouse**, the town's crown jewel. A number of films have been shot on location here. Most of Hanford's historic brick buildings along Court and 7th Sts date from the early 1900s and now house restaurants and shops. The town is great for strolling.

Learn more about the historic buildings at the **Hanford Carnegie Museum** (☎ 559-584-1367; 109 E 8th St; admission $2; noon-3pm Tue-Fri, noon-4pm Sat). Across from the courthouse is the **Fox Theatre** (☎ 559-584-7423; 326 N Irwin St), an eye-catching art deco venue dating from 1929 that regularly hosts live music.

Predating all these buildings is Hanford's **Taoist Temple** (☎ 559-582-4508; tours by appointment 2 weeks in advance), built in 1893 in **China Alley**, the heart of a once-bustling Chinatown. To reach China Alley from downtown, take 7th

CENTRAL VALLEY

STAYIN' ALIVE ON I-5

The ride from San Francisco to Los Angeles on I-5 – through the dreariest part of California – is something most people just want to get over with as painlessly as possible. Observing the speed limit means a six- or seven-hour drive. Stops for gas and food and a stretch of the legs are probably going to be necessary somewhere between Coalinga and Lebec.

For amusement, pull off at the **Tule Elk State Reserve** (☎ 661-764-6881), a few miles south of Bottonwillow. In late summer, the males lock horns to impress the gals.

Good refueling stops include **Harris Ranch Inn & Restaurant** (☎ 800-942-2333; 24505 W Dorris Ave, Coalinga; r $129-169, meals $28-42), which has high quality beef from the nearby cattle ranch in every cut imaginable. If the eating tires you out, you can stay a night in the posh ranch hotel, which has a 25m lap pool. For fast food try **In-N-Out Burger** (Hwy 41 at Bernard Dr, Kettleman City), an ever reliable quick-stop midway between SF and LA. It's far superior to McDonald's. There are other branches throughout California.

St east to Green St and turn left; it's immediately on your right.

Irwin St Inn (☎ 559-583-8000; 522 N Irwin St; r $89-99; P 🕸) is in a complex of beautiful Victorians with lush gardens and a peaceful courtyard. Rooms are tastefully done up without trying too hard to re-create 19th-century frills. There's also a restaurant.

Imperial Dynasty (☎ 559-582-0196; 406 China Alley; dishes $12-30; 🕑 Tue-Sun) sits next to the Taoist Temple but oddly enough serves upscale continental cuisine, steaks and seafood.

Superior Dairy (☎ 559-582-0481; 325 N Douty St), across the street from the Bastille, is a vintage 1929 ice-cream parlor; get a cone and sink into one of the pale-pink booths.

VISALIA

pop 96,900

Visalia is one of the valley's nicest towns and a good place to stay en route to Sequoia and Kings Canyon National Parks. Bypassed a century ago by the railroad (which goes through Hanford instead), the city is 5 miles east of Hwy 99, along Hwy 198. Its downtown – centered on the intersection of Court and Main Sts – has great old buildings and is a popular place to stroll, day or night.

Sights & Activities

The original Victorian and Craftsman-style homes in Visalia are real architectural gems and worth viewing on foot. Get details of a walking tour from the **Visalia Chamber of Commerce and Visitors Center** (☎ 559-734-5876, 877-847-2542; www.visaliatourism.com; 720 W Mineral King Ave; 🕑 8:30am-5pm Mon-Fri). Lovely examples are found north of Main St on both N Willis and Encina Sts.

The gloriously restored 1930 **Fox Theatre** (cnr W Main & Encina Sts) hosts assorted concerts and special events.

South of downtown on Hwy 63 (Mooney Blvd), shaded Mooney Grove Park is home to the **Tulare County Museum** (☎ 559-733-6616; park $5, museum free; 🕑 10am-4pm Mon, Thu & Fri, 1-4pm Sat & Sun), which has pioneer and Native American memorabilia.

About 7 miles east of Visalia is **Kaweah Oak Reserve**, home to 324 acres of valley oak trees, which once stretched from the Sierra to (long-gone) Tulare Lake in the valley. Nice for a short hike, it's also a rare glimpse into the valley's past before the orchards and vineyards took over. From Hwy 198, turn north onto Road 182; the park is about a half-mile along on your left.

Sleeping & Eating

Lamp Liter Inn (☎ 559-732-4511, 800-662-669; http://lampliter.net; 3300 W Mineral King Ave; r $72; P 🕸) Off Highway 198, this slightly older motel has been kept up well. Guest rooms look like middle class bedrooms from the early 1980s but are comfortable and quiet.

Spalding House (☎ 559-739-7877; www.thespaldinghouse.com; 631 N Encina; r $85-95; 🕸) This B&B has three classy suites, all with antique bed, sitting room and modern bath. The full-on breakfasts will get you going in the morning.

Vintage Press (☎ 559-733-3033; 216 N Willis; lunch $9-14, dinner mains $16-33) A cherished Visalia institution since 1966, Vintage Press is elegant, festive and upscale. Have a cocktail while you wait for excellent rack of lamb or filet mignon.

Mearle's Drive-In (☎ 559-734-4447; 604 S Mooney Blvd; meals $4-7; P) The Taj Mahal of classic drive-ins, Mearle's neon sign is flat out lovely to behold at sunset. Cheeseburgers, fries, shakes and other grease-pit fare are what you'll get here.

Java Jungle (☎ 559-732-5282; 208 W Main St) Main St has a couple of good coffeehouses, one being Java Jungle, where they roast their own beans.

Getting There & Away
Amtrak (☎ 559-582-5236) shuttles connect with the station in Hanford, by reservation only.

BAKERSFIELD
pop 261,000
At the southern end of the San Joaquin Valley lies Bakersfield, one of the valley's biggest towns and key agricultural centers. The region has seen its share of prosperity thanks not only to crops but also to oil. The Kern River oil field, developed in 1899, stretches from Oildale, just north of town, to Taft, some 30 miles west, and remains one of the biggest oil producers in the nation.

Though some parts of town are rather shabby, downtown is a surprisingly upbeat mix of restored buildings, county offices, restaurants and antique shops, such as the **Five and Dime** (cnr 19th St & K St) inside an original Woolworth's building. The 1930 Fox Theater hosts regular performances and the still impressive Padre Hotel is currently undergoing restoration. Near the freeway, Buck Owens' multi-million-dollar Crystal Palace is a raging success.

Orientation & Information
The Kern River flows along Bakersfield's northern edge, separating it from its blue-collar neighbor, Oildale, and a host of unsightly oil fields. Truxtun and Chester Aves are the main downtown thoroughfares.

The **Greater Bakersfield Convention and Visitors Bureau** (☎ 661-325-5051; www.bakersfieldcvb.org; 515 Truxtun Ave; ✆ 8:30am-5pm Mon-Fri) carries maps and loads of brochures, some with discounts to local attractions.

Sights
It's amazing how much history there is to explore everywhere you turn in Bakersfield. Old Town Kern, east of downtown around Baker and Sumner Sts, is a district that, while currently decaying, was a once vibrant and bustling centre. The **Bakersfield Historic Preservation Commission** (☎ 661-326-3765; www.bakersfieldcity.us/edcd/historic/walkingtours.htm) has put together walking tour brochures covering Old Town Kern as well as Bakersfield's historic downtown.

The **Kern County Museum** (☎ 661-852-5000; 3801 Chester Ave; adult/student $8/7; ✆ 10am-5pm Mon-Sat, noon-5pm Sun), north of downtown, is a worthwhile stop for kids, history buffs and music fans. The pioneer village has more than 50 restored and replicated buildings, including a hotel and a wooden oil derrick, spread over 16 shaded acres. An exhibit on the Bakersfield Sound highlights the local legends.

Surrounded by a small park and lovely sculpture garden, the newly expanded **Bakersfield Museum of Art** (☎ 661-323-7219; 1930 R St; adult/student $5/2; ✆ 10am-4pm Tue-Fri, noon-4pm Sat & Sun) has a strong, diverse schedule of permanent and rotating exhibits, highlighting regional artists but often tackling international issues and perspectives.

CENTRAL VALLEY

RACEWAYS
This being a town of good-ole boys, auto racing is really popular. Bakersfield's raceways are in full swing from March to November, and weekend events, some with high-profile sponsors, draw people from all over the state. Smaller races get a local crowd and can be equally thrilling. Ticket prices are between $9 and $12 (major events higher) and are usually available at the gate.

Bakersfield Speedway (☎ 661-393-3373; 5001 N Chester Ave Extension) has a one-third-mile clay oval track and has been hosting races since 1946. Follow Chester Ave north through Oildale.

The **Famoso Raceway** (☎ 661-399-2210) is a quarter-mile drag strip that hosts races most weekends and special vintage and custom events throughout the year. The raceway is about 15 miles north of Bakersfield. As you head north on Hwy 99, take the Hwy 46 exit, turn right onto Famoso Rd and go east for 4 miles.

Home to Nascar events, the **Mesa Marin Raceway** (☎ 661-366-5711) is a half-mile oval where cars do 25 to 100 laps at speeds way over 100mph. Races are held at 7:30pm Saturday nights.

DETOUR: WEEDPATCH LABOR CAMP

In the years following the Depression, Kern County boasted California's highest percentage of poor white farm laborers from the South and the Great Plains. Called Okies, whether they came from Oklahoma or not, they came with dreams of a new life in the fields and farms of the Golden State. The majority, though, found only migrant labor jobs and continued hardship.

Dating from 1935, this Farm Security Administration labor camp (the model for 'Weedpatch Camp' in *The Grapes of Wrath*) was one of about 16 in the US set up at the time to aid migrant workers – and it's the only one with any original buildings left. At the time of writing, the original structures were undergoing restoration, and some of the camp's newer buildings were still occupied by poor farm workers. The camp is a fascinating vision into the past – and a wake-up call to the continuing dichotomy between corporate agribusiness and its still-dirt-poor migrant workforce. **Tours** (☎ 661-832-1299) require advance arrangement.

From Bakersfield, take Hwy 58 east to Weedpatch Hwy; head south for about 7 miles, past Lamont; then turn left on Sunset Blvd, driving another mile. The buildings (the sign reads Arvin Farm Labor Center) are on your right. Please respect the privacy of the residents. **Dust Bowl Days** (www.weedpatchcamp.com) is a celebration of Okie history held here each October.

Sleeping

Best Western Crystal Palace (☎ 661-327-9651, 800-424-4900; 2620 Buck Owens Blvd; r $80; P ❄ ⚲) Next door to Buck Owens' night club, this Best Western has a stylish interior patio with a cool pool. Apart from that, you get what you'd expect from a Best Western.

California Inn (☎ 661-328-1100; www.cainn.net; 3400 Chester Lane; r $53-89; P ❄ ⚲) This modern hotel has large rooms, spa, sauna and pool (right off the parking lot but still pleasant). It's quiet, even though it's near Hwy 99.

Capri Motel (☎ 661-327-3577; 2020 Union Ave; r $40-55; P ❄) Old-school budget motels line Union Ave heading south from Hwy 178; some are sketchy, but among the more decent is the Capri.

Eating

Bakersfield is blessed with several traditional Basque restaurants, where food is served family-style in a series of courses including soup, salad, beans and thin slices of tangy beef tongue. All this comes *before* the main course, so you'd better be hungry. Mexican food is plentiful here too.

Wool Growers (☎ 661-327-9584; 620 E 19th St; lunch $7-14, dinner $14-21) Bakersfield's oldest Basque restaurant is a simple eating hall loaded with character. A fried chicken dinner will leave you full for a week.

Colima Mexican Restaurant (☎ 661-631-1188; 2000 Chester Ave; meals $5-9) This restaurant serves fajitas, *mole* (a sweet, chocolaty chili sauce) dinners and other specialties in a lively downtown setting.

La Fonda (☎ 661-325-1472; 1230 H St) Cheaper still is La Fonda, across from Bakersfield High School, where tasty, fresh tacos are just $1 (get three or four, as they're small).

24th Street Cafe (☎ 661-323-8801; 1415 24th St; meals $5-8) Trout and eggs is a local favorite at this popular café, though expect to wait for a table.

Entertainment

Buck Owens' Crystal Palace (☎ 661-328-7560; www .buckowens.com; 2800 Buck Owens Blvd) This venue, off Hwy 99 at the Rosedale Hwy exit, is a must-stop for country music fans. Looking like it belongs in Branson, Missouri, the flashy, Disney-esque joint is fun nonetheless. It regularly hosts touring country acts and Buck himself plays here every Friday and Saturday at 7:30pm ($6, reserve in advance to assure seating). Memorabilia lines the hallways too. The overpriced food is OK but nothing special.

Ethel's Old Corral (☎ 661-871-4136; 4310 Alfred Harrell Hwy) On the outskirts of town, north of Hwy 178, Ethel's is a friendly joint that features live music Friday and Sunday nights. Country bands frequently take the stage.

Trout's (☎ 661-399-6700; 805 N Chester Ave at Decatur St) The legendary Trout's, in Oildale, is a scratchy but still bustling cowboy bar that has survived intact for half a century. Crowds pack the place and dance to the music of Bobby Durham and the great Red Simpson, both one-time Bakersfield Sound hit makers who play there each week.

Fox Theater (☎ 661-635-0543; www.foxtheateronline
.com; 2001 H St) Downtown, the 1930 Fox Theater
is a restored art deco beauty. It hosts concerts, live performances and films.

Getting There & Around
From the **Amtrak station** (☎ 661-395-3175, 800-
872-7245; 601 Truxtun Ave at S St) trains head north
and Amtrak buses head to LA.

The **Greyhound** (☎ 661-327-5617, 800-229-9424;
1820 18th St) depot is downtown near the Padre
Hotel.

Airport Bus of Bakersfield (☎ 800-858-5000, 805-
395-0635; 2530 F St) runs a shuttle seven times
daily between Bakersfield and LAX ($27, 2½
hours).

Golden Empire Transit (GET; ☎ 661-869-2438;
fares 75¢) is the local bus system. Route 2 runs
north on Chester Ave to the Kern County
Museum and Oildale.

KERN RIVER
A half-century ago the Kern River originated on the slopes of Mt Whitney and
journeyed close to 170 miles before finally
settling into Buena Vista Lake in the Central Valley. Now, after its wild ride from
the high country – where the river drops
an incredible 60ft per mile – it's dammed
in several places and almost entirely tapped
by agricultural interests after hitting the
valley floor. Its upper reaches, though,
have been declared wild and scenic and
are hugely popular with white-water
enthusiasts.

Hwy 178 follows the dramatic **Kern River
Canyon**, making for a stunning scenic drive
through the lower reaches of Sequoia National Forest. East of the lake, Hwy 178
winds another 50 miles through a picturesque mixture of pine and Joshua trees before reaching Hwy 395.

The town of **Lake Isabella** is a strip of local
businesses on the south end of the lake.
Here Hwy 155 heads north, around the
west side of lake, to **Kernville**, a cute little
town straddling the Kern River and *the* hub
for rafting on the Kern. Normally serene,
the town swarms with visitors on summer
weekends. However, there's little protection
from the sun, and while the lake is popular for cooling off, note that the river's de-
ceptively strong currents can be extremely
dangerous – signs warn visitors to stay out,
advice best heeded.

The **Kernville Ranger Station** (☎ 760-376-3781;
105 Whitney Rd; ☉ 8am-5pm summer, 8:30am-4:30pm
Mon-Fri winter) has hiking and camping information on this area, as well as maps and
wilderness permits.

Rafting
The Upper Kern and Forks of the Kern
(both sections of the river north of Kernville) yield Class IV and V rapids during
spring runoff and offer some of the most
awe-inspiring white-water trips in the country. You'll need experience before tackling
these sections, though there are plenty more
opportunities for novices. Below Lake Isabella, the Kern is tamer and steadier.

About six rafting companies operate out
of Kernville; all offer competitive prices and
run trips from May to August, depending
on conditions. Excursions include popular
one-hour runs ($25), day-long Lower Kern
trips ($130 to $190) and multiday Forks of
the Kern wilderness experiences ($600 to
$920). Walk-ups are welcome and experi-
ence isn't necessary. Kids aged six and up
can usually participate too. Companies include **Sierra South** (☎ 760-376-3745, 800-457-2082;
www.sierrasouth.com; 11300 Kernville Rd); **Whitewater
Voyages** (☎ 800-400-7238, 660-376-8806; www.white
watervoyages.com) and **Mountain & River Adventures** (☎ 800-861-6553, 760-376-6553; www.mtnriver
.com; 11113 Kernville Rd).

Sleeping & Eating
Lake Isabella has motels, but Kernville's a
nicer location and rates here are still reasonable. Many of Kernville's motels have two-
day minimum stays on weekends.

Whispering Pines Lodge (☎ 760-376-3733; www
.kernvalley.com/whisperingpines; 13745 Sierra Way; r $149-
299; 🐾) This secluded B&B, blending rustic
character with luxurious comfort, is just
north of town.

McCambridge Lodge (☎ 760-376-2288; www.mc
cambridgelodge.com; 13525 Sierra Way; r $80-120) On
the hill above the square is this pleasant facility with river views.

USFS campgrounds (☎ 877-444-6777; sites $12-16)
These campgrounds line the 10 mile stretch
between Lake Isabella and Kernville, and several more lie north of Kernville on Mtn 99.

Ewings (125 Buena Vista Dr; meals $12-21) For an
ice-cold beer or sizzling steak dinner, check
out Ewings, a spacious lodge dating from
1956 with knockout river views.

Central Coast

After San Francisco and Los Angeles, the Central Coast is the top reason to visit California. Alternative-lifestyle guru Timothy Leary called California the 'nose-cone of the rocket' and this was certainly its tip when he and his band explored it physically, mentally and chemically at the start of the 1960s. Much of the mystique and lore of the state is here. The scenery is some of the world's most stunning, with magnificent redwood forests giving way to a craggy coast teeming with wildlife and interspersed with long beaches and pounding surf.

Monterey Bay delights with character-filled towns like Santa Cruz and Pacific Grove and natural beauty that includes starfish-filled tidepools and amazing sea life. The famous Hwy 1 clings to the rocky cliffs, passing through storied Big Sur on to the glories of Hearst Castle.

The warmth of Southern California can be felt starting in the historic college town of San Luis Obispo. The hills south of here are dotted with wineries that rival and even surpass those of Napa Valley. Santa Barbara may well be the ultimate stop, combining a superb beach with urban chic. Offshore, the Channel Islands preserve a California of 1000 years ago.

No trip to California is complete without time on the Central Coast. At the least, spend a couple of nights on Monterey Bay, see the aquarium and then take a day to drive south on Hwy 1. Add in another day for Hearst Castle and devote at least two to the wineries and Santa Barbara. Such a trip might just exceed those of Leary and his cohorts decades ago.

HIGHLIGHTS

- Plunging into the depths of undersea life at **Monterey Bay Aquarium** (p443)
- Experiencing the coastal lifestyle of frolicsome **Santa Cruz** (p434)
- Rocking and rolling along Hwy 1 through **Big Sur** (p454)
- Marveling at the grandiosity and fantasy of **Hearst Castle** (p461)
- Luxuriating in the culture and chic of **Santa Barbara** (p483)
- Following the **Sideways roads and wineries** (p482) of Santa Barbara County
- Enjoying the vibrant college life in **San Luis Obispo** (p466)
- Delving into **mission lore** (p476) along Hwy 101

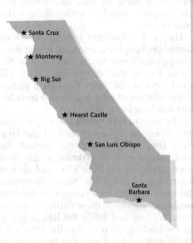

★ Santa Cruz

★ Monterey

★ Big Sur

★ Hearst Castle

★ San Luis Obispo

Santa Barbara ★

- AVERAGE TEMPS IN SANTA BARBARA: JAN 45/64°F, JUL 59/75°F

CENTRAL COAST

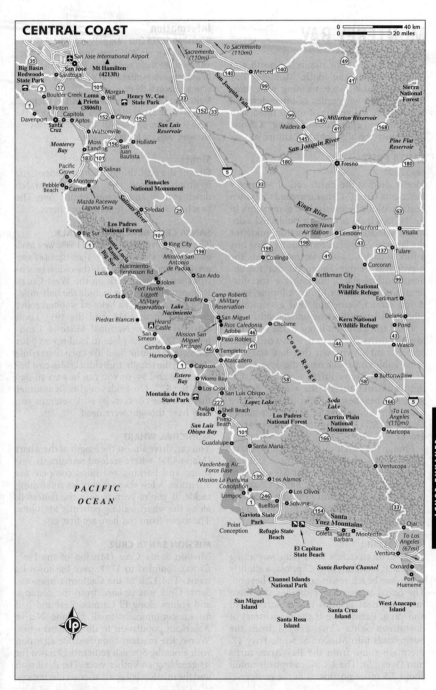

PACIFIC OCEAN

MONTEREY BAY

Anchored by Santa Cruz in the north and its namesake in the south, Monterey Bay is a remarkable place: teeming with marine life, lined with miles of often deserted beaches and a diversity of towns filled with character and appeal dotted along its shore. It's a must-see highlight of California.

SANTA CRUZ

pop 57,200

Ideally sited at the north end of Monterey Bay, Santa Cruz (SC) has marched to its own beat since long before the beat generation. In the 1970s a local newspaper published a do-it-yourself artificial-insemination guide for the large local lesbian community (first buy a turkey-baster…) and for many years the mayor was neither Democrat nor Republican (unthinkable!), but rather a 'socialist-feminist.' It's still cool to be a hippie, even if you scratch some and find a slumming Silicon Valley millionaire underneath.

Local ethos aside, it is one of the most enjoyable towns on the coast, with a delightful and vibrant downtown that has staged a remarkable comeback from the devastation of the 1989 Loma Prieta earthquake. On the waterfront there's the vintage boardwalk and beaches, while in the hills above town, the University of California Santa Cruz (UCSC) is surrounded by redwood groves.

Plunge the rich local brew of surfers, students, punks, characters and more and you may just need to add another day or two to your visit. If nothing else, Santa Cruz is a must-stop before or after the joys of Hwy 1 to the north and Monterey, Big Sur and the rest to the south.

Orientation

Santa Cruz stretches for a long way along the coast, blending into Capitola, a slightly lower-key beach resort, and Aptos beyond. The San Lorenzo River divides the town in an un-neat fashion into a sort of yin and yang. Pacific Ave is the main street of downtown Santa Cruz. Hwy 1 from the north leads into Mission St while Hwy 17, the main route from the Bay Area, turns into Ocean St. The UCSC campus is uphill about 2.5 miles northwest of the center.

Information

Bookshop Santa Cruz (Map p435; ☎ 831-423-0900; 1520 Pacific Ave; ☺ 10am-10pm) An excellent bookstore with a vast selection of new books, a few used ones, popular and unusual magazines and a café. There are several other bookshops in the city.

Santa Cruz County Conference & Visitors Council (Map p440; ☎ 831-425-1234; www.santacruz.org; 1211 Ocean St; ☺ 9am-5pm Mon-Sat, 10am-4pm Sun) Has brochures, maps and free Internet access.

Sights

One of the best things to do in Santa Cruz is simply to stroll, shop and people-watch downtown in and around Pacific Ave. The beach is a 10-minute walk from here.

SANTA CRUZ BEACH BOARDWALK

The 1906 **boardwalk** (☎ 831-423-5590; www.beach boardwalk.com; admission free; ☺ 11am-11pm daily summer, 11am-5pm Sat & Sun winter) is the oldest beach-front amusement park on the West Coast. Its most famous rides include the half-mile-long Giant Dipper, a beloved wooden roller coaster built in 1924, and the 1911 Looff carousel – both National Historic Landmarks. This is the place to load up on your life's quota of junk food like corn dogs while strolling the length. Individual rides cost between $2 and $4, or you can buy an all-day pass for $27. On Friday nights in summer there are free concerts by rock veterans you may have thought were dead.

MUNICIPAL WHARF

You can drive almost the length of the wharf (Map p435), where seafood restaurants, gift shops and barking sea lions compete for attention. A few shops rent poles and fishing tackle, if you're keen to join the fisherfolk along the wharf waiting patiently for a bite. The views from out here are first rate.

MISSION SANTA CRUZ

Mission Santa Cruz (Mission of the Holy Cross), founded in 1791, gave the town its name. The 12th of the California missions, Santa Cruz was isolated from the comings and goings along El Camino Real and had an uneconomically small Ohlone Native American population to do the hard work. Worse, the mission competed for attention with a nearby Spanish settlement known for its gambling and other vices. The devil won and the mission fell apart after secularization.

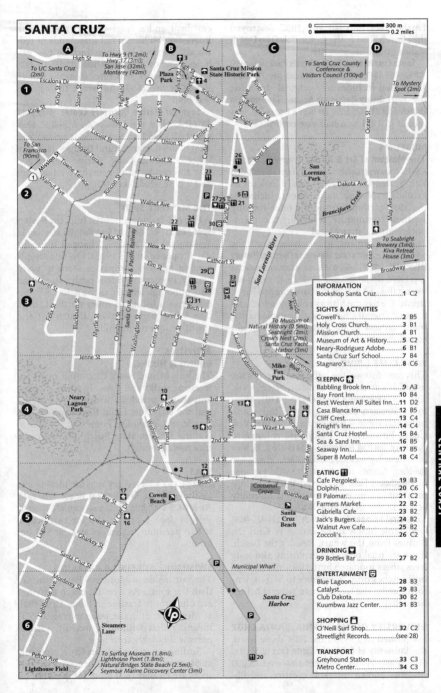

SANTA CRUZ

Earthquakes in 1840 and 1857 destroyed the church. Today the iconic **Holy Cross Church** stands on the original site.

Santa Cruz Mission State Historic Park (Map p435; ☎ 831-425-5849; 144 School St; admission free; ☺ 10am-4pm Thu-Sun) includes one original structure, the 1791 **Neary-Rodriguez Adobe**. The **mission church** (☎ 831-426-5686; cnr High & Emmet Sts) was rebuilt in 1931 as a half-size replica.

MUSEUMS

The **Museum of Art & History** (Map p435; ☎ 831-429-1964; www.santacruzmah.org; 705 Front St; adult/child $5/2; ☺ 11am-5pm Tue-Sun) is worth a look for its exhibits exploring local history, including the 1989 earthquake and the once-thriving Japanese community. It highlights contemporary artists, many local.

A large, cement, gray whale fronts the worthwhile **Santa Cruz Museum of Natural History** (Map p440; ☎ 831-420-6115; www.santacruzmuseums .org; 1305 E Cliff Dr; admission $2.50; ☺ 10am-5pm Tue-Sun) on the east side of the San Lorenzo River. Inside, the natural history collection includes a touch-friendly tidepool that explains the many critters living along the shore right across the street.

WEST CLIFF DRIVE

This road follows the cliffs southwest of the wharf. It's an excellent drive or, better, walk. The tip, **Lighthouse Point** (Map p440), overlooks **Steamers Lane**, one of the top – and most accessible – surfing spots on the West Coast. Fittingly, the lighthouse is home to the tiny **Surfing Museum** (☎ 831-420-6289; www .santacruzsurfingmuseum.org; admission free; ☺ noon-4pm Thu-Mon). Across the street, the wild expanse of **Lighthouse Field** was saved from development into a convention hotel by community action in the 1970s and '80s.

Natural Bridges State Beach (☎ 831-423-4609) is a scenic beach at the end of W Cliff Dr, 3 miles from the wharf. Besides the beach, there are tidal pools for exploring and leafy trees where monarch butterflies hibernate in big bunches from November to March. Unfortunately, the iconic main natural bridge has collapsed.

UNIVERSITY OF CALIFORNIA, SANTA CRUZ

Established in 1965 in the hills above town, the **University of California Santa Cruz** (UCSC; Map p440; ☎ 831-459-4008; www.ucsc.edu) has over 13,000 students known for their creative and lib-

eral bent and a rural campus dotted with interesting buildings and fine stands of redwoods. Campus buildings include two galleries, a renowned **arboretum** (☎ 831-427-2998) and a number of structures from the Cowell Ranch of the 1860s, on which the campus was built.

Seymour Marine Discovery Center (Map p440; ☎ 831-459-3800; near Delaware Ave & Swift St; adult/ student $5/3; ☺ 10am-5pm Tue-Sat, noon-5pm Sun), west of town near Natural Bridges, is part of UCSC's famous Long Marine Laboratory. The interactive exhibit include aquariums and a blue whale skeleton.

THE MYSTERY SPOT

A fine old-fashioned tourist trap, the **Mystery Spot** (☎ 831-423-8897; off Branciforte Dr; admission $5; ☺ 9am-7pm) has scarcely changed from the day it opened in the 1940s. On this steeply sloping hillside, compasses seem to point crazily, mysterious forces push you around and buildings lean at silly angles. All this nonsense is located 3 miles north of town; take Water St to Market St, turn left and continue up into the hills.

Activities

BIKING & HIKING

The hills behind Santa Cruz offer many interesting walks and rides. In town, a pleasant, easy trip follows winding W Cliff Dr and the coastline. From the boardwalk it's 1 mile to Lighthouse Point and 3 miles to Natural Bridges State Beach. It's especially nice toward sunset.

SPAS

Santa Cruz's New Agey spas are ideal places to unwind. At **Kiva Retreat House** (Map p440; ☎ 831-429-1142; http://kivaretreat.com; 702 Water St; ☺ noon-11pm), a private tub for two people is $20 per hour; massages start at $65 per hour.

SWIMMING, SURFING & KAYAKING

The north side of Monterey Bay is warmer than the south. As a result, beach activities are often more feasible in Santa Cruz than at Monterey. Still, the water averages 55°F, meaning that without a wetsuit, various parts will quickly turn blue.

Surfing is popular in Santa Cruz, especially at **Steamers Lane** (left). Other favorite surf spots are **Pleasure Point Beach** (Map p440), on

E Cliff Dr toward Capitola, and **Manresa State Beach** (see p440). Rent surfboards and related gear at **Cowell's** (Map p435; ☎ 831-427-2355; 30 Front St; per day $30; ⊙ 8am-6pm). The veterans at this shop have heaps of local knowledge.

Want to learn to surf? Both **Santa Cruz Surf School** (Map p435; ☎ 831-426-7072; www.santacruz surfschool.com; 322 Pacific Ave) or **Richard Schmidt Surf School** (☎ 831-423-0928; www.richardschmidt.com) will have you standing and surfing the first day out. Both charge $70 to $80 for beginner's lessons; all equipment is included.

Kayaking is a popular way to discover the kelp beds and craggy coastline. **Kayak Connection** (Map p440; ☎ 831-479-1121; 413 Lake Ave), at the Yacht Harbor, offers rentals ($40 per day) and tours.

WHALE-WATCHING & HARBOR CRUISES

Whale-watching trips, harbor cruises and fishing expeditions depart year-round from the municipal wharf. **Stagnaro's** (Map p435; ☎ 813-427-2334; www.stagnaros.com; cruises from $10) is a longstanding operator. Whale-watching trips run from December to April, though there's plenty of marine life to see on a summer bay cruise too. There's also a range of fishing trips offered.

Sleeping

Santa Cruz has a huge number of places to stay. Generally the best places to stay are those between downtown and the beach, giving you easy foot access to both. There's a plethora of uninteresting places further out along Ocean St. Note that some places by the boardwalk are pristine while others are dumps.

HOSTELS

Santa Cruz Hostel (Map p435; ☎ 831-423-8304; www.hi -santacruz.org; 321 Main St; dm/d $21/45; registration ⊙ 8-11am & 5-10pm) Budget travelers love this lovely hostel at the Carmelita Cottages. Not only is its garden setting lovely, it's just two blocks from the beach and five blocks from downtown. One bummer: the 11pm curfew. Make reservations.

B&BS

Cliff Crest (Map p435; ☎ 831-427-2609; www.cliffcrest inn.com; 407 Cliff St; r $95-245; 🞔 🖳) Close to the beach and boardwalk, Cliff Crest is an attractive and historic Victorian-era Queen Anne–style mansion with five rooms. The

decor is restrained while the garden is a treat.

Babbling Brook Inn (Map p435; ☎ 831-427-2437; www.innsbythesea.com; 1025 Laurel St; r $170-250; 🞔 🖳 🖳) The babble here comes not from a brook but a waterwheel on the grounds. It's not near the beach but it does have 13 French-inspired rooms, most having a gas fireplace, spa and deck. Breakfasts and afternoon wine are served.

MOTELS

Note that rates can vary by a factor of four or more between a wet winter weekday and a sunny summer weekend. For the latter, reserve.

Sea & Sand Inn (Map p435; ☎ 831-427-3400; www .santacruzmotels.com; 201 W Cliff Dr; r $100-360; 🖳) This is the place for ocean views. A neat and tidy establishment removed from the noisy boardwalk area and perched pleasantly on the cliff; every room looks onto the water. Some of the 20 rooms have whirlpools and fireplaces.

Casa Blanca Inn (Map p435; ☎ 831-423-1570, 800-644-1570; www.casablanca-santacruz.com; 101 Main St at Beach St; r $80-200; 🞔) Casa Blanca is one of the nicer beachside motels and is built around an old mansion. Most of its 39 uniquely furnished rooms have unobstructed ocean views. Some have whirlpools, kitchens and fireplaces.

Knights Inn (Map p435; ☎ 831-426-7574; www .knightsinn.com; 510 Leibrandt; r $40-180; 🞔 🖳) The charming owners make the stay at this simple place delightful. Furthermore, it's close to everything. The pool is small but there's always the ocean…

Seaway Inn (Map p435; ☎ 831-471-9004; www.sea wayinn.com; 176 W Cliff Dr; r $100-200; 🞔) Many of the brightly furnished rooms have views across the road to the bay. There are many patios and decks.

Bay Front Inn (Map p435; ☎ 831-423-8564; www.bay frontinnsc.com; 325 Pacific Ave; r $48-185; 🞔 🖳 🖳) Perfectly located, this 38-room modern motel is clean and comfortable.

Super 8 Motel (Map p435; ☎ 831-426-3707; www .super8.com; 338 Riverside Ave; r $50-200; 🞔 🖳) A typical, 24-room motel not far from the beach. There's no point passing up SC to hang out in the rooms, but some do have whirlpools.

Best Western All Suites Inn (Map p435; ☎ 831-458-9898; www.bestwestern.com; 500 Ocean St at Soquel Ave; r $90-210; 🞔 🖳 🖳) This is a good choice for business travelers on extended stays as every room is a suite with a kitchenette. There are other chain motels nearby.

CAMPING

There are many **campsites** (☎ reservations:800-444-7275; www.parks.ca.gov) at the state parks in the mountains and on the beach. In busy times be sure to reserve. Top spots include Big Basin Redwoods State Park (opposite); Henry Cowell Redwoods State Park (opposite); at **New Brighton State Beach** (Map p440; ☎ 831-464-6330) off Hwy 1 near Capitola; or at Sunset State Beach (p440) near Watsonville.

Eating

Pacific Ave is lined with casual eateries and cafés.

Gabriella Cafe (Map p435; ☎ 831-457-1677; 910 Cedar St; mains $15-25) This Mission-style gem is a tranquil candlelit restaurant. Chef Jim Denevan's menu is a constantly changing palette of local ingredients. Excellent wine list.

El Palomar (Map p435; ☎ 831-425-7575; 1336 Pacific Ave; meals $10-20) Consistently popular, El Palomar serves Mexican staples along with more inventive dishes – either way it's fresh and tasty. The tortillas are made fresh daily by charming women in the covered courtyard.

Crow's Nest (Map p440; ☎ 831-476-4560; www.crows nest-santacruz.com; 2218 E Cliff Rd; mains $12-30) Locals have been flocking to this waterfront place for years. There are two levels, a heated patio and a famous salad bar. The seafood is fresh and the steaks are large but your attention may be focused on the yacht-harbor traffic outside the window.

Cafe Pergolesi (☎ 831-426-1775; 418 Cedar St; snacks under $5; ☺ 9am-9pm; ☐) This landmark is in an old house that has a grand veranda overlooking the street, great cakes, teas, coffees and good beer on tap. Free wi-fi too.

Walnut Ave Cafe (☎ 831-457-2307; 106 Walnut Ave; meals $6-10; ☺ breakfast & lunch) Right in the center, this full-service place has great breakfasts, baked goods, sandwiches and salads. There are cool tables on the sidewalk.

Jack's Burgers (☎ 831-423-4421; 202 Lincoln St; burgers $4; ☺ lunch Mon-Sat) This bare-bones place with picnic tables serves up fantastic burgers.

Dolphin (Map p435; ☎ 831-426-5830; meals $9-16; ☺ breakfast, lunch & dinner) Way out at the end of the wharf, the Dolphin is a classic old seafood diner. The chow is fresh and the

chowder tops. Grab something from the take-out window and plop down at a picnic table with your new friends, the sea gulls.

Seabright Brewery (Map p440; ☎ 831-2739; 519 Seabright Ave; meals $8-12; ☺ 11-1am; ☐) This bright pub near the yacht harbor has decent food, excellent microbrewed beer, occasional live bands and a loud and crowded patio where you can use the free wi-fi.

Zoccoli's (Map p435; ☎ 831-423-1711; 1534 Pacific Ave; ☺ 9am-7pm) Zoccoli's is an authentic Italian deli where you can assemble a bravissimo picnic.

For organic fruits and vegetables and a taste of the local vibe, cruise by the **farmers market** (☎ 831-454-0566; cnr Lincoln & Center Sts; ☺ 2:30-6:30pm Wed).

Drinking

99 Bottles Bar (Map p435; ☎ 831-459-9999; 110 Walnut Ave; meals $8-10) A straightforward bar with, you guessed it, a whole lot of beer to choose from, including more than 40 on tap. Good tables outside.

The Crow's Nest restaurant has a popular and scenic bar. Pacific Ave downtown is also sprinkled with bars.

Entertainment

Metro Santa Cruz (www.mecruz.com) and *Good Times* (www.gtweekly.com) are free weeklies that do a good job of covering entertainment and the rest of the scene for Santa Cruz and south to Monterey.

Catalyst (Map p435; ☎ 831-423-1338; www.catalyst club.com; 1011 Pacific Ave) With an 800-seat capacity, Catalyst is a major Santa Cruz music venue; over the years it's hosted national acts from Gillian Welch to Black Uhuru to Nirvana. When there's no music, the upstairs pool room is still open.

Kuumbwa Jazz Center (Map p435; ☎ 831-427-2227; www.kuumbwajazz.org; 320 Cedar St) This has been one of the best live music venues in town since 1975, attracting big-name performers to its intimate room.

Club Dakota (Map p435; ☎ 831-454-9030; 1209 Pacific Ave) The sign at the entrance says it all: 'all lifestyles respected.' This popular local dance place has a classy bar and music that ranges from house to jazz.

Blue Lagoon (Map p435; ☺ 831-423-7117; 923 Pacific Ave) A small dance club lit by the glow from the bar. Sounds include hip-hop, trance, techno and retro.

Shopping

Downtown Santa Cruz boasts numerous locally owned stores selling real merchandise (as opposed to, say, a tea towel). You can spend several hours wandering Pacific Ave and the side streets.

O'Neill Surf Shop (Map p435; ☎ 831-469-4377; 110 Cooper St) This place is the mother ship for the locally based and internationally popular brand of surf wear and gear.

Streetlight Records (Map p435; ☎ 831-421-9200; 939 Pacific Ave) Streetlight is typical of several cool shops selling unusual and used CDs and records.

Getting There & Around

Santa Cruz is 20 miles from Silicon Valley on fast-moving and often perilous Hwy 17. It is 90 miles south and 43 miles north of Monterey on beautiful Hwy 1. Without your own wheels, the easiest way to reach Santa Cruz is on a bus.

Greyhound (☎ 831-423-1800; 425 Front St), next to the Metro Center, has daily buses to San Francisco ($11, three hours), Salinas ($13, 70 minutes) and Los Angeles ($43, 10 hours). To reach Monterey you'll need to change buses in Salinas (p475).

Santa Cruz Airporter (☎ 831-423-1214, 800-497-4997) runs shuttles to/from the airports at San Jose ($42) and San Francisco ($47).

Santa Cruz Metro (☎ 831-425-8600; www.scmtd .com) is the local public transit operation. It operates Hwy 17 Express buses from Santa Cruz to the San Jose CalTrain/Amtrak station (p183; $4). Metro also operates a thicket of bus services (tickets $1.50, day pass $4.50) throughout the county and is an excellent way to get around. Most routes converge on the Metro Center between Pacific and Front Sts downtown.

Useful routes follow. One-way trips cost $1; a day pass costs $3.

Bus No	Destination
3B	Natural Bridges State Beach
35	Felton, then on to Boulder Creek & Big Basin State Park
40 & 42	Davenport & the north coast beaches
69	Capitola Transit Center

SANTA CRUZ TO MONTEREY
Capitola

About 5 miles east of Santa Cruz is the little seaside town of Capitola, founded as a 19th-century vacation resort. Nestled quaintly between bluffs along Soquel Creek, it's quieter than Santa Cruz, and the crowds are more affluent and less apt to smoke things. Downtown, you'll find plenty of shops, galleries, B&Bs, restaurants and cute homes.

DETOUR: HIGHWAY 9

Hwy 9 is a gorgeous 34-mile road through the Santa Cruz mountains that links Santa Cruz with Saratoga in Silicon Valley. It's lined with cute little towns and parks and unlike Hwy 17, the pace is slow. Expect this detour to cheerfully consume a day.

Heading from Santa Cruz, it's 7 miles to **Felton**. Along the way you pass through **Henry Cowell Redwoods State Park** (☎ 831-335-4598; per vehicle $6) which has miles of hiking trails through some old groves of redwoods along the San Lorenzo River. In Felton, **Roaring Camp** (☎ 831-335-4400; www .roaringcamp.com; Mt Hermon Rd; adult/child from $18/12; ☺ vary by season) operates narrow-gauge trains up into the redwoods and a regular train that parallels Hwy 9 back to the Boardwalk in Santa Cruz.

Continuing on Hwy 9 for 6 miles, you pass through the village of **Ben Lomond** before reaching cute little **Boulder Creek**, the prettiest town on the road and a good place to try a café. Turn onto Hwy 236 and after twisting 17 miles, you'll reach **Big Basin Redwoods State Park** (☎ 831-335-3174; per vehicle $6) where there are 80,000 acres of old-growth coastal redwoods. A short circular trail from the parking area takes you past some of the largest ones. Better still, hike the amazing 12.5-mile **Skyline to the Sea trail**, which ends at Waddell Beach on the north coast of Santa Cruz County. You don't need a car for this; check the Santa Cruz Metro schedules carefully and you can ride up to Big Basin in the morning and get picked up at the beach in the afternoon.

From Big Basin you continue on Hwy 236 and rejoin Hwy 9. From here it is another 13 miles of mountain driving over the summit and down into genteel **Saratoga**, home to ladies who lunch and then buy antiques.

CENTRAL COAST

Keep in mind, though, that the streets can get crowded and parking isn't easy.

The **Capitola Chamber of Commerce** (☎ 831-475-6522; www.capitolachamber.com) has local tips and lodging information.

The **Begonia Festival** (☎ 831-476-3566), on Labor Day weekend, features a parade of flowered floats on Soquel Creek and celebrates the delicate plant that was once the town's main industry.

Possibly the best bakery in California is the legendary **Gayle's** (Map p440; ☎ 831-462-1200; 504 Bay Ave; ☒ 6:30am-8:30pm). Here you'll find everything from the finest Bear Claws (a breakfast pastry) you'll ever have to amazing cookies and elaborate tarts. Best of all there's a large deli area where you can assemble the beach picnic of your dreams.

South Santa Cruz County

Aptos is a cute little town with a very fun July 4th Parade (America's shortest). It's reached from the Aptos/Seacliff exit on Hwy 1. Nearby is **Seacliff Sate Beach** (☎ 831-685-6440; 201 State Park Dr; per vehicle $6) where the beach is fine but the real attraction is the 'cement boat,' a quixotic

freighter built from concrete that floated fine but had a star-crossed life which ended here on the coast as a fishing pier. South of the park are miles of free beaches.

Ten miles south of Santa Cruz, the La Selva Beach exit on Hwy 1 leads to **Manresa State Beach** (☎ 831-724-3750; per vehicle $6) and **Sunset State Beach** (☎ 831-763-7063; per vehicle $6) further south. At both, you'll have miles of sand and surf to yourself just a few yards from the parking lots.

Moss Landing & Elkhorn Slough

Hwy 1 returns to the coast at Moss Landing 25 miles south of Santa Cruz and 18 miles north of Monterey. Here there's a few interesting shops, some good cafés and a working fishing harbor all in the unfortunate shadow of a power plant. Nearby Elkhorn Slough is a federally protected water bird preserve popular with kayakers and walkers.

MONTEREY
pop 30,200

Monterey, together with its immediate neighbor Pacific Grove and posh Carmel to the

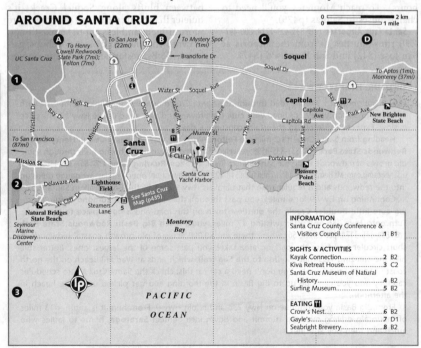

AROUND SANTA CRUZ

To Henry Cowell Redwoods State Park (7mi); Felton (7mi)
UC Santa Cruz
To San Jose (22mi)
To Mystery Spot (1mi)
Branciforte Dr
Soquel
Soquel Dr
To Aptos (1mi); Monterey (37mi)
Water St
Soquel Ave
High St
Capitola
Capitola Ave
Bay Ave
Park Ave
New Brighton State Beach
Western Dr
Bay Dr
Mission St
Ocean St
Seabright Ave
7th Ave
17th Ave
Capitola Rd
To San Francisco (87mi)
Santa Cruz
Murray St
41st Ave
Cliff Dr
Mission St
E Cliff Dr
Santa Cruz Yacht Harbor
Portola Dr
Pleasure Point Beach
Delaware Ave
Lighthouse Field
W Cliff Dr
Steamers Lane
See Santa Cruz Map (p435)
Natural Bridges State Beach
Seymour Marine Discovery Center
Monterey Bay
PACIFIC OCEAN

0 ———— 2 km
0 ———— 1 mile

INFORMATION
Santa Cruz County Conference & Visitors Council.....................1 B1

SIGHTS & ACTIVITIES
Kayak Connection........................2 B2
Kiva Retreat House.....................3 C2
Santa Cruz Museum of Natural History..................................4 B2
Surfing Museum.........................5 B2

EATING
Crow's Nest................................6 B2
Gayle's.......................................7 D1
Seabright Brewery.....................8 B2

CENTRAL COAST

south, forms the Monterey Peninsula, a place famous for its beauty, golf, galleries and aquarium.

Nowhere is evidence of the state's Hispanic heritage richer than in Monterey. The city has numerous lovingly restored adobe buildings from the Spanish and Mexican periods, and it's enlightening to spend a few hours wandering about the town's historic quarter. Less worthy of note are the tourist ghettos of Fisherman's Wharf and Cannery Row.

As you'll see at the amazing Monterey Bay Aquarium, Monterey Bay is one of the world's richest and most varied marine environments. It boasts dense kelp forests and a diverse range of marine life, including mammals such as sea otters, seals and sea lions, elephant seals, dolphins and whales.

Starting only a few hundred yards offshore from Moss Landing, the Monterey Canyon plummets to a depth of over 10,000ft. In summer the upwelling currents carry cold water from this deep submarine canyon, sending a rich supply of nutrients up toward the surface level to feed the bay's diverse marine life. These frigid currents also account for the bay's generally low water temperatures and the fog that often blankets the peninsula in summer.

History

The Ohlone tribe, who had been on the peninsula since around 500 BC, may have spotted Spanish explorer Juan Rodríguez Cabrillo, the first European visitor, who sailed by in 1542. He was followed in 1602 by Sebastián Vizcaíno, who landed near the site of today's downtown Monterey and named it after his patron, the Duke of Monte Rey. A long hiatus followed before the Spanish returned in 1770 to establish Monterey as their first presidio in Alta (Upper) California. The expedition was led by Gaspar de Portolá and accompanied by mission founder Padre Junípero Serra. A year later, Serra decided to separate church and state by shifting the mission to Carmel, a safe distance from the military presence.

Monterey became the capital of Alta California after Mexico broke from Spain in 1821. Freed from the tight Spanish trading constraints, it also became a bustling international trading port where East Coast Yankees mixed with Russian fur traders and seafarers carrying exotic goods from China.

The stars and stripes were temporarily raised over Monterey in 1842 when Commodore Thomas Jones, hearing a rumor that war had been declared between Mexico and the USA, took the town. A red-faced withdrawal took place a few days later when the rumor turned out to be false. When war really did break out in 1846, Commodore John Sloat's takeover was almost reluctant; he clearly did not want to repeat the mistake. The American takeover signaled an abrupt change in the town's fortunes, for San Jose soon replaced Monterey as the state capital, and the 1849 gold rush drained much of the remaining population.

The town spent 30 years as a forgotten backwater, its remaining residents eking out an existence from whaling, an industry replaced by tourism in the 1880s. After Southern Pacific Railroad entrepreneurs built a luxurious hotel, wealthy San Franciscans discovered Monterey as a convenient getaway.

Around the same time, fishermen began to capitalize on the teeming marine life in Monterey Bay, and the first sardine canneries soon opened. By the 1930s, Cannery Row had made the port the 'Sardine Capital of the World,' but overfishing and climatic changes caused the industry's sudden collapse in the 1950s. Fortunately, in more recent decades, the city has been able to net schools of tourists who flock to Monterey in greater numbers each year.

Orientation & Information

Monterey's historic downtown is a compact area surrounding Alvarado St, which ends with Portola and Custom House plazas, near Fisherman's Wharf. This area is known as Old Monterey, as distinct from Cannery Row, about a mile northwest. Cannery Row segues straight into Pacific Grove.

Bay Books (☎ 831-375-1855; 316 Alvarado St; ⏰ 7am-10pm) The best bookstore on the Monterey Peninsula with a superb range of books and a coffee bar.

Doctors on Duty (☎ 831-649-0770; 501 Lighthouse Ave; ⏰ 8am-8pm) Handles minor maladies.

Visitors center (☎ 831-649-1770, 888-221-1010; www.montereyinfo.org; cnr Camino El Estero & Franklin St; ⏰ 9am-5pm) Operated by Monterey County Convention and Visitors Bureau, this center is on the shore of El Estero Lake east of downtown. It has a free phone system for

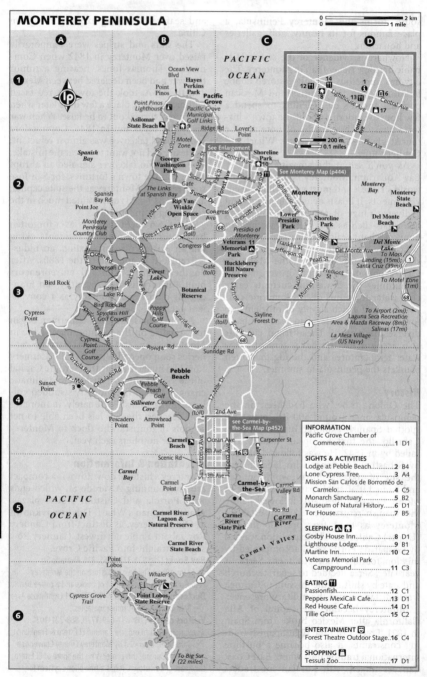

MONTEREY PENINSULA

0 _____ 2 km
0 _____ 1 mile

INFORMATION
Pacific Grove Chamber of
   Commerce.................................1 D1

SIGHTS & ACTIVITIES
Lodge at Pebble Beach..............2 B4
Lone Cypress Tree.....................3 A4
Mission San Carlos de Borroméo de
   Carmelo.................................4 C5
Monarch Sanctuary...................5 B2
Museum of Natural History........6 D1
Tor House.................................7 B5

SLEEPING
Gosby House Inn........................8 D1
Lighthouse Lodge......................9 B1
Martine Inn..............................10 C2
Veterans Memorial Park
   Campground..........................11 C3

EATING
Passionfish...............................12 C1
Peppers MexiCali Cafe...............13 D1
Red House Cafe.........................14 D1
Tillie Gort................................15 C2

ENTERTAINMENT
Forest Theatre Outdoor Stage....16 C4

SHOPPING
Tessuti Zoo..............................17 D1

CENTRAL COAST

checking room availability and prices at dozens of hotels and motels.

Visitors center (☎ 831-657-6400; 150 Olivier St; ☒ 8am-5pm Mon-Fri) Near the State Historic Park.

Sights

The entire Monterey Bay is part of the **Monterey Bay National Marine Sanctuary** (☎ 831-647-4201; www.mbnms.nos.noaa.gov), which extends from north of San Francisco south past San Simeon. The Bush administration has hinted that oil drilling may be necessary in this treasure to fuel the nation's unquenchable thirst for SUV-sustaining fuel.

MONTEREY BAY AQUARIUM

Monterey's most mesmerizing experience is a visit to this amazing **aquarium** (☎ 831-648-4888; www.montereybayaquarium.org; 886 Cannery Row; adult/child $22/11; ☒ 10am-6pm, 9:30am-6pm May-Sep), built on the site of what was once the city's largest sardine cannery (there are good displays on the industry). You'll encounter countless aquatic denizens, from slow-moving starfish and slimy sea slugs to animated sea lions and sea otters, all of which are part of the rich diversity of the Monterey Bay.

Among the many not-to-be-missed exhibits is the gigantic **kelp forest** in a three-story tank teeming with hundreds of animals – from sharks to sardines, all of which are hand-fed by a diver (at 11:30am and 4pm). It re-creates the very life you see out the windows in the bay. Even more fun are the sea otter–feeding sessions (at 10:30am, 1:30pm and 3:30pm). At other times, these critters can often be seen basking in the **Great Tide Pool** outside the aquarium, where they lounge around while they are readied for reintroduction to the wild.

Many people are astounded at the beauty of jellyfish in the **Drifters Gallery**. To see fish – including hammerhead sharks – that will outweigh you by many times, ponder the awesome **Outer Bay** tank.

Throughout the aquarium there are **touch pools**, where you can get close to sea cucumbers, bat rays and various tidepool creatures. Small children love **Splash Zone**, an interactive area. During the summer, the aquarium runs programs for kids that involve diving and sailing on the bay.

Allow at least three hours for your visit. To avoid long lines in summer, on weekends and holidays, get **tickets** (☎ 831-648-4937,

800-756-3737; transaction fee $3) in advance from hotels or via the Web or telephone. There are several shops, including a first-rate bookstore, and an excellent café. Before you leave, pick up the wallet-sized Seafood Watch, an essential seafood-dining guide to keeping fish populations sustainable.

MONTEREY STATE HISTORIC PARK

Old Monterey is home to an extraordinary assemblage of 19th-century brick and adobe buildings, administered as the Monterey State Historic Park and covered on a 2-mile self-guiding walking tour portentously called the **Path of History**. Admission to the buildings is free. After the aquarium this is a highlight of Monterey. You'll see more than 30 buildings, many with charming gardens and other features. Expect some buildings to be open while others aren't according to a capricious schedule dictated by draconian budget cuts by the governor.

Pick up a free brochure for a self-guided tour and find out what's open from the **park headquarters** (☎ 831-649-7118; Custom House Plaza; ☒ 10am-5pm) in the 1847 Pacific House. The latter also houses a **museum** (admission free) highlighting various facets of state history. You can join a docent-led 90-minute tour (adult/child $5/2; phone to confirm times), but the governor's budget cuts have put these in peril.

There are also separate tours of some of the individual houses. Pick up a current schedule at the park headquarters.

Custom House

In 1822, newly independent Mexico ended the Spanish trade monopoly but stipulated that any traders bringing goods to Alta California must first unload their cargoes at the **Monterey Custom House** (Custom House Plaza) for duty assessment. The restored 1827 building displays an exotic selection of the goods traders brought in to exchange for Californian cowhides, including rice and spices as well as such 'luxury' items as chandeliers, liquor, machinery and furniture. In 1846, the American flag was raised over the Custom House, and California was formally annexed from Mexico.

Casa Soberanes

A beautiful garden fronts **Casa Soberanes** (336 Pacific St), built in 1842 during the late

MONTEREY

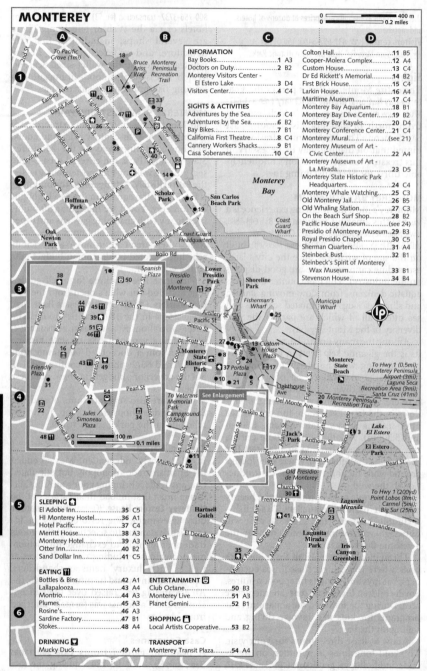

Monterey Bay

Coast Guard Wharf

Municipal Wharf

Monterey State Beach

To Hwy 1 (0.5mi);
Monterey Peninsula
Airport (3mi);
Laguna Seca
Recreation Area (9mi);
Santa Cruz (41mi)

Lake El Estero

El Estero Park

To Hwy 1 (200yd);
Point Lobos (8mi);
Carmel (5mi);
Big Sur (25mi)

Lagunita Miranda

Lagunita Mirada Park

Iris Canyon Greenbelt

See Enlargement

CENTRAL COAST

Mexican period. Across Pacific St, the large and colorful **Monterey Mural** mosaic, on the modern Monterey Conference Center, tells the history of Monterey.

Larkin House

Thomas Larkin arrived from New England in 1832 and made a fortune from the burgeoning regional trade. His fine 1842 **house** (cnr Calle Principal & Jefferson St) is a combination of New England design and adobe construction, known today as Monterey colonial. Larkin was US consul in Monterey during the US takeover and subsequently played an important role in the transition from Mexican to American rule.

Stevenson House

Robert Louis Stevenson came to Monterey in 1879 to meet with his wife-to-be, Fanny Osbourne. This building, then the French Hotel, was reputedly where he stayed while writing *Treasure Island*. The rooms were pretty primitive – they only cost about $2 a month – but he was still a penniless unknown at that time. The 1840 **building** (530 Houston St) was recently renovated and houses a superb collection of Stevenson memorabilia.

Cooper-Molera Complex

This spacious **adobe** (☎ 831-649-7111; 525 Polk St; ☒ 10am-4pm) was built between 1827 and 1900 by John Rogers Cooper (a sea captain from New England and harbormaster of Monterey) and three generations of his family. During those years, it was partitioned and extended, gardens were added, and it was eventually willed to the National Trust, which ensures it has more regular opening hours than other places. The bookshop and gardens are worth the stop.

OTHER HISTORIC BUILDINGS

Other structures along the Path of History include Monterey's **First Brick House** and the **Old Whaling Station** (both from 1847 and near Oliver St) – note the front walkway made of whalebone of the latter. The **California First Theatre** (cnr Pacific & Scott Sts) started out in 1844 as a saloon and lodging house; soldiers staying here are credited with staging California's first theatrical productions.

In 1849, California's state constitution was drawn up in **Colton Hall** (Civic Center on Pacific Ave), named for Walter Colton, navy chaplain

for Commodore Sloat. The upstairs room re-creates the chamber where the document was debated and drafted. The adjacent **Old Monterey Jail** is featured in John Steinbeck's *Tortilla Flat*.

The **Sherman Quarters** (Pacific St near Pearl St) was built by Thomas Larkin but takes its name from famed General Sherman of the Civil War, who lived there in 1847. The **Royal Presidio Chapel** (Church St), built of stone and adobe in 1795, was the military headquarters of Spanish and Mexican Monterey. The original mission church stood on this site in 1770 before being moved to Carmel. Until the 1820s the presidio's fortified walls embraced pretty much the entire town. As Monterey expanded, the old buildings were all gradually destroyed, leaving the chapel as a sole reminder of the old presidio's presence.

MARITIME MUSEUM

There is local naval history from the days of the early explorers to the 20th century at Monterey's **Maritime Museum** (☎ 831-372-2608; Stanton Center, 5 Custom House Plaza; adult/concession $8/6; ☒ 10am-5pm Thu-Tue). Highlights of the excellent collection include the Fresnel lens from Point Sur Lightstation, a great ship-in-a-bottle collection and interesting displays on Monterey's history, particularly of the rise and rapid fall of the sardine business.

PRESIDIO OF MONTEREY MUSEUM

This **museum** (☎ 831-646-3456; Corporal Ewing Rd, Bldg 113; admission free; ☒ 10am-4pm Thu-Sat, 1-4pm Sun, 10am-1pm Mon) is a good place to learn about Monterey's history from a military perspective covering the Native American, Mexican and American periods and up to the present. The museum stands on the grounds of the original fort, now home to the Defense Language Institute Foreign Language Center.

MONTEREY MUSEUM OF ART

With all the galleries, it's not surprising that Monterey has an excellent **art museum** (☎ 831-372-5477; adult/child $5/free; ☒ 11am-5pm Wed-Sat, 1-4pm Sun). In fact it has two locations with the same hours and you can visit both on the same ticket. The branch at the **Civic Center** (559 Pacific St) is particularly strong with regard to California painters and photographers, including Ansel Adams and Edward Weston.

The second site is in a charming villa called **La Mirada** (720 Via Mirada) whose humble adobe origins are well concealed indeed. It displays primarily selections from the museum's Asian collection and is backed by a lovely rose and rhododendron garden.

CANNERY ROW

John Steinbeck's novel *Cannery Row* immortalized the sardine-canning business that Monterey lived on for the first half of the 20th century. He describes Cannery Row as 'a poem, a stink, a grating noise, a quality of light, a tone, a habit, a nostalgia, a dream.' A bronze **bust** of the writer sits at the bottom of Prescott Ave.

Predictions that overfishing could decimate the business were ignored when the catch reached a peak of 250,000 tons in 1945. Just five years later, figures plummeted to 33,000 tons, and by 1951 most of the sardine canneries had closed, many of them mysteriously catching fire.

Today, Cannery Row is mostly a touristy nightmare of chain restaurants and souvenir shops selling fudge, candles, Christmas ornaments and suchlike thereof. There are a few exceptional places worth making time for, such as the aquarium, but mostly this is an area to avoid. 'Attractions' include **Steinbeck's Spirit of Monterey Wax Museum** (☎ 831-375-1010; 700 Cannery Row; adult/child $7/5; ☼ 10:30am-7pm), a hokey affair with more than a hundred life-sized wax figures.

Sadly, there's just too little effort made to celebrate the actual heritage of the place, which might make the rampant commercialism more palatable. But check out the **Cannery Workers Shacks** at the base of flowery Bruce Arliss Way with sober explanations of the hard lives led by the Filipino, Japanese and Spanish laborers. A little south, look for the **Dr Ed Rickett's Memorial** (Wave & Drake Sts), which marks the spot where the famous marine biologist and friend of Steinbeck died.

FISHERMAN'S WHARF

Like its larger namesake in San Francisco, the wharf is a tourist trap at heart. Noisy seals make regular visits to the wharf, and it's also the base for whale-watching expeditions (see opposite) and deep-sea fishing trips.

MAZDA RACEWAY LAGUNA SECA

Just off Hwy 68, about midway between Monterey and Salinas, the **Mazda Raceway Laguna Seca** (☎ 831-648-5111; www.laguna-seca.com) attracts racing fans with a year-round schedule of top-rated race car, vintage car and motorcycle events.

Activities

BIKING & HIKING

Thanks to stunning scenery and paved bike paths, cycling is a very popular peninsula activity. The paved **Monterey Peninsula Recreational Trail**, a former train line, travels for 18 car-free miles along the waterfront from Lovers Point in Pacific Grove to Seaside, passing by downtown and Cannery Row in Monterey.

Many people like to make the 20-mile round trip to Carmel by bike along 17-Mile Drive (p450). A grand 50-mile loop along the coast through Salinas is another option.

Lots of advice and maps are available from **Bay Bikes** (☎ 831-655-2453; 585 Cannery Row; ☼ 9am-7pm), where you can buy a bike, get one repaired or rent one starting at $6 per hour. The two locations of **Adventures by the Sea** (☎ 831-372-1807; Portola Plaza 201 Alvarado St; Cannery Row 299 Cannery Row) offer a similar service.

DIVING & SNORKELING

After seeing what awaits at the Monterey Bay Aquarium, you'll probably be ready to go diving or snorkeling. This is the place to do it; divers are drawn from around the world. Good spots for snorkeling and diving are off San Carlos Beach near the Coast Guard Wharf in Monterey; Lovers Point in Pacific Grove; and in the Point Lobos State Reserve (see p454).

One of the best places to organize a dive or snorkeling trip is at **Monterey Bay Dive Center** (☎ 831-656-0454; www.montereyscubadiving.com; 225 Cannery Row) offers instruction and equipment rental. Full standard dive outfits go for $69; snorkeling kits cost $39. Private guided tours cost $59/89 for a one-/two-tank dive. The shop can also advise on snorkeling in the shallow inlets of the bay.

SURFING & KAYAKING

The peninsula has some great surfing spots, though not usually for beginners. Strong rip currents and unpredictable rogue waves lie in wait for the unwary, not to mention the presence of those famous sharks. Local surfers vote Asilomar State Beach (in Pacific Grove) and Moss Landing (north of Monterey) as having the best and most

CENTRAL COAST

consistent breaks. For surf gear and rentals, head to **On the Beach** (☎ 831-646-9283; 693 Lighthouse Ave) near Cannery Row.

Monterey Bay Kayaks (☎ 800-649-5357; www.montereybaykayaks.com; 693 Del Monte Ave) rents open and closed kayaks from $30 per day, offers instruction courses every weekend and operates a range of natural history tours.

WHALE-WATCHING
You can spot whales off the coast of Monterey pretty much year-round. The season for blue and humpback whales runs from May to November, while gray whales pass by from mid-December to April. **Monterey Whale Watching** (☎ 831-372-2203;   www.montereywhalewatching.com; 96 Old Fisherman's Wharf; tours adult/child $35/25) boats leave daily on three-hour tours.

Festivals & Events
The Monterey Peninsula keeps an active schedule of festivals and special events that attract locals and visitors year-round. The wine and jazz festivals are two highlights worth reserving well in advance for.

AT&T Pebble Beach National Pro-Am (☎ 831-649-1533; www.attpbgolf.com) Famous golf tournament mixing pros and celebrities in late January or early February.

Monterey Wine Festival (☎ 800-656-4282; http://montereywine.com) April.

Concours d'Elegance (☎ 831-659-0663; www.pebblebeachconcours.net) Classic-car exhibit in August at Pebble Beach.

Monterey Jazz Festival (☎ 831-373-3366; www.montereyjazzfestival.org) September.

Sleeping
Monterey has accommodations geared for romancing couples, budget-conscious families and business travelers. Prices vary greatly by season and whether there is a special event in town. You can find places to stay around town. Generally there are a lot of cheap chain motels out east toward Seaside and downtown. The latter is also home to larger convention hotels while moving toward Cannery Row you find more intimate options.

One option you might consider is not staying in Monterey at all. Pacific Grove (p450) and Carmel (p452) both have more intimate places, while Salinas (p475) is great for those on a budget and Santa Cruz offers the most entertaining nightlife (p438). Skip the Embassy Suites in Seaside. It's an aesthetic blot on the landscape.

HOSTELS
HI Monterey Hostel (☎ 831-649-0375; www.montereyhostel.org; 778 Hawthorne St; dm $20; reception ⏱ 8-10am & 5-10pm) This bare-bones place (there are plastic chairs for lounging in the parking lot) is four blocks from the Monterey Bay Aquarium and Cannery Row. There's room for 45 and reservations are strongly recommended. To get there, take bus 1 from the Transit Center.

HOTELS & MOTELS
The cheapest accommodations are along Monterey's motel row, about 2.5 miles northeast of downtown on N Fremont St, east of Hwy 1 (take the Fremont St exit). Off-season prices average $60 to $90 in the midrange chain category.

Merritt House (☎ 831-6436-9686; www.merritthouseinn.com; 386 Pacific St; r $130-175; ✕ 🖳) Right in the historic district, this inn has three rooms in an old adobe building and 22 more in a modern addition. Rooms are large and many open onto gardens. Breakfast includes fresh muffins.

Monterey Hotel (☎ 831-375-3184, 800-727-0960; www.montereyhotel.com; 406 Alvarado St; r $70-300; ✕) This well-located 1904 hotel is grand in the traditional manner. Rooms are furnished in old-world style, and rates include a good-sized continental breakfast.

Hotel Pacific (☎ 831-373-5700, 800-554-5542; www.hotelpacific.com; 300 Pacific St; ste $190-400; ✕ 🖳) The Pacific features 105 spacious suites with elegant Spanish-style furniture, comfy feather beds, a large fireplace and a kitchenette. Rates include continental breakfast and afternoon cheese and fruit.

Sand Dollar Inn (☎ 831-372-7551, 800-982-1986; www.sanddollarinn.com; 755 Abrego St; r $90-190; 🐾 🖳) A friendly place with cheerfully decorated rooms. The Sand Dollar is close to the center and rates include a small breakfast.

El Adobe Inn (☎ 831-372-5409, 800-433-4732; www.el-adobe-inn.com; 936 Munras Ave; r $50-190) This inn offers basic accommodation with a bit of charm. It's a neat and well-kept property and rates include continental breakfast, free local calls and use of a hot tub. It's near the center and has a few cheapie neighbors as well.

Otter Inn (☎ 831-375-2299; www.otterinn.com; 571 Wave St; r $90-300; ✕) Close to Cannery Row, this modern motel has a range of cozy units. Some have fireplaces and whirlpools.

CAMPING

Veterans Memorial Park Campground (Map p442; ☎ 831-646-3865; sites per vehicle $20, walk-ins $5, 3-day maximum stay) This central municipal campground has 40 well-kept and mostly sunny nonreservable sites. Amenities include hot showers, flush toilets and lockers but not electric hookups. Coming from Hwy 1, take Hwy 68 to Skyline Forest Dr to Skyline Dr north. From downtown Monterey, follow Jefferson St west into the park.

Laguna Seca Recreation Area (☎ 831-755-4899, reservations 888-588-2267; Hwy 68; tent/RV sites $22/30) At the raceway, this county-run option is about 9 miles east of town en route to Salinas. It's a nicely maintained area with 175 spaces (102 with hookups), hot showers, flush toilets, picnic tables and fire pits.

Eating

Sardine Factory (☎ 831-373-3775; 701 Wave St; mains $20-40; �
 dinner) This is fine dining in the best of traditional manner. The seafood is perfectly fresh and perfectly prepared. The steaks are meltingly tender and the specials are always worth a try. Details like the garlic-anchovy dressing are superb. And the wine list? It's been winning awards for over a decade and features over 1300 selections (with some fascinating choices by the glass). But what makes it amazing is that a huge number are under $40 and the sommeliers are a chatty and unstuffy lot happy to recommend right into your budget. The bar is also a treat.

Montrio (☎ 831-648-8880; 414 Calle Principal; meals $25-35) An ever-trendy place in downtown Monterey with a hip interior that blends history and artistry. Beautiful people come to dine on an ever changing menu that mixes mostly organic foods from around the world, often in tapas-sized portions. It's Monterey's counterpoint to San Francisco.

Rosine's (☎ 831-375-1400; 434 Alvarado St; meals $6-9; �
 breakfast, lunch & dinner) Rosine's is a family-run coffee shop is about as good as it gets in the basic-food department. Eggs are cooked to perfection, sandwiches burst at the seams with quality and desserts are simply beauty to behold.

Stokes (☎ 831-373-1110; 500 Hartnell St; meals $10-30) This highly regarded restaurant is in a beautifully restored old adobe and is furnished to evoke the historic era. The varied menu focuses on rich, rustic flavors using local ingredients. Crab and steak are spe-

cialties but look for some of the more complex and creative dishes.

Lallapalooza (☎ 831-645-9036; 474 Alvarado St; mains $8-24; �
 dinner) There's trendy and innovative fare at this sprawling restaurant-cum-martini-bar. Updated versions of American classics, pizza and pasta are menu features.

Bottles & Bins (☎ 831-375-5488; 898 Lighthouse Ave; �
 10:30am-midnight) One of the best places to buy wine and unusual beers, this effervescent liquor store is also home to Karlen's Deli (meals $5 to $7; open for lunch Monday to Friday), where you can buy the fantastic fare prepared by Karlen Principie.

Plumes (☎ 831-373-4526; 400 Alvarado St; snacks $3; �
 6:30am-11pm) Plumes is a cool place to hang for a chat and a hot coffee. There's free wi-fi, sidewalk tables and good baked goods.

Drinking

Mucky Duck (☎ 831-655-3031; 479 Alvarado St) This lively English-style pub has a good backyard, lotsa beers on tap and some decent pub grub. There's live music (oldies to reggae) most nights.

Lallapalooza (☎ 831-645-9036; 474 Alvarado St) A hip restaurant-bar famous for its selection of martinis, it's popular after work.

Sardine Factory (☎ 831-373-3775; 701 Wave St) The bar at the legendary restaurant makes it worth venturing to Cannery Row after dark. There's good views and an exquisite selection of wines by the glass. Live piano music most nights too.

Entertainment

For comprehensive entertainment listings, pick up a free copy of the *Monterey County Weekly* (www.montereycountyweekly.com).

Monterey Live (☎ 831-646-1415; 414 Alvarado St) This small old adobe has been turned into a performance space where you can hear top local blues, jazz and other talents.

Planet Gemini (☎ 831-373-1449; www.planetgemini .com; 625 Cannery Row, 3rd fl) Planet Gemini draws a youthful clientele with its live music, comedy shows and 'alternative lifestyle' nights (usually Wednesday to Sunday).

Club Octane (☎ 831-646-9244; 321 Alvarado St) A 3rd-floor club in an otherwise humdrum commercial complex, Club Octane mixes live music and DJs. Expect anything from House to Top 40. Locals flock for metal nights featuring local group Retribution.

Shopping

You might want to save your energies for the galleries of Carmel or unusual shops of Santa Cruz, but one fun place to ponder is the **Local Artists Cooperative** (☎ 831-655-1267; 425 Cannery Row) which is just outside of the tourist-shop danger zone. Here 30 local artists of widely varying abilities have banded together to sell their wares at popular prices. A few can be found painting away right there.

Getting There & Away

Monterey Peninsula Airport (MRY; ☎ 831-648-7000; Olmsted Rd) handles flights operated by American Eagle (Los Angeles), America West (Las Vegas and Phoenix) and United Express (Los Angeles, San Francisco and Denver). It's 4 miles southeast of downtown off Hwy 68.

Monterey/Salinas Airbus (☎ 831-373-7777; www .montereyairbus.com) links those cities with the San Jose and San Francisco airports several times daily ($30 to $40).

If you aren't flying or don't have wheels, however, getting to the Monterey Peninsula can be a problem as Greyhound no longer serves the area. The best you can do is take Greyhound or Amtrak to Salinas (p475) 17 miles east of Monterey and then catch a local Monterey-Salinas Transit (MST) bus. It's also possible to spend a few hours on local buses getting from Santa Cruz to Monterey. Take the Santa Cruz Metro (p439) to the Watsonville transfer center and connect to MST bus 27.

Monterey is 120 miles south of San Francisco (scenic and slow by Hwy 1, quicker via Hwys 101 and 156). All major car-rental firms are at the airport.

Getting Around

Monterey-Salinas Transit (MST; ☎ 831-899-2555; www.mst.org) runs local buses in the region. Fares are $2 to $4 for one ride or $4.50 to $9 for a day pass depending on distance covered. Routes converge at the **Monterey Transit Plaza** (Jules Simoneau Plaza, Alvarado St).

Bus 20 makes the 50-minute run to/from Salinas every 30 to 60 minutes. Other useful routes:

Bus No	Destination
1	Cannery Row & Pacific Grove
4 & 5	Carmel
22	Big Sur via Carmel

Between late May and early September, you can take a free trolley-style bus that loops around downtown, Fisherman's Wharf and Cannery Row between 10am and 7pm.

PACIFIC GROVE
pop 16,000

Pacific Grove ('PG' to locals) is a tranquil community that began as a Methodist summer retreat in 1875. To this day, numerous stately Victorian homes line its nicely manicured residential streets. In summer, it hosts many tourists, but in winter PG hosts swarms of monarch butterflies, which make the local pine groves their temporary home. PG boasts a fun and thriving downtown and some of the area's best views of the bay and the ocean. For many it's the perfect respite from the Monterey-Carmel hubbub.

Orientation & Information

Central and Lighthouse Aves are PG's main commercial arteries; Lighthouse continues southeast to Monterey. The **chamber of commerce** (☎ 831-373-3304, 800-656-6650; www.pacificgrove .org; cnr Central & Forest Aves; ⏱ 9:30am-5pm Mon-Fri, 10am-3pm Sat) dispenses visitor information and brochures.

Sights & Activities

Appropriately named **Oceanview Blvd** affords fine views from Lover's Point west to Point Pinos. Here the road becomes the again appropriately named **Sunset Dr** with numerous turn-outs where you can enjoy the pounding surf, rocky outcrops and teaming tidal pools. The entire route is great for walking or cycling and many think it surpasses the 17-Mile Drive for beauty (p450).

PG's compact downtown is centered on Lighthouse and Forest Aves. It's well on its way to quaintness, but there are numerous little boutiques and antique stores that are worth a gander. One excellent place is **Tessuti Zoo** (☎ 831-648-1725; 171 Forest Ave) which is owned by a designer who handmakes funky items ranging from ponchos to lawn ornaments.

Fronted by a sculpture of a gray whale, the **Museum of Natural History** (☎ 831-648-3116; www .pgmuseum.org; 165 Forest Ave; admission free; ⏱ 10am-5pm Tue-Sun) has some old-fashioned exhibits about Big Sur, sea otters and the omnipresent monarch butterflies.

CENTRAL COAST

If you're in town during monarch season (roughly October to March), the best place to see them cluster by the millions is at the **Monarch Sanctuary**, a grove of pines on Ridge Rd off Lighthouse Ave (follow the signs). Note that one of the trees fell in 2004 crushing a tourist and the entire grove has become a center of controversy. The **Butterfly Parade**, marking the return of the monarchs to PG, is in early October.

At the northwestern end of Lighthouse Ave, on the tip of the Monterey Peninsula, you'll find **Point Pinos Lighthouse** (☎ 831-648-5716; adult/child $2/1; ☺ 1-4pm Thu-Mon), the oldest continuously operating lighthouse on the West Coast. It's been warning ships off this hazardous point since 1855. Inside are exhibits on its history and its failures: local shipwrecks.

Sleeping & Eating

There are several posh B&Bs in old mansions along Oceanview Blvd. Numerous modest motels cluster at the western end of Lighthouse Ave.

Martine Inn (☎ 831-373-3388, 800-852-5588; www .martineinn.com; 255 Ocean View Blvd; r $150-320; ☒ ☐) Martine Inn is one of several mansions lining the water. The 24 rooms are filled with antiques and other luxuries (some have fireplaces and/or stunning views). There's wine and appetizers at cocktail hour and you wake to a hearty breakfast. The aquarium is a 10-minute walk.

Gosby House Inn (☎ 831-375-1287, 800-527-8828; www.foursisters.com; 643 Lighthouse Ave; r $90-185; ☒ ☐) There's just a few too many teddy bears scattered about but otherwise this B&B is a fine choice in the heart of PG. Most of the 22 rooms have private bathrooms and there is a good breakfast in the morning and excellent cookies through the day.

Lighthouse Lodge (☎ 831-655-2111, 800-858-1249; www.lhls.com; 1150 & 1249 Lighthouse Ave; r $120-400; ☒ ☒) This motel is split into two parts, one an all-suites lodge and the other a more traditional motel. Units come in many sizes but are all well equipped and comfortable (some with fireplaces). The Pacific Ocean is just west and several other motels are nearby.

Passionfish (☎ 831-655-3311; www.passionfish.net; 701 Lighthouse Ave; meals $12-30; ☺ dinner) Passionfish is one of the finest fish restaurants in the region. Fresh, sustainable seafood is served in any number of inventive ways; there are

also slow-cooked meats and locally grown vegetables. Owner Ted Walther has built up a passionate following that extends well beyond PG.

Tillie Gort (☎ 831-373-0335; 111 Central Ave; meals $7-12; ☺ breakfast, lunch & dinner) This veteran goes back to the '60s and still is true to its hippie roots. There are lots of vegetarian items on a menu with global inspiration. Portions are hearty and the desserts are rather decadent. It's close to the aquarium.

Red House Cafe (☎ 831-643-1060; 662 Lighthouse Ave; meals $8-20; ☺ lunch & dinner Tue-Sun) This upscale café is in an 1895 house with a nice veranda. Always jammed with locals, you can enjoy dishes as diverse as unusual salads and steak frites.

Peppers MexiCali Cafe (☎ 831-373-6892; 170 Forest Ave; dishes $9-13; ☺ lunch & dinner Wed-Mon) Small and wooden-floored Peppers serves the gamut of Mexican classics as well as complex seafood dishes. There's a good wine and beer list.

Getting There & Away

MST bus 1 provides fast and frequent service to/from Cannery Row and downtown Monterey.

17-MILE DRIVE

Pacific Grove and Carmel are linked by the spectacularly scenic 17-Mile Drive, which meanders through Pebble Beach, a private resort and residential area that potently symbolizes the peninsula's affluence. Open sunrise to sunset, entry is controlled by the omnipresent **Pebble Beach Company** (☎ 831-647-7500; www.pebblebeach.com; per car $8.50). There are five gates; for the most scenic portion enter the Pacific Grove Gate off Sunset Dr and exit at the Carmel Gate. You'll shave about 7 miles off the route and at times the scenery will rival that which is free in PG.

Using the map provided when you pay to enter, you can easily pick out landmarks such as **Spanish Bay**, where explorer Gaspar de Portolá dropped anchor in 1769; treacherously rocky **Point Joe**, which in the past was often mistaken for the entrance to Monterey Bay and thus became the site of several shipwrecks; and **Bird Rock**, which is a bird and seal haven. Digital cameras capture billions of pixels daily at the **Lone Cypress**, the copyrighted symbol of the Pebble Beach Company that perches perfectly on a seaward rock. In fact it looks almost artificially perfect.

Besides the coast (or possibly instead of it), the real attractions here are the world-famous **golf courses** such as Spyglass Hill, Cypress Point and, of course, Pebble Beach. The latter (greens fee $425) was made famous by Bing Crosby's mixed professional and celebrity tournament that continues today under the guise of the AT&T Pebble Beach National Pro-Am (p447). It's easy to picture Jack Nicklaus driving down the spectacular 18th hole for a victory.

The renowned **Lodge at Pebble Beach** (☎ 831-624-3811; www.pebblebeach.com; r from $580; ✕ 🖳 🔊) is really the center of the drive and boasts world-class spas, restaurants, shops and much more. Everything is done just right and the most demanding of tastes are catered to. If you've forgotten to make reservations or rob a bank, you can still soak up the atmosphere in the art-filled public spaces and relax in a café.

CARMEL-BY-THE-SEA
pop 4400

Carmel began as a planned seaside resort in the 1880s and quickly established a reputation as a bohemian retreat. The artistic flavor survives in the more than 100 galleries that line the town's immaculate streets, but these days 'wealthy' and 'bourgeois' are just as descriptive. Carmel, with its picturesque homes, impressive coastal frontage and upscale shopping, positively glows with smugness. (Some of the sheen however is obscured by the nearly perpetual fog.)

The town's manicured appearance is ensured by strict local bylaws, which forbid neon signs, billboards and hot dog stands. Residents pick up their mail from the post office and houses have no street numbers, so addresses always specify the block and side of street. Even public phones, garbage cans and newspaper vending boxes are quaintly shingled.

If you are into galleries and shopping, you'll love Carmel as much as shade-loving flowers such as impatiens and hydrangeas; otherwise you may wish to check out its idiosyncratic charms (such as little alleys that lead to gardens) and keep moving.

Orientation & Information

Most of the shops, restaurants and motels are in the blocks around the intersection of Ocean Ave and San Carlos St.

The **Carmel Business Association** (☎ 831-624-2522, www.carmelcalifornia.com; San Carlos St near 6th Ave; ☻ 10am-5pm) distributes good town maps and information, though only about its members. The visitors centers in Monterey also handle Carmel.

The quixotic free weekly *Carmel Pine Cone* is packed with local personality and color. The police log is a comedy of manners.

Sights

Checking out the once modest cabins that have taken on the trappings of wealth along Carmel's tree-lined neighborhoods is reason enough to stroll outside of the shopping area. Better yet, go with a guide from the **Carmel Heritage Society** (☎ 831-624-4447; tours $10). The Society operates 90-minute walking tours at 9:30am on Saturday, which leave from **First Murphy House** (cnr 6th Ave & Lincoln St; ☻ 1-4pm, Wed-Sun), a former home with exhibits of local history and lore.

If you're afraid of sunburn, you'll love the **Carmel Beach**, a nice crescent of white sand.

MISSION SAN CARLOS DE BORROMÉO DE CARMELO

The original Monterey mission was established by Padre Serra in 1769, but poor soil forced the move to the riverside site in Carmel in 1771. Although the missionaries founded 20 other missions in California, this one remained Serra's base. He died here in 1784 and was buried in the mission church beside his compatriot, Padre Juan Crespi.

The mission church was originally built of wood, then replaced by an adobe structure and, in 1793, by the present stone church. In the 19th century, the mission went into decline; it was secularized in 1834 and virtually abandoned in 1836 when the padres moved to Monterey. The ruin was roofed over in 1884, which at least slowed the decay, but restoration didn't really commence until 1931. Today it is one of the most attractive and complete of the California missions; the arched basilica reeks of incense. Museum exhibits are scattered throughout the complex; the room attributed to Serra looks like something out of *The Good, The Bad And The Ugly*.

The **mission** (Map p442; ☎ 831-624-1271; 3080 Rio Rd; adult/child $5/1; ☻ 9:30am-5pm) is off Hwy 1 in southern Carmel.

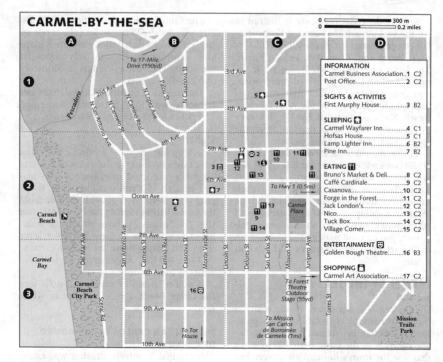

CARMEL-BY-THE-SEA

INFORMATION
Carmel Business Association..1 C2
Post Office............................2 C2

SIGHTS & ACTIVITIES
First Murphy House.............3 B2

SLEEPING
Carmel Wayfarer Inn...........4 C1
Hofsas House.....................5 C1
Lamp Lighter Inn................6 B2
Pine Inn...........................7 B2

EATING
Bruno's Market & Deli.........8 C2
Caffé Cardinale..................9 C2
Casanova........................10 C2
Forge in the Forest............11 C2
Jack London's...................12 C2
Nico..............................13 C2
Tuck Box........................14 C2
Village Corner..................15 C2

ENTERTAINMENT
Golden Bough Theatre........16 B3

SHOPPING
Carmel Art Association.......17 C2

TOR HOUSE

Poet Robinson Jeffers was one of the creators of the Carmel ethos, and his strikingly rugged home, the **Tor House** (Map p442; ☎ 831-624-1813; 26304 Ocean View Ave; tours adult/student $7/2; ☷ 10am-3pm Fri & Sat), off Scenic Ave, has become a pilgrimage point. Tours take in the house, which was a salon for a long list of creative types, as well as the gardens and a climb up Hawk Tower, inspired by ancient Irish stone towers.

CARMEL VALLEY

Go about two miles inland on Carmel Valley Rd and you'll hit sun almost every time. This Mediterranean-feeling valley is home to organic farms, upscale gated communities and posh garden shops. Scenic mountain roads lead over the hills to the Salinas Valley.

Sleeping

Accommodation is not cheap in Carmel – Motel 6s are definitely not welcome. Instead you'll find a slew of small boutique hotels and cozy B&Bs, many of which impose a two-night minimum stay on weekends and often fill up quickly, particularly in summer. As usual, rates vary greatly by season.

Carmel Wayfarer Inn (☎ 831-624-2711, 800-624-2711; www.carmelwayfarerinn.com; cnr Mission St & 4th Ave; r $90-230; ☒ ☐) This is a charming country inn dating back to 1919. None of the 16 rooms is the same and some have glorious sunset views. Rates include a tasty continental breakfast with homemade bread.

Hofsas House (☎ 831-624-2745, 800-221-2548; www .hofsashouse.com; San Carlos St near 4th Ave; r $85-250; ☐ ☒) Pink outside and frilly inside, the friendly Hofsas House has decent ocean views from the upper floors and large rooms, some with kitchenettes. But tub fans take note: some rooms only have showers.

Lamp Lighter Inn (☎ 831-624-7372; www.carmel lamplighter.com; Ocean Ave near Casanova St; r $145-325; ☒) All six rooms in these quaint cottages boast smart, contemporary decor that is a refreshing change from the potpourri elsewhere. Room sizes range from snug to spacious suites.

Pine Inn (☎ 831-624-3851, 800-228-3851; fax 831-624-3030; http://tallyho-inn.com; Ocean Ave & Lincoln St; r $135-295; ☒ ☐) Pine Inn has a pedigree going back

CENTRAL COAST

to 1889 and has a period elegance marked by red flock and brass trim. Antiques and cozy lighting conspire to create an ambience of comfort and style in the 49 rooms.

Eating & Drinking

Carmel's restaurant scene is a delight, with plenty of good places loaded with atmosphere (and usually an array of heaters over outside tables). Note that most restaurants stop serving dinner around 9pm.

Forge in the Forest (☎ 831-624-2233; cnr 5th Ave & Junípero St; mains $10-31) Many of the employees at the Forge are also the owners through a trust. They bring an enthusiasm to this fun place that's infectious. Dine on the well-heated and flower-bordered patio or on an antique table inside. The huge menu features great sandwiches, steaks and pizzas. The bar is a fine place for a drink.

Casanova (☎ 831-831-625-0501; 5th Ave btwn San Carlos & Mission Sts; mains $35-45) From the time you step past the home grown lavender and into this cottage until you get the bill, you'll know you are someplace special. The food and service is all high end and the seasonal menu blends French and California cuisines. Most ingredients are organic and sourced locally.

Nico (☎ 831-624-6545; San Carlos St & Ocean Ave; mains $10-20) This small Italian restaurant is run by the charming Enzo Ruben Nico. The menu has all the classics, including numerous pastas and pizza.

Caffé Cardinale (☎ 831-626-2095; Ocean Ave btwn San Carlos & Dolores Sts; snacks $3-8; ☺ 7am-4pm) This spot gets rave reviews for its rich coffee (roasted on the premises), but also does tasty baked goods, soups and panini sandwiches. It's tucked away in an alley off Ocean Ave.

Jack London's (☎ 831-624-2336; Dolores St btwn 5th & 6th Aves; dishes $6-20) In a walkway off Dolores St, Jack London's serves hot food until midnight. A Carmel mainstay since 1973, it pairs upscale pub grub (burgers, ribs) with a selection of microbrews and potent mixed drinks. With a cozy fireplace, the bar is a good place for just a drink.

Tuck Box (☎ 831-624-6365; Dolores St btwn Ocean & 7th Aves; meals $5-8; ☺ 7am-4pm) This is a snug British tea room in a small cottage that should be made out of gingerbread. People queue for its homemade scones and pies at afternoon tea.

Village Corner (☎ 831-624-3588; cnr Dolores St & 6th Ave; meals $9-23; ☺ breakfast, lunch & dinner) This classic California bistro has a lovely, flower-filled patio with an open-pit fire. The menu is long and portions are generous.

Bruno's Market & Deli (☎ 831-624-3821; cnr 6th Ave & Junípero St; meals $4-8; ☺ 7am-8pm) The best local grocery store, Bruno's has a superb deli for creating picnics. Daily lunch specials – many Mexican – are very popular.

Entertainment

Forest Theatre & Outdoor Stage (Map p442; ☎ 831-626-2845; www.foresttheaterguild.org; Mountain View btwn Forest & Guadalupe Sts) This venue was founded in 1910. Musicals, drama and comedies, as well as movie screenings, take place in a lovely setting surrounded by trees and anchored by two large fire pits.

Golden Bough Theatre (☎ 831-622-0100; Monte Verde St btwn 8th & 9th Aves) This is the home of the revered Pacific Repertory Theatre (www.pacrep.org), whose repertoire ranges from Shakespeare to contemporary works.

In July and August, Carmel hosts the well-respected **Carmel Bach Festival** (☎ 831-624-2046; www.bachfestival.org) at venues around town.

Shopping

Shopping is a favorite pastime for locals and visitors alike, and Carmel has plenty of outlets to satisfy the urge, with a particular abundance of galleries, boutiques and high-end specialty stores, including some national chains.

Many of Carmel's 100-plus galleries are laden with frolicking dolphin sculptures and oil paintings of local scenery (including golf courses). But serious browsers will be rewarded with persistence. The weighty and free *Carmel Gallery Guide* can help with your hunt. The **Carmel Art Association** (☎ 831-624-6176; www.carmelart.org; Dolores St btwn 5th & 6th Aves) has been showcasing the best of local artists since 1927 and is a good place to begin.

Getting There & Around

Carmel is only 5 miles south of Monterey by Hwy 1. MST buses 4 and 5 run north to Monterey (p449) and south to the mission. The 22 bus passes through en route to Big Sur. Free unlimited car parking can be found at **Vista Lobos Park** (cnr 3rd Ave & Torres St).

POINT LOBOS STATE RESERVE

About 4 miles south of Carmel, **Point Lobos** (☎ 831-624-4909; http://pt-lobos.parks.state.ca.us; per vehicle $8) has a dramatically rocky and convoluted coastline. It takes its name from the Punta de los Lobos Marinos, or the 'Point of the Sea Wolves,' named by the Spanish for the howls of the resident sea lions. Several short walks take in the wild and inspiring scenery. Favorite destinations include **Sea Lion Point** and **Devil's Cauldron**, the latter a whirlpool that gets splashy at high tide. At the end of the main road, **Bird Island** is good for birdwatching and for starting out on long hikes.

The kelp forest in **Whaler's Cove** is popular with divers and snorkelers, though reservations and **permits** (☎ 831-624-8413; per diving pair $10) are required .

BIG SUR TO SAN LUIS OBISPO

This is the Hwy 1 of a million dreams and a thousand car ads. The road follows the dramatic coast for 130 miles south until it joins with Hwy 101 at San Luis Obispo. Even if your driving skills are up for the myriad of hills and switchbacks, others aren't: expect to average under 40mph for the route. Parts of the road are battle-scarred, evidence of the constant struggle to keep it open after landslides and washouts.

BIG SUR

Big Sur is an experience rather than one tangible place. Its raw beauty is awe-inspiring, its quirky residents endearing. There are no traffic lights, banks or shopping centers, and when the sun goes down, the moon and stars are the only streetlights. And in summer even the streetlights go out as the coast is often shrouded in dense fog. If you have a choice, try visiting in the spring and fall when the crowds – and fog – are dispersed.

Although it's only 90 miles from Carmel to San Simeon, driving along this narrow two-lane highway is slow going. Allow at least four hours to cover the distance as you'll want to stop at the many state parks lining the road. Traveling after dark is perilous and futile, since you won't be able to see any of the countryside. Day or night, watch out for cyclists.

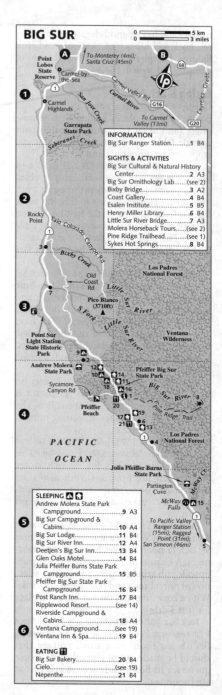

History

The Esselen people, known to date back at least 3000 years in the area, occupied settlements along the coast, surviving primarily on acorns, rabbit, deer, bear and sea mammals. They were wiped out by diseases brought by the Spanish before the first US settlers arrived.

Big Sur was named by the Spanish settlers living in Carmel's mission who referred to the unexplored wilderness as *el pais grande del sur* (the big country to the south). They named the two coastal rivers *el rio grande del sur* (the big river to the south) and *el rio chiquito del sur* (the little river to the south).

In 1852, John Rogers Cooper (also known as Juan Bautista Rogerio Cooper) filed claim to Rancho El Sur, stretching from Cooper Point to the mouth of the Little Sur River. Cooper Point and the headquarters for the ranch are now part of Andrew Molera State Park.

Homesteaders arrived in the early 1900s and supported the canning and lumbering industries. At the turn of the 20th century, Big Sur supported a larger population than it does today. Electricity arrived in the 1950s and TV reception in the 1980s.

In the 1950s and '60s, Big Sur became a favorite retreat for writers and artists, including Henry Miller, who lived here from 1947 to 1964, and Beat Generation members Lawrence Ferlinghetti and Jack Kerouac. The death of Hunter S Thompson in 2005 brought forth a score of articles recalling his raucous days here in the early 1960s. Today, Big Sur still attracts its share of New Age mystics, artists and eccentric types.

Orientation & Information

Visitors often wander into businesses along Hwy 1 and ask, 'How much further to Big Sur?' In fact, there is no *town* of Big Sur as such, though you may see the name on maps. Commercial activity is concentrated along the stretch between Andrew Molera State Park and Pfeiffer Big Sur State Park. Sometimes called 'The Village,' this is where you'll find many of the shops, restaurants and lodging options, including campgrounds; the post office is here as well.

Look for the free annual *Big Sur Guide* (www.bigsurcalifornia.org) published by the Big Sur Chamber of Commerce.

Just south of Pfeiffer Big Sur State Park is the **Big Sur Ranger Station** (☎ 831-667-2315; ☒ 8am-4:30pm), a good source for information and maps for Los Padres National Forest, the Ventana Wilderness and the state parks. In southern Big Sur, just south of the turnoff to the Nacimiento-Fergusson Rd (p459), is the **Pacific Valley Ranger Station** (☎ 805-927-4211; ☒ 9am-5pm).

Note that services here are distant. Road service is either in Monterey or Cambria. The nearest medical service is in Monterey (p441).

Sights & Activities

GARRAPATA STATE PARK

Although often overlooked, this **state park** (☎ 831-624-4909) is a pleasant spot fronting 2 miles of beach and laced with hiking trails running from the ocean into redwood groves. The **Soberanes Canyon Trail** and the **Rocky Ridge Trail** are among the more challenging routes. There's parking along Hwy 1, 7 miles south of Carmel.

BIXBY BRIDGE

A much photographed Big Sur landmark, Bixby Bridge spans Bixby Creek and is one of the world's highest single span bridges at 714ft long and 260ft high. Completed in 1932, it was built by prisoners eager to lop time off their sentences.

Before the bridge was constructed, travelers had to trek 14 miles inland on what's called the **Old Coast Rd**, which heads off east from Bixby Bridge's northern side and reconnects with Hwy 1 across from Andrew Molera State Park. This route is still navigable, but you'll need a vehicle that's comfortable off-road.

LITTLE SUR RIVER BRIDGE

Before rising to the lofty Hurricane Point headlands, Hwy 1 passes the low-lying Little Sur River Bridge. Here the Little Sur River makes a gentle sweep – a favorite subject for artists – before it meets the sea, turning the water bright blue with its heavy limestone deposits.

During the dry season the river forms a lagoon behind a sandbar. **Pico Blanco**, the white-and-green-striped mountain to the east, stands 3710ft tall and was revered by the Esselen people as the sacred birthplace of man and beast.

POINT SUR LIGHT STATION STATE HISTORIC PARK

About 19 miles south of Carmel, Point Sur is an imposing volcanic rock that looks like an island but is actually connected to land by a sandbar. Atop the rock, 361ft above the surf, is the 1899 **Point Sur Lightstation** (☎ 831-625-4419; tours adult/child $8/4), which remained in operation until 1974. Views and details of life here are engrossing, to partake you need to join a nonreservable three-hour tour. Tours meet at the farm gate on Hwy 1 and are at 10am and 2pm Saturday and 10am Sunday year-round. From April to October, there are also tours at 10am and 2pm on Wednesday, and in July and August, there is also one at 10am Thursday.

ANDREW MOLERA STATE PARK

A remote and wild setting, lots of wildlife and great beachcombing are among the assets of this **park** (☎ 831-667-2315; per vehicle $8; ☯ 8am-5pm), which once formed part of John Rogers Cooper's 9000-acre Rancho El Sur. The first-come, first-served, 24-hour **walk-in campground** (sites $9), a little under half a mile from the parking lot, has fire pits, vault toilets and drinking water. A gentle quarter-mile trail leads from the campground past sycamore trees and the **Cooper Cabin**, one of the oldest structures in Big Sur, to a beautiful beach where the Big Sur River runs into the ocean. From here, several trails head south along the bluffs above the beach.

Near the park entrance are several other interesting places. **Molera Horseback Tours** (☎ 831-625-5486, 800-942-5486; www.molerahorseback tours.com; ☯ Mar-Nov) offers a variety of guided trail rides from $25.

The Ventana Wilderness Society (see the boxed text, below) operates the **Big Sur Ornithology Lab** (☎ 831-624-1202) from a small shed. You can often find the naturalists here; they take justifiable pride in talking about their efforts to reintroduce the enormous California condor (24 and counting) and protect the myriad of other species locally.

Close by is the **Big Sur Cultural & Natural History Center** (☎ 831-455-9514), a historic place with erratic hours.

PFEIFFER BIG SUR STATE PARK

Named after Big Sur's first European settlers – Michael and Barbara Pfeiffer – who arrived in 1869, **Pfeiffer Big Sur State Park** (☎ 831-667-2315) is the largest state park in Big Sur. It occupies 964 acres of the former Pfeiffer Ranch Resort and contains the original homestead cabin and the graveyard where the Pfeiffers are buried. The rustic administration buildings and Big Sur Lodge (p458) were built in the 1930s by the Civilian Conservation Corps (CCC).

A 218-site **campground** (☎ reservations 800-444-7275; www.parks.ca.gov; sites $25-35) is beside the Big Sur River in a flat-bottomed valley shaded by redwood groves; facilities include showers and laundry. Hiking trails loop through the park and head into the adjacent Ventana Wilderness. Summer crowds are the drawback to this otherwise idyllic scene.

VENTANA WILDERNESS

The 167,000-acre Ventana Wilderness is the backcountry of the Big Sur coast. It lies within the northern part of Los Padres National Forest, which straddles the Santa Lucia Range and runs parallel to the coast for its entire length. Most of the wilderness is covered with oak and chaparral, though canyons cut by the Big Sur and Little Sur Rivers support virgin stands of coastal redwoods. Scattered pockets of the endemic Santa Lucia fir grow in rocky outcroppings at elevations above 5000ft.

The Ventana is especially popular with hikers and backpackers. There are 237 miles of trails with access to 55 designated backcountry trail camps. One favorite destination is **Sykes Hot Springs**, natural hot mineral pools (ranging from 98°F to 110°F) framed by redwoods, about 10 miles from the wilderness boundary via the **Pine Ridge Trail** – the gateway into the wilderness.

The trailhead is at the Big Sur Ranger Station, where you can also get backcountry ($5) and campfire (free) permits.

The **Ventana Wilderness Society** (☎ 877-897-7740; www.ventanaws.org) is a very active and knowledgeable private group that works to preserve the wilderness. Note that Ventana has the country's largest concentration of mountain lions (one cat per 10 sq miles). Try not to get acquainted. Also see p704 for advice on what to do if you encounter one.

CENTRAL COAST

Sycamore Canyon Rd winds 2 miles down to **Pfeiffer Beach**, a great spot.

HENRY MILLER LIBRARY

Housed amid gardens and sculptures, the **Henry Miller Library** (☎ 831-667-2574; www.henrymiller .org; suggested donation $1; ◷ generally 11am-6pm Thu-Sun) is Big Sur's most cultured venue. It was the home of Miller's great friend, the painter Emil White, until his death in 1989 and is now run by a nonprofit group. The library has all of Miller's written works, many of his paintings, translations of his books and a great collection of Big Sur and Beat Generation material. Grabbing a book and hanging out on the deck is encouraged and you can surf the net for free. Call ahead to check opening hours and see the website for a schedule numerous cultural events.

The library is a quarter of a mile past Nepenthe restaurant (p459).

COAST GALLERY

The **Coast Gallery** (☎ 831-667-2301; ◷ 9am-5pm) is a fairly commercial place. Pretty much everything is for sale although there is an exhibition of watercolors and artifacts related to Henry Miller. If you exhaust yourself in the candle studio, buy a sandwich and enjoy the nice ocean-view deck.

PARTINGTON COVE

From the western side of Hwy 1, a poorly marked steep dirt trail descends half a mile along Partington Creek to Partington Cove, named for a settler who built the first dock here in the 1880s. Originally, the cove was used for loading freight; during Prohibition it was an alleged landing spot for bootleggers. This is a beautiful and often overlooked section of Big Sur with great views, tide pools, swimming in the creek and lovely picnic spots. On the 1-mile loop you not only cross a cool bridge but also go through an even cooler tunnel.

The turnoff is inside a large hairpin turn 8 miles south of Nepenthe restaurant and 1.8 miles north of Julia Pfeiffer Burns State Park. There are turnouts for parking nearby.

JULIA PFEIFFER BURNS STATE PARK

Named for a Big Sur pioneer woman, this **park** (☎ 831-667-2315) hugs both sides of Hwy 1 and features redwood, tan oak, madrona and chaparral. At the park entrance (on the east

side of Hwy 1) are forested picnic grounds along McWay Creek and an old cabin (on the creek's northern side, just past the picnic area) that housed the Waters, the land's first homesteaders. The Ewoldsen Trail offers good views of the ocean and the Santa Lucia Range.

The park's highlight is California's only coastal waterfall (you'll recognize it from its starring role in stock photography), the 80ft **McWay Falls**, which drops straight into the sea. To reach the waterfall viewpoint, take the short Overlook Trail heading west and cross beneath Hwy 1. Continue a little further and you will find the evocative ruins of an old ranch. Nearby, two small walk-in **campgrounds** (☎ reservations 800-444-7275; www.parks.ca.gov; sites $15-20) sit on a semiprotected bluff. Camper registration is at Pfeiffer Big Sur State Park campground, about 12 miles north.

ESALEN INSTITUTE

Marked only by a lighted sign reading 'Esalen Institute, By Reservation Only,' the **Esalen Institute** (☎ 831-667-3000; www.esalen.org) is world renowned for its seminars and natural hot springs. Workshops deal with anything that 'promotes human values and potentials,' from African dance to yoga to exploring the inner game of golf. In business for decades, it's sort of the 'old timer' of the New Age. Things have changed a lot since Hunter S Thompson was the gun-toting caretaker here in 1960.

The Esalen baths are fed by a natural hot spring and sit on a ledge above the ocean, below the center's main building. The tubs are open to the public nightly from 1am to 3am (clothing optional). Call ahead.

When space is available (less than half the time), you can stay at Esalen without participating in a seminar. But the only way to do this is to stop in and ask at the guard house. Accommodations are in standard rooms sleeping up to three people (per person $150 to $180) or in four- to six-bed dorms (per person $105 to $110). The daily rates include three renowned and organic meals.

Esalen is 11 miles south of Nepenthe restaurant and 10 miles north of Lucia Lodge (p459).

Sleeping

There's as varied a choice of accommodation in Big Sur as there are views of the

CENTRAL COAST

ocean. Hotels and motels span the gamut from basic four walls and a mattress to the kind of storied resorts you drool over in a glossy magazine. What there isn't is a lot of rooms overall so demand often exceeds supply and prices go up further than a coast redwood. In summer and on weekends it's a good idea to reserve. Campers will find many pastoral options as well, and reserving is also advised.

There are additional sleeping options in the Southern Big Sur section (opposite).

INNS & RESORTS

With few exceptions, Big Sur's lodgings do not have TVs and rarely have telephones. This is where you come to escape the world.

Deetjen's Big Sur Inn (☎ 831-667-2377; www.deet jens.com; r $75-195) About a quarter of a mile south of the Henry Miller Library is this enchanting conglomeration of rustic rooms, redwoods and wisteria along Castro Creek. Built by a Norwegian immigrant in the early 1930s, each of the 20 rooms set in cabins still reflects his personality. You can chill the heck out here. The restaurant is excellent.

Post Ranch Inn (☎ 831-667-2200, 800-527-2200; www.postranchinn.com; r from $500) This architecturally lauded compound is about as good as it gets on the coast. The legendary inn pampers guests staying in the 30 individual units. Ocean-view rooms celebrate the sea while the tree houses have a little bit of sway supplied by your own motion. It's not stuffy, it is sublime.

Ventana Inn & Spa (☎ 831-667-2331, 800-628-6500; www.ventanainn.com; r from $420; 🖵 🖳) High above Hwy 1 and a grove of redwoods, Ventana exudes an aura of serenity and romance. The 60 rooms have been renovated and now feature lavish woodwork, plasma TVs and sybaritic bathrooms. There's also fireplaces and plush bathrobes. The complex includes a Japanese bathhouse, two pools and redesigned gardens highlighting indigenous plants. For fine food, visit its Cielo restaurant.

Ripplewood Resort (☎ 831-667-2242; www.ripple woodresort.com; cabins $75-135) Next to the Glen Oaks Motel, Ripplewood has struck a blow for fiscal equality by having the same rates year-round. Cabins vary in details: all have kitchens and private bathrooms, some have fireplaces. The cabins along the river are quiet and surrounded by redwoods, but those

on Hwy 1 can be noisy. Its café is good for breakfast and lunch.

Big Sur Lodge (☎ 831-667-3100, 800-424-4787; www .bigsurlodge.com; cottages $100-230; ☒ 🖳) This historic place, 26 miles south of Carmel, has 61 units in pretty cottages, all with a deck or a balcony. The pricier ones also have kitchens and/or a fireplace and sleep up to six people. There's a moderately priced restaurant and store.

Big Sur River Inn (☎ 831-667-2700, 800-548-3610; www.bigsurriverinn.com; r $85-225; 🖳) In business since 1888, this inn offers 20 comfy, country-style rooms in the Village. Facilities include a large heated pool and balconies overlooking the creek. There are several good eating options.

Glen Oaks Motel (☎ 831-667-2105; www.glenoaks bigsur.com; r $50-134, cottages $110-165) This motel in the Village has clean, airy and nicely furnished rooms, and cottages set amid trees and flowers. The bathrooms are quite good.

CAMPING

There's camping in three of Big Sur's state parks: Andrew Molera State Park (p456), Pfeiffer Big Sur State Park (p456) and Julia Pfeiffer Burns State Park (p457). There's also undeveloped backcountry camping available in Los Padres National Forest (p483) and Ventana Wilderness (p456). For specifics, check with the ranger stations in Big Sur, where you can also get an overnight parking permit ($5) and a free campfire permit.

Ventana Campground (☎ 831-667-2712; www.ven tanawildernesscampground.com; sites $27-40; ☯ Mar-Oct) Just south of Pfeiffer Big Sur State Park and set in a 40-acre redwood grove, this 80-site campground has beautiful secluded campsites with a lot of privacy. There's also a tiny general store. If you tire of campfire fare, you can head up the hill for a feast at Cielo restaurant.

Big Sur Campground & Cabins (☎ 831-667-2322; sites $25-29, tent cabins $54-59, cabins with bathroom & kitchen $95-225) This well-run option, in the Village, has 79 nice sites and small cabins shaded by mature redwoods right on the Big Sur River. The camping store stocks the basics, and there are laundry facilities, hot showers, volleyball and basketball courts and a playground.

Riverside Campground & Cabins (☎ 831-667-2414; sites $28, cabins $75-130) About a half-mile south of the Big Sur campground, this place is a more rustic but very pleasant option. You'll think you're back in the 1940s as you cross the crude causeway.

Eating

Whether you're staying or passing through, there's a number of good choices to eat in Big Sur.

Big Sur Bakery (☎ 831-667-0520; meals $10-32; ⏱ breakfast, lunch & dinner) In a warmly lit, ambience-laden old house behind a Shell gas station in the Village, this restaurant has a menu that changes through the day and by the day. The fare is basic eggs, burgers and steaks but it's done with flair and varies by what's in season. There are indeed some fine baked goods as well and a nice patio.

Deetjen's Big Sur Inn (☎ 831-667-2377; mains $17-30; ⏱ dinner) This atmospheric lodge has a cozy dining room serving up hearty fare from a daily menu. On one day it might feature organic steak and cassoulet, on another fresh wild salmon.

Cielo (☎ 831-667-4242; meals $12-40) Cielo, at the Ventana Inn & Spa, has a vast patio that's often sunny when the lower echelons are fogged in. The lofty views complement the modern California classics that are both artistic and tasty. Think Cobb salad and oak-grilled steak.

Big Sur River Inn (☎ 831-667-2700; mains $10-20; ⏱ breakfast, lunch & dinner) This inn has a woodsy old supper club with a deck overlooking the creek. The food is classic American.

Big Sur Burrito Bar (meals $6-8; ⏱ 7am-8pm) Next door in the inn's small market the bar, which makes burritos to your specifications, also has wraps and smoothies.

Nepenthe (☎ 831-667-2345; mains $13-32) South of Pfeiffer Big Sur State Park, this destination restaurant is known for its vivid gardens and breathtaking cliff-top location. Views are stunning from both the large outdoor terrace and through the panoramic windows in the bar and dining room. The food is tarted-up café classics. For cheaper eats and almost the same views, go downstairs to the outdoor Cafe Kevah (dishes $8 to $12), open for breakfast and lunch.

Getting There & Away

Although there are seasonal buses from Monterey to the northern sections of Big Sur, the area is best explored by car, since you'll be itching to stop frequently to take in the rugged beauty and stunning vistas that reveal themselves after every hairpin turn.

If you opt for public transit, MST bus 22 ($4, 75 minutes, twice daily) goes from Monterey (p449) via Carmel as far south as Nepenthe restaurant between late May to early September. The buses are equipped with bike racks.

SOUTHERN BIG SUR

With Carmel now over 40 miles behind you, Hwy 1 becomes even more sparsely populated. The 40-mile stretch south of Esalen to San Simeon is rugged and remote.

Certainly, you'll feel the solitude at the small and isolated **Lucia Lodge** (☎ 831-667-2391; www.lucialodge.com; r & cabins $125-250), perched about 400ft above the bay. It has a restaurant-lounge (meals $8 to $30) with an outdoor deck, dreamy views and a menu ranging from sandwiches to steak dinners. Some of the lodgings have amazing views.

Continuing south, you'll soon come to the turnoff for a narrow road snaking 2 miles up the hillside to the **New Camaldoli Hermitage** (☎ 831-667-2456). There are spectacular views along the way and picnic tables to enjoy them at leisure. About 30 monks live in this largely self-sufficient community, which at times welcomes pilgrims.

Limekiln State Park (☎ 831-667-2403; per vehicle $6) gets its name from the four remaining lime kilns originally built here in the 1880s to smelt local lime to powder. A half-mile trail through a new redwood grove leads to this historic site. Another short hike leads to a 100ft waterfall. The **campground** (☎ reservations 800-444-7275; www.parks.ca.gov; sites $20-25) sits right by the park entrance, tucked under a bridge next to the ocean; it has flush toilets and hot showers.

About 2 miles south, **Kirk Creek Campground** (☎ 805-434-1996; walk-ins $5, sites $20) is a US Forest Service (USFS) facility on a beautiful sunny bluff above the ocean. There are flush toilets but no showers.

Watch for the turnoff to the adventurous **Nacimiento-Fergusson Rd**, which cuts through the hills and connects with Hwy 101 after about 50 miles. A worthwhile stop en route is at the Mission San Antonio de Padua (p476). Slightly south of the intersection is the Pacific Valley Ranger Station (p455).

One of the nicest campgrounds in Southern Big Sur is the USFS **Plaskett Creek**

CENTRAL COAST

Campground (☎ 805-434-1996; sites $20, day-use $5), about 2 miles north of Jade Cove. It has 43 spacious first-come, first-served sites shaded by Monterey cypress. There are flush toilets but no showers. A short walk north is the turnoff for the **Sand Dollar Beach picnic area** (day use $5), from where it's about a five-minute walk down to the area's longest sandy beach.

Just south of Plaskett Creek is the most scenic stretch of southern Big Sur. In 1971, in the waters of **Jade Cove**, three divers recovered a 9000lb jade boulder that measured 8ft long and was valued at $180,000. People still comb the beach today. The best time to find jade, which is black or blue-green and looks dull until you dip it in water, is during low tide or after a big storm.

Next up is **Gorda** (Spanish for 'Fat'), named for an offshore outcropping that looks like a fat lady. It now serves as a beacon for tourists looking for snacks and a gas station

Your last – or first – taste of Big Sur rocky grandeur comes at **Ragged Point**, a craggy cliff outcropping with fabulous views of the coastline in both directions, about 15 miles north of San Simeon. It was originally part of the Hearst empire and is now occupied by the sprawling and expanding **Ragged Point Inn & Resort** (☎ 805-927-4502; www.raggedpointinn .com; r $100-250), which has comfortable rooms, some with views, and a restaurant (meals $8 to $25).

From this point south, the land is windswept and rolls gently and moodily down to the water.

PIEDRAS BLANCAS

The glories of Hearst Castle to the south now have some weighty competition: elephant seals. Weighing over two tons – about the same as the gas guzzling SUVs whizzing past on Hwy 1 – a colony has set up housekeeping 4.4 miles north of the castle entrance (coming from the north, look for the busy parking area).

Nearly extinct 100 years ago, these huge pinnipeds have made a remarkable comeback along California's coast. For the last several decades the last place to see these beasts was at heavily protected Año Nuevo State Park (p186) by Half Moon Bay.

Thanks to the elephant seals themselves you can now also see them anytime you want at their roadside retreat here. It's a bit

amusing that with the entire coast to choose from, this colony formed on a beach right on the road in 1992. Now during the peak seasons you can see upwards of 7500 in the coves and beaches. The seals are endlessly fascinating, with the behemoth bulls engaged in mock and sometimes real combat all the while making their odd guttural grunts not unlike that made by the space aliens in the cult movie *Repo Man*.

Watching them lumber around the beach, you'd never guess that they regularly dive deeper (more than 1 mile) and longer (80 minutes) than any other mammal. Here's the season for the seals:

■ November to December – Bull seals arrive at the beach, joining youngsters and moms.

■ January to April – Pregnant seals give birth, peaking in February; once delivered, the females mate with the waiting and rather anxious males.

■ May to August – Females wean pups and leave; pups teach themselves how to swim and leave as well; some older males hang around lounging on the sand.

■ September to October – Seals of all ages begin returning to molt and prepare for birthing and breeding.

Interpretative panels demystify the behavior of these humongous mammals. Better yet talk to one of the enthusiastic docents from **Friends of the Elephant Seal** (☎ 805-924-1628; www.elephantseal.org).

SAN SIMEON

pop 350

San Simeon began life in the 1850s as a whaling station. In 1865, George Hearst purchased 45,000 acres of land and established a beachside settlement on the western side of Hwy 1, across from today's entrance to Hearst Castle. The Julia Morgan houses (formerly inhabited by Hearst Castle staff) are now home to the cowboys who run the Hearst Corporation's 80,000-acre cattle ranch, a vast area mostly to the north of the castle. A recent deal with the state will allow for modest development here in return for keeping the entire ranch development free.

Adjacent to the houses, **William Randolph Hearst Memorial State Beach** has a pleasant sandy stretch with intermittent rock outcroppings, a rickety wooden pier (fishing permitted) and good places to picnic.

Three miles south of the original San Simeon (just outside the Hearst Corporation's property), the town of San Simeon is a 1-mile-long strip of unexciting motels and equally unimpressive restaurants on a bleak outcrop.

There are better places to stay in Cambria or points further south that are still close to Hearst Castle. If you must spend the night, try the friendly and simple **Courtesy Inn** (☎ 805-927-4691; www.courtesyinns.com; 9450 Castillo Dr; r $40-180; 🖳 🐾). Rooms are basic but it has an indoor pool.

HEARST CASTLE

The most important thing to know about Hearst Castle is that William Randolph Hearst was not very much like Charles Foster Kane in *Citizen Kane*. Not that he wasn't bombastic, conniving and much larger than life – he was – but from the 1920s through the 1940s he also had a ball: ever-enlarging his castle, constantly entertaining and running his media empire. The moody recluse of *Kane* he was definitely not.

Like Hearst's construction budget, the castle will devour as much of your time as you let it. It's grand, sumptuous, historic (beloved guest Winston Churchill penned anti-Nazi essays here in the 1930s) and will make you wish you had a spare billion or two so you could move in.

Perched high on a hill the castle is a monument to wealth and ambition. The estate sprawls out over 127 acres of lushly landscaped gardens, accentuated by shimmering pools and fountains and statues from ancient Greece and Moorish Spain. It has 165 rooms in four houses, all of them furnished with Italian and Spanish antiques and enhanced by 41 fireplaces and 61 bathrooms. There's a lavish private chapel and numerous entertainment rooms.

Hearst was a compulsive shopper of Europe's artistic glories, hoovering up artifacts, whole rooms and even entire monasteries, which his architect Julia Morgan artfully integrated into the whole.

Fortunately the entire complex is a state park which keeps excesses of crass commercialism to a minimum. Still you might want to try to bribe someone so you can take a dip in the stunning Neptune Pool.

Information

To see anything of **Hearst Castle** (☎ general information 805-927-2020, reservations 800-444-4445; www.hearstcastle.com), you will need to take a tour. For most of the year you will absolutely need reservations for these tours. In the peak summer months you'll need these a week or more in advance.

Tours start daily at 8:20am, with the last leaving at 3:20pm (sometimes later during summer). The weather can vary between the castle's hilltop location and the visitors center. The gloomy fog at the base can open up to blazing clear sunny skies up top, so dress with plenty of layers.

Getting to Hearst Castle without your own wheels can be a challenge. However San Luis Obispo's RTA (p469) makes two round-trips ($2.50, 90 minutes, Monday to Saturday) between San Luis Obispo (SLO) and the visitors center via Morro Bay and Cambria.

Tours

There are four **tours** (per tour adult/child $24/12 May-Sep, $20/10 Oct-Apr). For each you depart from the large and accommodating visitors center and make the 10-minute bus ride up the hill. No matter how many tours you go on you have to make the journey up and down each time, but the views are great and each time you'll see something new. The surrounding terrain is largely unspoiled and gives a feeling for California before the Europeans arrived. Each of the tours lasts about 1¾ hours.

It's best to start with **Tour 1**, aka the 'Experience Tour', as you get an overview of the estate and a chance to see a film about Hearst's life. This answers all the basic questions and prepares you to delve deeper. Unless you have just a passing interest in the castle, you'll likely be sucked into wanting to take more tours.

Tours 2, 3 and **4** are much less crowded than the Experience Tour and let you have more time talking with the professional guides, who love thoughtful and unusual questions. It is possible to do all four tours in one day, but this could leave you feeling like you carried one of the art treasures up the hill yourself. It's better to split your visit over two days. This gives you time for the good and free museum in the visitors center and allows you to explore some of Cambria to the south and the elephant seals to the north.

Splitting your visit also means you can have an enjoyable lunch. Facilities at the visitors center (there's no eating or drinking up the hill) are geared for industrial-sized mobs of visitors and are poor at best. It's better to get a picnic lunch in Cambria and enjoy it at the state beach across from the entrance to the visitors center.

Before you leave, take a moment to visit the often-overlooked museum area in the far back of the visitors center: it's worth it.

SAN SIMEON STATE PARK

This **park** (☎ 805-927-2035) embraces the **San Simeon Natural Preserve**, a popular wintering spot for monarch butterflies, and the **Pânu Cultural Preserve**, the site of archeological finds dating back 6000 years. A 3-mile trail meanders through the park, which is fringed by a long sandy beach. Camping is available at the 134-site **San Simeon Creek Campground** (☎ reservations 800-444-7275; www.parks.ca.gov; sites $20-25) with hot showers and flush toilets, and the undeveloped **Washburn Campground** (sites $11-15), with 60 sites, which are allocated on a first-come, first-served basis.

CAMBRIA

pop 5600

Cambria is a cute village that comes in three parts: the historic center a half-mile off Hwy 1 with cafés, bars, shops and restaurants along Main St; the newer center often called 'Cambria West', also on Main St but right off Hwy 1, which has more touristy shops and (surprise!) lots of real estate agents; and the motel-lined **Moonstone Beach** on a nice stretch of oceanfront. The first has the best nightlife, the last has good romantic walks along the rugged shore. It's named for the opalescent stones once abundant here.

For information, drop in at the **chamber of commerce** (☎ 805-927-3624; www.cambriachamber .org; 767 Main St; ✆ 9am-5pm Mon-Fri, noon-4pm Sat & Sun) in Cambria West.

Fans of the crazy and curious should make a beeline for **Nit Wit Ridge** (☎ 805-927-2690; 881 Hillcrest Dr; tours adult/child $10/5), a three-level house built entirely out of recycled materials – abalone shells to beer cans, tiles to toilet seats. This 'palace of junk' is the creation of one Arthur Harold Beal (aka Captain Nit Wit, aka Der Tinkerpaw) and was hand-built by him over a period of 51 years. Call to arrange tours.

South of Cambria, off Hwy 1, minuscule **Harmony** is a quirky slice of Americana. It consists of an old creamery housing artists' workshops and deserves a quick browse.

Sleeping & Eating

Cambria's choicest lodgings are along Moonstone Beach Dr, although they are quite strung out. The many choices in the historic center can be more affordable and you can walk to restaurants and bars.

Bluebird Inn (☎ 805-927-4634, 800-552-5434; www .bluebirdmotel.com; 1880 Main St; r $50-200; ⊠ 🖳) With a peaceful and fragrant garden overlooking a creek, the Bluebird has 46 artfully decorated rooms (complete with highspeed Internet), including some with a fireplace and private terrace or balcony.

Bridge Street Inn (☎ 805-927-7653; www.bridge streetinncambria.com; 4314 Bridge St; dm $20, r $40-70) This 1895 B&B cum hostel has character, charm and comfort at a great price. Breakfast is included as is use of the communal kitchen and parking. It's small, so reserve.

Cambria Shores Inn (☎ 805-927-8644, 800-433-9179; www.cambriashores.com; 6276 Moonstone Beach Dr; r $105-180; 🖳) The 24-room Cambria Shores looks like a motel but comes with B&B-type amenities such as fancy in-room breakfasts and an appetizer hour. Pets are pampered.

San Simeon Pines Seaside Resort (☎ 805-927-4648; www.sspines.com; 7200 Moonstone Beach Dr; r $100-180; ⊠ 🖳 🐕) At the northern end of the beach, this 58-room resort has woodsy rooms and that family vacation favorite: shuffleboard.

Robin's (☎ 805-927-5007; 4095 Burton Dr; meals $9-30) The finest place to eat locally, Robin's has been whipping up innovative cuisine using local ingredients for more than 20 years. The wine list celebrates the Central Coast. Dine inside, out in the lush garden or get something exquisite to go from the deli counter.

Wild Ginger (☎ 805-927-1001; 2380 Main St; meals $10-20; ✆ lunch & dinner Fri-Wed) This bright and cheery newcomer serves up fresh Asian fare that is perfectly seasoned and presented.

Linn's (☎ 805-927-0371; 2277 Main St; dishes $8-20; ✆ breakfast & lunch Mon-Sat, dinner daily) Linn's is a casual eatery famous for pot pies (and does a huge mail-order business in these), but the menu has many more offerings. The chef grows the berries used in the outlandish desserts.

Moonstone Beach Bar & Grill (☎ 805-927-3859; 6550 Moonstone Beach Dr; mains $20-25) The place that answers the question: 'Where can I go get a drink outside and watch the sun set over the Pacific?' The long menu features sandwiches, steaks and seafood.

ESTERO BAY

Estero Bay is a long, shallow, west-facing bay with Cayucos at its northern end and Montaña de Oro State Park at its southern end. Morro Bay, a deep inlet guarded by Morro Rock and separated from the ocean by a 12-mile-long sand spit, sits about halfway between the two and has most of Estero Bay's services and tourist activity. Morro Rock is the bay's unmistakable landmark, used as a navigation marker since the Portolá expedition in 1769.

San Luis Obispo's RTA (p469) bus 12 ($1 to $2.50, hourly 7am to 7pm, Monday to Saturday) travels up Hwy 1 from San Luis Obispo with stops in Los Osos and Morro Bay. Two runs every day continue on to Cayucos, Cambria and San Simeon. Fares vary by distance.

Cayucos
pop 3500

At the bay's northern end, small and slow-paced Cayucos (ki-*you*-kiss) preserves the look and feel of an old Western town. It's entering the modern age, however, as grand new homes front the broad white beach. The town is somewhat spread out but the compact center has a mix of antique stores and seafood shacks.

The town developed around the mouth of Cayucos Creek and a wharf and warehouse built by Captain James Cass in 1867. Ocean Ave, which parallels Hwy 1, is the main thoroughfare with historic store-fronts and most of the hotels and restaurants. At the town's northern end is the long pier, built in 1875, from which you can fish.

Cayucos' gentle waves are good for beginner surfers. **Cayucos Surf Company** (☎ 805-995-1000; 95 Cayucos Dr; ☇ 10am-6pm), just a few steps north of the pier, sells and rents surfboards (half-day $12) as well as wetsuits and boogie boards. Lessons are available.

Just half a block from the beach, **Tide Water Inn** (☎ 805-995-3670, 800-965-2699; www.tidewaterinn cayucos.com; 20 S Ocean Ave; r $55-150; ✗ ▣) is a

well-run, six-unit place with spacious rooms sporting flowery decor.

The sea-foam-green **Cayucos Pierpointe Inn** (☎ 805-995-3200; www.pierpointeinn.com; 181 Ocean Ave; r $100-300; ✗ ▣) matches the color of the surf right outside the door. Many of the rooms overlook the surf and pier, all have whirlpools, DVD-players and other luxuries.

Unpretentious, funky and eccentric, the **Sea Shanty** (☎ 805-995-3272; 296 S Ocean Ave; meals $6-20; ☇ breakfast, lunch & dinner) will quickly be your favorite place on the bay. Hang out in a booth or outside on the patio and enjoy excellent omelettes, burgers and fresh seafood. Banana Bama leads the line-up of killer desserts.

Hoppe's Garden Bistro (☎ 805-995-1006; 78 N Ocean Ave; mains $12-25; ☇ dinner Wed-Sun) features fresh seafood on its ambitious, seasonal menu. The wine list is long and you can have a elegant meal in the garden with the muted sound of the surf in the distance.

Morro Bay
pop 10,400

Still home to a large commercial fishing fleet, the biggest claim to fame of Morro Bay is its namesake Morro Rock, a 578ft peak that juts dramatically from the ocean floor just offshore. It's part of a chain of nine such volcanic rocks stretching between here and San Luis Obispo, which formed some 21 million years ago. Community action saved it from being pulverized into asphalt for strip malls.

Such action was too late, however, to save the town from a power plant's trio of cigarette-shaped smokestacks at the bay's northern end or the nuclear power plant a few miles to the south.

The bay itself is a giant estuary inhabited by two dozen threatened and endangered species, including the brown pelican, sea otter and steelhead trout. Morro Rock is home to peregrine falcons. In winter, about 120 migratory bird species make the bay their home.

Leading south from Morro Rock is the **Embarcadero**, a small waterfront boulevard lined with touristy shops and restaurants. It's the launching area for boat tours and the main stage of the popular Morro Bay Harbor Festival in October. The **chamber of commerce** (☎ 805-772-4467; www.morrobay.com; 845 Embarcadero; ☇ 10am-4pm Mon-Sat, 11am-3pm Sun) offers useful advice from its spot on the harbor.

CENTRAL COAST

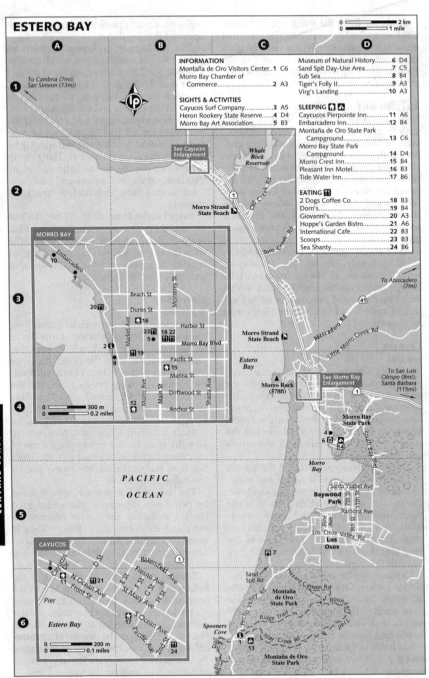

ESTERO BAY

0 —— 2 km
0 —— 1 mile

INFORMATION
Montaña de Oro Visitors Center..**1** C6
Morro Bay Chamber of
   Commerce............................**2** A3

SIGHTS & ACTIVITIES
Cayucos Surf Company.............**3** A5
Heron Rookery State Reserve......**4** D4
Morro Bay Art Association..........**5** B3

Museum of Natural History.........**6** D4
Sand Spit Day-Use Area............**7** C5
Sub Sea...................................**8** B4
Tiger's Folly II..........................**9** A3
Virg's Landing.........................**10** A3

SLEEPING 🏠 ⛺
Caycucos Pierpointe Inn...........**11** A6
Embarcadero Inn......................**12** B4
Montaña de Oro State Park
   Campground........................**13** C6
Morro Bay State Park
   Campground........................**14** D4
Morro Crest Inn.......................**15** B4
Pleasant Inn Motel....................**16** B3
Tide Water Inn........................**17** B6

EATING 🍴
2 Dogs Coffee Co....................**18** B3
Dorn's...................................**19** B4
Giovanni's..............................**20** A3
Hoppe's Garden Bistro..............**21** A6
International Cafe......................**22** B3
Scoops..................................**23** B3
Sea Shanty.............................**24** B6

To Cambria (7mi);
San Simeon (13mi)

Whale
Rock
Reservoir

See Cayucos
Enlargement

Old Creek Rd

Morro Strand
State Beach

Toro Creek Rd

To Atascadero
(7mi)

41

Atascadero Rd

Little Morro Creek Rd

MORRO BAY

Embarcadero
10
9

Beach St
Dunes St
20
23 18 22
2 5 •
8 19
Harbor St
Morro Bay Blvd
Pacific St
15
Marina St
Driftwood St
Anchor St

Monterey St
Market Ave
Morro Ave
Main St
Shasta Ave

0 —— 300 m
0 —— 0.2 miles

Morro Strand
State Beach

Estero
Bay

Morro Rock
(578ft)

See Morro Bay
Enlargement

To San Luis
Obispo (8mi);
Santa Barbara
(115mi)

1

Morro Bay
State Park

4 •
6 14

South Bay Blvd

Morro
Bay

Santa Ysabel Ave
Baywood
Park
7th St
11th St
Ramona Ave

Pine Ave

Los Osos Valley Rd
Los
Osos

**PACIFIC
OCEAN**

7

Sand
Spit Rd

Hazard Canyon Rd

Montaña
de Oro
State Park

Pecho Valley Rd

Ridge Trail

Boundary Trail

Islay Creek Rd

Spooners
Cove
1
13

Bluff Trail

Montaña de Oro
State Park

CAYUCOS

3
11

Cayucos Dr
N Ocean Ave
Front St
Pier

Bakersfield Ave
Fresno Ave
St Mary Ave
S Ocean Ave
Pacific Ave

D St
E St
F St
G St
H St
2nd St

21

17

24

Estero Bay

0 —— 200 m
0 —— 0.1 miles

CENTRAL COAST

Three blocks up the hill from the water, the traditional center of town has lured in free-spending sidewalk dawdlers with the ABCs (Antique shops, Boutiques and Curio vendors). These shops have brought life to **Main St** and this is the most interesting part of town. The **Morro Bay Art Association** (☎ 772-2504; 835 Main St; ⊙ noon-3pm) celebrates the burgeoning local arts scene. The fascinating **fishermen and farmers market** (☎ 805-772-4467; Main St near Morro Bay Blvd; ⊙ 3-6pm Sat) draws a crowd.

SIGHTS & ACTIVITIES

The 2700-acre **Morro Bay State Park** incorporates an 18-hole golf course, a marina and kayak rentals and a campground. Also here is the **Museum of Natural History** (☎ 805-772-2694; adult/child $3/1; ⊙ 10am-5pm), which recently underwent a massive expansion. There are 26 interactive exhibits showing how the forces of nature affect us all.

Just north of the museum is a eucalyptus grove that harbors the **Heron Rookery State Reserve**, one of the last remaining great blue heron rookeries in California; from late February to May, you can spot them feeding their young.

The incongruous paddle wheeler **Tiger's Folly II** (☎ 805-772-2257; 1205 Embarcadero; adult/child $12/6; ⊙ May-Sep) makes one-hour trips around the harbor.

For views of kelp forests and schools of fish, take a spin on **Sub Sea** (☎ 805-772-9463; 699 Embarcadero #9; adult/child $14/7; ⊙ May-Oct), a semi-submersible which plies the generally clear waters. You can also rent a kayak or canoe (per two hours $12) to check out the estuary, harbor and bay. Other places on the Embarcadero rent at similar rates.

Salty dogs ready to try sportfishing could book a trip with **Virg's Landing** (☎ 805-772-1222; 1215 Embarcadero; trips from $40). Trips include ones for rockfish and tuna. Virg's sells the required licenses.

SLEEPING

Motels cluster along Main and Harbor Sts. Rates drop in the off season, but make reservations in summer and for the Harbor Festival.

Pleasant Inn Motel (☎ 805-772-8521; www.pleasantinnmotel.com; 235 Harbor St; r $50-110; ✗) This is a flower-festooned place with 10 posy-patterned rooms, some with kitchens. Pets are welcome.

Morro Crest Inn (☎ 805-772-7740; www.morrocrestinn.com; 670 Main St; r $35-215) Some rooms have water views at this relaxed 17-room place near downtown. Rooms are large and some have refrigerators. There are similar properties nearby.

Embarcadero Inn (☎ 805-772-2700; www.embarcaderoinn.com; 456 Embarcadero; r $110-175; 🖳) Most of the large rooms have balconies with views of the rock and all feature upscale bathrooms, VCRs and refrigerators. Some also have gas fireplaces. You can hear the gentle clank-clank of boats in the harbor across the way.

Morro Bay State Park Campground (☎ 805-772-7434; ☎ reservations 800-444-7275; www.parks.ca.gov; sites $20-34) About 2 miles south of town, there are 117 beautiful sites fringed by eucalyptus and cypress trees here. It has hot water, and trails leading to the beach.

EATING

There are lots of predictable seafood places on the Embarcadero. But there are several good choices downtown.

Giovanni's (☎ 805-772-2255; 1001 Front St; meals $5-12; ⊙ 11am-7pm) This family-run place is a classic California seafood shack in every good sense of the word. Fish right off the boats is cooked a myriad of ways for you to eat on the waterfront deck. Inside there's a market with an amazing selection of smoked fish and other treats.

International Cafe (☎ 805-772-4727; 355 Morro Bay Blvd; meals $10-20; ⊙ lunch & dinner Wed-Sun) The largely French menu at this bright café has numerous global accents. Choose from crepes, sandwiches, steaks and more. Lots of local wines by the glass.

Dorn's (☎ 805-772-4415; 801 Market Ave; meals $10-25; ⊙ breakfast, lunch & dinner) Going strong since 1942, Dorn's (like a thousand other coastal places) is famous for its clam chowder. But it excels at fresh fish and has a good local wine list. It sits up the hill from the water.

2 Dogs' Coffee Co (☎ 805-927-7650; 844 Main St; snacks $2; ⊙ 6am-10pm; 🖳) This little place exudes the mellow vibe of the new generation of creative types that have discovered Morro Bay. Lots of tasty baked goods.

Scoops (☎ 805-772-3663; 857 Main St; shakes $3.75; ⊙ 11:30am-6pm Tue-Sun) This vintage ice-cream parlor does it right: real banana or strawberry milkshakes are just some of the scrumptious delights here.

Montaña de Oro State Park

About 6 miles southwest of Morro Bay, Montaña de Oro State Park covers about 8000 acres of undeveloped mountain and seaside terrain. Its coastal bluffs are a favorite spot for hiking, mountain-biking and horseback riding. The northern half of the park includes a row of sand dunes (some 85ft high) and the 4-mile-long sand spit that separates Morro Bay from the Pacific. The park's southern section consists of finger-like bluffs and an ancient marine terrace, which after seismic uplifting is now a series of 1000ft peaks. In spring the hills are blanketed by bright poppies, wild mustard and other wildflowers that give the park its name, meaning 'mountain of gold' in Spanish.

The park's **visitors center** (☎ 805-528-0513; ۝ 11am-3pm), a gorgeous 3 miles south of the park boundary, has an interpretive garden and serves as the ranger station and natural history museum. It sits right above **Spooners Cove**, once used by smugglers and now a beautiful sandy beach and picnic area. Several **hiking trails**, including the Bluff Trail, which skirts the cliffs and has beach access points, start from here. To get to the sand dunes, turn off onto Sand Spit Rd from the main park road to the **Sand Spit day-use area**, about 1.8 miles north of the visitors center.

Near the visitors center is the lovely and primitive **Montaña de Oro State Park Campground** (☎ 805-528-0513; reservations 800-444-7275; www.parks.ca.gov; sites $11-15) with 50 sites, each near the creek or against the hillside. Fees include use of picnic tables, fire rings, pit toilets and drinking water. There are more-remote walk-in sites further into the park.

The park is about 7 miles from Hwy 1. Exit at South Bay Blvd and follow the signs, which will lead you through the towns of Los Osos and Baywood Park.

SAN LUIS OBISPO

pop 43,700

San Luis Obispo (SLO; sun loo-*iss* obispo), inland from the coast, is a lively yet low-key town with a high quality of life and vibrant community spirit. Many people find its balance of urban pleasures and relaxed rural charm an ideal balance.

Like so many California cities, it grew up around a mission founded in 1772 by Padre Serra, which is still an active parish today. SLO is also home to the California Polytechnic State University (Cal Poly), which is renowned for its 'learning by doing' approach to education. Its 17,000 students inject a healthy dose of hubbub into city streets, pubs and cafés during the school year.

Thursday is a good day to visit SLO, when the famous **farmers market** (۝ 5-9pm) turns Higuera St near Mission Plaza, the main drag, and adjacent lanes into a giant street party. Barbecues belching smoke, strolling families and live music and entertainment make this one of the liveliest evenings you'll have anywhere in California.

SLO's reasonably priced accommodations and proximity to beaches, state parks and Hearst Castle (45 miles north on Hwy 1) make it a good Central Coast inland hub. It has long been a favorite stop-off for people making the journey between San Francisco and LA.

Orientation

SLO's compact downtown is bisected by the main commercial arteries of Higuera St, which travels one way going southwest, and Marsh St, parallel to Higuera St, running one way northeast. San Luis Obispo Creek, once used to irrigate mission orchards, flows through downtown parallel to Higuera St.

Information

Banks are along Higuera and Marsh Sts, near the main post office.

Chamber of commerce (☎ 805-781-2777; www.visitslo .com; 1039 Chorro St; ۝ 10am-5pm Sun-Wed, 10am-7pm Thu-Sat) Has plenty of free printed matter. You can use the free telephone to check for room availability at local hotels and motels.

Main post office (☎ 805-541-3062; cnr Marsh & Morro Sts)

Novel Experience (☎ 805-544-0150; 779 Higuera St) A small but good locally owned bookstore with many books and maps on the area.

SLO County General Hospital (☎ 805-781-4800; 2180 Johnson Ave; ۝ 24hr) Half a mile southeast of Monterey St.

Sights & Activities

SLO's attractions cluster around **Mission Plaza**, a shady oasis with restored adobes and fountains overlooking San Luis Obispo Creek, right in the heart of downtown.

The plaza is lorded over by the **Mission San Luis Obispo de Tolosa** (☎ 805-543-6850; museum suggested donation $2; ۝ 9am-5pm Apr-Oct, 9am-4pm Nov-Mar) on Monterey St between Chorro and

Broad Sts. The fifth of the California missions, it was established in 1772 and named for a French saint. Often called the 'Prince of the Missions,' its still-active church has an unusual L-shape with a flat open-beam ceiling and whitewashed walls decorated with the Stations of the Cross. An adjacent building contains an old-fashioned museum

about daily life during the Chumash and mission periods.

For a comprehensive survey of local history, check out the **San Luis Obispo County Historical Museum** (☎ 805-543-0638; 696 Monterey St; admission free; �},10am-4pm Wed-Sun), just southwest of the mission. It's housed in the 1905 Carnegie Library, an imposing stone structure.

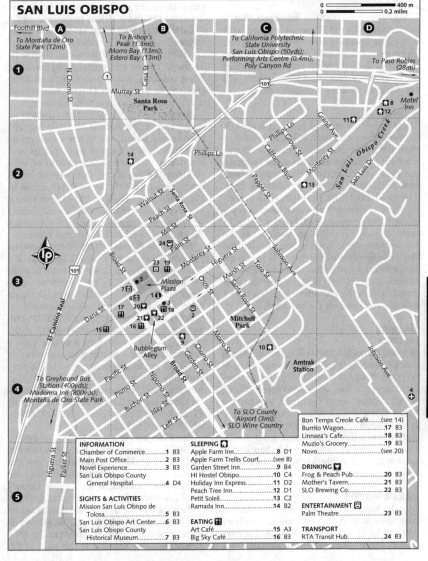

SAN LUIS OBISPO

INFORMATION
Chamber of Commerce.............**1** B3
Main Post Office.....................**2** B3
Novel Experience.....................**3** B3
San Luis Obispo County
 General Hospital.................**4** D4

SIGHTS & ACTIVITIES
Mission San Luis Obispo de
 Tolosa.............................**5** B3
San Luis Obispo Art Center.....**6** B3
San Luis Obispo County
 Historical Museum.............**7** B3

SLEEPING
Apple Farm Inn......................**8** D1
Apple Farm Trellis Court......(see 8)
Garden Street Inn..................**9** B4
HI Hostel Obispo.................**10** C4
Holiday Inn Express.............**11** D2
Peach Tree Inn....................**12** D1
Petit Soleil........................**13** C2
Ramada Inn.......................**14** B2

EATING
Art Café............................**15** A3
Big Sky Café......................**16** B3

Bon Temps Creole Café.......(see 14)
Burrito Wagon....................**17** B3
Linnaea's Cafe....................**18** B3
Muzio's Grocery..................**19** B3
Novo..............................(see 20)

DRINKING
Frog & Peach Pub................**20** B3
Mother's Tavern..................**21** B3
SLO Brewing Co..................**22** B3

ENTERTAINMENT
Palm Theatre......................**23** B3

TRANSPORT
RTA Transit Hub..................**24** B3

CENTRAL COAST

Strolling the downtown you will see a plethora of buildings dating from the 1800s.

Mission Plaza is bounded by the gentle San Luis Obispo Creek, which is lined with public art and is a nice spot for respite or a picnic. It leads straight to the **San Luis Obispo Art Center** (☎ 805-543-8562; 1010 Broad St; admission free; ☣ 11am-5pm Wed-Mon), a showcase for local artists as well as visiting exhibits from around California.

SLO's weirdest sight is **Bubblegum Alley**, a narrow walkway off Higuera blanketed with thousands of wads of discarded chewing gum. The origin of this local fetish may be murky, but fans will say the result embodies a certain impressionist artistic flair while others will say it simply makes a bad impression.

HIKING
There are plenty of good hikes around SLO, many of which start from Poly Canyon Rd on the Cal Poly campus. Hiking maps and parking information are available at the booth on the right as you enter the campus. **Bishop's Peak** (1559ft) is another popular day hike. The trail (about 2.5 miles) starts in a beautiful grove of live oaks and then heads steeply along rocky, exposed switchbacks, home to many lizards. Scramble up boulders at the top for panoramic views of San Luis Obispo Bay and the surrounding ranch land. To get to the hike, go northwest from downtown on Santa Rosa St (Hwy 1) for 1.5 miles, turn west onto Highland Dr and after a little less than 1 mile the road ends at the trailhead.

Sleeping
HOSTELS
HI Hostel Obispo (☎ 805-544-4678; www.hostelobispo .com; 1617 Santa Rosa St; dm $18-20, private r $45-60; check-in ☣ 7:30-10am & 4:30-10pm; 🖳) On a lovely tree-lined street is this avocado-colored hostel, a well-kept 20-room facility in a converted Victorian, which gives it a bit of a B&B feel. It's a one-minute walk from the Amtrak station and a five-minute walk from downtown. Amenities include a kitchen and a garden patio. For breakfast, there are often sourdough pancakes.

B&BS & MOTELS
Motels cluster along the northeastern end of Monterey St near Hwy 101 and at the Hwy 101 exit for Hwy 1 at Santa Rosa St. Tourism history buffs (all three of you) should check

out the shell of the Motel Inn, the world's very first motel right where Monterey St crosses Hwy 101.

Petit Soleil (☎ 805-549-0321; www.psslo.com; 1473 Monterey St; r $130-190; ✗ ✗) What a find! This French-themed 15-room charmer is run like a fine European B&B – which means plenty of comfort yet a minimum of Laura Ashley. The colors are as bright as Provence and you can soak up the sun on the patio. Breakfasts are exquisite and it's close to downtown.

Garden Street Inn (☎ 805-545-9802; www.garden streetinn.com; 1212 Garden St; r $145-210; ✗ ✗ 🖳) A carefully restored 1887 Victorian B&B with 13 theme rooms and suites. A big breakfast is served in a stylish room with original stained-glass windows. This is a relaxed and comfortable place close to downtown.

Madonna Inn (☎ 805-543-3000, 800-543-9666; www .madonnainn.com; 100 Madonna Rd; r $140-300; ✗) 'Goodness!' is but one of the more printable exclamations heard from guests and visitors at this bizarre fantasyland of wild and over-the-top décor, southwest of downtown. Don't miss (!) the waterfall urinal in the men's restroom. The 109 unique rooms are decorated in equally flamboyant themes including the Caveman Room, the Austrian Room, the Love Birds Room and more.

Holiday Inn Express (☎ 805-544-8600; www.hiex press.com; 1800 Monterey St; r $100-230; ✗ ✗ 🖳 🖳) This large 99-room modern motel is good for extended stays as the rooms are spacious and most have kitchenettes. There's a simple breakfast served in the morning.

Apple Farm Inn (☎ 805-544-2040, 800-374-3705; www.applefarm.com; 2015 Monterey St; r $150-400; ✗ ✗ 🖳 🖳) Pay your nightly fee and you've bought the farm – well at least one room of it. Grand gardens spread across this flowery and frilly 69-room motel near Hwy 101 that features a mill with water wheel. More modest rooms are available at the attached Apple Farm Trellis Court (rooms $80 to $240), which shares facilities.

Peach Tree Inn (☎ 805-543-3170, 800-227-6396; fax 805-543-7673; www.peachtreeinn.com; 2001 Monterey St; r $50-150; ✗ ✗ 🖳) Friendly and folksy, the 37 rooms here are quite nice and many are set right on the creek. Rates include a hearty breakfast with homemade breads.

Ramada Inn (☎ 805-544-2800; www.ramadainn .com; 1000 Olive St; r $70-200; ✗ ✗ 🖳 🖳) Grouped with some other modest motels at the Hwy 1 junction, the Ramada is the pick of the bunch for its 60 comfortable and well-equipped rooms. Some have kitchenettes. The restaurant, Bon Temps Creole Cafe, is a local fave.

Eating

SLO has a good range of restaurants, many using locally grown bounty.

Big Sky Cafe (☎ 805-545-5401; 1121 Broad St; meals $8-14; ☺ breakfast, lunch & dinner) A hip and friendly spot which serves global cuisine with a Southwestern bent. Breakfasts are excellent as are the sandwiches. Many love the noodle bowls. The lofty dining room is a good place for a creative coffee or a glass of wine.

Art Cafe (☎ 805-788-0330; 570 Higuera St; meals $6-20; ☺ breakfast & lunch daily, dinner Fri & Sat) Many of the good smells at this cute place come from the in-house bakery that produces treats such as spice white pepperjack bread and famous muffins. Salads, omelettes, sandwiches, steaks and such at night complete the menu. Art by patrons adorns the walls.

Novo (☎ 805-543-3986; 726 Higuera St; mains $10-25) Most of this popular place revolves around the multiple decks over-looking the creek. The fabulous atmosphere is complemented by the extensive menu of fresh Mediterranean fare. You can savor the view with a glass of wine and tapas.

Bon Temps Creole Cafe (☎ 805-544-2100; 1000 Olive St; meals $7-14; ☺ breakfast, lunch, dinner Wed-Sun) Perfectly placed for hungry road-trippers, this locally loved café is the real deal with a long list of New Orleans classics from po boys to shrimp Creole. Locally owned, it's in the Ramada Inn.

Linnaea's Cafe (☎ 805-541-5888; 1110 Garden St; meals $5-7; ☺ breakfast, lunch & dinner; ☐) A local institution, the short menu at this coffeehouse changes daily. The food is always spot-on fresh and at times whimsical (eg 'waffle night'). There's a good garden out back, wi-fi too.

Burrito Wagon (☎ 805-549-9966; 1024 Nipomo St; meals $4-7; ☺ lunch Mon-Sat) There's nothing mysterious about the menu at this friendly little place. Enjoy a superb burrito on the creekside patio.

Muzio's Grocery (☎ 805-543-0800; 870 Monterey St; sandwiches $6-8; ☺ 9am-6pm Mon-Sat) A classic old Italian deli that serves up tasty sandwiches you can enjoy in the shade of Mission Plaza.

Drinking

SLO Brewing Co (☎ 805-543-1843; 1119 Garden St) A popular brewpub whose homemade beers go well with the burgers, barbecue and grilled seafood served upstairs (meals $6 to $10) for lunch Wednesday to Sunday and dinner Tuesday to Sunday. Downstairs there's billiards and live music and deejays.

Frog & Peach Pub (☎ 805-595-3764; 728 Higuera St) This drinking spot wears the patina – and smell – of an old boozer with pride. Come for a pint of ale, a game of darts or the live music from reggae to rock.

Mother's Tavern (☎ 805-541-3853; 729 Higuera St; pub meals $6-20) An upscale pub that draws in the vaguely refined masses with good pub burgers, nachos and more plus frequent live music that include 'Big Band Sundays'.

Entertainment

Palm Theatre (☎ 805-541-5161; 817 Palm St; admission $7, Mon $5) An old-style independent movie house showing foreign and indie films.

Performing Arts Center (PAC; ☎ 805-756-2787; www.pacslo.org; 1 Grand Ave) This state-of-the-art facility, on the Cal Poly campus, is the town's main cultural venue and presents an eclectic schedule of concerts, theater, dance and other events.

Getting There & Around

The small **SLO County Airport** (SBP; ☎ 805-541-1038), 3 miles south of downtown between Hwy 1/101 and Broad St, is served by America West (Phoenix), American Eagle (Los Angeles) and United Express (LA & San Francisco).

Greyhound (☎ 805-543-2121; 150 South St) runs daily buses to Los Angeles ($27, five hours) via Santa Barbara ($18, two hours), and to San Francisco ($45, seven hours).

Amtrak (1011 Railroad Ave) has good train service at SLO. The *Pacific Surfliner* regional train serves Santa Barbara, Los Angeles and San Diego. The Seattle–LA *Coast Starlight* stops at SLO daily. There are several daily buses that link to regional trains in Santa Barbara and San Jose.

San Luis Obispo's **Regional Transit Authority** (RTA; ☎ 805-541-2228; www.slorta.org; fares $1-2.50) operates buses daily except Sunday across the region, including Paso Robles, San Simeon, Cambria, Morro Bay and the bay cities including Pismo Beach. Lines converge on the **transit hub** (cnr Palm & Osos Sts).

SAN LUIS OBISPO BAY

This broad bay is home to a string of laid-back, little beach towns: Avila, Shell Beach, Pismo Beach, Grover Beach and Oceano. The main industry here is tourism and there's plenty of opportunity for outdoor recreation, including fishing, bicycling, swimming and even clamming. If you're looking for a sandy respite from your trip, this is a good spot to break the journey.

San Luis Obispo's RTA operates buses from SLO to the bay cities including Pismo Beach. It also runs local buses for the acronym-challenged **South County Area Transit** (SCAT; ☎ 805-781-4472; www.scattransit.org; fare $1) that links all five bay towns.

Hwy 1 ends its brief relationship with Hwy 101 that began in SLO just south of Pismo Beach as it veers off to stay near the coast.

Avila Beach
pop 1250

Avila Beach has definitely had its ups and downs. In the late 1980s it was discovered that the soil under the town was massively contaminated with a toxic soup of petroleum products. For decades pipes from the nearby Unocal refinery and port (you can still see the pier) had been leaking into the soil. In 1999 Unocal began a legal settlement that involved tearing down the town and carting off the beach.

Today this nightmare is finally ending for the residents. There's a freshly built sea-front commercial district and new sand on the beaches. The question is: 'Will the crowds who once flocked here return?' Time will tell. In the meantime, it has a great old fishing pier and hot springs to delight you.

About 1 mile north of the new center is **Port San Luis**, a working fishing harbor. Enjoy panoramic bay views from the most authentic fishing pier on the coast, **Harford Pier**. It's home to an excellent fish restaurant, the **Olde Port Inn** (☎ 805-595-2515; mains $6-26). Its clam chowder and cioppino are standouts, and you can enjoy the views or watch the chefs hard at work in the open kitchen.

The pier is also home to fish markets that sell rockfish, sole, salmon or anything else right off the boats. If you'd like to try your own luck, **Patriot Sportfishing** (Hartford Pier; ☎ 805-595-7200; www.patriotsportfishing.com) rents out rods and tackle ($7) and leads deep-sea fishing trips.

Just south of Avila Beach, **Cave Landing** is a 150ft promontory that was used as a dock for large ships in the early 1900s. A rocky trail from the parking lot's southern end leads down to the cave and to **Pirate's Cove**, a beautiful sandy beach where clothing is optional and personal caution is urged.

In town, the **Inn at Avila Beach** (☎ 805-595-2300; www.avilabeachca.com; 256 Front St; r $80-200; ✗) has a cheerful mix of Mediterranean and Mexican styles, with vibrant colors, lots of hand-painted tiles, wrought iron and wood. There's a fun roof deck with good views and hammocks. Rooms span the gamut, so shop and compare.

The road out to Avila from Hwy 1/101, follows a lovely sycamore- and maple-lined glen. Along here at the amazing **Sycamore Mineral Springs Resort** (☎ 805-595-7302; www.sycamoresprings.com; 1215 Avila Beach Dr; r $165-330; ✗ ✗ ⌨ ⌨) guests melt away tensions in private hot mineral spas. The compound sprawls amongst gardens and hills and the rooms are luxurious. There is a good program of daily hikes in the surrounding countryside. **Gardens of Avila** (☎ 805-595-7365; meals $8-30), the resort's sophisticated restaurant, serves Pacific Rim cuisine best enjoyed on the lush rock-walled patio.

Even if you're not staying at the resort, you can treat yourself to a spa or a luxuriant soak in one of 20 private redwood **hot tubs** (per hr $20; ⏲ 24hr), discreetly scattered over a woodsy hillside.

Plebeians will enjoy the communal pool at the nearby **Avila Valley Hot Springs** (☎ 805-595-2359; 250 Avila Beach Dr; adult/child $8/6.50; ⏲ 8am-8pm), in operation since 1907. The adjacent **campground** (sites $30-45) has flush toilets, hot showers and hookups.

Shell Beach

Shell Beach is a residential community, which winds along the coast north of Pismo Beach. Businesses, including large motels, stretch along Shell Beach Rd. Ocean Blvd, lined with a grass parkway and picnic tables, gives access to the rocky beach with teeming tidepools.

Pismo Beach
pop 8200

Pismo Beach, the largest of the bay towns, is a conglomeration of tourist shops and cafés around Pismo Pier, on a wide sandy beach. The town is still called the 'Clam Capital

CENTRAL COAST

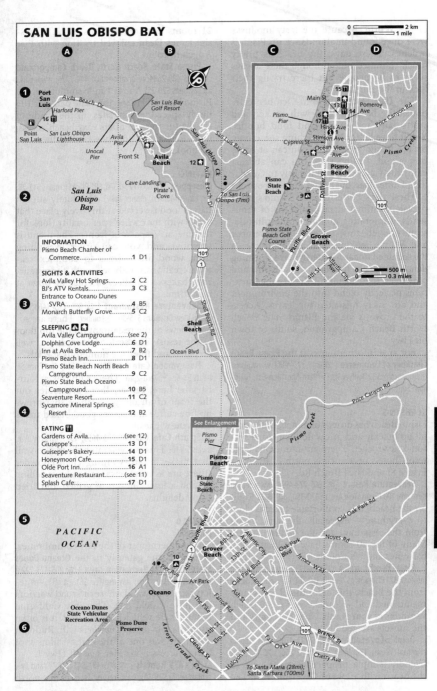

SAN LUIS OBISPO BAY

0 ——— 2 km
0 ——— 1 mile

INFORMATION
Pismo Beach Chamber of
   Commerce..............................**1** D1

SIGHTS & ACTIVITIES
Avila Valley Hot Springs...........**2** C2
BJ's ATV Rentals.......................**3** C3
Entrance to Oceano Dunes
   SVRA......................................**4** B5
Monarch Butterfly Grove.........**5** C2

SLEEPING
Avila Valley Campground........(see 2)
Dolphin Cove Lodge.................**6** D1
Inn at Avila Beach....................**7** B2
Pismo Beach Inn.......................**8** D1
Pismo State Beach North Beach
   Campground............................**9** C2
Pismo State Beach Oceano
   Campground...........................**10** B5
Seaventure Resort....................**11** C2
Sycamore Mineral Springs
   Resort...................................**12** B2

EATING
Gardens of Avila.....................(see 12)
Giuseppe's................................**13** D1
Guiseppe's Bakery....................**14** D1
Honeymoon Cafe......................**15** D1
Olde Port Inn...........................**16** A1
Seaventure Restaurant...........(see 11)
Splash Cafe..............................**17** D1

See Enlargement

0 ——— 500 m
0 ——— 0.3 miles

CENTRAL COAST

of the World' because the tasty mollusks were once found in abundance on Pismo's beaches. These days, the beach is pretty much clammed out, although there always seem to be people out there trying their luck in the muck.

The **Clam Festival** in mid-October celebrates the beloved clam with an arts and crafts fair, and music and food booths. You'll have better luck catching something off the Pismo Pier where you can at times rent a rod. Failing this, you can at least enjoy the views south all the way to Guadalupe Dunes (see the boxed text, opposite).

These days butterflies are Pismo's most prevalent animal attraction. Tens of thousands of migrating monarch butterflies descend upon the town between late November and March, making their winter home in the secluded **Monarch Butterfly Grove**. Forming dense clusters in the tops of eucalyptus and pine trees, these beautiful, dark orange creatures perfectly blend into the environment and are easily mistaken for leaves. Access to the grove is via the Pismo State Beach North Beach Campground, south of town off Hwy 1.

For area information visit the **Pismo Beach Chamber of Commerce** (☎ 805-773-4382; www.pismo chamber.com; 581 Dolliver St; ☺ 9am-5pm Mon-Sat, 10am-4pm Sun).

SLEEPING
Pismo Beach has dozens of motels, but rooms fill up quickly and prices do their usual seasonal sky-rocket. There are numerous large resort hotels on the cliffs north of town on Prince St and Shell Beach Rd.

Seaventure Resort (☎ 805-773-4994; www.seaven ture.com; 100 Ocean View Ave; r $120-350; ☐ ☒) Right on the beach, this comfortable place is close to everything – especially the surf. Views from the restaurant and the bar are superb. Many of the 50 rooms have thrilling vistas, balconies and whirlpools.

Pismo Beach Inn (☎ 805-773-1234; www.pismobeach inn.com; 371 Pismo St; r $70-180; ☒ ☐) Three blocks from the beach, this older motel is lovingly maintained and will make you recall beach vacations of your youth. Units are comfy and the sunsets are good.

Dolphin Cove Lodge (☎ 805-773-4706; www.dolphin covemotel.com; 170 Main St; r $70-200; ☒) This friendly, simple property is right next to the beach with views of the Pismo Pier. The

21 rooms have refrigerators. A bit of gossip: James Dean enjoyed trysting with Pier Angeli in room 8.

Pismo State Beach North Beach Campground (☎ 805-489-2684, reservations 800-444-7275; www.parks .ca.gov; sites $20-25) About 1 mile south from the Pismo Pier, off Hwy 1, this state park has 103 nicely spaced, grassy sites, in the shade of eucalyptus trees. It offers easy beach access, flush toilets and hot showers but there are no hookups.

EATING
Giuseppe's (☎ 805-773-2870; 891 Price St; mains $12-28; ☺ lunch Mon-Fri, dinner daily) Absolutely superb Italian food is served at this lively place that brims with the owner's personality (look for the line of Vespas out front). The menu is inventive and you can order everything from wood-fired pizzas to complex seasonal creations. One block south, the restaurant's bakery sells slices of amazing pizza at lunchtime.

Seaventure Restaurant (☎ 805-773-3463; 100 Ocean View Dr; mains $15-30; ☺ dinner) There are superb views at the restaurant on the top floor of the resort. The seafood is fresh and well prepared and there are numerous specials.

Honeymoon Cafe (☎ 805-773-5646; 999 Price St; treats $3-6; ☺ 7am-2pm) There's no hokey tourist vibe here; rather, there are tables out the front of an old gas station that brews up fine coffee and serves good baked treats and sandwiches.

Splash Cafe (☎ 805-773-4653; 197 Pomeroy Ave; meals $4-10) This is a veteran hole-in-the-wall that makes award-winning clam chowder (there are as many awards as places selling it) and a long line-up of grilled and fried briny delights.

Oceano
pop 4900
The southernmost of the bay communities, Oceano is the gateway to the **Oceano Dunes State Vehicular Recreation Area** (☎ 805-473-7223; www.ohv.parks.ca.gov; day-use fee $8), a 5½-mile-long stretch of sand where off-road warriors can have a field day. The only California beach where vehicles are allowed, it is often used as a movie set (*The Sheik* with Rudolph Valentino was one of the earliest films shot here). Access is via Pier Ave off Hwy 1.

BJ's ATV Rentals (☎ 805-481-5411; 197 Grand Ave; rentals per hr $25-50), in Grover Beach, just north

---

COMMANDMENTS IN THE DUNES

The mystery of the filming of the silent version of the *Ten Commandments* on the **Guadalupe Dunes** is in itself the stuff of a movie. In 1923 a huge Hollywood crew came to the sands for the filming of the scenes of the Jews in Egypt. Enormous sets were constructed complete with huge sphinxes and more.

After filming was complete, director Cecil B DeMille saved money by leaving the sets in place and simply had them buried in the sand. Over the following decades legends about the lost wonders of Egypt – albeit ones constructed from plaster, hay and paint – were common locally. DeMille himself told an interviewer while he was making his blockbuster 1956 version (the 1923 edition was also a blockbuster) that he worried that archaeologists digging in the dunes 1000 years hence would find an enormous mystery.

Still, knowledge of the exact location of the vast sets was lost and nobody could say for sure where to look in the 16 miles of shifting sands for a trace.

Starting in 1983 a team of film and archaeology buffs began looking for what has become known as the Lost City of DeMille. Numerous artifacts have been found and the location of the main structures pinpointed. Now all that needs to happen is for funds to be found to excavate the enormous sets, which are thought to be in good shape due to the protection of the sand.

You can see some of the recovered pieces and learn more about the project at the excellent **Dunes Center** (☎ 805-343-2455; www.dunescenter.org; 1055 Guadalupe St, Guadalupe; ☷ 10am-4pm Tue-Sun), which has exhibits about the ecology of the dunes as well. You can get loads more information on the excavations from the Lost City Project (www.lostcitydemille.com). The small farming community of Guadalupe is 20 miles south of Pismo Beach on Hwy 1. Entrance to the dunes is about 3 miles west of here.

---

of Oceano, will let you blow your socks off with dune-conquering ATV rentals.

Oceano has several campgrounds. **Pismo State Beach Oceano Campground** (☎ 805-489-2684, reservations 800-444-7275; www.parks.ca.gov; sites $20-34) has 82 sites on nicely kept grounds shaded by eucalyptus trees.

ALONG HIGHWAY 101

Traveling inland along Hwy 101 is a good alternative for people wanting to travel quickly between the Bay Area and Southern California. Although the landscape is not the striking scenery of Hwy 1, this historic road has a beauty of its own: from the fertile fields of Salinas immortalized by Steinbeck to the oak-dappled golden hills to the south. Along the way there are several emotive missions, amazing Pinnacles National Monument and lots of good wineries in and around Paso Robles.

If you are taking Hwy 1 in one direction, you certainly should consider Hwy 101 in the other. From the Bay Area you can reach San Luis Obispo in three hours, but although it takes longer, its worth it. If you don't have wheels you'll probably go this way anyway.

Both Greyhound and Amtrak link the north and the south via Hwy 101, the latter on the spectacular *Coast Starlight*.

GILROY

This Silicon Valley bedroom, 20 miles south of San Jose on Hwy 101, claims to be the garlic capital of the world (although subdivisions have replaced the fields). It celebrates this claim with the over-thronged annual **Gilroy Garlic Festival** (☎ 408-842-1625) on the last full weekend in July. It should be fun but isn't: 125,000 people eating mostly mediocre chow in the blazing sun is not a pretty sight.

Bonfant Gardens (☎ 408-840-7100; www.bonfante gardens.com; adult/child 3-6 $37/27; ☷ 10am-6pm Mon-Thu, 10am-7pm Fri, 10am-8pm Sat & Sun Jul & Aug, shorter daily hours Jun, Sat & Sun only May, Apr, Sep & Oct) is an unusual family theme park with a focus on food and plants rather than cartoon characters, rides that make you barf, or both. Family friendly to the extreme, this is best for folks who love herbs and flowers. Admission includes rides and attractions.

SAN JUAN BAUTISTA

In surprisingly neat San Juan Bautista, California's 15th mission is fronted by the only original Spanish plaza in the state. It's also perched right on the edge of the San Andreas Fault. Some of the climactic scenes in Alfred Hitchcock's *Vertigo* were set here.

San Juan Bautista is on Hwy 156 about 2 miles east of Hwy 101, south of Gilroy on the way to Salinas and Monterey. (South of Hwy 156 on Hwy 101 you pass through the majestic eucalyptus grove that James Stewart and Kim Novak drive through in *Vertigo*.) The town has many attractive old buildings, a few motels and a growing number of good restaurants and cafés along 3rd St. And note: that cock you hear crowing is one of the town's official roosters that are allowed by tradition to roam the streets at will.

Mission San Juan Bautista

The **mission** (☎ 831-623-4528; off 2nd St; donation requested; ☽ 9:30am-4:45pm) was founded in 1797, and construction of its church started in 1803. The church was built with three aisles, but at some point the outer aisles were walled off. They were destroyed in the 1906 earthquake and were not repaired until the 1970s, when the inner archways were opened up to make this the largest of California's mission churches. The bell tower was also added at that time. The climactic bell tower in *Vertigo* is just a special effect. Sorry.

In the Spanish era, the area had a large Native American population and over 4000 are buried in the old **cemetery** beside the mission. The ridge along the north side of the church is the actual line of the San Andreas Fault.

North of the cemetery, a section of the old El Camino Real (King's Highway) can be seen. This Spanish road, built to link the missions, was the state's first. In many places Hwy 101 still follows the original route.

The Plaza & Town

The buildings around the old Spanish plaza are part of **San Juan Bautista State Historic Park** (☎ 831-623-4526; adult/child $2/free; ☽ 10am-4:30pm). The **Plaza Hotel** started life as a single-story adobe building in 1814 and was enlarged and converted into a hotel in 1858. The adjacent **Castro House** was built for José Maria Castro, who led two successful revolts (in 1836 and 1848) against unpopular governors. In 1848, the house was bought by the Breen family, survivors of the Donner Party (see p348). The large blacksmith shop and the **Plaza Stable** hint at San Juan Bautista in

its heyday, when as many as 11 stagecoaches a day passed through. The railroad bypassed the town in 1876, and San Juan Bautista has remained sleepy until recently.

San Juan Bautista is becoming a popular place to visit even as the Bay Area's sprawl appears on the horizon. The result is that interesting cafés and the like are starting to appear; take a stroll down 3rd St.

The Mission-style **Posada de San Juan** (☎ 831-623-4030; 310 Fourth St; r $80-250; ☒) has 34 very atmospheric rooms in the center of town.

SALINAS
pop 152,000

Salinas is the birthplace of John Steinbeck and a major agricultural center whose top crop is the crunchy iceberg lettuce. From May to September, more than six million heads are harvested each day, a feat that's garnered the area the nickname 'the world's salad bowl.' Salinas makes a strong contrast with the conspicuous affluence of Monterey, a mere 17 miles to the west, a fact of life that helped shape Steinbeck's *East of Eden*. Its historic center stretches out along Main St, whose northern end is punctuated by the town's main attraction, the National Steinbeck Center. The addition of a 12-screen multiplex is a sign of a new, thriving downtown.

Pick up information and maps at the **Salinas Visitors Center** (☎ 831-424-7611; www.salinas chamber.com; 119 E Alisal St; ☽ 8:30am-5pm Mon-Fri), four blocks east of Main St.

Seasonal highlights include the huge **California Rodeo Salinas** (☎ 831-775-3100; www.carodeo .com), starting the third Thursday in July and the **California International Airshow** (☎ 888-845-7469; www.salinasairshow.com) in September or October.

Sights & Activities

The impressive **National Steinbeck Center** (☎ 831-796-3833; www.steinbeck.org; 1 Main St; adult/child $11/6; ☽ 10am-5pm) is a fitting homage to Salinas' Nobel Prize–winning native son, John Steinbeck (1902–68). Steinbeck's literary explorations were influenced and inspired by the people and daily life of the area; his observations on Cannery Row in Monterey resulted in the eponymous 1945 book.

The interactive exhibit chronicles the writer's life and works in a creative and engaging fashion. Each of seven theme galleries stages scenes from famous books such as *The Grapes of Wrath, East of Eden* and *Of Mice and Men*, incorporating quotes and artifacts such as letters and books. There's also a small theater showing film clips. Prized exhibits include Rocinante, the customized camper in which Steinbeck traveled around America while researching *Travels with Charley*. Take a moment and listen to his Nobel acceptance speech; it's grace and power combined.

Steinbeck was born and spent much of his boyhood in what is now **Steinbeck House** (☎ 831-424-2735; 132 Central Ave; ⏰ 11:30am-2pm), two blocks west of the center. It's now a twee lunch café. We're not sure he'd approve. He's buried in the family plot at **Garden of Memories Cemetery** (Abbott St & Romie Lane), 1 mile south of the center.

The Center has added a wing called 'Valley of the World', which looks at the politics and sweat of agriculture in the valley. Get even closer to your roughage with the popular **Ag Venture Tours** (☎ 831-384-7686; www.whps .com/agtours; tours from $55), which take an in-depth look at the fields and associated issues.

Sleeping

Salinas has plenty of budget motels, making it a less expensive base from which to explore the Monterey Peninsula.

Laurel Inn (☎ 831-449-2474; www.laurelinnmotel .com; 801 W Laurel Dr; r $60-140; ⊠ ☐ ⚊) This place is family-owned and a good choice if chains don't do it for you. The 146 rooms are clean and there's a large pool, hot tub and sauna for relaxing. It's at the Hwy 101 Laurel Dr exit.

The following three places are right off Hwy 101 at the Market St exit, where there are numerous chains, including an always-popular In-N-Out Burger.

Best Western Salinas Valley Inn & Suites (☎ 831-751-6411; www.bestwestern.com; 187 Kern St; r $70-300; ⊠ ⚊ ☐ ⚊) As posh as you can get next to the freeway, the larger rooms here are good for extended stays.

Comfort Inn (☎ 831-758-8850; www.comfortinn.com; 144 Kern St; r $70-230; ⚊ ☐) A basic place with 32 rooms in three stories.

Vagabond Inn (☎ 831-758-4693; www.vagabondinn .com; 131 Kern St; r $60-180; ⚊ ☐ ⚊) An immaculate place with 70 comfortable rooms.

Eating

If hunger strikes, you'll find several fine options along Main St near the Steinbeck Center, including the following two gems.

Hullaballoo (☎ 831-757-3663; 228 S Main St; lunch $7-18, dinner $8-25; ⏰ lunch Mon-Fri, dinner daily) There's a lively, artistic feel and a seasonally changing menu billed as 'bold American cooking'. Local produce is the basis for an eclectic menu popular with locals. So's the bar.

Monterey Coast Brewing (☎ 831-758-2337; 165 Main St; meals $8-16) This upscale microbrewery is part of the new life downtown. It has an attractive dining room where there's the expected large burgers and more.

Getting There & Away

Greyhound (☎ 831-424-4418; cnr Gabilan & Salinas Sts) has several daily runs to Santa Cruz and on Hwy 101 north to San Francisco and south to Los Angeles.

Amtrak (11 Station Pl at Railroad Ave) has a daily service on the Seattle–LA *Coast Starlight* as well as several daily buses connecting with regional train services in San Jose (p183) and Santa Barbara (p491).

MST bus (p449) 20 makes the 50-minute run to/from Monterey every 30 to 60 minutes. The Salinas Transit Center is one block west of the Steinbeck Center and two blocks south of the Amtrak station.

PINNACLES NATIONAL MONUMENT

This 24,000-acre **park** (☎ 831-389-4485; www.nps .gov/pinn; per vehicle $5) gets its name from the spires and crags that rise abruptly up to 1200ft over the oak- and chaparral-covered hills of the Salinas Valley. The rocks are remains of an ancient volcano that formed along the San Andreas Rift Zone about 23 million years ago. Their arches, spires and crags are the result of millions of years of erosion. The entire site is a study in stunning geological drama.

The rock formations divide the park into East Pinnacles and West Pinnacles. While there is no road connecting the two sides, you can hike from one to the other in about an hour.

Information, maps, books and bottled water are available from **Chaparral ranger station** (⏰ 9am-5pm) on the western side and **Bear Gulch Visitors Center** (⏰ 9am-5pm) on the eastern side. Note that trailheads can fill up quickly on pleasant weekends.

For West Pinnacles take Hwy 146 for 12 miles east off Hwy 101 at Soledad. The eastern entrance is accessed via lonely Hwy 25 in San Benito County.

CENTRAL COAST

Activities

Roads simply can't get to the heart of the monument, so to appreciate the Pinnacles' stark beauty you need to take a **hike**. Distances range from 1 to 10 miles and difficulty from easy to strenuous. Pick up a map at any local visitors center.

Among the park's main attractions are its two talus caves (formed by piles of large boulders), one of which – **Balconies Cave** – is always open for exploration. Scrambling through here is not an exercise recommended for the claustrophobic as it's pitch-black inside, making a flashlight essential (for sale at the visitors centers). Be prepared to get lost a bit. The cave is on a 2-mile loop from the Chaparral ranger station. The other cavern, **Bear Gulch Cave**, is closer to the east and closed at times so as not to disturb a resident colony of bats.

Other activities at the monumnet include **bird-watching** and **wildflower walks** in spring. Cycling is discouraged.

MISSION SAN ANTONIO DE PADUA

Remote and evocative, this large **mission** (☎ 831-385-4478; donation requested; ◷ 8am-6pm May-Oct, 8am-5pm Nov-Apr) is a must-see if you want to hear the whispers of the past and feel removed from modern life. Well, almost removed that is – the mission is in the middle of the mostly undeveloped Fort Hunter Ligget, an active army base. You'll pass a checkpoint on the way in.

The mission was founded in 1771 by Padre Serra and built with Native American labor from Salinas. The church is nicely restored to its 1813 appearance, with decorative flourishes adorning the whitewashed walls – note the wooden pulpit and elaborate canopied altar. A creaky door leads to a garden anchored by a fountain and ringed by tall cypress trees.

The museum has a good collection of Native American handiwork as well as such utilitarian items as an olive press, a loom and other equipment used in the mission's workshops. There's more to explore on the grounds, where you can see the remains of a grist mill, rip saw, corral, reservoir and irrigation system. Seldom crowded, you may have the vast site to yourself.

From the north, take the Jolon Rd exit (just before King City) off Hwy 101 and follow Jolon Rd (G14) 18 miles south to Mission Rd. From the south, take the Jolon Rd-G18 exit off Hwy 101 and head 22 miles northwest on Jolon Rd to Mission Rd.

You can also reach the mission from Hwy 1, about 30 miles away via rugged Nacimiento-Fergusson Rd.

LAKE NACIMIENTO

About 17 miles northwest of Paso Robles (reached via Lake Nacimiento Rd, clearly marked from Hwy 101), Lake Nacimiento is best visited on the way to or from Mission San Antonio de Padua, unless you are a water-skier, in which case it deserves priority status. With its sprawling inlets, the pine- and oak-fringed reservoir is considered one of the best water-skiing spots in the USA. The reservoir is crowded with boats from April to October, especially on weekends and holidays. Most lakeshore property is privately owned.

SAN MIGUEL
pop 1500

A small farming town right off Hwy 101, life here seems almost unchanged in decades. The star attraction is **Mission San Miguel Arcángel** (☎ 805-467-3256; 775 Mission St; donation requested; ◷ 9:30am-4pm), which suffered heart-breaking damage from the 2003 earthquake that hit Paso Robles 12 miles to the south. Previously it was one of the most accessible and one of the most authentic of the California missions. Established in 1797 as a stopover between Mission San Antonio de Padua and Mission San Luis Obispo de Tolosa, Mission San Miguel was number 16 in the chain of 21 missions. The current structure dates back to 1818 and, prior to the earthquake, had not been significantly altered.

Repairs are expected to last at least through 2007 and maybe much longer. In the meantime, the museum, living quarters, gardens and other areas are open. It's hoped the mission will eventually outlive the enormous cactus in front of the mission which was planted about the same time the mission was built.

A quarter-mile south of the mission is the **Rios Caledonia Adobe** (☎ 805-467-3357; 700 S Mission St; donation requested; ◷ 10am-4pm Wed-Sun), which stands on mission property that Governor Pio Pico illegally sold to Petronillo Rios in 1846. Using Chumash labor, Rios built the two-story adobe as a ranch headquarters and hacienda for his family, later turning it into a roadhouse on the stagecoach route between Los Angeles and San Francisco. Original adobe bricks are still visible.

PASO ROBLES

pop 22,500

About 30 miles north of San Luis Obispo, Paso Robles is at the heart of an agricultural region where grapes now constitute the biggest crop. Several dozen wineries along Hwy 46 produce a good number of increasingly respectable bottles. In addition, the Mediterranean climate is yielding other bounty: there's a fledging high-end olive-oil industry. Where you don't see grapes being planted look for young olive trees.

But everything going on in the ground is not good, on December 22, 2003, a 6.5-magnitude **earthquake** hit Paso Robles and hit hard. Several historic buildings were destroyed and dozens more were damaged. Even now, you'll see cracks and temporary braces on buildings throughout town. The town's historic core centers on Park and 12th Sts, where a few buildings are now missing. However, there are still numerous shops and cafés open and it makes a good place for a stroll.

The **chamber of commerce** (☎ 805-238-0506, 800-406-4040; www.pasorobleschamber.com; 1225 Park St; ⊙ 9am-4pm Mon-Fri) has maps and information.

Sample local history – of the non-earth-shaking variety – at the **El Paso Robles Area Pioneer Museum** (☎ 805-238-0506; 1225 Riverside Dr; admission free; ⊙ 1-4pm Thu-Sun). Lots of stuff that would have been carted away as junk just a few years ago has now found a home in this interesting compound, which puts the area's history into context.

About 25 miles east of Hwy 101, on Hwy 46 in **Cholame**, a monument is near the spot where James Dean fatally crashed his Porsche on September 30, 1955 at the age of 24. He'd only made three films.

Paso Robles Wine Country

The wine country surrounding Paso Robles is worth a day's exploration, as wineries here are generating a lot of buzz and it seems new ones are appearing almost daily. Most are concentrated along Hwy 46 west towards the coast, off Hwy 101 south of town. A few more line Hwy 46 east of town. **Paso Robles Vintners and Growers Association** (☎ 805-239-8463; www.pasowine.com) has an informative website .

Most vineyards have tasting rooms and free tours. Maps are available from the chamber of commerce and various businesses around town. Good stops going west include **Zenaida Cellars** (☎ 805-227-0382; 1550 Hwy 46 W; ⊙ 11am-5pm), which has a large, rustic style tasting room that's a fine venue for sampling its viogniers, syrahs and sangioveses, among others. Closer to the coast, **York Mountain Winery** (☎ 805-238-3925; 7505 York Mountain Rd; ⊙ 11am-4pm Thu-Mon), 7 miles west of Hwy 101 and off Hwy 46, is the oldest winery in the region and has a tasting room in an old log cabin. Try some of its award-winning pinot noirs.

About 3.5 miles east of Hwy 101, **Eberle Winery** (☎ 805-238-9607; 3810 Hwy 46 E; ⊙ 10am-5pm) has a lovely deck with vineyard views, and offers tours of its wine caves. The star here is cabernet sauvignon.

Sleeping & Eating

Paso Robles' accommodations are concentrated along Spring St, which is the town's main thoroughfare.

Paso Robles Inn (☎ 805-238-2660, 800-676-1713; www.pasoroblesinn.com; 1103 Spring St; r $95-245) This 108-room hotel in the town center is the pick of the lot by a long way. Sited above mineral hot springs, the hotel has more than 30 rooms with spas that let you take the waters in private. Many rooms feature fireplaces and 10 are in the original 1898 building. The vast gardens are intricately manicured.

Melody Ranch Motel (☎ 805-238-3911, 800-909-3911; 939 Spring St; r $48-70; ⊠ ⊡) There's just one story and it only has 19 rooms, but that small amount translates into small prices at this budgetary friend. Rooms are basic but you can take comfort in the small heated pool.

Adelaide Inn (☎ 805-238-2770, 800-549-7276; www .adelaideinn.com; 1215 Ysabel Ave; r $55-100; ⊠ ⊡) Surrounded by trees, this motel has a pool, spa and sauna for relaxing. The rooms are a bit generic, but they are well equipped with amenities like reclining chairs, refrigerators and more.

Good Ol' Burgers (☎ 805-239-5777; 305 Spring St; meals $4-6; ⊙ 9am-9pm) Don't even look at the fast-food joints at the Hwy 46 East junction with Hwy 101 or you may literally turn into a pillar of salt. Instead opt for this local favorite, which grills up damn fine burgers you can enjoy at tables outside. Before you go, pose for a silly photo with the cut-out characters.

Bistro Laurent (☎ 805-226-8191; 1202 Pine St; meals $10-25; ☯ lunch & dinner Mon-Sat) This vintage brick restaurant is helmed by Laurent Grangien, who brings a native expertise to the French menu. At lunch, the menu focuses on simple specials like seasonal salads and pizzas that will transport you to the Mediterranean via your shady garden table. At night, things are more complex; just be sure to save room for dessert.

Getting There & Away
Several **Greyhound** (☎ 805-238-1242; 845 9th St) Hwy 101 route buses stop daily. **Amtrak** (800 Pine St) has a daily service with the *Coast Starlight* as well as several buses that link to regional trains in Santa Barbara and San Jose.

San Luis Obispo's RTA (p469) bus 9 ($2.50, 90 minutes) travels north several times daily, Monday to Saturday, from SLO.

SANTA BARBARA AREA

Add the history and culture of Santa Barbara to viticultural and natural attractions, and there's a lot to do in this part of Southern California. Wineries are sprouting throughout the hills – this is *Sideways* country after all – and there's a lot of nature to explore. Untrammeled beaches abound and one glance off the Santa Barbara coast and you'll see the primitive Channel Islands National Park.

Whether you are looking for fine wine, a backcountry hike, a lie on a beach or a night out, you'll find it here.

LOMPOC
pop 41,000
If one were to describe Lompoc (pronounced *lahm*-poke), the largest town along Hwy 1 as it winds between Pismo Beach and Santa Barbara, in four words, they would be: mission, military, murals and flowers.

Vandenberg Air Force Base is used for launching commercial and military rockets. Closed to the public, it covers a vast part of the coast and supports this sprawling city characterized mostly by long stretches of undistinguished commercial development. Lompoc's old town, though – roughly where H St meets Ocean Ave – sports almost 30

large and varied murals painted on the sides of buildings.

Lompoc is embedded in a valley carpeted with commercial **flower fields** (larkspur, sweet peas, delphinium and many others), which erupt in a profusion of color, especially between June and August. Most of the fields cluster in the western section of town, west of Bailey Ave between Central and Ocean Aves.

Mission La Purísima Concepción
Around 3 miles northeast of Hwy 1 and the old town in Lompoc, this beautiful **mission** (☎ 805-733-3713; per car $4; ☯ 9am-5pm) was completely restored in the 1930s by the Civilian Conservation Corps (CCC). Its buildings are fully intact and decorated as they were in the mission period. The mission fields still support livestock, and the gardens are planted with medicinal plants and trees once used by the Chumash. Also here are fountains and ground-level troughs where women did the wash – one for the Native Americans and one for the mission women. With Mission San Antonio de Padua up north (p476), this mission is the most evocative of old California.

Surrounding the mission are 15 miles of hiking and horse trails. An new visitors center has good advice, but the exhibits are missing pending funding by the governor.

The mission is just off Hwy 246; look for the turnoff to Purisima Rd on the northern side of the highway and follow it for about 1 mile. From Old Town Lompoc, follow Ocean Ave east, which turns into Hwy 246.

BUELLTON
pop 3900
Sitting at the junction of Hwys 101 and 246, this town has two notable places to eat.

Yes it's hokey, and yes it has a cavernous gift shop but **Pea Soup Andersen's** (Map p480; ☎ 805-688-5581; www.peasoupandersens.net; meals $5-10; ☯ 7am-10pm) also delivers. Charming staff keep filling your bowl with excellent eponymous soup. Other items like burgers are spot on. And who can't be charmed by house characters Happea and Pea-Wee?

You'll be hard-pressed to find better steaks and chops *anywhere* than at **Hitching Post II** (Map p480; ☎ 805-688-06776; www.hitchingpost2.com; 406 E Hwy 246, Buellton; meals $20-35; ☯ dinner). This legendary, old-guard, dressed-down country

TWO HIDDEN BEACHES

South of Pismo Beach and west of Lompoc lie two excellent beaches well worth visiting.

Ocean Beach and **Surf Beach** are really one beach on the grounds of the huge Vandenberg Air Force Base. During the 9-mile drive west of Lompoc on Ocean Ave you'll pass mysterious-looking structures used to support launches of both spy and commercial satellites. At the coast you'll find parking for Ocean, then Surf Beach. The dunes are untrammeled, and there are good signs explaining the ecology of the nearby estuary. Surf Beach even boasts an Amtrak train station, but the schedules prohibit a day trip from LA since the *Coast Starlight* runs southbound in the morning and northbound at night. Be aware that the endangered snowy plover nests here. It's a tiny bird with a total population under 2000. The beaches usually close on weekdays from March to September to allow them some solitude. Because they are so skilled at camouflaging their nests in the sand, the average Frisbee-throwing Joe can easily trample them.

Five miles south of Lompoc on Hwy 1, look for Jalama Rd. Its 14 miles of twisting tarmac traverse pastoral ranch and farmlands. But the real reward is at the end of the road at Jalama Beach County Park. Utterly isolated, it's home to a terrific beachfront **campground** (day-use per vehicle $6, sites from $18). There are no reservations, but look for the 'campground full' sign, back at Hwy 1, and save yourself the 14-mile drive. To secure one of the private beachside sites, arrive near dawn. For information, phone ☎ 805-736-3504. A tiny store sells very fine cheeseburgers.

steakhouse serves locally raised meats and makes its own pinot noir (which is damn good, by the way). Make reservations.

SOLVANG
pop 5200

Three Danish farmers established a folk school in the Santa Ynez Valley to pass on their Danish traditions to future generations. Something seems to have been lost in the succeeding decades. Solvang (loosely meaning Sunny Field) today is the tourist trap to beat all tourist traps. It bills itself as 'authentic.'

Fudge shops abound and knick-knackeries peddling gee-gaws that have never been anywhere near Denmark jam the faux Scandinavian storefronts. It's a town that has given up any link to reality but one: profit (locals shop elsewhere).

The **Elverhøj Museum** (☎ 805-686-1211; cnr 2nd St & Elverhoy Way; donation requested; ☻ 12:30-4pm Wed-Sun) covers real Danish life in the area. Sadly, **Old Mission Santa Inés** (☎ 805-688-4815; 1760 Mission Dr; adult/child under 16 $3/free; ☻ 9am-5:30pm) shares the town's sense of history – it's been restored to death.

There are numerous places to stay. Many have large displays of teddy bears and Christmas ornaments for sale. Solvang's bakeries prove an irresistible draw for many, but actually aren't especially good. Fortunately, the **Solvang Restaurant** (☎ 805-688-4645;

1672 Copenhagen Dr; meals under $8; ☻ breakfast & lunch), delivers good food and cheer, serving *aeble-skiver* (ball-like pancakes dusted with powdered sugar) as well as typical diner fare.

Solvang is 3 miles east of Buellton along Hwy 246.

SANTA BARBARA WINE COUNTRY

Santa Barbara's Wine Country unfurls along winding country lanes amid oak-dotted rolling hills that stretch for miles. In the spring, when the grass is still green, wildflowers bloom a rainbow of colors; later in summer the grasses turn gold and brown, and make a shimmering sound when the wind blows through them. This is the California of old. Take your time. The hit movie *Sideways* was filmed throughout the region. See p482 for a guide to finding some of the most recognizable locations.

Orientation & Information

The Wine Country is north of Santa Barbara; you can get there in just under an hour, via Hwys 154 (San Marcos Pass Rd) and 101. The Santa Ynez Valley, where you'll find most of the wineries, lies south of the Santa Maria Valley. If you're tight on time, plan to see only the Santa Ynez Valley; if you've got the whole day, see both.

Hwy 246 runs east–west, via Solvang, across the bottom of the Santa Ynez Valley, but it's busier than the back roads and not as interesting. North–south secondary roads where you'll find good wineries include Alamo Pintado Rd from Hwy 246 to the town of Los Olivos, and Refugio Rd into neighboring Ballard.

The cute little Mayberry-like town of Los Olivos is a good place to stop for lunch, since it's essentially on the line between the Santa

Ynez Valley and the Santa Maria Valley. Grand Ave, the main street through town, heads south and turns into Alamo Pintado Rd. A great route to take from here is along the beautiful Foxen Canyon Wine Trail (opposite).

Santa Barbara Vintners' Association (☎ 805-668-0881, 800-218-0881; www.sbcountywines.com) pub-

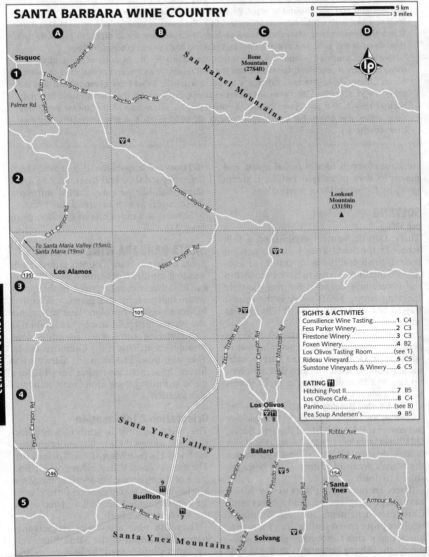

SANTA BARBARA WINE COUNTRY

SIGHTS & ACTIVITIES
Consilience Wine Tasting	**1** C4
Fess Parker Winery	**2** C3
Firestone Winery	**3** C3
Foxen Winery	**4** B2
Los Olivos Tasting Room	(see 1)
Rideau Vineyard	**5** C5
Sunstone Vineyards & Winery	**6** C5

EATING 🍴
Hitching Post II	**7** B5
Los Olivos Café	**8** C4
Panino	(see 8)
Pea Soup Andersen's	**9** B5

lishes a touring map of all the wineries in the area and has some useful information about the area on its website.

Santa Ynez Valley Wineries

Vineyards here are close in and around Hwy 246 as it runs east of Solvang for 6 miles to the junction with Hwy 154.

SUNSTONE VINEYARDS & WINERY

You'd swear you were in Provence at this destination **winery** (☎ 805-688-9463; www.sunstonewinery.com; 125 Refugio Rd; tastings $5; 🕐 10am-4pm) that looks like an 18th-century stone farmhouse. If you like merlot, this is the place. This entirely family-run estate is the closest winery to Santa Barbara (45 minutes), just south of Hwy 246.

RIDEAU VINEYARD

Inside a restored 1884 adobe house with a wraparound veranda and mature oaks out back, this **winery** (☎ 805-688-0717; www.rideauvineyard.com; 1562 Alamo Pintado Rd; tastings $7-10; 🕐 11am-5pm) was the first stagecoach stop in Los Olivos. Today people come for the Rhône varietals, good chardonnay and great syrah. This vineyard is north of Hwy 246 on the way to Los Olivos.

Los Olivos

The four-block main street in charming Los Olivos is lined with tasting rooms, shops, several restaurants, and a luxurious inn and full-service spa. The town is at the center of Wine Country with Hwy 154 passing right by.

If you're short on time but want to taste as many wines as possible, there are some good tasting rooms here.

Los Olivos Tasting Room (☎ 805-688-7406; www.losolivostastingroom.com; 2905 Grand Ave; 🕐 11am-5:30pm) The first independent tasting room in California sits right on the main drag and specializes in high-end pinot noir that you can't taste anywhere else.

Consilience Wine Tasting (☎ 805-691-1020; www.consiliencewines.com; 2933 Grand Ave; 🕐 11am-5pm) Specializes in vineyard-designated syrah and Rhône varietals, with some pinot noir and zinfandels as well.

EATING

This is an ideal place to have lunch and there are many choices.

Los Olivos Café (☎ 805-688-7265; 2879 Grand Ave; mains $10-25) There's a wine-tasting bar, a long list of vintages and a good Mediterranean-themed menu served both inside and out on the vine-covered porch. Order the meatballs.

Panino (☎ 805-688-9304; 2900 Grand Ave; meals $6-8; 🕐 9am-5pm) There are 10 different kinds of veggie sandwiches as well as special sandwiches, such as curried chicken, that you order at the counter and eat outside at an umbrella table. Good salads, too

Foxen Canyon Wine Trail

The very beautiful Foxen Canyon Wine Trail runs north from Hwy 154, just west of Los Olivos' main drag, and into the Santa Maria Valley, a more rural area with fewer visitors. It's a must-see for oenophiles or those wanting to get off the beaten path.

The Foxen Canyon Wine Trail follows Foxen Canyon Rd; most wineries are within

CENTRAL COAST

A SANTA BARBARA WINE COUNTRY PRIMER

Though large-scale winemaking has only been happening here since the 1980s, Santa Barbara's climate has always been perfect for growing grapes. Two parallel, east–west-trending mountain ranges (the Santa Ynez and the San Rafael) cradle the region and funnel coastal fog eastward off the Pacific into the valleys between. The further inland you go, the warmer it gets. At the shore, fog and low clouds can hover all day, keeping the weather downright chilly, even in July, while only a few miles inland, temperatures can soar a full 30°F hotter, sometimes approaching 100°F in mid-July. These delicately balanced microclimates support two major varieties of grape.

Near the coast in the Santa Maria Valley, pinot noir – a particularly fragile grape – and other Burgundian varieties thrive in the fog. Inland in the warmer Santa Ynez Valley, where there can be as much as a 50°F variance in temperatures from day to night, Rhône-style grapes do best; these include syrah, morvedre and viognier. (Bordeaux-style wines, such as cabernet franc and cabernet sauvignon, get a bad rap in Santa Barbara County, and are usually associated only with Napa, Sonoma and Alexander Valleys in Northern California. Nonetheless, there are a few pockets in the Santa Ynez Valley where you'll find some fine cabernet franc, often at good prices too.)

FINDING SIDEWAYS

The film *Sideways* was a surprise hit in 2004. Filmed entirely in and around Santa Barbara County, it follows two aging men as they come to terms with many of life's issues on what is supposed to be a last trip together before one, Jack, gets married. Things are never so simple, and Jack and his nebbish yet wine-loving buddy soon end up in a series of misadventures, sexual and otherwise.

Following in the footsteps of Miles and Jack has become quite popular. A *Sideways*-location map available at the Santa Barbara Visitors Center (p484) is a hot commodity. Some of this is driven by people who want to relive moments from the movie, but the greater motivator is simply the desire to see all the wonderful places showcased in the movie. The simple fact is that the misbehaving pair chose one of the most beautiful places in California to spend their week.

Buellton is the place to start your *Sideways* tour. Here Miles and Jack stayed at the otherwise unremarkable **Days Inn** (114 E Hwy 246) and walked to the **Hitching Post II** (p478) and their meeting with Maya.

Nearby **Solvang** is where the two have a declaratory breakfast at the **Solvang Restaurant** (p479). Between the two towns, the cars stopped on the side of Hwy 246 will signal **Ostrich Land** (☎ 805-686-9696) where you can see the huge birds day and night just as Miles and Jack do in the film.

The back roads of the Wine Country are mesmerizing with their color and Miles's red Saab convertible cruises most of them.

North of Buellton, Zaca Station Rd heads off Hwy 101 past the **Firestone Winery** (below) where the two couples – Jack (Thomas Haden Church) and Stephanie (Sandra Oh) as well as Miles (Paul Giamatti) and Maya (Virginia Madsen) – share some romantic moments in the perfectly lit cask room. A bit further, Foxen Canyon Rd is a star in its own right. The **Fess Parker Winery** (below) does almost too good a job in its role as the pedestrian Frass Canyon Winery (you know they make a mean Merlot). North, **Foxen Winery** (below) also does a star turn (it's is the tiny roadside place where Miles and Jack surreptitiously chug).

In the south, Foxen Canyon Rd ends at **Los Olivos** where the couples have a romantic meal at the **Los Olivos Cafe** (p481).

15 miles of Los Olivos. For the simplest loop, go up Foxen Canyon Rd to Sisquoc, a blink-and-miss-it community where several roads intersect. Turn left onto Palmer Rd, which will take you to Hwy 101 and south to Santa Barbara. Every time you stop at a winery, ask for directions.

WINERIES

Fess Parker Winery (☎ 805-688-1545; www.fessparker .com; 6200 Foxen Canyon Rd; tastings $7; ⏰ 11am-5pm Mon-Fri, 10am-5pm Sat & Sun) The two biggest wines here are Burgundy and Rhône. Afternoons and weekends get packed, when busloads turn up and it utterly resembles the crass Frass Canyon which it played in the film *Sideways*.

Foxen Winery (☎ 805-937-4251; www.foxenvineyard .com; 7200 Foxen Canyon Rd, Santa Maria; tastings per 5 wines $3-7; ⏰ noon-4pm Mon-Fri, 11am-4pm Sat & Sun) This is one of the finest, most diverse wineries in the county. Its tiny, dressed-down tasting room, with concrete floor and corrugated-metal roof, sits in one of the prettiest stretches of the Santa Maria Valley, near the north end of

Wine Country at mileage marker 16, about half an hour north of Los Olivos.

Firestone Winery (☎ 805-688-3940; www.firestone wine.com; 5000 Zaca Station Rd; ⏰ 10am-5pm) This pioneering winery is 3 miles south of Foxen Canyon Rd. The tasting area has both sweeping views and real emphasis on wine. Extraneous merchandising opportunities are eschewed. It's well regarded for its sauvignon blanc, which draws on Santa Ynez Valley grapes.

ALONG HIGHWAY 154

Highway 154 (San Marcos Pass Rd) heads south from Hwy 101 6 miles north of Buellton and passes Los Olivos. It bisects the Santa Barbara Wine Country and the Santa Ynez Valley before going through Los Padres National Forest and reaching Santa Barbara, having covered 35 miles of scenic driving.

Los Padres National Forest

Los Padres National Forest covers about two million acres of coastal mountains in various pockets stretching from the Carmel Valley to the western edge of Los Angeles County.

It's great for hiking, camping, horseback riding, mountain biking and other outdoor pursuits.

Not surprisingly, a good source of information is the **Los Padres National Forest Headquarters** (Map pp484-5; ☎ 805-968-6640; www.fs.fed.us /r5/lospadres; 6755 Hollister Ave; ☺ 8am-4:30pm Mon-Fri) in Goleta. If you're traveling by car, you must display a National Forest Adventure Pass (p60) in order to park in the forest. Passes cost $5 per day, and you can purchase them at the Forest Headquarters.

Paradise Rd, which crosses Hwy 154 north of San Marcos Pass, provides the best access to developed facilities in the forest. About 4 miles up the road there's a ranger station with posted maps and information. There are three **campgrounds** (sites $15) before the ranger station and one just beyond it. At Red Rocks (clearly marked from the ranger station), the Santa Ynez River deeply pools among rocks and waterfalls, creating a great swimming and sunning spot. Many hiking trails radiate out from here.

Chumash Painted Cave State Historic Park

This tiny **historic site** (☎ 805-733-3713; www.parks .ca.gov; ☺ dawn-dusk) shelters vivid pictographs painted by the Chumash over 400 years ago. The cave is protected by a metal screen, so a flashlight is helpful for getting a good view. Look for the turnoff to Painted Cave Rd, about 8 miles north of Santa Barbara; the last stretch of the road is narrow and steep.

SANTA BARBARA

pop 93,000

Is Santa Barbara California's best-smelling city? The jasmine, orange blossoms, hyacinth and more certainly do there part. Certainly it's fitting that Santa Barbara smells good, it's that kind of place.

Sandwiched between the Pacific Ocean and Santa Ynez Mountains, Santa Barbara is affluent and pretty, with red-tile roofs, white stucco and a seaside lassitude reminiscent of the Mediterranean. It's a highlight of the Central Coast and you should not whiz by on Hwy 101 without stopping. The problem will be getting back on the road.

Five colleges in the area, including the University of California at Santa Barbara (UCSB), give the town a youthful vivacity and balance its yachting and retirement communities. Downtown Santa Barbara has outstanding architectural integrity, a masterpiece of a courthouse, noteworthy cultural institutions, superb shopping and seductive nightlife.

History

Until about 200 years ago, Chumash people thrived in the Santa Barbara area, living in villages along the coast and in the Santa Ynez Mountains. In 1542, Juan Rodríguez Cabrillo entered the channel, put up a Spanish flag and went on his way. Sebastián Vizcaíno, a cartographer for the Duke of Monte Rey, landed in the harbor on December 4, 1602 (the feast day of St Barbara), and literally put Santa Barbara on the map. But being claimed and named by Spain didn't affect Santa Barbara's Chumash until the arrival of missionaries in the mid-1700s.

As elsewhere in California, the padres converted the Chumash, virtually enslaved them to construct the mission and presidio, and taught them to wear clothing and to change their traditional diet of acorn mush, roots and fish to meat. The Native Americans contracted European diseases and were decimated, though today the tribe is again very much alive and well.

Easterners started arriving in force with the 1849 gold rush, and by the late 1890s Santa Barbara was an established vacation spot for the rich, famous and creative. The American Film Company, founded at the corner of Mission and State Sts in 1910, was the largest in the world for about three of its 10 years in existence.

A disastrous 1925 earthquake proved ultimately to be a opportunity: tough laws were passed requiring that the town be rebuilt with its now characteristic faux-Mediterranean look. These dictates have mostly stayed in force.

Orientation

Downtown Santa Barbara is laid out in a square grid – its principal artery is State St, which runs roughly north–south. Lower State St (south of Ortega St) has a large concentration of cafés and bars, while upper State St (north of Ortega St) has most of the alluring shops and museums. Cabrillo Blvd hugs the coastline and turns into Coast Village Rd as it enters the eastern suburb of Montecito.

CENTRAL COAST

Santa Barbara is surrounded by small af-fluent communities: Hope Ranch to the west, Montecito and Summerland to the east. UCSB is just west of Hope Ranch in Isla Vista, and most of Santa Barbara's college crowd lives around the campus or in neighboring Go-leta. To the east is the enclave of Montecito, which outdoes even Santa Barbara in the posh department.

Information

BOOKSTORES

Chaucer's Books (Map pp484-5; ☎ 805-682-6782; 3321 State St) Best selection in town for any new book you could ever want.

Pacific Travelers Supply (Map p486; ☎ 805-963-4438; 12 W Anapamu St) The best spot in town to buy guidebooks and maps, as well as miscellaneous travelers' accessories.

INTERNET ACCESS

There are plenty of places around town for wi-fi access.

Fedex Kinko's (Map p486; ☎ 805-966-1114; 1030 State St; per min 25¢; ⊗ 9am-10pm) Has expensive computer access in a hot and stuffy area.

MEDICAL SERVICES

Santa Barbara Cottage Hospital (Map pp484-5; ☎ 805-682-7111; cnr Pueblo & Bath Sts; ⊗ 24hr) Full-service facility.

POST

Post office (Map p486; ☎ 805-564-2226; 836 Anacapa St; ⊗ 8am-6pm Mon-Fri, 9am-5pm Sat) Full-service.

TOURIST INFORMATION

Outdoors Santa Barbara Visitors Center (Map p486; ☎ 805-884-1475; 4th fl, 113 Harbor Way; ⊗ 11am-6pm) Activities-oriented branch that dispenses plenty of data about the Channel Islands National Park (p492) and Los Padres National Forest (p482). It has good views too.

Visitors bureau (Map p486; ☎ 805-965-3021; www .santabarbaraca.com; 1 Garden St; ⊗ 9am-5pm Mon-Sat, 10am-5pm Sun) Excellent service with maps, brochures and busy but helpful staff.

Sights

Santa Barbara has a lot of people with time on their hands, whether retired due to age, wealth or both, many volunteer at local museums and attractions. And while new-fangled cash registers may flummox, they

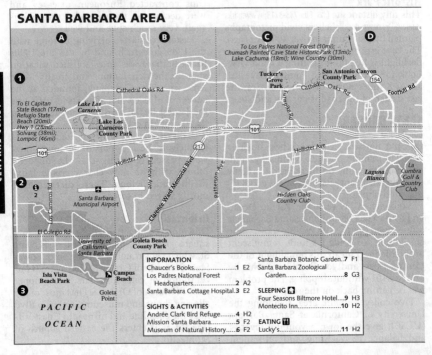

SANTA BARBARA AREA

To Los Padres National Forest (10mi);
Chumash Painted Cave State Historic Park (13mi);
Lake Cachuma (18mi); Wine Country (30mi)

To El Capitan State Beach (17mi); Refugio State Beach (20mi); Hwy 1 (28mi); Solvang (38mi); Lompoc (46mi)

Cathedral Oaks Rd

Tucker's Grove Park

San Antonio Canyon County Park

Foothill Rd

Lake Los Carneros

Lake Los Carneros County Park

Hollister Ave

Hollister Ave

Laguna Blanca

La Cumbra Golf & Country Club

Santa Barbara Municipal Airport

Hidden Oaks Country Club

El Colegio Rd

University of California, Santa Barbara

Goleta Beach County Park

Isla Vista Beach Park

Campus Beach

Goleta Point

PACIFIC

OCEAN

are often founts of knowledge and oral history.

SANTA BARBARA COUNTY COURTHOUSE

The magnificent 1929 **courthouse** (Map p486; ☎ 805-962-6464; 1100 Anacapa St; admission free; info desk ☯ 8:30am-4:30pm) is one sight not to be missed. Built in Spanish-Moorish Revival style, it features hand-painted ceilings, wrought-iron chandeliers and tiles from Tunisia and Spain. You're free to explore it on your own, but the best way to see it is on a free docent-led tour regularly at 2pm Monday to Saturday (and other times). Be sure to have a look at the mural room, and go up the 80ft clock tower for views of the city and ocean.

MISSION SANTA BARBARA

Called the 'Queen of the Missions,' **Mission Santa Barbara** (Map pp484-5; ☎ 805-682-4713; www .sbmission.org; 2201 Laguna St; adult/child $4/free; ☯ 9am-5pm) sits on a majestic perch half a mile north of downtown. It was established on December 4 (the feast day of St Barbara) in 1786, as the 10th California mission. The current stone version dates from 1820. Today, the

mission still functions as a Franciscan friary as well as a parish church and museum. The church features Chumash wall decorations and beautiful cloisters. To the side is an extensive cemetery where an estimated 4000 Chumash are buried in unmarked graves, in addition to elaborate mausoleums of early California settlers.

EL PRESIDIO DE SANTA BARBARA STATE HISTORIC PARK

One of four in California, the former Spanish **fort** (Map p486; ☎ 805-966-9719; E Cañon Perdido St btwn Anacapa & Santa Barbara Sts; adult/child $3/free; ☯ 10:30am-4:30pm) harbors structures even older than the mission. Founded in 1782 to protect the missions between Monterey and San Diego, the presidio also served as the social and political hub and as a stopping point for traveling Spanish military. Be sure to visit the chapel, with an interior that explodes in kaleidoscopic color and features some interesting trompe l'oeil effects. Restorations are ongoing, be sure to look at the El Cuartel fragment of the structure across Cañon Perdido St. It helps you visualize

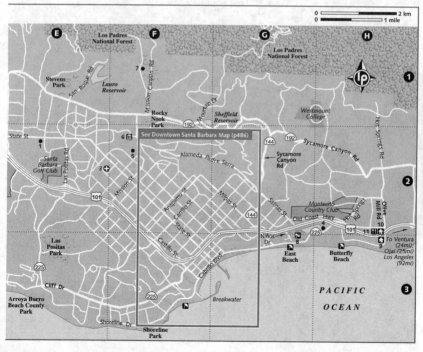

DOWNTOWN SANTA BARBARA

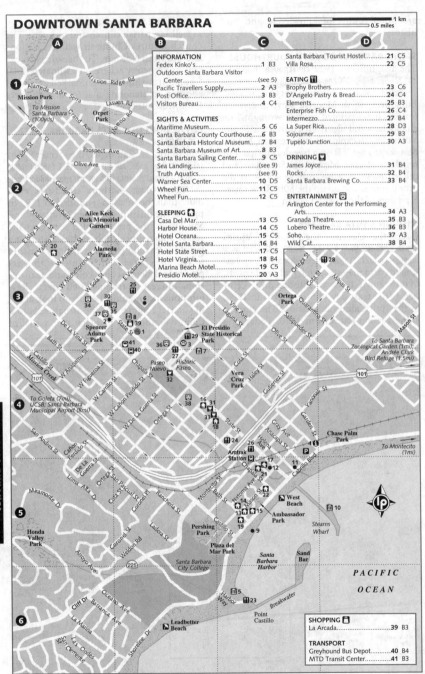

INFORMATION
Fedex Kinko's.................................1 B3
Outdoors Santa Barbara Visitor
  Center.....................................(see 5)
Pacific Travellers Supply..................2 A3
Post Office...................................3 B3
Visitors Bureau.............................4 C4

SIGHTS & ACTIVITIES
Maritime Museum...........................5 C6
Santa Barbara County Courthouse......6 B3
Santa Barbara Historical Museum.......7 B4
Santa Barbara Museum of Art............8 B3
Santa Barbara Sailing Center.............9 C5
Sea Landing................................(see 9)
Truth Aquatics.............................(see 9)
Warner Sea Center........................10 D5
Wheel Fun...................................11 C5
Wheel Fun...................................12 C5

SLEEPING 🛏
Casa Del Mar...............................13 C5
Harbor House..............................14 C5
Hotel Oceana..............................15 C5
Hotel Santa Barbara......................16 B4
Hotel State Street.........................17 C5
Hotel Virginia..............................18 B4
Marina Beach Motel.......................19 C5
Presidio Motel..............................20 A3

Santa Barbara Tourist Hostel............21 C5
Villa Rosa...................................22 C5

EATING 🍴
Brophy Brothers...........................23 C6
D'Angelo Pastry & Bread.................24 C4
Elements...................................25 B3
Enterprise Fish Co.........................26 C4
Intermezzo.................................27 B4
La Super Rica..............................28 D3
Sojourner...................................29 B3
Tupelo Junction...........................30 A3

DRINKING 🍷
James Joyce................................31 B4
Rocks......................................32 B4
Santa Barbara Brewing Co...............33 B4

ENTERTAINMENT 🎭
Arlington Center for the Performing
  Arts.......................................34 A3
Granada Theatre...........................35 B3
Lobero Theatre............................36 B3
Soho..37 A3
Wild Cat....................................38 B4

SHOPPING 🛍
La Arcada...................................39 B3

TRANSPORT
Greyhound Bus Depot....................40 B4
MTD Transit Center.......................41 B3

the original square shape now broken up by city streets.

SANTA BARBARA HISTORICAL MUSEUM
In an adobe complex, this engaging **museum** (☎ 805-966-1601; www.santabarbaramuseum.com; 136 E De La Guerra St; admission free; ☺ 10am-5pm Tue-Sat, noon-5pm Sun) has an exhaustive collection of local memorabilia which ranges from the mundane, such as antique furniture, to the intriguing, such as the intricately carved coffer that belonged to Padre Serra. You can also learn about Santa Barbara's involvement in toppling the last Chinese monarchy, a rather obscure chapter in history. In 30 minutes you can get a great local overview and there's a courtyard where you can digest it all.

SANTA BARBARA MUSEUM OF ART
This well-regarded **art museum** (Map p486; ☎ 805-963-4364; www.sbma.net; 1130 State St; adult/child $9/6, admission free Sun; ☺ 11am-5pm Tue-Sat, noon-5pm Sun) presents European and American hot shots – à la Monet, Matisse, Hopper and O'Keeffe – as well as Asian art, photography and classical sculpture. There's also an interactive children's gallery, a café and store.

SANTA BARBARA BOTANIC GARDEN
A mile north of the Museum of Natural History, this not-to-miss, 78-acre **botanic garden** (Map pp484-5; ☎ 805-682-4726; www.sbbg.org; 1212 Mission Canyon Rd; adult/child 13-17/child 5-12 $7/4/1; ☺ 9am-sunset) is devoted to California's native flora. About 5.5 miles of trails meander through cacti, redwoods, wildflowers and past the old mission dam, built by the Chumash to irrigate the mission's fields. Displays show how to plant a low-water garden, then you can buy the plants.

THE WATERFRONT
At its southern end, State St gives way to **Stearns Wharf** (Map p486), a rough, wooden pier with snack and souvenir shops. Built in 1872, it's the oldest continuously operating wharf on the West Coast. During the 1940s it was owned by Jimmy Cagney and his two brothers.

The wharf is home to a neat new attraction, the **Warner Sea Center** (☎ 805-962-2526; www.sbnature.org; adult/child $7/4; ☺ 10am-5pm), which has captivating hands-on exhibits and touch pools (the warty looking sea cucumber actu-

ally feels like velvet). It's all very well funded and it should be as its cost came from a tiny sliver of the profits from Ty Warner's Beanie Baby empire.

Southwest of the wharf along the harbor, the **Santa Barbara Maritime Museum** (☎ 805-962-8404; www.sbmm.org; 113 Harbor Way; adult/child $6/3; ☺ 10am-5pm) celebrates the town's seafaring history with memorabilia and hands-on exhibits. There's a good display about the 1923 Honda disaster, when the US Navy sailed seven new destroyers onto the rocks north of here.

Outside of the museum is a working yacht harbor that makes for an interesting stroll.

MUSEUM OF NATURAL HISTORY
Visit this **museum** (Map pp484-5; ☎ 805-682-4711; www.sbnature.org; 2559 Puesta del Sol Rd; adult/child $8/5; ☺ 10am-5pm), two blocks north of the mission, if only for its beautiful architecture and landscaping. Inside, the Chumash exhibit is worth a look, as is the complete skeleton of a blue whale, though other exhibits are dull. There's also a planetarium; the Warner Sea Center is an affiliate.

SANTA BARBARA ZOOLOGICAL GARDEN
The **zoo** (Map pp484-5; ☎ 805-962-5339; 500 Niños Dr; adult/child $9/7; ☺ 10am-5pm) has gorgeous gardens as well as 700 animals from around the world, including big cats, monkeys, elephants and giraffes. The 100-year-old vegetation was once part of a palatial estate.

Just east of the zoo, the **Andrée Clark Bird Refuge** (1400 E Cabrillo Blvd) consists of a lagoon, gardens and a path from which to observe nesting freshwater birds.

Activities
BEACHES
Long and sandy, **East Beach** (Map pp484-5) is the stretch between Stearns Wharf and Montecito; it's Santa Barbara's largest and most popular beach. At its eastern end, across from the Biltmore Hotel, Armani swimsuits and Gucci sunglasses abound at **Butterfly Beach**.

Between Stearns Wharf and the harbor, **West Beach** (Map p486) has calm water and is popular with families and tourists staying in nearby motels. On the other side of the harbor, **Leadbetter Beach** is a good spot for surfing and windsurfing, with access to a grassy picnic area atop the cliffs.

CENTRAL COAST

West of Santa Barbara near the junction of Cliff Dr and Las Positas Rd, **Arroyo Burro Beach County Park** (also called Hendry's; Map pp484–5) has a parking lot, picnic area and restaurant.

BOATING

Santa Barbara has a myriad of ways to enjoy the water. See p493 for details on trips to the Channel Islands.

Sea Landing (Map p486; ☎ 805-882-0088, 888-779-4425; www.condorcruises.com; 310 Cabrillo Blvd), on the beach at the foot of Bath St, rents kayaks, jet skis and jet boats and also operates whale-watching excursions (adult $35 to $70, child $18 to $40) to the Channel Islands aboard a stomach-friendly catamaran, *Condor Express*.

Santa Barbara Sailing Center (Map p486; ☎ 805-962-2826; www.sbsail.com; from adult/child $32/20; 133 Harbor Way), at Stearns Wharf, will take you sailing on a 50ft sailing catamaran (adult/child $32/20). If you want to pilot your own craft, it also rents paddleboats, motor boats, fishing boats and sailing boats.

CYCLING & SKATING

The Cabrillo Blvd **beachfront bike path** runs for 3 miles along the water, between Andrée Clark Bird Refuge and Leadbetter Beach. The **Goleta Bikeway** continues west to UCSB.

Wheel Fun (Map p486; ☎ 805-966-2282; www.wheelfunrentals.com; 22 State St & 101 State St) rents bikes from $10 per hour and in-line skates.

Tours

The **Red Tile Tour** is a self-guided 12-block walking tour that's an excellent way to take in all major downtown sights and historic landmarks, including the Santa Barbara County Courthouse, Museum of Art, Historical Museum and El Presidio. Pick up a free map from the visitors center.

Santa Barbara Trolley (☎ 805-965-0353; www.sbtrolley.com; adult/child $16/free) makes a narrated 105-minute loop past Stearns Wharf, the courthouse, the botanical garden, the mission and sights in between. Tickets are valid all day between 10am and 4pm, allowing you to get off and on as you please.

Festivals & Events

Santa Barbara throws a good party. For the current calendar of events, contact the visitors center.

Santa Barbara International Film Festival (☎ 805-963-0023; www.sbfilmfestival.org) New independent US and foreign films are shown from mid-January to early February.

Summer Solstice Parade (☎ 805-965-3396; www.solsticeparade.com) Kicking off the summer, this wildly popular and just plain wild parade in late June feels like something out of Burning Man (see p354).

Old Spanish Fiesta Days (☎ 805-962-8101; www.oldspanishdays-fiesta.org) The town gets packed in early August for this slightly overrated festival.

Sleeping

Don't show up in Santa Barbara and expect to find a cheap room at the last minute, especially on weekends. A bottom-of-the-heap dive motel that's $50 on weekdays can triple in price on a Saturday night. Because nights are generally cool, many places don't have air conditioning.

BUDGET

A number of fairly affordable motels, especially in the off season, cluster along upper State St near Las Positas Rd. Standards vary widely and some are rather a long way out.

Santa Barbara Tourist Hostel (Map p486; ☎ 805-963-0154; www.sbhostel.com; 134 Chapala St; dm r $22; private r $59-79; P ❑) Right next to the train station, this fun little hostel feels like a college dorm. In addition to having use of a kitchen, pool table, lockers, laundry and book exchange, you can rent in-line skates, bikes and boogie boards.

Hotel State Street (Map p486; ☎ 805-966-6586; fax 805-962-8459; 121 State St; r summer $50-70, winter $40-55) As fun and funky as you can get – it has origami hanging from the ceiling for goodness sakes. Rooms are spotless and many have big windows, a sink and TV, but no phone. It's only two blocks to the beach.

Presidio Motel (Map p486; ☎ 805963-1355; 1620 State St; r $50-90; P ✖ ❄ ❑) Not too far from the action, the Presidio is basic but clean and comfortable.

There is no campground anywhere near downtown Santa Barbara, but about 17 miles and 20 miles west of town, respectively, right on the beach off Hwy 101, are **El Capitan State Beach** and **Refugio State Beach** (☎ 805-968-1033, reservations 800-444-7275; www.parks.ca.gov; sites $20-25). Refugio is a popular surf spot and student hangout, while El Capitan, perched on low bluffs, is more popular with families. Amenities include flush toilets, hot showers, picnic tables and barbecues.

MIDRANGE

There's a school of midrange places in the blocks behind West Beach. Castillo St can be busy, streets such as Bath further in are not.

Hotel Santa Barbara (Map p486; ☎ 805-957-9300, 888-259-7700; www.hotelsantabarbara.com; 533 State St; r $160-260; P ☒ ☒ ☒) This bright and cheery classic from 1925 has 75 rooms that exude a beachy grace. Rattan and light woods mix with Mediterranean tonings. It's perfectly located.

Hotel Virginia (Map p486; ☎ 805-805-963-9757, 800-549-1700; www.hotelvirginia.com; 17 W Haley St; r $135-210; P ☒ ☒ ☒) This nearly 90-year-old hotel downplays its Holiday Inn Express affiliation. And why not? It has heaps of character (a tile-filled lobby with fountain) and 61 comfortable rooms that couldn't be better positioned.

Marina Beach Motel (Map p486; ☎ 805-963-8845; www.marinabeachmotel.com; 21 Bath St; r $100-210; P ☒ ☒ ☒) This old one-story courtyard-style motel has been done up inside and made bright. The 32 rooms are comfy and the grounds are pretty. There's wi-fi and free bike use.

Harbor House (Map p486; ☎ 805-962-9745; www.harborhouseinn.com; 104 Bath St; r $100-200; P ☒ ☒) Wrapped around a magnificent palm tree, this 10-room place serves banana bread at breakfast. Most rooms have kitchens; all have wi-fi.

Casa Del Mar (Map p486; ☎ 805-963-4418; www.casadelmar.com; 18 Bath St; r $130-200) Santa Barbara's trademark architectural style comes to the beach in the intimate Spanish-style inn right out of the 1920s. The 21 rooms vary greatly, some have kitchenettes or fireplaces, all have nice work areas and an un-motel feel.

Villa Rosa (Map p486; ☎ 805-966-0851; www.villarosainnsb.com; 15 Chapala St; r $150-300; P ☒ ☒ ☒) An 18-room inn surrounding a flower-festooned courtyard with swimming pool and whirlpool. It's pink stucco and balconies outside and spacious modern Spanish inside.

TOP END

Four Seasons Biltmore Hotel (Map pp484-5; ☎ 805-969-2261, 800-332-3442; www.fourseasons.com; 1260 Channel Dr; r $500-700; P ☒ ☒ ☒ ☒) The 1927 Biltmore is Santa Barbara's iconic beachfront resort, where rooms are decorated in retro-20s chic and every detail is perfect. Bathrooms have Mediterranean-style custom tiles and huge soaking tubs. Just wandering around the compound with its lush and lavish gardens is a delight.

Hotel Oceana (Map p486; ☎ 805-965-4577, 800-965-9776; www.hoteloceana.com; 202 W Cabrillo Blvd; r $230-400; P ☒ ☒ ☒) Take four modest beachfront motels, rebuild them with more than a dash of style and élan and you have the Oceana. The breezy and beautifully appointed rooms look onto West Beach and the classy palm-lined lawn. There are two pools and wi-fi throughout.

Montecito Inn (Map p486; ☎ 805-969-7854, 800-843-2017; www.montecitoinn.com; 1295 Coast Village Rd; r $130-300; P ☒ ☒) The Hollywood connection here stares you in the face from the time you enter. The model of Charlie Chaplin dressed as the Tramp honors his role as the lead investor in the hotel, which opened in 1928. It's a period piece throughout and the smallish but plush rooms are in the heart of toney Montecito.

Eating

Santa Barbara has much-lauded offerings for every budget.

BUDGET

Sojourner (Map p486; ☎ 805-965-7922; 134 E Cañon Perdido; dishes $4-12) This creative, mostly vegetarian place has tables outside. Everything seems to have an extra touch like the hint of orange in the iced tea or the balsamic black beans in the Cobb salad.

La Super Rica (Map p486; ☎ 805-963-4940; 622 N Milpas St; dishes under $6; ⏰ 11am-9pm) This was food guru Julia Child's favorite Mexican restaurant and Taco Hell it ain't. Order from the window, then join local families at the picnic-style tables for inventive yet simple fare that's absolutely fresh.

D'Angelo Pastry & Bread (Map p486; ☎ 805-962-5466; 25 W Gutierrez St; dishes under $7; ⏰ 7am-2pm) Come in the morning for fresh-from-the-oven flaky croissants, and big cups of strong coffee at this sidewalk café-cum-bakery. At lunch the sandwiches are equally sublime.

The **farmers market** (Map p486; ☎ 805-962-5354; 500 & 600 blocks of State St; ⏰ 3-7pm Tue), located on the blocks either side of Cota St, is an attraction in itself.

MIDRANGE

Elements (Map p486; ☎ 805-259-9279; 129 E Anapamu St; meals $10-30) In a Craftsman-style house with a patio across from the courthouse, this gem

CENTRAL COAST

Tupelo Junction (Map p486; ☎ 805-899-3100; 1218 State St; mains $7-22; ☺ breakfast, lunch & dinner) Southern-style comfort food is the specialty at this always-bustling and ever-expanding State St café, with an appealing menu that unsettles due to its allure. At breakfast, the choices include yummy takes on old standards such as the vanilla-dipped French toast with homemade berry syrup. Later in the day, you'll find it tough choosing between options such as ham hock gumbo and lobster pot pie.

of a restaurant serves classic American fare with real attention paid to details. Interesting salads and sandwiches at lunch, much more adventuresome fare at night.

Brophy Brothers (Map p486; ☎ 805-966-4418; 119 Harbor Way; mains $8-20) Right on the harbor this upstairs place delivers as expected on fresh seafood. Popular with skippers and their mates, it has tables on a balcony and a bar with seats facing the view.

TOP END

Bouchon (Map p486; ☎ 805-730-1160; 9 W Victoria St; mains $23-29; ☺ dinner) The perfect, unhurried, follow-up dinner to a day in Wine Country, convivial Bouchon's bright, flavorful California cooking uses only locally grown small-scale-farm produce and meats, which marry beautifully with the more than 50 local wines by the glass. For romance, book a table on the cozy candlelit patio.

Lucky's (Map pp484-5; ☎ 805-565-7540; 1279 Coast Village Rd; mains $20-50; ☺ dinner) Just know that have the best steak ever at Lucky's and you'll be able to rest in peace. Beef is cooked superbly at this high-end Montecito steakhouse with a crisp white interior and engaging service. Sides and salads don't shrink from being an assertive supporting cast.

Intermezzo (Map p486; ☎ 805-966-9463; 813 Anacapa St; mains $9-15) The casual Intermezzo has the sleek sophistication of a European bistro and a menu to match. There are many small plate choices and a myriad of wines by the glass in the seductive bar.

Enterprise Fish Co (Map p486; ☎ 805-962-3313; 225 State St; mains $12-25) Huge and open, this teaming fish place has a central kitchen where you can see the chefs work wonders with what's

fresh. Many choices are grilled and you can start off with heavenly lobster bisque.

Drinking

Santa Barbara's after-dark scene revolves around lower State St. Saturday nights here are rowdy. Places good for a drink that are listed under Eating are Brophy Brothers and Intermezzo.

James Joyce (Map p486; ☎ 805-962-2688; 513 State St) Free peanuts in the shell! A snacker's dream come true at this vaguely Irish-feeling pub that always a good place for a pint. On Saturday night, the house band featuring Dick LeGrand heats up the crowd with Dixieland jazz.

Santa Barbara Brewing Co (Map p486; ☎ 805-730-1040; 501 State St) Home to about a dozen microbrews on tap including the killer IPA Red Tide, it's amazingly hoppy. There's also a long menu of pub fare.

Rocks (Map p486; ☎ 805-884-1190; 801 State St) The patio at this slightly upscale place is a good place for eye-balling the State St action. Wide choice of well-poured drinks and wines by the glass.

Entertainment

The free weekly *Independent* (www.independent.com) has complete events listings and reviews. The *Santa Barbara News-Press* (www.newspress.com) has a daily events calendar and a Friday supplement called 'Scene' which has good dining reviews. There are numerous clubs on lower State St whose names and formats change on a whim.

CLUBS

Wild Cat (Map p486; ☎ 805-962-7970; 15 W Ortega St) Looking like a cross between a warehouse and a love den, Wild Cat is a 1970s revival lounge, with a diverse crowd shooting pool.

Soho (Map p486; ☎ 805-962-7776; www.sohosb.com; 1221 State St) Soho, above a McDonald's, has live bands nightly. Styles range from blues to funk to rock.

THEATRE & CLASSICAL MUSIC

Santa Barbara supports a variety of companies and historic venues.

Lobero Theatre (Map p486; ☎ 805-963-0761; 33 E Cañon Perdido St) This is one of California's oldest theaters (1873), and presents modern dance, ballet, chamber music and special events, often featuring internationally re-nowned top talent.

Granada Theatre (Map p486; ☎ 805-966-2324; 1216 State St) The Granada, built in 1930, is undergoing a lavish restoration. After 2006 it will be home to the Santa Barbara Symphony, opera and ballet.

Arlington Center for the Performing Arts (Map p486; ☎ 805-963-4408; 1317 State St) Another classic movie palace, home to the Santa Barbara Symphony until late 2006. It's a splendid place to see a film.

Shopping

State St has a fabulous range of shops and department stores. There are numerous stores run by local designers.

Paseo Nuevo (Map p486; btwn Cañon Perdido & Ortega Sts) This is an attractive outdoor mall anchored by Nordstrom and Macy's department stores, plus various retail chains.

La Arcada (Map p486; 1114 State St) Near Figueroa St, La Arcada is a historic red-tile passageway, which is filled with boutiques, restaurants and whimsical public art.

Historic Paseo (Map p486; State St), opposite Paseo Nuevo is another flower-festooned courtyard.

Getting There & Away

Santa Barbara Municipal Airport (SBA; Map pp484-5; ☎ 805-967-7111; 500 Fowler Rd), in Goleta some 8 miles west of downtown off Hwy 101, is a little gem with a beautiful, albeit slightly cramped design. American Eagle (Los Angeles), America West Express (Phoenix) and United Express (Denver, LA and San Francisco) are among the carriers with service. All major car-rental firms are here.

Santa Barbara Airbus (Map p486; ☎ 805-964-7759, 800-423-1618; www.santabarbaraairbus.com) shuttles between Los Angeles International Airport (LAX) and Santa Barbara (one way from $42, 2½ to three hours, 14 per day).

Greyhound (Map p486; ☎ 805-965-7551; 34 W Carrillo St) has up to nine daily buses to Los Angeles ($12, 2¼ to three hours) and up to five to San Francisco ($32, 7½ to nine hours), making stops along Hwy 101.

Amtrak (Map p486; 209 State St) operates from a beautifully restored station. Santa Barbara is a stop on the daily Seattle–LA *Coast Starlight*. It is the terminus for most of the frequent *Pacific Surfliner* regional trains to LA ($21, 2½ to three hours). One also goes north to San Luis Obispo ($22) and there are Amtrak buses north as well along Hwy 101 to San Jose.

Getting Around

The **Downtown-Waterfront Shuttle** route (25¢, every 10 minutes, 10am to 6pm) runs along State St to Stearns Wharf. A second route (25¢, every 30 minutes, 10am to 6pm) travels along the waterfront between the zoo and Harbor Way.

Santa Barbara Metropolitan Transit District (MTD; ☎ 805-683-3702; www.sbmtd.gov; $1.25) runs buses throughout the city and surrounding county. The **Transit Center** (Map p486; 1020 Chapala St) has details on routes and schedules.

OJAI

pop 8100

About 35 miles southeast of Santa Barbara and 14 miles inland from Ventura off Hwy 33, Ojai (pronounced *oh*-hi, meaning 'moon' to the Chumash) is a town that has long drawn artists and New Agers. Ojai is famous for the rosy glow that emanates both from its mountains at sunset – the so-called Pink Moment – and from the faces emerging from spa treatments. Many have been taken by the place, including Frank Capra who had the Ojai Valley represent the mythical Shangri-La in his 1937 movie *Lost Horizon*.

For information, go to the **Ojai Chamber of Commerce** (☎ 805-646-8126; www.ojaichamber.org; 150 W Ojai Ave; ⊙ 9:30am-4:30pm Mon-Fri, 10am-4pm Sat & Sun).

The Arcade Plaza, a maze of Mission revival-style buildings on Ojai Ave (the main thoroughfare), contains interesting shops, cafés and art galleries. **Bart's Books** (☎ 805-646-3755; 302 W Matilija St), one block north of Ojai Ave, is a large place with outdoor reading areas.

The well-maintained 9-mile **Ojai Valley Trail**, converted from old train routes, is popular with walkers, cyclists and equestrians.

The local star **Ojai Valley Inn & Spa** (☎ 805-646-5511, 800-422-6524; www.ojairesort.com; Country Club Rd; r from $250; ✕ ✖ 💻 🏊), on the western end of town, has been reborn after a total renovation. It's a gorgeous place to pamper yourself or let others do it for you. The golf course surrounds the lavish gardens and Mission-style architecture.

Farm Hostel (☎ 805-646-0311; www.hostelhandbook.com/farmhostel; PO Box 723, Ojai, CA 93024; dm $15;

P 🖳) allows you to connect with the land at this working family farm set in a large organic orchard, which reflects the serene and spiritual aura of Ojai. But note various idiosyncrasies: guests stay in gender-segregated dorms, the communal kitchen is meat-free, and guests need to show proof of international travel. It's 10 minutes from town; reservations by telephone are mandatory. Proof of international travel is also required. Free pickups from downtown Ventura.

Suzanne's Cuisine (☎ 805-640-1961; 502 W Ojai Ave; meals $10-30; ☪ lunch & dinner Wed-Mon) celebrates the produce of the valley. Creative salads and sandwiches mark lunch; dinner is more ambitious. The garden is scented by lavender.

The only direct bus service is from the city of Ventura. Take **SCAT** (☎ 805-487-4222; www.scat .org) bus 16 from Main & Figueroa Sts ($1.25, 45 minutes, hourly).

CHANNEL ISLANDS NATIONAL PARK

The Channel Islands is an eight-island chain lying off the coast from Newport Beach to Santa Barbara. The four northern islands – San Miguel, Santa Rosa, Santa Cruz and Anacapa – along with tiny Santa Barbara island 38 miles west of San Pedro comprise the Channel Islands National Park. The islands have unique flora and fauna and extensive tidepools and kelp forests. Here you'll find almost 150 mostly plant and a few animal species that are not found anywhere else in the world.

Originally inhabited by the Chumash and Gabrielino peoples (who were taken to the mainland missions in the early 1800s), the islands were owned by sheep ranchers and the US Navy until the mid-1970s, when conservation efforts began. San Miguel, Santa Rosa, Anacapa and Santa Barbara Islands are now administered by the National Park Service (NPS), which also controls 20% of Santa Cruz (the other 80% belongs to the Nature Conservancy).

Information

NPS runs the excellent **Channel Islands National Park Visitors Center** (☎ 805-658-5730; www.nps.gov /chis; 1901 Spinnaker Dr, Ventura; ☪ 8:30am-5pm). It is the primary resource center and has good natural-history displays, models of the islands and a three-story lookout from where you can see the islands on a clear day. Here too you can learn about attempts to restore

and preserve the islands, such as the current efforts to oust destructive feral pigs introduced years ago by settlers.

The center is at the far tip of Ventura Harbor, off Harbor Blvd southwest of Hwy 101.

The Islands

Anacapa, which is actually three separate islets, is the closest to the mainland and offers a nice, easy but memorable introduction to the islands' ecology. A visitors center and picnic area sit atop the island's narrow plateau. Snorkeling, diving, swimming and kayaking are all possible in the rich kelp beds surrounding the island.

Santa Cruz, the largest island, is laced with hiking trails and is probably the best island for exploring on your own. Popular activities include swimming, snorkeling, scuba diving and kayaking.

Beautiful sandy beaches, nearly 200 bird species and the Painted Cave are highlights on **Santa Rosa**, which is the best destination for longer trips.

San Miguel – the most remote of the four northern islands – offers solitude and a wilderness experience, but it's often shrouded in fog and is very windy. Some sections are off limits to prevent disruption of the fragile ecosystem. There are interesting natural formations (eg Caliche Forest, made of calcium-carbonate castings of trees) and an elephant seal colony at Point Bennett at various times during the year. Smaller colonies are on Santa Barbara and Santa Rosa Islands.

Santa Barbara is home to the humongous northern elephant seal and is a remote playground for birds and marine wildlife. Facilities include a visitors center and a primitive campground. Hikers, bird-watchers, divers, snorkelers and anglers will all find their fill here.

Beautiful any time of year, the islands receive most of their visitors between June and September; however, the nicest times to visit are during the spring-wildflower season (in April and May) and in September and October, when the weather conditions are the most calm.

Sleeping

All islands have primitive **campgrounds** (☎ reservations 800-365-2267; http://reservations.nps.gov; sites $10), which are open year-round. Each one has pit toilets and picnic tables, but you must take everything in (and out, including trash). Water is only available on Santa Rosa and Santa Cruz Islands. Due to fire danger, campfires are not allowed, but enclosed camp stoves are OK. Be prepared to carry your stuff a half to 1½ miles to the campground from the landing areas.

The campground on Santa Barbara is large, grassy and surrounded by hiking trails, while the one on Anacapa is high, rocky and isolated. Camping on San Miguel, with its unceasing wind, fog and volatile weather, is only for the hardy. Santa Rosa's campground is sheltered by a canyon with wonderful views of Santa Cruz, whose own site is within a eucalyptus grove. Del Norte, a backcountry campground on Santa Cruz, had just opened at the time of writing. It's in a shaded oak grove, a 3½-mile hike from the landing.

Getting There & Away

Two boat companies and one air operator offer camper transportation and excursions to the islands.

Island Packers (☎ 805-642-1393, recorded information 805-642-7688; www.islandpackers.com; 1691 Spinnaker Dr, Ventura), near the visitors center, offers numerous day trips and packages to all the islands. Rates begin at $42/25 per adult/child for the East Anacapa trip. Going to the other islands costs more and campers pay extra for their gear. Nonlanding whale-watching tours start at $26/17 for a 3½-hour gray whale trip (January to March).

Truth Aquatics (Map p486; ☎ 805-962-1127; www .truthaquatics.com; 301 W Cabrillo Blvd), the park's Santa Barbara-based operator, offers similar excursions as Island Packers.

Most trips require a minimum number of participants and may be canceled anytime due to surf and weather conditions. In any case, landing is never guaranteed, again because of changeable weather and surf conditions. Reservations are recommended for weekend, holiday and summer trips, and advance payment is required.

Those in a hurry or prone to seasickness might want to consider taking a 25-minute flight to Santa Rosa Island with **Channel Islands Aviation** (☎ 805-987-1301; adult/child $130/105) instead. Day trips leave year-round from the airports in Camarillo and Santa Barbara.

VENTURA
pop 103,000

Ventura, an agricultural and manufacturing center, makes up for its humble roots in its historic downtown along Main St, north of Hwy 101 via Seaward Ave. Here, you'll find a terrific assortment of ungentrified antique and thrift shops as well as used-book stores.

Ventura's mission roots remain in evidence at the **Mission San Buenaventura** (☎ 805-643-4318; 225 E Main St; donation requested; ☉ 10am-5pm Mon-Sat, 10am-4pm Sun), the last one founded by Padre Junípero Serra in 1782. The restored church is still home to an active congregation. A stroll around the complex is a tranquil experience, which leads you through a courtyard and a small museum, past statues of saints and 250-year-old paintings of the Stations of the Cross.

The mission's original foundations and related artifacts are among items on display in the nearby **Albinger Archaeological Museum** (☎ 805-648-5823; 113 E Main St; admission free; ☉ 10am-4pm Wed-Sun).

Across the street, **Ventura County Museum of History & Art** (☎ 805-653-0323; 100 E Main St; adult/child $4/1; ☉ 10am-5pm Tue-Sun) has an eclectic mix of exhibits. Highlights include some 300 quarter-life-sized historical figures, dressed in period costumes (by George Stuart), and an exhibit tracing Ventura's history back to the Chumash period.

Unwind from the past and hunt for bargains and treasure at **Anacapa Brew Pub** (☎ 805-643-2337; 472 E Main St; mains $8-18), which crafts its own microbrews and makes a fine pulled-pork sandwich.

Greyhound (☎ 805-653-0164; 291 E Thompson Blvd) runs buses daily from LA ($12, 2½ hours) en route to Santa Barbara ($8.50, 40 minutes). **Amtrak** (cnr Harbor Blvd & Figueroa) operates daily trains to Santa Barbara ($8.50, 40 minutes) and LA ($14, two hours).

CENTRAL COAST

Los Angeles

Whatever your version of the American Dream, the chances are good that some neighborhood, beach, event or chance encounter in Los Angeles will make it real for you. All you need is a credit card, car, beach towel, some lively curiosity and this book: LA will do the rest.

Looking for the edge? Visiting LA is like pushing the fast-forward button on the movie of your life. In this city swirling with energy and creativity, tomorrow's trends are born, nurtured and released. Relaxation? Beaches, parks and yoga studios help you on the tranquil path. Food and drink? Loosen your belt for boundary-pushing fusion cuisine, a United Nations of eateries and wines. Arts and architecture? Rejoice if the names Wright, Gehry and Greene & Greene mean anything to you, for LA is where they reached their heights. Music? Domingo to the Doors to Dr Dre. They either cut their musical teeth or conquered the world from here, or both.

There's one thing you won't need for your assault on LA's pleasures: your preconceptions. Locals knowingly smile at visitors who think they've already figured out the city: smog, traffic, celebrity murders, plastic culture and bosoms and the maddening hugeness of its featureless mass. That's it, right? So sorry, but so wrong. LA's truths aren't delivered in headlines or on a movie screen. They're in small portions at the street, personal and experiential levels. As with most exotic places of the world – and LA is one – you get back what you bring to the party.

HIGHLIGHTS

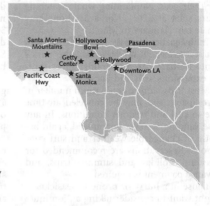

- Hot-rodding along breathtaking Pacific Coast Hwy to **Malibu** (p518), preferably on a sunny summer day
- Joining the locals for a picnic and a concert at the venerable **Hollywood Bowl** (p512)
- Exploring LA's 'wild' side on a trek through the **Santa Monica Mountains** (p530)
- Mingling with the beau monde in a hip **Hollywood bar or club** (p546)
- Dressing up for a day in **Pasadena** (p526), the ultimate culture vulture destination
- Admiring what $1 billion will buy at the exquisite **Getty Center** (p518)
- Taking a trip around the world and back in time in **Downtown LA** (p521)
- Immersing yourself in the sassy SoCal vibe in sophisticated **Santa Monica** (p518)

| ■ CITY/COUNTY POPULATION: 4/10.2 MILLION | ■ AVERAGE TEMPS: JAN 47/66°F, JUL 62/82°F |

HISTORY

Los Angeles' human history begins as early as 6000 BC, when the Gabrieleño and Chumash peoples occupied the region. Their hunter-gatherer existence ended in the late 18th century with the arrival of Spanish missionaries and pioneers, led by Padre Junípero Serra. Known as El Pueblo de la Reina de Los Angeles, the first civilian settlement became a thriving farming community but remained an isolated outpost for decades.

After Spain lost its hold on the territory to Mexico in 1821, many of that nation's citizens looked to California to quench their thirst for private land. By the mid-1830s, the missions had been secularized and their land divvied up into free land grants by Mexican governors, thus giving birth to the rancho (cattle ranch) system.

At the time of the Mexican–American War (1846–48), American soldiers encountered some resistance from General Andrés Pico and other Mexican commanders, but eventually LA came under US rule along with the rest of California. The city was incorporated on April 4, 1850.

A series of seminal events caused LA's population to swell to two million by 1930: the collapse of the Northern California Gold Rush in the 1850s, the arrival of the transcontinental railroad in the 1870s, the birth of the citrus industry in the late 1800s, the discovery of oil in 1892, the launch of the port of LA in 1907, the birth of the movie industry in 1908 and the opening of the LA Aqueduct in 1913.

Aside from motion pictures, few industries have had as strong an impact on LA as aviation. During WWI, the Lockheed brothers and Donald Douglas established aircraft manufacturing plants in LA. Two decades later, the aviation industry – helped along by billions of federal dollars for military contracts – helped to lift LA out of the Great Depression. Defense contracts continued to be a driving force behind the city's economy right until the end of the Cold War in 1990.

The deluge of new residents arriving after WWII shaped LA into the megalopolis of today, with its attendant problems, including suburban sprawl, air pollution and racial strife. Major riots in 1965 and 1992 created an abyss of distrust between the city's police department and various ethnic groups. A police corruption scandal in the late 1990s did nothing to alleviate tensions, although in 2002 the arrival of a new police chief, William Bratton of New York, did. Violent crime has dropped significantly on his watch and, despite isolated incidents of police brutality, he has earned the respect of most ethnic groups.

Ballistic population growth, pollution, traffic and soaring real-estate prices are among the problems that continue to cloud LA's sunny skies in the first decade of the new millennium. But with a strong economy, low unemployment and decreasing

LOS ANGELES IN...

Two Days

Fuel up with breakfast at the **Griddle Café** (p541) in West Hollywood, then drive west on Sunset to the **Getty Center** (p518). Head downhill to mansion-studded **Beverly Hills** (p516) and Rodeo Dr, then check out newly revitalized **Hollywood Blvd** (p511). Have sunset drinks at the hilltop **Yamashiro** (p546), then let your belly tell you where to go for dinner.

On the second day you're off to Downtown LA where your program might include **El Pueblo de Los Angeles** (p521), the **Cathedral of Our Lady of the Angels** (p522), **Walt Disney Concert Hall** (p523) and the **MOCA Grand Avenue** (p523). Spend the afternoon relaxing at **Venice Beach** (p519) and stroll along wild and wacky Ocean Front Walk. Catch the sunset from the Ferris wheel on the **Santa Monica Pier** (p519), then stay in Santa Monica for dinner.

Four Days

Make **Universal Studios Hollywood** (p528) the focus of your third day, then pack a picnic for a concert at the **Hollywood Bowl** (p512). For a change of pace on day four, drive up Pacific Coast Hwy to **Malibu** (p518), cut inland to **Malibu Creek State Park** (p530) and hike to the *M*A*S*H* filming site. Have dinner on the coast, then head to the **Sunset Strip** (p514) for one last night on the razzle.

crime rate, overall morale remains high. In May 2005, Angelenos elected Antonio Villaraigosa, the city's first Latino mayor since 1872. Perhaps even racial tensions will soon be a thing of the past.

ORIENTATION

Los Angeles may be vast and amorphous, but the areas of visitor interest are fairly well defined. About 12 miles inland, Downtown LA combines some great architecture and museums with global-village pizzazz thanks to such enclaves as Chinatown, Little Tokyo and El Pueblo de Los Angeles. Euroflavored Pasadena lies northeast of Downtown, while sprawling Hollywood with its hip 'hoods of Los Feliz and Silver Lake is to the northwest. West Hollywood is LA's center of urban chic and the gay and lesbian community. Most TV and movie studios are actually north of Hollywood in the San Fernando Valley.

South of Hollywood, Mid-City's main draw is Museum Row, while further west are ritzy Beverly Hills and the Westside communities of Westwood, home to University of California (UCLA); mansion-studded Bel Air; and Brentwood with the hilltop Getty Center. Of the beach towns, Santa Monica is the most tourist-friendly; but others include swish-but-low-key Malibu, bohemian Venice and bustling Long Beach.

Getting around is easiest by car, although public transport is usually adequate within specific neighborhoods. For information on traveling to and from Los Angeles International Airport (LAX), see p555.

Maps

A good map is as essential as sunscreen in LA. For navigating within specific neighborhoods the ones in this book should be sufficiently detailed. Otherwise, pick up a street map at gas stations, bookstores, convenience stores, supermarkets, tourist offices or a branch of the **American Automobile Association** (AAA; ☎ 800-874-7532; www.aaa.com). Lonely Planet's own laminated Los Angeles map is available in bookstores or at www.lonelyplanet.com.

INFORMATION
Bookstores

Outlets of chain stores Barnes & Noble and Borders abound throughout LA; check the

---

FREEWAY LOGIC

Angelenos live and die by their freeways and sooner or later you too will end up part of this metal cavalcade. It helps to know that most freeways have both a number and a name, which corresponds to where they're headed. However, to add to the confusion, freeways passing through Downtown usually have two names. The I-10, for instance, is called the Santa Monica Fwy west of the central city and the San Bernardino Fwy east of it. The I-5 heading north is the Golden State Fwy, heading south it's the Santa Ana Fwy. And the I-110 is both the Pasadena Fwy and the Harbor Fwy. Generally, freeways going east–west have even numbers, those running north–south have odd numbers.

Yellow Pages for locations. Listed here are our favorite indie bookstores, each with their own specialties and eclectic collections.

Bodhi Tree (Map pp504-5; ☎ 310-659-1733, 800-825-9798; 8585 Melrose Ave, West Hollywood) Celebrity-heavy dispensary of new and used spiritual tomes, soulful music and aura-enhancing incense. Psychic readings, too.

Book Soup (Map pp504-5; ☎ 310-659-3110; 8818 W Sunset Blvd, West Hollywood) Solid selection of entertainment, queer studies and fiction. Also great people-watching (high celeb quotient) and big-name book signings.

California Map & Travel Center (Map pp508-9; ☎ 310-396-6277; 3312 Pico Blvd, Santa Monica) Well-respected travel bookstore with frequent readings and slide shows.

Distant Lands (Map pp498-9; ☎ 626-449-3220; 56 S Raymond Ave, Pasadena) Treasure chest of travel books, guides and gadgets, including luggage and daypacks.

Equator Bookstore (Map pp508-9; ☎ 310-399-5544; 1103 Abbot Kinney Blvd, Venice) Rare and collectible books about art, surf culture, black studies, drugs and crime, and assorted offbeat subjects inside a gallery-style store.

Traveler's Bookcase (Map pp504-5; ☎ 323-655-0575; 8375 W 3rd St, Mid-City) Just what it says.

Vroman's (Map pp498-9; ☎ 626-449-3220; 695 E Colorado Blvd, Pasadena) Southern California's oldest bookstore (since 1894) and a favorite with local literati.

Emergency

Emergency number (☎ 911) For police, fire or ambulance service.
Police (☎ 800-275-5273) For nonemergency service.
Rape & Battering Hotline (☎ 800-656-4673)

Internet Access

Cybercafés are notoriously short-lived, so call ahead to confirm that the following are still in business. **Public libraries** (☎ 213-228-7272; www.lapl.org) also offer limited free Internet access. For branches call or log on to their website. For wi-fi locations, check www.jiwire.com.

Cyber Java (Map pp502-3; ☎ 323-466-5600; 7080 Hollywood Blvd, Hollywood; per 10 min $1.75, wi-fi free; ⏰ 7am-11:30pm)

Interactive Café (Map pp508-9; ☎ 310-395-5009; 215 Broadway, Santa Monica; per 10 min $1; ⏰ 6am-1am Sun-Thu, 6am-2am Fri & Sat)

Rooms Café (Map pp506-7; ☎ 310-445-3320; 1783 Westwood Blvd, Westwood; per hr $6; ⏰ 1pm-1am)

Internet Resources

@ LA (www.at-la.com) The ultimate Web portal to all things LA.

LA Blogs (www.lablogs.com) Gateway to LA-related blogs.

LA.com (www.la.com) Hip guide to shopping, eating and special events around town.

Los Angeles Almanac (www.laalmanac.com) All the facts and figures at your fingertips.

Los Angeles Convention and Visitors Bureau (www.visitlosangeles.info) Official website of the Los Angeles Convention & Visitors Bureau.

Media

For entertainment listings magazines, see p548.

KCRW 89.9 fm (www.kcrw.org) A National Public Radio (NPR) station with world music and intelligent talk.

KPFK 90.7 fm (www.kpfk.org) Part of the Pacific radio network; news and talk.

LA Weekly (www.laweekly.com) Free alternative news and listings magazine.

Los Angeles Magazine (www.losangelesmagazine .com) Glossy lifestyle monthly with useful restaurant guide.

Los Angeles Times (www.latimes.com) Nation's fourth-largest daily and winner of 35 Pulitzer Prizes, including five in 2004.

Medical Services

Cedars-Sinai Medical Center (Map pp504-5; ☎ 310-855-5000; 8700 Beverly Blvd, West Hollywood; ⏰ 24hr emergency room)

Los Angeles Free Clinic (☎ appointments at any branch 323-462-4158) Hollywood (Map pp502-3; 6043 Hollywood Blvd); Hollywood (Map pp502-3; 5205 Melrose Ave); Mid-City (Map pp504-5; 8405 Beverly Blvd) Medical and dental care, and counseling.

Sav-On Drugs (⏰ 24hr) Mid-City (Map pp504-5; ☎ 323-937-3019; 6360 W 3rd St); Santa Monica (Map pp508-9; ☎ 310-828-6456; 2505 Santa Monica Blvd) Pharmacy chain with dozens of branches across town; check the Yellow Pages for additional locations.

UCLA Medical Center (Map pp506-7; ☎ 310-825-9111; 10833 Le Conte Ave, Westwood; ⏰ 24hr emergency room)

Venice Family Clinic (Map pp508-9; ☎ 310-392-8630; 604 Rose Ave, Venice) Good for general health concerns, with payment on a sliding scale according to your means.

Women's Clinic (Map pp506-7; ☎ 310-203-8899; 9911 W Pico Blvd, Suite 500, Century City) Fees are calculated on a sliding scale according to your capacity to pay.

Money

American Express West Hollywood (Map pp504-5; ☎ 310-659-1682; 8493 W 3rd St; ⏰ 9am-6pm Mon-Fri, 10am-3pm Sat); Pasadena (Map pp498-9; ☎ 626-449-2281; 269 S Lake Ave; ⏰ 9am-6pm Mon-Fri, 10am-2pm Sat)

TravelEx (☎ 800-287-7362) West Hollywood (Map pp504-5; 806 Hilldale Ave, West Hollywood; ⏰ 9am-5pm Mon-Fri); Beverly Hills (Map pp506-7; 421 N Rodeo Dr, Beverly Hills; ⏰ 10am-6pm Mon-Fri)

Post

You're never far from a post office in LA. Call ☎ 800-275-8777 for the nearest branch.

Telephone

Thanks to the growth of electronic communication devices, LA County is now divided into five area codes; all telephone numbers in this chapter are accompanied by the appropriate area code.

Tourist Information

California Welcome Center (Map pp504-5; ☎ 310-854-7616; Beverly Center Mall, 8500 Beverly Blvd, West Hollywood; ⏰ 10am-6pm Mon-Sat, 11am-6pm Sun)

Downtown Los Angeles Visitor Information Center (Map pp500-1; ☎ 213-689-8822; www.visit losangeles.info; 685 S Figueroa St, Downtown; ⏰ 9am-5pm Mon-Fri)

Hollywood Visitors Center (Map pp502-3; ☎ 323-467-6412; Hollywood & Highland complex, 6801 Hollywood Blvd, Hollywood; ⏰ 10am-10pm Mon-Sat, 10am-7pm Sun)

Santa Monica Visitors Center (Map pp508-9; ☎ 310-393-7593; www.santamonica.com; 1920 Main St, Santa Monica; ⏰ 10am-6pm)

Santa Monica Visitors Kiosk (Map pp508-9; 1400 Ocean Ave, Santa Monica; ⏰ 10am-5pm Jun-Aug, 10am-4pm rest of year)

(Continued on page 511)

LOS AN

INFORMATION

American Express	(see 58)	
Distant Lands Bookstore	(see 24)	
Long Beach Visitor Information Kiosk	(see 3)	
Pasadena Central Library	(see 25)	
Pasadena Convention & Visitors Bureau	1	E2
Vroman's	2	E2

SIGHTS & ACTIVITIES (pp511–31)

Adamson House	(see 20)	
Aquarium of the Pacific	3	D4
Cabrillo Marine Aquarium	4	D5
California Institute of Technology	5	E2
El Mercado	6	D2
Escape on Horseback	7	B2
Forest Lawn Memorial Park - Glendale	8	D2
Gamble House	9	E1
Getty Center	10	C2
Getty Villa	11	B2
Huntington Library, Art Collections and Botanical Gardens	12	E2
Jet Propulsion Laboratory	13	E1
Kidspace Children's Museum	14	E2
Leimert Park Village	15	D3
Long Beach Museum of Art	16	E4
Los Angeles Maritime Museum	17	D5
Malibu Bluffs Park	18	A2
Malibu Colony	19	A2
Malibu Lagoon Museum	(see 20)	
Malibu Pier	20	B2
Mission San Fernando Rey de España	21	C1
Museum of Jurassic Technology	22	C2
Museum of Latin American Art	23	D4
New School of Cooking	(see 36)	
Norton Simon Museum	24	E2
Old Town Pasadena	24	E2
Pacific Asia Museum	25	E2
Palisades High	26	B2
Paramount Pictures	27	A2
Pasadena City Hall	(see 25)	
Pasadena Museum of California Art	(see 25)	
Pike at Rainbow Harbor	(see 3)	
Polytechnic High School	28	D4
Ports O' Call	(see 17)	
Queen Mary	29	D4
Rose Bowl Stadium	30	E1
San Gabriel Mission	31	E2
Santa Anita Park	32	E2
Scorpion	(see 29)	
Self-Help Graphics & Art	33	D2
Watts Towers	34	D3
Shoreline Village	35	D4
Sony Pictures Studios	36	C2
SS Lane Victory	37	D4
University of Southern California (USC)	38	D2
Vista del Arroyo Hotel	39	E2
Wayfarer's Chapel	40	C4
Will Rogers Ranch House	(see 41)	
Will Rogers State Historic Park	41	B2

SLEEPING (pp533–9)

Artists' Inn & Cottage B&B	42	E2
Beach House at Hermosa	43	C4
Best Western Sunrise Hotel	44	C4
Bissell House B&B	45	E2
Casa Malibu Inn	46	B2
Coast Hotel Long Beach	47	D4
Dockside Boat & Bed	48	D4
HI-Los Angeles–South Bay	49	D5
Malibu Country Inn	50	A2
Malibu Creek State Park Campground	51	A2
Queen Mary Hotel	(see 29)	
Ritz-Carlton Huntington Hotel & Spa	52	E2
Saga Motor Hotel	53	E2
Surf City Hostel	54	C4
Turret House	55	D4

EATING (pp540–6)

Alegria	56	D4
Bar Celona	(see 24)	
Belmont Brewing Company	57	E4
Burger Continental	58	E2
Café Bizou	(see 24)	
Geoffrey's	59	A2
Gina Lee's Bistro	60	C4
New Concept	61	D2
Saladang Song	62	E2
Uncle Bill's Pancake House	63	C3
Xiomara	(see 24)	

DRINKING (pp546–7)

705 Bar	64	C4
Alex's Bar	65	E4
Aloha Sharkeez	(see 64)	
Baja Sharkeez	66	C3

0   10 km
0   6 mi

E (2) To Wrightwood
Cogswell Reservoir
F
G San Gabriel Mountains
San Gabriel River
H

Angeles Crest Hwy   Red Box Rd

Mt Wilson Observatory
Mt Wilson (5710ft)
Angeles National Forest
San Gabriel Reservoir
Morris Reservoir
Mt San Antonio (Old Baldy; 10,064ft)

● 13   Arroyo Parkway
Brookside Park
Altadena
Colorado Blvd
Pasadena
San Antonio Heights
Foothill Fwy
Monrovia
Arcadia
Azusa
Glendora
Rancho Cucamonga
(30)
Upland
(66)

California Blvd
Los Angeles County Arboretum & Botanic Garden
Santa Fe Dam Recreation Area
Temple City
San Marino
Alhambra
San Gabriel
Pasadena Fwy
Monterey Park
Garvey Ave
Baldwin Park
El Monte
West Covina
Covina
Bonelli Regional County Park
Montclair
Ontario International Airport
Mission Blvd
Ontario
Pomona
To Big Bear Lake (55mi) Palm Springs (65mi)
(60)

Whittier Narrows Recreation Area
(10)
Atlantic Blvd
61
East Los Angeles
Industry
La Puente
San Bernardino Fwy
(10)
Diamond Bar
(57)
(71)
Chino
(83)
Norco

Pico Rivera
Downey
Santa Ana Fwy
San Gabriel River Fwy
Whittier
Schabarum Regional Park
Pomona Fwy
(60)
Rowland Heights
(57)
Diamond Bar
(142)
Carbon Canyon Rd
Chino Hills State Park
Prado Flood Control Basin
(3)

(710)
(5)
(605)
Norwalk
Paramount
La Mirada
La Habra Heights
Los Angeles County
Orange County
La Habra
Imperial Hwy
Brea
Richard Nixon Library
Yorba Linda Blvd
Yorba Linda
(90)
(71)
Corona

Artesia Fwy
Lakewood
Cerritos
Carson St
Long Beach Airport
Buena Park
Knott's Berry Farm
Lincoln Ave
CSU Fullerton
Fullerton
Riverside Fwy
Placentia
(91)
(91)
Santa Ana Mountains

San Gabriel River Fwy
(39)
Cypress
(5)
Anaheim
(57)
(55)
Villa Park
Irvine Regional Park
(231)
Cleveland National Forest
(4)

E Willow St
CSU Long Beach
(605)
Katella Ave
Stanton
Disneyland & Disney's California Adventure
Garden Grove
Garden Grove Fwy
(22)
(22)
Orange
Tustin

Belmont Shore
Naples
57
Westminster
Santa Ana
Irvine Transportation Corridor
(5)
Eastern Transportation Corridor

each Harbor
ong Beach
reakwater
Seal Beach Pier
Seal Beach National Wildlife Refuge
Beach Blvd
San Diego Fwy
(405)
Santa Ana River
San Pedro Bay

Bolsa Chica State Beach
San Pedro Bay
Pacific Coast Hwy
Huntington Beach
Huntington Pier
Huntington City Beach
Huntington State Beach
(1)
Irvine
John Wayne Airport (Orange County)
(55)
(73)
UC Irvine
Costa Mesa
Costa Mesa Fwy
Irvine Center Dr
(231)
(5)

Newport Beach
Newport Bay
Corona del Mar
Corona del Mar State Beach
Crystal Cove State Park
(73)

San Pedro Channel
Ferry to Catalina Island
(133)

Laguna Beach
Aliso Beach
Laguna Niguel
To Catalina Express Port – Dana Point (3mi)

(5)
(6)

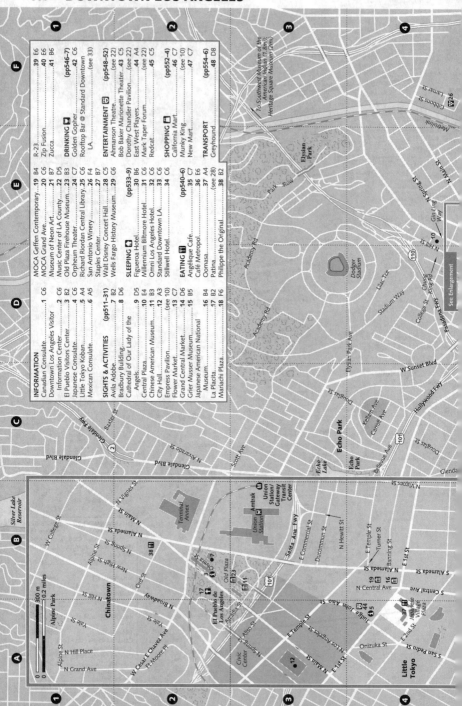

INFORMATION
Canadian Consulate.....1 C6
Downtown Los Angeles Visitor Information Center.....2 C6
El Pueblo Visitors Center.....3 B2
Japanese Consulate.....4 C6
Little Tokyo Koban.....5 A4
Mexican Consulate.....6 A5

SIGHTS & ACTIVITIES (pp511-31)
Avila Adobe.....7 B2
Bradbury Building.....8 D6
Cathedral of Our Lady of the Angels.....9 D5
Central Plaza.....10 E4
Chinese American Museum.....11 B3
City Hall.....12 A3
Empress Pavilion.....(see 10)
Flower Market.....13 C7
Grand Central Market.....14 D6
Grier Musser Museum.....15 B5
Japanese American National Museum.....16 B4
La Placita.....17 B2
Mariachi Plaza.....18 F6
MOCA Geffen Contemporary.....19 B4
MOCA Grand Ave.....20 C6
Museum of Neon Art.....21 B7
Music Center of LA County.....22 D5
Old Plaza Firehouse Museum.....23 B3
Orpheum Theater.....24 C7
Richard Riordan Central Library.....25 C6
San Antonio Winery.....26 F4
Staples Center.....27 B7
Walt Disney Concert Hall.....28 C5
Wells Fargo History Museum.....29 C6

SLEEPING (pp533-9)
Figueroa Hotel.....30 B6
Millennium Biltmore Hotel.....31 C6
Omni Los Angeles Hotel.....32 C6
Standard Downtown LA.....33 C6
Stillwell Hotel.....34 C7

EATING (pp540-6)
Angélique Cafe.....35 C7
Café Metropol.....36 E6
Oomasa.....37 A4
Patina.....(see 28)
Philippe the Original.....38 B2
R-23.....39 E6
Zip Fusion.....40 E6
Zucca.....41 B6

DRINKING (pp546-7)
Golden Gopher.....42 C6
Rooftop Bar @ Standard Downtown LA.....(see 33)

ENTERTAINMENT
Ahmanson Theatre.....(see 22)
Bob Baker Marionette Theater.....43 C5
Dorothy Chandler Pavilion.....44 A4
East West Players.....(see 22)
Mark Taper Forum.....45 C5
Redcat.....(see 28)

SHOPPING
California Mart.....46 C7
Munky King.....(see 10)
New Mart.....47 C7

TRANSPORT
Greyhound.....48 D8

0 _____ 1 km
0 _____ 0.5 miles

LP

Boyle
Heights

Chinatown

Little
Tokyo

Arts
District

Los Angeles River

Civic Center/
Tom Bradley

Pershing
Square

Financial
District

South
Park

Jewelry
District

Fashion
District

Los Angeles
Convention
Center

MacArthur
Park

Westlake

Los Angeles
Trade-Technical
College

Mount
St Mary's
College

A B C D

1

Universal Studios Hollywood

18

21

Brush Canyon

Hollywood Franklin Park

24

0   200 m
0   0.1 miles

Yucca St

Capitol Records Tower

N Redwood Dr
Hollyridge Dr

N Orange Dr

38 58
61
57 Hollywood & Highland 2

Hollywood/ Highland

Cherokee Ave

N Cahuenga Blvd

N Vine St

Hollywood/ Vine

Canyon Dr

Griffith Park

Western Canyon Dr

12
M 6
7 17 35

Hollywood Blvd

71
34
M

26
56

N Highland Ave

16

55
37

8
68

Schrader Blvd

63
28
3

69
59

Ivar Ave

43

Hollywood Library

Selma Ave

2

Hollywood Reservoir Dam

Mulholland Dr

Cahuenga Blvd E

Dearborn Dr

N Beachwood Dr

Runyon Canyon Park

Hollywood Hills

Metro Red Line

Cahuenga Blvd W

101

60

Outpost Dr

10
11

Ferndell Dr

3

Wattles Garden Park

Camrose Dr

14

Sycamore Ave

Hillcrest Rd

170

Hollywood Fwy

Scenic Gardens
49
25

Orchid Ave

Franklin Ave

22

19

27

N Vista St

Franklin Ave

Hollywood Blvd

See Enlargement

N Cahuenga Blvd

N Vine St

4
36

Hollywood/ Western
M

N Wilton Pl

44

N Western Ave

N Serrano Ave

1

4

30

N Curson Ave
N Gardner St
N Vista St
N Fuller Ave
N La Brea Ave
N Orange Dr

23
15

52

W Sunset Blvd

45

66 33

51

CBS Studios

N Cower St

N Bronson Ave

N Van Ness St

Hollywood

Delongpre Park

Fountain Ave

Hollywood Recreation Center

67

Santa Monica Blvd

Wilcox Ave

Cole Ave

N Cahuenga Blvd

N Vine St

50

El Centro Ave

13

2

N Oxford Ave

53

5

Warner Hollywood Studios

47

N Gardner St
N Vista St
N Market St
N Formosa Ave
N Sycamore Ave

Willoughby Ave

Waring Ave

Beth Olam Memorial Park

Paramount Studios

Poinsettia Recreation Center

Melrose Ave

Melrose/ La Brea

S Detroit St
S La Brea Ave

S Highland Ave
N Mc Cadden Pl
N Las Palmas Ave

N June St

Clinton St

Rosewood Ave

N Rossmore Ave

5

6

Pan Pacific Park

The Wilshire Country Club

Beverly Blvd

Robert Burns Park

0 _____ 1 km
0 _____ 0.5 miles

INFORMATION
Cyber Java..1 B4
Hollywood Visitors Center.....................2 A2
LA Gay & Lesbian Center.......................3 B2
Los Angeles Free Clinic - Hollywood
  Blvd...4 C4
Los Angeles Free Clinic - Melrose Ave...5 D5
Red Line Tours......................................6 B2

SIGHTS & ACTIVITIES (pp511–31)
Erotic Museum......................................7 B2
Frederick's of Hollywood Lingerie
  Museum...8 B2
Hollyhock House....................................9 E4
Hollywood Bowl...................................10 B3
Hollywood Bowl Museum.....................11 B3
Hollywood Entertainment Museum......12 A2
Hollywood Forever Cemetery...............13 C5
Hollywood Heritage Museum...............14 B3
Hollywood High School........................15 B4
Hollywood Museum..............................16 B2
Hollywood Pro Bicycles........................17 B2
Hollywood Sign....................................18 C1
Immaculate Heart High School.............19 D3
Marshall High School............................20 G3
Sunset Ranch Hollywood......................21 D1

SLEEPING (pp533–9)
Best Western Hollywood Hills Hotel......22 C3
Holiday Inn Express..............................23 B4

Hollywood Celebrity Hotel....................24 A1
Hollywood Hills Hotel...........................25 B3
Hollywood Roosevelt Hotel..................26 A2
Magic Castle Hotel...............................27 B4
USA Hostels–Hollywood.......................28 C2

EATING (pp540–6)
Cafe Stella...29 F5
Cheebo..30 A4
Cobras & Matadors..............................31 F4
El Conquistador....................................32 G5
Hungry Cat..33 C4
Kung Pao Kitty.....................................34 C2
Musso & Frank Grill.............................35 B2
Palms Thai..36 C4
Scooby's..37 B2
Vert...38 A1
Yuca's..39 F3
Zankou Chicken...................................40 E4

DRINKING (pp546–7)
4100 Bar..41 F5
Akbar...42 F4
Beauty Bar...43 C2
Blu Monkey Lounge..............................44 D4
Cat & Fiddle Pub..................................45 B4
Faultline...46 E6
Formosa Cafe.......................................47 A5
Good Luck Bar......................................48 F4
Yamashiro..49 B3

ENTERTAINMENT (pp548–52)
Actors' Gang Theatre...........................50 C5
American Cinematheque.................(see 55)
ArcLight & Cinerama Dome..................51 C4
Catalina Bar & Grill..............................52 B4
Dragonfly...53 B5
Echo...54 H6
Egyptian Theatre..................................55 B2
El Capitan Theatre................................56 A2
Grauman's Chinese Theatre..................57 A2
Highlands..58 A1
Hotel Café..59 C2
John Anson Ford Ampitheatre..............60 B3
Knitting Factory Hollywood.............(see 12)
Kodak Theatre......................................61 A1
Little Temple..62 F5
Nacional...63 C2
Spaceland...64 G5

SHOPPING (pp552–4)
American Apparel.................................65 F4
Amoeba Music.....................................66 C4
Aron's Records.....................................67 B5
Frederick's of Hollywood.................(see 8)
La Luz de Jesus...............................(see 70)
Larry Edmunds Bookshop....................68 B2
Panpipes Magickal Marketplace...........69 C2
Wacko..70 F4

TRANSPORT (pp554–6)
Greyhound..71 C2

INFORMATION
A Different Light..................(see 55)
American Express......................1 C5
Bodhi Tree.............................2 C4
Book Soup.............................3 B3
California Welcome Center.........4 C5
Cedars-Sinai Medical Center.....5 B5
Farmers Market Office..............6 D5
German Consulate....................7 D6
Los Angeles Free Clinic............8 C5
Sav-On Drugs.........................9 D5
South African Consulate..........10 D6
Traveler's Bookcase...............11 C5
TravelEx................................(see 57)
West Hollywood Convention &
  Visitors Bureau....................12 B4

SIGHTS & ACTIVITIES (pp511–31)
CBS Television City................13 D5
Crunch Gym..........................14 D3
Fairfax High School...............15 D4
Farmers Market....................16 D5
Hyatt Hotel..........................17 C3
La Brea Tar Pits....................18 D6
LACMA West.........................19 D6

Los Angeles County Museum
  of Art................................20 D6
MOCA Pacific Design Center....21 B4
Pacific Design Center...........(see 12)
Page Museum.......................(see 18)
Petersen Automotive Museum...22 D6
Porno Walk of Fame..............23 D3
Schindler House.....................24 C4

SLEEPING (pp533–9)
Alta Cienega Motel................25 C3
Beverly Laurel Hotel..............26 D5
Chamberlain West Hollywood...27 C3
Chateau Marmont.................28 C3
Elan Hotel Modern................29 C5
Farmer's Daughter Hotel........30 D5
Grafton on Sunset................31 C3
Le Montrose Suite Hotel........32 B4
Mondrian Hotel.....................33 C3
Orbit/Banana Bungalow
  Hollywood.........................34 C3
San Vicente Inn....................35 B4
Secret Garden B&B...............36 D2
Standard Hollywood..............37 C3

EATING 🍴 (pp540–6)
Angelini Osteria	38	E5
AOC	39	D5
Chao Krung	40	D5
Chaya Brasserie	41	B5
Cobras & Matadors	42	D5
Griddle Café	43	D3
Gumbo Pot	44	D5
La Terza	45	C5
Loteria! Grill	(see 44)	
Pink's Hot Dogs	46	E4
Real Food Daily	47	C4
Surya	48	D5
Swingers	(see 26)	
Tail O' the Pup	49	C4
Urth Caffe	50	C4
Xiomara	51	F4

DRINKING 🍷 (pp546–7)
Abbey	52	B4
Bar Marmont	(see 28)	
Factory/Ultra Suede	53	B4
Here Lounge	54	B4
Micky's	55	B4
Palms	56	C4
Rage	57	B4
Sky Bar	(see 33)	

ENTERTAINMENT 🎭 (pp548–52)
Celebration Theatre	58	E3
Comedy Store	59	C3
Conga Room	60	E6
Groundlings	61	E4
Grove	(see 63)	
House of Blues	62	C3
Pacific Theatres at the Grove	63	D5
Parlour Club	64	D3
Silent Movie Theatre	65	D4
Troubadour	66	B4
Viper Room	67	B3
Whisky-a-Go-Go	68	B3

SHOPPING 🛍 (pp552–4)
Baby Jane of Hollywood	69	D3
Baby Melt	(see 73)	
Fred Segal	70	D4
Head Line Records	71	D4
Kitson	72	B5
Melrose Trading Post	(see 15)	
Meltdown Comics & Collectibles	73	E3
Necromance	74	E4
Pleasure Chest	75	D3
Remix Vintage Shoes	(see 42)	
Turtle Beach Swimwear	76	C5
Wasteland	77	E4

A B C D

1

2

3

Bel Air

Philbert Dr

Bella Dr
Cielo Dr

Green
Acres Dr

Benedict Canyon Dr

39

30

46

St Cloud Rd

N Bel Air Rd

N Beverly Glen Blvd

21

16

St Pierre Rd

Bel Air Rd

31
18
38
13
8

Carolwood Dr

11 15 14
19

Chalon Rd

N Beverly Glen Blvd

36

Bellagio Rd

Bel Air
Country Club

**Holmby
Hills**

Monovale
Dr

W Sunset Blvd

Reservoir

De Neve Dr

Circle Dr E

17

Mapleton Dr

Charing
Cross Rd

29

Club View Dr

**Holmby
Park**

7

4

To Getty Center (0.1mi);
Skirball Cultural Center (3mi);
San Fernando Valley (5mi)

Cayley Ave

Westwood Plaza

34

University of
California,
Los Angeles
(UCLA)

37

Warner Ave

Comstock Ave

Los Angeles
Country Club

Circle Dr S

Westholme Ave

Hilgard Ave

Malcolm Ave

S Beverly Glen Blvd

24

5

Le Conte Ave

Los
Angeles
National
Cemetery

Weyburn Ave

Westwood

5

405

San Diego Fwy

Broxton Ave

P

Kinross
Ave

54
35

Thayer Ave

Glendon Ave

Lindbrook Dr

Wilshire Blvd

28

Selby Ave

Wellworth Ave

Malcolm Ave

Ohio Ave

S Santa Monica Blvd

2

**West Los Angeles
Veterans
Administration
Center**

2

Santa Monica Blvd

6

56

San Vicente Blvd

S Sepulveda Blvd

Veteran Ave

**Westwood
Park**

Westwood Blvd

3

To British Consulate (0.1mi);
Dutch Consulate (0.1mi); Italian
Consulate (0.8mi); New Zealand
Consulate (0.8mi)

61

0 — 1 km
0 — 0.5 miles

INFORMATION
Australian Consulate..............1 E5
French Consulate..................2 B5
Rooms Café.........................3 C6
TravelEx.............................4 F4
UCLA Medical Center..............5 C5
Women's Clinic....................6 F6

SIGHTS & ACTIVITIES (pp511–31)
Aaron Spelling Estate..............7 D4
Barbra Streisand's House..........8 D3
Beverly Hills High School..........9 E5
Bugsy Siegel's House.............10 E4
Burt Reynolds' House.............11 D3
Clara Bow's House................12 F4
Clark Gable's House..............13 D3
Diane Keaton's House.............14 D3
Elvis Presley's House.............15 D3
Errol Flynn's House...............16 C3
Franklin D Murphy Sculpture
   Garden.........................17 C4
George Harrison's House.....(see 11)
Gregory Peck's House............18 D3
Ira & George Gershwin's
   House..........................19 D3

Jack Benny's House..............20 E3
Johnny Weissmuller Estate......21 C3
Lana Turner's House.............22 E4
Lucille Ball's House.............23 E3
Mildred E Mathias Botanical
   Garden.........................24 C5
Museum of Television & Radio..25 F4
Museum of Tolerance...........26 F6
Peter 'Colombo' Falk's House...27 E3
Pierce Bros Westwood Memorial
   Park............................28 C5
Playboy Mansion................29 D3
Reagan Compound...............30 C2
Rod Stewart's House.............31 D3
Stan Laurel's House.............32 E4
Steve Martin House..............33 E4
UCLA Fowler Museum of Cultural
   History.........................34 C5
UCLA Hammer Museum..........35 C5
UCLA Hannah Carter Japanese
   Garden.........................36 C3
University of California, Los Angeles
   (UCLA)..........................37 C4
Walt Disney Estate..............38 D3
Westlake School for Girls........39 C2

SLEEPING (pp533–9)
Avalon Hotel.....................40 F5
Best Western Beverly Pavilion...41 G4
Beverly Hills Hotel..............42 G4
Beverly Hills Reeves Hotel......43 F5
Carlyle Inn......................44 H6
Crescent.........................45 F4
Hotel Bel-Air....................46 C3
Maison 140......................47 E5
Mosaic Hotel....................48 E5

EATING (pp540–6)
Crustacean.......................49 F4
Il Cielo...........................50 G4
Mako............................51 F5
Mulberry Street Pizzeria........52 F5
Nate 'n Al's......................53 F4
Native Foods....................54 C5
Real Food Daily..............(see 52)
Spago...........................55 G4
Taiko............................56 A6
Tamarin.........................57 G5
Urth Caffe.......................58 F5
Versailles........................59 H6
X'ian............................60 F4
Zankou Chicken.................61 C6

SHOPPING (pp552–4)
American Apparel................62 H4

INFORMATION
California Map & Travel Center	1 E4
Equator Bookstore	2 D6
Interactive Café	3 B7
Santa Monica Visitors Center	4 C5
Santa Monica Visitors Kiosk	5 B7
Sav-on Drugs	6 D3
Venice Family Clinic	7 D6

SIGHTS & ACTIVITIES (pp511–31)
Ballerina Clown	8 C6
Bergamot Station Arts Center	9 D4
Blazing Saddles	10 B5
Carousel	(see 15)
Chiat/Day Building	11 D6
Gold's Gym	12 D6
Santa Monica College	13 D4
Santa Monica High School	14 C5
Santa Monica Museum of Art	(see 9)
Santa Monica Pier Aquarium	15 B5
Spokes 'n Stuff	16 B5
University High School	17 E2
Yoga Works	18 C5

SLEEPING (pp533–9)
Ambrose	19 C3
Best Western Jamaica Bay Inn	20 E7
Cal Mar Hotel Suites	21 A6
Channel Road Inn B&B	22 A3
Georgian Hotel	23 B7
HI–Los Angeles–Santa Monica	24 B7
Inn at Venice Beach	25 D7
Sea Shore Motel	26 C6
Travelodge Santa Monica	27 E4
Venice Beach House	28 D7
Viceroy	29 C5

EATING (pp540–6)
Abbot's Pizza	30 D6
Beechwood	31 E7
Café Bizou	32 D4
Counter	33 E4
JiRaffe	34 B7
Joe's	35 D6
La Cabaña	36 D6
Mao's Kitchen	37 D7
Michael's	38 A6
Real Food Daily	39 B6
Rocca	40 B7
Swingers	41 C4
Urth Caffe	42 C5
Venice Cantina	43 D7
Wolfgang Puck Express	44 B7
Zip Fusion	45 F3

DRINKING (pp546–7)
Brig	46 D6
Chez Jay	47 C5
Galley	48 C5
Roosterfish	49 D6
Toppers	50 A6
Voda	51 B7
Ye Olde King's Head	52 B7

ENTERTAINMENT (pp548–52)
American Cinematheque	53 B3
Nuart Theatre	54 E2
Odyssey Theatre Ensemble	55 F3
Puppet and Magic Center	56 A7
Temple Bar	57 C4
Zanzibar	58 B6

SHOPPING (pp552–4)
DNA	59 D6
Fred Segal	60 B7
Hear Music	61 B7
Rhino Records	62 F2
Wasteland	63 B7

TRANSPORT (pp554–6)
| Route 66 | 64 E7 |

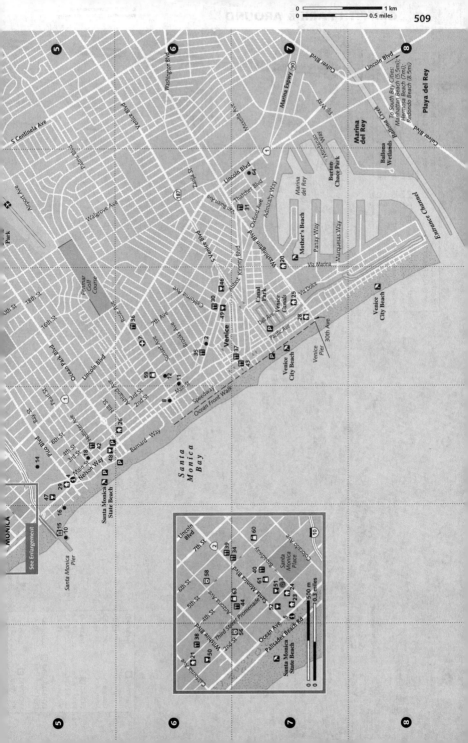

0 — 1 km
0 — 0.5 miles

MONICA

S Centinela Ave

Washington Blvd

Venice Blvd

Mildred Ave

Marina Expwy (90)

Culver Blvd

Lincoln Blvd

To South Bay Cities:
Manhattan Beach (5.5mi);
Hermosa Beach (7mi);
Redondo Beach (8.5mi)

Culver Blvd

Playa del Rey

Ballona Creek

Fiji Way

Marina
del Rey

Ballona
Wetlands

Mindanao Way

Burton
Chace Park

Park

Penmar Golf
Course

Walgrove Ave

Rose Ave

Zanja St

California Ave

Lincoln Blvd

Thatcher Blvd

Van Buren Ave

64

31

Oxford Ave

Admiralty Way

Marina
del Rey

Mother's Beach

Panay Way

Marquesas Way

Via Marina

20

25

Entrance Channel

7th Ave

Brooks Ave

S Venice Blvd

Abbot Kinney Blvd

Washington Blvd

Dell Ave

Pacific Ave

30

46

49

Canal
Park

Venice
Canals

Via Dolce

28

36

2

Venice

35

37

43

30th Ave

Venice Pier

Venice
City Beach

Venice
City Beach

Penmar Ave

Pico Blvd

Ocean Park Blvd

18th St

16th St

Main St

3rd Ave

Speedway

Ocean Front Walk

59

12

11

8

Santa
Monica
Bay

Pico Blvd

6th St

4th St

3rd St

Main St

Ashland Ave

Barnard Way

Nelson Way

14

29

4

47

16

10

15

Santa Monica
State Beach

18

42

48

26

MONICA

See Enlargement

Santa Monica Pier

See Enlargement

Lincoln Blvd

7th St

6th St

5th St

4th St

Arizona Ave

Wilshire Blvd

California Ave

2nd St

Ocean Ave

Santa Monica Blvd

Broadway

Colorado Ave

Palisades Beach Rd

Third Street Promenade

Santa
Monica
Place

Santa Monica
State Beach

(2)

(10)

60

39

34

58

59

63

44

40

61

52

3

51

23

24

5

50

38

21

56

0 — 500 m
0 — 0.3 miles

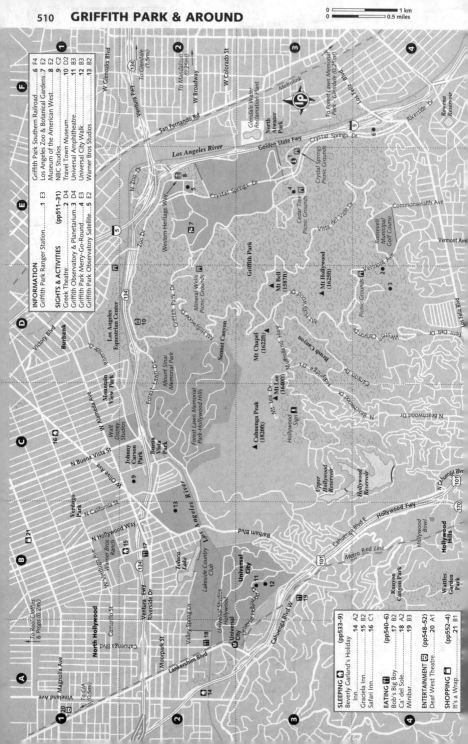

0 ━━━━━━ 1 km
0 ━━━━━━ 0.5 miles

INFORMATION
Griffith Park Ranger Station..............1 E3

SIGHTS & ACTIVITIES (pp511–31)
Greek Theatre...................................2 E3
Griffith Observatory & Planetarium..3 D4
Griffith Park Merry-Go-Round........4 E3
Griffith Park Observatory Satellite...5 E2

Griffith Park Southern Railroad.........6 F4
Los Angeles Zoo & Botanical Gardens...7 F2
Museum of the American West..........8 E2
NBC Studios.....................................9 C2
Travel Town Museum.......................10 D2
Universal Amphitheatre...................11 B3
Universal City Walk.........................12 B3
Warner Bros Studios........................13 B2

SLEEPING (pp533–9)
Beverly Garland's Holiday
Inn...14 A2
Graciela Inn...................................15 B2
Safari Inn......................................16 C1

EATING (pp540–6)
Bob's Big Boy...............................17 B2
Ca' del Sole.................................18 A2
Minibar.......................................19 B3

ENTERTAINMENT (pp548–52)
Deaf West Theatre........................20 A1

SHOPPING (pp552–4)
It's a Wrap...................................21 B1

(Continued from page 497)

DANGERS & ANNOYANCES

Walking around LA in the daytime is generally no problem, although extra caution should be exercised in East LA, Compton and Watts, sections which are plagued by gangs and drugs. Stay away from these areas after dark. Hollywood also yields dangers, especially in poorly lit side streets; ditto for Venice. Crime rates are lowest in Westside communities such as Westwood and Beverly Hills, as well as in the beach towns (except Venice) and Pasadena. Downtown LA is safe in the daytime, but as it basically empties out after sundown you don't really want to be walking around too much after dark. Downtown is also home to numerous homeless folks, especially on Skid Row, an area roughly bounded by 3rd, Alameda, 7th and Main Sts.

SIGHTS
Hollywood, Los Feliz & Silver Lake

Aging movie stars know that a facelift can quickly pump up a drooping career, and it seems the same can be done with LA's neighborhoods. The legendary **Hollywood Blvd** (Map pp502–3) in particular has been preened and spruced up in recent years, and even though it's still light years away from recapturing its Golden Age glamour (1920s–40s), at least some of the seediness is gone.

Historic movie palaces bask in restored glory, Metro Rail's Red Line makes access easy, some of LA's hottest bars and nightclubs have sprung up here, and even 'Oscar' has found a permanent home in the Kodak Theatre, part of a vast new shopping and entertainment complex called Hollywood & Highland.

The most interesting mile runs between La Brea Ave and Vine St, along the **Hollywood Walk of Fame**, which honors more than 2000 celebrities with brass stars embedded in the sidewalk. For interesting historical tidbits about local landmarks keep an eye out for the sign markers along here, or join a guided walking tour operated by Red Line Tours (p532).

Following Hollywood Blvd east beyond Hwy 101 (Hollywood Fwy) takes you to the neighborhoods of **Los Feliz** (loss *fee*-les) and **Silver Lake**, both boho-chic enclaves with

offbeat shopping, funky bars and a hopping cuisine scene.

The Metro Red Line (p556) serves central Hollywood (Hollywood/Highland station) and Los Feliz (Vermont/Sunset station) from Downtown LA and the San Fernando Valley. Pay-parking lots abound in the side streets; the cheapest we've found is the one on Cherokee Ave, just north of Hollywood Blvd, which charges $1 for the first two hours. The Hollywood & Highland parking garage charges $2 for four hours with validation (no purchase necessary) from any merchant within the mall or the Hollywood Visitors Center.

HOLLYWOOD BOULEVARD

The spark for the boulevard's rebirth was the construction of **Hollywood & Highland** (Map pp502–3; ☎ 323-467-6412; www.hollywoodandhighland.com; 6801 Hollywood Blvd; admission free; ⏱ 24hr), a big mall that's a perfect marriage of kitsch and commerce. Its focal point is **Babylon Court**, anchored by a preposterous triumphal arch (inspired by DW Griffith's 1916 movie *Intolerance*) that frames views of the Hollywood Sign. Part of the complex is the **Kodak Theatre** (☎ 323-308-6363; www.kodaktheatre.com; adult/child/student/senior $15/10/10/10; ⏱ 10:30am-4pm Jun-Aug, 10:30am-2:30pm rest of year), which hosts the Academy Awards and other star-studded events. Pricey 30-minute tours take you inside the auditorium, the VIP room and past an actual Oscar statuette. The first Academy Awards ceremony ever, by the way, was held diagonally across the street in the 1927 **Hollywood Roosevelt Hotel** (p534).

Hollywood & Highland mall dwarfs the 1927 **Grauman's Chinese Theatre** (Map pp502–3;

☎ 323-464-6266; 6925 Hollywood Blvd), famous for its forecourt where screen legends have left their imprint in cement: feet, hands and – in the case of Jimmy Durante – a protruding proboscis. Other classic movie palaces along here include the flamboyant 1926 **El Capitan Theatre** (Map pp502-3; ☎ 323-467-7674; 6838 Hollywood Blvd) and the 1922 **Egyptian Theatre** (Map pp502-3; ☎ 323-466-3456; 6712 Hollywood Blvd). The latter theatre is now the home of the nonprofit American Cinematheque (p548), which shows non-mainstream movies and, on weekends only, the one-hour documentary **Forever Hollywood** (adult/student/senior $9/8/8; ☽ 2pm & 3:30pm Sat & Sun).

Another way to time-travel through Hollywood history is by perusing the props, costumes, photos, posters, scripts and memorabilia at the **Hollywood Museum** (Map pp502-3; ☎ 323-464-7776; www.thehollywoodmuseum.com; 1660 N Highland Ave; adult/child/senior $15/12/12; ☽ 10am-5pm Thu-Sun), a veritable shrine to the stars – from Chaplin to DiCaprio. The basement holds Hannibal Lecter's original jail cell from the movie *Silence of the Lambs*.

For more film sets (from *Star Trek*, *X-Files* and *Cheers*), make a beeline to the **Hollywood Entertainment Museum** (Map pp502-3; ☎ 323-465-7900; www.hollywoodmuseum.com; 7021 Hollywood Blvd; adult/student/senior $12/5/10; ☽ 10am-6pm late May-early Sep, 11am-6pm Thu-Tue rest of year), which also offers a moderately interesting romp through the history and mystery of moviemaking, including the creation of special and sound effects.

East of Highland Ave, Hollywood Blvd's seedier side survives in numerous tattoo parlors and stripper supply stores, making it a suitable setting for the new **Erotic Museum** (Map pp502-3; ☎ 323-463-7684; www.theeroticmuseum.com; 6741 Hollywood Blvd; adult/student/senior $13/10/10; ☽ 11am-9pm Sun-Thu, 11am-midnight Fri & Sat). Inside are naughty sketches by Picasso, nude pictures of Marilyn, early John Holmes porn and changing exhibits ranging from silly to saucy to sexy that are not always worth the price of admission. And yes, you must be at least 18 to enter.

For another dose of titillation, drop by the **Lingerie Museum** (Map pp502-3; ☎ 323-957-5953; 6608 Hollywood Blvd; admission free; ☽ 10am-9pm Mon-Sat, 11am-7pm Sun), a small collection of the stars' undies in the back of the Frederick's of Hollywood store, which pioneered the thong, teddy and push-up bra.

HOLLYWOOD SIGN

LA's most recognizable landmark first appeared atop its hillside perch in 1923 as an advertising gimmick for a real-estate development. Each letter is 50ft tall and made of sheet metal. It's illegal to hike up to the sign, but there are many places where you can catch good views, including the Hollywood & Highland complex and the top of Beachwood Dr (Map pp502-3).

HOLLYWOOD BOWL & AROUND

Summer concerts at the **Hollywood Bowl** (Map pp502-3; ☎ 323-850-2000; www.hollywoodbowl.com; 2301 N Highland Ave; ☽ late Jun-Sep) have been a great LA tradition since 1922. It's the summer home of the LA Phil (p550) and also is host to big-name rock, jazz and blues acts. Many concertgoers come early to enjoy a pre-show picnic on the parklike grounds or in their seats (alcohol is allowed). For insight into the bowl's storied history visit the **Hollywood Bowl Museum** (Map pp502-3; ☎ 323-850-2058; www.hollywoodbowl.com/event/museum.cfm; 2301 N Highland Ave; admission free; ☽ 10am-showtime Mon-Sat, 4pm-showtime Sun late Jun–mid-Sep, 10am-4:30pm Tue-Sat rest of year).

South of here, next to a parking lot, is the **Hollywood Heritage Museum** (Map pp502-3; ☎ 323-874-2276; 2100 N Highland Ave; adult/child/senior $3/1/1; ☽ 11am-4pm Sat & Sun). It's inside the horse barn used by the movie pioneer Cecil B DeMille in 1913 and 1914 to shoot *The Squaw Man*, Hollywood's first feature-length film. Inside are exhibits on early filmmaking, including costumes, projectors and cameras, as well as a replica of DeMille's office.

HOLLYWOOD FOREVER CEMETERY

Next to Paramount Studios, this **cemetery** (Map pp502-3; ☎ 323-469-1181; www.hollywoodforever.com; 6000 Santa Monica Blvd; ☽ 8am-6pm) is crowded with famous 'immortals,' including Rudolph Valentino, Tyrone Power, Jayne Mansfield and Cecil B DeMille. Pick up a map ($5) at the **flower shop** (☽ 9am-5pm) near the entrance.

HOLLYHOCK HOUSE

In Los Feliz, surrounded by the sprawling Barnsdall Art Park, the **Hollyhock House** (Map pp502-3; ☎ 323-662-8139; www.hollyhockhouse.net; 4800 Hollywood Blvd; adult/student/senior $5/3/3; ☽ tours hourly 12:30am-3:30pm) is an early masterpiece by Frank Lloyd Wright. It marks his first attempt at creating an indoor–outdoor living space in

---

FAMOUS ALUMNI

Want to find out where your favorite celeb studied algebra and French? Visit any of the following high schools, community colleges and universities.

Beverly Hills High School (Map pp506-7; 241 S Moreno Dr, Beverly Hills) Nicolas Cage, Jamie Lee Curtis, Richard Dreyfuss, Angelina Jolie, Lenny Kravitz, Monica Lewinsky, Rob Reiner, David Schwimmer, Betty White.

Fairfax High (Map pp504-5; 7850 Melrose Ave, Mid-City) David Arquette, Flea (of Red Hot Chili Peppers), Al Franken, Demi Moore, Slash (of Guns N' Roses).

Hollywood High School (Map pp502-3; 1521 N Highland Ave, Hollywood) Carol Burnett, Judy Garland, James Garner, Barbara Hershey, John Ritter, Jason Robards, Mickey Rooney.

Immaculate Heart High (Map pp502-3; 5515 Franklin Ave, Hollywood) Tyra Banks, Natalie Cole, Mary Tyler Moore.

Marshall High (Map pp502-3; 3939 Tracy St, Silver Lake) Leonardo DiCaprio.

Palisades High (Map pp498-9; 15777 Boudoin St, Pacific Palisades) Jeff Bridges, Christie Brinkley, Katey Segal.

Polytechnic High (Map pp498-9; 1600 Atlantic Ave, Long Beach) Cameron Diaz, Snoop Doggy Dog, Marilyn Horne, Spike Lee.

Santa Monica College (Map pp508-9; 1900 Pico Blvd, Santa Monica) Buzz Aldrin, James Dean, Dustin Hoffman, Arnold Schwarzenegger, Hilary Swank.

Santa Monica High School (Map pp508-9; 601 Pico Blvd, Santa Monica) Glenn Ford, Robert Downey Jr, Rob Lowe, Sean Penn, Charlie Sheen.

University High School (Map pp508-9; 11800 Texas Ave, near Santa Monica) Jeff Bridges, James Brolin, Bridget Fonda, Marilyn Monroe, Randy Newman, Nancy Sinatra, Elizabeth Taylor, Tone Loc.

University of California, Los Angeles (UCLA; Map pp506-7; 405 Hilgard Ave, Westwood) Carol Burnett, Francis Ford Coppola, James Dean, Heather Locklear, Jim Morrison, Tim Robbins.

University of Southern California (USC; Map pp498-9; 3535 S Figueroa St, South Central) Neil Armstrong, Frank Gehry, Ron Howard, George Lucas, Tom Selleck, OJ Simpson, John Wayne, Robert Zemeckis.

Harvard-Westlake (formerly Westlake School for Girls; Map pp506-7; 700 N Faring Rd, Bel Air) Candice Bergen, Bridget Fonda, Tracy Nelson, Sally Ride, Shirley Temple.

---

harmony with LA's sunny climate, a style he later referred to as California Romanza. After a top-to-bottom five-year restoration, Hollyhock reopened for guided tours in mid-2005. The adjacent Municipal Art Gallery screens a documentary about the intricacies of the restoration.

Griffith Park

Sprawling **Griffith Park** (Map p510; ☎ 323-913-4688; www.laparks.org/dos/parks/griffithPK/griffith.htm; 4370 Crystal Springs Dr; admission free; ⏱ 6am-10pm), just to the north of Hollywood, is a thick spread of California oak, wild sage and manzanita that makes for a family-friendly escape from urbanity. At five times the size of New York's Central Park, Griffith Park embraces an outdoor theater, the city zoo, an observatory, two museums, golf courses, tennis courts, playgrounds, bridle paths, hiking trails and even the Hollywood Sign.

Kids love riding the richly festooned horses of the 1926 **Griffith Park Merry-Go-Round** (Map p510; ☎ 323-665-3051; Park Center; rides $1; ⏱ 11am-5pm May-Sep, Sat & Sun Oct-Apr), Park Center between the LA Zoo and Los Feliz park entrance, and

the vintage railcars and steam locomotives of the **Travel Town Museum** (Map p510; ☎ 323-662-5874; 5200 W Zoo Dr; admission free; ⏱ 10am-4pm Mon-Fri, 10am-5pm Sat & Sun). South of here, they can ride the **Griffith Park Southern Railroad** (Map p510; ☎ 323-664-6903; 4400 Crystal Springs Dr; adult/child/senior $2/2/1.50; ⏱ 10am-4:30pm Mon-Fri, 10am-5pm Sat & Sun), a miniature train chugging through a re-created old Western town and a Native American village.

Access to the park is easiest via the Griffith Park Dr or Zoo Dr exits off I-5 (Golden State Fwy). Parking is plentiful and free. For information and maps stop by the **Griffith Park Ranger Station** (Map p510; ☎ 323-665-5188; 4730 Crystal Springs Dr). Trails close at sunset.

GRIFFITH OBSERVATORY & PLANETARIUM

On the southern slopes of Mt Hollywood, the landmark 1935 **Griffith Observatory** (Map p510; ☎ 323-664-1181; www.griffithobs.org; 2800 E Observatory Rd) has been undergoing a multiyear overhaul and should reprise its 'starring' role as a window to the universe in late 2006. The distinctive domed building served as the backdrop for the switchblade fight in the James Dean flick *Rebel Without a Cause*. Until its reopening, stargazers can visit the **Griffith Park Observatory Satellite** (4800 Western Heritage Way; admission free; 1-10pm Tue-Fri, 10am-10pm Sat & Sun) near the Los Angeles Zoo. The temporary facility features exhibitions including meteorites and a Mars rock, planetarium shows and a telescope for viewing the moon and planets.

LOS ANGELES ZOO & BOTANICAL GARDENS
With its 1200 finned, feathered and furry friends, the **LA Zoo** (Map p510; ☎ 323-644-4200; www .lazoo.org; 5333 Zoo Dr; adult/child/senior $10/5/7; 10am-6pm Jul-early Sep, 10am-5pm rest of year) rarely fails to enthrall the little ones. What began in 1912 as a refuge for retired circus animals recently also won accreditation as a **botanical garden**. Still, it's definitely the zoo's animal magnetism that brings in the crowds. The crowd-pleasers include long-term resident Gita the elephant, playful chimpanzees, cuddly koalas and fierce komodo dragons. Tots gravitate toward **Adventure Island**, with its petting zoo and hands-on play stations, as well as the brand-new **Children's Discovery Center**.

MUSEUM OF THE AMERICAN WEST
Those keen on learning how the West was won will hit the mother lode at this delightful **museum** (Map p510; ☎ 323-667-2000; www.museum oftheamericanwest.org; 4700 Western Heritage Way; adult/ child/student/senior $7.50/3/5/5, admission after 4pm Thu free; 10am-5pm Tue, Wed & Fri-Sun, 10am-8pm Thu). Its 10 galleries engagingly combine scholarship and showmanship and are a veritable gold mine of Old West memorabilia. Combination tickets with the Southwest Museum of the American Indian (p528) are adult/child/student/senior $12/5/8/8.

West Hollywood
West Hollywood (WeHo) is an independent city that packs more personality into its 1.9 sq miles than most larger neighborhoods. It is the heart of gay and lesbian life in LA (p533), the center of Southern California's design community and the adopted home of about 6000 immigrants from the former Soviet Union who've turned eastern WeHo into 'little Russia.' LA's fabled nightlife mecca, the Sunset Strip, is its main artery.

Street parking is heavily restricted, but the structure at 8383 Santa Monica Blvd offers two hours of free parking in the daytime ($3 flat fee after 6pm). WeHo is also served by the DASH bus (p556).

SUNSET STRIP
The famed Sunset Strip – Sunset Blvd between Laurel Canyon Blvd and Doheny Dr – has been a favorite nighttime playground since the 1920s. The **Chateau Marmont** (p534) and clubs such as Ciro's (now the **Comedy Store**; p551), Mocambo and the Trocadero (both now defunct) were favorite hangouts for Hollywood high society, from Bogart to Bacall, Monroe to Sinatra. The '60s saw the opening of **Whisky-a-Go-Go** (Map pp504-5; ☎ 310-652-4202; 8901 W Sunset Blvd), America's first discotheque, the birthplace of go-go dancing and a launch pad for the Doors, who were the club's house band in 1966. Nearby is the **Hyatt Hotel** (☎ 323-656-1234; 8401 W Sunset Blvd), which earned the moniker 'Riot House' during the '70s when it was a favorite with Led Zeppelin and other raucous rock royalty. At one time, the band rented six floors and raced motorcycles in the hallways.

Today, the strip is still nightlife central, although it's lost much of its cutting edge. It's a visual cacophony dominated by billboards and giant advertising banners draped across building facades. The Whisky's still there, as is the Hyatt, but they've been eclipsed by such places as the **House of Blues** (p549); the jet-set **Mondrian Hotel** (p535), home of the übertrendy **Sky Bar** (p547); and the **Viper Room** (p549), until recently owned by Johnny Depp, where Tommy Lee attacked a paparazzo and, in 1993, actor River Phoenix overdosed.

PACIFIC DESIGN CENTER & AROUND
South of Sunset Strip, near the western end of trendy boutique-lined **Melrose Ave**, is the architecturally striking **Pacific Design Center** (PDC; Map pp504-5; ☎ 310-657-0800; 8687 Melrose Ave), with around 130 trade-only showrooms and the **West Hollywood Convention & Visitors Bureau** (Map pp504-5; ☎ 310-289-2525; www.visitwesthollywood .com; 8:30am-5:30pm Mon-Fri) on the mezzanine level. Outside, in a small pavilion, the **Museum of Contemporary Art** (MOCA; Map pp504-5; ☎ 213-626-6222; www.moca-la.org; admission free; 11am-5pm Tue, Wed & Fri, 11am-8pm Thu, 11am-6pm Sat & Sun), at the Pacific Design Center, presents rotating exhibits that tend to revolve around architecture and design themes. The surrounding **Avenues of Art & Design** invite strolling, people-watching and gallery hopping.

TOP FIVE THINGS TO DO WHEN IT RAINS

■ Catch a flick at the historic **Grauman's Chinese Theatre** (p548) or the futuristic **ArcLight** (p548)

■ Get in shape LA-style at the **Crunch Gym** (p530)

■ Watch favorite old broadcasts and discover new ones at the **Museum of Television & Radio** (p516)

■ Get lost in the amazing maze of **LACMA's** global art collection (below)

■ Dig up musical treasure at **Amoeba Music** and maybe even catch a live in-store gig (p553)

SCHINDLER HOUSE

The building that was the **home and studio** (Map pp504–5; ☎ 323-651-1510; www.makcenter.com; 835 N Kings Rd; $5, admission 4-6pm Fri free; ⊙ 11am-6pm Wed-Sun) of Vienna-born architect Rudolph Schindler (1887–1953) is one of the most celebrated private modernist residences in LA. Tours run on weekends, but you're free to look around at other times. Today it functions as a think tank and study center supporting current art and architecture issues.

Mid-City

Mid-City encompasses an amorphous area east of West Hollywood, south of Hollywood, west of Koreatown and north of I-10 (Santa Monica Fwy). A historic farmers market and a row of top-notch museums are its main attractions. There's plenty of street parking and validated parking at the farmers market. The main sights are served by DASH buses on the Fairfax route (p556).

FARMERS MARKET

Apples to zucchinis, you'll find these and then some at the landmark **farmers market** (Map pp504–5; ☎ 323-933-9211; www.farmersmarketla.com; 6333 W 3rd St; admission free; ⊙ 9am-9pm Mon-Fri, 9am-8pm Sat, 10am-7pm Sun), in business since 1934. Casual and kid-friendly, it's a fun place for a browse, snack or a spot of people-watching. Next door there's the **Grove** (Map pp504–5; ☎ 323-900-8080; www.thegrovela.com; 189 The Grove Dr), an attractive outdoor shopping mall built around a central plaza with a musical fountain.

North of the mall is **CBS Television City** (Map pp504–5; ☎ 323-575-2624; www.cbs.com; 7800 Beverly Blvd), where game shows, talk shows, soap operas and other programs are taped, often before a live audience. Check with the **CBS ticket office** (⊙ 9am-5pm Mon-Fri) or the farmers market office (near the clock tower on the market's north side) for free tickets.

LOS ANGELES COUNTY MUSEUM OF ART

Huge, compelling and global – **LACMA** (Map pp504–5; ☎ 323-857-6000; www.lacma.org; 5905 Wilshire Blvd; adult/child/student/senior $9/free/5/5, admission after 5pm free; ⊙ noon-8pm Mon, Tue & Thu, noon-9pm Fri, 11am-8pm Sat & Sun) is one of the country's top art museums. It brims with several millennia's worth of paintings, sculpture and decorative arts from around the world. Feast your eyes on works by Rembrandt, Cézanne or Magritte; marvel at ancient pottery, from China, Turkey or Iran; admire sculpture from Japan or photographs by Ansel Adams or Henri Cartier-Bresson. The museum also presents headline-grabbing touring exhibits such as the King Tut extravaganza in 2005. Audio guides are available for hire (adult/child $3/1). Check the museum's website or the listings magazines (p548) for film screenings, concerts and guided tours.

LA BREA TAR PITS & PAGE MUSEUM

Once upon a time, saber-toothed cats, mammoths, dire wolves and other extinct critters prowled the land that is now LA. Many of them met their maker between 40,000 and 10,000 years ago in gooey tar bubbling up from deep beneath the earth's surface along Wilshire Blvd, making the **La Brea Tar Pits** one of the world's most fecund and famous fossil sites.

The most spectacular excavations are on display at the **Page Museum** (Map pp504–5; ☎ 323-934-7243; www.tarpits.org; 5801 Wilshire Blvd; adult/child/student/senior $7/2/4.50/4.50; ⊙ 9:30am-5pm Mon-Fri, 10am-5pm Sat & Sun; Ⓟ). Every July and August you can observe scientists digging up treasure at **Pit 91** (admission free; ⊙ 10am-4pm Wed-Sun) on the museum grounds.

PETERSEN AUTOMOTIVE MUSEUM

LA's love affair with the automobile is celebrated at this fun **museum** (Map pp504–5;

LOS ANGELES

☎ 323-930-2277; www.petersen.org; 6060 Wilshire Blvd; adult/child/student/senior $10/3/5/5; ☺ 10am-6pm Tue-Sun; ℗). Even pedestrians will enjoy the walk-through LA streetscape that reveals the city as the birthplace of gas stations, billboards, strip malls, drive-in restaurants and drive-in movie theaters. Upstairs it's cars galore, from vintage wheels to hot rods, presented in changing exhibits. On the 3rd floor, a 'Discovery Center' play-fully teaches kids about science by way of the automobile.

Beverly Hills & Westside

The mere mention of Beverly Hills conjures images of fame and wealth reinforced ad nauseam by film and TV. Fact is, the reality is not so different from the myth. Stylish and sophisticated, this is indeed where the well-heeled frolic. Opulent mansions flank manicured grounds on tree-shaded avenues, especially north of **Sunset Blvd**, while hyper-posh **Rodeo Drive** is a three-block artery of style for the Prada and Gucci brigade that ranks right up there with the world's most expensive shopping strips. If you're into stargazing, you can follow the little tour in this book (opposite), take a guided bus tour (p532) or hope to espy a famous face at such hot spots as Spago (p543), Nate 'n Al (p542) or the Avalon Hotel (p536).

Several city-owned garages, including the one at 9510 Brighton Way near Rodeo Dr, offer two hours of free parking.

West of Beverly Hills, the neighborhoods of Westwood, Brentwood, Bel Air and Culver City are part of what is commonly referred to as the Westside. For tours of Sony Pictures Studios, see the boxed text, p529.

MUSEUM OF TELEVISION & RADIO

Fancy watching the pilot of *Bonanza* or *Star Trek*? How about the moon landing? These and thousands more classic TV and radio broadcasts are only the click of a mouse away in this sparkling **archive** (Map pp506-7; ☎ 310-786-1000; www.mtr.org; 465 N Beverly Dr; sug-gested donation adult/child/student/senior $10/5/8/8; ☺ noon-5pm Wed-Sun), where you can view or listen to your selections while seated at pri-vate consoles. The museum also presents daily screenings in its auditorium, seminars and the occasional live broadcast. Pick up a schedule at the information desk or call ☎ 310-786-1025.

MUSEUM OF TOLERANCE

Run by the Simon Wiesenthal Center, this **museum** (Map pp506-7; ☎ 310-553-8403; www.museum oftolerance.com; 9786 W Pico Blvd; adult/child/student/senior $10/7/7/8; ☺ 11:30am-6:30pm Mon-Thu, 11:30am-3pm Fri Nov-Mar, 11:30am-5pm Fri Apr-Oct, 11am-7:30pm Sun; ℗) uses interactive technology to make visitors confront racism and bigotry, although the focus is clearly on the Holocaust. Last entry is 2½ hours before closing.

A separate exhibit **Finding Our Families, Find-ing Ourselves** (adult/child/student/senior $8/6/6/7, combin-ation ticket with main museum $15/11/11/13; ☺ same as main museum) explores what it means to be an American and follows the personal histories of several celebrities, including Carlos San-tana and the poet Maya Angelou.

UNIVERSITY OF CALIFORNIA, LOS ANGELES

Westwood is practically synonymous with **UCLA** (Map pp506-7; ☎ 310-825-4321, tour reservations 310-825-8764; www.ucla.edu; 405 Hilgard Ave), the alma mater of Francis Ford Coppola, James Dean, Jim Morrison and several Nobel Prize laure-ates. Free student-guided tours are offered at 10:30am and 1:30pm Monday to Friday (reservations required).

If you're interested in the richly diverse arts, crafts and artifacts from non-Western cultures, stop by the **Fowler Museum of Cultural History** (Map pp506-7; ☎ 310-825-4361; www.fowler .ucla.edu; admission free; ☺ noon-5pm Wed & Fri-Sun, noon-8pm Thu). Garden retreats include the sprawl-ing **Franklin D Murphy Sculpture Garden**, which has dozens of works by Rodin, Moore, Calder and other American and European artists; the tranquil **Mildred E Mathias Botanical Garden** (Map pp506-7); and also the secluded **Han-nah Carter Japanese Garden** (Map pp506-7; ☎ 310-825-4574; www.japanesegarden.ucla.edu; 10619 Bellagio Rd; admission free; ☺ 10am-3pm Tue, Wed & Fri, reservations required).

UCLA HAMMER MUSEUM

South of the campus, in Westwood Village, this museum started as a mere vanity project for its main benefactor, the late oil tycoon Armand Hammer (1898–1990), but has since graduated to an increasingly well-respected contemporary and avant-garde art **museum** (Map pp506-7; ☎ 310-443-7000; www.hammer.ucla .edu; 10899 Wilshire Blvd; adult/child/student/senior $5/free/free/3, admission Thu free; ☺ 11am-7pm Tue, Wed, Fri & Sat, 11am-9pm Thu, 11am-5pm Sun; ℗). A selection from Hammer's collection of impressionists, Post-

TOUR OF THE STARS' HOMES

Seeing where the stars live – or lived – is a guilty pleasure easily indulged in during a visit to LA. Numerous tour companies specialize in celebrity tours, and maps to the stars' homes are sold all along Hollywood and Sunset Blvds, although they're often out-of-date. For those traveling with wheels, consider following this do-it-yourself tour of the glamorous, the notorious, the frivolous and the ostentatious. You'll see plenty of mansions protected by robotic cameras, armed guards and fierce dogs – look, but don't trespass. Budget about 90 minutes to two hours for this tour (see Map pp506–7).

Start your engine on Bedford Dr, a favorite with celebrities going back to the 1920s when original 'It' girl, **Clara Bow**, reputedly bedded the entire USC football team, including a linebacker named Marion Morrison (later John Wayne), in her home at 512 N Bedford Dr. **Stan Laurel** lived up the street at No 718 and **Steve Martin** once resided at No 721. **Lana Turner**'s one-time haunt, No 730, was where the film star's daughter stabbed her mother's abusive lover to death in 1958 (she was acquitted).

For more gore, turn left on Lomitas Ave, then right on N Linden Dr to No 810, where gangster **Bugsy Siegel** had a deadly encounter with a bullet back in 1947. Continue north to Sunset Blvd, turn right, then left on N Roxbury Dr for a great lineup of stars' homes, including those of **Lucille Ball** (No 1000), **Jack Benny** (No 1002), **Peter 'Columbo' Falk** (No 1004), **Ira and George Gershwin** (No 1019 and 1021, respectively) and **Diane Keaton** (No 1025).

Backtrack, turn right on Lexington Rd and right again on Ladera Dr, which veers left onto Monovale Dr; No 144 was **Elvis Presley's** home. Monovale merges with Carolwood Dr, another 'celebrity row.' The modest house at No 245 was occupied in happier times by **Burt Reynolds** and **Loni Anderson**, and before that by the late Beatle **George Harrison**. **Barbra Streisand** lived at No 301 and **Clark Gable** at No 325, not far from **Walt Disney**'s estate at No 355 (note the mouse-ear motif in the wrought-iron gate). **Gregory Peck** could be seen sauntering around No 375, while **Rod Stewart** had to keep fans away from his manse at No 391.

Turn around, follow Carolwood south to Sunset Blvd, turn right and then take the first marked left turn lane onto Charing Cross Rd, and watch out for 'bunnies' as you approach Hugh Hefner's **Playboy Mansion** at No 10236. The mansion is big but not as big as TV producer **Aaron Spelling**'s estate at 594 Mapleton Dr, adjacent to the Los Angeles Country Club (follow Charing Cross, then go left on Mapleton). The vanilla-colored chateau has 123 rooms and at one time was inhabited (not counting live-in staff) only by Spelling, his wife and their kids Tori and Randy. It is the largest private residence in all of LA.

Turn right on Club View Dr, right again on S Beverly Glen Blvd and across Sunset Blvd through the gates of swank Bel Air. Turn right on St Pierre Rd and follow it up and back down the hill. On your right at 486 St Pierre Rd is the abandoned hillside estate of **Johnny Weissmuller** of *Tarzan* fame. The actor used to keep in shape swimming in the moat-shaped pool surrounded by junglelike gardens. The house at 345 St Pierre Rd was where, in 1942, **Errol Flynn** allegedly raped a 17-year-old girl during a wild party; he was later acquitted. The incident gave birth to the expression 'in like Flynn,' referring to someone who's quick about getting the girl.

St Cloud Rd veers off to the right and skirts the vast Reagan compound. It was here that former-US President **Ronald Reagan** died in 2004. The original address was 666 Bel Air Rd, but superstitious Nancy had the number changed because of its satanic associations. Turning left and following Bel Air Rd south takes you back to Sunset Blvd.

---

impressionists and Old Masters is usually on view alongside changing exhibitions. A nice courtyard café opened in summer 2005.

PIERCE BROS WESTWOOD MEMORIAL PARK

This small and star-studded **cemetery** (Map pp506-7; ☎ 310-474-1570; 1218 Glendon Ave; admission free; ☽ 8am-sunset) is a bit hard to find – from

Wilshire Blvd, turn south onto Glendon Ave and look for the driveway immediately to your left. Marilyn Monroe is buried in an above-ground crypt next to an empty one reserved for Playboy owner Hugh Hefner. She's in good company for also planted here (in the ground) are Natalie Wood, Burt Lancaster, Walter Matthau, Jack Lemmon,

Roy Orbison and numerous other film and music legends.

GETTY CENTER

In the Santa Monica Mountains, high above the 405 Fwy, the billion-dollar **Getty Center** (Map pp498-9; ☎ 310-440-7300; www.getty.edu; 1200 Getty Center Dr; admission free; ⏰ 10am-6pm Sun & Tue-Thu, 10am-9pm Fri & Sat; Ⓟ) presents triple delights: a stellar art collection (Renaissance to David Hockney), the cutting-edge architecture of Richard Meier and the visual splendor of the seasonally changing gardens. On clear days, you can add breathtaking views of the city and ocean to the list. Even getting up to the 110-acre 'campus' aboard a driverless tram is fun.

The paintings collection is strongest when it comes to pre-20th-century Europeans, including famous canvasses by Van Gogh, Monet, Rembrandt and Titian. Tours, lectures and interactive technology, including audioguides ($3), make the art accessible to all, including children. A great time to visit is in the late afternoon after the crowds have thinned and you can watch the sunset while enjoying a picnic or a snack from a kiosk or the self-service café. Also check the Getty's cultural events calendar, which includes fabulous concerts, lectures and films (all free).

Both Metro bus 761 and the Big Blue Bus 14 stop at the Getty.

SKIRBALL CULTURAL CENTER

A cluster of galleries, performance spaces and educational facilities, the **Skirball** (☎ 310-440-4500; www.skirball.org; 2701 N Sepulveda Blvd; adult/child/student/senior $8/free/6/6; ⏰ noon-5pm Tue-Sat, 11am-5pm Sun) is a celebration of Jewish heritage, and the American Jewish experience in particular. The main exhibit, an engagingly presented pastiche of ceremonial objects, photographs, video, artifacts and archaeological finds, chronicles 4000 years of history, tradition, values and accomplishments of the Jewish people.

The Skirball also hosts traveling exhibits and has a packed schedule of lectures, concerts and performances. Zeidler's Café (mains $6 to $10) serves strictly kosher light California fare.

Malibu

Malibu hugs 27 miles of the Pacific Coast Hwy, a spectacular stretch of coastline right where the Santa Monica Mountains plunge into the ocean. There is no real center to it, but you'll find the greatest concentration of restaurants and shops near the century-old **Malibu Pier** (Map pp498-9).

Although it doesn't look terribly posh, Malibu is celebrity central and has been so since the early 1930s when money troubles forced landowner May Rindge to lease out property to her famous Hollywood friends. Clara Bow and Barbara Stanwyck were the first to stake out their turf in what became known as the **Malibu Colony**. Privacy-seeking celebs, including Tom Hanks and Barbra Streisand, still maintain homes in this gated and well-policed neighborhood. For good bird's-eye views, head a little up the coast to **Malibu Bluffs Park**. You're more likely to spot stars close up at the village-like **Malibu Country Mart** (Map pp498-9; 3835 Cross Creek Rd) and the more utilitarian **Malibu Colony Plaza** (Map pp498-9; 23841 W Malibu Rd).

The best way to really appreciate Malibu is through its natural assets. There are some fine beaches, including **Las Tunas**, **Point Dume**, **Zuma** and **Surfrider**, the last a world-famous surf spot. Rising behind Malibu is **Malibu Creek State Park**, part of the Santa Monica Mountains National Recreation Area and laced with hiking trails (p530).

Malibu's starring cultural attraction is the **Getty Villa** (Map pp498-9; ☎ 310-440-7300; www.getty.edu; 17985 Pacific Coast Hwy), which has undergone a massive eight-year revamp and should be open by the time you read this. Call or check the website for updates before heading out. The complex, centered around a replica of the Roman Villa dei Papiri, will showcase Getty's precious Greek, Roman and Etruscan antiquities. The rest of the Getty collection is in display at the hilltop Getty Center.

Other Malibu cultural sights include the **Adamson House** (Map pp498-9; ☎ 310-456-8432; www.adamsonhouse.org; 23200 Pacific Coast Hwy; adult/child $5/3; ⏰ 11am-2pm Wed-Sat), a beautiful Spanish-Moorish villa awash with locally made handpainted tiles. To learn more about the local history pop into the adjacent **Malibu Lagoon Museum** (Map pp498-9; ☎ 310-456-8432; admission free; ⏰ 11am-3pm Wed-Sat).

Santa Monica

The seaside city of Santa Monica is one of the most agreeable in LA, with an early-20th-

---

DETOUR: RONALD W REAGAN LIBRARY & MUSEUM

When Ronald Reagan, the country's 40th president, died on June 5, 2004, at age 93, he was buried in the shadow of his **presidential library** (☎ 800-998-7641; www.reaganlibrary.net; 40 Presidential Dr; adult/teen/senior $7/2/5; ☷ 10am-5pm) in Simi Valley, just across the Ventura county line. Love him or hate him, but the exhibits here are really quite fascinating. Galleries cover all phases of Reagan's life – from his childhood in Dixon, Illinois, through his early days in radio and acting, to his stint as governor of California – although the focus is obviously on his years as president (1980–88). The museum features re-creations of the Oval Office and the Cabinet Room, Reagan family memorabilia, gifts from heads of state and a nuclear cruise missile. The graffiti-covered chunk of the Berlin Wall never fails to impress either. To get there, take I-405 (San Diego Fwy) north to the 118 (Ronald Reagan Fwy) west; exit at Madera Rd South, turn right on Madera and continue straight for 3 miles to Presidential Dr.

---

century pier, pedestrian-friendly downtown, miles of sandy beaches and excellent shopping and dining. Once quaint and slightly wacky, it has evolved into a somewhat manicured beach town with cosmopolitan flair. For visitors, Santa Monica is a central, safe and fun base for exploring LA. Stop by either visitors center (p497) for maps and all sorts of information. Parking is free for two hours at four downtown public parking garages on 2nd and 4th Sts between Broadway and Wilshire Blvd.

The city's most recognizable landmark is the **Santa Monica Pier** (Map pp508-9; ☎ 310-458-8900; www.santamonicapier.org; admission free, unlimited rides under/over 42in tall $11/22; ☷ 24hr), the oldest amusement pier in California (1908). It has plenty of kid-friendly diversions, including a historic **carousel** and small **amusement park** with a solar-powered Ferris wheel, a roller-coaster and other rides each costing between $1.50 and $4.50.

Below the pier, the **Santa Monica Pier Aquarium** (Map pp508-9; ☎ 310-393-6149; admission by donation, suggested/minimum $5/1, children under 12 free; ☷ 2-6pm Tue-Fri, 12:30-6pm Sat & Sun) is the place for close encounters with jellyfish, small sharks and other critters residing in Santa Monica Bay.

Meandering right by the pier is the **South Bay Bicycle Trail** (p530), a paved bicycle and walking path. Bike or in-line skate rentals are available on the pier and at beachside kiosks.

A amble walk inland, the car-free **Third Street Promenade** – located between Wilshire Blvd and Broadway – is a great place for a stroll, a bite, a movie, a shopping spree and lots of free street entertainment, from flamenco guitarists to hip-hop crooners. It's

anchored by Santa Monica Pl, a shopping mall designed by Frank Gehry.

Fans of avant-garde art should continue inland for about 3 miles to the **Bergamot Station Arts Center** (Map pp508-9; 2525 Michigan Ave, enter from Cloverfield Blvd; ☷ 10am-6pm Tue-Sat; ☷), home to more than 30 galleries, shops, a café and the progressive **Santa Monica Museum of Art** (Map pp508-9; ☎ 310-586-6488; www.smmoa.org; admission by donation; ☷ 11am-6pm Tue-Sat).

Other Santa Monica neighborhoods suitable for strolling, shopping and dining are **Montana Ave** in the city's northern section and **Main St** on the southern end of town, near the border with Venice. Main St is connected to downtown by the electric Tide Shuttle (25¢ per ride).

Venice

If aliens landed on Venice's famous **Ocean Front Walk** (Map pp508-9; Venice Pier to Rose Ave; admission free; ☷ 24hr), they'd probably blend right into the human zoo of wannabe Schwarzeneggers, a Speedo-clad 'snake man' and a roller-skating Sikh minstrel. Known locally as Venice Boardwalk, this is the place to get your hair braided, skin tattooed or aura adjusted. It's a freak show that must be seen to be believed, preferably on a hot summer weekend when the scene is at its most surreal. Avoid the boardwalk after dark.

Venice was created in 1905 by eccentric tobacco heir Abbot Kinney as an amusement park, called 'Venice of America,' complete with a Ferris wheel, water ride and Italian *gondolieri* who poled visitors around canals. Most of the waterways vanished beneath roads later on, but some have been restored and are now flanked by flower-festooned villas. The **Venice Canal Walk** threads through

LOS AN

this idyllic neighborhood, easily accessed from either Venice or Washington Blvds.

Kinney may have been a little kooky but he unwittingly set the trend for 20th-century Venice, California. Counterculture royalty such as beatniks Lawrence Lipton and Stuart Perkoff and uber-hippie Jim Morrison made their homes here at one time. Today, Venice is still a cauldron of creativity, peopled by karmically correct New Agers, eternal hippies, cool-conscious musicians and even a few celebs, including Dennis Hopper, Anjelica Huston, Mira Sorvino and Julia Roberts.

Galleries, studios and public art abound, much of it with a predictably bizarre bent. Cases in point: Jonathan Borofsky's tutu-clad **Ballerina Clown** (Map pp508-9; Rose Ave & Main St) and Frank Gehry's **Chiat/Day Building** (Map pp508-9; 340 Main St), fronted by a three-story-tall pair of binoculars.

A fun place for a stroll is the mile-long stretch of **Abbot Kinney Blvd** between Venice Blvd and Main St, chockablock with boutiques, galleries, bars and restaurants.

South Bay & Palos Verdes

South of LA International, Santa Monica Bay is lined by a trio of all-American beach towns – **Manhattan Beach**, **Hermosa Beach** and **Redondo Beach** – with a distinctive laid-back vibe. Lovely, if not lavish, homes come all the way down to the gorgeous white beach, which is the prime attraction here and paralleled by the **South Bay Bicycle Trail** (p530).

The beaches run straight into the **Palos Verdes Peninsula**, a rocky precipice that's home to some of the richest and most exclusive communities in the LA area. A drive along Palos Verdes Dr takes you along some spectacular rugged coastline with sublime views of the ocean and Catalina Island. A worthwhile stop is at the 1949 **Wayfarers Chapel** (Map pp498-9; ☎ 310-377-7919; www.wayfarerschapel.org; 5755 Palos Verdes Dr S; admission free; ☼ 8am-5pm), an enchanting hillside structure surrounded by mature redwood trees and gardens. The work of Lloyd Wright, it is almost entirely made of glass and is one of LA's most popular spots for weddings.

San Pedro

San Pedro is a slow-paced harbor community on the edge of Worldport LA, the third-busiest container port after Singapore and Hong Kong. Nearly all the local sights are

along the waterfront and served by the electric Red Car trolley from Friday to Monday (all-day fare $1).

For a salty introduction to the region, visit the **Los Angeles Maritime Museum** (Map pp498-9; ☎ 310-548-7618; www.lamaritimemuseum.org; Berth 84; suggested donation $1; ☼ 10am-5pm Tue-Sat, noon-5pm Sun), which tells the story of the city's relationship with the sea and displays some great ship models, figureheads and navigational equipment. If you like to clamber around old ships, head a mile north to **SS Lane Victory** (Map pp498-9; ☎ 310-519-9545; www.lanevictory.org; Berth 94; adult/child $3/1; ☼ 9am-4pm), an immaculately restored WWII-era cargo ship. Just south of the Maritime Museum is touristy **Ports O' Call Village**, where you can grab a bite, hop on a port cruise or join a whale-watching trip (see p531 for details).

A short drive south takes you to the **Cabrillo Marine Aquarium** (Map pp498-9; ☎ 310-548-7562; www.cabrilloaq.org; 3720 Stephen White Dr; admission by donation, suggested adult/child $5/1; ☼ noon-5pm Tue-Fri, 10am-5pm Sat & Sun; Ⓟ), home to a parade of local oceanic denizens.

Long Beach

Long Beach, on the border with Orange County, has come a long way from its working-class oil and navy days, but gentrification hasn't completely spoiled its relaxed, small-town atmosphere – at least for now. Much of the action in its compact downtown centers on southern **Pine Ave**, which is chockablock with restaurants, nightclubs and bars. About 3 miles east of here are the upscale neighborhoods of Belmont Shore and canal-laced Naples, which can be explored aboard authentic **gondolas** (Map pp498-9; ☎ 562-433-9595; www.gondolagetawayinc.com; 5437 E Ocean Blvd; per couple $65).

Downtown Long Beach is the southern terminus of the Metro Blue Line. A shuttle service, called **Passport** (within downtown free, elsewhere 90¢), serves all major places of interest on four routes (free within downtown; 90¢ otherwise). A **Long Beach Visitor Information Kiosk** (Map pp498-9; ☎ 562-436-3645, 800-452-7829; ☼ 10am-5pm Jun-Sep, 10am-4pm Fri-Sun Oct-May) is right outside the Aquarium of the Pacific.

AQUARIUM OF THE PACIFIC & AROUND
One of the largest watery zoos in the country, the **Aquarium of the Pacific** (Map pp498-9; ☎ 562-590-3100; www.aquariumofpacific.org; 100 Aquar-

ium Way; adult/child/senior $19/11/15; ☺ 9am-6pm; Ⓟ)
is a joyful, high-tech romp through an intriguing underwater world. Its 12,500 creatures
hail from tepid Baja California, the frigid
northern Pacific, the coral reefs of the tropics
and the kelp forests swaying in local waters.
You can pet small sharks, observe the antics
of sea otters or be charmed by drifting sea
dragons.

At the nearby **Pike at Rainbow Harbor** development, the diversions include an antique
carousel, a fancy multiplex movie theater, a
GameWorks arcade and chain restaurants
galore. Further east is **Shoreline Village**, another shopping-and-dining complex that's
also a departure point for harbor and whale-
watching cruises (p531).

QUEEN MARY
Long Beach's flagship attraction is this elegant – and supposedly haunted – British
ocean liner (Map pp498-9; ☎ 562-435-3511; www.queen
mary.com; 1126 Queens Hwy; adult/child/senior $23/12/20;
☺ 10am-5pm Mon-Thu, 10am-6pm Fri-Sun, hours vary by
season; Ⓟ). Larger and more luxurious than
even the *Titanic*, the *Queen Mary* transported
royals, dignitaries, immigrants and troops
during its 1001 Atlantic crossings between
1936 and 1964. In Long Beach since 1967, it
is now a hotel and tourist attraction.

The basic admission includes a self-guided
tour as well as the tongue-in-cheek 'Ghosts
and Legends' special-effects tour. Other tours
are available.

Moored next to the *Queen Mary* is the
Scorpion (adult/child/senior $10/9/9), an authentic
Soviet submarine where you can clamber
around the claustrophobic interior.

MUSEUMS
In Long Beach's fledgling East Village Arts
District, the **Museum of Latin American Art** (Map
pp498-9; ☎ 562-437-1689; www.molaa.org; 628 Alami-
tos Ave; adult/child/student/senior $5/free/3/3, Fri free;
☺ 11:30am-7pm Tue-Fri, 11am-7pm Sat, 11am-6pm Sun)
is the only museum in the western USA to
exclusively showcase contemporary Latin
American art.

Sitting pretty on a waterfront bluff, the
Long Beach Museum of Art (Map pp498-9; ☎ 562-
439-2119; www.lbma.org; 2300 E Ocean Blvd; adult/child/
student/senior $5/free/4/4; ☺ 11am-5pm Tue, Wed &
Fri-Sun, 11am-8pm Thu) presents changing exhibitions mostly drawn from its collection of
American decorative arts, California Mod-

ernism, contemporary art (including video)
and early-20th-century European art.

Downtown
There's something afoot in Downtown LA
and adventurous urbanites are taking note.
A budding arts district with edgy galleries, stylish lofts reclaimed from aging office
buildings and new quirky bars and restaurants all fuel the buzz, as does headline-
grabbing architecture, most notably Frank
Gehry's Walt Disney Concert Hall. If you're
open-minded and don't mind a little grit
and grime here and there, Downtown is
your oyster. It's easily explored on foot or
by DASH minibuses (p556). Parking is
cheapest around Little Tokyo and in Chinatown (about $4 or $5 all day).

EL PUEBLO DE LOS ANGELES & AROUND
Compact, colorful and car-free, this state
historic park commemorates LA's founding and preserves the city's oldest buildings, most notably the 1818 **Avila Adobe** (Map
pp500-1; ☎ 213-628-1274; E-10 Olvera St; admission free;
☺ 10am-3pm). It's right on **Olvera St**, a block-
long, Mexican-flavored brick alley where
you can browse for tacky souvenirs, feast
on tacos and *tortas* (sandwiches), and peruse Chicano art.

Pick up a free self-guided tour pamphlet
at the **El Pueblo Visitors Center** (Map pp500-1;
☎ 213-628-1274; Sepulveda House, Olvera St; ☺ 10am-
3pm) or join a free guided tour leaving from
the **Old Plaza Firehouse Museum** at 10am, 11am
and noon Tuesday to Saturday.

Olvera St spills over into the **Old Plaza**,
the Pueblo's central square with a pretty
wrought-iron bandstand. Families stroll,
couples kiss and everyone seeks shade beneath the grand old Australian Moreton
Bay fig trees here. The little church across
the street, affectionately known as **La Placita**
(Map pp500-1; ☎ 213-629-3101; 535 N Main St; admission
free; ☺ 7am-7pm), meaning 'little plaza,' dates
from 1822 and is a sentimental favorite
with LA's Latino community. Peek inside
for a look at the gold-festooned altar and
nicely painted ceiling.

Southeast of the plaza looms the soaring
tower of **Union Station** (Map pp500-1; 800 N Alameda
St), built in 1939, the last of the grand railroad stations in the USA. It's a glamorous
exercise in Spanish-Mission and art deco,
and has a waiting room easily the size of

BLESSINGS BE UPON YE!

Catholics tend to be equal-opportunity blessers and nowhere are their blessings more quirkily bestowed than in LA. The city boasts not one but two festivals where soul-saving words fly as thick as fishwives' curses. The first, with origins in the 1700s, is the **Blessing of the Animals** (http://olvera-street.com/html/blessing_of_the_animals.html) which takes place in El Pueblo de Los Angeles the Saturday before Easter. Three-legged pit bulls, whacked-out monkeys, Chihuahuas in sombreros, banty roosters and iguanas: if it slithers, slimes, snarls, flies, crawls or hauls, your pet will receive an abundant blessing here from none other than Cardinal Roger Mahoney himself. Properly honored, it then enjoys the right to parade around with its owner, proudly displaying its feathers, fur or fangs. Artist Leo Politi has captured the goings-on in an endearing mural facing El Pueblo's Old Plaza.

Across town, the San Fernando Valley is the birthplace of the **Blessing of the Cars** (www.blessingofthecars.com), which was dreamed up a little over a decade ago by two Catholic sisters who were inordinately fond of both their cars and blessing things. Taking place in late July, the event has grown into one of the wildest scenes in LA. There are cars! cars! cars!, rock and roll, hot rod movies and a priest who will – if presumed upon – place holy water in your radiator. You'll see more tattoos on display than in the US Navy and more boobs clamoring for attention than in the US Senate. Lord help us!

a football field with the loftiness of a cathedral. The station has appeared in numerous movies, including *Guilty by Suspicion*, *Blade Runner* and *The Way We Were*.

The terminal stands on the spot of LA's original Chinatown, whose residents were forcibly relocated a few blocks north, along Broadway and Hill St. Today, the 'new' **Chinatown** is still a vibrant cultural and social hub of LA's Chinese Americans but of late has also begun registering on the radar of artists and hipsters from around town. Check out the galleries and eclectic stores in the historic **Central Plaza** (Map pp500-1; 900 block btwn Broadway & Hill St) and on nearby Chung King Rd.

The history of LA's Chinese Americans is engagingly commemorated in the **Chinese American Museum** (Map pp500-1; ☎ 213-485-8567; www.camla.org; 425 N Los Angeles St; adult/student/senior $3/2/2; 🕑 10am-3pm Tue-Sun), further south in El Pueblo. It's in the 1890 Garnier Building, once the original Chinatown's unofficial 'city hall.'

DODGER STADIUM

Just north of Chinatown sits one of the most beloved baseball parks, **Dodger Stadium** (Map pp500-1; ☎ 323-224-1448; 1000 Elysian Park Ave; tour adult/child 4-14 $8/4; 🕑 2pm Tue-Fri nongame days Apr-Sep), home of the Los Angeles Dodgers (p551). The one-hour tour takes you to the press box, the radio and TV booths, the Dodger dugout, the Dugout Club, a luxury suite and other 'horsehide and hickory' sites. Reservations required.

CITY HALL

LA's 1928 **City Hall** (Map pp500-1; ☎ 213-485-2121; 200 N Spring St; admission free; 🕑 8am-5pm Mon-Fri, free tours 9am-2pm) is the shining beacon in a sea of architectural mediocrity that marks the Civic Center area south of El Pueblo across the 101 Fwy (Hollywood Fwy). City Hall cameoed as the Daily Planet in the *Superman* TV series and got blown to bits in the 1953 sci-fi thriller *War of the Worlds*. If the smog isn't bad, you'll have great views from the wraparound Observation Deck. Enter on Spring St and be prepared to show ID and have your stuff x-rayed.

CATHEDRAL OF OUR LADY OF THE ANGELS

Downtown's new landmark **cathedral** (Map pp500-1; ☎ 213-680-5200; www.olacathedral.org; 555 W Temple St; admission free; 🕑 6:30am-6pm Mon-Fri, 9am-6pm Sat, 7am-6pm Sun, free tours 1pm Mon-Fri; P) is a monumental work by Spanish architect José Rafael Moneo. Behind its austere, ochre mantle awaits a vast hall of worship filled with plenty of original art and soft light filtering in through milky, alabaster windows. Gregory Peck is buried in the mausoleum. The cathedral store sells self-guided tour booklets ($2.50).

GRAND AVENUE CULTURAL CORRIDOR

Grand Avenue, on the northern edge of the Civic Center district, is being touted as the epicenter of Downtown revitalization and brims with architectural landmarks, museums and even a few good restaurants.

Walt Disney Concert Hall

Undisputed centerpiece along Grand Ave is this sparkling **concert venue** (Map pp500-1; ☎ 213-972-4399 ext 5; http://wdch.laphil.com; 111 S Grand Ave; self-guided audio tours adult/student/senior $10/8/8, guided tour $10; ☽ audio tours 9am-3pm non-matinee days, guided tours 10am-11:30am matinee days). Designed by Frank Gehry, the concert hall is a gravity-defying sculpture of curving and billowing stainless-steel walls that conjures visions of a ship adrift in a cosmic sea. The auditorium, meanwhile, feels like the inside of a finely crafted instrument, a cello perhaps, clad in walls of smooth Douglas fir. Disney Hall is the new home of the **Los Angeles Philharmonic** (p550), which used to play at the **Music Center of LA County** one block north of here.

MOCA Grand Avenue

A bit south of Disney Hall, this much-touted **museum** (Map pp500-1; ☎ 213-626-6222; www.moca -la.org; 250 S Grand Ave; adult/child/student/senior $8/ free/5/5, Thu free; ☽ 11am-5pm Mon & Fri, 11am-8pm Thu, 11am-6pm Sat & Sun) is a delicacy for contemporary art fans. Besides headline-grabbing special exhibits, it presents all the heavy hitters of the art world working from the 1940s to the present – from Andy Warhol to Cy Twombly. It's in a building by Arata Isozaki that many consider his masterpiece.

MOCA is shadowed by the glistening towers of California Plaza, a vast office complex that hosts the **Grand Performances** (www .grandperformances.org), one of the best free summer outdoor-performance series in town.

On the plaza's southeastern side is **Angels Flight**, a historic funicular that briefly revived in 1996 only to be mothballed five years later after a derailed car left one person dead and injured others. There are stairs down to Hill St and the wonderful **Grand Central Market**, although you may have to hopscotch around a few homeless folks to get there.

Wells Fargo History Museum

Continuing south along Grand Ave is the small but intriguing **Wells Fargo History Museum** (Map pp500-1; ☎ 213-253-7166; www.wellsfargo history.com/museums/lamuseum.html; 333 S Grand Ave; admission free; ☽ 9am-5pm Mon-Fri), which relives the Gold Rush era with an original Concord stagecoach, a 100oz gold nugget and a 19th-century bank office.

Richard Riordan Central Library

The 1922 **Richard Riordan Central Library** (Map pp500-1; ☎ 213-228-7000; www.lapl.org; 630 W 5th St; admission free; ☽ 10am-8pm Mon-Thu, 10am-6pm Fri & Sat, 1-5pm Sun, free tours 12:30pm Mon-Fri, 11am & 2pm Sat, 2pm Sun) was designed by Bertram Goodhue in quasi-Egyptian style. You can check email, read newspapers and magazines, browse the stacks, view the latest exhibits at the excellent Getty Gallery or the Photography Gallery, or grab a bite in the cafeteria. A modern wing was added in 1993, as was the **Maguire Gardens**, a small and tranquil park of sinuous walkways, pools, fountains and whimsical artwork.

Pershing Square & Around

A short stroll southwest of City Hall drops you right into Downtown's historic core anchored by **Pershing Square**, LA's oldest public park (1866), flanked on its north by the grand old **Millennium Biltmore Hotel** (p539).

Southwest of Pershing Sq, along Hill St, gold and diamonds are the main currency in the **Jewelry District**. For dazzling architecture, head one block northeast to Broadway, where the 1893 **Bradbury Building** (Map pp500-1; ☎ 213-626-1893; 304 S Broadway; admission free; ☽ 9am-6pm Mon-Fri, 9am-5pm Sat & Sun) is the undisputed crown jewel. Its red brick facade conceals a light-flooded, galleried atrium that has starred in many movies, most famously in *Blade Runner*. Across the street, the colorful and frenzied **Grand Central Market** (Map pp500-1; ☎ 213-624-2378; 317 S Broadway; ☽ 9am-6pm) is great for a browse or a snack.

Broadway also earned a spot on the National Register of Historic Places for its 11 lavish **movie palaces**, built between 1913 and 1931 in a marvelous hodgepodge of styles, from Spanish Gothic to French baroque. Some, such as the **Orpheum Theater** (Map pp500-1; 842 Broadway), have been gloriously restored and are now used for special screenings, parties and other events.

LITTLE TOKYO

Little Tokyo is the Japanese counterpart of Chinatown, with an attractive mix of traditional gardens, Buddhist temples, outdoor shopping malls and sushi bars. Stop into the visitors center, the **Little Tokyo Koban** (Map pp500-1; ☎ 213-613-1911; 307 E 1st St; ☽ 9am-6pm Mon-Sat) for maps and information. Otherwise, a great introduction to the area is the

DETOUR: SAN ANTONIO WINERY

Across LA's trickling 'river,' about 2 miles north of Union Station, is the **San Antonio Winery** (Map pp500-1; ☎ 323-223-1401; www .sanantoniowinery.com; 737 Lamar St; admission free; ☒ 10am-6pm Sun-Tue, 10am-7pm Wed-Sat), the last of what once used to be a flourishing local industry. It was founded in 1917 by Italian immigrant Santo Cambianica, whose descendants still make buttery chardonnay, velvety cabernet sauvignon and other vintages. You can sample some of them for free in the tasting room, enjoy a meal at the Italian restaurant, learn more about the noble grape at a wine seminar or take a free behind-the-scenes tour (call for times).

Japanese American National Museum (Map pp500-1; ☎ 213-625-0414; www.janm.org; 369 E 1st St; adult/child/student/senior $8/free/4/5, after 5pm Thu free; ☒ 10am-5pm Tue & Wed-Sun, 10am-8pm Thu). The galleries brim with objects of work and worship, photographs, art and even a uniform worn by *Star Trek* actor George Takei. Special focus is given to the painful chapter of the WWII internment camps.

Just north of here, the **MOCA Geffen Contemporary** (Map pp500-1; ☎ 213-626-6222; www.moca-la .org; 152 N Central Ave; adult/child/student/senior $8/free/5/5, Thu free; ☒ 11am-5pm Mon & Fri, 11am-8pm Thu, 11am-6pm Sat & Sun) is a subsidiary of the main museum on Grand Ave (p523) and presents mostly large-scale installations.

In the gritty, industrial section southeast of Little Tokyo, an increasingly lively **Arts District** is emerging ever so slowly. It's a young and adventurous crowd drawn to live and work in makeshift studios above abandoned warehouses and small factories. There's enough of them here to support a growing number of cafés, restaurants and shops.

SOUTH PARK

In the southwestern corner of Downtown, South Park is still a work in progress, but there are some pockets of new vitality here as well. One major catalyst has been the **Staples Center** (Map pp500-1; ☎ 213-742-7340; www .staplescenter.com; 1111 S Figueroa St), a saucer-shaped sports and entertainment arena with all the high-tech trappings. It's the home turf of the Los Angeles Lakers, Clippers and Sparks basketball teams, the Kings ice-hockey team and

the Avengers indoor-football team. When major headliners – from Bruce Springsteen to Britney Spears – are in town, they'll most likely perform at the Staples.

East of the arena, the **Museum of Neon Art** (MONA; Map pp500-1; ☎ 213-489-9918; www.neonmona .org; 501 W Olympic Blvd; adult/child/student/senior $5/free/3.50/3.50; ☒ 11am-5pm Wed-Sat, noon-5pm Sun) is a cool gallery highlighting neon, electric and kinetic art, including a serenely smiling Mona Lisa.

Continuing east on Olympic Blvd takes you straight into the heart of the **Fashion District** (Map pp500-1; ☎ 213-488-1153; www.fashiondistrict .org), a 90-block nirvana for bargain hunters, even if shopping around here is more Middle Eastern bazaar than American mall. The vast selection of samples, knockoffs and original designs will make your head spin.

Nearby, LA's **flower market** (Map pp500-1; ☎ 213-627-3696; Wall St; Mon-Fri $2, Sat $1; ☒ 8am-noon Mon, Wed & Fri, 6am-noon Tue, Thu & Sat), between 7th and 8th Sts, is the largest in the country and dates back to 1913.

Koreatown

Koreatown is a cacophonous, amorphous and steadily expanding area west of Downtown. Despite the moniker, most sights here actually have nothing to do with Korean culture, the lone exception being the **Korean American Museum** (☎ 213-388-4229; www.kamuseum .org; 4th fl, 3727 W 6th St; admission free; ☒ 11am-6pm Wed-Fri, 11am-3pm Sat).

Traveling west along Wilshire Blvd, a main artery, first takes you past **MacArthur Park** (Map pp500-1), an expanse of green that's gone from gritty to pretty following a recent refurbishment. Unfortunately, it still attracts a fair number of the down-and-out and, like all LA parks, should be avoided after dark.

Fans of Victoriana will get their fill at the nearby **Grier Musser Museum** (Map pp500-1; ☎ 213-413-1814; 403 S Bonnie Brae St; adult/child/student/senior $6/4/5/5; ☒ noon-4pm Wed-Sat), an immaculately restored turn-of-the-20th-century Queen Anne villa that's stuffed with period antiques and knickknacks.

Further west await a couple of delicacies for art deco buffs, the 1929 **Bullocks Wilshire Building** (☎ 213-738-8240; www.swlaw.edu/bullockswil shire; 3050 Wilshire Blvd), a former department store and now a law school, and the **Wiltern Theatre** (3790 Wilshire Blvd), an elegant music venue. In between is the 1922 **Ambassador Hotel** (3400

Wilshire Blvd), one of LA's oldest and grandest hotels and the site of the Robert F Kennedy assassination. It is slated to be largely demolished to make room for a new school.

In southern Koreatown, the Greek Orthodox **St Sophia Cathedral** (☎ 323-737-2424; www .stsophia.org; 1324 S Normandie Ave; admission free; ☯ 10am-4pm Tue-Fri, 10am-2pm Sat) is so lavishly decorated it inspires comparison to a giant's treasure chest, spilling over with gold, crystal and jewels.

Exposition Park

A couple of miles to the south of Downtown, the family-friendly **Exposition Park** (Map pp498–9) started as an agricultural fairground in 1872 and now contains three fine **museums**, a lovely **Rose Garden** (admission free; ☯ 9am-sunset mid-Mar–Dec) and the 1923 **Los Angeles Memorial Coliseum**. The latter hosted the 1932 and 1984 Summer Olympic Games, the 1959 baseball World Series and two Super Bowls.

The **University of Southern California** (USC; Map pp498-9; ☎ 213-740-5371, tours 213-740-6605; www .usc.edu; 3535 S Figueroa St), which counts George Lucas, John Wayne and Neil Armstrong among its alumni, is just north of Exposition Park.

The DASH bus 'F' (p556) from Downtown serves Exposition Park. There's parking ($6) on Figueroa at 39th St.

NATURAL HISTORY MUSEUM OF LOS ANGELES COUNTY

Take a spin around the world and back in time at this popular **museum** (NHM; Map pp500-1; ☎ 213-763-3466; www.nhm.org; 900 Exposition Blvd; adult/child/student/senior $9/2/6.50/6.50; ☯ 9:30am-5pm Mon-Fri, 10am-5pm Sat & Sun), inside a baronial building in Exposition Park's northwest corner. There is usually some special exhibit going on, but the permanent halls are also well worth a spin. Crowd-pleasers include stuffed African elephants, a Tyrannosaurus rex skull and the giant megamouth, one of the world's rarest sharks. Historical exhibits include prized Navajo texiles, baskets and jewelry in the **Hall of Native American Cultures**. The **Gem & Mineral Hall**, meanwhile, is a glittering spectacle with a walk-through gem tunnel and more gold than any other such collection in the USA. Kids love the hands-on **Discovery Center** and the **Insect Zoo** with its tarantulas, hissing cockroaches and other creepy-crawlies.

CALIFORNIA SCIENCE CENTER

If your memories of school science makes you groan, then a visit to this imaginative multimedia **museum** (Map pp500-1; ☎ 213-744-7400; www.casciencectr.org; 700 State Dr; admission free; ☯ 10am-5pm) should convince you that, gee, science *can* be fun. There's absolutely nothing stuffy about this place, where you can watch baby chicks hatch in an incubator, and you'll have plenty of buttons to push, lights to switch on and knobs to pull. During the school year, the center usually crawls with school kids on weekday mornings, so plan accordingly if you want a little more quiet.

Of the three main exhibition areas, **World of Life** focuses mostly on the human body. You can 'hop on' a red blood cell for a computer fly-through of the circulatory system, ask Gertie how long your colon really is and meet Tess, a giant techno-doll billed as '50ft of brains, beauty and biology.'

Virtual-reality games, high-tech simulations, laser animation and other gizmos and gadgets await in the **Creative World** exhibit, which zooms in on the tools and devices humans have invented in order to facilitate communication, transportation and construction.

In an adjacent building, spirits will soar in the **Air & Space Gallery** (Map pp500-1; ☯ 10am-1pm Mon-Fri, 11am-4pm Sat & Sun), where exhibits include the pioneering 1902 Wright Glider and the Soviet-made *Sputnik*, the first human-made object to orbit the earth in 1957.

The adjacent **IMAX** (p548) is a good place to relax and wind down at the end of an action-filled day.

CALIFORNIA AFRICAN AMERICAN MUSEUM

This acclaimed **museum** (Map pp500-1; ☎ 213-744-7432; www.caamuseum.org; 600 State Dr; admission free; ☯ 10am-4pm Wed-Sat) does an excellent job documenting African and African American art and history, especially as it pertains to California and other western states. An active lecture and performance schedule brings together the community and those wanting to gain a deeper understanding of what it means to be black in America.

South Central

The area south of Exposition Park is traditionally referred to as **South Central**. Gangs, drugs, poverty, crime and drive-by shootings are just a few of the negative images –

LOS AN

not entirely undeserved – associated with this district. Much of the area is bleak and foreboding, but there are also a few appealing pockets and sights.

WATTS TOWERS

South Central's beacon of pride, the **Watts Towers** (Map pp498-9; ☎ 213-847-4646; 1765 E 107th St; adult/child/teen/senior $5/free/3/3; ☉ 11am-2:30pm Fri, 10:30am-2:30pm Sat, 12:30-3pm Sun) rank among the world's greatest monuments of folk art. Italian immigrant Simon Rodia spent 33 years cobbling together this whimsical free-form sculpture from a motley assortment of found objects – green 7-Up bottles to sea shells, rocks to pottery. While here, sneak a peek inside the adjacent **Watts Towers Art Center** (Map pp498-9; ☎ 213-847-4646; admission free; ☉ 10am-4pm Tue-Sat, noon-4pm Sun).

LEIMERT PARK

About 2.5 miles west of Exposition Park, the Leimert (luh-*mert*) Park neighborhood has emerged as the cultural hub of LA's African American community. The action is centered in **Leimert Park Village**, especially along Degnan Blvd between 43rd St and the namesake park.

Sandwiched between restaurants, shops, coffeehouses and performance spaces along here is the **Museum in Black** (Map pp498-9; ☎ 323-292-9528; 4331 Degnan Blvd; admission free; ☉ 10am-6pm Tue-Sat). It combines a commercial African art gallery with a small but intriguing collection of segregation-era memorabilia (it's in the back, so you may have to ask to see it). Call ahead to confirm opening hours.

East Los Angeles

East of Downtown, the Los Angeles River is a bit like the US–Mexican border without the wall and the guards. Beyond the concrete gulch lies a sprawling neighborhood that's home to the largest concentration of Mexicans outside of Mexico, plus thousands of Latinos from Central and, to a lesser extent, South America. Life in the barrio is tough but lively. People shop in streets lined with *panaderías* (bakeries), *tiendas* (convenience stores) and stores selling *botánicas* (herbal cures). Brightly colored murals adorn many facades, but behind the color, life can be pretty grim. Unemployment is high, incomes are low and gang violence and poor schools ubiquitous.

There are no major tourist sights in this area, but Boyle Heights, the neighborhood closest to Downtown LA, has a few worthwhile stops. Here you'll find **Mariachi Plaza** (Map pp500-1; cnr Boyle Ave & 1st St), where traditional Mexican musicians dressed in fanciful suits and wide-brimmed hats mill beneath wall-sized murals waiting to be hired for restaurant or social events. A bit further east, **El Mercado** (Map pp498-9; 3425 E 1st St) is a wonderfully boisterous indoor market, where locals stock up on tortilla presses, pig bellies and toys. The upstairs restaurants are often packed, especially when there's live music.

North of here is one of LA's major Latino arts centers, **Self-Help Graphics & Art** (Map pp498-9; ☎ 323-881-6444; www.selfhelpgraphics.com; 3802 Cesar E Chavez Ave; admission free; ☉ 10am-4pm Tue-Sat, noon-4pm Sun), whose colorful facade is a mosaic of pottery and glass shards. The center was founded by a Franciscan nun in 1973 and has been nurturing and promoting Latino art ever since. The galleries and gift shops are well worth checking out.

Pasadena & Around

Resting below the lofty San Gabriel Mountains, Pasadena is a genteel city with old-time mansions, superb Craftsman architecture and fine-art museums. Every New Year's Day, it is thrust into the national spotlight during the **Rose Parade** (p532).

The main fun zone is **Old Town Pasadena**, a bustling 20-block shopping and entertainment district set up in successfully restored historic brick buildings along Colorado Blvd west of Arroyo Parkway. Another interesting strip, especially if you're into shopping, is **South Lake Ave**, about 1 mile east of here. About midway there you can start spending money at **Paseo Colorado**, an outdoor mall, or pick up information at the **Pasadena Convention & Visitors Bureau** (Map pp498-9; ☎ 626-795-9311, 800-307-7977; www.pasadenacal.com; 171 S Los Robles Ave; ☉ 8am-5pm Mon-Fri, 10am-4pm Sat).

Pasadena is surrounded by the numerous suburban communities of the San Gabriel Valley. It is served by the Metro Gold Line (p556) from Downtown LA. Pasadena ARTS buses (fare 50¢) plough around the city on seven different routes.

NORTON SIMON MUSEUM

Rodin's *The Thinker* outside this exquisite **museum** (Map pp498-9; ☎ 626-449-6840; www.norton

simon.org; 411 W Colorado Blvd; adult/child/student/senior $6/free/free/3; ☻ noon-6pm Wed, Thu & Sat-Mon, noon-9pm Fri; Ⓟ) is only a mind-teasing overture to the full symphony of art awaiting behind its doors. Norton Simon (1907–93) was an entrepreneur with the Midas touch and a collector with a passion for Western art. He amassed a respectable assortment of all the household names, from Rembrandt to Renoir, Raphael to Van Gogh, Botticelli to Picasso. The basement holds a sampling of Simon's secondary fancy: Indian and Southeast Asian sculpture. Western sculpture graces the gorgeous garden designed in the tradition of Monet's at Giverny, France. Audioguides rent for $3.

GAMBLE HOUSE
A masterpiece of Craftsman architecture, the **Gamble House** (Map pp498-9; ☎ 626-793-3334; www.gamblehouse.org; 4 Westmoreland Pl; tour adult/child/student/senior $8/free/free/5; ☻ noon-3pm Thu-Sun; Ⓟ) was created in 1908 by the style's prime practitioners, Charles and Henry Greene. One-hour tours give you close-ups of the beautiful woodwork, the iridescent stained glass and romantic design features such as outdoor sleeping porches. The house starred as the home of mad scientist Doc Brown (Christopher Lloyd) in the three *Back to the Future* movies.

Other Greene & Greene homes, including **Charles Greene's private residence** (368 Arroyo Tce), line nearby Arroyo Tce and Grand Ave. Pick up a self-guided walking tour pamphlet at the Gamble House bookstore.

ROSE BOWL STADIUM & BROOKSIDE PARK
One of LA's most venerable landmarks, the 1922 **Rose Bowl Stadium** (Map pp498-9; ☎ 626-577-3100; www.rosebowlstadium.com; 1001 Rose Bowl Dr) can seat up to 93,000 spectators and, every New Year's Day, hosts the famed Rose Bowl Game between two top-ranked college football teams. At other times, concerts, special events and a huge monthly **flea market** (p553) bring in the crowds.

The Rose Bowl is surrounded by **Brookside Park**, a broadening of the Arroyo Seco, a now-dry riverbed that runs from the San Gabriel Mountains to Downtown LA. It's a nice spot for hiking, cycling and picnicking. South of the stadium is the new **Kidspace Children's Museum** (p531), and beyond are the gracefully arched 1913 **Colorado St Bridge** and the former **Vista del Arroyo Hotel** (Map pp498-9; ☎ 626-441-2797;

125 S Grand Ave), a grand 1903 structure that now houses the Ninth Circuit Court of Appeals.

PASADENA CIVIC CENTER AREA
Pasadena's Civic Center, built in the 1920s, is a reflection of the great wealth and civic pride that have governed this city since its early days. Highlights include the Spanish Renaissance-style **City Hall** (Map pp498-9; 100 N Garfield Ave) and the **Central Library** (Map pp498-9; 285 E Walnut St).

A block east, in a Chinese-style mansion, the **Pacific Asia Museum** (Map pp498-9; ☎ 626-449-2742; www.pacificasiamuseum.org; 46 N Los Robles Ave; adult/student/senior $5/3/3; ☻ 10am-5pm Wed, Thu, Sat & Sun, 10am-8pm Fri) showcases five millennia worth of art and artifacts from Asia and the Pacific arranged around a koi pond. Just around the corner is the **Pasadena Museum of California Art** (Map pp498-9; ☎ 626-568-3665; www.pmcaonline.org; 490 E Union St; adult/child/student/senior $6/free/4/4; ☻ noon-5pm Wed-Sun), where exhibits focus on art, architecture and design created by California artists from 1850 to today.

CALIFORNIA INSTITUTE OF TECHNOLOGY
With 29 Nobel laureates among its faculty or alumni, it's no wonder that **Caltech** (Map pp498-9; ☎ 626-395-6327; www.caltech.edu; 551 S Hill Ave) is regarded with awe in academic circles (yes, Albert Einstein slept here). Free campus tours leave from the **visitors center** (355 S Holliston Ave) which also distributes free self-guided tour maps. Tours depart at 2pm, Monday to Friday, except on holidays, rainy days or during winter break.

The Caltech-operated **Jet Propulsion Laboratory** (JPL; www.jpl.nasa.gov), NASA's main center for robotic exploration of the solar system, is about 3.5 miles north of here but can only be visited on open-house days, usually in June. The website has dates and details about ongoing missions.

HUNTINGTON LIBRARY, ART COLLECTIONS AND BOTANICAL GARDENS
Urban LA feels a world away at this rarefied **country estate** (Map pp498-9; ☎ 626-405-2100; www.huntington.org; 1151 Oxford Rd; adult/child/student/senior $15/6/10/12; ☻ noon-4:30pm Tue-Fri, 10:30am-4:30pm Sat & Sun; Ⓟ), which was once owned by railroad tycoon Henry Huntington. Don't miss the Japanese Garden, the Desert Garden and the 1455 Gutenberg Bible in the library. The art gallery focuses mainly on 18th-century

British and French paintings and counts Thomas Gainsborough's famous *Blue Boy* among its most prized possessions.

The classic way to cap off a visit to the Huntington is with afternoon tea in the **Rose Garden Tea Room** (☎ reservations 626-683-8131). Next door is a self-service restaurant. Picnicking is not allowed.

SOUTHWEST MUSEUM OF THE AMERICAN INDIAN

LA's oldest **museum** (☎ 323-221-2164; www.south westmuseum.org; 234 Museum Dr; adult/child/student/senior $7.50/3/5/5; ☽ 10am-5pm Tue-Sun) holds one of the most formidable collections of Native American art and artifacts in the USA. The four permanent galleries focus on the traditions and cultures of tribal peoples in California, the Pacific Northwest, the Southwest and the Great Plains. This division lets you compare the traditions, rituals, clothing, crafts, religious ceremonies and social structures that developed in each of these areas. Highlights include magnificent feather headdresses, carved totem poles and jewelry. The museum also owns a prestigious basket collection with over 13,000 items. Combination tickets with the Museum of the American West (p514) are adult/child/student/senior $12/5/8/8.

HERITAGE SQUARE MUSEUM

Eight Victorian beauties dating from 1865 to 1914 were saved from the wrecking ball in the late 1960s and were literally airlifted to this village-like **outdoor museum** (☎ 626-449-0193; www.heritagesquare.org; 3800 Homer St; adult/child/senior $6/3/5; ☽ noon-5pm Fri-Sun), just off the Ave 43 exit of the I-110 (Pasadena Fwy). Highlights of the museum include the Italianate **Perry House**, the Queen Anne/Eastlake-style **Hale House** and the quirky Longfellow Hastings **Octagon House**. The grounds are open for self-guided tours. Tours of the interiors run on the hour from noon to 3pm.

SAN GABRIEL MISSION

About 3 miles southeast of central Pasadena, the city of San Gabriel is home to the fourth **mission** (Map pp498-9; ☎ 626-457-3035; www.san gabrielmission.org; 428 S Mission Dr; adult/child/senior $10/5/8; ☽ 9am-4:30pm) in the chain of 21 built in California. The church (1805) is a sturdy stone structure with numerous Spanish Moorish design accents, a copper baptismal font, an altar made in Mexico City in 1790

and carved statues of saints. Wandering the grounds takes you past the cemetery, original soap and tallow vats, and fountains. The **museum** contains Bibles, religious robes and Native American artifacts.

San Fernando Valley

The sprawling grid of suburbia known simply as 'the Valley' is home to most of the major movie studios, including Warner Bros, Disney and, of course, Universal. It also has the dubious distinction of being the world capital of the porn movie industry. Car culture was basically invented here, and the Valley takes credit for giving birth not only to the mini-mall but also to the drive-in movie theater, the drive-in bank and, of course, the drive-in restaurant. Note that temperatures here are usually 20°F higher – and pollution levels worse – than in areas further south. For studio tours, see the boxed text, opposite.

UNIVERSAL STUDIOS HOLLYWOOD

One of the world's oldest continuously operating movie studios, **Universal** Map p510; ☎ 818-622-3801; www.universalstudioshollywood.com; 100 Universal City Plaza; admission over/under 48in $53/43; ☽ vary by season; (P)) presents an entertaining mix of fairly tame – and sometimes dated – thrill rides and high-octane live action shows. It is a working studio, but chances of seeing any action, let alone a star, are slim to none.

Try to budget a full day, especially in summer. To beat the crowds, get there before the gates open or invest in the Front of Line Pass ($100) or the deluxe guided VIP Experience ($150). Some rides have minimum height requirements.

First-timers should head straight for the 45-minute narrated **Studio Tour** aboard a rickety tram that takes you past working soundstages to outdoor sets used in *Jurassic Park, Psycho* and other films. Also prepare to face down King Kong, brave a flash flood, and survive a shark attack and an 8.3-magnitude earthquake. It's a bit hokey, but fun.

Of the thrill rides at Universal, top billing goes to **Jurassic Park**, a gentle float through a prehistoric jungle with a rather 'raptor-ous' ending. **Revenge of the Mummy** is an indoor rollercoaster romp through 'Imhotep's Tomb' that at one point has you going backwards. The sentimental favorite is **Back to the Future**, where you'll be free-falling into volcanic tunnels, plunging down

STARGAZING

Hollywood hasn't been a promising place to bump into celebs since most of the studios moved north to the San Fernando Valley in the 1950s. To see particular TV stars, your best bet is to watch tapings of their shows. **Audiences Unlimited** (☎ 818-753-3470 ext 812; www.tvtickets.com) handles ticket distribution for dozens of shows, mostly sitcoms. Production season runs from August to March, and tickets are free. **CBS** (Map pp504–5; ☎ 323-575-2624; www.cbs.com; 7800 Beverly Blvd) distributes tickets directly.

With any luck, you might also run into stars while touring the actual studios where they work (note that there's usually no filming from June to August). The most extensive and authentic behind-the-scenes look is the 'VIP tour' run by **Warner Bros Studios** (Map p510; ☎ 818-972-8687; www.wbstudiotour.com; 3400 Riverside Dr, Burbank, San Fernando Valley; tour $39; ☺ 8:30am-4pm Mon-Fri; 🅿). This 2¼-hour romp around the historic studio kicks off with a video of WB's greatest hits (*Rebel Without a Cause, Harry Potter* etc) before you're whisked aboard a tram to sound stages, backlot sets and technical departments, including props, costumes and the paint shop. You can take pictures of the Batmobile in the Transportation Garage, see the Central Perk coffee shop set from *Friends* and observe sound artists at work. Tours conclude at the studio museum, a treasure trove of original props, sets, scripts and other memorabilia from movies and shows produced at the studio. A special Harry Potter exhibit runs throughout 2006. Tours leave roughly every half hour. Bring photo ID. Children under eight are not allowed.

Nearby, **NBC Studios** (Map p510; ☎ 818-840-3537; 3000 W Alameda Ave, Burbank, San Fernando Valley; tour adult/child $7.50/4.50; ☺ 9am-3pm Mon-Fri) runs tours that include a stop at the *Tonight Show* set. For tickets to *Tonight Show* tapings, call or check www.nbc.com/nbc/footer/Tickets.shtml.

On the Westside, in Culver City, you can tour **Sony Pictures Studios** (Map pp498-9; ☎ 323-520-8687; 10202 W Washington Blvd; tour $24; ☺ Mon-Fri), which was originally the venerable MGM, the studio that gave us *The Wizard of Oz* and *Ben Hur*. Movies and TV shows are still filmed here, including the studio's bread and butter, *Jeopardy*. Despite the historical MGM connection, the two-hour walking tour focuses mostly on Sony productions. Highlights include a visit to the *Jeopardy* set and sound stage 27 where *The Wizard of Oz* was filmed. Call for specific tour times; reservations are mandatory and children under 12 are not permitted. Bring photo ID.

---

glacial cliffs and colliding with dinosaurs while 'riding' aboard a Delorean.

Of the live shows, **Terminator 2: 3D** combines live action stunts with eye-popping digital imaging technology and stars none other than California governor Arnold Schwarzenegger. **Spider-Man Rocks** is a cutesy, fast-paced musical show with dance numbers and aerial acrobatics. The movie may have bombed, but the **Water World** show is a runaway hit with mind-boggling stunts that include giant fireballs and a crash-landing seaplane.

Snack food and drinks, including beer and margaritas, are available throughout the park, although you'll probably do better at the adjacent **Universal City Walk**, an unabashedly commercial fantasy promenade of restaurants, shops, bars and entertainment venues.

FOREST LAWN MEMORIAL PARK – GLENDALE

Often cheekily called the 'country club for the dead,' this humongous **cemetery** (Map pp498-9;

☎ 818-241-4151; 1712 S Glendale Ave, Glendale; ☺ 9am-5pm) is the final resting place of Clark Gable, Carole Lombard, Clara Bow, Walt Disney and numerous other Hollywood legends. There's plenty of repro art strewn about the grounds, including Michelangelo's *David* and a stained-glass rendition of Da Vinci's *Last Supper*. Despite the obvious kitsch factor, a visit here is fascinating, if only to catch a glimpse of the death culture so powerfully satirized in Evelyn Waugh's novel *The Loved One* (1948).

MISSION SAN FERNANDO REY DE ESPAÑA

This historic Spanish **mission** (Map pp498-9; ☎ 818-361-0186; 15151 San Fernando Mission Rd, Mission Hills; adult/child/senior $4/3/3; ☺ 9am-4:30pm) was the second built in the LA area (after the one in San Gabriel, opposite). The highlight is the 1822 convent, built with 4ft-thick adobe walls and Romanesque arches. Inside is an elaborate baroque altarpiece from Spain, and a small museum chronicling the mission's

LOS ANGELES

history. It's in the far northern Valley, near where the I-405 and Hwy 118 meet.

ACTIVITIES

Cycling & In-line Skating

The nicest place for skating or riding is along the paved **South Bay Bicycle Trail** that parallels the beach for 22 miles, from just north of Santa Monica to Torrance, with a detour around the yacht harbor at Marina del Rey. Mountain-bikers will find the **Santa Monica Mountains** (see right) a suitably challenging playground. *Mountain Biking in the Santa Monica Mountains* by Jim Hasenauer and Mark Langton is an excellent resource. You'll also find lots of good information at www .labikepaths.com. There are numerous bike-rental places throughout town, especially along the beaches. Here are a few:

Blazing Saddles (Map pp508-9; ☎ 310-393-9778; Santa Monica Pier, Santa Monica)

Hollywood Pro Bicycles (Map pp502-3; ☎ 323-466-5890; 6731 Hollywood Blvd, Hollywood)

Spokes 'n Stuff (Map pp508-9; ☎ 310-395-4748; 1700 Ocean Ave, Santa Monica) On the paved boardwalk below Loews Hotel.

Prices range from about $5 to $8 per hour and $10 to $30 per day (more for high-tech mountain bikes).

Fitness & Yoga

Many midrange and practically all top-end hotels have fitness centers, but for exercise classes or a fully fledged workout, try one of these places:

Crunch Gym (Map pp504-5; ☎ 323-654-4550; www .crunch.com; 8000 Sunset Blvd, West Hollywood; per day $24; ⏱ 5am-midnight Mon-Fri, 7am-10pm Sat & Sun) High-tech gym with cutting-edge classes such as Disco Yoga and Cycle Karaoke.

Gold's Gym (Map pp508-9; ☎ 310-392-6004; www .goldsgym.com; 360 Hampton Dr, Venice; per day $20; ⏱ 4am-midnight Mon-Fri, 5am-11pm Sat & Sun) Pump it up at Arnold's old gym.

Yoga Works (Map pp508-9; ☎ 310-393-5150; www .yogaworks.com; 2215 Main St, Santa Monica; per class $16) Popular place for doing the plough or sun salutation.

Hiking

Hiking may not be the obvious activity that comes to mind when thinking about LA, but there are actually a wealth of trails waiting for those wanting to experience the city's 'wild' side.

For a quick ramble, head to **Griffith Park** (p513) or to **Runyon Canyon** (Map p510; www.runyon -canyon.com), both just a hop, skip and jump from frenzied Hollywood Blvd. The latter is a favorite playground of hip and fitness-obsessed locals and their dogs, which roam mostly off-leash. You'll have fine views of the Hollywood Sign, the city and, on clear days, all the way to the beach. The southern trailhead is at the end of Fuller St, off Franklin Ave.

Runyon Canyon is on the eastern edge of the 150,000-acre **Santa Monica Mountains National Recreation Area** (Map pp498-9; ☎ 805-370-2301; www.nps.gov/samo). This hilly, tree- and chaparral-covered park follows the outline of Santa Monica Bay from just north of Santa Monica all the way north across the Ventura county line to Point Mugu. The 65-mile **Backbone Trail** covers its entire length, but there are also some scenic shorter hikes, especially in **Will Rogers State Historic Park** (Map pp498-9), **Topanga State Park** (Map pp498-9) and **Malibu Creek State Park** (Map pp498-9). The latter has a great trail leading to the set of the hit TV series *M*A*S*H*, where an old Jeep and other leftover relics rust serenely in the California sunshine. The trailhead is in the park's main parking lot on Malibu Canyon Rd, which is called Las Virgenes Rd if coming from Hwy 101 (Hollywood Fwy). Parking is $8. Malibu Creek also harbors the **Paramount Ranch** (Map pp498-9; ☎ 818-735-0896; Cornell Rd; ⏱ 8am-sunset), a historic movie ranch that has been used in countless features and TV shows. To get there catch Cornell Rd off Kanan Dume Dr or Mulholland Hwy. For more ideas, consult www.lamountains.com or Milt McAuley's *Hiking Trails of the Santa Monica Mountains*.

In 2005, the National Park Service introduced the **ParkLink Shuttle** (www.nps.gov/samo/shut tle; tickets $1), an air-conditioned bus that loops around the western half of the recreation area, stopping at many of the places mentioned above. Buses operate at 30-minute intervals on weekends between 8am and 5pm from October to March and from 8am to 8pm between April and September.

Horseback Riding

Leave the urban sprawl behind on the forested bridle trails of Griffith Park or Topanga Canyon. All rides are accompanied by an experienced equestrian wrangler.

TOP FIVE LA BEACHES

■ El Matador (Map pp498-9) Small beach hideaway hemmed in by battered rock cliffs and strewn with giant boulders. Wild surf; not suitable for children. Clothing optional.

■ Zuma (Map pp498-9) Gorgeous 2-mile long ribbon of sand with good water quality, excellent swimming and body surfing, and lots of tight bodies.

■ Malibu Lagoon/Surfrider (Map pp498-9) – Legendary surf beach with superb swells and extended rides. Water quality is only so-so. The lagoon is great for birdwatching.

■ Santa Monica (Map pp508-9) Extra-wide, hugely popular beach that's packed on weekends with families escaping the inland heat. Besides sand and ocean, attractions include the Santa Monica Pier (p519) and the paved shoreline path for strolling, in-line skating and cycling.

■ Venice (Map pp508-9) LA's most outlandish beach is paralleled by the Venice Boardwalk (p519) with its nonstop parade of friends and freaks. Drum circle in the sand on Sundays.

Escape on Horseback (Map pp498-9; ☎ 818-591-2032; www.losangeleshorsebackriding.com; 2623 Old Topanga Cyn Rd, Topanga Canyon) Guided tours, including full-moon rides.

Sunset Ranch Hollywood (Map pp502-3; ☎ 323-469-5450; www.sunsetranchhollywood.com; 3400 Beachwood Dr, Hollywood) Guided tours, including popular Friday-night dinner rides ($50, plus about $20 for food and tip), first-come, first-served.

Swimming & Surfing

Water temperatures become tolerable by late spring and peak at about 70°F in August and September. Water quality varies; for updated conditions check the 'Beach Report Card' at www.healthebay.org. Good surfing spots include Malibu Lagoon State Beach, aka Surf-rider Beach, and the Manhattan Beach pier.

Surfing novices can expect to pay about $70 to $100 for a two-hour private lesson or $40 to $60 for a group lesson, including board and wet suit. Contact these schools for details:

Learn to Surf LA (☎ 310-920-1265; www.learnto surfla.com)

Malibu Ocean Sports (☎ 877-952-9257; www.malibu oceansports.com)

Surf Academy (☎ 310-372-1036, 877-599-7873; www .surfacademy.org)

LOS ANGELES FOR CHILDREN

Traveling to LA with the rug rats tagging along is not a problem. Many museums and attractions have special kid-oriented exhibits, activities and workshops, but the excellent new **Kidspace Children's Museum** (Map pp498-9; ☎ 626-449-9144; www.kidspacemuseum.org; 480 N Arroyo Blvd, Pasadena; admission $8; ☼ 9:30am-5pm; P), with hands-on exhibits, outdoor areas and gar-

dens for exploring, is dedicated specifically to the younger set.

Kids love animals, of course, making the sprawling **Los Angeles Zoo** in family-friendly **Griffith Park** (p513) a sure winner. South of here, dinosaur fans gravitate to the **Natural History Museum of LA County** (p525), while budding scientists can have a field day next door at the **California Science Center** (p525).

Along the coast, the **Santa Monica Pier** (p519) has carnival rides and a small aquarium, but for a full 'fishy' immersion head south to the **Aquarium of the Pacific** (p520) in Long Beach, where you can even pet baby sharks. The latter city also has the grand **Queen Mary** (p521), where teens might get a kick out of the ghost tours.

The adorable singing and dancing marionettes at **Bob Baker Marionette Theater** (Map pp500-1; ☎ 213-250-9995; www.bobbakermarionettes .com; 1345 W 1st St; tickets $10; ☼ shows 10:30am Tue-Sat, 2:30pm Sat & Sun; P), near Downtown, have enthralled generations of Angelenos. A similarly magical experience awaits at **Puppet and Magic Center** (Map pp508-9; ☎ 310-656-0483; www .puppetmagic.com; 1255 2nd St, Santa Monica; tickets $6.50; ☼ shows 1pm Wed, 1pm & 3pm Sat & Sun).

Many hotels can provide referrals to reliable, qualified babysitter services.

TOURS

Architecture Tours (☎ 323-464-7866; www.architecture toursla.com) Tool around town taking in styles from Tudor to utopian.

Hornblower Cruises (☎ 310-301-6000; www.hornblower .com; cruises from $10) Harbor tours, brunch or dinner cruises, and whale-watching excursions (January-March). Boats depart from Marina del Rey, San Pedro and Long Beach.

LOS ANGELES

LOONY LOS ANGELES

Anything goes and anything sells in LA, a city that acts as a magnet for the wacky, the outlandish and the eccentric. Take, for instance, **Angelyne**, a self-styled vixen of indeterminable age famous for nothing but tooling around town in a pink Corvette convertible and erecting huge billboards featuring her scantily clad self. The Venice Boardwalk, no slouch in the strangeness department, has **Harry Perry**, a turbaned, roller-skating 'Kamakosmickrusader' (his word) who showers unsuspecting tourists with some pretty, shall we say, 'unique' guitar riffs. Both, of course, have their own Web pages (www.angelyne.com and www.venicebeachcalifornia.com, if you must know).

LA also has some pretty weird stores. **Necromance** (Map pp504-5; ☎ 323-934-8684; 7220 Melrose Ave, Hollywood/Mid-City) is a bazaar of the bizarre selling animal bones, frogs pickled in formaldehyde and vampire-repellent kits. Up the street, **Panpipes Magickal Marketplace** (Map pp502-3; ☎ 323-462-7078; 1641 Cahuenga Blvd, Hollywood) is LA's oldest occult and pagan supply shop (since 1961). Modern-day alchemist George Hiram Derby mixes more than 10,000 magical potions to help fix whatever ails you. And where else but LA would you find **Skeletons in the Closet** (☎ 323-343-0760; 1104 N Mission Rd, Downtown), a ghoulish gift shop operated by the LA County Coroners office as a fundraiser for an alternative youth sentencing program? Two floors above the morgue, its bestsellers include personalized toe-tags, body outline beach towels and travel garment 'body bags.'

Even museums get into the bizarro business in LA. Despite the name, the **Museum of Jurassic Technology** (Map pp498-9; ☎ 310-836-6131; www.mjt.org; 9341 Venice Blvd, Culver City; admission $4; ⊙ 2-8pm Thu, noon-6pm Fri-Sun) has nothing to do with dinosaurs and even less with technology. Instead, you'll find madness nibbling at your mind as you try to make sense of displays about Cameroonian stink ants, a tribute to trailer parks and a sculpture of the Pope squished into the eye of a needle. And please! Let us know if you figure out what it's *really* all about.

If the Hollywood Walk of Fame didn't get you hot and bothered, maybe the **Porno Walk of Fame** (Map pp504-5; 7734 Santa Monica Blvd, West Hollywood) will. Even those who wouldn't touch a porn movie with a 10-in pole probably know the names of such legendary hard-core divas and studs as Linda Lovelace and Harry Reems of *Deep Throat* fame. Alas, voyeuristic types expecting cement prints of performers' signature body parts may be disappointed: it's PG-rated hands and feet only.

LA has bars aplenty, of course, but none quite like **CIA** (☎ 818-506-6353; 11334 Burbank Blvd, North Hollywood), aka the California Institute of Abnormal Arts! Described as 'PT Barnum's bad acid trip,' this emporium is a warped celebration of fascinating freakishness with decor that looks like a train wreck of a traveling carnival from Mars. It's a Circus of the Sinister where girly shows, psycho sword-swallowers and the mortal remains of dead fairies and French clowns will have your skin crawling and your mind reeling.

Los Angeles Conservancy (☎ 213-623-2489; www.la conservancy.org; tours $10) Thematic walking tours, mostly of Downtown LA, with an architectural focus. Reservations required.

Red Line Tours (Map pp502-3; ☎ 323-402-1074; www.redlinetours.com; tours $20) 'Edutaining' walking tours of Hollywood and Downtown using headsets that cut out traffic noise.

Starline Tours (☎ 323-463-333, 800-959-3131; www .starlinetours.com; tours from $35) Your basic narrated bus tours of the city, stars' homes and theme parks.

FESTIVALS & EVENTS

LA has a packed calendar of annual festivals and special events. We've only got space for the all-time blockbusters, but for more ideas download the **LA Festival Calendar** (www.culturela .org, click on 'Events').

Rose Parade (☎ 626-449-4100; www.tournamentof roses.com) Cavalcade of flower-festooned floats along Pasadena's Colorado Blvd, followed by the Rose Bowl football game. Held on January 1.

Chinese New Year (☎ 213-680-0243, 213-617-0396) Colorful Dragon Parade, plus free entertainment, fireworks, food, games, carnival rides and other traditional revels in the heart of Chinatown during late January or early February.

Toyota Grand Prix of Long Beach (☎ 888-827-7333; www.longbeachgp.com) A week-long auto-racing spectacle in mid-April drawing world-class drivers.

Fiesta Broadway (☎ 310-914-0015; www.fiestabroad way.la) Huge Cinco de Mayo street fair along historic Broadway in Downtown on the last Sunday in April with performances by Latino stars.

Central Avenue Jazz Festival (☎ 213-485-2437; www.culturela.org;) In late July, this festival celebrates the period from the 1920s to the '50s when Central Ave was a hotbed of West Coast jazz; music, food, arts and crafts.

Sunset Junction Street Fair (☎ 323-661-7771; www .sunsetjunction.org) A mid-August street party celebrating Silver Lake's cultural wackiness with grub, libations and edgy bands.

Los Angeles County Fair (☎ 909-623-3111; www.fair plex.com) Carnival rides, livestock exhibits and live country entertainment in Pomona, in eastern LA County, in mid- to late September.

West Hollywood Halloween Carnival (☎ 323-848-6400; www.visitwesthollywood.com) Rambunctious street fair with eccentric, and occasionally X-rated, costumes along Santa Monica Blvd held on Halloween (Octocber 31).

Pasadena Doo Dah Parade (☎ 626-440-7379; www .pasadenadoodahparade.com) The Sunday before Thanks-giving this wacky parody of the traditional Rose Parade takes place on Colorado Blvd in Pasadena.

Griffith Park Light Festival (☎ 323-913-6488; www .laparks.org) Mile-long stretch of various holiday-themed light displays from 5pm to 10pm, late November to December 26. Walk or drive through slowly.

Hollywood Christmas Parade (☎ 323-469-2337; www.hollywoodchamber.net) Film and TV celebs ring in the season by waving at bystanders from flashy floats along Hollywood Blvd on the Sunday after Thanksgiving.

GAY & LESBIAN LOS ANGELES

LA is one of the country's gayest cities, with the rainbow flag flying especially proudly along Santa Monica Blvd in West Holly-wood (WeHo). Dozens of high-energy bars, cafés, restaurants, gyms and clubs flank this strip, turning it pretty much into a 24/7 fun zone. Most places cater to gay men, al-though there's plenty going on for lesbians and mixed audiences as well. Beauty reigns supreme in 'Boystown' and the intimidation factor can be high unless you're buff, bronzed and styled. Elsewhere, the gay scenes are considerably more laid-back and less body-conscious. Silver Lake, another major romp-ing ground, has a large leather and Levi's crowd and a few Latino bars. The beach towns, historically havens of queerness, have the most relaxed, neighborly scenes, especially in Santa Monica, Venice and Long Beach. Will Rogers Beach in Santa Monica is LA's most cruisey beach, especially toward the southern stretch. For ideas on where to go, see the boxed text, p549.

Freebie magazines containing up-to-date listings and news about the community are generally strewn about in bars, restaurants and gay-friendly establishments around

town. **A Different Light** (Map pp504-5; ☎ 310-854-6601; 8853 Santa Monica Blvd, West Hollywood) is LA's bastion of queer literature, nonfiction and magazines. Staff are chatty and women wel-come. The **LA Gay & Lesbian Center** (Map pp502-3; ☎ 323-993-7400; www.laglc.org; 1625 Schrader Blvd, Holly-wood; ⏰ 9am-8pm Mon-Fri, 9am-1pm Sat) is a one-stop service and health agency.

The festival season kicks off in late May with the **Long Beach Pride Celebration** (☎ 562-987-9191; www.longbeachpride.com), which basically serves as the warm-up for **LA Pride** (www.lapride .org), a three-day festival in mid-June with nonstop partying and a parade down Santa Monica Blvd. A few months later, on **Hal-loween** (October 31), the same street morphs into a veritable freak show bringing together tens of thousands of fancifully – and often erotically – costumed revelers of all sexual persuasions. **Outfest** (☎ 213-480-7088; www.outfest .org), held in July, is the biggest local festival for gay, lesbian, bisexual and transgender film and video.

SLEEPING

When picking a neighborhood for your stay, think about what type of experience you most want to have. For the beach life, base yourself in Santa Monica or Venice, which are fairly close to LAX. Urban explorers will find plenty of hot spots in West Hollywood, while Downtown is great for fans of history and architecture but pretty dead after dark. Central Hollywood provides easy access to the Metro Rail Red Line, but staying in posh Beverly Hills is certain to impress folks back home. Long Beach is handy for forays to Dis-neyland and Orange County. Some bargains notwithstanding, hotel rates in Los Angeles are higher than in other parts of California. Expect to pay between $100 and $200 a night for a midrange room. We've listed peak rates, so prices should drop in the off-season. The lodging tax is 12% to 14%. Unless noted oth-erwise, hotel parking is free.

Hollywood
BUDGET
USA Hostels–Hollywood (Map pp502-3; ☎ 323-462-3777, 800-524-6783; www.usahostels.com; 1624 Schrader Blvd; dm incl tax $22-25, r incl tax $59-65, discounts Oct-May; ▣) Energetic, well run and really central, this hostel is a convivial spot with plenty of parties and activities, a big kitchen and lots of freebies, including linen, pancake breakfast

Chateau Marmont (Map pp504-5; ☎ 323-656-1010, 800-242-8328; www.chateaumarmont.com; 8221 W Sunset Blvd; r $315, ste $350-510, bungalow $1500; **P** 🖵) Practically every celluloid luminary – from Greta Garbo to Gwyneth Paltrow – has enjoyed breakfast or drinks in the lobby bar, trysted in a bungalow or swum laps in the pool of this Hollywood landmark. Howard Hughes used to spy on bikini beauties from the balcony of his suite, which is now Bono's favorite. The superstitious might want to stay clear of Bungalow No 2 where John Belushi tossed back his final speedball in 1982. Free wi-fi.

and all-day coffee and tea. Each room has its own bathroom.

Hollywood Celebrity Hotel (Map pp502-3; ☎ 323-850-6464, 800-222-7017; www.hotelcelebrity.com; 1775 Orchid Ave; r incl breakfast $90-120; **P** 🗙 🖵) The sleek art deco–style lobby is a welcoming overture to this central, good-value property. The rooms can't quite carry the tune but most are large, clean and have comfy beds; some have full kitchens. The small fitness center and steam rooms are unexpected perks.

MIDRANGE

Magic Castle Hotel (Map pp502-3; ☎ 323-851-0800, 800-741-4915; www.magiccastlehotel.com; 7025 Franklin Ave; r $130-240; **P** 🗙 🗙 🖵 🖳) This mostly revamped stand-by now sparkles with contemporary furniture, attractive art and such luxe touches as comfy bathrobes and fancy bath amenities. Days start with freshly baked goods and gourmet coffee on your balcony (some rooms) or by the pool. The full-kitchen suites sleep up to six people.

Hollywood Hills Hotel (Map pp502-3; ☎ 323-874-5089, 800-741-4915; www.hollywoodhillshotel.com; 1999 N Sycamore Ave; r incl breakfast $160-240; **P** 🗙 🖳) City views, a curvy pool guarded by a pagoda and roomy digs with balcony and kitchen are among the assets at this older but well-kept property. It's up in the hills (just below Yamashiro bar-restaurant) yet still within walking distance of Hollywood Blvd. Check-in is at the Magic Castle Hotel.

Best Western Hollywood Hills Hotel (Map pp502-3; ☎ 323-464-5181, 800-287-1700; www.bestwestern.com; 6141 Franklin Ave; r $90-160; **P** 🗙 🖳) A central location, cleanliness and accommodating staff

are among the winning attributes of this family-run hotel. For more space and quiet get a room – all with fridge and microwave – in the back facing the sparkling tiled pool. The attached coffee shop is a hipster spot that's open until 3am.

Holiday Inn Express (Map pp502-3; ☎ 323-464-3242, 877-477-4674; www.holidayinnexpress.com; 1520 N La Brea Ave; r incl breakfast $130-200; **P** 🗙 🖳) This is an attractive-looking property with recently spiffed-up rooms and friendly staff. Light sleepers should request a room facing away from the street. Generous breakfast buffet (try the cinnamon rolls).

TOP END

Hollywood Roosevelt Hotel (Map pp502-3; ☎ 323-466-7000, 800-950-7667; www.hollywoodroosevelt.com; 7000 Hollywood Blvd; r $160-330, ste $550-2500; **P** 🗙 🖵 🖳) The current darling of the Hollywood in-crowd, this venerable old hotel has seen its share of elite players since the first Academy Awards were held here in 1929. It pairs a palatial Spanish lobby with rooms sporting a sleek Asian contemporary look. Marilyn Monroe shot her first commercial by the pool.

West Hollywood & Mid-City

BUDGET

Orbit/Banana Bungalow Hollywood (Map pp504-5; ☎ 323-655-1510, 800-446-7835; www.bananabungalow.com; 7950 Melrose Ave; dm incl tax $18-22, r incl tax $54-89; **P** 🖵) Mod decor, a hip location and small dorms with private baths are among the assets of this convivial hostel, which also has plenty of space for lounging and socializing. A café serves inexpensive breakfasts and dinners, but self-caterers will find only a microwave to work with.

Alta Cienega Motel (Map pp504-5; ☎ 310-652-5797; 1005 N La Cienega Blvd; r incl breakfast $60-70; **P** 🗙) Nothing distinguishes this basic motel from dozens of others in town, yet for Doors fans it's a place of pilgrimage: the 'Lizard King,' Jim Morrison, himself boozed and snoozed in room No 32 back in the late 1960s.

MIDRANGE

Secret Garden B&B (Map pp504-5; ☎ 323-656-3888, 877-732-4736; www.secretgardenbnb.com; 8039 Selma Ave; r incl breakfast $95-165; **P** 🗙 🖵) This pink Spanish Moorish jewel with its romantic Rapunzel tower and dreamy garden sits a mere block away from the velocity of the Sunset Strip. All five rooms bulge with character and eclectic furnishings, but for a treat book the free-standing guesthouse with slate floor, sleigh bed and Jacuzzi. Free wi-fi.

Farmer's Daughter Hotel (Map pp504-5; ☎ 323-937-3930, 800-334-1658; www.farmersdaughterhotel.com; 115 S Fairfax Ave; r $125-170; (P) ♦ ☐ ☒) After an extreme makeover, this LA fixture now sports a cheeky 'urban cowboy' look, complete with denim bedspreads and high-speed Internet and wi-fi access. The helpful staff are happy to clue you in about top spots at the farmers market and Grove mall across the street.

Standard Hollywood (Map pp504-5; ☎ 323-650-9090; www.standardhotel.com; 8300 W Sunset Blvd; r $145-225, ste $450; (P) ♦ ☐ ☒) This hipster haven seems stuck in perpetual party mode, so don't come here for a quiet night's sleep. Surprises abound, including a pool fringed by blue Astroturf, a barber who doubles as a tattoo artist and condoms in the minibar. At night the lobby morphs into a chic club lounge. The 24-hour coffee shop is a scene in itself.

Beverly Laurel Hotel (Map pp504-5; ☎ 323-651-2441, 800-962-3824; 8018 Beverly Blvd; r $90-105, with kitchenette extra $15; (P) ♦ ☒) Those wanting to ride the retro wave on a slim budget should check into one of the arty rooms at this classic 1950s motel near the farmers market. The attached Swingers diner (dishes $4 to 10) crawls with hipsters until the wee hours. Wi-fi is $10 per day.

Elan Hotel Modern (Map pp504-5; ☎ 323-658-6663, 888-611-0398; www.elanhotel.com; 8435 Beverly Blvd; r incl breakfast $135-215; (P) ♦ ☐) Never mind the bland facade, this place is packed with panache. The rooms, decked out in mellow natural tones, all sport plenty of beyond-standard-issue amenities, including Egyptian cotton sheets, goose-down comforters and fancy bath accoutrements. Ample breakfast, small fitness room and great dining and shopping nearby.

San Vicente Inn (Map pp504-5; ☎ 310-854-6915, 800-577-6915; www.gayresort.com/sanvicenteinn; 845 N San Vicente Blvd; r $70-300; (P) ♦ ☒) At LA's main men-only guesthouse, the rooms and cottages overlook a tropical garden and frolicking zones include a hot tub, sauna, pool and sundeck.

TOP-END
Le Montrose Suite Hotel (Map pp504-5; ☎ 310-855-1115, 800-776-0666; www.lemontrose.com; 900 Hammond St; ste $165-550; (P) ♦ ☐ ☒) Time at this stylish hideaway seems to move a bit slower than in the rest of LA. The newly spruced-up suites have sunken living rooms with gas fireplaces, and the larger ones also have a kitchenette and balcony. Feast on gourmet fare at the guest-only restaurant, then work off the indulgence in the rooftop pool (great views) or the health club.

Grafton on Sunset (Map pp504-5; ☎ 323-654-4600, 800-821-3660; www.graftononsunset.com; 8462 W Sunset Blvd; r $200-230, ste $250-350; (P) ♦ ☐ ☒) We like this charismatic boutique hotel for its pleasing Feng Shui aesthetic, enormous swimming pool and stylish rooms. Staying here puts you within a whisker of the strip's high-velocity club scene (ask the concierge about VIP access). The on-site Balboa steak house is popular with nonguests as well.

Chamberlain West Hollywood (Map pp504-5; ☎ 310-657-7400, 800-201-9652; www.chamberlainwesthollywood.com; 1000 Westmount Dr; ste $210-310; (P) ♦ ☐ ☒) The old Summerfield Suites has been transformed into LA's newest sleek boutique hotel by the skilled troupe behind Maison 140 (p536) and the Viceroy (p537). Each suite – clad in charcoal gray and other edgy hues – has a separate bedroom, fireplace, balcony and bevy of high-tech touches. Cool rooftop pool, too.

Mondrian Hotel (Map pp504-5; ☎ 323-650-8999, 800-525-8029; www.mondrianhotel.com; 8440 W Sunset Blvd; r $310-385, ste $370-570; (P) ♦ ☐ ☒) Like the gates to heaven, two giant metal doors, but no marquee, signal your arrival at LA's beacon for the rich and beautiful. The Philippe Starck–designed public spaces – the sleek lobby, the restaurant, the open-air Sky Bar (p547), the sexy swimming pool – are like stages where the auditioning never stops. Rooms are top-notch, the service only so-so. But heck, even the valets look like Calvin Klein models.

Beverly Hills & Westside
BUDGET
Beverly Hills Reeves Hotel (Map pp506-7; ☎ 310-271-3006; 120 S Reeves Dr; r incl breakfast $90-100; (P) ♦) Budget and Beverly Hills don't usually mix, except at this no-frills property in a converted apartment building on a quiet side street and within walking distance of ritzy Rodeo Dr. New management is making some upgrades but promised that prices would hold steady.

MIDRANGE

Maison 140 (Map pp506-7; ☎ 310-281-4000, 800-432-5444; www.maison140.com; 140 S Lasky Dr; r incl breakfast $170-240; Ⓟ ⌧ 🖳) This sensuous gem in the former home of silent-movie siren Lillian Gish cleverly marries French frivolity and Asian understatement in rooms that skimp on size but not on luxury. Rates include an evening wine reception and pool privileges at the top-end Avalon.

Crescent (Map pp506-7; ☎ 310-247-0505; www.crescentbh.com; 403 N Crescent Dr; r $165-225; Ⓟ ⌧ ⌧ 🖳) The new owners have spun this once dowdy property into a mod hot spot with a buzzing lobby-lounge-bar (ask for a room on the 2nd floor and in back if you're bothered by noise) and stylish indoor–outdoor restaurant, Boe. The chic rooms tend to be on the small side but the flat-screen TV, iPods and free wi-fi are all welcome hipster touches.

Best Western Beverly Pavilion (Map pp506-7; ☎ 310-273-1400, 800-441-5050; www.bestwestern.com; 9360 Wilshire Blvd; r $130-150; Ⓟ ⌧ 🖳) This nicely decorated property puts you in the poshest part of Beverly Hills yet has a price tag that is surprisingly modest. The rooftop pool is a stand-out, while rooms – mostly sheathed in pink and peach pastels – provide plenty of space and amenities.

Carlyle Inn (Map pp506-7; ☎ 310-275-4445, 800-322-7595; www.carlyle-inn.com; 1119 S Robertson Blvd; r $130-150; Ⓟ ⌧ 🖳) Named after a 19th-century poet, this breezy little spot wraps around a central courtyard dotted with umbrella-shaded tables perfect for enjoying the generous breakfast (daily) or afternoon wine and cheese (weekdays only). Rooms get a thumbs up for nice little extras such as comfy robes, VCRs and a small fridge.

TOP END

Hotel Bel-Air (Map pp506-7; ☎ 310-472-1211, 800-648-4097; www.hotelbelair.com; 701 N Stone Canyon Rd; r $400-575, ste $850-3500; Ⓟ ⌧ 🖳 🖳) An urge to splurge would be well directed toward this peaceful hideaway where every detail speaks of refinement and discretion is key. Rooms, each with private entrance and classy French country furnishings, are hugged by romantic gardens where white swans preen. If the price tag is too steep, come for afternoon tea or drinks in the fireplace bar.

Avalon Hotel (Map pp506-7; ☎ 310-277-5221, 800-535-4715; www.avalonbeverlyhills.com; 9400 W Olympic Blvd; r $200-370; Ⓟ ⌧ 🖳 🖳) Mid-century cool meets amenities fit for the new millennium at this hipper-than-thou boutique hotel. Rooms vamp it up with vintage Nelson bubble lamps and Eames cabinets, and the pool is as curvaceous as Marilyn Monroe, who once lived in this former apartment building. Trendy types sip their cosmos at the ultra-swank Blue on Blue restaurant-bar.

Mosaic Hotel (Map pp506-7; ☎ 310-278-0303, 800-463-4466; www.mosaichotel.com; 125 Spalding Dr; r $270-600; Ⓟ ⌧ 🖳 🖳) This gorgeous boutique hotel embraces you like a good friend the moment you enter the lobby with its stylish tile accents and integrated bar. Natural colors give the rooms a classic, timeless feel, while the Frette robes, Bulgari soaps and rainforest shower heads should feed luxury cravings.

Beverly Hills Hotel (Map pp506-7; ☎ 310-276-2251, 800-283-8885; www.beverlyhillshotel.com; 9641 Sunset Blvd; r $380-470, ste & bungalows $820-5000; Ⓟ ⌧ 🖳 🖳) If you fancy (and can afford) dwelling in the utmost of luxury in an ambience oozing opulence and infused with historical charm, this is your place.

Malibu

Leo Carrillo State Beach Campground (Map pp498-9; ☎ 818-880-0350, reservations 800-444-7275; 35000 W Pacific Coast Hwy; sites $13-20) This shady, kid-friendly site, around 28 miles northwest of Santa Monica, gets busy in summer, so book early, especially on weekends. It has 135 sites, flush toilets and coin-operated hot showers. A long sandy beach, offshore kelp beds and tide pools are all great places for exploring.

Casa Malibu Inn (Map pp498-9; ☎ 310-456-2219, 800-831-0858; casamalibu@earthlink.net; 22752 Pacific Coast Hwy; r $100-350; Ⓟ) This ultimate California Dreamin' getaway overlooks its own beach and has 21 attractive rooms orbiting a vine-festooned courtyard. The nicest ones have ocean views, private decks and fireplaces or kitchenettes. Lana Turner fans should book the Catalina Suite where the glamour queen once spent 18 months.

Malibu Country Inn (Map pp498-9; ☎ 310-457-9622, 800-386-6787; www.malibucountryinn.com; 6506 Westward Beach Rd; r Sun-Thu $140-230, Fri & Sat $180-265; Ⓟ ⌧ 🖳) This nicely restored 1943 Cape Cod–style inn is a quiet bluff-top retreat near Zuma Beach, about 7 miles north of the Malibu Pier. Each of the 16 rooms, set amid lush gardens, has a different decor and a private patio. The nicest have ocean views, fireplace and a Jacuzzi. Cute café too.

Santa Monica & Venice

BUDGET

Sea Shore Motel (Map pp508-9; ☎ 310-392-2787; www .seashoremotel.com; 2637 Main St, Santa Monica; r $90-110, ste $125-225; P X ⚐) This family-owned motel is one of a dying breed: a clean, budget-priced place mere steps from the beach, bars, boutiques and restaurants. The Spanish-tiled rooms are attractive enough, but the new lofty suites (sleeping up to four) with full kitchens and balconies are killer. Free wi-fi.

HI–Los Angeles–Santa Monica (Map pp508-9; ☎ 310-393-9913, 800-909-4776 ext 137; www.lahostels .org; 1436 2nd St, Santa Monica; members/nonmembers dm incl tax $28/31, r with shared bathroom $69/72; ⚐) This generic hostel may be low on charm, but the location – between the beach and Third Street Promenade – is the envy of much fancier places.

Travelodge Santa Monica (Map pp508-9; ☎ 310-450-5766, 800-231-7679; www.travelodge.com; 3102 W Pico Blvd, Santa Monica; r incl breakfast $64-104; P X) There's plenty to like besides the price about this chain entry next to a Trader Joe's super-market and steps from good restaurants. Rooms are large and spotless (many have kitchenettes) and the courtyard has a gas barbecue and picnic table for guests to use. The beach is about 2.5 miles away.

MIDRANGE

Channel Road Inn B&B (Map pp508-9; ☎ 310-459-1920; www.channelroadinn.com; 219 W Channel Rd, Santa Monica; r incl breakfast $165-375; P X ⚐) Upscale and romantic, this B&B has sumptuous, amenity-laden rooms facing either the ocean or the lovely garden. Breakfasts are gourmet affairs, and the afternoon tea and evening wine and cheese gatherings provide ample opportunity to mingle with fellow guests. Bicycles for taking a spin along the beach are available for free.

Venice Beach House (Map pp508-9; ☎ 310-823-1966; www.venicebeachhouse.com; 15 30th Ave, Venice; r $130, with private bathroom $170-195; P X) A block from the beach, this ivy-draped B&B in a 1911 Craftsman bungalow (listed on the National Register of Historic Places) is a welcoming old-California retreat with nine cozy rooms. The romantically inclined should book the James Peasgood room with its lofty wood ceiling and double Jacuzzi.

Ambrose (Map pp508-9; ☎ 310-315-1555, 877-262-7673; www.ambrosehotel.com; 1255 20th St, Santa Monica; r incl breakfast $175-225; P X X ⚐) This bliss-ful boutique hotel, about 20 blocks from the beach, beautifully blends Craftsman and Asian aesthetics. The spic-and-span rooms have high ceilings, dark-wood furniture and a fridge stocked with organic beverages. After indulging in a healthy buffet breakfast you can summon a London cab for a free ride to the beach.

Cal Mar Hotel Suites (Map pp508-9; ☎ 310-395-5555, 800-776-6007; www.calmarhotel.com; 220 California Ave, Santa Monica; ste $160-200; P X ⚐) The place may look hopelessly stuck in the disco decade, but who's to complain if a moderate tariff buys you a large suite with kitchen and a super-central, yet quiet location? It's a great choice for families and anyone in need of plenty of elbow room. The heated pool in its neat tropical setting comes in handy if the ocean's too cold for a swim.

Inn at Venice Beach (Map pp508-9; ☎ 310-821-2557, 800-828-0688; www.innatvenicebeach.com; 327 Washington Blvd, Venice; r incl breakfast $140-210; P X) Close to the beach, the Venice canals, and bars and restaurants, this pleasant inn sports a fresh and cheerful look. Rooms wrap around a central courtyard perfect for munching your morning muffins. Free wi-fi.

Best Western Jamaica Bay Inn (Map pp508-9; ☎ 310-823-5333, 888-823-5333; www.bestwestern.com; 4175 Admiralty Way, Marina del Rey; r $130-200; P X ⚐) Fronting sheltered Mother's Beach, this property is great for families and even has its own playground. Palm trees add a tropical touch and the rooms have bright bedspreads, framed art and private balconies (ask for one with ocean views). You can walk to restaurants and Venice Beach.

TOP END

Viceroy (Map pp508-9; ☎ 310-260-7500, 800-622-8711; www.viceroysantamonica.com; 1819 Ocean Ave, Santa Monica; r $110-150, ste $200-500; P X ⚐) Ignore the eyesore exterior and plunge headlong into this fabulous seaside outpost with its campy British Colonial design theme and wacky color palette from dolphin-gray to mamba-green. All the usual hot-spot trappings are here, from poolside cabanas to Italian designer linens, plus a bar and res-taurant bustling with socialites.

Georgian Hotel (Map pp508-9; ☎ 310-395-9945, 800-538-8147; www.georgianhotel.com; 1415 Ocean Ave, Santa Monica; r $200-340, ste $255-340; P X ⚐) This eye-catching art-deco landmark with its snug veranda for breakfast and sunset lounging has decor so Great Gatsby-esque that wearing a straw boater wouldn't feel out of place. The rooms, decked out in soothing earth tones, are surprisingly modern. Cute factor: the rubber duckie in the tub.

South Bay

Beach House at Hermosa (Map pp498-9; ☎ 310-374-3001, 888-895-4559; www.beach-house.com; 1300 The Strand, Hermosa Beach; r incl breakfast $210-360; P ☒ ☒) Whatever you've heard about California's laid-back lifestyle, this sparkling beachfront inn epitomizes it. Fall asleep to the sound of waves in large, lofty suites, each with private balconies and wood-burning fireplaces. The paved bikeway is right outside, and restaurants and nightlife only a quick stroll away.

Best Western Sunrise Hotel (Map pp498-9; ☎ 310-376-0746, 800-334-7384; www.bestwestern.com; 400 N Harbor Dr; r incl breakfast $120-150; P ☒ ☐ ☒) This sprawling place near the Redondo Beach marina breaks through the standard motel mold by offering make-your-own fresh waffles at breakfast, cookies and punch during the afternoon and free bicycle rentals. The cheerfully decorated rooms feature refrigerators and coffeemakers.

Surf City Hostel (Map pp498-9; ☎ 310-798-2323; www.surfcityhostel.ws; 26 Pier Ave, Hermosa Beach; dm incl breakfast $19, r incl breakfast $48; ☐) Right on Hermosa's Pier Ave and steps from the sand, this hostel puts the 'fun' in funky and is great for plugging straight into the SoCal beach scene. Halls, dorms and rooms are splashed with colorful murals.

San Pedro & Long Beach
BUDGET

HI–Los Angeles–South Bay (Map pp498-9; ☎ 310-831-8109, 800-909-4776; www.lahostels.org; 3601 S Gaffey St, No 613, San Pedro; member/nonmember dm $17/20, tr per person $20/22, d $40/42; ☺ May-Sep; P) You'll enjoy sweeping Pacific views from this bluff-top hostel with its nifty muraled walls, from African jungle to American jazz. The facilities include a big kitchen, a TV room and a guest laundry. Metro Bus 466 stops right outside.

MIDRANGE

Turret House (Map pp498-9; ☎ 562-624-1991, 888-488-7738; www.turrethouse.com; 556 Chestnut Ave, Long Beach; r incl breakfast $100-125; ☒) Owners Brian and Jeff (and their adorable dogs) have poured their hearts and cash into turning this little B&B into an oasis of charm. The stately

Victorian has five cozy rooms, each with fireplace, TV and bathroom with clawfoot tub. Rates include passes to a nearby gym, and there's a hot tub on the premises.

Coast Hotel Long Beach (Map pp498-9; ☎ 562-435-7676, 800-716-6199; www.coasthotels.com; 700 Queensway Dr, Long Beach; r $100-170; P ☒ ☐ ☒) Palm trees, a scenic waterfront location and a nice, spacious layout imbue this hotel with a relaxed resort feel. A few extra bucks buys a larger room with harbor-facing patio.

Queen Mary Hotel (Map pp498-9; ☎ 562-435-3511; www.queenmary.com; 1126 Queens Hwy, Long Beach; r $110-220, ste $450-650; P ☒) This grand ocean liner time-warps you back to a slower-paced era. The first-class staterooms have been nicely refurbished and brim with original art deco details (avoid the cheapest ones, which are on the inside). Rates include admission to guided tours (see p521).

TOP END

Dockside Boat & Bed (Map pp498-9; ☎ 562-436-3111, 800-436-2574; www.boatandbed.com; Rainbow Harbor, Dock 5, 316 E Shoreline Dr, Long Beach; r incl tax & breakfast $190-250; P ☒) Let the waves rock you to sleep as you snuggle up aboard your own private motor yacht, sailboat or 50ft Chinese junk. Boats are moored close to downtown Long Beach and they enjoy views of the *Queen Mary*. Breakfast is delivered directly to your vessel.

Downtown
BUDGET

Stillwell Hotel (Map pp500-1; ☎ 213-627-1151, 800-553-4774; www.stillwellh.qpg.com; 838 S Grand Ave; r $50-60; ☒ ☐) Nearly a century old, the Stillwell offers clean, no-nonsense rooms, good security and Hank's, a bar so noir it seems to have leapt out of the pages of a Raymond Chandler novel. The Staples Center and Los Angeles Convention Center are within walking distance.

MIDRANGE

Figueroa Hotel (Map pp500-1; ☎ 213-627-8971, 800-421-9092; www.figueroahotel.com; 939 S Figueroa St; r $120-225, ste $175-225; P ☒ ☒) This charmer near the Staples Center welcomes guests with a striking, Spanish-style lobby leading to a relaxing pool and outdoor bar. The Moroccan-themed rooms are nice but not all are equal, so check out a few before picking your favorite.

Standard Downtown LA (Map pp500-1; ☎ 213-892-8080; www.standardhotel.com; 550 S Flower St; r from $140; P ⊠ ⬛ ⬛) So LA it's almost a cliché, this hotel – cleverly converted from an old office building – goes after the same young, hip and shag-happy crowd as its Sunset Strip sister, Standard Hollywood (p535). Rooms feature platform beds and peek-through showers, and the rooftop pool bar (p547) has one of the city's most intense pick-up scenes.

Omni Los Angeles Hotel (Map pp500-1; ☎ 213-617-3300, 800-843-6664; www.omnihotels.com; 25 S Olive St; r $110-210; P ⊠ ⬛ ⬛) Modern and efficient, the Omni puts you within steps of major Downtown cultural hubs. Rooms are spacious and amenity-laden but can't quite shake that generic business-hotel feel. The rooftop pool, however, is a mighty fine unwinding spot indeed. Weekend rates sometimes drop below $100 (check the website).

TOP END

Millennium Biltmore Hotel (Map pp500-1; ☎ 213-624-1011, 800-245-8673; www.millenniumhotels.com; 506 S Grand Ave; r $160-360, ste from $460; P ⊠ ⬛ ⬛) Drenched in tradition and gold leaf, this palatial hotel has bedded a veritable galaxy of stars, presidents and royalty. Rooms, sheathed in soothing gold and blue hues, come with all the trappings, although some are surprisingly small. The art deco health club is so gorgeous, it takes the work out of workout.

Pasadena

BUDGET

Saga Motor Hotel (Map pp498-9; ☎ 626-795-0431, 800-793-7242; www.thesagamotorhotel.com; 1633 E Colorado Blvd; r incl breakfast $77-92, f incl breakfast $110-130; P ⊠ ⬛) One of the best bets on Pasadena's 'motel row,' this well-kept vintage inn has comfortable, spotless rooms. The nicest are near the good-sized pool orbited by plenty of chaises and chairs for soaking up the SoCal sunshine.

MIDRANGE

Bissell House B&B (Map pp498-9; ☎ 626-441-3535, 800-441-3530; www.bissellhouse.com; 201 S Orange Grove Blvd; r incl tax & breakfast $150-225; P ⊠ ⬛ ⬛) Sumptuous antiques, sparkling hardwood floors and a crackling fireplace make this 1887 Victorian B&B on 'Millionaire's Row' a bastion of warmth and hospitality. If you don't like flowery decor, book the Prince

Albert room. The Garden Room comes with a Jacuzzi for two.

Artists' Inn & Cottage B&B (Map pp498-9; ☎ 626-799-5668, 888-799-5668; www.artistsinns.com; 1038 Magnolia St; r incl tax & breakfast $120-205; P ⊠ ⬛ ⬛) Each of the six rooms and four suites in this lovely Victorian farmhouse in South Pasadena has decor inspired by Degas, Gauguin and other artists or artistic periods. Rooms in the cottage are quieter, and most suites have fireplaces and canopy beds. Days wind down with complimentary port and chocolates in the comfort of your room. Free wi-fi.

TOP END

Ritz-Carlton Huntington Hotel & Spa (Map pp498-9; ☎ 626-568-3900, 800-241-3333; www.ritzcarlton.com /hotels/hunting ton; 1401 S Oak Knoll Ave; r $265-395; P ⊠ ⬛ ⬛) If it weren't for the palm trees, you'd half expect this ultraposh hostelry to be a French country estate complete with rambling gardens, a huge pool and even a covered picture bridge. Rooms are lavishly dressed in regal reds or blues. Sunday brunch ($55) is a pricey but memorable treat.

San Fernando Valley

Safari Inn (Map p510; ☎ 818-845-8586, 800-716-6199; www.coasthotels.com; 1911 W Olive Ave, Burbank; r $90-130, f $170; P ⊠ ⬛) The classic 1950s neon sign is the only throwback to a bygone era at this friendly motel. Cheerful bedspreads and framed poster art add splashes of color to the nicely renovated rooms and family-friendly full-kitchen suites. It's reasonably close to Universal and NBC Studios.

Beverly Garland's Holiday Inn (Map p510; ☎ 818-980-8000, 800-476-9981; www.beverlygarland.com; 4222 Vineland Ave, North Hollywood; r $150-180, ste $220-275; P ⊠ ⬛ ⬛) Operated by Beverly Garland of TV and movie fame, this sprawling and nicely landscaped property is close to Universal Studios (free shuttles) and has its own pool and tennis courts. Families should ask about the kids' suites.

Graciela Inn (Map p510; ☎ 818-842-8887, 888-956-1900; www.thegraciela.com; 322 N Pass Ave, Burbank; r $160-220, ste $215-650; P ⊠ ⬛) This gracious boutique hotel near Warner Bros is a breath of fresh air in the charm-challenged Valley. The rooms are draped in soothing vanilla tones and feature ultracomfy beds, and the marble bathrooms have extra-big tubs. Enjoy great views from the rooftop sundeck with hot tub.

EATING

One thing's for sure: Angelenos are curious epicureans. No matter whether you fancy Korean *bulgoki* (barbecue), Ethiopian *watt* (stew), Mexican *carne asada* (grilled beef) or maybe just a good old-fashioned hamburger, you'll be sure to find the real thing among the city's gazillion eateries. Trendy types currently lust after adventurous Asian, brassy Nuevo Latino and unfussy bistro fare, preferably served in small-plate portions perfect for grazers and waist-watchers. No matter which part of town you find yourself in, there's simply no excuse for not eatin' good.

Reservations are recommended for dinner, especially at top-end places. Vegetarians and vegans should check out the options at www.vegparadise.com.

Hollywood, Los Feliz & Silver Lake
BUDGET

Yuca's (Map pp502-3; ☎ 323-662-1214; 2056 Hillhurst Ave, Los Feliz; mains $3-6; ☽ 11am-6pm Mon-Sat; ℗) Fresh ingredients, clever spicing and rock-bottom prices are what keep business constant at this tiny hut with a few parking-lot tables. Burritos, tacos and *tortas* all fly nonstop through the service window. Grab a cold one at the liquor store next door and dig in.

Scooby's (Map pp502-3; ☎ 323-468-3647; 6654 Hollywood Blvd, Hollywood; hot dogs $2.30-3.70; ☽ noon-10pm Sun-Thu, noon-2:30am Fri & Sat) Dressed in cheerful red, this hot-dog den serves up yummy gourmet wieners, but it's the fries – fresh, nicely crispy and paired with a mayo-based dipping sauce – that make us come back for more. Fresh lemonade, too.

Kung Pao Kitty (Map pp502-3; ☎ 323-465-0110; 6445 Hollywood Blvd; ☽ lunch Mon-Fri, dinner daily) No cat on the menu in this burgundy-walled Asian cantina where house music fills the lofty space. The MSG-free menu is heavy on typical Chinese dishes (Mongolian beef, *mu shu* pork, lemon chicken) but also throws in a few Thai-flavored options.

MIDRANGE

Cheebo (Map pp502-3; ☎ 323-850-7070; 7533 W Sunset Blvd, Hollywood; breakfast $5-9, lunch $8-14, dinner $10-26; ☽ 8am-11:30pm) This cheap and cheerful hipster joint is the go-to place for yummy organic pizzas topped creatively and delivered piping hot on wooden boards. Regulars are partial to the 'porkwich,' a winning combo of slow-roasted pork doused with

---

Manchego cheese, and 'da bomb,' a killer chocolate soufflé.

El Conquistador (Map pp502-3; ☎ 323-666-5136; 3701 W Sunset Blvd, Silver Lake; mains $9-13.50; ☽ lunch Wed-Sun, dinner daily) This wonderfully campy Mexican cantina is perfect for launching yourself into a night on the razzle. One margarita is all it takes to drown your sorrows, so be sure to fill your belly with tasty nachos, *chiles rellenos* (stuffed peppers, usually with cheese, but anything goes) and quesadillas to sustain your stamina through the night.

Hungry Cat (Map pp502-3; ☎ 323-462-2155; 1535 N Vine Ave, Hollywood; mains $14-22; ☽ dinner daily, brunch Sun) This kitty is small, sleek and hides out in the trendy Sunset & Vine complex (behind Schwab's). It fancies fresh seafood and will have you purring for such dishes as the tangy chorizo and clam stew, the hunky lobster roll or the portly crab cakes. Purists might prefer a portion of meaty peel 'n eat shrimp from the raw bar.

Cafe Stella (Map pp502-3; ☎ 323-666-0265; 3932 W Sunset Blvd, Silver Lake; mains $14-24; ☽ dinner Tue-Sat; ℗) This darling bistro, tucked away in a secluded courtyard at Sunset Junction (look for the red star on the rooftop), would not look out of place on Paris' Left Bank. The menu, with specials scribbled on a blackboard, features mostly classics such as tarragon chicken, steak *au poivre* and onion soup.

Palms Thai (Map pp502-3; ☎ 323-462-5073; 5273 Hollywood Blvd, Hollywood; mains $6-19; ⊙ 11am-2am) For some of the best Thai food in town head to this supper club, which is also famous for its hilarious (and actually quite good) Elvis impersonator. The huge menu has all the usual favorites, but you'll be amazed what they can do with frog, quail and jellyfish. It's located right in Thai Town in eastern Hollywood.

Vert (Map pp502-3; ☎ 323-491-1300; 4th fl, 6801 Hollywood Blvd, Hollywood; mains $10-26; ℗) Upstairs at Hollywood & Highland, Vert is Wolfgang Puck's paean to the Parisian brasserie with occasional flavor excursions to Italy and California. While sipping the signature Bellini (prosecco and green apple juice), look forward to steak *au poivre*, pan-roasted pork chops or even a classic Puck pizza.

TOP END
Musso & Frank Grill (Map pp502-3; ☎ 323-467-7788; 6667 Hollywood Blvd, Hollywood; mains $20-35; ⊙ Tue-Sat) Hollywood history hangs thickly in the air at the boulevard's oldest eatery. Waiters balance platters of steaks, chops, grilled liver and other dishes harking back to the days when cholesterol wasn't part of our vocabulary. For breakfast, which is served all day, try the signature flannel cakes (thin pancakes; $6). Service is smooth, and so are the martinis.

West Hollywood & Mid-City
BUDGET
Chao Krung (Map pp504-5; ☎ 323-932-9482; 111 N Fairfax Ave; lunch buffet $8-9, dinner mains $6-12) One visit and you're hooked on this authentic Thai dining shrine, one of the oldest in town. Mellifluous music fills the beautifully decorated dining room where servers clad in traditional outfits bring out fragrant curries, tangy pad thai and clever tofu-based dishes.

Griddle Café (Map pp504-5; ☎ 323-874-0377; 7916 W Sunset Blvd; dishes $6-9; ⊙ 8am-3pm) If you've greeted the day by peeling your lids back from crusty, bloodshot eyes, this scenester joint's high-octane coffee, wagon wheel–sized pancakes and tasty egg dishes will likely restore balance to your brain.

Swingers West Hollywood (Map pp504-5; ☎ 323-653-5858; 8020 Beverly Blvd; dishes $4-10; ⊙ 6:30am-4am); Santa Monica (Map pp508-9; ☎ 310-393-9793; 802 Broadway) If you're after Americana with a dollop of Hollywood, this diner is the genuine art-

icle. Its red plastic booths often fill with kool kids combating hunger pangs or hangovers. Servers in fishnet stockings and a certain, shall we say, sassy charm balance heaping platters of energy-restoring goodies while Little Richard makes the jukebox hop.

Wiener fans can compare notes at these two classic 'doggerias':
Pink's Hot Dogs (Map pp504-5; ☎ 323-931-4223; 709 N La Brea Ave; dishes $2.50-5.40; ⊙ 9:30am-2am Sun-Thu, 9:30am-3am Fri & Sat)
Tail O' the Pup (Map pp504-5; ☎ 310-652-4517; 329 N San Vicente Blvd; hot dogs $2.30-4.25; ⊙ 6:30am-5pm)

The original **farmers market** (Map pp504-5; 6333 W 3rd St) is a great spot for a casual meal any time of day, especially if the rug rats are tagging along. Favorite belly-filling stations include the **Gumbo Pot** (Map pp504-5; ☎ 323-933-0358; mains $4-8), whose southern food is so fingerlickin' good, Blanche Dubois might approve. If you've got a hankering for handmade, back-basics Mexican, there's no better place than **Lotería! Grill** (Map pp504-5; ☎ 323-930-2211; dishes $2.50-9).

MIDRANGE
Angelini Osteria (Map pp504-5; ☎ 323-297-0070; 7313 Beverly Blvd; mains $10-34; ⊙ lunch Tue-Fri, dinner Tue-Sun; ℗) The conversation flows as freely as the wine at this convivial eatery whose eclectic clientele share a passion for great Italian food with owner-chef Gino Angelini. Choose from soulful risottos, pungent pastas and delightful lamb chops. Price tags to match all budgets.

Surya (Map pp504-5; ☎ 323-653-5151; 8048 W 3rd St; mains $9-22; ⊙ lunch Mon-Fri, dinner daily; ℗) Curries are like culinary poetry at this upscale Indian restaurant dedicated to Surya, the Hindu god of the sun, which might explain the saffron-colored walls. Friendly waitstaff will happily help you navigate the menu, although your bill should always include an order of steamy naan and anything out of the tandoor (clay oven).

Cobras & Matadors Fairfax District (Map pp504-5; ☎ 323-932-6178; 7615 Beverly Blvd; tapas $4-12; ⊙ dinner; ℗); Los Feliz (Map pp502-3; ☎ 323-669-3922; 4655 Hollywood Blvd) Tables at this trendy tapas bar are squished together as tight as lovers, but scoring one can still be a tall order. If you pick up a bottle of vino at the shop next door, they waive the corkage fee. The branch in Los Feliz serves wine and beer.

Chaya Brasserie (Map pp504-5; ☎ 310-859-8833; 8741 Alden Dr; mains lunch $8-17, dinner $9-32; ☺ lunch Mon-Fri, dinner daily; 🅿) Chaya's menu is as tantalizing as the Zen-meets-industrial dining room where a small bamboo grove tickles the skylights. Chef Shigefumi Tachibe gives the culinary lead to Mediterranean cuisine with supporting roles assigned to Japan, China and other Asian countries. It is advisable to reserve.

Urth Caffe West Hollywood (Map pp504-5; ☎ 310-659-0628; 8565 Melrose Ave; mains $7-15; ☺ 6am-midnight); Beverly Hills (Map pp506-7; ☎ 310-205-9311; 267 S Beverly Dr); Santa Monica (Map pp508-9; ☎ 310-314-7040; 2327 Main St) The West Hollywood branch, a megahip hangout near the Pacific Design Center, has been packed with hotties, producers and gawkers for more than a decade. The organic teas and coffees are all primo quality but it's the see-and-be-seen patio that gives this place its edge. For sustenance, try the pastries, salads and sandwiches.

TOP END

AOC (Map pp504-5; ☎ 323-653-6359; 8022 W 3rd St; dishes $4-14; ☺ dinner) The small-plate menu at this stomping ground of the rich, lithe and silicone-enhanced will have you noshing happily on sweaty cheeses, homemade charcuterie and such richly nuanced morsels as braised pork cheeks. Huge list of wines by the glass.

La Terza (Map pp504-5; ☎ 323-782-8384; 8384 W 3rd St; mains $18-35; ☺ 7am-2:30pm & 5:30-11pm) Few new restaurants land with as much authority as La Terza, which instantly impressed Italophiles with its sophisticated comfort food. The spotlight shines on grilled and rotisserie meats but the pastas and fish dishes are executed with the same perfection, as are the desserts.

Xiomara Hollywood (Map pp504-5; ☎ 323-461-0601; 6101 Melrose Ave; mains lunch $11-25, mains dinner $17-33; ☺ 11:30am-11pm Mon-Fri, 8:30am-11pm Sat & Sun; 🅿); Pasadena (Map pp498-9; ☎ 626-796-2520; 69 N Raymond Ave) The old Havana décor of the West Hollywood branch is the perfect foil for the flavor explosions churned out by this humming Nuevo Latino bistro. Nurse one of the excellent minty *mojitos* while trying to pick through the varied menu, where the inky bean soup, the *arroz frito* (fried rice) and the shredded pork leg are all stars of the show. The three-course $14 lunches are a steal.

Beverly Hills & Westside

BUDGET

Native Foods (Map pp506-7; ☎ 310-209-1055; 1110-1/2 Gayley Ave, Westwood; dishes $5-10; ☺ 11am-10pm) No animal products will ever find their way into this vegan haven. The tempeh and *seitan* (wheat gluten meat substitute) are homemade and turned into such globally inspired fare as Jamaican jerk salad and Ghandi curry. Popular for take-out, too.

Other good nosh spots:

Mulberry Street Pizzeria (Map pp506-7; ☎ 310-247-8100; 240 S Beverly Dr, Beverly Hills; pizza $2.50-25) Little slices of heaven – New York-style.

Versailles (Map pp506-7; ☎ 310-558-3168; 10319 Venice Blvd, Culver City; mains $6-11; 🅿) Country-style Cuban at its finest.

Zankou Chicken Westwood (Map pp506-7; ☎ 310-444-0550; 1716 Sepulveda Blvd, near Westwood; dishes $2.50-8; ☺ 10am-11pm; 🅿); Los Feliz (Map pp502-3; ☎ 323-655-7845; 5065 W Sunset Blvd) Lip-smacking rotisserie chicken best paired with vampire-repellent garlic sauce.

MIDRANGE

Mako (Map pp506-7; ☎ 310-288-8338; 225 S Beverly Dr, Beverly Hills; mains lunch $10-13, dinner small plates $4-13; ☺ lunch Wed-Fri, dinner Mon-Sat; 🅿) Champion chef Makoto Tanaka wows patrons with his personal spin on the Asian fusion at this minimalist-chic restaurant. The small-plate menu is ideal for sampling flavors and textures, from snow-crab tempura to Asian risotto and crispy oysters. At lunchtime most people order the 'Bento Box' filled with whatever inspires Makoto that day.

Xi'an (Map pp506-7; ☎ 310-275-3345; 362 N Cañon Dr, Beverly Hills; mains $9-16) Named for the ancient Chinese city (pronounced *shee*-an), this bustling and stylish eatery lets health- and waist-conscious patrons dip into a pool of mostly low-fat exotic dishes such as black peppercorn chicken and poached cod in black bean sauce. Local ingredients are used whenever possible, but MSG is a no-no.

Nate 'n Al's (Map pp506-7; ☎ 310-274-0101; 414 N Beverly Dr, Beverly Hills; dishes $8-15; ☺ 7:30am-8:45pm Sun-Fri, 7:30am-9:30pm Sat) It's not much to look at, but this landmark deli will have you gobbling what may quite possibly be the best pastrami on rye, lox on bagels and chicken soup this side of Manhattan. With a little luck, you'll even get a free helping of star sightings.

Il Cielo (Map pp506-7; ☎ 310-276-9990; 9018 Burton Way, Beverly Hills; mains $12-30; ☺ Mon-Sat) Candles, Chianti and a courtyard table are all you need for a romantic night out with your significant other at this classy yet cozy *ristorante*. The food is solid, not exceptional, but the attentive waitstaff and the setting ensure an unforgettable night.

Taiko (Map pp506-7; ☎ 310-207-7782; 11677 San Vicente Blvd, Brentwood; mains $7-20; (P)) This prim Japanese café inside a stylish Brentwood mall is the place to slurp succulently flavored soba and udon soups, either hot or cold, or dig into delectable rice bowls topped with a variety of meats and vegetables. Prepare for a wait: low prices and top quality are an irresistible combo.

TOP END

Spago (Map pp506-7; ☎ 310-385-0880; 176 N Cañon Dr, Beverly Hills; mains lunch $14-27, dinner $26-36; ⊙ lunch Mon-Sat, dinner daily; (P)) Wolfgang Puck's flagship emporium has long been tops for A-list celebrity-spotting and fancy eating. Try to score a table on the lovely patio and prepare your taste buds to do cartwheels as chef Lee Hefter digs deep into his repertory to give pork chops, porcini and pasta the gourmet treatment. Even dessert is worth the hip-expanding indulgence. Reservations essential.

Crustacean (Map pp506-7; ☎ 310-205-8990; 9646 Little Santa Monica Blvd, Beverly Hills; mains $18-38) A beautiful place where design features include a sunken aquarium in which plump koi lazily tumble. Seafood reigns supreme here, with top honors going to the whole-roasted Dungeness crab treated to an aromatic balm of 'secret spices.'

Malibu

Neptune's Net (Map pp498-9; ☎ 310-457-3095; 42505 Pacific Coast Hwy; meals $7-12; ⊙ 10:30am-8pm Apr-Oct, 10:30am-7pm Nov-Mar, 10:30am-9pm Fri year-round; (P)) This landmark shack with an ocean-view patio serves up delicious shrimp, crab, oysters and other seafood straight from the sea tank. Fans include everyone from Harley riders to beach bums and families. It's way up the coast, just shy of the Ventura County line.

Geoffrey's (Map pp498-9; ☎ 310-457-1519; 27400 Pacific Coast Hwy; mains lunch $14-24, dinner $18-36; (P)) This posh player in northern Malibu possesses just the right mix of assets to ensure it'll never go out of style: the Pacific Ocean as a front yard, nicely executed Cal-Asian cuisine, and a regular clutch of celebrity patrons.

In short, it's the perfect date spot, especially at night when romance rules.

Santa Monica & Venice
BUDGET

Counter (Map pp508-9; ☎ 310-399-8383; 2901 Ocean Park Blvd, Santa Monica; burgers from $6.50; ⊙ 11am-10pm) Let your creativity fly at this crisp postmodern patty-and-bun joint where you can build your own gourmet burger by choosing your favorite bread, cheese, topping and sauce. The basket of delicious fries – a steal at just $2 – easily feeds two or three.

Mao's Kitchen (Map pp508-9; ☎ 310-581-8305; 1512 Pacific Ave, Venice; mains $5-10; ⊙ 11:30am-10:30pm Sun-Thu, 11:30am-3am Fri & Sat) Mao said, 'Serve the people!' and that's just what the folks at this boldly pigmented eatery do. Everything's made to order from fresh ingredients and comes hot, cheap and in heaps. Add a small salad for just $1.

Abbot's Pizza (Map pp508-9; ☎ 310-396-7334; 1407 Abbot Kinney Blvd, Venice; slices $2.50-3, pizzas $12.50-20) Join the leagues of surfers, students and urbanites at this little walk-in joint for its addictive bagel-crust pizzas. Go classic with pepperoni and sausage or gourmet with wild mushroom, barbecue chicken or olive pesto.

Real Food Daily Santa Monica (Map pp508-9; ☎ 310-451-7544; 514 Santa Monica Blvd; mains $6-12); West Hollywood (Map pp504-5; ☎ 310-289-9910; 414 N La Cienega Blvd); Beverly Hills (Map pp506-7; ☎ 310-858-0880; 242 S Beverly Dr) Tempted by tempeh? Salivating for *seitan*? Vegan cooking queen Ann Gentry sure knows how to give these meat subs the gourmet treatment. Start things off with lentil-walnut pâté, move on to the vegan club sandwich with Caesar salad, then finish up with a rich tofu cheesecake. The Beverly Hills branch is certified kosher.

If you're looking for quick food fix, check out the options at the bilevel food court at 1315 Third Street Promenade in Santa Monica. Our favorites include the Chinese place on the ground floor (try the roast pork) and **Wolfgang Puck Express** (Map pp508-9; ☎ 310-576-4770; 1315 Third St Promenade; mains $7-10), which makes tasty Chinese chicken salad and wood-fired pizza.

MIDRANGE

Beechwood (Map pp508-9; ☎ 310-448-8884; 822 Washington Blvd, Venice; mains $15-25; ⊙ dinner) With its warm woods, cool patio lounge and toasty fire pit, this sophisticated Venice hangout

LOS ANGELES

is clearly a winner in the looks department. The updated American bistro fare convinces too, especially the small-plate bar menu, although the service needs work.

Rocca (Map pp508-9; ☎ 310-395-6765; 1432 4th St, Santa Monica; mains $6-15; ☾ dinner) Just one block from bustling Third St Promenade is this two-story gem of a trattoria with a wall of wine and a Romeo and Juliet–style balcony. Chef Don Dickman finds endless ways to spin fresh ingredients into tasty dishes, ranging from the rustic (ricotta gnocchi with oxtail ragout) to the refined (slow-roasted salmon). There's a new menu daily.

La Cabaña (Map pp508-9; ☎ 310-392-6161; 738 Rose Ave, Venice; mains $7-14; ☾ 11am-3am) There's always a party going on in this cozy Mexican cottage with lots of dark nooks and crannies and a brick patio (smoking allowed). The food's good but pretty standard, but the margaritas are not. Friendly servers will let you linger until you've sopped up the last delicious drop.

Café Bizou Santa Monica (Map pp508-9; ☎ 310-582-8203; Water Garden, 2450 Colorado Ave; mains lunch $11-16, dinner $13-20; ☾ lunch Mon-Fri, dinner Tue-Sun, brunch Sun); Pasadena (Map pp498-9; ☎ 626-792-9923; 91 N Raymond Ave) As dependable as April rain in Paris, this French bistro is on the speed dial of many local budget gourmets. The menu is more country than *haute* with tender roast chicken, steak *au poivre* and veal sweetbreads all jockeying for your attention. Soup or salad costs just $1 extra.

Venice Cantina (Map pp508-9; ☎ 310-399-8420; 23 Windward Ave, Venice; mains $8-22; ☾ lunch Sat & Sun, dinner daily) This high-octane hot spot just off the Venice Boardwalk usually fills with shiny happy patrons knocking back potent tequila and sinking their teeth into intrepidly flavored Mexican fare.

TOP END

Joe's (Map pp508-9; ☎ 310-399-5811; 1023 Abbot Kinney Blvd, Venice; mains lunch $10-14, dinner $21-26, 4- or 5-course menus $50-60; ☾ Tue-Sun; Ⓟ) Like a good wine, this charmingly unpretentious restaurant only seems to get better with age. Owner-chef Joe Miller consistently serves great and gimmick-free Cal-French food. The choicest tables are out on the patio with its waterfall fountain.

Michael's (Map pp508-9; ☎ 310-451-0843; 1147 3rd St, Santa Monica; mains lunch $15-25, dinner $25-40; ☾ lunch Mon-Fri, dinner Mon-Sat; Ⓟ) Food fanciers

with deep pockets have long been partial to the inspired food of Michael McCarty, one of the pioneers of California cuisine. Dishes like grilled *loup de mer* and oven-roasted lobster taste even better if you manage to snag a table in the oh-so-romantic garden. Reservations essential.

JiRaffe (Map pp508-9; ☎ 310-917-6671; 502 Santa Monica Blvd, Santa Monica; mains lunch $10-12.50, dinner $22-29) Surfer-chef Raphael Lunetta honed his culinary craft in Paris and now regales diners with flawless Cal-French cuisine. The menu changes regularly, but the signature roast-beet salad and caramelized pork chops never go out of fashion.

South Bay & Long Beach

Gina Lee's Bistro (Map pp498-9; ☎ 310-375-4462; Riviera Plaza, 211 Palos Verdes Blvd, Redondo Beach; mains $8-21; ☾ dinner Tue-Sun; Ⓟ) The strip-mall location may not dazzle but Gina's imaginative Asian fusion fare does. Dishes borrow from China, Japan and Korea but are prepared California-style with little fat, super-fresh ingredients and robust flavors. Try the plump wontons, juicy *ponzu* catfish and other intriguing palate pleasers.

Alegria (Map pp498-9; ☎ 562-436-3388; 115 Pine Ave, Long Beach; tapas $6-11, mains $15-20; Ⓟ) The trippy, technicolor mosaic floor, trompe l'oeil murals and an eccentric art nouveau bar form an appropriately spirited backdrop to Alegria's vivid Latino cuisine. The tapas menu is great for grazers and the paella a feast for both eyes and stomach. There's even live flamenco some nights.

Belmont Brewing Company (Map pp498-9; ☎ 562-433-3891; 25 39th Place, Belmont; mains $10-20) This bustling brew-pub has a great outdoor deck (overlooking the Belmont Pier – perfect for watching sunsets), handcrafted brews and a well-priced menu that goes far beyond pub grub. You can even go *haute* with such dishes as seafood Leo, a fishy bonanza packaged in filo pastry.

Uncle Bill's Pancake House (Map pp498-9; ☎ 310-545-5177; 1305 N Highland Ave, Manhattan Beach; mains $3-7.50; ☾ closes at 2pm) Despite the name, this breakfast legend serves much more than just pancakes (although they're great; try the macadamia-nut version). Grab a table on the ocean-view patio, and then ponder whether to go for classic eggs and bacon or the Istanbul omelette (made with turkey – get it?).

Downtown

BUDGET

Angélique Cafe (Map pp500-1; ☎ 213-623-8698; 840 S Spring St; dishes $6-10; ☻ 7am-4pm Mon-Sat) After a browse around the Fashion District, lug your bags to this charming French café to refuel on toothsome *frites*, crispy salads, skinny sandwiches and classic bistro fare. Owner-chef Bruno's pâtés, sold here for a few dollars per pound, pop up at premium prices in swank restaurants around town.

Philippe the Original (Map pp500-1; ☎ 213-628-3781; 1001 N Alameda St; sandwiches $5; ☻ 6am-10pm) From cops to couples, they all flock to this legendary 'home of the French dip sandwich' with a pedigree going back to 1908. Do as millions have done before you and order a crusty roll filled with your choice of meat and hunker down at the tables parked on the sawdust-covered floor. Coffee is just 9¢ (and that's no misprint). Cash only.

Grand Central Market (Map pp500-1; ☎ 213-624-2378; 317 S Broadway; meals $2-7; ☻ 9am-6pm; P) This historic indoor market is perfect for sopping up Downtown's mélange of ethnicities, languages and cuisines. Just wander along the aisles and pick a place that looks good or head straight to Maria's Pescado Frito (central aisle) for great fish tacos and ceviche tostadas; Gaucho (facing Broadway) for lobster empanadas and bulging sandwiches; or China Café (upper level, near Hill St) for sinus-clearing chicken soup or heaping plates of chow mein.

MIDRANGE

Empress Pavilion (Map pp500-1; ☎ 213-617-9898; 3rd fl, Bamboo Plaza, 988 N Hill St; dim sum per plate $2-5, dinner $20-25; ☻ 9am-10pm; P) Other Chinatown places do dim sum, but regulars swear by this Hong Kong–style banquet hall with seating for a small village (500 people, to be exact). Dumplings, wontons, pot stickers, short ribs, barbecued pork and other delicacies just fly off the carts wheeled right to your table by a small army of servers.

Café Metropol (Map pp500-1; ☎ 213-613-1537; 923 E 3rd St; mains $7-15; ☻ 8am-10pm Mon-Sat; P) You'll have to get off the beaten path to track down this Euro-flavored Arts District bistro, but the gourmet sandwiches, organic salads and yummy pizzas make the trip well worth your while. Busiest at lunchtime, it's an airy space of industrial elegance where bold canvases brighten the brick walls.

Zip Fusion Downtown (Map pp500-1; ☎ 213-680-3770; 744 E 3rd St; mains $8-17; ☻ lunch Mon-Fri, dinner Mon-Sat); Westside (Map pp508-9; ☎ 310-575-3636; 11301 W Olympic Blvd) The chatter of happy patrons wafts around the gallery-like dining room or the bougainvillea-filled patio of this Arts District restaurant. The boundary-pushing fusion fare features such eye-and-palate candy as the 'alba-cado' – intricately spiced albacore tuna enclosed by waferthin avocado slices. The seaweed salad and the spicy calamari are other good choices.

Zucca (Map pp500-1; ☎ 213-614-7800; 801 S Figueroa St; mains lunch $9-17, dinner $11-30; ☻ lunch Mon-Fri, dinner Sat & Sun) A grown-up, big-city flair pervades this latest Joachim Splichal outpost which takes you on a culinary journey around the boot. Some of the tastiest dishes feature *zucca*, which is Italian for pumpkin. Try the pizza crowned with roast pumpkin or the pumpkin tortellini. During happy hour (4pm to 7pm Monday to Friday) appetizers and drinks are just $4.

Oomasa (Map pp500-1; ☎ 213-623-9048; 100 Japanese Village Plaza; mains lunch $9-13, dinner $10-20; ☻ Wed-Mon) This long-standing Little Tokyo restaurant, with its giant horseshoe-shaped bar, is a haven for sushi purists. From dark-red tuna to marbled salmon, it's all super-fresh, expertly cut (if a bit on the chintzy side), affordably priced and best enjoyed while snuggled into one of the old-timey booths.

TOP END

Patina (Map pp500-1; ☎ 213-972-3331; 141 S Grand Ave; mains lunch $18-30, dinner $33-40; ☻ lunch Mon-Fri, dinner daily; P) The flagship restaurant of culinary wunderkind Joachim Splichal is now in stunning new digs at the Walt Disney Concert Hall. Tantalize your tongue with such unique compositions as blue-crab mango cannelloni or Peking duck with caramelized Belgian endives. Or go all out and order the chef's menu (lunch/dinner $50/100).

R-23 (Map pp500-1; ☎ 213-687-7178; 923 E 2nd St; mains lunch $10-15, dinner $40-60; ☻ lunch Mon-Fri, dinner daily; P) Hidden in the bowels of the gritty Arts District, R-23 is a fantasy come true for serious sushi aficionados. Not even the bold art and bizarre Frank Gehry–designed corrugated cardboard chairs can distract from the exquisite and ultrafresh piscine treats prepared by a team of sushi masters. The green-tea cheesecake makes for a fitting finish.

Pasadena & Around

Bar Celona (Map pp498-9; ☎ 626-405-1000; 46 E Colorado Blvd, Pasadena; tapas $4-7, mains lunch $5-14, dinner $16-23; **P**) The Rioja-tinted walls offer a fiery backdrop for the taste-bud teasers streaming from the kitchen at this classy tapas place. Pick your way around the tapas menu or dig into big platters of paella or slow-cooked boneless short ribs. Either way, your belly will think it's fiesta time.

Saladang Song (Map pp498-9; ☎ 626-793-5200; 383 S Fair Oaks Ave, Pasadena; mains $6-17; ⏲ 6:30am-10pm) Soaring concrete walls with artsy, cut-out steel insets hem in the outdoor dining room of this modern Thai temple. Even simple curries become extraordinary here, while the unusual breakfast soups offer a nice change from the eggs-and-bacon routine. Some diners prefer the original Saladang next door, which has a more traditional menu.

Burger Continental (Map pp498-9; ☎ 626-792-6634; 535 S Lake Ave, Pasadena; breakfast/lunch buffet $5/8, all-you-can-eat Sunday brunch $14, dishes $5-15; ⏲ 7am-11pm; **P**) What sounds like a patty-and-bun joint is in reality Pasadena's most beloved Middle Eastern nosh spot. Nibble on classic hummus, dig into sizzling kebab dinners or go adventurous with the Moon of Tunis platter (chicken, gyros and shrimp in filo). Live bands and belly dancers provide candy for ears and eyes. Great patio.

New Concept (Map pp498-9; ☎ 626-282-6800; 700 S Atlantic Blvd, Monterey Park; mains $9-20) Sinophiles tired of the *kung pao* school of Chinese cooking know that for the best food they must travel to the far east – of LA that is. At this buzzy eatery the chef whips up boundary-pushing feasts, usually with delicious results, even if some sound like a Fear Factor challenge (snow frog fat soup anyone?).

San Fernando Valley

Minibar (Map p510; ☎ 323-882-6965; 3413 Cahuenga Blvd W, Universal City; small plates $5-16; ⏲ dinner; **P**) Not too far from Universal Studios, this fun restaurant-lounge with *Back-to-the-Future* decor churns out small plates with big flavor. Join the plugged-in crowd feasting on a global piñata of flavors, from Thai ceviche to salmon-brie strudel to Moroccan-spiced chicken wings.

Mandaloun (☎ 818-507-1900; 141 S Maryland St, Glendale; mains $10-22; **P**) Everything at this upscale Lebanese restaurant happens on a grand scale. Owner Ara Kalfayan greets you with a *big* smile, seats you in a *big* dining room and brings you a *big* menu. Before long, you're devouring *big* portions of sublime kebabs, lamb chops, tabbouli and other tasty fare. It also has belly dancing on weekends and water pipes on the patio.

Ca' del Sole (Map p510; ☎ 818-985-4669; 4100 Cahuenga Blvd, North Hollywood; mains $10-20; ⏲ lunch Sun-Fri, dinner daily; **P**) Near Universal Studios, the 'house of the sun' is one of the Valley's most attractive restaurants, a veritable slice of Venice complete with fireplaces and romantic patio. Much of the chef's imagination has gone into the tantalizing antipasto menu, which may feature pan-roasted quail, homemade pork-and-fennel sausage or octopus salad.

Bob's Big Boy (Map p510; ☎ 818-843-9334; 4211 Riverside Dr, Burbank; meals $6-9; ⏲ 24hr; **P**) This landmark coffee shop is a classic fill-me-up stop.

DRINKING

LA is prime sipping territory, whether your taste runs to Budweiser or three-olive martinis. Hollywood Blvd and the Sunset Strip are classic bar-hopping grounds, but there's plenty of good drinking going on in the beach cities and Downtown as well.

Hollywood, Los Feliz & Silver Lake

Formosa Cafe (Map pp502-3; ☎ 323-850-9050; 7156 Santa Monica Blvd, Hollywood; **P**) Bogie and Bacall used to knock 'em back at this watering hole, making it a great place for sopping up some Hollywood nostalgia along with your cocktail. Mai tais and martinis are the beverages of choice. Smoking patio.

4100 Bar (Map pp502-3; ☎ 323-666-4460; 4100 W Sunset Blvd, Silver Lake) An unpretentious, omnisexual and artsy crowd sidles up to the oval bar of this vibrant Silver Lake hangout. The bartenders have been around the block once or twice.

Good Luck Bar (Map pp502-3; ☎ 323-666-3524; 1514 Hillhurst Ave, Los Feliz; **P**) The clientele is cool, the jukebox loud and the drinks are seductively strong at this cultish watering hole decked out in Chinese opium-den carmine red. The baby-blue Yee Mee Loo and Chinese herb-based whiskey are popular choices.

Yamashiro (Map pp502-3; ☎ 323-466-5125; 1999 N Sycamore Ave, Hollywood; **P**) Sure, this landmark Japanese palace is also a restaurant, but we think the classy bar is simply the perfect spot for romantic tête-à-têtes, with the entire city glittering below.

Blu Monkey Lounge (Map pp502-3; ☎ 323-957-9000; 5521 Hollywood Blvd, Hollywood; P) Hollywood bars without attitude are about as rare as blue monkeys, so this is a refreshing find. DJs spin a head-bobbing mix of drum and bass, rock and world music as the crowd gets comfortable on thick sofas or at the shiny walnut bar amid sizzling Moroccan-themed decor.

Cat & Fiddle Pub (Map pp502-3; ☎ 323-468-3800; 6530 W Sunset Blvd, Hollywood; ⏱ 11:30am-2am; P) Order up a pint, grab an outdoor table in the fountain courtyard and enjoy Sunday twilight jazz radio broadcasts at this ever-popular pub, a favorite among expat Brits.

Beauty Bar (Map pp502-3; ☎ 323-468-3800; 1638 N Cahuenga Blvd, Hollywood) At this pint-sized cocktail bar, decorated with hair-salon paraphernalia from the Kennedy era, you can sip your martini, get your nails done or peruse the hipster crowd while seated in swivel chairs beneath plastic hair dryers.

Sky Bar (Map pp504-5; ☎ 323-848-6025; 8440 W Sunset Blvd, West Hollywood) The poolside bar at the Mondrian Hotel (p535) has made a virtue out of snobbery. Unless you're exceptionally pretty, rich or are staying at the hotel, chances are relatively slim that you'll be imbibing expensive drinks (from plastic cups no less, because of the pool) with the ultimate in-crowd.

Santa Monica & Venice

Voda (Map pp508-9; ☎ 310-394-9774; 1449 2nd St, Santa Monica) Voda is chic, small and filled with flattering candlelight, making it a top date spot. The house beverage – vodka – turns up in any number of fruit-infused drinks capably mixed by a crew of congenial barkeeps.

Ye Olde King's Head (Map pp508-9; ☎ 310-451-1402; 116 Santa Monica Blvd, Santa Monica) This is the unofficial headquarters of the Westside's big British expat community, complete with darts, soccer on TV and the best fish and chips in town.

Brig (Map pp508-9; ☎ 310-399-7537; 1515 Abbot Kinney Blvd, Venice; P) This one-time pool hall is now an electronica den with an up-to-the-minute design and a crowd of grown-up beach bums, arty professionals and professional artists.

Toppers (Map pp508-9; ☎ 310-393-8080; 1111 2nd St, Santa Monica; P) Enjoy knock-out sunset views, potent margaritas and a tasty selection of inexpensive appetizers at this penthouse bar at the top of the Radisson-Huntley Hotel. Getting up there aboard a glass-encased outside elevator is half the fun. Women: check out the restroom with its surreal 'toilet-with-a-view.'

If you like bars that ooze history, pop into **Chez Jay** (Map pp508-9; ☎ 310-395-1741; 1657 Ocean Ave, Santa Monica) or the **Galley** (Map pp508-9; ☎ 310-452-1934; 2442 Main St, Santa Monica), both classic watering holes with campy nautical themes.

South Bay & Long Beach

705 Bar (Map pp498-9; ☎ 310-372-9705; 705 Pier Ave, Hermosa Beach) More sophisticated than most beachside watering holes, 705 combines a lounge, sushi bar (but eat elsewhere) and live music club under one roof.

Aloha Sharkeez (Map pp498-9 ☎ 310-374-7823; 52 Pier Ave, Hermosa Beach) It's always fiesta time at this 'Animal-House-by-the-sea,' where potent libations and an abundance of bare skin help fan the party. It's west of 705 Bar.

Baja Sharkeez (Map pp498-9; ☎ 310-545-6563; 3801 Highland Ave) The action is just as wild and wacky here as at sister property Aloha Sharkeez.

Alex's Bar (Map pp498-9; ☎ 562-434-8292; 2913 E Anaheim St, Long Beach) This punk hole is as alternative as it gets in Long Beach. Cheap drinks, free wireless Internet access with purchase and occasional live bands. Enter from the back.

Downtown

Rooftop Bar @ Standard Downtown LA (Map pp500-1; ☎ 213-892-8080; 550 S Flower St; P) The scene at this outdoor lounge, swimming in a sea of skyscrapers, is libidinous, intense and more than a bit surreal. There are vibrating waterbed pods for lounging, hot-bod servers and a pool for cooling off if it all gets too steamy. Velvet rope on weekends.

Golden Gopher (Map pp500-1; ☎ 213-614-8001; 417 W 8th St) Downtown hipsters are the core clientele of this campy glamour lounge in a somewhat scary neighborhood. Gopher lamps bathe the place in mellow lighting that makes everyone look good and there are lots of couches for relaxing, in case your brain isn't handling that third martini. Those who haven't had enough at closing time can stock up for later at the in-house liquor store.

ENTERTAINMENT

LA's party scene is lively, progressive and multifaceted. You can hobnob with hipsters at a trendy dance club, groove to experimental sounds in an underground bar, skate along the cutting edge at a multimedia event in an abandoned warehouse or treat your ears to a concert by the LA Philharmonic. Mainstream, offbeat and fringe theater and performance art all thrive, as do the comedy clubs. Seeing a movie, not surprisingly, has become a luxe event with stadium-style multiplex theaters offering giant screens, total surround-sound and comfy leather seats.

The freebie *LA Weekly* and the *Los Angeles Times* Calendar section (especially Thursday's tabloid-sized pullout) are your best sources for plugging into the local scene. Buy your tickets at the box office or through **Ticketmaster** (☎ 213-480-3232; www.ticketmaster.com). Half-price tickets to many shows are sold online by **LAStageTIX** (www.theatrela.org).

Cinemas

Movie ticket prices have soared in recent years, now fetching anywhere between $10 and $15, a little less before 6pm. Tickets for most theaters can be prebooked through: **Moviefone** (☎ from any LA area code 777-3456)
ArcLight (Map pp502-3; ☎ 323-464-4226; www.arclightcinemas.com; 6360 W Sunset Blvd, Hollywood; **P**)
Pick your flick from the airport-style 'departure board' at this stylish, ultramodern multiplex that hosts the occasional film festival.
El Capitan Theatre (Map pp502-3; ☎ 323-347-7674; 6838 Hollywood Blvd, Hollywood) Lavish historic theater showing mostly first-run Disney movies, often preceded by live show extravaganzas.
Grauman's Chinese Theatre (Map pp502-3; ☎ 323-464-8111; 6925 Hollywood Blvd, Hollywood) An Industry favorite for glitzy movie premieres.
American Cinematheque (☎ 323-466-3456; www.americancinematheque.com) Hollywood (Map pp502-3; 6712 Hollywood Blvd); Santa Monica (Map pp508-9; 1328 Montana Ave) Eclectic film fare from around the world for serious cinephiles, often followed by discussions with actors or directors associated with the movie.
Pacific Theatres at the Grove (Map pp504-5; ☎ 323-692-0829; www.thegrovela.com; 189 The Grove Dr, Mid-City; **P**) A posh place to catch the latest Hollywood blockbuster.
Silent Movie Theatre (Map pp504-5; ☎ 323-655-2520; www.silentmovietheatre.com; 611 N Fairfax Ave, Mid-City; admission varies, usually adult/student $15/10) 'Silents are golden' at this unique theater where screenings are accompanied by live music.

Nuart Theatre (Map pp508-9; ☎ 310-478-6379; www.landmarktheatres.com; 11272 Santa Monica Blvd, near Westwood) The best in offbeat and cult flicks, including the camp classic, *The Rocky Horror Picture Show* every Saturday at midnight.
California Science Center IMAX (Map pp500-1; ☎ 323-724-3623; www.californiasciencecenter.org/Imax/Features/Features.php; Exposition Park, 700 State Dr, near Downtown; adult/child/student/senior $7.50/4.50/5.50/5.50) Nature-themed films for the entire family.

Live Music

Big-name acts appear at numerous venues around town, including the **Staples Center** (Map pp500-1; ☎ 213-742-7340; www.staplescenter.com; 1111 S Figueroa St, Downtown); the **Universal Amphitheatre** (Map pp510; ☎ 818-622-4440; www.hob.com; 100 Universal City Plaza, Universal City; **P**), next to Universal Studios Hollywood; the historic **Wiltern Theater** (☎ 380-5005; 3790 Wilshire Blvd), near Downtown; and, in summer, the Hollywood Bowl (p512) and the **Greek Theatre** (Map pp510; ☎ 323-665-1927; www.greektheatrela.com; 2700 N Vermont Ave, Griffith Park; **P**). For world music, check out what's playing at the intimate outdoor **John Anson Ford Amphitheatre** (Map pp502-3; ☎ 323-461-3673; 2580 E Cahuenga Blvd, Hollywood; ☼ May-Oct; **P**).

Following are some of our favorite live-music clubs. Cover charges vary widely – some gigs are free, but most average between $5 and $10. Unless noted, venues are open nightly and only open to those 21 or older. Also check the listings mags for free concerts playing at Amoeba Music (p553).
Knitting Factory Hollywood (Map pp502-3; ☎ 323-463-0204; 7021 Hollywood Blvd, Hollywood) This bastion of indie bands welcomes patrons of all ages and offers up top-notch world music, progressive jazz and other alterna-sounds. Headliners take the main stage, the rest make do with the intimate AlterKnit Lounge.
Troubadour (Map pp504-5; ☎ 310-276-6168; 9081 Santa Monica Blvd, West Hollywood; ☼ Mon-Sat) The Troub did its part in catapulting the Eagles and Tom Waits to stardom, and it's still a great place to catch tomorrow's headliners. The all-ages policy ensures a mixed crowd that's refreshingly low on attitude. Mondays are free.
Spaceland (Map pp502-3; ☎ 323-661-4380; 1717 Silver Lake Blvd, Silver Lake; **P**) Mostly local alt-rock, indie, skate-punk and electrotrash bands take the stage here in the hopes of making it big. Beck and The Eels played some of their early gigs here.

OUT & ABOUT IN LA

West Hollywood is LA's most sizzling gay and lesbian party zone, but there are plenty of happening places to be found in Silver Lake and the beach towns as well. Here are some of our favorites:

Abbey (Map pp504-5; ☎ 310-289-8410; www.abbeyfoodandbar.com; 692 N Robertson Blvd, West Hollywood; mains $9-13; ⏲ 8am-2am, breakfast to 2pm) From its beginnings as a humble coffeehouse, the Abbey has grown into WeHo's funnest, coolest and most varied club, bar and restaurant. Take your pick from many spaces, which range from outdoor patio to chill room and your own private divan. On weekend nights, they're all busy.

Factory/Ultra Suede (Map pp504-5; ☎ 310-659-4551; www.factorynightclubla.com; 652 La Peer Dr, West Hollywood; P) This giant double club has an edgy New York feel and sports different stripes nightly. On Friday night, the Girl Bar (at the Factory) is the preferred playground of fashion-forward femmes, while male hot bods strut their stuff on Saturdays. Music-wise, anything goes here as long as it's got a good beat.

Here Lounge (Map pp504-5; ☎ 310-360-8455; www.herelounge.com; 696 N Robertson Blvd, West Hollywood) This is WeHo's premier venue for S&M (standing and modeling, that is). It's chic and angular, with lots of smooth surfaces – and that goes for both the men *and* the setting. Thursday's Fuse night draws luscious lipstick lesbians.

Rage (Map pp504-5; ☎ 310-652-7055; 8911 Santa Monica Blvd, West Hollywood; ⏲ 11:30am-2am) This pulsating double-decker bar and dance club for boy pals has a rotating roster of DJs spinning house, R&B, hip-hop, funk and other sounds. There's no cover for Monday's Alternative Night, while 18+ Tuesdays bring in the younger set.

Micky's (Map pp504-5; ☎ 310-657-1176; 8857 Santa Monica Blvd, West Hollywood; ⏲ noon-2am) Not far from Rage, it's 'raining men' at this posing, preening and cruising club where nonstop high-energy dance music translates into an electric party atmosphere. Frequent drinks specials help break down any residual inhibitions.

Palms (Map pp504-5; ☎ 310-652-6188; 8572 Santa Monica Blvd, West Hollywood) This scene staple has been keeping lesbians happy for over three decades and even gets the occasional celebrity drop-in, as in Melissa Etheridge or Ellen DeGeneres. Beer is the beverage of choice and the Beer Bust Sundays are legendary.

Roosterfish (Map pp508-9; ☎ 310-392-2123; www.roosterfishbar.com; 1302 Abbot Kinney Blvd, Venice; ⏲ 11am-2am) This friendly, been-there-forever kind of bar still manages to stay current and cool. It's the type of place where you can strike up new friendships while playing pool, shooting electronic darts or nursing your drink. Friday is the busiest night, or go for the Sunday afternoon barbecue.

Faultline (Map pp502-3; ☎ 323-660-0889; 4216 Melrose Ave, Silver Lake; ⏲ 6pm-2am Tue-Fri, 2pm-2am Sat & Sun) This indoor-outdoor venue is party central for manly men with nary a twink in sight. Take off your shirt and head to the beer bust on Sunday afternoon (it's an institution), but get there early or expect a long wait.

Akbar (Map pp502-3; ☎ 323-665-6810; 4356 W Sunset Blvd, Silver Lake) Best jukebox in town, Casbah-style atmosphere and a great mix of people that's been known to change from hour to hour – gay, straight, on the fence or just hip, but not too-hip-for-thou.

Catalina Bar & Grill (Map pp502-3; ☎ 323-466-2210; 6725 W Sunset Blvd, Hollywood; cover $10-18, plus dinner or 2 drinks; ⏲ Tue-Sun) LA's premier jazz club has moved into new, slicker and more spacious digs but nothing's changed about Catalina Popescu's top-notch booking policy, which has included heavies like Wynton Marsalis and Chick Korea.

Conga Room (Map pp504-5; ☎ 323-938-1696; www.congaroom.com; 5364 Wilshire Blvd, Mid-City; ⏲ Thu-Sat; P) Ladies in their spiky heels and nattily dressed gents whirl around to the salsa beat at this upscale club with the slightly decadent feel of prerevolution Havana. Come early for dance lessons or dinner at La Boca restaurant.

Temple Bar (Map pp508-9; ☎ 310-393-6611; 1026 Wilshire Blvd, Santa Monica; P) At one of the more happening hangouts west of Holly-wood the bands are hit-or-miss, but the Temple's drinks are strong, the crowd's heavy on the eye candy and the ambience is fairly relaxed.

Babe & Ricky's (Map pp498-9; ☎ 323-295-9112; 4339 Leimert Blvd, Leimert Park) Mama Laura has presided over LA's oldest blues club for nearly four decades. The Monday-night jam session, with free food, often brings the house down.

Also try:

Hotel Cafe (Map pp502-3; ☎ 323-461-2040; 1623 1/2 N Cahuenga Blvd, Hollywood) Intimate space for handmade music by talented singer-songwriters.

House of Blues (Map pp504-5; ☎ 323-848-5100; www.hob.com; 8430 W Sunset Blvd, West Hollywood; P) The original branch.

Viper Room (Map pp504-5; ☎ 310-358-1880; 8852 W Sunset Blvd, West Hollywood; P) Celebrity-heavy.

Dance Clubs

If you want all your clichés about LA confirmed, look no further than a nightclub in Hollywood or West Hollywood. Come armed with a hot bod, a healthy attitude or a fat wallet in order to impress the armoire-sized goons presiding over the velvet rope. Clubs elsewhere are considerably more laid-back, but most require you to be at least 21 (bring picture ID). Cover ranges from $5 to $20. Doors are usually open from 9pm to 2am.

Highlands (Map pp502-3; ☎ 323-461-9800; 6801 Hollywood Blvd, Hollywood) The mall-setting of this club could be a turnoff if the mall wasn't the splashy Hollywood & Highland fun complex. It's a huge place with seven bars, a restaurant and lots of shiny, happy and barely legal people. The multiple balconies are perfect for smoking, stargazing and scanning the LA skyline.

Nacional (Map pp502-3; ☎ 323-962-7712; 1645 Wilcox Ave, Hollywood; ☽ Tue-Sat; ℗) Another entry in Hollywood's growing cadre of mega-clubs, this one has a seductive prerevolution-Cuba theme with fiery mood lighting and loungy Bauhaus-style furniture. A picky door policy keeps out any weekend warriors that don't fit the profile (whatever that may be).

Parlour Club (Map pp504-5; ☎ 323-650-7968; 7702 Santa Monica Blvd, West Hollywood) We can't guarantee that, as you're reading this, this cozy dive still does Punk Rock Karaoke, Milkshoot comedy nights and Bricktops! (a 1920s Berlin cabaret hosted by Vaginal Davis, LA's fave drag queen), but it's sure to be something similarly wacky.

Zanzibar (Map pp508-9; ☎ 310-451-2221; 1301 5th St, Santa Monica; ☽ Tue-Sun) Jason Bentley and Garth Trinidad are among the spinmeisters working their turntable magic (deep house, dubbed-out funk, retro jazz) at this Santa Monica lounge with sultry African-themed decor. The wraparound bar is great for socializing, while the comfy couches invite canoodling.

Also recommended:

Dragonfly (Map pp502-3; ☎ 323-466-6111; 6510 Santa Monica Blvd, Hollywood; ℗) Hardcore party chamber with theme nights ranging from laid-back reggae to sexy sounds for the fetish set.

Echo (Map pp502-3; ☎ 213-413-8200; 1822 W Sunset Blvd, near Silver Lake) Divey hangout that's a favorite with Eastside hipsters hungry for an eclectic alchemy of sound.

Little Temple (Map pp502-3; ☎ 323-660-4540; 4519 Santa Monica Blvd, Silver Lake; ☽ Tue-Sun; ℗) The Eastside cousin of Santa Monica's Temple Bar (p549), this lounge is perfect for anyone with a yen for Zen and soulful sounds.

Performing Arts

Los Angeles Philharmonic (Map pp500-1; ☎ 323-850-2000; www.laphil.org; 111 S Grand Ave, Downtown; tickets $15-120; ℗) Led by Esa Pekka-Salonen, the world-class LA Phil performs classics and cutting-edge compositions at the Walt Disney Concert Hall from October to June (see p523).

Hollywood Bowl (Map pp502-3; ☎ 323-850-2000; www.hollywoodbowl.com; 2301 N Highland Ave, Hollywood; tickets $1-105; ☽ late Jun-Sep; ℗) This historic natural amphitheater is the LA Phil's summer home and also a stellar place to catch big-name rock, jazz, blues and pop acts. Do as the locals do and come early for a pre-show picnic (alcohol is allowed).

Los Angeles Opera (Map pp500-1; ☎ 213-972-8001; www.laopera.com; Dorothy Chandler Pavilion, 135 N Grand Ave, Downtown; tickets $30-190; ℗) Star tenor Plácido Domingo presides over the LA Opera, whose productions range from real crowd-pleasers to rarely performed esoteric works.

Redcat (Map pp500-1; ☎ 213-237-2800; www.redcat.org; 631 W 2nd St, Downtown; ℗) Part of the Walt Disney Concert Hall complex, this venue presents a global feast of avant-garde and experimental theater, performance art, dance, readings, film and video.

Theater

Mark Taper Forum (Map pp500-1; ☎ 213-628-2772; www.taperahmanson.com; 135 N Grand Ave, Downtown; ℗) The Taper is the home base of the Center Theatre Group, one of SoCal's leading resident ensembles. It has developed numerous new plays, most famously Tony Kushner's *Angels in America*. Ask about public rush tickets ($12).

Actors' Gang Theatre (Map pp502-3; ☎ 323-465-0566; www.theactorsgang.com; 6209 Santa Monica Blvd, Hollywood; tickets $20-25; ℗) The 'Gang' was founded in 1981 by Tim Robbins and other renegade UCLA acting-school grads. Its daring and offbeat reinterpretations of classics have a loyal following, although it's the bold new works developed at ensemble workshops that give the troupe its edge.

Odyssey Theatre Ensemble (Map pp508-9; ☎ 310-477-2055; www.odysseytheatre.com; 2055 S Sepulveda Blvd, near Westwood; tickets $20-25; ℗) This well-respected ensemble presents new work, updates the classics and develops its own plays in a ho-hum three-stage space housing three 99-seat theaters under one roof.

East West Players (Map pp500-1; ☎ 213-625-4397; www.eastwestplayers.org; 120 N Judge John Aiso St, Little Tokyo, Downtown; tickets $23-38; **P**) Founded in 1965, this pioneering Asian-American ensemble presents modern classics as well as premieres by local playwrights. Alumni have gone on to win Tony, Emmy and Academy awards.

Will Geer Theatricum Botanicum (Map pp498-9; ☎ 310-455-3723; www.theatricum.com; 1419 N Topanga Canyon Blvd, north of Santa Monica; tickets $11-25; Jun-Oct; **P**) This magical natural outdoor amphitheatre was founded by Will Geer (TV's Grandpa Walton) and takes on Shakespeare, Dylan Thomas, Tennessee Williams and other American and European writers.

Other thespian venues:

Ahmanson Theatre (Map pp500-1; ☎ 213-628-2772; www.taperahmanson.com; Music Center of LA County, 135 N Grand Ave, Downtown; tickets $20-80; **P**) Mostly bigtime Broadway-style musicals and visiting blockbusters.

Deaf West Theatre (Map p510; ☎ 818-762-2773; www.deafwest.org; 5112 Lankershim Blvd, North Hollywood, San Fernando Valley; tickets vary) Hearing-impaired actors perform classic and contemporary plays in sign language with voice interpretation and/or supertitles.

Celebration Theatre (Map pp504-5; ☎ 323-957-1884; www.celebrationtheatre.com; 7051 Santa Monica Blvd, West Hollywood) One of the nation's leading producers of gay and lesbian plays, winning dozens of awards.

Comedy

Comedy clubs often fill up so make reservations or show up early for decent seats. At clubs serving full menus, the best seats are reserved for dinner patrons. If you're not eating, many clubs require a two-drink minimum order on top of the cover charge (usually $10 to $20). Except where noted, you must be 21 or older to get in.

Comedy & Magic Club (Map pp504-5; ☎ 310-372-1193; www.comedyandmagicclub.com; 1018 Hermosa Ave, Hermosa Beach) Headliners such as Bill Maher and Bob Saget serve up yucks at this fine South Bay venue, although it is best known as the place where Jay Leno tests out his *Tonight Show* shtick most Sunday nights. Reservations required and partons must be 18 years old.

Groundlings (Map pp504-5; ☎ 323-934-4747; www .groundlings.com; 7307 Melrose Ave, Mid-City; all ages; **P**)

This improv school and company has tickled people's funny bones for over 30 years and launched the careers of Lisa Kudrow, Jon Lovitz, Will Ferrell and other top talent. Improv night on Thursday brings together the main company, alumni and surprise guests.

Comedy Store (Map pp504-5; ☎ 323-656-6225; www .thecomedystore.com; 8433 W Sunset Blvd, West Hollywood) From Chris Tucker to Whoopi Goldberg, there's hardly a famous comic alive that has not at some point performed at this classic, which was a gangster hangout in an earlier life. Pauly Shore's mom, Mitzi, has presided over the joint for about three decades.

Sports

BASEBALL

Since moving here from Brooklyn in 1958, the **LA Dodgers** (www.dodgers.com) have become synonymous with LA baseball. The team plays from April to October at Dodger Stadium (p522).

BASKETBALL

They may have lost some of their hustle, but the **LA Lakers** (www.nba.com/lakers) still pack 'em into the sparkling **Staples Center** (Map pp500-1; ☎ 213-742-7340; www.staplescenter.com; 1111 S Figueroa St, Downtown), which is also home to the city's second men's NBA team, the historically mediocre **LA Clippers** (www.nba.com/clippers), and the considerably more successful women's team, the **LA Sparks** (www.wnba.com/sparks). The WNBA season (late May to August) follows the regular men's NBA season (October to April). Lakers tickets are hardest to come by and are mostly sold through **Ticketmaster** (☎ 213-480-3232; www.ticketmaster.com).

ICE HOCKEY

The **LA Kings** (www.lakings.com) play in the National Hockey League (NHL), whose regular season runs from October to April, followed by the play-offs. Home games take place at the Staples Center.

SOCCER

Major League Soccer (MLS) may not yet be huge with general audiences but *futból* definitely enjoys a passionate following among LA's Latino population. The city's moderately successful **LA Galaxy** (www.lagalaxy.com) was joined by a second franchise in 2005, the **Club Deportivo Chivas USA** (http://chivas.usa.mlsnet.com/MLS /cdc/). Teams play from April to October in the slick new **Home Depot Center** (Map pp498-9; 18400 Avalon Blvd; P), in the southern LA suburb of Carson (take the Avalon exit off I-405).

SHOPPING

LA is a great place to shop, and we're not just talking malls (although there are plenty of good ones around). No matter whether you're a penny-pincher or a power shopper, you'll find lots of opportunities to drop some cash around town.

Fashion-forward fashionistas flock to **Robertson Blvd** (btwn N Beverly & W 3rd St) or **Melrose Ave** (btwn San Vicente & La Brea) in West Hollywood, while bargain hunters haunt Downtown's Fashion District. If money is no object, Beverly Hills beckons with international couture, jewelry and antiques, especially along Rodeo Dr, which is ground central for groovy tunes, while east of here Silver Lake has cool kitsch and collectibles, especially around **Sunset Junction** (Hollywood & Sunset Blvds). Santa Monica has good boutique shopping on Tony Montana Ave and eclectic Main St, while the chain store brigade (Gap to Sephora) has taken over Third Street Promenade. In nearby Venice, you'll find cheap and crazy knickknacks along the Venice Boardwalk, although locals prefer Abbot Kinney Blvd with its fun mix of art, fashion and New Age emporiums.

Fashion

Fred Segal West Hollywood (Map pp504-5; ☎ 323-651-4129; 8100 Melrose Ave; P); Santa Monica (Map pp508-9; ☎ 310-458-9940; 500 Broadway; P) Cameron and Gwyneth are among the stars kitted out at this kingpin of LA fashion boutiques where

you can also stock up on beauty products, sunglasses, gifts and other essentials.

Kitson (Map pp504-5; ☎ 310-859-2652; 115 S Robertson Blvd, West Hollywood) If you like to stay ahead of the fashion curve, pop into this hip haven chock-full of tomorrow's outfits and accessories, many of them by local labels. It's a major stop for celebs on a shopping prowl.

Wasteland Mid-City (Map pp504-5; ☎ 323-653-3028; 7428 Melrose Ave); Santa Monica (Map pp508-9; ☎ 310-395-2620; 1338 4th St) This warehouse-sized space has glamour gowns, velvet suits and other vintage outfits going back to the '40s, plus rows of racks packed with contemporary styles, all in great condition.

DNA (Map pp508-9; ☎ 310-399-0341; 411 Rose Ave, Venice; P) Tiny DNA is jam-packed with a small but choice assortment of hip garb for men and women, much of it with a stylish European flair, by both local and national designers.

American Apparel (www.americanapparel.net; ☼ 11am-10pm Mon-Thu, 11am-11pm Fri & Sat, noon-8pm Sun) Beverly Hills (Map pp506-7; ☎ 310-274-6292; 104 N Robertson Blvd); Hollywood (Map pp502-3; ☎ 323-465-6312; 6922 Hollywood Blvd) AA's stylish logo-free T-shirts, tank tops, skirts and shorts – available in bold popsicle colors – may not be for brand-name bunnies but they are all made locally in a sweatshop-free facility. The website lists other branches of this fast-growing chain.

Remix Vintage Shoes (Map pp504-5; ☎ 323-936-6210; 7605 Beverly Blvd, Mid-City; P) This handsome store is stocked with never-worn vintage footwear from the 1920s to the '70s. If you need a pair of wingtips or wedgies to complete your retro look, this is the place to go.

TINSELTOWN TREASURES

So you've stood in Tom Cruise's footsteps at Grauman's Chinese Theatre, dined at the table at Spago once occupied by Britney Spears and seen Ashton Kutcher in the flesh during a taping of the *Tonight Show*. To keep the tinsel glittering for a bit longer, pick up a souvenir from one of these stores, all of which stock a bit more than plastic Oscar statuettes and Hollywood Sign fridge magnets.

It's a Wrap (Map p510; ☎ 818-567-7366; 3315 W Magnolia Ave, Burbank) Tank tops to tuxedos worn by actors, extras and cameos working on TV or movies and sold at steep discounts.

Larry Edmunds Bookshop (Map pp502-3; ☎ 323-463-3273; 6644 Hollywood Blvd, Hollywood) Longtime purveyor of scripts, posters, stills and books about movies, theater and TV.

Reel Clothes & Props (☎ 818-508-7762; 5525 Cahuenga Blvd, North Hollywood; ☼ Mon-Sat) Movie wardrobes plus truckloads of props, including lamps, picture frames and ashtrays; about half a mile north of the North Hollywood subway station.

Baby Jane of Hollywood (Map pp504-5; ☎ 323-848-7080; 7985 Santa Monica Blvd, West Hollywood; ☼ noon-8pm; P) The go-to place for famous autographs, vintage movie posters or even topless pictures of Dame Julie Andrews.

Turtle Beach Swimwear (Map pp504-5; ☎ 310-652-6039; 320 N La Cienega Blvd, West Hollywood) This little shop will have you looking good poolside with its big selection of mix-and-match tops and bottoms. Tankinis to push-ups, thongs to boy shorts in nylon, cotton, velvet, crochet – you name it, it's here.

Flea Markets

Melrose Trading Post (Map pp504-5; 7850 Melrose Ave; admission $2; ☉ 9am-5pm Sun; P) Small but choice, this market at Fairfax High School has about 100 purveyors feeding the current retro frenzy with funky and often quite bizarre stuff – from '40s glamour gowns to mermaid swizzle sticks.

Pasadena City College Flea Market (Map pp498-9; 1570 E Colorado Blvd, Pasadena; admission free; ☉ 8am-3pm 1st Sun of the month; P) With over 450 vendors, this market has plenty in store for treasure hunters and is more manageable than the Rose Bowl. The music section is legendary.

Rose Bowl Flea Market (Map pp498-9; Rose Bowl, 1001 Rose Bowl Dr, Pasadena; admission $7-20; ☉ 5am-4:30pm 2nd Sun of the month; P) This is the mother of all flea markets with over 2200 vendors. True pros show up at 5am (when admission is $20), flashlight in hand, to ferret out the best stuff.

Music

Amoeba Music (Map pp502-3; ☎ 323-245-6400; 6400 W Sunset Blvd, Hollywood; ☉ 10:30am-10pm Mon-Sat, 11am-9pm Sun; P) Hailing from San Francisco, Amoeba has made a big splash in Hollywood. All-star staff and listening stations help you sort through over half a million new and used CDs, DVDs, videos and vinyl. Check the *LA Weekly* for free in-store live shows.

LA'S FASHION DISTRICT DEMYSTIFIED

Bargain hunters from throughout the city flock to this frantic 90-block warren of fashion (p524) in southwestern Downtown every day of the week. Shopping here can be a lot of fun but first-timers often find the area bewildering and overwhelming. For orientation, you can print out a self-guided tour of the area from www.fashiondistrict.org. Serious shoppers can contact **Urban Shopping Adventures** (☎ 213-683-9715) for a guided tour led by people who know the district inside-out. Basically, the area is subdivided into several distinct retail areas:

- Women – Los Angeles St between Olympic and Pico Blvds, 11th St between Los Angeles and San Julian Sts
- Children – Wall St between 12th St and Pico Blvd
- Men and bridal – Los Angeles St between 7th and 9th Sts
- Textiles – 8th St between Santee and Wall Sts
- Jewelry and accessories – Santee St between Olympic Blvd and 11th St
- Designer knockoffs – Santee & New Alleys (enter on 11th St between Maple and Santee Aves)

Shops with signs reading 'Wholesale Only' or *'Mayoreo'* are off limits to the public. Leave your credit cards at home because most vendors will only accept cash. Haggling is OK, but don't expect to get more than 10% or 20% off. There are usually no refunds or exchanges, so choose carefully and make sure the item is in good condition (many items sold here are 'seconds,' meaning they're slightly flawed). Most stores don't have dressing rooms. Hours are generally 9am to 5pm Monday to Saturday; many stores are closed on Sunday except those on Santee Alley.

Clued-in fashionistas in town on the last Friday of the month can snap up amazing deals when dozens of designer showrooms – Betsey Johnson to Von Dutch – open to the public for just a few hours to unload samples and overstock. Prices are below wholesale and sometimes bargaining can yield extra savings. Sales take place from 9am to 3pm at the **New Mart** (Map pp500-1; ☎ 213-627-0671; 127 E 9th St), which specializes in contemporary and young designers, and across the street at the **California Mart** (Map pp500-1; ☎ 213-630-3600; 110 E 9th St), which is one of the largest apparel marts in the country with 1500 showrooms. Come early and bring cash. Not all showrooms are open every time, but there's always plenty to browse through. Note that sales are sometimes cancelled during fashion trade shows or around holidays. Always call ahead to confirm.

Aron's Records (Map pp502-3; ☎ 323-469-4700; 1150 N Highland Ave, Hollywood; ☯ 10am-10pm Mon-Thu, 10am-midnight Fri & Sat; (P)) The grand-daddy among LA's sound boutiques, Aron's has been unloading cool tunes since 1965. New and used, indie or mainstream, vinyl and CD, you'll find it here, mostly at excellent prices.

Hear Music (Map pp508-9; ☎ 310-319-9527; 1429 Third St Promenade, Santa Monica; ☯ 11am-11pm Sun-Thu, 11am-midnight Fri & Sat) This former indie store is now in cahoots with Starbucks but still specializes in choice grown-up sounds – from electronica to blues, world music to jazz. You can test-listen over 10,000 CDs and even burn your own favorite compilation.

For more cool tunes:

Head Line Records (Map pp504-5; ☎ 323-655-2125; 7706 Melrose Ave, Mid-City; ☯ noon-8pm) The ultimate source for punk and hardcore.

Rhino Records (Map pp508-9; ☎ 310-474-8685; 2028 Westwood Blvd, Westwood; ☯ 10:30am-10pm Mon-Sat, noon-5:30pm Sun; (P)) Gives serious collectors itchy fingers.

Offbeat Stuff

Wacko/La Luz de Jesus (Map pp502-3; ☎ 323-663-0122; 4633 Hollywood Blvd, Silver Lake; ☯ 11am-7pm Mon-Wed, 11am-9pm Thu-Sat, noon-6pm Sun) Billy Shire's emporium of camp and kitsch has been a fun browse for over three decades. Pick up hula-girl swizzle sticks, a Frida Kahlo mesh bag, an inflatable globe or other, well, wacky stuff. In back is La Luz de Jesus, one of LA's top lowbrow art galleries.

Munky King (Map pp500-1; ☎ 213-620-8787; 441 Gin Ling Way, Downtown; ☯ noon-7pm Sun-Thu, noon-8pm Fri & Sat) This toy temple with a twist specializes in independent designer playthings from around the world, including Ugly Dolls, urban vinyl toys from Hong Kong and Kubricks from Japan.

Meltdown Comics & Collectibles (Map pp504-5; ☎ 323-851-7283; 7522 W Sunset Blvd, West Hollywood; ☯ 11am-10pm) LA's coolest comics store beckons with indie and mainstream books, from Japanese manga to graphic novels by Daniel Clowes of *Ghost World* fame. The Baby Melt department stocks rad stuff for kids.

Pleasure Chest (Map pp504-5; ☎ 323-650-1022; 7733 Santa Monica Blvd, West Hollywood; ☯ 10am-midnight Sun-Wed, 10am-1am Thu, 10am-2am Fri & Sat; (P)) This kingdom of kinkiness is filled with sexual hardware catering to every conceivable fantasy and fetish, though more of the naughty than the nice variety.

GETTING THERE & AWAY
Air

The main gateway to LA is **Los Angeles International Airport** (LAX; Map pp498-9; ☎ 310-646-5252; www.lawa.org), right on the coast not far south of Santa Monica and Venice. Its eight terminals are built around a horseshoe-shaped bi-level traffic loop. Ticketing and check-in are on the upper (departure) level, while baggage-claim areas are on the lower (arrival) level. The hub for most international airlines is the Tom Bradley International Terminal.

To travel between terminals, board the free Shuttle 'A' beneath the 'Shuttle' sign outside each terminal on the lower level. Hotel shuttles stop here as well. A free minibus for the mobility-impaired can be ordered by calling ☎ 310-646-6402.

Domestic flights operated by Alaska, Aloha, America West, American, Southwest and United also use the **Bob Hope Airport** (Map pp498-9; ☎ 818-840-8840, 800-835-9287; www.burbankairport.com) in Burbank, in the San Fernando Valley, which is handy if you're headed for Hollywood, Downtown or Pasadena.

To the south, on the border with Orange County, **Long Beach Airport** (Map pp498-9; ☎ 562-570-2600; www.longbeach.gov/airport) is convenient for Disneyland and is served by Alaska, American, America West and Jet Blue.

Ontario International Airport (Map pp498-9; ☎ 909-937-2700; www.lawa.org/ont), approximately 35 miles east of Downtown LA, is another regional landing base.

Bus

The main bus terminal for **Greyhound** (Map pp500-1; ☎ 213-629-8421; 1716 E 7th St) is in an unsavory part of Downtown, so avoid arriving after dark. Bus 58 makes the 10-minute trip to the transit plaza at Union Station with onward service across town, including Metro Rail's Red Line to Hollywood. Some Greyhound buses go directly to the terminal in **Hollywood** (Map pp502-3; ☎ 323-466-6381; 1715 N Cahuenga Blvd) and a few also pass through **Pasadena** (Map pp498-9; ☎ 626-792-5116; 645 E Walnut St) and **Long Beach** (Map pp498-9; ☎ 562-218-3011; 1498 Long Beach Blvd).

Greyhound buses serve San Diego at least hourly ($16, 2¼ to four hours) and there are up to eight buses to/from Santa Barbara ($12, 2¼ to three hours). Services to/from San Francisco run almost hourly ($43, 7½ to 12½ hours). There are also frequent departures to Anaheim and Disneyland ($8.50, one hour). For general information about Greyhound travel, see p719 and p721.

Car & Motorcycle

All the major international car-rental agencies have branches at LAX and throughout Los Angeles (see p724 for central reservation numbers). If you haven't prebooked, use the courtesy phones in the arrival areas at LAX. Offices and lots are outside the airport, but each company provides free shuttles to take you there.

For Harley rentals, check **Eagle Rider** (Map pp498-9; ☎ 310-536-6777; www.eaglerider.com; 11860 S La Cienega Blvd, Hawthorne; 9am-5pm) or **Route 66** (Map pp508-9; ☎ 310-578-0112, 888-434-4473; 4161 Lincoln Blvd, Marina del Rey; 9am-6pm Tue-Sat, 10am-5pm Sun & Mon). Rates range from $75 to $135 a day, with discounts for longer rentals.

Train

Amtrak trains roll into Downtown's historic **Union Station** (Map pp500-1; ☎ 800-872-7245; 800 N Alameda St). The *Pacific Surfliner* travels daily to San Diego ($26, 2¾ hours), Santa Barbara ($17, 2½ hours) and San Luis Obispo ($25, 5½ hours). See p726 for full details. Amtrak cross-country *Coast Starlight*, *Southwest Chief* and *Sunset Limited* trains also depart from Union Station (see p719).

GETTING AROUND
To/From the Airports
LOS ANGELES INTERNATIONAL AIRPORT
Door-to-door shuttles, such as those operated by **Prime Time** (☎ 800-473-3743) and **Super Shuttle** (☎ 310-782-6600), leave from the lower level of all terminals. Typical fares to Santa Monica, Hollywood or Downtown are $18, $23 and $14, respectively. Practically all airport-area hotels and some hostels have arrangements with shuttle companies for free or discounted pick-ups. The **Airport Bus** (☎ 714-978-8855) travels hourly or half-hourly from LAX to the main Disneyland resorts for $19 one way or $28 round-trip.

Curbside dispatchers will summon a taxi for you. Fares average $20 to $25 to Santa Monica, $25 to $35 to Downtown or Hollywood, and up to $80 to Disneyland.

Using public transportation is slower and less convenient but cheaper. From outside any terminal catch a free Shuttle C bus to the

LAX Transit Center, the hub for buses serving all of LA. Trip planning help is available at ☎ 800-266-6883 or www.metro.net.

Popular routes include (trip times given are approximate and depend on traffic):
Downtown Metro Buses 42a or 439 West; $1.25; 1½ hours
Hollywood Metro bus 42a West to Overhill/La Brea, transfer to Metro bus 212 North; $2.50; 1½ hours
Venice & Santa Monica Big Blue Bus 3; $0.75; 30 to 50 minutes

BOB HOPE AIRPORT
For door-to-door shuttle companies, see LAX information. Typical shuttle fares to Hollywood, Downtown or Pasadena are $20, $24 and $22, respectively. Cabs charge about $20, $30 and $40, respectively. Metro Bus 163 South goes to Hollywood (40 minutes), while Downtown is served by Metro Bus 94 South (one hour).

LONG BEACH AIRPORT
Shuttle service (see LAX for contact information) costs $34 to Disneyland, $51 to Downtown LA and $28 to Manhattan Beach. Cabs cost $45, $65 and $40, respectively. Long Beach Transit Bus No 111 South makes the trip to the Transit Mall in downtown Long Beach in about 45 minutes. From here you can catch the Metro Blue Line to Downtown LA and points beyond.

Bicycle
Most buses are equipped with bike racks and bikes ride for free, although you must securely load and unload it yourself. Bikes are also allowed on Metro Rail trains except during rush hour (6:30am to 8:30am and 4:30pm to 6:30pm, Monday to Friday). For rental places, see p530.

Car & Motorcycle
Unless time is no factor – or money is extremely tight – you're going to want to spend some time behind the wheel, although this means contending with some of the worst traffic in the country. Avoid rush hour (7am to 9am and 3:30pm to 6pm).

Parking at motels and cheaper hotels is usually free, while fancier ones charge anywhere from $8 to $25 for the privilege. Valet parking at nicer restaurants and hotels is commonplace.

For local parking suggestions, see the introductions to individual neighborhoods in the Sights section.

Public Transportation
METRO
LA's main public transportation agency is **Metro** (☎ 800-266-6883; www.metro.net), which operates about 200 bus lines as well as four rail lines:

Red Line Downtown LA's Union Station to North Hollywood, via central Hollywood and Universal Studios.

Blue Line Downtown to Long Beach.

Gold Line Union Station to Pasadena.

Green Line Norwalk to Redondo Beach.

Tickets cost $1.25 per boarding or $3 for a day pass with unlimited rides. Bus drivers sell single tickets and day passes (exact fare required), while train tickets are available from vending machines at each station. Call the toll-free number or check the website for trip planning help.

LOCAL BUSES
Some neighborhoods are served by local **DASH minibuses** (☎ your area code + 808-2273; www.ladottran sit.com). Here are some of the useful routes (fare per boarding 75¢):

Beachwood Canyon Route Useful for close-ups of the Hollywood Sign, runs from Hollywood Blvd up Beachwood Dr.

Downtown Routes Six separate routes, hitting all the hot spots, including Chinatown, City Hall, Little Tokyo, the Financial District and Exposition Park.

Fairfax Route Makes a loop taking in the Beverly Center mall, the Pacific Design Center, the farmers market, LACMA and other museums on the Miracle Mile.

Hollywood/West Hollywood Route Connects Hollywood & Highland with the Beverly Center along Sunset Blvd (including Sunset Strip) and La Cienega Blvd.

Santa Monica-based **Big Blue Bus** (☎ 310-451-5444; www.bigbluebus.com) serves much of western LA, including Santa Monica, Venice, Westwood and LAX (75¢). Its express bus 10 runs from Santa Monica to Downtown LA ($1.75).

Taxi
Except for those taxis lined up outside airports, train stations, bus stations and major hotels, cabbies only respond to phone calls. The fares are metered and are $2 at flag fall plus $1.80 per mile. Some recommended companies:

Checker (☎ 800-300-5007)

Independent (☎ 800-521-8294)

Yellow Cab (☎ 800-200-1085)

AROUND LOS ANGELES

CATALINA ISLAND
pop 4000

Mediterranean-flavored Catalina Island is a world removed from the bustle of LA and a popular day trip or overnight getaway. It is part of the Channel Islands, a chain of semisubmerged mountains off the coast of Southern California. Catalina has a unique ecosystem and rather tumultuous history. Before appearing on the radar screen of vacationers in the late 19th century, it went through phases as a hangout for sea-otter poachers, smugglers and Union soldiers. Chewing-gum magnate William Wrigley Jr (1861–1932) purchased the place in 1919 and brought his baseball team, the Chicago Cubs, here for spring training. Most of the island's interior of sun-baked hillsides, valleys and canyons is owned by the Santa Catalina Island Conservancy, which ensures that most of it remains free of development.

Catalina's main tourist season is June to September, when prices soar and the island seems to sink from the load of day-trippers. Consider spending the night, as the ambience goes from frantic to romantic in no time.

Orientation
Nearly all tourist activity concentrates in the pint-sized port town of Avalon, where a yacht-studded harbor hems in a tiny downtown with shops, hotels and restaurants. The only other settlement is remote Two Harbors in the backcountry, which has a general store, dive and kayak center, snack bar and lodge.

Information
Catalina Visitors Bureau (☎ 310-510-1520; www .catalina.com; Green Pier, Avalon; ☺ varies)

Post office (Arcade btwn Sumner Ave & Metropole St)

Public Library (☺ 1-7pm Tue-Thu, 10am-4pm Fri & Sat; ☐) Internet free.

Tradewinds Gift Shop & Internet Café (☎ 310-510-0010; 119 Sumner Ave; per 15 min $3; ☺ 8am-10pm Jun-Aug, 8am-7pm Sep-May)

US Bank (Crescent Ave & Metropole St) 24hr ATM.

Sights
Avalon's most recognizable landmark is the art deco **Casino** (1 Casino Way), which has great murals, a theater with a twinkling domed ceiling and a giant ballroom where, throughout

the 1930s and '40s, ladies and gents jived and jitterbugged to big-band music. The theater now shows first-run Hollywood movies ($8), but to see the upstairs dance hall you must join an amusing one-hour tour ($14.50). Tour tickets also include admission to the **Catalina Island Museum** (☎ 310-510-2414; www.cata linamuseum.org; 1 Casino Way; adult/child/senior $4/1/3; 🕙 10am-4pm, 10am-5pm Jul & Aug, Wed-Mon Jan-Mar), which has modest exhibits about milestones in the island's history, including its role during WWII and the Chicago Cubs era.

About 1.5 miles inland from Avalon harbor is the peaceful **Wrigley Memorial & Botanical Garden** (☎ 310-510-2595; 1400 Avalon Canyon Rd; admission $5; 🕙 9am-4pm), which has sweeping views, a monument awash with handmade local tile and impressive gardens showcasing cacti, succulents and several plants unique to the island.

Catalina's hilly interior is a protected **nature preserve** and may only be explored on foot or mountain bike (permit required; see right) or on an organized tour (see p558). Although the landscape appears to be barren, it actually teems with plant life and animals,

and you'll enjoy plenty of memorable views of the rugged coast and sandy coves. If you're lucky, you'll even run into the resident herd of bison, who are descended from those left behind from a 1924 movie shoot.

Activities
HIKING & MOUNTAIN-BIKING

Escape Avalon's stifling crowds by hitting the trails. The trailheads closest to town are above Hermit Gulch campground and behind the Wrigley Memorial. Pick up maps and free but compulsory permits at the **Catalina Island Conservancy** (☎ 310-510-2595; www.cata linaconservancy.com; 125 Claressa St; 🕙 8:30am-3:30pm Sep-May, 8:30am-4:30pm Jun-Aug). Permits are also available at Two Harbors and the airport. Mountain-bike permits cost $20 for two days or $60 per year.

WATER SPORTS

Avalon's sliver of a beach along Crescent Ave gets packed, and it's not much better at palm tree–lined **Descanso Beach** (admission $2), a beach club with a bar and restaurant that's a short walk north of the Casino. **Descanso Beach Ocean**

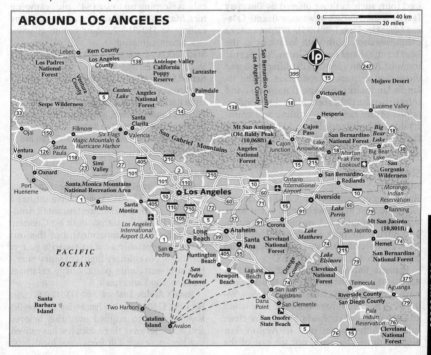

AROUND LOS ANGELES

0 —— 40 km
0 —— 20 miles

Sports (☎ 310-510-1226; www.kayakcatalinaisland.com) rents snorkeling gear and kayaks, and also runs guided kayaking tours and kayak camping trips. Paddling out from here quickly gets you away from the sun-worshipping hordes and to the quiet coves of Catalina's rocky coastline. This is some of the finest kayaking anywhere in Southern California.

Snorkeling is pretty good at Descanso as well, but other spots include Lovers' Cove, just south of the Avalon boat terminal, and Casino Point Marine Park behind the Casino, which is also the best shore dive. Both are protected marine preserves where schools of sardines flit through thick kelp beds and majestic golden garibaldi cruise serenely. Outfitters that offer equipment, guided snorkeling trips and offshore dives include **Catalina Divers Supply** (☎ 310-510-0330; www.catalinadiverssupply.com), on the Green Pier, and the **Catalina Dive Shop** (☎ 877-766-7535; www.catalinadiveshop.com), near the boat terminal. Guided dive tours start at $85, including all gear.

Tours

The easiest way to see Catalina is on an organized tour, such as those offered by **Discovery Tours** (☎ 310-510-2500; www.scico.com) and **Catalina Adventure Tours** (☎ 310-510-2888; www.catalinaadventuretours.com), both with locations at the boat terminal and on the Green Pier. Scenic tours of Avalon (about $15) offer postcard views and a quick introduction to the island's landmarks, history, flora, fauna and infrastructure. Other options include explorations of the canyons, coastline and countryside of the interior (from $31) and of the fish-rich underwater gardens seen from a glass-bottom boat (from $11).

Sleeping

HOTELS

Rates vary enormously on Catalina. Generally, prices go up on weekends, when some properties impose a two-night minimum, and during the peak season (roughly from May to September). Rates listed below drop 30% to 60% the rest of the year.

Hermosa Hotel & Cottages (☎ 310-510-1010, 888-684-1313; www.hermosahotel.com; 131 Metropole St; r with shared bath $35-70, cottage with private bath $65-90; ✗) The small, bare-bones rooms won't cause you fits of euphoria but they're clean and the only budget pick in Avalon. For slightly more character, opt for one of the

cute cottages (some with kitchens) flanking a bougainvillea-draped courtyard.

La Paloma & Las Flores (☎ 310-510-1505, 800-310-1505; Sunny Lane; cottage $140-160, r $190-220) Tucked at the end of a quiet lane, this delightful, flower-filled hideaway exudes Old Catalina charm. Retreat to vintage cottages with kitchen or newer rooms with double whirlpool tubs and balconies. The fountain-studded patio is great for curling up with a book or preparing a feast on the barbecue.

Villa Portofino (☎ 310-510-0555, 888-510-0555; 111 Crescent Ave; r $95-195, ste $160-380; ✗ ✗) Rooms here hit the mark in terms of comfort, decor and amenities, but it's really the rooftop sundeck with gorgeous bay views that is the trump card. Rates include a light breakfast.

CAMPING

Catalina has one campground in Avalon and four in the interior. Per night camping fees are $12 for adults and $6 for children. Tent ($16) and sleeping bag ($11) rentals are available at Little Harbor, Two Harbors and Hermit Gulch; the latter two also have tent cabins sleeping up to six ($45, plus camping fee). Mandatory reservations can be made by calling ☎ 310-510-7254 or online at www .scico.com/camping.

Black Jack In the mountains, hike 1.5 miles from Airport Shuttle or Safari Bus drop-off.

Hermit Gulch Around 1.5 miles inland from the Avalon boat landing, served by Avalon Trolley.

Little Harbor Beach-adjacent, served by Safari Bus.

Parson's Landing Remote, primitive beachfront sites that are a 7-mile hike from Two Harbors.

Two Harbors Ocean views, short uphill walk from Two Harbors boat landing.

Eating

Café Prego (☎ 310-510-1218; 603 Crescent Ave; pasta $11-19, meat & fish $17-33; ☽ dinner) Avalon has a number of good Italian restaurants (Antonio's and Villa Portofino, both on Crescent Ave, are also recommended), but this one fits as comfortably as your favorite pair of flip-flops. No culinary flights of fancy here – just soul-sustaining pasta, crispy calamari, fresh seafood and steak.

Rosie's Avalon Seafood (☎ 310-510-0197; Green Pier; dishes $2.50-10; ☽ 7am-7pm Jun-Sep, 8am-6pm Oct-May) Rosie, who reigned over this beloved fish shack for over three decades, has retired, but her successor still feeds loyal locals with dock-fresh fish tacos, fried calamari, halibut sandwiches and other simple, fishy fare.

Pancake Cottage (☎ 310-510-0726; 118 Catalina St; dishes $5-10; ☽ 6:30am-1:30pm) Fans of big American breakfasts regularly crowd the counter and pink Formica tables at this local favorite. The menu, with its gazillion variations of waffles, omelettes, pancakes and egg dishes, will make your head spin.

Other tummy-pleasers:

Catalina Country Club Restaurant (☎ 310-510-7404; 1 Country Club Dr; mains lunch $8-12, dinner $20-35) Creative California fusion.

Casino Dock Café (☎ 310-510-2755; 1 Casino Way; dishes $5-10; ☽ 8:30am-7pm Apr-Nov) Casual waterfront hangout.

Getting There & Away

Catalina Express (☎ 310-519-1212, 800-481-3470; www.catalinaexpress.com; round-trip about $50) operates frequent scheduled ferries to Avalon from San Pedro (Map pp498–9; 1¼ hours), Long Beach (Map pp498–9) and Dana Point (Map pp498–9; Orange County, 1½ hours), and to Two Harbors from San Pedro (1½ hours) only.

The **Marina Flyer** (☎ 310-305-7250; www.catalina ferries.com; round trip $63) makes one or two departures daily from Fisherman's Wharf in Marina del Rey to Avalon (1¼ hours) and Two Harbors (one hour).

From Newport Beach in Orange County, the **Catalina Flyer** (☎ 949-673-5245; www.caladventures .com; round-trip $44) also goes to Avalon once daily (1¼ hours).

Fifteen-minute helicopter rides with the **Island Express** (☎ 310-510-2525; www.islandexpress .com) depart from the boat terminals in San Pedro (Map pp498–9) and next to the *Queen Mary* in Long Beach (Map pp498–9), and cost $76/144 one way/round trip.

Getting Around

Most places in Avalon are reached within a five- or 10-minute walk. The Avalon Trolley operates along two routes, passing all major sights and landmarks; tickets cost $1.50 per ride or $5 for a day pass.

Brown's Bikes (☎ 310-510-0986; www.catalinabik ing.com), near the boat terminal, repairs, sells and rents ($12 to $21) beach cruisers and mountain bikes.

To get into the backcountry, board the **Airport Shuttle** (☎ 310-510-0143; round trip $17) leaving up to six times daily. Reservations

are required. The **Safari Bus Shuttle** (☎ 310-510-8687; ☽ mid-Jun–early Sep) connects Avalon and Two Harbors via the airport and also stops at trailheads for campgrounds. Fares depend on distance traveled; Avalon to Two Harbors is $23.50 each way. Buy tickets at any Discovery Tours office.

SIX FLAGS MAGIC MOUNTAIN & HURRICANE HARBOR

Velocity is king at **Six Flags Magic Mountain** (☎ 661-255-4111, 818-367-5965; www.sixflags.com/parks /magicmountain; 26101 Magic Mountain Parkway, Valencia; adult/child under 4ft/senior $48/30/30; ☽ from 10am Apr-early Sep, Sat & Sun only mid-Sep–Mar, closing times vary from 6pm-midnight), where you can go up, down and inside-out faster and in more baffling ways than anywhere besides a space shuttle.

The ever-growing arsenal of rides, shows and attractions includes 16 roller-coasters likely to scare the bejeezus out of most of us. Ride the aptly named **Scream**, which goes through seven loops, including a zero-gravity roll and a dive loop with you sitting – feet dangling – in a floorless car. **Flashback** deals you six spiral hairpin drops, while **Viper** drops 188ft into a double-boomerang turn that can be most unpleasant if you're not ready for it. If you've got a stomach of steel, don't miss **X**, where you ride in cars that spin around themselves while hurtling forward and plummeting all at once.

Note that children under 4ft are not allowed on many of the fiercest rides. In fact, in summer, a better place to take the little ones might be right next door to **Six Flags Hurricane Harbor** (☎ 661-255-4100, 818-367-5965; www .sixflags.com/parks/hurricaneharborla; 26101 Magic Mountain Parkway; adult/child under 4ft/senior $24/17/17; ☽ 10am Jun-Aug, Sat & Sun only May & Sep, closing times vary). At this jungle-themed water park you can keep cool frolicking in fanciful lagoons and churning wave pools, plunging down wicked speed slides or getting pummeled on rafting rides.

Combination tickets to both parks are $57 (no discounts) and can be used on the same day or on separate days.

The parks are about 30 miles north of LA, right off the Magic Mountain Parkway exit off I-5 (Golden State Fwy). If you don't have your own vehicle, it's easiest to join one of the organized tours. Just look for flyers in your hotel.

BIG BEAR LAKE

pop 21,000

Big Bear Lake (elevation 6750ft) is a family-friendly four-season playground, drawing ski bums and boarders in winter and hikers, mountain-bikers and water-sports enthusiasts the rest of the year. About 110 miles northeast of LA, it's a quick and popular getaway not only for Angelenos but also for people from other Southland cities and even Las Vegas.

Big Bear is on the scenic **Rim of the World Drive** (Hwys 18 and 38), a panorama-filled road that climbs, curves and meanders through the **San Bernardino National Forest** for about 87 miles from the town of San Bernardino. Past Big Bear it plunges back down through canyons and chaparral to Redlands. Views are spectacular on clear days and downright depressing on smoggy ones. The forest is hugely popular with weekend warriors, but from Monday to Thursday you'll often have trails and facilities to yourself and can also benefit from lower accommodation prices.

Orientation

Most of Big Bear is sandwiched between the lake's south shore and the mountains. The main thoroughfare is Big Bear Blvd (Hwy 18), which is lined by motels, cabins and other businesses. It skirts the pedestrian-friendly 'Village,' which has cutesy shops, restaurants and the tourist office. The ski resorts are east of the Village. North Shore Blvd (Hwy 38) is quieter and provides access to campgrounds and hiking and mountain-biking trails.

Information

Drivers need to obtain a National Forest Adventure Pass if parking on forest land. See p60 for details. Passes are available at the Big Bear Discovery Center.

INTERNET ACCESS

Cyberland (☎ 909-866-1999; 42001 Big Bear Blvd; per 30 min $2.25; ☒ 5-9:30pm Mon-Thu, 5-11pm Fri, 10:30am-11pm Sat & Sun)

MEDICAL SERVICES

Urgent Care (☎ 909-878-3696; 41949 Big Bear Blvd)

POST

Post office (cnr Big Bear Lake & Pine Knot Dr)

TOURIST INFORMATION

Big Bear Discovery Center (☎ 909-382-2790; www.bigbeardiscoverycenter.com; North Shore Dr, Fawnskin; ☒ 8am-6pm May-Oct, 8am-4:30pm Nov-Apr) Outdoor information, exhibits and guided tours. Issues the National Forest Adventure Pass.

Big Bear Lake Resort Association (☎ 909-866-7000, 800-424-4232; www.bigbear.com; 630 Bartlett Rd; ☒ 8am-5pm Mon-Fri, 9am-5pm Sat & Sun) Maps, information and room reservations.

Activities

SKIING

With an 8000ft ridge rising above the lake's southern side, Big Bear usually gets snow between mid-December and March or April and has two ski mountains, **Bear Mountain** (off Hwy 18) and **Snow Summit** (☎ 909-866-5766; www.bigbearmountainresorts.com; off Hwy 18; lift ticket half-/full-day $36/48). Bear Mountain, the higher of the two has a vertical drop of 1665ft (1200ft at Snow Summit), and is an all-mountain freestyle park with 150 jumps, 80 jibs and two pipes across 195 acres. At Snow Summit the focus is more on traditional downhill skiing with trails for all levels of experience, although boarders are welcome too. More than two thirds of the trails are for intermediate and advanced skiers, and there's night skiing as well. Altogether the mountains are laced with over 60 runs and served by 24 lifts, including four high-speed quads. One tickets buys access to both resorts, which are linked by a free shuttle. Complete ski and boot rentals range from $15 to $25.

HIKING

In summer, people trade their ski boots for hiking boots and hit the forest trails. If you only have time for one short hike, make it the Castle Rock Trail, which is 2.4-mile round trip and offers superb views. The first half-mile is pretty steep but the trail flattens out somewhat after that. The trailhead is off Hwy 18 on the western end of the lake. Also popular is the moderate Cougar Crest Trail (5 miles round-trip), starting near the Discovery Center, which links up with the Pacific Crest Trail (PCT) after about 2 miles and offers views of the lake and Holcomb Valley. Most people continue eastward for another half-mile to the top of Bertha Peak (8502ft) for a 360-degree view of Bear Valley, Holcomb Valley and the Mojave Desert.

MOUNTAIN-BIKING

Big Bear is mountain-biking mecca with over 100 miles of trails for cross-country adventure. It hosts several pro and amateur races each year. A good place to get your feet in gear is along the aptly named 9-mile **Grandview Loop**, which starts at the top of Snow Summit, easily reached via the **Scenic Sky Chair** (all-day pass $20). If you just want to go up for the views or to hike, it's $7, or $10 round trip. One of the best single-track rides is the intermediate 13-mile **Grout Bay Trail**, which starts on the north shore. For more experienced bikers, Delamar Mountain, Holcomb Valley and Van Duesen Canyon off Hwy 38 are popular destinations. **Bear Valley Bikes** (☎ 909-866-8000; 40298 Big Bear Blvd; half-/full-day from $25/35), near the Alpine Slide (see below), is a good rental place.

WATER SPORTS

In summer, Big Bear Lake provides a cool respite from the heat. **Swim Beach**, near the Village, has lifeguards and is popular with families. For a bit more privacy, rent a boat, kayak or waverunner and get out on the water. A pretty destination is **Boulder Bay** near the lake's western end. Rentals are available at several marinas, including **Holloway's** (☎ 909-866-5706; www.bigbearboating.com; 398 Edgemoor Rd), about 1 mile west of the Village.

The lake teems with fish, but catching them is not always easy. Those bent on success should sign up with **Cantrell Guide Service** (☎ 909-585-4017), which guarantees anglers their catch – or your money back. You'll need a fishing license, available at sporting stores around town, and $75 per hour for the boat, with a three-hour minimum.

Great for families is the **Alpine Slide** (☎ 909-866-4626; www.alpineslidebigbear.com; Big Bear Blvd), a small fun park with a water slide, wheeled downhill bobsled ride, go-cart track and miniature golf course.

TOURS

Take a 20-mile self-guided tour through the Holcomb Valley, the site of Southern California's biggest Gold Rush in the early 1860s on the Gold Fever Trail. The dirt road is negotiable by mountain bikes and practically all vehicles. Budget two to four hours, stops included. The Big Bear Discovery Center has a free pamphlet describing 12 sites of interest along this route.

Take the interpretive **Off-Road Adventures** (☎ 909-585-1036; www.offroadadventure.com) tour ($50) if you prefer to let someone else do the driving. The company offers other tour options as well.

Another fun backcountry destination is Butler Peak a mountain top crowned by a historic fire lookout tower, from where you have tremendous panoramic views. You'll need a mountain bike or high-clearance vehicle to get there, or join a guided tour ($30) offered by the Discovery Center (9am to noon on Saturday).

Between late December and March, a flock of bald eagles makes Big Bear their winter home. The Discovery Center **Eagle Tour** (☺ 9am-noon Sat late Dec–mid-Mar; $30) combines an educational slide program with an eagle-spotting outing.

Sleeping

The Big Bear Lake Resort Association books accommodations for $10 per reservation.

CABINS & INNS

Rates listed below are for wintertime, which is peak season in Big Bear; they drop by about 40% in spring and fall and 20% in summer.

Knickerbocker Mansion (☎ 909-878-9190, 800-388-4179; www.knickerbockermansion.com; 869 Knickerbocker Rd; r $115-225; ✗) Innkeepers Thomas and Stanley have poured their hearts into this ornate B&B with nine rooms and two suites inside a hand-built 1920s log home and a converted carriage house. The breakfasts are to-die-for.

Grey Squirrel Resort (☎ 909-866-4335, 800-381-5569; www.greysquirrel.com; 39372 Big Bear Blvd; r $120-190; ⬤) Set amid the pines, this delightful resort has a big assortment of classic mountain cabins that make for idyllic getaways year-round. Most have a kitchen and the nicest come with a fireplace, sundeck and Jacuzzi.

Honey Bear Lodge (☎ 909-866-7825, 800-628-8714; www.honeybearlodge.com; 40994 Pennsylvania Ave; r $75-200) In a quiet, woodsy spot close to the Village, this friendly, low-key lodge has all types of accommodations, including lofts, rustic cabins and Jacuzzi rooms. Even the economy units have a TV, microwave, refrigerator and fireplace.

Northwoods Resort (☎ 909-866-3121, 800-866-3121; www.northwoodsresort.com; 40650 Village Dr; r $100-215; ✗ ⬤) If you like to have the amenities of

A TOWERING EXPERIENCE

Jack Kerouac spent a summer as a forest fire lookout during the dharma-seeking days of 1950s American bohemia. Half a century later you too can get a taste of the experience during a night at the **Morton Peak Fire Lookout** (midweek/weekends $75/85) in the San Bernardino Forest.

Back in 2001, the US Forest Service condemned the tower for demolition along with six others nearby. Loath to see a vital part of forest history disappear into memory, the San Bernardino National Forest Association corralled a league of volunteers who meticulously restored the lookouts and maintain them to this day. To help fund the project, they opened up the one on Morton Peak to the curious, stargazers and solitude-seekers.

Getting to the lookout means lurching up a chaparral-cloaked mountain on a steep, rocky dirt road better suited for mules and encountering a gate with padlocks as intricate as the Gordian knot. Your destination is a 30ft steel tower where volunteers arrive in the morning to keep their sharp-eyed vigil for destructive forest fires. High above the smog-shrouded Inland Empire, the lookout is small and sparse – you are in somebody's office, after all – but there's a bed, wraparound windows and an observation deck. It's quiet and peaceful, the silence cut only by screeching jays and buzzing insects. On clear nights, the stargazing is as good as it gets this close to a metropolitan area.

The lookout is off Hwy 38, about 10 miles east of Redlands. Stays are similar to primitive camping since you have to truck in everything from water to food to flashlights. You'll be given detailed instructions and directions when making reservations, which are handled by the Big Bear Lake Resort Association (p560).

a modern hotel, this one is your best bet. Rooms are heavily decorated and comfortable, although the walls are surprisingly thin. The large pool, heated year-round, is a sweet kicking-back spot. The restaurant (mains lunch $9 to $13, dinner $14 to $30) has lots of palate-pleasers and nice tables on the pond-adjacent patio.

Castlewood Theme Cottages (☎ 909-866-2720; www.castlewoodcottages.com; 547 Main St; r $90-200; ✗) Bored with bland motel rooms? Then let your fantasies go wild in these well-crafted, clean and amazingly detailed cabins, complete with Jacuzzi tubs and costumes. Let your inner Tarzan roar, fancy yourself a damsel in distress or cavort amongst woodland fairy-folk. It's cheesy, wacky and, oddly, fun. Kids are not allowed.

Adventure Hostel (☎ 909-866-8900, 866-866-5255; www.adventurehostel.com; 527 Knickerbocker Rd; dm $20-25, r $40-120; ▣) Closed for remodeling at the time of writing, this place may have reopened by the time you're reading this. Call ahead.

CAMPING

Big Bear has five **US Forest Service campgrounds** (USFS; ☎ 800-444-6777; www.reserveusa.com) called Pineknot, Serrano, Hanna Flat, Big Pine Flat and Holcomb Valley. All but the latter have potable water and flush toilets and are open from spring until fall (exact times vary each year). Serrano near the Discovery Center is the biggest campground. Except for Pineknot all are on the north shore.

Eating

Mandoline (☎ 909-866-4200; 40701 Village Dr; lunch $11-15, dinner $14-29) The Village's best eatery puts clever, globally inspired spins on pasta and grilled foods in a setting that combines antler chandeliers with hip black tablecloths without looking ridiculous.

Grizzly Manor Cafe (☎ 909-866-6226; 41268 Big Bear Blvd; meals under $10; ☺ 6am-2pm Mon-Fri, 7am-2pm Sat & Sun) You'll feel like you're part of a backwoods sitcom at this buzzy locals' hangout, about a quarter mile east of the Village, where the breakfasts are bear-sized, the staff irreverent, the walls covered with whacky stickers and the prices small.

Old Country Inn (☎ 909-866-5600; 41126 Big Bear Blvd; mains breakfast & lunch $9-13, dinner $14-26; ☺ 8am-9pm) This place puts the accent on hearty American and German fare, although there's plenty of seafood to accommodate noncarnivores. You'll be dining under the mournful eyes of mounted stags and elk. Good breakfasts, too.

Sonora Cantina (☎ 909-866-8202; 41144 Big Bear Blvd; dishes $5-14) Next to the Old Country Inn, this restaurant brings the cheerful aesthetics of Mexico to the mountains and serves gussied-up staples (burritos and tacos) plus great fajitas and tequila lime chicken.

Self-caterers can stock up at **Vons** (42170 Big Bear Blvd) and **Stater Bros** (42171 Big Bear Blvd), across from each other near the lake's eastern end. For fresh produce your best bet is **Forest Farms** (41078 Big Bear Blvd), about 0.25 miles east of the Village.

Getting There & Away

Big Bear is on Hwy 18, which heads north of Hwy 30 in San Bernardino. A quicker approach is via Hwy 330, which starts in Highland and intersects with Hwy 18 in Running Springs. If you don't like serpentine mountain roads, pick up Hwy 38 near Redlands, which is longer but easier on the queasy.

Mountain Area Regional Transit Authority (Marta; ☎ 909-878-5200; www.marta.cc) buses connect Big Bear with the Greyhound bus station in San Bernardino ($5). On weekends and holidays, it also operates a trolley around town (single ride/day pass $1/3).

Orange County

What, exactly, lies beyond the 'Orange Curtain'? More than Disneyland, it turns out. Orange County occupies one of the most inviting stretches of the Southern California coast, especially at Laguna Beach, where hills, canyons and dramatic bluffs meet a sparkling blue Pacific. Huntington Beach is the cradle of California's surf culture, while Newport Beach, its more affluent neighbor to the south, has put the finishing touches on the attitude of entitled nonchalance that defines the SoCal beach scene. And don't miss San Juan Capistrano. While many of California's missions are poured concrete re-creations, this one is the real McCoy – and lovely to behold.

Angelenos came up the 'Orange Curtain' to distinguish themselves from their neighbors to the south (whom they see as neo-cons in Hummers, with Stepford wives riding shotgun). There's no denying either the county's long history of reactionary politics or its distinctly sanitized aesthetic; it prizes shiny malls and easy parking over messy city life. To get up to speed on the 'hurray for me, screw you' attitude of the county's wildly affluent beach towns, check out the TV series *The OC* – an over-the-top (but often dead-on) take on life in the rich lane.

As you move back from the coast, the social reality grows more complex and, depending on your tastes, more interesting. Just south of Disneyland lies Santa Ana, whose overwhelmingly Latino population supports a vital downtown – and regularly votes Democratic. Just up the road is Westminster, known as 'Little Saigon' due to its largely Vietnamese-American population.

Still, Mickey and the gang are far and away the county's biggest draw. Whether you're a true believer or merely an aficionado of kitsch, Disneyland is the OC's must-see.

HIGHLIGHTS

- Walking the perimeter of quaint **Balboa Island** (p579) before taking the ferry ride to the beaches of **Balboa Peninsula** (p578)

- Setting the teeth achatter on **Disneyland's Space Mountain** (p568) then sticking around for the nightly fireworks display

- Watching the sun dip below the horizon from any clifftop in **Laguna Beach** (p581)

- Boning up on surfing history at the **International Surfing Museum** (p576) in **Huntington Beach**

- Getting buzzed on Vietnamese coffee in a strip mall café in **Westminster's Little Saigon** (p574)

■ AVERAGE TEMPS IN ORANGE COUNTY: JAN 35/65°F, JUL 59/79°F

Information

Most of Orange County's cities maintain visitor bureaus, but for general area information, stop in at the new **California Welcome Center** (☎ 714-667-0400; 2800 N Main St) in the MainPlace mall in Santa Ana off the Main St exit of the I-5, at the intersection with Hwy 22. The office is on the lower level, near the southwest outside entrance.

Getting There & Around

AIR

If you're heading to Disneyland or the Orange County beaches, you can avoid the always-busy Los Angeles International Airport (LAX) by flying into the easy-to-navigate **John Wayne Airport** (SNA; ☎ 949-252-5200;

www.ocair.com) in Santa Ana. The airport is 8 miles inland from Newport Beach, via Hwy 55, near the junction of I-405 (San Diego Fwy). Airlines serving Orange County include Alaska, Aloha, America West, American, Continental, Delta, Frontier, Midwest, Northwest, Southwest and United.

Long Beach Airport (LGB; ☎ 562-570-2600; www .longbeach.gov/airport), to the north just across the county line, is a handy alternative.

BUS

For getting around by public transportation, the **Orange County Transportation Authority** (OCTA; ☎ 714-636-7433; www.octa.net; info line ☯ 5am-10pm Mon-Fri, 7am-7pm Sat & Sun) operates a fleet of buses serving towns and destinations

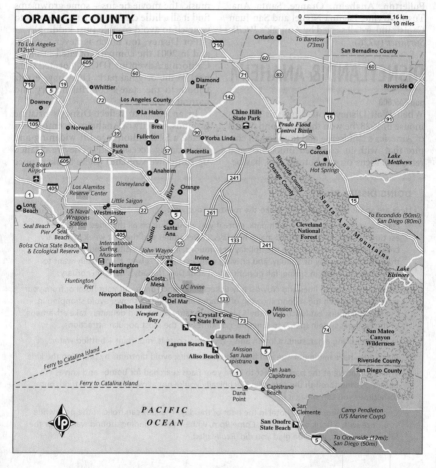

ORANGE COUNTY

throughout the county. The fare is $1.25 per ride or $3 for a day pass. Both types of tickets are sold onboard and you'll need exact change. Free OCTA bus system maps and schedules are available at train stations, most chambers of commerce and online. You can get schedule information by phone, but there is no after-hours automated phone service, so call before it closes.

CAR
The easiest way to get around Orange County is by car, but avoid driving on the freeways during the morning and afternoon rush hours (7am to 10am and 3pm to 7pm).

TRAIN
Fullerton, Anaheim, Orange, Santa Ana, Tustin, Irvine, Laguna Niguel and San Juan Capistrano are all served by Amtrak's *Pacific Surfliner* (p726).

DISNEYLAND & ANAHEIM

pop 345,000
When Walt Disney trotted out his famous mouse in 1928, he won the hearts and minds of America's children – and founded an empire that, with its conjured innocence and relentless focus on the bottom line, has be-come synonymous with America itself. After conquering publishing, film and TV, Disney decided to give physical form to his imaginary world. He opened Disneyland in 1955 and, a half-century later, the crowds – and profits – are bigger than ever.

As you approach the gates, loudspeakers inform you that you're about to have the 'happiest day of your life.' Warning: this may be an exaggeration. Still, you can't help but be amazed by this alternate universe, where each detail has been carefully 'imagineered,' from the pastel sidewalks to the personal hygiene of the park's 21,000 employees (called 'cast members' in Disney-speak). While kids tend to swoon over it all – the costumed greeters, the singsong music, the movie tie-ins – some grown-ups find it all a little creepy. Keep such doubts to yourself to avoid trouble (just kidding).

For Disney, too much is never enough, and in 2001 the company opened Disney's California Adventure (DCA). Located right next to the original park, DCA pays ersatz tribute to the state's colorful history and natural wonders.

In an effort to reflect Disney's pristine grounds, the city of Anaheim recently completed a $4.2 billion face-lift widening and landscaping access roads. They've cleaned up run-down stretches where hookers once

---

DOING DISNEY RIGHT

Here are some tips to help you make the most of your visit:

- Plan on at least one day for each park, more if you want to go on all the rides. Lines are longest during summer and around major holidays. In December and the first week of January crowds pack the resort to see the holiday decorations. In general, visiting midweek is better than Friday, Saturday or Sunday, and arriving early in the day is best. If you really want to avoid crowds, come in spring, fall or right after Labor Day. Nobody's here in February.

- Other ways to avoid lines and crowds: buy tickets in advance online, at your hotel or from your travel agent; watch the second showing of parades and other live shows; avoid shopping in the evening hours; eat lunch early (by 11am) or late (after 3pm). And definitely take advantage of the Fastpass system (p567) to schedule ride times for the most popular attractions.

- In summer bring a hat, suntan lotion and – if cutting costs is important – bottled water.

- Many rides have minimum age and height requirements; avoid tantrums by prepping the kids.

- When you arrive at the park, expect to have your bags searched for bombs and knives etc before passing through the turnstiles. Technically you're not allowed to bring in food, but sometimes you can sneak it in.

- Consider returning to your hotel in the heat of the day. The kids can frolic in the pool while you doze with a book on your face. Come 9pm, while you're standing around waiting for the fireworks display, you'll be glad you did. *Really* glad.

catered to over-tired dads. And they've established the first police force in the US devoted specifically to guarding tourists (they call it 'tourist-oriented policing').

INFORMATION
Medical Services
Western Medical Center Anaheim (☎ 714-533-6220; 1025 S Anaheim Blvd; ☯ 24hr)

Money
In Disneyland, the Bank of Main Street has foreign currency exchange and basic services. In Disney's California Adventure park, head to the Guest Relations lobby.

Tickets & Opening Hours
Both parks are open 365 days a year, but park hours depend on the marketing department's projected attendance numbers. During peak season (mid-June to early September) Disneyland's hours are usually 8am to midnight. The rest of the year it's open from 10am to 8pm or until 10pm. DCA closes at 10pm in summer, earlier in the off-season. Check on the current schedule at ☎ 714-781-4565 or

☎ 714-781-7290 (live assistance) or on http://disneyland.disney.go.com.

One-day admission to *either* Disneyland or DCA costs $56 for adults, $46 for children aged three to nine. To visit *both* parks in one day costs $76/66 per adult/child. Multi-Day Park Hopper Tickets cost $105/85 for two days, $139/109 for three days, $159/129 for four days, and $169/139 for five days of admission within a two-week period. Ticket prices increase annually so check the website for the latest information or to buy tickets.

Disney has a free Fastpass system, which pre-assigns specific boarding times for selected attractions, significantly cutting wait times. Look for ticket machines near the entrances to the rides. Simply show up at the time printed on the ticket and go straight to the Fastpass line instead of the regular line. There's still a wait, but it'll be much shorter. It's worth noting you can only get one Fastpass at a time.

Better yet, if you're alone, ask the attendant at the entrance to each attraction if there's a single-rider line; often you can head right to the front of the queue.

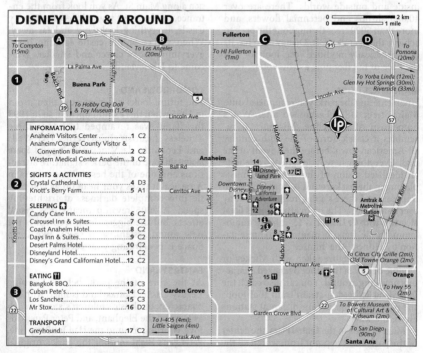

DISNEYLAND & AROUND

0 —— 2 km
0 —— 1 mile

INFORMATION
Anaheim Visitors Center 1 C2
Anaheim/Orange County Visitor &
  Convention Bureau....................2 C2
Western Medical Center Anaheim....3 C2

SIGHTS & ACTIVITIES
Crystal Cathedral...........................4 D3
Knott's Berry Farm.........................5 A1

SLEEPING
Candy Cane Inn.............................6 C2
Carousel Inn & Suites.....................7 C2
Coast Anaheim Hotel......................8 C2
Days Inn & Suites...........................9 C2
Desert Palms Hotel.......................10 C2
Disneyland Hotel..........................11 C2
Disney's Grand Californian Hotel....12 C2

EATING
Bangkok BBQ...............................13 C3
Cuban Pete's................................14 C2
Los Sanchez.................................15 C3
Mr Stox.......................................16 D2

TRANSPORT
Greyhound...................................17 C2

ORANGE COUNTY

Tourist Information

Anaheim Visitors Center (☎ 877-991-4636; www .anaheimvisitorscenter.com; 640 W Katella Ave; ☿ 8am-8pm) Inside the Jolly Roger Hotel, with information on countywide lodging, dining and transportation, as well as Internet kiosks (33¢/$20 per minute/hour). The staff will help you book lodging and will answer questions via telephone.

SIGHTS & ACTIVITIES
Disneyland Park

As you walk through the gates of **Disneyland** (☎ recorded info 714-781-4565, live assistance 714-781-7290; www.disneyland.com), a giant floral Mickey Mouse blooms before you. A sign above the nearby archway reads 'Here you leave today and enter the world of yesterday, tomorrow and fantasy' – a rather garbled notion if you stop and think about it, but a delight to the millions of children who visit every year. This is their park, but adults who willingly suspend disbelief also succumb to the 'magic of Disney.'

Notice that the park has no outside visual intrusions. You can't see out and nobody can see in. The Disneyland Railroad and the wall of foliage mark 'the berm' between the inside and outside worlds. There are over 40,000 shrubs and perennial flowers, and more than 5000 trees throughout the park to achieve the overall effect. Disney even has its own genetically modified rose; look for it at the base of the flag pole as you enter.

MAIN STREET USA

Upon entering the park, you're funneled onto Main Street USA. Fashioned after Walt's hometown of Marceline, Missouri, it resembles a classic turn-of-the-20th-century all-American town, before the advent of the mall. Everything here is designed to celebrate an idealized vision of the USA. The music playing in the background is from American musicals and there's a flag-retreat ceremony every afternoon. The main attraction is **Great Moments with Mr Lincoln**, a 15-minute audio-'animatronic' (talking mannequin) presentation by Honest Abe 'himself.'

Have your picture taken with Mickey or Minnie or any of the other oversized characters prancing around. You can also catch the **Disneyland Railroad**, a steam train that loops the park and stops at four different stations along the way.

Main St ends in the **Central Plaza**, the center of the park and the point from which all the

---

SLIPPING YOU A MICKEY

As you wander through the Disneyland Resort, try to find the 'hidden Mickeys.' Throughout the parks and in Downtown Disney, the distinctive outline of Mickey Mouse's head and ears is hidden in unexpected places. Atop flag poles, on painted signs, in filigree, at entrance gates – they're everywhere, you just have to train your eye to find them. Here's one to get you started: after you pass through the turnstiles at Disneyland, turn right and look at the fanciful woodwork in the white-washed sign atop the stroller- and wheelchair-rental station. The distinctive three circles are carved out of the wood.

'lands' extend (eg Frontierland and Tomorrowland). Lording it over the plaza is **Sleeping Beauty Castle**. Inside the iconic structure (which was fashioned after a real castle in southern Germany), dolls and big books tell the story of Sleeping Beauty.

Pay attention to the wonderful **optical illusion** along Main St. As you look from the entrance, up the street toward Sleeping Beauty Castle, everything looks big and far away. When you're at the castle looking back, everything looks closer and smaller. Welcome to Disneyland.

TOMORROWLAND

The future looks different now than it did in 1955 when this exhibit opened, so in 1998 this 'land' was revamped to honor three 'timeless' futurists: Jules Verne, HG Wells and Leonardo da Vinci. Don't miss **Space Mountain**, one of the park's signature attractions and one of the best roller coasters in America. It takes your head off as you hurtle into complete darkness at frightening speed. A 2005 revamp means new visual effects, but the biggest improvement is the new sound system, so it seems like Deep Space is penetrating your eardrums.

FANTASYLAND

At the core of the park, behind Sleeping Beauty Castle, Fantasyland is filled with the characters of classic children's stories, such as Dumbo the Elephant, and Peter Pan. Kids love whirling around the **Mad Tea Party** ride. **Peter Pan's Flight**, one of the park's original attractions, takes you floating through the air in a galleon. If you only see one attraction in Fantasyland, visit **It's a Small World**, a boat ride past hundreds of animatronic children (representing many of the world's cultures) all singing the song of the same name.

MICKEY'S TOONTOWN

At the northern end of the park, beyond Fantasyland, Mickey's Toontown is the province of the elementary-school set. This is where Mickey and Minnie make their home (separately, of course; this *is* Disneyland), Donald keeps his boat and Goofy has a Bounce House.

FRONTIERLAND

Frontierland gives a Disney nod to the Old West. This is a low-key area of the park, and even small children will emerge unshaken after a ride on the **Big Thunder Mountain Railroad** roller coaster. **Rivers of America** pays tribute to 19th-century river culture, with **Tom Sawyer's Island** in the middle of the water. Take **Tom Sawyer's Raft** to the island, where kids can play in the woods.

ADVENTURELAND

Dedicated to exploration and adventure, Adventureland is very loosely based on Southeast Asia and Africa. The hands-down highlight is the jungle-themed **Indiana Jones Adventure**. Enormous Humvee-type vehicles lurch and jerk as they re-create stunts from the famous film trilogy. (Look closely at Indie during the ride: is he real or animatronic?) Nearby, little ones love climbing the stairways of **Tarzan's Treehouse**.

NEW ORLEANS SQUARE

Adjacent to Adventureland, New Orleans Square is a refrain of that city's French Quarter, minus the marauding drunks. **Pirates of the Caribbean**, the longest ride in Disneyland (17 minutes), opened in 1967 and was the first addition to the original park. You'll float through the subterranean haunts of tawdry pirates, where buccaneers' skeletons perch atop their mounds of booty. This is the only ride in the park that addresses sex ('Buy a Bride') – blame it on the '60s. At the **Haunted Mansion**, '999 happy haunts' – spirits and goblins, shades and ghosts – evanesce while you ride in a cocoon-like car through web-covered graveyards of dancing skel-

etons. The Disneyland Railroad stops at New Orleans Square.

CRITTER COUNTRY

Tucked behind the Haunted Mansion, Critter Country is home to both Winnie the Pooh and **Splash Mountain**, a flume ride through the story of Brer Rabbit and Brer Bear, based on the controversial film *Song of the South*. Stuffed-animal characters sing and dance as you float by. Right at the big descent, a camera snaps your picture. Some visitors to the park lift their shirts, earning the ride the nickname 'Flash Mountain.'

SHOWS & PARADES

Verify all show times once you arrive in the park; also see p570 for events at DCA.

In summer look for **fireworks** above the park, nightly around 9:30pm. (During winter, snow falls after the fireworks; check schedules for locations.) The **Parade of the Stars** featuring famous Disney characters takes place twice daily during the high season.

Snow White, the musical, tells the famous story on stage, several times daily in the Fantasyland Theatre. No tickets necessary; line up 15 to 30 minutes before show time for good seats.

Fantasmic!, an outdoor extravaganza of gigantic proportions held on Rivers of America across from New Orleans Square, may be the best show of all. It pulls out all the stops, using full-size ships, lasers and pyrotechnics (at one point the water catches fire). Arrive early to scope seats – the best are down the front by the water – or splurge and reserve the oh-so-civilized balcony seating upstairs in New Orleans Square, which includes premium show seating, coffee and desserts. **Premium seating tickets** (☎ 714-781-4400; adult/child $56/46) can be reserved up to 30 days in advance. Ordinary seats are included in the price of park admission.

Disney's California Adventure

Whereas Disneyland is all about make-believe, Disney's California Adventure (DCA) is about a real place – at least the Disney version thereof. Devoted to both California's history and its natural wonders, DCA covers more acres than Disneyland and feels less crowded, especially on summer afternoons. Perhaps because DCA was built in conjunction with other major corporations, parts feel more like a shopping mall than a unified theme park, but like all things Disney, it's a work in progress.

SUNSHINE PLAZA

The entrance to DCA sits directly opposite the entrance to Disneyland and was designed to look like an old-fashioned painted-collage postcard. As you pass through the turnstiles, note the gorgeous mosaics on either side of the entrance. One represents Northern California, the other Southern California. After passing under the Golden Gate Bridge, you'll arrive at Sunshine Plaza, where a 50ft-tall sun made of gold titanium 'shines' all the time because heliostats direct the rays of the real sun onto the Disney sun. Close your eyes and stand in the plaza, and you'll hear the simulated sound of the surf as produced by the plaza's fountain, a neat trick.

HOLLYWOOD PICTURES BACKLOT

Designed to look like the backlot of a Hollywood studio, this attraction includes a mishmash of building styles, with everything from a Frank Lloyd Wright knock-off to a Pantages-style theater. If you're early, you'll have an unobstructed view of the forced-perspective mural at the end of the street, a sky-and-land backdrop that looks, at least in photographs, like the street keeps going. In the air-conditioned **Animation Building** you can put your voice into a Disney film and find out which Disney character you're most like – perfect for little ones. Across the street you can see Kermit at **Muppet Vision 3D**. The big attraction, though, is the 183ft-tall **Twilight Zone Tower of Terror**, which is essentially a drop down an elevator chute in a haunted hotel.

A BUG'S LAND

Here the attractions, designed in conjunction with Pixar Studios after its film *A Bug's Life*, attempt to see the world from the insect's point of view. Kids can splash around the 'irrigation systems' at **Bountiful Valley Farm**, but the best attraction is the 3D **It's Tough to Be a Bug**. Hilarious and oddly touching, it packs some unexpected tactile surprises. Other good rides include **Heimlich's Chew Chew Train** and the **Drive 'em Buggies** bumper cars.

GOLDEN STATE

Broken into sections that recognize California's cultural achievements, the Golden State has several distinct areas. **Condor Flats**, a nod to the state's aerospace industry, features **Soarin' Over California**, a virtual hang gliding ride using IMAX technology. Keep your nostrils open for the smell of the sea, orange groves and pine forests. **Grizzly River Run** takes you 'rafting' down a faux Sierra Nevada river; you *will* get wet so try it when it's warm. Raise a glass to the Napa Valley at the **Golden Vine Winery**. At the Palace of Fine Arts in 'San Francisco,' check out **Golden Dreams**, where an eerie embodiment of Whoopi Goldberg takes you on a 22-minute film journey through California's history.

PARADISE PIER

Paradise Pier is an amalgam of California's beachside amusement piers, like the ones in Santa Monica and Newport Beach. The **California Screamin'** roller coaster occupies 10 acres and resembles an old wooden coaster, but it's got a state-of-the-art, smooth-as-silk steel track; the beginning of the ride feels like you're being shot out of a cannon. Awesome. For more bird's-eye views of the park, head to the **Sun Wheel**, a giant Ferris wheel where each gondola pitches and yaws as it makes its grand circuit.

SHOWS & PARADES

The premier show at DCA is **Aladdin**, a 40-minute one-act musical extravaganza, based on the movie of the same name. It's in the Hyperion Theater on the Hollywood Studios Backlot. Arrive 30 to 60 minutes early to get good seats. Sit in the mezzanine for the best view of the flying carpet.

In the evening the **Electrical Parade** ends the day at DCA, with thousands of tiny colored chase lights blinking on fabulous floats.

Downtown Disney

The quarter-mile-long pedestrian mall that is Downtown Disney feels longer than it is, mostly because it's packed with stores, restaurants, entertainment venues and, in summer, hordes of people. Don't expect mom-and-pop shops with individual character here. On summer evenings, musicians perform outside.

SLEEPING

Anaheim gets most hotel business from Disneyland tourism, but the city is also a year-round convention destination, and room rates spike accordingly. Prices listed are for standard double rooms during high season. Expect discounts of up to 40% or more outside summer and holiday weekends. Many hotels and motels have family rooms that sleep up to six people, though expect to pay somewhat more for the right.

Budget
Days Inn & Suites (☎ 714-971-5000, 800-416-7583; www.daysinnanaheimresort.com; 2029 S Harbor Blvd; r $75-95; ✗ ☐ ☎) Built in 2003, this well-maintained modern motel has refrigerators and microwaves in every room, plus on-site laundry facilities. Rates include continental breakfast and you can walk to Disneyland in 20 minutes.

HI Fullerton (☎ 714-738-3721, 800-909-4776, ext 138; www.hiusa.org; 1700 N Harbor Blvd, Fullerton; dm members/nonmembers $20/23; ☀ Jun-Sep; P ✗) About 5 miles north of Disneyland, this clean and friendly summer-only facility is inside a Mediterranean home with just 20 beds in three dorms (no private rooms). Free wireless access and kitchen facilities. The office closes at 11pm but 24-hour access is available. Bus 47 runs to the hostel from the Anaheim Greyhound station; from the Amtrak station, take bus 43. To/from Disneyland also take bus 43.

Midrange
Candy Cane Inn (☎ 714-774-5284, 800-345-7057; www.candycaneinn.net; 1747 S Harbor Blvd; r $159; ✗ ☎) This oh-so-cute motel has welcoming grounds bursting with blooming flowers. Rooms have all the mod-cons, plus down comforters and plantation shutters. The hotel is adjacent to the main gate to Disneyland. Top choice.

Carousel Inn & Suites (☎ 714-758-0444, 800-854-6767; www.carouselinnandsuites.com; 1530 S Harbor Blvd; r $99, ste $129-179; ✗ ☎) Just over the berm from Disneyland, this otherwise standard four-story motel makes an effort to look good, with upgraded furniture and pots of flowers hanging from its exterior corridors' wrought-iron railings. The rooftop pool has great views of Disneyland's fireworks. Suites sleep four to eight people.

Coast Anaheim Hotel (☎ 714-750-1811, 800-663-1144; www.coasthotels.com; 1855 S Harbor Blvd; r $129; ✗ ☐ ☎) You can see the fireworks over Disneyland from some upper-floor rooms in this 13-story hotel with a hot tub and large

pool surrounded by palm trees. There's also a bar, restaurant and coffee shop. It's a 10-minute walk to the park.

Desert Palms Hotel (☎ 714-535-1133, 800-788-0466; www.desertpalmshotel.com; 631 W Katella Ave; r $135; ✗ ☐ ☎) A five-story all-suites hotel, the Desert Palms has rooms with microwaves and refrigerators. Downstairs there's a bar, restaurant, fitness center, hot tub and continental breakfast in the morning. Some rooms sleep six.

Top End
For the full Disney experience, stay right at the **resort** (☎ reservations 714-956-6425, 800-225-2024; http://disneyland.disney.go.com). One-night stays are expensive, but rates fluctuate almost daily.

Disney's Grand Californian Hotel (☎ 714-635-2300; 1600 S Disneyland Dr; r $300-350; ✗ ☐ ☎) Giant timber beams rise six stories in the cathedral-like lobby, a monument to the American Arts and Crafts movement and the top choice for lodging at Disneyland. Rooms have cushy amenities, such as triple-sheeted beds, and outside there's a redwood water slide into the pool. At night kids can wind down with bedtime stories by the lobby's giant stone hearth.

Disneyland Hotel (☎ 714-778-6600; 1150 Magic Way; r $235-270; ✗ ☐ ☎) The park's original hotel hasn't lost its sleek appeal, though its two towers feel retro-mod. Turn off the lights in your room and Tinkerbell's pixie dust glows in the dark on the walls. Geared especially toward families, the hotel has good-sized rooms, some of which sleep four or more. Outside there's a great pool – the best of the three hotels – with a 110ft waterslide.

EATING
At both Disneyland and DCA, park maps indicate restaurants and cafés where you can find healthy foods and vegetarian options; look for the red apple icon.

Disneyland Park
Besides the following sit-down options, each 'land' has several cafeteria-style options.

Blue Bayou (☎ 714-781-3463; New Orleans Sq; mains lunch $10-18, dinner $23-37) Surrounded by the 'bayou' inside Pirates of the Caribbean, this place is famous for its Monte Cristo sandwiches at lunch, and Creole and Cajun specialties at dinner. Make reservations.

ORANGE COUNTY

River Belle Terrace (☎ 714-781-3463; Frontierland; mains under $12; ☟ 10am-3pm Mon-Thu, 9am-9pm Fri-Sun) Kids love the Mickey Mouse pancakes at breakfast, served until 11:30am.

Disney's California Adventure

Besides the following options, there is a good food court at Pacific Wharf.

Trattoria at Golden Vine Winery (☎ 714-781-3463; mains $5-15; ☟ 11am-6pm) DCA's best place for a relaxing sit-down lunch serves surprisingly inexpensive and wonderfully appetizing Italian pasta, salads and gourmet sandwiches.

Vineyard Room (☎ 714-781-3463; kids' meals $6-7, 3-/4-course prix fixe $43/56; ☟ dinner Thu-Sun) DCA's white-tablecloth dining room serves contemporary Cal-Italian cuisine in three- or four-course set menus, from polenta and portobello to prosciutto and veal.

Downtown Disney

La Brea Bakery (☎ 714-490-0233; mains breakfast $7-9, lunch & dinner $8-20; ☟ breakfast, lunch & dinner) This branch of one of LA's top bakeries serves up great sandwiches and salads.

Napa Rose (☎ reservations 714-956-6755; Grand California Hotel, 1600 S Disneyland Dr, Downtown Disney; mains $24-40, 4-course prix fixe $65, with wine $100; ☟ dinner) Disney's – and one of OC's – finest restaurants occupies a soaring Craftsman-style dining room overlooking DCA's Grizzly Peak. There's a special emphasis on pairing native ingredients with native wines. Splurge on the four-course meal. Reservations strongly recommended.

Around Disneyland

Bangkok BBQ (☎ 714-534-4490; 12541 S Harbor Blvd, Garden Grove; mains lunch $5, dinner $7-10; ☟ lunch Mon-Fri, dinner daily) A bowl of soup and a rice plate at lunch costs just $5 at this strip-mall Thai joint with friendly service; dinners don't cost much more.

Los Sanchez (☎ 714-971-5883; 12151 S Harbor Blvd, Garden Grove; mains around $9; ☟ 9am-10pm Sun-Thu, 9am-11pm Fri & Sat) The cooking is fiery and delicious at this big, family-owned, order-at-the-counter Mexican joint. Try the *carne asada* (grilled, chopped beef served with rice, beans and tortillas), shrimp *rancheros* (shrimp in garlic, olive oil and wine) or seafood *tostada*. If you don't recognize the names, there's a picture of every dish on the wall. It's one block south of Chapman Ave.

Cuban Pete's (☎ 714-490-2020; 1050 W Ball Rd; mains lunch $11, dinner $11-20; ☟ lunch Thu-Sun, dinner daily) Outside it looks like a witch's castle, but inside it's all woodsy and decorated with photos of Old Havana. The Cuban and Caribbean cooking is richly spiced, but there's also a kids' menu. There's live music Thursday to Saturday nights; call ahead to confirm.

Mr Stox (☎ 714-634-2994; 1105 E Katella Ave; mains lunch $15-25, dinner $19-36; ☟ lunch Mon-Fri, dinner daily) Mr Stox serves some of Anaheim's best Cal-American cooking in a clubby atmosphere with oval booths and thick carpeting. The chef bakes five different breads daily. Wear nice shoes and make reservations.

GETTING THERE & AWAY

Air

See p565 for information on air connections. The **Airport Bus** (☎ info 714-938-8937; www.airportbus.com) runs between Disneyland-area hotels and Los Angeles International Airport (LAX) at least hourly ($19/28 one way/roundtrip). It also serves John Wayne Airport (SNA) in Santa Ana ($14/24).

Bus

Frequent departures are available with **Greyhound** (☎ 714-999-1256; 100 W Winston Rd) to/from downtown LA ($8.50, one hour) and to San Diego ($16, two to three hours).

Car

The Anaheim Resort is just off I-5 on Harbor Blvd, about 30 miles south of downtown LA. The park is roughly bordered by Ball Rd, Disneyland Dr, Harbor Blvd and Katella Ave.

Arriving at Disneyland and DCA is like arriving at an airport. Giant easy-to-read overhead signs indicate ramps to take for the theme parks, hotels or Anaheim's streets. The system is remarkably ordered.

PARKING

All-day parking costs $9, cash only. Enter the 'Mickey & Friends' parking structure from southbound Disneyland Dr at Ball Rd. (It's the largest parking structure in the world, with a capacity of 10,300 vehicles.) Take the tram to reach the parks; follow signs. The lots stay open until two hours after the parks close.

The parking lots for Downtown Disney are reserved for shoppers and have a different rate structure: the first three hours are free, with an additional two more free hours if you have a validation from a table-service restaurant or the movie theater. After that you'll pay $6 per hour, up to $30 a day. Downtown Disney also has valet parking for an additional $6, plus tip. Cash only.

Train

The depot next to Angels Stadium is where **Amtrak** (☎ 714-385-1448; 2150 E Katella Ave) trains stop. Tickets to/from LA's Union Station are $10 (45 minutes), to San Diego it's $21 (two hours).

GETTING AROUND
Bus

The bus company **Anaheim Resort Transit** (ART; ☎ 888-364-2787; www.rideart.org) provides frequent service to/from Disneyland from hotels in the immediate area, saving headaches parking and walking. An all-day pass costs $3 per day. You must buy the pass before boarding; pick one up at one of a dozen kiosks or online. Otherwise it's $3 per one-way trip.

Many hotels and motels have free shuttles to Disneyland and other area attractions.

Monorail

Take the monorail from Tomorrowland to the Disneyland Hotel, across from Downtown Disney, and save about 20 minutes of walking time, more if you have little ones in tow. The ride is free for holders of Disneyland tickets for the day of the ticket.

AROUND DISNEYLAND

As you drive along the interchangeable boulevards that radiate out from Disneyland, the whole region looks like a giant strip mall. Fair enough, but if you know where to look, you can find some interesting oases of humanity made all the more intriguing by the suburban desert that surrounds them. Besides Knott's Berry Farm – a mellower version of Disneyland – there's plenty to please hunters of kitsch, from charming Old Towne Orange to the aggressively futuristic Crystal Cathedral of televangelist Robert Schuller.

KNOTT'S BERRY FARM

Though Disneyland gets all the accolades, **Knott's** (☎ 714-220-5200; www.knotts.com; 8039 Beach

---

DETOUR: RICHARD NIXON LIBRARY

Ever wonder just who Richard Nixon really was? You may not find the answer, but you'll certainly gain new insight into the man at the **Richard Nixon Presidential Library & Birthplace** (☎ 714-993-5075; www .nixonlibrary.org; 18001 Yorba Linda Blvd, Yorba Linda; adult/child 7-11/student/senior $8/3/5/6; ☼ 10am-5pm Mon-Sat, 11am-5pm Sun), which displays everything from the dress that Pat wore at the 1973 inaugural to the pistol given to Nixon by Elvis Presley. You can watch a film called *Never Give Up: Richard Nixon in the Arena*, listen to carefully edited White House tapes from the Watergate era, and view the telephone used to communicate with Apollo 11 astronauts while they were on the moon. There's also a 70ft-long doll-house-like replica of the Nixon White House, as well as a re-creation of the Lincoln Sitting Room, Nixon's favorite room in the house. The library is located in Yorba Linda, in northeastern Orange County. To get there, exit east on Yorba Linda Blvd from Hwy 57 and continue straight to the library.

Blvd, Buena Park; adult/child 3-11 $45/15) was the first theme park in America. Just 4 miles northwest of Anaheim off the I-5, Knott's is smaller and less frenetic than the Disneyland parks, but it's lots of fun, especially for families with pre-teen children. The park opened in 1932, when Mr Knott's boysenberries (a blackberry-raspberry hybrid) and Mrs Knott's fried-chicken dinners attracted crowds of local farmhands. Mr Knott, a rabid anti-communist, built an imitation ghost town to keep his wife's guests entertained. Eventually they hired local carnival rides and charged admission – bread, circuses and capitalism all rolled into one.

These days, it's the thrill rides that draw most people to Knott's. The newest of the bunch is **Xcelerator**, a '50s themed roller coaster that blasts you from 0mph to 82mph in only 2.3 seconds. The teeth-chattering **GhostRider** is one of the best wooden roller coasters in California. It hurtles along a neck-breaking 4530ft track, at one point plunging 108ft with a G-force of 3.14. Expect long lines. The **Perilous Plunge** is the tallest water ride in the world. It catapults up 127ft, then drops down a 115ft-long water chute at an insane 75-degree angle. You *will* get soaked. **Supreme Scream** drops 25 stories at 50mph with a G-force of four, bouncing back upward with a G-force of -1.5, all in about 45 seconds.

In October Knott's hosts what is regarded as SoCal's best and scariest Halloween party. Professional costumed performers haunt the park, special rides and attractions go up for the occasion, and park lights are dimmed or turned off entirely.

HOBBY CITY DOLL & TOY MUSEUM

A bit of Americana kitsch 2 miles south of Knott's, Hobby City is a cluster of 20 specialty art and craft shops, including a Native American store in a log cabin and shops that sell stuffed bears, model trains and model cars; there's even one that sells reptiles. The **Doll & Toy Museum** (☎ 714-527-2323; 1238 S Beach Blvd; adult/child $2/1; ☻ 10am-5pm), housed in a half-scale model of the White House, offers the best entertainment value here. Along with every type of Barbie doll ever made, the museum has Russian dolls from the 1800s. Its toy replicas of TV, movie and sports personalities, rock stars and presidents present an interesting survey of pop culture in the US over the last 60 years.

BOWERS MUSEUM OF CULTURAL ART & KIDSEUM

In a gracious 1932 Mission-style complex in Santa Ana, this exquisite **museum** (☎ 714-567-3600; www.bowers.org; 2002 N Main St; permanent collection $5, major shows adult/student/senior $19/14/14; ☻ 10am-4pm Tue-Sun) has a rich permanent collection of pre-Columbian, African, Oceanic and Native American art, but gets its biggest crowds with its tantalizing and high-quality special exhibits (which require separate tickets; call ahead for prices).

The Bowers has a great indoor-outdoor restaurant called **Tangata** (☎ 714-550-0906; mains $8-17; ☻ lunch Tue-Sun). It features a Mediterranean menu masterminded by LA star chef Joachim Splichal.

The **Kidseum** (☎ 714-480-1520; www.bowers.org /kidseum/kidseum.asp; 1802 N Main St; admission $5; ☻ 12-4pm Sat & Sun), one block south, keeps youngsters entertained with 11,000 sq ft of hands-on exhibits on world cultures. The museum is also open weekdays in summer – call ahead for details.

CRYSTAL CATHEDRAL

You needn't agree with televangelist Robert Schuller's teachings or be an 'Hour of Power' fan to appreciate the architecture of the **Crystal Cathedral** (☎ 714-971-4000; www.crystalcathedral.org; 12141 Lewis St), in Garden Grove, about 2 miles southeast of Disneyland. A cross between an office complex and a science-fiction movie set, the cathedral is built in the shape of a four-pointed star and boasts 10,661 windows, seating for 3000 and a 16,000-pipe organ.

Designed by Cleveland-born Philip Johnson, international-style architect turned postmodernist, the church anchors a vast campus of gardens, reflecting pools, fountains and sculpture. Explore on your own or take a free 30-minute tour (offered regularly from 9am to 3:30pm Monday to Saturday).

ORANGE
Population 138,000

The historic center of the city of Orange, about 6 miles southeast of Disneyland, offers a lovely break from inland OC's strip malls and cookie-cutter homes. Known as Old Towne Orange, it was originally laid out by Alfred Chapman and Andrew Glassell who, in 1869, received the 1 sq mi piece of real estate in lieu of legal fees. Built around a pretty plaza at the intersection of Chapman Ave and Glassell Sts, it's the best and most concentrated collection of antiques, collectibles and consignment shops in Orange County. Unfortunately, some dealers may try to pass off replicas as antiques: *caveat emptor*.

Citrus City Grille (☎ 714-639-9600; 122 N Glassell St; mains lunch $10-15, dinner $15-30; ☻ lunch & dinner Mon-Sat) is pricey and noisy, but the food's terrific at this Cal-American grill. It specializes in comfort food, from pot roast with Burgundy-wine sauce to ravioli with gorgonzola alfredo.

For entertainment, try **Lucky Strike Lanes** (☎ 714-937-5263; Block at Orange, 20 City Blvd West; game/shoe rental $7/4; ☻ 11am-2am), a stylin' bowling alley and pool hall decked out incongruously – yet so very SoCal – with low-slung Naugahyde sofas, Chinese lanterns and halogen-spot lighting. On weekends call to reserve a table or lane.

LITTLE SAIGON

The city of Westminster, southwest of Anaheim near the junction of I-405 and Hwy 22, is home to a large Vietnamese popula-

---

DETOUR: GLEN IVY HOT SPRINGS

Soak away your troubles at this lovely **day spa** (☎ 888-258-2683; www.glenivy.com; 25000 Glen Ivy Rd; admission Mon-Thu $35, Fri-Sun & holidays $48; ⊙ 9:30am-6pm Apr-Oct, 9:30am-5pm Nov-Mar). Nicknamed 'Club Mud,' it has 15 pools and spas filled with naturally heated mineral water, surrounded by 5 acres of landscaped grounds profuse with bougainvillea, eucalyptus and palm trees. You can wallow in the water, lounge in the saunas or steam rooms, take an aqua aerobics class, treat yourself to a massage (for an extra fee) or swim some laps in a larger swimming pool.

The best thing, though, is the red-clay mud pool. Like a prehistoric animal wandering into the tar pits, you first soak yourself in muck. Then, apply what amounts to a full-body mask by grabbing chunks of clay and smearing them all over your body before lounging in the sun until it's baked on to your skin. Minimum age for entry is 16.

The spa is in Corona, technically just east of Orange County in Riverside County. To get there, exit I-15 at Temescal Canyon Rd, turn right and drive 1 mile to Glen Ivy Rd, then right again and go straight to the end.

---

tion, which has carved out its own vibrant commercial district around the intersection of Bolsa and Brookhurst Aves. At its heart is the **Asian Garden Mall** (☎ 714-842-8018; 9200 Bolsa Ave), a behemoth of a structure packed with 300 ethnic boutiques, including herbalists and jade jewelers.

One of the best of the many casual eateries here is **Pho 79** (☎ 714-893-1883; dishes $4-15), on the lower level toward the mall's north entrance. It has a great variety of noodle and vegetable dishes and the *pho ga* (chicken noodle soup) is superb, especially on a cold day.

Across the street, the **New Saigon Mall Cultural Court** marries commercialism and spirituality with its impressive display of statues and murals.

ORANGE COUNTY BEACHES

The OC coast consists of a string of beaches that start off just fine but grow increasingly inviting as you move south toward Laguna Beach. Average incomes are directly proportional to the beach's aesthetics; by the time you reach Newport Beach (by car of course, only suckers take public transportation) you may find yourself surrounded by Mercedes convertibles and Cadillac SUVs. You can feel the conservative crackle in the open-air malls, though in Laguna Beach a thriving arts scene as well as the county's most visible gay and lesbian community temper the right-wing tendencies. Surfers

rule the sands as well as the waves, especially at Huntington Beach, North America's unofficial surfing capital.

In summer, accommodations book up far in advance, prices rise and some properties impose minimum two- or three-night stays.

SEAL BEACH
pop 24,100

Refreshingly noncorporatized, Seal Beach has a great beach and an inviting downtown area. The town stretches along a few blocks of Main St, between Ocean Ave, which skirts the beach, and Pacific Coast Hwy. Along Main, you'll find restaurants and some interesting mom-and-pop antique and consignment clothing stores. Like most SoCal towns, Seal Beach has a split personality: aside from being a carefree little beach community, it's also home to a huge US naval weapons station and to Leisure World, one of SoCal's first, and most exclusive, retirement communities.

Main St spills into **Seal Beach Pier**, which extends 1885ft out over the ocean. The beach faces south here and, except for the off-shore oil rigs (which locals seem to easily tune out), it's very pleasant. The mild surf makes it a great place to ride your first long board.

There are no budget options in town (head to Huntington Beach instead). However, the **Seal Beach Inn & Gardens** (☎ 562-493-2416, 800-443-3292; www.sealbeachinn.com; 212 5th St; r $140-180; ⚿), built in 1924, features mature landscaping and cozy, antique-filled rooms ranged around a central courtyard. There's chess in the library, tea in the parlor and a pool in the small backyard – all one block from the beach.

Walt's Wharf (☎ 562-598-4433; 201 Main St; mains lunch $8-15, dinner $12-25) is everybody's favorite for fresh fish – some people even come from LA. Walt's gets packed on weekends, and you can't make reservations, but it's worth the long wait for the oak fire–grilled seafood and steaks, served with delicious sauces. There's a huge selection of wines by the glass, and if you can't wait for a table, eat at the bar.

HUNTINGTON BEACH
pop 201,000

Welcome to 'Surf City, USA,' where according to the Jan and Dean song, there are 'two girls for every boy.' These days the ratio is more like one-to-one, and the town has developed into a string of graceless tract homes – until you reach the beach, that is, which remains the unofficial headquarters of California surfing. Buyers for major retailers come here to see what surfers are wearing, then market the look for mass consumption. In fact, the town owes its very existence to a potent combination of surfing and salesmanship. In order to attract homebuyers, mega-developer Henry Huntington imported Hawaiian-Irish surfing star George Freeth to give surfing demonstrations in 1907, an event considered the birth of the mainland surf scene.

Huntington Beach Convention and Visitors Bureau (☎ 714-969-3492; www.surfcityusa.com; 301 Main St, Suite 208; ◯ 9am-5pm Mon-Fri) provides tourists maps and other information.

Sights & Activities
SURFING

Note that surfing in Huntington Beach (HB) is competitive. Control your long board or draw ire from locals, who pride themselves on being aggro (surfspeak for aggressive). For lessons (and a bodyguard), check out **M&M Surfing School** (☎ 714-846-7873; www.mmsurfingschool.com), which offers five-day surf intensives for about $225; it also gives single-day instruction for $60 to $80. **HB Wahine** (☎ 714-596-2696; www.hbwahine.com) is a great women-only surf school and costs $40 per hour for private lessons and up to $250 for a five-day course.

INTERNATIONAL SURFING MUSEUM

Back from the sands, this **museum** (☎ 714-960-3483; www.surfingmuseum.org; 411 Olive St; adult/discount

$2/1; ◯ noon-5pm summer, Wed-Sun rest of the year), off Main St, is a mecca for surf-culture enthusiasts. Exhibits chronicle the sport's history with photos, early surfboards, surf wear, and surf music recordings by the Beach Boys, Jan and Dean, and the Ventures. There's also an interesting display about the women of surf.

BOLSA CHICA STATE ECOLOGICAL RESERVE

As you head north toward Seal Beach, Pacific Coast Hwy looks out onto **Bolsa Chica State Ecological Reserve** (☎ 714-840-1575; www.amigosdebolsachica.org), which looks rather desolate (especially with the few small oil wells scattered about), but actually teems with bird life. Terns, mergansers, pelicans, pintails, grebes and endangered Belding's savannah sparrows congregate among the pickleweed and cordgrass in a restored salt marsh. A 1.5-mile loop trail starts from the parking lot on Pacific Coast Hwy.

Sleeping

Colonial Inn Hostel (☎ 714-536-3315; www.huntingtonbeachhostel.com; 421 8th St; dm per night/week $21/130, d $50; ☐) In a 1906 home three blocks from the beach, the area's only hostel is a peach of a place. Dorms sleep three to eight people, and communal areas include a nice kitchen, a living room and a backyard. There's also a laundry and free surfboard and bike rentals.

Sun'n'Sands Motel (☎ 714-536-2543; www.sunnsands.com; 1102 PCH; r $149-189; ☐) Rates spike absurdly high in summer for this nothing-special, mom-and-pop motel, but its location across from the beach lets them get away with it.

Hotel Huntington Beach (☎ 714-891-0123, 877-891-0123; www.hotelhb.com; 7667 Center Ave; r $109-139; ☒ ☒ ☐ ☒) This eight-story hotel, which looks like an office building, is decidedly sans personality, but the clean rooms are perfect for get-up-and-go travelers and the hot tub is a perk.

Hyatt Regency Huntington Beach (☎ 714-698-1234, 800-633-7313; www.huntingtonbeach.hyatt.com; 21500 Pacific Coast Hwy; r $265-305; ☒ ☐ ☒) It looks like an ersatz Spanish-style condo complex on steroids, but the deluxe rooms are inviting and impeccably maintained; there's also a good spa.

Eating

Wahoo (☎ 714-536-2050; 120 Main St; mains under $10) The fish comes flame-broiled or spicy-blackened at HB's favorite for cheap eats.

BEHIND THE ORANGE CURTAIN

In 1946, Orange County sent native son Richard Nixon to Congress, where he raised red-baiting to a fine art. By the early 1960s, OC high school students were being excused from classes to attend the so-called Southern California School of Anti-Communism. When B-movie actor Ronald Reagan ran successfully for governor in 1966, the county provided key support, as they did in 1980, when he was elected president. And today, when right-wing politicians need to fill their coffers, they head straight to OC.

Indeed, the county has invented its own special brand of conservatism – a sometimes uneasy amalgam of Christian fundamentalism, antigovernment libertarianism and immigrant bashing. Historians have come up with a number of theories to explain this rightward tilt. Since the early 20th century, its beach towns have attracted the affluent, who have a natural stake in the status quo. During the Cold War, a number of aerospace and other military suppliers relocated to OC. Since most people vote with their pocketbooks, residents naturally preferred Republicans, which in turn reinforced the conservative zeitgeist. Historians also point to 'white flight' – conservative LA residents who 'escaped' city life in the wake of the 1965 Watts race riots.

These days, Republicans hold a strong 3-2 advantage over Democrats in party affiliation, but changing demographics, in particular high rates of immigration from Mexico, are helping Democrats win seats that used to be safely Republican. The watershed came in 1996 when Democrat Loretta Sanchez ousted ultra-conservative Robert 'B-1 Bob' Dornan from his US Congressional seat. Nevertheless, the county remains a powerful voice in defining the national conservative agenda, thanks to the wealth – and ideological fervor – of its core constituency.

Order at the counter, then chow down beneath fluorescent lights.

Sugar Shack (☎ 714-536-0355; 213 Main St; mains $5-8; ☖ breakfast & lunch) Get here at 6am to watch surfer dudes don their wet suits. Breakfast served all day. Expect a wait for this HB institution.

What the Pho (☎ 714-536-4370; 300 Pacific Coast Highway; dishes $7-9; ☖ 11am-10pm Mon-Tue, Thu-Sun) It's all-you-can-eat *pho* (Vietnamese noodle soup) for just $8 at this friendly eatery. It opened in 2005 but is quickly becoming a favorite for hungry surfers. And you gotta love that name.

Duke's (☎ 714-374-6446; 317 Pacific Coast Hwy; mains $17-25; ☖ lunch Tue-Sat, dinner daily) This beachside restaurant honors Hawaiian surfing great Duke Kahanamoku with a good Hawaiian menu, but what you come for is the beachside location.

Drinking

It's easy to find a bar in HB. Walk up Main St and you'll spot them all.

Huntington Beach Beer Co (☎ 714-960-5343; 201 Main St, 2nd fl) This cavernous brew pub specializes in ales and has eight giant, stainless-steel kettles brewing it all the time. There's also good pub grub and on most weekend nights there are DJs or live music.

Bulldog Hookah and Havana Corner Smoke Lounge (☎ 714-267-4569; 417 Main St; ☖ 2-11:30pm Sun-Thu, 1pm-1am Fri & Sat) Finally a place for smokers. HB's mellowest crowd lazes on sofas, puffing on cigars and toking on hookahs while watching *The Simpsons* and playing chess. You must be 18 to enter.

NEWPORT BEACH
pop 83,000

Newport Beach has two things going for it: a superb stretch of coast and lots and lots of money. Its citizens, uniformly fresh-faced and sun-kissed, are the last word in resort wear. You'll be hard-pressed to find even one brooding, pimply-faced smoker in a too-large sweater. And if you're seen walking along one of the access roads, don't be surprised if a passing SUV recommends that you 'Get a car, loser!'

Why have all these rich people chosen to live here? Because, despite all the glitzy development, the local environment is particularly lovely. The city surrounds a pretty natural harbor that doubles as one of the largest pleasure craft harbors in the US. Balboa Peninsula, which faces the harbor on one side and the open ocean on the other, is less ritzy than the rest of the city, but its wide beaches are terrific.

Newport Beach Conference and Visitors Bureau (☎ 800-942-6278; www.newportbeach-cvb.com, 110 Newport Center Dr, Suite 120; ☼ 8am-5pm Mon-Fri) provides maps, brochures and other tourist information at its main office near Fashion Island.

Sights

BALBOA PENINSULA
Six miles long and a quarter of a mile wide, the Balboa Peninsula has a white-sand beach on its ocean side and a number of stylish homes, including the 1926 **Lovell House** (1242 W Ocean Front). Designed by seminal modernist architect, Rudolph Schindler, it was built using site-cast concrete frames with wood. Hotels, restaurants and bars cluster around the peninsula's two piers: **Newport Pier**, near

its western end, and **Balboa Pier** at the eastern end. The oceanfront strip teems with beach-goers, and the people-ogling is great.

Opposite the Balboa Pier on the harbor side of the peninsula, the **Balboa Fun Zone** (☎ 949-673-0408; www.thebalboafunzone.com; 603 E Bay Ave; ☼ 11am-8pm Sun-Thu, 11am-10pm Fri & Sat) has been around since 1936. There's a small Ferris wheel, arcade games, touristy shops and restaurants, as well as the landmark 1905 **Balboa Pavilion**, which is beautifully illuminated at night. Look for stands selling the local delicacy: frozen bananas dipped in chocolate and rolled in nuts.

At the very tip of the peninsula, by the West Jetty, the **Wedge** is a bodysurfing and knee-boarding spot famous for its perfectly

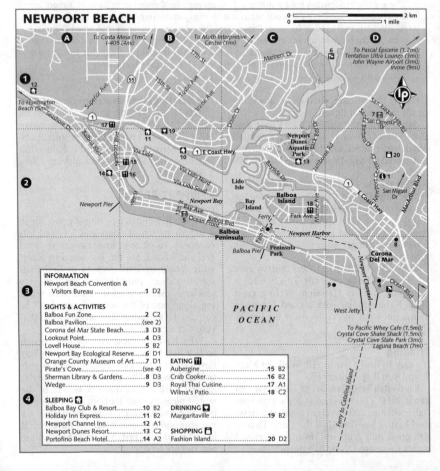

NEWPORT BEACH

INFORMATION
Newport Beach Convention &
  Visitors Bureau 1 D2

SIGHTS & ACTIVITIES
Balboa Fun Zone...........................2 C2
Balboa Pavilion............................(see 2)
Corona del Mar State Beach..........3 D3
Lookout Point...............................4 D3
Lovell House................................5 B2
Newport Bay Ecological Reserve....6 D1
Orange County Museum of Art......7 D1
Pirate's Cove...............................(see 4)
Sherman Library & Gardens...........8 D3
Wedge..9 D3

SLEEPING
Balboa Bay Club & Resort............10 B2
Holiday Inn Express......................11 B2
Newport Channel Inn....................12 A1
Newport Dunes Resort..................13 C2
Portofino Beach Hotel..................14 A2

EATING
Aubergine.....................................15 B2
Crab Cooker.................................16 B2
Royal Thai Cuisine........................17 A1
Wilma's Patio...............................18 C2

DRINKING
Margaritaville...............................19 B2

SHOPPING
Fashion Island.............................20 D2

hollow waves that can get up to 30ft high. Beware: the waves are shore-breakers.

BALBOA ISLAND
In the middle of the harbor sits the island that time forgot. Its streets are still largely lined with tightly clustered cottages built in the 1920s and '30s when this was a summer getaway from LA. That said, from the promenade that circles the island (and makes a terrific car-free stroll or jog), you can see right into the marble-and-glass monsters that have gone up along the waterfront. The whole place is like a rich, conservative, Midwestern suburb, but with much better weather. The island is connected to the Fun Zone via a tiny car and passenger **ferry** (car & driver $1.50, per person $0.60; ☺ 5:30am-2:30am). It lands at Agate Ave, about 11 blocks west of Marine Ave, the main drag lined with cutesy stores and restaurants.

ORANGE COUNTY MUSEUM OF ART
Near Fashion Island, this **museum** (☎ 949-759-1122; www.ocma.net; 850 San Clemente Dr; adult/child under 12/student $10/free/8; ☺ 11am-5pm Tue-Sun, 11am-8pm Thu) provides a survey of California art as well as remarkably cutting-edge contemporary exhibits.

CORONA DEL MAR
A ritzy bedroom community favored by the skirt-and-sweater crowd, Corona del Mar occupies the privileged eastern flank of the Newport Channel. It includes a high-end stretch of Pacific Coast Hwy, with trendy shops and restaurants, as well as **Corona del Mar State Beach** (☎ 949-644-3151; ☺ 5am-10pm), which lies at the foot of rocky cliffs.

Lookout Point sits above the beach along Ocean Blvd. Locals throw sunset cocktail parties here, though be discreet with your chardonnay: technically open containers are illegal. Stairs lead to **Pirate's Cove**, which has a great, waveless beach. Scenes from *Gilligan's Island* were shot here.

Corona del Mar's prize attraction is the **Sherman Library & Gardens** (☎ 949-673-2261; www.slgardens.org; 2647 E Coast Hwy; adult/child $3/1, Mon admission free; ☺ gardens 10:30am-4pm, library 9am-4:30pm Tue-Thu). The gardens are manicured and lush, with profuse orchids, a koi pond and a garden for the visually impaired. The small research library holds a wealth of California historical documents, as well as

paintings by early California landscape artists.

CRYSTAL COVE STATE PARK
The 3.5 miles of open beach and 2000 acres of undeveloped woodland at this state **beach** (☎ 949-494-3539; www.parks.ca.gov; Pacific Coast Highway) let you forget you're in a crowded metropolitan area, at least once you get past the parking lots and stake out a place on the sand. Everyone thought the hilltops were part of the state park until the Irvine Company, the actual landowner, bulldozed them to make room for McMansions that are the dream of many an OC resident. For a more discreet, short-term stay reserve one of the park's inland campsites with **Reserve America** (☎ 800-444-7275; www.reserveamerica.com; sites $15).

NEWPORT BAY ECOLOGICAL RESERVE
Inland from the harbor, where run-off from the San Bernardino Mountains meets the sea, the brackish water of the Newport Bay Ecological Reserve supports more than 200 species of birds. This is one of the few estuaries in Southern California that has been preserved, and it's an important stopover on the Pacific Flyway (see the boxed text, p287). The **Muth Interpretive Center** (☎ 949-923-2290; 2301 University Dr), near Irvine Ave, has displays and information about the 752-acre reserve; call for hours. For guided tours with naturalists (including kayak and canoe tours), contact the **Newport Bay Naturalists & Friends** (☎ 949-640-6746; www.newportbay.org).

Sleeping
Rates drop by as much as 40% or more in winter. Rates listed are for high season.

Newport Channel Inn (☎ 949-642-3030, 800-255-8614; www.newportchannelinn.com; 6030 W Coast Hwy; r $109-139; ⊠) Right on the busy highway but just one block from the beach, this spotless motel has large rooms that sleep two to seven people. Great service, friendly owners.

Holiday Inn Express (☎ 949-722-2999, 800-633-3199; www.ichotelsgroup.com; 2300 W Coast Hwy; r $128-170; ⌨ ⌨) Brand new in 2004, its spotless rooms have up-to-date furnishings and extras such as microwaves and refrigerators. For a midrange chain property, it's great.

Newport Dunes Resort (☎ 949-729-3863, 800-765-7661; www.newportdunes.com; 1131 Back Bay Dr; cottages $125-295; ⌨ ⌨) Welcome to RV heaven. Besides hookups, this place has a pool, spa, game rooms and a small beach on one of Newport's brackish lagoons. For those without a Winnebago, the cottages are a good deal, especially off-season.

Portofino Beach Hotel (☎ 949-673-7030, 800-571-8749; www.portofinobeachhotel.com; 2306 W Oceanfront; r $180-350; ⏅) You can't beat the location of this small, old-fashioned beachside hotel decorated with cabbage-rose wallpaper. Rooms, all with marble baths, are smallish. Some have ocean views, but the quietest ones are at the back.

Balboa Bay Club & Resort (☎ 949-645-5000, 888-445-7153; www.balboabayclub.com; 1221 W Coast Hwy; r $295-450; ⏅ 🖳 🏊) Humphrey Bogart courted Lauren Bacall at this harborside luxury resort, back when it was still a private yacht club. Now there's a new hotel attached to the historic building, and its discreet architecture complements the craftsmanship of the yachts moored outside. Rooms have topflight amenities; book one on the waterside.

Eating

Wilma's Patio (☎ 949-675-5542; 203 Marine Ave; burgers $8-12, mains $9-25; ⏅ breakfast, lunch & dinner) Wilma's is a family-style institution on Balboa Island serving high-quality diner food in one of the island's original 1920s cottages.

Pascal Épicerie (☎ 949-261-9041; 1000 Bristol North; sandwiches $6-8; ⏅ 7am-7pm Mon-Sat, 8am-4pm Sun) This is not SoCal fusion, it's a classic French

market. Great to-go sandwiches and salads at very reasonable prices.

Pacific Whey Cafe (☎ 949-715-2200; 97961 Pacific Coast Hwy; dishes $8-12; ⏅ breakfast & lunch) Lauded as Newport's best bakery, this place has pricey but excellent baked goods as well as breakfast platters and Provençale-inspired salads and sandwiches.

Crystal Cove Shake Shack (☎ 949-497-9666; 7703 E Coast Hwy) Stop for a date shake on your way to the park. They're dee-lish.

Crab Cooker (☎ 949-673-0100; 2200 Newport Blvd; mains lunch $9-20, dinner $12-26) Expect a wait at this always-busy fish joint, which serves great seafood and fresh crab on paper plates to an always-appreciative crowd in flipflops and jeans. Good chowder, too.

Royal Thai Cuisine (☎ 949-645-8424; 4001 West Coast Hwy; mains $9-19) Gracious service, a smart dining room and consistently delicious cooking distinguish this as the top Thai eatery in Newport. There's a good $9 lunch special.

Aubergine (☎ 949-723-4150; 508 29th St; mains $36-42, 9-course prix-fixe menu $115; ⏅ dinner Tue-Sun) Regularly rated OC's best, the French-inspired menu changes daily to accommodate the freshest ingredients. There's also a stunning selection of wine and cheese.

Drinking

Tentation Ultra Lounge (☎ 949-660-1010; www.ten restaurantgroup.com/tentation; 4647 Macarthur Blvd; admis-

---

DETOUR: COSTA MESA

Despite the name, Costa Mesa has no coastline to speak of, but does it ever have shopping. **South Coast Plaza** (☎ 800-782-8888; www.southcoastplaza.com; 3333 Bristol St) defines the OC shopping scene (exit I-405 at Bristol). But don't call it a mall, please – it's a 'shopping resort.' Disagreements over nomenclature aside, one thing's for sure: South Coast Plaza grosses more than any other shopping center in the USA. Boutiques by the likes of Chanel and Ralph Lauren do their part to keep the numbers high. Bigger stores include Saks Fifth Avenue, Nordstrom, Macy's, Crate & Barrel and even lowly Sears.

If this is too much mall – er, shopping resort – for you, consider a visit to the **Lab** (www.thelab .com; 2930 Bristol St). Conceived in 1993 and charged with the unlikely task of bringing 'urban culture' to unapologetically suburban OC, the so-called anti-mall occupies a refurbished factory filled with 'alternative,' youth-oriented stores. But whaddya know? OC alternative culture also manifests itself in chains – Na Na, Urban Outfitters etc. Still, the sleek design and pastel-free crowd is a refreshing departure from the county's other blonder-than-thou malls.

And as if shopping weren't enough, Costa Mesa also has culture. In fact, it's become the arts center of Orange County, thanks to the **Orange County Performing Arts Center** (☎ 714-556-2787; www.ocpac.org; 600 Town Center Dr), which draws international performing-arts luminaries and professional Broadway roadshows. Check the calendar before you head to Southern California, and you might get to see the likes of the American Ballet Theater or Dianne Reeves. It is also home to the widely acclaimed **South Coast Repertory** (☎ 714-708-5555; www.scr.org).

sion $20; ☾ 8pm-2am Thu-Sat) Newport's current hotspot aims to please with multistory waterfalls, onyx bar, chill alcoves and cigar patio. But what makes this place oh-so OC is the pride with which members of both sexes proudly show off their gym-sculpted bodies.

Margaritaville (☎ 949-631-8220; 2332 W Coast Hwy; ☾ 11:30am-1:30am) This good-times standby serves up killer margaritas ($4), good Mexican grub (mains around $10), and live music every night of the week.

Shopping
There is a string of tiny boutiques along Pacific Coast Hwy in Corona del Mar. On Balboa Island, Marine Ave is lined with unassuming (but not cheap) shops in a village-like atmosphere.

However, **Fashion Island** (☎ 949-721-2000; 550 Newport Center Dr; ☾ 10am-9pm Mon-Fri, 11am-7pm Sat, 11am-6pm Sun) – sometimes referred to as 'Fascist Island' – is the draw for serious shopping. It's an indoor-outdoor mall with more than 200 midrange to upper-end retail stores, among them Bloomingdale's, Neiman Marcus, Macy's Women and Robinsons-May. And it's got a good food court.

Getting Around
OCTA bus 71 stops at the corner of Pacific Coast Hwy and Hwy 55 and goes south to the end of the Balboa Peninsula. Bus 57 goes north to South Coast Plaza in Costa Mesa.

LAGUNA BEACH
pop 25,000
Which do you prefer, art or nature? In Laguna Beach, you don't have to choose. Locals liken their town to the French Riviera, which is a fair comparison, what with the wooded hillsides, seaside cliffs, pristine beaches and azure waves. This is, hands down, the most beautiful stretch of coast south of Los Angeles.

The town's natural beauty was like a siren call for San Francisco artist Norman St Clair, who discovered Laguna around 1910 and stayed on to paint its surf, cliffs and hills. His enthusiasm attracted other artists influenced by French impressionism who came to be known as the 'plein air' ('open air') school. By the late '20s, more than half of the town's 300 residents were artists.

Real-estate prices make such hopeful ratios impossible these days. Still, public art

graces the streets and parks, dozens of galleries feature local artists and the city hosts several renowned festivals (see p583).

Partly tucked into canyons and partly arrayed on oceanfront bluffs, Laguna is also a refreshing change from OC's beige-box architecture, with a combination of classic Craftsman cabins and bold (if at times garish) modern homes. There's even a distinct downtown, known as the 'Village,' with shops, art galleries and restaurants, many hidden in courtyards and housed in funky little shacks. Forest Ave has the highest concentration of chic boutiques.

While Laguna swells with tourists on summer weekends, there's plenty of uncrowded sand, even on the busiest days, once you move away from downtown and the adjacent Main Beach.

Orientation & Information
Laguna stretches for about 7 miles along Pacific Coast Hwy. Shops, restaurants and bars are concentrated along a 0.25-mile stretch in the Village, along three parallel streets: Broadway, Ocean Ave and Forest Ave. The town gets packed in summer.

Note that Hwy 1 goes by several names in Laguna Beach. South of Broadway, downtown's main street, it's called South Coast Hwy; north of Broadway it's North Coast Hwy; and you'll hear locals call it Pacific Coast Hwy or simply PCH.

Laguna Beach Visitors Center (☎ 800-877-1115; www.lagunabeachinfo.org; 252 Broadway; ☾ 9am-5pm Mon-Fri) provides maps, brochures, and other information.

Sights & Activities
LAGUNA ART MUSEUM
This breezy **museum** (☎ 949-494-8971; www.lagunaartmuseum.org; 307 Cliff Dr; adult/child under 12/student $9/free/7; ☾ 11am-5pm) has changing exhibits usually featuring one or two California artists, plus a permanent collection heavy on California landscapes, vintage photographs and works by early Laguna artists. The museum also makes an effort to support new artists.

BEACHES
Laguna Beach has 30 public beaches and coves. Though many are hidden from view by multimillion-dollar homes, most beaches are accessible by stairs off Pacific Coast

Hwy; just look for the 'beach access' signs. Be prepared to pass through people's backyards to reach the sand.

Main Beach has volleyball and basketball courts, and is the best beach for swimming. Northwest of Main Beach, the area is too rocky to surf; tidepooling is best. (Tidepool etiquette: tread carefully and don't pick anything up that you find living in the rocks.)

Just northwest of Main Beach, stroll the grassy, bluff-top **Heisler Park** for sweeping views of the craggy coves and deep-blue sea. Bring your camera. Drop down below the park to **Diver's Cove**, a deep, protected inlet popular with snorkelers and, of course, divers. Northwest of town, **Crescent Bay** has

big hollow waves good for bodysurfing, but parking is difficult here; try the bluffs atop the beach.

About 1 mile south of the Village, **Victoria Beach** has volleyball courts and **La Tour**, a Rapunzel's tower-like structure from 1926. Take the stairs down Victoria Dr; there's limited parking on Pacific Coast Hwy. Nearby **Aliso Beach** has a fair amount of parking and is popular with surfers.

COURSES
If you plan to cook for yourself in Laguna, consider a class at the **Laguna Culinary Arts** (☎ 949-494-0745; www.lagunaculinaryarts.com; 550 S Coast Hwy), which has both introductory three-hour classes as well as daylong and multi-

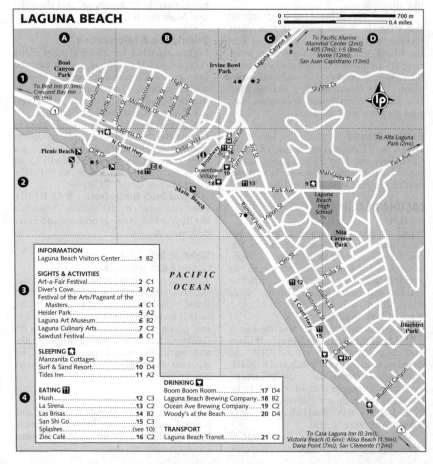

LAGUNA BEACH

0 ——— 700 m
0 ——— 0.4 miles

INFORMATION
Laguna Beach Visitors Center..........1 B2

SIGHTS & ACTIVITIES
Art-a-Fair Festival..............................2 C1
Diver's Cove.....................................3 A2
Festival of the Arts/Pageant of the
    Masters.......................................4 C1
Heisler Park.....................................5 A2
Laguna Art Museum..........................6 B2
Laguna Culinary Arts.........................7 C2
Sawdust Festival...............................8 C1

SLEEPING
Manzanita Cottages...........................9 C2
Surf & Sand Resort...........................10 D4
Tides Inn...11 A2

EATING
Hush..12 C3
La Sirena..13 C2
Las Brisas.......................................14 B2
San Shi Go......................................15 C3
Splashes....................................(see 10)
Zinc Café..16 C2

DRINKING
Boom Boom Room...........................17 D4
Laguna Beach Brewing Company...18 B2
Ocean Ave Brewing Company.......19 C2
Woody's at the Beach.....................20 D4

TRANSPORT
Laguna Beach Transit.....................21 C2

day options. Call for schedule and price information.

Sleeping

There are no budget lodgings in Laguna in summer, but it's the best place in OC for charming, non-corporate digs. Listed here are summer rates; come fall, they drop significantly. Reservations are recommended; book well in advance for stays in July and August.

Casa Laguna Inn (☎ 949-494-2996, 800-233-0449; www.casalaguna.com; 2510 S Coast Hwy; r $210-310; ☒ ☐ ☒) Laguna's B&B gem is built around a historic 1920s Mission revival house surrounded by lush, manicured, mature plantings. Rooms are inside former artists' bungalows built in the 1930s and '40s; all have delicious beds, some have Jacuzzi tubs. There's full breakfast, and evening wine and cheese. Delightful.

Manzanita Cottages (☎ 949-661-2533, 877-661-2533; www.nwo.com/thecottages; 732 Manzanita Dr; apartments $175, cottages $250; ☐) These oh-so-cute bungalows, up the hill from downtown, were designed in the 1920s by a Hollywood producer and they retain all their original romantic charm. Each has a gas fireplace and full kitchen. Lovely gardens, too. Re-

serve in advance. There's always a minimum two-night stay; in summer it's a week. Also budget for the $75 cleaning fee.

Tides Inn (☎ 949-494-2494, 888-777-2107; www.tides laguna.com; 460 N Coast Hwy; r $110-225; ☐ ☒) For Laguna, this place is a bargain, especially considering its tasteful and comfortable rooms, convenient location three blocks north of the Village and friendly service. Some rooms have kitchenettes and ocean views.

Crescent Bay Inn (☎ 949-494-2508, 888-494-2508; www.crescentbayinn.com; 1435 N Coast Hwy; r $105-145) What this vintage-'50s motel lacks in amenities it makes up for in value. Some units have kitchenettes. And several even have ocean views.

Surf & Sand Resort (☎ 949-497-4477, 800-524-8621; www.surfandsandresort.com; 1555 S Coast Hwy; r from $260; ☒ ☐ ☒) All but three of the 165 rooms at this great-for-a-splurge, sparkling seaside resort have full ocean views – you'll be lulled to sleep by the crashing of waves. Common areas are breezy and understated, while rooms feature soothing colors and ultra-comfy beds. There's also a full-service spa.

Eating

Zinc Café (☎ 949-494-6302; 350 Ocean Ave; dishes $5-8; ☼ breakfast & lunch) Locals say Zinc is the

---

LAGUNA ART FESTIVALS

Laguna Beach's landmark event is the **Festival of the Arts** (☎ 800-487-3378; www.foapom.com; 650 Laguna Canyon Rd; adult/student/senior $7/4/4; ☼ from 10am Jul & Aug), a seven-week juried exhibit of 160 artists whose work varies from paintings to handcrafted furniture to scrimshaw. Begun in 1932 by local artists who needed to drum up buyers, the festival now attracts patrons and tourists from around the world. In addition to the art, there are free daily artists' workshops, a children's art gallery and live entertainment.

The most thrilling part of the fair, a tremendous experience that will leave you rubbing your eyes in disbelief, is the **Pageant of the Masters** (☎ 800-487-3378; admission $15-300), where human models blend seamlessly into re-creations of famous paintings. It began in 1933 as a sideshow to the main festival. Tickets are hard to secure; they generally go on sale around the beginning of December of the previous year and sell out before the year is out. You may be able to snag last-minute cancellations at the gate. Nightly performances begin at 8:30pm.

In the '60s, Laguna Beach artists who didn't make the grade for the juried exhibition started their own festival to take advantage of the art seekers passing through town. They set up directly across from the festival, mocking its formal atmosphere by scattering sawdust on the ground. Thus, the so-called **Sawdust Festival** (☎ 949-494-3030; www.sawdustfestival.org; 935 Laguna Canyon Rd; adult/child/senior $7/2/5.50; ☼ 10am-10pm) was born. Ironically enough, it's juried now, but you can still find arts and crafts that are both utilitarian and affordable.

A third art happening, the **Art-A-Fair Festival** (☎ 949-494-4514; www.art-a-fair.com; 777 Laguna Canyon Rd; adult/student/senior $6/3/3; ☼ 10am-9pm Sun-Thu, 10am-10pm Fri & Sat) runs simultaneously. It's a nationally juried show focused mainly on watercolors, pastels and oil paintings, but expect to see some photography, jewelry, ceramics and other arts and crafts, too.

thing they miss most when they leave Laguna. Maybe it's the happy-making tomato-colored walls inside or the serene terrace outside. The vegetarian menu – including egg dishes, pizzas and sandwiches – places emphasis on fresh ingredients.

La Sirena (☎ 949-497-8226; 347 Mermaid St; dishes $4-10; ◷ 11am-9pm Mon-Sat) Hole-in-the-wall La Sirena shines for its bargain-basement prices and knockout contemporary Mexican specialties (think crunchy jicama and zingy salsa, not fat-laden refries with melted yellow cheese).

San Shi Go (☎ 949-494-1551; 1100 S Coast Hwy; mains $9-17; ◷ lunch Tue-Fri, dinner daily) A favorite local hangout for its clean, white decor, good sushi and killer views. It's hidden upstairs in an undistinguished mall, but worth seeking out.

Las Brisas (☎ 949-497-5434; 361 Cliff Dr; mains lunch $9-17, dinner $17-29; ◷ breakfast, lunch & dinner) Come here for one of Laguna's best views. Sip margaritas while you stare at the crashing waves from the glassed-in patio on the bluff, or book a table in the dining room. You won't long remember your Mexican-seafood meal, but the image of the coast will leave an indelible impression. Cocktail hour gets packed; make reservations.

Hush (☎ 949-497-3616; 858 S Coast Hwy; mains $26-38; ◷ dinner) Laguna's favorite for hipsters with cash to burn, and their parents. Macaroni and cheese comes with lobster and crayfish while pork chops are wrapped delightfully in sage.

Drinking & Entertainment

Splashes (☎ 949-497-4477; Surf & Sand Resort, 1555 S Coast Hwy) Perched at the bottom of a dramatic cliff right above the sand this is, hands down, the most dramatic beachside bar in the state. Come with your wallet, because prices are as breathless as the beauteous ocean views.

Woody's at the Beach (☎ 949-376-8809; 1305 S Coast Hwy) Laguna Beach has the only gay venues for miles around. Woody's offers surprisingly great food and a fun bar scene for the OC gay-on-the-go set.

Boom Boom Room (☎ 949-494-7588; 1401 S Coast Hwy; ◷ Tue-Sun) Across the street from Woody's, at the Coast Inn, this place is a dance club on Wednesday, Friday and Saturday, and charges $5 after 9pm.

For pub grub and microbrews head to **Laguna Beach Brewing Company** (☎ 949-494-2739; 422 S Coast Hwy), which has live music Thursday to Sunday, or the **Ocean Ave Brewing Company** (☎ 949-497-3381; 237 Ocean Ave; ◷ Tue-Sun).

Getting There & Around

To reach Laguna Beach from the I-405, take Hwy 133 (Laguna Canyon Rd) southwest. Laguna is served by OCTA bus 1, which runs along the coast from Long Beach to San Clemente.

Laguna is hemmed in by steep canyons, and parking is a perpetual problem. Pack quarters to feed the meters. If you're spending the night, leave your car at the hotel and ride the local bus. Parking lots in the village charge $10 or more per entry and fill up early in the day during summer. Pacific Coast Hwy through town moves slowly in summer, especially in the afternoon on weekends; allow extra time. If you can't find parking downtown, drive to the north end of town by the beach and ride the bus.

Laguna Beach Transit (☎ 949-497-0746; 300 block of Broadway) has its central bus depot on Broadway, just north of the visitors bureau in the heart of the Village. It operates three routes at hourly intervals (approximately 7am to 6pm Monday to Friday, 9am to 6pm Saturday). Routes are color-coded and easy to follow, but they're subject to change. For tourists, the most important route is the one that runs north–south along Pacific Coast Hwy. Pick up a brochure and schedule at your hotel or the visitors bureau. Rides cost 75¢. There is no Sunday service.

If you're planning a trip to Catalina Island (p556), you can pick up the ferry 8 miles south of Laguna Beach in Dana Point.

SAN JUAN CAPISTRANO

Famous around the world for the swallows that return from their winter migration on the same day every year (March 19 to be exact), the small town of San Juan Capistrano is also home to the 'jewel of the California missions.'

Located about 10 miles southeast and inland of Laguna Beach, the beautiful **Mission San Juan Capistrano** (☎ 949-234-1300; www.mission sjc.com; 31882 Camino Capistrano; adult/child/senior $6/4/5; ◷ 8:30am-5pm) was built around a series of 18th-century arcades, each of which enclose charming fountains and lush gardens that range from rose to cactus to water lilies. The charming Serra Chapel – whitewashed outside and decorated with vivid frescoes inside –

is considered the oldest building in California. It's the only chapel still standing in which Father Junípero Serra gave Mass. He founded the mission on November 1, 1776 and tended it personally for many years. The mission's gift shop has a good collection of books on early California and mission history.

To celebrate the swallows' return from their South American sojourn, the city puts on the **Festival of the Swallows** every year on March 19. The birds nest in the walls of the mission until around October 23. They're best observed at feeding time, usually early in the morning and late afternoon to early evening.

Sleeping & Eating

Mission Inn (☎ 949-234-0249, 866-234-0249; www .missioninnsjc.com; 26891 Ortega Hwy; r $165-195; ☒ ☐ ☒) is, that's right, a Mission-style motel that has been tastefully updated. Rooms are plush, the grounds are gardenlike, and it's just down the street from the mission.

Señor Pedro's (dishes $5; 31721 Camino Capistrano; ☒ 10am-8pm) is the place to go for cheap Mexican eats. It serves plentiful if uninspired grub

just across the street from the mission entrance.

El Adobe (☎ 949-493-1163; 31891 Camino Capistrano; mains lunch $12-15, dinner $14-20) is more upscale with its pretty (you guessed it) Mission-style dining rooms and bar.

Coach House (☎ 949-496-8930; www.thecoachhouse .com; 33157 Camino Capistrano), is worth a visit if you are around during the evening. Check the line-up at the a legendary live entertainment venue featuring a roster of local and regional rock and alternative bands.

Getting There & Away

From Laguna Beach, take OCTA bus 1 south to K-Mart Plaza, then connect to bus 191/A in the direction of Mission Viejo, which drops you near the mission ($2, about one hour).

The Amtrak depot is one block south and west of the mission; it would be perfectly reasonable to arrive by train from LA or San Diego in time for lunch, visit the mission and be back in the city for dinner.

Drivers should exit I-5 at Ortega Hwy and head west for about a quarter of a mile.

San Diego Area

While LA and Frisco duke it out for top-dog status, California's third city kicks back and enjoys the show from extremely agreeable digs just up from the Mexico border. With 70 miles of coastline and America's most enviable climate, San Diegans have nothing to prove; they're too busy enjoying themselves. In an age when even relaxation comes prepackaged, the beaches of San Diego are among the last places in America where you can still experience 'mellow' in its natural habitat.

If you're hungry for high culture, San Diego still can't compete with LA or San Francisco, but you may be surprised by a new crackle in the city's zeitgeist. Fueled by its cutting-edge biotech sector and a tremendous boom in real-estate values, San Diego's red-hot economy is attracting new blood – and a new sense of style – to a population long dominated by retirees and military types.

Beyond sun and sand, San Diego County has something to distract all comers: two of the world's great zoos, one of the country's largest urban parks with a whole raft of fine museums and theaters, a New Orleans–style party scene, excellent food for all budgets, and scuba diving, hiking and hang gliding. North of the city, a series of seaside communities attracts equal numbers of gnarly surfers and game retirees. Inland from San Diego, desertlike valleys, fragrant with orange blossoms in spring, give way first to pine-covered mountains and then, almost instantly, to stark but beautiful deserts.

HIGHLIGHTS

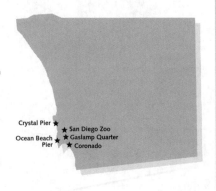

- Watching the sunset – and hearing the crowd break out in applause – at **Crystal Pier** (p607) in Pacific Beach

- Standing in the towering aviary at the **San Diego Zoo** (p599) as fearless birds of all shades flit about

- Slaloming through the pilings of **Ocean Beach Pier** (p606), or watching others do the same

- Whooping it up in the **Gaslamp Quarter** (p591), San Diego's equivalent of Bourbon Street

- Getting lost in the Victorian maze that is **Hotel del Coronado** (p603) before reaching its gorgeous beach

Crystal Pier ★

★ San Diego Zoo

Ocean Beach ★ ★ Gaslamp Quarter
Pier ★ ★ Coronado

- AVERAGE TEMPS IN SAN DIEGO: JAN 48/64°F, JUL 66/75°F

SAN DIEGO

pop 1.3 million

Some people say San Diego lacks weather, but the city's residents seem to be surviving just fine without it. In fact it's the mildness of the climate that, above all, defines the city. Though it's big (and growing fast), San Diego manages to hang on to a resort feel even amid the skyscrapers and brick facades of its revamped downtown. A huge influx of visitors helps add to the vacation atmosphere, from party-hearty undergrads to boozy conventioneers. San Diego is also a favorite for family vacations, what with kid-positive attractions like SeaWorld and the city's world-famous zoo.

San Diego has reserved plenty of outdoor space to enjoy the weather, from beaches and boardwalks to the fields and footpaths of sprawling Balboa Park. This is a place where life is lived outdoors, so it's not surprising that fitness is a religion. Sit at a café long enough, and you are bound to hear talk of 10K races, if not triathlons.

While the rest of California went into a holding pattern when the Internet bubble went bust, San Diego's economy kept quietly growing. The sustained boom has helped bring a new dynamism to a culture where tastes were once largely defined by military retirees – think khaki and plaid. San Diego won't seduce you like San Francisco or wow you like Yosemite, but life here is so unrelentingly pleasant that you might not care either way.

HISTORY

Humans have been enjoying San Diego's climate since at least 18,000 BC, if the middens (ancient refuse heaps) that litter the region are any proof. By the time Spanish explorer Juan Rodríguez Cabrillo became the first European to sail into San Diego Bay in 1542, the region was divided peaceably between the native Kumeyaay and Luiseño/Juaneño peoples. Their way of life continued undisturbed until Junípero Serra and Gaspar de Portola arrived in 1769. They founded a mission and a military fort on the hill now known as the Presidio, making

SAN DIEGO AREA

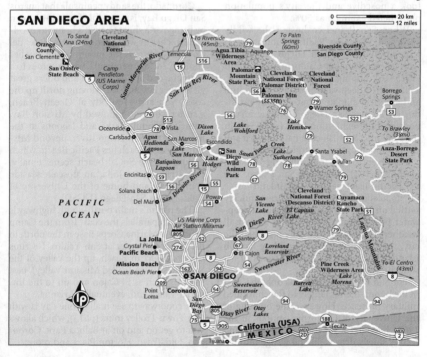

SAN DIEGO AREA

it the first permanent European settlement in California.

When the United States took California from Mexico in the 1840s, San Diego remained little more than a ramshackle village. But William Heath Davis, a San Francisco property speculator, knew there was a fortune to be made. In the 1850s, he bought 160 acres of bayfront property and erected prefabricated houses, a wharf and warehouses. 'Davis' Folly' eventually went bust, but only because he was ahead of this time. Just a decade later, another San Francisco speculator acquired 960 acres of waterfront land and promoted it as 'New Town.' This time the idea stuck, and Alonzo E Horton became a rich man.

The discovery of gold in the hills east of San Diego in 1869 certainly helped. The ensuing rush brought the railroad to San Diego in 1884, and also led to the development of a classic Wild West culture, with saloons, gambling houses and brothels hidden behind the respectable Victorian facades of the city's Gaslamp Quarter. But when the gold played out, the economy took a nosedive and the city's population plummeted as much as 50%.

When San Francisco hosted the wildly successful Panama-Pacific International Exposition (1914), San Diego responded with its own Panama-California Exposition (1915–16), hoping to attract investment to a city with a deepwater port, a railroad hub and a perfect climate – but virtually no industry. To give San Diego a unique image, boosters built exhibition halls (see p595) in the romantic, Spanish colonial style that still defines much of the city today.

However it was the bombing of Pearl Harbor in 1941 that made San Diego. The US Pacific Fleet needed a mainland home for its headquarters. The top brass quickly settled on San Diego, whose excellent deepwater port affords protection in almost all weather. The military literally reshaped the city, dredging the harbor, building landfill islands, and constructing vast tracts of instant housing.

For San Diego, the war was only the start of the boom, thanks largely to the continued military presence. However, the opening of the University of California campus in the 1960s heralded a new era as students and faculty slowly drove a liberal wedge into the city's homogenous, flag-and-family culture. The university, especially strong in the sciences, has also been a fine incubator for the biotech sector. The military still plays a major role in San Diego County, accounting for at least a fourth of its economic activity.

ORIENTATION

San Diego is user friendly, geographically speaking. The airport, train station and bus terminal are within, or very close to, the city center. Downtown consists of a compact grid of streets east of San Diego Bay and encompasses the Gaslamp Quarter, the Embarcadero and Little Italy. All are within walking distance of each other.

On a bluff north of downtown sit Balboa Park and the famous San Diego Zoo. At the northwest edge of the park lie the Uptown and Hillcrest districts, headquarters of the city's large gay and lesbian community. Keep heading northwest from Hillcrest and you arrive in Old Town, site of San Diego's original settlement. Above Old Town, Presidio Hill and park overlooks Mission Valley, now a freeway and a commercial corridor.

Coronado, the sandy peninsula that guards San Diego Bay, is accessible from downtown by bridge or a short ferry; it's home to excellent beaches as well as the famous Hotel del Coronado. Across the mouth of the bay lies another, rockier peninsula, which comes to a dramatic end at Point Loma and offers great views over city and sea. Moving north up the coast, you arrive quickly at Ocean Beach, a surfer's delight, followed by Mission Bay, with its tranquil parks and lagoons at the mouth of the San Diego River. Beyond Mission Bay and Beach lies Pacific Beach, which epitomizes the SoCal beach scene. Finally, you arrive in La Jolla, an upscale seaside community and home of the University of California at San Diego (UCSD).

The region's main north–south highway is I-5, which parallels the coast from the Camp Pendleton Marine Corps Base in the north to the Mexican border at San Ysidro. I-8 runs east from Ocean Beach, up the valley of the San Diego River (called Mission Valley), past suburbs such as El Cajon and on to the Imperial Valley and, eventually, Arizona.

A good way to see it all in one day is with Old Town Trolley tours (p613), which allows you to get on and off at Balboa Park, Coronado, Old Town, Horton Plaza and more.

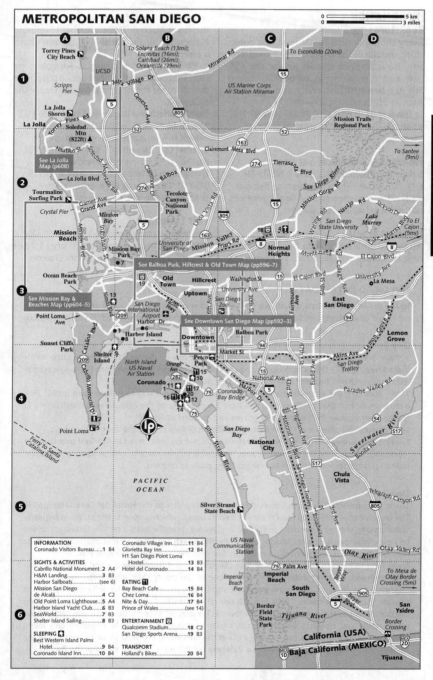

METROPOLITAN SAN DIEGO

SAN DIEGO AREA

INFORMATION
Coronado Visitors Bureau......1 B4

SIGHTS & ACTIVITIES
Cabrillo National Monument..2 A4
H&M Landing.........................3 B3
Harbor Sailboats...............(see 6)
Mission San Diego
de Alcalá.............................4 C2
Old Point Loma Lighthouse....5 A4
Harbor Island Yacht Club......6 B3
SeaWorld.............................7 B3
Shelter Island Sailing............8 B3

SLEEPING
Best Western Island Palms
Hotel..................................9 B4
Coronado Island Inn..........10 B4

Coronado Village Inn...........11 B4
Glorietta Bay Inn.................12 B4
H1 San Diego Point Loma
Hostel..............................13 B3
Hotel del Coronado.............14 B4

EATING
Bay Beach Cafe...................15 B4
Chez Loma..........................16 B4
Nite & Day..........................17 B4
Prince of Wales...............(see 14)

ENTERTAINMENT
Qualcomm Stadium.............18 C2
San Diego Sports Arena.......19 B3

TRANSPORT
Holland's Bikes....................20 B4

INFORMATION
Bookstores

Every shopping mall has at least one bookstore, usually of the large, chain-owned variety. Book hounds should peruse the old, new and rare offerings of bookstores on 5th Ave between University and Robinson Aves in Hillcrest.

Le Travel Store (Map pp592-3; ☎ 619-544-0005; 745 4th Ave) Excellent selection of maps, travel guides and accessories. Helpful staff.

Emergency & Medical Services

Scripps Mercy Hospital (Map pp596-7; ☎ 619-294-8111; 4077 5th Ave; ☯ 24hr) An urgent-care clinic operates in addition to an emergency room. For nonemergencies, call the clinic and inquire about wait times.

Internet Access

All public libraries provide free Internet access; no library card required. You can make reservations one day in advance by calling the main library. There are also 15-minute express terminals available if you don't have a reservation.

You can pay to log on at Kinko's copy stores throughout the city; check a telephone directory for the nearest location. Or try the following:

David's Coffeehouse (Map pp596-7; ☎ 619-296-4173; 3766 5th Ave, Hillcrest; ☯ 7am-11pm Sun-Thu, 7am-midnight Fri & Sat) Internet access while you sip coffee.

Internet Cafe (Map pp592-3; ☎ 619-702-2233; 800 Broadway at 8th Ave; per hr $8) Downtown.

Living Room Coffeehouse (Map pp596-7; ☎ 619-295-7911; 1417 University Ave, Hillcrest; ☯ 6am-midnight) Another coffeehouse with connections.

Left Luggage

Greyhound station (Map pp592-3; ☎ 619-239-3266; 120 W Broadway) Luggage storage costs $3 for the first three hours with a $5 maximum the first day; then $5 per day.

SAN DIEGO IN TWO DAYS

To see the best of the best in just two days, here is a reasonable itinerary. Admittedly, access to a car would dramatically simplify matters, but public transportation can work too if you plan ahead.

Day 1:

9:30am: Start off with breakfast and espresso drinks at one of the outdoor cafés on Little Italy's **India Street** (p594). Then check out the neighboring boutiques for insight into the long-overdue style makeover this flag-and-family city is finally getting.

11am: Walk past the Victorian mansions of Bankers Hill on your way to **Balboa Park** (p595). Pick a museum or two that interests you, and have lunch at one of the cafés or restaurants along El Prado. Then explore the surrounding groves and gardens at leisure.

2pm: Devote the afternoon to the **San Diego Zoo** (p599) – among the best in the world.

Evening: For dinner and – if you're up for it – a night out on town, head to the **Gaslamp Quarter** (opposite). It's touristy but the restaurants, most with terrace seating, can be good; the people-watching is great; and the partying ranges from posh to raucous.

Day 2

10am: After breakfast, head to Coronado Island, in particular to the **Hotel del Coronado** (p603). The Queen Anne–style hotel itself is a jewel, and its beach, which is open to the public, is regularly voted among the most beautiful in California. Have lunch at the hotel's terrace restaurant or the less expensive poolside grill. Sounds stuffy? **Pacific Beach** (p607) is a great alternative, with its over-the-top SoCal surf scene. Cruise Garnet Ave and the area around Crystal Pier.

3pm: Time to head to **Hillcrest** (p602), San Diego's gay and lesbian mecca and most bohemian neighborhood. Go thrift-shopping or hang in one of the comfy cafés along 5th Ave.

Sunset: A trip to San Diego must include a stroll through downtown **La Jolla** (p609), with its upscale shops and elegant, 1920s Spanish revival landmarks. Follow this up with a walk along the oceanfront as the sun starts to dip below the horizon. As evening descends you can let your wallet guide you either to one of the city's gastronomical palaces, or to cheap(er) eats along Girard Ave. Afterwards, you can join the PYTs at the bars along Prospect St, or sip martinis in the refined old-world lobby of the lovely **La Valencia** (p616), with its killer views of the Pacific.

Libraries
Main library (Map pp592-3; ☎ 619-236-5800; www
.sannet.gov/public-library; 820 E St; ☾ noon-8pm Mon
& Wed, 9:30am-5:30pm Tue & Thu-Sat, 1-5pm Sun) About
two blocks east of the Gaslamp Quarter. There are smaller
branch libraries (check the *Yellow Pages*).

Media
KPBS 89.5FM Public radio, high-quality news and
information.
San Diego Reader What's happening in town, particularly on the active music, art and theater scenes; pick up
a free copy at convenience stores and cafés. It comes out
every Thursday.
San Diego Union-Tribune The reasonably good local daily.

Money
You'll find ATMs throughout San Diego.
Travelex (Map pp592-3; ☎ 619-235-0901; 177 Horton
Plaza; ☾ 10am-6pm Mon-Fri, 10am-4pm Sat, 11am-4pm
Sun) For foreign-currency exchange.

Post
For local post office locations, call ☎ 800-
275-8777 or log on to www.usps.com.
Downtown post office (Map pp592-3; ☎ 619-232-
8612; 815 E St; ☾ 8:30am-5pm Mon-Fri)
Midway postal station (Map pp596-7; ☎ 619-758-
7101; 2535 Midway Dr, San Diego, CA 92138; ☾ 7am-11pm
Mon, 8am-11pm Tue-Fri, 8am-4pm Sat) Receives poste-
restante (general-delivery) mail.

Tourist Information
International Visitors Information Center (Map
pp592-3; ☎ 619-236-1212; 1040-1/3 W Broadway at
Harbor Dr; ☾ 9am-5pm daily Jun-Aug & Thu-Tue Sep-
May) The on-site official visitors center for the city sits
across from Broadway Pier, along the Embarcadero.
Old Town State Historic Park Visitor Center
(Map pp596-7; ☎ 619-220-5422; www.parks.ca.gov;
☾ 10am-5pm) For information about state parks in San
Diego County, head to the Robinson-Rose House at the end
of the plaza in Old Town.
San Diego Convention & Visitors Bureau
(☎ 619-236-1212; www.sandiego.org) The city's official
visitor-information source will send a complimentary
vacation-planning guide anywhere in the world. Provides
online hotel reservations and discount vacation packages.

DANGERS & ANNOYANCES
Areas of interest to visitors are quite well defined and mostly within easy reach of downtown by foot or by public transportation. San
Diego is a fairly safe city, though you should
be cautious venturing east of about 6th Ave

in downtown, especially after dark. Hostile
panhandling is the most common problem.
Also steer clear of Balboa Park after dark.

SIGHTS
Downtown
If you want to see evidence of San Diego's
booming economy, just scan the downtown
skyline. At the time of research, it was a web
of construction cranes working feverishly
to complete million-dollar McMansions in
the sky.

Just south of the city's stretch of skyscrapers lies the historic Gaslamp Quarter, which,
with its countless restaurants, nightclubs and
bars, is California's answer to New Orleans'
Bourbon Street. Closer to the bay and near
the city's mammoth convention center looms
Petco, San Diego's new, state-of-the-art baseball stadium, which has helped seal the remarkable renewal of the entire downtown.
To the west lies the Embarcadero district, a
fine place for a bayfront jog or promenade.
A short walk north lands you in Little Italy,
where mom-and-pop eateries alternate with
high-end design stores.

GASLAMP QUARTER
Founded by the San Francisco speculator
Alonzo Horton in 1867, the Gaslamp Quarter has, almost since its inception, catered
to the vices of travelers. During San Diego's
Gold Rush of the 1870s, the neighborhood
quickly degenerated into a string of saloons,
bordellos, gambling halls and opium dens.

Ironically, the quarter's very seediness
provided the roots of its recent renaissance.
In San Diego's postwar boom, the lovely
Victorian and beaux arts buildings were left
to molder while the rest of downtown was
razed and rebuilt. When developers started
to eye the area in the early 1980s, preserva-
tionists organized to save the old brick and
stone facades from the wrecking ball. The
city eventually signed on to the effort, con-
tributing trees, benches, wide brick sidewalks and replica 19th-century gas lamps.

These days, the Gaslamp Quarter is again
the focus of the city's nightlife, though of a
significantly tamer variety. Tables from upmarket restaurants spill out onto sidewalks,
ideal people-watching on warm evenings.
As the night progresses and drinks continue
to flow, sailors vie with fraternity brothers
for the attention of young ladies – and vice

DOWNTOWN SAN DIEGO

SAN DIEGO AREA

INFORMATION
Downtown Post Office..............**1** F5
International Visitors Information
  Center.............................**2** B4
Internet Cafe.......................**3** F4
Le Travel Store.....................**4** E5
Main Library........................**5** F5
Travelex............................**6** E5

SIGHTS & ACTIVITIES
Gaslamp Books & Antiques........**7** E6
Hornblower Cruises.................**8** B4
Horton Plaza........................**9** D5
Maritime Museum...................**10** A3
Museum of Contemporary Art
  Downtown..........................**11** C4
Our Lady of the Rosary Catholic
  Church.............................**12** C2
San Diego Aircraft Carrier
  Museum.............................**13** B5
San Diego Children's Museum/
  Museo de los Niños **14** D6
San Diego Chinese Historical
  Museum.............................**15** E6
San Diego Harbor Excursion....**16** B4
William Heath Davis House........**17** E6

ENTERTAINMENT 🎭
Civic Theatre......................**42** E4
Gaslamp 15.........................**43** E5
San Diego Symphony............**44** F4
SiDE Bar............................**45** E6
Times Arts Tix.....................**46** E4
UA Horton Plaza..................(see 9)

SHOPPING 🛍
KADD................................**47** B1
Seaport Village....................**48** B6

TRANSPORT
Bike Cab Co........................**49** E6
California Rent a Car............**50** B1
Ferry Landing......................**51** A4
Greyhound Station...............**52** D4
Santa Fe Depot....................**53** C4
Transit Store.......................**54** D4
West Coast Rent a Car..........**55** B1

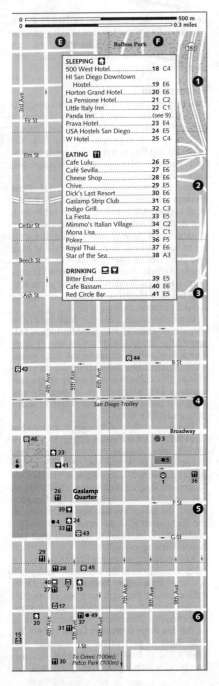

SLEEPING
500 West Hotel............................18 C4
HI San Diego Downtown
  Hostel..................................19 E6
Horton Grand Hotel..............20 E6
La Pensione Hotel...................21 C2
Little Italy Inn..........................22 C1
Panda Inn............................(see 9)
Prava Hotel..............................23 E4
USA Hostels San Diego..........24 E5
W Hotel....................................25 C4

EATING
Cafe Lulu.................................26 E5
Café Sevilla.............................27 E6
Cheese Shop...........................28 E6
Chive.......................................29 E5
Dick's Last Resort...................30 E6
Gaslamp Strip Club................31 E6
Indigo Grill..............................32 C3
La Fiesta..................................33 E5
Mimmo's Italian Village.........34 C2
Mona Lisa................................35 C1
Pokez......................................36 F5
Royal Thai...............................37 E6
Star of the Sea........................38 A3

DRINKING
Bitter End................................39 E5
Cafe Bassam...........................40 E6
Red Circle Bar.........................41 E5

SAN DIEGO AREA

versa. And the neighborhood still offers a small but potent dose of sleaze, including a scattering of adult entertainment shops and some very downmarket hotels.

William Heath Davis House (Map pp592-3; ☎ 619-233-4692; cnr Island St & 5th Ave; ☉ Mon-Fri 10am-2pm, 10am-4pm Sat, noon-4pm Sun) is one of 14 prefabricated houses that Davis, San Diego's original real estate developer, had shipped here from Maine in 1850. Today the house contains a small museum with 19th-century furnishings. At 11am each Saturday, the Gaslamp Quarter Historical Foundation offers a two-hour guided walking tour from here (adult/concession $5/3).

Gaslamp Books & Antiques (Map pp592-3; ☎ 619-237-1492; 413 Market St; admission free) doubles as a museum, displaying all manner of memorabilia that the owner has collected during his 50-plus years in San Diego. Check out the Wyatt Earp room, which pays homage to the famous Wild West figure. He ran several hooch joints in the neighborhood during San Diego's Gold Rush.

For an insight into the city's Chinese-American community, check out the **San Diego Chinese Historical Museum** (Map pp592-3; ☎ 619-338-9888; 404 3rd Ave; admission $2; ☉ 10:30am-4pm Tue-Sat, noon-4pm Sun), which is located in the heart of San Diego's former Chinatown. It occupies the attractive Chinese Mission Building, constructed in the 1920s, as well as a contemporary annexe that was completed in 2004.

HORTON PLAZA

Like brash, '80s-style postmodernism? Then you'll love this downtown **megamall** (Map pp592-3; ☎ 619-238-1596; Horton Plaza; ☉ 10am-9pm Mon-Fri, 10am-7pm Sat, 11am-6pm Sun). From outside, it's an uninviting monolith that, critics say, turns its back on downtown. Inside it's a playful jumble that's supposed to imitate an authentic urban space. Toy-town arches, asymmetrical balconies and a five-floor, open-air atrium can make you feel you're walking through an MC Escher drawing rather than an actual city.

City planners can debate whether it was worth $140 million and the leveling of seven city blocks, but no one can doubt that it marries convenience and amusement, with one-stop access to a multiscreen cinema complex, two live theaters, dozens of restaurants and cafés, a top-floor food court and

140 shops. Experience the suburbs without ever leaving downtown.

The main pedestrian entrance is on Broadway. Parking is validated with purchase.

MUSEUM OF CONTEMPORARY ART (MCA) – DOWNTOWN

Opposite the train station and adjacent to the San Diego Trolley stop, the **MCA** (Map pp592-3; ☎ 619-234-1001; 1001 Kettner Blvd; admission free; ◷ 11am-5pm Thu-Tue) is the downtown branch of the respected La Jolla–based institution that has brought groundbreaking art to San Diegans since the 1960s. The ever-changing exhibits of painting and sculpture are publicized widely (see the *Reader* or call the gallery).

SAN DIEGO CHILDREN'S MUSEUM/ MUSEO DE LOS NIÑOS

Kids can get down and dirty at this interactive **museum** (Map pp592-3; ☎ 619-233-5437; 200 Island Ave; adult/child under 3 $6/free; ◷ 10am-4pm Tue-Sat), whose mission is to unlock kids' hidden talents. Activities include giant construction toys, spaces for painting and modeling, storytelling, music and a stage with costumes for impromptu theater. At the time of writing, the museum was closed for a major makeover, with no fixed date for reopening. However, the offices remain open, so you can call for updates.

LITTLE ITALY

Italian immigrants, mostly fishermen, began settling this pleasant rise of land just up San Diego Bay in the 19th century. The tight-knit community had its heyday in the 1920s, when Prohibition opened up new business opportunities (read 'bootlegging'). Unfortunately, the construction of I-5, completed in 1962, tore apart the fabric of the community.

Nevertheless, the hardiest of the old family businesses have survived and, thanks to the city's recent urban renaissance, they've gained a brand-new clientele. Now old-world grocery stores alternate with slick cafés and high-end boutiques. For an antidote to the hectic Gaslamp Quarter, head to the sunny side of **India Street** (Map pp592–3) for a glass of Chianti.

When you've had your fill, consider ducking into **Our Lady of the Rosary Catholic Church** (Map pp592-3; cnr State & Date Sts), which still presides over Little Italy's social life. Its rich ceiling murals, painted by an Italian flown in especially for the job, are worth a gander. Across the street in Amici Park, you can still watch locals play bocce, an Italian form of outdoor bowling.

Embarcadero

Heading west from downtown, you cross the tram tracks and enter a 500yd-wide stretch of landfill that culminates with the Embarcadero. This wide pedestrian strip hugs the bay, offering fine water views, green spaces, and pleasant if impersonal restaurants, hotels and cafés.

Start your harborside stroll at the **Maritime Museum** (Map pp592-3; ☎ 619-234-9153; 1492 N Harbor Dr; all 3 vessels adult/child/senior $10/8/8; ◷ 9am-8pm), just north of Ash St. The 100ft masts of the square-rigger *Star of India* make the museum easy to find. Built on the Isle of Man and launched in 1863, the tall ship plied the England–India trade route, carried immigrants to New Zealand, became a trading ship based in Hawaii and, finally, worked the Alaskan salmon fisheries.

Continue south, past the dock for cruise megaships, to the euphemistically named **Seaport Village** (Map pp592-3; ☎ 619-235-4014; ◷ 10am-10pm summer), which caters to the huge ocean liners berthed nearby. Neither a port nor a village, this collection of novelty shops, restaurants and snack outlets is touristy and twee, but not a bad place for souvenir shopping and a bite to eat.

The main attraction, though, is the new **San Diego Aircraft Carrier Museum** (Map pp592-3; ☎ 619-544-9600; www.midway.org; Navy Pier; adult/child/senior & student $15/8/10; ◷ 10am-5pm; P) aboard the decommissioned USS *Midway*, the Navy's longest-serving aircraft carrier (1945–91). A self-guided audio-tour takes in the berthing spaces, the galley, the sick bay and, of course, the flight deck with its restored aircraft, including an F-14 Tomcat. Allow at least two hours. Parking costs $10.

Keep heading down the Embarcadero as it takes a turn toward the southeast, and you'll arrive at **Embarcadero Marina Park** – with its public fishing pier and an open-air amphitheater that presents free concerts on summer evenings. From here you'll see the 'sails' of the **San Diego Convention Center** (☎ 619-525-5000). Built as part of the city's highly successful bid to host major conventions, this complex, which opened in 1989, was designed by Canadian avant-garde architect Arthur Erickson and is said to have been inspired by an ocean liner.

Balboa Park

When, in 1868, city planners first set aside the land for this rambling 1400-acre park, it was a forbidding landscape of bare hilltops and snake-filled gullies above Horton's fledgling New Town. Today, it's one of the country's largest and finest urban parks, with flower gardens and shaded walks, tennis courts and swimming pools, museums and theaters, a velodrome, nine- and 18-hole golf courses, an outdoor organ and one of the world's great zoos.

Balboa Park is the ideal place to see San Diegans at play – jogging, strolling, in-line skating, catching rays, playing catch. With the city's fine weather and its people's preoccupation with the body beautiful, the park gets plenty of use.

In addition, the park is one of San Diego's premier cultural centers, with a cluster of theaters and museums arrayed along the extraordinary El Prado promenade. Nearby is a faithful reconstruction of Shakespeare's Old Globe theater, and a short walk to the north is the world-famous San Diego Zoo.

To visit all the museums and attractions would take two days, so it's a good idea to plan your visit. Note that many museums are closed Monday, and several per week (on a rotating basis) are free Tuesday.

The **Balboa Park Information Center** (Map pp596-7; ☎ 619-239-0512; 1549 El Prado; 🕑 9am-4pm) is in the House of Hospitality and has a good park map and helpful staff selling the Balboa Passport (single entry to 13 of the park's museums for one week) for $30.

Balboa Park is easily reached from downtown on bus 7, 7A or 7B along Park Blvd. By car, Park Blvd provides easy access to free parking areas near the majority of exhibits, but the most scenic approach is over the Cabrillo Bridge. From the west, El Prado is an extension of Laurel St, which crosses Cabrillo Bridge with the Cabrillo Fwy 120ft below.

The free Balboa Park Tram stops at various points on a continuous loop through the main areas of the park. (It's actually a bus rather than a tram and is not to be confused with the Old Town Trolley tour bus.) But walk if you can; the park is such a pleasant place for a stroll.

THE LEGACY OF KATE SESSIONS

Kate O Sessions graduated in botany from the University of California at Berkeley in 1881, a time when few women attended college and even fewer studied the natural sciences. She came to San Diego as a teacher but soon began working as a horticulturist, establishing gardens for the fashionable homes of the city's emerging elite. In 1892, in need of space for a nursery, she proposed an unusual deal to city officials: she would have the use of 30 acres of city-owned Balboa Park for her nursery in return for planting 100 trees a year and donating 300 others for placement throughout San Diego. The city agreed to the arrangement, and Kate Sessions more than fulfilled her side of the bargain. Within 10 years, Balboa Park had shade trees, lawns, paths and flowerbeds. Grateful San Diegans soon began referring to her as 'The Mother of Balboa Park.'

EL PRADO

Originally built for the 1915–16 Panama-California Exposition, these Spanish colonial buildings are particularly beautiful in the morning and evening, when the sun sweeps across their richly ornamented facades. The original exposition halls, which were mostly constructed out of stucco, chicken wire, plaster, hemp and horsehair, were only meant to be temporary. However, they proved so popular that, over the years, they have been gradually replaced with durable concrete replicas.

California Building & Museum of Man

As you enter Balboa Park via Laurel St, you cross the picturesque Cabrillo Bridge and then pass under an archway and into an area called the California Quadrangle, with the **Museum of Man** (Map pp596-7; ☎ 619-239-2001; www.museumofman.org; adult/child under 6/child 6-17/senior $6/free/3/5; 🕑 10am-4:30pm) on its northern side. This was the main entrance for the 1915 exposition, and the building was said to be inspired by the churrigueresque church of Tepotzotlán near Mexico City. The single **Tower of California**, richly decorated with blue and yellow tiles, has become a symbol of San Diego itself. The museum specializes in Native American artifacts, in particular from the American Southwest.

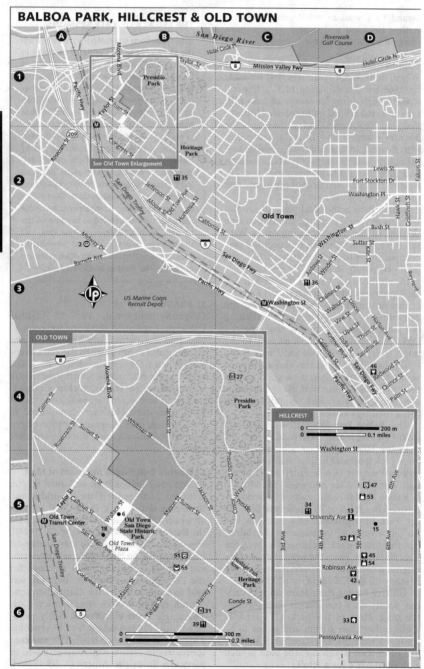

BALBOA PARK, HILLCREST & OLD TOWN

SAN DIEGO AREA

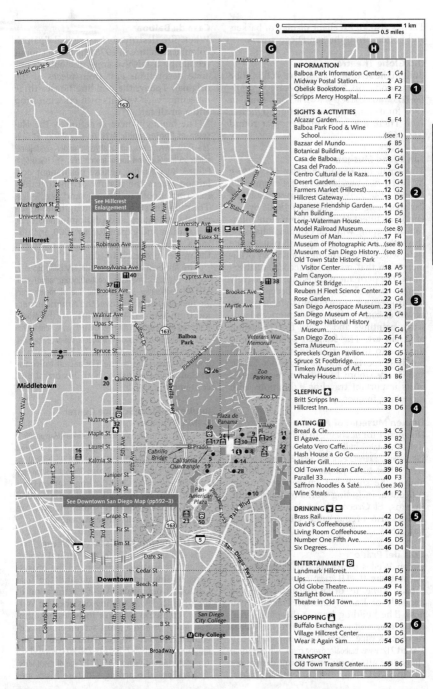

INFORMATION
Balboa Park Information Center...1 G4
Midway Postal Station..............2 A3
Obelisk Bookstore....................3 F2
Scripps Mercy Hospital.............4 F2

SIGHTS & ACTIVITIES
Alcazar Garden.......................5 F4
Balboa Park Food & Wine
  School.............................(see 1)
Bazaar del Mundo....................6 B5
Botanical Building....................7 G4
Casa de Balboa......................8 G4
Casa del Prado......................9 G4
Centro Cultural de la Raza........10 G5
Desert Garden......................11 G4
Farmers Market (Hillcrest).......12 G2
Hillcrest Gateway...................13 D5
Japanese Friendship Garden....14 G4
Kahn Building.......................15 G4
Long-Waterman House............16 E4
Model Railroad Museum.........(see 8)
Museum of Man....................17 F4
Museum of Photographic Arts...(see 8)
Museum of San Diego History...(see 8)
Old Town State Historic Park
  Visitor Center.....................18 A5
Palm Canyon........................19 F5
Quince St Bridge....................20 E4
Reuben H Fleet Science Center..21 G4
Rose Garden.........................22 G4
San Diego Aerospace Museum..23 F5
San Diego Museum of Art........24 G4
San Diego National History
  Museum............................25 G4
San Diego Zoo......................26 F4
Serra Museum.......................27 C4
Spreckels Organ Pavilion.........28 G5
Spruce St Footbridge..............29 E3
Timken Museum of Art............30 G4
Whaley House........................31 B6

SLEEPING 🛏
Britt Scripps Inn......................32 E4
Hillcrest Inn...........................33 D6

EATING 🍴
Bread & Cie..........................34 C5
El Agave..............................35 B2
Gelato Vero Caffe..................36 C3
Hash House a Go Go...............37 E3
Islander Grill........................38 G3
Old Town Mexican Cafe..........39 B6
Parallel 33............................40 F3
Saffron Noodles & Saté..........(see 36)
Wine Steals..........................41 F2

DRINKING 🍷
Brass Rail.............................42 D6
David's Coffeehouse..............43 D6
Living Room Coffeehouse........44 G2
Number One Fifth Ave............45 D5
Six Degrees..........................46 D4

ENTERTAINMENT 🎭
Landmark Hillcrest.................47 D5
Lips....................................48 F4
Old Globe Theatre..................49 F4
Starlight Bowl.......................50 F5
Theatre in Old Town...............51 B5

SHOPPING 🛍
Buffalo Exchange....................52 D5
Village Hillcrest Center............53 D5
Wear it Again Sam.................54 D6

TRANSPORT
Old Town Transit Center..........55 B6

There's also an excellent display of baskets and pottery from the San Diego area.

Old Globe Theatre
Built in the style of Shakespeare's Old Globe in London, this **theater** (Map pp596-7; ☎ 619-239-2255; www.oldglobe.org) won a Tony award in 1984 for its ongoing contribution to theater arts. There are performances year-round (see p620).

San Diego Museum of Art
This small but elegant **museum** (Map pp596-7; ☎ 619-232-7931; www.sdmart.org; adult/child/youth 18-24/senior $9/4/7/7; ⏰ 10am-6pm Tue-Sun, 10am-9pm Thu) was designed in the early 1920s by San Diego architect William Templeton Johnson. In keeping with the exhibition halls, he chose the 16th-century Spanish plateresque style, which gets its name from heavy ornamentation that resembles decorated silverwork. The permanent collection has no truly famous works, but includes a decent survey of European art, from Giotto to Josef Albers, as well as some noteworthy American landscape paintings and a very fine collection of Asian art. The **Sculpture Garden**, behind the café to the west of the main museum building, sports works of Alexander Calder and Henry Moore. In addition, the museum hosts important traveling exhibitions with increasing frequency.

Timken Museum of Art
Distinctive for *not* being in imitation Spanish style, this 1965 **building** (Map pp596-7; ☎ 619-239-5548; www.timkenmuseum.org; 1500 El Prado; admission free; ⏰ 10am-4:30pm Tue-Sat, 1:30-4:30pm Sun Oct-Aug) houses the small but impressive Putnam collection, including works by Rembrandt, Rubens, El Greco, Cézanne and Pissarro. There's also a remarkable selection of Russian icons.

Casa del Prado
Orson Welles used this lavish **Spanish colonial structure** (1549 El Prado) as a backdrop in *Citizen Kane,* its ornate facade expressing the folly of Kane's unbridled acquisitiveness. The building houses the park's visitors center and is also home to the **Balboa Park Food & Wine School** (Map pp596-7; ☎ 619-557-9441 ext 212; www.balboafoodwine.com), where local chefs give afternoon or evening demos for $39 to $75. Call for the current schedule.

Casa de Balboa
When fire destroyed the original Spanish colonial structure in 1978, the city set about rebuilding a faithful copy, including concrete decorations cast from pieces of the original. Today, the building houses three museums, each with its own museum shop and a small café.

The highlight here is definitely the **Museum of Photographic Arts** (Map pp596-7; ☎ 619-238-7559; www.mopa.org; adult/child under 12/student/senior $6/free/4/4, 2nd Tue of month free; ⏰ 10am-5pm Fri-Wed, 10am-9pm Thu), whose permanent collection traces the history of photography in terms of both technology and aesthetics. The museum's particular strength lies in social documentary and photojournalism. A renovation and expansion in 2000, including a state-of-the-art theater, has extended the museum's reach to film.

The **Museum of San Diego History** (Map pp596-7; ☎ 619-232-6203; www.sandiegohistory.org; adult/youth 13-17/student/senior $6/2/5/5, 2nd Tue of month free; ⏰ 10am-5pm) exhibits cover the American period from about 1848. Downstairs, the **Model Railroad Museum** (☎ 619-696-0199; www.sdmodelrailroadm.com; adult/child under 15/student/senior $5/free/3/4, 1st Tue of month free; ⏰ 10am-4pm Tue-Fri, 10am-5pm Sat & Sun) has working models of actual railroads in Southern California, both historical and contemporary.

Reuben H Fleet Science Center & IMAX Theater
This is an interactive **science center** (Map pp596-7; ☎ 619-238-1233; www.rhfleet.org; adult/child 3-12/senior $6.75/5.50/6, with 1 IMAX film $11.75/9.75/8.75; ⏰ 9:30am-5pm Mon-Thu, 9:30am-9pm Fri, 9:30am-8pm Sat, 9:30am-6pm Sun) geared for kids, but the huge-screen Omnimax, with its hemispherical, wraparound screen and 152-speaker sound system, can provide a fun jolt to any age group.

San Diego Natural History Museum
Kids dig this temple to the natural world, which has a particular focus on the ecosystems of southern California and the Baja California peninsula. A 2001 renovation of the original 1933 building designed by William Templeton Johnson includes beautiful new galleries and a giant-screen cinema devoted exclusively to the natural world. The **museum** (Map pp596-7; ☎ 619-232-3821; www.sdnhm.org; adult/child 3-17/senior $9/5/6, 1st Tue of month free; ⏰ 10am-5pm) also arranges nature hikes and

field trips in Balboa Park and throughout San Diego County.

JAPANESE FRIENDSHIP GARDEN

What began as a teahouse for the Panama-California Exposition, just south of the Casa del Prado, has slowly grown into a serene group of **Japanese gardens** (Map pp596-7; ☎ 619-231-0048; www.niwa.org; adult/student/senior $3/2/2.50; ⏰ 10am-4pm Tue-Sun), including winding paths, koi-stocked ponds, a Zen garden and an elegant garden pavilion constructed in the traditional Japanese style.

SPRECKELS ORGAN PAVILION

Heading south from Plaza de Panama, you can't miss the extravagantly curved colonnade that provides shelter for one of the world's largest **outdoor organs** (Map pp596-7). Donated by the Spreckels family of sugar fortune and fame, the organ has some 4400 pipes, the smallest the size of a pencil and the largest nearly 10m long. Free concerts are held at 2pm every Sunday, and at 7:30pm Monday from mid-June to August.

SAN DIEGO AEROSPACE MUSEUM

In a distinctive round structure at the end of Pan American Plaza, this **museum** (Map pp596-7; ☎ 619-234-8291; www.aerospacemuseum.org; adult/child 6-17/student/senior $9/4/7/7; ⏰ 10am-4:30pm, 10am-5pm Jun-Aug) houses a small but interesting collection that ranges from the balloon age to the space age and includes a host of Charles Lindbergh memorabilia. Don't miss the Cold War display in the courtyard, in which a US Phantom jet pursues a Russian MiG-17 between art deco lamp standards.

At the adjacent Starlight Bowl, the **Starlight Opera** (Map pp596-7; ☎ 619-544-7800; www.starlight theatre.com) presents musicals and light opera outdoors from July to September.

CENTRO CULTURAL DE LA RAZA

Devoted to Mexican and Native American art, this **cultural center** (Map pp596-7; ☎ 619-235-6135; www.centroraza.com; 2125 Park Blvd; donation requested; ⏰ noon-5pm Thu-Sun), sits on the fringe of the main museum area (easiest access is via Park Blvd). The round, steel building is actually a converted water tank beautifully decked out by Chicano muralists. Inside, temporary exhibits of contemporary Chicano and indigenous artwork can be very powerful.

GARDENS OF BALBOA PARK

Balboa Park is home to a remarkable variety of flora, from desert cactus to subtropical ferns. To learn more about the gardens, consider one of the free weekly Offshoot Tours, conducted every Saturday by park horticulturists from mid-January to Thanksgiving. The **Park & Recreation Department** (☎ 619-235-1122) has more information. Reservations are not required – be at the front of the Botanical Building by 10am.

If you're exploring on your own, don't miss the **Alcazar Garden**, a formal Spanish-style garden; **Palm Canyon**, which has more than 50 species of palms; the **Australian Garden**; the **Rose Garden**; the **Desert Garden**, which is best in the spring; and **Florida Canyon**, which gives an idea of the San Diego landscape before the Spanish settlement. The Natural History Museum runs guided walks in the canyon. Call for details.

SAN DIEGO ZOO

Packed into 100 acres of exceedingly clever design in the northwestern corner of Balboa Park, the **zoo** (Map pp596-7; ☎ 619-231-1515; www .sandiegozoo.org; adult/child $21/14, deluxe package $32/20; ⏰ 9am) is a compendium of some of nature's largest, smallest, noblest, oddest and most endangered creatures, from pandas to anacondas, gorillas to pygmy marmosets. The zoo provides shelter to some 4000 animals in all, representing more than 800 species.

It is not only the sheer size of its collection that makes this zoo special. Over the years it has also pioneered ways to house and display animals that mimic their natural habitat, leading to a revolution in zoo design and, so the argument goes, to happier animals. The zoo also plays a major role in the protection of endangered species. If you were a zoo animal, this is the gig you'd want.

In its efforts to re-create those habitats, the zoo has also become one of the country's great botanical gardens. Experts trick San Diego's near-desert climate to yield everything from bamboo and eucalyptus to mini-African and Asian rain forests. The plants don't just provide pleasant cover for cages and fences; many are grown specifically to feed the zoo's more finicky eaters.

A big, free, parking lot is off Park Blvd. Bus 7 will get you there from downtown. The zoo is open daily at 9am, but closing times vary with the season; call for current

SAN DIEGO AREA

SAN DIEGO AREA

IT TAKES ALL KINDS

San Diego Zoo owes its origins to the 1915–16 Panama-California Exposition, when caged lions and other East African fauna were shipped in to provide that 'authentic' Panama-California feel.

Hearing the roar of one of the lions, Dr Harry Wegeforth, a prominent local, exclaimed 'Wouldn't it be wonderful to have a zoo in San Diego? I believe I'll build one.' He started a campaign in the press and formed the Zoological Society of San Diego. Meanwhile, he pulled strings at City Hall and suddenly all those caged animals were quarantined. It was very clever move, since now they were forbidden to leave San Diego. So with the stroke of a pen, Wegeforth had his menagerie.

The zoo maintained a similarly unorthodox approach to expanding its collections. Rattlesnakes caught in Balboa Park were traded for animals from other zoos. The US Navy contributed an assortment of animals that had been adopted as mascots but could no longer be kept on ships. After WWII, the zoo played a key role in rebuilding devastated European zoos.

The Zoological Society continued at the forefront of zoo management with the introduction of 'bioclimatic' habitats, which allow a number of different types of animals to share a simulated natural environment. In the 1960s the society started work on an 1800-acre Wild Animal Park (p623), 32 miles north of the city, which now provides free-range areas for many large species.

---

hours. If you would like to leave the zoo and return, staff will stamp your hand.

The 'deluxe admission package' includes a 40-minute guided bus tour and a round-trip aerial tram ride on the Skyfari cable car. The extras probably aren't worth it, unless you have sore feet or are in a hurry. Discount coupons are widely available from San Diego magazines, weekly newspapers and coupon books at hotels and information centers. A combined ticket to visit both the San Diego Zoo and the Wild Animal Park within a five-day period costs $54/34.

It's wise to arrive early, as many of the animals are most active in the morning, and a number of them are fed between 9am and 11am. Animal shows are held in the two amphitheaters (no extra charge), and they're usually entertaining, especially for kids. The Skyfari cable car goes right across the park and can save you some walking time, though there may be a line to get on. From late June to early September, the zoo is open until 9pm and has special exhibits that focus on nocturnal creatures.

Extensive facilities are provided for disabled visitors. For specific questions, call ahead.

Zoo Highlights
Most visitors will have their own favorites. The uncannily human pandas are a perennial crowd-pleaser. The koalas are so popular that Australians may be surprised to find them an unofficial symbol of San Diego. Less cuddly is the Komodo dragon, an Indo-nesian lizard that grows up to 10ft long and strides around the reptile house in a very menacing manner indeed.

Gorilla Tropics, **Hippo Beach** and **Polar Bear Plunge** all provide excellent views of animals in action thanks to all-glass walls. **Tiger River**, a remarkable re-creation of an Asian rain forest, is the home of some pretty fearsome striped cats. Arboreal orangutans and sia-mangs peacefully coexist in **Absolutely Apes**, another re-creation of an Asian rain forest. And don't miss the vast **Scripps Aviary** and **Owens Rain Forest Aviary**, where carefully placed feeders (and remarkably fearless birds) allow close-up viewing.

The zoo has also expanded its entertainment and educational role in the community with the opening of a **children's zoo exhibit** (where youngsters can pet small critters) and of outdoor theaters for animal shows. Both children and adults will enjoy the animal nursery, where you can see the zoo's newest arrivals.

Mission San Diego de Alcalá
Though the first California mission was established on Presidio Hill, Padre Junípero Serra decided in 1773 to move upriver several miles, closer to a better water supply and more arable land.

In 1784 the missionaries built a solid adobe and timber church, but it was destroyed by an earthquake in 1803. The church was promptly rebuilt, and at least some of it still stands on a slope overlooking Mission Valley. With the end of the mission system in the

1830s, the buildings were turned over to the Mexican government and fell into disrepair. Some accounts say that they were reduced to a facade and a few crumbling walls by the 1920s. Extensive reconstruction began in 1931, and the pretty white church and the buildings you see now are the result of the thorough restoration.

The **mission visitors center** (Map p589; ☎ 619-281-8449; 10818 San Diego Mission Rd; adult/student/senior $3/2/2; ☺ 9am-5pm) has friendly, informative staff. It is two blocks north of I-8, between I-15 and Mission Gorge Rd. You can take the trolley to the Mission stop, walk two blocks north and turn right onto San Diego Mission Rd.

Old Town

Until the 1860s, the city of San Diego was little more than a cluster of wood and adobe buildings just below Presidio Hill. Today this area is called Old Town, although it is neither very old (most of the buildings are reconstructions), nor exactly a town (more like a leafy suburb). Still, it's a more-or-less faithful copy of San Diego's original nucleus, offering a pleasant pedestrian plaza, a number of restaurants and cafés, and a good opportunity to explore San Diego's early days.

The **Old Town State Historic Park visitor center** (Map pp596-7; ☎ 619-220-5422; Robinson-Rose House; ☺ 10am-5pm) is at the southern end of the plaza. It has informative staff and houses a California history slide show and memorabilia. If you're particularly interested in the historical background, take a guided tour, which leaves from the visitor center at 2pm daily (there's also an 11am tour if enough people show up).

The **Bazaar del Mundo**, just off the plaza's northwest corner, is a pleasant if twee collection of restaurants and import shops, most open until 9pm, with goods imported from around the world. Along San Diego Ave, on the southern side of the plaza, is a row of small, historical-looking buildings (only one is authentically old), some of which house souvenir and gift shops.

Two blocks from the Old Town perimeter sits **Whaley House** (Map pp596-7; ☎ 619-297-7511; 2482 San Diego Ave; admission $5; ☺ 10am-4:30pm Wed-Mon), a lovely Victorian mansion and the city's oldest brick building. Over the years it has served as courthouse, theater and private residence, and it was *officially* certified as haunted by the US Department of Commerce in the early 1960s. Inside is a collection of period furniture and clothing.

In 1769 Padre Junípero Serra and Gaspar de Portolá established the first Spanish settlement in California on **Presidio Hill**, overlooking the valley of the San Diego River. The walk from Old Town along Mason St rewards you with excellent views of San Diego Bay and Mission Valley. A large cross, made with tiles from the original mission, commemorates Padre Serra. American forces occupied the hill in 1846, during the Mexican–American War, and named it Fort Stockton, for American commander Robert Stockton. A flagpole, cannon, some plaques and earthen walls now form the **Fort Stockton Memorial**. The nearby **El Charro Statue**, a bicentennial gift to the city from Mexico, depicts a Mexican cowboy on horseback. Nothing remains of the original Presidio structures, but archaeological digs are under way.

The **Serra Museum** (Map pp596-7; ☎ 619-297-3258; 2727 Presidio Dr; adult/child $5/2; ☺ 10am-4:30pm)

NO BULL

Bungee jumping isn't getting you high like it used to? Consider a turn in the bullring. If you're in San Diego it's possible, thanks to America's first bullfight school and proximity to the Mexican border, where bullfighting is actually legal. The **California Academy of Tauromaquia** (☎ 619-709-0664; www.bullfightschool.com) offers introductory weekend and intensive, weeklong courses, both of which have you in the ring before you know it. No animals die or are even harmed – actually, you face cows that are being tested to see if they should be bred to produce fightworthy bulls. But don't think Bessie the Cow – these girls are fierce attack animals. Plan on biting the dust. Generally, training starts in San Diego, and then when you're ready (often after just one evening), you head across the border to face the fierce *vacas* (cows). A nice bonus: the ranch has stunning vistas of the mountains that surround the border town of Tecate. Schedules and availability vary. Email the school coordinator at bullfightschool@yahoo.com for more information.

is a well-preserved Spanish colonial–style structure designed by William Templeton Johnson in 1929. The museum has a small but interesting collection of artifacts and pictures from the Mission, Mexican and American periods.

The Old Town Transit Center, on the trolley line at Taylor St at the northwestern edge of Old Town, is a stop for the *Coaster* commuter train, the San Diego Trolley (orange and blue lines) and buses 4 and 5 from downtown; Old Town Trolley tours stop southeast of the plaza on Twiggs St.

Uptown & Hillcrest

Without being too precise (San Diegans certainly aren't), Uptown consists roughly of the triangle north of downtown, east of Old Town and south of Mission Valley. As you head north from downtown along the west side of Balboa Park, you arrive at a series of bluffs that, in the late 19th century, became San Diego's most fashionable neighborhood – only those who owned a horse-drawn carriage could afford to live here. Known as Bankers Hill after some of the wealthy residents, these upscale heights had unobstructed views of the bay and Point

Loma before I-5 went up. Easily recognized by its towers, gables, bay windows and veranda, it was once the home of former California governor Robert Waterman.

As you head northward toward Hillcrest (where the real action is), consider a detour across the 375ft **Spruce Street Footbridge** (Map pp596–7). Note that the 1912 suspension bridge, built over a deep canyon between Front and Brant Sts, wriggles beneath your feet. But don't worry; it was designed that way. The nearby **Quince Street Bridge**, between 4th and 3rd Aves, is a wood-trestle structure built in 1905 and refurbished in 1988 after community activists vigorously protested its slated demolition.

Just up from the northwestern corner of Balboa Park, you hit **Hillcrest** (Map pp596–7), the heart of Uptown (buses 1, 3 and 25 go to/from downtown along 4th and 5th Aves). The neighborhood began its life in the early 20th century as a modest middle-class suburb. Today, it's San Diego's most bohemian district, with a decidedly urban feel despite the suburban visuals. It's also the headquarters of the city's gay and lesbian community. University and 5th Aves are lined with coffeehouses, fashion-forward thrift shops

---

GAY & LESBIAN SAN DIEGO

Ironically, many historians trace the roots of San Diego's thriving gay community to the city's strong military presence. During WWII, gay men from around the country left the relative isolation of their hometowns and, amid the enforced intimacy of military life, were suddenly able to create strong if clandestine social networks. When the war was over, these new friends often settled in the cities where they were decommissioned, including San Francisco and San Diego.

In the late 1960s, a newly politicized gay community began to make the Hillcrest neighborhood its unofficial headquarters. Here you'll find the highest concentration of bars, restaurants, cafés and bookstores catering to lesbians and gays. The scene is generally more casual and friendly than in San Francisco and LA, with more of a hometown feel. A great time to visit is during **San Diego Gay Pride** (☎ 619-297-7683; www.sdpride.org), which takes place in Hillcrest and Balboa Park at the end of July. For more complete listings and events, get a copy of *Buzz* and the *Gay and Lesbian Times*, both widely available in the neighborhood. You can also check out the following:

David's Coffeehouse (Map pp596–7; ☎ 619-296-4173; 3766 5th Ave, Hillcrest; 7am-11pm Sun-Thu, 7am-midnight Fri & Sat) Homey Hillcrest classic.

Obelisk Bookstore (Map pp596–7; ☎ 619-297-4171; 1029 University Ave; 10am-10pm Mon-Fri, 10am-11pm Fri & Sat, 11am-10pm Sun) Caters particularly to gay, lesbian, bisexual and transgender readers.

Brass Rail (Map pp596–7; ☎ 619-298-2233; 3796 5th Ave) The city's oldest gay bar has a different music style nightly, from Latin to African to Top 40.

Number One Fifth Ave (Map pp596–7; ☎ 619-299-1911; 3845 5th Ave) If you're looking for a friendly neighborhood joint, this is the place.

Six Degrees (Map pp596–7; ☎ 619-296-6789; 3175 India St) San Diego's best lesbian bar has a different theme every night, from football to Goth. It's famous for its Sunday barbecues with cheap burgers and beer on the patio. Call ahead to see what's doing.

and excellent restaurants in all price ranges. These commercial streets, with their neon-enhanced, 1950s facades, have a campy, small-town feel. The leafy side streets, with their Craftsman-style cottages, take you back to the 1920s.

Begin your tour at the **Hillcrest Gateway** (Map pp596–7), which arches over University Ave at 5th Ave. Not far away, on 5th Ave between University Ave and Washington St, is the **Village Hillcrest Center** (Map pp596–7), with its colorful postmodern architecture. There you will find the multiplex **Landmark Hillcrest Cinema** (Map pp596–7) and restaurants and shops, as well as News Etc, a newsstand with a great selection. Go east on University Ave to see the 1919 **Kahn Building** (Map pp596–7) at No 535; it is an original Hillcrest commercial building with a kitschy (and distinctly fruity) facade. Then head south on 5th Ave to find a variety of cafés, friendly gay bars, vintage clothing shops and independent bookstores, many with a good selection of nonmainstream publications.

Hillcrest's **farmers market** (Map pp596-7; 5th Ave, cnr Normal & Lincoln Sts; 9am-1pm Sun) is a fun place to people-watch and buy fresh produce.

Coronado

Just across the bay from downtown, **Coronado** (Map p589) provides natural protection to San Diego's port – and just as carefully guards its own prosperously conservative ambience. Locals call it an island, but that's just wishful thinking. Although it's administratively separated from San Diego, it's connected to the mainland by the spectacular, 2.12-mile Coronado Bay Bridge (opened in 1969), as well as by a long, narrow spit of sand known as the Silver Strand. The large North Island US Naval Air Station occupies a northern tip of the island.

There are two reasons to come to Coronado Island: the remarkable Hotel del Coronado (known as 'the Del') and the stunning strand it sits on.

The **Coronado Visitors Bureau** (Map p589; 619-437-8788; www.coronadovisitors.com; 1100 Orange Ave; 9am-5pm Mon-Fri, 10am-5pm Sat, 11am-4pm Sun) has information and conducts a walking tour ($12), starting from the **Glorietta Bay Inn** (Map p589; 1630 Glorietta Blvd), near Silver Strand Blvd, at 11am Tuesday, Thursday and Saturday. The 90-minute route takes in many of Coronado's most interesting sights.

Even the famously fussy Henry James couldn't help but love the **Hotel del Coronado**, affectionately known as the Del. On leave from his self-imposed exile in London, the novelist effused that the hotel's gardens 'raged' under the raw California sun. The hotel's main building, which opened in 1888, is a sprawling timber palace with billowing turrets, dramatic ballrooms and nearly 700 rooms, all connected by a dazzling maze of dark corridors, bright courtyards, and elegantly carved stairways.

It's believed that Edward (then Prince of Wales) first met Mrs Simpson (then Mrs Spenser) at the Del in 1920, though the two did not become an item until some years later. However, the Del achieved its widest exposure in the 1959 movie *Some Like It Hot,* which earned its lasting association with Marilyn Monroe. Even today, the hotel remains the choice for heads of state; every American president since Lyndon Johnson has stayed here.

Cars with driver only pay a $1 toll when coming over the bridge to Coronado, but it's free for vehicles with passengers. Buses 901, 902 and 903 from downtown run the length of Orange Ave to the Hotel del Coronado.

A regular ferry ($2.25) operates hourly between Broadway Pier and Coronado. A **water taxi** (619-235-8294) makes a regular connection between Seaport Village and Coronado, where it stops at the Ferry Landing Marketplace and Glorietta Bay. It also makes on-call trips to Shelter Island, Harbor Island, Chula Vista and South Bay (from $5 per person, runs 2pm to 10pm Monday to Friday, and 11am to 11pm weekends). Rent a bike at Coronado's Ferry Landing Marketplace ($5 per hour) or bring one on the ferry for 50¢. Alternatively, use the electric Coronado Shuttle to get around (free). The Old Town Trolley tour stops in front of Mc P's Irish Pub, on Orange Ave at 11th St.

Point Loma

On the southern tip of Point Loma, the strategically placed peninsula that provides shelter to San Diego Bay, you'll find **Cabrillo National Monument** (Map p589; bus 26 from downtown; admission per car/person $5/3; 9am-5pm, 9am-6pm in summer), offering fine views across the bay to San Diego's downtown. It's also the best place in San Diego to see the gray whale migration (January to March) from land. The

MISSION BAY & THE BEACHES

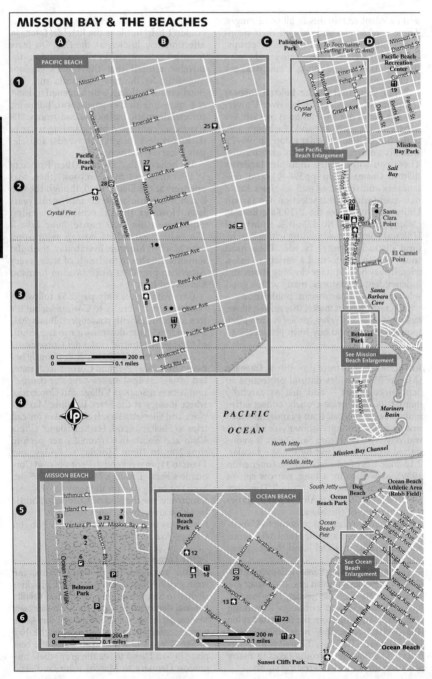

SAN DIEGO AREA

A **B** **C** **D**

PACIFIC BEACH

Missouri St
Diamond St
Emerald St
Felspar St
25
Bayard St
Cass St
Garnet Ave
27
Hornblend St
Mission Blvd
28
10
Crystal Pier
Ocean Front Walk
Grand Ave
26
Pacific Beach Park
1
Thomas Ave
Reed Ave
9
8
5 Oliver Ave
17
Pacific Beach Dr
15
Wavecrest Ct
Santa Rita Pl

0 — 200 m
0 — 0.1 miles

Palisades Park
To Tourmaline Surfing Park (0.4mi)
Missouri St
Diamond St
Pacific Beach Recreation Center
Emerald St
Felspar St
Ocean Blvd
Garnet Ave
19
Cass St
Grand Ave
Dawes St
Everts St
Fanuel St
Crystal Pier
Mission Blvd

See Pacific Beach Enlargement

Mission Bay Park
Sail Bay
20
4 Santa Clara Point
24 **30**
Santa Clara Pl
Bayside Ln
Strand Way
El Carmel Pl
El Carmel Point
Santa Barbara Cove

Belmont Park

See Mission Beach Enlargement

Mission Blvd
Mariners Basin

PACIFIC OCEAN

North Jetty
Mission Bay Channel
Middle Jetty

South Jetty Dog Beach
Ocean Beach Park
Ocean Beach Athletic Area (Robb Field)
Spray St
Ocean Beach Pier
Abbott St
Muir Ave
Lotus Ave
Voltaire St
Long Branch Ave
Brighton Ave
Cape May Ave
Saratoga Ave
Santa Monica
Newport Ave
Niagara Ave
Narragansett Ave
Del Monte Ave
Cable St
Sunset Cliffs Blvd

See Ocean Beach Enlargement

MISSION BEACH

Isthmus Ct
Island Ct
33
32 **7**
Ventura Pl Mission Bay Dr
2
Ocean Front Walk
6
Mission Blvd
P
Belmont Park
P

0 — 200 m
0 — 0.1 miles

OCEAN BEACH

Ocean Beach Park
Abbott St
12
Bacon St
Saratoga Ave
Santa Monica Ave
31 **18**
29
Cable St
Newport Ave
13
22
Niagara Ave
23

0 — 200 m
0 — 0.1 miles

Ocean Beach
11
Bermuda Ave
Sunset Cliffs Park

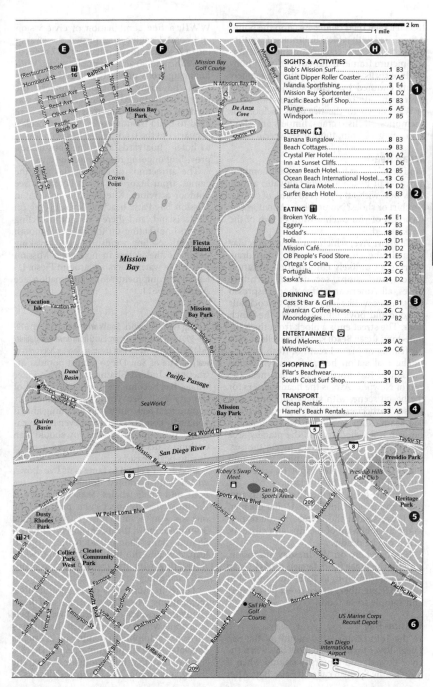

SAN DIEGO AREA

SIGHTS & ACTIVITIES
Bob's Mission Surf.............................1 B3
Giant Dipper Roller Coaster.............2 A5
Islandia Sportfishing.........................3 E4
Mission Bay Sportcenter...................4 D2
Pacific Beach Surf Shop....................5 B3
Plunge..6 A5
Windsport...7 B5

SLEEPING
Banana Bungalow..............................8 B3
Beach Cottages.................................9 B3
Crystal Pier Hotel............................10 A2
Inn at Sunset Cliffs.........................11 D6
Ocean Beach Hotel.........................12 B5
Ocean Beach International Hostel...13 C6
Santa Clara Motel............................14 D2
Surfer Beach Hotel..........................15 B3

EATING
Broken Yolk.....................................16 E1
Eggery...17 B3
Hodad's..18 B6
Isola..19 D1
Mission Café....................................20 D2
OB People's Food Store...................21 E5
Ortega's Cocina..............................22 C6
Portugalia.......................................23 C6
Saska's..24 D2

DRINKING
Cass St Bar & Grill..........................25 B1
Javanican Coffee House..................26 C2
Moondoggies...................................27 B2

ENTERTAINMENT
Blind Melons...................................28 A2
Winston's..29 C6

SHOPPING
Pilar's Beachwear............................30 D2
South Coast Surf Shop....................31 B6

TRANSPORT
Cheap Rentals.................................32 A5
Hamel's Beach Rentals....................33 A5

1854 **Old Point Loma Lighthouse**, atop the point, is furnished with typical lighthouse furniture from the late 19th century, including lamps and picture frames hand-covered with hundreds of shells – testimony to the long, lonely nights endured by lighthouse keepers. On the ocean side of the point, you can drive or walk down to the **tide pools** to look for anemones, starfish, crabs, limpets and dead man's fingers (thin, tubular seaweed).

Ocean Beach

San Diego's most bohemian seaside community, Ocean Beach actively cultivates a mellow vibe – without trying too hard, of course. No shirt or shoes? No problem. And don't be surprised if you catch a whiff or two of the wacky weed.

Newport Ave, which runs perpendicular from the beach, serves as the main drag, offering an unlikely combination of tattoo parlors, surf shops, secondhand furniture stores, all-American coffee shops, espresso joints and cavelike bars serving up cocktails to good old boys lubing up for the lunch hour. The street ends a block from the half-mile-long **Ocean Beach Pier**, an excellent spot for fishing or just a breath of fresh air.

The real action here, of course, lies on the sands. Just north of the pier, near the end of Newport Ave, is the headquarters for the beach scene, with volleyball courts and sunset barbecues. Further up you'll reach **Dog Beach** (Map pp604–5), where pooches can run unleashed around the marshy area where the San Diego River meets the sea. A few blocks south of the pier, you'll find **Sunset Cliffs Park**, a great spot to watch the sun dipping below the horizon.

There are good surf breaks at the cliffs and, to the south, off Point Loma. Under the pier, the brave slalom the pilings. If you're new to the area, beware of the rips and currents, which can be deadly.

If you're here on Wednesday afternoon, stop by the **Ocean Beach farmers market** (Map pp604–5, from 4pm to 7pm, and until 8pm June to September) to see street performers and sample fresh food.

Mission Bay

In the 18th century, the mouth of the San Diego River formed a shallow bay when the river flowed, and a marshy swamp when it didn't – the Spanish called it False Bay. After WWII, a fine combination of civic vision and coastal engineering turned the swamp into a 7-sq-mile playground, with 27 miles of shoreline and 90 acres of public parks. With financing from public bonds and expertise from the Army Corps of Engineers, the river was channeled to the sea, the bay was dredged and millions of tons of sludge were used to build islands, coves and peninsulas. A quarter of the land created has been leased to hotels, boatyards and other businesses, providing ongoing revenue for the city.

The attractions of Mission Bay run the gamut, from luxurious resort hotels to free outdoor activities. Kite flying is popular in Mission Bay Park, beach volleyball is big on Fiesta Island, and there's delightful cycling and in-line skating on the miles of smooth bike paths. Sailing, windsurfing and kayaking dominate the waters in northwest Mission Bay, while water-skiers zip around Fiesta Island. For equipment-rental information, see Activities, p611.

SEAWORLD

Along with the zoo, **SeaWorld** (Map p589; ☎ 619-226-3901; www.seaworld.com; bus 9 from downtown; adult/child $51/41; ☒ 9am-11pm summer, shorter hours rest of year) is one of San Diego's most popular attractions. Indeed Shamu, the park's killer whale, has become an unofficial symbol of the city itself. SeaWorld has a shamelessly commercial feel, but it's entertaining and, if you really concentrate, it can even be educational. Its popularity means you should plan on long waits for rides, shows and exhibits during peak seasons.

SeaWorld's claim to fame is its live shows, which feature trained dolphins, seals, sea lions and killer whales. **Shamu Adventure** is the most visually spectacular program, the one you won't want to miss. Throughout the 30-minute show, the three star performers – Shamu, Baby Shamu and Namu – glide, leap, dive and flip through the water while interacting with the trainer, the audience and each other.

There are numerous other aquariumlike installations where you can see and learn about underwater creatures, as well as petting pools where you can touch the slippery surface of a dolphin or manta ray. In **Penguin Encounter**, several penguin species share a habitat that faithfully simulates Antarctic living conditions. You'll also see dozens of sharks as you walk through a 57ft acrylic tube at **Shark Encounter**. Species include black-tip, whitetip, reef and sand tiger sharks, some impressively large. Amusement park–style rides include **Journey to Atlantis**, a combination flume ride and roller coaster, and **Wild Arctic**, a simulated helicopter flight.

Prepare yourself for deafeningly loud advertisements while you wait to see Shamu, and there's a corporate logo on everything in sight. Still, SeaWorld manages to do its share for animal conservation, rescue, rehabilitation, breeding and research.

At the regular admission price, you may have an expensive day. Discount coupons are available, and buying tickets online gives you 10% off, but the extras add up – parking costs $7 and food is expensive ($3 for a 20oz bottle of water). Ways to get the best value: a re-entry stamp (you can go out for a break and return later – good during late-opening hours in summer); a combination ticket, also good for Universal Studios (in Los Angeles); and a two-day ticket, only $4 more than a regular one.

The park is easy to find by car – take Sea World Dr off I-5 less than a mile north of where it intersects with I-8. Take bus 9 from downtown. Tickets sales end 1½ hours before closing time.

Mission Beach & Pacific Beach

You've got to love a place where people gather each evening to cheer the sun as it dips down into the Pacific. Between the South Mission Jetty and Pacific Beach Point stretch 3 miles of unadulterated SoCal beach scene. **Ocean Front Walk** (Map pp604–5), the beachfront boardwalk, bristles year-round with joggers, in-line skaters and cyclists – the perfect place for scantily clad pretty people–watching. Back from the beach, Mission Blvd, which runs up and down the coast, consists of block after block of surf shops, burger joints, beer busts and '60s-style motels.

Down at the Mission Beach end, beach bums pool their resources to rent small houses and apartments for the summer season. Here, the hedonism is concentrated in a narrow strip between the ocean and Mission Bay.

The surf is a beach break, good for beginners, bodyboarders and bodysurfers.

The family-style **Belmont Park** (Map pp604-5; ☎ 858-488-0668; admission free) has been on Mis-sion Beach since 1925. When it was threatened with demolition in the mid-1990s, concerted community action saved the large indoor pool known as the **Plunge** (Map pp604–5) and the classic wooden **giant dipper roller coaster** ($3.50; operates from 11am), which will shake the teeth right out of your mouth. It's free to enter Belmont Park; you pay for the rides individually ($2 to $4).

Up in Pacific Beach (or PB) the activity spreads farther inland, especially along **Garnet Ave** (Map pp604–5), with well-stocked bars, restaurants and vintage clothing stores. At the ocean end of Garnet Ave, **Crystal Pier** is worth a gander. Built in the 1920s, it's still home to San Diego's quirkiest hotel (p616), which consists of a cluster of rustic cabins built out over the waves .

Surfing is more demanding around Crystal Pier, where the waves are steep and fast. Tourmaline Surfing Park (Map p589), at the far northern end of the beach, is particularly popular with longboarders. For information on equipment rentals, see p611.

To get around, consider renting a bike or in-line skates (see p622). **Cheap Rentals** (Map pp604-5; ☎ 800-941-7761, 858-488-2453; www.cheap-rentals.com; 3221 Mission Blvd; ⏰ 9am-7pm daily Mar-Aug, 9am-5pm Mon- Fri Sep-Feb) has low prices and rents everything from bikes (per two hours/full day about $10/20) and skates to baby joggers; it also accepts advance reservations, crucial in summer if you sleep late.

La Jolla

With immaculate parks, upscale boutiques, sandy coves and turquoise waters, you can understand why locals say La Jolla is Spanish for 'the jewel.' Some challenge this claim, saying that the indigenous peoples who inhabited the area until the mid-19th century called it 'Mut la Hoya, la Hoya' – the place of many caves. Either way, it's pronounced 'la *hoy*-ya' and is a great place to spend a day – more if you can afford it.

Technically part of San Diego, La Jolla definitely feels like a world apart, both because of its radical affluence as well as its privileged location above San Diego's most photogenic stretch of coast. The neighborhood first became fashionable when Ellen Browning Scripps moved in to here in 1897. The newspaper heiress acquired much of the land along Prospect St, which she subsequently donated to various community

SAN DIEGO AREA

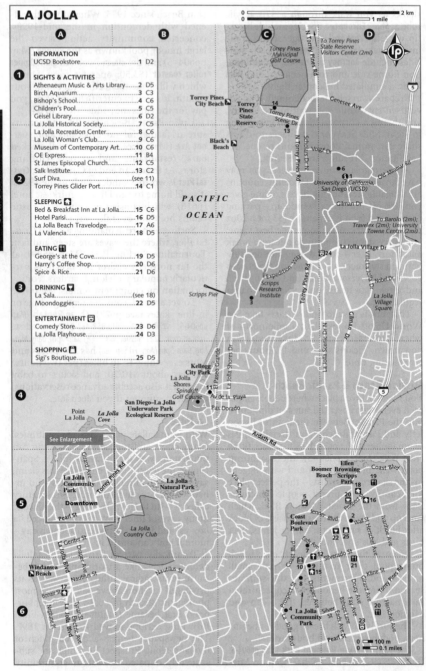

LA JOLLA

0 _____ 2 km
0 _____ 1 mile

INFORMATION
UCSD Bookstore................................1 D2

SIGHTS & ACTIVITIES
Athenaeum Music & Arts Library.......2 D5
Birch Aquarium.................................3 C3
Bishop's School.................................4 C6
Children's Pool.................................5 C5
Geisel Library....................................6 D2
La Jolla Historical Society...................7 C5
La Jolla Recreation Center..................8 C6
La Jolla Woman's Club.......................9 C6
Museum of Contemporary Art.........10 C6
OE Express.......................................11 B4
St James Episcopal Church................12 C5
Salk Institute...................................13 C2
Surf Diva....................................(see 11)
Torrey Pines Glider Port...................14 C1

SLEEPING
Bed & Breakfast Inn at La Jolla........15 C6
Hotel Parisi.....................................16 D5
La Jolla Beach Travelodge................17 A6
La Valencia.....................................18 D5

EATING
George's at the Cove.......................19 D5
Harry's Coffee Shop........................20 D6
Spice & Rice...................................21 D6

DRINKING
La Sala....................................(see 18)
Moondoggies.................................22 D5

ENTERTAINMENT
Comedy Store.................................23 D6
La Jolla Playhouse..........................24 D3

SHOPPING
Sigi's Boutique...............................25 D5

Torrey Pines
Municipal
Golf Course

To Torrey Pines
State Reserve
Visitors Center (2mi)

Torrey Pines
City Beach

Torrey
Pines
State
Reserve

Genesee Ave

Torrey Pines
Scenic Dr

Black's
Beach

University of California,
San Diego (UCSD)

Gilman Dr

To Barola (2mi);
Travelex (2mi); University
Towne Centre (2mi)

La Jolla Village Dr

PACIFIC
OCEAN

Expedition Way

Scripps
Research
Institute

La Jolla
Village
Square

Scripps Pier

La Jolla Scenic Dr N

Gilman Dr

Kellogg
City Park

La Jolla
Shores
Spindrift
Golf Course

El Paseo Grande

La Jolla Shores Dr

Av de la Playa

Pas Dorado

San Diego–La Jolla
Underwater Park
Ecological Reserve

Ardath Rd

Point
La Jolla

La Jolla
Cove

See Enlargement

La Jolla
Community
Park

Girard Ave

Torrey Pines Rd

La Jolla
Natural Park

Via Capri

Downtown

Pearl St

La Jolla
Country Club

La Jolla Blvd

La Genter St

Draper Ave

Nautilus St

Windansea
Beach

Bonair St

Tyian St

La Jolla Electric Ave

La Jolla Blvd

Neptune Pl

Boomer
Beach

Ellen
Browning
Scripps
Park

Coast Blvd

Coast
Boulevard
Park

Jenner Blvd

Prospect St

Wall St

Ivanhoe Ave

Herschel Ave

Back Ave

Coast Blvd

Silverado St

Girard Ave

Fay Ave

Kline St

Drury Ave

Torrey Pines Rd

Herschel Ave

Prospect St

La Jolla
Community
Park

Draper Ave

Silver St

Bishops Ln

Eads Ave

Pearl Ave

0 ___ 100 m
0 ___ 0.1 miles

uses, including **Bishop's School** (Map p608; cnr Prospect St & La Jolla Blvd) and the **La Jolla Woman's Club** (Map p608; 715 Silverado St). She also hired Irving Gill to set the architectural tone of the community – an elegant if unadorned Mediterranean style characterized by arches, colonnades, palm trees, red-tile roofs and pale stucco.

Bus 34 connects La Jolla to downtown via the Old Town Transit Center.

DOWNTOWN LA JOLLA
The compact downtown, known affectionately as 'the Village,' sits atop a bluff lapped by ocean waves. Regrettably, there is little interaction between downtown and the sea, though you can catch lovely glimpses of Pacific blue between buildings. The main thoroughfares, Prospect St and Girard Ave, are San Diego's favorite places for high-end shopping. Galleries offer up paintings, sculpture and decorative items (a few too many involving whale themes), while gaps between stores such as Banana Republic and Armani Exchange are filled by some interesting independent purveyors of clothing, furniture and jewelry.

For a tour of old La Jolla, start off at the **Athenaeum Music & Arts Library** (Map p608; ☎ 858-454-5872; www.ljathenaeum.org; 1008 Wall St; ⚐ 10am-5:30pm Tue-Sat, 10am-8:30 Wed). Housed in a compact but graceful Spanish renaissance structure near the intersection of Prospect and Girard, the library hosts small art exhibits and concerts. You can also read daily newspapers here from around the globe. Next, head southwest along Prospect St. until you reach No 780 – a cottage once owned by Ellen Browning Scripps. Around the corner, the **La Jolla Historical Society** (Map p608; ☎ 858-459-5335; Eads Ave; ⚐ noon-4:30pm Tue-Thu) has vintage photos and beach memorabilia – think old bathing costumes, lifeguard buoys and the like. Further down Prospect St, you will find St James Episcopal Church, the La Jolla Recreation Center and the Bishop's School, all of which date from the early 20th century.

Just across the street from the church stands the small but excellent **Museum of Contemporary Art** (MCA: Map p608; ☎ 858-454-3541; www.mcasd.org; 700 Prospect St; admission $6, 3rd Tue of month free; ⚐ 11am-5pm Mon, Tue & Fri-Sun, 11am-7pm Thu). Besides a regular collection especially strong in minimalist, pop and California art, the museum regularly hosts world-class

temporary exhibitions. Originally designed by Irving Gill in 1916 as the home of Ellen Browning Scripps, the building was extensively renovated by the postmodern master Robert Venturi.

THE COAST
Private property along the coast of La Jolla restricts coastal access, and parking is very limited in places, but there is a wonderful walking path that skirts the shoreline for half a mile. The path's western end begins at the **Children's Pool** (Map p608), where a jetty (funded by none other than Ellen Browning Scripps) protects the beach from big waves.

Originally intended to give La Jolla's youth a safe place to frolic, the beach is now more popular with sea lions, which you can view up close as they lounge on the shore. Atop Point La Jolla, at the path's eastern end, **Ellen Browning Scripps Park** (Map p608) is a tidy expanse of green lawns and palm trees, with views of **La Jolla Cove** to the north. The cove's gem of a beach provides access to some of the best snorkeling around; it's also popular with rough-water swimmers.

Look for the white buoys offshore from Point La Jolla north to Scripps Pier (visible to the north) that mark the **San Diego–La Jolla Underwater Park Ecological Reserve** (Map p608), a protected zone with a variety of marine life, kelp forests, reefs and canyons (see p612). Waves have carved caves into the sandstone cliffs east of the cove.

If you like to surf and know what you're doing, head to **Windansea Beach** (Map p608), 2 miles south of downtown (take La Jolla Blvd south and turn west on Nautilus St). However, some of the locals at Windansea are aggressive toward outsiders. If you brave their ire, you'll find that the surf's consistent peak (a powerful reef break that's not for beginners) works best at medium to low tide. You'll find a more civilized welcome immediately south at **Big Rock**, California's version of Hawaii's Pipeline, which has steep, hollow, gnarly tubes. The name comes from the large chunk of reef protruding just offshore – a great spot for tide pooling at low tide.

LA JOLLA SHORES
Called 'the Shores,' this area northeast of La Jolla Cove is where La Jolla's cliffs meet the wide, sandy beaches that stretch north to Del Mar. To reach the **beach** (Map p608),

take La Jolla Shores Dr north from Torrey Pines Rd and turn west onto Ave de la Playa. The waves here are gentle enough for beginner surfers, and kayakers can launch from the shore without much problem.

Some of the best beaches in the county are north of the Shores in **Torrey Pines City Park** (Map p608), which covers the coastline from the Salk Institute up to the Torrey Pines State Reserve. At extreme low tides (about twice a year), you can walk from the Shores north to Del Mar along the beach. The **Torrey Pines Glider Port** (Map p608), at the end of Torrey Pines Scenic Dr, is the place for hang gliders and paragliders to launch themselves into the sea breezes that rise over the high cliffs. It's a beautiful sight – tandem flights are available if you can't resist trying it (p613). Down below is the predominantly gay **Black's Beach** (Map p608), where bathing suits are technically required, but in practice are very much optional.

BIRCH AQUARIUM AT SCRIPPS

Marine scientists were working here as early as 1910 and, helped by donations from the ever-generous Scripps family, it has grown to one of the world's largest marine research institutions. It is now part of UCSD, and its pier is a landmark on the La Jolla coast.

Birch Aquarium (Map p608; ☎ 858-534-3474; www .aquarium.ucsd.edu; 2300 Exhibition Way; adult/child $10/ 6.50; ⏰ 9am-5pm), off N Torrey Pines Rd, has brilliant displays about the marine sciences and of marine life. The **Hall of Fishes** has more than 30 fish tanks, simulating marine environments from the Pacific Northwest to the tropics. For an extra $4, take **Morphis: Movieride**, a hydraulic-motion ride with accompanying video that simulates swimming with dolphins; it's really cool if you're 12. If you're interested in studying oceanography or seeing the campus, get the self-guided campus-tour brochure. For the aquarium, take bus 34 from downtown and La Jolla.

SALK INSTITUTE

In 1960 Jonas Salk, the pioneer of polio prevention, founded the **Salk Institute** (Map p608; ☎ 858-453-4100; www.salk.edu; 10010 N Torrey Pines Rd) for biological and biomedical research. San Diego County donated 27 acres of land, the March of Dimes provided financial support and Louis Kahn designed the building. Completed in 1965, it is a masterpiece of modern

architecture, with its classically proportioned travertine marble plaza and cubist, mirror-glass laboratory blocks framing a perfect view of the Pacific. Regrettably, the outside walls have grown rather pitted and discolored over time. The Salk Institute attracts the best scientists to work in a research-only environment. The facilities have been expanded, with new laboratories designed by Jack McAllister, a follower of Kahn's work. You can tour the Salk Institute free with a volunteer guide most days; call in advance. Buses 41 and 301 go along N Torrey Pines Rd.

TORREY PINES STATE RESERVE

Encompassing the land between N Torrey Pines Rd and the ocean from the Torrey Pines Glider Port to Del Mar, this **reserve** (Map p608; ☎ 858-755-2063; www.torreypine.org; ⏰ 9am-sunset) preserves the last mainland stands of the Torrey pine *(Pinus torreyana)*, a species adapted to sparse rainfall and sandy, stony soils. Steep sandstone gullies are eroded into wonderfully textured surfaces, and the views over the ocean and north to Oceanside are superb, especially at sunset.

The main access road, Torrey Pines Scenic Dr, off N Torrey Pines Rd (buses 41 and 301) at the reserve's northern end, leads to a simple adobe – built as a lodge in 1922 by (drum roll) Ellen Browning Scripps – which now acts as a **visitors center**, with good displays on the local flora and fauna. Rangers lead nature walks from here at 10am and 2pm on weekends.

Parking costs $6 per car, but admission is free if you enter on foot. Several walking trails wind through the reserve and down to the beach. If you want to hike, park near the driving range on N Torrey Pines Rd and take the paved path northwest until you reach a box of trail maps at the beginning of the Broken Arrow Trail.

UNIVERSITY OF CALIFORNIA, SAN DIEGO

The University of California's San Diego campus was established in 1960 and now has more than 18,000 students as well as a sterling academic reputation, particularly for its math and science programs. It lies on rolling coastal hills in a parklike setting, with many tall and fragrant eucalyptus trees. Its most distinctive structure is the **Geisel Library** (Map p608, formerly the Central Library), an upside-down pyramid of glass and concrete whose namesake, Theodor Geisel, is better known as Dr Seuss, creator of the *Cat in the Hat*. He and his wife have contributed substantially to the library, and there is a collection of his drawings and books on the ground level.

From the eastern side of the library's second level, an allegorical snake created by artist Alexis Smith winds around a native California plant garden, past an enormous marble copy of John Milton's *Paradise Lost*. The piece is part of the **Stuart Collection** of outdoor sculptures spread around campus. Other works include Niki de Saint Phalle's *Sun God*, Bruce Nauman's *Vices & Virtue* (which spells out seven of each in huge neon letters), Robert Irwin's very blue *Fence* and a forest of talking trees. Most installations are near the Geisel Library, and details are available from the Visual Arts Building or the Price Center, where the **UCSD bookstore** (Map p608; ☎ 858-534-7323) has excellent stock and helpful staff. In the Mandell Weiss Center for the Performing Arts is **La Jolla Playhouse** (Map p608; ☎ 858-550-1010), known for its high-quality productions.

The best access to campus is off of La Jolla Village Dr or N Torrey Pines Rd (buses 41 and 301 from downtown); parking is free on weekends.

SOLEDAD MOUNTAIN
For a 360-degree view of La Jolla, take Nautilus St east from La Jolla Blvd, turn left on La Jolla Scenic Dr and follow it to **Soledad Mountain Park** (Map p589). The large cross on top was the subject of an unsuccessful lawsuit in the late 1960s – residents objected to the sectarian religious symbol on publicly owned land.

ACTIVITIES
If you love surf and sky, you'll go nuts in coastal San Diego. Carry your swimsuit at all times; you never know when the beach will beckon. For information on biking, see p622.

Surfing
A good number of San Diegans moved here for the surfing, and boy is it good. But the water can get crowded. Several spots, particularly Sunset Cliffs and Windansea, are somewhat 'owned' by locals – which means they'll heckle you to death unless you're an

awesome surfer – but in general, San Diego is a great place for surfers of any skill level.

Fall brings the strong swells and offshore Santa Ana winds. In summer swells come from the south and southwest, and in winter from the west and northwest. Spring brings more frequent onshore winds, but the surfing can still be good. For the latest beach, weather and surf reports, call **City Lifeguard** (☎ 619-221-8824).

Beginners looking to rent equipment should head to Mission or Pacific Beaches, where the waves are gentle. North of the Crystal Pier, Tourmaline Surfing Park is an especially good place to take your first strokes. **Pacific Beach Surf Shop** (Map p608; ☎ 858-373-1138; www.pacificbeachsurfshop.com; 4150 Mission Blvd, Suite 161, Pacific Beach) provides instruction through its Pacific Beach Surf School. It has friendly service, and also rents wetsuits and both soft (foam) and hard (fiberglass) boards. Call ahead. Also check out **Bob's Mission Surf** (Map p608; ☎ 858-483-8837; www.missionsurf.com; 4320 Mission Blvd, Pacific Beach). Rental rates at both vary depending on the quality of the equipment, but generally soft boards cost about $10 to $16 per half-day, $15 to $25 per full day; wet suits cost $5 per hour, $10 per half-day. For 90-minute lessons expect to pay $70 (including equipment) for one person, with discounts for additional people.

In La Jolla, the wonderful women at **Surf Diva** (Map p608; ☎ 858-454-8273; www.surfdiva.com; 2160 Av de la Playa) offer two-day weekend workshops for gals (only) of all ages for between $95 and $130.

The best surf breaks, from south to north, are (see Map p589) at Imperial Beach (especially in winter); Point Loma (reef breaks, which are less accessible but less crowded; best during winter); Sunset Cliffs in Ocean Beach; Pacific Beach; Big Rock (California's Pipeline); Windansea (hot reef break, best at medium to low tide); La Jolla Shores (beach break, best in winter); and Black's Beach (a fast, powerful wave). In North County (Map p625), there are breaks at Cardiff State Beach, San Elijo State Beach, Swami's, Carlsbad State Beach and Oceanside.

The bodysurfing is good at Coronado, Pacific Beach, Boomer Beach near La Jolla Cove (for the experienced only, best with a big swell) and La Jolla Shores. To get into the whomp (the forceful tubes that break directly onshore), know what you're doing and head to Windansea or the beach at the end of Sea Lane (both in La Jolla).

Diving & Snorkeling

Off the coast of San Diego County, divers will find kelp beds, shipwrecks (including the *Yukon*, a WWII destroyer), and canyons deep enough to host bat rays, octopus and squid. For current conditions, call ☎ 619-221-8824. You'll find some of California's best and most accessible (no boat needed) diving in the **San Diego–La Jolla Underwater Park Ecological Reserve** (Map p608), accessible from La Jolla Cove. With an average depth of 20ft, the 6000 acres of look-but-don't-touch underwater real estate are great for snorkeling, too. Ever-present are the spectacular, bright orange garibaldi fish, a protected species (there's a $500 fine for poaching one). Further out, you'll see forests of giant California kelp (which can increase its length by up to 3ft per day) and the 100ft-deep La Jolla Canyon.

A number of commercial outfits conduct scuba courses, sell or rent equipment, fill tanks and run boat trips to nearby wrecks and islands. A snorkel and fins cost around $10; scuba-gear rental packages cost about $65; and certification and open-water dives run about $375 for the first person, with discounts for additional people. Closest to the water, **OE Express** (Map p608; ☎ 858-454-6195; www.oeexpress.com; 2158 Av de la Playa) is a full-service PADI dive shop in La Jolla Shores that provides rentals and instruction.

Fishing

A state fishing license is required for people over 16 years old, except when fishing from an ocean pier. A **recorded service** (☎ 619-465-3474) provides fishing information.

The most popular public fishing piers are Imperial Beach Municipal Pier, Embarcadero Fishing Pier at the Marina Park, Shelter Island Fishing Pier, Ocean Beach Pier and Crystal Pier at Pacific Beach (see Map p589). The best time of year for pier fishing is from about April to October. Offshore catches can include barracuda, bass and yellowtail. In summer albacore is a special attraction.

Many companies run daily fishing trips year-round (half-day trip per adult/child around $37/27). Prices for full-day trips (per adult $75 to $150, child $50 to $100) depend on how far off the coast you go. A

license costs an extra $11 per person, and you can rent full tackle for a half-day for $9. Most also offer overnight and three-day trips, plus special charters for large groups. The most reputable include the following: **H&M Landing** (Map p589; ☎ 619-222-1144; www.hmlanding.com; 2803 Emerson St) On Shelter Island.
Islandia Sportfishing (Map p589; ☎ 619-222-1164; www.islandiasportfishing.com; 1551 West Mission Bay Dr)

Boating

Rent power and sailboats, rowboats, kayaks and canoes on Mission Bay. Try **Mission Bay Sportcenter** (☎ 858-488-1004; www.missionbaysportcenter.com; 1010 Santa Clara Pl).

Ocean kayaking is a good way to see sealife and explore cliffs and caves inaccessible from land. **Family Kayak** (☎ 619-282-3520; www.familykayak.com) has guided single- and multiday trips and classes, both from $55 for three hours. Call for details. It's easy to explore the caves and cliffs around La Jolla from the boat launch of **OE Express** (Map p608; ☎ 858-454-6195; www.oeexpress.com; 2158 Av de la Playa; 2hr kayak rental single/double $28/45) in La Jolla Shores. It also guides tours. If you want to rent a kayak in Mission Bay, call **Windsport** (Map pp604-5; ☎ 888-488-4642; www.windsport.net; 844 W Mission Bay Dr; per hr single/double about $15/20), across from the roller coaster.

Experienced sailors can charter yachts and sailboats for trips on San Diego Bay and out into the Pacific. Quite a few charter companies are based around Shelter and Harbor Islands (on the west side of San Diego Bay near the airport), including the following:
Harbor Sailboats (Map p589; ☎ 619-291-9568, 800-854-6625; www.harborsailboats.com; 2040 Harbor Island Dr, Suite 104)
Harbor Island Yacht Club (Map p589; ☎ 619-291-7245, 800-553-7245; www.sdyc.com; 1880 Harbor Island Dr)
Shelter Island Sailing (Map p589; ☎ 619-222-0351; www.shelterislandsailing.com; 2240 Shelter Island Dr)

Whale-Watching

Gray whales pass San Diego between mid-December and late February on their way south to Baja California and again in mid-March on their way back to Alaskan waters. Their 12,000-mile round-trip journey is the longest migration of any mammal on earth.

Cabrillo National Monument (p603) is the best place to see the whales from land, where you'll also find exhibits, whale-related ranger programs and a shelter from which to watch the whales breach (bring binoculars). If you

SAN DIEGO FOR CHILDREN

San Diego may be America's most kid-friendly destination. Like everything in San Diego, this virtue begins with the fine weather. Except for a few months in winter, you won't be subject to hours of disappointed whining as rain lashes the window of your hotel room. No need for plan Bs or rainchecks. In addition, the city has a number of attractions that send kids into ecstasy while keeping parents more than entertained. The most famous include the **San Diego Zoo** (p599), the **San Diego Wild Animal Park** (p623) and SeaWorld (p606). Balboa Park has two kid-friendly science museums, the **Reuben H Fleet Science Center** (p598) and the **San Diego Natural History Museum** (p598), both offering entertaining educational films on screens large enough to mesmerize audiences of all ages. The park also has plenty of space for running around and expelling excess ya-yas. The **San Diego Children's Museum** (p594) was undergoing renovation at the time of writing but may reopen in 2006.

And of course there are always the **beaches**, where you can build sandcastles for the price of a plastic bucket. Be aware, however, that some beaches have high waves and strong currents, and plan accordingly. The beaches of Mission Bay (p606) are always a safe option.

---

find yourself further north, Torrey Pines State Reserve (p610) and La Jolla Cove (p609) are also good spots for whale-watching.

Half-day whale-watching boat trips are offered by all of the companies that run daily fishing trips. The trips generally cost $20/15 per adult/child for a three-hour excursion, and the companies will even give you a free pass to return again if you don't spot any whales. Look for coupons and special offers in the *Reader* (available in convenience stores and cafés).

Hang Gliding

Glider riders hang at **Torrey Pines Glider Port** (Map p608; ☎ 858-452-9858; www.flytorrey.com; 2800 Torrey Pines Scenic Dr; tandem hang-glider flights per person per 20min $150), in La Jolla, a world-famous gliding location. This is also one of the best gliding schools in the country; if you've ever wanted to learn to glide, here's your chance.

Experienced pilots can join in if they have a USHGA Hang 4 rating and take out an associate membership of the Torrey Pines Hang Glider Association.

TOURS

To get the lay of the land begin your visit with a tour, then return to the sights that interest you most.

Old Town Trolley Tours (☎ 619-298-8687, 800-868-7482; per day adult/child 4-12 $15/28) Makes a loop around the main attractions near downtown and in Coronado inside an open-air trolley. Best of all, you can get on or off at any number of stops, staying to look around as long as you wish. Not to be confused with the Metropolitan Transit System's trolleys, which run on rails, the Old Town Trolley is a green

and orange bus styled after an old-fashioned streetcar. Tickets are good for unlimited all-day travel. Tours start at 9am and run every 30 minutes or so until 7pm. You can start at any trolley stop (they're well marked with orange and are usually next to a regular San Diego Transit bus stop). The tours are a great introduction to the city, and the commentary is entertaining.

San Diego Scenic Tours (☎ 858-273-8687; www.sandiegoscenictours.com; adult $28-56, child 3-11 $14-28) Leads half- and full-day bus tours around San Diego and Tijuana, some of which build in time to shop and dine. You can combine some tours with a harbor cruise.

Both **Hornblower Cruises** (Map pp592-3; ☎ 888-467-6256; www.hornblower.com) and **San Diego Harbor Excursion** (Map pp592-3; ☎ 800-442-7847, 619-234-4111; www.sdhe.com) operate boat tours of San Diego Harbor. One- and two-hour sightseeing tours (adult $15 to $20, child $7.50 to $10) leave from the Embarcadero (near the *Star of India*). Nightly dinner-dance cruises are about $55 per person ($60 Friday and Saturday) and whale-watching excursions run in season.

FESTIVALS & EVENTS

For the most current list, contact the San Diego Convention & Visitors Bureau.

Ocean Beach Kite Festival (☎ 858-274-2016) Kite-making, decorating, flying and competitions at Ocean Beach on the first Saturday in March.

San Diego Crew Classic (☎ 619-225-0300; www.crewclassic.org) The national college rowing regatta takes places in early April at Crown Point Shores Park in Mission Bay.

San Diego County Fair (☎ 858-755-1161; www.sdfair.com) Huge county fair held from mid-June to July 4;

features headline acts and hundreds of carnival rides and shows at the Del Mar Fairgrounds in Del Mar.

US Open Sandcastle Competition (☎ 619-424-6663; www.usopensandcastle.com) You won't believe what can be made out of sand at the amazing sandcastle-building competition held mid-July in Imperial Beach, south of Coronado.

Del Mar Horse Racing (☎ 858-755-1141; www.dmtc .com) The well-heeled bet on the horses, 'where the turf meets the sea,' at Del Mar Fairgrounds, from mid-July to early September.

San Diego Gay Pride (☎ 619-297-7683; www.sdpride .org) The city's gay community celebrates in Hillcrest and Balboa Park at the end of July.

Summerfest Chamber Music Festival (☎ 858-459-3728; www.ljcms.org) La Jolla hosts this two-week series in August with international performers.

Old Globe Festival (☎ 619-239-2255; www.oldglobe .org) Renowned Shakespeare festival at the Old Globe Theatre (p620) in Balboa Park during August.

San Diego Street Scene (☎ 800-260-9985; www .street-scene.com) California's largest outdoor music festival takes place downtown in late August.

Thunderboat Regatta (☎ 619-225-9160; www .thunderboats.net) Some of the fastest boats in the world compete on Mission Bay in mid-September.

Fleet Week (☎ 800-353-3793; www.fleetweeksandiego .org) The US military shows its might in a parade of ships and the signature Blue Angels air show from mid- to late September.

December Nights (☎ 619-239-0512; www.balboapark .org) Call in advance for the schedule of events in Balboa Park; the festival includes crafts, carols and a candlelight parade in the park.

Harbor Parade of Lights (☎ Oct-Dec only 619-224-2240; www.sdparadeoflights.org) Dozens of decorated, illuminated boats float in procession on the harbor on two Sunday evenings in December.

Las Posadas & Luminaries (☎ 619-291-4903; www .oldtownsandiego.org) This traditional Latin Christmas celebration in Old Town reenacts Mary and Joseph seeking shelter.

SLEEPING

High-season summer tariffs for double-occupancy rooms are listed in this section; suites cost more. The prices drop significantly between September and June, often by 40% or more.

Downtown

Despite its recent popularity, downtown still has some great, quirky budget options. It's also where you'll find the bulk of the city's high-end palaces.

BUDGET
La Pensione Hotel (Map pp592-3; ☎ 619-236-8000, 800-232-4683; www.lapensionehotel.com; 606 W Date St; r $75; P ☐) Rooms have a queen-size bed and private bathroom at this four-story hotel in Little Italy, within walking distance of most downtown attractions. A great bargain.

   HI San Diego Downtown Hostel (Map pp592-3; ☎ 619-525-1531; www.sandiegohostels.org; 521 Market St; dm members/nonmembers $19/26, s/d/tr $47/57/64; ☐) Centrally located in the Gaslamp Quarter, this HI facility is handy to public transportation and nightlife. It provides breakfast, basic dorm rooms, good kitchen facilities and 24-hour access.

   USA Hostels San Diego (Map pp592-3; ☎ 619-232-3100, 800-438-8622; www.usahostels.com; 726 5th Ave; dm/d incl breakfast $22/57; ☐) This Victorian-era hotel has been refitted with six-bed dorms, some doubles and a pleasant lounge and kitchen. It's right in the Gaslamp Quarter and so can be a bit noisy, but the crowd doesn't seem to mind.

MIDRANGE & TOP END
Little Italy Inn (Map pp592-3; ☎ 619-230-1600, 800-518-9930; www.littleitalyhotel.com; 505 E Grape St; r $110-220; P ☒) It may lie in the shadow of the I-5, but this small, charming hotel somehow manages to be serene anyway. Rooms are all tastefully appointed. Some of them have shared bathrooms, others in-room spa baths. Recommended.

   W Hotel (Map pp592-3; ☎ 619-231-8220, 888-625-5144; www.whotels.com; 421 West B St; r from $240; P

🗷 💻 🕾) San Diego's hippest high-end option includes a rooftop beach (the sand is heated, no less). On weekends the slick lobby turns into a nightclub, complete with house-spinning DJ. But don't worry, there is plenty of soundproofing, and the beds are engineered for exquisite comfort.

Omni Hotel (Map pp592-3; ☎ 619-231-6664, 800-843-6664; www.omnihotels.com; 675 L St; r from $329; 🅿 🗷 💻 🕾) Linked by a skyway to Petco Park, this 38-story megalith is San Diego's newest sleek marble getaway. Check out the rooftop deck with heated pool.

Prava Hotel (Map pp592-3; ☎ 619-233-3300; www.pravahotel.com; 911 5th Ave; r $140-190; 🅿 🗷 💻 🕾) Rooms are huge at this boutique hotel with pull-out sofas for extra guests, kitchenettes with blenders for cocktails, and king-size beds made up with Egyptian cotton sheets.

Horton Grand Hotel (Map pp592-3; ☎ 619-544-1886, 800-542-1886; www.hortongrand.com; 311 Island Ave; r $189; 🅿 🗷 💻) Some rooms in this turn-of-the-century brick hotel have wrought-iron balconies on the street, but the quietest face the inner courtyard. All are decorated in Victoriana and have gas fireplaces.

Hillcrest

Britt Scripps Inn (Map pp596-7; ☎ 888-881-1991; www.brittscripps.com; 406 Maple St; r from $295; 🅿 💻) This new Victorian B&B overlooks the downtown area from Banker's Hill and offers fantastic gourmet breakfasts, afternoon wine and hors d'oeuvres, and luxuriously appointed rooms.

Hillcrest Inn (Map pp596-7; ☎ 619-293-7078, 800-258-2280; www.hillcrestinn.net; 3754 5th Ave; r from $70) Given its location right in the heart of Hillcrest and crawling distance from the bars, this inn offers great value. Its motel rooms surround a central courtyard and there's a Jacuzzi, but neither air-con nor a pool. It's primarily a gay hotel that also welcomes straight guests, but not children.

Coronado

Hotel del Coronado (Map p589; ☎ 619-435-6611, 800-468-3533; www.hoteldel.com; 1500 Orange Ave; r $280-505; 🅿 🗷 💻 🕾) San Diego's iconic hotel, the 'Del' combines history (p603), luxury and access to the city's most stunning beach. Amenities include tennis courts, a pool, full-service spa, shops, restaurants, manicured grounds and a white-sand beach at the edge of the Pacific. However, half the accommo-

dations are not in the main Victorian-era hotel, but in an adjacent seven-story building constructed in the 1970s. For a sense of place, book a room in the original hotel.

Coronado Village Inn (Map p589; ☎ 619-435-9318; www.coronadovillageinn.com; 1017 Park Pl; r $105) The top budget choice in pricey Coronado, this 15-room 1928 hotel has no amenities, such as air-conditioning or big bathrooms, but its tidy rooms and location – two blocks from the beach, half a block to shops and restaurants – more than compensate. It even includes a self-serve continental breakfast.

Coronado Island Inn (Map p589; ☎ 619-435-0935, 888-436-0935; www.coronadoinn.com; 301 Orange Ave; r $105-125; 🅿 🕾) Some of the standard-issue rooms have kitchens; all have access to the pool at the motel's sister property across the street. Price includes breakfast.

Point Loma

HI San Diego Point Loma Hostel (Map p589; ☎ 619-223-4778; www.sandiegohostels.org; 3790 Udall St; dm incl breakfast members/nonmembers $19/22, r $48; 💻) It's a 20-minute walk from the heart of Ocean Beach to this HI hostel in Loma Portal, which is near a market and launderette. Buses 23 (from downtown, weekdays only) and 35 (from Old Town), run along nearby Voltaire St. No lockout times.

Best Western Island Palms Hotel (Map p589; ☎ 619-222-0561; www.islandpalms.com; 2051 Shelter Island Dr; r $159-180; 🅿 🗷 💻 🕾) The Island Palms is a small Polynesian-themed resort hotel fronting the yacht harbor, with comfortable, well-maintained upper-end-chain-motel-style rooms; those with a marina view cost $180, a bargain in these parts. Free bike rentals, too.

Ocean Beach

Ocean Beach (OB) is under the outbound flight path of jets departing from San Diego airport; pack earplugs.

Inn at Sunset Cliffs (Map pp604-5; ☎ 619-222-7901, 866-786-2543; www.innatsunsetcliffs.com; 1370 Sunset Cliffs Blvd; r from $150; 🅿 🕾) Right on the ocean at the north end of Sunset Cliffs, this motel has a garden that bursts with roses and a terrace with great ocean views. Some rooms have full kitchens. Ask about discounts.

Ocean Beach International Hostel (Map pp604-5; ☎ 619-223-7873, 800-339-7263; www.californiahostels.com; 4961 Newport Ave; dm $16-20, r $20-25; 💻) The cheapest option is only a couple of blocks from the ocean; it's a friendly, fun place that's popular with Europeans. Bus 35 from downtown passes Newport Ave a block east of the hostel.

Ocean Beach Hotel (Map pp604-5; ☎ 619-223-7191; www.obhotel.com; 5080 Newport Ave; r with ocean view $130-175, without $99-130; Ⓟ) Walk everywhere in OB from this three-story motel on the beach. Rooms are small, but have refrigerators and microwaves.

Mission Beach & Pacific Beach

Pacific Beach (PB) has most of the beachside accommodations. Motels provide better value in winter than summer, when rates are high and availability scarce (if not specified, summer rates are listed here).

Crystal Pier Hotel (Map pp604-5; ☎ 858-483-6983, 800-748-5894; www.crystalpier.com; 4500 Ocean Blvd; cottages summer $270-420, winter $225-355; Ⓟ) Unlike anyplace else in San Diego, Crystal Pier has cottages built right on the pier above the water. All have full ocean views and kitchens, but the original 1936 clapboard units are the best – though the newer, larger cottages sleep more people. For stays between July and December, book on the morning of January 1; for January to June, book on November 15 (keep hitting redial on the phone; it's worth the hours of aggravation). Minimum-stay requirements vary by season.

Banana Bungalow (Map pp604-5; ☎ 858-273-3060; www.bananabungalow.com; 707 Reed Ave; dm/r incl breakfast $24/75; Ⓠ) Reasonably clean, beach-party atmosphere, and communal patio right on the boardwalk.

Santa Clara Motel (Map pp604-5; ☎ 858-488-1193; 839 Santa Clara Pl; r $75-110; Ⓟ) This bare-bones motel in Mission Beach has brusque service, and you can't reserve in advance, but rates are the cheapest you'll find.

Beach Cottages (Map pp604-5; ☎ 858-483-7440; 4255 Ocean Blvd; r $120-180, cottages from $230; Ⓟ Ⓧ Ⓠ Ⓡ) Family-owned and operated, the place encompasses both plain motel rooms and cozy 1940s beachfront cottages. The price is right for groups who secure a cottage. Book well in advance.

Surfer Beach Hotel (Map pp604-5; ☎ 858-483-7070, 800-787-3373; www.surferbeachhotel.com; 711 Pacific Beach Dr; r $199; Ⓟ Ⓧ Ⓡ) This formerly undistinguished '60s motel just got a jazzy facelift. All rooms have pillow-top beds; most have ocean-view balconies. The beachside pool is heated year-round.

La Jolla

It's hard to find a room here under $100, even on weekdays off-season. The least expensive are on La Jolla Blvd, south of town. Longer stays yield lower rates.

Bed & Breakfast Inn at La Jolla (Map p608; ☎ 858-456-2066; www.innlajolla.com; 7753 Draper Ave; r $180-300; Ⓟ Ⓧ) Book ahead at this classy B&B. Designed in 1913 by Irving Gill, it was home to John Philip Sousa in the 1920s. Now it's one of San Diego's top B&Bs, and has rooms with noncheesy antiques. Some also have balconies and ocean views.

La Valencia (Map p608; ☎ 858-454-0771, 800-451-0772; www.lavalencia.com; 1132 Prospect St; r $275-550; Ⓟ Ⓧ Ⓠ Ⓡ) Called La Jolla's 'living room,' this pink Mediterranean palace spills down the hillside toward the ocean. Even if you can't afford to sleep with the 1926 ghosts of Depression-era Hollywood, tour the garden and then have a drink in the elegant Spanish revival lounge.

La Jolla Beach Travelodge (Map p608; ☎ 858-454-0716, 800-454-4361; www.lajollatravelodge.com; 6750 La Jolla Blvd; r $120-200; Ⓟ Ⓧ Ⓠ Ⓡ) Near Windansea Beach, this motel offers amenities like a heated pool, a Jacuzzi, and refrigerators and microwaves in every room, all at bargain prices – by La Jolla standards anyway.

Hotel Parisi (Map p608; ☎ 858-454-1511, 877-472-7474; www.hotelparisi.com; 1111 Prospect St; r $295-495; Ⓟ Ⓧ Ⓠ) Despite its self-conscious beauty (think an Armani suit made with 5% Lycra), the Parisi is one of San Diego's top boutique hotels for sumptuous rooms and contemporary style.

EATING

You can eat very well in San Diego, and at all price ranges. The city has an array of ethnic restaurants (though admittedly not as rich as in Los Angeles or San Francisco), good pub grub and Americana, California foodie venues that emphasize organic ingredients and rigorous freshness, and a generous sprinkling of super-refined temples of gastronomy.

Downtown & Embarcadero

Because of their proximity to the convention center, the restaurants here cater to an expense-account crowd and can be overpriced for dinner. Some are mainly daytime operations, while others provide entertainment well into the night.

BUDGET

Cafe Lulu (Map pp592-3; ☎ 619-238-0114; 419 F St; light mains $4-8; ☻ 9am-1am Sun-Thu, 9am-2:30am Fri & Sat) Linger over lattes or merlot at this hip café, and refuel on sandwiches, cheese boards and cakes. Open late. Outside seating.

Pokez (Map pp592-3; ☎ 619-702-7160; 947 E St; ☻ 10am-9pm Mon-Fri, 9am-9pm Sat & Sun) This SoCal burrito joint with an East Village soul caters to punks and suits alike. Good vegetarian dishes as well as *carne asada* (grilled beef) and enchiladas.

Dick's Last Resort (Map pp592-3; ☎ 619-231-9100; 345 4th Ave; mains $6-12; ☻ 11am-1:30am) A big frat party where revelers converse full voice while guzzling beer and downing fried foods.

Royal Thai (Map pp592-3; ☎ 619-230-842; cnr 5th & Island Aves; mains $7-13, lunch specials $8) A casually elegant eatery inside a building that's been an Asian restaurant ever since it opened its doors as Nanking Cafe in 1912.

Panda Inn (Map pp592-3; ☎ 619-233-7800; Horton Plaza, top fl; mains $10-15, lunch specials $8; ☻ 11am-10pm) Don't confuse this place with Panda Express, even though it's in the Horton Plaza food court. Its Mandarin and Szechuan special-ties make it one of the city's best places for Chinese.

Mimmo's Italian Village (Map pp592-3; ☎ 619-239-3710; 1743 India St; mains under $10; ☻ Mon-Sat 8am-4pm) In a cavernous building decorated to the hilt, Mimmo's deli serves salads, hot and cold sandwiches and lunch specials, such as lasagna and eggplant parmigiana.

Mona Lisa (Map pp592-3; ☎ 619-234-4893; 2061 India St; mains $9-16; ☻ lunch Mon-Sat, dinner daily) Aside from delicious and hearty meals (try the cannelloni), Mona Lisa also makes some of the best sandwiches in town, and sells im-ported Italian specialty foods at its market and deli.

MIDRANGE & TOP END

La Fiesta (Map pp592-3; ☎ 619-233-7800; 628 5th Ave; mains lunch $10-16, dinner $18; ☻ 11am-11:30pm) Chef Raul Delgadillo turns out creative takes on the food of Mexico City and surrounding regions.

Gaslamp Strip Club (Map pp592-3; ☎ 619-231-3140; 340 5th Ave; mains $10-20; ☻ dinner) Despite the name and the policy of refusing entry to anyone under 21, there's no live girls at this retro-Vegas dining steakhouse. Good steaks are a relative bargain, and the atmosphere is young and exuberant.

Café Sevilla (Map pp592-3; ☎ 619-233-5979; 555 4th Ave; tapas $5-8, mains $15-23; ☻ dinner) The tapas and Spanish food are good, but the truly delicious thing at Sevilla is its live tango and flamenco performances, which include a three-course meal for $40 per person, Friday to Sunday. Book in advance. Otherwise, there's music (and sangria) nightly in the tapas bar.

Star of the Sea (Map pp592-3; ☎ 619-232-7408; 1360 N Harbor Dr; mains $26-36; ☻ dinner) San Diego's top special-occasion seafood restaurant, where artful French-California presentations of expertly prepared fish are complemented by an elegant white-tablecloth dining room and mesmerizing water views. Reserve in advance; request a window table.

Indigo Grill (Map pp592-3; ☎ 619-234-6802; 1536 India St; mains $18-28; ☻ lunch Mon-Fri, dinner daily) Talk about fusion – chef Deborah Scott has won fame for her Oaxacan-Alaskan cook-ing, as in Mexican-Arctic. (Think fire and ice, spicy and sweet.) The vibe is convivial and relaxed, and sharing of huge dinner portions is encouraged. Make reservations.

Balboa Park

A great neighborhood for both delicious cheapies and high-end foodie meccas.

Islander Grill (Map pp596-7; ☎ 619-297-3929; 3645 Park Blvd; mains $7; ☻ 11am-8pm Mon-Sat, 11am-7pm Sun) Distinctively tart Guamanian barbecue served with red rice seasoned with adobo seeds. The Islander is located next to the lobby of a seedy hotel.

Wine Steals (Map pp596-7; ☎ 619-295-1188; 1243 University Ave; cheese & charcuterie boards $10-12; ☻ 2-10pm Mon-Thu, 2pm-midnight Fri & Sat) A convivial neighborhood place that specializes in fine but inexpensive wines (half a pour $1.50 to $2.50, glass $3 to $8), which you can pair with cheese-charcuterie boards.

Old Town

Most Old Town eateries serve unexciting Mexican fare in contrived digs, although good food, strong margaritas and outdoor seating can add up to a pleasant evening.

Old Town Mexican Cafe (Map pp596-7; ☎ 619-297-4330; 2489 San Diego Ave; mains around $9; ☻ 7am-midnight) Famous for its freshly made tortillas and *machacas* (shredded pork with onions and peppers). Serves breakfast.

Saffron Noodles & Saté (Map pp596-7; ☎ 619-574-7737; 3737 India St; mains $5-9; ☻ 10:30am-9pm Mon-Sat, 10:30am-8pm Sun) Fresh, healthy, delicious and cheap. What's not to like here? Dig into big bowls of steaming noodle soup or a plate of stir-fried noodles with plenty of al dente veggies.

El Agave (Map pp596-7; ☎ 619-220-0692; 2304 San Diego Ave; mains lunch $12-19, dinner $18-30) White-tablecloth Mexican for cognoscenti. The *mole* – a sauce that is made with chilies and chocolate – is superb, and you can choose from an astonishing 1200 different tequilas. Make reservations.

Gelato Vero Caffe (Map pp596-7; ☎ 619-295-9269; cnr Washington & India Sts; gelato per oz 59¢; ☾ 6am-midnight Sun-Thu, 7am-1am Fri & Sat) True Italian-style gelato, and among San Diego's best.

Hillcrest

Hillcrest is a great place to eat, whether you are looking for hangover hash or haute cuisine. Places tend to be more casual than downtown – and better value.

Bread & Cie (Map pp596-7; ☎ 619-683-9322; 350 University Ave; pastries $2-4, sandwiches $5-8; ☾ 7am-7pm Mon-Fri, 7am-6pm Sat, 8am-6pm Sun) Some of San Diego's best pastries and bread (including anise and fig, kalamata and black olive, and three-raisin), plus great sandwiches such as curried-chicken salad.

Hash House a Go Go (Map pp596-7; ☎ 619-298-4646; 3628 5th Ave; breakfast mains $6-14; ☾ breakfast, lunch & dinner) Serving the biggest – and among the best – breakfasts in San Diego, including scrumptious biscuits and gravy, towering benedicts and, of course, six kinds of hash.

Parallel 33 (Map pp596-7; ☎ 619-260-0033; 741 W Washington St; mains $18-27; ☾ dinner Mon-Sat) A smart, casual neighborhood spot, where the chef skillfully fuses the cuisines of the globe's 33°N latitude. Expect savory and sweet combinations from Morocco, Lebanon, India, China, Japan – and San Diego, which also lies at this latitude. Reserve a table.

Coronado

Nite & Day (Map p589; ☎ 619-435-9776; 847 Orange Ave; dishes under $8; ☾ 24hr) A refreshing change of pace in squeaky-clean Coronado, this eat-at-the-counter greasy spoon serves breakfast 'round the clock.

Bay Beach Cafe (Map p589; ☎ 619-435-4900; 1201 1st St; mains lunch $10-11, dinner $16-19; ☾ 11am-9pm, brunch Sat & Sun) Strategically located on the water with views across the bay to the downtown skyline, with good sandwiches and grill food.

Chez Loma (Map p589; ☎ 619-435-0661; 1132 Loma Ave; mains $20-29; ☾ dinner daily, brunch Sun) Inside an 1899 cottage, this cozy bistro serves updated versions of beef bourguignon, roast duckling and seafood cassoulet. For a bargain, come before 6pm for the $25 three-course, prix fixe menu.

Prince of Wales (Map p589; ☎ 619-522-8490; Hotel del Coronado, 1500 Orange Ave; mains $28-40; ☾ dinner Tue-Sun) Sup at a table overlooking the sea at one of San Diego's cushiest, and best, restaurants, with a French-inspired menu and creative young chef who spares no expense to get the finest ingredients.

Ocean Beach

OB is the place to go for cheap eats. Most places are concentrated on Newport Ave.

OB People's Food Store (Map pp604-5; ☎ 619-224-1387; 4765 Voltaire St; most light mains under $5; ☾ 8am-9pm) For vegetarian groceries, check out this organic cooperative with bulk foods, fresh soups and excellent premade sandwiches, salads and wraps. No meat.

Hodad's (Map pp604-5; ☎ 619-224-4623; 5010 Newport Ave; burgers around $5) OB's legendary burger joint serves great shakes and succulent hamburgers wrapped in paper. No shirt, no shoes, no problem.

Ortega's Cocina (Map pp604-5; ☎ 619-222-4205; 4888 Newport Ave; mains $5-9; ☾ breakfast, lunch & dinner Wed-Mon) Ortega's is so popular that people queue up for a spot at the counter. Seafood is the specialty, but all its soulful, classic Mexican dishes are delicious.

Portugalia (Map pp604-5; ☎ 619-222-7678; 4839 Newport Ave; mains lunch $6-9, dinner $17-20; ☾ 11am-10pm Tue-Sun) Classic Portuguese dishes like kale soup, salt cod and grilled meats are popular with Point Loma's large Portuguese population.

Mission Beach & Pacific Beach

You can eat well for not a lot of money at these two beach communities. Both locations have a young, mostly local scene; PB has the bulk of the restaurants, especially along Garnet Ave.

Eggery (Map pp604-5; ☎ 858-274-3122; 4150 Mission Blvd; mains $6-8; ☾ breakfast & lunch) Head to the Eggery in the morning. It has no view, but makes one of the best breakfasts at the beach; try the French toast.

Broken Yolk (Map pp604-5; ☎ 858-270-9655; 1851 Garnet Ave; mains $5-9; ☾ breakfast & lunch) If you're cruising Garnet, the Broken Yolk cooks up 47 omelette specials.

Mission Café (Map p604-5; ☎ 858-488-9060; 3795 Mission Blvd; dishes $6-9; ☺ breakfast & lunch) A PB favorite for its casual atmosphere and healthy version of comfort food with distinct Latin and Asian touches.

Saska's (Map pp604-5; ☎ 858-488-7311; 3768 Mission Blvd; pastas $9-12, mains $12-20) Seems like the whole Saska family is employed at this pleasant steak and pasta joint. Soak up alcohol with light meals ($8) served until 2am.

Isola (Map pp604-5; ☎ 858-274-7014; 1269 Garnet Ave; small plates $6-14; ☺ dinner) Down good tapas with white sangria while watching the upscale end of PB's postbeach scene.

La Jolla

La Jolla is a major haute-cuisine outpost, but there are some good budget options too.

Harry's Coffee Shop (Map p608; ☎ 858-454-7381; 7545 Girard Ave; dishes $6-11; ☺ 6am-3pm) Classic coffee shop with vinyl booths and a posse of regulars, from blue-haired socialites to sports celebs.

Spice & Rice (Map p608; ☎ 858-456-0466; 7734 Girard Ave; mains $12-16) A healthy but delicious take on Thai classics. Portions are generous, and the lunch menu, with soup and appetizer, is a bargain at $7.50.

Barolo (☎ 858-622-1202; 8935 Towne Center Dr; mains $11-20; ☺ lunch Mon-Fri, dinner daily) Don't let its shopping-center location put you off this gem. Barolo serves authentic Italian cooking, including homemade pasta, prepared by an off-the-boat chef.

George's at the Cove (Map p608; ☎ 858-454-4244; 1250 Prospect St; mains $26-42; ☺ dinner) Sweeping ocean vistas complement the artistry on the plate at La Jolla's top special-occasion restaurant. Chef Trey Fochee's Euro-Cal cuisine ranks among San Diego's best. There is a cheaper (mains $15 to $20) bistro upstairs, also with killer views.

DRINKING
Cafés

Cafe Bassam (Map pp592-3; ☎ 619-557-0173; 401 Market St; ☺ 8am-1:30am) Smoker-friendly cigar bar and café offers up espresso drinks and 150 different teas amid the owner's quirky memorabilia.

Javanican Coffee House (Map pp604-5; ☎ 858-483-8035; 4338 Cass St, Pacific Beach; ☺ 6am-10pm) Occupying a lovely Craftsman cottage and

a pair of flowery outdoor patios, this is hands-down San Diego's prettiest place to get buzzed on caffeine. There's also live music many evenings.

Also recommended:

David's Coffeehouse (Map pp596-7; ☎ 619-296-4173; 3766 5th Ave, Hillcrest; ☺ 7am-11pm Sun-Thu, 7am-midnight Fri & Sat) Outside patio.

Living Room Coffeehouse (Map p608; ☎ 858-459-1187; 1010 Prospect St, La Jolla; ☺ 6:30am-midnight) The La Jolla branch of the popular Hillcrest area café (p590).

Bars

Most of the bars in Hillcrest are gay. For a complete list, check out *Buzz* and the *Gay & Lesbian Times*, both widely available in the neighborhood.

DOWNTOWN

In the center of the city's straight nightlife, the line between restaurant, bar and club often gets blurry after 10pm.

Bitter End (Map pp592-3; ☎ 619-338-9300; 770 5th Ave) The crowd wears khakis and drinks martinis at this former brothel that has been turned into an atmospheric watering hole. There's an extensive selection of beers on tap. Dancing downstairs.

Red Circle Bar (Map pp592-3; ☎ 619-234-9211; 420 E St) Order a martini, raise your pinkie and peruse the Soviet-era memorabilia and lissome crowd bathed in sexy red lighting at this trendy Russian-themed boîte. The bar serves more than 100 varieties of vodka.

PACIFIC BEACH

Moondoggies (Map pp604-5; ☎ 858-483-6550; 832 Garnet Ave) Next door to Club Tremors, Moondoggies has a large patio, big-screen TVs, pool tables, good food and an extensive tap selection; there's a second location in La Jolla.

Cass Street Bar & Grill (Map pp604-5; ☎ 858-270-1320; 744 Ventura Pl, Mission Beach) This PB classic attracts young and old alike with its 16 beers on top and complete lack of attitude.

LA JOLLA

Moondoggies (Map p608; ☎ 858-454-9722; 909 Prospect St, 2nd fl) Frat boys do shots at this bar, where there's dancing to hip-hop and Top 40 after 10pm Thursday to Saturday.

La Sala (Map p608; ☎ 858-454-0771; La Valencia Hotel, 1132 Prospect St) For civilized cocktails or Sunday-afternoon Bloody Marys, visit the romantic, ocean-view lobby bar of La Valencia Hotel, which becomes a piano lounge on Friday and Saturday evenings.

ENTERTAINMENT

The free weekly *San Diego Reader* and *San Diego Union Tribune*'s Night & Day section hit the stands each Thursday – both have comprehensive entertainment listings. The nightlife scene for lesbians and gay men is small but lively, and – predictably – concentrated in Hillcrest.

Times Arts Tix (Map pp592-3; ☎ 619-497-5000), in the little Horton Plaza Park on Broadway, sells half-price tickets for same-day evening or next-day matinee performances in theater, music and dance, as well as full-price tickets to most major events in the area.

Nightclubs & Live Music

SiDE Bar (Map pp592-3; ☎ 619-696-0946; 536 Market St) This Gaslamp Quarter institution perennially snags San Diego's PYTs. Not on the guest list? Dress up, not down, to get past the bouncers.

W Hotel (Map pp592-3; ☎ 619-231-8220, 888-625-5144; www.whotels.com; 421 West B St) The silicone set twirls its Vuitton on the catwalk of the W Hotel (p614) on Thursday, Friday and Saturday nights. Occasionally, dumbfounded guests must show their key to get past the bouncers.

Lips (Map pp596-7; ☎ 619-295-7900; 2770 5th Ave, Hillcrest) The cross-dressing waitresses double as performers at this restaurant-nightclub. Those with egos of steel should check out 'Bitchy Bingo' on Wednesdays. Fun.

Blind Melons (Map pp604-5; ☎ 858-483-7844; 710 Garnet Ave, Pacific Beach) The club books a solid lineup of blues musicians with the occasional rock act thrown in for good measure.

Winston's (Map pp604-5; ☎ 619-222-6822; 1921 Bacon St, Ocean Beach) Bands play most nights, often live reggae. On Sunday there's a football party. Mondays a Grateful Dead cover band draws stoners and Jerry-o-philics.

Comedy Store (Map p608; ☎ 858-454-9176; 916 Pearl St, La Jolla) One of the area's most established comedy venues also serves meals and drinks.

Classical Music & Opera

San Diego Opera (☎ 619-533-7000) This fine company performs from January to May at the Civic Theatre (Map pp592–3).

San Diego Symphony (Map pp592-3; ☎ 619-235-0804; www.sandiegosymphony.com; 750 B St) This accomplished symphony presents classical and family concerts at the Civic Center, as well as the innovative Light Bulb Series, an interactive program intended to demystify classical music.

In summer the symphony moves outdoors to the **Navy Pier** (Map pp592-3; 960 N Harbor Dr) for its more light-hearted Summer Pops season.

Cinema

Landmark Hillcrest (Map pp596-7; ☎ 619-819-0236; 3965 5th Ave) Regularly shows new art and foreign films as well as classics.

The main downtown cinemas, which both show current-release movies:

Gaslamp 15 (Map pp592-3; ☎ 619-232-0400; 701 5th St) Pacific Theater's elegant new venue.

UA Horton Plaza (Map pp592-3; ☎ 800-326-3264; Horton Plaza)

Theater

Theater thrives in San Diego and is one of the city's greatest cultural attractions. Book tickets from the theaters or with one of the agencies listed in the introduction to this section. Venues include the following:

Civic Theatre (Map pp592-3; ☎ 619-570-1100; 1100 3rd Ave) For Broadway musicals and opera.

La Jolla Playhouse (Map p608; ☎ 619-550-1010; www.lajollaplayhouse.com; UCSD) Classic and contemporary plays.

Old Globe Theatre (Map pp596-7; ☎ 619-239-2255; www.oldglobe.org; 1363 Old Globe Way; tickets $17-55) Mostly Shakespeare.

San Diego Repertory Theatre (Map pp592-3; ☎ 619-544-1000; www.sandiegorep.com; 79 Horton Plaza) Regional and avant-garde works.

Theatre in Old Town (Map pp596-7; ☎ 619-688-2494; www.theatreinoldtown.com; 4040 Twiggs St) Musical theater.

Sports

Petco Park (Map p589; ☎ 619-795-5000, for tickets 877-374-2784; www.padres.com; 100 Park Blvd; tickets $6-49) The San Diego Padres Major League Baseball team began the 2004 season in this new stadium right in the middle of downtown San Diego. Baseball season goes from April to September.

Qualcomm Stadium (Map p589; ☎ 858-874-4500, for tickets 619-220-8497; www.chargers.com; 9449 Friars Rd; tickets from $25) The San Diego Chargers National Football League team plays here in Mission Valley (there's a San Diego Trolley stop right in front). Football season is from August to January.

San Diego Sports Arena (Map p589; ☎ 619-224-4171; 3500 Sports Arena Blvd) This is where the San Diego Sockers play soccer and the San Diego Gulls play ice hockey. It's also the venue for any big rock concerts visiting town. Be aware that the neighborhood may be a little rough after dark.

SHOPPING

You can usually rely on gift shops at the museums and major attractions for decent souvenirs: a stuffed Shamu from SeaWorld, a rubber snake from the zoo, or a historical reprint from the Museum of San Diego History. For quick access to a huge quantity of mid- to high-end chain stores, head to downtown's Horton Plaza Center (p593). Little Italy has become the de facto design district, with some great home furnishings as well as personal accessories. La Jolla is the place to go for jewels and couture, particularly along Girard Ave and Prospect St. For bikinis and surfboards, head to Garnet Ave in Pacific Beach or Newport Ave in Ocean Beach. They also have good thrift and vintage shops, but the best are along Hillcrest's 5th Ave.

KADD (Map pp592-3; ☎ 619-546-5121; www.kettner artanddesigndistrict.com) The Kettner Art & Design District consists of independent purveyors of fine art and home furnishing, from leather couches to hand-blown glass, all clustered within a few blocks of Little Italy's main drag.

Wear It Again Sam (Map pp596-7; ☎ 619-299-0185; 3823 5th Ave) There are several cool thrift stores on 5th Ave, but this place sells the best vintage gear – and it's well organized.

Pilar's Beachwear (Map pp604-5; ☎ 858-488-3056; 3745 Mission Blvd, Mission Beach) For swimwear, women should head to Pilar's, which has all the latest styles in all sizes.

South Coast Surf Shop (Map pp604-5; ☎ 619-223-7017; 5023 Newport Ave, Ocean Beach) Apathetic surfer dudes man the counter at this beach-apparel and surf-gear shop that carries a good selection of Quiksilver, Hurley, Billabong and O'Neill for men and women.

Buffalo Exchange (Map pp596-7; ☎ 858-273-6227; 1007 Garnet Ave) If you need something to wear to dinner, Buffalo carries a good selection of contemporary and vintage fashions, including designer labels.

Kobey's Swap Meet (Map p589; ☎ 619-523-2700, 619-224-4176; parking lot, San Diego Sports Arena; admission 50¢ Fri, $1 Sat & Sun; ⊙ 7am-3pm Fri-Sun) A massive flea market, this is the place to get really cheap stuff. On sale are new and used items, including sunglasses, clothing, jewelry, produce, flowers and plants, tools and furniture.

Sigi's Boutique (Map p608; ☎ 858-454-7244; 7888 Girard Ave) Sigi's is where La Jolla ladies prefer to get their European couture.

GETTING THERE & AWAY
Air
Most flights into **San Diego International Airport** (SAN; Map p589; ☎ 619-231-2100; www.san.org), about 3 miles west of downtown, are domestic. Coming in from overseas, you'll most likely change flights – and clear US Customs – at one of the major US gateway airports, such as LA, Chicago or Miami.

The standard one-way fare between LA and San Diego is about $75. The flight from LA takes only about 35 minutes; the drive is around two hours. Rental-car prices are about the same in both cities.

If you're flying to/from other US cities, it's almost as cheap to fly to/from San Diego as it is to LA. Airlines serving San Diego include Aeromexico, America West, American, Continental, Delta, Northwest, Southwest and US Airways. For contact details see p716.

Bus
Greyhound (Map pp592-3; ☎ 800-231-2222, 619-239-3266; 120 W Broadway) serves San Diego from cities all over North America. The station has luggage lockers ($5 per day) and telephones.

To and from LA (one way/round trip $16/27, 2¼ to four hours, almost every half hour) trip times vary depending on the number of stops en route. There is a bus to Anaheim, the home of Disneyland, which runs nine times per day for the same prices (and about the same trip duration).

Services between San Francisco and San Diego (one way/round trip $57/11, 11 hours, nine daily) usually require a transfer in LA. There is one daily bus to Las Vegas and seven more that require you to change in either LA or San Bernardino ($49/95, 7½ to 12½ hours).

Greyhound also has direct services from San Diego to Tijuana, across the border in Mexico (one way/round trip $7/9, one hour, hourly on the half hour), where you can connect to other buses serving destinations throughout Mexico.

There are also seven daily buses to Calexico, inland on the US side of the border, across from Mexicali. The trip takes three hours and costs one way/round trip $24/40. Services from Calexico are limited to two buses a day.

Train

Amtrak (☎ 800-872-7245; www.amtrak.com) trains arrive at and depart from the **Santa Fe train depot** (Map pp592-3; 1050 Kettner Blvd) at the western end of C St. The *Pacific Surfliner* makes up to 11 round trips to LA ($21, 2½ hours); as many as five trains continue on to Santa Barbara ($32 each way, 5½ hours).

For travel to San Francisco take the *Pacific Surfliner* to LA, where you can catch the *Coast Starlight* to Oakland, with onward motor-coach service to San Francisco ($88, 14 hours). Services to other parts of the USA also require a change in LA.

GETTING AROUND

Many people get around by car, but you can reach most places on public transportation. Metropolitan buses and the trolley lines are run by Metropolitan Transit Service (MTS), and several other bus companies serve surrounding areas. All sorts of local public-transportation tickets, maps and information are available from the **Transit Store** (Map pp592-3; ☎ 619-234-1060; 102 Broadway at 1st Ave; ⏰ 9am-5pm Mon-Fri). It sells the Day Tripper Transit Pass ($5/15 for one day/four consecutive days), which is good for unlimited travel on local buses, the trolley and bay ferry.

To/From the Airport

Bus 992 – nicknamed the *Flyer* – operates at 10- to 15-minute intervals between the airport and downtown (adult/senior $2.25/1). Buses leave between 5am and 1am and make several stops along Broadway before heading north on Harbor Dr to the airport.

Several companies operate door-to-door shuttles from all three airport terminals. Per-person fares depend on the distance traveled; figure on about $10 to Old Town or downtown and $16 to La Jolla. For some of the shorter trips, taxis charge only slightly more and may therefore be preferable, especially if there's more than one of you traveling.

If you're going *to* the airport, call the shuttle company a day or so ahead to make arrangements for a pick-up time and location. **Cloud 9 Shuttle** (☎ 619-505-4950, 800-974-8885) is the most established company. There are other companies as well:
Airport Shuttle (☎ 619-234-4403)
Seaside Shuttle (☎ 619-281-6451)
Xpress Shuttle (☎ 619-295-1900)

Bicycle

Some areas around San Diego are great for biking, particularly Pacific Beach, Mission Beach, Mission Bay and Coronado.

All public buses are equipped with bike racks and will transport two-wheelers free. Inform the driver before boarding, then stow your bike on the rack on the tail end of the bus. For more information telephone ☎ 619-685-4900.

The following outfits all rent various types of bicycles, from mountain and road bikes to kids' bikes and cruisers. In general, expect to pay about $5 per hour, $10 to $14 per half-day (four hours) and $14 to $25 per day.
Bike Cab Co (Map pp592-3; ☎ 888-245-3222; 523 Island Ave)
Cheap Rentals (Map pp604-5; ☎ 800-941-7761; 3221 Mission Blvd, Mission Beach)
Hamel's Beach Rentals (Map pp604-5; ☎ 858-488-5050; 704 Ventura Place, Mission Beach)
Holland's Bike (Map pp604-5; ☎ 619-435-3153; 977 Orange Ave, Coronado)

Boat

A regular ferry ($2.25) runs hourly between Broadway Pier and Coronado. A **water taxi** (☎ 619-235-8294; per person from $5) makes a regular connection between Seaport Village and Coronado, where it stops at the Ferry Landing Marketplace and Glorietta Bay. The service runs 2pm to 10pm Monday to Friday and 11am to 11pm Saturday and Sunday. It also makes on-call trips to Shelter Island, Harbor Island, Chula Vista and South Bay.

Bus

MTS covers most of the metropolitan area, North County, La Jolla and the beaches and is most convenient if you're going to/from downtown and not staying out late at night. Get the free *Regional Transit Map* from the Transit Store.

For route and fare information, call **MTS** (☎ 619-233-3004, 800-266-6883, 24hr recorded info 619-

DETOUR: SAN DIEGO WILD ANIMAL PARK

Since the early 1960s, the San Diego Zoological Society has been developing the **Wild Animal Park** (Map p587; ☎ 760-747-8702; www.sandiegozoo.org; 15500 San Pasquale Valley Rd; adult/child 3-11 $28.50/17.50; ☷ 9am-8pm summer, 9am-4pm rest of year), an 1800-acre, open-range zoo where herds of giraffes, zebras, rhinos and other animals roam the open valley floor. Currently you can take a 50-minute ride (there are plans for a new, faster tram) around the preserves on the Wgasa Bush monorail (actually an open-sided electric tram), which gives great views of the animals and includes interesting commentary. Since the monorail makes a loop, sit on the right side (inside the loop) for the best viewing. The animals look wonderful in the wide, open spaces, though often you can't get as close to them as you can in a regular zoo.

Over 500 animals are born here every year. At the Petting Kraal you can touch some of the youngest. Animal shows are held in a number of areas, between 11am and 4:30pm daily; pick up a map and a schedule as you enter.

The park has all services, from souvenir shops to places to eat (with choices for vegetarians). It's just north of Hwy 78, 5 miles east of I-15 from the Via Rancho Parkway exit. Plan 45 minutes transit by car from San Diego, except in rush hour when that figure can double. Bus 386 will get you there from the Escondido Transit Center, Monday to Saturday, but it's a long, involved process getting back; you're better off going by car. For bus information contact **North San Diego County Transit District** (☎ 619-233-3004, from North County 800-266-6883; www.gonctd.com).

The park remains open an hour after the entrance gates close. Admission includes the monorail and all shows. Discount coupons are widely available. A combined ticket to visit the San Diego Zoo and Wild Animal Park within a five-day period costs $56/38 per adult/child. Parking is $6 extra. For a real safari experience, photo caravan tours drive right up alongside the animals, but they're pricey, and reservations are required; there are also night tours available at different times of year – call the park to inquire. There are also facilities for disabled visitors; call ☎ 760-738-5067 for information.

685-4900; ☷ 5:30am-8:30pm Mon-Fri, 8am-5pm Sat & Sun). For route planning via the Internet, go to www.sdcommute.com.

Tickets cost $1.75 for most trips, including a transfer that is good for up to two hours; on express routes it's $2.50. Exact fare is required.

Useful routes to/from downtown:

Route No	Destination
3	Balboa Park, UCSD
4	National City
5	Old Town, Little Italy
7	Seaport Village, Balboa Park
25	Mission Valley, Fashion Valley, Hillcrest
30	Pacific Beach, University Towne Centre
34	Sports Arena, Mission Beach, Belmont Park, Pacific Beach, Stephen Birch Aquarium, UCSD, University Towne Centre
35	Ocean Beach
901	Coronado

Car

All the big-name rental companies have convenient desks at the airport, but lesser-known ones can be cheaper. It's definitely worth shopping around and haggling – prices vary widely, even from day to day within the same company. The western terminal at the airport has free direct phones to a number of car-rental companies – you can call several and then get a courtesy bus to the company of your choice. Also, car rentals are as cheap or cheaper in LA, so it might be preferable to get one there.

For contact details of the big-name rental companies, including Avis, Budget and Hertz, see p724. Some of the smaller, independent companies – such as **California Rent a Car** (Map pp592-3; ☎ 619-238-9999; 904 W Grape St) and **West Coast Rent a Car** (Map pp592-3; ☎ 619-544-0606; 834 W Grape St), both in Little Italy – may have lower rates and offer more relaxed conditions.

Taxi

Fares are around $2.20 to start, and then are about $2.30 per mile. Some established companies:

American Cab (☎ 619-292-1111)
Orange Cab (☎ 619-291-4444)
San Diego Cab (☎ 619-226-7294)
Yellow Cab (☎ 619-239-8061)

SAN DIEGO AREA

Train

A commuter train service, the *Coaster*, leaves the Santa Fe train depot (Map pp592–3) and runs up the coast to North County, with stops in Solana Beach, Encinitas, Carlsbad and Oceanside. In the metropolitan area, it stops at the Sorrento Valley station (where there's a connecting shuttle to UCSD) and Old Town. Tickets are available from vending machines at stations and must be validated prior to boarding. Fares range from $3.75 to $5.25; machines give change.

There are 11 daily trains in each direction Monday to Friday; the first trains leave Oceanside at 5:23am and the Santa Fe depot at 6:33am; the last ones depart at 5:28pm and 6:45pm, respectively. On Saturday, there are four trains only.

For information, contact **Regional Transit** (☎ 619-233-3004, from North County 800-266-6883; www.sdcommute.com).

Trolley

Two trolley lines run to/from the downtown terminal near the Santa Fe train depot (see Map p589). The Blue Line goes south to the San Ysidro border and north to Old Town, then continues east to Qualcomm Stadium. From the stadium you can catch the Green Line all the way through Mission Valley to Mission San Diego and on to Santee. The Orange Line goes east, past the Convention Center to El Cajon and Santee. Trolleys run between 4:20am and 2:20am daily at 15-minute intervals during the day, and every 30 minutes in the evening. The Blue Line continues running all night on Saturday.

Fares vary with distance ($1.25 to $3). Tickets are dispensed from vending machines on the station platforms and are valid for two hours from the time of validation. Machines give change. For information, contact **Regional Transit** (☎ 619-233-3004, from North County 800-266-6883; www.sdcommute.com).

NORTH COUNTY COAST

A little north of La Jolla, the coastal cliffs shrink quickly, making way for a series of wide, inviting beaches that stretch nearly unbroken all the way to Camp Pendleton, the huge military base that takes up the northwest corner of the county.

Known simply as 'North County,' this region resembles the San Diego of 40 years ago, though more and more development, especially east of I-5, has turned it into a giant bedroom community. Though there is not much to distinguish one town from the next, this is a great place for a lazy soak in the laid-back SoCal scene. And San Diego is never far away. Via I-5 in nonrush-hour traffic, Del Mar is only 20 to 30 minutes from San Diego, Oceanside 45 to 60 minutes; so you can zip in for a citified afternoon or evening.

Information

The **San Diego North County Convention & Visitors Bureau** (☎ 760-745-4741, 800-848-3336; www.sandiego north.com; 360 N Escondido Blvd), in Escondido, is an excellent source for information on all of North County, including inland locations. Request a free visitors guide.

Getting There & Around

From the south, take N Torrey Pines Rd to Del Mar for the most scenic approach to North County. Continue along the coast on S21 (which changes its name from Camino del Mar to Pacific Coast Hwy to Old Hwy 101, going north). The I-5 is quicker and continues to LA. If possible, avoid driving during rush hour (7am to 10am and 3pm to 7pm Monday to Friday).

Bus 101 departs from University Towne Centre near La Jolla and follows the coastal road to Oceanside, while bus 310 operates an express service up I-5; for information call the **North County Transit District** (NCTD; ☎ 760-966-6500; www.gonctd.com). The NCTD also operates the *Coaster* commuter train, which originates in San Diego, and makes stops in Solana Beach, Encinitas, Carlsbad and Oceanside. All NCTD buses and trains have bike racks. Greyhound buses stop at Oceanside and San Diego, but nowhere in between.

DEL MAR

pop 4400

The ritziest of North County's seaside suburbs, Del Mar has good (if rather pricey) restaurants, high-end boutiques and a fabled horse-racing track, which is also the site of the annual county fair in June. Downtown Del Mar (sometimes called 'the village') extends for about a mile along Camino del Mar. At its hub, where 15th St crosses Camino del Mar, the tasteful Del Mar Plaza

NORTH COUNTY COAST

0 ——————— 10 km
0 ——————— 6 miles

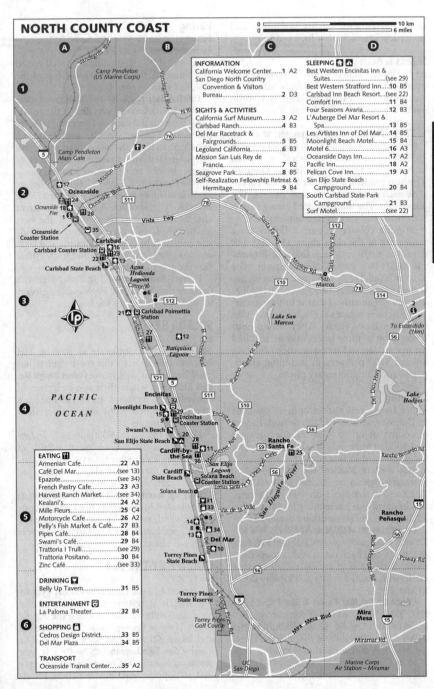

SAN DIEGO AREA

INFORMATION

California Welcome Center......**1** A2	
San Diego North Country Convention & Visitors Bureau......**2** D3	

SIGHTS & ACTIVITIES

California Surf Museum.........**3** A2	
Carlsbad Ranch.....................**4** B3	
Del Mar Racetrack & Fairgrounds......**5** B5	
Legoland California...............**6** B3	
Mission San Luis Rey de Francia.....**7** B2	
Seagrove Park.....................**8** B5	
Self-Realization Fellowship Retreat & Hermitage.....**9** B4	

SLEEPING

Best Western Encinitas Inn & Suites.....(see 29)	
Best Western Stratford Inn....**10** B5	
Carlsbad Inn Beach Resort...(see 22)	
Comfort Inn...........................**11** B4	
Four Seasons Avaria.............**12** B3	
L'Auberge Del Mar Resort & Spa.....**13** B5	
Les Artistes Inn of Del Mar....**14** B5	
Moonlight Beach Motel.........**15** B4	
Motel 6...............................**16** A3	
Oceanside Days Inn.............**17** A2	
Pacific Inn..........................**18** A3	
Pelican Cove Inn..................**19** A3	
San Elijo State Beach Campground.....**20** B4	
South Carlsbad State Park Campground.....**21** B3	
Surf Motel..........................(see 22)	

EATING

Armenian Cafe.....................**22** A3	
Café Del Mar......................(see 13)	
Epazote..............................(see 34)	
French Pastry Cafe...............**23** A3	
Harvest Ranch Market..........(see 34)	
Kealani's.............................**24** A2	
Mille Fleurs.........................**25** C4	
Motorcycle Cafe..................**26** A2	
Pelly's Fish Market & Café....**27** B3	
Pipes Café...........................**28** B4	
Swami's Café.......................**29** B4	
Trattoria I Trulli...................(see 29)	
Trattoria Positano................**30** B4	
Zinc Café............................(see 33)	

DRINKING

Belly Up Tavern....................**31** B5	

ENTERTAINMENT

La Paloma Theater...............**32** B4	

SHOPPING

Cedros Design District..........**33** B5	
Del Mar Plaza.....................**34** B5	

TRANSPORT

Oceanside Transit Center.....**35** A2	

boasts restaurants, quality boutiques and upper-level terraces that look out to sea.

Sights & Activities

At the beach end of 15th St, **Seagrove Park** overlooks the ocean. This little stretch of well-groomed beachfront lawn is favorite gathering place for locals and a good spot for a picnic.

The **Del Mar Racetrack & Fairgrounds** (☎ 858-755-1141; www.dmtc.com; admission $3-8) was founded in 1937 by a number of Hollywood luminaries, including Bing Crosby and Jimmy Durante. The lush gardens and pink, Mediterranean-style architecture are a visual delight. Get gussied up. The thoroughbred racing season runs from mid-July to mid-September.

Brightly colored hot-air balloons are a trademark of the skies above Del Mar. For a sunset flight, contact **California Dreamin'** (☎ 800-373-3359; www.californiadreamin.com). The *Reader* (available in cafés and convenience stores) carries other balloon-company listings and frequently contains hot-air excursion discount coupons. Flights usually take off at sunrise or sunset. They last an hour (though up to three hours may be required for instruction and transportation) and cost around $200 per person, including champagne and complimentary photo.

Sleeping

There are no real budget options available in Del Mar, at least in high season. Expect discounts of up to 40% outside summer and holiday weekends for all North County lodgings listed in this book.

Best Western Stratford Inn (☎ 858-755-1501; www.stratfordinndelmar.com; 710 Camino Del Mar; r $150-220; 🗟) A motel complex with well-kept rooms, the Stratford also has laundry facilities, a few kitchenettes and some distant ocean views.

Les Artistes Inn of Del Mar (☎ 858-755-4646, 800-223-8449; www.lesartistesinn.com; 1702 Coast Blvd; d $95, ste $130-185; ✖) Each room at this souped-up motel is devoted to an early-20th-century artist, with framed prints and kitschy decor to match.

L'Auberge Del Mar Resort & Spa (☎ 858-245-9757, 800-553-1336; www.laubergedelmar.com; 1540 Camino Del Mar; r $249-490; 🗖 🗟) Rebuilt in the 1990s on the grounds of the historic Hotel del Mar, L'Auberge continues its long tradition of European-style elegance, including full-service spa and lovely gardens.

Eating

Epazote (☎ 858-259-9966; 1555 Camino Del Mar; mains lunch $10-14, dinner $17-26) The Southwestern-style tapas and spit-grilled cuisine are well spiced and flavorful; the view from the top of the Del Mar Plaza is even better.

Café Del Mar (☎ 858-481-1133; 1247 Camino Del Mar; mains lunch $9-13, dinner $11-20) Dine in the courtyard, beneath the canopy of a coral tree, on mains-sized salads (try the warm chicken salad), pizza from the wood-fired oven, and simple grilled and roasted meats. Lots of veggie choices, too. Smoking section.

Mille Fleurs (☎ 858-756-3085; 6009 Paseo Delicias, Rancho Santa Fe; www.millefleurs.com; mains lunch $20-25, dinner $30-35; 🕑 lunch Mon-Fri, dinner daily) German chef Martin Woesle runs one of the best kitchens in California, delivering up exquisite French cuisine with California and German touches. As the name suggests, edible flowers grace many dishes.

Harvest Ranch Market (☎ 858-847-0555; 1555 Camino Del Mar; 🕑 8am-9pm) High-quality groceries and sandwiches for the beach.

SOLANA BEACH

pop 13,400

Solana Beach is not quite as posh as Del Mar, its neighbor to the south, but it has good beaches as well as the **Cedros Design District** (Cedros Ave), where there is a collection of home-furnishing stores, art and architecture studios, antiques shops and handcrafted-clothing boutiques.

Zinc Café (☎ 858-793-5436; mains $5-7; 🕑 7am-5pm) Order at the counter or sit outside at this all-veg café, which serves an Italian-influenced menu that also includes fine salads, vegetarian chili and pizza.

Belly Up Tavern (☎ 858-481-9022, 858-481-8140; 143 S Cedros Ave) Music lovers flock to this converted warehouse and bar that consistently books good bands, from jazz to funk. Covers vary; call ahead.

CARDIFF-BY-THE-SEA

pop 62,000

Shortened to just 'Cardiff' by most people, this stretch of restaurants, surf shops and New Age–style businesses along the Pacific Coast Hwy is known both for its surfing and its consciously laid-back lifestyle. The nearby **San Elijo Lagoon** (☎ 760-436-3944; www.sanelijo.org) is a 1000-acre ecological preserve that is popular with bird-watchers for its

SAN DIEGO AREA

abundance of herons, coots, terns, ducks, egrets and about 250 more species. A 7-mile network of trails leads through the area. At **Cardiff State Beach** (☎ 760-753-5091; www.parks .ca.gov; ☼ 7am-sunset), just south of Cardiff-by-the-Sea, the surf break on the reef is mostly popular with longboarders. Parking costs $6. A little further north, San Elijo State Beach has good winter waves.

Sleeping & Eating

Comfort Inn (☎ 760-944-0427, 800-424-6423; www .choicehotels.com; 1661 Villa Cardiff Dr; r incl breakfast $150; ☒ ☒) This faux-Tudor motel just off I-5 offers comfortable rooms that sleep up to four people.

San Elijo State Beach Campground (☎ 760-753-5091, reservations 800-444-7275; tent/RV sites in summer $26/39) Overlooks the surf at the end of Birmingham Dr. Also has free wireless.

Pipes Café (☎ 760-632-0056; 121 Liverpool Ave; mains $5-7; ☼ 7am-3pm) Barefoot surfers chow down egg burritos and scrambles here before hitting the water. At lunch there are sandwiches, too. A wall mural details North County surfing.

Trattoria Positano (☎ 760-632-0111; 2171 San Elijo Ave; mains $11-29; ☼ lunch Mon-Sat, dinner daily) For white-tablecloth Italian food book a table at this homey mom-and-pop trattoria, one block inland from the highway.

ENCINITAS

pop 62,700

Since Paramahansa Yoganada founded his **Self-Realization Fellowship Retreat & Hermitage** here in 1937, the town has been a magnet for healers and seekers. The gold lotus domes of the hermitage – conspicuous on Old Hwy 101 (S21) – mark the southern end of Encinitas, as well as the turnout for **Swami's**, a powerful reef break favored by territorial locals. If you practice yoga or meditation, check out the hermitage's **Meditation Garden** (☎ 760-753-2888; 215 K St; ☼ 9am-5pm Tue-Sat, 11am-5pm Sun), which has wonderful ocean vistas; the entrance is west of Old Hwy 101 (S21).

The heart of Encinitas lies north of the hermitage between E and D Sts. Apart from the outdoor cafés, bars, restaurants and surf shops, the town's main attraction is **La Paloma Theater** (☎ 760-436-7469; 471 S Coast Hwy 101), built in 1928. La Paloma shows current movies nightly.

Sleeping & Eating

Moonlight Beach Motel (☎ 760-753-0623, 800-323-1259; www.moonlightbeachmotel.com; 233 2nd St; r $110-125; ☒) Upstairs rooms have private decks and partial ocean views at this homey motel, 1½ blocks from the sea. Not all rooms have air-con; some could use upgrading, but they are clean and quiet.

Best Western Encinitas Inn & Suites (☎ 760-942-7455, 866-326-4648; www.bwencinitas.com; 85 Encinitas Blvd; r $145-170) If you wear nail polish or white pants, you'll be better off at this hotel, which has all modern conveniences and up-to-date furnishings.

Swami's Café (☎ 760-944-0612; 1163 S Coast Hwy; mains $4-7; ☼ breakfast & lunch) For breakfast burritos, stir-fries, salads and smoothies, you can't beat Swami's. Lots for vegetarians.

Trattoria I Trulli (☎ 760-943-6800; 830 S Coast Hwy; mains $11-20) One taste of the homemade gnocchi, ravioli or lasagna, and you'll know why this home-style Italian trattoria is always packed. Make reservations.

CARLSBAD

pop 95,100

Besides fine beaches, the town is home to the kitschy but fun Legoland. Carlsbad got its start when train service arrived in the 1880s. As a result, it has a solid downtown of four square blocks rather than stretching along the highway like most North County towns. Early homesteader John Frazier, a former ship's captain, claimed his well water had identical mineral content to the spa water of Karlsbad (hence the town's name), in Bohemia (now the Czech Republic). Now, people come for the waves rather than the waters.

Sights & Activities

LEGOLAND CALIFORNIA

Modeled loosely after the original in Denmark, **Legoland California** (☎ 760-918-5346; www .lego.com/legoland/california; ☼ 10am-5pm daily summer, 10am-8pm daily mid-Jun–late-Aug, Thu-Mon fall-spring; adult/child 3-12 $47/39, 2-day tickets $55/47) is a fantasy environment built entirely of those little colored plastic building blocks that many of us grew up with. Highlights include **Miniland**, in which the skylines of major metropolitan cities have been spectacularly re-created entirely of Lego. There are also lots of activities geared specifically to kids, such as face painting, boat rides and scaled-down roller coasters.

To get to Legoland, take the Legoland/ Cannon Rd exit off I-5 and follow the signs. From downtown Carlsbad or downtown San Diego, take the *Coaster* to the Carlsbad Village Station; from here bus 344 goes straight to the park. Call to inquire about discounts.

CARLSBAD RANCH

From mid-March to early May, the 50-acre flower fields of **Carlsbad Ranch** (☎ 760-431-0352; http://visit.theflowerfields.com; adult/child $8/5; 9am-5pm) turn into vibrating, Technicolor sea of carmine, saffron and snow white ranunculus blossoms. The fields are two blocks east of I-5; take the Palomar Airport Rd exit, go east, then left on Paseo del Norte Rd – look for the windmill. Call for an events schedule.

BATIQUITOS LAGOON

One of the last remaining tidal wetlands in California, Batiquitos Lagoon separates Carlsbad from Encinitas. A self-guided tour lets you explore area plants, including the prickly pear cactus, coastal sage scrub and eucalyptus trees, as well as lagoon birds, such as the great heron and the snowy egret. The **Nature Center** (☎ 760-931-0800; www.batiquitos foundation.org; noon-4pm Wed-Fri, 10am-2pm Sat & Sun) is a short walk into the park from the end of Gabbiano Lane in Carlsbad.

Sleeping

Pelican Cove Inn (☎ 888-735-2683; www.pelican-cove .com; 320 Walnut Ave; r $90-210) A comfortable, if highly floral, B&B 220yd from the beach. All rooms have fireplaces, some have spa baths.

Motel 6 (☎ 760-434-7135; www.motel6.com; 1006 Carlsbad Village Dr; s $50-64, d $56-70) For no-frills lodging, you won't find cheaper in North County.

Surf Motel (☎ 760-729-7961, 800-523-9170; www .surfmotelcarlsbad.com; 3136 Carlsbad Blvd; d $90-100;) The second-cheapest place in town has thin pillows and more-or-less clean rooms.

Carlsbad Inn Beach Resort (☎ 760-434-7020, 800-235-393; 3075 Carlsbad Blvd; r $205-290;) A faux-Tudor hotel cum time-share property on the beachfront offering organized activities from ceramics to ping-pong tourneys.

Four Seasons Aviara (☎ 760-603-6800, 800-332-3442; www.fourseasons.com/aviara; 7100 Four Seasons Point; r from $375;) Superb service and top-flight amenities at this world-class spa, though aesthetically it's a gated community on steroids.

South Carlsbad State Park Campground (☎ 760-438-3143, reservations 800-444-7275; tent sites $16-21, RV sites $26-31) Three miles south of downtown, this has 222 tent and RV sites.

Eating

Armenian Cafe (☎ 760-720-2233; 3126 Carlsbad Blvd; mains $8-15; 8am-9pm) Come here for the delicious dolmas and kebabs with garlic dip – and strong-as-the-devil coffee. Rounding out the picture are outdoor seating, partial ocean views and belly dancing on Friday and Saturday nights.

French Pastry Cafe (☎ 760-729-2241; 1005 Carlsbad Village Dr; mains $6; 7am-6pm) Great pit stop just off I-5, to pick up classic French baked goods fresh daily, as well as have omelettes, salads and panini for breakfast and lunch.

Pelly's Fish Market & Café (☎ 760-431-8454; 7110 Av Encinas; dishes $5-12; 10am-7pm Mon-Sat, 10am-6pm Sun) Order at the counter at this shopping-center fish market that grills freshly caught seafood and serves mm-mm-good chowder in paper bowls. Next to Ralph's supermarket, off Poinsettia Ave Exit from I-5.

OCEANSIDE
pop 175,000

Just outside the giant Camp Pendleton Marine Base, Oceanside lacks the charm of Encinitas and Carlsbad, but the wide beaches and fine surf continue unabated. Amtrak, Greyhound, the *Coaster* and MTS buses all stop at the **Oceanside Transit Center** (235 S Tremont St).

The **California Welcome Center** (☎ 760-721-1101, 800-350-7873; www.visitcwc.com; 928 N Coast Hwy; 9am-5pm) has helpful staff and coupons for local attractions, as well as maps and information for the San Diego area and the entire state.

Sights & Activities

The wooden **Oceanside Pier**, which extends more than 1900ft out to sea, is so long that an **electric shuttle** transports people to the end (50¢). You'll also find bait-and-tackle shops, with poles to rent and lights for night fishing. Two major surf competitions – the West Coast Pro-Am and the National Scholastic Surf Association (NSSA) – take place near the pier in June.

See a history of surf contests at the wonderful **California Surf Museum** (☎ 760-721-6876; www.surfmuseum.org; 223 N Coast Hwy; admission free; 10am-4pm). Displays include the whopping

---

DETOUR: SAN DIEGO BACKCOUNTRY

While inland San Diego County lacks the drama of the Sierra or Yosemite, its pine-covered mountains and valleys of fragrant orange groves make for a tranquil day or weekend getaway, though you will need a car to make the trip worthwhile.

On Rte 78 about 45 miles, or a one-hour drive, northeast of San Diego, the town of **Julian** (Map p587) was the center of the region's 1870s Gold Rush. These days, it's known for its quaint inns, Victorian storefronts and apple pie. Opened by a former slave, the 1897 **Julian Hotel** (☎ 760-765-0201, 800-734-5854; www.julianhotel.com; 2032 Main St; r from $145-200) has period furnishings and generous breakfasts. Reservations are strongly recommended, especially at weekends. For pie, check out the **Julian Pie Company** (☎ 760-765-2449; 2225 Main St; ☺ 9am-5pm). Note that Julian also makes a great base to explore the adjacent Anza Borrego Desert State Park (p649).

About 15 miles North of Julian just of Rte 76, the 6140ft **Palomar Mountain** is the centerpiece of three promontories that make up the 25-mile-long Palomar Range. Orange groves give way to dense forests of pine, oak, fir and cedar, and the peaks even receive several feet of snow a year. It's also home to the 200in Hale telescope (in use since 1948) at the **Palomar Observatory** (☎ 760-742-2119; admission free; ☺ museum & viewing platform usually 9am-4pm. Within **Palomar Mountain State Park** (☎ 760-742-3462; day-use fee $4), you can camp at **Doane Valley Campground** (☎ reservations 800-444-7275; tent & RV sites $14). Reservations are recommended. You can also stay on the valley floor at the **Lazy H Ranch** (☎ 760-742-3669; www.lazyhranchresort.com; 16787 Hwy 76; d $60-70, with bathroom $90-100; ☒ ☒). The rooms need upgrading and regular airings, but the grounds are pretty, and there is a homey restaurant attached.

Just south of Julian lies **Cuyamaca Rancho State Park** (☎ 760-765-0755; www.cuyamaca.statepark .org). Once a green oasis between dry coastland and inland desert, 90% of its trees – oak, willow, sycamore and pine – were destroyed in a devastating 2003 fire. It's open once again, though most of its trails pass through a haunting landscape of charred stumps.

Just east of the park lies the **Sunrise Hwy** (County Rd S1), which runs along the crest of the **Laguna Mountains**. The Lagunas support a wonderful array of plant and animal life, including Jeffrey and Coulter pines as well as coyotes, mountain lions and foxes. But the real draw here is the view from the crest down onto the 6000ft drop to the Anza-Borrego Desert (p649) below – you can often see the Salton Sea (p649), 60 miles away to the northeast. Along the Sunrise Hwy, the **Laguna Mountain Lodge** (☎ 619-445-2342; www.lagunamountain.com; r $60, cabins $80-135) rents rustic, somewhat bare-bones cabins and has a good selection of maps, books and groceries.

8ft-long, 85lb redwood board that once belonged to Baird Fraser, plus photos and surf memorabilia of Duke Kahanamoku, the Olympic gold-medal swimmer and surfer who died in 1968.

Little remains from the 1880s, when the new Santa Fe coastal railway came through Oceanside, but a few buildings designed by Irving Gill and Julia Morgan still stand. The Welcome Center has a pamphlet describing a self-guided history walk.

Four miles inland lies **Mission San Luis Rey de Francia** (☎ 760-757-3651; www.sanluisrey.org; 4050 Mission Ave, Hwy 76; adult/child $5/3; ☺ 10am-4pm), the largest California mission and the most successful in recruiting Native American converts. After the Mexican government secularized the missions, San Luis fell into ruin; only the adobe walls of the 1811 church are original. Inside the build-

ing there are displays on work and life in the mission, with some original religious art and artifacts.

Sleeping & Eating

There are lots of budget motels, though they fill up on summer weekends.

Pacific Inn (☎ 760-722-1781; www.pacificinn.net; s/d $65/85; ☒) A good bargain at the north end of town, with microwave, refrigerator and VCR available.

Oceanside Days Inn (☎ 760-722-7661; www.daysinn .com; r $85-120) For a basic motel, the mattresses are surprisingly good. Near the Oceanside Harbor Dr exit.

Motorcycle Cafe (☎ 760-433-1829; 624 S Coast Hwy; 6-11am Mon, 6am-4pm Tue-Wed, 6am-9pm Thu, 6am-6pm Fri, 7am-6pm Sat & Sun) A fun place to pick up some deli food, espresso drinks or Harley gear. The quirky hours are proof this place is family-run. On Thursday there is an all-you-can-eat barbecue dinner ($7), a favorite of local bikers.

Kealani's (☎ 760-722-5642; 207 N Coast Hwy at Mission; mains $4-6; ⏰ 11am-8pm Mon & Tue, 11am-6pm Wed, 11am-8pm Thu-Sat) Traditional Hawaiian plate lunches, such as teriyaki chicken and grilled mahimahi, made right. All come with rice and macaroni salad.

TIJUANA, MEXICO

pop 1.5 million

Americans have long used Tijuana as a quick escape from moral norms, and SoCal teens, like their predecessors during Prohibition, still pour across the border for booze, boobs and debauchery. The once-notorious Avenida (Av) Revolución – aka La Revo – is still one of the wildest streets in North America, its curio stores overflowing with kitschy souvenirs while strip-club touts bark at every passerby.

But these days, Tijuana (pronounced tee-*hwah*-na and sometimes called 'TJ' north of the border) is no longer beholden to thirsty gringos. In the wake of the North American Free Trade Agreement, the city has grown spectacularly as new businesses – particularly *maquiladoras* (assembly plants) – continue to open every month. At the same time, Tijuana – now Mexico's fourth-largest city, and one of its richest – is home to an increasingly sophisticated cultural scene, from music to food, as well as having a high concentration of universities and other academic institutions. However, the newfound wealth is, ironically, accompanied by desperate poverty, as the rural poor who arrive daily outpace both jobs and city services.

Just over the US border from San Diego's southern suburbs, the two cities are so interdependent that they can almost be regarded as a single urban region. Indeed, San Diego promotes Tijuana as one of its own tourist attractions, and depends on the border town for a steady supply of cheap labor. Still, there is no getting around what novelist T Coraghessan Boyle dubbed the 'Tortilla Curtain' in his novel of the same name (see the boxed text, p632), the forbidding, 150-mile-long, chain-link fence that runs like a scar from the Pacific right to the banks of the Colorado River.

ORIENTATION

Tijuana parallels the US border for about 12 miles. Downtown Tijuana (also called Zona Centro) is a 10- to 15-minute walk southwest of the San Ysidro border crossing and consists of a grid pattern of north–south *avenidas* (avenues) and east–west *calles* (streets). Most streets have numbers that are more frequently used than their names, which is why this chapter usually includes both. Av Revolución (La Revo), five blocks to the west, is the city's main tourist artery.

INFORMATION
Emergency & Medical Services
Tijuana now has a central number for all kinds of emergencies (☎ 066), including crime, fire and medical.

Central police station (Av Constitución 1616) At the corner of Calle 8a (Hidalgo) in the Zona Centro; the fire station is next door.

Hospital General (☎ 664-684-0922; Av Centenario 10851) North of Río Tijuana, this is the most central medical center with an emergency room.

Internet Access
Vacanett (Calle 7a 8150; per hr US$1; ⏰ 9am-10pm)

Worldnet (Calle 2a 8174; per hr US$1; ⏰ 24hr)

Money
Everyone accepts (even prefers) US dollars. It's best to carry small bills; otherwise you may end up receiving change in Mexican currency at a poor exchange rate. Numerous *casas de cambio* (currency-exchange houses) will change money and traveler's checks at almost any hour. Banks, though slower and more bureaucratic, offer slightly better rates; most also have ATMs, which is generally the cheapest and most convenient solution.

Beware of cambiums on the US side, some of which advertise 'no commission' on exchanges of pesos for US dollars but charge up to 8% for converting US-dollar cash or traveler's checks into pesos. Change money on the Mexican side instead.

Tourist Information
Tijuana Convention & Visitors Bureau (☎ 664-683-1405; ⏰ 8am-5pm Mon-Thu, 8am-7pm Fri & Sat, 8am-3pm Sun) There's a branch just south of the pedestrian border crossing.

Tijuana Secretary of Tourism (☎ 664-685-2210; ⏰ 10am-4pm Mon-Thu, 10am-7pm Fri-Sun) On Av Revolución between Calles 3a and 4a.

Visas & Immigration

US citizens or permanent residents not intending to go past the border zone (that is, beyond Ensenada), or to stay in the border zone for more than 72 hours, don't need a visa or even a passport to enter Tijuana. Do, however, bring some form of identification with your photo on it. Non-Americans can be subject to a full immigration interrogation upon returning to the USA, so bring your passport and US visa (if you need one).

DANGERS & ANNOYANCES

'Coyotes' and *polleros* (human smugglers) and their clients congregate along the river, west of San Ysidro crossing. After dark, avoid this area as well as Colonia Libertad, east

of the crossing. Theft, pickpocketing, short-changing, bill-padding and the addition of 'gringo-tax' are not uncommon in Tijuana.

Car theft is a big problem in Tijuana. Don't leave anything valuable looking in your car, and park in a guarded garage or lot – not on the street (even if you have a car alarm).

The Zona Norte, Tijuana's seedy red-light district west of Av Revolución and north of Calle 1a (Artículo 123), is not recommended for foreigners lacking street savvy, at least after dark. City officials prefer not to dwell on its continued existence, but the area is still of sufficient economic importance that authorities cannot, or will not, eradicate it. Neonlit Calle Coahuila is especially notorious for its street prostitution and hardcore clubs.

SAN DIEGO AREA

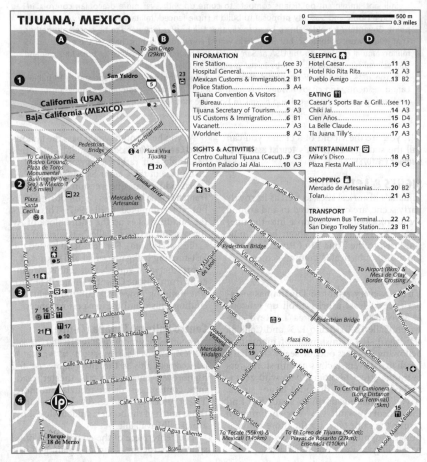

TIJUANA, MEXICO

0 — 500 m
0 — 0.3 miles

INFORMATION	
Fire Station..........................(see 3)	
Hospital General..........................1 D4	
Mexican Customs & Immigration..2 B1	
Police Station..........................3 A4	
Tijuana Convention & Visitors	
Bureau..........................4 B2	
Tijuana Secretary of Tourism......5 A3	
US Customs & Immigration......6 B1	
Vacanett..........................7 A3	
Worldnet..........................8 A2	

SIGHTS & ACTIVITIES	
Centro Cultural Tijuana (Cecut)..9 C3	
Frontón Palacio Jai Alai............10 A3	

SLEEPING	
Hotel Caesar..........................11 A3	
Hotel Rio Rita Rita..............12 A3	
Pueblo Amigo 13 B2	

EATING	
Caesar's Sports Bar & Grill...(see 11)	
Chiki Jai..........................14 A3	
Cien Años..........................15 D4	
La Belle Claude..................16 A3	
Tía Juana Tilly's..................17 A3	

ENTERTAINMENT	
Mike's Disco.......................18 A3	
Plaza Fiesta Mall..................19 C4	

SHOPPING	
Mercado de Artesanias..........20 B2	
Tolan..........................21 A3	

TRANSPORT	
Downtown Bus Terminal.......22 A2	
San Diego Trolley Station......23 B1	

THE POROUS BORDER

Despite hundreds of miles of chain link, reinforced concrete and razor-sharp wire, California's border with Mexico has always been, and will no doubt remain, a porous affair. The economic pressures driving Mexicans north, and political pressures to send them south again, make the border a hotly contested region, especially the stretch that divides San Diego County from Tijuana.

In 1994 the Clinton administration initiated Operation Gatekeeper, a costly effort to curb illegal immigration employing a metal fence, a huge contingent of border-patrol agents and sophisticated equipment such as infrared scopes and ground sensors. But many experts claim these efforts are just a public-relations gimmick to reassure US citizens that the border is 'secure' while US businesses can still benefit from the influx of cheap labor. Immigrants have simply been forced to cross the deserts to the east, they say, where vast expanses and temperatures that soar to 110°F cause hundreds of deaths each year from heat exposure and dehydration. Even with such risks, unauthorized crossings are rising, not falling. In 2004, it is estimated that more than a million people entered this way, up from about 750,000 in the late 1990s. In 2005, a group of calling themselves Minutemen complicated matters further by insisting on patrolling the borders themselves in Texas, New Mexico and Arizona.

Still, anti-immigrant politicians compete to come up with ever more draconian controls, including a Homeland Security proposal to build a triple-fenced, militarized security zone. At one point, Governor Ah-nold went so far as to say that the border may need to be closed altogether. That might work as rhetoric, but San Diego would come to a crashing halt. Of the estimated 45 million annual entries into the USA at San Ysidro, the majority are workers (of both Mexican and US nationality) commuting to jobs in the greater San Diego area.

In the 2004 film *A Day Without a Mexican*, a mysterious 'fog' whisks away the state's 14 million Latino residents, and chaos ensues. It is a satirical but ultimately profound examination of the vital role of immigrants, legal and illegal, in both the state's economy and its very way of life.

If you are the victim of a crime, you can call the state government's **tourist assistance number** (☎ 078).

SIGHTS & ACTIVITIES

Tijuana's historical sites, as well as its rowdy party scene, are concentrated in and around Av Revolución. For a glimpse into the finer things in Tijuana, head about half a mile southeast to the Zona Río ('River District'), the more sophisticated cultural center.

La Revo

Virtually every visitor to Tijuana has to experience at least a brief stroll up raucous **Av Revolución**, also known as 'La Revo,' between Calle 1a (Artículo 123) and Calle 8a (Hidalgo). It's a mishmash of nightclubs, bellowing hawkers outside seedy strip bars, brash taxi drivers, tacky souvenir stores, restaurants, street photographers with zebra-striped burros, and discount liquor stores. If you're walking north to south but find the sensory assault too overwhelming to return the same way, try the more conventional shopping street of Av Constitución, paralleling La Revo one block west.

As you head south, you'll pass the famous **Hotel Caesar** (Av Revolución 827). Built in 1930, this venerable – if rather shopworn – hotel is birthplace of the Caesar Salad (see p69).

An oddly baroque version of art deco, **Frontón Palacio Jai Alai** was begun during 1926 but not completed until 1947. This striking building takes up the entire block of Av Revolución between Calle 7a (Galeana) and Calle 8a (Hidalgo). For decades it hosted the fast-moving ball game of jai alai – kind of a hybrid between squash and tennis, originating from Basque Country (in north Spain). The building now hosts cultural events including music and theater performances.

Centro Cultural Tijuana (Cecut)

An aggressively modern **cultural center** (☎ 664-687-9695; www.cecut.gob.mx; Paseo de los Héroes at Av Independencia), this is the city's showcase for highbrow events – concerts, theater, readings, conferences, dance recitals and more. Ticket prices vary but tend to be lower than those north of the border; student discounts are usually available.

The centerpiece of the complex is a huge spherical structure – sort of a giant golf ball that locals have dubbed La Bola (the ball). Inside is the **Cine Planetario** (adult/student US$4/2, Tuesday and Wednesday 2-for-1), a popular Omnimax-style theater showing a changing roster of films – usually in Spanish – on a 180-degree screen.

The state-of-the-art **Museo de las Californias** (☎ 664-687-9641/42; admission US$2; ☼ 10am-6pm Tue-Fri, 10am-7pm Sat & Sun) provides an excellent history of Baja California from prehistoric times to the present, including the earliest Spanish expeditions, the Mission period, the Treaty of Hidalgo, the irrigation of the Colorado River delta and the advent of the railroad.

Bullfights

Bullfights (corridas) take place on Sunday afternoons every two or three weeks from the last weekend in April to late September/early October. For schedules and information in English, see www.tjbullfight.com.

Of the town's two bullrings, the larger, more spectacular venue is the **Plaza de Toros Monumental**, the renowned bullring-by-the-sea in Playas de Tijuana, only a short distance from the border fence. The other is **El Toreo de Tijuana** (Blvd Agua Caliente), between central Tijuana and the Hipódromo de Agua Caliente racetrack. Spring bullfights take place at El Toreo, which has room for 12,000 spectators. In July or August, corridas move to the ring in Playas, which holds up to 25,000 people.

Tickets are available at the bullrings daily from noon to 6pm and from 10am on the day of the corrida. In the USA you can also buy tickets through **Five Star Tours** (☎ 619-232-5049, 800-553-8687; www.fivestartours.com) online or at the San Diego office (in the Santa Fe Depot Amtrak station; Map pp592–3). Prices range from $15 for general admission to $100 or more for prime seats in the shade. Five Star also offers round-trip transportation from its offices for $20.

SLEEPING

While budget accommodations are more rustic than in San Diego, they're also significantly cheaper. Midrange hotels are also less expensive than equivalent lodgings north of the border. Avoid the really cheap hotels in the Zona Norte, Tijuana's red-light district.

Hotel Rio Rita Rita (☎ 664-685-7777, 685-8810; rio rita@bc.cablemas.com; Av Revolución 968; s/d $53/59) This fine option, in the middle of La Revo, has spotless rooms with cable TV, carpet and

fans. Rooms over the strip have balconies but get noisy from weekend revelry outside.

Hotel Caesar (☎ 664-685-1606; Av Revolución 1079; s/d $28/32) Historic bullfighting posters grace this Tijuana classic, where it is said the Caesar Salad got its start (see p69). It's seen better days, but the price and location are right. Ask for a room off Av Revolución if you have plans to sleep.

Pueblo Amigo (☎ 664-683-5030, in the USA 800-386-6985; www.hotelpuebloamigo.com; Via Oriente 9211; r/ste US$152/392; P ☒ 🖳) This is a modern, well-landscaped hotel with state-of-the-art rooms and all the usual amenities. Adjacent to the high-end mall of the same name.

EATING

Most restaurants on Av Revolución cater to tourists, serving the usual Mexican dishes, while the city's best restaurants are in the Zona Río and along Blvd Agua Caliente.

Tía Juana Tilly's (☎ 664-685-6024; Av Revolución at Calle 7a; mains US$5-10) Can't go wrong here; classic Mexican food served up to gringos in a festive, cantina-like atmosphere.

La Belle Claude (☎ 664-685-0744; Calle 7a 8186; ☼ 8am-11pm) Just off Av Revolución, this civilized French-style bakery serves up traditional sweets as well as good espresso drinks.

Chiki Jai (☎ 664-685-4955; Av Revolución 1388; mains US$9) Thanks to its always good Spanish/Basque seafood, the small, friendly Chiki Jai has been packed with patrons since 1947.

Cien Años (☎ 664-634-3039; Av José María Velasco 1407; mains US$12-20) One of Tijuana's temples of alta cocina (haute cuisine), Cien Años is worth the splurge. The chefs have dug deep into a box of ancient Mexican recipes, some going back to the Aztecs and Mayans, and have devised some unusual concoctions (how does 'spinal marrow soup' sound?). It's a formal place – no shorts, jeans or T-shirts.

DRINKING & ENTERTAINMENT

If you want to down Jell-O shots while waiters blow whistles in your ears, head to Av Revolución. Just listen to what's pumping out of the sound system, then pick your party.

Mike's Disco (☎ 664-685-3534; Av Revolución 1220) The perennial favorite for gay men, with drag shows starting most nights at midnight.

Plaza Fiesta Mall (Independencia at Guadalupe Victoria) Or you could head to the Zona Río to check out this mall. What La Revo is to gringos, this is to locals, with a dozen or so bars and restaurants where you can knock back a few tequilas and hear the local rock and DJ talent thrash (or spin) it out.

SHOPPING

Many Americans make regular trips across the border to purchase prescription drugs, which are significantly cheaper here. Other popular buys include leather goods, pottery and other handicrafts and, of course, tequila. Each person returning to the USA is allowed to bring $400 worth of duty-free goods back across the border.

Tolan (☎ 644-688-3637; Av Revolución 1471; ☼ 11am-5pm Mon-Sat) Founded by a prominent local artisan, this quirky collection of Mexican handicrafts is the most sophisticated in the town. Prices aren't cheap, but quality's high.

Mercado de Artesanías (Plaza Viva Tijuana) This is the first big outdoor market you will encounter when coming over the border by foot. You'll find TJ's biggest concentration of souvenirs, crafts and curios, most of them mass-produced. If you see something you like, bargain for it.

GETTING THERE & AROUND

If you are coming from San Diego and don't plan to venture further than Tijuana itself, your best bet is to drive to San Ysidro and park your car in one of the many lots near the border. Alternatively, San Diego's trolley will take you straight to the border crossing from downtown. Then cross the border by foot. Traffic congestion at the border can be unbelievable, and driving in Mexico requires special insurance. Details follow.

Once you arrive on the other side of the border, don't let the number of waiting taxis intimidate you. Most sites in Tijuana are within an easy, 20-minute walk from the crossing. Just follow the blue and white signs reading 'Centro Downtown' through Plaza Viva Tijuana, take another pedestrian bridge across Río Tijuana and walk a further couple of blocks to the northern end of Av Revolución. If you do take a taxi, be sure to establish a price before entering.

Air

Flights to other Mexican cities can be much cheaper from **Aeropuerto Internacional Abelardo L Rodríguez** (☎ 683-24-18), right on the international border in the suburb of Mesa de Otay, 6 miles east of downtown. To US cities, it is

better to fly from San Diego, since it is generally cheaper and there are more services.

Bus

Greyhound buses to and from both Los Angeles ($21, four hours) and San Diego ($7, one hour) serve Tijuana's **main terminal** (☎ 664-688-0752; cnr Av Madero & Calle 1a) almost hourly between about 5:30am and 12:30am. Note that buses can also experience punishing delays crossing back into the USA.

Car

If you're going to Tijuana for just one day, don't drive your car – the traffic is frenetic, parking is competitive and there's likely to be a long wait to cross back into the USA, especially at rush hour and the beginning and end of holiday weekends. It's far better to drive to San Ysidro (exit I-5 at the last exit before the border), leave your car in a day parking lot (about $7) and cross the border on foot.

If you take your car, be aware that Mexican law recognizes only Mexican *seguro* (car insurance), so a US or Canadian policy won't suffice. Driving in Mexico without Mexican insurance is extremely foolish and can land you in jail. Entering Tijuana from San Diego, you'll find many insurance offices right at the Via de San Ysidro and Camino de la Plaza exits off I-5. Daily rates vary depending on the value of your car, deductible, liability coverage and the number of days you'll be in Mexico. Expect to pay a minimum of $10 to $15 per day, with discounts possible for additional days. For real-time quotes from multiple companies, check on www.mexpro.com. Most major US insurance companies and the American Automobile Association (AAA) also arrange coverage.

Trolley

The trolley is a great way to get to Tijuana. It runs from downtown San Diego to San Ysidro ($3, about 30 minutes) every 15 minutes from about 5am to midnight. From the San Ysidro stop, take the pedestrian bridge over the road and go through the turnstile into Mexico. You don't need a taxi to get to Av Revolución. Just follow the blue and white signs to 'Centro Downtown' through the largely deserted tourist trap of Plaza Viva Tijuana, across a second pedestrian bridge over Río Tijuana and walk another couple of blocks.

California Deserts

California's outback is where the Wild West lives on. Though spliced by ribbons of interstate, the desert state of mind is as far from Los Angeles as Shangri-La. It's the lair of escapists, hedonists, rabble-rousing ranchers, prophetic environmentalists, Native American tribes, eccentric folk artists and daredevil test pilots. If coastal California is a misleading dream manufactured in Hollywood, then the desert is the Golden State's jaw-dropping biblical reality. People come here to seek healing hot springs, to dig gold out of the bowels of the earth, even to play God by creating miraculous oases of green.

Hunter S Thompson famously wrote, 'We were somewhere around Barstow on the edge of the desert when the drugs began to take hold.' Luckily, you won't need a suitcase full of illegal substances just to relive his joyride. The desert landscape itself is a hallucinogen, with vast expanses of sand interrupted only by the seeming mirages of mountain peaks. Once you flee the subdivisions encircling the celebrity playground of Palm Springs, the Mojave and Sonoran Deserts stretch as far as the eye can see: south down Mexico way, east to the neon lights of Las Vegas and north to the snowy Sierra Nevada range.

On long, lonely stretches of road between desert outposts, such as on tumbleweed-ridden Route 66, the solitude is as refreshing as ice. Singing sand dunes near Death Valley, the Mojave National Preserve's volcanic cinder cones, marble-like boulders across Joshua Tree National Park, and remote tracks to lush palm canyons in Anza-Borrego Desert State Park – all will test your limits as they soothe your soul. Rejuvenation, even rebirth, happens here.

CALIFORNIA DESERTS

HIGHLIGHTS

- Surfing sand dunes and witnessing wildflowers blossoming in **Death Valley National Park** (p666)
- Rock climbing and hiking to palm oases in **Joshua Tree National Park** (p654)
- Roaming where camels once trod in the **Mojave National Preserve** (p662)
- Rediscovering America's 'Mother Road' on retro **Route 66** (p664)
- Ascending through five climatic zones in 15 minutes on the **Palm Springs Aerial Tram** (p639)
- Leaving the highway behind in rugged **Anza-Borrego Desert State Park** (p649)

★ Death Valley National Park

★ Mojave National Preserve

★ Route 66

★ Palm Springs

★ Joshua Tree National Park

★ Anza-Borrego Desert State Park

■ AVERAGE TEMPS IN PALM SPRINGS: JAN 43/70°F, JUL 76/108°F

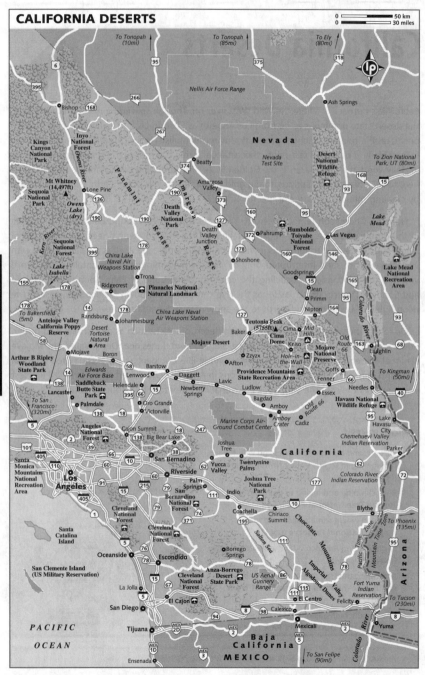

CALIFORNIA DESERTS

0 ——— 50 km
0 ——— 30 miles

CALIFORNIA DESERTS

History

Since ancient times, indigenous tribes have lived in those corners of the desert where springs, streams or lakes can sustain them. For early European explorers, such as Juan Bautista de Anza and Jedediah Smith, the desert was a barrier to the more habitable West Coast. The trails they pioneered can still be traced. Miners also came and went, establishing towns that died as the minerals played out, leaving their skeletons and stories scattered in the sand. After the turn of the 20th century, cities arose only where there were dependable water supplies. Military bases took over after WWII, when General Patton rolled tanks and trained troops in the eastern Mojave. Although not welcomed by some ranchers, hunters and OHV (off-highway vehicle) enthusiasts, the 1994 California Desert Protection Act created parks and reserved millions of acres of wilderness.

Geography

Over one quarter of California is desert. In the state's southeast corner is the 'low desert,' often called the Colorado Desert since it's near the Colorado River. It's actually part of the Sonoran Desert, most of which lies in Arizona and Mexico. Further north near the Sierra Nevada range is the 'high desert.' Named the Mojave, it extends into Arizona, Nevada and Utah. The low desert has few peaks over 1000ft. The high desert averages over 2000ft, yet Death Valley drops almost 300ft below sea level. In all cases, the term 'desert' means the same: a place that gets, on average, less than 10in of annual rainfall. Both deserts get surprisingly cold in winter and after sunset. Temperatures commonly drop below freezing on a January night, when snowcapped mountain peaks surround some of the hottest valleys. Snow is less common at lower elevations, but snow-covered Joshua trees,

---

DESERT SURVIVAL 101

The desert is an unforgiving place, but if you take precautions you'll have nothing to fear.

The biggest concern? Water. Plan on carrying and drinking at least a gallon of water per day, double if you're exercising or boozing it up. Summer temperatures can reach over 125°F, but you won't always feel yourself sweat in low humidity. Eat salty foods and consume sports drinks high in sodium and potassium. See p730 for more information on heat stroke.

Gas stations are few and far between. A backcountry drive can turn disastrous if the car breaks down or gets stuck in sand. Be sure your vehicle is in good condition, know how to do basic repairs and don't push it beyond its limits. An underinflated tire can overheat very quickly, although drivers of 4WD vehicles may let some air out of their tires when driving in rocky or sandy areas.

Watch the temperature gauge of your car. If it starts to heat up, turn off the air-conditioning, turn on the heater and roll down the windows. If that doesn't work, pull over, face the front of the car into the wind, carefully pop the hood and keep the car idling. If the engine continues to get hotter, shut off the car immediately to prevent serious damage.

A short walk can turn fatal if you get lost or injured. Always tell someone where you're going and when you'll be back. If you become hopelessly lost on foot, seek the closest shady spot and stay put. You'll only get dehydrated and exhausted by walking around. Always carry a compass and map, and know how to use them; GPS units are helpful, but batteries die and units can malfunction. Cell phones won't work in many areas. Carry a small mirror, matches and even flares to signal for help. A tent or groundsheet provides vital sun protection and increases your visibility. Also useful: a flashlight, pocketknife, first-aid kit, and extra food and water.

Flooding can occur after heavy rains, even if the downpour is miles away. Don't camp or park in streambeds or washes. There are hundreds of abandoned mineral mines in the deserts. Watch out for holes, which are easy to fall into. Never enter old mines as the shaft's supporting timbers have usually deteriorated and the air may contain poisonous gases.

Black widows, scorpions, rattlesnakes and centipedes are venomous but unlikely to attack. Be sure to check your shoes before putting them on in the morning, and don't leave your bag unzipped outside overnight. Obviously, cacti have spikes. Less obvious are their tiny barbs, which make the spikes difficult to extract. Bring strong tweezers or pliers, and avoid hiking in shorts.

palms and cacti are not unheard of on the desert floor.

Flora & Fauna

The distinction between the two deserts is really one of ecology. Straddling the transition zone is Joshua Tree National Park. The low desert is characterized by cacti, particularly the cholla and ocotillo. The most distinctive high-desert plant is the Joshua tree, seen throughout the Mojave, but only one variety is native: the California fan palm, which grows in desert oases fed by natural springs and small streams. The palm oases of Anza-Borrego Desert State Park are popular with ornithologists. The desert supports a good deal of wildlife, too, but much of it is nocturnal. Wildflowers bloom in spring.

PALM SPRINGS & COACHELLA VALLEY

pop 45,000

Resort hounds love Palm Springs. About 3.5 million visitors come here each year, mostly in the cooler months of October through April, to play golf and tennis and enjoy the desert climate of the Coachella Valley, the 300 sq mile valley stretching eastward from Palm Springs.

From spring-break college kids meandering the streets of downtown, to circuit-party gay boys lounging by swimming pools, to LA matrons recovering from face-lifts behind the bougainvillea-covered walls of gated compounds, people are here to relax.

HISTORY

For over 1000 years, Cahuilla tribespeople occupied canyons on the southwestern edge of the Coachella Valley, where permanent streams flowed from the San Jacinto Mountains. The early Spanish explorers called the hot springs where the city of Palm Springs now stands Agua Caliente (hot water), later used to refer to the local Cahuilla band.

In 1876, the federal government divided the valley into a checkerboard. Odd-numbered sections were granted to the Southern Pacific Railroad, while the even-numbered sections were given to the Agua Caliente as their reservation. Not until the 1940s did surveys establish the boundaries.

By then much of the Native American land had been built on, though the local tribes today are quite wealthy.

At the southern end of the valley, Indio began as a construction camp for the railway and its artesian water was tapped to irrigate crops. Date palms from Algeria were imported in 1890 and have become the valley's major crop, along with citrus fruits and table grapes. The whole valley was developed first as farmland, later with health spas, hotels and resorts. In the 1920s, Palm Springs (PS) became a winter playground for Hollywood stars, many of whom built mid-century modern homes here in the 1940s and '50s. PS's popularity faded in the late '60s, but today it's back on the map.

ORIENTATION

Palm Springs has a compact downtown area, centered on about four blocks of Palm Canyon Dr, with shops, banks, restaurants and a few sights. In this area, traffic goes south on Palm Canyon Dr and north on Indian Canyon Dr. Tahquitz Canyon Way divides street addresses into north and south. At the south end of town, Palm Canyon Dr abruptly turns eastward and becomes E Palm Canyon Dr.

Going southeast down the Coachella Valley, Cathedral City, Rancho Mirage and Palm Desert sprawl into one another. At the far end of the valley, blue-collar Indio is a railroad and agricultural town. Going up and down the valley, it's often quicker to take I-10 than to follow Hwy 111 through miles of suburbs and dozens of traffic lights. North of I-10 lies the dusty enclave of Desert Hot Springs.

INFORMATION

In summer, many places close or at least keep shorter hours, so always call ahead.

Bookstores

Celebrity Books (Map p642; ☎ 760-320-6575; 182 N Palm Canyon Dr; ☒ 10am-6pm Mon-Wed, 10am-9pm Thu-Sat, some Sun) Hollywood pulp, true crime, star biographies and autograph signings.

Emergency & Medical Services

Desert Regional Medical Center (Map p642; ☎ 760-323-6511, emergency room 760-323-6251; 1150 N Indian Canyon Dr) Twenty-four hour emergency care.
Emergency number (☎ 911)

Palm Springs Police (☎ 760-323-8116) For nonlife-threatening situations.

Internet Access
LalaJava (Map p642; ☎ 760-325-3494; 300 N Palm Canyon Dr; per 30 min $4; ✆ 6am-6pm) Internet terminals and wi-fi.
Palm Springs Public Library (Map p642; ☎ 760-322-7323; www.palmspringslibrary.org; 300 S Sunrise Way; access free; ✆ 9am-8pm Mon & Tue, 9am-5:30pm Wed, Thu & Sat, 10am-5:30pm Fri) Walk-in Internet access.

Money
Anderson Travel (Map p642; ☎ 760-325-2001, 800-952-5068; 700 E Tahquitz Canyon Way; ✆ 8:30am-5pm Mon-Fri) American Express representative for foreign currency exchange.

Media
Desert Post Weekly A free alternative newspaper.
Desert Sun (www.thedesertsun.com) Daily newspaper.
KWXY 1340AM, 98.5FM Campy cocktail music that matches Palm Springs perfectly.

Post
Palm Springs Post Office (Map p642; ☎ 800-275-8777; 333 E Amado Rd; ✆ 8am-5pm Mon-Fri, 9am-3pm Sat) The city's main post office.

Tourist Information
Palm Springs Official Visitor Center (Map pp640-1; ☎ 760-778-8418, 800-347-7746; www.palm-springs.org; 2901 N Palm Canyon Dr; ✆ 9am-5pm) North of downtown, at the tramway turnoff; provides free hotel bookings, tourist publications and maps.
Uptown Visitors Center (Map p642; ☎ 760-327-2828; 777 N Palm Canyon Dr; ✆ 8am-5pm Mon-Fri) Smaller than the main visitors center.

SIGHTS
The most fascinating sights are not in downtown Palm Springs.

Palm Springs Aerial Tram
The highlight of any visit is a trip in this revolving **cable car** (Map pp640-1; ☎ 760-325-1391, 888-515-8726; www.pstramway.com; 1 Tramway Rd; adult/child 3-12/senior $21.50/14.50/19.50; ✆ departures 10am-8pm Mon-Fri, 8am-8pm Sat & Sun, last tram back down 9:45pm), which climbs nearly 6000 vertical feet through five visibly different vegetation belts, from the Sonoran desert floor up into the San Jacinto Mountains. It's about 30°F cooler as you step out into alpine forest at the top, so bring some warm clothing.

The top of the tramway has a bar, a cafeteria, an observation area, natural history exhibits and a theater showing documentary films. The views over the valley are brilliant from the restaurant, **Elevations** (☎ 760-327-1590; mains lunch/dinner from $13/21; ✆ noon-3pm & 4pm-8:30pm), which has a meat and seafood menu. Reservations are recommended.

Allow time at the top of the ride to enjoy the 13,000-acre **Mt San Jacinto State Park** (Map pp640-1; ☎ 951-659-2607; www.sanjac.statepark.org). There are over 50 miles of hiking trails, including a nontechnical 11-mile round-trip route up to the San Jacinto peak (10,834ft). Anyone heading into the backcountry (even for a few hours) must register for a wilderness permit at the ranger station in Long Valley, 0.3 miles from the upper tram station. Pick up maps, brochures and guided-walk schedules at the upper tram station's information center. Outside, the **Adventure Center** rents snowshoes, snow tubes and cross-country skis until 3:30pm daily in season, usually mid-November to mid-April.

It takes about three hours to park, ride the tram and take a leisurely stroll around the top. To reach the tramway, head north from downtown on Palm Canyon Dr to Tramway Rd, turn left and continue on for 4 miles to the valley station.

Living Desert Zoo & Gardens
At this amazing **zoo** (Map pp640-1; ☎ 760-346-5694; www.livingdesert.org; 47-900 Portola Ave, Palm Desert; adult/child 3-12/senior & AAA members $11/6.50/9.50, in summer $8/4.50/8, shuttle $5; ✆ 8am-1:30pm mid-Jun–Aug, 9am-5pm Sep–mid-Jun) you'll see a wide variety of desert plants and animals, plus terrific exhibits on geology and Native American culture. Highlights are a walk-through wildlife hospital and an African-themed village with a fair-trade market, eateries and a storytelling grove. Bring hiking shoes to explore the miles of wilderness trails. Overnight 'Starry Safaris' **camp-outs** (adult/child 7-12 $95/65) are perfect for families. The zoo is a 30-minute drive from Palm Springs and last admissions are 30 minutes to an hour before closing.

Tahquitz Canyon
Reopened for self-guided tours after having been off-limits to independent exploration for more than 30 years, **Tahquitz Canyon** (Map p642; ☎ 760-416-7044; www.tahquitzcanyon.com; 500 W Mesquite Ave; adult/child under 13 $12.50/6;

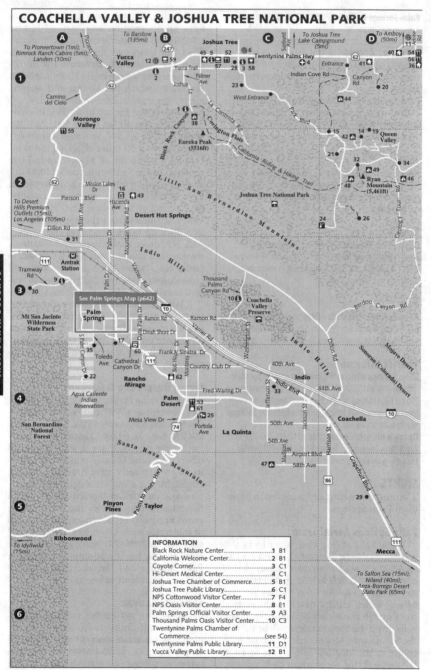

COACHELLA VALLEY & JOSHUA TREE NATIONAL PARK

INFORMATION	
Black Rock Nature Center...................1	B1
California Welcome Center................2	B1
Coyote Corner....................................3	C1
Hi-Desert Medical Center.................4	C1
Joshua Tree Chamber of Commerce...5	B1
Joshua Tree Public Library................6	C1
NPS Cottonwood Visitor Center.......7	F4
NPS Oasis Visitor Center..................8	E1
Palm Springs Official Visitor Center...9	A3
Thousand Palms Oasis Visitor Center...10	C3
Twentynine Palms Chamber of	
Commerce...................................(see 54)	
Twentynine Palms Public Library......11	D1
Yucca Valley Public Library...............12	B1

CALIFORNIA DESERTS

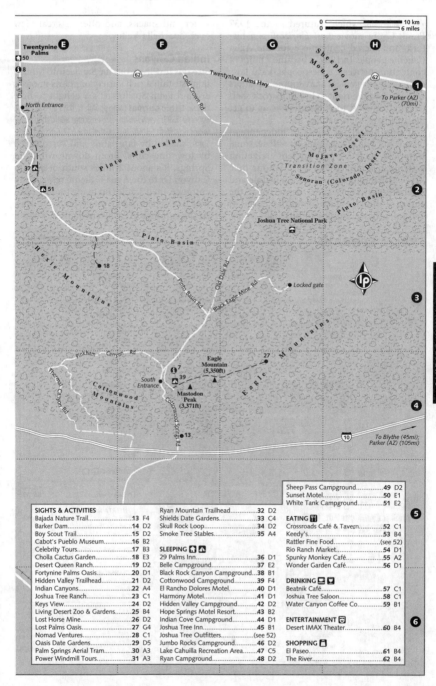

Sheep Pass Campground.............**49** D2
Sunset Motel.............................**50** E1
White Tank Campground............**51** E2

SIGHTS & ACTIVITIES
Bajada Nature Trail.....................**13** F4
Barker Dam................................**14** D2
Boy Scout Trail..........................**15** D2
Cabot's Pueblo Museum.............**16** B2
Celebrity Tours..........................**17** B3
Cholla Cactus Garden.................**18** E3
Desert Queen Ranch...................**19** D2
Fortynine Palms Oasis.................**20** D1
Hidden Valley Trailhead..............**21** D2
Indian Canyons..........................**22** A4
Joshua Tree Ranch......................**23** C1
Keys View..................................**24** D2
Living Desert Zoo & Gardens......**25** B4
Lost Horse Mine.........................**26** D2
Lost Palms Oasis.........................**27** G4
Nomad Ventures.........................**28** C1
Oasis Date Gardens.....................**29** D5
Palm Springs Aerial Tram............**30** A3
Power Windmill Tours.................**31** A3

Ryan Mountain Trailhead............**32** D2
Shields Date Gardens..................**33** C4
Skull Rock Loop..........................**34** D2
Smoke Tree Stables.....................**35** A4

SLEEPING
29 Palms Inn...............................**36** D1
Belle Campground.......................**37** E2
Black Rock Canyon Campground..**38** B1
Cottonwood Campground............**39** F4
El Rancho Dolores Motel..............**40** D1
Harmony Motel...........................**41** D1
Hidden Valley Campground.........**42** D2
Hope Springs Motel Resort..........**43** B2
Indian Cove Campground.............**44** D1
Joshua Tree Inn...........................**45** B1
Joshua Tree Outfitters.............(see 52)
Jumbo Rocks Campground...........**46** D2
Lake Cahuilla Recreation Area......**47** C5
Ryan Campground.......................**48** D2

EATING
Crossroads Café & Tavern............**52** C1
Keedy's.......................................**53** B4
Rattler Fine Food....................(see 52)
Rio Ranch Market........................**54** D1
Spunky Monkey Café...................**55** A2
Wonder Garden Café...................**56** D1

DRINKING
Beatnik Café................................**57** C1
Joshua Tree Saloon......................**58** C1
Water Canyon Coffee Co..............**59** B1

ENTERTAINMENT
Desert IMAX Theater...................**60** B4

SHOPPING
El Paseo......................................**61** B4
The River.....................................**62** B4

CALIFORNIA DESERTS

⊙ 7:30am-5pm), which featured in the 1937 Frank Capra movie *Lost Horizon*, is a historic and sacred centerpiece for the Agua Caliente people. In 1969, it became a point of contention between tribespeople, local law-enforcement agencies and hippie squatters who claimed the right to live in its rock shelters and caves. It took the tribe years to get the area back to its natural state.

It's no longer off-limits to independent hikers, but you also can see its 60ft seasonal waterfall, rock art and ancient irrigation system on a guided 2-mile, 2½-hour hike led by tribal rangers; call for a schedule and reservations. The visitors center near the entrance shows a video about the legend of Tahquitz, has cultural exhibits, sells maps,

water and snacks, and offers a great view over Coachella Valley.

Indian Canyons

Streams flowing from the San Jacinto Mountains sustain a rich variety of plants in oases around Palm Springs. It's a delight to hike these three **canyons** (Map pp640-1; ☎ 760-325-3400, 800-790-3398; www.indian-canyons.com; adult/child 6-12/ senior & student $8/4/6, incl guided tour $11/6/8; ⊙ 8am-5pm), shaded by fan palms and surrounded by towering cliffs. From downtown Palm Springs, it's about 2 miles south of S Palm Canyon Dr to the Agua Caliente reservation entrance, then 3 miles up to the trading post, which sells hats, water, maps, books and art. At the entrance to each canyon there's a trail

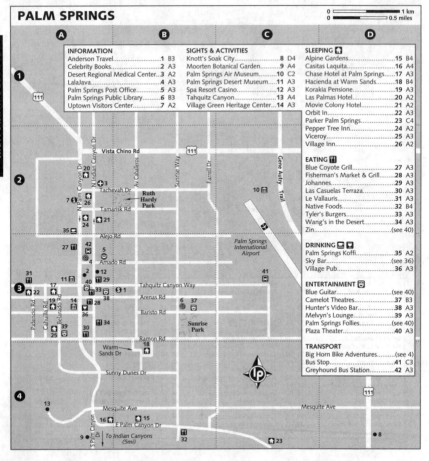

PALM SPRINGS

INFORMATION	
Anderson Travel	1 B3
Celebrity Books	2 A3
Desert Regional Medical Center	3 A2
LalaJava	4 A3
Palm Springs Post Office	5 A3
Palm Springs Public Library	6 B3
Uptown Visitors Center	7 A2

SIGHTS & ACTIVITIES	
Knott's Soak City	8 D4
Moorten Botanical Garden	9 A4
Palm Springs Air Museum	10 C2
Palm Springs Desert Museum	11 A3
Spa Resort Casino	12 A3
Tahquitz Canyon	13 A4
Village Green Heritage Center	14 A3

SLEEPING 🏠	
Alpine Gardens	15 B4
Casitas Laquita	16 A4
Chase Hotel at Palm Springs	17 A3
Hacienda at Warm Sands	18 B4
Korakia Pensione	19 A3
Las Palmas Hotel	20 A2
Movie Colony Hotel	21 A2
Orbit In	22 A3
Parker Palm Springs	23 C4
Pepper Tree Inn	24 A2
Viceroy	25 A3
Village Inn	26 A2

EATING 🍴	
Blue Coyote Grill	27 A3
Fisherman's Market & Grill	28 A3
Johannes	29 A3
Las Casuelas Terraza	30 A3
Le Vallauris	31 A3
Native Foods	32 B4
Tyler's Burgers	33 A3
Wang's in the Desert	34 A3
Zin	(see 40)

DRINKING 🍷 🍸	
Palm Springs Koffi	35 A2
Sky Bar	(see 36)
Village Pub	36 A3

ENTERTAINMENT 🎭	
Blue Guitar	(see 40)
Camelot Theatres	37 B3
Hunter's Video Bar	38 A3
Melvyn's Lounge	39 A3
Palm Springs Follies	(see 40)
Plaza Theater	40 A3

TRANSPORT	
Big Horn Bike Adventures	(see 4)
Bus Stop	41 C3
Greyhound Bus Station	42 A3

CALIFORNIA DESERTS

post with a map and information about that particular hike. To reserve a ranger-led interpretive walk, call ☎ 760-416-7044.

En route to the canyons, stop off at family-run **Moorten Botanical Garden** (Map pp640-1; ☎ 760-327-6555; 1701 S Palm Canyon Dr; adult/child $3/1.50; ☺ 9am-4:30pm Mon-Sat, 10am-4pm Sun), which displays over 3000 varieties of desert plants.

Village Green Heritage Center
Surrounding this grassy little **square** (Map p642; ☎ 760-323-8297; 221 S Palm Canyon Dr) downtown are **Ruddy's General Store** (admission 95¢; ☺ 10am-4pm Thu-Sun Oct-Jun, 10am-4pm Sat & Sun Jul-Sep), a reproduction of a 1930s general store, and the 1884 **McCallum Adobe** (admission $1; ☺ 10am-4pm Thu-Sat, noon-3pm Wed & Sun mid-Oct–May), a historical museum inside Palm Springs' oldest building. The **Agua Caliente Cultural Museum** (☎ 760-323-0151; www.accmuseum.org; donations welcome; ☺ 10am-5pm Wed-Sat, 10am-noon Sun) has exhibits on the local tribe's history and offers educational workshops. It will relocate to the southeast corner of Tahquitz Canyon Way and Hermosa Dr as soon as 2008.

Palm Springs Desert Museum
Downtown, this **museum** (Map p642; ☎ 760-325-7186; www.psmuseum.org; 101 Museum Dr; adult/child 6-17/senior $12.50/5/10.50, 4-8pm Thu free; ☺ 10am-5pm Tue, Wed, Fri-Sun, noon-8pm Thu Oct-May, Wed-Sun Jun-Sep) has

a small collection of 20th-century art and contemporary exhibitions from around the Southwest. Outside there's a sculpture garden with desert plants. Call for schedules of free docent tours.

Palm Springs Air Museum
Adjacent to the airport, this **museum** (Map p642; ☎ 760-778-6262; www.air-museum.org; 745 N Gene Autry Trail; adult/child 6-12/family $10/5/20; ☺ 10am-5pm) has an exceptional collection of WWII aircraft and flight memorabilia, a movie theater, family activities and occasionally flying demonstrations.

Coachella Valley Preserve
This preserve abuts a national wildlife refuge that is home to the Coachella Valley fringe-toed lizard. **Thousand Palms Oasis** (Map pp640-1; ☎ 760-348-5278; www.fws.gov/pacific/saltonsea/Coachella/CV_recreation.html; Thousand Palms Canyon Rd; ☺ dawn-dusk), off I-10 exit Ramon Rd, has a 2-mile round-trip nature trail that crosses over the San Andreas Fault, passing by dozens of desert plant species. Pick up a trail brochure at the **visitor center** (☺ 8am-noon), about 10 miles east of Palm Springs.

ACTIVITIES
On a hot day, kids go nuts at **Knott's Soak City** (Map p642; ☎ 760-327-0499; www.knotts.com/soakcity;

QUIRKY PALM SPRINGS

Cabot's Pueblo Museum (Map pp640-1; ☎ 760-329-7610; www.cabotsmuseum.org; 67-616 E Desert Ave, Desert Hot Springs; tour adult/child 6-16/senior $6/4/5; ☺ 10am-3pm Fri & Sat Oct-May) Inside a rambling 1913 adobe house built by a wealthy East Coaster who traded high society for the solitude of the desert, this quirky museum displays Native American basketry and pottery, Alaskan artifacts and turn-of-the-20th-century photos. Contact the museum for directions and tour schedules.

Palm Springs Follies (Map p642; ☎ 760-327-0225; www.psfollies.com; Plaza Theatre, 128 S Palm Canyon Dr; tickets $40-93; ☺ Nov-May) This Ziegfeld Follies–style revue includes music, dancing, showgirls and comedy. The twist? Many of the performers are as old as the theater – all are over 50, some as old as 80. But this is by no means amateur hour. Palm Springs can pull some big names out of its celebrity closet. Reservations recommended.

Shields (Map pp640-1; ☎ 760-347-7768; 80-225 Hwy 111, Indio; ☺ 9am-5pm) In business since the 1950s, this date garden continuously shows the film, *The Romance and Sex Life of the Date*.

Oasis (Map pp640-1; ☎ 760-399-5665, 800-827-8017; 59-111 Hwy 111, Thermal; ☺ 8am-5:30pm Mon-Fri, 9am-5:30pm Sat & Sun) Between Indio and the Salton Sea (p649), Oasis is a more welcoming place to pick up gift boxes and date milkshakes.

Spa Resort Casino (Map p642; ☎ 888-999-1995; www.sparesortcasino.com; hotel 100 N Indian Canyon Dr, casino 401 E Amado Rd; day pass $35; ☺ spa 8am-7pm, casino 24hr) The valley's original hot springs are now part of the Native American–owned casino. Choose from a variety of expensive wraps, scrubs and rubs.

The town of **Desert Hot Springs** (Map pp640-1; ☎ 760-329-6403; www.deserthotsprings.com), north of I-10, has cheaper spa pools.

1500 S Gene Autry Trail; adult/child 3-11 $26/15, after 3pm $16/12; ☑ daily Jun-Aug, hours vary mid-Mar–Sep), a water park with an 800,000-gallon wave pool, towering water slides and beaches.

Golf
Golf is huge here, with more than 100 public, semiprivate, private and resort golf courses in and around Palm Springs. It takes a million gallons of water per day to irrigate them, so eco-conscious travelers may want to pass on playing here. Greens fees run from $50 to $250, depending on the course, season, time and day of the week. **Stand-By Golf** (Map pp640-1; ☎ 760-321-2665, 866-224-2665; www.standbygolf.com; ☑ 7am-9pm) provides guaranteed tee times, at a discount, for same-day or next-day play.

Horseback Riding
Close to Indian Canyons, **Smoke Tree Stables** (Map pp640-1; ☎ 760-327-1372, 800-787-3922; www.smoke treeranch.net; 2500 Toledo Ave; ☑ Nov-Apr) arranges daily trail rides, from one-hour outings to all-day treks. The cost is about $35 per hour for novice or experienced riders. Call ahead to secure a spot.

Hiking
In addition to the desert and canyon walks described earlier, you can hike to the top of the tramway (p639) via the **Skyline Trail**. This is an extremely challenging, 11-mile climb through multiple climatic zones with an 8000ft elevation gain. It's recommended only for the very fit who can spend a whole day. Be prepared for snow any time of year. Allow seven to 11 hours, bring extra water and start at the trailhead near the Palm Springs Desert Museum (p643). Enjoy the stellar views, then ride the tram back down.

TOURS
Fans of modernism can pick up *A Map of Palm Springs Modern* ($5), by the **Palm Springs Modern Committee** (www.psmodcom.com). The *Palm Springs Map of the Stars' Homes* ($5) takes you to the abodes of the city's rich and famous, but sometimes you will only see the bougainvillea-covered walls. Both maps are sold at visitors centers. You'll need a car for either self-guided tour.

Celebrity Tours (☎ 760-770-2700; www.celebrity-tours .com; Vons Rimrock Plaza, 4751 E Palm Canyon Dr; adult/child/senior 1hr tour $22/12/20, 2½hr tour $27/14/25) Catch up on the gossip and glamour of Palm Springs on a bus tour.

You can do it yourself with a map from the visitors center, but then you won't get the amusing commentary and juicy dish.
Desert Adventures (☎ 760-324-5337, 888-440-5337; www.red-jeep.com; 2/3/4hr tour $70/90/100) Guided jeep tours of the Joshua Tree backcountry, along the San Andreas Fault and to other hard-to-reach areas.
Palm Springs Modern Tours (Map pp640-1; ☎ 760-318-6118; psmoderntours@aol.com; 3hr tour $55) This van tour pays special attention to the 1950s and '60s, when architects such as Richard Neutra and Albert Frey were major players on the scene.
Power Windmill Tours (Map pp640-1; ☎ 760-251-1997, reservations 760-320-1365; www.windmilltours.com; 90min tour adult/child/senior $23/10/20) Off I-10 exit Indian Ave, then 1.3 miles west on 20th Ave. If the gigantic windmills outside Palm Springs off I-10 have captivated your imagination, go behind the scenes (and hang onto your hats!).
Trail Discovery (☎ 760-325-4453, 888-867-2327; www.palmspringshiking.com) Educational guided hikes locally and in Joshua Tree National Park; call for prices.

FESTIVALS & EVENTS
Every Thursday evening, downtown Palm Canyon Dr is closed to traffic for live music, food vendors, and art and handicraft booths. Go gallery-hopping on North Palm Canyon Dr on the first Friday of every month. For a complete calendar of events, including jazz festivals and celebrity golf tournaments, contact either visitors center.
Coachella Valley Music & Arts Festival (☎ 213-480-3232; www.coachella.com; 1-/2-day tickets $81/152) In late April or early May, Indio's Empire Polo Club hosts one of the hottest music festivals of its kind, with hip indie no-names to pop idols appearing on stage.
National Date Festival (☎ 760-863-8247, 800-811-3247; Riverside County Fairgrounds, 46-350 Arabia St, Indio; adult/child 5-12/senior $7/5/6) Old-fashioned carnival fun with camel and ostrich races in mid- to late February.
Palm Springs International Film Festival (☎ 760-322-2930, 800-898-7256; www.psfilmfest.org; ticket prices vary) In early January this Hollywood star–studded film festival shows over 200 films from more than 60 countries.

SLEEPING
Many of the accommodations are expensive resort-style hotels. There are a few bargains to be had, notably at small, independent places. You'll find many 'inns' and 'lodges' since the word 'motel' seems to have a bad connotation around here. Air-con rooms, cable TV and swimming pools are the norm. Many places serve Continental breakfast of varying quality. More than a few have rooms with full or partial kitchens. Summer

rates are much lower than in peak winter season. The main visitor center operates a no-fee lodging reservation service.

Budget

MOTELS

Chain motels cluster at the southern end of downtown Palm Springs and along I-10 toward Indio.

Alpine Gardens (Map p642; ☎ 760-323-2231, 888-299-7455; www.alpinegardens.com; 1586 E Palm Canyon Dr; r $50-95, ste incl kitchen $80-125; ⊠ ⊠ ⊠) All 10 rooms at this beautifully landscaped, impeccably kept 1950s motel have redwood-beamed ceilings, refrigerators, and slightly kitsch but extremely charming furnishings. It's tops in its class.

Village Inn (Map p642; ☎ 760-320-8622, 866-320-8622; www.palmspringsvillageinn.com; 855 N Indian Canyon Dr; d $45-120, q $65-150; ⊠ ⊠ ⊠) All rooms have VCRs and refrigerators at this clean and well-maintained 16-unit motel north of town, though the mattresses are a bit soft. Still, it's a cozy bargain. Pets are welcome with advance notice.

CAMPING

There are several recreational vehicle (RV) parks around the valley. Mt San Jacinto State Park (p639) has primitive wilderness campsites.

Lake Cahuilla Recreation Area (Map pp640-1; ☎ 760-564-4712, 800-234-7275; www.riversidecountyparks.org; 58-75 Jefferson St, La Quinta; tent & RV sites $13-18; ☾ daily Oct-Apr, Fri-Mon May-Sep, main gate locked 10pm-6am; ⊠) This quiet park is south of Hwy 111 at the western end of 58th Ave. It has shoreline sites (no swimming, but there's a pool), showers and picnic facilities. Reserve ahead in winter.

Midrange

Shelling out a little more may put you within walking distance of downtown.

Chase Hotel at Palm Springs (Map p642; ☎ 760-320-8866, 877-532-4273; www.chasehotelpalmsprings.com; 200 W Arenas Rd; d $80-140, ste $120-170; ⊠ ⊡ ⊠) A classic mid-century modern motel complex with large open spaces, the Chase has immaculately kept, oversized rooms decorated with contemporary furnishings. Great value, friendly service and afternoon cookies make it one of the most popular hotels in town.

Pepper Tree Inn (Map p642; ☎ 760-318-9850, 866-887-8733; www.peppertreepalmsprings.com; 622 N Palm

Canyon Dr; d $80-200, ste $165-300; ⊠ ⊠ ⊠) Big, modern rooms in Spanish style all have mini-refrigerators; some have Jacuzzis, private patios, fireplaces, even mountain views. Quaint touches include ceiling fans and plantation shutters, plus a breezy, natural atmosphere north of downtown.

Movie Colony Hotel (Map p642; ☎ 760-320-6340, 888-953-5700; www.moviecolonyhotel.com; 726 N Indian Canyon Dr; d $130-290, ste $200-290; ⊠ ⊠) The little luxuries – high-thread-count sheets, CD/DVD players and chaise lounges – make all the difference at this minimalist hideaway. The two-story townhouses have private poolside seating or a patio terrace. Guests enjoy free wi-fi and California wines by the glass firepit.

Orbit In (Map p642; ☎ 760-323-3585, 877-996-7248; www.orbitin.com; 562 W Arenas Rd; r $150-310; ⊠ ⊠) Hip, stylish and retro, the Orbit's ultra lounge rooms are outfitted with high-end original pieces of mid-century modern furniture, and amenities like a movie and book library, high-speed Internet access and a guests-only cocktail hour.

Hope Springs Motel Resort (Map pp640-1; ☎ 760-329-4003; www.hopespringsresort.com; 68075 Club Circle Dr, Desert Hot Springs, exit 1-10 at Palm Dr; d $135-185; ⊠ ⊠) This modernist's mecca north of Palm Springs has great views, 10 impeccably stylish rooms with kitchens, and a natural hot spring that flows through three relaxing pools. No pets, no kids.

Top End

If you're going to splash out in the deserts, Palm Springs is the place to do it.

Viceroy (Map p642; ☎ 760-320-4117, 800-237-3687; www.viceroypalmsprings.com; 415 S Belardo Rd; d $100-360; ❌ ❧) It's a sexy property with a modern Palm Springs aesthetic. Wear a slinky cocktail dress and blend right in at this chic miniresort done up in black, white and lemon yellow (think Austin Powers meets Givenchy). There's also a full-service spa, as well as a fab Cal-French restaurant for a white-linen luncheon or swanky supper. Whirlpool villas are the crème de la crème.

Korakia Pensione (Map p642; ☎ 760-864-6411; www.korakia.com; 257 S Patencio Rd; r & ste $140-300, houses $300-600; ❌ ❧) A Moroccan-style villa built in the 1920s, Korakia is a romantic gem, although its offbeat style is not for everyone. It's so authentically decked out that you might think you detect saffron in the air. The antique-filled rooms have feather beds with luxurious linens, and stone entrances that echo the inn's fountain courtyards. Bring groceries and you'll never have to leave.

EATING

Palm Springs isn't what you'd call a 'foodie town.' It's better known for cocktails than dining. Still, you can find good eats just a block or two off the main drag of Palm Canyon Dr. Other powerhouse restaurants are off Hwy 111 through the valley, especially in Rancho Mirage.

Budget

Tyler's Burgers (Map p642; ☎ 760-325-2990; 149 S Indian Canyon Dr; items $2-8; ❧ 11am-4pm) If you're hungry for a damn fine burger, this famed locals' spot is inside an adobe hut with a parking lot patio. Expect a wait at lunchtime, but it's so worth it. Order a root-beer float.

Keedy's (Map pp640-1; ☎ 760-346-6492; 73-633 Hwy 111; mains $5-10; ⏰ 5:30am-3pm Mon-Sat, 5.30am-2pm Sun) In hoity-toity Palm Desert, old-fashioned Keedy's fountain grill serves straightforward 1950s diner fare: eggs, pancakes, hamburgers and milkshakes. It's a handy break from shopping or on the way to the zoo.

Midrange

Fisherman's Market & Grill (☎ 760-327-1766; 235 S Indian Canyon Dr; meals $6-25, early-bird dinner 4-6:30pm Mon-Thu $8; ⏰ 11:30am-9pm Mon-Sat, noon-8pm Sun) This venue grills fantastically fresh fish or shellfish (from Hawaiian *ono* to *ahi* sashimi), served as a salad, sandwich, taco or with coleslaw and chips or rice. Domestic beer is a mere $2.50 and the key lime cheesecake gets rave reviews. Take-out available.

Blue Coyote Grill (Map p642; ☎ 760-327-1196; 445 N Palm Canyon Dr; meals $10-25; ⏰ 11am-10pm Sun-Thu, 11am-11pm Fri & Sat) The flower-laden courtyard tables are the most coveted at this lively cantina serving citrus- and spice-laden Mexican and Southwestern standards, but the real standout is the legendary Wild Coyote margarita.

Native Foods (Map p642; ☎ 760-416-0070; Smoke Tree Village, 1775 E Palm Canyon Dr; mains $8-12; ⏰ 11:30am-9:30pm Mon-Sat) There's great vegan fare at this LA import, and it's worth a special trip for a half dozen kinds of veggie burgers, Southwestern salads and sizzling hot rice bowls (after 5pm), all served in a candlelit and natural-wood setting.

Wang's in the Desert (Map p642; ☎ 760-325-9264; 424 S Indian Canyon Dr; mains $13-18; ⏰ dinner) A stream runs through this watered-down, pan-Asian restaurant, where the minimalist decor, giant cocktails and friendly service draw big crowds for the scene, but not necessarily for the Californicized cooking. Come early or make reservations.

Top End

Zin (Map p642; ☎ 760-322-6300; 198 S Palm Canyon Dr; mains $16-27; ⏰ dinner) Casual white-tablecloth bistro, Zin serves surprisingly good food, given its location on the tourist strip. An American-Belgian menu shows off escargots, steaks, monkfish and homemade pastries. Big portions, neighborly service and a handpicked wine list are all stars.

Johannes (Map p642; ☎ 760-778-0017; 196 S Indian Canyon Dr; mains $22-34; ⏰ dinner Tue-Sun) The chef-owner's Austrian roots shine through

the contemporary Euro-Cal cuisine (think almond-crusted venison) at this spartan, special-occasion spot for diners who like imaginative cooking without a lot of fuss. The black mussels are delish.

Le Vallauris (Map p642; ☎ 760-325-5059; 385 W Tahquitz Canyon Way; mains lunch $13-26, dinner $23-38, steak prix fixe $60-75, Sun brunch $38; ⏰ lunch & dinner Sep-Jun) Le Vallauris serves perfectly crafted contemporary-French haute cuisine. Though lovely, the stately dining room is a bit stiff; for maximum romance, dine alfresco beneath giant ficus trees. Wear high heels or a jacket.

DRINKING

Palm Springs Koffi (Map p642; ☎ 760-416-2244; The Corridor, 515 N Palm Canyon Dr; ⏰ 6am-7pm) Tucked among the art galleries, this local independent java bar serves strong organic coffee.

Sky Bar (Map p642; ☎ 760-325-5200; The Deck, 262 S Palm Canyon Dr; ⏰ 11:30am-12:30am) Overlooking the mountains from a 2nd-floor cocktail lounge, this bar is best for happy hour.

Village Pub (Map p642; ☎ 760-323-3265; 266 S Palm Canyon Dr) Casual Village Pub has live music, dancing, darts and pool tables.

ENTERTAINMENT

Meandering on foot along Palm Canyon Dr downtown is entertaining on almost any given night, or place your bets at the Spa Resort Casino (p643).

Blue Guitar (Map p642; ☎ 760-327-1549; www.blueguitarpalmsprings.com; 120 S Palm Canyon Dr; cover Fri & Sat $10) Hear live jazz and blues upstairs Friday to Sunday nights, at this musician-owned venue next door to the Plaza Theater. The jukebox has soul, blues and jazz.

Melvyn's Lounge (Map p642; ☎ 760-325-0046; Ingleside Inn, 200 W Ramon Rd) There's music and dancing to piano and vocals every night at this old-guard standby, popular that attracts retired celebs and hipsters of all stripes. Sunday afternoon jazz jam sessions are a long-standing tradition. Shine your shoes.

Camelot Theatres (Map p642; ☎ 760-325-6565; 2300 Baristo Rd; adult/senior $8/6, before 2pm $5.50) The desert's premier art house cinema for foreign and indie flicks has a full bar and café.

Desert IMAX Theatre (☎ 760-324-7333; Hwy 111 & Cathedral Canyon Dr, Cathedral City; tickets $7-10) Big-screen Hollywood and 3D movies, as well as virtual-reality IMAX ridefilms, are shown here.

CALIFORNIA DESERTS

SHOPPING

You'll still find fabulous modern design and consignment galleries in Palm Springs, especially on N Palm Canyon Dr. But major retailers that once had stores in Palm Springs have moved to the malls around Palm Desert.

River (Map pp640-1; ☎ 760-341-2711; cnr Hwy 111 & Bob Hope Dr, Rancho Mirage; ☻ 11am-9pm) This midrange shopping mall with a big movie complex is a possible stop en route to the malls of Palm Desert.

El Paseo (Map pp640-1; ☎ 877-735-7273; El Paseo, Palm Desert; ☻ hrs vary) For serious shopping at high-end retailers, head to El Paseo, the main shopping street in Palm Desert, dubbed the Rodeo Dr of the desert. El Paseo runs parallel to Hwy 111, one block south of the highway, about 13 miles southeast of Palm Springs.

Desert Hills Premium Outlets (☎ 951-849-6641; 48400 Seminole Dr, Cabazon; ☻ 10am-8pm Sun-Thu, 10am-9pm Fri, 9am-9pm Sat) Twenty minutes northwest of Palm Springs, off the Fields Rd exit on I-10, this place has retail outlets from Polo to Prada, plus department-store discounts like Off 5th and from Barney's New York.

GETTING THERE & AWAY
Air

Convenient to downtown, **Palm Springs International Airport** (Map pp640-1; ☎ 760-318-3800; www.palmspringsairport.com; 3400 E Tahquitz Canyon Way) is served by Alaska, America West, American, Continental, Delta, Harmony Airways, Horizon Air, Northwest (seasonally), Sun Country, United and WestJet. For more airline information, see p715.

Bus & Train

Greyhound (Map p642; ☎ 800-231-2222; www.greyhound.com; 311 N Indian Canyon Dr; ☻ 8am-6pm) has several daily buses to and from LA ($23, 2¾ to 3¾ hours). Buy your ticket on board when the bus station is closed.

Amtrak (Map pp640-1; ☎ 800-872-7245; www.amtrak.com; cnr Indian Canyon Dr & I-10) runs trains to and from LA (one-way $15 to $30, depending on type of ticket) on Wednesday, Friday and Sunday. Thruway buses provide service on other days; reservations required. Buses pick up at the SunBus airport stop at 3400 Tahquitz Canyon Way. Trains often run late.

Car & Motorcycle

From LA take I-10, the main route into and through the Coachella Valley; the trip to Palm Springs takes about two hours. The more scenic Palms to Pines Hwy leaves the interstate at Banning and heads southeast via Hwys 243 and 74 to Palm Desert, from where Hwy 111 slowly connects west to Palm Springs.

GETTING AROUND
To/From the Airport

Unless your hotel provides airport transfers, plan to take a taxi, which costs at least $10 to downtown Palm Springs. SunBus 24 stops outside the airport.

Airport parking costs $1 per 20 minutes (daily maximum $8).

If you're going to one of the communities outside Palm Springs, call for advance shuttle reservations:

At Your Service (☎ 760-343-0666, 888-700-7888)
Desert Valley Shuttle (☎ 760-251-4020, 800-413-3999)

Bicycle

Palm Springs and the valley have an excellent network of bike paths that are great for tooling around. **Big Horn Bike Adventures** (Map pp640-1; ☎ 760-325-3367; 302 N Palm Canyon Dr; rental per hr $6-12; ☻ 8am-4pm Mon, Tue & Thu-Sat, 10am-4pm Sun, fall-spring) rents bikes downtown. Ask about daily and weekly rates.

Bus

Powered by alternative fuels, **SunBus** (☎ 760-343-3451, 800-347-8628; www.sunline.org), the local bus service, will take you around the valley, albeit slowly, from about 5am to 10pm. Route 111 follows Hwy 111 between Palm Springs and Indio (1½ hours). The standard fare is $1 (exact change required), plus 25¢ for a transfer. Buses have air-con, wheelchair lifts and a two-bicycle rack.

Car

Though you can walk to most sights downtown, you'll need a car to get around the valley. Major rental-car companies (p724) all have desks at the airport in Palm Springs.

Taxi

On weekends in downtown Palm Springs you can often flag a taxi. Otherwise, you'll need to call. If you know you're going to need one at a certain time – say, to go to the airport in the morning – book in advance.

Ace Taxi (☎ 760-835-2445)
American Cab (☎ 760-775-1477)
Yellow Cab (☎ 760-345-8398)

DETOUR: IMPERIAL VALLEY & SALTON SEA

The rich agricultural district of the Imperial Valley is a monument to vision and pioneering enterprise, but only those with an interest in irrigation and agribusiness, odd Americana culture or vast expanses of nothingness will find much to see.

The soil is rich in alluvial deposits from the ancient course of the Colorado River, and its agricultural potential was recognized by Europeans as early as the 1850s, though Native Americans had been cultivating crops here for centuries. Because the area is actually below sea level, water flowing down the Colorado River to the Gulf of California was able to be channeled via the Alamo watercourse, through Mexican territory, then back north into the valley as of 1901.

In 1905, the Colorado River flooded, its water flowing uncontrolled through the canals and into the Imperial Valley. It took 18 months, 1500 workers, $12 million and half a million tons of rock to put the Colorado River back on course. The previously dry Salton Sink became a lake, 45 miles long and 17 miles wide. It had no natural outlet and, as evaporation reduced its size, the natural salt levels became more concentrated. It became an inland sea, with its surface over 200ft below the sea level and its water 25% more salty than the Pacific Ocean.

The **Salton Sea** (www.saltonsea.ca.gov) looks intriguing on a map but is uninspiring in reality. Swimming is unpleasant – the water is murky and the salt stings the eyes – and not recommended at the southern end of the sea because of pollution. The only reason to visit is to see migratory and endangered water bird species, including snow geese, California brown pelicans, bald eagles and peregrine falcons. Right on the Pacific Flyway, the **Sonny Bono Salton Sea National Wildlife Refuge** (☎ 760-348-5278; http://saltonsea.fws.gov; 906 W Sinclair Rd; ☼ dawn-dusk, visitors center 7am-3:30pm Mon-Fri year-round, 8am-4:30pm Sat & Sun Nov-Mar) is 4 miles west of Hwy 111 between Niland and Calipatria.

The **Salton Sea State Recreation Area** (☎ 760-393-3052; www.saltonsea.statepark.org; Hwy 111; day-use fee $6, tent/RV sites $17/23), 25 miles south of Indio on the sea's north shore, has several campgrounds. The best is first-come, first-served Mecca Beach, a mile south of headquarters and the visitors center. Just south of Bombay Beach, east of Hwy 11 off Hot Mineral Spa Rd, are several desert hot-springs RV parks.

One other eccentric site worth turning off Hwy 111 to see is **Salvation Mountain**, a 100ft-high hill of concrete and hand-mixed adobe and covered with eccentric Christ-themed folk art. It's the continual life work of Leonard Knight, who has been living behind his mountain and touching up its acrylic cloak since 1985. Turn east off the highway at Niland, drive 5 miles and you can't miss it.

ANZA-BORREGO DESERT

This untamed desert – centered on 600,000-acre Anza-Borrego Desert State Park – has some of the most spectacular scenery and wildlife in southeastern California. While it lacks the magnetism and facilities of Death Valley or Joshua Tree, it has myriad untrammeled byways to explore, all within reach of the retro delights of Borrego Springs resort.

The human history here goes back more than 10,000 years, as recorded by Native American petroglyphs. Spanish explorer Juan Bautista de Anza passed through in the mid-1770s, pioneering a colonial trail from Mexico. *Borrego* is the Spanish word referring to the millions of Peninsular bighorn sheep that once ranged here as far south as Baja California. Now only a few hundred survive, mostly inside state park refuges.

The enormous and little-developed Anza-Borrego Desert State Park (the largest in the USA outside of Alaska) occupies over a fifth of San Diego County. Depending on winter rains, the park's spring wildflowers can be absolutely stunning. The flowers blossom in late February at lower elevations and reach their best over the next two months at successively higher levels, but the peak typically lasts less than two weeks. Summers start in May here in the low desert and are extremely hot, more so than in Joshua Tree. The average daily maximum temperature in July is 107°F, but it can reach 125°F.

ORIENTATION

If you're short on time or if it's your first visit to the park, head for Borrego Springs (population 3000). Its easy-to-reach sights – including Borrego Palm Canyon and the Borrego Badlands – are fairly representative

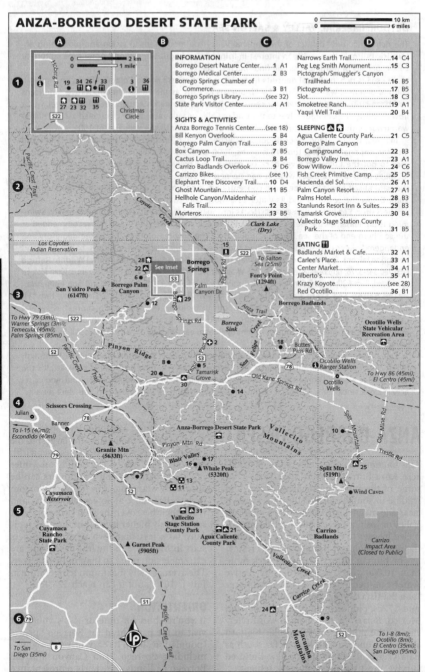

ANZA-BORREGO DESERT STATE PARK

INFORMATION
Borrego Desert Nature Center......1 A1
Borrego Medical Center................2 B3
Borrego Springs Chamber of
  Commerce.................................3 B1
Borrego Springs Library.............(see 32)
State Park Visitor Center..............4 A1

SIGHTS & ACTIVITIES
Anza Borrego Tennis Center......(see 18)
Bill Kenyon Overlook....................5 B4
Borrego Palm Canyon Trail...........6 B3
Box Canyon..................................7 B5
Cactus Loop Trail..........................8 B4
Carrizo Badlands Overlook...........9 D6
Carrizzo Bikes..........................(see 1)
Elephant Tree Discovery Trail.....10 D4
Ghost Mountain..........................11 B5
Hellhole Canyon/Maidenhair
  Falls Trail................................12 B3
Morteros....................................13 B5

Narrows Earth Trail....................14 C4
Peg Leg Smith Monument...........15 C3
Pictograph/Smuggler's Canyon
  Trailhead..............................16 B5
Pictographs...............................17 B5
Slot...18 C3
Smoketree Ranch.......................19 A1
Yaqui Well Trail..........................20 B4

SLEEPING
Agua Caliente County Park.........21 C5
Borrego Palm Canyon
  Campground..........................22 B3
Borrego Valley Inn.....................23 A1
Bow Willow...............................24 C6
Fish Creek Primitive Camp.........25 D5
Hacienda del Sol.......................26 A1
Palm Canyon Resort..................27 A1
Palms Hotel..............................28 B3
Stanlunds Resort Inn & Suites....29 B3
Tamarisk Grove.........................30 B4
Vallecito Stage Station County
  Park......................................31 B5

EATING
Badlands Market & Cafe............32 A1
Carlee's Place............................33 A1
Center Market...........................34 A1
Jilberto's...................................35 A1
Krazy Koyote..........................(see 28)
Red Ocotillo..............................36 B1

of the park as a whole. There are peaceful nature hikes and camping just over Yaqui Pass, south of town. Further east beyond Ocotillo Wells, the Split Mountain area offers interesting geology and spectacular wind caves. The desert's southernmost region, including Blair Valley, is the least visited and has few facilities. Besides the solitude, its attractions include canyons, hot springs and historic sites.

To explore the park in-depth, buy Earthwalk Press' waterproof, six-color and topographic *Anza-Borrego Desert Region Recreation Map* ($9).

INFORMATION

You'll find ATMs, banks, gas stations and a post office in Borrego Springs. There are also gas stations in the towns of Julian, Ocotillo Wells and Ocotillo.

Anza-Borrego Institute (☎ 760-767-0445; www .theabf.org) Offers a variety of lectures and field trips in the area, and an info-packed website.

Borrego Desert Nature Center (☎ 760-767-3098; www.california-desert.org; 652 Palm Canyon Dr; 9am-5pm Sun-Thu, 9am-7pm Fri & Sat) Excellent bookshop run by Anza-Borrego Desert Natural History Association (ABDHA). Pick up the *Sand Paper* newsletter or go online to find out about lectures, courses, hiking and bird-watching tours, and volunteer field trips.

Borrego Medical Center (☎ 760-767-5051; 4343 Yaqui Pass Rd; 8:15am-5pm Mon-Fri) Urgent-care services.

Borrego Springs Chamber of Commerce (☎ 760-767-5555, 800-559-5524; www.borregosprings.org; 786 Palm Canyon Dr; 9am-4pm Mon-Fri) Tourist information brochures.

Borrego Springs Library (☎ 760-767-5761; 652 Palm Canyon Dr; access free; 9am-4pm Tue & Fri, 10am-6pm Wed & Thu, 9am-3pm Sat) Walk-in Internet access.

Emergency (☎ 911) Cell phones won't work except in more populated areas, such as Borrego Springs.

State Park Visitor Center (☎ 760-767-4205; west end of Palm Canyon Dr, Borrego Springs; 9am-5pm Oct-May, 9am-5pm Sat, Sun & holidays only Jun-Sep) Outside are plants that you'll encounter in the park. Inside, a small theater shows a short slide show on the park, and there are free natural history exhibits, as well as naturalist talks and guided hikes. Pick up the free park magazine, which has a handy hiking-trail guide and map.

Wildflower Hotline (☎ 760-767-4684) Find out when peak blossoms are expected.

SIGHTS

Many of the most awesome attractions of **Anza-Borrego Desert State Park** (www.anzaborrego

.statepark.org, http://parks.ca.gov; admission free; 24hr) are only accessible by dirt roads. To find out which ones require 4WD vehicles or are currently impassable, check the signboard inside the visitors center. Free self-guiding trail brochures are available here, but not at the trailheads.

Around Borrego Springs

The popular **Borrego Palm Canyon Trail**, a 3-mile loop starting at the campground near the visitors center, climbs to a native palm grove, a delightful oasis in the dry, rocky countryside. The challenging **Maidenhair Falls Trail** starts from the Hellhole Canyon parking area, a mile west of Borrego Springs on S22, and climbs 3 miles each way past several palm oases to a seasonal waterfall that supports birds and a variety of plants.

Northeast of Borrego Springs, where S22 takes a 90-degree turn to the east, there's an obscure pile of rocks just north of the road. This, the **Peg Leg Smith Monument** memorializes Thomas Long 'Peg Leg' Smith – mountain man, fur trapper, fighter, horse thief, con artist and Wild West legend – who passed through Borrego Springs in the early 19th century and allegedly picked up some rocks that were later found to be pure gold. Strangely, when he returned during the Gold Rush era, he was unable to find the lode. Nevertheless, he told lots of prospectors about it (often in exchange for a few drinks), and many came to search for the lost gold.

A 4-mile dirt road, usually passable without a 4WD, goes south of S22 to **Font's Point**, which offers a spectacular panorama over the Borrego Valley to the west and the Borrego Badlands to the south. You'll be amazed when the desert seemingly drops from beneath your feet. The easy-to-miss turnoff is 3.7 miles east of the monument.

Around Tamarisk Grove

Coming from Borrego Springs over Yaqui Pass, a 1-mile loop starts at the primitive campground and passes several species of cacti en route to **Bill Kenyon Overlook**, with sprawling views of San Felipe Wash and the Pinyon Mountains.

Lower down, opposite Tamarisk Grove campground, are two short nature trails: the 1-mile **Cactus Loop Trail** and 1.6-mile **Yaqui Well Trail**, which also has labeled desert plants, including honey mesquite and agave, and leads to a natural water hole that attracts a rich variety of birds and other wildlife.

The 0.5-mile **Narrows Earth Trail** is a geologist's walk in a fault zone. The trailhead is off Hwy 78, about 4.5 miles east of Tamarisk Grove.

East to Split Mountain

Six miles south of Hwy 78 at Ocotillo Wells, paved Split Mountain Rd takes you past the mile-long dirt road turnoff to the **Elephant Tree Discovery Trail**, a sandy 1.5-mile loop past ocotillo plants and the rare elephant tree, whose short, shrubby trunks and waving branches are said to resemble an elephant. Related to frankincense and myrrh, these fragrant trees were thought not to exist in the Colorado Desert until a full-fledged hunt found them in 1937.

About 4 miles further south along Split Mountain Rd is a dirt-road turnoff for Fish Creek primitive campground. Another 4 miles brings you to **Split Mountain**. The road – popular with 4WD enthusiasts – goes right between 600ft-high walls created by earthquakes and erosion. The gorge is about 2 miles long from north to south. At the far end, the steep **Wind Caves Trail** scrambles a mile up to delicate caves carved into sandstone outcroppings by the wind.

Back on Hwy 78, 5 miles west of Ocotillo Wells, look for the turnoff for Buttes Pass Rd. Drive 1 mile, turn left at the junction and after less than another mile, park where the road turns sharply to the left. From there, it's a 1.5-mile hike through **The Slot**, an extremely narrow canyon wedged in by boulders, ending with a view.

South to Ocotillo

Around 5 miles below Scissors Crossing, where S2 crosses Hwy 78, is the turnoff to **Blair Valley**, known for its morteros (rock hollows used for grinding seeds) on the site of an ancient Kumeyaay village. The valley is about 4 miles east of S2 along a dirt road. A steep, mile-long trail climbs **Ghost Mountain**, to the ruins of the 1930s adobe homestead of an eccentric Australian artist and his reclusive family. You can see a boulder covered in Native Californian pictographs 1 mile along the **Smuggler's Canyon Trail**, which starts 1.6 miles further east in the valley.

Next up, **Box Canyon** marks the intersection of several skeins of area history, including

the pioneer Southern Emigrant Trail, also used in the mid-19th century by the Mormon Battalion, Butterfield Overland stagecoaches from Missouri and many who came to California seeking gold.

You can see a replica of a historic stage station in a green valley further south at **Vallecito Stage Station County Park** (opposite), and four miles down the road, take a hot-springs dip at **Agua Caliente County Park** (opposite). For information on these two parks, which are closed in summer, call ☎ 858-694-3049.

Continuing south on S2, you'll leave the crowds behind and pass dusty pull-offs for short hikes to palm grove oases and the stunning **Carrizo Badlands Overlook**. If you make it all the way down to Ocotillo, you can drive a few miles north on dirt Shell Canyon Rd to **Fossil Canyon**.

ACTIVITIES

The park offers many more hiking trails and 4WD roads than those described earlier. It's also renowned for **stargazing** – purchase sky charts in Borrego Springs.

Cycling

Both paved and dirt 4WD roads are open to bikes. Popular routes are the downhill Grapevine Canyon, relatively flat Blair Valley, steep and demanding Oriflamme Canyon, and other canyon loops in the Carrizo Badlands.

Carrizo Bikes (☎ 760-767-3872; 648 Palm Canyon Dr, Borrego Springs) rents mountain bikes.

Horseback Riding

The **Smoketree Ranch** (☎ 760-767-5850; www.smoke treearabianranch.com; 302 Palm Canyon Dr, Borrego Springs; pony ride $30, guided tours $100-240) leads guided rides on Arabian horses in the desert, as well as the mountains around Julian (p629) during summer.

Golf & Tennis

There are several championship golf courses in Borrego Springs. You can rent a tennis court at some country clubs or the **Anza Borrego Tennis Center** (☎ 760-767-0577; 286 Palm Canyon Dr; day pass incl pool access adult/child $10/5, equipment rental $6; ☾ seasonal hrs vary).

TOURS

The best guided hikes and field trips are led by the nonprofit Anza-Borrego Institute and Anza-Borrego Natural History Association, as well as state park rangers.

California Overland (☎ 760-767-1232, 866-639-7567; www.californiaoverland.com) Uses old military trucks for guided 4WD tours of the park; call for rates.

Ranchita Bike & Hike (☎ 760-782-3900; www.ranchita bikehike.com; tour incl snacks $65-75) Offers morning and dusk downhill mountain-bike trips.

FESTIVALS & EVENTS

Grapefruit Festival Family fun in late February.

Peg Leg Liars Contest On the first Saturday night in April, the Western tradition of telling tall tales lives on. Anyone can enter, so long as the story is about gold mining in the Southwest, is less than five minutes long and is anything but the truth.

Borrego Days In late October there's a beer garden.

SLEEPING

For a cooler retreat, especially in summer, there are some good-value accommodations outside the park in Julian (p629), which is about an hour's drive southwest of Borrego Springs.

Budget

All campfires must be in metal containers; wood gathering is prohibited.

Bow Willow Campground (sites $7) Off S2 in the southern part of the park, Bow Willow has only 16 sites, with water, pit toilets, tables and fire pits.

Agua Caliente County Park (☎ 858-565-3600, 877-565-3600; www.sdcounty.ca.gov/parks; 39555 Rte S2; day-use fee $5, tent sites $14-18; ☿ Sep-May) A better choice for RVers than Bow Willow. Agua Caliente has indoor-outdoor natural hot springs pools, hiking trails and horseshoe pits. Call for pool hours.

Vallecito Stage Station County Park (☎ 858-565-3600, 877-565-3600; www.sdcounty.ca.gov/parks; 37349 Rte S2; tent sites $12; ☿ Sep-May) Tent-friendly is nearby Agua Caliente and is a better choice for campers.

Developed camping facilities are found at **Borrego Palm Canyon** (☎ reservations 800-444-7275; www.reserveamerica.com; 200 Palm Canyon Dr; tent/RV sites $20/29), near the visitors center, and smaller 27-site **Tamarisk Grove** (☎ reservations 800-444-7275; www.reserveamerica.com; off Hwy 78; sites $20; ☿ Nov-May), a quiet spot 13 miles south of Borrego Springs. There are also several free primitive campgrounds in the park, which have pit toilets but no water. With a free permit, backcountry camping is allowed anywhere in the park that's off-road and more than 100ft from a water source.

Midrange & Top End

All of these are in Borrego Springs. In summer, rates drop and some places even close. Motels can be overpriced.

Borrego Valley Inn (☎ 760-767-0311, 800-333-5810; www.borregovalleyinn.com; 405 Palm Canyon Dr; r incl breakfast $130-220; ☒ ☒ ☒) This petite inn, with its contemporary Southwestern-style architecture, has the feel of an intimate spa resort, just perfect for adults. One pool is clothing-optional. There's free wi-fi in the guest cocktail lounge. Expect to hear some traffic noise in your room.

Palm Canyon Resort (☎ 760-767-5341, 800-242-0044; www.pcresort.com; 221 Palm Canyon Dr; RV sites $30, r $70-195; ☒ ☒) Spend a little more than at the motels and you'll get a comfy, if dull room with free high-speed Internet access and two pools to choose from at this family-friendly place near the visitors center. There's an on-site restaurant, store and self-serve laundry.

Palms Hotel (☎ 760-767-7788, 800-519-2624; www.thepalmsatindianhead.com; 2220 Hoberg Rd; r $80-230; ☒ ☒) Hidden a mile north of Palm Canyon Dr, the Palms is a mid-century modern masterpiece. Aside from having the town's biggest pool, where movie stars once frolicked, it has direct access to the park. Unfortunately, the place gets mixed reviews since the substandard service and ill-maintained rooms (with no phones) don't measure up. The front desk is often deserted.

Hacienda del Sol (☎ 760-767-5442; www.hacienda delsol-borrego.com; 610 Palm Canyon Dr; d $70, kitchenette duplexes & cottages $100-130; ☒ ☒) The family-owned Hacienda has fresh rooms with cable TV and in-room coffeemakers.

Stanlunds Resort Inn & Suites (☎ 760-767-5501; www.standlunds.com; 2771 Borrego Springs Rd; d incl breakfast $75-150) Smaller, simpler Stanlunds is pet-friendly. Some rooms have kitchenettes, and all rooms have free wi-fi, but no phones.

EATING

There are few places to eat in Borrego Springs. In summer many places keep shorter hours.

Red Ocotillo (☎ 760-767-7400; 818 Palm Canyon Dr; mains $6-10; ☿ 7am-2pm daily, dinner from 5pm Wed-Sun) In a historic Quonset hut on the east side of town, this anonymous café (the sign simply says 'Eat') is an oasis. Fuel up on homemade coffee cake, breakfast skillets,

CALIFORNIA DESERTS

creative sandwiches and bottomless cups of coffee. There's a shady patio and free wi-fi.

Krazy Koyote (☎ 760-767-7788; Palms Hotel, 2220 Hoberg Rd; mains $17-50; ⏲ dinner) At this posh, poolside grill there is Southwestern- and American-style cooking, including prime steaks and lobster. The lounge atmosphere is more fabulous than the food, with boudoir lamps and chill-out tunes, plus panoramic views over the desert.

Carlee's Place (☎ 760-767-3262; 660 Palm Canyon Dr; lunch $6-12, dinner mains $12-25; ⏲ 11am-9pm, bar until late) Locals pick Carlee's, near Christmas Circle, for its burgers, salads, pasta and steak dinners, though the pool table, karaoke and dive-bar atmosphere are big draws, too. The cheapskate's alternative is Jilberto's taco shop, across the street.

Badlands Market & Cafe (☎ 760-767-4058; The Mall, 561 Palm Canyon Dr; snacks $2-4, sandwiches $5-7; ⏲ 8am-3pm) Globally minded desert cuisine with a gourmet twist, from morning espresso and pastries to fresh salads and sandwiches. Where else are you going to get smoked chicken and feta on pita bread? Take-out available.

Center Market (☎ 760-767-3311; 590 Palm Canyon Dr; ⏲ 8:30am-6:30pm Mon-Sat, 8.30am-5pm Sun) Stocks groceries, water and camping supplies.

From Tamarisk Grove, it's a curvy 20-mile drive west, past Scissors Crossing, to the small town of Julian (p629), famed for its apple pie and hearty, frontier-style eateries. Coming from LA, you'll find wine-tasting rooms and quaint restaurants among the antiques shops of historic Temecula, about 90 minutes northwest of Julian on I-15.

GETTING THERE & AROUND

By car from Palm Springs, take I-10 east to Indio, Hwy 86 south along the Salton Sea (p649) and turn west on S22; the 85-mile drive to Borrego Springs takes around two hours. From LA, take I-10 east to I-15 south, Hwy 79 east from Temecula past Warner Springs, then S2 and S22 to Borrego Springs; a 150-mile (three-hour) total trip. From San Diego, there are a few routes. One way is to follow I-8 east to scenic Hwy 79, which winds north through Cuyamaca Rancho State Park to Julian, then Hwy 78 east and S3 north over Yaqui Pass to Borrego Springs, a 90-mile (2½-hour) trip. Winding S2 also heads north from I-8 at Ocotillo and connects to Hwy 78 after about 45 miles.

San Diego's Metropolitan Transit Service (☎ 619-233-3004, 800-266-6883) operates a limited (nondaily) bus route from Ramona to Borrego Springs via Julian, with occasional stops in Ocotillo Wells and along S2 to Agua Caliente. To get to here from San Diego, though, you'll need to transfer buses at least twice, in Escondido and Ramona. For fare information, bus schedules and bicycle rack reservations, phone ☎ 800-858-0291.

JOSHUA TREE NATIONAL PARK

Joshua Tree National Park straddles the transition zone between the Colorado Desert and the higher, cooler Mojave Desert, where distinctive Joshua trees, so named by Mormon settlers who saw the branches as reaching up toward heaven, grow. In spring some trees bloom dramatically with a profusion of creamy-white blossoms. Every child of the '80s already knows what these strange trees look like, thanks to Irish rockers U2, who stayed here while they worked on their masterpiece.

The park's wonderfully shaped rocky outcroppings draw world-class climbers, who know 'J-Tree' as the best place to climb in California. Backpackers are less enthusiastic, as there is no natural water flow, but day hikers and campers enjoy the chance to scramble up, down and around the giant boulders and palm oases, while mountain-bikers are hypnotized by desert vistas as seen from dirt 4WD roads.

Summer temperatures climb above 100°F, while the average daytime highs in winter hover above 60°F, which is the same as the overnight low in summer. AT higher elevations, such as Keys Point (5185ft), it can be over 10° cooler year-round and receive more precipitation, even snow. Wildflowers bloom at varying elevations between February and May.

HISTORY

Successive Native American cultures inhabited this area for thousands of years. Villages were founded near desert oases and tribespeople harvested desert plants for food, medicine and building materials, as well as hunted wildlife such as bighorn sheep.

Starting in the mid-19th century, miners and ranchers arrived.

This area was also the birthplace of the California desert-conservation movement, when a Southern belle called Minerva Hamilton Hoyt founded the International Deserts Conservation League and campaigned until President Franklin D Roosevelt created Joshua Tree National Monument in 1936. The 1994 California Desert Protection Act turned it into a national park.

ORIENTATION

Twentynine Palms Hwy (Hwy 62) borders the north side of the park, I-10 the south side. From south of the Twentynine Palms area, Pinto Basin Rd drops into the Pinto Basin and leads to Cottonwood Spring, connecting the northern and southern entrances of the park. Park Blvd winds east to west through the area known locally as 'Wonderland of Rocks,' all the way to the west entrance station.

Everything else sprawls along Twentynine Palms Hwy. East of Yucca Valley, the town of Joshua Tree is just outside the park's western entrance. It has the most soul of any town near the park – look out for steel sculptures by Simi Dabah (www.gallery29.com/simi). By the park's northern entrance, the town of Twentynine Palms, also favored by a few artists and writers, serves the park and the nearby Marine Corps Air Ground Combat Center (don't freak out if you hear a big kaboom!).

The NPS park map won't suffice for much more than a day trip. National Geographic's topographic, waterproof and tear-resistant *Trails Illustrated: Joshua Tree National Park* ($9.95) shows 4WD roads, hiking trails and more.

INFORMATION

The NPS website has extensive information on the **Joshua Tree National Park** (www.nps.gov/jotr; 7-day entry pass per car/motorcycle & bicycle $10/5; 24hr), from activities and accessibility to weather and wildflowers. At the park's entrance gates, rangers provide a handy foldout map brochure and an informative park newspaper.

Pick up food, water and gasoline in the nearby towns of Joshua Tree, Twentynine Palms or Yucca Valley, which all have post offices, banks and 24-hour ATMs.

Emergency & Medical Services

Emergency numbers (911, 909-383-5651) Cell-phone coverage is almost nonexistent in the park. You'll find emergency phones at the Intersection Rock parking area (near Hidden Valley campground) and at Indian Cove ranger station.
Hi-Desert Medical Center (760-366-3711, emergency room 760-366-6126; www.hdmc.org; 6601 Whitefeather Rd, Joshua Tree; 8am-5:30pm) 24-hour emergency room.

Internet Access

Beatnik Café (p660; per 15min/1hr $2/6) Self-serve Internet terminals.
Joshua Tree Outfitters (p658; per 15min $2)
San Bernardino County Libraries (access free; closed Sun) Joshua Tree (760-366-8615; 6465 Park Blvd); Twentynine Palms (760-367-9519; 6078 Adobe Rd); Yucca Valley (760-228-5455; 57098 Twentynine Palms Hwy) Hours vary.

Tourist Information

California Welcome Center (760-365-5464; 56711 Twentynine Palms Hwy, Yucca Valley; 8:30am-5:30pm) Free tourist publications and maps.
Coyote Corner (760-366-9683; www.joshuatreecoyotecorner.com; 6535 Park Blvd, Joshua Tree; 9am-7pm) Camping supplies, maps, books, coin-operated showers and free water.
Joshua Tree Chamber of Commerce (760-366-3723; www.joshuatreechamber.org; 61325 Twentynine Palms Hwy, Joshua Tree; 10am-3pm Mon-Fri) Some local information.
Joshua Tree National Park Association (760-367-5525; www.joshuatree.org) Runs visitors center bookstores and Desert Institute (760-367-5535) field trips and classes ($45 to $100).
NPS Cottonwood Visitor Center (Pinto Basin Rd; 8am-4pm) A few miles inside the park's southern entrance, it has on-duty rangers, small exhibits, and sells books, maps and gifts.
NPS Oasis Visitor Center (760-367-5500; Utah Trail; 8am-5pm) Stock up on books and maps at park headquarters, up the road from the northern entrance station. Free interpretive programs include videos, ranger talks, junior ranger workbooks for kids, and monthly stargazing parties held on the Saturday closest to the new moon.
Twentynine Palms Chamber of Commerce (760-367-3445; www.29chamber.com; 6455A Mesquite Ave; 9am-3pm Mon-Fri Jun-Aug, 9am-5pm Sep-May) Has a few brochures.
Twentynine Palms Convention & Visitors Bureau (www.visit29.org) Comprehensive online guide to 'California's outback,' with photos.

CALIFORNIA DESERTS

SIGHTS

You really have to get away from your car to appreciate the psychedelic landscapes and unlimited horizons. If you're short on time, the 0.25-mile **Skull Rock Loop** is an easy walk starting in Jumbo Rocks campground, at the east edge of the Wonderland of Rocks. Just west of Twentynine Palms, from the end of Canyon Rd, a 3-mile round-trip hike leads to quiet **Fortynine Palms Oasis**.

Oasis of Mara

Behind the visitors center outside the north entrance station, this natural oasis has the original 29 palm trees for which the nearby town is named. They were planted by the Serrano tribespeople who once lived here. It's one of a handful of desert fan palm oases in the park. The Pinto Mountain Fault, a small branch of the San Andreas Fault (which forms the park's southern boundary), runs through the oasis, as does a 0.5-mile nature trail that's wheelchair-accessible.

The Valleys

Those who enjoy history and local lore should take a tour of the **Desert Queen Ranch** (☎ 760-367-5555; adult/child 6-11 $5/2.50; ☼ 90 min tour 1pm Mon-Fri, 10am & 1pm Sat & Sun Oct-May) in Queen Valley. Russian immigrant William Keys built a homestead here on 160 acres in 1917 and over the next 60 years forged a full working ranch, school, store and workshop out of the harsh desert.

Amazingly, everything still stands pretty much as it did when Keys died in 1969. Reservations for the half-mile walking tour are recommended; book over the phone or in person at the Oasis Visitor Center. To get to the tour start point, take the turnoff east of Hidden Valley campground and follow the dirt road 2 miles north to the gate.

To the west near shady **Hidden Valley**, a popular rock-climbing area, take a 1.1-mile walk past petroglyphs to **Barker Dam**, a watering hole for birds and other desert wildlife. On the west side of Park Blvd, a 1-mile nature trail starts at the Hidden Valley picnic area.

East of Queen Valley, intrepid travelers with 4WD vehicles or mountain bikes can detour off Park Blvd onto **Geology Tour Road**, an 18-mile field trip down into and around Pleasant Valley. Stop by the visitors center to pick up a self-guiding brochure and to ask about current road conditions.

The Mountains

Detour south off Park Blvd and follow the paved road for 5.5 miles until it ends at **Keys View**, a high point overlooking the entire Coachella Valley and the San Bernardino Mountains. You can even observe the San Andreas fault from here.

On the way back, a dirt road turnoff leads east for just over a mile to the trailhead parking area for the 4-mile round-trip hike to **Lost Horse Mine** (5278ft), which stands in ruins up on a mountaintop. Allow at least three hours.

More ruins and 360-degree views await atop **Ryan Mountain** (5461ft), a 3-mile round-trip climb that starts back on Park Blvd near Sheep Pass campground.

Black Rock Canyon

With a family-friendly campground, this area in the far northwest of the park is a good place for outdoor novices. Stop by the **Black Rock Nature Center** (☎ 760-367-3001; Joshua Lane; ☼ 8am-4pm Sat-Thu, noon-8pm Fri Oct-May) for a self-guiding brochure to the 1.3-mile **Hi-View Nature Trail** loop, which blossoms hugely in spring. The 5.5-mile **Panorama Loop** starts at the campground and climbs to viewpoints.

Black Rock is an alternative base for backcountry excursions, such as an athletic 10-mile round-trip hike to **Eureka Peak** (5516ft) which follows part of the California Riding and Hiking Trail and a steep 4WD road. Another way into the **Covington Flats** area, which boasts the park's biggest Joshua trees, is via unpaved La Contenta Rd further east.

Cottonwood Spring

Cottonwood Spring is at the far southern edge of the park. While most visitors give it a passing glance, it hides some of the lushest scenery in the park. You can stroll down the wash on a mile-long nature trail or tackle the 3-mile round-trip up **Mastodon Peak** for views over the Salton Sea (p649). But the park's best hiking trail is a 7.5-mile round-trip to **Lost Palms Oasis**, a remote canyon filled with palm trees; the hike to the overlook is fairly flat, followed by fun boulder scrambling.

To get to the spring from the north entrance station, take Park Blvd south and drive straight onto Pinto Basin Rd, which winds for 30 miles down into the low desert. Take a break at the **Cholla Cactus Garden**, where a quarter-mile loop leads around waving

---

TOP 10 WEIRDEST PLACES IN THE CALIFORNIA DESERTS

The unique part of traveling in the desert is meeting its eccentric characters, such as at these places.

Pioneertown (p659) A Hollywood movie set with a time-warped life of its own.

Exotic World Burlesque Museum & Striptease Hall of Fame (p665) A socialist, feminist history lesson for us all.

Integratron (☎ 760-364-3126; www.integratron.com; Landers, CA; tour per person $15, minimum $60; ☺ by appointment) Built by a man who worked with Howard Hughes, this acoustically perfect dome sits on a magnetic vortex northwest of Joshua Tree. It was designed as a rejuvenation chamber and time machine. Call ahead for a personal tour or a sonic healing bath. Check the website for special events like UFO symposiums.

Amargosa Opera House (p674) If she builds it, they will come .

Rhyolite's Goldwell Open-Air Museum (p674) Is that a prospector and a penguin on the horizon?

Salton Sea (p649) The desert's accidental, irresistible seashore.

Salvation Mountain (p649) One old man's wacky evangelical dream.

Trona Pinnacles (p675) On the way to Trona town, with its rough Finish Line saloon.

Felicity (☎ 760-572-0100; www.felicityusa.com; off I-8 exit 164; ☺ Dec-Mar) Eight miles west of Yuma, AZ, tour the 'official center of the world,' as proclaimed by a children's book author, then gawk at the spiral staircase from the Eiffel Tower now ascending nowhere and granite walls in the desert that are etched with eclectic scenes from world history.

Mojave Phone Booth (p664) RIP.

---

ocotillo plants and jumping 'teddy bear' cholla.

Beyond the spring, just inside the park's southern boundary, **Bajada Nature Trail** is a quarter-mile paved loop that ambles into the Sonoran Desert.

ACTIVITIES

For guided horseback rides, saddle up at **Joshua Tree 'JT' Ranch** (☎ 760-366-5357; www.joshua treeranch.com; 8651 Quail Spring Rd, Joshua Tree; per hr $35), near the west entrance station.

Rock Climbing

From boulders to cracks to multipitch faces, there are thousands of established routes here. The longest climbs are not much more than 100ft or so, but there are many challenging technical routes, and most can be easily top-roped for training. Some of the most popular climbs are in the **Hidden Valley** area.

A specialized climbing book, such as *The Trad Guide to Joshua Tree* by Diane and Charlie Winger, is a must. Connect with the cyber climbing community at www.climbing jtree.com. For a day or weekend of instruction or a private guided climb, contact locally based **Joshua Tree Rock Climbing School** (☎ 760-366-4745; 800-890-4745; www.joshuatreerock climbing.com; classes from $110).

The nearby town of Joshua Tree is a launching pad for climbers. **Nomad Ventures** (☎ 760-366-4684; www.nomadventures.com; 61795

Twentynine Palms Hwy; ☺ 8am-6pm Mon-Thu, 8am-8pm Fri & Sat, 8am-7pm Sun) is the place to buy the latest gear. Coyote Corner (p655) also carries climbing books and route diaries.

Hiking

To protect plantlife and keep the desert from blowing away, always stay on established trails. Longer hikes present a challenge because of the need to carry water: one to two gallons per person per day. Overnight backcountry hikers must register at one of 12 backcountry boards throughout the park. Cars left overnight that are not registered at a designated parking area may be cited or towed.

The well-traveled, 16-mile **Boy Scout Trail** (Map pp640–1) through the Wonderland of Rocks starts from either the Indian Cove or Keys West backcountry board, and you'll need two cars. A 35-mile stretch of the **California Riding & Hiking Trail** passes through the park and nearby **Eureka Peak** (opposite).

Cycling

Bicycles must stay on established paved and dirt roads, not on trails. A mountain bike or at least a hybrid is necessary for the park's many unpaved roads. Favorite routes are the challenging 20-mile **Pinkham Canyon Road**, which begins at the Cottonwood Visitor Center, and the long-distance **Old Dale Road** and **Black Eagle Mine Road**, which start

6.5 miles north of there. The **Queen Valley** road network is a more gentle set of trails with bike racks along the way, but it's busy with cars, as is **Geology Tour Road** (p656). **Covington Flats** (p656) is a wide-open network of dirt roads.

FESTIVALS & EVENTS

Contact the towns' chambers of commerce for more info.

EarthWorks Now (www.cmccd.edu/faculty/sdowner) The biennial environmental art exhibition takes place in March and April.

Turtle Days Street Fair Joshua Tree town, April

Joshua Tree Music Festival (www.joshuatreemusic festival.com; day pass $25-30) In May this upstart fest happens out at Joshua Lake Campground.

Gem & Mineral Jamboree Joshua Tree town, October

Gram Parsons Festival Joshua Tree town, October

Wild West Coyote Fest Joshua Tree town, October

Pioneer Days Twentynine Palms puts on this Western-themed event in October.

Weed Show Wacky found art sculptures are on display in Twentynine Palms in November.

SLEEPING

There are no lodges in the park, only campgrounds. There are many more chain motels and hotels on Twentynine Palms Hwy in Yucca Valley and between Joshua Tree and Twentynine Palms.

Budget

Rent camping gear – from tents, bags and solar showers to stoves and coolers – from **Joshua Tree Outfitters** (☎ 760-366-1848, 888-366-1848; www.joshuatreeoutfitters.com; 61707 Twentynine Palms Hwy; ⊙ 9am-5pm Mon, Tue, Thu & Fri, 9am-6pm Sat, 8am-6pm Sun).

There are nine campgrounds (sites $5) open year-round in the park. Hidden Valley, Ryan, Sheep Pass, Jumbo Rocks, Belle and White Tank are available on a first-come, first-served basis, as is Cottonwood (sites $10). At busy times, find a site before noon and stake your claim. Group-oriented Black Rock Canyon and Indian Cove have sites ($10) by reservation only. Call ☎ 800-365-2267 or visit http://reservations.nps.gov.

Water is available at Black Rock Canyon and Cottonwood. All other campgrounds have pit toilets, picnic tables and fireplaces, but no water. Jumbo Rocks has sheltered rock alcoves that act as the perfect sunset/sunrise–viewing platforms, but Belle and White Tank also have views. Hidden Valley is busy. Cottonwood is popular with RVs.

Backcountry camping is permitted in the park, but not less than a mile from the nearest road, or 500ft from the nearest trail, and not in any wash or day-use area. Required self-registration is free at backcountry boards also used by hikers (p657). Campfires are forbidden.

Five miles north from Twentynine Palms Hwy, the family-run **Joshua Tree Lake Campground** (☎ 760-366-1213; www.jtlake.com; 2601 Sunfair Rd; tent & RV sites $9, walk-in shower $3) offers hot showers, laundry, a general store, horseshoes and fishing.

Midrange & Top End

Twentynine Palms has most of the accommodations near the park. Joshua Tree has fewer places, but more diversity. There's often a two-night minimum stay, especially on weekends. Check with the chambers of commerce for more lodging options, including vacation rental houses.

29 Palms Inn (☎ 760-367-3505; www.29palmsinn .com; 73950 Inn Ave, Twentynine Palms; d $50-155, q $125-295; ✖ ▯ ▣) Around the Oasis of Mara, this charming collection of old adobe-and-wood cabins, bungalows and houses is the best place to stay in Twentynine Palms. Some have decks and fireplaces, perfect on a cool desert evening. Continental breakfast is included and features scratch muffins.

Spin & Margie's Desert Hide-a-Way (☎ 760-366-9124; www.deserthideaway.com; ste $115-150; ✖ ▣) Every boldly colorful, snappy-looking suite has its own kitchen, TV/VCR and stereo at this delightful hacienda-style inn, situated on three fenced-in acres in Joshua Tree. Charming, knowledgeable and gregarious owners ensure a relaxed visit.

Harmony Motel (☎ 760-367-3351; www.harmony motel.com; 71161 Twentynine Palms Hwy, Twentynine Palms; s/d/q $50/60/80; ✖ ▣ ▯ ▣) An eccentric spot on the western edge of Twentynine Palms where U2 stayed. This back-to-basics 1950s motel has a small pool, communal kitchen, large rooms (but no TVs), gorgeous views, and nooks for reading or meditating. Expect traffic noise, especially in the cabin, which sleeps three.

Rosebud Ruby Star (☎ 760-366-4676, 877-887-7370; www.rosebudrubystar.com; s/d $140/155, bunkhouse $165-200, houses $220-585; ⊙ Sep-Jun; ✖) Just south of Joshua Tree near the western entrance of

DETOUR: PIONEERTOWN

From Hwy 62 (Twentynine Palms Hwy) in the town of Yucca Valley, head 5 miles north along Pioneertown Rd, and you'll drive straight into the past.

Pioneertown (www.pioneertown.com; admission free) was built as a Hollywood movie backdrop in 1946 and has hardly changed since. The main street (Mane St) is lined with buildings that were used in countless Western movies and TV shows. You can witness a 'real' Old West–style gunfight in the street here at 2:30pm on Saturdays and Sundays from April to October; it's a little cheesy, but kids love it. Whenever they're open, definitely check out **Pioneer Bowl** (☎ 760-365-3615; ☾ usually 11am-7pm Sat & Sun), an old-fashioned bowling alley built for Roy Rogers in 1947 that has an amazing collection of vintage pinball games, and the **Red Dog Saloon**.

Make it a point to visit **Pappy & Harriet's Pioneertown Palace** (☎ 760-365-5956; www.pappy andharriets.com; 53688 Pioneertown Rd; mains lunch $6-10, dinner $8-25; ☾ 5pm-late Mon, 11am-late Thu-Sun), a real honky-tonk. Expect plenty of cowboy hats, cheap beer, real Tex-Mex food (mesquite-fired beef and chicken slathered with barbecue sauce) – portions are huge, but the kitchen closes at 9:30pm. Weekend reservations recommended. Best of all, there's free live music every night it's open. Call ahead for the show calendar: sometimes big names, from Shelby Lynne to Cracker to the Donnas, perform and you'll need tickets.

To avoid driving in a binge-induced coma, you can sleep where movie stars slept at **Pioneertown Motel** (☎ 760-365-4879, 888-365-4879; www.pioneertownmotel.com; 5040 Curtis Rd; RV sites $10, d $55-65; ☒), where rooms have kitchenettes and satellite TV, or **Rimrock Ranch Cabins** (below).

the park, this out-of-the-way Western-style charmer has two lovingly decorated guest rooms, a comfy ranch bunkhouse that sleeps up to five people, and two houses (go for the adobe retreat) that sleep up to seven people. There are no TVs or phones.

Rimrock Ranch Cabins (☎ 760-228-1297; www.rim rockranchcabins.com; 50857 Burns Canyon Rd, Pioneertown; cabins $100-155; ☒ ☒) For an off-the-beaten-path hideaway where time slows down and tensions melt away, book a cabin at Rimrock, approximately 20 minutes from Joshua Tree. Built in the 1940s as the area's first homestead, its four cabins each come with a full kitchen and a private patio, perfect for stargazing.

Joshua Tree Inn (☎ 760-366-1188; www.joshuatree inn.com; 61259 Twentynine Palms Hwy, Joshua Tree; r incl breakfast $75-145; ☒ ☒) Alt-country pioneer and 1970s rock legend Gram Parsons overdosed in this large U-shaped motel in Joshua Tree (and his fans still flock here to stay in Room 8). It's an OK place to stay, with a communal living room and a fireplace.

More money-saving options:

Sunset Motel (☎ 760-367-3484; www.sunsetmotel29 .com; 73842 Twentynine Palms Hwy, Twentynine Palms; r $37-55; ☐ ☒ ☒) Clean and friendly; full kitchens available.

El Rancho Dolores Motel (☎ 760-367-3528; www .virtual29.com/a-z/dolores; 73352 Twentynine Palms Hwy, Twentynine Palms; r $35-80; ☒ ☒) Large pool, some kitchenette suites.

EATING

Twentynine Palms has OK food, but – other than the 29 Palms Inn – not much character. Places in Joshua Tree have microbrews, live music and vegan food.

Budget

Crossroads Cafe & Tavern (☎ 760-366-5414; 61715 Twentynine Palms Hwy, Joshua Tree; mains $3-10; ☾ 7am-8pm Sun-Tue & Thu, 7am-9pm Fri & Sat) A warm, cozy and rustic-looking joint with consistently good food, Crossroads serves healthy breakfasts, huge sandwiches, big salads, tasty dinner specials, smoothies, espresso drinks, beer and wine.

Wonder Garden Café (☎ 760-367-2429; 73511 Twentynine Palms Hwy, Twentynine Palms; dishes $3-8; ☾ 8am-4pm Mon-Sat) Attached to a natural foods market, this laidback café has a shady outdoor back patio where you can nosh on breakfast pastries, vegetarian soups and sandwiches, or a delicious cup o' somethin' from the juice and smoothie bar.

Rattler Fine Food (☎ 760-366-1898; 61705 Twentynine Palms Hwy, Joshua Tree; dishes $2-9; ☾ 9am-5:30pm mid-Sep–June) This tiny gourmet specialty-food store makes terrific take-out foods and boxed lunches. Superb artisanal cheeses, prosciutto, affordable wines, delicious salads and killer brownies.

Along the Twentynine Palms Hwy are several supermarkets, especially in the Yucca

Valley. **Rio Ranch Market** (☎ 760-367-7216; 73544 Twentynine Palms Hwy, Twentynine Palms; ❤ 7am-10pm) is nearest the park's north entrance station.

Midrange & Top End

29 Palms Inn (☎ 760-367-3505; 73950 Inn Ave, Twentynine Palms; mains lunch $7-10, dinner $14-23; ❤ 11am-2pm & 5-9pm Mon-Thu, 11am-2pm & 5-9:30pm Fri & Sat, 9am-2pm & 5-9pm Sun) The oasis inn makes its own bread and desserts, grills great steaks and serves a variety of daily specials. Lunch brings fresh sandwiches and salads. It's well worth a detour, so make reservations.

Spunky Monkey Café (☎ 760-363-7372; 49700 Twentynine Palms Hwy, Morongo Valley; mains $7.50-12; ❤ 8am-9pm) En route to or from Palm Springs, stop off at this roadside kitchen in Morongo Valley for fabulous plates of daring pastas, fresh salads, awesome smoothies, espresso and free wi-fi.

DRINKING

Joshua Tree Saloon (☎ 760-366-2250; 61835 Twentynine Palms Hwy, Joshua Tree) If it's pool tables, karaoke and live rock bands you're after, the ol' Joshua Tree Saloon is nearby the Crossroads Cafe and Tavern.

Beatnik Café (☎ 760-366-2090; www.jtbeat.com; 61597 Twentynine Palms Hwy, Joshua Tree; ❤ 11am-midnight Sun-Thu, 11am-2am Fri & Sat) A community coffeehouse, hippie Beatnik has live acoustic music, film nights and poetry readings.

Water Canyon Coffee Co (☎ 760-365-7771; 55844 Twentynine Palms, Yucca Valley; ❤ 7am-9pm Sun-Thu, 9am-10pm Fri & Sat) In Old Town, hipsters hang at this coffeehouse for its live acoustic sounds, rich coffee, art and free wi-fi.

GETTING THERE & AROUND

Rent a car in Palm Springs or LA. For general rental information and agencies, see p724. From LA, the trip takes two to three hours via I-10 then Hwy 62; from Palm Springs, it takes an hour. For the southern entrance to the park, exit 1-10 about 25 miles east of Indio. Drive defensively on the 15-mile stretch of Twentynine Palms Hwy between Joshua Tree and Twentynine Palms.

Morongo Basin Transit Authority (☎ 760-366-2395, 800-794-6282; www.mbtabus.com) runs local buses along the Twentynine Palms Hwy ($1 to $2) and limited commuter services to Palm Springs (one way/round-trip $10/15). Call ahead to check fares (exact change only) and schedules.

Inside the park, bikes are a great way to get around. Just hop on your two-wheeled steed to get from your campground to any destination and you'll have gorgeous scenery along the way. Otherwise, you've got to drive.

MOJAVE DESERT

The Mojave Desert covers a vast region, from urban areas on the northern edge of LA County to the remote, sparsely populated country of the Mojave National Preserve. Most people just pass through corners of the desert in Death Valley or Las Vegas, but there's a lot more worth stopping for here.

The Upper Mojave is a harsh land, with sporadic mining settlements and vast areas set aside for weapons and aerospace testing. Driving around Mojave town, you might mistake it for a huge international airport, but all those airliners are actually in storage, since the dry desert air minimizes the deterioration.

Southeast of Mojave, **Edwards Air Force Base** (☎ 661-277-3512; www.edwards.af.mil) is a flight test facility for the US Air Force, NASA and civilian aircraft, and a training school for test pilots with the 'right stuff.' It was here that Chuck Yeager flew the world's first supersonic flight; the first space shuttles glided in after their missions; and in 2004, SpaceShipOne became the first civilian aircraft to reach suborbital altitudes – twice. At press time, the base was open to visitors on a limited basis.

BARSTOW

pop 23,600

At the junction of I-40 and I-15, sleepy Barstow is about halfway between LA and Las Vegas. Lots of travelers break their journey here. They're not looking for charm, nor will they find any.

History

This area has been a desert travelers' crossroads for centuries. The Spanish priest Francisco Garcès came through in 1776, and the Old Spanish Trail passed nearby. By the 1860s, settlers on the Mojave River were selling supplies to California immigrants. Mines were founded in the hills. Barstow, named after a railway executive, got going as a railroad junction after 1886. It was

DETOUR: ANTELOPE VALLEY

The Antelope Valley is dead flat, and it's difficult to see a valley, much less an antelope. But in spring, the valley bursts with spectacular fields of native California poppies, like a vision out of the *Wizard of Oz*.

The **Antelope Valley California Poppy Reserve** (☎ 661-724-1180; www.parks.ca.gov; Lancaster Rd & 150th St W; admission per vehicle $5; 🕐 dawn-dusk) outlines 7 miles of easy walks among the wildflowers, starting from the **interpretive center** (🕐 10am-4pm Mon-Fri, 9am-5pm Sat & Sun in season). To get here, exit Hwy 14 in Lancaster at Avenue I, then drive 15 miles west. Another five miles further, **Arthur B Ripley Desert Woodland State Park** (☎ 661-942-0662; Lancaster Rd, at 210th St W; admission free; 🕐 dawn-dusk) has precious stands of Joshua trees and native junipers.

About 17 miles east of Lancaster, the **Antelope Valley Indian Museum** (☎ 661-942-0662; www .avim.av.org; Ave 'M' E; adult/child under 16 $1/free; 🕐 11am-4pm Sat & Sun late Sep–mid-Jun), between 150th & 170th Sts, has Native American artifacts from California and across the Southwest. From Hwy 14, go east on Ave K and follow the signs to a Swiss-style chalet up among the boulders on the north side of the road. You can camp among Joshua trees and desert tortoises at nearby **Saddleback Butte State Park** (☎ 661-942-0662; Ave 'J' E; sites $12), east of 170th St.

Lancaster's motels are east of Hwy 14 on Ave K and the Sierra Hwy. **Whole Wheatery** (☎ 661-945-0773; 44264 10th St W; 🕐 9am-7pm Mon-Fri, 9am-6pm Sat, 11am-5pm Sun, café 10:30am-4pm Mon-Sat, 11am-4pm Sun) is the Mojave's healthiest grab-and-go food emporium.

also a major rest stop for travelers along old Route 66. Today it serves a couple of military bases, as well as being the unofficial capital of the Mojave Desert.

Information

Barstow Area Chamber of Commerce (☎ 760-256-8617, 888-422-7786; www.barstowchamber.com; Casa Del Desierto, 681 N 1st Ave) Free brochures galore.

California Welcome Center (☎ 760-253-4782; Tanger Outlet Center, 2796 Tanger Way, off I-15; 🕐 9am-6pm) Pitiful selection of tourist brochures and books.

Desert Discovery Center (☎ 760-252-6060; www .discoverytrails.org; 831 Barstow Rd, off I-15; 🕐 11am-4pm Tue-Sat) Cooperative BLM, NPS and nonprofit educational center. Stop in to see the second-largest meteorite (6070lb) ever found in the USA.

Highway Radio (98.1FM) Mojave traffic and weather updates every half-hour.

Sights & Activities

Murals optimistically adorn boarded-up buildings downtown. North of Main St over the train tracks is historic **Casa Del Desierto** (681 N 1st Ave), a 1911 Harvey House designed by the famed Southwestern architect Mary Jane Coulter. Inside is the artistic **Route 66 'The Mother Road' Museum** (☎ 760-255-1890; www .route66museum.org; admission by donation; 🕐 11am-4pm Fri-Sun) and the **Western America Railroad Museum** (☎ 760-256-9276; www.barstowrailmuseum.org; admission by donation; 🕐 11am-4pm Fri-Sun), with memorabilia and a growing stock collection.

Near the Desert Discovery Center, off I-15 at the Barstow Rd exit, the **Mojave River Valley Museum** (☎ 760-256-5452; www.wemweb.com /mrvm; 270 E Virginia Way; admission free; 🕐 11am-4pm) focuses on local history, culture and natural science. Its bookstore is easily best in the region.

Sleeping

Only when the Mojave freezes over will there be a lack of rooms in Barstow. Check yourself into any of dozens of budget motels strung along E Main St, most with doubles under $40.

Desert Inn (☎ 760-256-2146; fax 760-256-3244; 1100 E Main St; d $30-45; 🏊 📶) For a little more money, you can get yourself a few more creature comforts here at this motor court, with spacious rooms. More upscale chain motels stand at the ready nearby.

Oak Tree Inn (☎ 760-254-1148; www.oaktreeinn.net; 35450 Yermo Rd; d $65-85; ❌ 📶 📶) A better midrange bargain than most places in Barstow, this comfy upscale motel 8 miles east of town, off I-15 exit at Ghost Town Rd, even offers free wi-fi for guests.

Eating & Drinking

Di Napoli's Firehouse (☎ 760-256-1094; 1358 E Main St; meals $8-15; 🕐 10am-9pm Mon-Sat) A charmingly old-school Italian joint in a strip mall, the friendly family's servers dish up minestrone soup so hearty it could fuel an expedition,

---

CAMELS IN THE MOJAVE

The old Mojave Rd was first blazed by Spanish missionaries, traders and fur trappers such as Jedediah Smith traveling along the same path of watering holes used by Native American tribes to reach the California coast from the Colorado River.

Between the Mexican–American and Civil Wars, the USA established a string of military outposts in the Mojave. In the late 1850s, General Edward Fitzgerald Beale led an expedition of Tunisian camels through the desert, but they scared the living daylights out of local ranch horses. So the idea of using them to defend the Southwest was abandoned, as were the forts.

When the Santa Fe Railway started running in the late 1880s, traffic along the Mojave Rd died out. But intrepid travelers can still drive it today. North of Mid Hills, Cedar Canyon Rd follows an easy, graded dirt section of the old road for a short ways. To drive the entire 140 miles, plan on three days to make the 4WD trip west from the Colorado River nearby Laughlin (p697) to Afton Canyon, passing desert oases, dry lakebeds and historical ruins.

You'll need a topographic map and the essential *Mojave Road Guide* ($20) by Dennis Casebier, which shows you how to navigate by rock cairns and is full of desert survival information (see p637). Order it from the Mojave Desert Heritage & Cultural Association (p665) or buy a copy at visitors centers in the preserve. Taking the road is best in dry, cool autumn weather.

---

plus gigantic calzones, pastas, chicken parmesan and salads.

Idle Spurs Steakhouse (☎ 760-256-8888; 690 Old Hwy 58, off I-15; mains lunch $8-14, dinner $12-35; ☷ 11am-4pm Mon-Fri, 4-9pm daily) In the saddle since the 1950s, this casual spot with an atrium patio and full bar east of town is a fave with RVers. Get yer prime rib, lobster and shrimp Louie here, folks.

Peggy Sue's Nifty Fifties Diner (☎ 760-254-3370; 35654 Yermo Rd; mains $6-12; ☷ 6am-9pm Sun-Thu, 6am-10pm Fri & Sat) A 15-minute drive north of Barstow, off I-15 exit at Ghost Town Rd, Peggy Sue's has thick milkshakes, chicken-fried steaks, a pizza parlor, a nostalgic candy store and a video arcade full of teens from the nearby military base. It's rowdy.

Entertainment
A classic from the 1960s, the **Skyline Drive-In** (☎ 760-256-3333; 31175 Old Hwy 58, off I-15; adult/child under 12 $5/free) is one of only two dozen drive-in movie theaters left in California. It shows two double features daily.

Getting There & Around
You'll need a car to get around the Barstow area. Some major car-rental agencies (p724) have offices in town.

Greyhound (☎ 800-231-2222; www.greyhound.com) buses from LA ($25, 2½ to 4½ hours), Las Vegas ($29, 2¾ hours), Palm Springs ($29, 4¾ to 5¾ hours) and San Diego ($29, 4½ to 6¼ hours) arrive at a **station** (☎ 760-256-8757; 1611 E Main St; ☷ 9am-6pm Mon-Sat, 7:30am-4:30pm

Sun) east of downtown, near many of the motels.

One **Amtrak** (☎ 800-872-7245; www.amtrak.com) train, the *Southwest Chief*, stops at Barstow's historic **railroad station** (685 N 1st Ave; ☷ 9am-11:30pm), but schedules are inconvenient and trains often run late. This route travels west to San Bernardino ($18, two hours) and LA ($27, 3¾ to 4½ hours), and east to Needles ($30, 2½ to three hours). There is no staffed ticket office. Thruway bus services depart from the Greyhound bus station to Bakersfield ($20, three hours), for rail connections north to San Francisco and beyond.

MOJAVE NATIONAL PRESERVE
Created as part of the 1994 California Desert Protection Act, this free preserve contains 1.5 million acres of sand dunes, Joshua trees, volcanic outcroppings and stunning rock formations – sort of like Death Valley and Joshua Tree National Parks rolled into one, but with far fewer people. Bighorn sheep, desert tortoise and wily coyote are frequently sighted, especially around dusk and in the early morning. Daytime temperatures hover above 100°F from May to September, then hang around 50°F in winter, when snowstorms are not unheard of. Strong winds are usual in autumn and spring.

Information
To explore everywhere in the Mojave National Preserve, buy *Mojave National Preserve: A Visitor's Guide* by Cheri Rae.

Cima post office (☎ 800-275-8777; 1 Northside Kelso–Cima Rd; ⊙ 9:30am-1:30pm Mon-Sat)
Highway Radio (99.7FM) Along the I-15 corridor, broadcasts Mojave traffic and weather updates every half-hour.
Hole-in-the-Wall Information Center (☎ 760-928-2572; ⊙ 9am-4pm Fri-Sun May-Sep, 9am-4pm Wed-Sun Oct-Apr) Off Black Canyon Rd, 20 miles north of I-40. Seasonal ranger-led programs and info on weather and road conditions.
Kelso Depot Visitor Center (☎ 760-252-6161; Kelso–Cima Rd, at Kelbaker Rd; ⊙ 9am-5pm) Interpretive displays, and excellent maps and books for sale inside a restored 1920s railroad depot.
Nipton Trading Post (☎ 702-856-2335; 107355 Nipton Rd, Nipton; ⊙ 8am-6pm) Books, maps, groceries, water and 24-hour self-serve laundry.

Sights & Activities

You can spend an entire day or just a few hours driving around the free **preserve** (www.nps.gov/moja; admission free; ⊙ 24hr), taking in its sights and exploring some of them on foot.

Coming from Barstow, take the Afton Rd exit off I-15 and drive a graded gravel road for 3 miles to **Afton Canyon**, the terminus of the Mojave Rd. Or take the Zzyzx Rd exit, 6 miles west of Baker, and follow a washboard gravel road 4 miles down to dry **Soda Lake**. On the site of a mid-20th-century mineral-springs resort run by Doc Springer, aka the 'King of Quacks,' California State University's solar-powered **Desert Studies Center** (☎ 909-880-5975; http://biology.fullerton.edu/facilities/dsc/zzyzx.html; courses $190-295) offers all-inclusive weekend courses.

Visible to the south from I-15, **Cima Dome** is a 1500ft hunk of granite spiked with volcanic cinder cones and crusty outcroppings of basalt left by lava that flowed from over seven million years to around 10,000 years ago. At one point the number of cones is so great that they are protected as the **Cinder Cones National Natural Landmark**. On Kelbaker Rd, you can see this anciently charred landscape up close, or take the 4-mile round-trip hike up **Teutonia Peak** (5755ft), which starts off Cima Rd, 6 miles north of Cima. It wanders through the world's largest Joshua Tree forest.

On Black Canyon Rd, east of Kelso–Cima Rd, is the heart of the preserve – the **Hole-in-the-Wall** formation. These vertical walls of tuff (pronounced 'toof'), which look something like cliffs made of unpolished marble, are thought to be from a powerful volcanic eruption that blasted rocks across the landscape some 18.5 million years ago. Explore the nature trails, then ask the rangers if **Wild Horse Canyon Road**, a gorgeous 9.5-mile drive up to Mid Hills, is currently passable. If you have two cars, an 8-mile hiking trail starts at Mid Hills and heads back downhill to Hole-in-the-Wall.

Three miles west of Kelbaker Road, the weathered **Kelso Dunes** rise up to 600ft above the Devil's Playground. Like Death Valley's Eureka Dunes (p671), these 'booming' dunes can produce a musical sound when sand slips down their faces – try running down 'em to jumpstart the effect. The dunes are a 3-mile round-trip hike from the parking area.

Over to the east, the Providence Mountains create an impressive wall of rocky peaks. In the Spring Mountains National Recreation Area, **Mitchell Caverns** (☎ 760-928-2586; www.parks.ca.gov; adult/child 6-16 $4/2; ⊙ tours daily Sep-May, Sat & Sun Jun-Aug) are known for their driplike formations called speleothems. The tours often sell out early. Call for current schedules and make reservations at least two weeks in advance. Short nature hikes commence nearby. The caverns are 6 miles west of Essex Rd, off I-40.

Sleeping

The few budget motels in Baker are best avoided. The old Route 66 town of Needles (p665), southeast of the preserve, has better budget motels from $25.

Hotel Nipton B&B (☎ 760-856-2335; www.nipton.com; 107355 Nipton Rd; tent sites $15, incl breakfast ecolodge d $60, hotel d $70; ⊙ check-in until 6pm; ⊠) Their slogan is 'conveniently located in the middle of nowhere.' In the northeastern corner of the preserve, this early 20th-century railroad town has all the peace you could ever ask for. Historic B&B rooms and ecotents (with electricity and platform beds) share garden hot tubs under the stars; campers enjoy hot showers. Free wi-fi for guests. Check-in at the trading post.

Primm Valley Resort (☎ 800-386-7867; www.primadonna.com; 31900 Las Vegas Blvd S, Primm; r from $43; ⊠ ⊠) On the far side of the California–Nevada state line, off I-15 at exit 1, this polished convention hotel and casino stands next to an enormous outlet shopping mall and has rooms with all the perks.

Primm Valley Resort also handles reservations for two other casino hotels.
Buffalo Bill's (r from $36) Family-friendly Buffalo Bill's is next door.

THE MOJAVE PHONE BOOTH

If a phone rang in the middle of the Mojave Desert, and someone was around to answer it, does that mean it still exists? Sadly, no.

Called the loneliest phone booth in the world, there once was a bullet-ridden payphone on Aiken Mine Rd, 15 miles from the nearest highway. It was marked on AAA maps only as 'Telephone.' After seeing it mentioned in a magazine, artist Godfrey Daniels became curious enough to call the phone booth every day until local miner Lorene Caffee finally answered. He chronicled their 1997 conversation online (www.deuceofclubs.com/moj/mojave.htm).

The phone booth soon became a cult attraction. People from Vietnam to Germany would call the pay phone at all hours of the day or night. Burning Man festival-goers and other indie travelers would stop by just to answer the ringing phone. It even cameoed in an *X-Files* episode.

And then it disappeared. In 2000, PacBell and the National Park Service agreed to remove it. The NPS alleged that all the traffic was negatively affecting the environment. To some, the phone booth symbolized a greater controversy over land-use rights in the Mojave National Preserve. It seemed that everyday folks had lost out to the feds – again.

And even though there'd still be someone there to hear it ring, the phone booth is gone.

Whiskey Pete's (r from $27) The well-worn Whiskey Pete's is across the Interstate.

First-come, first-served sites with pit toilets and running water are available at the park's two **NPS Campgrounds** (☎ 760-928-2572; tent & RV sites $12). Hole-in-the-Wall has 35 sites surrounded by rocky desert landscape, while Mid Hills has 26 sites (no RVs) set among pine and juniper trees.

Eating & Drinking

There are dozens of predictable dining options at Primm's casino hotels.

Whistlestop Oasis (☎ 760-856-1045; 107355 Nipton Rd, Nipton; breakfast & lunch $4.50-8.50, dinner $8-25; ☺ usually 10am-7pm) This unlikely gourmands' haven serves up scrumptious pork chops, sandwiches and more. There's just one cook in the kitchen, so go ahead – have an ice-cold beer and shoot some stick while you wait.

Mad Greek (☎ 760-733-4354; 72112 Baker Blvd, Baker; meals $7-14; ☺ 24hr) Near to the world's largest thermometer in Baker, these gyros, Greek salads, strawberry shakes and desserts galore are easily the best food along I-15 for over 100 miles. It's worth stopping in even if you're just barreling through from LA to Vegas.

Pioneer Saloon (☎ 702-874-9362; ☺ 11am-late) About 10 miles north of the California border on I-15 is the enclave of Jean. Turn off at Nevada Landing, a steamboat-style casino hotel, for the 7-mile trip west on NV 161 to Goodsprings, where this little roadside shack dates from 1913 (which makes it southern

Nevada's oldest bar). Riddled with bullet holes, the saloon still boasts a vintage cherrywood bar and movie-star memorabilia.

Getting There & Away

Entrance roads to the north side of the preserve are along I-15 between Barstow and the Nevada state line, especially near Baker, an hour's drive east of Barstow and 90 minutes southwest of Las Vegas. Entrances to the south side of the preserve off I-40 are closer to the dunes and caverns. On the return trip, take Route 66.

ROUTE 66

Never has a highway been so symbolic as Route 66, now bypassed by the interstate system. Snaking across the belly of America, it connected the prairie capital of Chicago with distant Los Angeles in 1926. Along the way, lightning-bug towns sprouted up with neon signs, motor courts and drive-in theaters. Every year another landmark goes up for sale, but more are rescued from ruin.

Route 66 was not built on a surveyor's straight line. Instead it linked existing highways and rural roads, earning the moniker 'Main Street of America.' The 'Mother Road' came into is own during the Depression, when thousands of migrants escaped the Dust Bowl by slogging westward in beatup old jalopies painted with 'California or Bust' signs, *Grapes of Wrath*–style.

In southeastern California, Route 66 mostly follows the National Old Trails Hwy, which is prone to potholes and big bumps, but doesn't normally require 4WD. The **California Route 66 Preservation Foundation** (☎ 760-868-3320; www.cart66pf.org) website has news, special events and a virtual tour. Turn-by-turn driving directions are available at www.historic66.com.

Needles to Barstow

Start near the intersection of I-40 and Hwy 95 in Needles, named after nearby mountain spires. Drive downtown on Front St past the old mule-train wagon and 1920s Palm Motel alongside the railroad tracks to El Garces, a 1908 Harvey House undergoing restorations. Then head west on Broadway and left onto Needles Hwy.

Vintage motels stand on the western outskirts of town, where you'll join I-40 westbound. Exit at US 95 and drive north for 6 miles, then turn west at the railroad tracks toward **Goffs**, where the **Mojave Desert Heritage & Cultural Association** (☎ 760-733-4482; www.mdhca.org; 37198 Lanfair Rd; ☉ by appointment only) conducts tours of a 1914 schoolhouse. Back on Goffs Rd, drive past **Fenner**, which has a pricey gas station, to the south side of I-40.

Curve right onto the National Old Trails Hwy, which barrels through more desert ghost towns in backward alphabetical order. You'll pass **Essex** (where you can detour to the Mojave National Preserve, p662), **Danby**, **Cadiz** and **Bagdad** before reaching newly revived **Amboy**, famous for its 'Roy's Motel & Café' sign. (This is the turnoff south to Joshua Tree National Park, p654). West of town is **Amboy Crater**, a symmetrical 250ft-high cinder cone. It's a scramble up the volcano's west side (don't do it in high winds or summer heat).

Keep driving west, past haunting ruins spliced in among the majestic landscape. At **Ludlow**, turn right onto Crucero Rd, pass under I-40, then turn west on the frontage road. After several bumpy miles, turn left at Lavic Rd. Cross back over I-40, then drive west on the National Old Trails Hwy to **Newberry Springs**, where the **Bagdad Café** (☎ 760-257-3101; 46548 National Trails Hwy; meals $5-10; ☉ 7am-6pm Sun-Thu) was renamed after the 1988 indie flick.

Cross under I-40, then go west to **Daggett**, with its small **museum** (☎ 760-254-2629; http://mojavedesert.net/daggett/index.html; 33703 2nd St; donations welcome; ☉ usually 1-4pm Sat & Sun) and the

historic **Stone Hotel**, where desert adventurers like Death Valley Scotty once stayed. Rejoin I-40 into Barstow.

Barstow to San Bernardino

On the western outskirts of Barstow, Main St becomes the National Old Trails Hwy, which winds westward through **Lenwood** and **Helendale**. Call for directions to the va-va-va-voom **Exotic World Burlesque Museum & Striptease Hall of Fame** (☎ 760-243-5261; www.exoticworldusa.org; admission $5; ☉ 10am-4pm Tue-Sun), owned by a former Marilyn Monroe impersonator. Look out for a folk-art collection of glass bottles, telephone poles and road signs, on the way into **Oro Grande**, with its **Iron Hog Saloon** (☎ 760-843-8004; 20848 National Trails Hwy). Even cowboy Roy Rogers used to stop by this old shack.

Cross the Mojave River on a steel-truss bridge, following D St into **Victorville**, where Westerns were once filmed. Opposite the transportation center, poke around the **California Route 66 Museum** (☎ 760-951-0436; www.califrt66museum.org; 16825 D St; donations welcome; ☉ 10am-4pm Mon & Thu-Sat, 11am-3pm Sun). Turn right onto 7th St. Drive past the county fairgrounds, home to the Route 66 Raceway, veering onto Palmdale Rd by the Interstate.

Take I-15 south across the Cajon Summit, passing by the landmark 1950s **Summit Inn** (☎ 760-949-8688; 5960 Mariposa Rd, Oak Hills; meals $4-8; ☉ 8am-8pm Sun-Thu, 8am-9pm Fri & Sat), a truck stop with antique gas pumps and a lunch counter that serves ostrich burgers and date shakes. At Cleghorn, exit at Cajon Blvd and trundle south along an ancient section of the Mother Road. Rejoin I-15 at Kenwood Ave and drive southbound onto I-215, exiting right away at Devore. A short dead-end road leads north to the **Screaming Chicken Saloon** (☎ 909-880-0056; 18169 Cajon Blvd), a biker bar.

Follow Cajon Blvd further south into San Bernardino, where you can drive by the **First McDonald's Museum** (☎ 909-885-6324; www.route-66.com/mcdonalds; 1398 N 'E' St; admission free; ☉ 10am-5pm), which has historic Route 66 exhibits. The **Inland Empire 66ers** (☎ 909-888-9922; www.ie66ers.com; 280 S 'E' St; tickets $5-8; ☉ Apr-Sep) play minor league baseball at Arrowhead Park. Take 5th St west of downtown, curving onto Foothill Blvd past the kooky **Wigwam Motel** (☎ 909-875-3005; www.wigwammotel.com; 2728 W Foothill Blvd; s/d from $50/60) and **Giant Orange** (15395 Foothill Blvd).

CALIFORNIA DESERTS

California's first winery was founded in Rancho Cucamonga. On the western outskirts of town are two retro steakhouses, the rustic **Sycamore Inn** (☎ 909-982-1104; www .thesycamoreinn.com; 8318 Foothill Blvd; mains $18-36; 5-9pm Mon-Sat, 4-9pm Sun) and the **Magic Lamp Inn** (☎ 909-981-8659; www.themagiclampinn.com; 8189 Foothill Blvd; mains $15-25; lunch Tue-Fri, dinner Tue-Sun), with a fabulous neon sign and dancing most evenings.

In the college town of Claremont, **Rancho Santa Ana Botanic Garden** (☎ 909-625-8767; 1500 N College Ave; admission $4; 8am-5pm) claims the world's largest collection of Californian plants, including wildflowers, palms and cacti. At Glendora, divert briefly onto Alosta Ave by driving straight ahead. The brick **20th Century Motor Lodge** (☎ 626-335-3348; 1345 E Route 66; d from $50; P) has a swimming pool with mountain views. Further west, the **Hat** (☎ 626-857-0017; 611 W Route 66; meals $5-10; 11am-1am) has made famous pastrami sandwiches since 1951.

Back on Foothill Blvd, wind west through Azusa past the dead Foothill Drive-in Theatre into Irwindale, where Foothill Blvd changes into Huntington Dr. Drive west through Duarte, where the **Route 66 Roadhouse & Tavern** (☎ 626-357-4210; 1846 E Huntington Dr; until 2am) has live music.

Keep going west under I-210 into Arcadia. The Marx Brothers' *A Day at the Races* was filmed at **Santa Anita Race Track** (☎ 626-574-7223, tour reservations 626-574-6677; www.santaanita.com; 285 W Huntington Dr; tours free, race entry $5-8.50), the home of the legendary Seabiscuit. Thoroughbreds race here from 26 Dec through late April and again in the fall. During race season, tram tours take you to the jockeys' room and training areas. Reservations are required for tours.

Veer right onto Colorado Pl, then straight onto Colorado Blvd. Drive west into Pasadena and stop off for an egg cream at the nostalgic soda fountain of **Fair Oaks Pharmacy** (☎ 626-799-1414; 1526 Mission St; items $2-7; 9am-8pm Mon-Thu, 9am-9pm Fri & Sat, 11am-8pm Sun) before braving traffic on the final stretch through Los Angeles.

Head south on I-110, exiting onto Sunset Blvd. After a few miles, turn left onto Manzanita Blvd and cruise west along Santa Monica Blvd, which will deliver you to the road's end at the Pacific Ocean by Santa Monica Pier (p519).

DEATH VALLEY

The name itself evokes all that is harsh, hot and hellish in the deserts of the imagination, a punishing, barren and lifeless place of Old Testament severity. Yet it acts like a siren's call on travelers, who find an endless geological wonderland to explore here.

DEATH VALLEY NATIONAL PARK

Death Valley National Park, the largest national park in the continental USA, covers an enormous area – more than 5000 sq miles – that includes other valleys and mountain ranges to the north. Created as part of the 1994 California Desert Protection Act, its primary reason for being is conservation, not tourism. Inside this amazing natural playground, you'll find musical sand dunes, mosaic marbled canyons, boulders that appear to race across the sunbaked desert floor, extinct volcanic craters, palm-shaded oases and dozens of rare wildlife species that exist nowhere else in the world.

The actual valley is about 140 miles north to south and 10 miles to 20 miles wide, with the Panamint Range on its western side and the Amargosa Range on its eastern side. But it's not a true valley – it's a basin formed by earthquake fault lines. The valley floor and the mountain range are joined as a single geological structure, which is slowly rotating: as the valley floor continually sinks, runoff from erosion in the encircling mountains fills Death Valley like an hourglass. Around Badwater, the lowest elevation in the continental USA, the sediment layer could be 9000ft deep.

The rock formations you see today were created by geological events that occurred as long as 500 million years ago. Extensive faulting and fracturing allows some of the oldest rocks to be visible on the earth's surface, when normally they would be hidden deep underground. Limestone and sandstone were formed on an ancient seabed and slowly lifted by movement in the earth's crust. The rock strata were bent, folded and cracked as converging tectonic plates pushed up mountain ranges. These stresses led to a period of volcanic activity, explosively distributing ash and cinders that provided much of the rich coloring seen in the valley.

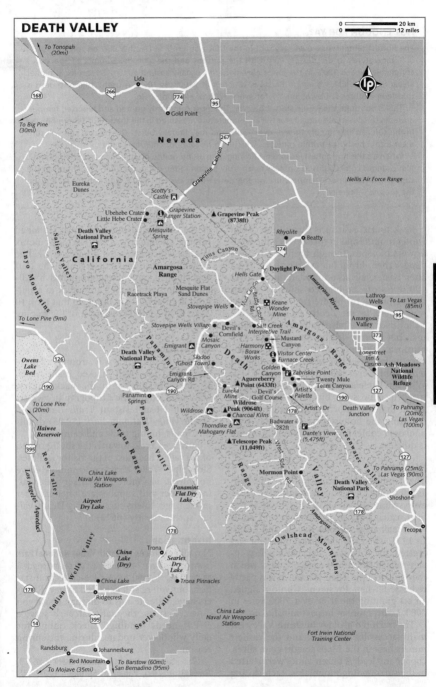

HOT ENOUGH FOR YA?

The hottest temperature ever recorded in the USA was 134°F in Death Valley on July 10, 1913.

Temperatures in the deserts vary with the seasons and the altitude. Summer temperatures commonly exceed 120°F in the lower elevations. It's usually around 10° to 15°F cooler at higher elevations. The July average in Barstow, which is at 2100ft, is 102°F. A useful rule of thumb is that temperatures fall by about 1°F for every 300ft of elevation gain.

This is not quite the whole story, however. The most commonly quoted and reported temperatures in the desert are actually for the air temperature measured in the shade. But a thermometer in the sun can rise rapidly to well over 150°F and may literally burst. The blazing sun will turn a car into a hothouse within minutes, which can be fatal for children or pets.

When it's this hot, adhesives soften, chewing gum disintegrates, plastics melt and photographic film changes color. Exposed surfaces reach truly blistering temperatures after a few hours in the sun. When the surface temperature on the desert floor exceeds 200°F, you can fry an egg on the ground – literally!

Peak tourist season is during the cooler winter months and in spring when the wildflowers blossom, though flash floods are a danger then. From late March to the week after Easter, all accommodations for over 100 miles can be booked solid for weeks, campgrounds fill before noon and people wait hours to see Scotty's Castle. Death Valley used to be practically empty in summer, but recently it's become popular with European travelers who are keen to experience hellaciously hot weather. The highest temperature ever recorded here was 134°F. With a reliable air-conditioned car, a summer trip is possible, but only if you sightsee in the early morning and late evening, spending the hottest part of the day by a pool or at cooler higher elevations. Autumn is quietest.

History

The Timbisha Shoshone lived in the Panamint Range for centuries, visiting the valley every winter to gather acorns, hunt waterfowl, catch pupfish in marshes and cultivate small areas of corn, squash and beans. In 1933, when the national monument was created, the tribe was allocated a paltry 40-acre village site near Furnace Creek, which they still occupy. Their grievance was partly redressed when President Clinton signed an act granting the tribe over 7000 acres in 2000. Learn more at http://timbisha.org.

The fractured geology of Death Valley left many accessible minerals, and the earliest miners here in the 1860s sought gold, silver, copper and lead. A dozen mines were started in the surrounding mountains, each closing

as the ore played out. The most sustained mining operation was the Harmony Borax Works, which extracted borate, an alkaline mineral used to make detergents. The stuff was shipped out in wagons pulled by 20-mule teams and hauled 165 miles to a railhead at Mojave, a grueling trip that took 10 days. By the late 1920s, most of the mining had ceased.

Orientation

It's easy to find your way around, as there are only a few, well-marked main roads. If you're heading into the backcountry, National Geographic's topographic, waterproof and tear-resistant *Trails Illustrated: Death Valley National Park* ($9.95) details dirt roads, hiking trails and camping.

Furnace Creek, towards the southern end of the valley, has most of the visitor facilities. Stovepipe Wells, about a 30-minute drive northwest, has more limited services. Gas, food, water and supplies are often cheaper in the larger towns surrounding Death Valley, such as Beatty (p673).

Information

Not all entrances to **Death Valley National Park** (www.nps.gov/deva; 7-day entry pass per car/motorcycle & bicycle $10/5; ⊙ 24hr) have a fee-collection station, but you're still expected to pay. Rangers have better things to do than chase you down. Besides, the national park service (NPS) needs funding. Check online for daily wildflower updates during the spring season.

Gas stations are in **Furnace Creek** (☎ 760-786-2343; ⊙ 24hr), **Panamint Springs** (☎ 775-482-

7680; 🕑 24hr), **Scotty's Castle** (☎ 760-786-2325; 🕑 9am-5:30pm), and **Stovepipe Wells** (☎ 760-786-2387; 🕑 seasonal, hours vary). For towing and auto repairs after hours, call **Furnace Creek** (☎ 760-786-2345).

BOOKSTORES
Death Valley Natural History Association (☎ 800-478-8564) Operates nonprofit bookstores at Furnace Creek and Scotty's Castle.

EMERGENCY & MEDICAL SERVICES
The nearest hospital emergency rooms are hours away in Ridgecrest (p675) and Tonopah, 90 miles north of Beatty.
Emergency number (☎ 911) Cell-phone coverage is almost nonexistent. Pay phones at Furnace Creek, Stovepipe Wells and Scotty's Castle may not accept coins, so bring a phonecard.
Medical clinic (☎ 775-553-2208; 250 S Irving St, Beatty; 🕑 8am-noon & 1-5pm Mon-Fri).

INTERNET RESOURCES
Death Valley (www.death-valley.us) Head here for the locals' persepectives.
National Parks Services (www.nps.gov/deva) Information on national parks including Death Valley.

MONEY
There are ATMs at Furnace Creek and Stovepipe Wells.

POST
Post office (☎ 800-275-8555; Hwy 190, Furnace Creek; 🕑 8:30am-5pm Mon-Fri)

TOURIST INFORMATION
Furnace Creek Visitors Center (☎ 760-786-3200; Hwy 190; 🕑 8am-5pm) Has a small museum on the natural and human history of the valley, an excellent selection of books, maps and information, and a moderately interesting slide show every half-hour. Check out the schedules of other free ranger-led interpretive programs from late November to late April. Free handouts on everything from 4WD roads to desert geology are available, plus junior ranger activity workbooks for kids.

Sights
You really can't do it all in a single day, even if you start out very early in the morning, which is always a good thing to do in the desert. A peaceful overnight stay in or near the park ensures you'll see the stunning sunset and sunrise. Always carry one gallon of water per person, plus more to splash over the radiator if your car overheats. Heat and dehydration kill more quickly than most visitors think.

There are many interesting side trips along the edges of the valley and in the surrounding mountains. Before starting out, always check with the Furnace Creek Visitors Center for an update on road conditions and informational handouts. During summer, stick to paved roads only and strictly limit your exertions (eg hiking).

AROUND FURNACE CREEK
Start by driving up to **Dante's View** (5475ft), where the view is absolutely brilliant at sunrise or sunset. En route, detour at **Twenty Mule**

DEATH IN THE VALLEY
A small band of pioneer '49ers first wandered into this valley after they separated from a larger emigrant group that was crossing Utah along the Old Spanish Trail, taking a sensible southern route to avoid repeating the Donner party disaster of 1846–47, which was caused by crossing the Sierra in winter (p348).

Taking what they hoped would be a shortcut to the California goldfields, the small party struggled across the Nevada desert for a month before entering this valley from the east and arriving near Furnace Creek on Christmas Eve in 1849. They crossed the valley floor, but couldn't get their wagons over the Panamint Range.

While most of the party sheltered near a water hole, two young men were sent to scout for a route west over the mountains. Meanwhile, the rest of the party split up. Only two families waited for the scouts, who eventually returned, after 26 days in the wilderness. Everyone slaughtered their oxen, burned their wagons and walked out of the valley along the route now called Emigrant Canyon.

As they left, one woman reputedly looked back and uttered the words 'Good-bye, death valley.' Ironically, the most life-threatening part of their journey – walking across the rest of the Mojave – was yet to come.

Team Canyon, a windy one-way loop through an ancient lakebed – it will make you feel like an ant. Heading back down toward the valley, it's a short walk out to **Zabriskie Point**, where you can scramble down into the eroded badlands. With a good sense of orientation, make the 4-mile round-trip hike over to Golden Canyon (see below).

Take a break at Furnace Creek Ranch and sit in some shade. The **Borax Museum** (☎ 760-786-2345; admission $2; ☺ 9am-4pm Oct-May), past the restaurants, will tell you all about the stuff, and there's a collection of old coaches and wagons out back. The Furnace Creek visitors center is just up the road. A short drive north is the short interpretive trail through the ruins of **Harmony Borax Works**, where you can drive through **Mustard Canyon**.

HIGHWAY 178 TO BADWATER BASIN

A few miles south of Furnace Creek is **Golden Canyon**, where a self-guided interpretive trail winds for a mile up to the now-oxidized iron cliffs of **Red Cathedral**. You can keep going up to Zabriskie Point, for a hardy 4-mile round-trip. A more challenging canyon scramble goes up **Desolation Narrows** to an overlook of colorful badlands, but you'll need a good topo map for it. Take the unsigned dirt road turnoff 4 miles south of the Hwy 178/190 junction, and stay to the left.

Further south on Hwy 178 is the turnoff for the **Artist's Drive** scenic loop through an alluvial fan, with the **Artist's Palette** of colorful exposed minerals and volcanic ash. Driving south again on Hwy 190, the valley floor to the west is filled with lumps of crystallized salt in what is nicknamed the **Devil's Golf Course**. East of the road, stretch your legs with a 1-mile walk to the **Natural Bridge**.

The lowest elevation in the US is at notorious Badwater (282ft below sea level), a little further south. Walk out onto the boardwalk next to the constantly evaporating bed of salty, mineralized water that's otherwordly in its beauty. To delve deeper into the valley, drive 27 miles south past Mormon Point, then turn right onto 40-mile dirt **West Side Road**, which heads back north past 4WD turnoffs to several side canyons and meets Hwy 178 just south of the end of Artist's Dr.

AROUND STOVEPIPE WELLS

Heading north along Hwy 190 from Furnace Creek, turn right onto Beatty Cutoff Rd, from where a rough road leads to the ruins of **Keane Wonder Mine**.

If you continue north to **Hells Gate**, then turn right and drive east over **Daylight Pass** (4316ft), Hwy 374 takes you out of the valley, past the turnoffs to Leadfield and Rhyolite ghost towns, into Beatty (p673). The Leadfield turnoff is the start of a 27-mile, one-way scenic road that drops ruggedly down through spectacular **Titus Canyon**, passing petroglyphs at Klare Spring, to the floor of Death Valley. It's often only passable for 4WD vehicles and may be closed at any time, so call the visitors center before making the trip.

Back on Hwy 190, just north of Beatty Cutoff Rd, is the half-mile **Salt Creek Interpretive Trail**. In late winter or early spring, rare pupfish splash in the stream alongside the boardwalk. Beyond the next junction are the original **Stovepipe Wells**, marked by miners traveling between Rhyolite and Skidoo (see below) who pounded old stovepipes into the sand at these now-dry watering holes. Keep going north to peek at the mouth of dramatic Titus Canyon or to tour Scotty's Castle (opposite).

Heading back down the valley, turn west onto Hwy 190 toward **Stovepipe Wells Village**. Watch for a camera-icon sign and a pull off on the north side of the road, from where you can walk (as long as it's not hot) out into the scenic **Mesquite Flat sand dunes**. Only do this when the sun is low in the sky, which also makes the dunes more photogenic. It's even more fun on a full-moon night. On the south side of the road, look for the field of arrow weed clumps called the **Devil's Cornfield**.

Just west of the village, which was the site of the valley's original 1920s tourist resort (nicknamed 'Bungalette City'), is a 3-mile gravel road leading to **Mosaic Canyon**, where you can push yourself up a sinuous, polished slot canyon.

EMIGRANT CANYON ROAD

Eight miles west of Stovepipe Wells, this scenic road winds past turnoffs to **Skidoo** mining town site, a 4WD trek to jaw-dropping views of the Sierra Nevada, or to **Eureka Mine**, beyond which **Aguereberry Point** has 6500ft-deep views east into Death Valley. Back on the main road, it's a steep climb over Emigrant Pass (5318ft). Further along, turn left up Wildrose Canyon to reach the **charcoal kilns**, a line of large, stone, beehive-shaped structures used by 19th century miners to make fuel for smelting silver ore. The landscape is subalpine, with forests of piñon pine and juniper, and can be covered with winter snow.

SCOTTY'S CASTLE
Walter E Scott, alias 'Death Valley Scotty,' was the quintessential tall-tale teller who captivated people with his fanciful stories of gold. His most lucrative friendship was with Albert and Bessie Johnson, insurance magnates from Chicago. Despite knowing Scotty was a freeloading liar, they bankrolled the construction of this elaborate home that eventually became their main residence. Restored to the 1930s era, inside the historic house are sheepskin drapes, carved California redwood, handmade tiles, elaborately wrought iron, woven Shoshone baskets and a bellowing pipe organ upstairs.

To get the full story about **Scotty's Castle** (☎ 760-786-2392; Hwy 267; adult/child 6-15/senior $11/6/9; ☼ 7:30am-6pm, tours 9am-5pm, ticket office opens 8:30am), take one of the guided 'Living History' tours. More technically minded 'Underground Mysteries' tours happen four times daily. All tickets are first-come, first-served, so there can be a long wait (or they may sell out completely). If you just want a glimpse of the place, the grounds are free for exploring and the free visitors center exhibits bits and pieces from the past. Nearly 3000ft above sea level and noticeably cooler than the valley floor, the palm-shaded lawns make for a picturesque escape from the midday heat. Scotty's Castle is a 90-minute drive north of Furnace Creek.

GRAPEVINE JUNCTION
Three miles west of Scotty's Castle, turn west toward 770ft-deep **Ubehebe Crater**, caused by the explosive meeting of fiery magma with cool groundwater. You can loop around its half-mile-wide rim and over to younger and smaller **Little Hebe Crater**.

The mysterious **Racetrack Playa** is a 28-mile trip south of Ubehebe Crater, over a tire-shredding dirt road that requires 4WD. From the natural 'grandstand,' you can see large rocks that appear to have moved on their own across this mud flat, making long, faint tracks in the sunbaked surface. Scientific theories abound, but nothing has been proven.

Want more 4WD adventure? Between the craters and Grapevine Junction, a graded dirt road heads north out past Crankshaft Junction (slow down, then turn left) and Hanging Canyon (hang another left afterward) to **Eureka Dunes**, California's tallest, 45 miles away. Rising almost 700ft from a dry lakebed, these are some of the world's only dunes to have 'singing sands,' which sound deep bass notes during sandslides. An easier approach to Eureka Valley is from Big Pine (p403), from where it's 28 miles along a paved road, then 21 miles of roughly graded dirt to the dunes.

Activities
HIKING
Stop by the Furnace Creek visitors center for helpful trail handouts and backcountry registration forms. As well as the shorter interpretive trails and canyon walks described earlier, there are two tougher hiking trails, too. From the charcoal kilns off Wildrose Canyon Rd, **Wildrose Peak** (9064ft) is an 8.4-mile round-trip, with a healthy elevation gain of 2200ft. But the most demanding trail climbs 3000ft from Mahogany Flat to the summit of **Telescope Peak** (11,049ft). Allow seven to nine hours for the 14-mile round trip, and don't attempt it in winter unless you're fully equipped for snow and are an experienced ice climber. The last stretch of road to the trailhead might be too rough for a 2WD car, so you may have to start walking from the charcoal kilns, adding 1.5 miles and another 2000ft of elevation each way.

HORSEBACK RIDING
Back at the ranch, **Furnace Creek Stables** (☎ 760-786-3339; Hwy 190; 1hr/2hr ride $35/50; ☼ Oct–mid-May) arranges three horseback rides daily, except during summer; best are the monthly full-moon rides.

GOLF
For novelty's sake, you can play a round at historic **Furnace Creek Golf Course** (☎ 760-786-2301; Hwy 190; greens fees $55; ☼ mid-Oct–early May), the world's lowest-elevation course.

Festivals & Events
Badwater (www.badwater.com) Staged at the suicidal height of summer in mid-July, Badwater is a 130-mile ultramarathon from Badwater Basin to the portals of Mt Whitney (p405).

Death Valley '49ers (www.deathvalley49ers.org) In early November, the '49ers host a historical encampment at Furnace Creek, featuring cowboy poetry, campfire sing-alongs, pioneer costumes and a Western art and photography show. Show up early to see wagon trains and horseback riders thunder in.

Sleeping

Non-camping accommodations in the central valley are overpriced, though beautifully situated. If you want a roof over your head, you'll find better value in towns around Death Valley (p674).

BUDGET

Inside the park, **NPS campgrounds** (☎ reservations 800-365-2267; http://reservations.nps.gov; most tent & RV sites $10-16) are first-come, first-served. Reservations are accepted only for Furnace Creek arrivals between mid-October and mid-May.

During summer, it's just too hot to camp on the valley floor, while at the higher elevations campgrounds may get snowed in during the winter period. Only Furnace Creek (crowded, little shade, mostly RVs), Mesquite Spring (an oasis near Scotty's Castle) and free Wildrose (high in the Panamint Range, no RVs) campgrounds are open year-round.

Campgrounds at Stovepipe Wells and Sunset near Furnace Creek are like roadside gravel parking lots, lacking much shade but with plenty of RVs. Texas Springs, set on a hillside above Furnace Creek, has more shade.

Southwest of Stovepipe Wells, free Emigrant campground (2100ft) has 10 first-come, first-served tent sites; it's cooler and has views down to the valley.

In the Panamint Range are three free tent-only campgrounds with about 40 total sites. Water should be available except in winter at Wildrose (4100ft). Thorndike (7400ft) and Mahogany Flat (8200ft) are generally open between March and November, but you may need to use a 4WD to reach them during spring and fall.

Free backcountry camping is allowed in most parts of the park at least 2 miles from the nearest developed area or paved road and 200yd from any water source. Note the old mining areas are for day-use only. Stop by the visitors center for more info and to pick up a voluntary permit.

MIDRANGE & TOP END

The central park lodges are run by Xanterra for reservations call ☎ 303-297-275 or 800-236-7916.

Furnace Creek Inn (☎ 760-786-2345; www.furnacecreekresort.com; Hwy 190; r $235-335, ste $350-390; ❄ mid-Oct–mid-May; ✗ ❄ ⊑) This adobe hotel is on a hillside near the ranch. Its elegant, Mission-style buildings dating from 1927 are set among palm-shaded garden terraces. Elemental rooms with cable TV and Nintendo are overpriced, but the peaceful atmosphere is priceless. Facilities include tennis courts and a springwater-fed swimming pool with gorgeous valley views.

Furnace Creek Ranch (☎ 760-786-2345; www.furnacecreekresort.com; Hwy 190; cabins $105-125, motel r $135-180; ✗ ❄ ⊑) Popular with families, this dusty ranch is a short walk south of the visitors center, near the general store. It has ordinary cabins and motel rooms, which are a comfortable step above Stovepipe Wells, though not as peaceful. Facilities include tennis courts and swimming pools.

Stovepipe Wells Village (☎ 760-786-2387; www.stovepipewells.com; Hwy 190; RV sites with full hookups $23, r $63-103; ❄ ⊑) Basically, it's just a roadside motel with a small swimming pool, yet it has more quirky character than Furnace Creek. Rooms are small and a bit worn (no phones or TVs), but they're definitely the best bargain in the valley itself.

Panamint Springs Resort (☎ 775-482-7680; www.deathvalley.com; Hwy 190; tent & RV sites $12-25, d $65-80, tr $95, 2-bedroom cottage $140; ❄) Barely inside the park's western boundary, this charmer of a budget motel is perched at a cooler elevation (2000ft), about 30 miles west of Stovepipe Wells. Basic rooms are in small cabins arranged quaintly like a 1930s-style motor court behind the café.

Eating

Toll Road Restaurant (☎ 760-786-2387; Stovepipe Wells Village; breakfast & lunch $5-8, dinner mains $10-23; ❄ 7am-10am, 11:30am-2pm & 5:30-9pm) Above-par cowboy cooking inside a ranch house that has a fireplace, Native American blankets, and wooden chairs and tables that really feel like the Old West. Classic pancake breakfasts go like gangbusters, and at dinner there are meaty mains, an unlimited salad-bar special and key lime pie for dessert.

Furnace Creek Inn (☎ 760-786-2345; mains lunch $10, dinner $20-30; ❄ lunch & dinner mid-May–mid-Oct)

The inn's elegant dining room atop the oasis serves only so-so food, such as grilled vegetables over polenta and filet mignon. Instead order appetizers a la carte at the casual bar, which also has an excellent wine list. Afternoon tea and Sunday brunch are far finer affairs.

Forty Niner Cafe & Wrangler Steak House (☎ 760-786-2345; Furnace Creek Ranch; mains $8-25; ♥ café 7am-9pm Oct-May, 10am-9pm Nov-Apr, steakhouse 5-9pm Oct-May, 6-9:30pm Nov-Apr) Often very long waits for only average American food, yet it's always crowded. Portions are huge at both the cafe and more ambitious steakhouse, but avoid the Wrangler's breakfast and lunch buffet.

Stovepipe Wells Village sells limited grocery items and camping supplies at its **general store** (♥ seasonal hrs vary). Furnace Creek Ranch has a more balanced (but equally expensive) selection at its **general store** (♥ 7am-9pm). There's a fast-food snack bar at Scotty's Castle (p671).

Panamint Springs' friendly **café** (meals $5-20; ♥ breakfast, lunch & dinner) cooks three square meals a day and has barbecues outdoors in summer.

Drinking

Corkscrew Saloon (♥ noon-midnight Sun-Thu, noon-1am Fri & Sat) In Furnace Creek, the busy Corkscrew has pool tables, all kinds of firewaters, televised sports and pub grub like buffalo wings.

Bad Water Saloon (♥ 5:30-9pm Sun-Thu, 5.30-11pm Fri & Sat) At Stovepipe Wells, the divey Bad Water has Skynyrd on the jukebox and a pool table.

A Panamint Springs Resort, you can crack open a microbrew and toast the panoramic views from the front porch.

Getting There & Around

There is no public transportation to Death Valley, though a few charter bus tours operate from Las Vegas.

All of the roads into Death Valley offer spectacular views. Driving west or north into the valley from US-95 (Nevada) or I-15 (California) respectively takes you past high desert scenery that could easily fit into Mongolia or Patagonia. Driving out of the valley via Panamint Springs, along Hwy 190, is breathtaking when you can see the entire Sierra Nevada stretched out in front of you.

Gas is expensive in the park, so fill up your tank beforehand. Furnace Creek's visitors center is about 110 miles (2½ to 3 hours) from Baker or 145 miles (three to 3½ hours) from Las Vegas. Bicycles are only allowed on park roads open to vehicle traffic.

AROUND DEATH VALLEY

If you're going to be exploring for more than a day, it's probably best to stay inside the park, as any of these satellite towns is a fairly long haul from Furnace Creek. Alternatively, it's feasible to spend each night in a different park gateway town, commuting into a different section of the park each day. Visitor information boards in Death Valley list motels in small towns not reviewed here. Dusty Baker (p663) is about 50 miles south of Tecopa. Heading toward the Sierras, Lone Pine (p404) is over an hour's drive west of Panamint Springs. Pahrump, a good-sized casino town, is 60 miles east from Furnace Creek, at the intersection of Hwys 160 and 372 in Nevada.

Beatty, Nevada
pop 980

Just 40 miles from Furnace Creek, this historic Bullfrog mining district boomtown is your best bet for cheap digs, a friendly beer and little gambling.

ORIENTATION & INFORMATION

Everything is close to the main crossroads, including a bank and the helpful **chamber of commerce** (☎ 775-553-2424, 866-736-3716; www .beattynevada.org; 119 Main St; ♥ 10am-2pm). The **NPS Information Center** (☎ 775-553-2200; 307 Main St; ♥ 8am-4pm Sat-Wed) is near the museum. The **public library** (☎ 775-553-2257; 4th & Ward Sts; ♥ 10am-4pm Mon, Wed & Thu, noon-7pm Tue, 10am-noon Sat) offers free wi-fi and Internet terminals. There's a 24-hour gas station up by the Stagecoach Hotel.

SIGHTS & ACTIVITIES

Worth a stop is the **Beatty Museum** (☎ 775-553-2303; 417 Main St; admission by donation; ♥ 10am-4pm Mon-Fri, 10am-2pm Sat), where you will be amazed by artifacts from the old mining days, all cheerfully explained by the curator.

A few miles west is the ghost town of **Rhyolite** (www.rhyolitesite.com; Hwy 374; donations welcome; ♥ 24hr). Don't overlook the 1906 'bottle house' or the skeletal remains of a three-story bank. Also on-site is the bizarre **Goldwell Open-Air Museum** (www.goldwellmuseum.org; admission free; 24hr) of installation art begun by Belgian artist Albert Szukalski in 1984.

Five miles north, **Bailey's Hot Springs** (775-553-2395; Hwy 95 N; entry $6; pools 8am-8pm) has three natural mineral pools in two antique bathhouses inside a 1906 railroad depot. It's past the sign for Angel's Ladies brothel.

FESTIVALS & EVENTS

Railroad Days Historic-themed festival in early June.

Fourth of July An old-fashioned celebration that turns up potato-sack races and fireworks.

Flap Jack Burro Races, Quirky festival held in October. Jockeys load up the pack animals with prospecting equipment, race them around a course and then cook a special pancake breakfast – for the animals.

SLEEPING & EATING

The roadside RV campsites at Bailey's Hot Springs cost $16 per night (tents OK).

Exchange Club Casino (775-553-2368, 888-561-2333; www.exchangeclubcasino.com; 119 Main St; r $41-68;) A historic gambling hall that's been around since 1906 has slightly larger rooms, with refrigerators, out back. Its c-1890 bar is a good place to belly up, and its 24-hour restaurant (meals $2 to $20) has a cowboy menu of burgers, steaks and sandwiches.

Stagecoach Hotel (775-553-2419, 800-424-4946; pitboss@casinocity.com; 900 E Hwy 95 N; r from $45;) A mile north of the main intersection, these spruced-up rooms are bland (and so are the restaurants), but they're just about the most comfy in town.

Motel 6 (775-553-9090; 550 Hwy 95 N; s/d from $38/44) Cookie-cutter Motel 6 is nearby the Stagecoach.

Phoenix Inn (775-553-2250, 800-845-7401; 350 S 1st St; r incl breakfast from $35;) Adequate, if a bit shabby, rooms are inside double-wide trailers, found a few blocks off the main street. The management is welcoming, if a bit eccentric.

Happy Burro Hostel (775-553-9130; 100 Main St; dm $15, r $35;) Very small rooms are inside this former brothel. The shared space downstairs is cozy, but pretty cramped, too. It'll do in a pinch, if you don't need amenities.

DRINKING

Sourdough Saloon (775-553-2266; noon-midnight) Across the street from the Exchange Club Casino, which also has a bar, the Sour-

dough has nickel video poker, pool tables and pizza.

Amargosa Valley

Marked as Death Valley Junction on the map, where Hwys 127 and 190 collide 30 miles east of Furnace Creek, is ghostly **Amargosa Opera House & Hotel** (760-852-4441; www.amargosa-opera-house.com; r $49-66;). It's presided over by eccentric Marta Becket, a Broadway dancer who almost single-handedly revived this abandoned mining settlement after her car broke down here in 1967.

Built by the Pacific Coast Borax Company in the 1920s, the Mission-style arcade has extremely basic motel rooms, some with boudoir lamps and murals (no TVs or phones). Reservations are required, as reception closes early.

The historic opera house has a trompe l'oeil audience painted by Marta herself, who performs heartbreakingly corny dance-and-mime shows (adult/child 5-12 $15/12; Oct-May). Check out the award-winning documentary *Amargosa* (www.amargosafilm.com), sold in the gift shop.

Northeast of the highway junction, **Ash Meadows National Wildlife Refuge** (775-372-5435; http://desertcomplex.fws.gov/ashmeadows; admission free; 8am-4pm) is an oasis for endangered pupfish, rare waterbirds, desert mammals and reptiles, which can be seen along the Crystal Springs Boardwalk Trail. The headquarters are 5 miles east of Hwy 373, or 6 miles north of Hwy 190. The refuge also contains a small detached area of the national park, mysterious **Devil's Hole**.

Just north of the California–Nevada border, **Longstreet Inn & Casino** (775-372-1777, 800-508-9493; 4400 S Hwy 373; RV sites $16, r from $60;) is a hard-edged place for locals and bus package tourists to gamble and drink. You can grab a bite or gas up here, too.

Shoshone

pop 70

It's 55 miles via the shorter, northern route from Furnace Creek through Death Valley Junction to Shoshone, but most folks take the 72-mile scenic route through Badwater Basin instead. Look for an old Chevy parked outside the **Shoshone Museum** (760-852-4414; admission by donation; 9:30am-5pm), which has unusual desert history exhibits, opposite the **general store** (760-852-4242) and gas station.

Shoshone Inn (☎ 760-852-4335; www.shoshonevillage .com; Hwy 127; d incl tax $64-80; 🄳 🄰) has basic 1950s motel rooms with TVs and phones (some have kitchenettes). Rates include access to a small, old natural hot-springs pool. The **Shoshone RV park** (☎ 760-852-4569; tent & RV sites $15-20) is just north of town.

Solar-powered **Café Çest Si Bon** (☎ 760-852-4307; 118 Hwy 127; dishes $2-6; 🕑 7am-5pm Wed-Mon) Internet café is an alternative community hub. The genial owner makes a mean espresso, with gourmet baked goods and vegetarian breakfasts and lunches on the menu.

Tecopa

About 10 miles south of Shoshone, east of Hwy 127, is this small hot-springs habitat, named after a peace-making Paiute chief. It's a favorite haunt of 'snowbird' RVers during winter. Rejuvenate yourself in the simple, sex-segregated bathhouses of **Tecopa Hot Springs Resort** (☎ 760-852-4420; www.tecopahotsprings.org; Tecopa Hot Springs Rd; entry $5, tent & RV sites $14-20, r $45-55, cabin with kitchenette $65; 🕑 6am-10pm Oct-May; 🄰).

Nearby, several private RV campgrounds are open year-round. **Delight's Hot Springs Resort** (☎ 760-852-4343, 800-928-8808; www.delight shotspringsresort.com; 368 Tecopa Hot Springs Rd; entry $10, RV sites $25, d $60, cabin $75; 🄰) has a few 1930s cabins and motel rooms, plus four private hot-springs bathhouses (two sans roofs).

HI Desertaire Hostel (☎ 760-852-4580, 877-907-1265; www.desertairehostel.com; 2000 Old Spanish Trail Hwy; dm $15-18, r $40-50; 🄳 🄰) has sex-segregated dorms and private rooms in trailers. There's a self-catering communal kitchen, BBQ grills and a tower platform for sleeping out under the stars. Reservations are required, even if that means just calling ahead from the road.

Outside town, the beautiful oasis of **China Ranch Date Farm** (☎ 760-852-4415; www.chinaranch .com; 🕑 9am-5pm) is a family-run venture. Follow the Old Spanish Trail Hwy east of Tecopa Hot Springs Rd, turn right on Furnace Creek Rd and follow the signs. Mmm, fresh-baked date bread. If you enjoy the bird-watching and hiking trails into Amargosa Canyon, stay overnight in a simple cottage room at the **Ranch House Inn** (☎ 760-852-4360; www.ranchhouse inn.com; d/tr/q incl breakfast $100/130/160; 🄳).

Ridgecrest

pop 25,000

Ridgecrest is the last sizable town before Death Valley if you're coming from or going

to the Sierra. About 125 miles from Furnace Creek, it exists only because of the million-acre China Lake Naval Air Weapons Station along its eastern edge. You can stock up on information, gas and supplies here, but it's not a pretty place.

SIGHTS & ACTIVITIES

Also the Northern Mojave Visitor Center, the **Maturango Museum** (☎ 760-375-6900; www.matu rango.org; 100 E Las Flores Ave, cnr China Lake Blvd; adult/child under 6/senior & student $4/free/2; 🕑 10am-5pm) is an excellent resource for area information, with loads of free handouts in the lobby. Kid-centric exhibits focus on natural science, Native Californians and military technology. The shop sells maps, books and videos.

US citizens (guest passes available at the gate) can visit the **US Naval Museum of Armament & Technology** (☎ 760-939-3530; www.chinalake museum.org; admission free; 🕑 10am-4:30pm Mon-Fri) on the military base.

About 4 miles east of town off Ridgecrest Blvd (Hwy 178) stands the **BLM Wild Horse & Burro Corral** (☎ 800-951-8720; www.blm.gov/whb; Randsburg–Wash Rd; admission free; 🕑 7am-4pm Mon-Fri). Bring some apples and carrots to feed the frisky equines.

Detour further east to the **Trona Pinnacles**, an awesome national landmark, where tufa spires rise out of an ancient lakebed in an alien fashion. Déjà vu? You may have already seen this place in that '60s TV show *Lost in Space* or the movie *Star Trek V: The Final Frontier*. Look for the turnoff from Hwy 178, about 7.5 miles east of Trona–Red Mountain Rd. From there, it's 5 miles along a dirt road, usually accessible to 2WD vehicles.

Around 15 miles further east along Hwy 178, the hard-scrabble mining town of **Trona** hosts an annual fossickers' festival, **Gem-o-Rama** (☎ 760-372-5356), every October. You can drink with some odd characters at Trona's roadside **saloon**.

About 20 miles to the south of Ridgecrest on Hwy 395, **Randsburg** (www.randsburg.com) is a 'living ghost town,' where you can poke around a tiny **historical museum** (🕑 10am-4pm Sat, Sun & holidays), an antiques shop, a saloon and an opera house café, or even stay overnight in the lone hotel.

SLEEPING & EATING

Stay overnight only if you have to. There are a half dozen chain motels, hotels and all

CALIFORNIA DESERTS

SLOW: DESERT TORTOISE X-ING

The valleys of the Mojave are the abode of the desert tortoise, which can live for up to 80 years, munching on wildflowers and grasses. With its canteen-like bladder, it can go up to a year without drinking. Using its strong hind legs, it burrows to hibernate in winter and also to lay eggs. The sex of the hatchlings is determined by temperature: cooler for males, hotter for females.

Habitat loss and disease have decimated the desert tortoise population. They like to rest in the shade under parked cars, and are often hit by high-speed, off-road drivers. If you see a tortoise in danger, call a ranger. It's illegal for you to pick one up, as a frightened tortoise may urinate on an attacker, making it likely that it will die of dehydration later before the next rain.

About a 90-minute drive southwest of Ridgecrest, the **Desert Tortoise Natural Area** (☎ 951-683-3872; www.tortoise-tracks.org; admission free; ☽ 24hr) has self-guiding trails where you can get a glimpse of these threatened herbivores. Visit between mid-March and mid-June, when a naturalist is on-site. The refuge is 4 miles northeast of California City, off unpaved Randsburg–Mojave Rd.

---

kinds of eateries on China Lake Blvd, south of Inyokern Rd (Hwy 178). For more options, contact the **Ridgecrest Area Convention & Visitors Bureau** (☎ 760-375-8331, 800-847-4830; www.visitdeserts.com; 128 E California Ave; ☽ 9am-5pm Mon-Fri).

BevLen Haus B&B (☎ 760-375-1988, 800-375-1989; www.bevlen.com; 809 N Sanders St; s $55, d $65-75; ☽ reception 3-8pm; ⊠) This European-style B&B is filled with small rooms and antiques, but there's a friendly atmosphere and an out-

door hot tub. It's located one block west of China Lake Blvd.

Rose Garden Inn & Suites (☎ 760-375-6777; fax 760 375 9077; 329 E Ridgecrest Blvd; s/d from $27/44; ⊠) Just a few blocks east of China Lake Blvd, on the way toward the park, this decent budget motel has a bonus: a '50s-themed diner (☽ 6am to 2pm) next door.

You can meet some odd characters at Trona's roadside **Finish Line Saloon** (☎ 760-372-4427; 8293 Trona Rd).

Las Vegas Valley

You know you're in Nevada when even roadside gas stations have slot machines.

As ambitious as a starlet vying for your affections, outrageous Las Vegas is a wild ride, a fantasy land that'll never let you down. According to Hollywood legend, some ramshackle gambling houses, tumbleweeds and cacti were all there was the day mobster Benjamin 'Bugsy' Siegel drove out into the Mojave Desert and decided to raise a glamorous, tropical-themed casino under the searing sun. Nobody thought that anyone would ever come here. But they couldn't have been more wrong, baby.

In Sin City, fate is decided by the spin of a roulette wheel. It's a place where the poor feel rich and the rich lose thousands. In this high-octane desert oasis, all that glitters is likely gold. Glamour's sweet stench is as thick as the cigarette smoke rolling off a blue-haired grandmother's fingers feeding nickels into the slot machine while slugging gin-and-tonics. Vegas wasn't built to last, but ironically it does. Like the shifting sand dunes that encircle it, what's hot and what's not can change in the blink of an eye here. Thankfully, what never changes is the eternal cool of the city itself.

Every decade has just made Vegas more of a boomtown than ever before. But time is irrelevant in this town. There are no clocks, just never-ending buffets and ever-flowing drinks. Acrobats spiral above the blackjack tables at Circus Circus, fountains burst outside the Bellagio, and go-go dancers heat up ultra lounges at megaresorts such as the MGM Grand. A bible-toting Elvis kisses a giddy couple that just pledged eternity in the Graceland Wedding Chapel. Nothing on the Strip ever stops, nor do the vintage gambling halls on Fremont Street in old downtown, and neither should you.

Welcome to fabulous Las Vegas, where everyone lives like the King.

HIGHLIGHTS

- Gambling and cruising casino megaresorts on the **Strip** (p681)
- Thrill-seeking atop the **Stratosphere Tower** (p684)
- Living Old Vegas at the **Fremont Street Experience** (p684)
- Boozin' (p691) and shakin' your booty till dawn (p692)
- Scrambling around **Red Rock Canyon** (p696) and the **Valley of Fire** (p697)

Red Rock
Canyon
★

Fremont
Street
★

★
Valley
of Fire

★
The
Strip

■ AVERAGE TEMPS: JAN 34/58°F, JUL 74/106°F

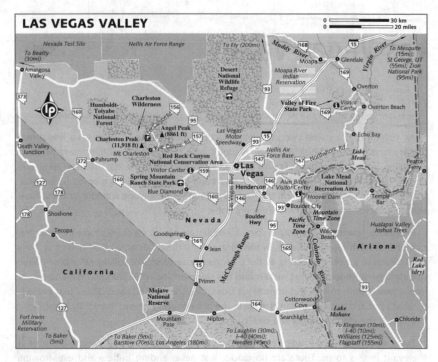

LAS VEGAS VALLEY

LAS VEGAS VALLEY

LAS VEGAS

pop 560,000

HISTORY

Unlike the rest of the ruin-laden Southwest, traces of early history are scarce in this town. Southern Paiutes inhabited the valley around Las Vegas for almost a millennium before the Spanish Trail blazed through this last, final area of the country to be encountered by Anglos.

In 1829 Rafael Rivera, a scout for a Mexican trading expedition, discovered a spring in this valley, after which it became known as *las vegas* ('the meadows'). Hell-bent on doing God's work in Native American country, Mormon missionaries arrived from Salt Lake City in 1855; their small fort was abandoned just three years later. After the Civil War ended in 1865, Octavius Decatur Gass transformed the fort into a flourishing ranch.

On May 15, 1905, the railroad company auctioned off the Las Vegas townsite. The infamous red-light district, Block 16, survived

Nevada's 1911 ban on gambling (lifted in 1931) and the supposedly dry years of Prohibition. Quickie divorces, legalized prostitution and championship boxing all proved Depression-proof bets. New Deal dollars for projects like the Hoover Dam kept flowing into coffers right through WWII.

In 1941, Thomas Hull opened the city's first casino hotel, El Rancho Vegas, along the two-lane Los Angeles highway that eventually became Las Vegas Blvd. Most of the Strip's phenomenal development occurred after WWII, though, when air-conditioning and a reliable water supply made life in the desert bearable. Mobster Benjamin 'Bugsy' Siegel took over the $6-million Flamingo hotel in 1946. Big-name entertainers like Frank Sinatra and Liberace arrived at the same time as topless French showgirls in the early 1950s. The '50s also ushered in the Cold War and atomic bomb blasts at the Nevada Test Site.

The high-profile purchase of the Desert Inn in 1966 by eccentric billionaire Howard Hughes gave the gambling industry a much-needed patina of legitimacy, which quickly

LAS VEGAS BY THE NUMBERS

- Metro-area population: 1.8 million
- Annual number of visitors: over 35 million
- Marriage licenses issued each year: 120,000
- Cost of a drink while you're gambling: free
- Steak-and-eggs graveyard special: from $5
- Miles of neon tubing on the Strip: about 15,000
- Number of sunny days per year: over 300
- Average visitor's gambling budget: $500
- Height of the Stratosphere Tower: 1149ft
- Biggest slot machine pay-out: almost $40 million

paved the way for a corporate building bonanza in the late 1960s and early '70s. The 1990s saw the Strip get even bigger, when the debut of the MGM Grand signaled the dawn of the megaresort era.

ORIENTATION

Disorientation is a constant risk, whether while searching for your room, wending your way through a purposefully confusing casino, or just trying to remember where you parked the car. McCarran International Airport is southeast of the Strip off I-215; take a taxi or a shuttle. Greyhound buses arrive downtown at the Plaza. For details on transportation, see p695.

I-15 parallels the entire length of the Strip, a 3-mile stretch of Las Vegas Blvd, which begins at the Stratosphere and runs south past Mandalay Bay. Downtown sits at the far north end of Las Vegas Blvd, with the Fremont Street Experience streaking down the middle of Glitter Gulch. A desolate area along Las Vegas Blvd, known as 'Naked City,' links downtown with the Strip.

More giant casino hotels are found east of the Strip along Paradise Rd by the University of Nevada at Las Vegas (UNLV) campus; west of I-15, mostly on Flamingo Rd; and east of downtown on the Boulder Hwy, the slow, scenic route to Hoover Dam. The outlying metro area consists of strip malls

and sprawling suburbs, such as fast-growing Henderson.

Maps
Detailed maps of the city are sold at hotels, gas stations and newsstands. The **Nevada Commission on Tourism** (www.travelnevada.com) distributes a free state map which has regional insets, a distance chart, and a list of tourism offices, attractions, recreational areas and campgrounds.

INFORMATION
Bookstores
Gambler's Book Shop (Map p685; ☎ 702-382-7555, 800-522-1777; www.gamblersbook.com; 630 S 11th St; ☺ 9am-5pm Mon-Sat) Stocks just about every book ever written on gambling.
Reading Room (Map p682; ☎ 702-632-9374; Mandalay Place, 3930 Las Vegas Blvd S; ☺ 8am-11pm Sun-Thu, 8am-midnight Fri & Sat) Indie bookshop for local-interest titles, guidebooks and maps.

Emergency
Police, fire, ambulance (☎ 911) Emergencies only.
Police (☎ 311) Nonemergency.
Rape Crisis Hotline (☎ 702-366-1640)

Internet Access
Most Las Vegas hotels have business centers that charge an arm and a leg for 24/7 Internet access. The best wi-fi hotspots are off-Strip at the airport and Las Vegas Convention Center.
Clark County Public Library (Map p685; ☎ 702-734-7323; www.lvccld.org; 833 Las Vegas Blvd N; ☺ 9am-9pm Mon-Thu, 10am-6pm Fri-Sun) Free Internet access with photo ID.
Cyber Stop (Map p682; ☎ 702-736-4782; www.cyberstopinc.com; Hawaiian Marketplace, 3743 Las Vegas Blvd S; per 30min/hr $8/12; ☺ 7am-2:30am) One of dozens of Internet cafés inside the Strip's tourist shops.
FedEx Kinko's (Map p682; ☎ 702-951-2400; www.fedexkinkos.com; 395 Hughes Center Dr; per min 25¢; ☺ 24hr) Between the Strip and the convention center.

Internet Resources
Las Vegas Advisor (www.lasvegasadvisor.com) Free information for serious gamblers.
Las Vegas on 25¢ a Day (www.bigempire.com/vegas) A hilarious cheapskate's guide.
Only Vegas (www.visitlasvegas.com) The Las Vegas Convention & Visitors Authority's official website for visitors.
VEGAS.com (www.vegas.com) Encyclopedic information, but watch out for advertorials.

LAS VEGAS IN...

One Day
Cruise the **Strip** (opposite), then hit the megaresorts for a taste of high-roller action. Ride the monorail between casinos, with stops for shopping. As the sun sets, zoom up the **Stratosphere** (p684) for thrilling rides. Fire up the night at an ultra lounge (p691), then party until dawn.

Two Days
Nobody's an early riser in Vegas. Shake off the Rabelaisian fête of the night before just in time for a breakfast **buffet** (p690). Indulge at a **spa** (p684) or chill poolside at your hotel – it's going to be another late night. Rent a **convertible** (p696) and roll west to **Red Rock Canyon** (p696). After a cat-nap, dine at a celebrity chef's **restaurant** (p689), then catch a late show or hit the **clubs** (p692).

Three Days
Sleep in again, then spend the afternoon at one of Vegas' **quirky attractions** (p685). Score a dinner reservation at **Rosemary's** (p691), then head downtown to see where it all began. Check out the **Fremont Street Experience** (p684) and the Neonopolis. After midnight, let it ride on the Strip one last time, dropping by **Mr Lucky's** (p691) for a graveyard special before sunrise.

Media
Published daily, the conservative **Las Vegas Review-Journal** (www.lvrj.com), includes Friday's *Neon* entertainment guide. **CityLife** (www.lvcitylife.com) and **Las Vegas Weekly** (www.lasvegasweekly.com) are free alternative weeklies. Free tourist glossies containing valuable discount coupons are **What's On** (www.ilovevegas.com), **Showbiz Weekly** (www.lvshowbiz.com) and **Today in Las Vegas** (www.todayinlv.com).

Medical Services
CVS (Map p682; ☎ 702-262-9028; 3758 Las Vegas Blvd S; 🕑 24hr) Pharmacy.
Harmon Medical Center (Map p682; ☎ 702-796-1116; 150 E Harmon Ave; 🕑 24hr) Offers courtesy vans from the Strip and translation services.
McCarran Quick Care (☎ 702-383-3600; www.umc-cares.org; 1769 E Russell Rd; 🕑 8am-7:30pm) Urgent-care clinic just east of the airport.
University Medical Center of Southern Nevada (Map p685; ☎ 702-383-2000, emergency 702-383-2661; 1800 W Charleston Blvd; 🕑 24hr) Nevada's most advanced trauma center.
Walgreens (Map p682; ☎ 702-739-9645; 3765 Las Vegas Blvd S; 🕑 24hr) Pharmacy.

Money
Fees imposed by casinos to exchange foreign currency at their ATMs are much higher than at banks. **American Express** (Map p682; ☎ 702-739-8474; Fashion Show Mall, 3200 S Las Vegas Blvd; 🕑 9am-9pm Mon-Fri, 10am-8pm Sat, 11am-6pm Sun) charges competitive rates for foreign currency exchange.

A 7.5% retail sales tax applies to most goods and services. A 9% hotel tax is added to all room rates. Drinks are usually complimentary while you're gambling, but tip the cocktail waitress at least $1 per drink or round. It's also polite to 'toke,' or tip, your dealer if you are winning. At buffet dining rooms, leave your server $1 per person on the table.

Every casino hotel, bank and most convenience stores have ATMs. Transaction fees start at $3 inside the gaming areas. You can avoid these surcharges by using your debit card to get cash when making a purchase at Walgreens pharmacy.

Post
Convenient full-service **post offices** (☎ 800-275-8777; www.usps.com):
Downtown (Map p685; 201 Las Vegas Blvd S; 🕑 8:30am-5pm Mon-Fri)
McCarran airport (Map p682; 5795 Paradise Rd; 🕑 9am-1pm & 2-5pm Mon-Fri)
West of the Strip (Map p682; 3100 S Industrial Rd; 🕑 8:30am-6pm Mon-Fri, 9am-3pm Sat)

Telephone
The area code for Clark County, including Las Vegas city district, is ☎ 702. Using cell phones all race and sports books is strictly prohibited.
Cyber Stop (☎ 702-736-4782; www.cyberstopinc.com; Hawaiian Marketplace, 3743 Las Vegas Blvd S) Rents Nokia handsets.

Tourist Information

Las Vegas Convention & Visitors Authority (LVCVA; Map p682; ☎ 702-892-7575, 877-847-4858; www.visitlas vegas.com; 3150 Paradise Rd; ☼ 8am-5pm) The city's official tourist office, opposite the Las Vegas Convention Center. The hotline has 24-hour recorded information.

Nevada Commission on Tourism (www.travelnevada .com) Statewide welcome centers, including at the California state line in Primm, off I-15 at exit 1.

DANGERS & ANNOYANCES

Violent crime is not likely to affect many tourists, but theft of property is common. Police and private security officers are out in force downtown on the Fremont Street Experience and on the Strip, where surveillance cameras are omnipresent. Las Vegas Blvd between downtown and the north end of the Strip is shady. Fremont Street east of Las Vegas Blvd is also unsavory.

SIGHTS

Open for business 24/7/365 is the rule at casino hotels and megaresorts – many don't even bother with locks on their doors. Unless otherwise noted, admission is free.

The Strip

Las Vegas Blvd, aka the Strip, is continually reinventing itself. Every megaresort is an attraction, and there's plenty on offer besides gambling. With each new development it's more spectacular – and more of a spectacle.

CENTER STRIP

Here are the casino showpieces everyone comes to see. You'll experience pirate battles, fountain shows and erupting volcanoes. The main 'Four Corners' intersection is at Flamingo Blvd.

Inspired by the beauty of the lakeside Italian village, the $1.6 billion **Bellagio** (Map p682; ☎ 702-693-7111; www.bellagio.com; 3600 Las Vegas Blvd S) is Vegas' opulent, if parvenu, pleasure palazzo. Dancing fountains put on a choreographed show every half hour until midnight for gawking visitors strolling the Strip. The **Bellagio Gallery of Fine Art** (Map p682; ☎ 702-693-7871, 877-957-9777; adult/student & senior $15/12; ☼ 9am-9:30pm) hosts traveling museum exhibitions.

Thanks to continuing megabuck renovations, the city's kitschy, Greco-Roman fantasy land, **Caesars Palace** (Map p682; ☎ 702-731-7110; www.caesarspalace.com; 3570 Las Vegas Blvd S) is as quintessentially Vegas as ever. Bar girls roam the

gaming areas in skimpy togas, and out front are the same fountains daredevil Evil Knievel failed to jump on his motorcycle in 1967.

Back in 1946, the **Flamingo** (Map p682; ☎ 702-733-3111; www.flamingolasvegas.com; 3555 Las Vegas Blvd S) was the talk of the town. Even its janitors wore tuxedos. Its walk-through wildlife habitat is filled with Chilean flamingos, exotic birds, ornamental koi and tropical plants.

The **Venetian** (Map p682; ☎ 702-414-1000; www .venetian.com; 3355 Las Vegas Blvd S; gondola ride adult/child/ couple from $12.50/5/50) is a replica of La Repubblica Serenissima ('Most Serene Republic'), reputed to be the home of the world's first casino. Masterpieces are displayed at the **Guggenheim Hermitage** (Map p682; ☎ 702-414-2440; www.guggenheimlasvegas.org; adult/student & child/senior $19/14.50/16.50; ☼ 9:30am-8:30pm) art museum, designed by Rem Koolhaas. Outside, next to the Rialto Bridge, is **Madame Tussauds Wax Museum** (Map p682; ☎ 702-862-7800; www.madametussaudslv.com; adult/child/senior & student $23/13/18; ☼ 10am-10pm), where you can play poker with a replica of Ben Affleck and a live-action dealer.

The Polynesian-inspired **Mirage** (Map p682; ☎ 702-791-7111; www.mirage.com; 3400 Las Vegas Blvd S) is replete with a rain-forest atrium, saltwater aquariums, a royal white tiger habitat and a fiery 100ft artificial volcano out front that erupts every 15 minutes from 7pm till midnight. Next door, the swashbuckling **TI** (Treasure Island; Map p682; ☎ 702-894-7111; www.treasure island.com; 3300 Las Vegas Blvd S) has reinvented itself, trying to put the 'sin' back in casino with its racy, yet silly 'Sirens of TI' show, during which pyrotechnics explode several times nightly.

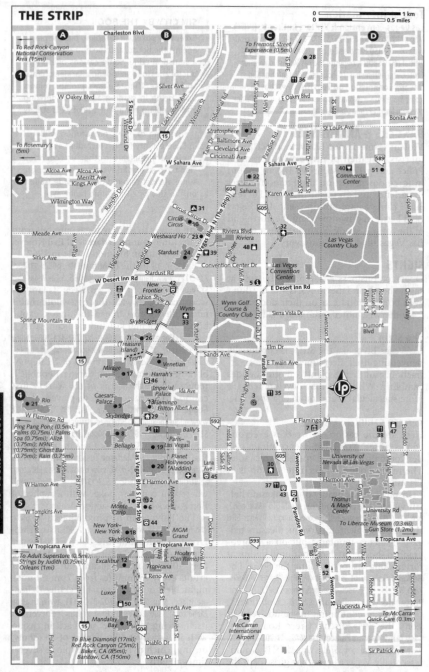

THE STRIP

0 ————————— 1 km
0 ————————— 0.5 miles

A **B** **C** **D**

1

Charleston Blvd

To Red Rock Canyon
National Conservation
Area (15mi)

To Fremont Street
Experience (0.5mi)

● 28

🏨 36

Silver Ave

W Oakey Blvd

E Oakey Blvd

Bonita Ave

2

St Louis Ave

Stratosphere ● 25

Baltimore Ave
Cleveland Ave
Cincinnati Ave

40 🛏 ● 51
Commercial
Center

W Sahara Ave

E Sahara Ave

● 22

Alcoa Ave   Alcoa Ave
Merritt Ave
Kings Ave

Sahara

Karen Ave

Wilmington Way

3

Meade Ave

Circus Circus Dr
Circus 🏨 31
Circus ● 10

Riviera Blvd
Riviera

32

Las Vegas
Country Club

Sirius Ave

Westward Ho ● 23

48 🏨

Stardust ● 24

🛏 39

Las Vegas
Convention
Center

Spring Mountain Rd

W Desert Inn Rd

Stardust Rd

Convention Center Dr

Mel Ave

E Desert Inn Rd

5 ℹ

Rome St
Brussels St
Athens St

New
Frontier
🏛 11

42

Fashion Show Dr

Sierra Vista Dr

Dumont
Blvd

Oneida Way

🛏 49

Wynn
● 33

Wynn Golf
Course &
Country Club

Skybridges

Elm Dr

TI
(Treasure
Island)
● 26
Tram

27

Venetian

Sands Ave

E Twain Ave

🏨 35

4

Mirage
● 17

Harrah's
🛏 46
Imperial
Palace
13 ●
Flamingo

Ida Ave

Albert Ave

3
@

● 21
Rio

Caesars
Palace
● 9

Hilton

34 🛏

Skybridges

Bally's

Paris–
Las Vegas

E Flamingo Rd

7 🏛

🏨 38   ● 47

Escondido

Ping Pang Pong (0.5mi);
Palms (0.75mi); Palms
Spa (0.75mi); Alizé
(0.75mi); N9NE
(0.75mi); Ghost Bar
(0.75mi); Rain (0.75mi)

● 8

Bellagio

● 19

● 20

Planet
Hollywood
(Aladdin)
⊕ 4

30

University of
Nevada at Las Vegas

5

W Harmon Ave

E Harmon Ave

Lana
Ave

🛏 45

37 🛏

43

Harmon Ave

Thomas
& Mack
Center

University Rd

W Tompkins Ave

● 1
● 6

● 2

Monte
Carlo

44

16

MGM
Grand

41

To Liberace Museum (0.3mi);
Gun Store (1.2mi)

New York–
New York
● 18

Skybridges

W Tropicana Ave

E Tropicana Ave

E Tropicana Ave

To Adult Superstore (0.5mi);
Strings by Judith (0.75mi);
Orleans (1mi)

Excalibur 12

Hooters
(San Remo)

● 52

Tropicana

E Reno Ave

Luxor

14

W Hacienda Ave

🛏 50

Hacienda Ave

To McCarran
Quick Care (0.3mi)

Mandalay
Bay ● 15

6

To Blue Diamond (17mi);
Red Rock Canyon (25mi);
Baker, CA (85mi);
Barstow, CA (150mi)

Diablo Dr

Dewey Dr

McCarran
International
Airport

Sir Patrick Ave

LAS VEGAS VALLEY

Back south of the Flamingo, **Paris–Las Vegas** (Map p682; ☎ 702-946-7000; www.parislasvegas.com; 3655 Las Vegas Blvd S) has an ersatz **Eiffel Tower** (Map p682; adult/child 6-12/senior Sun-Thu $9/7/7, Fri & Sat $12/10/10; ✆ 10am-1am) with a glass elevator and an observation deck.

SOUTH STRIP
The South Strip neighborhood is attracting ever more of a crowd, especially to its after-dark haunts.

The mini-megapolis of **New York–New York** (Map p682; ☎ 702-740-6969; www.nynyhotelcasino.com; 3790 Las Vegas Blvd S) features scaled-down replicas of the Big Apple's skyline, Statue of Liberty and Brooklyn Bridge, plus a bumpy rollercoaster, **Manhattan Express** (Map p682; ride $12.50; ✆ 10:30am-11pm Sun-Thu, 10:30am-midnight Fri & Sat), inside the kiddie heaven of the **Coney Island Emporium** (Map p682; ✆ 8am-midnight Sun-

Thu, 8am-2am Fri & Sat), which features over 200 video arcade games.

The $1 billion **MGM Grand** (Map p682; ☎ 702-891-7777; www.mgmgrand.com; 3799 Las Vegas Blvd S) retains the 'world's largest hotel' title. At the Stripside entrance, it's impossible to miss the signature 100,000lb lion surrounded by spritzing fountains. Other 'Maximum Vegas' attractions include a $9 million live lion habitat, flashy entertainment and gourmet restaurants.

The standout daytime attraction at **Mandalay Bay** (Map p682; ☎ 720-632-7777; www.mandalaybay.com; 3950 Las Vegas Blvd S) is the **Shark Reef** (Map p682; adult/child $16/10; ✆ 10am-11pm, last admission 10pm), a 1.6 million gallon walk-through aquarium with over a thousand species, including jellyfish, moray eels and stingrays. Like the MGM Grand, dining and nightlife are M-Bay's biggest draws.

LAS VEGAS VALLEY

THE SPA WHO LOVED ME

Vegas' splendid spas are perfect for pampering and detoxing. Day-use fees are $20 to $35; treatments run from $100 to $200 per hour (book ahead). Some spas are reserved for hotel guests only on weekends.

bathhouse (Map p682; ☎ 877-632-9636; THEhotel, Mandalay Bay, 3950 Las Vegas Blvd S; ☯ 6am-9:30pm) A multimillion dollar minimalist temple, it offers 'aromapothecary' massage oils, Asian tea baths, fruit-pulp facials, a redwood sauna and plunge pools. Ask about sunrise yoga on Mandalay Beach.

Palms Spa (☎ 702-942-7777; Palms, 4321 W Flamingo Rd; ☯ 6am-8pm) Ultra-soft 'cashwear' robes, hot stone massage and 'margarita madness' skin care – oh, it's trendy to the max. Relax by the lushly landscaped pool before hitting the hotel's leather-walled tattoo studio.

Paris Spa by Mandara (Map p682; ☎ 702-946-4366; Paris–Las Vegas, 3655 Las Vegas Blvd S; ☯ 6am-7pm) With Matisse-styled tiling, this full-service salon and spa has Euro and Balinese influences. The most luxurious treatment rooms have handcrafted tropical hardwood, artworks and silk carpets.

Rock Spa (Map p682; ☎ 702-693-5522; Hard Rock, 4455 Paradise Rd; ☯ 6am-10pm) The celebrity stylist here has tousled the heads of David Bowie and Isabella Rossellini. The spa has soothing, natural wood, rock and water elements, while the state-of-the-art health club hosts boxing classes.

Modeled after Egypt's ancient city on the Nile, **Luxor** (Map p682; ☎ 702-262-4000; www.luxor .com; 3900 Las Vegas Blvd S) is guarded by a crouching sphinx. At the apex of its 30 story black-glass pyramid is the world's most powerful beacon, visible by astronauts in space. Exquisite reproductions of artifacts discovered by English archaeologist Howard Carter during his 1922 excavation of the tomb of Tutankhamun, are seen inside the overpriced **King Tut Museum** (Map p682; admission $10; ☯ 9am-5pm).

NORTH STRIP
The North Strip is where you'll find survivors from the old Rat Pack days. You gotta love the landmark 188ft sign outside the **Stardust** (Map p682; ☎ 702-732-6111; www.stardustlv.com; 3000 Las Vegas Blvd S), which continues to lure fans of bygone Vegas.

Circus Circus (Map p682; ☎ 702-734-0410; www .circuscircus.com; 2880 Las Vegas Blvd S) is a strange world in itself. Trapeze artists, high-wire workers, jugglers and unicyclists perform above the casino floor every half hour until midnight. Its **Adventuredome** (Map p682; ☎ 702-794-3939; www.adventuredome.com; per ride $4-6, day pass $15-23) is jam-packed with amusements. Back on the Strip, grab a few 75¢ beers and $1 half-pound hot dogs at **Slots A' Fun** (Map p682; ☎ 702-734-0410; 2890 Las Vegas Blvd S), then enjoy the laughable lounge acts.

Further north, Moroccan-themed **Sahara** (Map p682; ☎ 702-737-2111; www.saharavegas.com; 2535 Las Vegas Blvd S) is one of the few old-Vegas carpet joints to have survived the megaresort onslaught. Jump on the Strip's best roller-

coaster, **Speed** (Map p682; ☯ 11am-midnight), or virtually race a Formula One car at **Las Vegas Cyber Speedway** (Map p682; ☯ noon-9pm Mon-Thu, noon-10pm Fri & Sat, 11am-9pm Sun); each ride costs $10, or it's $15 for both.

The soaring **Stratosphere Tower** (Map p682; ☎ 702-380-7777; www.stratospherehotel.com; 2000 Las Vegas Blvd S; elevator adult/senior $10/6, elevator & thrill rides $25) has some of the highest thrill rides in the world (Insanity and Big Shot are best). Also reached by America's fastest elevators are a revolving restaurant, circular bar, and panoramic indoor and outdoor viewing decks.

Downtown
Downtown casino hotels are the city's oldest, a jumble of blazing neon, red velvet and fading carpet, once known as Glitter Gulch. The city's original quarter attracts far fewer onlookers and is preferred by serious gamblers who find white tigers and faux volcanoes beneath them. The smoky, low-ceilinged casinos have changed little over the years – and that's the whole point.

FREMONT STREET EXPERIENCE
By 1995, Vegas' downtown had lost nearly all of its tourists to the rapidly developing Strip. Always ready for a gamble, downtown boosters installed a 1400ft-long arched steel canopy along Fremont Street to make a five block–long **pedestrian mall** (Map p685; www.vegas experience.com; Fremont Street; ☯ shows hourly 8pm-midnight) between Main St and Las Vegas Blvd. The cheesy light-and-sound show enhanced by 550,000 watts of wraparound sound is

enough to stop most people (particularly drunks) in their tracks. The latest addition is a superbig Viva Vision screen, featuring 12.5 million synchronized LEDs.

You can easily stroll between half a dozen gaming joints here. Don't miss the gigantic 61lb 11oz **Hand of Faith** (Map p685), the heftiest chunk of gold ever found, off the lobby of the luxe **Golden Nugget** (Map p685; ☎ 702-385-7111; www.goldennugget.com; 129 E Fremont Street). **Binion's** (Map p685; ☎ 702-382-1600; www.binions.com; 128 E Fremont Street), opened in 1951 by notorious Texan gambler Benny Binion, has a high-stakes poker room. It's where real Nevada cowboys gamble.

The **Neonopolis** (Map p685; ☎ 702-477-0470; http://neonopolis.com) has a multiplex cinema; Jillian's for bowling, billiards and video games; a nostalgic gambling museum (p686); and a collection of vintage neon signs in the central courtyard. Sparkling genie lamps, glowing martini glasses and 1940s motel marquees also brighten smaller displays just off Fremont Street further west. Look for 1950s landmark Vegas Vic and latter-day Vegas Vickie kicking up her heels above a strip club.

MAIN STREET STATION

The opulent Victorian-styled **casino hotel** (Map p685; ☎ 702-387-1896; www.mainstreetcasino.com; 200 N Main St) boasts an extensive collection of antiques, architectural artifacts and other collectibles – pick up a free guide brochure in the lobby. Outside to the south is Buffalo Bill Cody's private railcar, which he used to travel the USA with his Wild West Show until his death in 1917.

QUIRKY LAS VEGAS

Atomic Testing Museum (Map p682; ☎ 702-794-5161; www.atomictestingmuseum.org; Desert Research Institute, 755 E Flamingo Rd; adult/child under 7/child 7-17/senior $10/free/7/7; ☺ 9am-5pm Mon-Sat, 1-4pm Sun) During the atomic heyday of the 1950s, gamblers and tourists downtown watched as mushroom clouds rose behind Fremont Street, and the city even crowned a Miss Atomic Bomb. Buy your tickets at the replica Nevada Test Site guard station, then watch a historical film inside the Ground Zero Theater, which mimics a concrete test bunker.

Elvis-A-Rama Museum (Map p682; ☎ 702-309-7200; www.elvisarama.com; 3401 Industrial Rd; admission $13, tribute show combo ticket $27; ☺ 10am-6pm) Elvis may have left the building, but the largest private collection of

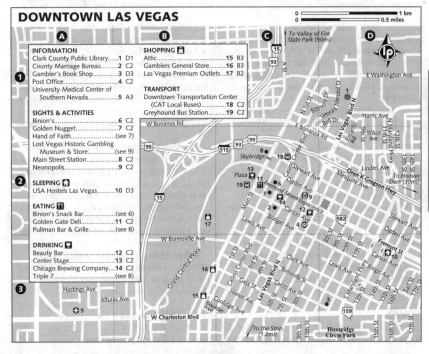

DOWNTOWN LAS VEGAS

INFORMATION
Clark County Public Library......1 D1
County Marriage Bureau.........2 C2
Gambler's Book Shop.............3 D3
Post Office.............................4 C2
University Medical Center of
  Southern Nevada................5 A3

SIGHTS & ACTIVITIES
Binion's...............................6 C2
Golden Nugget....................7 C2
Hand of Faith.................(see 7)
Lost Vegas Historic Gambling
  Museum & Store...........(see 9)
Main Street Station.............8 C2
Neonopolis..........................9 C2

SLEEPING
USA Hostels Las Vegas........10 D3

EATING
Binion's Snack Bar...........(see 6)
Golden Gate Deli................11 C2
Pullman Bar & Grille.......(see 8)

DRINKING
Beauty Bar..........................12 C2
Center Stage.......................13 C2
Chicago Brewing Company....14 C2
Triple 7...........................(see 8)

SHOPPING
Attic....................................15 B3
Gamblers General Store........16 B3
Las Vegas Premium Outlets...17 B2

TRANSPORT
Downtown Transportation Center
  (CAT Local Buses)..............18 C2
Greyhound Bus Station.........19 C2

LAS VEGAS FOR KIDS

With increasing frequency, casino hotels are prohibiting strollers on their grounds. State law prohibits people under age 21 from being in gaming areas and under 18s on the Strip after 9pm on weekends or holidays unless accompanied by a parent or guardian.

But not every gaming establishment looks upon children as unprofitable monkeys. Some of the best bets for families:

- Circus Circus (p684) – The original family-friendly casino hotel is the most crowded with tots to teens, including the Adventuredome.
- Excalibur (Map p682; ☎ 702-597-7777; www.excalibur.com; 3850 Las Vegas Blvd S) – For kids of all ages, with the Fantasy Faire Midway, free entertainment on the Court Jester's Stage and the rowdy Tournament of Kings dinner show.
- New York–New York (p683) – Coney Island Emporium, the Manhattan Express rollercoaster, Houdini's Magic Shop and eateries that won't break the bank.
- Stratosphere (p684) – The best thrill rides in town, plus Roxy's Diner.
- Luxor (p684) – Video games fit for a Pharaoh, an IMAX cinema and ride films, and the quirky King Tut Museum.
- Orleans (p689) – The closest off-Strip casino hotel for families, with bowling, cinemas and on-site babysitting.

Elsewhere, there's no shortage of video arcades, movie theaters and other attractions where discounts for children are readily available. You can ask for a licensed and bonded babysitting service, which hotel concierges can recommend. Many agencies send someone right to your hotel room. Click to www.lasvegaskids.net for more info and advice.

his memorabilia is still here at this cheesy museum. Call for schedules of Elvis impersonator shows and Strip shuttles.

Liberace Museum (☎ 702-798-5595; www.liberace.org; 1775 E Tropicana Ave; adult/child under 11/senior & student $12/free/8.50; ⊗ 10am-5pm Mon-Sat, noon-4pm Sun) For connoisseurs of bizarre extravagance, this creepy memorial museum is a must-do. A tribute to 'Mr Showmanship,' it houses the most flamboyant cars, outrageous costumes and ornate pianos you'll ever see. Call for schedules of free tours, given by his passionate fans.

Lost Vegas Historic Gambling Museum & Store (Map p685; ☎ 702-385-1883; www.neonopolis.com; Neonopolis, 450 E Fremont Street; adult/senior $2.50/1.50; ⊗ 11am-9pm Sun-Thu, 11am-10pm Fri & Sat) Pleasantly jumbled displays of Old Vegas memorabilia: historic photographs, pulp tabloid clippings and vintage gaming chips from casinos that have since been blown up. Under 16 not admitted.

Viva Las Vegas Wedding Chapel (Map p682; ☎ 702-384-0771, 800-574-4450; www.vivalasvegasweddings.com; 1205 Las Vegas Blvd S) Even if you're not contemplating tying the knot, it's worth a peek inside this little chapel to loooove to see if anyone is getting married – the public is welcome and ceremonies are broadcast live online.

TOURS

Most tours appeal to seniors who prefer to leave the driving to others, but they do ease logistical hassles. Free Strip hotel pick-ups and drop-offs are included in many rates. Check online for discounts.

Black Canyon River Adventures (☎ 702-294-1414, 800-455-3490; www.blackcanyonadventures.com; adult/child 5-12/child 13-15 $73/45/70, incl transportation from Las Vegas $106/78/103) Three-hour motor-assisted raft floats down the Colorado River. Boats launch from the base of Hoover Dam, with stops for swimming and lunch en route.

Down River Outfitters (☎ 702-293-1190, 800-748-3702; www.downriveroutfitters.com; guided tour $150, canoe & kayak rental per day $45-55) All-day guided canoe and kayak trips for small groups from the base of Hoover Dam.

Gray Line (☎ 702-384-1234, 800-634-6579; www.grayline.com; tours $35-140) The granddaddy of large-group coach sightseeing tours runs popular nighttime city tours and a variety of excursions, including to Hoover Dam and the Grand Canyon.

Papillon Helicopter Flights (☎ 702-736-7243, 888-635-7272; www.papillon.com; tours $55-350) Vegas' oldest helicopter-flightseeing outfitter offers after-dark flyovers of the Strip and Grand Canyon tours.

FESTIVALS & EVENTS

Contact the LVCVA (p681) for up-to-date information on annual events.

LAS VEGAS VALLEY

MARRIAGES MADE IN SIN CITY

If you're looking to get hitched, first go to the **county marriage bureau** (☎ 702-455-4415; 200 S 3rd St; ☽ 8am-midnight Mon-Thu, 8am Fri-midnight Sun, 24hr on holidays) for a license ($55). Choices for the perfect spot to say 'I do' are endless. Expect to pay from $200 for a basic wedding service, including a limo ride to the chapel. Don't expect much ceremony, though: there's probably another couple, hearts bursting with love, in line right behind you.

Laughlin Desert Challenge Short, brutal off-road races in mid-January.

Colorado River Bluegrass Festival Old-timey bands down by the river in Laughlin during February.

St Patrick's Day Fremont Street throws a party every year on March 17.

NASCAR Weekend Over 140,000 fans descend on the Las Vegas Motor Speedway (Map p678) in March.

Mardi Gras New Orleans–style carnival held at the wrong time (April), but it's still a riot.

Lei Day A Polynesian and Pacific Rim block party downtown on May 1.

Cinco de Mayo Mexican Independence Day (May 5) is celebrated citywide.

CineVegas Sin City's premier film festival lights up the Palms casino hotel during June.

World Series of Poker High rollers vie for millions in June and July.

4th of July Choose from Clark County's rockin' 'Red, White 'N Boom,' the Las Vegas Philharmonic's 'Star Spangled Spectacular' or Boulder City's old-fashioned Damboree.

Oktoberfest Bouts of drinking (endorsed by real Bavarians!) across the valley for the month.

Aviation Nation Top-gun military and civilian air show in November at Nellis Air Force Base (Map p678), near the speedway.

National Finals Rodeo Ten days of steer wrestling and bull riding at UNLV's Thomas and Mack Center in December.

New Year's Eve The Strip sees the biggest crush of humanity this side of Times Square.

SLEEPING

If you're going to splurge anywhere on your vacation, Vegas is the place to do it. Hotels are over-the-top glamorous and ridiculously luxurious; even midrange ones give you lots of bang for your buck. Every place reviewed here offers at least one swimming pool, aircon, fee-based Internet access and free self-parking.

Avoid visiting during big conventions. Colossal crowds can be annoying, hotels jack-up room rates and standard rooms are scarce. Contact the LVCVA (p681) for a list of convention dates and for help booking accommodations. The slowest times of year are usually the hottest summer months, July and August, and after New Year's through February. In general, rates are lowest Sunday to Thursday, with weekend rates easily double or triple and may require a two-night minimum stay. Motel prices are less variable, but they still tend to be higher on Friday and Saturday nights. With all that in mind, don't take our prices as gospel.

Whatever you do, do *not* arrive without a reservation, at least for the first night. You'd be amazed how often every room – even in Laughlin, 100 miles away – is booked solid.

The Strip
BUDGET

Sahara (Map p682; ☎ 702-737-2111, 888-696-2121; www.saharavegas.com; 2535 Las Vegas Blvd S; r weekday/weekend from $50/90) A delightfully tacky Moroccan theme pervades this vintage 1950s hotel (p684). The atmosphere doesn't churn up a whole lot of excitement, but does contain simple, comfortable rooms that are among the city's better bargains. It's on the monorail line.

Barbary Coast (Map p682; ☎ 702-737-7111, 888-227-2279; www.barbarycoastcasino.com; 3595 Las Vegas Blvd S; r weekday/weekend from $40/100) With basic rooms smack bang mid-Strip, the Barbary is the Strip's worst-kept secret. It's great value that features charming Victorian-era decor, so it's often tough to secure a bed – or a parking space.

Circus Circus (Map p682; ☎ 702-734-0410, 877-224-7287; www.circuscircus-lasvegas.com; 2880 Las Vegas Blvd S; r weekday/weekend from $50/80) Most of the rooms

---

LIGHT ME UP, BABY

A common complaint registered by Californians is that 'smoke-free' and 'Las Vegas' are rarely in the same sentence: there are ashtrays at every telephone, elevator, pool and shower, in toilets and taxis. Token nonsmoking sections exist at some restaurants, and most hotels claim to offer nonsmoking rooms, but don't expect either to be free of a whiff (or much worse) of cigarettes.

---

at this family favorite casino hotel (p684) are nonsmoking and have sofas and balconies. The suites, like clowns, come in varying shapes and sizes. Avoid the motel-style Manor rooms out back, which unusually (for Vegas) have refrigerators.

Stratosphere (Map p682; ☎ 702-380-7777, 800-998-6937; www.stratospherehotel.com; 2000 Las Vegas Blvd S; r weekday/weekend from $35/55, extended check-out $20-30) Warning! Your room is not the neck-craning Stratosphere tower, but rather in a smaller building at the base of the spire. This crowded hotel is remote, but perks include a free laundry room and fitness center.

KOA RV Park (Map p682; ☎ 702-733-9707, 800-562-7270; www.koa.com; 500 Circus Circus Dr; sites $22-82) Circus Circus also has an RV park with 24-hour check-in and wi-fi Internet access; pets OK.

MIDRANGE
Many places listed here would fall into the luxury bracket elsewhere.

MGM Grand (Map p682; ☎ 702-891-7777, 877-880-0880; www.mgmgrand.com; 3799 Las Vegas Blvd S; r weekday/weekend from $90/200) There's plenty to choose from at the world's largest hotel (p683), but is bigger better? Luxurious suites, with multiple bathrooms and patio whirlpools, can be a bargain. Standard rooms have Hollywood bungalow decor. The sprawling pool complex and after-dark entertainment are both knock-outs.

New York–New York (Map p682; ☎ 702-740-6969, 888-693-6763; www.nynyhotelcasino.com; 3790 Las Vegas Blvd S; r weekday/weekend from $80/120) Classy and freshly remodeled rooms have black marble-topped sinks and comfy beds. The cheapest ones are rather tiny (just what one would expect in NYC). Avoid noisy lower-level rooms facing the rollercoaster (p683).

Luxor (Map p682; ☎ 702-262-4100, 888-777-0188; www.luxor.com; 3900 Las Vegas Blvd S; r weekday/weekend from $80/150) Featuring art deco Egyptian furnishings and marble bathrooms, Luxor's rooms are one of Vegas' best midrange deals. Ones in the newer tower often have better views than those in the pyramid (p684), though the latter have slanted windows (but no bathtubs).

TI (Treasure Island; Map p682; ☎ 702-894-7111, 800-288-7206; www.treasureisland.com; 3300 Las Vegas Blvd S; r weekday/weekend from $90/160) The rooms in this casino (p681) feel deceptively expansive, thanks to floor-to-ceiling windows. Recent grown-up additions include deluxe poolside

> ### AUTHOR'S CHOICE
> **THEhotel** (Map p682; ☎ 702-632-7777, 877-632-7800; www.mandalaybay.com; Mandalay Bay, 3950 Las Vegas Blvd S; ste weekday/weekend from $150/200) Kick back with your entourage at THEhotel, at least for the moment. Enter the high-ceilinged lobby off Mandalay Bay's casino floor, then zoom up to your expansive, chic suite with a wet bar, plasma TV, living area and deep soaking tub.

cabanas amidst waterfalls and lush greenery, and a huge party-friendly hot tub.

Flamingo (Map p682; ☎ 702-733-3111, 888-308-8899; www.flamingolasvegas.com; 3555 Las Vegas Blvd S; r weekday/weekend from $80/150) The hotel part of the Flamingo complex (p681) attracts faithful flocks for two good reasons: price and location. The tropical-themed abodes are tiny, with diminutive bathrooms and worn decor. Spend a bit more of your bankroll for a minisuite.

TOP END
True luxury comes cheaper here than almost anywhere else in the world. Impeccable service, 24/7 can-do concierge pampering and expedited airport check-in are par for the course.

Wynn (Map p682; ☎ 702-770-7100, 888-320-9966; www.wynnlasvegas.com; 3131 Las Vegas Blvd S; r weekday/weekend from $219/299, ste from $359) Vegas' newest haute, copper-tinted high-rise hides deluxe resort rooms that are bigger than some studio apartments, with high thread-count linens, sofas, flat-screen high-definition TVs, Turkish towels and all the little luxuries. Salon suites enjoy floor-to-ceiling views and VIP check-in.

Venetian (Map p682; ☎ 702-414-1000, 877-857-1861; www.venetian.com; 3355 Las Vegas Blvd S; ste weekday/weekend from $170/200) Fronted by flowing canals and graceful arched bridges, the Venetian's (p681) 700 sq ft 'standard' rooms are anything but. In fact, they're the largest and most luxurious in town. The Venezia Tower boasts a private garden pool and exclusive concierge.

Bellagio (Map p682; ☎ 702-693-7111, 888-987-3456; www.bellagio.com; 3600 Las Vegas Blvd S; r weekday/weekend from $160/200) If anything in Vegas is truly spectacular, then this luxe five-diamond casino destination (p681) is it. The lake-view rooms looking onto the Bellagio's famous fountains are most in demand. A spa tower is the lavish icing atop this Italian cake.

Downtown

Golden Nugget (Map p685; ☎ 702-385-7111, 800-846-5336; www.goldennugget.com; 129 E Fremont Street; r weekday/weekend from $60/80, apt ste from $275) Downtown's swankest 'carpet joint' owes its newfound panache to Fox's *Casino* reality TV show. Oversized standard rooms, with half-canopy beds and marble everywhere, are decadent. Service is top-notch.

USA Hostels Las Vegas (Map p685; ☎ 702-385-1150, 800-550-8958; www.usahostels.com; 1322 E Fremont Street; incl breakfast dm $15-23, d $39-54) It's in a crappy part of downtown, but has accommodating staff and facilities (including a pool, Jacuzzi and bar). Call for free pick up from the Greyhound station. Americans must have an out-of-state college ID and may be asked for proof of international travel.

UNLV & East of the Strip

Hard Rock (Map p682; ☎ 702-693-5544, 800-473-7625; www.hardrockhotel.com; 4455 Paradise Rd; r weekday/weekend from $99/259) Rock on. Hip rooms are as boldly done as the rest of this vainglorious shrine to rock and roll, which pulls in a moneyed crowd mainly from Southern California. French doors reveal expansive views to grace the stylish Euro-minimalist rooms. Suites are even sexier. Some caveats: service can be half-assed, and overbooking is common.

Las Vegas Hilton (Map p682; ☎ 702-732-5301, 888-732-7117; www.lvhilton.com; 3000 Paradise Rd; r weekday/weekend from $70/110) There's nothing memorable about this contemporary hotel near the Las Vegas Convention Center, but it's certainly convenient to the monorail. Sprawling rooms have deeper-than-usual bathtubs and panoramic desert-view windows.

West of the Strip

Palms (☎ 702-942-7777, 866-942-7770; www.palms.com; 4321 W Flamingo Rd; r weekday/weekend from $99/330) The post–*Real World* Palms attracts a flashy crowd and has become a favorite with celebs such as Britney Spears (she spent her *first* wedding night here). Spacious rooms have comfy king-size beds. Playpen suites are tailored for bachelor/bachelorette parties.

Orleans (☎ 702-365-7111, 800-675-3267; www.orleanscasino.com; 4500 W Tropicana Ave; r weekday/

weekend from $40/110) Hundreds of tastefully appointed French-provincial rooms are actually 450 sq ft 'petite suites' with oversized tubs. A spa, fitness center, on-site child care and the best bowling alley in town round out the family fun.

EATING

Sin City is an unmatched eating adventure – and an expensive one. Since Wolfgang Puck brought Spago to Caesars in 1992, celebrity Iron Chefs have taken up residence in nearly every megaresort. With so many star-struck tables to choose from, stakes are high and there are many overhyped eating gambles. Book in advance for upscale restaurants and inquire about dress codes. Loss-leader meal deals still exist, mostly downtown, although every casino hotel on the Strip also has a buffet and 24-hour coffee shop. Vegas' restaurants alone could be fodder for an entire book. We've listed a few of our favorites, but there are many, many more.

In these reviews, budget means mains up to $15 and top-end means mains over $30.

The Strip

BUDGET

Canter's Deli (Map p682; ☎ 702-894-7111; TI (Treasure Island), 3300 Las Vegas Blvd S; meals $8-15; ☺ 11am-midnight) At this landmark LA-import delicatessen, slide onto a seat at the stainless-steel counter or nab a mod booth for authentic Jewish deli fare that's as good as it gets.

Village Eateries (Map p682; ☎ 702-740-6969; New York–New York, 3790 Las Vegas Blvd S; meals $6-12) The cobblestone streets of Greenwich Village are bursting with incredibly tasty options such as Greenberg & Sons Deli, Fulton's Fish Frye, Jodi Maroni's Sausage Kingdom and Chin Chin Café.

MIDRANGE

Mon Ami Gabi (Map p682; ☎ 702-944-4224; Paris–Las Vegas, 3655 Las Vegas Blvd S; mains $10-29; ☺ 11am-2:30pm, 5-11pm Sun-Thu, 5pm-midnight Fri & Sat) Think charming Champs Élysées bistro. This elevated patio seating in the shadow of the Eiffel Tower is just about the only Stripside alfresco dining and is great for people watching. There's a raw seafood bar and the steak frites are *parfait*. Good, reasonable wine list.

Fix (Map p682; ☎ 702-693-8400; Bellagio, 3600 Las Vegas Blvd S; mains $20-30; ☺ 5pm-midnight Sun-Thu, 5pm-2am Fri & Sat) A vibrant and warm space cut

---

TOP FIVE RABELAISIAN FEASTS

When it comes to all-you-can-eat buffets, the old adage 'you get what you pay for' was never truer; classier hotels have better buffets. Expect to pay $7 to $15 for breakfast, $10 to $20 for lunch (more for weekend champagne brunch) and $15 to $25 for dinner.

Bally's Sterling Brunch (Map p682; ☎ 702-967-7999; Bally's, 3645 Las Vegas Blvd S; brunch $58; 🕑 9:30am-2:30pm Sun) Indulge in the best brunch in town. Ice sculptures and lavish flower arrangements add to the rich ambiance, while selections like broiled lobster, caviar and French champagne never stop flowing.

Le Village Buffet (Map p682; ☎ 702-946-7000; Paris–Las Vegas, 3655 Las Vegas Blvd S; 🕑 breakfast, lunch & dinner) Fresh fruit and cheeses, pastries and seafood make this a great value. Breakfast is *magnifique*.

The Buffet (Map p682; ☎ 702-693-7111; Bellagio, 3600 Las Vegas Blvd S; 🕑 breakfast, lunch & dinner) This classy, live-action buffet features a sumptuous spread of crowd-pleasing dishes from around the world. Go for dinner.

House of Blues (Map p682; ☎ 702-632-7600; Mandalay Bay, 3950 Las Vegas Blvd S; adult/child under 12 $39/20; 🕑 seatings 10am & 1pm Sun) The Sunday gospel brunch comes with live music, unlimited champagne and down-home Southern favorites. Buy tickets in advance.

Carnival World Buffet (☎ 702-252-7777; Rio, 3700 W Flamingo Rd; 🕑 breakfast, lunch & dinner) Food from Europe, Asia and the Americas is showcased at this lavish off-Strip buffet, with seafood as the dinner specialty, along with house-made desserts. There's a free shuttle from Harrah's.

---

from tropical hardwoods. A three-course *prix fixe* menu ($40) offers such goodies as roasted tomato soup with a grilled-cheese sandwich, chicken with smoked mash and a choco-java 'shake & cake' for dessert.

Olives (Map p682; ☎ 702-693-8181; Bellagio, 3600 S Las Vegas Blvd; mains lunch $16-25, dinner $25-46; 🕑 11am-10:30pm) Bostonian chef Todd English dishes up homage to the life-giving fruit. Flatbread pizzas, house-made pastas and flame-licked meats get top billing. Patio tables overlook the Bellagio's Lake Como. There's a good wine list and flamboyant desserts.

Mesa Grill (Map p682; ☎ 877-346-4642; Caesars Palace, 3570 Las Vegas Blvd S; mains lunch $13-20, dinner $25-45; 🕑 lunch Mon-Fri, brunch 10:30am-3pm Sat & Sun, dinner daily) While star chef Bobby Flay doesn't cook on the premises, his signature menu of Southwestern fusion fare is spicy and satisfying. Whether it's a sweet potato tamale with crushed pecan butter, blue corn pancakes or spice-rubbed pork tenderloin, this is iron-clad value.

RM (Map p682; ☎ 702-632-9300; Mandalay Place, 3930 Las Vegas Blvd S; mains $19-52; 🕑 restaurant dinner, café 11am-3pm & 5-11pm Sun-Thu, 11am-midnight Fri & Sat) From NY chef Rick Moonen, American seafood dishes, such as cajun popcorn and Maine lobster, come with comfort-food sides like gourmet mac and cheese and beer parings. The downstairs café with rich mahogany tables offers a raw bar and a 'biscuit bar' serving seafood salads.

Okada (☎ 702-770-3320; Wynn, 3131 Las Vegas Blvd S; mains $16-29; 🕑 dinner) At this combination sushi

bar, *robatayaki* (choose-your-own-adventure teppanyaki) and teppanyaki grill overlooking the lagoon, sushi maestro Takashi Yagahashi exhibits mastery of Eurasian twists on Japanese classics, like red miso bouillabaisse or tea-smoked Maine lobster with marinated beets. Go for the bento box special.

TOP END

Alex (Map p682; ☎ 702-770-3300; Wynn, 3131 Las Vegas Blvd S; prix fixe $110-235; 🕑 dinner) Award-winning chef Alessandro Stratta stretches his wings at this haute French restaurant, with high-concept dishes like foie gras ravioli and giant clams with caramelized fennel, sour orange and mint, plus some Asian influences. No casual attire.

Fleur de Lys (Map p682; ☎ 702-632-9400; www.fleurdelyssf.com; Mandalay Bay, 3950 Las Vegas Blvd S; prix fixe $74-94; 🕑 dinner) It doesn't have the famous wine tower of Charlie Palmer's Aureole next door, but famed French chef Hubert Keller has built an equally soaring space to enhance his creative seasonal tasting menus with creative vegetarian options.

Eiffel Tower Restaurant (Map p682; ☎ 702-948-6937; Paris–Las Vegas, 3655 Las Vegas Blvd S; dishes from $30; 🕑 dinner) The adage about the better the view, the worse the food doesn't apply here. Views of the Strip and the Bellagio's fountains are as breathtaking as near-perfect renditions of haute classics like foie gras. The chef's tasting menu is recommended. Good wine list. Reservations are required; dress is business casual.

Downtown

Famous cheap eats down on Fremont St include 99¢ shrimp cocktails from the **Golden Gate deli** (Map p685; ☽ 11am-2:30am) and old-fashioned burgers from Binion's Snack Bar (Map p685).

Pullman Bar & Grille (Map p685; ☎ 702-387-1896; Main St Station, 200 N Main St; mains $20-40; ☽ dinner Wed-Sat) A well-kept secret, the clubby Pullman has the finest Black Angus beef and seafood specialties, and a good wine list, amidst gorgeous carved wood paneling and priceless antiques. The centerpiece namesake is a 1926 Pullman train car, now a cigar lounge.

Florida Café (Map p682; ☎ 702-385-3013; Howard Johnson's, 1401 Las Vegas Blvd S; mains $5-16; ☽ 7am-10pm) The hub of Naked City's Cuban community is advertised on bus stops all over town, but don't let that dissuade you from the authentic shredded steak, fried pork and seasoned chicken with yellow rice. *Café con leche* (coffee with milk), flan and *batidos* (tropical shakes) are superb.

UNLV & East of the Strip

Firefly (Map p682; ☎ 702-369-3971; Citibank Plaza, 3900 Paradise Rd; dishes $3-10, mains $10-20; ☽ lunch Mon-Fri, dinner 5pm-2am Sun-Thu, 5pm-3am Fri & Sat) Firefly is always hopping. Spain shakes hands with Asia, as chorizo clams jostle alongside shrimp potstickers. The backlit bar pours sangria and lychee-infused vodka, while turntablists or live Brazilian bands perform.

Mr Lucky's (Map p682; ☎ 702-693-5000; Hard Rock, 4455 Paradise Rd; dishes $5-10; ☽ 24hr) Though the Hard Rock has more famous eateries, such as Nobu and Simon Kitchen & Bar, this all-hours diner is just steps away from the happening casino floor. The comfort food menu doesn't list the $7.77 surf-and-turf special: a juicy 8oz steak, three jumbo shrimp and starchy sides.

Paymon's Mediterranean Café (Map p682; ☎ 702-731-6030; 4147 S Maryland Pkwy; dishes $6-10; ☽ 11am-1am Mon-Thu, 11am-3am Fri & Sat) One of the city's few veggie spots, serving up baked eggplant with fresh garlic, hummus, tabouli and baba ghanoush. Carnivores get kebab sandwiches, gyros or rotisserie lamb. The adjacent Hookah Lounge is a tranquil spot to chill with a water pipe and a fig-flavored cocktail.

West of the Strip

N9NE (☎ 702-933-9900; Palms, 4321 W Flamingo Rd; mains $28-42; ☽ dinner) A sexy mod steakhouse

---

> ### AUTHOR'S CHOICE
>
> **Rosemary's** (☎ 702-869-2251; 8125 W Sahara Ave; 3-course prix fixe lunch/dinner $21/40; ☽ lunch Mon-Fri, dinner daily) Words fail to describe the epicurean ecstasy you'll encounter here. Yes, it's a very long drive from the Strip. But once you bite into heavenly offerings like Texas BBQ shrimp with blue cheese 'slaw, roasted chestnut soup or Creole honey mustard–glazed salmon, you'll forget about everything else. Wine and beer pairings make each course sublime.

packed with celebs. The dramatically lit room centers on the champagne caviar bar, while the Chicago-style aged steaks and chops are ordered up along with everything from oysters Rockefeller to sashimi.

Alizé (☎ 702-951-7000; 56th fl, Palms, 4321 W Flamingo Rd; mains $28-55; ☽ dinner) Local chef André Rochat's top-drawer gourmet room is named after the gentle French Mediterranean trade wind. The panoramic floor-to-ceiling views are stunning, just like the haute French cuisine and impressive wine tower.

Ping Pang Pong (☎ 702-367-7111; Gold Coast, 4000 W Flamingo Rd; mains $7-30; ☽ 5pm-3am) The name's fun to say, isn't it? Designed by star chef Kevin Wu, a wok-tossed menu ranges across the regions of China, from Cantonese roast chicken to Beijing seafood stew. Service is fast and furious at this casual spot.

DRINKING

Angling for a free drink? Most booze consumption takes place while staring down slot machines and gaming tables. But hotel megaresort bars and ultra lounges, plus a few independent watering holes, offer plenty of diversity. You'll never be left out to dry in Vegas.

Ghost Bar (☎ 702-942-7777; Palms, 4321 W Flamingo Rd; cover $10-20; ☽ 8pm-4am) A clubby crowd, often thick with celebs, packs this 55th-floor ultra lounge. DJs spin pop while patrons sip overpriced cocktails amidst the sky-high 360-degree panoramas and sci-fi decor.

Tabú (Map p682; ☎ 702-891-7183; MGM Grand, 3799 Las Vegas Blvd S; cover $10-20; ☽ 10pm-dawn Tue-Sun) Stylish indulgence and sensual sophistication rule at Vegas' original ultra lounge. DJs spin to an interactive backdrop; stunning model/hostesses mix the cocktails tableside.

LAS VEGAS VALLEY

Also check out the glowing lotus blossom and go-go girls inside the MGM's Teatro.

Mix (Map p682; ☎ 702-632-9500; 64th fl, Mandalay Bay, 3950 Las Vegas Blvd S; cover after 10pm $20-25; ☾ 5pm-1am Sun-Thu, 5pm-2am Fri & Sat) This is *the* place to grab sunset cocktails. The glassed-in elevator has amazing views, and that's before you glimpse the mod interior design and the champagne bar.

Caramel (Map p682; ☎ 702-693-8300; Bellagio, 3600 Las Vegas Blvd S; ☾ 5pm-4am) This buttery yellow and rich chocolate lounge shakes a mean martini while DJs spin retro tunes to 21st-century hip-hop. The velvet curtains, leather couches, handblown glass sculptures and plasma TVs will keep you mesmerized. The Bellagio's Fontana Bar patio overlooks the fountains.

rumjungle (Map p682; ☎ 702-632-7408; Mandalay Bay, 3950 Las Vegas Blvd S; no cover before 11pm; ☾ until 2am Sun, Tue & Wed, until 4am Mon & Thu-Sat) Take a seat for a dark, light or spicy rum flight from the 100-bottle tower. A headless statue of Lenin invites comrades next door behind the blood-red curtains of Red Square, with its solid ice bar and specialty vodkas.

Napoleon's (Map p682; ☎ 702-946-7000; Paris–Las Vegas, 3645 Las Vegas Blvd S; ☾ 4pm-2am) Whisk yourself off to a never-neverland of 19th-century France, with overstuffed sofas and over 100 types of bubbly, including vintage Dom Perignon. A cigar humidor, dueling pianos and a happy-hour carving station make it worth a detour.

Nine Fine Irishmen (Map p682; ☎ 702-740-6969; New York–New York, 3790 Las Vegas Blvd S; ☾ 11am-11pm Mon-Fri, 9am-11pm Sat & Sun) Built in Ireland and shipped over to America, this pub has semiprivate booths, open-air tables next to Brooklyn Bridge and live entertainment.

ESPN Zone (Map p682; ☎ 702-933-3776; New York–New York, 3790 Las Vegas Blvd S; ☾ 11:30am-midnight Mon-Thu, 11:30am-1am Fri, 11am-1am Sat, 11am-midnight Sun) A sports fan's wildest dream come true. ESPN Zone has 'Zone Throne' viewing stations and state-of-the-art sports games and duckpin bowling upstairs.

Fireside Lounge (Map p682; ☎ 702-735-4177; Peppermill, 2985 Las Vegas Blvd S; ☾ 24hr) The Strip's most unlikely romantic hideaway is inside a retro coffee shop. Courting couples flock here for the sunken fire pit and cozy nooks built for cuddling. Skip the food – sup a Scorpion.

Beauty Bar (Map p685; ☎ 702-598-1965; 517 E Fremont Street; cover $5-15; ☾ 5pm-4am Wed-Fri, 9pm-4am Tue, Sat & Sun) The fad that started in New York, then spread to San Francisco and LA, has arrived in Vegas. The bar is actually the salvaged innards of a 1950s New Jersey beauty salon. Swill a cocktail while you get a manicure demo and chill out with the hip DJs.

Triple 7 (Map p685; ☎ 702-387-1896; Main St Station, 200 N Main St; ☾ 24hr) Locals crowd this cavernous spot for happy hour and graveyard specials. It has a sushi and oyster bar, draught homebrews and cheap pub grub.

Chicago Brewing Company (Map p685; ☎ 702-385-4011; Four Queens, 202 E Fremont Street; ☾ 11:30am-1am) With just a dozen bar stools set up in front of video poker machines, this friendly place overlooks the casino floor. The pizza ain't like in the Windy City, but the beer sampler ($5) should be enough to satisfy you, with Ultimate Weiss, Black Star, Red Rocker and Old Town Brown.

Center Stage (Map p685; ☎ 702-386-2512; Plaza, 1 Main St; ☾ 4pm-midnight) With its signature glass dome hovering at eye level with the Fremont Street Experience, this hideaway has a nightly lounge singer and piano player. Dress up so you don't feel out of place.

ENTERTAINMENT

Vegas is the original Disneyland for adults. Prostitution may be illegal, but there are plenty of strip clubs offering the illusion of sex on demand. Production shows are big business, too, from Cirque du Soleil to cheesy showgirls to the celebrity impersonators at the Imperial Palace. If you are not picky, save money at the Strip's half-price **ticket booths** (Map p682; ☾ noon-9pm) at the Fashion Show Mall and the big Coca-Cola bottle near MGM Grand. Call **Ticketmaster** (☎ 702-474-4000; www.ticketmaster.com) for music and sports events, including championship boxing at Mandalay Bay, the MGM Grand and the Orleans. Call **Fandango** (☎ 800-326-3264; www.fandango.com) for cinema listings.

Clubs

Little expense has been spared to bring clubs at the Strip's megaresorts on par with New York and Los Angeles. Most dance clubs are open from 10pm to 3am later in the week.

Pure (Map p682; ☎ 702-731-7873; Caesars Palace, 3570 Las Vegas Blvd S; cover $10-30; ☾ 10pm-dawn Fri-Tue) With the most immovable bouncers in Vegas, this modern-chic space is the hottest club on the Strip. Crowds of fine young thangs

---

GAY & LESBIAN LAS VEGAS

Queer Las Vegas exists, but it's largely unmapped. Public displays of affection (whether gay or straight) aren't very common, or appreciated by the moral majority in this conservative town.

Kräve (Map p682; ☎ 702-836-0830; Desert Passage, 3663 Las Vegas Blvd S; cover $10-20; ☾ 10pm-6am Fri & Sat, 6pm-4am Sun), off Harmon Ave, is the hottest nightclub, and the only one on the Strip.

The flamboyant Fruit Loop area, a mile east of the Strip near UNLV, is the queer epicenter. **Hamburger Mary's** (Map p682; ☎ 702-735-4400; 4503 Paradise Rd; ☾ 11am-1am) restaurant has trivia, karaoke, TV and bingo nights. **Gipsy** (Map p682; ☎ 702-731-1919; 4605 Paradise Rd; cover $5-10; ☾ 9pm-late) nightclub often has drag shows.

Pick up free copies of **Bugle QVEGAS** (www.qvegas.com) and **Out Las Vegas** (www.outlasvegas.com) at the **Pride Factory** (Map p682; ☎ 702-444-1291; Commercial Center, 953 E Sahara Ave; ☾ 10am-midnight) café.

---

lounge inside a labyrinth of rooms that make it feel like LA, especially now that the Pussycat Dolls Lounge has arrived. Dress to kill.

Rain (☎ 702-942-6832; Palms, 4321 W Flamingo Rd; cover $10-25; ☾ 11pm-late Thu-Sat) Britney Spears threw an impromptu concert when partying at this ostentatious club. Enter through a bright futuristic tunnel and be immersed in color and motion. The bamboo dance floor appears to float on a bed of fountains, with drama-queen fog and pyrotechnics.

Tangerine (Map p682; ☎ 702-992-7970; TI (Treasure Island), 3300 S Las Vegas Blvd; cover $20-40; ☾ 10pm-4am Tue-Sat) TI turns up the heat with its new orange-flavored lounge and nightclub. DJs spin pop, house and hip-hop, while burlesque dancers heat up the bartop hourly. The outdoor patio is a gorgeous place to sip.

Forty Deuce (Map p682; ☎ 702-632-9442; Mandalay Place, 3930 Las Vegas Blvd S; cover $10-25; ☾ 10pm-4am Wed & Sun, 10pm-6am Thu-Sat) A speakeasy vibe pervades this hidden club, where you can feast your eyes on the smoking-hot traditional burlesque acts backed by a brassy, three-piece band. Acts appear on stage every 90 minutes or so.

Gilley's (Map p682; ☎ 702-794-8434; New Frontier, 3120 Las Vegas Blvd; cover up to $10; ☾ 4pm-late) Yee-haw! The Strip's only country-and-western dance hall and saloon, with a lusty, mostly male crowd coming for the bikini mud wrestling and mechanical bull riding. It's named after the Houston honky-tonk featured in *Urban Cowboy*, starring John Travolta.

Ice (Map p682; ☎ 702-699-9888; 200 E Harmon Ave; cover $5-20; ☾ 10pm-4pm Wed, 10pm-6am Fri & Sat) Stellar DJs spin at this off-Strip jewel box, home to internationally renowned 'Godskitchen' events on Saturday nights. Deep house, trance and techno play in the main

multistoried dance hall, while the sidecar lounge heaves with hip-hop, retro '80s and mash-ups.

Live Music

House of Blues (Map p682; ☎ 702-632-7600; Mandalay Bay, 3950 Las Vegas Blvd S; tickets $15-100) Blues is the tip of the hog at this Mississippi Delta juke joint. Seating is limited, so show up early if you want to take a load off. The sightlines are good and the outside folk art is übercool. Monday and Tuesday nights, the restaurant features free 'Rock Star Karaoke' with a live band.

Joint (Map p682; ☎ 702-693-5066; Hard Rock, 4455 Paradise Rd; tickets $25-100) Concerts at this intimate venue feel like private shows, even when Bob Dylan or the Rolling Stones are in town. Most shows are standing room only, with reservable VIP balcony seats upstairs.

Double Down Saloon (Map p682; ☎ 702-791-5775; 4640 Paradise Rd; ☾ 24hr) You just gotta love a dive whose tangy, blood-red house drink is named Ass Juice. The jukebox vibrates with New Orleans jazz, British punk, Chicago blues and surf-guitar king Dick Dale. There's never a cover charge and they don't accept credit cards. Live local bands go on stage around 10pm almost every night.

Comedy

Big-name comedians headline at the Las Vegas Hilton, MGM Grand, Flamingo and Stardust.

Second City (Map p682; ☎ 702-733-3333, 800-221-7299; Flamingo, 3555 Las Vegas Blvd S; admission $33; ☾ performances 8pm daily, also 10:30pm Fri & Sat) For the best-value sketch comedy acts in the city, try this national chain theater. It goes totally 'scriptless' on Wednesday.

LAS VEGAS VALLEY

The Improv (Map p682; ☎ 702-369-5223; Harrah's, 3475 Las Vegas Blvd S; admission $25; ☼ performances 8:30pm & 10:30pm Tue-Sun) Harrah casino's well-established showcase spotlights touring stand-up headliners *du jour*.

SHOPPING

The metro area has over 40 million sq ft of retail space.

Malls

Most casino shops are open from 10am to 11pm (until midnight on Friday and Saturday nights).

Forum Shops (Map p682; ☎ 702-893-4800; Caesars Palace, 3500 Las Vegas Blvd S) Franklins fly out of Fendi bags fast here at the nation's most profitable consumer playground. In the mélange of 150 shops are catwalk wonders Armani, Escada, Versace and MAC Cosmetics. Don't miss Caesars' Exotic Cars showroom, the Playboy boutique or the high-tech gizmos at Sony Style.

Grand Canal Shoppes (Map p682; ☎ 702-414-4500; Venetian, 3355 Las Vegas Blvd S) Living statues, jugglers and mezzosopranos perform on cobblestone walkways that wind past 80 upscale shops like Ann Taylor, Banana Republic, Godiva, Kenneth Cole and Jimmy Choo.

Fashion Show Mall (Map p682; ☎ 702-369-0704; 3200 Las Vegas Blvd S; ☼ 10am-9pm Mon-Fri, 10am-8pm Sat, 11am-6pm Sun) Nevada's biggest and flashiest – and the Strip's only – mall is anchored by seven major department stores. Models hit the runway almost daily while movie stars shop at Talulah G boutique. 'The Cloud' multimedia shade canopy is out front.

Wynn Esplanade (Map p682; ☎ 702-770-7000; 3131 Las Vegas Blvd S) Wynn has lured high-end retailers such as Oscar de la Renta, Jean-Paul Gaultier, Cartier and Manolo Blahnik to a 75,000-sq-ft concourse of consumer bliss. After you hit the jackpot, take a test drive at the Ferarri-Maserati dealership.

Via Bellagio (Map p682; ☎ 702-693-7111; Bellagio, 3600 Las Vegas Blvd S) Bellagio's swish indoor promenade is home to the who's who of the fashion world: Armani, Chanel, Dior, Gucci, Hermés, Prada, Tiffany and Yves Saint Laurent. Fred Leighton has the world's most prestigious collection of antique jewelry.

Mandalay Place (Map p682; ☎ 702-632-7777; 3930 Las Vegas Blvd S) Beteewn Mandalay Bay and the Luxor, M-Bay's upscale promenade houses a few dozen, fashion-forward boutiques, in-

cluding Samantha Chang, Sauvage, GF Ferre, Oilily and super-mod 55° Wine + Design.

Hard Rock (Map p682; ☎ 702-693-5000; 4455 Paradise Rd) The casino hotel's gift shop has limited-edition rock and roll collectibles, but why stop there? Love Jones has imported lingerie; Cuba Libre cigar humidor serves specialty martinis, scotch and cognac; and Rocks, a 24-hour jewelry store, sells diamonds anytime.

Las Vegas Premium Outlets (Map p685; ☎ 702-474-7500; 875 S Grand Central Pkwy; ☼ 10am-9pm Mon-Sat, 10am-8pm Sun) The most upscale of Vegas' outlets features 120 high-end names like Armani Exchange, Dolce & Gabbana, Guess, Kenneth Cole and Polo Ralph Lauren, alongside more casual brands like Levi's.

Desert Passage (Map p682; ☎ 888-800-8284; Planet Hollywood-Aladdin, 3663 Las Vegas Blvd S) Aladdin's upscale North African–themed marketplace has a rainy harbor and 140 retailers with an emphasis on jewelry, gifts and women's apparel. Pedicabs await to transport all the baggage-laden shoppers along the 1.2-mile-long shopping arcade to remote parking.

Clothing

Buffalo Exchange (Map p682; ☎ 702-791-3960; 4110 S Maryland Pkwy; ☼ 10am-8pm Mon-Sat, 11am-7pm Sun) Trade in your nearly new garb for cash or credit at this second-hand chain. They've combed through the dingy thrift store stuff and culled only the best 1940-70s vintage fashions, clubwear, costuming goodies and designer duds. A real find.

Attic (Map p685; ☎ 702-388-4088; 1018 S Main St; ☼ 9am-5pm Mon-Sat) A $1 'lifetime pass' is required to enter this vintage emporium, but it's worth it. The 1st floor is mostly furnishings. Upstairs, the 1960s and '70s are strengths, with a smaller pre-1950s selection and a cool retro coffee bar.

Cowtown Boots (Map p682; ☎ 702-737-8469; 2989 Paradise Rd; ☼ 10am-7pm Mon-Sat, 10am-5pm Sun) A Western-wear wonderland for rattlesnake, ostrich, crocodile, eel and more exotically skinned boots. An expertly crafted and hand-trimmed pair is easily worth the $100 or more you'll pay.

Strings by Judith (☎ 702-873-7820; 4970 Arville St; ☼ 10am-9pm) It should come as no surprise that the adult apparel business is ba-bah-booming. All those hard-working dancers obviously don't have time to make their own G-strings and tasseled undies. This industrial warehouse outfits you from head to toe, with almost nothing in between.

Specialty Shops

Houdini's Magic Shop (Map p682; ☎ 702-740-6969; New York–New York, 3790 Las Vegas Blvd S; ☺ 9am-midnight) The legendary escape artist's legacy lives on at this shop packed with gags, pranks, magic tricks and 'zines. Magicians perform for wide-eyed crowds. Every purchase includes a free private lesson.

Gamblers General Store (Map p685; ☎ 702-382-9903; 800 S Main St; ☺ 9am-5pm) This store boasts one of the largest inventories of slot machines in Nevada, with new models and beautiful vintage machines, and loads of gambling paraphernalia.

Gun Store (☎ 702-454-1110; 2900 E Tropicana Ave; ☺ 9am-6:30pm) Attention wannabe Schwarzeneggers: this high-powered shop offers you the chance to fire off live submachine gun rounds in its indoor range, not to mention the massive cache of weapons for sale.

Adult Superstore (☎ 702-798-0144; 3850 W Tropicana Ave; ☺ 24hr) Popular with couples, this huge, well-lit porn warehouse has more pussies than the SPCA: books, magazines, videos, tasteful 'marital enhancement products,' and titillating accessories.

GETTING THERE & AWAY
Air

Las Vegas has direct flights from most US cities and from a few Canadian, European and Asian gateways. Arriving via a package that includes airfare and accommodations is sometimes the best deal. Check casino and airline websites and newspaper travel sections for specials.

Just a crap shoot from the south end of the Strip, **McCarran International Airport** (LAS; Map p682; ☎ 702-261-5211; www.mccarran.com) has ATMs, a bank, post office, 24-hour fitness center (day pass $10), free wi-fi, tourist information and slot machines. Free shuttles link domestic and international terminals. Short-term metered parking costs 25¢ per 10 minutes.

Bus & Train

Downtown, **Greyhound** (Map p685; ☎ 702-384-9561, 800-231-2222; www.greyhound.com; 200 S Main St) has buses to and from Los Angeles ($29 to $40, five to seven hours), San Diego ($39 to $49, 7¾ to 9½ hours), San Francisco ($49 to $70, .13¾ to 16½ hours) and Reno ($39

to $71, 20 to 22½ hours). Ask at the hostels about backpacker shuttles.

Talk of reviving the **Amtrak** (☎ 800-872-7245; www.amtrak.com) train services persists, but for now the closest stations are in Kingman, AZ (105 miles away), Needles, CA (p665), and Barstow, CA (p660).

Greyhound provides connecting Thruway bus services daily.

Car & Motorcycle

The main roads are I-15 to and from California, and US 95, the chief north–south artery to Reno, 450 miles away (a 6½-hour drive). US Hwy 93 leads east from downtown to Hoover Dam; I-215 goes by McCarran Airport. It takes about four to five hours to get here from Los Angeles (270 miles); 4½ to 5½ hours from San Diego (330 miles); and nine to 10 hours from San Francisco (570 miles). On weekends and holidays, trip times can double or even triple. For road condition updates, phone ☎ 877-687-6237 for Nevada and ☎ 800-427-7623 for California. Along I-15, Highway Radio (98.1FM and 99.7FM) has traffic and weather updates every 30 minutes.

GETTING AROUND
To/From the Airport

Taxi fares to Strip hotels (30 minutes in heavy traffic) run $10 to $20, or to downtown $15 to $25, cash only. Fare gouging ('long-hauling') through the airport connector tunnel instead of using Paradise Rd is common. Most airport shuttles operate from 7am to midnight, but some run 24 hours. They charge $5 per person to the Strip, $6 to downtown or off-Strip hotels. Some hotels offer free airport pick-up and return. If you're traveling light and staying on Fremont Street, city bus 109 ($1.25, 35 minutes) runs 24/7 to the Downtown Transportation Center (DTC).

Bus

Local buses operated by **Citizens Area Transit** (CAT; ☎ 702-228-7433, 800-228-3911; www.catride.com) run from 5:30am to 1:30am daily, with the most popular Strip and downtown routes running 24/7. The fare is $1.25, except on Las Vegas Blvd bus 301 and express bus 302 ($2); exact change is required. Free transfers and day passes ($5) are available from drivers.

Car & Motorcycle

Booking ahead rental cars gets you the best rates, with the airport being cheaper than downtown or the Strip. Las Vegas is a way more expensive place to rent a car than California. See p724 for rental companies and policies.

For something glamorous, ring **Rent-A-Vette** (Map p682; ☎ 800-372-1981; www.rent-a-vette .com; 5021 Swenson St). Corvettes and exotic convertibles easily fetch $200 or more per day. **Las Vegas Motorcycle Rentals** (Map p682; ☎ 877-571-7174; www.lvhd.com; 2605 S Eastern Ave) rents Harleys from $90 to $155 per day, including unlimited mileage.

Traffic moves along at a decent clip, except during morning and afternoon rush hours and on weekend nights, especially along the Strip. Work out in advance which cross street will bring you closest to your destination and utilize alternate routes like Industrial Rd and Paradise Rd. Tune to 970AM for traffic updates.

There's free self-parking everywhere on the Strip. For valet parking, there's no charge (but tip $2 when your keys are returned). The downtown casino hotels offer free self-parking (four-hour maximum stay) if you validate the parking stub inside the casino (no purchase required).

Monorail & Tram

The **monorail** (☎ 702-699-8299; rides $3, 1/3-day pass $10/25; ☼ 7am-2am) links properties along the Strip corridor. Currently monorail stations are at MGM Grand; Bally's/Paris–Las Vegas; Flamingo/Caesars Palace; Harrah's/Imperial Palace; Convention Center; Las Vegas Hilton; and the Sahara. A discounted 10-ride ticket ($20) can be used by multiple riders.

There are free private trams that connect TI (Treasure Island) and the Mirage; the Excalibur, Luxor and Mandalay Bay; and the Monte Carlo and the Bellagio (may be suspended).

Taxi

Taxi stands are found at casino hotels, but it's impossible to hail one on the Strip. The fares (cash only) are metered. A 4½-mile lift along the entire Strip runs between $10 and $15 (plus tip), depending on traffic. Reputable companies include **Yellow/Checker/Star** (☎ 702-873-2000).

AROUND LAS VEGAS

You don't have to go as far as the Grand Canyon or Utah's Zion National Park just to experience the natural glories of the American Southwest.

RED ROCK CANYON NATIONAL CONSERVATION AREA

The startling contrast between the artificial neon of Vegas and the awesome splendor of this conservation area (Map p678), a 20-mile drive west of the Strip, can't be exaggerated. It's especially impressive around sunrise or sunset.

A 13-mile, one-way **scenic loop drive** (☼ 6am-dusk) passes striking features, with access to hiking trails and world-class rock climbing routes. Pay the day-use fee ($5) at the entrance station, then stop by the **visitor center** (☎ 702-515-5367; www.redrockcanyonlv.org; ☼ 8:30am-4:30pm), which has free maps and brochures, natural history exhibits and information about all kinds of activities.

You can rent mountain bikes in Blue Diamond at **McGhie's Bike Outpost** (☎ 702-875-4820; www.bikeoutpost.com; rental per day $35, guided tour $109; ☼ Wed-Sun), en route from the Strip. Horseback trips with **Silver State Tours** (☎ 702-798-7788; www.silverstatetours.com; guided rides $28-115) depart from historic Spring Mountain Ranch State Park, also nearby.

First-come, first-served free campsites with water and pit toilets are available at **Red Rock Canyon Campground** (☎ 702-515-5352; ☼ Sep-May), 2 miles east of the visitor center.

From the Strip, you can take I-15 south, exit Blue Diamond Rd (NV 160) westbound, then veer right onto NV 159. On the return trip, take NV 159 east, which turns into W Charleston Blvd.

HOOVER DAM

The 726ft-high, concrete Hoover Dam (Map p678) was once the tallest dam in the world. Its has a striking art deco beauty, with an imposing, graceful curve backed by the brilliant blue waters of Lake Mead. A New Deal project, construction of the dam in the 1930s provided much-needed employment as the country struggled through the Great Depression.

The recommended **Discovery Tour** (☎ 702-294-3517, reservations 866-291-8687; adult/child 7-16/

LAS VEGAS VALLEY

senior & military $10/5/8; ☼ 9am-4:45pm) starts below ground at the **Hoover Dam Visitor Center** (www .usbr.gov/lc/hooverdam) with a short video. Then ride the elevators 50 stories down to the dam's massive power generators, each of which could power a city of 100,000 people. Above ground, 30ft-high **Winged Figures of the Republic** memorializes the men who built this engineering triumph. Arrive early in the day to avoid long lines.

From the Strip, take I-15 south to I-215 and continue on to I-515/US 93 and 95 past Boulder City, which has motels, cafés and the **Hoover Dam Museum** (☎ 702-294-1988; Boulder Dam Hotel, 1305 Arizona St; admission $2; ☼ 10am-5pm Mon-Sat, noon-5pm Sun).

Approaching the dam, park in the multi-level garage ($5, cash only) before you reach the Arizona state line.

LAKE MEAD NATIONAL RECREATION AREA

This sprawling **national recreation area** (Map p678; www.nps.gov/lame; 5-day entry pass $5), encompasses 110-mile long Lake Mead, 67-mile long Lake Mohave and many miles of desert.

Lake Mead has year-round boat cruises, swimming, waterskiing and even scuba diving. The **Alan Bible Visitor Center** (☎ 702-293-8990; ☼ 8:30am-4:30pm) is located 4 miles west of Hoover Dam. **Lakeshore Scenic Drive** winds around the lake, passing campgrounds, hiking trailheads and marinas, becoming **Northshore Road** about halfway to Valley of Fire State Park.

South of Hoover Dam past Lake Mojave on US 95, **Laughlin** is a gambling gulch with old-fashioned casino hotels along the west bank of the Colorado River. **Golden Nugget Laughlin** (☎ 702-298-7111, 800-950-7700; www.golden nugget.com; 2300 S Casino Dr; r weekday/weekend from $21/92) has the poshest rooms and dining. Laughlin is 100 miles southeast of Las Vegas, just 25 miles north of Needles, CA (p665).

VALLEY OF FIRE STATE PARK

Near the north end of Lake Mead, this **state park** (Map p678; admission $6) is a masterpiece of desert scenery, with psychedelic sandstone carved in fantastical shapes by wind and water. Plentiful petroglyphs are a reminder of early Native American tribes who dwelled here.

NV 169 runs through the park, right past the **visitor center** (☎ 702-397-2088; http://parks.nv .gov/vf.htm; ☼ 8:30am-4:30pm), which has excellent exhibits, general information and hiking suggestions. The winding side road to **White Domes** passes scenic **Rainbow Vista** and the 3-mile round-trip hiking trailhead to **Fire Canyon** and **Silica Dome**, where Captain Kirk perished in *Star Trek: Generations*.

The valley is at its most fiery at dawn and dusk, so consider staying overnight in one of the two first-come, first-served **campgrounds** (sites incl admission $14; ☼ year-round), which have water, toilets, showers and barbecue grills.

The quickest route to the park from Las Vegas is I-15 to NV 169, which takes about an hour.

LAS VEGAS VALLEY

Directory

CONTENTS

ACCOMMODATIONS

California offers all types of places to unpack your suitcase, from hostels, campgrounds and B&Bs to chain motels, hotels and luxury resorts. Reservations are a good idea, especially if you're traveling in the busy summer season (June to September). Rooms can also be scarce and prices high around major holidays (see p706).

Prices listed in this book are for peak-season travel (usually summer) and, unless stated otherwise, do not include taxes.

This book categorizes accommodations as budget, midrange and top end. Budget recommendations won't put you more than $90 (per double) out of pocket and will have you checking in at hostels, motels, basic hotels and campgrounds. Midrange accommodations generally offer the best value for

money, which is why most of our listings fall into this category. Expect to pay between $90 and $175 for a clean, comfortable and decent-sized double room with at least a modicum of style, a private bathroom and a slew of amenities, including cable TV, direct-dial telephone, a coffeemaker, perhaps a microwave and a small refrigerator. Many midrange properties also have swimming pools and communal Jacuzzi tubs.

Top end properties (costing $175 and up per double) offer an international standard of amenities and perhaps a scenic location, special decor or historical ambience. Swimming pools are pretty standard and facilities such as saunas, fitness rooms and business centers are common. Unless you're going to use these facilities, though, it's rarely worth the extra cost over midrange hotels.

Note that we've had to stretch these definitions a bit in expensive cities, most notably Los Angeles and San Francisco, where 'budget' can mean paying up to $100 per double and 'midrange' places can end up costing up as much as $200.

Smoking rooms are becoming increasingly rare in health-conscious California. Where they exist, they are often in less desirable locations or the last to receive renovations.

Smokefree properties are identified with the nonsmoking icon ( ) throughout this book. Some owners levy a hefty 'clean-up fee' on guests who smoke inside their nonsmoking rooms.

More and more properties are offering free or fee-based wireless Internet access (wi-fi). Those with Internet access for guests who aren't traveling with their own gear are designated with the Internet icon ( ).

Prices listed in this book do not – and in fact cannot – take into account seasonal variations or promotional discounts. Many establishments drop prices in the low season, especially in winter (except in the desert and the ski areas). City hotels geared to the suit brigade often try to lure leisure travelers with weekend specials. Membership in the **American Automobile Association** (AAA; ☎ 800-874-7532; www.aaa.com) or another automobile club, the **American Association of Retired Persons** (AARP; ☎ 800-687-2277; www.aarp.org) and other organizations may get you modest savings (usually around 10%) at any time of the year. Also look out for freebie ad rags packed with hotel discount coupons at gas stations and tourist offices.

The online agencies such as www.orbitz.com, www.expedia.com, www.travelocity.com and www.hotel.com may offer you a better rate than what you'd get if you booked directly with the hotel. A handy Web resource is **TripAdvisor** (www.tripadvisor.com), which features both reader and published reviews, and also simultaneously searches for rates offered by the aforementioned agencies for some of the properties. For an even more exhaustive rate comparison, try **Travelaxe** (www.travelaxe.com), which has several filters to help you narrow down your search (eg distance from the town center or airport, price, comfort level). It requires a free software download (spyware-free, so they say). You should also check out hotel websites for special online rates or packages.

B&Bs

Bed-and-breakfast lodging is usually high-end accommodations in converted private homes, typically fine old Victorians or other heritage buildings. Owners take great pride in decorating the guest rooms and common areas and a personal interest in ensuring that you enjoy your stay. People in need of lots of privacy may find B&Bs a bit too intimate.

Rates typically include a lavish, home-cooked breakfast. Amenities vary widely, but rooms with TV and telephone are the exception; the cheapest units share bathroom facilities. Most B&Bs require advance reservations, though some will accommodate the occasional drop-in guest. Smoking is generally prohibited and minimum stays are common in peak season and on weekends.

Many places belong to the **California Association of Bed & Breakfast Inns** (☎ 831-462-9191; www.cabbi.com).

Camping

Camping in California is so much more than just a cheap way to spend the night. The nicest sites have you waking up to breezy ocean views, shimmering lakes, splendid rock formations or a canopy of pines. Many campgrounds, especially in the mountains and in northern California, are closed in winter. Actual opening and closing dates vary slightly each year, depending on weather conditions.

Basic campsites usually have fire pits, picnic benches and access to drinking water and pit or vault toilets. These are most common in national forests managed by the United States Forest Service (USFS) and on Bureau of Land Management (BLM) land. Campgrounds in state and national parks tend to have more amenities, including flush toilets, sometimes hot showers and RV (recreational vehicle) hookups. Private campgrounds are usually close to cities and cater more to the RV crowd.

Most campgrounds accept reservations for all or some of their sites. The following websites let you search for locations, check availability, book a site, view maps and get driving directions.

National Park Service (☎ 800-365-2267, outside the USA 301-722-1257; http://reservations.nps.gov) Free campsite reservations in national parks; up to five months in advance on the fifth of each month. For Yosemite, call ☎ 800-436-7275.

National Recreation Reservation Service (NRRS; ☎ 877-444-6777, outside the USA 518-885-3639; www.reserveusa.com; per reservation $9) Reservations for campgrounds in national forests and on BLM land; up to 240 days in advance.

Reserve America (☎ 800-444-7275, outside the USA 916-638-5883; www.reserveamerica.com; per reservation $7.50) Reservations for camping in national forests, California state parks and private sites; up to seven months in advance.

DIRECTORY

THE CHAIN GANG

For additional chain hotels and motels not included in this guide, call these numbers:

Budget

Clarion Hotel (☎ 877-424-6423; www.clarion hotel.com)

Comfort Inn (☎ 877-424-6423; www.comfortinn .com)

Days Inn (☎ 800-329-7466; www.daysinn.com)

Econo Lodge (☎ 877-424-6423; www.econolodge .com)

Howard Johnson (☎ 800-446-4656; www.hojo.com)

Motel 6 (☎ 800-466-8356; www.motel6.com)

Quality Inn & Suites (☎ 877-424-6423; www .qualityinn.com)

Super 8 (☎ 800-800-8000; www.super8.com)

Travelodge (☎ 800-578-7878; www.travelodge.com)

Midrange

Best Western (☎ 800-780-7234; www.best western.com)

Embassy Suites (☎ 800-362-2779; www.embassy suites.com)

Fairfield Inn (☎ 800-228-2800; www.fairfieldinn .com)

Hampton Inn (☎ 800-426-7866; www.hampton inn.com)

Hilton (☎ 800-445-8667; www.hilton.com)

Holiday Inn (☎ 800-465-4329; www.holiday-inn.com)

Hyatt (☎ 888-591-1234; www.hyatt.com)

Marriott (☎ 888-236-2427; www.marriott.com)

Radisson (☎ 888-201-1718; www.radisson.com)

Ramada (☎ 800-272-6232; www.ramada.com)

Sheraton (☎ 888-625-5144; www.sheraton.com)

Westin (☎ 800-228-3000; www.westin.com)

Top End

Four Seasons (☎ 800-819-5053; www.fourseasons .com)

Ritz-Carlton (☎ 800-241-3333; www.ritz carlton.com)

St Regis (☎ 800-598-1863; www.stregis.com)

W Hotels (☎ 888-625-5144; www.whotels.com)

Hostels

California has 22 hostels affiliated with **Hostelling International** (☎ reservations 800-909-4776; www.hiusa.org), as well as a growing number of independent hostels, particularly in the cities. Indies tend to have a more convivial vibe, with regular guest parties and other organized events and activities. Some hostels include a light breakfast in their rates, arrange local tours or will pick up guests at transportation hubs. Some say they accept only international visitors (basically to keep out destitute locals), but Americans who look like they are travelers should not have a problem, especially during the slower months.

Besides dorms of varying sizes, many hostels have private rooms for couples and families, although bathrooms are usually shared. Other typical features include a communal kitchen, lockers, Internet access, a laundry room and a common room with TV, games and books.

Rates range from $14 to $27, tax included. HI hostels offer discounts to HI members. Reservations are always a good idea, especially during summer. Most hostels take bookings online and by phone, fax, mail or email. Many independent hostels belong to reservation services such as www.hostels .com, www.backpackers.com and www.hos telworld.com, which may offer lower rates than the hostels directly.

Hotels & Motels

Hotels differ from motels in that they don't surround a parking lot and usually have some sort of a lobby. Hotels may provide extra services such as laundry, but such conveniences usually come at a price. If you walk in without reservations, always ask to see a room before paying for it, especially at motels.

Rooms are often priced by the size and number of beds, rather than the number of occupants. A room with one double or queen-size bed usually costs the same for one or two people, while a room with a king-size bed or two double beds costs more. Rooms with two doubles can accommodate up to four people, making them a cost-saving choice for families and small groups. A small surcharge often applies to the third and fourth person, but children under a certain age (this varies) often stay free. Cribs or rollaway beds usually incur an extra charge.

Room location may also affect the price; recently renovated or larger rooms, or those with a nice view, are likely to cost more. Hotels facing a noisy street may charge extra for quieter rooms.

Many hotels offer suites for people in need of more elbow room. While this should technically get you at least two rooms, one of them a bedroom, this is not always the case as some properties simply call their larger rooms 'suites' or 'junior suites.' Always ask about a suite's size and layout before booking.

The rates increasingly include breakfast, which may be just a stale donut and wimpy coffee, an all-out gourmet affair with fresh croissants and homemade jam, or anything in between.

Make reservations at chain hotels by calling their central reservation lines (see the boxed text, opposite), but to learn about specific amenities and possible local promotions, call the property directly. Every listing in this book includes local direct numbers.

Resorts

One type of accommodation California has plenty of is full-service luxury resorts, usually with integrated spas offering the latest in pampering techniques. For busy urbanites they serve as quick getaways, places that offer a respite from the rat race and restore balance to body and soul. Luxury resorts are normally so attractive that they're often destinations in themselves.

Expect very comfortable, attractively designed rooms with quality furnishings and outfitted with pillow-top mattresses, fancy linens, down comforters and fluffy terrycloth bathrobes. Services include in-room massages, shoeshine and evening turndown; some of these require an extra fee. High-caliber restaurants serving three meals a day are commonplace, as are bars.

ACTIVITIES

For outdoor enthusiasts California offers the mother lode of possibilities. No matter what kind of activity gets you off that couch, you'll be able to pursue it in this land of lakes and rivers, ocean and mountains, deserts and forests. Everywhere you go, you'll find outfitters and local operators eager to gear you up. Flip the page to the California Outdoors chapter

for an overview of the main types of active pursuits that await in the Golden State.

BUSINESS HOURS

Standard business hours, including for most government offices, are 9am to 5pm Monday to Friday. Bank hours are usually from 9am to 5pm weekdays and many branches are also open on Saturday, usually from 9am to 2pm. Post offices do business from 8am to 4pm or 5:30pm weekdays, and many are open from 8am to 2pm on Saturday.

Restaurants typically serve lunch from 11:30am to 2:30pm and dinner from 5:30pm to 10pm daily. Pubs and bars welcome patrons from around 5pm until 2am nightly, while music and dance clubs open doors at 8pm or 9pm, though many on Friday and Saturday only. Most close at 2am, but if business is buzzing they may keep going until 3am or 4am.

Most shops open their doors around 10am, although noon is quite common for boutiques and art galleries. Closing time is anywhere from 5pm or 6pm to 9pm in shopping malls. Typical Sunday hours are noon to 5pm (until 6pm in malls). Convenience stores and supermarkets often don't close until 10pm or midnight and may even stay open around the clock, especially in the cities.

Any variations on the above are noted in individual reviews.

CHILDREN

California is a tailor-made destination for traveling with kids. Just be sure you involve the little ones in the day-to-day trip planning and don't pack the schedule too full. Lonely Planet's *Travel with Children* offers a wealth of tips and tricks on the subject. The websites www.travelwithyourkids.com and www.flyingwithkids.com are also good general resources.

Practicalities

Children enjoy a wide range of discounts for everything from museum admissions to bus fares and motel stays. The definition of a 'child' varies – in some places anyone under 18 is eligible, while others put the cut-off at age six. Airlines usually allow infants (up to the age of two) to fly for free, while older children requiring a seat of their

DIRECTORY

own qualify for reduced fares. Many also offer special kids' meals, although you need to pre-order them.

Hotels and motels commonly have rooms with two double beds or a double and a sofa bed, which are ideal for families. Even those that don't can bring in rollaway beds, usually for a small extra charge. Some properties offer 'kids stay free' promotions, although this may apply only if no extra bedding is required. Some B&Bs don't welcome children.

Larger hotels often have a babysitting service, and other hotels may be able to help you make arrangements. Alternatively, look in the *Yellow Pages* for local agencies. Be sure to ask whether the sitters are licensed, what they charge per hour, whether there's a minimum fee and whether they charge extra for meals and transportation.

It's perfectly fine to bring your kids, even toddlers, along to casual restaurants (although not to upscale ones at dinnertime) and for daytime events. Most eateries have high chairs, and if they don't have a specific children's menu, they can usually make a kid-tailored meal. For more details, see p72.

In vehicles, any child under the age of six or weighing less than 60lb must be restrained in a child safety or booster seat. Most car-rental firms rent these for about $8 per day, but it is essential that you book them in advance.

Baby food, infant formulas, soy and cow's milk, disposable diapers (nappies) and all other necessities are all widely available in drugstores and supermarkets. Breastfeeding in public is legal, although most women are discreet about it. Public toilets – in airports, stores, shopping malls, movie theaters etc – usually have nappy-changing tables.

Sights & Activities

It's easy to keep kids entertained no matter where you travel in California. The great outdoors yields endless possibilities. A day spent swimming, bodysurfing, snorkeling, bicycling, kayaking, horseback riding, walking or otherwise engaging in physical activity is sure to send the little ones quickly off to dreamland by day's end. The national and state parks run 'Junior Ranger' and other programs specially geared to children. Check http://kids.parks.ca.gov and www.nps.gov/learn for details. Outfitters and tour operators may also have dedicated kids' tours.

Even in the cities there's usually no shortage of entertaining options. Take them to parks, playgrounds, swimming pools, zoos or child-friendly museums. For specific suggestions, check out the City for Children sections in the destination chapters or the kid-themed Itinerary on p26. In addition, most tourist offices can lead you to local resources for children's programs, childcare facilities and pediatricians.

For more ideas also have a look at the articles available on www.thefamilytravelfiles .com/state/california.asp.

CLIMATE CHARTS

The climate charts provide a snapshot of California's weather patterns. For general advice on climate and the best times to travel in the state, see p16.

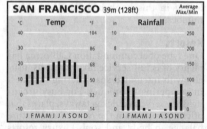

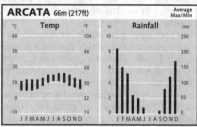

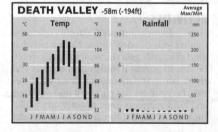

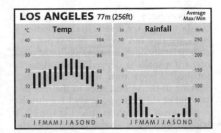

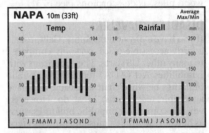

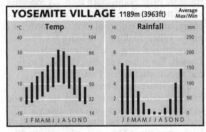

COURSES
For cooking courses, see p73.

DANGERS & ANNOYANCES
By and large, California is not a dangerous place. The most headline-grabbing problem is violent crime, but what the news often fails to convey is that the majority of incidents take place in areas where few travelers would venture anyway. Wildlife may pose some danger, and of course there is the dramatic, albeit unlikely, possibility of a natural disaster, such as an earthquake. Prepare for the worst, but expect the best.

Crime
Travelers will rarely get tricked, conned or attacked simply because they're tourists. Potential violence is a problem for all but there's really no need to be overly worried. Most cities have some 'bad neighborhoods,' which should be avoided, particularly after

dark. The Dangers & Annoyances sections in the destination chapters provide some details, and you could also quiz hotel staff or police officers about the latest no-go zones. Outside the cities, crime of all kinds drops dramatically.

To minimize the risk of trouble always maintain your street smarts and an awareness of your surroundings. Exercise particular caution in parking areas at night. Try to use ATMs in well-lit and well-trafficked areas. Don't carry lots of cash; keep the bulk of your money and your passport in a money belt inside your clothes; stash valuables inside your room safe, or the hotel safe. If your car is bumped from behind by another vehicle in a remote area, try to keep going to a well-lit area, gas station or even a police station.

If a mugger accosts you, there's no fail-safe policy. Handing over whatever the mugger wants may prevent serious injury, and having a separate amount of money in a front pocket, which can be handed over quickly, is often recommended. Muggers are not too happy to find their victims penniless.

That said – don't dwell on crime. The American media tend to blow crime out of proportion, giving the impression that you're going to get shot if you set foot on the wrong street. Don't panic. Protect yourself as best you can, then focus your awareness on having a great trip. You'll save yourself a lot of unnecessary mental anguish.

Earthquakes
Earthquakes happen all the time but most are so tiny, it takes sensitive seismological instruments even to register them. Chances of getting caught in a serious shaker are minuscule, but here are a few pointers on what to do (and not to do), just in case. Basically, if indoors, get under a desk, table or doorway. Protect your head and stay clear of windows, mirrors or anything that might fall. Don't head for elevators or go running into the street. If you're in a shopping mall or large public building, expect the alarm and/or sprinkler systems to come on.

If outdoors, get away from any buildings, trees and power lines. If you are driving, pull over to the side of the road away from bridges, overpasses and power lines. Stay inside the car until the shaking stops. If you're on a sidewalk close to buildings, duck into a doorway to protect yourself from falling

DIRECTORY

bricks, glass and debris. Prepare for after-shocks. Use the telephone only if absolutely necessary. Turn on the radio and listen for bulletins.

Scams

There are no scams unique to California. A healthy skepticism is your best defense. In restaurants it pays to study your final bill as some servers have been observed slipping in extra charges or adding their tip to the final tally without telling you (thereby hoping for a double tip). European visitors, who are per-ceived as cheap tippers, are especially prone to falling victim to this annoying practice.

Swimming

Popular beaches are patrolled by lifeguards, but even so some of them can be dangerous places to swim if you aren't used to the con-ditions. Rip currents are the main problem. If you find yourself being carried offshore by a rip, the important thing is to just keep afloat; don't panic or try to swim against the current, which will quickly exhaust you. In most cases, the current stops within a couple of hundred feet from the shore and you can then swim parallel to the shore for a while to get out of the rip and make your way back to land.

Wildlife

Wild animals, including squirrels, can be potentially dangerous if you invade their turf. Feeding them or getting too close will make them lose their innate fear of people – and eventually their lives to park rangers.

Bears – always on the lookout for an easy snack – often find campgrounds simply ir-resistible. The boxed text (p66) has full de-tails on how to avoid encounters and what to do if they happen anyway.

California is home to an estimated 4000 to 6000 mountain lions (also called cougars or pumas), which live in forests and mountains, especially in areas teeming with deer, which includes some areas in the desert and near the coast. Attacks on humans are extremely rare. If you encounter one, face the animal and retreat slowly trying to appear large by raising your arms or grabbing a stick. If at-tacked, you'll need to fight back aggressively, shouting and throwing rocks at it.

From spring to fall, encounters with rattle-snakes – California's only venomous snake –

are a possibility. Rattler country ranges from coastal areas to the deserts to the mountains. Bites are rare (an average of 800 per year, ending fatally once or twice) and most often occur if a snake is stepped on or otherwise touched. Always wear hiking boots when walking in the woods, stick to the trail and stay out of tall grass and heavy underbrush.

The most dangerous spider is the black widow, which often hides under rocks and wood piles, as do scorpions (see p731).

DISABLED TRAVELERS

If you have a physical disability, California is a fairly accessible place, certainly compared to many other US states. The Americans with Disabilities Act (ADA) requires that public buildings be wheelchair accessible and have accessible rest rooms. Most do. However, when it comes to nonpublic buildings, such as hotels, restaurants, museums and theaters, there are no guarantees. In theory, properties built after January 26, 1993 must be ADA compliant, but sadly violations are common-place. When making a lodging reservation, always make your particular needs clearly known. For other venues, call ahead to find out about what access issues to expect.

Many buses and trains have wheelchair lifts, and telephone companies are required to provide relay operators (available via TTY numbers) for the hearing impaired. Many banks provide ATM instructions in Braille, and you'll find dropped curbs at most in-tersections and sometimes audible crossing signals as well. The major car-rental agencies offer hand-controlled vehicles and vans with wheelchair lifts at no extra charge, but you *must* reserve them well in advance.

All the big airlines, Greyhound buses and Amtrak trains can accommodate people with disabilities, although they usually need at least a day or two advance notice. Just describe your specific needs when making reservations. Seeing-eye dogs are permitted to accompany passengers.

Most national and state parks and rec-reation areas have paved or boardwalk-style nature trails. For free admission to national parks, blind or permanently disabled US citizens and permanent residents can get a Golden Access Passport (p63).

There are a number of organizations and tour providers that specialize in serving disabled travelers:

INTERNET MOBILITY

Various organizations publish regional access guides, including:

A Wheelchair Rider's Guide: Los Angeles and Orange County Coast (http://www.scc .ca.gov/Wheel/index.html) Free download.

Access Guide: In San Diego (www.accessan diego.org) Order booklet for $5.

Access Northern California (www.access nca.com)

Theme Park Access Guide (www.mouse planet.com/tag/dlintro.htm) An insider's view of Disneyland and other parks 'on wheels.'

Access-Able Travel Source (☎ 303-232-2979; www .access-able.com) An excellent website with useful links.

Mobility International (www.miusa.org) UK (☎ 020-7403-5688); USA (☎ 541-343-1284) Advises disabled travelers on mobility issues and runs an educational exchange program.

Moss Rehabilitation Hospital's Travel Information Service (www.mossresourcenet.org/travel.htm) Lists extensive useful contacts.

New Directions (☎ 805-967-2841, 888-967-2841; www .newdirectionstravel.com) Specializes in developmentally disabled travelers.

Society for Accessible Travel & Hospitality (SATH; ☎ 212-447-7284; www.sath.org) Lots of useful links and information for disabled travelers.

DISCOUNT CARDS

If Southern California's theme parks are the focus of your trip, a **Southern California CityPass** (www.citypass.com) may be a wise investment. Passes cost $185 for adults and $127 for children ages three to nine, and buy three-day admission to Disneyland and Disney's California Adventure, one-day admission each to Knott's Berry Farm and SeaWorld and another day at either the San Diego Zoo or the San Diego Wild Animal Park. Passes are valid for 14 days from the day of the first use and may be purchased online or at any of the attractions. The total savings are $80 for adults and $55 for children. The Hollywood CityPass (p511) and the San Francisco CityPass (p90) offer similar schemes.

Members of AARP (see Senior Cards) and of the **American Automobile Association** (AAA; ☎ 800-874-7532; www.aaa.com) or its foreign affiliates get small discounts (usually 10%) in many places. Just make it a habit to ask

every time you book a room, reserve a car, order a meal or pay an entrance fee, especially since these discounts are not usually advertised.

Also look for out discount coupons and magazines in tourist offices, hotels, gas stations and newspapers. Be aware that discounts may have restrictions and conditions or may not be valid at peak times, so always read the fine print. Online hotel discount coupons can be obtained through **Roomsaver** (www.roomsaver.com).

Senior Cards

People over the age of 65 (sometimes 55, 60 or 62) often qualify for the same discounts as students; any identification showing your birth date should suffice as proof of age. Members of the **American Association of Retired Persons** (AARP; ☎ 800-687-2277; www.aarp.org), an advocacy group for Americans 50 years and older, qualify for small discounts (usually 10%) at many hotels and venues.

Student & Youth Cards

If you're a full-time student, never leave home without an **International Student Identity Card** (ISIC; www.isiccard.com), which entitles you to discounts on movie and theater tickets, travel insurance and admission to museums and other attractions. For nonstudents under 26, the same organization also issues the International Youth Travel Card (IYTC), which offers many of the same savings and benefits. You can apply for either on the website or through student unions, hosteling organizations and youth-oriented travel agencies such as STA Travel.

International and US students can also buy the **Student Advantage Card** (☎ 877-256-4672; www.studentadvantage.com) for $20 per year for 15% savings on Amtrak and Greyhound plus discounts up to 50% at participating hotels, shops and airlines.

FESTIVALS & EVENTS

California has a wonderfully packed schedule of festivals and special events happening throughout the year. To find out what's scheduled during your visit, have a look at www.culturecalifornia.com. Many of the major festivities are mentioned in the destination chapters of this book, usually under a Festivals & Events headline. See p532 for major LA festivals, p108 for San Francisco festivals and p613 for San Diego festivals. For our Top 10 festivals, see p18.

Listed below are festivals that are celebrated California-wide, although with more fanfare and enthusiasm in some places than in others.

Chinese New Year Happy New Year: parades, fire-crackers and fortune cookies in late January or early February.

Valentine's Day Catch the love bug: roses, candies and kisses on February 14.

St Patrick's Day Hail to the saint: wear green on March 17 – or else.

Cinco de Mayo Viva Mexico: margaritas, music, merriment on May 5.

Memorial Day Summer is here: flags, patriotism and picnics in late May.

Gay Pride Month Coming out: floats, costumes and craziness throughout June.

Independence Day Red, white & blue: parade, fireworks and barbecues for July 4.

Halloween Trick or treat: costumes, candy and kookiness on October 31.

Day of the Dead Blessings upon ye: skulls, skeletons and memories on November 2.

Thanksgiving Gobble, gobble: pilgrims, turkey and football in late November.

Chanukah (dates vary) Jewish Festival of Lights: candles, latkes and gelt. Dates vary, but often in late November or early December.

New Year's Eve Let's celebrate: parties, friends and champagne.

FOOD

This guide includes eating options to match all tastes and travel budgets. Budget eateries include takeouts, delis, cafés, snack bars, markets and basic restaurants where you can fill up for $10 or less. At the midrange establishments, you usually get tablecloths, full menus, beer and wine lists and main courses from $10 to $20. Top-end places tend to be full gourmet affairs with fussy service, creative and freshly prepared food and matching wine lists; expect mains to start at $20. Remember that your final tally will be swelled by the sales tax, which ranges from 7.25% to 8.75%, depending on the city, and by a tip of 15% to 20%.

Since most restaurants serve lunch and dinner daily, we've spelled out only deviations from this basic rule in our reviews.

Smoking is not allowed inside restaurants, but some have patios or sidewalk tables where lighting up may still be tolerated.

GAY & LESBIAN TRAVELERS

California is a magnet for gay travelers with major hot spots being the Castro in San Francisco, West Hollywood (WeHo) and Silver Lake in Los Angeles, the Hillcrest area of San Diego and the desert oasis of Palm Springs. All of these hubs have humming nightlife scenes, magazines, associations and support groups, and major Gay Pride celebrations. As elsewhere, the scene is predominantly male oriented, although lesbians won't feel left out. LA's Long Beach and Orange County's Laguna Beach also have small gay communities, and Guerneville in the Russian River Valley is a popular destination as well. For an overview of the LA scene, see p549; for San Francisco, flick to p109. Palm Springs is covered on p646, Las Vegas on p693 and San Diego on p602.

California offers gays and lesbians extensive domestic rights but stops short of the legalization of gay marriage and civil unions. Registered couples enjoy practically all spousal rights available under state law, although they cannot file a joint tax return. For more on the subject, see p76.

Check **Damron** (www.damron.com), which publishes the classic gay travel guides, including *Men's Travel Guide* and *Women's Traveler*. Damron's *Accommodations* lists gay-owned and gay-friendly hotels, B&Bs and guesthouses nationwide. **Out & About** (www.gay.com /travel/outandabout) publishes downloadable guides with lots of juicy information about numerous destinations, including all the major ones in California.

If you find yourself in need of counseling or referrals of any kind, contact the **Gay & Lesbian National Hotline** (☎ 888-843-4564; www.glnh .org; ✉ 4pm-midnight Mon-Fri, noon-5pm Sat).

Other good resources:

Gay.com (www.gay.com) Major web portal with travel, health, shopping and other coverage.

Gay Travelocity (www.travelocity.com/gaytravel) Gay-specific articles, listings and hotels.

Out Traveler (www.outtraveler.com) Bimonthly magazine; free subscription to e-newsletter.

Purple Roofs (www.purpleroofs.com) Great online directory of gay and lesbian accommodations.

HOLIDAYS
Public Holidays

On the following national holidays banks, schools and government offices (including post offices) remain closed, and transportation, museums and other services operate on a Sunday schedule. Holidays falling on a weekend are usually observed the following Monday.

New Year's Day January 1
Martin Luther King Jr Day Third Monday in January
Presidents' Day Third Monday in February
Easter A Friday and Sunday in March or April
Memorial Day Last Monday in May
Independence Day July 4 (aka the Fourth of July)
Labor Day First Monday in September
Columbus Day Second Monday in October
Veterans' Day November 11
Thanksgiving Day Fourth Thursday in November
Christmas Day December 25

School Holidays

Colleges take a one- or two-week 'spring break' around Easter, sometime in March or April. Although California is currently not one of the superhot destinations for libidinous students to let loose, some hotels may hike up prices during this time. School summer vacations run from late June to early September, making July and August the busiest travel months.

INSURANCE

No matter how long or short your trip, make sure you have adequate travel insurance. At a minimum you need coverage for medical emergencies and treatment (see p728).

You should also consider coverage for luggage theft or loss. If you already have health insurance or a homeowners or renters policy, check what they will cover and only get supplemental insurance to protect against the rest. If you have prepaid a large portion of your vacation, trip cancellation insurance is a worthwhile expense.

For information about what type of insurance you need while driving in California, see p723.

Agencies offering comprehensive travel insurance include the following:

1 Cover (☎ 1300-368-344; www.1cover.com.au) Australia-based agency.
Quoteline Direct (☎ 0870-444-0870; www.quoteline direct.co.uk) Compares quotes from 30 UK-based insurance companies.
Squaremouth.com (☎ 866-874-7226; www.square mouth.com) Compares more than 100 US-based travel-insurance plans.
Travel Insurance Online (☎ 0870-755-6101; www .travel-insurance-online.com) UK-based.

World Travel Center (☎ 402-343-3699, 866-979-6753; www.worldtravelcenter.com) Global insurance-policy search.

INTERNATIONAL VISITORS
Entering the Country

Getting into the USA can be a bureaucratic nightmare, especially as the rules keep changing. For up-to-date information about entry requirements and eligibility, we highly recommend checking with a US consulate in your home country. For background information, also check the visa website of the **US Department of State** (www.unitedstatesvisas.gov) and the travel section of the **US Customs & Border Protection** (www.cbp.gov).

In 2004, the US Department of Homeland Security introduced a new set of security measures called US-VISIT. Upon arrival in the USA, all visitors will be photographed and have their index fingers scanned. Eventually, this biometric data will be matched when you leave the USA. The goal is to ensure that the person who entered the country is the same as the one leaving it and to catch people who've overstayed the terms of their admission. For full details about US-VISIT, check with a US consulate or www.dhs.gov/us-visit.

PASSPORTS & VISAS

Under the US Visa Waiver Program, visas are currently not required for citizens of 27 countries for stays up to 90 days (no extensions allowed) as long as they have a machine-readable passport (MRP). If you don't have an MRP, you will need a visa to enter the USA.

If you're getting a new passport, note that requirements are even tighter. Under current regulations, passports issued between October 26, 2005 and October 25, 2006 must be machine-readable and feature a digital photograph on the data page. Passports issued after October 25, 2006 must be machine-readable and also include an integrated chip with biometric information from the data pages.

If you have a passport issued *before* October 26, 2005 it will still be accepted for travel as long as it's machine-readable. In other words, there is *no* need to get a new passport until your current one expires.

Canadian citizens are technically exempt from both visa and passport requirements but official proof of citizenship with photo

ID is necessary. Valid documents include a birth certificate, a citizenship certificate or a passport.

Citizens from all nonvisa-waiver countries need to apply for a visa in their home country. The process costs a nonrefundable $100, involves a personal interview and can take several weeks, so you should apply as early as possible.

Again, we'd like to stress that this information, while accurate at press time, may change. Always get the latest scoop from your nearest US consulate.

Customs

Non-US citizens or permanent residents over the age of 21 may bring 1L of alcohol, 200 cigarettes or 50 cigars or 2kg of smoking tobacco, and $100 worth of gifts into the USA without paying duty. An additional 100 cigars may be brought in under your gift exemption.

Amounts in excess of $10,000 in cash, traveler's checks, money orders and other cash equivalents must be declared. Unless you're curious about US jails, don't even think about bringing in illegal drugs.

California is an important agricultural state. In order to prevent the spread of pests and diseases certain food items (including meats, fresh fruit and vegetables) may not be brought into the state. Bakery items, chocolates and hard-cured cheeses are admissible.

If you drive into California across the border from Mexico or the neighboring states of Oregon, Nevada and Arizona, you may have to stop for a quick inspection and questioning by officials of the California Department of Food and Agriculture.

For complete information, visit the US Customs and Border Protection website at www.cbp.gov.

Embassies & Consulates
US EMBASSIES & CONSULATES

Visas and other travel-related documents are handled by consulates, not embassies. While the US embassy is located in your country's capital city, the US also maintains consulates in many other major cities. To find the US consulate nearest to you, contact the US embassy in your country. If your country isn't listed here, see www.travel.state .gov/visa/questions_embassy.html.

Australia (☎ 02-6214-5600; http://canberra.usembassy .gov; Moonah Pl, Yarralumla, ACT 2600)
Canada (☎ 613-238-5335; www.usembassycanada.gov; 490 Sussex Dr, Ottawa, Ontario K1N 1G8)
France (☎ 01-43-12-22-22; www.amb-usa.fr; 2 ave Gabriel, 75008 Paris)
Germany (☎ 030-830-50; www.usembassy.de; Neustädtische Kirchstrasse 4-5, 10117 Berlin)
Ireland (☎ 01-668-8777; http://dublin.usembassy.gov; 42 Elgin Rd, Dublin 4)
Israel (☎ 03-519-7575; www.usembassy-israel.org.il; 71 Hayarkon St, Tel Aviv 63903)
Italy (☎ 06-467-41; www.usembassy.it; Via Veneto 119/A, 00187 Rome)
Japan (☎ 03-3224-5000; http://tokyo.usembassy.gov; 1-10-5 Akasaka, Minato-ku, Tokyo 107-8420)
The Netherlands (☎ 070-310-9209; http://nether lands.usembassy.gov; Lange Voorhout 102, 2514 EJ The Hague)
New Zealand (☎ 04-462-6000; http://usembassy.org.nz; 29 Fitzherbert Tce, Thorndon, Wellington)
UK (☎ 020-7499-9000; www.usembassy.org.uk; 24 Grosvenor Sq, London W1A 1AE)

CONSULATES IN CALIFORNIA

Most foreign embassies are in Washington, DC, but many countries, including the following, have consular offices in California, usually in Los Angeles and San Francisco. For additional countries, visit www.ss.ca.gov /business/ibrp/fgncons.htm.

Australia Los Angeles (Map pp506-7; ☎ 310-229-4800; 2049 Century Park E, 19th fl); San Francisco (Map pp80-1; ☎ 415-243-2072; 625 Market St, Suite 20)
Canada (Map pp500-1; ☎ 213-346-2700; 550 S Hope St, 9th fl, Los Angeles)
France Los Angeles (Map pp506-7; ☎ 310-235-3200; 10990 Wilshire Blvd, Suite 300); San Francisco (Map pp80-1; ☎ 415-397-4330; 540 Bush St)
Germany Los Angeles (Map pp504-5; ☎ 323-930-2703; 6222 Wilshire Blvd, Suite 500); San Francisco (Map pp86-7; ☎ 415-775-1061; 1960 Jackson St)
Italy Los Angeles (☎ 310-826-5998; 12400 Wilshire Blvd, Suite 300); San Francisco (Map pp86-7; ☎ 415-931-4924; 2590 Webster St)
Japan Los Angeles (Map pp500-1; ☎ 213-617-6700; 350 S Grand Ave, Suite 1700); San Francisco (Map pp80-1; ☎ 415-777-3533; 50 Fremont St, Suite 2300)
Mexico Los Angeles (Map pp500-1; ☎ 213-351-6815; 2401 W 6th St); San Francisco (Map pp80-1; ☎ 415-392-5554; 532 Folsom St)
New Zealand (☎ 310-207-1605; 12400 Wilshire Blvd, Suite 1150, Los Angeles)
South Africa (Map pp504-5; ☎ 310-651-5902; 6300 Wilshire Blvd, Suite 600, Los Angeles)

UK Los Angeles (☎ 310-477-3322; 11766 Wilshire Blvd, Suite 400); San Francisco (Map pp80-1; ☎ 415-981-3030; 1 Sansome St, Suite 850)

Money

US coins come in 1¢ (penny), 5¢ (nickel), 10¢ (dime) and 25¢ (quarter) pieces, while paper currency comes in $1, $5, $10, $20, $50 and $100 denominations. Some vendors may be reluctant to accept a $100 bill for small purchases.

The US dollar is generally a stable currency. It lost some of its value against the euro after 9/11, but slowly started gaining against the European currency in 2005. See the exchange-rate table on the inside front cover for some guidelines. For an overview of how much things cost in California, see the information on p17.

You can exchange money at airports, some banks and currency-exchange offices such as American Express and Travelex. Always ask about rates and fees. In rural areas, exchanging money may be a problem, so be sure you have plenty of cash, a credit card or US-dollar traveler's checks on hand.

Usually the best and quickest way to obtain cash is using ATMs, which are ubiquitous and accessible around the clock. Almost all accept cards from the international Cirrus, Plus, Star and Maestro networks. Keep in mind that most ATMs charge a service fee of $1.50 per transaction and that your own bank may impose additional charges.

Credit cards are almost universally accepted and, in fact, you will find it hard or impossible to rent a car, book a room or order tickets over the phone without one. A credit card may also be vital in emergencies. Most ATMs also spit out cash if you use your credit card, but it's expensive because, in addition to a steep service fee, you'll be charged interest immediately on the entire statement period's balance (ie there's no grace period as with purchases).

For exact fees, check with your bank or credit-card company.

When it comes to traveler's checks, American Express and VISA are the most widely known issuers. Buying them online through such agents as **Travelex** (www.travelex.com) or **American Express** (www.americanexpress.com) may be cheaper than going through your bank. Restaurants, hotels and most shops generally accept US-dollar traveler's checks, as they would cash, but small businesses, markets and fast-food chains may refuse them.

Post

The **US Postal Service** (USPS; ☎ 800-275-8777; www .usps.com) is inexpensive and reliable. Call the toll-free number for the nearest branch, including those that accept general delivery mail (poste restante). There is no charge for this service, but you must show photo identification when picking up mail. Post offices will hold mail for 10 days.

At the time of publication, standard letters up to 1oz (about 30g) cost 37¢ within the US, 60¢ to Canada and Mexico and 80¢ to all other countries. Rates for postcards are 23¢, 50¢ and 70¢, respectively. Postal rates increase by a penny or more every few years. For other rates, zip (postal) codes and general information, stop by any post office, call the toll-free number or visit the website.

Telephone

PAY PHONES

In the age of cell phones, public pay phones are becoming a dying breed. Those still around are usually coin-operated, although some accept credit cards. Really fancy ones (such as those at airports) have data ports so you can access the Internet using your laptop. Local calls usually cost 35¢ minimum and increase with the distance and length of call. For long-distance calls, you'll likely be better off using a prepaid phonecard available in convenience stores, supermarkets, newsstands and electronics stores. Be sure to read the fine print before buying such a card as many contain hidden charges such as 'activation fees' or a per-call 'connection fee.' However, a surcharge of about 30¢ or 50¢ for calls made from pay phones is normal.

AREA CODES

US phone numbers consist of a three-digit area code followed by a seven-digit local number. When dialing a number within the same area code, just punch in the seven-digit number. Long-distance calls must be preceded by ☎ 1. For direct international calls, dial ☎ 011 plus the country code plus the area code plus the local phone number. If you're calling from abroad the country code for the USA is ☎ 1.

For local directory assistance, dial ☎ 411. For directory assistance outside your area code, dial ☎1 plus the area code, plus ☎555-1212; this call is charged as a long-distance call. For international directory assistance, dial ☎00.

Tollfree numbers begin with ☎800, ☎866, ☎877 or ☎888 and must be preceded by ☎1. Most can be used within the entire USA, some only work within California, and others only go through when calling from outside California. To find any tollfree number, call ☎800-555-1212 (no charge).

CELL PHONES (MOBILE PHONES)

The only foreign phones that work in North America are international triband models, operating on GSM 1900 as well as on GSM 900/1800. If you have such a phone, check with your service provider about using it in the USA, but be aware that calls will be more expensive than using your home network.

If you don't have an international phone, you can rent one from such online companies as **Planet Omni** (www.planetomni.com) or **World Cell** (www.worldcell.com). If you prefer to rent a phone from a bricks-and-mortar store, try **TripTel** (☎877-874-7835; www.triptel.com), which has a branch at the **Los Angeles International Airport** (Map pp498–9), outside the customs gate in the Tom Bradley International terminal. There's another in **San Francisco** (1525 Van Ness Ave). Pricing plans vary, but generally this is an expensive option.

It might work out cheaper to buy a pre-paid SIM chip for the USA, which you insert into your international mobile phone to get a local phone number, voice mail and, usually, lower rates. Planet Omni as well as **Teles-**tial (www.telestial.com) are among the companies offering this service.

Time

California is in the Pacific time zone, which is Greenwich mean time minus eight hours.

When it's noon in California, it's 3pm in New York, 8pm in London and 6am (the next day) in Sydney or Auckland.

In 2006, daylight saving time comes into effect on the first Sunday of April, when the clocks are put forward one hour, and ends on the last Sunday in October. Starting in 2007, it will begin on the second Sunday in March and end on the first Sunday in November.

INTERNET ACCESS

Surfing the Web and checking email is rarely a problem while traveling in California. Access is usually free at public libraries but downsides may include registration requirements, time limits, queues and slow connections. Otherwise, Internet cafés are plentiful and are listed in the Information sections of the destination chapters; expect to pay between $5 and $12 for one hour of online time. Hostels and hotels offering guest terminals with Internet access are identified in this book with an Internet icon (▣).

If you're traveling with your own laptop or personal digital assistant (PDA), you'll find that most hotels have technology that lets you connect in the comfort of your room. High-speed access is especially common in hotels courting a business clientele and many properties including, increasingly, motels, now also offer wi-fi. Some airports, including San Francisco International and Reno/Tahoe

---

WIRELESS IN THE WILDERNESS

Time was when folks went to the woods to get away from their 'day-to-day' routine and connect instead with nature and their own thoughts and feelings. Well, apparently no more. California State Parks – and others across the country – are reporting that people aren't coming to the parks as they used to because they lack 'connectivity.' So the parks are wiring up for wireless. Soon you'll be able to sit beneath a giant redwood tree, boot up and download stock quotes, email and clips from *Three Stooges* classics. Don't worry if you miss the mating rituals of those rare hummingbirds or the sight of a trout breaking the stillness of a deep river pool. Just Google 'em! After all – and according to a 17-year-old code writer – 'The great outdoors is waaay overrated.'

Wireless Internet connections are available in 85 California state parks, including Pfeiffer Big Sur State Park (p456), Sutter's Fort State Historic Park (p411) and Henry Cowell Redwoods State Park (p439). For a list, go to www.parks.ca.gov and type 'wireless' into the search function. You'll need your own wi-fi–enabled laptop or PDA. The cost is $8 per day or $20 per month. Most hot spots are at the campgrounds.

International, are also wireless hot spots, as are some of the state parks throughout California (see the boxed text, opposite). To find wireless hot spots anywhere, try the directories at www.wi-fihotspotlist.com/browse/ca and www.hotspot-locations.com.

Beware of digital phones without built-in data ports, which may fry your modem unless you're using a digital-to-analog converter. Depending on where you bought your laptop, you also need adapters for US electrical outlets and telephone sockets. Both are available in larger electronics stores.

For more information on traveling with a portable computer and the gadgets you might need to help you get online, see www.igo.com or www.teleadapt.com.

See p19 for websites that might be useful when traveling in California.

LEGAL MATTERS

If you are stopped by the police, remain courteous at all times and, if driving, keep your hands where the cop can see them, ie atop the steering wheel. Don't get out of the car unless asked. There is no system of paying fines on the spot. Attempting to pay the fine to the officer is frowned upon at best and may lead to a charge of attempted bribery. For traffic offenses, the police officer will explain the options to you. There is usually a 30-day period to pay a fine. Most matters can be handled by mail.

If you are arrested for more serious offenses, you have the right to remain silent and are presumed innocent until proven guilty. There is no legal reason to speak to a police officer if you don't wish, but never walk away from one until given permission. Everyone arrested is legally allowed to make one phone call and the right to representation by an attorney. If you don't have a lawyer, friend or family member to help you, call the nearest consulate. The police will give you the number upon request. If you can't afford a lawyer, a public defender will be appointed to you free of charge.

When driving in California, you'll need to carry your driver's license (p722) as well as proof of registration. Be sure to obey the road rules carefully (p725). The highest permissible blood-alcohol limit is 0.08%. Driving while under the influence (DUI) is a serious offense that incurs stiff fines, a suspended license, higher insurance premiums

---

THE LEGAL AGE FOR...

- Drinking alcohol: 21
- Driving a car: 16
- Military service: 17
- Sexual consent: 18
- Smoking tobacco: 18
- Voting in an election: 18

---

and other nasty consequences. Consuming alcohol anywhere other than at a residence or licensed premises is also a no-no, which puts parks, beaches and much of the rest of the great outdoors off-limits (campgrounds are ok, for now). It is also illegal to carry open containers of alcohol inside a vehicle, even if they are empty. Containers that are full and sealed may be carried, but if they have ever been opened they must be stored in the trunk.

Possession of under 1oz of marijuana is a misdemeanor in California, and though it is punishable by up to one year in jail, a fine is more likely for first-time offenders. Possession of any other drug, including cocaine, ecstasy, LSD, heroin, hashish or more than an ounce of weed, is a felony punishable by lengthy jail sentences, depending on the circumstances. For foreigners, conviction of any drug offense is grounds for deportation.

If you find yourself in an emergency, dial ☎ 911. For nonemergency police assistance, call directory assistance for the number of the nearest local police station.

MAPS

Most visitors centers distribute free (but often very basic) town maps. For car touring, you'll need detailed road maps or an atlas, such as those published by Rand McNally. Members of the **American Automobile Association** (AAA; ☎ 800-874-7532; www.aaa.com) or one of its international affiliates, can get AAA's high-quality and frequently updated maps for free from any local office. Bookstores and tourist offices usually stock a good assortment of maps, while newsagents and gas stations have a more limited selection. For downloadable maps and driving directions try **Mapquest** (www.mapquest.com) or **Yahoo! Maps** (http://maps.yahoo.com). For details about hiking maps, see p62.

DIRECTORY

PHOTOGRAPHY

If photography means only digital to you, you need only go to www.malektips.com for advice on how to keep your pixels poppin' in nearly every situation you can imagine. If you still have one of those 'traditional' cameras with actual film, keep in mind that for general shooting – either prints or slides – 100 ASA film is the most useful and versatile as it gives you good color and enough speed to capture most situations. If you plan to shoot in dark areas or in brightly lit night scenes without a tripod, switch to 400 ASA. For slides, Fuji Velvia and Kodak E100VS are easy to process and provide good quality. For print film, you can't beat Kodak Gold or Fuji.

Film can be damaged by excessive heat, so avoid leaving your camera and film in the car (this goes for digital cameras too). Carry spare batteries to avoid disappointment when your camera dies in the middle of nowhere. With any new camera, practice before leaving for your trip.

Drugstores are good places to get your film processed cheaply. If you drop it off by noon, you can usually pick it up the next day. A roll of 100 ASA 35mm color film with 24 exposures will cost about $6 to get processed. One-hour processing services charge up to $11 per 24-exposure roll.

For some tips on how to take good pictures while on the road, check out Lonely Planet's *Travel Photography: A Guide to Taking Better Pictures.*

SHOPPING

Californians spend a lot of time spending their money and there's certainly no shortage of big malls, department stores, outlet centers, boutiques and markets to help them do it. To many visitors the sheer variety and quantity of consumer goods can be as staggering as it is tempting. There's really nothing you can't buy here, be it computers or couture, flip-flops or funky designer outfits, anime DVDs or sex toys, surf gear or antiques.

Orange County has the biggest concentration of glitzy malls, especially in Costa Mesa (p580), while Los Angeles (p552) is best for boutiques stocked with tomorrow's fashions and also has unique items such as clothing worn by the stars. San Francisco (p130) is another great shopping town, especially when it comes to vintage clothing, collectibles and quirky, unusual items. Las Vegas (p694) and Palm Springs (p648) have some of the best outlet malls, while places with local artist communities, such as Laguna Beach (p581) and Carmel (p453), are good for picking up originals. Rural towns, especially in the desert or mountain areas, are usually best for digging up Americana and Old West paraphernalia.

If you're keen on Native American items, like rugs, jewelry or artwork, be aware that much of the stuff sold in stores and trading posts is mass produced. Genuine products usually have a tag or stamps identifying them as 'Indian handmade' while imitations will say something like 'Indian style.' Be conscious of who's doing the selling and ask a lot of questions. Who made the item? What tribe is the artist from? What kinds of materials were used? A reputable dealer will know the answers and happily talk about their origin.

SOLO TRAVELERS

There are no particular problems or difficulties traveling alone in California. Although it is not for everybody, a major advantage is the freedom to do anything and to go anywhere you want whenever you want.

Americans are generally friendly and easy to talk to. Women don't need to be afraid of initiating conversation, even with men. Unless you're overtly coquettish, it most likely won't be interpreted as a sexual advance. Hostels are great places for hooking up with other people, as are guided tours, major tourist attractions and Internet cafés. Unless you're a total loner, you'll soon meet people with whom to share travel trips or go sightseeing, bar hopping or out to a movie.

In general, don't advertise where you're staying or that you're traveling alone. When going for a long hike, let someone else know about your intended whereabouts in case something should happen to you. Carrying a cell phone can be a lifesaver in this situation and other emergencies.

Some issues of safety are slightly different for women than they are for men – see opposite for more specific information.

TIPPING

Tipping is an American practice that is not really an option – the service has to be absolutely appalling to consider not tipping. In a restaurant, tip your server at least 15% of the bill. In bars at least $1 a round is customary.

To tip a cabbie, add at least 10% (starting at $1, even for fares under $6) to the taxi fare. Hotel porters who carry bags a long way expect $3 to $5, or tip $1 per bag. Valet parking is worth about a $1 to $2 tip, to be given when your car is safely returned to you.

TOURIST INFORMATION

California has no tourist offices in other countries, but the state-funded **California Tourism** (☎ 800-462-2543; www.visitcalifornia.com) operates an excellent website packed with useful pretrip planning information. The office will also mail out a free information package, including a magazine-sized visitors guide, although the website has just about all the same information, without all the paper.

The state government also operates 11 **California Welcome Centers** (www.visitcwc.com) in Los Angeles (p497), Oceanside (near San Diego; p628), Santa Ana (Orange County; p565), Yucca Valley (near Joshua Tree National Park; p655), Barstow (near Mojave National Preserve; p661), Merced (west of Yosemite National Park; p425), San Francisco (p91), Auburn (Gold Country; p318), Anderson (in the Shasta Cascade; p284), Santa Rosa (Wine Country; p210) and Arcata (North Coast, p269).

Almost every city and town has a local visitors center or a chamber of commerce where you can pick up maps, brochures and information.

TOURS

Backroads (☎ 510-527-1555, 800-462-2848; www.backroads.com) Active guided and self-guided deluxe tours of the Wine Country, Death Valley, Yosemite or Santa Barbara, many combining hiking, biking and kayaking (six-day tours $1400 to $2500).

California Dreamin' (☎ 626-533-5529, 866-440-4440; www.caldreamin.com) One- and two-week van tours ($510/1025) from LA to the blockbuster parks and cities, including Yosemite, San Francisco and Vegas. Camp or sleep in hostels; meals are included.

Eagle Rider (☎ 310-536-6777; www.eaglerider.com /tours.html) Guided and self-guided motorcycle tours, including six-day California Dreamin' from LA to San Francisco (from $1450) and the eight-day Gold Rush tour to Yosemite and NoCal (from $2500). Rates include Harleys, lodging and some meals.

Elderhostel (☎ 877-426-8056; www.elderhostel.org) This nonprofit organization offers guided tours throughout the world, including Southern California, for active people over 55. Includes bus and walking tours.

Incredible Adventures (☎ 415-642-7378, 800-777-8464; www.tmltours.com) Operates one- and two-day trips to Yosemite, the Wine Country and Tahoe (for skiing) from San Francisco ($75 to $270) and to the Grand Canyon, Bryce and Zion from Las Vegas ($130 to $210).

Sun Trek (☎ 707-523-1800, 800-786-8735; www.suntrek.com) Various small-size camping tours around California and beyond leaving from LA and San Francisco. One-week tours start at $550, plus a food contribution.

WOMEN TRAVELERS

California is generally a safe place to travel for women, even alone and in the cities. Of course, this doesn't mean you can let your guard down and blindly entrust your life to every stranger. Simply use the same common sense you would at home.

Going alone to cafés and restaurants is perfectly acceptable, although how comfortable you feel depends entirely on you. In bars and nightclubs, solo women are likely to attract attention from men, but if you don't want company, most will respect a firm 'no thank you.' If you feel threatened, protesting loudly will often make the offender slink away with embarrassment – or will at least spur other people to come to your defense.

The website www.journeywoman.com facilitates women exchanging travel tips and includes links to other sites. Another good source is **Her Own Way** (www.voyage.gc.ca/main/pubs /PDF/her_own_way-en.pdf), an online booklet published by the Canadian government but filled with lots of good general travel advice useful for any woman.

Although physical attack is unlikely, it does, of course, happen. If you are assaulted, you could call the **police** (☎ 911), although you do not need to do so in order to seek help. Many women prefer first to contact a women's or rape crisis center whose staff can help you deal with emotional and physical issues surrounding an assault. They can make referrals to medical, legal and social service providers as well as useful organizations and support groups. To find one near you, call the 24-hour **National Sexual Assault Hotline** (☎ 800-656-4673; www.rainn.org).

WORK

If you are not a US citizen or permanent resident, there's a lot of red tape involved in getting a work permit and rather severe penalties (a heavy fine for your employer, deportation for yourself) if you're caught working illegally. To work in the USA legally, you'll need to apply for a work visa with an American embassy before leaving home.

The type of visa you require depends on the length of your stay and the type of work. A J1 visa, for exchange students, is issued to young people (age limits vary) for student vacation employment, work in summer camps and short-term traineeships with a specific employer. Organizations that can help with obtaining such a visa include the **American Institute for Foreign** **Study** (AIFS; ☎ 800-727-2437; www.aifs.com) and the **Council on International Education and Exchange** (CIEE; ☎ 800-407-8839; www.ciee.org).

For nonstudent jobs, temporary or permanent, you need to be sponsored by a US employer who will have to arrange one of the various H-category visas. These are not easy to obtain, since the employer has to prove that no US citizen or permanent resident is available to do the job. Seasonal work is possible in national parks and other tourist sites, especially ski areas.

Transportation

GETTING THERE & AWAY

AIR

In the post–9/11 world, increased security measures at airports have become commonplace. Typical procedures now include having checked luggage subjected to high-level x-rays, taking off your shoes and turning on your laptop computer to show that it's real. The government's **Transport Security Administration** (TSA; www.tsa.gov/public) is constantly refining the list of what may and may not be taken on board. At the time of research, you're free to lug tweezers, nail files and plastic knives in your carry-on luggage, but please stash your saber and ice axe in your checked suitcase.

THINGS CHANGE...

The information in this chapter is particularly vulnerable to change. Check directly with the airline or a travel agent to make sure you understand how a fare (and the ticket you may buy) works and be aware of the security requirements for international travel. Shop carefully. The details given in this chapter should be regarded as pointers and are not a substitute for your own careful, up-to-date research.

Due to the rise of theft from baggage by airport employees, TSA has approved specific locks, which can be safely opened and locked again by screeners using special tools. For all the latest rules and requirements, consult the TSA's website.

Airports & Airlines

If you're traveling to California from overseas, you'll most likely first land on US soil at **Los Angeles International Airport** (code LAX; ☎ 310-646-5252; www.lawa.org), one of the world's busiest, or at **San Francisco International Airport** (code SFO; ☎ 650-821-8211; www.flysfo.com). Both airports also handle domestic arrivals, although in some instances flying into one of the following regional airports may be cheaper and more convenient to your final destination. See the regional chapters for details.

Arcata/Eureka Airport (code ACV; ☎ 707-839-5401; www.co.humboldt.ca.us/aviation)

Bob Hope Airport (code BUR; ☎ 818-840-8840, 800-835-9287; www.burbankairport.com) In Burbank, Los Angeles County.

John Wayne Airport (code SNA; ☎ 949-252-5200; www.ocair.com) In Santa Ana, Orange County.

Long Beach Airport (code LGB; ☎ 562-570-2600; www.longbeach.gov/airport) In southern LA County.

McCarran International (code LAS; ☎ 702-261-5211; www.mccarran.com) In Las Vegas.

Monterey Peninsula Airport (code MRY; ☎ 831-648-7000; www.montereyairport.com)

Oakland International (code OAK; ☎ 510-563-3300; www.flyoakland.com) Near San Francisco.

Ontario International Airport (code ONT; ☎ 909-937-2700, 866-456-3900; www.lawa.org/ont) In Riverside County, east of LA.

Palm Springs International Airport (code PSP; ☎ 760-318-3800; www.palmspringsairport.com)

Redding (code RDD; ☎ 530-224-4321; www.ci.redding.ca.us/airports/rma/rma.htm)

Reno-Tahoe International (code RNO; ☎ 775-328-6870; www.renoairport.com)

Sacramento International Airport (code SMF; ☎ 916-929-5411; www.sacairports.org/int)

San Diego International Airport (code SAN; ☎ 619-231-2100; www.san.org)

San Jose International (code SJC; ☎ 408-277-4759; www.sjc.org)

San Luis Obispo County Airport (code SBP; ☎ 805-541-1038; www.sloairport.com)

Santa Barbara Municipal Airport (code SBA; ☎ 805-967-7111; www.flysba.com)

Major domestic and international carriers serving California include the following:

US AIRLINES

AirTran (code FL; ☎ 800-247-8726; www.airtran.com; hub Atlanta)

Alaska Air/Horizon Air (codes AS & QX; ☎ 800-426-0333; www.alaskaair.com; hub Seattle)

America West (code HP; ☎ 800-235-9292; www.americawest.com; hub Phoenix)

American Airlines (code AA; ☎ 800-433-7300; www.aa.com; hub Dallas–Fort Worth)

Continental (code CO; ☎ 800-525-0280; www.continental.com; hub Houston)

Delta (code DL; ☎ 800-221-1212; www.delta.com; hub Atlanta)

Frontier Air (code F9; ☎ 800-432-1359; www.frontierairlines.com; hub Denver)

Jet Blue (code B6; ☎ 800-538-2583; www.jetblue.com; hub JFK, New York)

Midwest Airlines (code YX; ☎ 800-452-2022; www.midwestairlines.com; hub Milwaukee)

Northwest Airlines (code NW; ☎ 800-225-2525; www.nwa.com; hub Minneapolis–St Paul)

Southwest (code WN; ☎ 800-435-9792; www.southwest.com; hub Love Field, Dallas)

United Airlines (code UA; ☎ 800-241-6522, 800-538-2929; www.united.com; hub Chicago O'Hare)

US Airways (code US; ☎ 800-428-4322; www.usairways.com; hubs Charlotte, Philadelphia)

INTERNATIONAL AIRLINES

Aer Lingus (code EI; ☎ 800-474-7424; www.aerlingus.com; hub Dublin)

Aeromexico (code AM; ☎ 800-237-6639; www.aeromexico.com; hub Mexico City)

Air Canada (code AC; ☎ 888-247-2262; www.aircanada.com; hub Pearson, Toronto)

Air France (code AF; ☎ 800-237-2747; www.airfrance.com; hub Charles de Gaulle, Paris)

Air New Zealand (code NZ; ☎ 800-262-1234; www.airnewzealand.com; hub Auckland)

Alitalia (code AZ; ☎ 800-223-5730; www.alitalia.com; hubs Fiumicino, Rome; Malpensa, Milan)

ANA (code NH; ☎ 800-235-9262; www.fly-ana.com; hub Narita, Tokyo)

Asiana (code OZ; ☎ 800-227-4262; www.flyasiana.com; hub Incheon, Seoul)

ATA (code TZ; ☎ 800-435-9282; www.ata.com; hub Midway, Chicago)

British Airways (code BA; ☎ 800-247-9297; www.britishairways.com; hub Heathrow, London)

Cathay Pacific (code CX; ☎ 800-228-4297; www.cathaypacific.com; hub Hong Kong)

EVA Air (code BR; ☎ 800-695-1188; www.evaair.com; hub Chiang Kai-Shek, Taipei)

Iberia (code IB; ☎ 800-772-4642; www.iberia.com; hub Barajas, Madrid)

Japan Airlines (code JL; ☎ 800-525-3663; www.japanair.com; hub Narita, Tokyo)

KLM (code KL; ☎ 800-374-7747; www.klm.com; hub Schiphol, Amsterdam)

Lufthansa (code LH; ☎ 800-645-3880; www.lufthansa.com; hub Frankfurt)

Mexicana (code MX; ☎ 800-531-7921; www.mexicana.com; hub Mexico City)

Philippine Airlines (code PR; ☎ 800-435-9725; www.philippineair.com; hub Manila)

Qantas (code QF; ☎ 800-227-4500; www.qantas.com; hub Sydney)

Singapore Airlines (code SQ; ☎ 800-742-3333; www.singaporeair.com; hub Changi, Singapore)

Virgin Atlantic (code VS; ☎ 800-862-8621; www.virgin-atlantic.com; hubs Heathrow, London; Gatwick, London)

WestJet (code WS; ☎ 888-937-8538; www.westjet.com; hub Calgary)

Tickets

Everybody loves a bargain and timing is key when it comes to snapping up cheap airfares. You can generally save a bundle by booking early, traveling midweek (Tuesday to Thursday) or flying in the late evening or early morning. Some airlines offer lower fares if you stay over a Saturday.

Your best friend in ferreting out deals is the Internet. Start by checking fares at online travel agencies such as Expedia, Opodo or Zuji, then run the same flight request through metasearch engines such as **SideStep** (www.sidestep.com), **Kayak** (www.kayak.com), **Mobissimo** (www.mobissimo.com), **Qixo** (www.qixo.com) or **Farechase** (www.farechase.com). These so-called aggregators find the lowest fares by combing the websites of major airlines, online consolidators, online travel agencies and low-cost carriers.

Another interesting site is **ITA Software** (www.itasoftware.com), a search matrix that finds the cheapest fare on a particular day or within a 30-day period, sorts results by price and alerts you to potential downsides such as long layovers, tight connections or overnight travel.

If you're flexible, you might be able to save a bundle through **Priceline** (www.priceline.com) and **Hotwire** (www.hotwire.com), where you set your own price and see if any airline bites. The downside is that the airline and departure times won't be revealed until after you've bought the ticket.

Many airlines now guarantee that you'll find the lowest fare on their own websites, so it may pay to check these out as well, especially to see if any promotional fares are available. One way to learn about latebreaking bargain fares is by signing on to free weekly email newsletters put out by the airlines. Even the old-fashioned newspaper can yield deals, especially in times of fare wars. And don't forget about travel agents, who can be especially helpful when planning extensive trips or complicated routes.

COURIER FLIGHTS

If you're on a flexible schedule and traveling solo, flying as a courier might save you a bundle. Couriers accompany freight to its destination in exchange for a discounted ticket. You don't have to handle any shipment personally but simply deliver the freight papers to a representative of the courier company at your destination. Your luggage is limited to carry-on and there may also be other restrictions, such as the length of your stay.

The **International Association of Air Travel Couriers** (IAATC; ☎ 352-475-1584; www.courier.org) and **Air Courier Association** (ACA; ☎ 800-282-1202; www.aircourier.org) are both US-based central clearinghouses that keep track of routes offered by courier companies; membership is required. IAATC also has an office in the **UK** (☎ 0800-0746 481; www.aircourier.co.uk).

INTERCONTINENTAL (RTW) TICKETS

Round-the-world (RTW) tickets are great if you want to visit other places besides California. They're usually more expensive than a simple round-trip ticket, but the extra stops are pretty cheap. They're of most value for trips combining California with Europe, Asia or Australasia. RTW itineraries that include South America or Africa as well as North America are substantially more expensive.

Official airline RTW tickets are usually put together by a combination of airlines or

an entire alliance and permit you to fly to a specified number of stops and/or a maximum mileage, so long as you don't backtrack. Tickets are usually valid for one year. An alternative type of RTW ticket is one put together by a travel agent using a combination of discounted tickets.

Most RTW fares restrict the number of stops within the USA. The cheapest RTW fares permit only one stop; others will allow two or more. Some airlines 'black out' a few heavily traveled routes (like Honolulu to Tokyo). In most cases a 14-day advance purchase is required. After the ticket is purchased, dates can usually be changed without penalty, and tickets can be rewritten to add or delete stops for an extra charge.

For more details and tickets, check out these websites:

Air Brokers (www.airbrokers.com)
Air Treks (www.airtreks.com)
Circle the Planet (www.circletheplanet.com)
Just Fares (www.justfares.com)

Asia

Tokyo, Seoul, Bangkok and Hong Kong are among the Asian cities that have good flight connections to Los Angeles (LA) and San Francisco (SF). Many flights go via Honolulu, but stopovers usually cost extra. Compare prices from the following agencies:

Asia Travel Mart (www.asiatravelmart.com)
Bezurk (www.bezurk.com)
Farenet (www.fare.net)
STA Travel Bangkok (☎ 02-236-0262; www.statravel.co.th); Hong Kong (☎ 2736-1618; www.statravel.com.hk); Singapore (☎ 6737-7188; www.statravel.com.sg); Tokyo (☎ 03-5391-2922; www.statravel.co.jp)
Zuji (www.zuji.com)

Australia & New Zealand

The dominant carriers from down under are Air New Zealand and Qantas, but United Airlines, US Airways and American Airlines also fly across the Pacific Ocean. Flights to San Francisco from New Zealand often go via Japan. Canvass the following agents for fares:

Flight Centre Australia (☎ 133-133; www.flightcentre.com.au) NZ (☎ 0800-243-544; www.flightcentre.co.nz)
STA Travel Australia (☎ 1300-733-035; www.statravel.com.au) NZ (☎ 0508-782-872; www.statravel.co.nz)
Travel.com Australia (☎ 1300-130-482; www.travel.com.au); NZ (☎ 0800-468-332; www.travel.co.nz)
Zuji (www.zuji.com)

TRANSPORTATION

TRANSPORTATION

Canada
Air Canada, American Airlines, United Airlines, America West and Canadian discount carrier WestJet all offer a regular nonstop service to LAX from most major Canadian cities. WestJet also flies to Palm Springs from Calgary and Vancouver. The main carriers serving San Francisco are Air Canada, United and Air New Zealand.

Travel CUTS (☎ 866-246-9762; www.travelcuts.com) is Canada's national student travel agency. Online agencies include www.expedia.ca and www.travelocity.ca.

Continental Europe
Many airlines, including Air France, Alitalia, Delta, Lufthansa, Iberia, United and US Airways have direct flights to LA and San Francisco from major European cities. Many other international and US airlines fly to a gateway city (usually Chicago or Miami), from where you can continue on domestic flights. Try the following travel agents:

France
Anyway (☎ 0892-302-301; www.anyway.fr)
Easyvols (☎ 0899-700-207; www.easyvols.fr)
Lastminute (☎ 0899-78-5000; www.fr.lastminute.com)
Nouvelles Frontières (☎ 0825-000-747;
www.nouvelles-frontieres.fr)
Opodo (www.opodo.fr)
OTU Voyages (www.otu.fr) Specializes in student and youth travelers.

Germany
Expedia (www.expedia.de)
Just Travel (☎ 089-747-3330; www.justtravel.de) English-language agency.
Lastminute (☎ 01805-777-257; www.de.lastminute.com)
Opodo (www.opodo.de)
STA Travel (☎ 069-7430-3292; www.statravel.de)

Italy
E-Viaggi (www.eviaggi.com)
CTS Viaggi (www.cts.it) Student and youth specialists.

Netherlands
Airfair (☎ 020-620-5121; www.airfair.nl)

Spain
Barcelo Viajes (☎ 902-116-226; www.barceloviajes.com)

Mexico
Aeromexico and Mexicana are among the airlines with frequent flights to Los Angeles

from most major Mexican cities. Aeromexico has flights to Ontario and San Diego as well. San Francisco is primarily served by United Airlines and Mexicana. Also look into flights to Tijuana, just across the border from San Diego, which may actually be cheaper.

UK & Ireland
One of the busiest and most competitive air sectors in the world is between the UK and the USA. American Airlines, British Airways, Continental, United Airlines and Virgin Atlantic all operate direct flights from London to Los Angeles. All but American also fly nonstop to San Francisco. Aer Lingus and American Airlines fly nonstop from Dublin to LA, although you'll find more choices and probably cheaper fares by going via London.

Besides the travel agencies listed here, also look for special deals in the travel pages of the weekend broadsheet newspapers or in *Time Out*, the *Evening Standard* and the free magazine *TNT*.

Ebookers (www.ebookers.com)
Flight Centre (☎ 0870-499-0040; www.flightcentre.co.uk)
Last Minute (www.lastminute.com)
Opodo (www.opodo.co.uk)
Quest Travel (☎ 0870-442-3542; www.questtravel.com)
STA Travel (☎ 0870-1-600-599; www.statravel.co.uk)
Trailfinders (☎ 0845-058-5858; www.trailfinders.co.uk)
Travel Bag (☎ 0800-082-5000; www.travelbag.co.uk)

Elsewhere in the USA
Domestic airfares fluctuate hugely depending on the season, day of the week, length of stay and flexibility of the tickets for changes and refunds. Still, nothing determines fares more than demand, and when business is slow, airlines lower fares to fill seats. Discount carriers such as AirTran, America West, Frontier Air, Jet Blue and Southwest have been giving the big guys, including United Airlines, American Airlines and US Airways, a run for their money. Recommended online agencies:

Cheap Air (www.cheapair.com)
Cheap Tickets (www.cheaptickets.com)
Expedia (www.expedia.com)
Lowest Fare (www.lowestfare.com)
Orbitz (www.orbitz.com)
STA Travel (www.sta.com)
Student Universe (www.studentuniverse.com)
Travelocity (www.travelocity.com)
Travelzoo (www.travelzoo.com)

LAND
Border Crossings
San Ysidro on the US–Mexican border between San Diego and Tijuana is the world's busiest border crossing. Travel into Mexico is usually not a problem but coming back into the USA almost always entails a long wait, especially if you're driving. The US Department of Homeland Security maintains a very useful website at http://apps .cbp.gov/bwt showing the current border wait times. If you are not a US citizen or permanent resident, be sure to bring all of the necessary documents (p707). For more details on traveling between San Diego and Tijuana, see p634.

BUS
There are lots Mexican bus companies – including Autobuses ABC, Elite and Estrellas del Pacifico – with services to Tijuana or Mexicali, from where you can catch a Greyhound bus for onward travel to points within California. Within Canada, Greyhound Canada operates the largest bus route network. It's affiliated with US-based Greyhound and you usually have to transfer to one of their buses at the border. For visa and passport requirements, see p707.

CAR & MOTORCYCLE
If you're driving into the USA from Canada or Mexico, bring your vehicle's registration papers, liability insurance and driver's license. Some car rental agencies allow their vehicles to be taken into Mexico for a hefty insurance surcharge (about $25 per day).

TRAIN
Amtrak operates one daily service from Vancouver, Canada, to Seattle where you can catch the *Coast Starlight* to numerous destinations in the Golden State. There is no train service operating between California and Mexico.

Bus
Greyhound (☎ 800-231-2222; www.greyhound.com) has reduced its routes considerably but is the king of the bus world in the USA. Its nationwide route system serves about 2000 destinations, including dozens in California. See the following table for sample fares. For more general information about Greyhound, including how to buy tickets, costs, reservations and bus passes, see p721.

Route	Adult Fare	Duration	Frequency
Albuquerque–Las Vegas	$72	12½-15½hr	3 daily, change in Flagstaff
Phoenix–LA	$39	6½-10hr	up to 8 buses daily
Portland–Sacramento	$59	13hr	up to 6 direct buses daily
Salt Lake City–San Francisco	$80	16hr	3 direct buses daily

Car & Motorcycle
The main freeways connecting California with the rest of the country are the I-10 from points east such as Albuquerque and Phoenix, the I-15 from Las Vegas, the I-80 from Salt Lake City and the I-5 from Portland and Seattle. The quality of the roads is universally excellent. For road rules and potential road hazards, see p725.

Train
Amtrak (☎ 800-872-7245; www.amtrak.com) operates a fairly extensive rail system throughout the USA. The trains are comfortable, if a bit slow, and are equipped with dining and lounge cars on long-distance routes. California is served by four interstate Amtrak trains:
California Zephyr Daily service between Chicago and Emeryville, near San Francisco, via Omaha, Denver and Salt Lake City.
Coast Starlight Travels along the West Coast daily from Seattle to LA (from $126, 35 hours) via Portland, Sacramento and Oakland.
Southwest Chief Daily departures between Chicago and LA (from $191, 43 hours) via Kansas City, Albuquerque and Flagstaff.
Sunset Limited Thrice-weekly service between Orlando and LA (from $128, 68 hours) via Tucson, El Paso and New Orleans.

See p726 for details about Amtrak services within California, how to buy tickets and the California Rail Pass.

If California is part of a wider US itinerary, Amtrak's North America Pass may be a ticket to savings. Overseas travelers may also want to look into the various USA Rail Pass options. Call, check the website or consult a travel agent to determine which one best suits your needs.

GETTING AROUND

AIR

Flying within California is convenient if your time is limited and you want to cover great distances quickly. Besides the big international airports in San Francisco and Los Angeles, flights also depart from smaller regional airports, including Redding, Sacramento, Oakland, San Jose, San Luis Obispo, Monterey, Burbank, Ontario, Long Beach, Orange County and San Diego. For details about services, see p715 and the relevant destination chapters.

The best fares are usually available on major routes with hourly services or better. These include SF–LA, SF–Burbank, SF–Orange County, SF–San Diego, SF–Reno, Oakland–LA and LA–Las Vegas. It's possible to just show up at the airport, buy your ticket and hop on, though the best fares usually require advance purchase. Flights to smaller destinations tend to be fairly pricey because fewer airlines compete for your travel dollars. See p716 for more about buying tickets – much of the same advice applies for domestic travel.

Airlines in California

Several major US carriers fly within California. Flights are often operated by their regional subsidiaries, such as American Eagle, United Express/Skywest and American West Express. Alaska Air and its partner airline Horizon Air have possibly the most extensive intra-California networks, even serving Redding and Eureka/Arcata in northern California. The most popular low-cost airline is Southwest. Contact information for any of these airlines is listed on p716.

BICYCLE

In theory, cycling around California is a great, nonpolluting way to get around the state. In reality, though, the distances involved make it hard to cover a lot of the state and some of the more mountainous regions require a very high level of fitness. Cycling in the desert in summer is brutal and not recommended. Some cities have designated bicycle lanes, but you really want to have your wits about you when venturing out into heavy traffic.

Cyclists must follow the same rules of the road as vehicles, but don't expect drivers to always respect your right of way. Helmets may give you a bad hair day but using one is not only the smart thing to do but is mandatory for anyone under 18. Cycling is permitted on all roads and highways – even along freeways if there's no suitable alternative such as a smaller parallel road; all mandatory exits are marked. With hust the occasional exception there is no off-road mountain-biking in wilderness areas or in national parks, though bikes are allowed on national forest and BLM single-track trails. Trail etiquette requires cyclists to yield to other users.

Emergency roadside assistance is available from the **Better World Club** (☎ 866-238-1137; www.betterworldclub.com). Membership costs $40 per year, plus a $10 enrolment fee, and entitles you to two free pickups and transportation to the nearest repair shop, or home, within a 30-mile radius.

Most airlines will carry your bike in place of a checked bag without charge on international flights, although it may have to be in a box. On domestic flights there's usually a fee of about $80. Check before you buy the ticket.

Members of the **League of American Bicyclists** (LAB; ☎ 202-822-1333; www.bikeleague.org) may transport their bikes free on selected airlines. See the website for details about this program as well as bicycle routes, special events, local clubs and tons of helpful tips on safe biking, maintenance and things to do prior to a big trip.

Greyhound buses will carry bicycles as luggage for about $15 to $25, provided the bicycle is disassembled and placed in a box (usually available at terminals for $10).

Most of Amtrak's *Pacific Surfliner* and *Capitol Corridor* trains feature special racks where you can secure your bike unboxed, but be sure to reserve a spot when making your ticket reservation. There's a fee of $5 to $10, depending on the destination. On trains without racks, bikes must be put in a box and checked as luggage (fee $5, box $10). Not all stations or trains have checked baggage service.

Bicycle theft is fairly common, so protect yours with a heavy-duty bicycle lock and park in well-lit, busy areas. Some parking garages have special bike-parking areas. If possible, bring your bike inside your hotel room at night.

Rental

Outfitters renting bicycles from an hour to several weeks exist in practically all towns and cities; many are listed throughout this book. Rentals start at about $10 per day for touring bikes and $20 for mountain bikes, usually including helmet and a lock. Most companies require a security deposit ranging from $20 to $200.

Purchase

Buying a bicycle is easy, as is – usually – reselling it before you leave. Specialist bike shops have the best selection and advice, but general sporting-goods stores may have lower prices. Some bicycle stores and rental outfitters also sell used bicycles. To sniff out the best bargains, scour flea markets, garage sales and thrift shops, study the notice boards in hostels and universities or check the online listings at www.craigslist.com. These will also be the best places to sell your bike, although stores selling used bikes may also buy one from you.

BOAT

Boating is not an option for getting around California, although there are a few local services, notably to Catalina Island off the coast of Los Angeles. On San Francisco Bay, ferry routes operate between San Francisco and Sausalito, Tiburon, Larkspur, Oakland, Alameda and Vallejo. There are some small ferries and water taxis operating in San Diego Bay. Details are given in the relevant chapters.

BUS

Within California, buses operated by **Greyhound** (☎ 800-231-2222; www.greyhound.com) provide an economical and environmentally friendly way to travel between major cities and to points along the coast, but they won't get you off the beaten path or into parks and forests. Frequency of service varies from 'rarely' to 'constantly,' but main routes have a service every hour or so, including a few nonstop express buses. Stopovers are allowed on full-fare tickets only.

US customers can purchase tickets online, over the telephone and in person at a terminal. If you order them at least 10 days in advance, they'll be mailed to you (US and Canadian addresses only) or you can pick them up at the terminal with proper identification. Non-US customers must buy tickets at the terminal.

Greyhound is most popular with the less-affluent strata of American society, but by international standards the service is really quite good. There's only one class and buses are generally comfortable, reliable and clean. Amenities may include lavatories, reclining seats, air-conditioning (bring a sweater). Smoking on board is prohibited. On longer journeys, buses make meal stops every few hours, usually at highway service stations where the food tends to be bad and over-priced; you're better off bringing your own sustenance.

Bus stations are often dreary places located in sketchy areas. This is especially true of LA (see p554).

Greyhound can accommodate disabled travelers, but you should make your needs known either at the time of booking or by calling ☎ 800-752-4841 at least 48 hours in advance of travel.

Bus Passes

For those planning on making the bus their main method of travel to, from and around California, Greyhound offers a variety of unlimited travel passes (called Discovery Pass or Domestic Ameripass). These are available for periods ranging from seven to 60 consecutive days and cost from $249 to $689. Seniors over 62 (p705) and students with an ISIC or Student Advantage Card (p705) qualify for a 15% discount, while children under 12 pay half price. Also check the website for special promotions.

Passes may be bought at Greyhound terminals up to the departure date and online at least two weeks prior to the first day of travel.

Overseas travelers qualify for the slightly cheaper international versions of the passes, which are sold worldwide through selected ticket agents and online at least 21 days before your first Greyhound trip. You can look up the nearest agent in your home country on the website. If you're already in the USA, you can still buy the Domestic Ameripass.

Costs

Greyhound is the cheapest method of getting around and there are ways to trim costs even further. A round trip is generally cheaper than two one-way tickets. Children under 12 save 40% when accompanied by a passenger paying the full adult fare. Seniors get 5% off, while students in possession of a Student Advantage Card (p705) save 15% on the full fare.

Other promotions, including advance purchase or companion fares, become available all the time, although they may come with restrictions or blackout periods. Simply ask or check the website for the latest deals. For specific route and fare information, see the Getting There & Away sections of the destination chapters. See the following table for some sample fares.

Route	Standard Adult Fare	Duration	Frequency
Arcata–Oakland	$35	7hr	1 daily
LA–Anaheim	$8.50	¾hr	up to 7 daily
LA–Palm Springs	$21	3-3½hr	up to 5 direct daily
LA–San Diego	$16	2¼-4hr	up to 24 daily
Las Vegas–San Diego	$49	8hr	up to 2 direct, 9 indirect daily
San Diego–Anaheim (Disneyland)	$16	2¼-2½	up to 7 daily
San Francisco–LA	$43	7½-12½hr	up to 15 daily
Santa Barbara–LA	$12	2¼-3hr	up to 8 daily

Reservations

Greyhound does not take reservations and even buying tickets in advance does not guarantee you a seat on any particular bus. Show up 45 minutes to one hour prior to the scheduled departure and chances are pretty good you'll get on. Allow more time on Friday and Sunday afternoons and around holidays.

CAR & MOTORCYCLE
Automobile Associations

For long road trips, an auto club membership is an excellent thing to have. The **American Automobile Association** (AAA; ☎ 800-874-7532; www .aaa.com), which has branches throughout the country, is the main auto club in the USA. Many AAA services, including 24-hour **emergency roadside assistance** (☎ 800-222-4357), are also available to members of its international affiliates such as CAA in Canada, AA in the UK and ADAC in Germany. The club also offers free trip-planning advice and maps,

travel-agency services and a range of discounts on hotels, car rentals, Amtrak tickets, admissions etc.

In recent years, Better World Club (p720), which donates 1% of annual revenue to environmental cleanup efforts, has emerged as an alternative association. It offers service throughout the USA and Canada and also operates a roadside assistance program for bicycles.

Bring Your Own Vehicle

Requirements for bringing your car to the USA from Canada or Mexico are briefly discussed on p719. Forget about shipping your car from overseas unless you're actually moving to the USA. Otherwise, it simply does not make economic sense and you'll be better off renting one in-country.

Driver's License

Visitors can legally drive in California for up to 12 months with their home driver's license. For non-US visitors an International Driving Permit (IDP) is not compulsory but it could give you greater credibility with the traffic police. It may also be required when you are renting a vehicle, especially if your home license is not in English or doesn't have a photograph. IDPs are easy to obtain. Just grab a passport photo and your home license and stop by your local automobile association, which will make you one for a small fee. Always carry your home license along with the IDP.

Fuel & Spare Parts

Gas stations in California, practically all of which are self-service, are ubiquitous except in sparsely populated mountain and desert areas where you might want to carry a filled gas canister as a backup. Gas is sold in gallons (1 gallon equals 3.78L). At the time of going to press the California average price for midgrade fuel was around $2.38 per gallon. Prices are generally higher in the national parks and in remote mountain and desert areas.

Finding spare parts should not be a problem, especially in the cities, although actual availability depends on the age and model of your car. Always bring some tools and a spare tire and be sure to have an emergency roadside assistance number in case your car breaks down.

ROAD DISTANCES (MILES)

Distances are approximate

	Anaheim	Arcata	Bakersfield	Death Valley	Las Vegas	Los Angeles	Monterey	Napa	Palm Springs	Redding	Sacramento	San Diego	San Francisco	San Luis Obispo	Santa Barbara	Sth Lake Tahoe	Yosemite
Anaheim	---																
Arcata	710	---															
Bakersfield	135	585	---														
Death Valley	285	740	235	---													
Las Vegas	265	870	285	140	---												
Los Angeles	25	680	110	290	270	---											
Monterey	370	390	235	480	520	330	---										
Napa	435	265	300	545	585	395	150	---									
Palm Springs	90	790	215	300	280	110	435	505	---								
Redding	570	140	445	600	730	540	315	190	650	---							
Sacramento	410	300	285	440	570	385	185	60	490	160	---						
San Diego	95	800	230	350	330	120	450	515	140	660	500	---					
San Francisco	405	275	280	530	570	380	120	45	485	215	85	500	---				
San Luis Obispo	225	505	120	385	460	200	150	260	305	425	295	315	230	---			
Santa Barbara	125	610	145	375	355	95	260	365	200	530	400	220	335	105	---		
Sth Lake Tahoe	505	400	390	355	470	480	280	155	585	260	100	598	185	395	500	---	
Yosemite	340	480	210	305	490	315	185	210	420	340	180	435	195	236	350	195	---

Insurance

California law requires liability insurance for all vehicles, which covers you if you injure another person in an accident. The minimum for bodily injury liability is $15,000 for one person or $30,000 for all injuries in one accident. You also have to carry at least $5000 of property damage liability. Car-rental contracts do not automatically include basic liability insurance, so be sure to ask. Liability insurance policies available through the rental companies usually provide coverage for up to $1 million as well as protection against damage or injury to you inflicted by uninsured or underinsured drivers. Taking out this insurance inflates daily rental costs by about $12.

Insurance against damage to the car itself, called Collision Damage Waiver (CDW) or Loss Damage Waiver (LDW), reduces or eliminates the amount you'll have to reimburse the rental company in case of an accident. Although it is optional, driving without a waiver is not recommended, even though it adds a rather steep $9 to $15 to your daily tab. If you don't have this cover-

age, you accept responsibility for all damages to the rental car.

Depending on your personal vehicle-insurance policy or travel-insurance policy, you may be covered for liability and CDW/LDW when you rent a car. Be sure to check details with your agent.

Some credit cards, especially the gold and platinum versions, cover CDW/LDW for a certain rental period if you use the card to pay for the entire rental and decline the policy offered by the rental company. Always check with your card issuer to see what coverage it provides in California.

Personal Accident Insurance (PAI) covers you and any passenger(s) for medical costs incurred as a result of an accident. If your travel insurance or your health-insurance policy at home does this as well (and most do, but check), then this is one expense (about $5 per day) you can do without.

Parking

Parking is usually plentiful and free in small towns and rural areas and scarce and expensive in the bigger cities. In Los Angeles

TRANSPORTATION

and San Francisco, for instance, you can expect to pay as much as $25 for the privilege of leaving your car in a lot or garage overnight. Valet parking at nicer hotels and restaurants is commonplace in those cities as well, especially in trendy areas.

When parking in the street, study sign posts for parking restrictions, such as street cleaning hours and areas reserved for residents. Don't park within 15ft of a fire hydrant and definitely be aware of painted colored curbs:

Red No parking or stopping anytime.
Yellow Stopping no longer than the posted time and only for loading or unloading passengers or freight.
White Stopping only for picking up or dropping off passengers or mail.
Green Parking for a limited time indicated on nearby signs.
Blue Parking for the disabled only (permit required).

Rental

CARS

As anywhere, rates for car rentals vary considerably by model and pick-up location, but with advance reservations you should be able to get an economy-size vehicle from about $25 per day or $150 a week, plus insurance and taxes. If you belong to an auto club, ask about discounts. It's also worth asking whether car rentals are eligible for frequent-flyer miles.

Rates generally include unlimited mileage, but expect surcharges for rentals originating at airports and train stations, as well as for additional drivers and one-way rentals. Child or infant safety seats are compulsory (reserve at the time of booking) and cost about $8 per day or $40 per week.

In order to rent your own wheels you generally need to be at least 25 years old and hold a valid driver's license and a major credit card. Some companies may rent to drivers between the ages of 21 and 24 for an additional charge (about $15 to $25 per day). If you don't have a credit card, you may be able to make a large cash deposit.

Here is a list of the major international car-rental companies with dozens of branches throughout California.

Alamo (☎ 800-327-9633; www.alamo.com)
Avis (☎ 800-331-1212; www.avis.com)
Budget (☎ 800-527-0700; www.budget.com)
Dollar (☎ 800-800-4000; www.dollar.com)
Enterprise (☎ 800-325-8007; www.enterprise.com)
Hertz (☎ 800-654-3131; www.hertz.com)

National (☎ 800-227-7368; www.nationalcar.com)
Thrifty (☎ 800-367-2277; www.thrifty.com)

You might get a better deal through online agencies, such as **Expedia** (www.expedia.com) or **Travelocity** (www.travelocity.com), or consolidators such as www.carrentals.com. Independent local agencies may offer lower rates, so it's worth looking into that as well. They're also more likely to rent to drivers under 25 and to accept cash or travelers checks as a deposit. About 300 independent agencies are represented by **Car Rental Express** (☎ 604-714-5911, 888-557-8188; www.carrentalexpress.com).

Overseas travelers should look into prepaid deals or fly-drive packages arranged in your home country, which often work out cheaper than on-the-spot rentals.

MOTORCYCLES

Motorcycle rentals and insurance are not cheap, especially if you've got 'Harley hunger.' Small bikes, such as the Harley's Sportster 883, go for about $75 per day; three-day or one-week rentals cost around $210 or $455 respectively. Larger models, such as the Fat Boy, go for about $130, $345 or $750. Security deposits range from $1000 to $3000 (credit card required). Rates usually include helmets, unlimited miles and minimum liability insurance; collision insurance (CDW) costs extra. One-way rentals typically incur a hefty surcharge.

Eagle Rider (☎ 310-536-6777, 888-900-9901; www .eaglerider.com) Nationwide company with 10 outlets in California, including Los Angeles, San Francisco, Palm Springs and San Diego.
Moturis (☎ 800-890-2909; www.moturis.com) Also rents recreational vehicles (RVs).

RECREATIONAL VEHICLES

Traveling by recreational vehicle (RV) is a popular way of exploring California and great for those keen on getting away from the major population centers and into the forest, mountains or desert. For the widest choice, book as early as possible. Costs vary by size and model, but you can generally expect to pay from $100 per day for a small campervan sleeping two or three adults to as much as $300 for a mansion on wheels for up to seven people. Diesel-fueled RVs have considerably lower running costs. Your travel agency back home may have the best deals, or contact these companies directly:

Cruise America (☎ 480-464-7300, 800-671-8042; www.cruiseamerica.com) Also rents motorcycles.
El Monte RV (☎ 888-337-2214; www.elmonterv.com)
Happy Travel Campers (☎ 310-675-1335, 800-370-1262; www.camperusa.com)
RV Central (☎ 909-613-0562; www.rvcentral.com)

Road Conditions & Hazards

For up-to-date highway conditions in California, including road closures, dial ☎ 800-427-7623 or check www.dot.ca.gov/hq/roadinfo. For Nevada roads, call ☎ 877-687-6237 or go to www.nevadadot.com/traveler/roads.

Most roadway dangers in California can be avoided with simple common sense and courteous driving. But there are a few issues to bear in mind, especially when traveling in snow country. In general, make sure your vehicle is in top shape and equipped with emergency supplies such as a flashlight, a warm blanket, water and snacks and an ice scraper. Heavy snow may close roads or require the fitting of tire chains. Ideally, carry your own chains and learn how to use them before you hit the road. Otherwise, chains can usually be bought in the nearest town; don't expect bargains. Most rental-car companies don't permit the use of chains.

In deserts and range country, deer and other wild animals may insist on sharing the road with you, so keep your eyes peeled. Also look out for fallen rocks, which may seriously damage or even disable your car if struck. In coastal areas, especially in Northern California, thick fog may make driving difficult at times. Slow down and be extra alert or, if it's too soupy, get off the road.

For special tips on driving in the desert, see the boxed text, p637.

Road Rules

Californians drive on the right-hand side of the road. The use of seat belts and infant and child safety seats is required at all times, while motorcyclists must wear helmets.

Distances and speed limits are shown in miles. Unless otherwise posted, the speed limit is 65mph on freeways, 55mph on two-lane undivided highways, 35mph on major city streets and 25mph in business and residential districts and near schools. It's forbidden to pass a school bus when its rear red lights are flashing.

Except where indicated, turning right at red lights after coming to a full stop is permitted so long as you don't impede intersecting traffic, which has the right of way. Talking on a cell phone while driving is still legal in California. At four-way stop signs, cars proceed in the order in which they arrived. If two cars arrive simultaneously, the one on the right has the right of way. When emergency vehicles (ie police, fire or ambulance) approach from either direction, pull over to get out of their way.

On freeways, slower cars may be passed on either the left or the right lane. If two cars are trying to get into the same central lane, the one on the right has priority. The lanes marked with a diamond symbol are reserved for cars with multiple occupants. California has strict antilittering laws, and throwing trash from a vehicle can incur a fine up to $1000.

For full details, consult the *California Driver Handbook* or the *California Motorcycle Handbook,* which may be picked up at no cost from any Department of Motor Vehicles office or downloaded from www .dmv.ca.gov/pubs/pubs.htm. For details about penalties for drinking and driving, see p711.

HITCHHIKING

Hitchhiking is never entirely safe anywhere in the world and we don't recommend it. Quite frankly, it's also fairly uncommon in modern-day America where hitchers are generally viewed with suspicion. In urbanized areas you'll find few motorists willing to stop for a thumb, although the practice may be more accepted in remote, rural areas where public transport is sporadic or nonexistent. Generally speaking, you can hitchhike on roads and highways; on freeways you must stand at the on-ramp. Use extreme caution, both when hitchhiking and picking up hitchhikers.

If you're undeterred by the potential risk, you may at least want to familiarize yourself with conditions in California by checking out digihitch (www.digihitch.com), a community website and portal that posts safety tips, specific road advice, links and stories. It also has a ride-board that connects travelers with others going to the same destination. You can advertise a ride yourself or make arrangements with drivers. Other Web-based ride-boards include www.eride share.com and www.craigslist.com/rid.

TRANSPORTATION

LOCAL TRANSPORTATION

Check the Getting Around sections of the destination chapters for details about specific local transportation options.

Bicycle

Cycling may be a feasible way of getting around in some of the smaller towns but it is not really recommended in such traffic-dense areas as LA, San Francisco (think about those hills!) and San Diego. According to the League of American Bicyclists, Palo Alto, Santa Barbara, Davis and Chico are the most bicycle-friendly communities in California.

Bicycles may often be transported on public transportation at certain times of day. Rental stations are listed throughout this book. Also see p720 and p58.

Bus

Buses are the most ubiquitous form of public transportation and practically all towns have their own system. Some lines are commuter oriented and offer only limited or no service at all in the evenings and on weekends.

Subway & Light Rail

Los Angeles has Metro Rail, a combination subway–light-rail network, while *Metrolink* is a system of commuter trains linking LA with the surrounding counties. San Diego operates a trolley to the Mexican border and the *Coaster* commuter trains along the coast between Oceanside and downtown. Getting around San Francisco and the East Bay is a snap aboard superefficient BART.

Taxi

Taxis are metered, with charges from $1.50 to $2.50 at flag fall, plus $1.20 to $2 per mile. There may be an extra charge for handling baggage and drivers expect a tip of 10% to 15%. In many cities, including Los Angeles, it isn't customary to hail a cruising cab. Instead you phone ahead for one; numbers of local companies are listed throughout this book or look under 'Taxi' in the *Yellow Pages*.

TRAIN

Amtrak (☎ 800-872-7245; www.amtrak.com) operates train services throughout California. At some stations, the trains are met by motorcoaches (called Amtrak Thruways) for onward connections to smaller destinations. Travel on these buses is only permitted in conjunction with a train ticket.

A pleasant way to travel along the coast between San Diego and San Luis Obispo (SLO) is aboard the *Pacific Surfliner*. The sleek, double-decker cars have comfortable seats with panoramic windows, and there's a café car as well. Business-class seats feature nifty little video screens, slightly more legroom and outlets for plugging in laptops or other electrical devices. Up to 11 trains daily ply the San Diego–LA route (via Anaheim, home of Disneyland), with as many as five trains continuing north to Santa Barbara via Oxnard and Ventura. Two trains usually plunge on to San Luis Obispo. The trip itself, which hugs the coastline for much of the way, is a treat because of the beautiful scenery.

Amtrak also operates two other intra-California lines. The *Capitol Corridor* links communities in the eastern San Francisco Bay area (including Oakland, Berkeley and Emeryville with Sacramento several times daily. From here, a few trains as well as Thruway buses continue south to San Jose, north to Auburn in the Gold Country and east to Truckee and Reno near Lake Tahoe.

The third train is the *San Joaquins*, which has several departures daily between Oakland and Bakersfield as well as Sacramento and Bakersfield. Stops along the way include Merced, with onward service to Yosemite National Park. From Bakersfield, buses leave for Santa Barbara, Las Vegas, Los Angeles and Anaheim.

Of Amtrak's long-distance trains (p719) the *Coast Starlight* provides the most extensive intra-California service as it chugs pretty much along the entire length of the state. Major stops include Los Angeles, Santa Barbara, San Luis Obispo, Paso Robles, San Jose, Oakland, Sacramento and Redding.

The *California Zephyr*, which travels between Emeryville/San Francisco and Chicago, passes through Truckee and Reno, where you can catch a local bus service to Lake Tahoe.

Costs

Tickets can be purchased in person, by telephone and online. Fares depend on the day of travel, the route, the type of seating and other factors. See the following table for sample standard adult fares. The fares are slightly

---

ALL ABOARD THE CHOO-CHOO

Riding the rails has a certain romantic aura, especially when the train in question is of vintage stock or chugs through particularly scenic terrain. Here are some of the nicest routes in California, all of which operate as tourist attractions:

Napa Valley Wine Train Traveling in style between Napa and St Helena (p191).
Old Sacramento Train Travel along the Sacramento River from Old Sacramento (p411).
Railtown 1897 Steam Train A scenic trip through Gold Country from Jamestown (p329).
Roaring Camp Railroads Narrow-gauge train rides through the redwoods (p439).
Skunk Train Chugs between Willits and Fort Bragg on the North Coast (p245).
Sugar Pine Railroad A narrow-gauge spin around the woods just south of Yosemite (p372).

---

higher between late May and early September. Round-trip tickets cost the same as two one-way tickets.

Route	Fare	Duration
Emeryville/San Francisco–Merced	from $25	3hr
Emeryville/San Francisco–Truckee	$44	5½hr
LA–Santa Barbara	$17/$28	2½hr
San Diego–LA	$26/$38	2¾hr
San Diego–Santa Barbara	$26/$41	5½hr

Seniors over 62 and students with a Student Advantage Card (p705) receive a 15% discount, while up to two children aged two to 15 and accompanied by an adult get 50% off. Children under two travel for free. AAA members enjoy 10% off regular fares. Special promotions can become available at any time, so be sure to ask or check the website.

Reservations

Reservations can be made any time from 11 months in advance to the day of departure. In summer and around holidays, some trains fill up quickly, so book seats as far in advance as possible.

Train Passes

Amtrak's California Rail Pass costs $159 ($80 for children aged two to 15) and is valid for seven days of travel within a 21-day period. It is valid on the *Capitol Corridor, Pacific Surfliner, San Joaquins* and most connecting thruway services as well as the *Coast Starlight* between Los Angeles and Dunsmuir. Passes may only be purchased by phone or in person and you must make seat reservations for each leg of travel.

Health Dr David Goldberg

CONTENTS

Generally speaking, California is a healthy place to visit. No prevalent diseases or risks are associated with traveling here, and the USA is well served by hospitals.

BEFORE YOU GO

INSURANCE

Because of the high cost of health care, international travelers should take out comprehensive travel insurance before they leave home. If you have a choice between lower or higher medical expense options, take the higher one for visiting the USA.

Bring any medications you may need in their original containers, clearly labeled. A signed, dated letter from your physician that describes all medical conditions and medications, including generic names, is also a good idea.

If your health insurance does not cover you for medical expenses abroad, consider supplemental insurance. Check the **Lonely** **Planet website** (www.lonelyplanet.com) for more information. Find out in advance if your insurance plan will make payments directly to providers or reimburse you later for overseas health expenditures.

RECOMMENDED VACCINATIONS

No special vaccines are required or recommended for travel to the USA. All travelers should be up-to-date on routine immunizations: tetanus-diphtheria, measles, chicken pox and influenza.

MEDICAL CHECKLIST

Recommended items for a personal medical kit:

- acetaminophen (Tylenol) or aspirin
- anti-inflammatory drugs (eg ibuprofen)
- antihistamines (for hay fever and allergic reactions)
- antibacterial ointment (eg Bactroban) for cuts and abrasions
- steroid cream or cortisone (for poison ivy and other allergic rashes)
- bandages, gauze, gauze rolls
- adhesive or paper tape
- scissors, safety pins, tweezers
- thermometer
- pocket knife
- DEET-containing insect repellent for the skin
- permethrin-containing insect spray for clothing, tents and bed nets
- sunblock

INTERNET RESOURCES

There is a wealth of travel health advice on the Internet. The World Health Organization

Vaccine	Recommended for	Dosage	Side effects
tetanus-diphtheria	all travelers who haven't had booster within 10 years	one dose lasts 10 years	soreness at injection site
measles	travelers born after 1956 who've had only one measles vaccination	one dose	fever; rash; joint pains; allergic reactions
chicken pox	travelers who've never had chicken pox	two doses a month apart	fever; mild case of chicken pox
influenza	all travelers during flu season (Nov through Mar)	one dose	soreness at the injection site; fever

publishes a superb book, called *International Travel and Health*, which is revised annually and is available online at no cost at www .who.int/ith. Another website of general interest is MD Travel Health at www.mdtravel health.com, which provides complete travel health recommendations for every country, updated daily, also at no cost.

It's usually a good idea to consult your government's travel health website before departure, if one is available:

Australia (www.smartraveller.com.au)
Canada (www.hc-sc.gc.ca/english/index.html)
UK (www.doh.gov.uk/traveladvice/index.htm)
United States (www.cdc.gov/travel)

IN CALIFORNIA

AVAILABILITY & COST OF HEALTH CARE

In general, if you have a medical emergency, your best bet is to find the nearest hospital and go to its emergency room (ER). If the problem isn't urgent, you can call a nearby hospital and ask for a referral to a local physician, which is usually cheaper than a trip to the emergency room. In a serious emergency, call ☎ 911 for an ambulance to take you to the nearest ER. Many city hospitals have 'urgent care clinics' designed to deal with walk-in clients with less-than-catastrophic injuries and illnesses. Note that these are for-profit centers and they tend to perform large numbers of expensive tests, even for minor illnesses.

Pharmacies are abundantly supplied, but you may find some medications that are available over the counter in your home country require a prescription in the USA. As always, if you don't have insurance to cover the cost of prescriptions, they can be shockingly expensive.

INFECTIOUS DISEASES

In addition to more common ailments, there are several infectious diseases that may be acquired by mosquito or tick bites.

Giardiasis

This parasitic infection of the small intestine occurs throughout North America and the world. Symptoms may include nausea, bloating, cramps, and diarrhea, and may last for weeks. To protect yourself from giardia, you should avoid drinking directly from

---

TRADITIONAL MEDICINE

American health-food stores and many of the regular groceries abound with so-called 'natural' remedies. These are a few of the more successful ones, in our opinion. They're not guaranteed, of course, but they may work great. You never know…

Problem	Treatment
jet lag	melatonin
mosquito bite	oil of eucalyptus
motion sickness	ginger

---

lakes, ponds, streams and rivers, which may be contaminated by animal or human feces. The infection can also be transmitted from person to person if proper hand washing is not performed. Giardiasis is easily diagnosed by a stool test and readily treated with antibiotics.

HIV/AIDS

As with most parts of the world, HIV infection occurs throughout the USA. You should never assume, on the basis of someone's background or appearance, that they're free of this or any other sexually transmitted disease. Be sure to use a condom for all sexual encounters.

West Nile Virus

This virus was unknown in the USA until a few years ago, but has now been reported in almost all 50 states. The virus is transmitted by culex mosquitoes, which are active in late summer and early fall and generally bite after dusk. Most infections are mild or asymptomatic, but the virus may infect the central nervous system leading to fever, headache, confusion, lethargy, coma and sometimes death. There is no treatment for West Nile virus. For the latest update on the areas affected by West Nile, go to the **US Geological Survey website** (http://westnilemaps.usgs.gov).

ENVIRONMENTAL HAZARDS
Altitude Sickness

Visitors from lower elevations undergo rather dramatic physiological changes as they adapt to high altitudes, and while the side-effects are usually mild, they can be dangerous if ignored. Some people – age and fitness level are not predictors of who these will be – will feel the effects of altitude strongly, while others won't even notice.

Symptoms, which tend to manifest after four days and continue for about two weeks, may include headache, fatigue, loss of appetite, nausea, sleeplessness, increased urination and sometimes hyperventilation due to over-exertion. More severe cases (usually affecting hikers over 10,000ft who don't take time to acclimatize) display extreme disorientation, breathing problems and vomiting. These people should descend immediately and get to a hospital.

To avoid the discomfort characterizing the milder symptoms, drink plenty of water (dehydration exacerbates the symptoms) and take it easy. Schedule a nap if you have a sleepless night and put off serious hiking and biking for a few days, if possible. A mild painkiller like aspirin should take care of the headache.

Dehydration

Visitors to the desert may not realize how much water they're losing, as sweat evaporates almost immediately and increased urination (to help the blood process oxygen more efficiently) can go unnoticed. The prudent tourist will make sure to drink more water than usual – think a gallon a day if you're active. Parents can carry fruit and fruit juices to help keep kids hydrated.

Severe dehydration can easily cause disorientation and confusion, and even day hikers have gotten lost and died because they ignored their thirst. So bring plenty of water, even on short hikes, and drink it!

Heat Exhaustion & Heat Stroke

Dehydration or salt deficiency can cause heat exhaustion. Take time to acclimatize to high temperatures and make sure you get enough liquids. Salt deficiency is characterized by fatigue, lethargy, headaches, giddiness and muscle cramps. Salt tablets may help. Vomiting or diarrhea can also deplete your liquid and salt levels. Anhydrotic heat exhaustion, caused by the inability to sweat, is quite rare. Unlike other forms of heat exhaustion, it may strike people who have been in a hot climate for some time, rather than newcomers. Always use water bottles on long trips. One gallon of water per person per day is recommended if hiking.

Long, continuous exposure to high temperatures can lead to the sometimes-fatal condition of heat stroke, which occurs when the body's heat-regulating mechanism breaks down and the body temperature rises to dangerous levels. Hospitalization is essential for extreme cases, meanwhile get out of the sun, remove clothing, cover the body with a wet sheet or towel and fan continually.

Hypothermia

Skiers and winter hikers will find that temperatures in the mountains or desert can quickly drop below freezing. A sudden soaking or even high winds can lower your body temperature rapidly. Travel with a partner whenever possible.

Seek shelter when bad weather is unavoidable. Woolen clothing and synthetics, which retain warmth even when wet, are superior to cottons. Carry a good-quality sleeping bag and high-energy, easily digestible snacks like chocolate or dried fruit.

The symptoms of hypothermia are exhaustion, numbness, shivering, slurred speech, irrational or violent behavior, lethargy, stumbling, dizzy spells, muscle cramps and violent bursts of energy. Get hypothermia victims out of bad weather and into dry, warm clothing. Give hot liquids (not alcohol) and high-calorie, easily digestible food. In advanced stages place victims in warm sleeping bags and get in with them. Do not rub victims.

Animal Bites

Do not attempt to pet, handle or feed any wild animal, no matter how cuddly it looks; most injuries from animals are directly related to people trying to do just that.

Any bite or scratch by a mammal, including bats, should be promptly and thoroughly cleansed with large amounts of soap and water, followed by application of an antiseptic such as iodine or alcohol. The local health authorities should be contacted immediately for possible post-exposure rabies treatment, whether or not you have been immunized against rabies. It may also be advisable to start an antibiotic, since wounds caused by animal bites and scratches frequently become infected.

Mosquito Bites

When mosquitoes are present, keep yourself covered (wear long sleeves, long pants, hats and shoes rather than sandals) and apply a good insect repellent, preferably one containing DEET, to exposed skin and clothing. Don't overuse the stuff, though, because neurologic toxicity – though uncommon – has been reported from DEET, especially in children. DEET-containing compounds should not be used at all on kids under age two.

Insect repellents containing certain botanical products, including oil of eucalyptus and soybean oil, are effective but last only 1½ to two hours. Products based on citronella are not effective.

Tick Bites

Ticks are parasitic arachnids that may be present in the brush, forest and grasslands, where hikers often get them on their legs or in their boots. Adult ticks suck blood from hosts by burrowing into the skin and can carry infections such as Lyme disease.

Always check your body for ticks after walking through high grass or thickly forested area. If ticks are found unattached, they can simply be brushed off. If a tick is found attached, press down around the tick's head with tweezers, grab the head and gently pull upwards – do not twist it. (If no tweezers are available, use your fingers, but protect them from contamination with a piece of tissue or paper.) Do not rub oil, alcohol or petroleum jelly on it. If you get sick in the next couple of weeks, consult a doctor.

Snakebites

There are several varieties of venomous snakes in the USA, but unlike those in other countries they do not cause instantaneous death and antivenins are available. Rattlesnake bites are fairly common. First aid is to place a light constricting bandage over the bite, keep the wounded part below the level of the heart and move it as little as pos-

sible. Stay calm and get to a medical facility as soon as possible. Bring the dead snake for identification if you can, but don't risk being bitten again. Do not use the mythic 'cut an X and suck out the venom' trick, as this causes more damage to snakebite victims than the bites themselves.

Many snakebites result from people picking up the snake, either out of bravado or mistakenly assuming that the animal was dead. Keep a healthy distance away from snakes and watch where you step.

Spider & Scorpion Bites

Although there are many species of spiders in California (check out www.calpoison.org for a list of potential biters), one of the most common biting spiders is the black widow. This spider is black or brown in color, measuring about 15mm in body length, with a shiny top, fat body and a distinctive red or orange hourglass figure on its underside. It's usually found in barns, woodpiles, sheds, harvested crops and bowls of outdoor toilets.

If bitten by a black widow, you should apply ice or cold packs and immediately go to the nearest emergency room. Complications of a black widow bite may include muscle spasms, breathing difficulties and high blood pressure.

If stung by a scorpion, you should immediately apply ice or a cold pack, immobilize the affected body part and go to the nearest emergency room. To prevent scorpion stings, be sure to inspect and shake out clothing, shoes and sleeping bags before use, and wear gloves and protective clothing when working around piles of wood or leaves.

Poison Control Centers have staff available 24 hours a day and advise about bites, stings and ingested poisons of all kinds. Call ☎ 800-222-1222 anywhere in California for the one nearest you.

HEALTH

Behind the Scenes

THIS BOOK

This 4th edition of *California* was researched and written by Andrea Schulte-Peevers (coordinator), Sara Benson, Tom Downs, Robert Landon, Suzanne Plank, Ryan Ver Berkmoes and John A Vlahides. The Health chapter was adapted from material by Dr David Goldberg. Mark Morford contributed the What Is Burning Man? boxed text and Heather Harrison the Gay San Francisco boxed text. Andrea Schulte-Peevers coordinated and co-wrote the 2nd and 3rd editions of this book. This guidebook was commissioned in Lonely Planet's Oakland office and produced by the following:

Commissioning Editor Suki Gear
Coordinating Editor Yvonne Byron
Coordinating Cartographer Julie Sheridan
Coordinating Layout Designer Jacqui Saunders
Managing Cartographer Alison Lyall
Assisting Editors Janet Austin, Jackey Coyle, Justin Flynn, Lauren Rollheiser, Jeanette Wall
Assisting Cartographers Barbara Benson, Julie Dodkins, Owen Eszeki, Anneka Imkamp, Lyndell Stringer
Cover Designer James Hardy
Project Managers Brigitte Ellemor, Glenn van der Knijff

Thanks to Sally Darmody, Bruce Evans, Adriana Mammarella, Wibowo Rusli, Sarah Sloane, China Williams, Celia Wood

THANKS from the Authors

Andrea Schulte-Peevers A small army of folks deserves a heartfelt thank you, starting with Suki Gear for again entrusting me with this gig and my

fellow authors for making this job go so smoothly, with a special nod to John Vlahides for so generously sharing his insider knowledge of Tahoe ski resorts. Big thanks also to Frank Ruiz for revealing all his favorite Tahoe places and to Kurt Wolff, whose Yosemite National Park guide provided the inspiration for the park's write-up in this book. Other capable folks who've shared their knowledge and wisdom along the way include Cay Lepre, Kirstin Cattell, Katrina Paz, Ronele Klingensmith, Mary Ann McAuliffe, Erin Wallace, Kerri Holden, Alexandra Picavet, Caroline McGrath, Douglas Shaw and Dan McKernan – great big thanks to all of you. Finally, a gold medal to David, my husband, soul mate and companion in travel and life.

Sara Benson Thanks to Las Vegas PR gurus Stephanie Heller, Gina Boccadoro, Kate Turner, Victoria Kent, Marc Jay and Jana Blackburn. Authors Becca Blond and Kim Grant generously gave advice, and buddies Amy Lowe and Josh Lucas kept me sane on the road. Thanks to coordinating author Andrea Schulte-Peevers for answering dozens of questions with grace and skill, and to commissioning editor Suki Gear for hiring me to write about my favorite haunts in the California deserts.

Tom Downs I'd like to thank my travel partners, Fawn, Mai, Lana and Liam, for keeping an eye out for interesting things along the road and for not crying too much. Also, thanks for understanding when I stopped bringing you along. Thanks as well to Suki Gear for hiring me, to Andrea Schulte-Peevers, with whom I always wanted to work, and to the

---

THE LONELY PLANET STORY

The story begins with a classic travel adventure: Tony and Maureen Wheeler's 1972 journey across Europe and Asia to Australia. There was no useful information about the overland trail then, so Tony and Maureen published the first Lonely Planet guidebook to meet a growing need.

From a kitchen table, Lonely Planet has grown to become the largest independent travel publisher in the world, with offices in Melbourne (Australia), Oakland (USA) and London (UK). Today Lonely Planet guidebooks cover the globe. There is an ever-growing list of books and information in a variety of media. Some things haven't changed. The main aim is still to make it possible for adventurous travelers to get out there – to explore and better understand the world.

At Lonely Planet we believe travelers can make a positive contribution to the countries they visit – if they respect their host communities and spend their money wisely. Every year 5% of company profit is donated to charities around the world.

patient and helpful Californians who answered my questions along the way. These include Sam Parker of Modesto, that flowery old dame at the Merced tourist office, Peepin' Tom Thumb (alias of an actual guy) of San Jose and Maureen Bing of San Rafael. Huge thanks also must go to editor Yvonne Byron and cartographer Julie Sheridan, who do such polished work in Lonely Planet's Melbourne office.

Robert Landon First, thanks to all the people who shared their expertise on the ground. Jamie Lynn Sigler, Chris Donovan and Suzanne Van Cleve were extremely helpful in San Diego. In Orange County, Julia and Ken Lupton Reinhart provided both insider insights and truly familial hospitality. My stay with them was, as always, a delight. I can't fail to mention Suki Gear, first for hiring me and second for providing such an intelligent and thoughtful brief. Paulo Gonçalves once again kept me well fed in all ways during the writing process. And thanks once again to Carlos Ponce, who ensured that the lifelong spoiling of Manuel and Simon (domestic shorthairs) continued uninterrupted in my absence.

Suzanne Plank Thanks Suki Gear for your guidance. Andrea Schulte-Peevers, thanks so much for your support. Among the many helpful, warm souls I met on the road, I am especially grateful to Susan and Brady Stewart, Teresa and (phantom chef extraordinaire) Greg Ramsey, Carter Fleming, Kerrie Wilson, Judy Yzquierdo Morris, Belinda R and Theresa Baird. Robert in Lassen, thanks for the Geology 101 intro. Ana, I'll be back with the snowfall. Finally, I'm most appreciative of my brilliant, hilarious sidekick, navigator, editor and favorite friend Marty Jones for making my planet far from lonely.

Ryan Ver Berkmoes I'm indebted to many for the California experience I got to celebrate in writing this book. My parents, sister and Dr Otto were there at the start. Later, while my hair was both still on my head and a prepubescent blond, I enjoyed many endless beach days with the Aptos gang. In high school I enjoyed the close companionship of many in the 1978 class at Marello Preparatory High School including Joe Sciacca, Robert Silva, the late Dan Pelton (of the water wheel clan), Matt Camarlinghi, Michael Howe et al. In writing this book, there are many who were kind and helpful, but I want to reserve special thanks to the curators at the amazing National Steinbeck Center in Salinas. I first read *Travels with Charley* when I was 13. It changed my life and it was a dream come true to see Rocinante in person. Almost as neat as my California girl, Erin Corrigan.

John A Vlahides Andy Moore, how can it be that I've never properly thanked you, in print, for giving me my first travel-writing gig? I'm forever indebted. Thanks also to my ever-fab commissioning editor Suki Gear and supercool coordinating author Andrea Schulte-Peevers for their kindness and guidance. For help pointing me in the right direction on the road, I'm especially grateful to Tyffani Peters, Sherry Sue Huss, Brenda Bouillerce, Debra Stegman, Lori Chambers, Tony Smithers, Doug White, Garret Murphy, Lynn Kennelly, Stacy Lewis, Suzanne Guido and Carole Saville. You're wonderful! Thanks again.

THANKS from Lonely Planet

Many thanks to the hundreds of travellers who used the last edition and wrote to us with helpful hints, useful advice and interesting anecdotes:

A Ida Aarving, Trygve Anderson, Jessica Andrews **B** Elise Baril, George Baxter Smith, Bruce K Belknap, Jeffrey Bell, Joseph Blum, Jenny Bourke, Matthias Bode, Darryl Brock **C** Jennifer Charpentier, Beng Wan Chua, Kate Claisse, Liz Clark, John Cojeen, Caroline Coppin, Rupert Cousens, Paul Crowe **D** Siobhain Danaher, B Dark, Rosalie de Boer, Christina Demetriou, Richard Desomme, AB DiLucente, Dennis DiLucente, Guy Dowman **E** Patrick Easterling, Nivine Emeran, Pat Eyre **F** Colin Falls, Sean Fargo, Jean Feilmoser, Matthew Fennessy, Elsa Flores, Andy Foltz, Eleanor Friedman, Jean Fruend **G** Nicolas Gaere,

---

SEND US YOUR FEEDBACK

We love to hear from travelers – your comments keep us on our toes and help make our books better. Our well-traveled team reads every word on what you loved or loathed about this book. Although we cannot reply individually to postal submissions, we always guarantee that your feedback goes straight to the appropriate authors, in time for the next edition. Each person who sends us information is thanked in the next edition – and the most useful submissions are rewarded with a free book.

To send us your updates – and find out about Lonely Planet events, newsletters and travel news – visit our award-winning website: **www.lonelyplanet.com/feedback**.

Note: We may edit, reproduce and incorporate your comments in Lonely Planet products such as guidebooks, websites and digital products, so let us know if you don't want your comments reproduced or your name acknowledged. For a copy of our privacy policy visit www.lonelyplanet.com/privacy.

BEHIND THE SCENES

Joe Ganesh, Len Gierach, Emma Giesen, Laura Guidali, Joost Groot, Iris Gumm **H** Stuart Hale, Ian Harris, Kay Harry, David & Mairin Herman, Bruce Hicks, Ian Hicks, Marese Hickey, BJ Hill, Trevor Humphreys, Garrit Huysman **I** Eleanor, Christopher & Susannah Inglis **J** Jane James, Fabricio Jimenez, Darryl Jones, Andreas Johns, Gretchen Joseph, Christiane Jung **K** Beth A Kaplan, Udo Keil, Christy Khattab, Don Kilburg **L** Judy Lake, John Lam, SW Lam, Nancy Lee, Celine Lescaut, Derek Lycke **M** Youval Marks, Elona Masson, Kate Mathhams, Jade Mawbey, Eugene McAuley, Daniel McChesney Young, Pete McCusker, Joseph McKenzie, Guy Melvin III, Christian Mena, Rich Mick, John Mitchell, Fiona Mocatta, Heather Monell, Mark Morgan, TRW Moore, Peter Mynors **N** Joe Nekrasz, Lucy Newman **O** Leah Oehlert, Alex Oestreicher **P** Marco Pace, Michelle Pauling, Katerina Pavlou, Eliza Penrose, Grace PerLee, Martin Plant **R** Donna Reddin, Donna Regan, Gerry Renshaw, Maxine Ressler, Brett Rhodes, AN Richmond, Vittorio Riguzzi, Sarah Robinson, Jan Roehlk, Ben Roman, Claudia Royston, Rob Ruschak **S** Sean Savage, Petra Schneider, Christina Schulte, Don Shirley **T** Ken Tanji, Mark Terry, Joanne Thomson, Brian Tiernan, Dawn Toles, Jane Toon, Corinne Turton **V** Craig & Linda Vandermeer **W** Darien Werfhorst, Wolfgang Wilfling, Duncan Williamson **Y** Andrew Young, Mary Young **Z** Adriana Zambojova

ACKNOWLEDGMENTS

Many thanks to the following for the use of their content:

Globe on back cover © Mountain High Maps 1993 Digital Wisdom, Inc.

Map data contained in Geography of California map © Mountain High Maps 1993 Digital Wisdom, Inc.

Index

000 Map pages
000 Photograph pages

000 Map pages
000 Photograph pages

INDEX

INDEX

INDEX

752

MAP LEGEND
ROUTES

Tollway	One-Way Street
Freeway	Street Mall/Steps
Primary Road	Tunnel
Secondary Road	Walking Tour
Tertiary Road	Walking Tour Detour
Lane	Walking Trail
Under Construction	Walking Path
Track	Pedestrian Overpass
Unsealed Road	

TRANSPORT

Ferry	Rail
Metro	Rail (Underground)
Monorail	Tram
Bus Route	Cable Car, Funicular

HYDROGRAPHY

River, Creek	Canal
Intermittent River	Water
Swamp	Lake (Dry)
Mangrove	Lake (Salt)
Reef	Mudflats

BOUNDARIES

International	Regional, Suburb
State, Provincial	Ancient Wall
Disputed	Cliff
Marine Park	

AREA FEATURES

Airport	Land
Area of Interest	Mall
Beach, Desert	Market
Building	Park
Campus	Reservation
Cemetery, Christian	Rocks
Cemetery, Other	Sports
Forest	Urban

POPULATION

✪ CAPITAL (NATIONAL)	◉ CAPITAL (STATE)
● Large City	● Medium City
● Small City	● Town, Village

SYMBOLS

Sights/Activities
- Beach
- Castle, Fortress
- Christian
- Diving, Snorkeling
- Hindu
- Monument
- Museum, Gallery
- Point of Interest
- Pool
- Ruin
- Skiing
- Trail Head
- Winery, Vineyard
- Zoo, Bird Sanctuary

Eating
- Eating

Drinking
- Drinking
- Café

Entertainment
- Entertainment

Shopping
- Shopping

Sleeping
- Sleeping
- Camping

Transport
- Airport, Airfield
- Bus Station
- Cycling, Bicycle Path
- General Transport
- Parking Area
- Petrol Station
- Taxi Rank

Information
- Bank, ATM
- Embassy/Consulate
- Hospital, Medical
- Information
- Internet Facilities
- Police Station
- Post Office, GPO
- Telephone
- Toilets

Geographic
- Lighthouse
- Lookout
- Mountain, Volcano
- National Park
- Pass, Canyon
- Picnic Area
- River Flow
- Shelter, Hut
- Spot Height

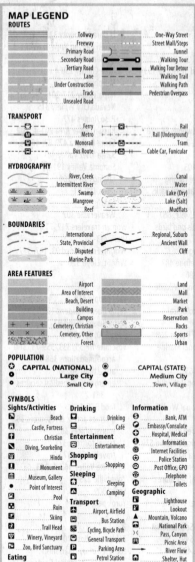

LONELY PLANET OFFICES

Australia
Head Office
Locked Bag 1, Footscray, Victoria 3011
☎ 03 8379 8000, fax 03 8379 8111
talk2us@lonelyplanet.com.au

USA
150 Linden St, Oakland, CA 94607
☎ 510 893 8555, toll free 800 275 8555
fax 510 893 8572
info@lonelyplanet.com

UK
72-82 Rosebery Ave,
Clerkenwell, London EC1R 4RW
☎ 020 7841 9000, fax 020 7841 9001
go@lonelyplanet.co.uk

Published by Lonely Planet Publications Pty Ltd
ABN 36 005 607 983
© Lonely Planet Publications Pty Ltd 2006
© photographers as indicated 2006

Cover photographs by Lonely Planet Images: Surfboard on classic car, Huntington Beach, Christina Lease (front); Flexing at Muscle Beach, Los Angeles, David Peevers (back). Many of the images in this guide are available for licensing from Lonely Planet Images: www.lonelyplanetimages.com.